AUSTRALIAN FISHING

Edited by
Jack Pollard

Recent books by Jack Pollard

When Stumps Were Drawn (ed., 1985)
Australian Rugby Union: The Game and the Players (1984)
Tribute to Lillee and Chappell (1984)
The Pictorial History of Australian Cricket (1983)
Australian Cricket: The Game and the Players (1982)
The Pictorial History of Australian Horse Racing (1981)

ANGUS & ROBERTSON PUBLISHERS
Unit 4, Eden Park, 31 Waterloo Road,
North Ryde, NSW, Australia 2113, and
16 Golden Square, London W1R 4BN,
United Kingdom

This book is copyright.
Apart from any fair dealing for the
purposes of private study, research,
criticism or review, as permitted
under the Copyright Act, no part may
be reproduced by any process without
written permission. Inquiries should
be addressed to the publishers.

First published in Australia in 1969
Revised edition first published in Australia
by Angus & Robertson Publishers in 1986

Copyright © Jack Pollard 1986

National Library of Australia
Cataloguing-in-publication data.

Australian fishing.-
  Bibliography.
  Includes index.
  ISBN 0 207 15161 X

  1. Fishing — Australia. I. Pollard, Jack, 1926-
799.1'2'0994

Typeset in 10/11 Zapf Book Light by
Graphicraft Typesetters Ltd, Hong Kong
Printed in Australia by Globe Press

CONTENTS

Preface .... *page v*
Australian Fishing .... *page 1*
Maps .... *following page 393*
Acknowledgements .... *page 909*
Bibliography .... *page 910*
Index *of scientific names* ...... *page 911*
Index *of common names* ...... *page 915*

PREFACE

Since it first appeared in 1969, this book has been in such regular demand that there has been little opportunity to revise and update it. A succession of reprints demonstrated that the original idea of providing a comprehensive look at fishing for sport right around Australia had succeeded beyond even the most optimistic forecasts. This time, however, the book has been completely reshaped to cover the most recent developments in fishing research and in tackle and angling techniques.

The fish do not change, of course, but our knowledge of them, and of the best ways to catch them, constantly improves. Rangoon rods and split cane blanks have virtually disappeared and sales people talk about graphite. Metrication has come to the sport, while a growing band of biologists has expanded the scientific knowledge of fishes. Favoured fishing spots have disappeared and new ones have opened up.

In fully revising the book and catering for all these changes, the original aim of offering help to all types of sports fishermen has been retained. Whether they are weekend fishermen, once-a-year holiday handliners, deep-sea devotees, beach or freshwater anglers, or those who simply dangle a line from wharves or breakwaters, every fisherman will find something of real value in this book.

More than 3000 species of fish have now been identified in Australian waters; to include an entry on all of them would require several volumes. We have chosen instead to include fishes the average angler is most likely to encounter. The space allocated to each fish has been judged by its popularity. Thus snapper, a fine table fish which occupies anglers in all States, receives detailed coverage, while Bombay duck, a fish anglers mostly sight on Chinese restaurant menus, earns only a small entry.

The well-known problem of determining the common name acceptable in all parts of Australia of many species, and sometimes the scientific name as well, has caused much heartache. Many efforts have been made to standardize common names. After 16 years' preliminary work, a conference of experts from all States was held in 1963. Among the names decided on then was mulloway, and that is the name we have used in listing this fish, although we know that it is more generally spoken of by anglers as jewfish.

An invaluable feature of this revised edition is the index of common and scientific names, which will enable readers to find information on a fish that may be discussed in the text under a name unfamiliar to them.

In addition, fish have been grouped in families instead of being scattered all over the book. Thus striped marlin, blue marlin and black marlin are together under billfish, the soles and flounders are under flatfish, and rainbow and brown trout can be found under "T" for trout. Readers puzzled about the group in which a particular species may be found, can turn to the index to find the page on which it appears.

The confusion over the name of a fish in no way detracts from the pleasure of catching a good one. Anglers reeling in a fish they may call a nigger or a blackfish, never think that what they really have on the line is a luderick. A good fish is a good fish, and more worthy if it fights spiritedly.

There have been big changes in the various State fisheries departments since this book first appeared. The expertise of the scientists involved with our fish fauna has improved dramatically, as have their numbers. Some exciting programmes in fisheries' research are under way, but, more importantly, some very talented young people are now training.

Queensland, South Australia and Tasmania now have splendid books on the fishes of their States and these should be commended to all sports fishermen. Victoria has a book on inland fishing, but so far Western Australia and New South Wales have not published books to complete the set. The success of the State handbooks so far published indicates a sad gap that anglers would like to see filled.

All the people who have contributed to this edition of the book are regarded as authorities in their fields. Their work has combined to present the most comprehensive guide to successful fishing so far published in Australia. The methods they advocate will help novices and veterans alike.

JACK POLLARD
Sydney 1986

A

ABALONE

An edible mollusc; a gastropod of the genus *Haliotis*, with a single, ear-shaped shell lined with mother of pearl. The abalone thickly inhabits rocky foreshores along the Australian coast from Newcastle to Western Australia. It clings to rocks, seaweed beds and suchlike in very shallow waters and to reefs in deeper waters close to shore but avoids sandy surfaces, which do not permit a secure suction grip.

Abalone found in shallow waters average 10 to 12.5 cm in size but those inhabiting greater depths grow to 17.5 to 20 cm. The mollusc is considered a great delicacy, particularly in Asiatic countries, to which Australia exports it in large quantities. Because it usually does not appear above the low tidal level abalone hunting is the exclusive preserve of skindivers, but it remains a community resource, which some State governments allow to be freely exploited. New South Wales authorities have suggested a $10,000 licence fee for lucrative abalone leases, but Tasmania gives them away free, including one to an enterprise which makes $400,000 a year. Amateur anglers in N.S.W. have a bag limit of 15 abalone per day; Victorians 10 per day.

It is not difficult to obtain with deft handling of a tool called an abiron, similar in design and size to a paint scraper. The hunter dislodges the abalone by sliding the abiron between its body and the surface to which it clings. This must be done quickly and surely because, if alerted to approaching danger, the abalone so increases its suction that it is almost impossible to move. Though the abalone is still abundant, professional skindivers seeking it for export and local markets are reported to be thinning out the species throughout its habitat. It costs $40,000 to set up as an abalone hunter with boat, gear, trailer and so on, and most average $20,000 a year in earnings—not enough considering the long-term damage to hearing, bone disorders, and the now proven brain damage that can result.

Professionals prefer the deeper waters as their hunting grounds because this is where the biggest specimens are found. Usually they hunt in pairs using a hooker, a device

A ■ ABORIGINAL fishing methods

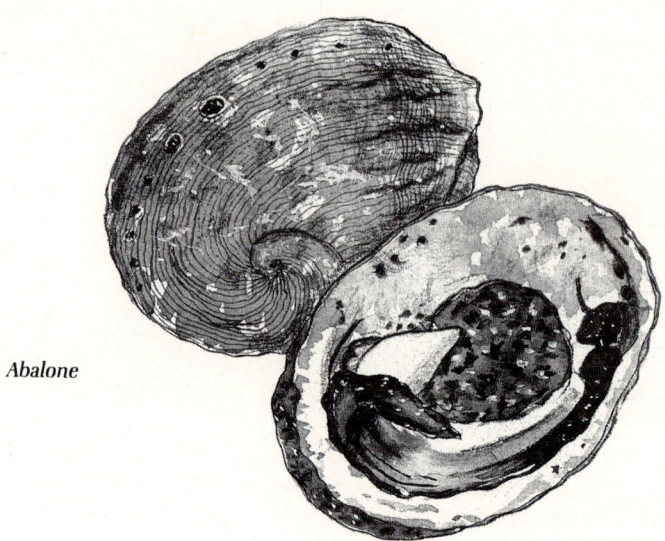

Abalone

which pumps air to them through individual pipelines, on the same principle as that used to supply air to deep sea divers. As each man fills his bag with abalone he releases a small parachute to carry it to the surface where a colleague, operating the air pump in a boat, unloads it. The diver then hauls down the bag by means of an attached line and proceeds to fill it again. Thus, with an adequate air supply and a means of continually delivering the catch, the divers can remain underwater for long periods.

The abalone cannot be eaten raw but it may be cooked in a variety of ways. The simplest method is to remove the flesh with a sharp knife, trim off the black edges, slice it horizontally to make two pancake portions, wrap it in cloth and pound it with a mallet and then fry it in butter for about 30 seconds. A Chinese method for removing the black coating is to put the abalone (free of shell and stomach) into a dish and sprinkle each layer generously with salt. Leave refrigerated for 24 hours and then scrub with a coarse brush under cold running water until the black is rubbed off.

See Cookery.

ABORIGINAL fishing methods These varied from the simple expedient of wading into the water and catching fish by hand to conventional hooking, netting or spearing, or the building of elaborate traps or the use of plant poisons. The methods used often displayed great understanding of natural resources and of the habits of fish. Those Aborigines who lived mainly on fish were described as being of better physique than the inland tribes who were confined to eating the animals and plants of the drier areas.

ABORIGINAL fishing methods ■ A

Hooks and lures

One of the crudest methods of angling was to transfix an earthworm on a piece of fine cane attached to string. This method was widely used for catching eels, which fix their teeth firmly enough in their prey to be jerked ashore by a pull on the string. A lure for catching small fish was made from the web of a large bush spider dipped in the dead spider's abdomen to make it more sticky. The lure was then capable of holding any small fish that bit at it. Hooks were made of shell, bone or hardwood, often jointed with resin to obtain a barbed effect but sometimes merely pointed at both ends. Fishing with these hooks and lines was usually done from canoes, being regarded as women's work by the tribes of south-eastern Australia. After the arrival of white men, hooks were often beaten out of nails or wire. Prawns or shellfish, often well chewed beforehand, were used as bait. Hooks were sometimes rubbed with corpse fat or sweat from the armpit as a magic to make them more effective. The people of Cape York and the Torres Strait islands practise a remarkable method of fishing using a sucker-fish *Echeneis*. The sucker disc at the top of this fish's head can be detached easily by the fish itself swimming forwards but grips so tightly that the body will tear apart before the fish can be removed backwards. The suckerfish is commonly used to catch turtles. The fish is released with a line fastened around its tail in an area where turtles have been sighted. The feel of the line indicates when the fish has fastened on its quarry. One of the fishermen may then dive into the water and secure a stronger line to the turtle or else it may be harpooned from the canoe.

Aboriginal women holding turtles and snakes caught with their bare hands in a lily-filled lagoon.

A ABORIGINAL fishing methods

Spears and harpoons
Fish were speared from rocks or in the shallow water of rivers and lagoons. In some cases the men dived in and speared the fish underwater. A shorter form of spear was used for this skin-diving which was popular in the Murray River area and on the Queensland coast. The spears or harpoons varied according to locality from a simple timber lance sharpened to a fire-hardened point, to a many-pronged or barbed harpoon some 3 to 4.5 m in length. Suitably shaped fragments of stone, bone or hardwood were used as points or barbs, mounted and secured to the shafts with gum and sinew bindings. Fishing spears were made with up to six prongs of hardwood held in place by similar means. A popular type of spear in Victoria and New South Wales consisted of a long reed fitted with a sharp bone or wood point. Fish-spearing was often carried out at night by the light of torches or of a fire lit on the riverbank. Torches were made of bundles of sticks tied together and the men would wade into the water, with a torch in one hand and a spear in the other.

Nets and baskets
Among the many uses of the Aboriginal woman's dilly-bag was that of a fishing-net by which small fish were scooped from streams. Skilfully-made woven nets were commonly used for catching larger species. These nets were made of bark, roots or other plant fibre, chewed and split into threads with the finger-nails, then spun into twine by rubbing the threads against the thigh. This twine was then tied into nets by means of a stitch similar to that of European net-makers although made in a different way. The nets were made in many different shapes as dip nets or two-winged types, drum nets or large hauling nets like those known to European fishermen as seine nets. Queensland Aborigines used hollow logs to trap crayfish and eels. A sophistication of this method was the weaving of basket-traps from strands of lawyer cane.

Dams and fish-traps
A tribe would combine to drive fish into shallow water for capture both in waterholes and on the seashore. A variation of this method had the women rolling bundles of dry grass or leafy boughs to drive the fish before them. Complete dams were built across rivers in order to trap fish in times of floods. The fence of brushwood or tea-tree was supported by a strong log construction of posts and rails with an opening on either hand in which nets were secured. These devices were the beginnings of the permanent fish trap, an example of which remains at Brewarrina, on the Barwon, in western New South Wales. It is a dam consisting of a series of convoluted stone walls forming a maze of pools and narrow passages.

Natural poisons
Stirring up the mud at the bottom of a water-hole and spearing, clubbing or netting the fish that rose to clearer water

was another ancient ploy. From this it was only one more cunning step to using bark, leaves, roots or seeds from a score of different plants and trees to poison the water and stupefy the fish. The species employed depended on locality. *Barringtonia asiatica*, for example, is a tree growing conveniently to hand on Australia's tropic beaches. More deadly, however, were the roots of the *Derris* species of which one part in a thousand parts of water is sufficient to kill fish. For this reason *Derris trifoliolata* is known colloquially in New Guinea as dynamite plant. Other trees and bushes used included the *Tephrosia purpurea* of New South Wales and South Australia, the *Planchonia careya* or cocky apple and various acacias and eucalypts. Branches of the small tree *Duboisia myoporoides*, a relative of the pituri tree widely distributed over eastern Australia, were thrown into pools in order to catch eels. The usual method of applying the poison was to take the leaves, stems, roots or seeds of the plants and pound them to fragments. These fragments were either scattered broadcast in the water or placed in small nets and swirled about in the same manner as teabags. The poisonous juices, while killing the fish, did not affect their wholesomeness as food.

Traditional Aboriginal spears are often a simple lance made from gum wood or a reed with a sharpened piece of stone, bone or hardwood attached by sinew bindings to form the striking tip.

ALBACORE See Tunas.

AMBERJACK *Seriola dumerilii:* Sometimes classified as *Seriola purpurascens* or commonly called yellow banded amberjack. A close relative of the yellowtail kingfish and generally confused with it by anglers and commercial fishermen.

It does not venture into the southern temperate waters to the same extent as the kingfish and is found mainly on the east coast of Queensland, where it appears to be in greatest numbers south of the Tropic of Capricorn. Apparently there is good reason to assume that it is also found on the west coast of Western Australia, for anglers' descriptions of big fish taken there fit this species rather than the samson, which they were supposed to be. Amberjack grow to 35 kg.

It is difficult to distinguish the amberjack from the yellowfin kingfish until the two are put side by side for comparison. The amberjack is purplish-brown on the upper body and the kingfish purplish-blue with a green tinge on the head. The broad lateral stripe along the side is a dull, dirty-yellow whereas on the kingfish it is bright yellow. The belly is creamy-white whereas on the kingfish it is silvery-white. On the amberjack the fins are olive-blue to dark blue, the anal fin is edged with white and the tail fin shows some yellow tones. On the kingfish the pectoral and dorsal fins are bluish-grey and the others, particularly the tail fin, are yellow. The first dorsal fin on the amberjack is decidedly higher, and the ventral fins slightly longer than those of the kingfish.

Like the kingfish, the amberjack is taken both on the surface and at the bottom around the offshore reefs. It does not grow to the same maximum size but is credited with reaching 1.5 m and 35 kg. It is fished for in the same manner as the kingfish and has a similar reputation as a fast and stubborn fighter and may as a last resort take to the kelp or coral at the bottom. Although it is sold in southern Queensland as 'samson', it is not highly rated as a fish food, the larger specimens becoming hard and dry.

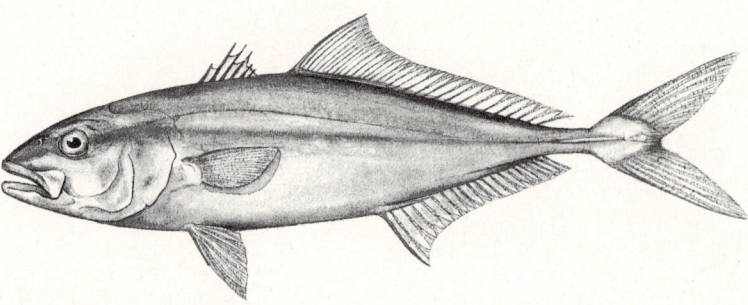

Amberjack

ANATOMY of fish

All fish are vertebrates, possessing some kind of backbone. This backbone is known as the notochord and in primitive fish it is not bone at all but a tube of gristle. In the teleost, this tube is calcified and broken up into a series of cylindrical segments upon which the skull, ribs, spines and other body bones are anchored.

The formation and shape of these bones depends on the action of the muscles, which are divided along the body into interconnected segments called myotomes. It is these muscles which deposit dissolved calcium in such a manner as to strengthen and confirm the shape of the fish without restricting its movements.

The manner in which the bony skeleton has evolved is seen in the development of young fish. At the larval stage, the fish is merely muscular tissue. For bone to develop, it is necessary for the larvae to be swimming freely in the water.

GENERAL EXTERNAL FEATURES OF A BONY FISH

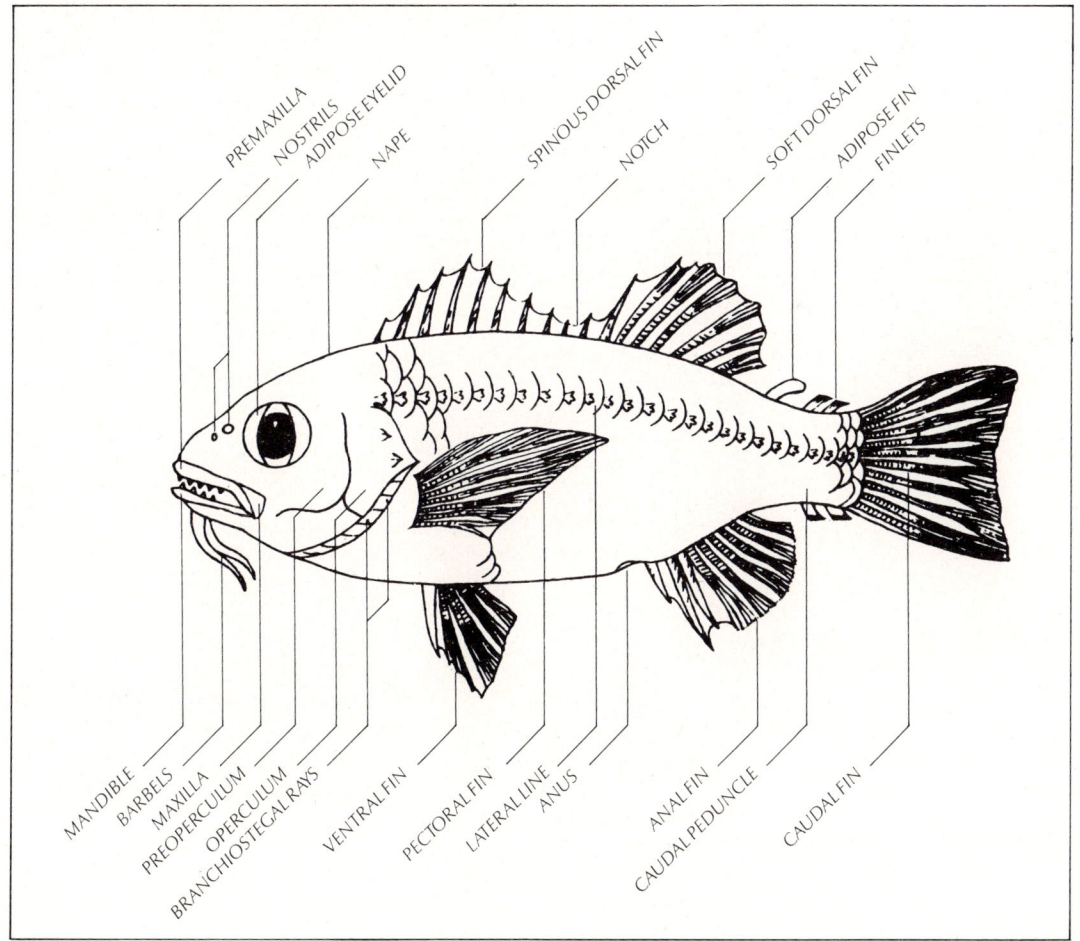

The strength of bone produced varies with species. Herrings and pilchards for instance have flexible bones that cannot restrict the movements of the fish while at the other end of the scale, in fish such as the perch, the bones become rigid enough to control the working of the muscles.

Water pressure is one of the main factors in deciding the shape of the head as well as the body. Fish of the deep sea have their skull almost completely flattened, while the heads of the swift swimmers of the surface waters are streamlined to a point. Other factors in shaping the head are balance, which causes the skull to be bent downwards on the vertebrae, as in the john dory, and the size and working of the mouth.

Tools for swimming
Fins are swimming tools created from skin and muscle by the body of the young fish beating against the water. Larvae of some species of bony fish develop a fold of skin around the vertical margin of the body. Muscle cells collect in this area and grow into rods of cartilage called radials which support the fin and upon which the fin rays develop.

The distribution and size of the fins is conditioned by body movement, the fin rays failing to grow well when movement is rapid while the radials are pressed out beyond the margin of the body. This development is seen in the fins of sharks and the tails of eels. Fin-rays of swift swimming fish such as salmon and herring are shorter than those of slower moving species in which some of the rays may be converted into spines of bone.

Distribution and positioning of the fins is also decided by muscular movement. Fish that wriggle or swim with gentle wavy motions like the flatfish have almost continuous fins around the body margin. In other fish these fins are restricted by areas of strong muscular action to the dorsal fin on the back of the fish and the anal fin of the underbelly. In many species a small adipose fin occurs behind the dorsal, which is itself often split in two.

As well as these vertical fins, the majority of fish—but not all—grow two sets of paired fins, the pectorals and ventrals. The pectorals, as their name (the Latin word for breast) implies, are usually above and ahead of the ventrals, situated behind the gills, one on either side of the body. The ventrals are generally set close together in front of the vent. These fins, like the dorsals and anals, include sharp spines as well as soft rays, in some species.

The spines are for use as weapons but the fins are mainly designed for propulsion, direction and balance. Propulsion is usually the business of the muscular tail, or caudal fin; other fins are also used by some fish. Sea horses, for instance, progress by rapid movements of the dorsals and pectorals. Other species flap their dorsal and anal fins, while skates and rays wing their way through the seas on enlarged pectorals.

Walking fish make use of pectorals and ventrals as well as their tails.

The shape of the tail fin is a major factor in balance. Because they have no buoyant swim bladder, sharks develop what are called asymmetrical or heterocercal caudal fins. To counteract the weight of the head, the notochord extends to the tip of the tail, the fin lobe forming entirely beneath it. The pectoral fins are set low so that the combined effect is to lift the shark.

The swim bladder is a gas bag of membrane situated at the centre of gravity of the fish. A delicate mechanism of the inner ear controls the volume of air in the bladder according to the depth at which the fish are swimming. Consequently the weight of the fish is automatically cancelled out by the buoyancy of the swim bladder and it floats. Not so the shark, which must keep moving or else it will sink.

All the bony fish possess—or have possessed—swim bladders and therefore their fin mechanism is quite different. The caudal fin is split into more or less equal lobes at the end of the vertebrae in the type of tail described as homocercal. As the pectoral fins are not needed to keep the head up, they can be set higher on the sides of the fish for use as brakes or paddles.

However, the shape of the symmetrical homocercal tail fins vary greatly in area, width and degree of fork. Widely forked or lunate tails, such as those of the swordfish, tuna or wahoo indicate the fast distance swimmer. Fan-shaped tails, like that of the barracuda, mark the sprinters for they give greater initial speed while creating more drag.

The number of soft rays and hard spines, given in Arabic and Roman numerals respectively, in each of the fins is part of experts' formulae for describing individual species.

Scales tell age
Generally fish are covered with slime, skin and scales. However, the scales are not all the same nor do all fish possess them. The slime is produced from mucous glands in the epidermis or thin layer of outer skin covering the scales. Its purpose is to protect the fish against fungi and other parasites.

In many fish, these mucous glands are seen as a lateral line running midway along both sides of the body. Here the glands are developed as sense organs acting as delicate pressure gauges to warn the fish of depths, currents and other changes in the water.

The scales, also produced by the skin, take a variety of forms—placoid or toothlike, as in sharks, ganoid or platelike, cycloid (smooth and round) or cetenoid (rough). All are composed of bony substance—the placoid scales growing rather like teeth—and are translucent or glassy.

Scales grow with the fish and show rings which mark off the year's growth. In this way it is possible to tell the age of the fish and, according to the distance between the rings, whether conditions were good or bad for growth. The ear-stones or otoliths give similar indications.

Scales assist in giving a silvery appearance by reflecting light, although the white or silver appearance of a fish's belly is mainly due to particles of a substance called guanin deposited in the skin. These particles are known as iridocytes because of their glitter.

Experts describe fish by counting the scales along the lateral line and down the transverse line from the start of the dorsal fin to the centre of the belly. On fish like the herring which show no lateral line, the count is made between shoulder and tail where the line would otherwise occur.

Messages in colour

The real colouring matter in fish is found as pigment-containing cells or chromatophores in the skin. These cells have the power of concentrating or spreading the pigment—which may be red or black, yellow or blue and blended in various proportions and combinations. This power is controlled by the nervous system so that fish may change their colour for various reasons.

One of these reasons is camouflage. This may take the form of colours which merge into the background or disguise the true shape of the fish or colours that mimic some other fish. Another important use of colour is for recognition either for mating within the species or living as a scavenger or lodger in association with some other species.

Not all camouflage is intentional or voluntary, however. Most surface fish, especially in cooler waters, are dark on the back and pale on the belly where the iridocytes form a dense layer. This is due to the influence of light rays in encouraging the development of pigment cells. In a similar way, the fish of sunlit tropic seas show a wealth of brilliant colour.

The variation in body colouring caused by sunlight has the useful consequence of camouflaging the fish when viewed from either above or below.

Sense and sight

As fish dress in varied colours, it follows that they can see colours. In fact the colour vision of some shallow water species seems to be the most precise and delicate of any living creature judging by the way they can alter their body colouring to match their surroundings.

The fact that trout take artificial flies according to their colour is often quoted, but the colour vision of fish has been scientifically proved by laboratory tests with food of different colours.

That is not to say all fish can see colour for there is great variety in the quality of vision possessed by various species. The eyes of fish differ from those of human beings in having a globular lens of fixed size which is unlikely to give a very sharp or distinct image. In addition most fish cannot focus both eyes on an object at the same time, so that the sense of distance or perspective cannot be very accurate.

Flatfish such as the soles and flounders are a jump ahead in this respect. At the time when the larval fish adopts horizontal life on the sea bottom, one eye moves around—or maybe through—the head to line up with the other. By this means distance vision is greatly improved.

Fish, with a few exceptions, have no eyelids, so they never close their eyes. At intervals they rest motionless in the water in a sort of trance which is the equivalent of human sleep. But they do not sleep soundly and are roused at the slightest disturbance of the water.

The senses of fish are more acute in this respect because the whole skin is pervaded with nerve organs similar to the taste buds of the human mouth. Some of these organs in fish also respond to taste or smell, but those of the lateral line detect vibrations in the water, changes in currents and assist balance.

The brain itself is more simple in fish than in any other creatures with backbones. It is developed mainly in the parts associated with smell, taste, sight, respiration, balance and posture. The cerebellum, which is the part of the brain regulating the two last-named senses, is less well-developed in bottom-living fish. Fish feel pain, but not as acutely as humans.

The brains of sharks and rays appear to be superior to those of most other fish. Sharks are attracted over distances as great as a mile by the smell of blood in the water. Many other fish detect their food by smell although the exercise of this sense varies considerably. Some species also flee from the scent of their enemies and of the fright substance released by the tissues of wounded fish.

Can fish hear and talk?
Fish have no outer ears but the enclosed organs situated on either side of the head behind the eyes respond to sound waves in the water. These vary from the primitive ears of the hagfish and lampreys to the more complicated mechanism of the teleosts. Experiments have shown that the bony fish respond to sound vibrations between 40 and 15,000 a second, hearing ranges from around 30 to 30,000 vibrations a second.

This capability varies considerably with species owing to the variations in ear mechanism, the fish who hear best being those whose ears are coupled to their swim bladder.

It therefore follows that those fish which make noises are heard by their fellows. The many Australian species of grunters make the noise from which they are named by vibrating the swim bladder. Some fish, like the old wife, grumble when disturbed, others squeak or make drumming sounds. The mouth, gill-covers and spines are used for this purpose as well as the swim bladder.

In some species the making of noises is connected with courtship and the breeding season, the male and female holding a kind of conversation. Noises are also used to frighten enemies and attract friends. River catfish in muddy water are believed to communicate in this way.

The fish's body at work
Fish feed on almost anything and everything in the sea—plankton, seaweed, molluscs, crustaceans and other fish, either as eggs, larvae or adult. As a result great diversity is seen in their teeth, which may be large and dagger-like, flattened for crushing, or like combs and bristles. Teeth occur on the tongue and in the throat as well as the jaws.

Few fish chew their food and some swallow it alive. Some chase their prey, others lie in wait and trap it. One very peculiar species of deep-sea fish extends its stomach outside its body to take in creatures far larger than itself.

Digestion takes place in the stomach and intestines, which are longer in weedeaters and mudsifters than flesheaters. The speed of digestion varies considerably, some fish taking long rests between meals.

Insects form a great part of the diet of freshwater fish, either immature wrigglers in the water or windblown adults on the surface. But the archer fish of northern Australia carries its hunting a stage further by expertly shooting down flies with a jet of water, at distances of up to 1.5 m.

Fish are said to be cold-blooded because the temperature of their blood fluctuates according to their surroundings. Consequently fish in general can cope with extremes of heat and cold, although a number of species are adapted to life in specific conditions, such as freshwater or tropical marine fish.

With a few exceptions, the blood of fish is red and contains haemoglobin. Water drawn in at the mouth is forced out over the gill filaments so that the dissolved oxygen can be absorbed by the haemoglobin through the thin tissue of the gills.

The blood circulates forwards ventrally and backwards dorsally through a network of veins. It carries oxygen from the gills to the body tissues and returns waste carbon dioxide to the gills. It also conveys nutrients from the intestine to the liver, although the circulatory system varies a good deal in different species.

Considerable variation also exists in the construction of the heart, although the general principles of operation are similar. Blood is pumped by the muscular ventricle through the ventral aorta to the gills. Valves which vary in number according to species, control the direction of flow. Oxygenated blood from the gills is distributed through the dorsal aorta, eventually returning to the ventricle by way of the posterior chamber of the heart, the sinus venosus.

However, red blood only amounts to about two per cent of the body weight. Many important circulatory functions in feeding and cleansing the body are carried out by the lymph, a watery liquid which substitutes for red blood in many larval fish.

The lymph also provides a second means of respiration for those species which gulp air into the swim bladder. Other fish manage to breathe atmospheric air by modifications of the gills.

The main function of the kidneys is to regulate the salt solutions of the body. In freshwater fish the problem is to retain salts and get rid of excess water, while in sea fish the problem is reversed, the body fluids being less salt than the sea. Excess salt is shed by means of special cells on the gills. Sharks and rays do not have this problem, their body tissues being saltier than the sea.

Growth, reproduction and other factors are controlled by hormone-producing endocrine glands as in the higher animals. Some species of marine fish are unique in possessing light-producing organs known as photophores. The light is produced either by the action of the substances luciferin and luciferase in special glands or by a culture of luminous bacteria.

Some of the rays, such as the numbfish of Australia, eels and catfish carry electricity-producing organs called electroplaxes on the head or body. Many other fish contain poisons either in the spines or body tissues, some of which are deadly to man.

Reproduction

Fish employ two methods of reproduction, the laying and fertilizing of eggs or the live birth of young following fertilization of the female through bodily contact with the male. The great majority of the teleosts are egg layers although in certain species the anal fin has evolved into a male sexual organ.

In general, fish eggs are fertilized after being laid by the female, either as pelagic eggs left floating in the currents or demersal eggs stuck to the sea floor. In most species this spawning takes place at fixed seasons and in fixed places, once a year in the cooler waters but often twice in the tropics. Spawning causes some species to undertake extensive migrations from the rivers to the sea or from the sea to the rivers in search of conditions chosen by instinct.

Once the eggs are fertilized some species pay no more attention to them. In others, the males—almost always the males—carefully choose the site for a nest built from weed or stones. They then guard both nest and eggs against intruders. In a few species parental care is taken to the extent of carrying the eggs in the mouth for safety, while the male pipefish and sea horses tuck the eggs in a pouch on their bodies until they hatch.

Size of families and parental care show a direct relationship. Fish that pay little attention to their offspring usually produce a large number of eggs, often in the order of millions, compared to the few hundred produced by careful parents and even smaller numbers of those whose young are born alive.

Some species lay eggs in strings or masses of mucus, sometimes floating on the surface or attached to water plants. The eggs of the Queensland lungfish are like those of frogs and the larva has similarity in appearance to a tadpole. In the tadpole, however, the back legs are the first to appear whereas the young lungfish develops its pectoral fins first.

In many species, the larvae or young fish look very different from their parents. Young eels, for instance, called *Leptocephalus* larvae or glass eels, are transparent blue-eyed creatures only a few inches long.

Most fish display little difference in appearance between the sexes, although some species show colour changes in the breeding season. The ovaries (hard roes) of the females and the testes (soft roes) of the males are paired organs adjoining the kidneys. In some species, ducts from either side unite in a single opening or join with the duct from the kidneys. In other species, the ripening eggs are shed into the abdominal cavity and escape through special pores.

Some of the sea-perches and the lampreys are self-fertilizing. Hermaphrodite individuals of other species sometimes also occur. On the other hand, the most extraordinary difference in the sexes is found in the deep-sea anglerfish of the Pacific and elsewhere.

The male fish has no angling device and is much smaller than the female. He grows special clutching teeth with which to grip her body. The couple is so united that the male shares the female's blood supply and is entirely parasitic on her. The female, in a sense, becomes self-fertilizing, an obvious advantage for breeding in the ocean depths.

Fish grow throughout their lives although the rate of growth slows down with age. The largest known fish is the whale shark *Rhincodon typus* which commonly grows more than 15 m in length. The smallest is a freshwater goby of the Philippine Islands, less than 1.2 cm long when fully grown.

See Evolution of fish.

BILL MYATT

ANCHOVY A sub-family of small fish, which in one species or another are found all around the Australian coast. They are gregarious by nature and usually are seen in big shoals, sometimes in tremendous quantities moving closely packed together. Some authorities predict considerable commercial interest in these fish in the future, but at present they are taken only for the manufacture of a small amount of fish paste and as bait, mainly for the barracouta fishermen. Because of the small turnover in this country canned anchovies, used for savouries etc, are still imported.

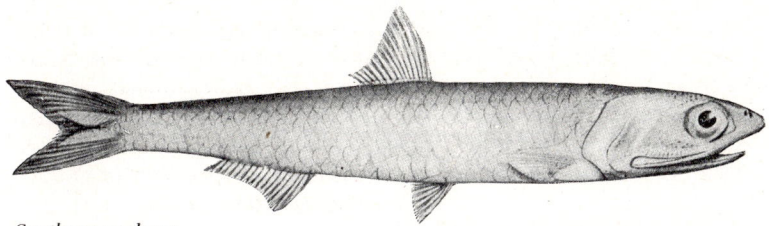

Southern anchovy

Local anchovies have been found to be highly suitable for processing, and some authorities have claimed that they are of better flavour than their European counterparts. Commercial interests obviously may focus on our sub-tropical species, for in winter they shoal off the Queensland and north Australian coasts in great quantities.

Members of this group of fish are often confused with the sprats and pilchards, but the anchovies mostly are semi-transparent or translucent and have a very large gape to their undershot mouths, which extend back to the vicinity of the rear edge of the gill covers, and in one species reaches beyond them. When a shoal of fish is seen feeding voraciously on small fry, anglers mostly assume that they are pursuing whitebait, but examination of regurgitated fish usually reveals that they were feasting on anchovies, sprats, smelts or herrings.

Anchovies abound on the large estuaries, big inlets and other sheltered waters rather than the open sea. They shoal offshore in the winter and with the coming of spring they make their way back into the more spacious inlets to spawn there in the summer. The young fish remain in the upper reaches of the bays until they are about two years old, and are approximately 8 cm long before they begin to move toward the entrance. It is usually only in their third winter, when they are two-and-a-half years old, and up to 11.25 cm long that they venture to sea to shoal. In northern waters they apparently spawn much earlier, and often in the open sea, particularly in the more sheltered waters behind the Great Barrier Reef.

The southern anchovy, *Engraulis australis*, may be found in most of our coastal waters south of the Tropic of Capricorn. It grows to 15 cm but those seen in shoals in the open sea mostly average 7.5 to 10 cm. The smaller specimens are semi-transparent or translucent, with a broad silver stripe along the side. The large fish become greenish-silver to purplish-green on the back and silver on the belly, with the band still visible along each side. Specimens often may be seen trapped in rock pools or stranded on a beach where tailor or other predators had pursued them so closely as to frighten them into leaping ashore.

Not much research has been done on distribution of this species, but it is known to appear in considerable quantities off places such as the far south coast of New South Wales;

Lakes Entrance, Western Port Bay and Port Phillip in Victoria; St Helens and Devonport in Tasmania; in the St Vincent and Spencer Gulfs (particularly off Franklin Harbour) in South Australia and at a number of spots on the Western Australian coast. It is in evidence far up the western coast and doubtless sufficient would be found in all States to make it interesting commercially if markets were available. It is mainly used at present as bait in the tuna fishery.

Relatively small quantities are caught with ring nets and used for bait. These nets form hoops up to 3 m in diameter and are lowered a metre or so into the water. Anchovies, sometimes mixed with pilchards and sprats, are enticed into the net with a berley of bread, pollard or boiled potato. Once there the nets are quickly raised and enclose them. Larger quantities have been taken in beach-sieves of fine mesh, and in improved surface trawls. Commercial fishermen handling them in greater quantities have made big catches by shining powerful lights on the water at night to attract them *en masse* and hold them while a suitable lampa net is run around them.

Marshall lists six species of anchovy from Queensland and north Australian waters. Of these, probably the most common is Hamilton's anchovy, *Thrissa hamiltoni*, which grows to as much as 20 cm. It is found in the estuaries and along the shores in great numbers on most of the Queensland coast. The estuary anchovy, *Thrissina aestuaria*, may be seen on the coast all year round, particularly in the more southerly waters of Queensland. It comes into the rivers in winter and may be seen shoaling around jetties, and is frequently taken in prawn nets. It grows to 20 cm but is mostly seen in much smaller sizes.

De Vis' anchovy, *Stolephorus devisi*, grows to around 12.5 cm and is seen in great numbers in north Australian waters, particularly in the Gulf of Carpentaria. It occurs in somewhat lesser quantities right down the coast to Moreton Bay.

The gulf anchovy, *Stolephorus carpentariae*, which appears to be a much smaller species, up to 5 cm, is present in quantities in the waters of the far north.

The whiskered anchovy, *Thrissa setirostris*, has a long barbel-like ray projecting back on both sides from the rear of its upper jaws. It grows to 20 cm but is comparatively rare.

ANGELFISH   Family Pomacanthidae: Beautiful, short, deep tropical fish of brilliant colouring and designs which, says Whitley, surpass those of birds and butterflies in good looks. They are indeed close allies of the butterfly fish. There are at least a dozen species in Australian tropical waters, the largest reaching 60 cm and all of them varying in colouring and growth. They are very popular in aquariums and have appeared in their glory in dozens of books and magazines illustrating the striking colouring of Barrier Reef fish. Whitley in his book, *Marine Fishes* *of Australia*, tells of one angelfish in Zanzibar that was found to have the markings on its tail corresponding with the Arabic letters for 'There is no God but Allah,' with 'A Warning from Allah' on the other side. The fish, originally worth a penny, brought 5000 rupees.

Centropyge bicolor: Small but very lovely fish of the Queensland coral reefs. Their bodies are divided into two complementary colour patterns. The rear half of the body is vivid black or violet-black and the front half or anterior half of the fish is lemon-yellow or gold. There is a prominent black band above the eyes. They reach 10 to 15 cm. — **Black and gold angelfish**

Pomacanthus imperator: Superb example of the species, of regal colouring, found on the coral reefs of north Queensland, growing to 35 cm. They seldom venture south of the Tropic of Capricorn. They are golden-brown in colour, with numerous narrow yellow or orange bands. These bands run in a vivid series of circles in young fish but as the fish mature they become horizontal and the colouring lightens. — **Emperor angelfish**

Chaetodontophus duboulayi: Seldom found south of the Tropic of Capricorn, these lovely fish grace the waters of north Queensland. The body is a purplish-brown or black with a golden head and body. They grow to 25 cm. — **Scribbled angelfish**

Euxiphipops sexstriatus: A common Barrier Reef variety, with a more sharply defined, less attractive snout than others of the species. They have a broad band of white across the head and are golden-brown or golden-green in colour. The dark bands that give them their name stretch across the body from top to bottom. They grow to 50 cm and are surprisingly good table fish. — **Six-banded angelfish**

Pomacanthus semicirculatus: Another Barrier Reef member of the family, mostly black in colour with vivid transverse white bands, alternately wide then narrow. These bands, very prominent in the young, fade until they disappear as the fish grows. They reach 35 cm. — **Zebra angelfish**

ANGLERFISH

Grotesque, scaleless fish, rasping to touch, with mouths invariably pointing upwards, and so well camouflaged that they can easily remain concealed in weed and rubble. The fish seldom grow longer than 15 cm but have eaten fish within 2.5 cm of their own length. The anglers do this with their own fishing lure—a first spine that has moved forward to the snout to produce a fish's fishing rod. Many of the angler fish caught lack this fishing lure which indicates they do not always outwit the small fish on which they prey.

Shore anglerfish, Atennariidae, hide or walk among rocks

A ■ AQUATIC insects

Tasselled anglerfish

and reeds. They have a fine fishing rod and two separate blunt dorsal spines over the head. Each pectoral fin is complete and they generally harmonize with their surroundings. There are more than 20 kinds of inshore anglerfish in the various States, and they are most prevalent in Western Australia and Queensland. Oceanic anglerfish, Ceratiidae, lack ventral fins. The females have long, slender fishing rods, whereas the males have no lure, are much smaller, and develop clutching 'teeth' outside the teeth of the jaws which are moved by the bone and the muscles that normally would support a dorsal fin ray. They attach themselves to the head or body of the female, eventually becoming a parasite. Australia has two genera, *Ceratias* with a long, slender fishing rod and two dorsal caruncles, and *Cryptopsaras*, with a very short rod and three caruncles and luminous nobs on the caudal rays.

AQUATIC insects Although the great majority of insects are terrestrial, a number are aquatic, occurring almost entirely in freshwater, where they feature largely in the diets of fish. Five insect orders are entirely aquatic and seven others contain families or genera that are primarily aquatic. Insects are distinguished from other aquatic animals by possessing a three-segmented thorax typically bearing three pairs of legs and, in the adult, two pairs of wings. Such features are often recognizable in immature development stages.

All the orders of winged insects pass through development stages which differ in appearance. Many groups have the wings developing externally as pads which increase in size at each moult. In this type of development, called gradual metamorphosis, the young are designated as nymphs. The orders Ephemeroptera, Odonata, Hemiptera and Plecoptera are insects of this type. In other orders the wings develop internally for several stages and are then everted as external pads in the last pre-adult stage. This type of development is known as complete metamorphosis and the early stages without wing pads are termed larvae, with the final pre-adult stage with wing pads, being known as the pupa. The orders Coleoptera, Trichoptera and Diptera are aquatic insects of this type.

Each group of insects is most abundant in certain types of habitat. Dragonflies Odonata, are predominantly stillwater species, although also common in streams. Stoneflies Plecoptera and mayflies Ephemeroptera, are predominantly running water forms. Caddis flies Trichoptera, beetles Coleoptera, bugs Hemiptera, and other groups are abundant in both lakes and streams.

In only the aquatic beetles and bugs are both adults and nymphs or larvae, of some species, adapted for living in the water. In other groups the immature stages live in the water and the adults and sometimes the pupae also, are terrestrial. Certain water bugs such as the 'water-striders' or 'water boatmen' live on the surface of the water and are termed semi-aquatic.

The orders of principal importance to the angler are:

Mayfly

Ephemeroptera: The scientific name of this order is derived from the Greek *ephemeros* meaning lasting only a day, and *pteron* meaning wing. This is an apt derivation, as some adults live for less than a day. Uniquely, among insects, there are two winged stages after the nymph. The first is commonly known to anglers as the 'dun' and the second as the 'spinner'. Mayflies are particularly well known to fly fishermen as hatches often produce spectacular trout 'rises'. Both the dun and spinner are delicate insects with multi-veined translucent, or transparent wings. Both have vestigial mouthparts only, and do not feed.

The nymphal stages are always aquatic and are mainly found in all types of running water. Some species do, however, occur in still water and are common in many shallow Tasmanian lakes renowned for fly fishing. The nymphs can be immediately distinguished from other aquatic insects by the presence of external gills on the abdomen, unpaired rather than paired claws on the tip of each leg and an enlarged thorax. Full grown nymphs rarely exceed 2.5 cm in length.

TWO MAYFLY NYMPHS

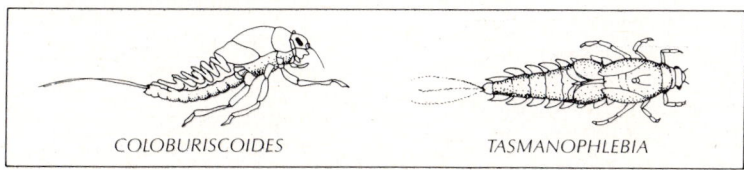

COLOBURISCOIDES   TASMANOPHLEBIA

Some are sedentary but others have very active habits and feature prominently in the diets of trout and native fishes such as Macquarie perch.

Approximately 80 Australian species are known so far but undoubtedly many have yet to be described. Five families are cosmopolitan and occur in all States.

Stonefly Plecoptera: Most adults are sombrely coloured insects that occur on rocks and vegetation bordering upland streams and around lakes with rocky shores. A few are brightly coloured. The adult has characteristic long antennae, wings, which when mature are folded flat on top of the abdomen, and usually two long 'tails' or cerci. They are uncommon and live for a relatively short time. However, the nymphs are frequently recorded and live for many months.

All Australian stonefly nymphs are fully aquatic. They have typically well developed legs, a distinct head and two long cerci (tails) at the posterior end of the abdomen. The older nymphs possess wing-pads. Nymphs are usually to be found in fast-flowing streams and the unsheltered edges of lakes. They can be collected by lifting stones from the bottom and examining the undersurface.

Stoneflies occur only in eastern, south-eastern and south-western Australia, including Tasmania. Four families are represented in Australia and over 60 species have been described. Further species probably await identification.

Dragonfly Odonata: It is difficult to mistake an adult dragonfly for any other insect as their medium to large size, bright colours and their quick darting flight, are very distinctive. The adult typically possesses slender legs, large compound eyes, a long slender body, and narrow wings with a network of many cross-veins.

The larvae of all Australian Odonata are aquatic. There is a series of stages, known as instars, during which the larvae assume the structure of the adult. The larger nymphs are commonly known to the angler as mudeyes. The length of the larval life varies from less than one to perhaps several years. Some Australian species can utilize pools and the like and persist for only a few months, whereas others take at least three years to mature. The final instar leaves the water and crawls a short distance from the edge before giving rise to the adult by splitting the skin and emerging from its larval case. The remnants of the last larval skins can often be seen in hundreds along the edges of lakes and streams.

All the larvae are carnivorous and possess mouthparts capable of being extended very rapidly to grasp their prey. They are not active animals and rely on stealth, rather than speed, when hunting. The majority clamber or crawl among submerged plants or detritus, but some burrow. They occur in all types of fresh water but generally favour sluggish rivers and

DRAGONFLY LARVAE FROM VARIOUS FAMILIES

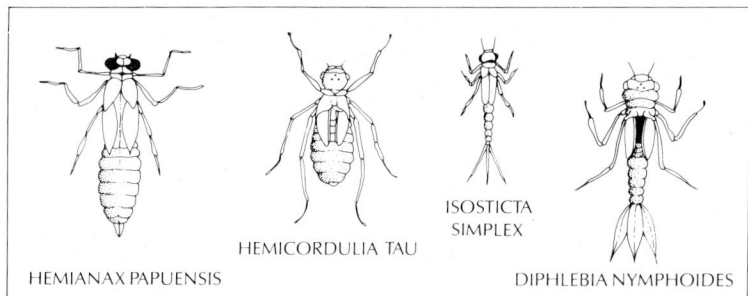

enclosed waters rather than swift-flowing streams, and are major dietary components for many fish species. The vast mudeye population of the new Lake Pedder in Tasmania has resulted in the lake's providing spectacular fly fishing for brown trout.

Australia is extremely rich in Odonatan fauna, having over 250 species, most of which occur in tropical and subtropical climates. The wing span of the adults varies from less than 2.5 cm to slightly over 15 cm.

Trichoptera: Small to medium-sized insects with long antennae and large compound eyes. They are very similar in appearance to small moths, having hairy and scaly wings, and are usually sombrely coloured. The adults are short-lived and are mostly nocturnal in habits, although some species are active during the day. The period November to March is the time when most adults occur. The adults of some species emerge over a limited time and when doing so often cause the good 'rises' so beloved by fly fishermen. Such an example was the famous Shannon Rise in Tasmania, caused by the short period of emergence of huge numbers of *Asmicridea grisea*, the Shannon moth. This species is presently being studied with a view to its establishment in other waters.

The eggs, larvae and pupae of almost all Trichoptera are aquatic. The larvae are the longest lived stage and the pupae have a relatively short life. Many larvae build protective cases out of a wide range of materials such as sand, gravel, twigs, leaves and grass. The cases have a variety of shapes; being square, conical, helical or otherwise. Some larvae can swim with their case but the majority are bottom-dwelling animals.

Caddis fly

CADDIS FLY LARVAL TYPES

A ■ AQUATIC insects

There are two principal types of larvae, one of which has a portable case and occurs in still waters. The other has no case, or possesses a fixed retreat, and is common in running waters.

Larvae occur in fast and slow-flowing streams and in many bodies of still water but are not usually found in very small pools, or polluted water. In many waters trichoptera larvae form important dietary components of fish, frogs, dragonfly nymphs and other aquatic organisms. Many wet fly patterns imitate caddis larvae. The Trichoptera are widespread throughout Australia, with 24 families encompassing 405 species.

Water bug Hemiptera: The majority of hemipterae are terrestrial and comparatively few are wholly, or semi-aquatic. They can be easily recognized by their mouthparts, modified to form a piercing and sucking tube or beak. Some species are minute but others measure up to several centimetres in length. Fifteen families are associated with Australian inland waters and these may be conveniently divided into three groups: shore-living families of only semi-aquatic habit; families restricted to the water surface; and families leading a completely submerged existence. The majority of aquatic hemipterae are carnivorous and feed by sucking body fluids from their prey, while others pierce plant stems.

The family Gerridae contains the 'pond-skaters' or 'water-striders'. They are long-legged, active bugs and frequently occur as small groups which when disturbed will scatter in all directions. Their length does not exceed 1.2 cm. The families Corixidae and Notonectidae contain those bugs commonly referred to as 'water-boatmen'. The bugs in the latter family are also called 'backswimmers' owing to their rapid underwater swimming movements which take place whilst the animal is upside down. Both families feature largely in the diet of fish. The insects are dependent upon atmospheric oxygen for respiration and carry air-reservoirs with them when diving. Once again, they rarely exceed 1.2 cm in length. The majority of species are good fliers.

TYPES OF WATER BUG

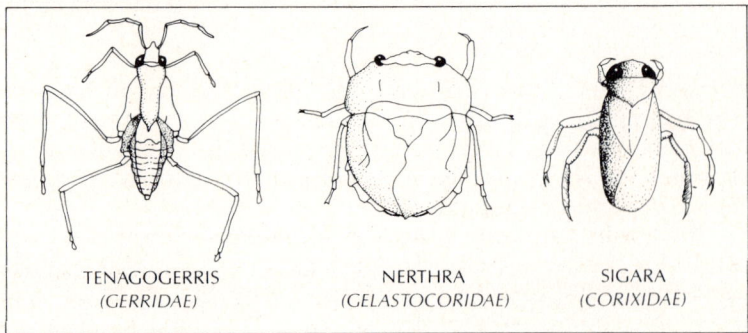

TENAGOGERRIS (GERRIDAE)   NERTHRA (GELASTOCORIDAE)   SIGARA (CORIXIDAE)

The family Nepidae contains those bugs known as 'water-scorpions'. They occur in slow-flowing or still waters and are sluggish animals, but feed voraciously, grasping the prey with their modified forelegs. The family Belostomatidae contains the 'giant water-bugs' some of which exceed 7.5 cm in length. Frogs and fish often form part of their diet. Such insects should be handled with care as their beaks can inflict a painful stab. Other families contain small bugs of little interest to the angler.

Coleoptera: The order Coleoptera is of immense size, encompassing in excess of 150 families. Less than 20 families are associated with inland waters and 14 are represented in Australia. Adult beetles are easily distinguished from the bugs by the structure of their first pair of wings, which are modified to form a protective sheath. When at rest a longitudinal suture or seam is formed. The anterior wings cannot be folded over one another. The mouthparts of adult beetles are modified for biting. In size, adults range from 1 mm to in excess of 2.5 cm, and exhibit various modifications for swimming.

Most adults and larvae rely on atmospheric oxygen for respiration and must continually renew their supplies. Some species possess an air reservoir. Water beetles occur in a wide variety of habitats ranging from fast-flowing mountain streams to still waters. They occur throughout Australia. The families most commonly occurring in the diets of the large freshwater fish are the Gyrinidae, Dysticidae and Hydrophilidae.

Gyrinida, as their name implies, skim rapidly on the surface in a whirling fashion and are commonly known as 'whirligig beetles'. They occur predominantly around the edges of still or slow-flowing waters and are found throughout Australia. They are dark-coloured, smooth, oval-shaped and up to 2.5 cm long.

The Dytiscidae is a large family with over 200 species occuring in Australia. They exhibit a considerable range of coloration and vary in length from less than 6 mm to over 2.5 cm. Their hind legs act as oars and are fringed. They are voracious predators and the adults can ingest solid food. Tadpoles, frogs and fish fry fall prey to larger species. Dytiscida occur in both still or flowing waters and are found throughout Australia.

Diptera: This group can conveniently be referred to as 'two-winged flies' and includes midges and mosquitoes. The majority of Diptera families are terrestrial but there are many families whose immature stages are in part aquatic. Very few adult Diptera are aquatic.

The adults have only a single pair of wings, compound eyes, and mouthparts usually modified as a piercing and sucking structure. The larvae are typically worm-like and are very common components of the fish diet. The majority of larvae

Water beetle

LARVAL WATER BEETLES

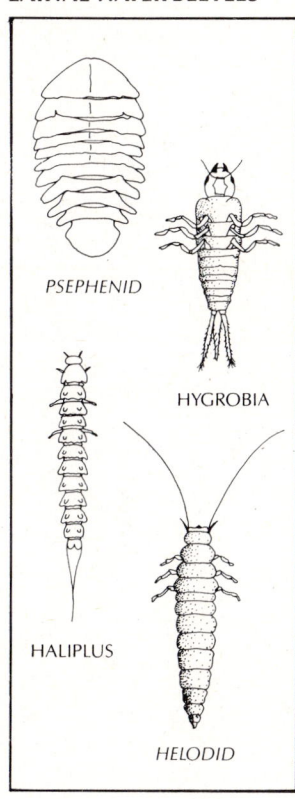

Midge, mosquito

A ■ AQUATIC insects

DIPTERAN LARVAE

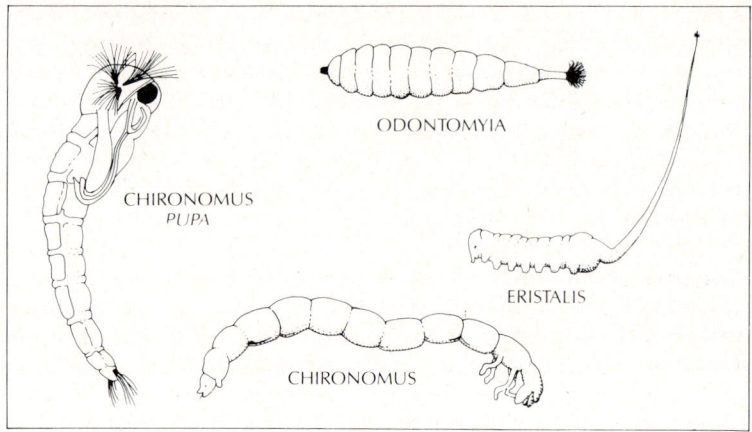

are dependent upon atmospheric oxygen, but some can utilize dissolved oxygen and thus remain submerged indefinitely. The families of most importance to anglers are the Tipulidae, Culicidae and Chironomidae.

Tipulida are commonly known as 'crane flies' or 'daddy long legs'. There are a great number of Australian species, comparatively few of which spend part of their life cycles in water. The length of aquatic larvae may reach 5 cm and both they and the adults frequently comprise food for fish.

Adults of the family Culicidae are known as mosquitoes and as such have probably caught the attention of more Australian anglers than any other insect. The larvae and pupae are extremely common in most inland waters. The majority of larvae are pelagic, floating just beneath the surface, but some are bottom-dwellers. Both larvae and pupae are relatively small and as such do not frequently occur in the diet of large fish. Nevertheless they comprise one of the most important foods to the juveniles of the majority of Australian inland fish. Many larvae are dependent upon atmospheric oxygen and thus remain just below the surface. When disturbed they characteristically move quickly to the bottom, a habit which has earned them the common name 'wrigglers'. The pupae are also active but persist for a relatively short time.

Chironomida adults are usually known as 'gnats' or 'midges'. Their larvae are also extremely common and occur in all sorts of waters. Such larvae are distinctly worm-like and are often white, green, yellow or deep red in colour, the latter being commonly known as 'blood-worms'. They are mainly herbivorous and exhibit varying habits. The pupae are similar to those of the mosquitoes but few are active, the majority being fastened to submerged surfaces. The adults are frequently encountered in large numbers near lakes or streams. Little is known of the life-cycle of Australian species.

RICHARD TILZEY

ARCHER fish

Toxotes chatareus also known as the rifle fish and spotty. Anglers have a kindred soul in this alert little huntsman. Although his reputation is built on the habit of shooting down insects with a jet of water that he can propel to a height of 60 to 90 cm, the archer fish is an omnivorous feeder which eats small fish, shrimps, insects which fall into the stream and certain types of berry from overhanging bushes. The waters inhabited by archer fish usually contain larger fish, so it is rarely fished for except in fun. In size, it has never been known to exceed half a kilogram or 30 cm, and its range is strictly tropical—north Queensland to upper Western Australia.

A typical observation of its feeding method under natural conditions was made on the Gregory River in the western Gulf of Carpentaria. A dead log overhanging the stream was festooned with a hatch of small grey bugs each night and at day rifle fish would congregate beneath the log to shoot down the crawling bugs with accuracy, at a range of one metre. The tiny globule of water would spatter the log, and a swift race for the fallen bug would follow. The fish must position its body in order to aim the jet of water along a narrow funnel inside the mouth. Propulsion is achieved by a swift compression of the gill cover. A straight back and upward-sloping mouth assist in feeding on insects. A small quantity of sand or finely-shredded bread thrown on the water usually brings them to the surface.

The river range of rifle fish extends from salt water to hundreds of miles up freshwater rivers, including lagoons and swamps which have access to rivers only during the wet season. They have been popular as aquarium fish in the smaller sizes, and can be conditioned to perform such mini-feats as shooting food from their owner's extended finger. Breeding is thought to be irregular rather than seasonal, as tiny specimens down to 1.5 cm length have been seen as late as November, before wet season rains trigger the breeding of many other tropical species. Temperature tolerance is geared to the tropics, and they will not survive southern winters unless in a heated pool, at about 25 degrees C.

Archer fish

Being active feeders, archer fish are strong and active fighters for their size—stronger, considering their weight than bream or bass. They are mostly caught accidentally by anglers seeking barramundi, mangrove jacks, jungle perch and freshwater grunters, and on the lines used have little chance to show their ability as a game fish. The larger specimens are fair quality table fish but not outstanding.

A second species, *Toxotes jaculator*, is found in Australia only in the far northern waters and is mainly confined to saltwater bays and estuaries. It grows to 25 cm.

Tackle, baits and hooks
Since it feeds in this fashion, the archer fish is easily seen and fished for. It is supremely observant and always curious, and often leaps for a fly or small lure or bait that is swung on a rod just over the water. Rifle fish can be caught, in fact, without getting the bait wet, by holding just about 2.5 cm above the surface. It has proved vulnerable to small surface lures with a strong action and to floating insect baits. A suitable hook is a No. 1 suicide for adults or a No. 4 for smaller fish, with the barb to facilitate release, since few anglers keep these fish for the table.

ARROW worms Small, transparent creatures up to 4 cm in length armed with spiny jaws that are used to spear the smaller organisms on which they feed. They live entirely amongst the plankton of the sea and are unrelated to any other marine creatures. They are placed in an exclusive group known as Chaetognatha and form a considerable part of the diet of many fishes.

ARTIFICIAL reefs With most species of marine fish the greater concentrations are usually found on or in the vicinity of underwater reefs. For instance: off the Sydney metropolitan area, where extensive reefs are particularly scarce, offshore anglers tend to congregate at weekends over the rough bottom off Longreef, the underwater plateau at The Peak or the rock patches away down near Stanwell Park.

Reefs attract more fish and a greater variety of species than sandflats or muddy bottoms, for a number of reasons. They provide shelter from currents and predators, and promote the growth of algae and seaweeds. These induce the production of plankton and minute marine creatures which provide food for crustaceans and small fish. These, in turn, give sustenance to larger fish, which follow the rule of nature in lingering where there is good food and shelter.

Considerable experiment has been carried out overseas, mainly in the U.S.A. and Japan, on improvement of fishing conditions by the construction of artificial reefs. A great deal of data is now available which shows beyond doubt that such work does give a very worthwhile improvement in angling

Lake Burley Griffin, which is open to lure, bait and fly fishing all year round, is popular with junior anglers.

mously in diverting fishing pressure away from fragile mountain streams and other areas more suited to and useful for those truly dedicated to sport fishing.

In the early 1980s local authorities have scaled down stocking of the lake with trout in an attempt to develop larger populations of golden perch and Murray cod and the hope that these native species will breed and develop into a self-sustaining population. This experiment is still in progress, the spin-off for anglers being reasonably large numbers of the native fish available for sport angling. Although the lake is open to lure, bait and fly angling on a year-round basis, it commonly is too turbid for lure and fly fishing except at the Scrivener Dam end and much of the fishing is bait fishing by necessity. Despite this, the area is exceedingly heavily used and is popular as a fun fishery, even though most of the catch consists of European carp during the winter period when the native fish largely become inactive.

Googong Reservoir

Formed in 1977 by placing a dam across the Queanbeyan River a short distance above Queanbeyan, Googong Reservoir and surrounds are managed by the Department of Territories together with fisheries in the A.C.T., but New South Wales angling laws are applied.

Although the reservoir is a terminal storage, meaning that water is taken directly from the lake to the taps of consumers,

A ■ AUSTRALIAN Capital Territory

the water is fully treated, both chemically and physically, immediately after withdrawal and before despatch to town systems. This means that it can be used for angling, provided some firm management guidelines are followed. These are explained in special brochures printed and distributed to anglers by the Department of Territories. Briefly, the reservoir is open to angling only during certain hours, typically 8.00 a.m. to 6.00 p.m. during winter and 7.00 a.m. to 8.00 p.m. during summer. No camping is allowed in the area and health and sanitation regulations are strictly policed. Anglers are expected to take home with them all materials they bring in, and to reinforce both the need for and seriousness of this management, the authority does not provide litter bins.

Lure, fly and bait fishing is allowed all year round. The reservoir contains excellent populations of brown and rainbow trout, with a marked preponderance of the latter, resulting from both natural and stocked supplies. Silver and golden perch, together with Murray cod, have been stocked in recent years and are growing extremely well, despite the fact that the region is considered to be at or above the known altitudinal limit for these species. Small numbers of goldfish also exist in the area but to date there has been no sign of European carp in the reservoir.

All the fish grow quickly and are in excellent health. Rainbows and browns exceeding 4 kg have been taken, although the average size of the fish is considerably less than this and in 1986 appeared to be declining. Silver perch at two to three years of age are mostly around 0.5 to 1 kg. Golden perch show much faster growth and reach greater maximum weight. Those stocked three or four years ago now weigh from 2 to 3.5 kg and some outstanding specimens have been taken on lure, bait and fly. Murray cod are growing at a modest rate, the largest now about 4 to 6 kg after three to four years.

The reservoir is generally clear throughout the year and if it becomes turbid following heavy flooding it clears quickly. Accordingly it is a favoured fishery with locals and is heavily used. Despite this it remains extremely productive and is undoubtedly the premier fishery of the region. It is also a remarkable success story in itself, as it represents the first and possibly the only terminal water storage of this type in Australia to be used for controlled recreational angling. Hopefully it will pave the way for many similar reservoirs throughout Australia to be used in this manner, with appropriate management care and control, and the strong co-operation of regional anglers.

The reservoir is accessible only via two roads: a main access road in the north and London Bridge Road in the south. A water quality protection zone near the dam wall and the offtake tower is closed to angling at all times. Boating is allowed but power boating is prohibited. Electric motors may be used and are extremely popular.

Lake Ginninderra

Approximately similar to Lake Burley Griffin in intent and usage, Lake Ginninderra is only about one-seventh the size. It has a surface area of 105 ha, a shoreline of 9.7 km, an average depth of 4.5 m and a maximum depth of 13 m. It was first filled in 1976 and was formed by damming a small local stream, Ginninderra Creek, in the heart of the Territory's third city, Belconnen. It serves Belconnen residents in exactly the same way that Lake Burley Griffin serves Canberra's visitors and residents, but is somewhat cleaner, less turbid during part of the year, and apparently more suited to the growth of trout and native fish.

Stocking experiments have shown that both brown and rainbow trout grow extremely well in the lake; so too have golden perch and Murray cod. Golden perch stocked between 1980 and 1985 have grown rapidly and numerous specimens exceeding 3 to 4 kg have been taken, the largest recorded to 1985 weighing 6.7 kg. Murray cod stocked during the same period now weigh up to 14 kg and are still growing at a highly satisfying rate.

Lure, fly and bait fishing are allowed, but since again turbidity resulting from local stormwater run-off is a major problem, lure and fly fishing can be practised seriously only intermittently during the year. Despite this the lake is extremely popular as a productive, easily accessible urban fishery and is regarded as a pronounced success. The lake, predictably, contains goldfish and large numbers of European carp but not redfin perch.

Angling regulations

The angling regulations in New South Wales and the A.C.T. are basically similar, the major exception being that an inland angling licence is required in New South Wales but not in the Territory.

In the A.C.T. most streams can be fished only during the open season, from approximately the Saturday nearest to 1 October to the Sunday nearest 1 June, using only flies and lures and only a single rod and line, held in the hand. Exceptions to this are Lake Burley Griffin and Lake Ginninderra, where live bait in addition to flies and lures may be used, and where the waters may be fished all the year round. In addition, the Molonglo River downstream from Coppins Crossing, and the Murrumbidgee River can be fished with lure, flies or bait; a rod and line held in the hand, plus two set lines, may be used.

In Googong Reservoir, New South Wales angling regulations apply, in addition to management controls over access and boating.

Bryan Pratt

B

BAIT Selection of the right bait, skilful arrangement of it on the hook, and wise presentation of it to the fish, remain the most important of all the angling arts. Bait comprises anything that can be placed on a hook to entice fish to bite, but the choices fall into three basic categories; artificial bait, live bait and dead bait. The quality, condition and use of bait is probably the most important single factor in sport fishing success.

All good fishermen give careful consideration to which bait they use and how they present it, emphasizing with every good catch that they are aware of the feeding habits of the fish available.

Most beginners buy their bait from shops and seafood outlets, but as their skill improves more and more accept the challenge of collecting their own. Finally, the skill in gathering the right bait matches that of catching fish, and is just as satisfying. For regular fishermen, the costs of every fishing outing can be sharply cut by collecting bait instead of buying it at the local tackle shop or boat shed.

Fish bait

Most fish are carnivorous and eat a lot of smaller whole fish. Most are also cannibalistic and eagerly finish off the remains of a relative left by predators. Fish baits that can be used to catch other fish are virtually limitless, ranging from tiny yellowtail or cowanyoung to bonito, small luderick, mackerel, mullet, tailor, salmon and tuna. Small bait fish such as pilchards, garfish and anchovy are excellent all-round bait and can be treated in a variety of ways. Pilchards and garfish are best presented on a gang of three or four hooks linked together by passing the point and barb through the eye of the adjoining hooks. This allows the bait to be trolled at low speeds without breaking up and overcomes the tendency of the soft skin to tear. Anchovy are best presented on a two-hook rig or by placing three or four on a hook placed through the eyes. Another successful method is to insert the point of the hook through the anchovy's mouth, feeding up the hook until the anchovy covers the shank and eye of the hook. Anchovies rigged in this way with a running lead above the bait or with a bottom lead are responsible for a lot of big catches of trevally, turrum and samson fish. Cast out with a rod and reel from a beach into a high tide or low tide gutter they yield many good flathead.

Whole garfish on four ganged hooks can be trolled behind a boat, cast from rocks or beach with a bait-spinning rod and threadline reel, and are very effective on sidecast reels. Even marlin have succumbed to the four-hook garfish rig, and excellent bream, flathead, snapper, tailor, mackerel, salmon, tuna, bonito and trevally are regular victims. Pieces of garfish or fish with sections stripped along the body and allowed to flap are equally efficient. For large pilchards three or four 4/0 hooks work well when left to float under a bobby float. Smaller pilchards can be baited on a single hook, with the shank passing through the body and secured by a half hitch around the tail.

Equipment for bait

Good yabby pumps cost little more than $20 and are a sound investment when weighed against the frequent purchase of prawns, anchovy, squid and other bait. Prawn scoops are also inexpensive and very effective in gathering small bait fish such as yellowtail and poddy mullet. Cast nets have proved a good investment for amateur fishermen in Queensland and the Northern Territory, but are illegal in New South Wales. At many fishing hotspots simple spears are now available that will impale octopus and crabs.

Bait buckets that can be worn on a belt or carried in a boat are indispensable, and aerators, battery-operated aids to keeping bait fish alive, are becoming increasingly popular. Fishermen who use live bait regularly usually prefer to use a live bait tank in their boats rather than a bucket, for these tanks can hold up to a hundred bait fish that can be kept alive for a considerable time with submerged pumps.

Squid and cuttlefish

Splendid baits for many species and particularly for bream, tailor, snapper, mulloway and flathead. The ideal form are the baby squid that can be used whole. The larger squid can be cut up and used as strip bait, but it has poor storing qualities unless it is salted. Cuttlefish are big squid-like creatures distinguished from squid by the broad, pithy backbone that often is washed up on our beaches. The cuttlefish makes ideal bait for reef fish. Squid-catching is usually a night-time activity with the squid taken on home-made jigs containing four or five hooks. The squid are attracted from the shadows by the simple method of flashing a light on the hooks. Estuary regulars soon learn that when squid are present there usually are good fish about, too.

Prawns

The most widely used of all baits, relished by most saltwater fish, but almost impossible to keep fresh. They must be snap-frozen while still fresh or they become discoloured and spongy. Dark, tough king prawns are best and if the heads are removed soon after capture they can be readily preserved in bran or bread crumbs. Live prawns can provide deadly bait, so it pays to personally collect them and keep them alive in saltwater or in a bag of damp weed. The prawn looks more natural to fish if the hook is passed through the tip of the tail from above and brought through the butt from beneath so that it lies straight along the shank. Some good fishermen prefer to use the hook like a needle, by threading the line through the thorax and pushing the point of the hook up through the tail from beneath.

Weed and cabbage

Luderick are vegetarians and usually are caught on weed that can be bought at baitshops, but it is best collected fresh. It grows on rocks and timbers. There are two common varieties: the long, stranded, mosslike form that often is described as grass, and the softer form that is akin to lettuce. The trick in baiting hooks with green weed is to drape it over the hook so that in the water it fluffs out but stays on. Use four or five strands a few centimetres long. Hold a couple of centimetres of it along the hook shank, with the hook vertical. Twist the other end around the line three or four times above the eye or flat of the hook and continue twisting it down the shank of the hook to the bend. Finally, nip off the trailing ends after passing them over the point of the hook, leaving a couple of centimetres of weed below the bend.

Beach, blood and sand worms

Beach worms are taken from the sand after it has been washed by the surf, usually with a 'stink' bait of very old fish attached to a stout cord. The worms are detected by the ripples they make in the receding wash. They are caught by coaxing them to raise their heads and bite on the bait and are taken with special pliers or with bare fingers. They should be rolled in dry sand when caught to remove the slime and placed in a tin or bag with cool sand. Blood worms are harder, more brittle wrigglers, brownish-red in colour, and they shed blood if broken. They are collected by digging with a garden spade in the upper reaches of estuary flats. They are seldom more than 12 cm long, but will stay alive for long periods if kept in a cool place. Sand worms, also known as squirt or pump worms, are smaller than beach or blood worms and are found in large numbers in sand-lined burrows in muddy flats. They are thin and delicate, pink to light red in colour, and are first-class bait for whiting. They are usually taken with yabby pumps. They are too small for thick hooks and are not used for bait for any of our larger fish.

METHODS OF BAITING

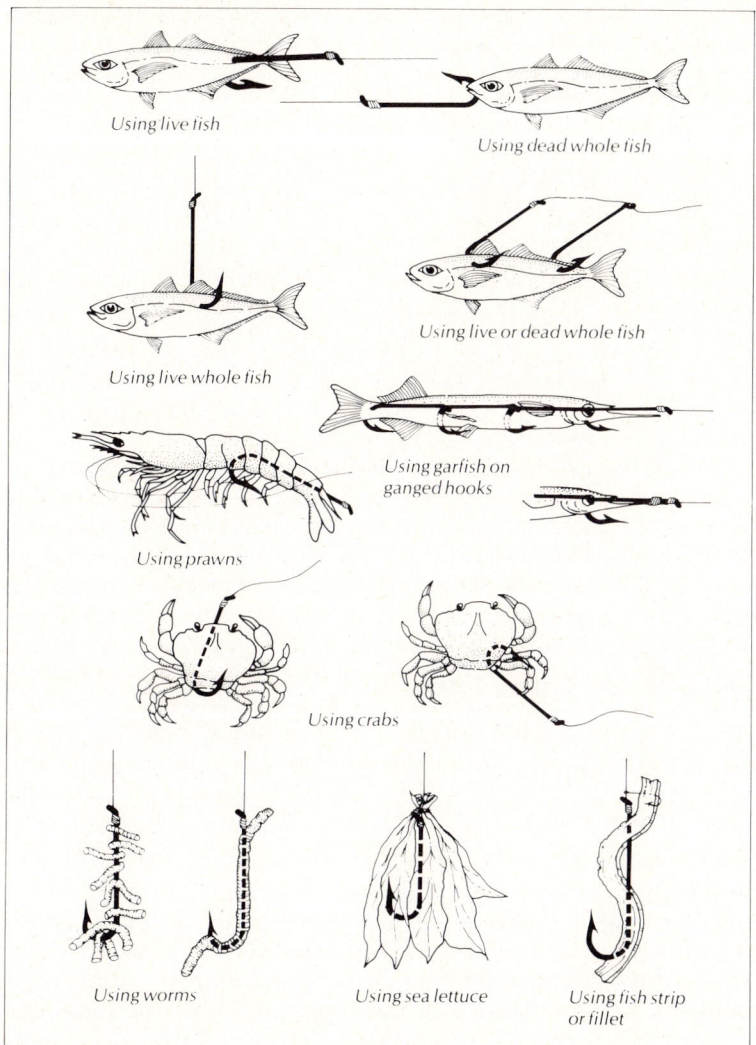

Pipis
Large bivalve molluscs that are found in large quantities in the sand under surf on the larger ocean beaches. They are often exposed by receding waves but can be located by digging in the sand and water until their hard shells are felt. Cracked out of their shells, they make a large bait attractive to whiting, salmon, bream, flathead and dart. They are known in Victoria as cockles and in South Australia as Goolwa cockles. Pipi is the Maori name for them.

Mussels and cockles
The black mussels that cluster around jetty piles are regarded as top quality bream bait. They are black or purple bivalves, a

CUNJEVOI

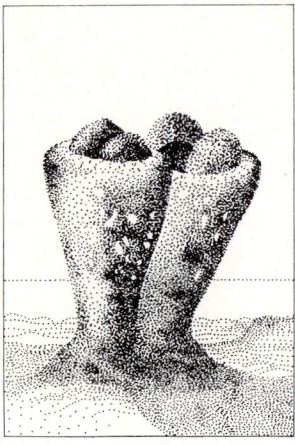

soft bait that can be toughened by pickling in salt and sugar. Another ideal bream bait is the fluted cockle which corresponds closely to the southern pipi.

Cunje and crabs

Cunjevoi is the large, leathery ascidian that grows on ocean rocks between high and low tide levels. Cunje usually squirts water when disturbed and can be torn from the rocks with a cunje hook or tomahawk. It is an excellent bait for rock fishing. When pickers are at work, they usually only leave two tough hooks on a cunje bait. Fishermen use the mouths to provide a good hold for their hooks, passing the hook down through one mouth, with the barb held in the other. Cunje that has been allowed to dry out in the sun is harder to remove from the hook. The Australian coast and the rivers and waterholes of the north are well populated with a variety of crabs that all make good baits. Black crabs are plentiful but they are not as effective as the fleshy green crabs or the big red and brown crabs that live in the crevices of rocks under cunje lower down in the water. Ghost crabs, sand crabs, soldier crabs and hermit crabs all provide excellent bait, particularly if they are found with soft shells after moulting. The flesh of the big mud crab is good bait when carved up but most people find them too appetizing to use as bait.

Freshwater fishing baits

All the main species of Australian freshwater fish relish earthworms, the traditional bait for all inland anglers. The lively red worm found in gardens usually is a better bait than the pale, creamy pink variety. The huge earthworms of black-soil plains areas are far superior to garden wrigglers and most homesteads boast a patch where they can be dug up, usually under the woodheap or down beside a barn. The giant earthworms of the Gippsland Lakes districts of Victoria provide outstanding bait. Among the best places to find good worms for bait are at the water's edge at night when the water level is rising on new lakes and dams.

Witchetty grubs

Experienced inland fishermen use a piece of wire with a corkscrew end to screw down into holes tenanted by witchetty grubs. They are the larvae of big jewel beetles and large moths and occur alongside big rivers, usually close to large gum trees. Witchetty grubs are excellent bait for cod, yellowbelly, catfish and redfin.

Yabbies

Yabbies are freshwater crayfish, frequently confused with saltwater sand shrimps of the same name. They inhabit waterholes, dams and inland bore drains, and are easily taken with a length of prawn netting, or by using a wire-netting yabby rake. They can also be coaxed up with hunks of meat on a string, with the angler slipping a piece of net under them.

They should be kept in a tub containing grass and bushes until used as bait for cod, yellowbelly, redfin and trout.

Wood grubs, mussels and frogs
Split open most riverside logs and stumps and you will find wood grubs, an ideal bait for catfish, cod, yellowbelly, redfin and trout. The big brown mussels that are found in the mud under water in our big rivers are also splendid bait. They can be gathered by simply feeling for them with bare feet and tossing them out on to the bank. There are numerous frogs in inland districts, but the speckled brown one found along the water's edge is the best bait. They can be located under logs or picked up at night in the beam of a good lamp.

Recommended baits are provided in the entries on all popular species. Artificial baits are discussed in the sections on the various forms of fishing or in the entry on tackle.

BAITFISH, Red

Emmelichthys nitidus: Dark red or pink-coloured fish of the open sea which make unpredictable appearances in such huge schools they turn the ocean red. Tunas and barracoutas feed voraciously on them. They are distributed from Western Australia across southern Australia to Tasmania and up the east coast to Queensland, and also turn up in New Zealand. They average between 30 and 40 cm in Australian waters but reach 60 cm overseas. They are also known as picarel, pearl fish and red herring. They have a savoury smell and may be canned or eaten fresh.

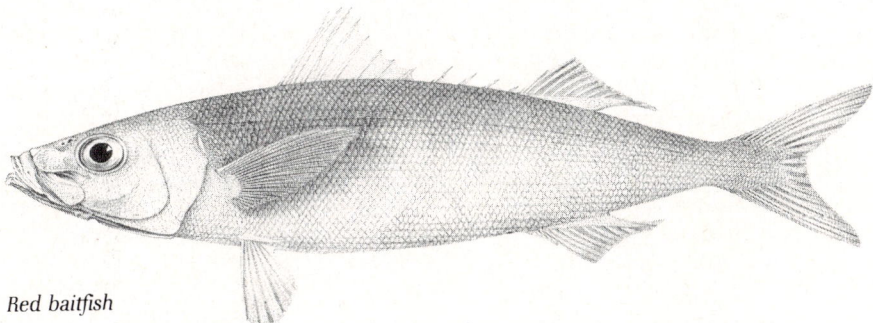

Red baitfish

BALDFISH

Rouleina eucla: Weak, flaccid fish with scales curiously absent from their heads but with scaly bodies. There is no adipose dorsal fin and the fish is heavy with blacks and blues. They have almost no angling value whatsoever and are only found more than 800 m down by deep-sea trawling expeditions. They average about 30 to 40 cm in length. In some baldfish, little luminous organs called photophores stud the sides and shine in the dark.

BANDFISH Family Cepolidae: Narrow fish with dorsal and anal fins running almost the length of their bodies, which frequent deep, temperate coastal waters. They grow to 40 cm and are found in Western Australia, South Australia, New South Wales and Queensland. They are mainly notable for a swimming action in which they adopt an S-shaped position, with the head forward, and for their habit of burrowing into the sand by sucking it up. They come in deep reds and pinks and there are at least two species in Australian waters.

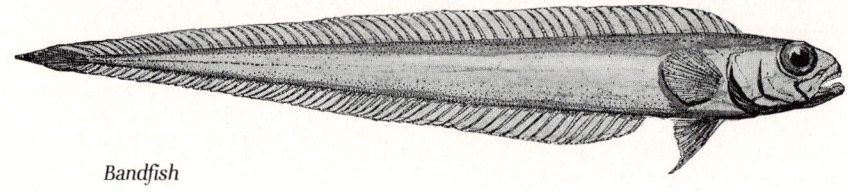

Bandfish

BARRACONDA See Barracouta.

BARRACOUTA *Leionura atun:* A splendid sporting fish which will slash at anything that glitters or jump clear of the water in pursuit of lures trolled behind boats. It is a commercial food fish, in no way related to the barracuda *Agrioposphyraena barracuda* with which it is repeatedly confused. The barracouta is abundant in the southern hemisphere, ranging widely from southern Australia, both islands of New Zealand, where it is particularly plentiful, south of Cook Strait, South Africa, Argentina, Chile and Patagonia. It is not a barracuda, which is called sea pike or dingo fish in Australia, but is related to the great mackerel family and its allies. The nearest relatives in Australian and New Zealand waters are the barraconda, oilfish, frostfish and hairtail. It is known as snoek in South Africa and sierra in South American waters.

Pioneer Australian fishermen considered that in appearance and habits it closely resembled the barracuda of the eastern Atlantic and Mediterranean. They applied the name 'barracouta' to the fish and thus began the confusion which has gone on ever since. Two distinct species are found in Australian and New Zealand waters, the common barracouta *Leionura atun* and the king barracouta or barraconda, *Rexea solandri*. The common barracouta is a pelagic travelling in shoals, and has been known to grow to 135 cm and 5.5 kg but most of those taken average 90 cm and between 1.4 and 2 kg. It has three vicious big teeth under its upper front lip, followed by rows of very sharp, flat cutting teeth in each jaw.

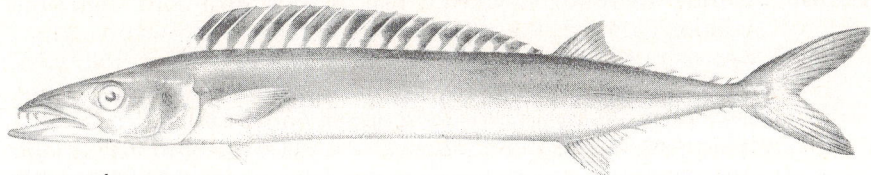

Common barracouta

The common barracouta's main dorsal fin is unusually long and black in colour. It is immediately followed by the second dorsal which balances up with the anal fin, each being followed by five or six detached finlets as seen on the tuna and Spanish mackerel. The tail is deeply forked, and like the pectoral and second dorsal its rear marginal edges are black. Its body is steel-blue to blue-black above, merging to silver on the lower sides and belly. The skin is smooth and covered with small scales, which are easily detached and come off freely on the hands when it is being handled. When freshly caught, the eyes are pale gold.

Although they are basically surface pelagics, the 'coutas' are met in shoals at all depths down to 75 m. Very large shoals of these fish stretching for as far as 30 km have been seen in Bass Strait and around Tasmania when they have been following up and feeding on whitebait or similar small fry.

Small schools have made their way as far north as Moreton Bay in Queensland, but for angling purposes they are at times reasonably plentiful on the New South Wales coast from Eden down to Green Cape and Gabo. Only moderate quantities are taken on the southern and south-eastern coast of Western Australia, and they are only plentiful in the south-eastern waters of South Australia. The main fisheries, which yield such tremendous quantities, are around Tasmania, though there is also a very important 'couta' fishing area on the coast of Victoria where the area of big catches is fairly closely concentrated in that big inlet off Bass Strait that lies between Wilson's Promontory and Cape Otway, off the entrances to Port Phillip and Westernport Bay.

Like other pelagics, such as the tailor and bonito, the barracouta that are caught seem to travel and feed close to the coast. Most are caught within 8 km and very few outside 16 km from the shore. Their food consists mainly of small fish such as whitebait, pilchards, anchovies, sprats, herrings, mackerel, young salmon and even young barracouta. At times they feed very extensively on krill, the prawn-like creatures up to 4 cm long that are found in ocean plankton. These fish are active, savage hunters and are driven on by a voracious appetite. It is not unusual for one to take after a small fish and pursue it for a considerable distance, sometimes shooting out of the water again and again after it as it leaps in terror. On occasions one has been found to be so intent on the chase that it has leapt into a boat after its prey.

B ■ BARRACOUTA

King barracouta

These fish differ in many ways from their more common relative, although there is some superficial resemblance. They are easily distinguished by the deeper and heavier body, the very large eye and the clearly discernible black patch on the forward top corner of the long dorsal fin. They are much more colourful fish. They are iridescent blue on the back and upper body and silver down below. The second dorsal, anal and tail fins are bright orange. They have two large fang-like teeth in the front of their lower jaws, as well as the usual three in the top. There is only one semi-detached finlet behind the second dorsal or anal fins, instead of the five or six clearly detached ones as seen on the more elongated relative. And the king barracouta is rather unusual in that it has two easily discernible lateral lines, the upper one running along high up on the back to end under the second dorsal, and the lower one running from the pectoral fin to the tail.

The king barracouta are fairly plentiful around New Zealand, where they generally are known as the southern kingfish, and occur in somewhat lesser quantities on the coasts of Tasmania and southern New South Wales. They have been known to grow to about 130 cm. According to T. C. Roughley's *Fish and Fisheries of Australia*, up until about 1880 this species was very plentiful on the coasts of Tasmania and the south coast of New South Wales. At one time it was one of the most important food fish from Tasmanian waters and also an important one in the Sydney market, where it was sold as 'hake'. In those days it was not unusual for three or four men, catching fish from 3 to 4 kg, to take over 2.5 tonnes in a night.

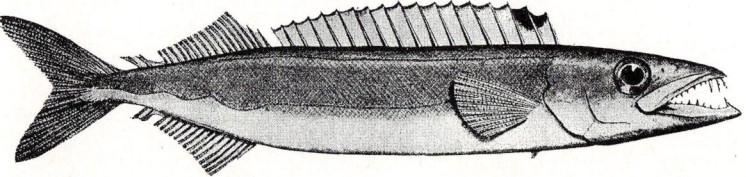

King barracouta

'Couta' lures

In selecting lures it should be borne in mind that the couta's teeth are particularly sharp and strong, so only the most durable of the plastics can be expected to withstand them for a reasonable period of service. When the fish are not biting enthusiastically a small piece of fish strip or a piece of couta gill placed on the hook behind the lure may induce them to strike more readily. In casting from the rocks it is necessary to use the larger and heavier lures to get out far enough to be among the fish. In spinning from a kellicked or drifting boat lighter lures are permissible, for with a little action the fish may be induced to approach quite near to the craft.

Most sportfishing for barracouta is done from boats.

In the old days hooks decorated with red or white cloth, red wool, pork rind, cow hide, shark skin, feathers or white bone were trolled behind the boat. Today more sophisticated tackle is used, metal jigs, plastic jigs, plastic squid and nylon jigs. Some anglers troll with strips of fish or small whole fish on a pair of 8/0 carlisle hooks with the barb of one hooked through the eye of the other. In all couta fishing there is a high loss of tackle and wire traces are essential.

Although most barracouta are caught by trolling well out from the shore, land-based anglers have been becoming more and more interested in recent years. Good catches are occasionally taken from jetties, piers and rocky vantage points. In season, some anglers specialize in spinning for them with surf casting gear and heavy metal lures. Others go after them with lighter threadline reels and plastic wobblers, wrigglers and plugs.

Bait-fishing for 'couta'
For casting with spinning gear from the jetties or rocks it is necessary to use one of the big conical casting floats which have a thin brass tube running through them. This is arranged on a running rig so that when it is cast out the light sinker pulls the bait down about 2 m below it. Bait can consist of a pilchard, herring, small yellowtail, king prawn, squid or a strip of fish such as salmon, bonito, blue mackerel, whiting, mullet or ruff. Bait fishing with a similar rig may be carried out from a boat by casting out or letting the float drift away with the wind or current.

A method of fishing deeper with bait is used with the aid of a heavier sinker and a large strip of bait or a small whole fish. The bait is allowed to sink to the bottom and then retrieved fast by 'jiggling' as employed in fishing for pike. The line is retrieved with one hand and then the other, the arms being thrown out sideways from the body to give the bait a wriggling motion as it comes up through the water.

When they are on the bite, barracouta give plenty of action and a lot of excitement. But always remember that a live specimen can be dangerous to handle, for its teeth can inflict serious damage on the hands or fingers. It is usual to crack each one on the head with a heavy waddy or 'billy' with sufficient force to ensure that it is quite dead before attempting to unhook it.

BARRACUDA

Family Sphyraenidae: Barracuda have featured in adventure stories for so long most people believe them to be vicious predators given to looking for nothing but vulnerable swimmers. In fact, the big sea-pike is predatory to the same extent as many other fish. No attack on a human has ever been recorded in Australian waters, except when the fish was first wounded with a spear gun, and in fact most overseas attacks appear to be a single slice at something like the moving foot of a swimmer. This is possibly a conditioned reflex of the kind which can cause fish to strike an unlikely lure. Whether by accident or design, the attacks can be serious for the victim—barracuda have some of the best teeth in the business and it is on record that they have caused deaths in the Americas and Fiji. Anglers usually treat them with respect, as the fish will often snap suddenly after being landed, a trait of some other species such as tailor, sharks and mangrove jacks.

The barracuda of our semi-tropical waters appear to breed in tidal creeks. At least, that is where large numbers of small fish are found. They can sometimes be caught in schools, one after another, but in general the adults are solitary fish. Anglers mostly take one or two while trying for something else. More rarely, it is possible to see and stalk a barracuda in clear coral waters, and thus watch the inherent savagery of the fish or test its powerful fighting ability on a line.

For male anglers, the biggest barracuda on the Game Fishing Association of Australia's record charts in 1985 was Peter Owen's 30.84 kg catch on a 10 kg line at Cairns in October 1973. But this was surpassed by Anne See Poy's women's record of 32 kg in the same line class at Yammacutta Reef, Innisfail, Queensland, in August 1979.

As table fish, barracuda of north Australia are unpopular in the larger sizes. Many anglers eat the smaller fish of a few kilograms weight but ignore the others, which appear to be likely causes of the food poisoning ailment known as ciguatera. This is mainly a poison of reef fish, and anglers are generally safe in eating barracuda caught in mangrove creeks or over sandflats, but it never is entirely without risk to make a series of meals from the one big fish.

Barracuda habitat
Barracuda go where the food is plentiful and are caught over a more extensive range than is realized. Large solitary fish are sometimes taken on the slopes of the continental shelf, though they are more common over reefs with a substantial fish population. They take almost any kind of moving lure or bait, strike fast, and leap well. The fighting ability of the larger species is on a par with that of Spanish mackerel, and wire is needed as a trace to counteract the large pointed teeth. Although they are clean fighters, in not deliberately running for cover when hooked, they sometimes cut an angler off on rocks or oyster shells when making their first frantic run.

One of the usual methods of taking barracuda is by trolling on light tackle over weedbeds, flats and even in the deeper water. They can be taken in the bays and estuaries around the mouths of creeks, from the shallower waters around ocean headlands and particularly when fishing close to cover for other species. The big fish of the Great Barrier Reef usually are taken by trolling Drone spoons or garfish on heavy lines over or around the coral reefs. Some are caught by reef fishing.

Pick-handle barracuda

Sphyraena jello: Also known as 'jello's barracuda', 'dingo-fish', 'sea-pike' and 'pick-handle'. It is found throughout north Australian and Barrier Reef waters. It has been credited with growing to 2.4 m, though those taken by the mackerel fishermen average about 90 cm, and one exceeding 120 cm would be considered large. It is purplish-brown to greenish-brown on the upper body and silvery below. There are more than a dozen dark stripes on its sides which slant rearwards as they descend below the lateral line, though they may be indistinct in some large specimens.

The pick-handle barracuda can be distinguished from the giant barracuda by its more upright teeth; the lower teeth of the giant barracuda slope backwards. It is not highly rated as a table fish as the flesh is coarse and pulpy.

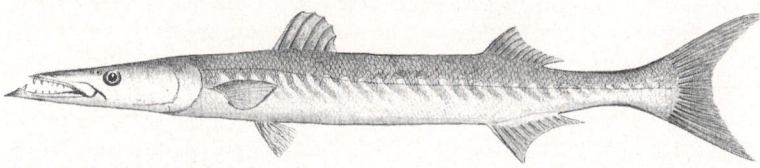

Pick-handle barracuda

Giant barracuda

Agrioposphyraena barracuda: Another big and dangerous predator which is easily confused with the previously described species and is therefore also known under colloquial names such as 'dingo-fish', 'sea-pike' and 'pick-handle'. It has been known to grow to 2.4 m and over 45 kg, but one 1.5 m long is difficult to handle, with its powerful tail, array of awesome teeth and habit of snapping at anything within range as it thrashes about.

It is dull blue-grey on the upper body and silvery below. There are about 18 dark grey cross-bands on the back, which slant forward as they descend to the lateral line. It may be distinguished from the pick-handle barracuda, *S. jello*, on the following points: its larger teeth in the lower jaw are vertical, it has about 18 as against 12 or 14 stripes, its stripes slant forward as they descend and do not extend below the lateral line, and the first two dorsal spines are of equal length whereas in *S. jello* the second spine is longer than the first.

The big barracudas cannot be regarded as good food-fish. Some are highly odorous when caught. Their flesh is coarse and either rank or flavourless. They do not store well and some quickly go pulpy. With large specimens there may be danger of the fish-poisoning known as ciguatera.

Barracuda tackle and techniques

Despite their awesome teeth and powerful muscle, barracuda of average size are not difficult fish to land on light tackle. They can be fished for with a moving bait, linked hooks in a garfish bait suited to tailor being an excellent choice, and a typical outfit would be as follows: The angler's usual boat or

B ■ BARRACUDINA

A wire trace is often needed to counteract the sharp teeth of the barracuda.

casting rod and reel, preferably a rod with a firm action; line of not less than 5.5 kg test, a 30 cm wire trace added; lures such as a feather jig, chrome spoon or plastic wobbler; or baits such as live prawn, fish or garfish on linked 4/0 hooks. Heavier line and big hooks with a short wire trace would be required for the larger species, particularly for the big fish found out around the reefs.

The difficulty with barracuda is turning them on their first, or striking run, especially close to rocks, for they can cut the line on that first lightning burst through the water. However, once the run is over, and the first few leaps are out of the way, the fight quickly subsides to a series of head-thrashing struggles at the surface, and some tired runs which are easily controlled.

See Pike.

BARRACUDINA Small, slender, rare fish of the family Paralepididae, with large eyes and teeth similar to those in the barracuda. Barracudinas are fish for collectors only, although several species have been found in Australia. They are colourless, with dark blotches along the belly, growing to 6 cm. Whitley gives their range as eastern Australia, from the Tasman to the Coral Sea, Indian Ocean and the South Sea Islands, except for the areas

BARRAMUNDI

south of India, where there is a gap in their known distribution. They inhabit the mid-oceans, he says, and have been reported hanging head-downward. They are related to cucumber fish.

Lates calcarifer: Giant perch is one of the greatest sportfish, and to many anglers represents close to an ideal opponent. Originally these fish were numerous throughout tropical Australia, but overfishing and other pressures have reduced them to a stage where they are no longer of major economic importance and the Northern Territory has placed an annual four-month ban from October 1 on commercial fishing for barramundi. The ban also applies to amateurs. Barramundi are inevitably good for debate wherever anglers gather. They are an impulsive and voracious feeder, given to stages of unpredictable behaviour. Quite often they behave predictably, too, so fishermen can easily disagree about them. On several points, however, the verdict is unanimous. They are big, handsome and powerful fighters which usually leap when hooked and which test sporting tackle to the fullest. As the number one food fish in Queensland, they are avidly sought by anglers. More than 2 million tonnes of barramundi were removed from Northern Territory waters before the ban was imposed.

There has never been serious argument about the name of barramundi, although a certain amount of confusion has persisted. In all areas where they are found, they are known as barramundi, so while the scientifically correct 'giant perch' or 'palmer' might still be heard in some quarters, it is never used by anglers at large. On the Dawson River a totally different species is known as a 'Dawson barramundi' or 'spotted barramundi'. This is *Scleropages leichardti*, known throughout tropical Australia as the saratoga (*which see*) or saratoda. It is a relatively primitive species bearing no relationship to barramundi.

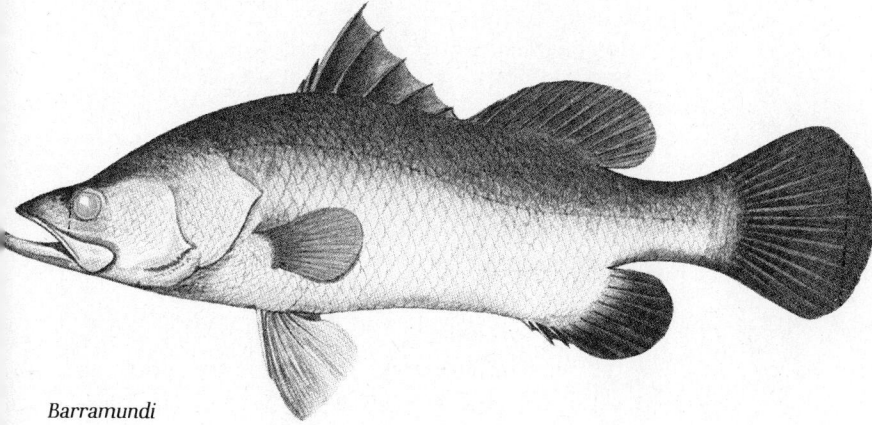

Barramundi

B ■ BARRAMUNDI

The habitat of barramundi corresponds very closely with that of the American snook, and the fish occupies the same ecological niche, a predator in both estuarine and fresh water. Under good conditions the average weight of fish taken by anglers is about 3.5 kg, although this figure has fallen in coastal areas of Queensland. The Game Fishing Association of Australia recognizes the 16.8 kg barramundi caught by Len Evans at Peron Island, Northern Territory, in May 1982 as the record for the 6 kg class.

It is difficult to define the exact stage of scarcity of barramundi in a meaningful way for visitors. In certain sections of Cape York and the Northern Territory the barramundi is in danger, but in the populated coastal areas of Queensland it could be said that an angler with barramundi experience should be able to locate at least one barramundi during a day's fishing. This could be compared with catches of bass or trout anglers who should find a good many more fish in the same length of time.

Causes of barramundi decline

These are well established and authenticated by research. They include the usual processes of pollution, siltation and overfishing. A primary reason is the biology of the fish itself, which makes it vulnerable to the factors listed. Barramundi breed by travelling to river mouths each wet season, normally starting about late November. Fish travel downstream to breed, and the heaviest netting and fishing takes place during this breeding movement. The theory is simple: when it rains, place nets across the rivers and catch the fish as they travel down to breed. Coincident with the breeding, the end-of-year flushing of sugar mill effluents, with a nil oxygen content, kills large numbers of fish, including other species.

The picture is not completely black. Progressive sugar mill managements, aware of the high mortality, are moving to block off effluent chemicals from the rivers. Two schools of thought on the future of barramundi are evident. One takes the line that the species has been reduced so drastically in numbers that it is not important any longer as a commercial species; the other argues that the fish could be rehabilitated by control of sugar mill pollution and the strict policing of the closed season while fish are breeding. Anglers, being born optimists, prefer the second line of thought, and the scarcity of fish does not stop them fishing for barramundi. The methods used are as diverse as can be imagined, but generally they are taken on large artificial lures or on live baits of prawn or mullet.

Barramundi tackle In Queensland, anglers generally use a strong spinning outfit with either a geared baitcaster or a fixed spool reel, with tubular rods from 1.5 to 2 m in length. A typical outfit would be a stiff, fast-action baitcaster with strong geared reel, 6 to 8

This barramundi was taken on a light line in rarely fished Northern Territory waters.

kg nylon line, 30 cm clip wire trace, and a wobbling minnow-type plastic lure such as the reb 2, killer or large bellbrook. Lures are mostly 'toughened up' before use with stronger than usual split rings and hooks.

The movement of the fish during the wet season can be used to avoid the taking of fish which have not yet spawned. In a typical year, an angler fishing with lures in February could take estuarine 'barra' around the mouths of tidal creeks on the last of a falling tide. However, a sudden flood might release lagoon fish from inland which would need to be left alone for a few weeks to complete their spawning cycle, the saltwater barramundi having generally spawned in December. For the sake of simplicity, the October 1 to January 31 closed season should be effective in increasing numbers of spawned fish.

The best locations under present conditions include creek and river mouths during the summer months, the junctions with smaller creeks and lagoons while water is still running at the latter stages of the Wet, and lagoons and freshwater river reaches around rock bars, logs and other cover during the winter or Dry season.

Barramundi are extremely active fish and often travel many

B ■ BARRAMUNDI

kilometres on a single tide, feeding on mullet and prawns as they forage upstream on a rising tide, or waiting around the mouth of a creek in a backwater for food flushed out by a falling tide. There is nothing very original in this method of finding food, and in practice many other species do exactly the same thing. An angler fishing for barramundi usually takes mangrove jacks, estuary cod, small barracuda, trevally and archer fish as a matter of course, and will catch more fish of other species than barramundi in salt water. In freshwater rivers and lagoons barramundi are often the dominant species, and large catches can be made in isolated areas without any other species being taken. In a typical river such as the Burdekin, anglers in fresh water expect as many black bream, *Hephaestus* spp., as barramundi when using light tackle lures.

Barramundi make an excellent post-graduate fish for bass anglers, as techniques and tackle are very similar. The difference is only in the average size and power of the fish, and here again anglers will argue. A typical debate is on the subject of line test, for a 5 kg barramundi may break a 7 kg test in a few seconds or succumb to a 4 kg test. This depends on terrain. In clear water, devoid of snags or oyster-studded rocks, a light line is all that is necessary. The more difficult fishing grounds will call for heavier tackle or greater care in casting, or both. Some may not be difficult fish to land for the average angler new to the species, others can be incredibly tough opponents.

The truth lies in between. This very active species can be encountered under an incredible variety of conditions. An angler may be lucky with a few around the snags, or unfortunate with some in open water. Experts who have caught hundreds of barramundi on sporting tackle cheerfully expect to meet both Jekyll and Hyde in the barramundi they hook. A fat lagoon fish can be a real slob, one from fast, clean tidal water can be a shocking blast of action. The average fish is fast, strong, and spectacular, but is not unbeatable. A check on the experience of one noted angler showed that half the barramundi hooked on light gear in the previous few weeks had escaped. This does not mean anglers do not enjoy runs of greater success than failure. This is the reason for the high regard for this species among sportsmen who do not mind being beaten by good fish.

Locating barramundi

Where to go for barramundi is optional. To enjoy the fishing under natural conditions in isolated tropical rivers is the easy way to find them—the tough part is only the travel to the tropical paradise. Anglers from Rockhampton north work each river and creek on its merits, and Queensland east coast rivers are therefore the most accessible and the most heavily fished. The upper reaches of most longer rivers are largely empty of barramundi, the prime areas ranging from creek mouths to the freshwater and brackish stretches within tidal influence. In some streams such as the Burdekin, freshwater fishing above tidal influence can be quite good, using stream tactics almost identical to those used on bass. Gulf country rivers are often muddy and almost unfishable, although this again varies from place to place. Streams such as the Staaten are usually relatively clear, and in fact may be fished almost as a flathead spinner would do over tidal sandflats. Predictable lagoon fishing is at its best in the top end of the Northern Territory, where rivers—mainly the Daly, East Alligator and Victoria—are also bountiful fish producers which will yield a good day's catch to the keen angler.

Spinning
Tackle must be strong, tough and durable. Typical outfits are: Firm action 2 m tubular rod; saltwater mitchell or similar quality fixed spool reel with capacity of about 180 m by 7 kg monofilament; 30 cm wire trace; large reb 2, killer or bellbrook lures fitted with 2X strong triple hooks and heavy duty split rings.

Baitcasting
Firm action 1.8 m tubular rod; strong baitcasting reel; line and lure as above.

Sidecasting
Rod at least 2.5 m long fitted with 15 cm reel, other tackle as before. This outfit may be fished profitably with a live bait, which can be fished under a float or else on the drift, without a sinker. A typical method is to moor a boat upstream of snags or rocks, and drift the live bait towards the cover, allowing no slack line. Barramundi do not 'bite' a live bait—they strike it hard, so the sidecast form of fishing involves constant readiness.

See Cookery.

BASS

Macquaria novemaculeata: The bass is one of the few sporting fish to have achieved legal recognition as a sporting species. It cannot be sold commercially in Australia, an indication of the rare respect and concern shown for it. Anglers understand this concern, for few fish can match the bass in sporting quality. Its range extends from Tin Can Bay in Queensland to the Glenelg and Hopkins rivers in western Victoria, coinciding with the greatest population of anglers. It is most commonly fished for in the beautiful coastal streams of our eastern watershed.

The scenery and atmosphere of the Australian bush, however hackneyed it may be to mention it, are a basic part of the charm of bass fishing. Other pleasing elements are the handy size range of adult fish, running from 0.5 kg to a very rare 3 kg;

BASS

Australian bass

the fact that it will take a wide range of lures if the angler can present them well enough; that it is a prime table fish; and that it is a clean and powerful fighter. Lastly, it is an intelligent and wary fish which repays close study. Unless a bass angler pays close attention to his fishing, he will not catch very many bass. The challenge and stimulus of the bass puts bass anglers among Australia's most dedicated sportsmen.

There has long been argument among scientists and others as to whether two species or varieties exist. In 1910, David Stead maintained that there were two, and nominated similar reasons to those put forward 50 years later by fisheries researcher, Neville Williams. The Queensland fisheries consultant, Hamar Midgley, kept records over a period of 15 years on populations and types, and his claim as a result that male fish were smaller, and outnumbered females three to one, was subsequently accepted by other scientists.

Recent research, particularly by L. S. Llewellyn, of the New South Wales State Fisheries and M. C. MacDonald, of the Australian National University, has shown conclusively that *Macquaria novemaculeata* is a separate species to estuarine perch, *Macquaria colonorum*, with which it is often confused. Llewellyn and MacDonald classified both as members of the family Percichthyidae, which also includes Murray cod, trout cod, golden perch and Macquarie perch. The range of bass on a typical healthy river extends from the mouth to the upper reaches, immediately below the first impassable waterfall. This also embraces water varying from totally salt to pure fresh. Local conditions vary greatly, as do the streams. There are great differences between the volcanic flaw that is the deep Glenelg, the shallow mouth of the Snowy and the swollen country streams of Queensland. The fish adapt to these conditions and so do the anglers.

The methods which have developed in Australian bass fishing owe as much to Australia's pioneers as they do to imported ideas. Early settlers discovered that cedar plugs fitted with hooks, and sometimes with a light propeller, were a fit substitute for frog, prawn or live insect baits. Lures were being used for bass 70 years ago. With the post-war expansion of techniques and lure types, anglers generally forget that baits remain an easy and effective tool for bass.

Bait fishing for bass

Assuming an angler wishes to learn bass fishing from the ground up, bait is the best introduction. The fish are active predators given to feeding on live creatures—fish, prawns and similar crustacea from below the surface, and on frogs, cicadas, grasshoppers and crickets which fall from overhead shrubbery. For this reason, bass angling with bait is based inflexibly on live bait fished in a lively fashion. Bass can be caught by many means, but the only one which consistently fails is by using a sinker and allowing a dead bait to lie on the bottom. A catfish or eel may find it, but the odds against a bass are long indeed. On the other hand, a live prawn hooked transversely through the body and cast in beside a log or under an overhanging tree, with or without a float, is terrific. The flicking of the tail which accompanies the struggle of a prawn will call fish from some distance off, and they will not hesitate.

The same applies to the small brown frogs which bushmen have used for so many years. Prawns and frogs are active and agile, and therefore easily seen by the fish. Other insect baits, notably cicadas and crickets, are equally effective if fished with a little movement of the rod. Baits may be fished either with a float or without, but a running float (i.e., one which can move freely up to a stop on the line) allows the angler to set the bait depth as required, and also to jiggle it without disturbing the water. A float also allows a light bait to be cast a greater distance. A suitable hook size is 2/0 French.

A challenging fighting fish, the Australian bass bites just as well on live bait as on lures.

For bait fishing, the most suitable outfit is one which permits the easiest casting using a light line. A fixed spool reel filled with 4.5 kg line is typical, on a spinning rod about 200 m in length. This kind of outfit is versatile enough for bait fishing, and is also useful with lures. For maximum utility, the rod should be a good tubular glass and the reel a reputable brand suited for light saltwater angling as well. This is necessary since much bass fishing is done in salt water, and since corrosion will affect it less than a light freshwater reel.

Bait fishing soon teaches an angler where the fish live. A deep pool at the bottom of a run of rapids, with an overhanging bank; beneath sunken logs and under overhanging trees such as willows—a tree which provides splendid sub-surface cover for fish; at the mouths of tributary creeks; in beside rock faces and among sunken boulders. A bass angler is always an explorer, and one hears continually of new and isolated streams which someone discovers for the first time as a haven for unwary big fish.

Lure fishing for bass

This has the appeal of spectacle and action and is better sport than bait fishing, though it is doubtful if more fish could be caught on lures than on live bait. The only problem to live bait is keeping it that way—catching it and carrying it. Lures do not have to be fed, aerated or even caught. However, many beginner anglers start first on lures without learning the useful lessons of bait fishing, and without the experience in bait presentation lure fishing can be misdirected and unrewarding.

The commonest lures are those with a weight close to 15 g with a plastic body and an inclined bib which causes them to wobble when retrieved through the water. The hydrodynamics of various lures causes a tremendous variety of possible action styles with this kind of lure. So many are made that the choice can be bewildering. It is unlikely that colour variations have much influence on bass, other than making lures more visible under certain conditions. It is a sound idea to use colours and patterns with some resemblance to natural foods, especially if the lure is an imitation of some bait or other—such as a frog or a minnow.

Imported American bass lures show tremendous ingenuity in design and certainly catch bass, but it is an error to give too much credit to a lure and too little to the angler who presented it well enough to fool the fish. Bearing this in mind, wobbling lures which have long been recognized for their bass-killing virtues include the following:

Bellbrook

Brown scale and other natural patterns in floater, midget, deep diver and swayback designs. These lures were introduced to Australians by the late Bill Southam, and have been of tremendous importance on the Australian angling scene.

Flopy
Medium size, green or brown. These lures are lightweight floaters with an adjustable and breakable bib, and spares should be purchased with the lure. In daylight they are usually set to run deep, and at night can be set to retrieve close to the surface. With a slow retrieve and the rod tip held high, they may be worked as a surface lure. Apart from a strong wobbling action, the flopy is so light in proportion to size that it 'plops' lightly into the surface and is said to aid lifelike presentation. A smaller and a larger model flopy also has these adherents, but the 7 g lure is the most popular.

Abu killer
Minnow type lures of great versatility which can be used on bass known to feed on minnows. The smaller size killer is the most useful for bass. It is a sinking lure with a strong action which can be enhanced by an irregular retrieve. In deeper water, use is made of the sinking characteristic to work it more deeply.

Reb 2
Well-made American lures which include a variety of sizes and types. All are floaters, but some carry longer bibs to ensure deeper action. One shallow lure, known as the half back, has been effective as a late afternoon and night lure.

Cello
A cellular plastic floating lure in natural colour combinations, with the same lightweight 'plop' on the surface as the flopy, which gives best results on a slow retrieve, broken by short jerks on the rod. Again, late afternoon.

Surface poppers
Nowhere in fishing is American inventiveness seen to greater advantage. The earliest popper imports to succeed included Crazy Crawlers and Jitterbugs, and these are still popular—sure sign of basic utility. Small versions of the wounded spook, poppers by Helin and Arbogast, tiny torpedo, lucky thirteen, hula popper and a host of others are available and will catch fish. The only limitation to their effectiveness is on other species. They are not effective on trout or redfin, or on inland species. In effect, apart from the tropics and certain forms of saltwater fishing, poppers remain bass specialists.

Spoons
Especially in running water, light spoons are effective on bass. The hardy imp spoon and the stainless steel wonder wobbler are inexpensive and durable. An effective technique in clear water is to fish the spoon close to the bottom, with a bouncing retrieve.

Spinners
Trout spinners of similar weight to the wobbling lures—between 7 and 20 g—can be used on the same rods. Celtas,

mitchells, wonder spinners, veltics and wonder hotshots are typical. One special situation in which spinners are effective on bass is late afternoon fishing in moving water, usually at the head of a deep pool.

Bass rods and reels
Bass fishing calls up all the skills of hand and eye, and success in the final analysis goes to the angler who can present his bait or lure in front of a feeding fish. There are no short cuts to this. It is easy to short cut the method, say by settling on a live prawn for bait or a flopy for a lure. Many good anglers use nothing but floater bellbrooks or one kind of surface popper, and get fish with them because they fish so effectively. One method for instance, is used among willows in brackish water, by casting through the branches from a drifting boat. All the methods depend for their success, apart from finding bass under cover, in casting as close to that cover as possible. This means accurate casting—accuracy of the kind just not needed in estuary or surf or lake fishing. It comes with practice, and with a certain kind of rod and reel—the baitcaster. This is usually a pistolgrip rod not more than 1.8 m in length fitted with a light geared reel. Casting with these is controlled by the thumb, and anglers enjoy the accurate casting of lures so much that some enthusiasts forget the main purpose of the sport, namely catching fish. Longer spinning rods, of 2 m length with a fixed spool reel, give moderate accuracy and greater distance. Bait rods can be longer, especially where live baits and floats are used.

Australian bass flies
The story of bass fishing in Australia is not complete without reference to fly fishing. The most successful 'flies' are bulky hair frogs with an appearance designed to give the fish an impression of a genuine meal. Light poppers can also be used, but smaller flies result only in smaller bass. Fly fishermen often find a good bass stream too densely timbered for their back cast. Flies can be worked, however, in many cases from a drifting boat, with resulting battles which allow the bass to show its true worth as a fighting opponent.

Typical bass streams
These include the Noosa and Maroochy Rivers, Richmond, Clarence, Macleay, Shoalhaven, Clyde (New South Wales); Snowy and Glenelg (Victoria). Many of the shorter streams, such as those of Gippsland, produce fantastic sport. The present trend, however, is to an increasing exploration of tidal reaches with bass lures cast to shoreline cover—regions of river where bait methods are usually aimed at whiting and bream, in clear water rather than among the snags. Much of the best bass fishing may still be waiting to be exploited.

Within the range indicated at the beginning of this article, any coastal stream or swamp is worth prospecting for bass.

Streams of moderate size are best fished by paddling or drifting a boat along in mid-stream and casting to likely cover at the bank on either side. The dense scrub or blackberries along some streams make this the only practicable course. Those anglers who go deep into the bush and fish among the snags in the higher reaches of the coastal rivers and their tributaries often experience good sport with the larger fish.

The Shakespeare battery-operated twelve volt electric outboard motor enables the working of a boat in bass water with the minimum of noise or disturbance to alarm the fish.

For Sand bass and Red bass, see Saltwater bass.

See Cookery.

BATFISH

Mostly crescent-shaped fish of the family Platacidae in which mature fish are completely different in appearance from the young fish. Their deep bodies and slow swimming make them highly vulnerable to spearfishermen. Seldom caught by anglers, though they are fairly common in tropical waters of Queensland and Western Australia and will bite readily on peeled prawns. The species is distinguished by the dark brown vertical bands, which become fainter with age.

Hump-headed batfish

Platax batavianus: A common fish among northern reefs and coastal waters sometimes confused with wrasse because of the humps that appear on their heads as they age. They grow to 4.5 kg and 55 cm and are greyish on top and silvery beneath, with characteristic wide vertical bands across the cheeks. Fully grown their depth equals their length but they are not satisfactory table fish.

Silver batfish

Monodactylus argenteus: A deep-bodied fish which enters fresh water but prefers salt water. They are popular aquarium fish because of the wide colour variations they pass through as they grow. Found in New South Wales, Queensland and the Northern Territory.
Common in estuaries.

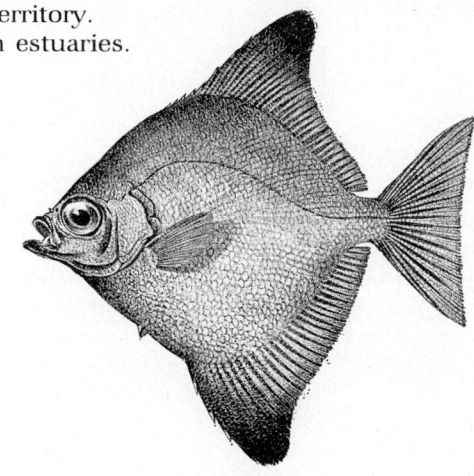

Silver batfish

Long-finned batfish *Platax pinnatus:* Crescent-shaped oddities that occur in rivers, estuaries and coastal waters of Western Australia, around our tropical coasts to New South Wales, and are probably most abundant in Queensland. They grow to 75 cm, and a weight of 22 kg, but are scarce beyond 50 cm. They have very small mouths for fish of this size. Marshall gives their colouring as blackish-brown, tinged with purple. The young are reddish-brown with three diffused black bands and with the anterior dorsal and anal rays prolonged. They are easily camouflaged by the debris and leaves in which they float.

BEACH fishing See *Surf fishing*.

BELLOWSFISH Deep-bodied fish of the family Macrorhamphosidae which resemble related pipefish and seahorses, with their mouths at the end of a tube-like snout. At least nine species are found in Australia. They are abundant in deep water off southern Australia and New Zealand, but are very rarely caught by anglers. Their mouths prevent them taking the hook and because of the depths they inhabit trawlermen are encountering them regularly. Whitley suggests that they get their name from the closeness with which they resemble the old-fashioned bellows for blowing fires.

Banded bellowsfish *Centriscops humerosus:* A deep-water inhabitant taken in depths up to 800 m, with bodies that are covered in small spiny scales. Their bodies are extremely deep and strongly compressed and there are two rows of tough, bony plates embedded in the skin on the shoulder. The dorsal fin is divided between an anterior spiny portion which carries a long serrated spine, and a posterior portion comprising soft rays. They are orange-pink, with five oblique dark bars. They have been noted in New South Wales, Victoria, Tasmania, South Australia and Western Australia. They grow to 22 cm.

Banded bellowsfish

Crested bellowsfish

Notopogon lilliei: A deep-bodied, compressed specimen, orange-pink on the back and silvery-white beneath, with characteristic white, smoky lines edging the bony shoulder plates, and a dark, silver-bordered band across the body. They reach 30 cm in length and are found between 90 and 180 m in Western Australia, South Australia, Tasmania, Victoria and New South Wales. Their heads are covered with close-set spines, and the dorsal fin is divided into two parts, an anterior spiny portion and a posterior portion of soft rays.

BERLEYING

A technique of attracting fish, usually from some distance away, to the bait by scattering concoctions of fish food in the water. Berley depends for success on its scent luring the fish to its source. Veteran anglers often guard the ingredients of successful berley as if they were atomic formulae. Berleying is known as chumming in America, where it is regarded as non-sporting when used on sharks. In New Zealand and other countries it is called ground-baiting.

Berley ranges from the beginner's use of bread crumbs to the deep sea angler's use of decayed animal carcasses. It can comprise sea-lettuce or green weed mixed with sand, normal baits mixed with carrying agents such as pulped bread, pollard or bran; chicken or turkey pellets, boiled fish heads, filleted bones, garden worms, chopped corn beef or the entrails of other fish. As the scent of berley provides its attraction to fish, there has long been a fallacy among anglers that the foulest smelling berley works best.

The Western Australian dinghy fisherman heading a few hundred metres offshore to catch herring, tommy ruff, garfish or trevally nearly always carries berley. The basic ingredient of most Western Australian berley is whale oil. If it is not available, shark liver oil or neat's-foot oil, or even olive oil may be used. Fishermen have found that herring, eternally hungry for oil, will swarm happily in an oilstream from a bottle of brilliantine hair tonic. Whale oil and pollard attract herring, garfish and trevally. The whale oil and pollard may be mixed into a slush with boiled fish and potatoes and other ingredients and sloshed overboard at intervals. It may be kneaded into dough to wrap above the bait as an extra incentive or pressed into a coil of wire known as a berley cage.

Handfuls of old whitebait or mulies may be squashed up by hand and dribbled over the side into the water to attract trevally. Crunched up cray, prawn or crab shells are excellent trevally berley. Some anglers pour a mixture of fat and whale oil over road metal stones and throw them overboard. A foul mixture may be dangled alongside in an old stocking and occasionally jiggled up and down. An old singlet liberally doused in whale oil and hung from the gunwales produces a long shimmering slick along which come dancing herring and garfish. A few puffs of dry pollard ladled over the slick make it the more enticing. Butchers' cracklings—the residue of boiled

B ■ BERLEYING

BERLEY RIG

This home-made berley rig is anchored so it cannot move, and the top tin acts as a marker buoy. Water movement releases berley from the tins.

dripping—are used as part of a never-failing herring berley.

Many fishermen spend hours preparing berley for their berley pot; cooking meat pieces secured from local fish shops, removing the bigger bones and grinding the remainder into a paste. Some avoid the splashing noise that might frighten fish by lowering their berley over the side in paper bags attached to old lines. When they have the berley in the right position they jerk the line which breaks open the sodden bag. A stone placed in the bag with the berley, takes it down and makes sure the bag ruptures.

Anglers frequently follow the rule of berleying with similar elements to the hook-bait. If they are using weed bait, they berley with a weed mixture. If they are fishing with prawns they berley with a prawn concoction. Some even have been known to feed maggots with liver to form the bait and then to berley with ordinary maggots.

In game fishing, berleying is a highly controversial subject and many Australian deep sea exponents are strongly opposed to the International Game Fishing Association's ban on the use of mammal meat berley in shark fishing. The ban is intended to prevent anglers increasing the weight of sharks following their lures by giving them an outsized feed of whale meat, offal oozing with blood, or whatever else takes the angler's or the shark's fancy. The Australian view is that the reasons behind the ban only apply to small sharks and certainly not to the 1000 to 2000 kilogram specimens found in Australian waters.

Techniques for dispersing berley

Apart from the paper bag method mentioned, there are numerous ways of casting berley upon the water being fished, all of them dependent on the fishing location and the quarry. Positioning of the boat is important to success, as is the judgement of currents and winds if the berleying is done from a pier or from rocks. Basically, anglers think in terms of surface berley or bottom berley, and use the appropriate berley when fishing for surface fish or bottom fish.

On deep reefs when hunting bottom species, it is essential to get the berley down to where the fish are, either by mixing the berley with tiny pebbles, sending it down in a berley bag, or lowering it in a weighted tin punctured in numerous places to allow the berley or its scent to escape gradually. It is wise to ration the dispersal of berley so that it will last whatever period the angler expects to fish, berleying say at 40 minute intervals through a day. One method that works sometimes when a boat is kellicked by the bow is to hang the berley bag from there and then to fish over the stern.

Game fishermen berley for yellowfin tuna either while drifting or by kellicking the boat over a reef. A deep cylindrical chum pot, perforated with many holes, is attached at the stern with its bottom about 20 to 25 cm below water level. A limited amount of tuna, bonito or salmon is thrown in and chopped fine by jabbing it with a chumming spade, which is a sharp blade set axially on the end of a long handle. With the roll and pitch of the boat, water washes in and out of the holes in the pot and carries out juices and pieces of berley. These wash around and drift away from the boat, and soon a long oil slick may be seen leading away from it. When cruising fish or sharks strike this they usually follow it to its source. Part of the catch of tuna or other fish is put on ice or refrigerated for use as berley on the next outing.

In the estuaries, bays and tidal lakes of the south-eastern coast the 'blackfish' anglers berley luderick with finely chopped greenweed mixed in sand. The weed is gathered from where it grows on rocks, shells and sticks in the backwaters of the big inlets or along the rivers. It is sold as a standard bait item in tackle shops and bait bars. Half a kilogram, finely chopped, is more than sufficient to mix with a bucket of damp sand. Often it is used in conjunction with crumbed stale bread. Luderick are fished for with a strand of the same weed as bait.

Luderick anglers working from the ocean rocks mostly berley and fish with the green sea-cabbage or lettuce *Ulva lactuca*. This is currycombed off the rock surface, often by scuffing with the iron cleats on the angler's boots, so that when the waves run in over the rocks the backwash carries it out and down to the fish. In the same way, rock-blackfish (black drummer) and the big silver drummer are berleyed with crumbed stale bread and fished for with selected pieces of bread crust or cunje.

Where a current is running shallowly across a sandbank anglers sometimes succeed in berleying whiting by stirring up the sand with their feet. Either this releases small marine organisms from the sand or the fish come looking for the disturbance in hope that it may do just that. Rock fish may be enticed by throwing in crushed shellfish, sea urchins, cunje, or crab tit-bits, but this is a location where berley usually attracts more rubbish, in the way of green eels and wirrahs, than good edible fish.

BILLFISH

The term now in international use—and Australian ichthyologists are pleased to follow suit in the interests of uniform usage—to describe swordfish, spearfish, sailfish and marlins. All members of the billfish group are good fish, all provide exciting sport fishing, and most spawn in summer, apparently leaving their eggs in the open sea. Females in the group can produce up to 100-200 million eggs, which allows for a high mortality rate.

The fisherman recognizes members of the group immediately from the upper jaw which is prolonged into a spear or bill and by their unrivalled fighting qualities. They are probably the most spectacular fish in the sea to catch; most possess tremendous speed and endurance, and are not discouraged in protracted fights with fishermen. It is on record that a swordfish which attacked a boat penetrated its planking to a depth of 67.5 cm. The piece of pierced planking is in the British Museum of Natural History. Scientists have estimated that marlin and broadbill swordfish, the fastest fish in the sea, can reach speeds of between 80 and 95 km/h.

In 1860, New Zealand scientist Dr Fred Knox dissected a broadbill swordfish and observed that the supra-spinal rays of the dorsal fin had become modified and bifid so that they formed a trough or socket in which the dorsal fin could be moved at will. The fish could, by muscular effort, erect or depress the fin and make it rigid on the vertical plane. Thus it acted as a vane or rudder to keep the fish on a straight course after it had aimed itself at its victim.

The most up to date revision of billfishes was provided by Dr Izumi Nakamura at an international symposium in Hawaii in 1972. He recognized 11 species of billfishes, the swordfish *Xiphias gladius*, the Atlantic sailfish *Istiophorus albicans*, the Pacific sailfish *Istiophorus platypterus*, three species of spearfish *Tetrapturus* sp., the white marlin of the Atlantic *Tetrapturus albidus*, the striped marlin of the Indo-Pacific *Tetrapturus audax*, the blue marlins *Makaira inazara* and *Makaira nigricans*, and the black marlin *Makaira indica*. Some scientists, however, only recognize one species of sailfish and one species of blue marlin.

In Australia the striped marlin and the Indo-Pacific black marlin have been recognized since the start of game fishing around 1930, but the presence of a third species was recognized by several game fishermen from Bermagui to Port Stephens from about 1937 on. This was loosely termed a blue marlin, mainly on account of the supposed blue colouring. Much the same thing happened in New Zealand where boatmen had also recognized a third marlin and this too was called a blue marlin. Athel D'Ombrain recognized a different type of marlin at Port Stephens and notified Gilbert P. Whitley, then Curator of Fishes at the Australian Museum, Sydney. When the late John K. Howard came to Australia in 1953 he visited D'Ombrain at Port Stephens where he hoped to fish for marlin. Owing to rough weather Howard was unable to go out, but he did discuss the third marlin. He then went to Bermagui where he landed a 182 kg marlin which several local fishermen believed was a Pacific blue marlin. Whitley later classified this as a 'Howard marlin' and the Port Stephens one as a 'D'Ombrain marlin.' It is now generally considered that D'Ombrain's marlin is a colour variant of the black marlin and Howard's marlin is the true Pacific blue marlin.

Since then many marlin have been caught and recorded as blue marlin but the first authenticated capture of this species in Australia was made by Bob Dyer of the Sydney Game Fishing Club about 16 km off Sydney Heads on 17 April 1968, at

The Peak. This was a fine 139 kg fish taken on 22 kg test line, and it resembled in every detail many that Dyer had seen brought in at Hawaii.

The colouring of marlin is an unreliable means of identification. Marlin and many other fish often go through rapid colour changes, possibly from excitement, or from the effects of fighting to get free of a line. Most experienced fishermen have seen the rapid changing of colour on a marlin brought quickly into the cockpit of a boat. It runs from beautiful blue, through coppery green to pale blue, and silver, before fading away to the drab brownish grey to black. In the water near the boat, the refraction of light and the angle the fish is swimming against the sun have diverse effects on the general colour. Stripes or spots are more reliable as they can be regular and fairly reliable in colour, but the general overall colour is unreliable.

Another small marlin D'Ombrain sent to Whitley was caught by Mrs Ron Duncan off Port Stephens. It was identified as a short-billed spearfish, *Tetrapturus angustirostris*. Whitley considered this was almost certainly the young of the black marlin, but it is now known that the short-billed spearfish is one of three closely related species occurring throughout the world's oceans. In recent years the short-billed spearfish has been caught off Port Stephens, Ulladulla, Eden and Narooma.

Black marlin

Makaira indica: A marine fish found mainly in the Pacific and Indian Oceans, of high commercial value to Japanese, Korean and other long-line fishermen. The Pacific black marlin has always been regarded as the most prized game fish in Australian waters, mainly because of its great fighting qualities and also because of its large size. It is identified by its short, thick, and sometimes upturned bill and a very heavily-built body which is deep and in big fish rather humped at the shoulders, tapering off towards the tail. It is this shoulder hump that partly distinguishes it from the blue marlin.

The black marlin has no marks or colour bands on the body in death, and the main identification is the pectoral fin which is rigidly erect and cannot be laid down alongside the body. In adults, however, in specimens less than 20 kg, this fin is quite flexible. The name black marlin is an unfortunate choice as this magnificent fish is a striking slate blue on top, when seen fighting in the sea, going to a lighter blue about the centre of the body and changing to silvery white underneath. Large fish seem to lack the colours of smaller young fish. Often pale blue stripes show on the sides when the fish is active but they disappear after death.

The silver-white belly of fresh specimens leads to the Japanese name for the fish, *shirokajiki*, white marlin, and the Chinese, *pu-pi*, white skin. Occasional black marlin turn a uniform bronze shade when they come from the water, but this quickly fades. The pelvic fins of the black marlin (the

B ■ BILLFISH

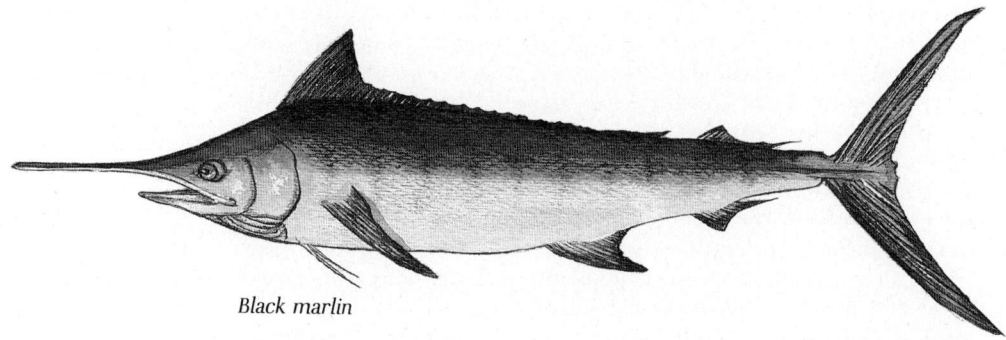

Black marlin

straplike fins under the 'chin' of all billfish except swordfish) are shorter than in other marlins, generally less than 30 cm long whatever the size of the fish. All its fins are dark. The flesh is always light pink. The female grows to a far bigger size than the male. The black marlin has attracted leading overseas game fishermen to Cairns, where a 611 kg specimen was landed in November 1979. Small black marlin of 50 kg or less have provided excellent sport from Coolangatta to Cairns. The Australian record of 654.08 kg by Michael Magrath off Cairns in 1973 was 53.53 kg short of the world record of 707.61 kg.

The black marlin is caught either by trolling or drifting, trolling being the most popular method; but the presence of whalers and other species of sharks in Australian waters makes drifting less practical. Fish such as bonito *Sarda chiliensis australis*, yellow-tailed kingfish *Seriola lalandi*, and Australian salmon *Arripis trutta* (the kahawai of New Zealand), are the main baits used, but any fish that trolls well can be employed. In Cairns mullet is used with very good results. But large rainbow runners, wahoo and Spanish mackerel, which are caught outside the Reef and rigged on a bridle, are considered the best baits for that area.

Trolling live bait
In trolling, the roughness of the sea usually dictates the speed at which trolling is done and the weight of the bait used. Normally a speed of four to six knots is a good trolling speed, as the bait should plane along the surface and not twist or revolve underneath. An alternative method is to troll a live salmon or other fish such as slimy mackerel or yellowtail at a very slow speed, allowing the baitfish to sink well below the surface and be trolled more or less in the natural, upright position. Live bait can also be used when drifting, but not all fish will stand this treatment. Yellow-tailed kingfish are very good for this type of baiting.

Lures for marlin fishing have become increasingly popular. Plastic squid, knuckleheads and the recently developed 'Hawaiian eye' are among the best. Using lures, it is better to fish from the rod direct rather than from an outrigger, as the hook must be driven in at the strike. The drag is set fairly strongly for this reason, and higher speeds are necessary, up to 10 or 12 knots. But with big black marlin it has been found all around the world that it is almost impossible to get one to take a lure. Lures are acceptable to small black marlin but the really big fish like a bait, and a big bait at that. Bait fish of 3 to 5 kg are used on the marlin grounds 56 km out from Cairns, rigged with the bridle type rig. The fish is trolled slowly, giving it a natural swimming appearance. The black marlin is carnivorous, feeding on large invertebrates. Stomach contents have varied from large tuna to squid. Some stomachs contain the bills of very small billfish, possibly baby marlin.

Black marlin usually fight deep down, often not jumping when hooked, or not for some time afterwards. Some do not jump at all but may come to the surface and thrash about at the trace with their bill. They have great reserve strength and unless hooked deep in the stomach fight doggedly to the end.

Black marlin have always outnumbered striped marlin in Australian waters. In New Zealand the opposite is true, with striped marlin outnumbering the black marlin by a very large margin. There have been seasons in New Zealand when no black marlin were taken. Figures from the Bay of Islands since 1924 show wide fluctuations.

In 1940, 40 black marlin were caught off Bermagui and they averaged 105 kg in weight, including a 308 kg fish caught by C. B. A. Straling, of Ceylon. This remained an Australian record for 26 years until beaten at Cairns by the first marlin to be caught in Australia to weigh over 450 kg (1000 lb). This was taken in September 1968, on a 36 kg breaking strain line, by Bob Walker, and weighed 480 kg, only 1 kg short of Richard Oback's world record for this line. The present Australian record chart includes a black marlin of 600.10 kg by Georgette Douwma off Cairns in 1977, which is also a world record for a 37 kg line.

Much the same thing happened in New Zealand, where a black marlin of 442 kg (976 pounds) was captured off Cape Brett by Capt. Laurie Mitchell in 1926. This stood as a world record, also for 26 years, until broken, off Cabo Blanco, Peru, by Alfred C. Glassell jr on 7 August 1952, with a fish of 464 kg (1025 lb).* The record was broken no less than seven times there in one year and the same fisherman now holds the world all-tackle record with a mighty 706 kg (1560 lb)* marlin measuring 4.6 m taken on a 60 kg line.

Maximum sizes of black marlin
A black marlin of 555 kg was washed up on the beach at Eden, New South Wales and another of nearly 4.5 m came ashore at Stockton Beach in 1967. Expert Athel D'Ombrain took measurements of this fish and estimated its weight at over 770 kg. Elsewhere in the world black marlin of 900 kg have been reported and one of 1019 kg was harpooned off Cabo Blanco.

*World records are still judged in imperial weights.

The prediction by Peter Goadby in Athel D'Ombrain's book *Game Fishing off the Australian Coast*, published in 1957, that Cairns and the water round Ribbon Reefs off Cooktown would produce the best game fishing in Australia, has proved correct, and it will be intriguing to see how long this lasts, as experience at several other great fishing grounds around the world has indicated that these really big fish of the species may be rapidly fished out. This pattern may not apply there because of the abundant food available to all fish off the Great Barrier Reef and also because Japanese longliners have been excluded from fishing near the Reef since 1981.

Habits and distribution

The spawning season for black marlin is in the summer or warmer months of the year. In the western Pacific fish with running roe and milt have been recorded from July to December. Very little reliable research has been done on the species, though it is known that the young of between 9 and 13 kg are already typical black marlin although they possess a relatively higher dorsal fin and flexible pectoral fins. Evidence is accumulating from the tagging of hundreds of marlin each year that extensive migrations are undertaken by marlin of all sizes, and that mixing of marlin from all over the Pacific may regularly occur. As tuna up to 70 kg have been found in the stomachs of black marlin it is obvious few fish in the seas are fast enough to escape them when they are really hungry. Japanese love the delicious pink meat of the black marlin and use it extensively in fish sausages. It is eaten cooked or raw.

The Pacific black marlin is distributed all down the east coast of Australia, from Cape York to Mallacoota, and also off North Island, New Zealand, at Cape Brett and the Bay of Plenty. It is common to all the islands north of Australia and spreads right across the Pacific Ocean and throughout the Indian Ocean. There appears to be a migratory stock of small fish which works its way down our eastern coastline, appearing off Port Stephens, Sydney and Bermagui towards the end of December. They are most plentiful in February and into March, but stragglers have been recorded in most months of the year and some may stay about our coastline for long periods. Mid-August to the first week in December has been the season for black marlin off Cairns, but further experience may yet show that other times also yield fish.

Blue marlin *Makaira nigricans:* The commonest marlin taken in equatorial Pacific waters by commercial long line fleets. There is frequent confusion in identifying this gamefish. Some experts believed New Zealand to be the extreme limit of the blue marlin's range and were dubious of them being caught off Australia but we now know that some blue marlin are caught off eastern Australia each year.

However, blue marlin take the same food as black and

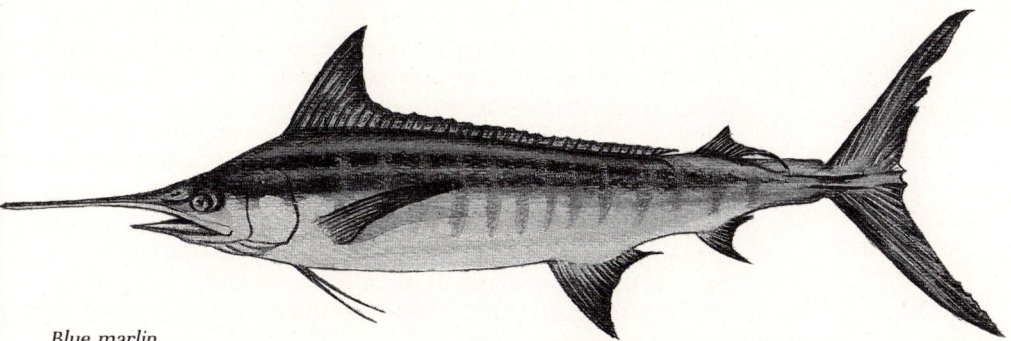

Blue marlin

striped marlin. Given extremely warm-water conditions, it is probable that these fish with a minimum temperature requirement of 22 degrees C do straggle into Australian waters, particularly off north Queensland. In the warm habitat they prefer, they frequently grow even bigger than the black marlin. Hawaiian commercial fishermen have taken blue marlin up to 820 kg, and there have been reliable records of blue marlin weighing more than 220 kg off Sydney.

Blue marlin are only occasionally taken in New Zealand, where the first recorded was as late as the 1951–52 season. New Zealand's best year for blues was in 1962–63 when 10 fish were boated. On average they are fairly heavy fish, 160 to 200 kg, with a few 270 to 300 kg. The largest, 460 kg, was landed in 1968 and is the heaviest marlin caught in New Zealand waters and second to the world's best blue. All New Zealand's blue marlin were taken on a bait trolled in the ordinary way. The largest blue marlin so far landed by an Australian angler was 319 kg by Sir Garrick Agnew off Rottnest Island in 1983, whereas the world record stands at 624.14 kg.

Blue marlin resemble black more than striped marlin, although stripes are often quite noticeable on them. These stripes fade when the fish has been dead some time. The tail is wide and almost identical in shape to that of the black. The dorsal is higher than on the black, but not as high as on striped marlin. The pectorals fold in alongside the body and this is the key point in many ways, in identifying blue marlin, as the black's pectoral is rigid and will not fold alongside the body. The blue marlin's spear is long, more rounded in section than on the striped marlin, but not quite as big or heavy as on the black.

Blue marlin do not have the depth of body at the shoulders that black marlin have, but are thick and heavy on the sides. The under jaws are not as long as those of striped marlin and fit close to the underside of the upper jaws.

The breeding season for blue marlin has not been firmly fixed. Males with free-running milt have been taken in the tropics almost throughout the year. There is also evidence of males spending much of the year segregated from females.

New Zealander Neil Illingworth, in researching his book *Fighting Fins*, which is a history of New Zealand game fishing, looked at hundreds of photographs of marlin caught there since 1924. None of the photographs showed a fish that could even remotely be considered a blue marlin. This does not, of course, rule out the possibility of some blue marlin having been identified as striped marlin in the days before the 1951–52 season when blue marlin were positively identified in New Zealand waters. The curious aspect of all this is that now New Zealand boatmen and regular game anglers have seen both blue and striped marlin together, they have no difficulty distinguishing both species at a glance.

Baiting techniques for these fish have remained the same for years and the well-known New Zealand rig, used extensively in Australia, is the accepted method. In this method the hook is set into the bait pointing to the tail, the trace being brought back along the fish, lightly tied down with a final tie at the nose or front of the bait. If marlin take the trolled bait cleanly on the strike, and are able to swallow the fish (the ties having broken) they must be hooked, but often they get this in the throat or gills, which can spoil the fight.

Striped marlin *Tetrapturus audax:* An exciting, valuable commercial and sport fish from the Indian and Pacific Oceans. In some years, the striped marlin is almost as plentiful as the black marlin off New South Wales. In 1940, when 40 black marlin were captured off Bermagui, New South Wales, 33 striped marlin were taken, and these had the same average weight of 105 kg as the blacks. Although they are known to reach 440 kg, 90 to 135 kg is the average size.

Apart from the very prominent 14 lavender coloured stripes which extend well across the body, the striped marlin is easily distinguished from the Pacific black marlin by its much more slender shape, the long narrow bill as compared to the short stout bill of the black, and the pectoral fin which can be folded flat alongside the body. It is a beautiful cobalt blue, turning to silvery white on the belly. The high, pointed dorsal fin extends right down the back to the second dorsal fin, and is a dark blue, often with purple spots at its base. This very high fin, often as high as the body is deep, is the true distinguishing feature of this species.

The striped marlin is without doubt the most spectacular of all the marlins when hooked. From the moment one is hooked it mostly races wildly over the sea making 20 to 30 mighty leaps, in which it shoots out a shower of foaming spray, shakes its whole body, and flaps its pectoral fins, before crashing back again in a smother of spray. Then it may do four or five long, low greyhound leaps, with the head hunched and long thin beak pointing down, before diving deep to carry on the fight, first on one side of the boat, then doubling back on its tracks to fight on the other side. They also jump clear of the

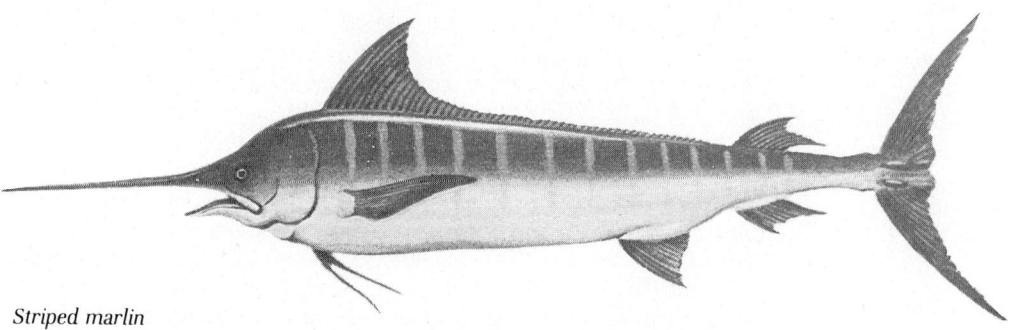

Striped marlin

sea at times for no apparent reason, but this could be because they are chasing fish or possibly evading something chasing them. Speeds of fish are very hard to estimate accurately but it has been stated that striped marlin can attain a speed of 95 km/h. This is doubtful, but they could reach 55 to 65 km/h when swimming free.

Lures for striped marlin
Like the black marlin, they can be taken either while trolling or drifting, and the same kind of baits will catch them. They are sometimes even taken on dead shark baits. They are much more easily taken on lures and will go for white, red, or green feather lures, plastic squids, or knuckleheads. It is not uncommon for two to swim together and when one is hooked the other will follow it around, even coming up to the boat just prior to the captured fish being gaffed. New Zealand boatmen keep a second line ready and throw this over on the instant the first fish is gaffed, frequently picking up the other fish. The same thing has been done off Port Stephens, New South Wales, on one or two occasions. At times they swim in quite large schools. Fifty-two were counted off Port Stephens one day when the sea was very calm.

In New Zealand the striped marlin makes up by far the greatest percentage of marlin captured. From 1924 to 1957, 5587 striped marlin were captured, compared to 336 black marlin, by the Bay of Islands Swordfish Club (which does not take into account captures in the Bay of Plenty area). Off the Australian eastern coast the reverse is the case, as striped marlin are now a comparative rarity. Striped marlin around 23 kg are frequently taken by commercial mackerel trollers working the southern inshore reefs in autumn. The biggest striped marlin so far caught by an Australian angler was 166 kg by David Eley off Bermagui in 1982.

Why the scarcity?
March seems to be the best month for striped marlin in New Zealand, but they appear later at Port Stephens, sometimes not being noted until late in May. The first marlin caught off Sydney in any year invariably is a large striped marlin, usually in October. Many more probably could be caught then if they

B ▪ BILLFISH

were fished for in earnest. Still-fishing with balloons or floats has become popular overseas but these methods have not found favour in Australia and New Zealand.

Sailfish *Istiophorus platypterus:* The sailfish is common along the northern parts of Queensland, particularly in Great Barrier Reef waters and also off Cape Moreton in Southern Queensland and Exmouth in Western Australia. It is more frequently found around the islands north of Australia but many are seen and captured around Cairns and southwards to Gladstone. It has been taken in impressive sizes in Western Australian waters. In New South Wales waters it is only an occasional visitor, at least as far south as Port Stephens where several have been taken by game fishermen and professionals. In New Zealand a sailfish was chased ashore at Pataua, near Whangarei, in 1948.

As a result of tagging sailfish in Florida, it has been found that there is no great migration of these fish and many stay where they are all summer. Thus it is possible that much the same happens in Australian waters, and with the Great Barrier Reef as a breeding ground those areas perhaps may yet reward game-fishermen with more sailfish than have ever been taken elsewhere. Certainly, large numbers of juveniles appear in July each year off Dunk Island.

Sailfish, like marlin, come to the surface at times to feed, and no doubt feast on the vast schools of pilchards, sprats, garfish, and other surface fish. However, they have been found (like marlin) with many bottom-dwelling fish in their stomachs and no doubt they get much of their food from the bottom.

The sailfish is easily distinguished from the marlin by the magnificent sail-like dorsal fin from which it gets its name. It is easily distinguished by the very slender body and the long slender bill.

The sailfish's general colour is brilliant blue from the sail down to the mid-line of the body, where it turns to silver and white. The dorsal fin is spotted freely with blue or black spots, and broken lines of greyish-blue cross the body from behind the gill cover to the tail. It does not grow to anything like the great size of the marlins, as 83 kg is the Australian record for a rod and line, and most taken off Australian waters are under 45 kg. Anglers who catch a sailfish over 54 kg should start

Sailfish

checking in the record books. A sailfish of 79.83 kg was caught off Bagagbag Island, Papua New Guinea, in 1974 by John Barlow, but the biggest from Australian waters was 78 kg by Bronwyn Dowson in 1983 off Cairns.

A magnificent fighting fish on light tackle, the sailfish puts on a great show of spectacular leaping, but in doing this soon wears itself out. In Hawaii, Florida, Cape Moreton (Queensland) and many other places, the fish are not gaffed, but are taken by the beak with a gloved hand, tagged, and released, providing they are not in a dying state. Strip baits are greatly favoured in American waters for catching sailfish, but they will take small marlin baits of whole fish, and plastic lures quite readily at times.

Like other billfishes, the sailfish when very young has no resemblance at all to the adult fish. A post-larval fish of 8 mm has huge eyes, two serrated spines protruding from each side of the gill covers, and strong teeth in the short upper and lower jaws. At about 20 mm, it starts to develop the dorsal fin and the upper jaw starts to lengthen.

Feeding habits
Sailfish congregate in numbers when large schools of pilchard-type fish or oceanic toadfish are travelling on or near the surface. They adopt the same technique used by bluefin tuna, circling the school of milling fish and gradually forcing them into a tighter circle. Then one or two will break off and swim slowly through the mass, slashing vigorously right and left with the bill, killing or stunning numbers of fish. Then they turn and swim down to collect the slowly sinking pilchards or toadfish. Tuna do the same, but dash madly through a school and do not go about the job in as leisurely a fashion as sailfish.

The story that sailfish erect their dorsal fins and sail merrily along the surface in great numbers, like some fishy armada, is a stretch of the imagination. They certainly do erect these fins at times on the surface, just as a striped marlin will, but when travelling on the surface usually show only the upper lobe of the tail. They have been observed to erect the giant fin underwater to scare bait into tighter groups.

Sailfish should not be fished for on heavy tackle, lines with a breaking strain of 10 to 15 kg are all that are needed, and even a 2 kg breaking strain is used. However, unless an area is located where these fish are sure to be found to the exclusion of others, the risk of hooking on to a very large marlin must be taken.

Pacific short-billed spearfish

Tetrapturus angustirostris: A small specimen of the short-billed spearfish was caught by Mr Ron Duncan off Port Stephens. The fish weighed about 22 kg and was 150 cm in length. This specimen was sent down to the Australian Museum which recorded: 'It is nearest to the short-billed spearfish *Pseudohistiophorus angustirostris* and agrees very

B ▪ BILLFISH

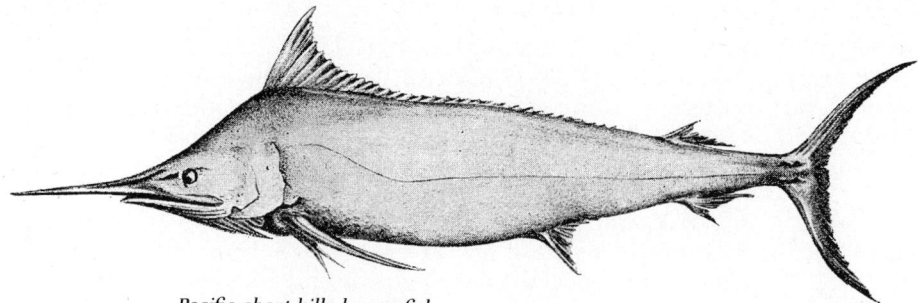

Pacific short-billed spearfish

well with smaller specimens we have here of that species from India, and the Northern Territory.' Since then several have been caught off New South Wales, especially off Ulladulla.

This fish is a greyish-blue in colour above, whitish below, some with up to about 20 stripes down the back, extending about one-third of the depth of the fish, instead of most of the way down as in the striped marlin. The first dorsal fin is dark, not spotted, sometimes with light proximal area. Specimens in the Australian Museum are from north-western Australia, northern Australia and New South Wales. Northern fish appear in August to early October; and those in New South Wales in December, February and April. They take a trolled bait, similar to those used for other species of marlin or lures similar to those for other tunas and billfish.

A capture by R. McKay in Western Australia led Whitley to think that this fish is the young of the black marlin, but this is not the case.

Broadbill swordfish *Xiphias gladius:* A highly prized commercial food fish hunted by professionals in specially equipped boats in many parts of the world, and an exciting, challenging sport fish. Although the broadbill, also known as the swordfish, has been sighted in Australian waters and found washed up on our beaches, it has only rarely been caught by an Australian game fisherman on rod and reel, but never heavier than the breaking strain used. The recorded strandings have ranged from Western Australia to the eastern coastline, always on surf beaches. Among sightings by game fishermen, the Port Stephens area has predominated. Col. Bruce Steer saw one in 1939 off Morna Point; Nelson Mitchell, a professional fisherman, identified one also near Morna Point; and Athel D'Ombrain and Dr A. B. K. Watkins recognized one a few kilometres north of the same area in 1947. They have also been seen off the Gold Coast and commercial line fishermen catch occasional specimens off the New South Wales south coast.

A small specimen was taken by professional fisherman Jack Jensen off Port Stephens and a beautiful little 3 kg fish was taken by professional fisherman Joe Cain off Port Stephens in 1965 on a handline. In 1966, two men found a good sized broadbill washing ashore in the breakers at Nobbys Beach,

Broadbill swordfish

Newcastle. The surge was too great and they had to let it go, but it washed up dead next day. Many of these prized game fish are taken on the Japanese longline boats operating wide out off the Queensland and New South Wales coasts, up to 4.5 m in length, and it is rather strange that after nearly 50 years of game fishing no angler has yet landed a big one.

In 1982, Sydney game fisherman John O'Brien made a concerted effort to catch a broadbill off Jervis Bay. He brought a large one to gaff, but the hook pulled, and he finally boated one of 15 kg on 60 kg tackle.

Broadbill distribution

This difficulty in catching a broadbill in Australian waters is all the more extraordinary considering the wide distribution of the fish in temperate and tropical seas. It is distinguished at once from the marlins by the long flat sword which is very broad across, far longer than the head behind it and not rounded as in the marlins. It has only one dorsal fin which is fixed and cannot fold down, one anal fin, and no ventral fins. The tail joint, known as the caudal peduncle, is very broad across and has a single keel fin. It's been described as 'varying from bronze above and whitish below to greyish-blue or black above and light below'. It is found off Japan, Formosa, the Philippine Islands, Hawaii, New Zealand, Australia, from California to Peru and Chile, from Newfoundland south to Cuba, Scandinavia to Portugal, Iceland and the Baltic Sea, Straits of Gibraltar and the Mediterranean, the Black Sea and from Cape Province, off Africa, around the tip and north to Durban, Madagascar and Reunion Island.

Special broadbill techniques

They are very wary fish and must be fished for with quite a different technique from that employed on marlin, with the bait drawn across the path of a fish while it is 'finning out' on the surface. Apart from their great strength and fighting ability the fish, according to Zane Grey, have very soft mouths and hooks pull out more easily.

On a 54-day angling operation off northern Chile in 1954 the Lou Marron team, fishing from the specially designed launch *Explorer*, on an assignment carried out for the University of

Miami, sighted 93 broadbill. Baits were presented to 56 and 27 strikes were obtained. Of these 17 fish were hooked but only 11 landed.

Broadbill are taken by professionals in some countries while the fish is finning along on the surface usually in a calm sea. A special 'pulpit' extends well out from the bow of the boat and the fish is approached quietly from behind and harpooned. Game fishermen also have to use special rigs. The bait, a fish such as a mackerel or small tuna, is cut open and two hooks set in the flesh and then sewn up. The bait is not trolled behind as for marlin or other game fish but is kept ready, attached to the line, until the broadbill is seen swimming on the surface. It is then carefully taken across its path of travel so that the bait is presented in front of the fish and only just moving. Although there is a special technique for catching them, many broadbill have been caught while drifting or trolling for other game fish.

A recently developed technique is to fish deep at night, using squid baits suspended under 'cyalume' light sticks. This method is used in Florida and was modified by John O'Brien for his venture.

New Zealand has quite a few recorded captures, among them a 239 kg fish taken by the legendary Zane Grey in 1926, and a 300 kg specimen captured off Cape Brett by that famous game fisherman from London, H. White-Wickham, on 9 January 1928. New Zealand also can boast of an incredible fishing feat—Donald Heatly, fishing from the launch *Abalone* off Mayor Island in January 1968, hooked a giant broadbill estimated at over 450 kg and played it for 32 hours. He hooked it at 3.30 p.m. on Sunday and lost it at 11.30 p.m. on Monday, when he was late reaching the brake and the line snapped in the double tackle. It's probable that this fish was foul-hooked, possibly through throwing the bait early in the fight and getting hooked in the tail or body. If it had been hooked in the mouth the hook probably would have pulled out during such a long fight. A fish hooked deep in the stomach would have been affected by the loss of blood and probably died down deep near the bottom.

The world record broadbill catch was by Lou Marron with a 4.48 m fish he caught off Iquique, Chile, on 7 May 1953, which weighed 536 kg (1182 lb). It was caught on a 60 kg breaking strain line.

Julian Pepperell

BLACK bream *See Bream. See also Macquarie perch.*

BLACKFISH, River *Gadopsis marmoratus:* A unique species also known as the freshwater blackfish, 'slippery' or 'slimy'. This fish belongs to an order of fish found nowhere else in the world but

River blackfish

Tasmania, Victoria and the Murray-Darling system. It is brown to brownish olive-green in colour, mottled with dark blotches, sometimes almost black. Yellow on the underside, often with purple overtones in the ventral area. The scales are very small. In the south it grows larger and darker than those anglers catch north of the Dividing Range. In New South Wales blackfish rarely exceed 30 cm in length and 280 g in weight but in southern Victoria and Tasmania they can exceed 60 cm and 5 kg.

River blackfish are believed to have evolved thousands of years ago when Tasmania was part of the Australian mainland, infiltrating from Tasmanian streams into Victorian waters and north into the Murray and its tributaries. The fish that remained in Tasmania and those in southern Victoria continued to grow to average size, but those in the Murray and northern streams became smaller. Thousands of blackfish were hauled from creeks, when Victoria was an infant colony, by farmers who learned that they provided excellent eating and were very easily caught. The ease with which the smaller blackfish could be caught and the introduction of that fast, voracious feeder the trout, saw blackfish numbers dwindle alarmingly. In rivers where they once were common they have now been hunted out by the trout and confined to the pools of the smaller tributaries. Blackfish, like trout, feed principally on insects such as caddis larvae, beetles, small shrimps and crustaceans.

They spawn mainly in late spring and early summer. Little is known of their biology but eggs are few and large, similar in size to trout eggs. A fish of 224 g to 280 g produces about 500 eggs. It is fairly certain that breeding occurs in ponds. The eggs are demersal. For centuries it apparently avoided the more open sunlit waters, remaining hidden in the dark recesses of overgrown creeks. For its size, the blackfish has very good angling qualities. It is largely nocturnal, biting best at dusk and at sunrise.

Northern blackfish are rarely found away from stream debris or submerged tree roots, the only dark spots remaining in open sunlit waters. The southern species can still live in dark overgrown pools. Most biologists lean to the view that although the northern blackfish enjoys far better feeding conditions than those in the south the warmer water temperature causes them to remain small in size. It seems that the blackfish can only reach its optimum weight in cold, clear, well-sheltered waters.

The blackfish always has a large amount of slime on its body. Trying to remove the hook from a large blackfish while holding it in the hand provides problems even for experienced anglers.

Blackfish habits

Blackfish are also much softer and lighter in the flesh than trout and a 1 kg blackfish will look as big as a 1.5 kg trout. Small blackfish bite eagerly at times and it was common only a few years ago for anglers to fill a sugar bag in an evening's fishing. The larger specimens take the bait with more care and if the line does not run freely they will drop the bait as quickly as any big trout. Thus it is essential to let the line run freely and avoid using sinkers after the bigger specimens.

Tackle for blackfish

In the still waters of the pools, a light trout rod, a 2 kg line and a No. 4 to 6 hook with two split shot 1 m above it, is the best rig. When fishing for big blackfish use small yabbies, mudeyes or wood grubs. Earthworms are good but too often they attract those nuisances of the blackfish streams: the galaxias minnows. If, in the faster waters of the streams, it is necessary to use a small round sinker, this should be rigged so that the line runs freely through it. A single split shot nipped on the line 90 cm above the hook will prevent the sinker sliding down to the hook eye.

In those streams where the bed is like a weed jungle, the bait is likely to be lost and a float is needed. Choose a narrow-bodied one like the porcupine quill or the pencil float. These dive under the surface without too much resistance and this is important when you are fishing for big blackfish. Blackfish bite best at night or in early evening, but good catches can be had by day in those creeks that wind through deep gullies overgrown with tree fern and bracken. During a fresh when the stream is slightly discoloured, the blackfish will bite ravenously. Under these conditions ordinary earthworms are the best bait. However, if the stream is badly discoloured the blackfish will go off the bite and stay off until the stream begins to clear.

BLACKFISH, Rock *Girella elevata:* A valued sportfish in New South Wales, the only State in which it is found. Also known as black drummer and pigfish. Similar in appearance to the drummer, it is often taken by anglers fishing for silver drummer. The flesh is white and tender if it is eaten soon after being caught, and is of splendid table quality.

Rock blackfish are plentiful around rocks in estuaries and right along the New South Wales coast. Spearfishermen have a far better chance of luring them away from the rocky ledges and caves which they inhabit, than anglers. They are very powerful swimmers who head straight for hideouts among

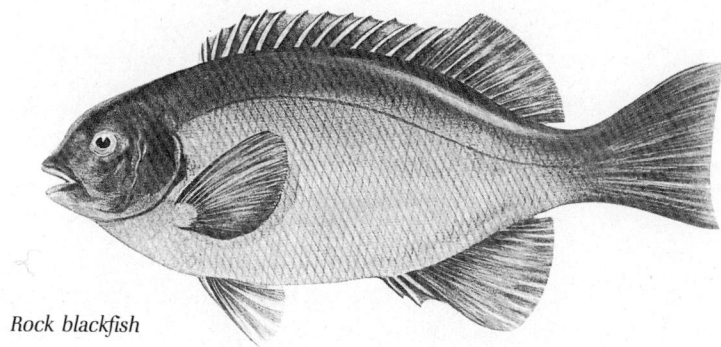

Rock blackfish

rocky crevices when they are hooked and from there become very difficult to dislodge.

They are carnivorous on occasions and will take baits such as prawns, cunjevoi, crabs and fish flesh, but they feed mainly on weed; Roughley recommended cabbage weed mixed with bread, soaked in water and squeezed tight on the hook. But heavy tackle is essential, for rock blackfish are determined fighters.

There is very little reliable information on the weight and length to which rock blackfish grow because of the confusion among sport fishermen between this fish and the drummer. Roughley put its limits at 75 cm and 6.5 kg but veteran anglers are inclined to set its maximum weight nearer to 3.5 kg. The confusion is unfortunate as drummer and rock blackfish are easy to identify. The rock blackfish is a very dark black-brown; drummer are much lighter with longitudinal stripes on their backs. In the drummer, the soft portions of the dorsal and anal fins are narrow and practically straight. In the rock blackfish, they are prominent and rounded.

See Luderick.

BLENNY

A group of carnivorous fish of the family Blenniidae and the related Clinidae, Ophiclinidae and Tripterygiidae, that are too small to concern anglers but attract considerable attention from scientists because of their strange habits and anatomy. Many small boys know them well, and catch them by hand in rock pools. They are quaint little creatures that seldom grow longer than a few centimetres. They are widespread in both islands of New Zealand and throughout Australia.

Some blennies leave the water to sun themselves on rocks, hopping about on their fins, but they soon scamper back into the water when disturbed. There they hide under stones and rocks, feeding on small marine animals. New Zealanders sometimes refer to blennies as weedfish, twisters or cockabullies. One Australian variety is known as the jumping joey because of its ability to scramble over weeds and rocks.

B ■ BLENNY

Oyster blenny

Oyster blenny *Blennechis anolius:* These queer little fish take their name from their habit of sheltering in empty oyster shells and depositing eggs therein, guarding them until they hatch. They have long canine teeth on each side of the jaw. The larger specimens have a crest on the head and extended or produced rays. They average around 7 cm in length but are brave enough to bite a hand that seeks to disturb the eggs. Oyster blennies are found in Queensland, New South Wales, Victoria and South Australia.

Jumping joey *Lepidoblennius haplodactylus:* One of the 30 species of clinid blennies which are found around weeds and rocks in the southern half of Australia. They have bare heads, velvety teeth and grow to 12.5 cm. They are creamy-grey in colour with black spots on the sides and curved stripes below. Also known as the jumping blenny or the basking blenny from its penchant for skittering about the rocks above the water to sunbake.

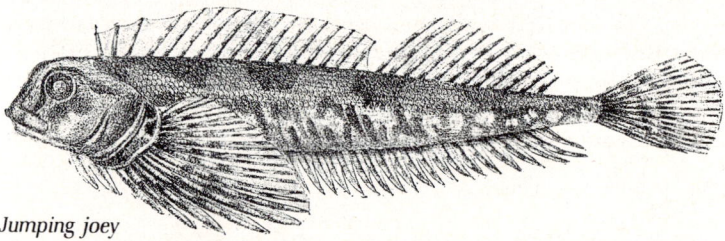
Jumping joey

Eel blenny *Peronedys anguillaris:* A South Australian blenny found only in St Vincent Gulf which can be distinguished from an eel by the dorsal fin and the large gill openings. Also known as shanny, eel codlet or gunnel. Seldom seen by fishermen but of great interest to naturalists. They are black or chestnut brown on top, with pale yellow or pink sides and yellowish-brown heads, and reach 12.5 cm.

Snake blenny Ophiclinidae: These are found along the shorelines of New South Wales, Victoria, Tasmania and South Australia, where they include the black-backed snake blenny *Ophiclinus gracilis*; the dusky snake blenny *Ophiclinus aethiops*; the Adelaide snake blenny *Ophiclinus antarcticus*; the snake blenny *Ophiclinops pardalis*; and the variegated snake blenny

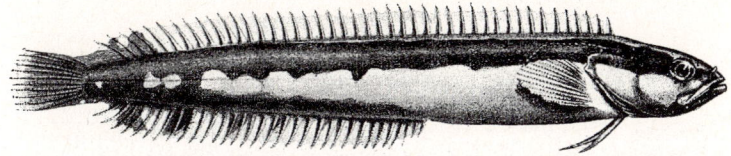

Black-backed snake blenny

Ophiclinops varius. Very little research has been done on these blennies and most of them have been identified by single specimens.

Threefin blenny

Tripterygion spp: A common New Zealand blenny found in several varieties around reefs and rock pools. They come in several colours, brown, grey, reddish-brown, with silvery markings or brown bars. They are mostly seen at low tide and take their name from the dorsal fin that is divided into three parts, the first short and low, the second long and evenly arched, and third short, first rays highest. They grow to 15 cm and are also found in Western Australia and South Australia.

Hairtail blenny

Xiphasia setifer: Probably the biggest of all blennies, growing to 50 cm. The extended tail is tipped by hair-like threads.

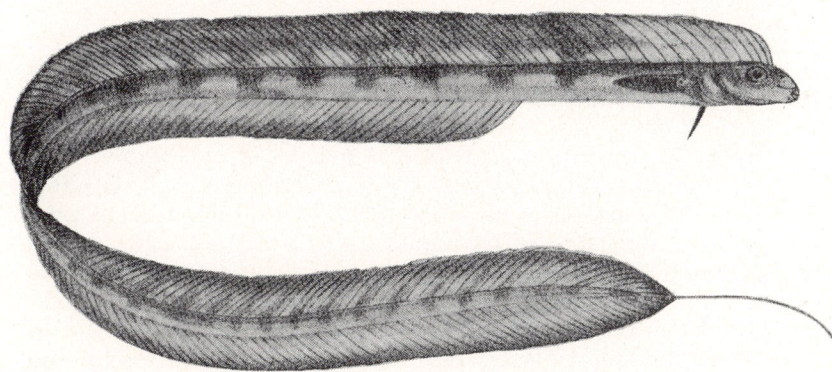

Hairtail blenny

Saltlickers

Istiblennius edentulus: A northern variety of blenny also known as reef blenny or grasshopper fish. There are, according to Whitley, about 16 species distributed in tropical Australia, where they skip around mudflats and rocks rather like the mudskipper (which see). They are blunt-nosed little fish with wide, vacant eyes and many of them have a clear division or notch between the spines and rays of the dorsal membrane. They reach 17 cm.

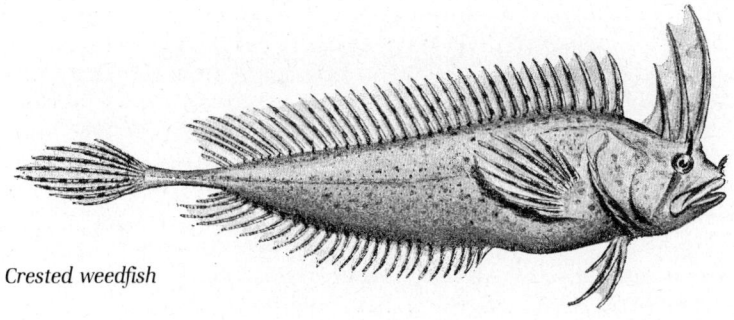

Crested weedfish

Weedfish Clinid blennies with strange crested heads and two dorsal fins which may be partly joined, usually similar in colour to the weeds in which they live. They are poor swimmers and move about on their claw-like ventral fins. They are found only in the southern half of Australia. They include the weed fish *Petraites heptaeolus*, the common weedfish *Clinus perspicillatus* and the crested weedfish *Cristiceps australis*. The most common is probably the crested weedfish, light green in colour with six vertical bands and a dark bar above the eye. They are found in beds of sea grass *Zostera* and grow to 22 cm. The young are born alive.

BLUDGER *See Trevallies.*

BLUEBOTTLE or Portuguese man-o'-war *Physalia* species are mostly known in the English tongue as the Portuguese man-o'-war but generally referred to among anglers along the eastern Australian coastline as the bluebottle. Despite the fact that this animal is well-known and occurs in vast numbers at times—appearing in plague proportions every few years for a few days—there remain large gaps in our knowledge of its habits and life-history. This makes attempts to predict its numbers incalculable, and the hazards involved immense, and efforts to prevent such plagues are at present impossible.

The air-water interface of the open sea has been considered by some authors as an ecological niche, and is clearly one with very distinct features. A number of animals live there permanently, or spend most of their lives there, and these may have special adaptations. Among the inhabitants of this niche are the bubble snail, the paper nautilus, various crustaceans and various siphonophores, but not all of these are permanent inhabitants. *Physalia* is one of the floating siphonophores, a specialized group of coelenterates, which includes also *Velella*, the by-the-wind sailor, and *Porpita*, a disc-like colonial form the size of a penny. The floating wind-directed fauna has been named the 'pleuston' by the Russian ecologist Savilov. This ecological 'niche' is certainly a hazardous one, as its inhabitants are exposed not only to predation from above and below, but also to the battering of the waves and the dangers of stranding along shores. It is this stranding which makes *Physalia* such a pest to *Homo aquaticus* because of its considerable stinging abilities, but cannot be of any survival value to the *Physalia* itself.

Very few animals use coelenterates as a principal food source, possibly because of their unpleasant stinging power, together with their low food value. Coelenterates also appear to be remarkably free from parasites. However, in a number of instances there is a distinct fauna, mostly fish, associated with a species of jellyfish. Other coelenterates also have distinct associated organisms, probably among the best known being some of the larger sea anemone and the fish which live among their tentacles. Why some fish can do this, while others are instantly killed by the stinging apparatus of the tentacles, remains still largely unclarified. In some cases the situation is utilized by the coelenterate's associate for shelter, as far as can be determined, but in other cases the relationship is more complex. The associate of the coelenterate is usually a fish, but in one recorded Australian instance the large jellyfish *Pseudorhiza haeckeli* had sheltering underneath it a number of small clear hydroid jellyfish, *Eirene menoni*.

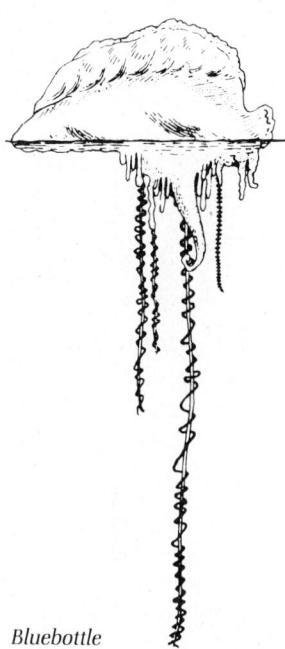
Bluebottle

The classic case of jellyfish-fish symbiosis (living together) is that of *Physalia* with *Nomeus gronovii*, a small pelagic fish which swims among the tentacles of its siphonophore 'host'. The question of the degree of, and possible mechanisms for, immunity is too long a subject to be discussed here, but can be studied further in other publications. The situation is, however, a complex one, as *Nomeus* does feed upon the tentacles of *Physalia*, and in its turn *Physalia* can sting *Nomeus* fatally and digest it.

Turtles appear to be among the more important natural enemies of coelenterates, as there are records of turtles eating *Physalia*, and also the lethal box-jelly or sea-wasp *Chironex fleckeri*. More observations on this predation by turtles in the Indo-Pacific region are, however, required.

For many years sailors have noted the *Physalia*'s peculiar habit of sailing at an angle to the wind, and in fact the name Portuguese man-o'-war is believed to have been given because of the resemblance of the float or pneumatophore to the lateen sail of the caravel, a fast and successful light ship introduced by the Portuguese in the reign of Henry the Navigator.

Specimens of *Physalia* have this float, a medusoid form which has been inflated by a gas-gland, projecting to either the left (left-handed) or the right (right-handed) when the animal is under the influence of the wind, and in different areas the strange 'navies' of the man-o'-war carry different proportions of the right-handed and left-handed forms. (Another siphonophore, *Velella*, also occurs in mirror-image

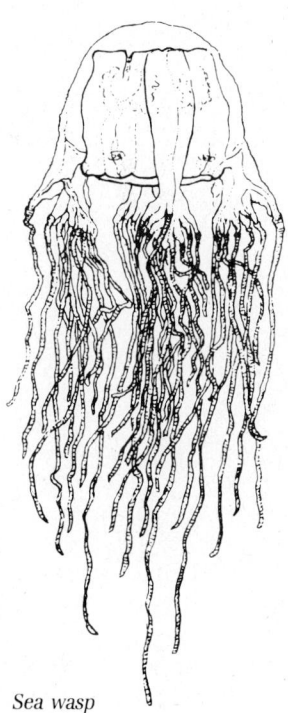
Sea wasp

forms with opposite sailing characteristics.) The left-handed *Physalia* sails to the right of the wind direction, and vice-versa. In the laboratory, or in beach-stranded specimens, the left- or right-handedness of a specimen can be recognized from the fact that the bulge of the specimen, with its various polyp-forms and tentacles, drags to the rear, serving in fact as a drogue or sea-anchor.

Another motion seen in *Physalia* under aquarium or other still conditions is that of rolling or somersaulting. This is possibly due to the animal being unstable if there is no breeze. Some authors do not accept the old sailors' explanation that the animal is 'tacking'. Whatever its explanation, it certainly has the effect of keeping the float wetted.

The feeding habits of the Portuguese man-o'-war have been studied more particularly in the Atlantic, and there it has been found that it feeds mainly on flying fish, mackerel and other surface-swimming fish which collide with it. Immediately this occurs the fish succumbs to the injection of poison by the thousands of nematocysts, the tentacle contracts (this is the main tentacle or 'fishing-tentacle', of which there is usually only one in the Pacific forms of *Physalia*, but several in the Atlantic form) and the fish is drawn up towards the float. The mouths of the hundreds of feeding polyps then open upon the prey and digestion begins. In the laboratory it has been found that in the presence of glutathione, a simplified amino-acid derivative, the mouths of the feeding polyps open widely.

Each specimen of *Physalia* is not a single animal in the ordinary sense; it is, instead, a group of organisms which has developed from a single egg and is living a colonial existence. One member of the group is expanded by the gas-gland to a float, which then bears beneath it not only tentacles, but polyps specialized for feeding, the gastrozooids; others specialized for reproduction, the gonozooids, which are actually adult forms; as well as dactylozooids bearing the tentacles. Despite a number of careful studies, there are a number of morphological features of the Portuguese man-o'-war still remaining to be elucidated. The structure of an adult *Physalia* is exceedingly complex, and in addition there are many features of its behaviour and physiology which need classification. Although each specimen of *Physalia* is made up of a number of adult and larval forms, each specimen is either male or female, and the two sexes are separate. The shedding of eggs and sperm has not as yet been observed, and so far specimens below 1 mm in length have not been described.

The stinging abilities of *Physalia* have been known for centuries, and an early account of them is mentioned in *Hakluyt's Voyages*, 1579. During the period of European exploration of the oceans *Physalia* became well-known to sailors, and in fact this was why deaths from the little-known box-jellies (sea wasps) in the tropical Indo-West Pacific zone came to be attributed by many authors to *Physalia*. Despite its considerable stinging power, no human fatality has with certainty been attributed to stinging by *Physalia*. Earlier claims of deaths from *Physalia* of swimmers in New South Wales have not been substantiated on critical examination.

Among early studies on the stings of *Physalia* are two by naturalists with Australian connections. Sir Joseph Banks made observations on the stinging powers of *Physalia*, being the first to observe the 'millions of fine white threads' which pierced the skin, arising out of 'little knobbs or beads' which were in fact the tentacular nematocyst capsules. The diagram with this article shows the spherical capsules and the threads they shoot out when in contact with suitable prey material. Banks also made observations on the sailing character of *Physalia*, and in addition recorded that an albatross he shot disgorged large amounts of *Physalia* it had consumed. A century later, Dr George Bennett also made observations on the stinging powers of *Physalia*.

The nematocysts in *Physalia* occur in different sites of the various appendages, but the ones of interest to swimmers occur only on the main fishing tentacles, where they are grouped in bean-like packets strung consecutively along. The nematocysts occur in two different sizes, but their action is fundamentally the same. On appropriate stimulation the internally coiled threads turn inside-out like a sock, and, on full evagination, discharge their venom. This poison is still under study by various laboratories, and appears to be a protein complex with added factors, but its full nature is not yet known. One of the major problems has been to get enough purified venom, free from contaminants, corresponding to the actual contents of the capsule. Possibly the differing sizes and kinds of nematocysts in these coelenterates contain fundamentally different types of toxins, as their differing effects appear to indicate; this is a subject still being explored.

The best first-aid treatment for the sting victim is vinegar, which neutralizes the toxins. If the sting is a severe one, however, medical attention should be sought.

DR RONALD V. SOUTHCOTT

BLUEBOTTLE fish

Slight little fish of the family Nomeidae, which have achieved a strange affinity with the bluebottle (*which see*) or Portuguese man-o'-war and are immune to the poison in its tentacles. Bluebottle fish are the same bright blue on top as the bluebottle, and live on pieces of food left by the bluebottle. They travel with the bluebottle in groups up to a dozen and never leave it. When the bluebottle is washed ashore, the bluebottle fish that accompanied it through the sea, are found close by on the beach. They grow to 15 cm and are distributed in temperate waters in Queensland and Western Australia, and sometimes when the weather is warm they occur in New South Wales.

BLUEFISH *Girella cyanea:* A pretty violet-blue fish studded with flecks of gold which inhabits the warm northern waters off New Zealand, usually around off-shore islands and rocky headlands. A close relation of luderick and drummer. Plentiful at Norfolk Island and Lord Howe Island, where they are watched by many impressed tourists. Once frequently caught off the New South Wales coast, but now extremely rare there.

Bluefish have a stout shape and are identified by teeth that have three points each. They are caught on set lines or in nets in New Zealand, and will take most fish baits. They are an abundant species which frequently appear in large numbers, cruising about the bottom, feeding among kelp beds. Berley will sometimes bring them to the surface, and they then provide quite exciting angling. Like luderick, they are particularly partial to weed, but their mouths are bigger than luderick and they will take hooks up to 4/0.

BOARFISH Spiny-finned, deep-bodied fish of the family Histiopteridae, with streaming fins and often with tube-like snouts. Plentiful in several species around Australia at depths which generally puts them beyond the reach of anglers. They are a major part of trawling catches, however, rivalling such species as nannygai, flathead, snapper and jackass fish in numbers. Their flesh is excellent eating.

Boarfish grow to 90 cm and 8 kg and are most abundant in the Great Australian Bight. A few stragglers swim into north coast harbours, but mostly they are deepwater fish found between 250 and 550 m down. The young are usually banded. One rare specimen, the roseate boarfish *Antigonia rubicunda* found only in the Capricorns, is rose-pink in colour with darker bands, but according to Marshall only two of these have been noted. There is frequently a big variation in the shape of juveniles and adults.

Big-spined boarfish *Undecimus hendecacanthus:* A deepwater variety that has been trawled at 275 to 350 m in the Great Australian Bight. Known to be found in New South Wales, Victoria and South Australia and almost certainly extends into Western Australia. Grows to 25 cm. Has a very compressed body, with a flattened ventral fin, but the snout is not as flute-like as in others of the species. The lips are very thick and fleshy, the mouth small, and the eye is about one-third the size of the whole head. The dorsal fins and anal spines are very powerful, the caudal fin truncate, and the whole body is covered with small scales.

Giant boarfish *Paristiopterus labiosus:* Probably the biggest of all boarfish, growing to 90 cm, with specimens over 60 cm uncommon. Found in Western Australia, South Australia, Victoria, Tasmania and New South Wales and regarded as outstanding eating. There is quite a marked difference between the young and adult in this variety. The young have deep, compressed bodies

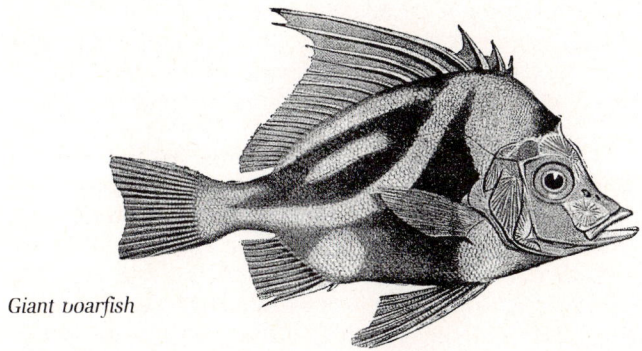

Giant boarfish

covered with three oblique dark bands. As they grow the dark bands completely disappear and the reddish-brown colour of the adult predominates. Adults have far more slender bodies. Both juveniles and adults have very strong spines and are covered with very small scales.

Paristiopterus gallipavo: A plentiful variety in the Great Australian Bight, with prominent thick lips and a robust, elongated body. The spinous dorsal fin is preceded by two long spines, the longest of which is three times the length of the longest ray. They are pearly grey in colour, with a pinkish head, and the whole body is studded with yellow spots. They reach 90 cm and are distributed in Western Australia, South Australia, Victoria, Tasmania and New South Wales.

Yellow-spotted boarfish

Pentaceropsis recurvirostris: A very distinctive fish with a flute-like snout, a tough, compressed and very deep body, and jaws with rows of coarse, pointed teeth. Found in New South Wales, Victoria, Tasmania, South Australia and Western Australia. The body colour is salmon pink, with three oblique dark bars across the whole body. They grow to 60 cm and 6.5 kg and Scott says they are excellent eating. There is a big variation in their body shape and in the outlines of their fins as they mature. Like all other boarfish they have characteristic streaming fins, with the dorsal particularly strong.

Long-snouted boarfish

Long-snouted boarfish

BOATS Used by sportsmen for sea, lake and river fishing, boats vary so greatly they defy precise classification. The majority, from 2 m dinghies to 18 m cruisers, are powered by either outboard or inboard motors or both. Some of these craft are seaworthy in all conditions but most are not.

Open boats, usually the most convenient for fishing parties, are only safe at sea in relatively calm weather. The motor also must be powerful enough to contend with currents, winds and tides and to bring the boat back to port without running out of fuel. Fuel consumption at sea is much more variable than on land owing to these factors. Adverse winds and tides can drastically reduce a boat's range, especially one that is underpowered from the start.

See Safety in angling.

Choice of a boat

The main qualifying factors determining the choice of a fishing craft are the depth of the buyer's pocket and the sort of fishing for which the boat will be used. Powered boats can be bought for hundreds of dollars or thousands of dollars depending on size or other requirements. The man who intends fishing in shallow and sheltered inland waters may be satisfied with an easily portable inflated rubber life raft fitted with a small outboard motor or the humble rowboat or dinghy.

Apart from being sound and watertight, the most desirable feature of any rowboat is that it should move easily through the water. This ability to transform the impulses of the oars into a smooth continuous motion is built into the shape and balance of the boat. The badly-made rowboat progresses with a jerky motion guaranteed to tire out the strongest rower.

The quality of a rowboat in this respect is best determined by a practical test and the fisherman who expects to do a good deal of rowing should try his boat before he buys it. Although an outboard motor is now available for even the smallest of craft, it is wise to keep a pair of oars in the boat.

A 2 m dinghy is rather cramped in space and fishermen, even on inland waters, prefer something larger. The answer is the utility boat, usually an open craft powered by either an inboard or outboard motor, 4 m to 9 m in length.

The utility is an ideal fishing boat, its open construction allowing ample space for four, six or more fishermen and their gear. Excellent for harbours and estuaries, it is usually manoeuvrable enough for smaller rivers and creeks. Utilities are often taken to sea, but are not seaworthy in all conditions.

The man who wants to go sea fishing regularly or can afford comfort on his week-end fishing trips will pick the cabin launch or cruiser. They are available in even greater variety of size and style than the utilities and runabouts, ranging from 5 m to 18 m or more in length and 20 to 80 km/h in speed.

Seaworthiness varies with size, shape and power although even a half-cabin 5 m launch is safe enough when properly handled. By the nature of its construction the cabin cruiser is not as stable in rough seas as a sailing craft of similar size.

In such conditions, the powered craft relies on its motor to maintain steerage-way so that it quarters the seas—that is to say, meets the waves diagonally. In this way seaworthiness is relative to the range and reliability of the boat's engines.

Outboard motors are more portable, convenient and easy to maintain. Consequently most of the smaller cruisers are powered by one or two outboard motors mounted on the transom. When buying an outboard bear in mind that the size of the motor must suit the boat. In general four-cycle motors are more suitable for sea fishing than two strokes, being better capable of being run at the low speeds necessary for trolling.

Most of the cruisers fitted with inboard motors are larger and more powerful than the outboard types and therefore better sea boats. Diesel engines are usually more expensive than those using petrol, but safer and cheaper to operate.

Although light metal alloys, plastics and fibreglass are now commonly used for utility boats and the smaller cruisers, the larger boats are still usually built of wood, fine timbers such as mahogany and teak being used for the more costly craft.

Metal and fibreglass hulls are much less trouble to maintain than marine plywood or wooden planking, but since both metal and fibreglass are heavier than water, sufficient flotation material must be built into the boat to ensure safety. This is a point that should be kept in mind when buying a second-hand or backyard-built boat.

Used boats are generally a better buy than used cars, but there are sufficient pitfalls—dry rot, borers and engine condition, for example—to justify having a second-hand boat thoroughly examined by an expert before you buy it.

Where will your boat be kept? Storage and maintenance are two factors which must not be overlooked. The utility or smaller outboard cruiser can be towed on a trailer and stored at home, distance and traffic conditions permitting. Moorings must be rented and slipway facilities available for larger boats.

Maintenance
Every boat with timber in its construction must be inspected regularly for dry rot. This is a fungus contagion causing decay in wood and the only way to get rid of it is to replace the affected timber.

A musty smell, discoloured or flaking paintwork and disintegration are the signs of dry rot at work. It is most liable to occur in craft unprotected from rain or washed down with the garden hose. The rot settles in damp spots left by fresh water. It cannot grow in salt water. Scattering salt in the bilges is a preventative. So is good ventilation. Boat covers can create the conditions in which dry rot thrives. Similarly, damp clothing, ropes, life jackets should never be left in the boat.

All the metal parts of a boat are subject to corrosion,

B ■ BOATS

TYPES OF ANCHORS

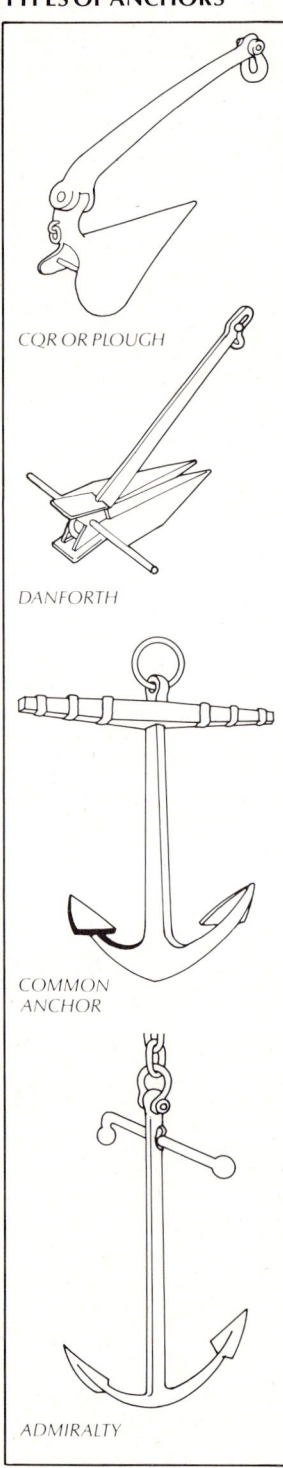

CQR OR PLOUGH

DANFORTH

COMMON ANCHOR

ADMIRALTY

particularly below the waterline, where a special type of corrosion known as electrolysis occurs. This results from electrical reactions between certain metals—copper reacting with zinc, for instance—and the softer metal being eaten away. This can be prevented by attaching a zinc plate to the boat in any area where electrolysis might take place.

Copper is preferable to galvanized iron for all fittings. Rusted screws or nails will show as discoloured spots in the paintwork and should be either replaced completely or cleaned and treated with anticorrosive compound.

Boats must be repainted regularly and recaulked as necessary. Careful preparation is the basis of good painting, cutting back the old paint to a clean sound foundation. Non-skid paint or paint mixed with sand should always be used on decks. A neatly painted, accurate waterline has more uses than merely improving the appearance of your craft. It tells you at once whether all is well with your boat's balance and buoyancy.

Rust also can spoil a boat's engine, particularly internal rust in the water jacket which may cause either the jacket or cylinder wall to burst when the engine is under stress. Stop leaks from the water jacket because a leaky jacket will rust.

Major repairs to an engine are best left to a skilled mechanic but every boat owner should carry an instruction book and essential spare parts which he can replace in an emergency.

Trouble-free motors are maintained by regular cleaning and changing the oil, looking after batteries, never revving up a cold engine but allowing it to warm gradually. A little extra thought and care for your boat when it is laid up will also pay dividends the following summer.

Equipment

Each Australian State lays down regulations for safety equipment in boats and publications stating the official requirements can be obtained on request. In general these consist of life jackets, fire extinguishers, foghorn, navigation lights, bilge pump, oars, a couple of anchors and distress flares. Common sense will also suggest a spare coil of strong line, emergency flashlights, tool and first aid kits, food and water supplies. A radio transceiver is almost an essential in any seagoing boat and an ordinary metal water bucket has saved lives before today as we shall see later.

Harbour rules

Various harbour regulations covering speed, anchorages and so forth are in force around the Australian coast and it is every boatman's duty to acquaint himself with them. Entry to harbour is marked by black conical buoys on the starboard (right) and red can buoys on the port (left). Black and white striped buoys mark the centre line.

The rule of giving way to the right applies at sea just as it does on land. A boat propelled by sails or by oars has right of way over a power boat on all occasions. Vessels meeting pass on their port sides while vessels crossing go across the stern of the boat having the right of way.

Docking and anchoring

A boatman uses wind and current to bring his craft alongside a dock or mooring float. The boat must have sufficient steerage way for the bow to be pointed either into the wind or the current, whichever is the stronger. In this way control of the craft is maintained. An onshore wind or current is allowed to drift the boat into position.

All boats should carry at least two anchors and a line at least ten times the length of the boat. If the line is too short, the anchor may not hold properly. It should be long enough to allow the anchor flukes to become well embedded and more than strong enough to withstand the weight of the craft.

A variety of anchors are available to suit different sizes of boat and various types of seabed. Unless the anchorage allows space for the boat to swing, it will be necessary to set an anchor at the stern as well as the bow. These anchors should line up the boat in the direction of the prevailing current or wind. An anchor light should be shown at night.

Anchors can drag at times. Check this by taking the bearings of two or three landmarks in different directions ashore. If the relative positions of these landmarks change, you may be sure that your anchor is not set firmly.

Everyone who goes to sea should have at least an elementary knowledge of navigation. This involves the ability to read charts and to understand the compass well enough to plot a course. In order to do this it is necessary to correct the variation caused by the difference between true North and magnetic North and the deviation caused by magnetic interference within the boat itself. When these adjustments have been made correctly, the answer is the course on which the boat should be steered to reach a given destination.

Weather

Every boatman should take care to obtain the latest information from the Weather Bureau before going to sea. This particularly applies to hobby fishermen whose boats and seamanship may not be the best for coping with rough weather.

Changes in the weather are the results of vast movements in the atmosphere. Warm air rises, cold air descends. Winds rush into areas of low pressure. Warm air blowing over a chilly sea produces fog.

The sky warns the seafarer ahead of a change in the weather. Wind draws a shadow across a bright blue sky and rain darkens that shadow. The depth of the clouds is a clue to the strength of the coming storm. Dark ragged clouds and rising waves are nature's warning to head for shore.

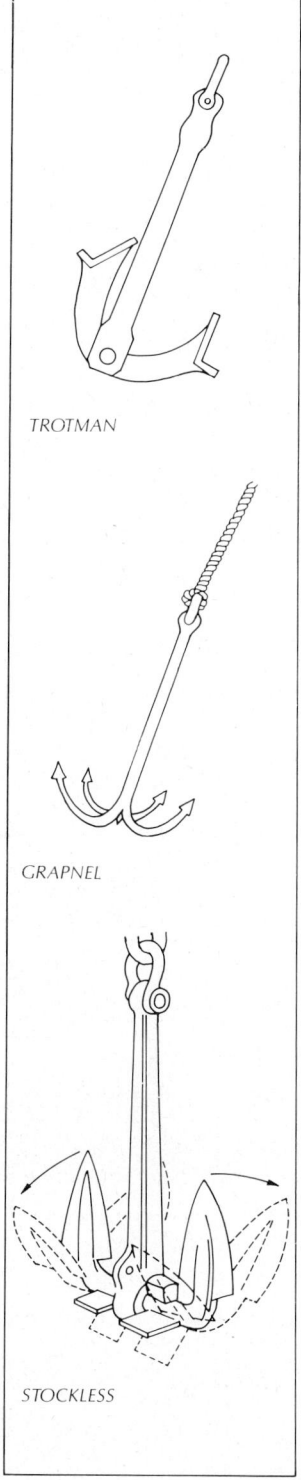

TROTMAN

GRAPNEL

STOCKLESS

A boat caught in a squall may be saved by an ordinary bucket securely tied to a long line. The bucket can then be pressed into service as an emergency rudder if it is hung over the stern and manoeuvred from side to side. It can be let out from the bow as a sea anchor to hold the boat's head into the sea. Finally it can be slung from the middle of the line beneath the boat amidships to act as a false keel and give increased stability.

In a crisis, flares or oily rags set on fire in a metal dish are an effective way of calling for help. Petrol-soaked rags which burn with a clear flame should be substituted at night.

Together with storms, fire is the boatman's worst enemy. Good ventilation to clear petrol fumes, equipping an inboard engine with a flame arrestor, prevention of petrol leaks and the use of proper marine cooking appliances are all measures that cut down fire risks.

Reasonable precautions such as a complete ban on smoking, stoves and all use of electricity will obviate most of the dangers of fuelling. Spilled petrol should always be washed away and a careful check made for petrol fumes below decks before the engine is restarted.

Game fishing

Aristocrats of the sporting fishing fleet are the ocean-going game fishing cruisers. These are often luxury craft costing up to $300,000 or more, equipped with running-water bait tanks and outriggers for trolling. They offer the ultimate in fishing comfort, with refrigerators, gas stoves, electric light, comfortable cabins and a spacious cockpit with swivel chairs.

A medium-sized game fishing boat such as this is well-equipped and comfortable for open sea fishing.

BOMBAY duck

Harpodon translucens: A flabby, unattractive fish which forms the oriental dish known as Bombay duck and is served in Chinese food in Australia, usually in a curry. The young are transparent with minute black spots. The adults are milky opalescent pink below and greenish above with minute dark spots on all parts of the body. It has a very small eye, a large mouth with long teeth and lateral line extending beyond the fork of the tail.

Maryborough fishermen call it the 'ghost grinner'. Found in the Northern Territory, north-western Australia and Queensland. Grows to about 40 cm and 1.8 kg.

BONEFISH

Albula vulpes: A shy, fast and specialized fish of the shallow water, the bonefish has almost completely resisted the efforts of Australia's anglers, and so occupies a unique niche in Australian fishing. It is here, it has been caught by anglers, but it remains an enigma. It is likely that bonefish may yet be mastered in the wide, spreading sandflats of the Barrier Reef. The preferred habitat is clear or moderately clear water over a rich marl—marl being a food-rich combination of sand and mud which settles quickly after being disturbed. Bonefish are not known to favour turbid water, and this keeps them out from the inshore waters of most of the tropical coastline. Typical bottoms are usually patterned with weedbeds interspersed with open sand, and well supplied with prawns, crabs, mussels and similar shellfish, including oysters.

It follows that such rich feeding grounds attract large numbers of other species. On a visit to a likely Australian bonefish ground, American angler Peter Wright had problems with the sheer numbers of other species. To catch bonefish successfully it is necessary to largely avoid other species. Mr Wright described the habitat as ideal, and saw several fish which could have been bonefish, as well as hosts of mullet, small queenfish, trevallies, turrum, barracuda, rays and sharks.

Bonefish

Feeding habits

The bonefish is a finely-boned animal which feeds by grubbing for shellfish on the bottom, crushing the shells with powerful jaws, and then swallowing the shell animal while discarding the broken shell. It also takes crabs and prawns freely. The same strength of muscle which makes it a non-stop fighter makes it a popular and expensive marlin bait, which can be towed for long hours behind game boats without wearing out.

One problem facing anglers interested in bonefish is the correct identification of a fish when it is still some distance off. Protective coloration is so good that often all that can be seen from a boat is a slight shadow on the bottom, and it is easy to mistake other species, such as mullet and barracuda, for bonefish. It is safe to say the breakthrough will only be made by a persistent angler willing to spend time making mistakes and then rectifying them. The wary nature of a fast, observant fish in clear shallow water makes it a tougher opponent than most anglers appreciate.

Pole-boating for bonefish

The normal method of bonefishing suited to Australian conditions is for a shallow-draft outboard boat to be drifted or poled across a flat. There are usually two occupants, one an angler ready to fish and the other the man on the pole. Both wear polaroid glasses for improved vision. The chief virtue of a pole, usually 3.5 m in length, is that it allows the user to stand up high on the bow and so to see better while moving the boat. Most craft, such as aluminium dinghies, pole better from the bow. Alternatively, one may row while the angler stands on the bow and gives directions. The outboard may not be used while fishing, as the bonefish is one species which reacts adversely to sound. The chief use of the motor is in travelling to and from the fishing grounds.

Bonefishing technique

The rod is usually at least a 2 m tubular fitted with a large saltwater spinning reel, with a capacity of at least 180 m of 5 kg line and a reliable braking system. Anglers new to bonefish are advised to fish not less than 4 kg test until experience is built up. In some cases, where fish are larger than average, it may be necessary to use a leader of up to 135 kg test, about 60 cm long, which can be used to hold the fish in the final stages of capture—for which a landing net is an asset. Lighter lines tied direct to the hook can involve hour-long fights. No sinkers are used, owing to the shy nature of the fish, though a couple of small split shots may be clamped close to the hook. The hook should be of 1/0 or 2/0 size, carefully sharpened and preferably in a strong pattern—a 2/0 stainless steel is a good choice. The bait is best fished live, and a live prawn or crab is ideal. When a cruising fish is sighted, the bait is cast ahead of and to the side of the course of the fish, as quietly as possible, and then drawn

A rare photograph of a bonefish.

towards the path of the fish. When it moves in, the angler strikes on the first nibble. The fish will reject the bait as soon as it crushes it and encounters the hook.

Bonefish do not jump. In shallow water, the first run of a hooked fish may be for 180 m, with a pronounced bow wave and a jet of spray flying from the curling line. Working the line back to the reel and coping with subsequent runs will keep the angler fully occupied for anything up to half an hour. One angler who captured a 2.5 kg bonefish on 1.5 kg test monofilament took 54 minutes to do the job, and ended by virtually jumping on the fish to grab it, since it was still swimming too strongly to be held in place by the line.

Alternative methods of angling include saltwater fly fishing, which calls for a strong saltwater fly rod and a weight-forward fly line which can 'shoot' (pull out more line as it is projected). Casts to 30 m can be made with this kind of tackle. Saltwater flies in patterns such as hagen sands, pink shrimp, homer rhodes and philips pink are used on bonefish. This is considered one of the finest forms of the angling art, calling for the best that any sportsman can offer.

See Tunas.

BONITO

BOXFISH Oddly-shaped, vividly-coloured fish of the sub-order Ostracioidei represented by two families in Australian waters. They are also known as cowfish, trunk or coffer fish, and in Western Australia they carry the erroneous name of stonefish. They are mostly found in water of 180 m or more and take their name from the covering of tough shell or carapace that protects them from predators. The shell does not develop around the fins, gill-slits or mouth, and the tail has only isolated plates that allow movement. Their flesh is poisonous. Whitley says they are claimed to pass a poisonous secretion into the water so that they cannot be kept with other fish in aquariums.

Boxfish have teeth pushed together, but each jaw has 10 or 12 conical teeth set in separate sockets. They are mostly taken by trawlers and dredges but will take a hook. They feed on shells, crabs, pieces of small fish, plankton and weeds. Their colour varies with sex, but they are mostly brown or olive-green in body colour, with striking spots, stripes and other markings. They range from 12 to 45 cm and average 1 kg.

Boxfish of the family Ostraciontidae, an order which includes cowfish and turret fish, are distributed around tropical Australia, the Indian and Pacific oceans. The colder-water members of the Acaranidae from the southern waters of Australia are considered to be more colourful, and are mentioned in the writings of early naturalists.

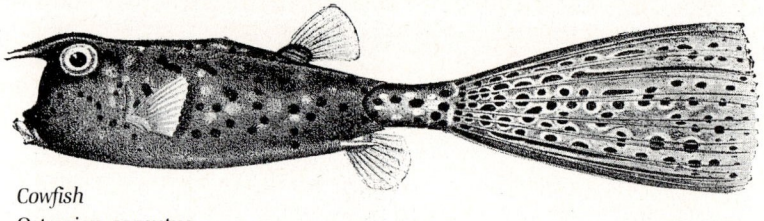

Cowfish
Ostracion cornutus

Blue-spotted boxfish *Ostracion tuberculatus:* A very common variety in Queensland reef waters which is distributed right down the Queensland coast. Exceptionally speedy swimmers with a wide range outside Australia. They are olive green in colour with yellow fins and grow to 45 cm.

Robust boxfish *Strophiurichthys robustus:* A yellow-brown fish with large black spots on the back and upper sides that is found in tropical Australian waters at depths down to 275 m. Marshall says it is common to find it among the catches of prawn-trawlers operating from Coolangatta. Reaches 25 cm.

Small-nosed boxfish *Rhynchostracion nasus:* A bone-coloured variety with vivid dark brown spots and prominent mouth. The young are frequently a bright orange-yellow, with black spots. Found in Western Australia, and through the Pacific to Malaya and right across the Indian Ocean. Rare in Queensland. Grows to 22 cm.

Anoplocapros lenticularis: A far more compressed, shorter, deeper bodied fish than tropical varieties. The dorsal is well back, just in advance of the anal fin, the pectoral is short and the caudal rounded. The mouth is very small. Yellow in colour with dark grey areas on the back. Ranges from Western Australia to South Australia and New South Wales. Reaches 30 cm.

Smooth boxfish

Capropygia unistriata: A deepwater variety with a short, deep body and a single dorsal set well back near the origin of the anal fin. Pale yellow in colour. Smaller at a maximum of 12.5 cm than other boxfish. Found in Western Australia and South Australia in deep water.

Spiny boxfish

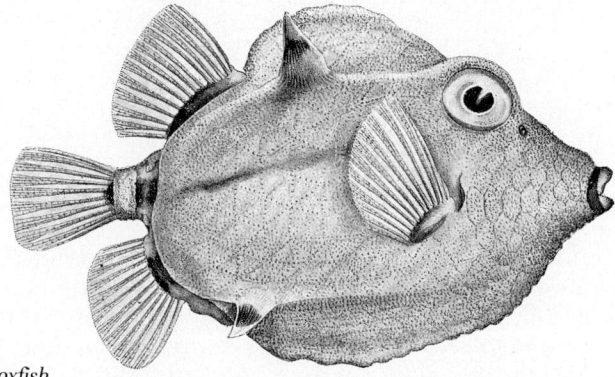

Spiny boxfish

Stone or cement structures also known as seawalls have become so numerous around the Australian coastline they present a new challenge for sports fishermen. Most have been built to make the entrance to coastal harbours and rivers safer, with the breakwater extending into the sea. They are at precisely the spot where fish leave and enter and offer protection for smaller fish. There are some famous fishing breakwaters around Australia such as the wall at Harrington, New South Wales, and the one formed by extensions to the runway into Botany Bay at Sydney's Kingsford Smith airport. Breakwaters at Nelsons Bay, north of Sydney, Evans Head, Yamba and Tweed Heads become very crowded fishing spots when good fish are running. In Western Australia catches of salmon, tailor and tommy ruff taken off locations like the Fremantle breakwater are legendary. The breakwaters at Mackay and Townsville in Queensland have a similar reputation for producing abundant hauls, particularly at the end of a flood.

BREAKWATER fishing

Many breakwaters are built across the natural flow of rivers, causing sandspits and islands to build up inside the river mouth. On the seaward side of the wall the river flow slows down and this allows a bar to be formed that becomes a

Breakwater safety

hazard for small boats. Many fatalities have stemmed from ignorance of these hazards by careless navigators. Fishermen who venture on to breakwaters should ensure that they are wearing non-slip footwear. They should beware of wet and slippery rocks. Waterproof jackets are essential when high seas are running. Waves that break over seawalls and disperse into holes and cracks give the fisherman who falls into the water as he scurries back little chance of avoiding injury. Wherever there is a likelihood of taking a fish larger than a rod and line can lift a gaff is essential. A lot of men have drowned trying to bring in big fish without a gaff.

Breakwater species Mulloway, bream, luderick, tailor, dusky flathead and salmon are the main targets of breakwater fishermen, but small tuna, Spanish mackerel, and drummer are also taken in numbers. Mulloway require strong rods and lines and respond best to live baits. Sinkers up to 110 g are often needed to prevent the bait washing back on to the rocks. After a flood when small schools of mullet or garfish try to re-enter rivers, mulloway wait for them at the end of the breakwaters. In these conditions, the mulloway will take surface lures, especially white feathers. Bream fishermen should carefully assess the run of the water alongside breakwaters. When there is little or no tidal run, small sinkers should be used, but as the movement of the water increases so should the weight of the sinkers, for it is essential to keep the bait down. Even then be prepared for snags. Some bream fishermen boost their holiday fun by positioning their boats just off breakwaters where the water is calm. Casting towards the breakwater at night they catch a lot of fish. Sizeable breakwaters also provide good conditions inside estuaries where luderick and dusky flathead flourish. Drifting from a boat with live yellowtail for bait can be highly productive.

Between February and April tailor are frequently caught from the sea end of breakwaters by fishermen using rods 4 or 5 m long with 7 kg lines and heavy fish baits or metal spinners. The technique required is to keep the bait used active to suggest the movements of a small fish in the water. The well known east coast fisherman Les Firth has for years used a stale bread rig for bream with outstanding success. Before he goes out on to the breakwater or seawall Firth prepares a dozen or two three-hook rigs with chunks of bread on them. He casts well out, playing the rig back towards the breakwater and by the time the bread softens enough to slip from the hooks, the bream have usually bitten.

BREAM Cunning, fickle members of the scavenging family Sparidae which occur all around the Australian coast in a variety of species, and, because of their caution in approaching bait, provide consistent tests of the angler's skill. A splendid table fish much sought by anglers, but no relation to the European bream, which is a freshwater carp of the family Cyprinidae. None of the Australian species of bream occur in New Zealand, where snapper, lacking the hump-heads of mature Australian snapper, are sometimes called bream. The New Zealand black perch or parore is also known in some areas as black bream, and the bull-headed, swallow-tailed rays bream is sometimes labelled sea bream.

Bream are known by a multiplicity of local names, including black, bluenose, bony, cockney, emperor, freshwater, government, hump-headed, Murray, pikey, red, sea, silver, southern, spangled, emperor, surf, yellowfin, Cape Moreton, sea, creek, red, coral, grunter, kelp, rays, slater, snapper, stinging, thick-lip, yellow-banded butterfly and yellow-lip butterfly bream. In fact, there are just six distinct bream species in Australian waters: black bream, southern bream, tarwhine, pikey bream, yellowfin bream and the uncommon hump-headed rays bream, each of them with several aliases. Red bream are young snapper. Research completed by N.S.W. Fisheries biologist Stuart Rowland in 1980 showed that the two common angling and commercial species were black bream *Acanthopagrus butcheri*, and yellowfin bream *Acanthopagrus australis*. Both are endemic to Australia.

Bream are generally olive and silvery in colour with darker bands running from head to tail. The sea run varieties are lighter in colour than the specimens of shaded waters. They mature at 15 to 20 cm in 2 to 3 years and mostly spawn in river mouths in winter. Outstanding specimens reach 50 to 60 cm. They have steep snout profiles and a single dorsal fin.

All bream become extremely perceptive as they mature. They have fine teeth which project from their lips and they use these to tear, hold or rip at food. They habitually approach baits warily, testing an edge to assess if the baits are attached to anything. They will seize on loose handfuls of prawns but as soon as the prawns are put on a hook will swim away from them. When they are extremely hungry, they mostly try to nip pieces off a bait or shake it free of the hook. Seldom will they swallow it.

To overcome this caution, experienced anglers use extremely light lines for breaming, to allow the fish to run without feeling any drag on the line. Trying to stop this run on a light line so that the hook is set in the fish's mouth soon exposes any weaknesses in the angler's technique. Though bream may become suspicious of a heavy sinker set back along the line, they will frequently take a bait with a small sinker set alongside the bait. If bream swallow the bait, the danger moment for the angler comes when he tries to stop the fish's initial fast rush.

When to fish for bream

Bream can be caught at any time of the day, but the angler's chances are far better at night when they venture into shallower water and become markedly less suspicious. They prefer the dark and rarely bite well in moonlight, or when the sun is bright overhead. They are far more plentiful on dull winter days than in summer sunshine.

Black bream sometimes bite best in the period before slack tide, southern bream midway through the flood tide, but when it is dark and conditions are calm they may contradict this by biting at any stage of the tide. They are extremely sensitive to noise and will scare off at the sound of a dropped oar or when a foot dislodges a stone from a river bank.

Where to fish for bream
Bream are mostly bottom feeders that seek out marine worms, crustaceans, shellfish, green weed and small fish. In waters where there are extensive oyster beds, they do considerable damage to these shellfish. They will feed in fairly open water but they have a fondness, too, for logs, weed beds, bridge piles and roots of trees. A favourite spot for big bream is around and among submerged tea-trees.

The flats around the mouths of rivers, usually found at the end of a beach, are good bream spots, particularly straight after the sandbar that often blocks such a river is swept away by floodwaters or by storm-driven tides. Some estuaries provide good fast-water breaming when the tide is running strong. This hides the angler from the feeding fish and scours out food, but it has the disadvantage that a big sinker has to be used. In some saltwater lakes and inlets it is possible to find spots where there are large areas of weed that hold numerous items on which bream feed. In these areas, bream often feed at mid-water and bottom baits can be forgotten.

For rock-hoppers, bream often can be taken where the waters spill back from rock platforms and ledges into gutters. Here the bream pick up worms, shellfish and crabs pounded out of the rock crevices. But they are fish which roam all types of coastal water, and they can be taken from jetties, breakwaters or from boats. In boats the angler is wise to spread wet bags along the spots where he puts down his gear and where he places his feet so that all noise is muffled.

In the summer when the sun is on the water, bream fishing is very patchy, but as soon as the evening comes or the clouds obscure the sun the bream will feed ravenously. Most bream fishermen prefer a slight breeze, just enough to ripple the surface. A light wind that blows straight up an estuary, hurrying the incoming tide is the best one for bream fishing.

It is unwise to try and skulldrag a big bream, whether the angler is fishing the surf or the rock areas. A big bream, immediately it feels the hook and the restraining line, will attempt to swim parallel to the beach and a 4.5 kg line is not equal to dragging a fish of this shape against strong currents. Play the fish until it is exhausted and then let a strong wash and a steady strain on the line bring it in.

Black bream

Acanthopagrus butcheri: Also known as sea bream, silver bream, surf bream and yellowfin bream. Primarily an estuary fish, important both to commercial fishermen who take it in seine nets, meshing nets and wire-netting traps, and to the saltwater angler. It ranges from Shark Bay in Western Australia to Myall Lakes in New South Wales and is the common bream species found in the Gippsland Lakes in Victoria. Its colour varies according to its environment. In the lakes and estuaries, which are often discoloured by floodwaters, the black bream is a golden bronze or an olive green. In the waters of the surf or outside of the river mouths where the black bream feeds over clean sand it tends to become silvery in appearance.

For a period of 51 years the largest bream recorded captured by an Australian angler was one of 3.3 kg caught by F. Negus at Baldface Point, Georges River, New South Wales, in 1916. Then, in 1967, N. Beckhouse caught a yellowfin bream weighing 3.7 kg, with a length of 55 cm and girth of 50 cm, at Lake Macquarie, near Newcastle. Larger fish of the species have been netted by commercial fishermen.

Splendid black bream fishing is to be had during the dark nights of winter, and while they will feed at almost any stage of the tide, they bite best from half flood through to the first part of the ebb. When feeding through the day the black bream congregate in the deep holes of the lake or estuary or in the deep channels in the surf zone, but at night they move into the shallows where excellent fishing can often be found in water only a metre deep. They sometimes will take almost any meat offered and at other times they become very choosy.

Black bream have a more torpedo-shaped body and flatter snout than yellowfin bream and the ventral fins are always dark. They prefer saline waters and are common.

Black bream

Yellowfin bream

Acanthopagrus australis: Also known as black bream and silver bream, the yellowfin bream is generally a silver colour with greenish tints on the back and sides. But the main difference between the black bream and the yellowfin bream, as far as the angler is concerned, is that the yellowfin bream does not venture out of the estuary even in the spawning season. It is not caught in the surf, the bays or the sea. And while it is sometimes difficult trying to define an estuary, we can take it that the yellowfin bream is strictly an estuarine fish.

The yellowfin bream ranges from Townsville in north Queensland to Victoria's Gippsland Lakes. It is also found in the Tasmanian estuaries. It grows to 2.5 kg or more but anything over 1.2 kg is a good catch these days. Most of those caught average between 150 and 650 g.

Although yellowfin bream have been caught on most of the baits used for black bream, the best baits are shrimps, softworms, sand worms, yabbies, softshell clams, small fish, shellfish and crabs (whole or cut). It does not eat oysters like black bream simply because oysters are uncommon in southern waters.

Yellowfin bream have a deeper body than black bream, with a higher forehead or snout. They have yellow ventral fins which may be pale or lack yellow colouring, depending on the type of habitat. Yellowfin bream will venture into fresh water. They spawn at the mouths of estuaries in winter.

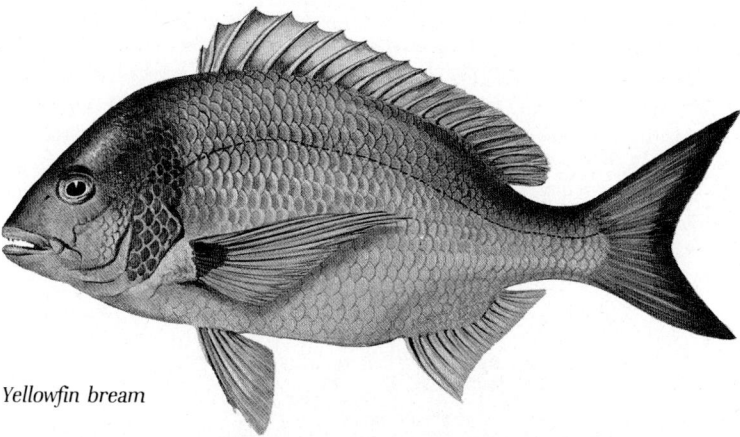

Yellowfin bream

Hybrid bream Distribution of black bream and yellowfin bream overlaps between the Gippsland Lakes and Myall Lake, and both can be caught in the same estuaries, for example, Gippsland Lakes, Wallaga Lake, Wongonga River, Bermagui River, Myall Lake. Although there is a large population of black bream in Myall Lake, their numbers decline in proportion to yellowfin bream as one proceeds up the coast from the Gippsland Lakes. Intermediate specimens are caught, particularly on the N.S.W. south coast around Narooma and Bermagui. Stuart Rowland's research on the east coast showed that these intermediate bream were hybrids.

Apart from first generation hybrids, later generation or backcross hybrids were found but they were small in numbers, which indicated a hybrid breakdown is occurring.

Although the breeding of black bream and yellowfin bream normally occurs at different times and places, when the two species become trapped in a lake closed to the sea, as can happen in the Narooma area, their breeding seasons change slightly and overlap. This makes possible the interbreeding of these closely related species and the formation of hybrid bream.

Pikey bream

Acanthopagrus berda: A tropical species, usually dark grey to black in colour with a tinge of purple to brass. Some taken from mangrove-lined creeks are almost black. An exceptionally long and stout second spine on the anal fin gave the fish its name. The black marks at the base of the pectoral fin usually found on other bream are completely absent from pikey bream. It ranges from Darwin to the Burdekin River in Queensland, and is the common bream of north Queensland where it is easily taken by handlining close to jetty piles or from creek banks by anglers using small sinkers and cut baits of mullet, garfish or other small fish.

The pikey bream grows to about 40 cm in Australian waters but a specimen of twice this length has been recorded from Indian waters. This fish provides excellent evening fishing in South Africa.

The best places to find pikey bream are in the tidal creeks, along the mangrove flats and in the vicinity of rocks, jetties and piers in the bays. Ordinary bream tackle, baits, and methods are used to catch this species. It is as delicious as black bream and southern bream.

Pikey bream

B ■ BREAM

Tarwhine *Rhabdosargus sarba:* An important member of the bream family, prized as a food fish. The body of the tarwhine is silvery in colour. The centre of each scale is golden and this forms longitudinal golden bands on the back and upper part of the sides. The dorsal on the head is golden brown. It is often confused with black bream, though it has a more convex rounded head, is smaller than black bream, and has those distinctive golden streaks which the black bream lacks.

On the eastern Australian coast the tarwhine ranges from Townsville in Queensland to the Gippsland Lakes in Victoria. An occasional specimen has been taken at other places along the Victorian coast. The tarwhine grows to about 40 cm and 2 kg. In South Africa specimens up to 11 kg in weight have been recorded. Although the Australian tarwhine is relatively small it fights strongly because of its deep body, especially in the surf.

In Victoria the best bait seems to be a small crab, but in New South Wales small fish and marine worms are used successfully. In Queensland, anglers favour fresh prawns, yabbies and sea worms. In Western Australia, the tarwhine ranges from Albany, where some excellent catches are taken, to Shark Bay.

The same tackle, baits and methods can be used for tarwhine as are used for black bream or southern bream. May, June and July are the best months. The most noticeable feature when fishing for this fish is the way it usually bites: instead of the 'pick-up and run' generally associated with bream fishing, the tarwhine takes the bait with two or three sharp, hard tugs. Many anglers consider it a better fighter than the bream.

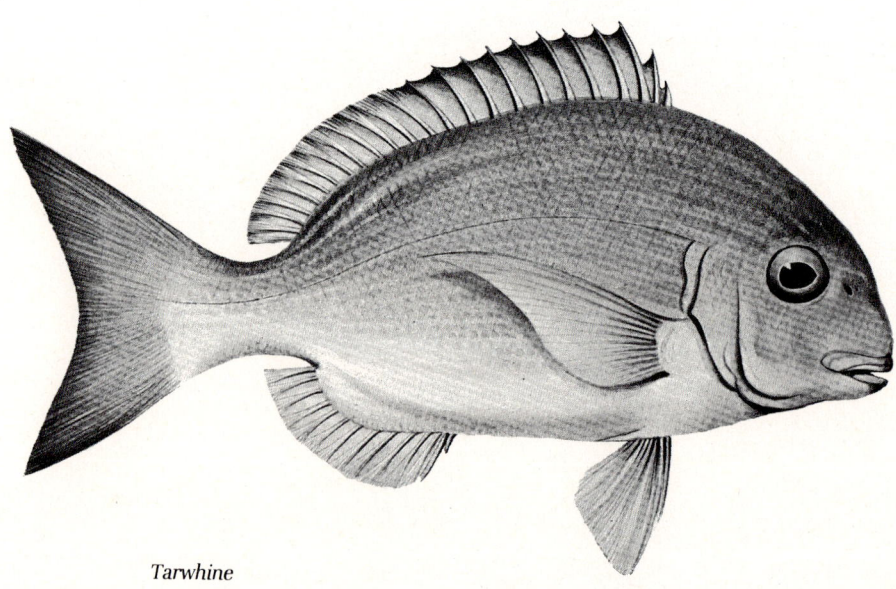

Tarwhine

Rays bream

Brama brama: An uncommon open sea species found in South Australian waters that normally frequents very deep water of 180 m or more. Its appearances are spasmodic and only seldom does it enter bays. Rays bream are more often found stranded on beaches than on the end of an angler's line. They have a very steep snout profile with an oblique, protruding lip, and their single dorsal fins and anal fins are covered in scales. Little is known about them, though it is certain they take squid and small fish.

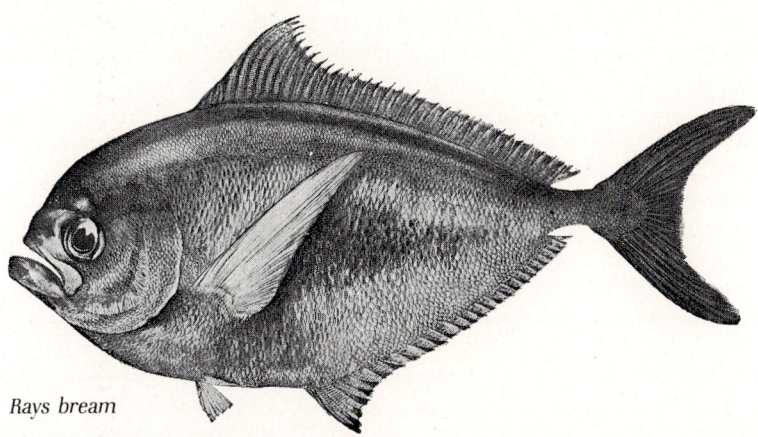

Rays bream

Bream fishing techniques

The most successful, and consequently the most popular, method of fishing for bream in the estuaries is to use the running-sinker rig. A small sinker is slid onto the 3 to 4 kg line and a 1 m nylon leader of about 2 to 2.5 kg is tied to the extreme end of the line. To the end of the leader is tied a single hook, ranging from size 4 to 1/0. To prevent the sinker sliding down onto the leader a single shot is nipped on close to the joining knot. This rig can be used in all bream fishing where normal conditions are found.

There are, however, many estuaries where the river, lake, inlet or estuary flat has a bed of thick, sticky mud. Any sinker used, no matter how light, will either sink into the mud or become stuck to it. Every bream that attempts to run with the bait is lost because the resisting line pulls the bait out of its mouth. Now the logical thing to do is to fish without a sinker, using a small light hook, a light bait that would drift around at mid-water or to use a float that would hold the bait off the bottom. But unfortunately nearly all estuaries have strong currents running through them and only in certain spots can the 'no-sinker' or 'float' method be used.

The secret of fishing these mud-bottomed areas, where there is a strong tidal flow, is to rig the sinker in such a way that it does not matter whether it sinks into the mud or sticks to it. And the way to do this is to slide a small split ring on to the main line and to attach the sinker to it by a 15 cm length of nylon. The end of the line is tied to another split ring of the same size, and to this split ring is tied the 1 m nylon leader with the hook at the end. This rig is the same as the normal bream rig except that the sinker itself does not run along the line; only the split ring to which it is attached does. If the sinker slides into the mud or becomes stuck to it, the line and the leader and the hook can all move freely.

Because of the difficulty of casting the standard running-sinker rig any distance, particularly on windy days, anglers who fish from jetties, breakwaters and beaches have worked out another rig which allows the sinker to move along the line and yet is easy to cast. On this rig the sinker is allowed to run right down the line and leader to the hook eye. So, on this rig no split shot or split ring is used as a stop. The slight resistance this rig imparts to the bait is said to be an advantage, as this resistance would be felt by a bream picking up a crab from the sea or river bed.

Although a midwater bait has long been used by boat anglers to catch bream, it is obvious that this method was only made practicable for bank anglers by the introduction of the threadline reel. In boat fishing it was a simple method to drop the bait and float over the side and wait for a bite. But bank fishing with a float that had to be cast some distance over weed beds posed a very difficult problem. When sufficient weight was added to a light bait like shrimp, a large float had to be used and in quiet waters this scared the scales off every decent sized bream in the area. With threadline tackle the angler can use a light float, a couple of split shot and two or three shrimps and can cast far enough to catch bream feeding at midwater.

Fishing for bream in the surf
It is hopeless trying to catch bream in a surf so violent that the sea is thick with churned-up sand, drifting weed and waving kelp. Strong off shore winds that produce a dead-flat surf are not conducive to good fishing either. What the surf man wants is plenty of lively water without the drifting sand and weed. In this kind of water the bream take the bait freely.

As in all other kinds of bream fishing, the best time to fish the surf is during a run-in tide of an early morning, late evening or at night. During the night the bream come in the flood tide and will feed in water right under the angler's feet. The best spots are in the channels, the gutters and along the edges of the sandbanks. Surf bream can be just as choosey as the bream of the estuary but they will take almost as wide a variety of baits: crabs (whole or cut), yabbies, beach worms, nippers, prawns, garfish, pilchards, and sand sprats.

The most suitable tackle is a light surf rod of about 3 m, a threadline reel and a 4.5 kg line. If a running sinker can be used, it can be rigged either to run right down to the hook or it can be stopped 25 to 60 cm from the hook. The size of the hook used is chosen to suit the bait used, sizes ranging from No. 1 to 2/0. Mustad Beak hooks are usually preferred. Rock fishermen use the same tackle and baits and fish in much the same areas as the surf man.

Estuary breaming
As the southern coastline faces every point of the compass it is obvious that there is no wind from any one quarter that will bring good bream fishing to all our estuaries. On most occasions an easterly wind will put the fish off the bite no matter where the angler is fishing. As a general rule a south to south-westerly brings the best fishing along the Victorian and South Australian coasts, although the force of the wind is important. A very strong wind can ruin estuary fishing by lifting the silt found in most of them.

The bream fishermen usually claim that the wind that blows straight up the estuary, the same time as the run-in tide, is the one that brings the best fishing. If the angler is fishing a late afternoon after a sunny day, and the tide begins to run-in about 4.30 p.m., accompanied by a freshening tail wind, he can expect a good bag of bream before the dark sets in. Tides play an important part in all estuary fishing but to the bream fisherman a high tide is as important as clear water is to the fly fisher. At low tide the estuary may be almost emptied of water; the deep holes may be seen, and many sand banks and mud flats exposed to the air. The water at low tide in these shallow estuaries is usually too hot for bream fishing on a summer's day, and the angler may be restricted to the early morning, late evening or at night.

When the first ripple of the flood tide runs into the estuary some good bream fishing may be had if the waters already in the estuary are deep. In the shallower waters the angler will have to wait until almost full flood before the bream really begin to bite. At high tide all the mud flats are covered and only the highest sand bars are exposed. The weed beds along the margins of the estuary are again under water and big bream search among them for shrimps and small fish.

For the first few hours after discoloured waters reach the estuary, after heavy rains, the bream bite well, even on ordinary garden worms. But it does not take much of this flood water to put the fish off the bite. If the incoming tides are strong enough to push back the discoloured waters, good fishing will probably be found at this period. But what usually happens is that the flood waters not only prevent the tides from entering the estuary but they discolour the waters for some distance off shore. Heavy flooding may ruin all fishing for a week or so.

In the estuaries, the most frequently used rig is the running-sinker rig with the 1 m leader and No. 4 to 1/0 hook, tied below the sinker.

BULLROUT *Notesthes robusta:* Of the 40 members of the family Scorpaenidae found in Australia, most are marine, but the bullrout spends most of its time in freshwater streams of the eastern seaboard descending into estuaries during heavy rain to cause considerable problems for commercial net fishermen. They are impressive camouflaged fish of basic black and yellow colouring, densely marbled in reddish-brown, dark brown and grey. They grow to 30 cm and make superb aquarium fish. Bullrout are fish of outstanding table quality but are rarely eaten because of the stings they inflict on the unwary. Treatment for the stings inflicted on amateur fishermen is to immerse the inflicted area in hot water and bathe it in Condy's crystals (potassium permanganate) or ammonia. The sting comes from venomous spines on the head and along the back.

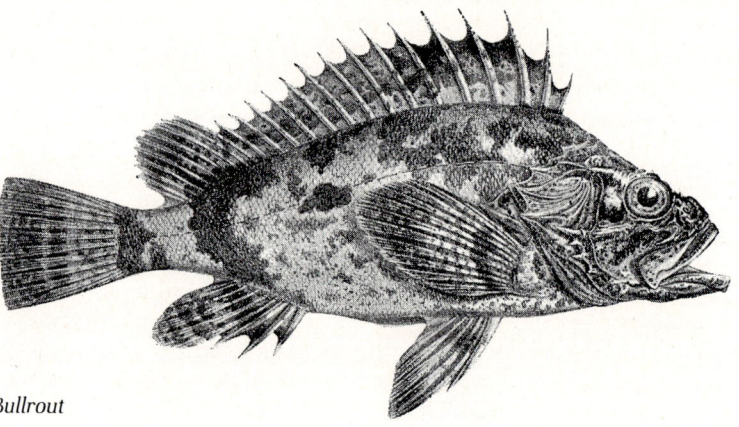

Bullrout

BULLSEYE A common cold-weather group of reddish-pink, large-eyed, deep-bodied fish of the family Priacanthidae. They have very small scales and a protruding lower jaw that makes the mouth opening almost vertical. Also known as big eyes, they are found right along the Queensland coast and into New South Wales, and are particularly plentiful in Queensland's shallow bays in winter months. South Queensland anglers catch them from piers and jetties or around rocky ledges at night, the best of them between 30 and 35 cm. They are not considered good eating but Grant says their flavour improves if they are steamed and not fried. Red bullseye, *Priacanthus macracanthus*, is probably the most abundant of the family and is noted for its large glowing eye. The eye pupil is black, surrounded by scarlet. The fins are red or pink and inside the mouth red. They swim in circles when hooked and are said to grunt when caught. In northern Queensland waters, the red bullseye is supplanted by the spotted-finned bullseye, *Priacanthus tayenus*, which has a similar deep-bodied appearance and grows to around the same size.

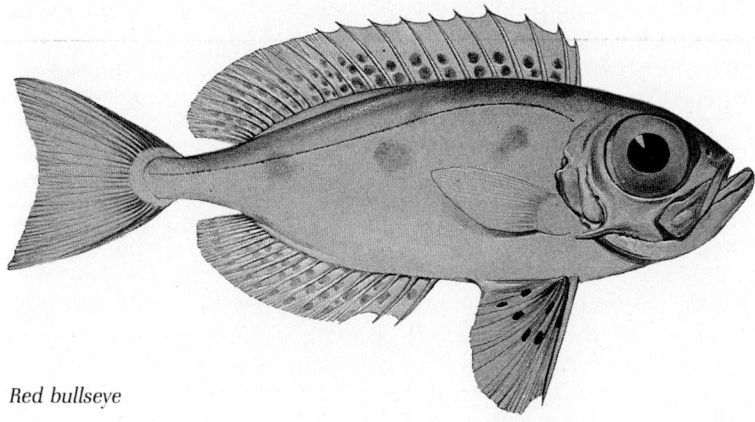

Red bullseye

BUTTERFISH

A common Queensland fish of the family Chaetodontidae which inhabits shallow sand flats and bays in sizeable shoals. They are good table fish but suffer from a prejudice among some anglers who appear unaware that they should be bled promptly after capture. Butterfish should be carefully handled as the wounds caused by their strong dorsal spines are very painful, but not fatal.

Several fish are loosely called butterfish, including the john dory. The true butterfish, *Selenotoca multifasciata*, is caught in estuarine waters, creeks and rivers by anglers using baits of moss, weed, peeled prawns and dough. They grow to around 30 cm, are found mostly in northern waters, and are silvery in appearance having a greenish back with dark vertical bars and spots.

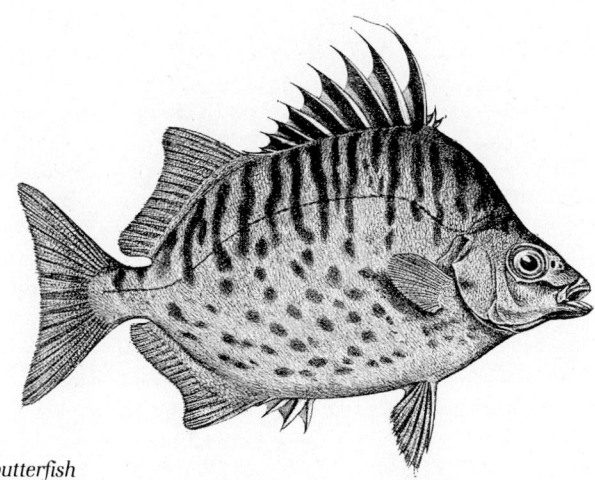

True butterfish

B ■ BUTTERFISH

Southern butterfish *Selenotoca multifasciata* variety *aetatevarians:* Grow to about 40 cm and are common in southern Queensland estuaries and bays and in Western Australia. They are green along the upper sides and back, silvery below, with thick dark green vertical bands or spots, and stripes below the belly. They are a good food fish if they are bled quickly but the flesh is soft.

Spotted butterfish *Scatophagus argus:* Are deep-bodied fish which can inflict a sting that remains painful for several hours. They are caught in inshore coastal waters and grow to 35 cm. Despite the danger of stings, they are highly popular aquarium fish because of their colouring. Juveniles are vividly marked with dark vertical bands over an orange body. Adults have a greenish-grey body on top, and silvery to yellow underneath, and are covered in dark spots. They can adapt to fresh water.

Striped butterfish or scat *Selenotoca multifasciata:* Is a freshwater variety which also inhabits saltwater sandflats. The fish have what Whitley calls curious helmet-like headbones, and at 5 to 12 cm they are scats that are suitable for aquariums. They are quite striking fish the colour of butter, with black stripes or bars and light spots underneath. They are distributed in New South Wales, Queensland, the Northern Territory and Western Australia and like others in the family have dangerous spines.

C

CADDIS fly *See* Aquatic insects.

CARDINAL fish *See* Gobbleguts; Mouth almighty.

CARP Only three of the world's 1500 odd species of carp are found in Australian waters, and all are poor sporting fish introduced by well-meaning people unaware that they would come to be regarded as pests by a majority of anglers in the waters of their adoption. All who have eaten these fish regard them as unacceptable table fare, coarse in texture and very bony, but they are favoured by some Europeans who believe eating carp boosts their virility. To Australian anglers, their best use is as live bait for Murray cod.

Carp, first introduced to Australia in 1876 by the Geelong and Western District Acclimatization Society, are freshwater fish of still and slow-flowing pools, billabongs and rivers. They feed on plants, insects and crustaceans, and are fish of extreme hardiness that can tolerate turbid conditions and high water temperatures that kill the native fish. They are abundant in Australian rivers west of the Great Dividing Range and in some coastal rivers of south-east Queensland. Anglers dislike them not only because of their poor table quality but because they root about in the mud in confined water creating disordered conditions and because of a belief, probably false, that carp devour the eggs of other fish.

In Britain specimens have been caught that exceeded 18 kg, and such trophy fish are eagerly sought by sport fishermen using specialized tackle and methods. There are no records of large carp being caught in Australia, which does not mean that they do not exist, for no very large fish were caught in Britain until anglers began a very specialized search for them in recent years.

Prussian carp or common carp *Cyprinus carpio:* These fish are known to attain a weight of 27 kg. They are characterized by a long dorsal fin, large scales, and four barbels (whiskers) on the mouth, a feature not shared by the other two species. They do not appear to be present in the numbers of the other two.

Crucian carp *Carassius carassius:* Also known as golden carp. They attain a weight of 2.5 kg and a length of 40 cm in Europe, but do not grow so large here. They are easily distinguished from the common carp by their smaller scales and the absence of barbels. They vary in colour from dull greenish-grey above with silvery sides to brilliant pinkish-red, and some are mottled halfway between these colours.

Goldfish *Carassius auratus:* Often cultivated in ponds and aquariums because of their attractiveness. Their length is usually only around 8 cm, although a specimen caught in Queensland and preserved in the Australian Museum is 30 cm long. Colours may be silver, gold, red or white. In the wild they frequently revert back to their feral colouring of greenish black, and then are often confused with the crucian carp, to which they are closely related. Gold and red fish are often referred to as 'golden carp'.

Besides being extremely hardy, goldfish breed prolifically, and are present in vast numbers in some waters, but because of their generally small size they are largely ignored for food and also sport. Examination of stomach contents of trout from Lake Burley Griffin, Australian Capital Territory, and Oberon Dam, New South Wales, show that they are an important item of food for these fish, and undoubtedly they play an important part in the attaining of such good condition by these trout.

The three species of carp are easily caught on light tackle, using either worms or bread for bait. The very large fish taken in Europe in recent years have almost all been taken on floating breadcrust after 'berleying' the area for days with bread. Carp are sometimes found rising to natural flies, and then can be taken by fly fishing methods, the larger fish providing good sport.

See Tench.

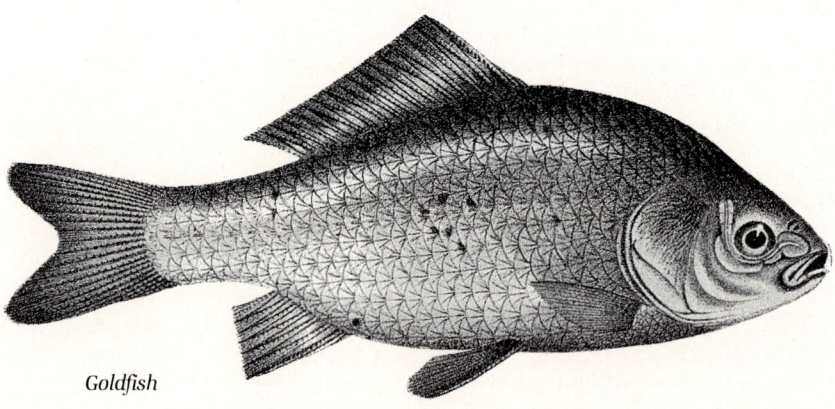

Goldfish

CASTING a fly

From the strictly practical point of view, flycasting is the basis of all fly fishing, for fly fishing consists of presenting an artificial fly to a fish in such a manner that it is accepted as something good to eat. This means that the angler must be at a reasonable distance from the fish, or at least well hidden, and the fly must arrive in a way that is completely natural. A variety of techniques have been developed over the years to accomplish this, and these are collectively known as 'fly-casting'.

The three aims of a flycaster are: delicacy of presentation, accuracy and distance, in that order.

All casting techniques consist of storing energy in the rod by bending it so that when it unbends the released energy is used to throw the flyline, and with it the fly, forward. It is important to realize that it is this controlled bending and unbending of the rod that shoots the line and fly forward, and not just the strength of the angler's arm. A direct analogy is the storing of energy in a bow by bending it, so that when the string is released the straightening limbs hurl the arrow forward.

In flycasting, the rod is made to bend by two procedures. (1) The application of leverage with the rod hand, i.e. by waving the rod back and forth so that it is made to flex and straighten, or 'work'. (From the feel and appearance of a rod working in this way a skilled caster can tell what type of fishing a rod is suited for, and what size line is best for it.) (2) By loading. The weight used for loading is the flyline, which is why flylines are so heavy in comparison to ordinary lines. (Flylines come in different weights to suit different rods and types of fishing. If a line is too heavy the rod will not be able to throw it very far, and if too light it will not enable the rod to work properly. Many modern manufacturers mark their rods with the recommended line size.)

Correct grip
The hand that holds the rod is called the 'rod hand'. The other is consequently the 'line hand'. The rod is held as a hammer is held, but with the thumb on top. A correct grip is important, for it is the drive of the thumb on the forward cast that supplies much of the loading to modern 'fast' rods.

False casting
Pull a metre or so of line off the reel and out through the guides. Then, holding the rod correctly, swish it back and forth in an upright arc so that the line is made to stream through the air parallel to the ground. When this can be done successfully, pull a couple more metres of line off the reel and let the weight of the line already in the air pull it out through the guides. This is called 'false casting', and is an exercise often practised by fly fishermen. In actual fishing it plays an important part in feeding out line, changing direction, keeping dry flies buoyant etc.

C ■ CASTING a fly

GRIPPING A FLY ROD

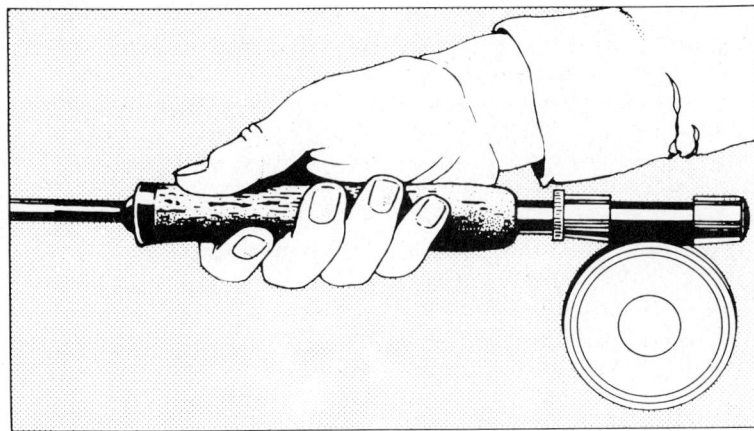

Hold the rod firmly, with the fingers spread and the thumb on top so that the hand will have complete control.

Leverage

On the forward movements of all casting techniques leverage is applied to the rod by the thumb on top and the little finger underneath the handle. The rod is not merely held in the hand, rather leverage is applied, in much the same way that leverage is applied to a hammer when driving a nail into a wall. During the back cast leverage is applied with the forefinger underneath the top of the handle, and the heel of the hand on top of the butt. It is necessary, particularly for tournament casters, to have a clear understanding of how leverage is applied. But this leverage is by no means the whole of the force applied in making a cast. As the line is picked up off the water, or otherwise brought into a backcast, the casting hand moves back toward the angler's shoulder. On the forward cast the hand pushes the rod butt firmly forward so that the force acting to load the spring of the rod is a combination of leverage and forward push. In making the push, the hand should move smoothly forward in a horizontal plane, the movement coming from the shoulder rather than a mere bending of the elbow. This smooth forward push of the rod hand is one of the main factors in smooth flycasting.

Side cast When some feel for the rod and line has been achieved through false casting on a horizontal plane, it is time to practise making true casts. This should be done over water. It is a good idea to start with the side cast, where the rod is worked parallel to the ground so that the line flies low over the surface of the water. If a white fly is used, it is possible to watch the line and fly, and so see where improvement may be required to iron out any troubles.

Stand with your left side to the water and false cast so that as the line goes to the right (back cast) it extends over the land, and as it goes to your left (forward cast) it extends over the water. When making a true forward cast the rod is extended fully with a spearing-thrust and pointed in the direction the line is to go, and the line allowed to drop to the water in a fully extended position. The final spearing-thrust is most important, for this is what makes the difference between a false cast and a true cast. This method of casting, with the rod parallel to the ground and moving at the angler's side, is known as side casting. It is used when the fly has to be cast under an overhanging obstruction, such as a willow.

From the side cast the novice should progress to the overhead cast. The overhead cast is the basic cast; most other techniques are variations of it. Whereas the side cast is practised in a horizontal plane, the overhead cast is made with the rod working in a plane vertical to the ground, as follows. The back cast of an average overhead cast begins with 6 to 9 m of line extended on the water. The angler faces the direction he intends to cast with his left foot forward if he holds the rod in his right hand. Stance is as a boxer or fencer stands. He reaches forward with the rod until it almost touches the water and ensures that there is no slack between the rod tip and the line on the water. A rod cannot be loaded with slack line. When all the slack line has been gathered in with the line hand it is dropped on the ground and the line hand grasps the line to ensure that no slack line will run out through the guides when the rod is lifted during the cast. From this position the back cast is made by lifting the rod to a position directly overhead. This is accomplished by a snap of the wrist, the elbow staying relaxed by the caster's side, leverage being applied with the forefinger below the top of the rod handle, and the heel of the hand at the butt.

Overhead cast

1 At the beginning of the back cast, the line hand hauls in slack and maintains tension on the line. The line hand is raised towards the rod at the end of the back cast, ready to pull the line down during the forward cast.
2 Stand in a relaxed manner, allowing the rod to do the work. During the back cast, the forefinger applies pressure by lifting under the rod handle; during the forward cast, the thumb presses the rod forward.

THE OVERHEAD CAST

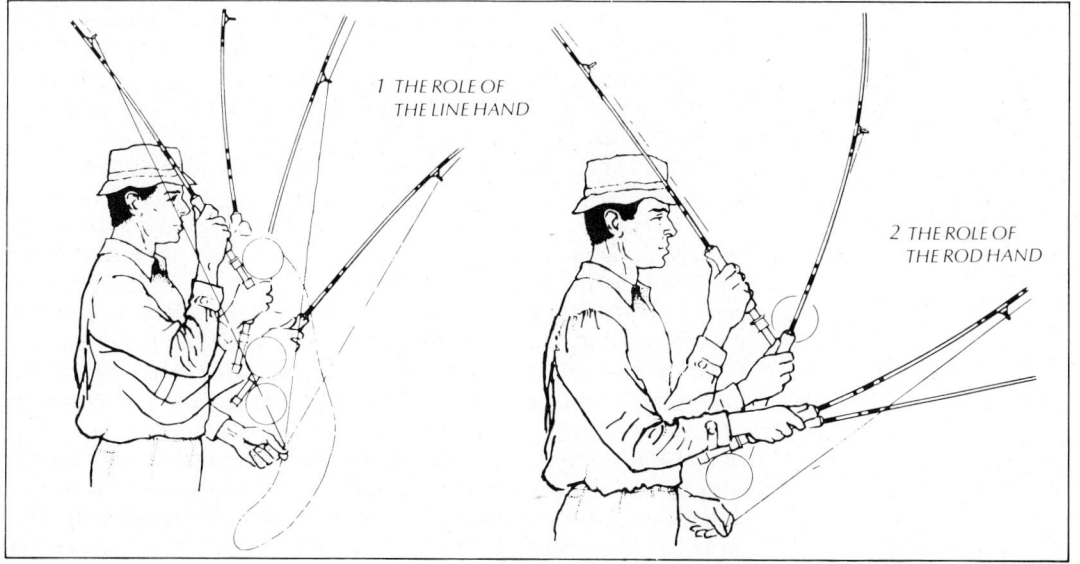

1 THE ROLE OF THE LINE HAND

2 THE ROLE OF THE ROD HAND

C ■ CASTING a fly

The cast begins slowly so that the line is lifted smoothly off the water, and accelerates so that the line is thrown up and back. The rod is stopped when pointing vertically overhead, but on longer casts momentum carries it back a little further. One of the most common mistakes made by casters is to carry the rod back too far, which causes the line to travel back too low and so foul on bushes or earth. Simultaneously with this movement of the rod the line hand pulls slightly on the line, keeping it tight and adding speed to it. This is called hauling, and is very important when casting long distances, as it greatly adds to the speed and momentum of the line.

The caster now pauses as the line flies back to straighten out behind. The longer the line being back cast, the longer the caster has to wait. Experienced casters wait for the straightening line to tug the rod tip back, and begin their forward cast at this moment, which has the effect of adding extra loading to the rod. If the pause is too long then the line will commence to drop and slacken, and so will be difficult to gather into the forward cast. If on the other hand the forward cast is commenced too soon, then the line will crack like a whip, and the fly may be broken off. So it is just as the backwards-flying line straightens out behind that the forward cast begins.

The caster pushes his hand out as he snaps his wrist forward, applying force with his thumb on top of the rod handle and levering back with the little finger underneath. The weight and momentum of the line, which has just reached maximum extension behind, loads the rod so that it flexes backwards. As the rod is snapped forward and so loaded, it is extended with a spearing thrust in the direction the line is to be cast. Simultaneously the line hand tugs on the line to tighten it as in the backcast. As the rod straightens forward, it unloads and throws the line. If the caster releases the line that is held in his line hand at the moment that the forward flying line achieves maximum velocity, then the momentum of line will be great enough to pull extra line up off the ground and out through the guides. This is called 'shooting line', and is the method of lengthening successive casts. A caster who wishes to extend line quickly will pull a great deal of line off the reel and onto the ground, and will then execute continuous overhead false casts, shooting line into each forward false cast until enough is in the air, when the final delivery cast is made.

With modern 'fast' fly rods the casting action is almost all with the wrist, unlike older slower rods with which it was the custom to use little wrist action, and much more elbow. An accomplished caster can throw 18 or 20 m of line using only wrist action, and practically no elbow, shoulder or body movement, using a modern fast-action rod designed for normal fishing. Using the 'double haul' technique, hereafter described, wherein elbow, shoulder and body movement, and 'line hauling' are all utilized to achieve maximum distance, casts out to the vicinity of 30 m can be made, and even further if special lines are used.

The two main faults to be avoided when overhead casting are: (a) Carrying the rod tip back too far at the end of the back cast, resulting in a dropping line, and (b) not timing the forward cast to begin just as the line straightens out behind.

Finer points
At the beginning of the forward cast it is important that the line should be picked up smoothly off the water so that any fish nearby are not disturbed. This is accomplished by:
(1) Gently lifting the rod straight up before the powered section of the back cast begins. This lifts the line off the water without disturbance.
(2) By making a forward roll cast before beginning the back cast (*see Roll cast*).
(3) By holding the rod parallel to the water and flicking it quickly up and down, which causes the line to jump off the water. Similarly the line and fly must land gently on the water when being presented to a fish. There are two methods of ensuring this:
(1) By shooting line. When the line is allowed to shoot the last couple of metres all its energy is used in pulling line out through the rod guides, and so it falls gently on the water.
(2) The jerk-stop. In this the line is aimed 90 to 120 cm above and beyond the target. As the shooting line comes up off the ground it passes over the line hand. As the line nears the end of the 'shoot' the line hand grasps it and jerks it to a stop. Thus the belly of the line cannot continue forward, but the leader end of the fly line will continue to turn over, and just as this is completed the caster reaches forward with the rod and the line is lowered gently to the water. This method allows gentle presentation of the fly even with a forward taper or level line, which are designed to throw big lures such as salmon flies or bass bugs, and are not suited for delicate presentation such as is needed with a dry fly or nymph.

Back-hand side cast

A side cast made with the rod on the linehand side of the body, used when occasion demands.

'L' turn side cast

This is used when an angler has a fish directly in front of him, but cannot make a normal back cast because of surrounding trees, and cannot roll cast because he is too high above the water. It is essentially a side cast in which the line is false cast left and right of the angler, parallel to the bank, and at right angles to the direction it is to be finally cast. When enough line has been extended a final back cast is made, still at right angles to the direction the final delivery cast is to go, and then the final cast is made directly at the fish. It should be realised that a line will always go in the direction the rod is pointed during the powered section of the delivery.

Steeple cast A variation of the overhead cast used when a nearby obstruction behind the angler blocks a normal back cast. The back cast, instead of being thrown backwards, is thrown directly upwards. This is done by lifting the whole arm directly upwards during the powered section of the back cast and exaggerating the final snap of the wrist. When the line has extended overhead, the rod is smoothly drawn down and then extended into the forward cast. The line tends to drop sooner than with a normal overhead cast, and so hit the water too hard, so the forward cast must be aimed higher than usual to compensate.

Galway cast This is used on small streams where the trees etc. on each side form a tunnel overhead through which the back cast must be thrown. The angler pivots his hips so that he can look behind as he makes the back cast, and then pivots forward again in time to make the forward cast.

Double-haul This was developed for distance tournament casting. It is a development of, and in many ways an exaggeration of, the overhead cast. It is most useful when fishing big water such as lakes and large pools.

The cast begins with the caster's feet well apart and his weight on the forward foot. When making the back cast he sways onto his rear foot, and then forwards again during the forward cast. Full use of shoulder, elbow and wrist movement is made, and the rod is carried back further than in an ordinary overhead back cast. The line is 'hauled' as far as possible during the powered sections of the forward and back casts, adding enormously to the line speed and rod loading. The greatest difficulty anglers have when first attempting the double haul is in reaching the line hand up to the rod in preparation for the haul during the forward cast. This must be done smoothly, so that no slack develops between the line hand and the butt guide on the rod.

During forward cast the angler sways forward and 'punches' the rod forward with a spearing-thrust that ends with the rod arm and rod fully extended. Simultaneously the line hand hauls the line down and back, ending with the line arm fully extended behind the caster's back. When the line reaches maximum velocity from the unloading of the rod, it is released and allowed to 'shoot'. Top tournament casters using tournament rods and lines may shoot more than 30 m of line. A good caster using standard fishing tackle, that is a 2.5 m rod weighing approximately 100 g and a HCH line, will lift about 18 m of line off the water and into the back cast, and will then shoot 12 m of line into the forward cast, when using the double haul. This is a very long cast by the standards of a generation ago.

Serpentine cast

This is not a cast proper, but describes the way the line is laid on the water to prevent 'drag' when a cast has to be made over water that is moving at different speeds. (If a portion of the flyline is lying on water that is moving faster than that on which the fly rests, then it will communicate this faster movement to the fly, which will then drag across the surface, alerting and frightening the fish.) The fly is aimed a little higher than usual, and lightly jerked to a stop so that the line rebounds slightly towards the caster. This causes the leader to fall on the water with curves in it, in a 'serpentine' manner. A dragging line must pull these curves straight before the fly can drag, and so there is an extra margin of safety.

Catapult cast

This is used when the only approach to a fish is through thick brush where no orthodox cast can be made. It is of short range and poor accuracy. The fly is held by the bend of the hook between the thumb and forefinger of the line hand, and the line is clipped to the rod with the forefinger of the rod hand. The rod is held pointing away from the fish and bent by pulling on the fly, which is then released and the rod pointed at the fish with spearing-thrust. As the rod straightens it will throw the line.

A trout angler casts in the middle of a Snowy Mountains stream.

C ■ CASTING a fly

Switch cast Little used today as it has been superseded by the roll cast. It was developed for use by salmon fishermen when a normal back cast was blocked by vegetation or rocks. Line is shaken out through the guides until a lot of slack hangs between the rod tip and the line on the water. This slack line is then flicked back behind the caster without any attempt to lift the fly off the water. As it billows back a forward cast is made, so the billow is rolled forward in a large loop along the water's surface. It is necessary to continue the forward cast further down into the water than is usual with an overhead cast, and timing is important, for the rod has to be loaded with the line just as it billows backwards.

Roll cast The most useful cast after the overhead cast. It is capable of delivering a long line accurately and is particularly useful on bushy mountain streams because it entails no back cast to tangle in the wilderness behind. It is the easiest of all fly casting techniques to learn.

The cast is best described with 12 m of line already on the water. The caster stands with feet well apart as in the double haul. The rod is drawn slowly back to the position where a normal overhead back cast begins, the caster's weight being on his rear foot. The line droops from the tip of the backtilted rod to the water. The caster's weight is now transferred to his forward foot, and the rod is extended with a spearing-thrust. Shoulder force is used to drive through the thumb. The casting action is followed through further than with the overhead casts, ending with the rod practically touching the water. The line is not cast forward as in the overhead casts, rather it is rolled across the water's surface in much the same way as a loop is thrown along a rope on the ground by a child. When the loop unrolls and reaches the end of the flyline it uncurls to deliver the fly.

Line is extended by pulling extra line off the reel before each cast and dropping it on the water. The adhesion of the extended fly line to the water allows this extra line to be pulled out through the rod guides as the rod is lifted up and back in preparation for the forward cast.

Side roll cast This is used when casting into the wind. Usually the wind is less strong near the water, and a cast made with the rod held almost horizontally will take advantage of this. The side roll cast is also made back-handed when occasion demands.

Roll cast pick-up Is used when fishing fast water that brings the flyline quickly back downstream. It saves gathering in a lot of slack which subsequently has to be cast out again. As the floating line comes back to the angler it is thrown forward with a roll cast that is aimed higher than usual, and as it uncurls in the air it is then gathered into a normal back cast and then thrown forward with the usual overhead forward cast.

CASTING in tournaments

Many anglers become very skilled in casting and this is the basis of many competitions. The contests cover the throwing of a fly or plug with rod and reel for accuracy or distance, either on dry land or on the water. The sport began with fishermen eager to learn how to handle their gear more efficiently but has progressed into a highly competitive game (for men or women) of its own. Contests are held in flycasting, plug accuracy and plug distance casting (plug casting is known internationally as skish casting) and weight-distance casting, each of which has several different sections. Australia has casting clubs in every State, although not all of them are affiliated to the Australian Casting Association. Local performances compare well in accuracy tests with the best achieved overseas but are lagging in distance casting.

First casting in Australia

The first casting tournaments were held in 1939. The Australian Casting Association was formed in Victoria in 1947 with Theo Brunn president but Australian championships were not organized until 1951. In 1952 Australia made enquiries about affiliating with other casting countries, with Bill Southam playing a leading role. The outcome was an international conference in 1955 in Europe at which the International Casting Federation was formed. The first World Casting Championships were held at Hanover, Germany, in 1957, when world flycasting titles were begun. In October 1959, Australia staged the first world surf casting championships at Moorebank, New South Wales, much of the work falling on Alyn B. Walker.

C ■ CASTING in tournaments

Australian casting records

Joe Carnemolla held most of the national records—he made casts approaching 170 m with a light line—just after the war but in the 1970s Sydney salesman, John Bethune, established himself as Australia's best caster. Bethune held many Australian records and State records. The Australian distance record stands at 191.72 m by Victorian R. Reeves in 1979—compared with the world record of 300 m set in South Africa. In accuracy casting events casters are permitted three casts at wooden discs 75 cm in diameter and 45 cm above ground at ranges varying from 12 to 15 m. Up to five points are given for the first cast, three for the second and two for the third. The possible maximums vary according to the weight of plug or fly used.

WEIGHT OR SURF CASTING

56 Gram Stationary Spool Distance: *E. Whittam* Vic. 169.50 m 107.83
Artificial Bait Distance: *E. Whittam* Vic. 165.73 m 30.5.82
Surf Spinner Distance: *E. Whittam* Vic. 194.64 m 30.5.82
Level Line Distance: 112 grams. *I. Cameron* NSW 184.88 m 25.11.79
56 Gram Multiplier Level Line Distance: *E. Whittam* Vic. 176.39 m 10.7.83
Artificial Bait Accuracy: *C. Edgar* NSW 113 points 5.3.72

PLUG CASTING

18 Gram Double Handed Spinning Distance: *D. Pettie* Vic. 134.80 m 26.10.80
7.5 Gram Single Handed Spinning Distance: *R. Reeves* Vic. 94.03 m Nov. 1981
18 Gram Multiplier Accuracy Skish: *H. Crystal* NSW 90 points 11.4.82
7.5 Gram Spinning Accuracy Skish: *P. Hayes* Vic. 95 points 29.3.81
18 Gram Double Handed Multiplier Distance: *D. Pettie* Vic. 124.07 m 26.10.80
7.5 Gram Spinning Accuracy Arenburg: *P. Hayes* Vic. 100 points 8.3.81

FLY CASTING

ICF Skish Fly Accuracy: *All achieved possible 100 points*
R. Reeves Vic. 8.5.76; *R. Foy* Vic. 23.10.77; *P. Hayes* Vic. 1.4.78; *P. Jones* Vic. 1.6.78; *R. Peach* Vic. 23.7.78; *J. Rumpf* Vic. 4.3.79; *R. Heath* Vic. 6.6.82; *E. Whittam* Vic. 14.10.84

ACA Wet Fly Accuracy: *All achieved possible 50 points*
H. Jenkins Vic. 22.9.79; *P. Forster* Vic. 21.10.79; *R. Heath* Vic. 3.2.80; *R. W. Ricketts* Vic. 18.5.80; *R. Peach* Vic. 18.5.80; *B. Jones* Vic. 4.10.80; *E. A. Barkley* Vic. 14.2.81; *C. J. Brittain* Vic. 7.11.81; *R. Callaghan* Vic. 4.9.82; *G. Latter* Vic. 3.10.82

ACA Dry Fly Accuracy: *All achieved possible 50 points*
P. Jones Vic. 19.5.79; *W. J. Sanderson* Vic. 20.5.79; *P. Hayes* Vic. 10.6.79; *J. Waters* Vic. 24.6.79; *E. A. Barkley* Vic. 28.7.79; *P. Wilson* Vic 5.8.79; *B. Jones* Vic. 22.9.79; *K. Kelynack* Vic. 16.9.79; *R. Heath* Vic. 18.5.80; *R. W. Ricketts* Vic. 18.5.80; *C. J. Brittain* Vic. 17.8.80; *J. F. Phelan* Vic. 5.7.81; *R. Dodds* Vic. 24.7.82; *F. Eva* Vic. 17.7.83; *D. Rogers* Vic. 2.10.83

ICF Single Handed Distance: *J. Rumpf* Vic. 68.32 m 12.2.77

ICF Double Handed Distance: *R. Reeves* Vic. 76.40 m 12.2.77

ICF Fisherman's Accuracy and Distance: *R. Reeves* Vic. 191.72 pts 12.5.79

When the sport began, Australian women competed against men in distance tests but they now concentrate on accuracy.

CATFISH

An extensive group, represented by more than 1000 species around the world, all of them with mouths encircled with barbels or whiskers. They belong to the family Siluroidea and are well distributed in both marine and fresh water in Australia, where they are among the most common inland fish. Whitley sorts the Australian catfish into either fork-tailed or eel-tailed species. Though they mostly do not look imposing, they are good table fish. Many catfish have acute hearing, with the swim bladder linked to the ear.

Marine catfish

Most catfish provide splendid sport on light gear. They are found in estuaries and in the open sea, and when they are skinned and filleted, the smaller specimens usually are good eating. Some make a hoarse grunting sound when landed.

Blue catfish

Neoarius australis: Very common in estuaries and rivers in Australia's north, entering fresh waters above the tidal limits. They are particularly prevalent in the Noosa lakes of southern Queensland and in Moreton Bay, where they often have to be cut from nets. On capture their three serrated spines, one dorsal and two pectoral, lock into position. They are a bluish-purple on top, with greenish reflections, colours that fade quickly after death. They reach 4 kg and 70 cm, and are pleasing table fare if the fillets are skinned before cooking. Pieces of blue catfish provide excellent bait for crabs.

Salmon catfish

Netuma thalassina: This fork-tailed variety grows to over 9 kg and 90 cm and uses its big fins and tail to good effect. They are found in north Australian waters and as far south as Brisbane on the Queensland coast, and to Geraldton on the Western Australian coast. Their colour varies from silver-grey to brown or even red, and appears to change to suit their environment. They are excellent eating when skinned.

Salmon catfish

C ■ CATFISH

Eel-tailed catfish

Plotosus anguillaris: A plentiful fish of the estuaries, rivers and coastal waters of the north. They should be very carefully handled for their spines can inflict a painful wound. So anglers often stab them to the wharf or decking with a knife. They occur in large shoals and are taken in numbers by trawlers. The biggest reach 90 cm. They are also known as striped catfish because of the whitish stripes that run right along the body. They are best fished for on chained hooks or with a wire trace.

Catfish have a fondness for prawns, but pick at almost any fish bait. The adults bite readily, taking whole small herring, whiting and mullet and even catfish. They need 5/0 to 8/0 hooks. Those found in estuaries will take spoons, wobblers and plugs.

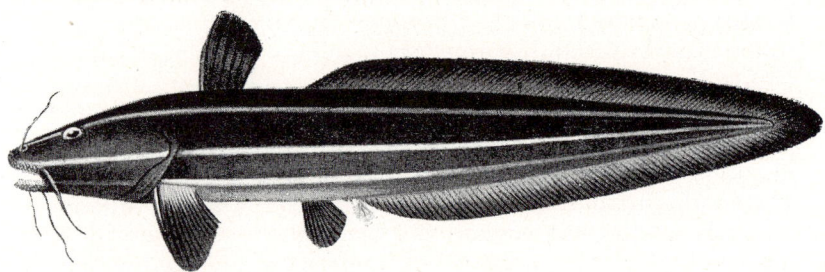

Eel-tailed catfish

Freshwater catfish

Part of a large group of fish of the family Plotosidae that are armed with strong barbed spines in their pectoral and dorsal fins and can inflict severe wounds if they are carelessly handled. The group has a characteristic mouth in both freshwater and marine species. The mouth is encircled by long feelers or barbels providing the resemblance to a cat. They are scaleless and slimy and often repugnant to those unaware of their good edible qualities. Whitley called them the vacuum cleaners of the rivers because they eat everything from mud to cowdung.

Freshwater catfish occur in tropical and subtropical waters. They are easily distinguished from salmon catfishes by their tapered and rounded, rather than forked, tails. They spawn as temperatures rise in spring and summer, with one of the adults remaining at the nest until eggs hatch. They provide good sport on light fishing gear, breed and flourish in ponds, but do not often survive in temperatures below 4 degrees C. Because of their excellent eating qualities they show potential for fish farming if public prejudice can be overcome.

The most common of Australia's freshwater catfish is *Tandanus tandanus* first discovered by T. L. Mitchell in the Namoi River in New South Wales in 1831. It is commonly known as landau, dewfish, jewfish, eelfish, kenaru and eel-tail catfish. Lesser-known but closely related species include *T. bostocki*

Freshwater catfish
Tandanus tandanus

from south-western Australia and *T. rendahli* from the Northern Territory. Other freshwater catfish include the straight-backed catfish *Neosilurus mortoni*, *N. hyrtlii*, *N. brevidorsalis* and *N. ater ater* from central and northern Australia. Catfish are called cobbler in Western Australia.

Freshwater catfish are related to the two well-known groups of marine catfish, the eel-tailed and the fork-tailed, and are characterized by the same sensitive barbels or 'whiskers' surrounding the mouth and by the presence of a barbed locking spine on the first dorsal fin and each pectoral fin. Venom is injected through a fine poison duct and the spine can inflict a painful but not fatal wound.

Freshwater eel-tail catfish are usually grey and mottled with dark brown to black spots when young. The larger fish may have an olive green or brown background but this is usually a purple or reddish-brown colour and rather mottled. The belly is white and the fish has no scales.

Eel-tail catfish were once one of Australia's most common native freshwater fish, inhabiting coastal rivers and streams, inland waterways, dams and reservoirs, in an area covering much of Queensland, New South Wales, Victoria and South Australia. They were particularly widespread in the Murray-Darling River system and formed a valuable part of the commercial freshwater fishing industry, but there has been a fall recently in catfish marketed in Australia. Since the development of irrigation schemes and the widespread occurrence of carp and redfin perch, catfish stocks have declined rapidly and they are now rare in much of the Murray, Murrumbidgee and Lachlan Rivers, and have disappeared completely from many of the smaller rivers, creeks and enclosed waters. However, they are still plentiful in the Darling River and its more northern tributaries where redfin and carp have not yet become well established. Only one species, *Cnidoglanis macrocephalus*, has been found in Tasmania.

They have not, however, been fished out in Western Australia. Wherever an angler drops a line once he gets north of Onslow he is likely to land catfish, long, streamlined silver fighters with a forked tail and three poisonous spikes. They extend far into Western Australian freshwater rivers and inland pools and will take any flesh bait. Freshwater catfish bite best in the west on grasshoppers and will often strike at slow-action lures. The majority of catfish caught in Western Australian tidal creeks average 0.5 kg, but one big fellow caught off Wyndham Jetty in Cambridge Gulf was said to weigh 27 kg.

Northerners seem to nourish the same hatred of eel-tail catfish that southern Western Australian anglers held for cobblers many years ago. Today the cobbler, or southern eel-tail catfish, is a prime market fish and eagerly sought by anglers. The northern catfish has not quite the same delicious flavour as the southern cobbler, but its thick steaks, if filleted and grilled with a slice or two of onion, are as tasty as any good fish.

Habitat and baits
Catfish are bottom-feeding fish which eat a wide variety of invertebrates, notably shrimps, yabbies, mussels and worms, but probably have a very wide dietary range and have even been observed to eat cow-dung at cattle drinking points. They prefer creeks, backwaters and billabongs to swift-flowing rivers and commonly remain in enclosed waters for long periods where they may attain great size. They are found sheltering near or under willow trees and can be caught quite close to the bank. Normally the species does not exceed 1 m in length and 7 kg. Specimens taken by anglers are usually in the 0.5 to 2.5 kg range. They take a bait freely but unfortunately do not appear to accept artificial lures of any type. They give fair sport on light tackle, but are sluggish when taken on heavy gear.

The edible qualities of freshwater catfish are high, but there is intense popular opposition to the fish when it is displayed in shop windows. This probably results from the unfamiliar appearance of the eight barbels surrounding the mouth, the slippery, eel-like body and the extensive fin formation which many people find repugnant. When the fish are skinned, however, both the appearance and taste are enhanced and they are highly valued as a table fish. As they become scarcer their commercial distribution is becoming limited to those country towns close to where the fish are caught.

Catfish can be skinned quite easily if they are immersed (the body section only, not the head) in boiling water for about one minute. This causes the skin to loosen considerably and it can be removed with a sharp knife.

Freshwater eel-tail catfish have an interesting breeding pattern which has now been well documented. The fish form a depression up to 2 m in diameter on a sandy or muddy bottom or sometimes in gravel in clear water. Pebbles and small sticks are carried by mouth to the nest. The eggs are guarded by the male. Courtship procedure is fairly elaborate.

Eggs are up to 3.2 mm in diameter, and are spherical, light green in colour, non-adhesive and demersal. A fish of 1.5 kg can produce approximately 20,000 eggs. Hatching occurs at about seven days at temperatures of 20 to 25 degrees C. They are notably hardy fish that can withstand high water temperatures and do not readily develop fungi infections.

CEPHALOPODS

A group of mollusca which includes octopus, squid and cuttlefish. Anglers prize all three as very good bait (which see).

Cuttlefish

Common all around Australia and resembles squid in appearance. Its body contains a large shell, to the under side of which is appended a horny growth. The shell from dead cuttlefish is frequently found on seashores and has a place in shell collections. Cuttlefish inhabits shallow water, in which it swims with a series of rapid forward movements interrupted by periods of hovering. While hovering it is easily caught by hand if approached with caution. Like squid, cuttlefish makes excellent bait. Octopus, squid and cuttlefish are edible. Indeed, all are considered great delicacies when expertly prepared.

Octopus

The zoological name of one genus of eight-armed Cephalopoda, a class of mollusca with tentacles surrounding the mouth, and with a highly developed nervous system. More than 140 species of octopus have been scientifically classified throughout the world but research work on Cephalopoda in Australian waters has been extremely limited since the 1920s. Consequently, scientific knowledge of local species is largely limited to the most common varieties inhabiting inter-tidal and sub-tidal waters. These are *Octopus australis* and the larger *Octopus pallidus*, known respectively to anglers as the brown octopus and the white, or pink, octopus, and *Hapalochlaena maculosa*, or blue ringed octopus, notorious for its deadly poison which has caused two human deaths in east coast waters in recent years.

Normally *Octopus australis* is of mottled brown colour on the upper side of its body and tentacles and creamy white, or buff, on the under side.

The dreaded *Hapalochlaena maculosa* inhabits sub-tidal waters and thus is often exposed on foreshores at low tide. It then takes shelter beneath rocks and in shallow pools. Although its poison can be fatal to humans the danger of *Hapalochlaena maculosa* has been greatly exaggerated in the general opinion of marine biologists. Doubtless the peril of physical contact with the species has been somewhat over rated because of publicity that attended the deaths of humans from the poison. While handling should be avoided, it is stressed that it is not an aggressive creature and will attack only when disturbed. There is little danger that it will bite if trodden upon, for its mouth, through which it injects poison,

CEPHALOPODS

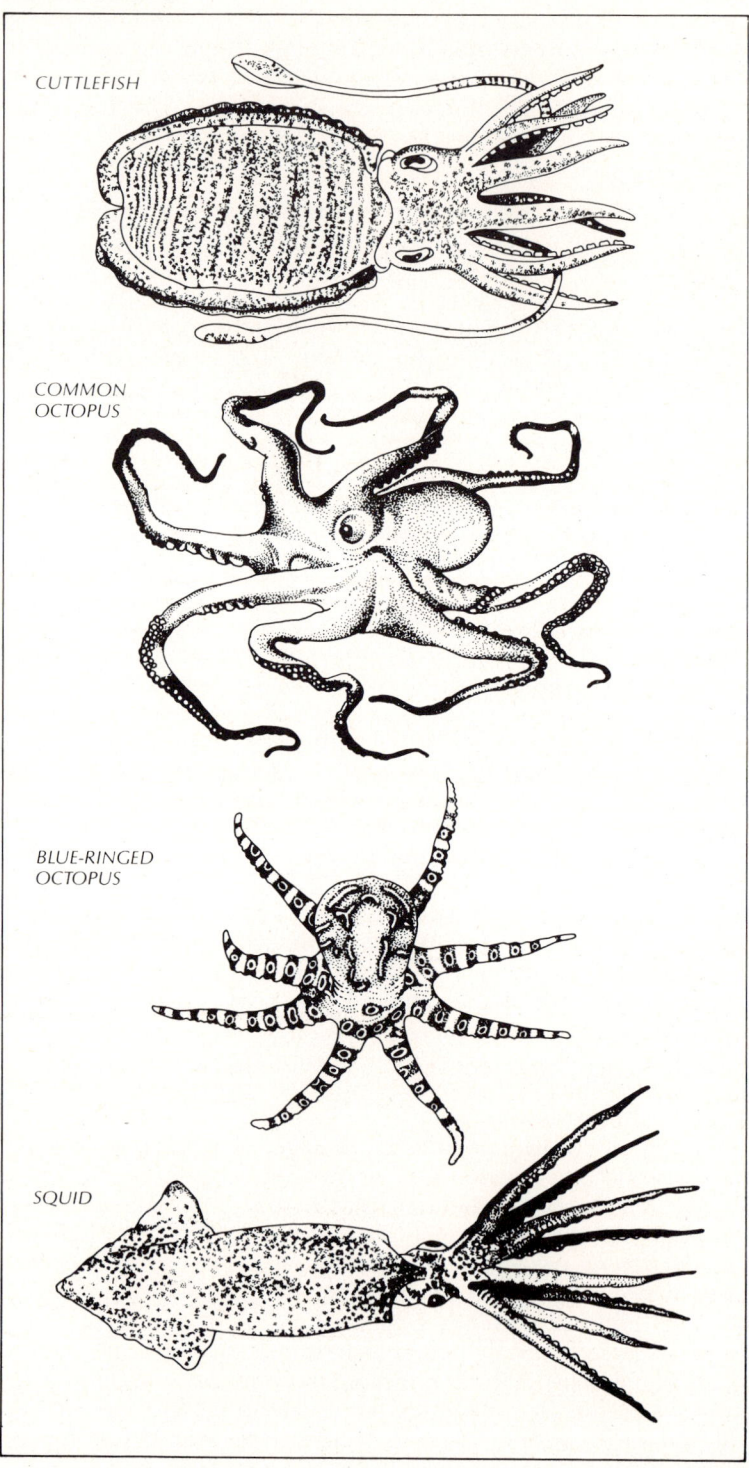

is beneath its body. *Hapalochlaena maculosa* is of brownish colour. Blue rings, from which it derives its popular name, appear only when it is aroused and about to attack. It grows to only about half the size of *Octopus australis*.

All three types of octopus occur along the whole Australian coastline. Octopuses are not habitually free swimmers, generally moving on sea bottoms or rocks by means of their arms. But they propel themselves through the water by using their funnels through which they draw in and expel water with jet force. Although mainly inhabiting shallow coastal waters certain forms prefer very deep water. The greatest depth at which a specimen has been taken is 3500 m.

Squid

This occurs in a large number of species in waters around most of Australia. The commonest variety, *Nototodarus gouldi*, abounds on the coasts of New South Wales and southern Australia, including Tasmania and the Great Australian Bight. It prefers oceanic waters, rarely appearing in harbours, bays or estuaries. It is a free swimmer, propelling itself by means of the water jet system. Though normally of very light grey, or off-white colour, speckled with dark spots, it very rapidly changes colour patterns when feeding, mating, endangered and so on. Squid is rarely taken on a hook but is trawled up in large numbers by commercial fishing craft and thus is readily available for purchase as bait.

CHANDA perches

Small, deep-bodied river fishes of the family Ambassidae represented by only a few species in Australia. Net fishermen dislike them because their fine spines get stuck in nets and have to be picked out by hand. They are attractive aquarium fish, also known as silver spray or doody. Whitley said *Ambassis* was a classical name meaning 'two sous', a trifling amount in French coinage suggesting they were virtually worthless as human food. The joke was carried further when one tiny tropical specimen found in Australia's north was named *Denariusa*, the penny fish. They prey on mosquito larvae efficiently. They occur in such numbers in Malaysia that they are used to manure crops.

Giant perchlet

Parambassis gulliveri: The largest of the family found in the rivers of the Atherton Tablelands and the Gulf of Carpentaria, which grow to around 30 cm. Fish of 20 cm are regarded as worthwhile table fare. They are yellowish-brown in colour with silvery reflections, and dark narrow lines follow the rows of scales along their upper body. Internal organs show through the skin of juveniles.

Western chanda perch

Ambassis castelnaui: A yellowish-silver variety that grows to 27 cm but averages around 18 cm. Their range includes the warmer waters of the Murray-Darling system in New South

Wales, Victoria and South Australia. They are also found in Queensland and the Northern Territory. They have small black flecks on the fins and survive well in captivity. Like the olive perchlet *Ambassis nigripinnis*, the network perchlet *Ambassis macleayi*, and the glassy perchlet *Ambassis agassizi*, the western chanda perch are important food for larger predatory fish.

CHINAMAN fish A reef fish of the family Lutjanidae which are poisonous for at least part of the year and should be treated as highly dangerous to eat by all anglers. Some anglers have eaten it without ill-effect but they are undoubtedly one of the fish that cause ciguatera (*see Poisoning*). Chinaman fish grow to just over 1 m and 15 kg and are easily identified by the deep pit just in front of the eyes. The young are roseate, with a yellowish tint and wavy blue-green bands. Adults have a pink or crimson-pink body, with obscure vertical bars and fine yellow lines about the head. They are found only in Queensland and the Northern Territory, usually close to rocks or coral.

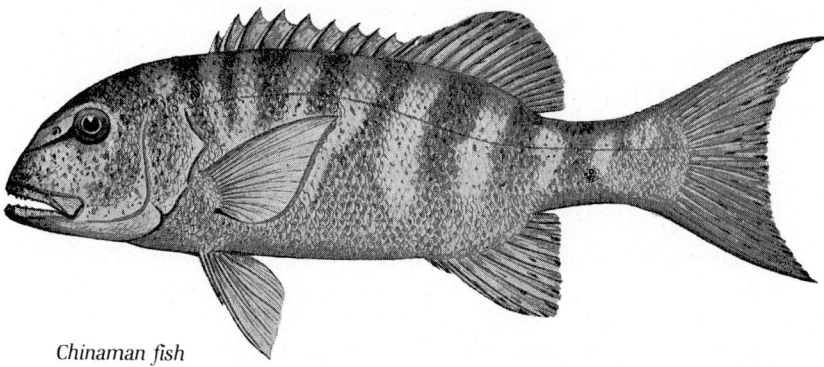

Chinaman fish

CLIFF-TOP fishing Australia's rugged coastline has provided challenging fishing locations for sportsmen since the days of the early settlers, particularly in places where the continental shelf is wide. Early cliff-top fishermen relied on sturdy hand lines and heavy sinkers but in the 1980s cliff-top fishermen depend on specially designed rods and powerful sidecast reels to keep their lines clear of the edge and provide the essential casting distance and strength to bring up a big fish.

Cliff-top fishing is extremely popular around Sydney, where the lofty cliffs south of Sydney Harbour are easily accessible and extend as far south as Nowra. Victorians, too, have outstanding cliff-top locations along the Port Campbell National Park, which attracts many amateur fishermen. Both these areas—and indeed all cliff-top hotspots—are at their best when heavy seas pound the rocks and wash food for fish into the sea. At these times when other forms of fishing are impossible the cliff-top angler often enjoys prolific catches.

CLIFF-TOP fishing ■ C

Australia's rugged coastline, such as near Sydney, provides the best cliff-top fishing when seas are heavy, but care must be taken to avoid injury.

Every year, however, dozens of cliff-top fishermen are injured or drowned because they had not observed elementary safety precautions.

Winds that are simply fresh breezes at sea level can assume gale force up on the cliffs. Non-slip footwear is essential. In New South Wales, where the cliffs often are sandstone eroded by centuries of saltwater and industrial pollution, selection of the right spots in which to fish the cliffs is essential. Anglers should avoid the thin jutting edges and overhangs that are common on these cliffs. Protection from the wind on very squally days is important, as is the selection of a platform from which the current will take out the rig.

Cliff-top tackle

A sturdy, long rod capable of lifting fish of 4 kg to 5 kg is essential. The line should be of at least 9 kg (20 lb) breaking strain, but most experienced cliff-top fishermen use even heavier line. Brightly coloured bobby corks that can be seen from the cliff-top are an advantage. Baits and hook rigs are the same as for conventional fishing but weed and cabbage clearly have preference for the fish that feed off the edge of the rocks below, such as blackfish, luderick and wirrah. The 'E' series sidecast reels have been designed specially for rock fishing and the unusual drag system is ideal for cliff-top fishing. A smooth running drag with handles mounted on the spool enables the user to stop winding if he tires in winching up his fish, a big asset on very high cliffs.

Ideal cliff-top locations

Probably the best fishing spots during heavy weather are those where off shore reefs break up the seas. This provides large areas of swirling white water to cast into without the hazards of combating big, pounding waves. Rock blackfish, trevally, tailor and salmon are often found at these spots. Backward-sloping submerged ledges with channels of deeper water at the base of the cliff offer bream and snapper, for these places produce abundant fish food. Avoid exposed cliff-top locations on squally days because of the risk of being blown off the edge. If you are caught on an open cliff-top during a severe squall lie flat on the ground until it eases.

See Continental shelf.

CLINGFISH

Fairly widespread fish with large suckers or adhesive discs on the underside of the belly which they use to attach themselves to rocks or the undersides of stones. They belong in Australia to the family Gobiesocidae, and about 10 species are present. They are also a common species in both the North and South islands of New Zealand, living on small crabs, shrimps and other small crustaceans which they take with sudden, short rushes from cover. They are also known as suckerfin.

Clingfish have slimy, scaleless heads, and short slender bodies. The sucker pads are formed by folds in the belly. They are found in the southern half of Australia in rock pools just above or below the tidal zone and when disturbed they will often move over the rocks to attach themselves to the hand. They come in a variety of colours, pinks, reds, purples, greens and yellows and are often mottled brown.

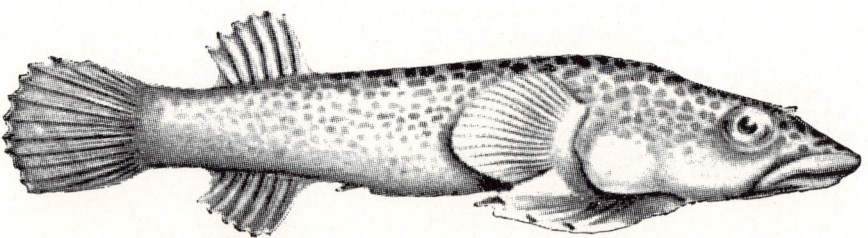

Broad-headed clingfish

The best-known Australian species include the cardinal clingfish *Creocele cardinalis*, the broad-headed clingfish *Cochleoceps spatula*, and the Tasmanian clingfish *Apasmogaster tasmaniensis*, which is perhaps the most vividly marked clingfish, with a number of brown vertical bars across a green body. They are found in Western Australia, South Australia, Victoria, Tasmania and New South Wales, and grow to 7 cm.

See Kingfish, Black.

COBIA

COD

Although Australians and New Zealanders call many fish cod the majority of them are not cod at all. Murray cod, black rock cod, blue cod, coral cod, scorpion cod, spotted cod, humpback cod and many others are all misleading names for fish of other families, most of them warmer-water varieties. Western Australians even call barramundi cod and have several quaint local names such as white flowered, black rankin and the wire-netting cod. True cod of the family Gadidae are confined to the colder regions of southern Australia and New Zealand.

Cods are highly important commercial fish in Europe, where Gadidae such as haddock, hake, ling and English whiting (unrelated to Australian whiting), provide food for millions of people. In Australia, codfish are small in size and numbers and are restricted to two main species and a few deep-water varieties. They all have barbels on the chin.

Ling

Eel-like fish with large gill openings; come in several varieties and are also known in some areas as beardies. The most common ling is *Lotella callarias*, which is found around rocky locations in southern Australia. They are caught on hand lines, grow to 50 cm, but their flesh is too flabby to be good eating. *Genypterus blacodes* is another ling common in cooler Australian waters and is the main species of ling in New Zealand. They reach 90 cm and 1.8 kg and are good eating but their eel-like appearance prevents many anglers from trying them. The banded ling, *Genypterus microstomus*, occurs in Western Australia, South Australia and Tasmania.

Ling
Lotella callarias

Red cod

Physiculus bachus: Are cod common to Tasmanian and Victorian waters but only seen along the south coast of New South Wales and Western Australia. They grow to 45 cm and 1.7 kg, averaging 1.2 kg and are caught in Victoria with nets and lines and in Tasmania on set lines. They are not considered good eating fish. They are grey to reddish above and pink or white

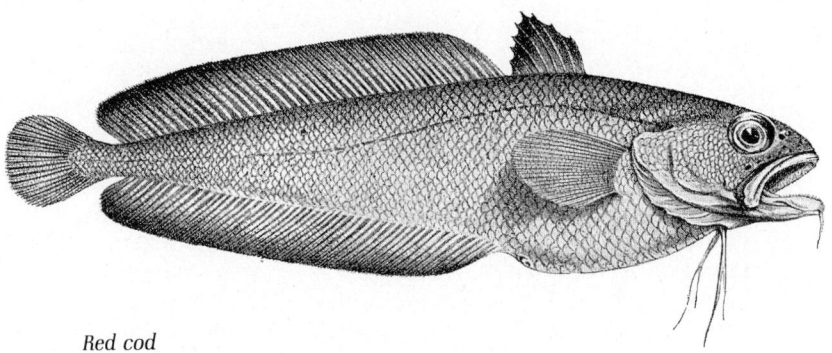

Red cod

below, turning red after death. The red cod has been marketed in small quantities in Tasmania since colonial days but its presence in South Australia is doubtful.

CONGOLLI *Pseudaphritis urvillii:* A small native Australian fish found in estuarine rivers of Tasmania and the southern coast of the mainland. Aborigines who were catching congolli when the First Fleet arrived, called it tupong. It is known in South Australia and Tasmania as the sandy. Other local names include sand trout, freshwater flathead, and marble fish. The last two names are descriptive. The congolli is long and lean, straight-backed, with widely separated first and second dorsal fins. Distinguishing features include the small mouth, eyes set close together near the front of the head, weak spines in the first dorsal fin, long second dorsal of soft rays, even longer anal fin, and bases of pectoral and ventral fins set forward of back edge of gill covers.

Although the fish is known to attain 35 cm in length, it takes more than four years to reach that size. They can move from the sea to fresh water without adverse effect. It is described as 'a fairly well-flavoured table fish'. In South Australia it is sometimes used as live bait.

Colour varies in different specimens, or even in an individual fish, according to surroundings. Thus one specimen is described as reddish-brown clouded and marbled with greenish-brown on the back and yellow-white below, while another is dark blue to purple above and silver below. Most congolli show dark blotches on the back and some a dark stripe below the lateral line connected at intervals by crossbars to a broken stripe on the abdomen. All the fins may be spotted except the ventrals. The anal fin is pink.

The heads of the majority of the fish are colourfully marked in purple and red, with a dusky bar below the yellow eye. Whether the colour variations seen in individual congolli have any significance is a matter of conjecture. Changes in colour between marine and freshwater specimens have not been clearly established.

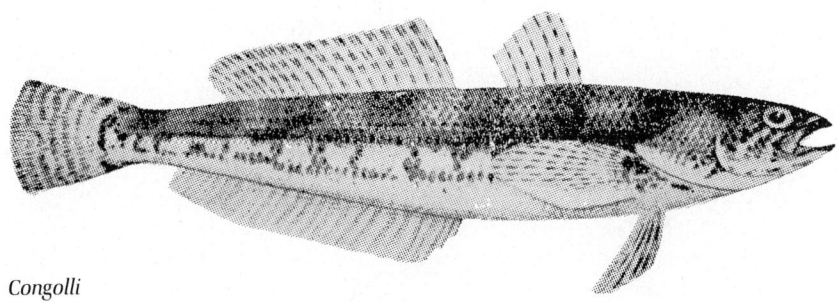
Congolli

Migration of congolli down to the Murray mouth has been observed during June, July and August. It is thought to spawn in coastal waters. River works, pollution and the competition of introduced species are combining to exterminate the congolli, which once had an extensive range. It is now almost unknown in New South Wales.

CONTINENTAL shelf

The term used for the area of shallow sea surrounding all land masses. It is the result of either erosion or deposition accompanied by wave action. On a world average continental shelves are a little over 120 m in depth and 65 km in width. Shelves are widest off coasts where large rivers or glaciers exist or have existed in the past; they are often narrowest on coasts exposed to strong ocean currents.

The continental shelf is of importance to the fishermen because it is the area of the sea richest in marine life and the spawning ground of many fish species. In areas of coral growth the shelf is marked by reef limestone terraces caused by the changing sea levels of the ice age.

A depth of 180 m (the 100 fathom line) is traditionally regarded as marking the division between the continental shelf and the continental slope, this being the depth at which surface wave action ceases. The continental slope is the area of seabed descending at varying degrees of steepness to the depths of the ocean basins.

These slopes are not always even, many showing mounds and ridges or the puzzling features known as submarine canyons, which seem to have been created by past or present rivers. At their deepest these canyons may dip over a thousand metres below the surrounding seabed. Features of this type are found south of Kangaroo Island, off the South Australian coast, and off Morobe, in eastern New Guinea.

South of Capricorn, Australia possesses only a narrow continental shelf, widest in the Great Australian Bight and in the Bass Strait where it links Tasmania with the mainland. Off Sydney the shelf is no more than 32 km wide, probably owing to heavy faulting of the foundation rocks, whereas in the Bight it increases to more than 240 km in width.

Above the tropic, the shelf broadens considerably off the north-western and south-eastern coasts. It continues across a neck more than 1200 km wide beneath the Gulf of Carpentaria and the Arafura Sea to join New Guinea with the Australian land mass. Coral growth is possible over most of this area and on the eastern side of the continent ideal conditions resulting from the equatorial current have created the 2016 km long Great Barrier Reef in a period of little more than 10,000 years.

Off the north coast of Western Australia, by contrast, more sluggish ocean movements and very low rainfall have discouraged coral growth and reefs have not formed to the same extent. Most of the reefs are submerged, only isolated coral masses, such as the Cartier, Ashmore, Fantome, Troubador, Seringapatam and Scott Reefs, appearing above the surface.

On the eastern coast of Queensland the main formations in the Great Barrier Reef are laid bare at low tides. Between them and the mainland there is a semi-sheltered band of continental shelf at an average depth of about 30 m, varying from 240 to 16 km in width. In the north there are long sections where two parallel lines of coral reefs form inner and outer lanes of continental shelf, varying from a few kilometres to as much as 32 km wide. On the ocean side of the outer reefs the seabed drops away sharply into the depths.

Owing to the comparative narrowness of the continental shelf in many places, Australia's commercial fishing resources are restricted in comparison with those of other countries. The British Isles, for instance, enjoys resources a hundred times greater. On grounds capable of being trawled off Australia, the story is one of periods of overfishing followed by scarcity. Facilities for fishing as a sport are unsurpassed, however, particularly in the coral seas.

Under international law, a twelve mile (19 km) zone of the continental shelf surrounding the coastline is regarded as being Australian territory. It is generally agreed that exploitation of the seabed up to the 180 m (100 fathom) line is the right of the nation whose territory borders it. Since November 1979, Australia has claimed territorial rights to seas up to three nautical miles from her shores and fishing rights on waters up to 200 nautical miles offshore. Countries such as Korea and Japan are sometimes granted licences to fish inside these limits if the areas are not fished by Australians.

COOKERY

Anglers have a big advantage over those who buy fish in the markets or from shops both in the range of fish which they can eat and in the freshness with which they can bring the fish to the table. They have the chance to sample first-rate table fish which may not be commercially sound propositions and thus never reach the markets. They can cook their catch on the bank or bring it home, but either way the fish will be far fresher and tastier than those non-anglers buy in the shops.

COOKERY ■ C

Fish have always been an important item in the diets of Australians; rich in vitamins and containing the vitamins A and D, easily digested, invaluable in feeding the sick, appetising to young children, equally as satisfying for quickly served meals presented by hard-pressed wives as for lavish banquets. As every fisherman knows, the fish always tastes better if you have caught it yourself.

Preparation of fish for cooking

Cleaning
Lay the fish on its side and with a sharp knife cut in front and behind the gills, then down the belly to the vent. Slit under the gills and remove with entrails. Wash well in water, rubbing off any of the black lining. For blackfish you will need a nail brush and salt.

Skinning
Place the cleaned fish on a flat surface and hold it firmly, using a little salt on your fingers to stop them slipping. With a sharp knife, make an incision around the neck and remove the pectoral fin. Slide the knife between the skin and the flesh to separate them slightly, then grasp the skin with your fingers and draw it back. Sever the skin at the tail and repeat on the other side.

For flatfish, such as sole, make a cut at the tail and pull the skin quickly and firmly towards the head.

SKINNING A FISH

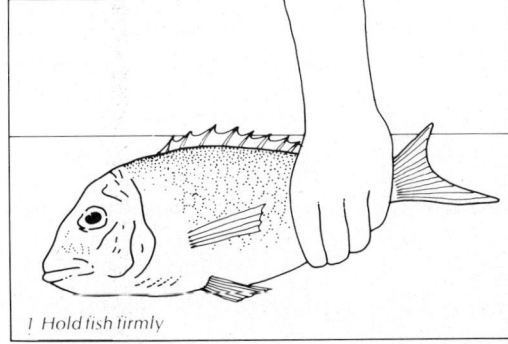
1 Hold fish firmly

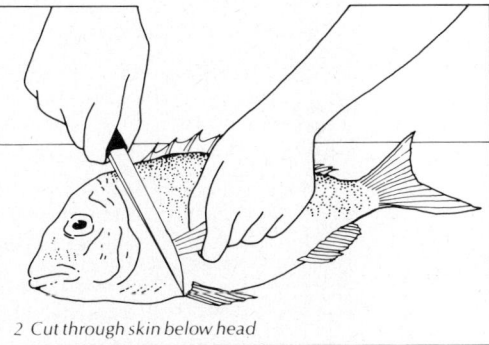
2 Cut through skin below head

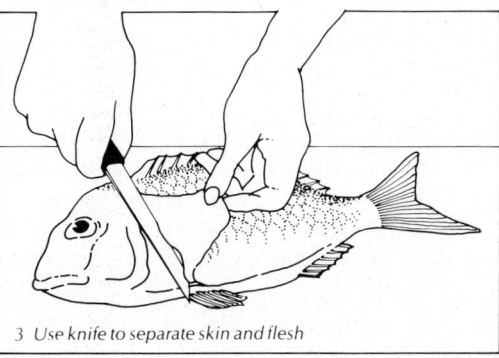
3 Use knife to separate skin and flesh

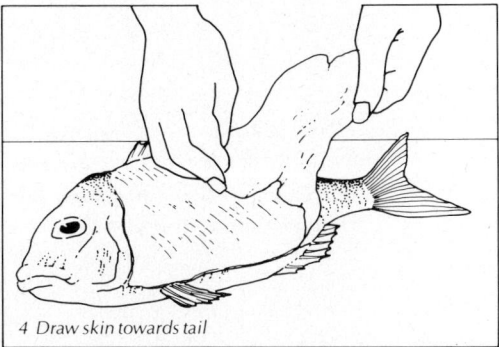
4 Draw skin towards tail

C ■ COOKERY

FILLETING A FISH

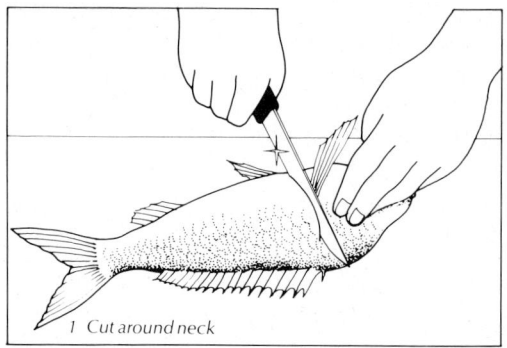
1 Cut around neck

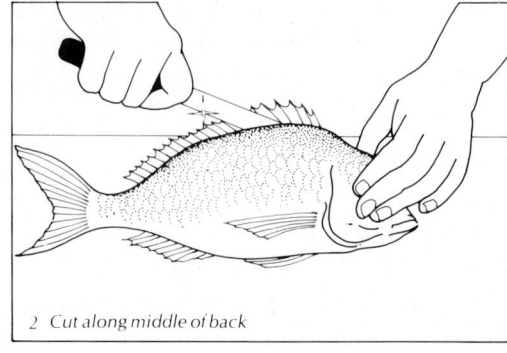
2 Cut along middle of back

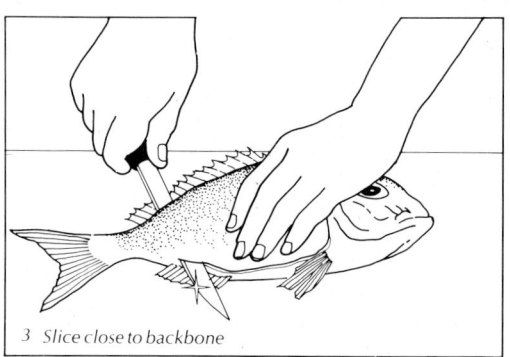
3 Slice close to backbone

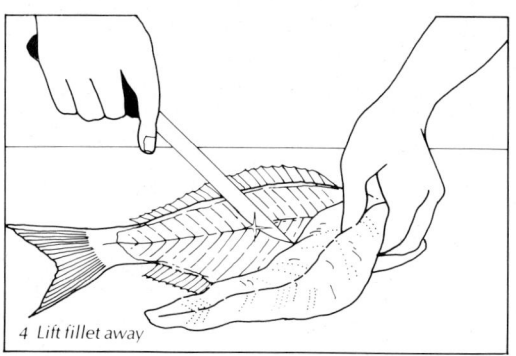
4 Lift fillet away

Filleting
Lay the cleaned fish on a flat surface and using a sharp filleting knife cut down to the bone around the neck and along the middle of the back. Starting at the neck, slice the upper side of the flesh cleanly from the backbone, keeping the knife as close to the bone as possible. Turn the fish over and repeat on the other side. Remove the small bones along the side of the fish separately.

Barbecued whole fish
For campers-out or for one-day fishing trips, try cooking your catch on an outdoor barbecue. There is nothing that can quite equal the flavour of fresh fish cooked outdoors. Teraglin, a good eating fish, similar to snapper, mulloway (jewfish), and bass (or freshwater perch) are some of the fish suitable for barbecuing.

1 whole fish, weighing about 2 kg
4 tablespoons butter
1 teaspoon salt
pepper
2 teaspoons ground coriander
1 teaspoon ground cumin
fresh banana leaves or large sheet heavy foil

Clean and scale fish. Slash flesh in 5 cm wide strips down to the bone. Blend butter with salt, pepper, coriander and cumin. Spread in the slashes on both sides of the fish. Pour boiling water over banana leaves to soften, and remove the centre rib from the leaves. It is a good idea to put a long skewer lengthwise through the fish to hold it firmly while turning. Wrap fish in banana leaves, then in heavy foil. Put on grid over hot coals. Allow 30 minutes to cook, turning fish every 5 minutes. *Serves 4 to 6.*

A 1 kg fish will take about 20 minutes, a 2.5 to 3.5 kg fish will take about 45 minutes.

NOTE: *3 teaspoons of curry powder and a good squeeze of lemon may be used instead of the coriander and cumin. If preferred, try one of the following butters to spread on the fish.*

Savoury butters and sauces to serve with fish
The flavour of fried, grilled, baked or poached fish is enhanced when accompanied by a sauce or flavoured butter. These following recipes (except the caper sauce) can be made ahead and kept chilled for several days. They make a quick and easy variation to fish dishes—especially for holidaying anglers bringing in a big catch.

To 4 tablespoons creamed butter add any of the following:

Anchovy butter: Pound 4 anchovy fillets to a paste (or use 1 teaspoon anchovy paste), add 1 teaspoon lemon juice and pepper to taste.

Horseradish butter: Add ½ to 1 tablespoon bottled horseradish, salt and lemon juice to taste.

Mustard butter 1: Add ½ teaspoon dry mustard blended with 2 teaspoons tarragon vinegar and salt to taste. Excellent for smoked fish.

Maître d'hôtel butter: Add 2 teaspoons chopped parsley, salt, freshly ground pepper, 1 tablespoon lemon juice.

Garlic butter: To 4 tablespoons butter add 2 cloves garlic, crushed, the juice of ½ lemon, 1 teaspoon salt and a good pinch of cayenne.

Mustard butter 2: Add 2 teaspoons dry mustard, 1 teaspoon salt and a dash of Worcestershire sauce to 4 tablespoons butter.

Herb butter: Add 2 teaspoons chopped parsley, 1 teaspoon each dried marjoram and thyme (or dill), 1 teaspoon salt and a good squeeze of lemon to 4 tablespoons butter.

Tartare sauce

½ cup homemade or bottled mayonnaise
1 teaspoon chopped capers
1 teaspoon chopped gherkins
a little prepared mustard
salt and pepper to taste

Blend all ingredients well together and serve cold.

Caper sauce

2 tablespoons butter
2 teaspoons capers
1 hard-boiled egg, chopped
2 anchovy fillets, chopped
freshly ground pepper
1 teaspoon lemon juice

Heat butter until a golden brown colour. Add capers, egg, anchovy fillets and pepper. Cook 2 to 3 minutes then stir in lemon juice and pour over the fish.

Sour cream sauce

½ cup commercial sour cream
salt and pepper
few chopped capers
1 to 2 teaspoons grated onion
lemon juice to taste

Mix all ingredients well together and chill. Serve with cold fish and fish salads. If liked grated cucumber may be added.

Beginner's bisque

A simple, but delicious dish which enables inexperienced cooks to exploit Australia's wealth of crabmeat, prawns and oysters in one highly satisfying meal.

1 cup chicken stock
2 tablespoons heavy cream
½ cup milk
1 teaspoon butter
100 g oysters
½ teaspoon Worcestershire sauce
dash cayenne pepper
140 g crabmeat
140 g prawns
2-3 tablespoons dry sherry
dash nutmeg
paprika

Combine stock in large saucepan with cream, milk, butter, oyster juice, sauce and pepper. Bring to simmering point and remove from heat. Flake crabmeat, chop prawns, halve oysters and add these to liquid, simmering for 15 minutes. Remove and add sherry and nutmeg. Serve hot, sprinkled with paprika.

Bouillabaisse

The famous soup/stew, originated in the South of France on the Mediterranean coast. The fishermen's wives made soup with the unsold portion of the catch. The variety of fish and the native flair for good food resulted in Bouillabaisse, which is considered by many connoisseurs as the greatest soup of all. Our seafood is different but the principle is the same. Use as wide an assortment of seafood as possible, the bulk of it firm-fleshed fish. All the following are suitable: Murray perch, Murray cod, snapper fillets, whiting, mullet, pike, trout, jewfish, john dory, flathead, bream, mackerel, kingfish, morwong, trevally. The soup is cooked rapidly, releasing the natural oils from the fish to give the soup its characteristic consistency. Small delicate fish are added at the end.

1 kg mixed pieces of fish
1 uncooked lobster or 500 g prawns
3 onions, peeled and finely sliced
4 cloves of garlic, crushed
3 tomatoes, peeled and seeded
1 bouquet garni (bunch of herbs and celery tops)
1 sprig of fennel, optional
¼ teaspoon grated nutmeg
¼ teaspoon saffron
1 piece orange peel
¼ cup olive oil
¼ cup of white wine
¾ cup of hot water or stock made from fish heads
2 teaspoons chopped parsley
salt and pepper
slices of stale bread or rolls

Wash and trim fish and if using lobster cut into pieces and leave in shell. Put onions, garlic, tomatoes, bouquet garni, nutmeg, fennel, saffron and orange peel in a large saucepan and put lobster and firmer kinds of fish on top. Add oil, wine and water or stock. Add salt to taste. Bring to the boil and continue to boil rapidly for 5 minutes. Put in the softer fish (e.g. trout, whiting, mullet, john dory) and an extra ½ cup water and boil for another 5 minutes or until all fish are tender but not overcooked and falling apart. Total cooking time should not exceed 15 minutes. Add more salt and pepper to taste. Remove the fennel, bouquet garni and orange peel. Put slices of bread in a tureen or soup bowl and pour the liquid over. Arrange fish pieces in another dish and sprinkle with parsley. The diner blends the soup and fish according to taste or the Bouillabaisse may be served in 2 courses—the liquid first with the bread and fish as a second course (with potatoes if desired). *Serves 6.*

Deep fried fish

Use fish fillets or small whole fish previously coated in any of the following ways: dip into milk, then plain flour seasoned with salt and pepper; or dust with plain flour, then dip into batter; or coat lightly with plain flour, brush with beaten egg and roll in breadcrumbs. A coating is essential to keep flesh moist and succulent and to give a crisp outer layer.

To fry: Use sufficient oil or fat to cover fish. It must be hot enough to seal the coating, preserving all natural juices in the fish. Test temperature of fat by dropping in a 2.5 cm square of bread; it should brown in one minute. Add fish (take care not to overcrowd pan) and fry until golden and cooked. Fish fillets take 3 to 4 minutes each side, small whole fish—about 8 minutes. Drain and serve immediately with French fried potatoes and lemon wedges.

NOTE: For deep fried whole fish, it may be necessary to lower heat once the outside is golden.

Batter

1 cup S.R. flour *30 g butter or 1 tablespoon oil*
½ teaspoon salt *1 egg white, optional*
¾ cup water

Sift flour and salt into a bowl, make a well in the centre. Pour in water and melted butter. Stir well, with a wooden spoon, incorporating the flour gradually into the liquids in centre. Allow to stand for 1 hour or longer. If using egg white, beat stiffly and fold into batter. Use for frying fish fillets, but coat the fish in a little flour before dipping into the batter. Fry in about 5 cm of hot oil until golden on both sides.

Escabouche

This recipe is particularly good for fishermen if they get a good catch because the sauce preserves the fish with or without refrigeration for several days.

1 kg fish fillets (bream, morwong, or trevally)
1 cup plain flour
pinch salt
2 tablespoons oil

150 ml tepid water
1 egg white
extra flour for coating
olive oil for frying

Sauce
1 cup Hock or Chablis
1 cup white wine vinegar
1 cup olive oil

1 teaspoon salt
6 whole peppercorns

Pickles
250 g finely sliced carrots, turnips, onions, green beans
1 red pepper, sliced
1 green pepper, sliced

1 tablespoon sugar
300 ml white vinegar
2 cloves of garlic

Cut the fish fillets into pieces 2 to 4 cm square. Sift flour and salt into a bowl, make a well in the centre, add the oil and water. Stir flour in gradually using a wooden spoon and beat to a smooth batter. Stand for an hour if possible. If necessary, add a little more water to make a thin batter. Beat egg white and stir in very lightly just before using. Roll fish pieces in a little flour, dip into batter and fry in oil until golden brown. Drain on absorbent paper and cool. Put into an earthenware or glass bowl.

Sauce: Mix together all ingredients and pour over fish.

Pickles: Put vegetables into saucepan, add sugar, vinegar and garlic. Bring to the boil and cook for 3 minutes. Cool. Drain and pour over fish. Serve cold with salads. *Serves 4 to 6.*

Fish à la meunière
This is a simple and ideal way of cooking delicate fish like sole, flounder, bream, whiting, trout or john dory and can be easily done outdoors over an open fire. The fish is usually filleted but small fish may be left whole.

plain flour
salt and pepper
2 tablespoons clarified butter (or half butter, half oil)

juice of one lemon
1 tablespoon chopped parsley
6 fillets fish
lemon wedges for serving

Season flour with salt and pepper and use to coat fish lightly. Heat half the butter in a frying pan. There should be enough to coat the bottom of the pan. Melt slowly but do not allow to colour. When hot, place fish in it and cook one side to a delicate brown for about 3 minutes, turn and cook other side. Whole fish will take about 6 minutes each side, depending on the thickness of the fish. Arrange on serving plate and keep warm. Add 30 g butter to the pan and while foaming add the strained lemon juice and the chopped parsley. Cook to a rich hazelnut brown and immediately pour over the fish and serve at once with lemon wedges. *Serves 4 to 6.*

Fish soufflé
For the fisherman with a flair for experimentation in the kitchen.

2 cups cooked fish of your choice	½ cup stale breadcrumbs
paprika	½ cup milk
2 teaspoons lemon juice	3 eggs
¼ teaspoon salt	

Thoroughly rinse the fish, removing bones and skin, separate into flakes and add paprika, lemon juice and salt. Cook breadcrumbs in milk for five minutes, add fish and egg yolks beaten until thick and lemon-coloured. Then cut and fold in egg whites, beaten until stiff. Turn into a buttered dish, set in pan of hot water, and bake in a moderate oven until firm.

Island baked fish in foil
A simple method for preparing fish that can be done outdoors, over a barbecue or open fire or indoors, in the oven. Choose small fish like whiting, bream, sand mullet, leatherjacket or flathead. Fish fillets and steaks may also be prepared in the same way, allowing 15 to 20 minutes to cook.

6 small whole fish	salt and pepper
4 tablespoons butter	½ teaspoon ground ginger
2 teaspoons soy sauce	banana or spinach leaves
juice of 1 lemon	heavy foil

Clean and wash fish. Put butter, soy sauce and lemon juice into a small pan and stir over gentle heat until melted. Use to brush the fish inside and out. Season inside of fish with salt, pepper and ginger, sprinkling a little more on top. Cut squares of foil large enough to wrap each fish securely. (If using banana leaves, soak in boiling water for 5 minutes. If using spinach leaves, wash well.)

Place a piece of banana leaf or spinach leaves on foil to cover, arrange fish on top then cover with another leaf. Wrap up, turning in ends and folding securely. Place in a shallow baking tray and cook in a moderate oven (175 degrees C) for 30 to 40 minutes, or over glowing coals of barbecue for 20 to 30 minutes.

NOTE: The leaves impart a special flavour and keep the fish moist, but if they are unavailable, cook the fish in the same way but make sure the foil is very well buttered to prevent fish sticking.

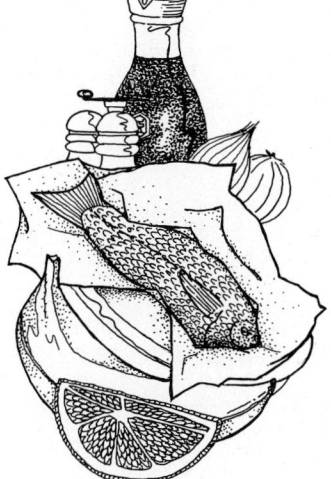

Pickled fish
Select a firm, white fish from your catch for this unusual hot day dish, recommended as an alternative to a salad.

1 fresh fish	3 large onions
flour	300 ml vinegar
salt	1 tablespoon cornflour
oil for frying	1 tablespoon curry powder

Cut the fish into neat pieces, dry, sprinkle with a little flour and salt, and fry. Cut up the onions and boil until soft. Strain off the water, cover the onions with vinegar and boil up again. Mix the cornflour and curry powder and use to thicken the onions and vinegar. Place alternate layers of fish and onion mixture in a dish and serve cold.

Tahitian fish salad

In Tahiti the fish is 'cooked' in lime or lemon juice. The fish is cut into dice and marinated in lemon juice which turns the flesh white and it will look and flake like cooked fish. Absolutely fresh fish must be used for this salad and it can be cut up and marinated in the lemon juice when freshly caught, ready to add the coconut cream on arrival home. Bream and snapper are suitable for this salad because of their superb tender texture and delicate flavour.

2 kg fish fillets
juice of 3 lemons
2 cups coconut cream

2 medium sized onions, peeled and finely sliced
salt and pepper to taste

Remove all skin and bones from fish and cut into small dice. Put into a plastic or glass bowl and pour the lemon juice over. Cover and leave in a cool place for 3 hours, turning with a wooden spoon or plastic spatula from time to time. Avoid using metal utensils. When fish is white and opaque, squeeze out all the liquid. Put into a clean bowl, add sliced onion and seasoning. Stir in the coconut cream and toss to coat well. Serve cold. *Serves 6 to 8.*

Coconut cream: For every 2 cups desiccated coconut add 2 cups of milk. Put into a saucepan and bring slowly to the boil. Cool, and if you have an electric blender, whiz for a few seconds at high speed. Strain through a muslin-lined strainer and squeeze out the milk.

NOTE: *Coconut cream is obtainable in a concentrated block from some delicatessen stores.*

Abalone

Also known as mutton fish, this shellfish is fast becoming a popular delicacy. It is abundant in the south coast of New South Wales, where it is caught professionally and canned for overseas trade. It is a member of the large marine snail family closely related to the paua shell of New Zealand and should be 10 to 18 cm long, enclosed in a shell that is inlaid with mother of pearl.

To prepare: Cut abalone out of shell, discard the stomach. Wash in salt water and cut away the black frill. Either peel off the 'heel' or sucking pad, with a knife, or rub against the rocks. A Chinese method for removing the black coating is to put the abalone (free of shell and stomach) into a dish and sprinkle each layer generously with salt. Leave refrigerated for 24 hours and then scrub with a coarse brush under cold running water until all the black is rubbed off.

Abalone steaks: It is essential for the abalone to be fresh when cooked in the following way. In fact it is ideal cooked at the seaside. Overcooking will cause a tough result.

Cut abalone into 1 cm slices and pound with a mallet or heavy knife, taking care not to tear the fibres. Wash well and dry thoroughly. Season with salt and roll in a little plain flour to give a light coating. In a frying pan heat about 1 tablespoon of butter or oil and when hot, add the abalone, one layer at a time and fry quickly, about 30 seconds each side until golden brown. Serve immediately.

NOTE: *The slices may be marinated for 15 minutes before cooking in a mixture of 2 teaspoons salt, 1 teaspoon paprika and 2 tablespoons lemon juice for added flavour.*

Chinese style: This method of boiling abalone enhances the flavour and results in a different texture, firm and yet tender. It is sliced thinly and used for soups and braises.

Braised abalone with oyster sauce

500 g fresh abalone, cleaned
2 shallots, peeled
3 level teaspoons salt
2 tablespoons dry sherry
2.5 cm green ginger, peeled and sliced.

Sauce

1 tablespoon oil
1 clove garlic
3 teaspoons Chinese Oyster Sauce
2 teaspoons cornflour
¼ cup liquid in which abalone was cooked.

Put abalone into a large saucepan with shallots, salt, sherry and ginger. Add enough water to cover and simmer gently for 2 to 3 hours (depending on size of abalone) or until tender when tested with a fine skewer. Cool in liquid, then slice thinly.

Sauce: Heat oil, add crushed garlic and cook 1 minute without allowing garlic to brown. Add abalone slices and Chinese Oyster Sauce. Cook for 5 minutes, stirring constantly. Blend cornflour with a little of the liquid, stir into remaining liquid, then add to abalone in pan. Stir until sauce boils and thickens. Simmer the sauce for 2 minutes and serve with boiled rice. Serves 4.

Australian dories

John dory, the best known member of the family, is a fine food fish and can be cooked either in fillets or whole. It is a thin, almost weed-like fish when viewed head-on, with ragged fins, but the flesh is firm and delicate. Other smaller Australian dories are the shiny mirror dory and the silver dory and several deep-sea forms notable for their very large eyes. Whitley said the dark thumbprints on each side of the dories suggested that this was the fish taken by St Peter for the tribute money (*Matthew xvii, 27*).

Barbecued john dory

1 cup plain flour
salt and pepper
dory fillets or whole fish
1 tablespoon butter
1 lemon
chopped parsley

An ideal fish for outdoor cooking over an open fire. First season the flour with salt and pepper and coat the fish with it. Melt the butter in a frying pan, without burning it. When the butter is hot, place the fish in it, cooking each side for 3 or 4 minutes, depending on the thickness of the fish. When the fish is cooked, drop in remaining butter and while it is foaming, add lemon juice and parsley.

Barramundi

Barramundi (Palmer perch or giant perch) is renowned as one of the choicest eating fish in Australian waters. Supplies of this fish are frozen in steaks and fillets and shipped all over Australia for wholesale and retail trade.

The Aborigines used to wrap the fish in leaves of wild ginger plant and bake it in hot ashes, which is said to be the best method of cooking the fish. However the following recipe, although very simple, is excellent. The flesh is flaky and white with a fine flavour.

Fried barramundi steaks

4 barramundi steaks, 2.5 cm thick
salt and pepper
plain flour
oil for frying
60 g butter
1 dessertspoon lemon juice
lemon wedges for serving, optional

Season fish steaks with salt and pepper. Coat with flour, then dip into milk. Heat enough oil in a frying pan to fully cover the bottom of pan. Add fish and fry until golden on both sides. Lower heat and cook 2 to 3 minutes until the flesh flakes easily. Test the thickest part of the fish with a fork. Lift onto a serving plate. Pour off oil from pan and add the butter. Heat until a rich hazelnut brown, add lemon juice and immediately pour over fish and serve garnished with lemon wedges if desired.

Bass

Bass cannot be sold commercially in Australia, but are one of our outstanding sporting fish, a quarry that rewards the successful amateur fisherman with a fine meal.

Baked bass bordelaise

fillets of bass
salt and pepper
cooked rice
parsley

Sprinkle bass fillets with salt and pepper, put into a shallow pan covered with buttered paper or foil, and bake for 12 minutes in a fairly hot oven. Arrange in a rice border, garnish with parsley, and serve with the Bordelaise sauce.

Bordelaise sauce

1 shallot
1 sliced onion
2 sliced carrots
parsley
bay leaf
a few peppercorns
1 clove
2 tablespoons butter
beef cubes, or beef extract

Bordelaise is one of many choices of fish sauces, prepared by cooking the chopped shallots, sliced onion and carrot, parsley, bay leaf, peppercorn and a clove for about 8 minutes with butter until well browned. Add to this a brown sauce stock or the beef cubes or extract and simmer for 8 minutes before straining.

Crayfish

Technically, Australia does not have a true lobster, though restaurants do their best to hide the fact. But we do have a variety of succulent sea and freshwater crayfish. Indeed, most inland lakes, dams, rivers and ponds are inhabited by crays that provide the basis for this gastronomic delight.

Cootamundra crayfish

butter
oil
cornflour
3 tablespoons tomato sauce
1 tablespoon Worcestershire sauce
crayfish meat
large lemon
cayenne pepper
breadcrumbs

Make a cup of white sauce with part butter, part oil and part cornflour, adding Worcestershire sauce and tomato sauce. Dice the crayfish meat and soak in the lemon juice. Sprinkle it with a spoonful of cayenne pepper and tip it into the sauce. Bring to the boil, stirring constantly. Pour into a shallow fireproof dish and sprinkle with breadcrumbs, dot with butter and brown in the oven.

Murray cod

Murray Cod is one of the best eating freshwater fish in Australia. It has a distinctive flavour, a tender flaky flesh and adapts itself to a wide variety of dishes. Fillets or steaks of Murray cod may be poached, cooked in soup, fried à la meunière or coated with crumbs and then fried in hot oil.

Because of the layer of fat found between the skin and flesh of this fish, some people consider the fish too fatty for frying. To remove fat, skin the fish and, using the back of the knife, scrape away the fatty layer. If possible leave the fish in the refrigerator overnight before skinning.

Poached Murray cod

2 to 2.5 kg Murray cod
2.5 to 3 litres water
1½ tablespoons salt
bunch herbs, optional
3 tablespoons vinegar (or 4 slices lemon)
6 peppercorns
1 bay leaf

Clean and scale fish. Put water, salt, herbs, vinegar, peppercorns and bay leaf into a large pan and simmer gently for 20 to 30 minutes. Cool lightly, place a small rack in pan and lay the fish on rack. There should be enough liquid to cover the fish. Simmer gently about 30 to 40 minutes, until flesh is tender when tested. Insert skewer in thickest part of the fish—if it comes out easily the fish is cooked.

Serve the Murray cod hot with tartare or caper sauce or one of the flavoured butters.

NOTE: If serving the fish cold, cool in liquid. The poaching liquid may be 1 part wine to 2 parts water.

Oysters

To open oysters, put a thin flat knife under the back end of the right valve and push forward until it cuts the strong muscle which holds the shells together. As soon as this is done, the right valve can be raised and separated from the left. There is a knack to it, which a little rehearsing can produce. To clean oysters, put the oysters in a strainer over a bucket or bowl. Pour cold water over the shells and this will loosen the shells slightly. Pick over the oysters to remove bits of shell or weed. To parboil oysters, drop them in a saucepan with water and liquid drained from them. Heat and cook only until the oysters are plump and the edges begin to curl.

Oyster fricassee

3 cups oysters
milk or cream
2 tablespoons butter
2 tablespoons flour
¼ teaspoon salt
few grains cayenne
1 teaspoon parsley, finely chopped
1 egg, slightly beaten

Parboil oysters and add enough cream to oyster juice to make a cupful. Melt butter, add flour, and slowly pour on hot liquid. Stir until thickened and add salt, cayenne pepper, parsley, oysters and egg.

Oyster pie

Line a shallow pie plate with pastry, fill with oysters (not more than two layers), sprinkle with salt and pepper, dot with butter, cover with pastry, prick and bake in a hot oven until brown. (This is delicious served with ham.)

Snapper

Possibly the most popular eating fish in Australia, snapper has a delicate flavour and a flaky, firm texture.

Baked snapper and oysters

1 snapper, about 1 kg
2 slices bread
2 lemons
30 bottled oysters
1 onion, peeled and finely chopped
1 clove garlic, crushed
1 tomato
salt and pepper to taste
1 cup white wine (Hock or Chablis)
½ cup olive oil
parsley

Oyster sauce

2 tablespoons butter
2 tablespoons plain flour
fish stock or water
150 ml cream
salt and pepper

Clean and prepare snapper. Soak bread (crusts removed) in the juice of one lemon and half of the oyster liquid. Add onion, garlic, chopped tomato, half the oysters, salt and pepper. Fill into fish and sew up the cavity, or skewer together. Cut a slit across the fish on both sides—through to the bone to allow heat to penetrate right through the fish. Arrange fish in a buttered baking dish. Pour the wine and oil over and bake in a moderate oven (170 degrees C) for 30 minutes, until fish is cooked and flakes easily. Drain off liquid. Garnish with parsley and serve with Oyster sauce. *Serves 6.*

Sauce: Melt butter, add flour and cook, stirring, over gentle heat until it just starts to turn golden. Combine remaining oyster liquor and the strained liquid in which the fish was cooked. Add enough fish stock or water to make 450 ml. Gradually blend into the flour mixture. Stir constantly over medium heat until sauce thickens. Season to taste with salt and pepper and just before serving blend in the remaining oysters. Basically, this is sauce flavoured with oysters. It may also be flavoured with anchovies or chopped prawns.

Spanish mackerel

This firm textured fish with a dry quality and notable flavour is excellent for smoking and also for use in curries, casseroles and soups. Of the 4 types of Spanish mackerel, the narrow-banded mackerel is considered to have the superior flavour. Kingfish may be substituted for mackerel.

Mackerel curry

1 kg Spanish mackerel steaks
juice of ½ lemon
1 teaspoon turmeric
3 teaspoons salt
oil for frying
2 large onions, finely chopped
4 cloves of garlic, finely chopped
2.5 cm green ginger, grated
3 teaspoons curry powder
½ teaspoon chilli powder, optional
2 tablespoons vinegar or lemon juice
1½ cups coconut milk

Wash fish steaks well, rub over with lemon juice, then sprinkle evenly with turmeric and 2 teaspoons of the salt. Allow to stand for ten minutes. Dab with paper towels. Heat enough oil in frying pan to well cover base. Add fish and fry until golden on both sides. Drain and place aside.

Heat 2 tablespoons oil in a large saucepan. Add onion, garlic and ginger and fry gently until soft and lightly browned. Add curry powder and stir over heat 1 minute, then add remaining 1 teaspoon salt, chilli powder, vinegar (or lemon juice) and coconut milk. Cover and simmer for 20 minutes, then add fish and simmer a further 10 to 15 minutes. Serve with boiled rice. *Serves 4 to 6.*

C ■ COOKERY

Trout Trout flesh has a slight orange-pink to deep pink colour and they have a distinctive but not strong flavour. Simple ways of cooking trout like Fish à la meunière are suitable. Use small trout or if the fish are large, cut into fillets.

For a gourmet touch add a few blanched and halved almonds to the butter.

Smoking: Smoked trout is popular with keen fishermen because it gives a characteristic smoke flavour and improves the eating qualities of the fish. Devices for smoking fish are available from leading sports stores and will hold 3 to 4 fish. Trout scales do not come loose in cooking, so the fish is filleted and smoked with skin and scales attached. Smoked trout is generally served skinned and filleted, with lemon and a sauce of 1 teaspoon of bottled horseradish relish blended with ½ cup whipped cream—or bottled tartare sauce.

Baked trout

When preparing trout it is important to see that the gills have been cut away as these will give the fish a bitter taste.

2 trout
salt and pepper
few sprigs of parsley
few sprigs dill or thyme, optional

4 tablespoons butter
2 shallots or 2 spring onions peeled and sliced
1 bay leaf

Wipe trout and season well with salt and pepper. Place parsley and dill in the cavities. Grease a baking dish well with 1 tablespoon butter, place the fish in dish and top with shallots and the crumbled bay leaf. Pour over rest of melted butter. Cover loosely with buttered foil or greaseproof paper and bake in a moderate oven 20 to 25 minutes.

Barbecue grilled trout

Prepare the barbecue or open fire (or use a grill set at medium). Season trout well with salt and pepper. Cut rind off bacon and wrap one rasher around each fish, then arrange the fish in a fold-over gridiron. Brush with plenty of melted butter. When fire is reduced to glowing coals start cooking trout, turning often and brushing constantly with butter, for 8 to 10 minutes or until fish flakes easily. The following sauce adds piquant flavour to the trout and keeps the flesh moist and succulent. Use this sauce instead of butter when grilling fish, if preferred.

½ cup oil
juice of 2 lemons
freshly ground pepper

2 teaspoons soy or Worcestershire sauce
1 teaspoon salt

Beat all ingredients well together and use to brush over trout while cooking.

Whitebait

A tiny transparent fish, the whitebait is netted in shoals near mouths of streams and rivers. In season it is considered a great delicacy and is now sold commercially in tins as well as in fish shops.

Whitebait fritters

4 tablespoons flour
1 egg
½ cup tepid milk
1 tablespoon oil
pinch salt and pepper
2 cups whitebait

Mix salt with sieved flour, make a well in the centre and break in an egg. Add milk gradually, then oil, beating continuously with a wooden spoon until surface of batter is covered with bubbles. Stand for 1 hour. Add whitebait to batter and stir. Drop tablespoons of mixture into pan of hot deep oil and fry 2 to 3 minutes or until golden brown. Drain on soft paper and sprinkle with a little pepper and salt. Serve immediately on a hot dish.

Whitebait and breadcrumb fritters

125 to 250 g raw whitebait
2 eggs
1 teaspoon salt
2 tablespoons fine soft white breadcrumbs
pepper

Beat eggs well. Add other ingredients and blend well. Drop tablespoons of mixture into pan with thin layer of hot butter. Fry and turn like pikelets. Serve hot with lemon.

Creamed whitebait

tin of whitebait	1 cup milk
1 tablespoon butter	salt and cayenne pepper
1 tablespoon flour	1 tablespoon whipped cream

Immerse tin of whitebait in boiling water for 10 minutes. Melt butter and stir in flour. Add seasoning and milk gradually. Simmer for 5 minutes. Add cream. Open tin and pile fish in centre of hot dish. Pour sauce over fish and serve with fingers of toast or fried bread.

Whitebait tart

2 tablespoons butter	1 teaspoon chopped chives
2 tablespoons flour	1 teaspoon chopped parsley
½ teaspoon salt	1 hard boiled egg, chopped
⅛ teaspoon pepper	125 g whitebait
1 cup milk	flaky pastry
2 teaspoons lemon juice	

Melt butter. Add flour and seasonings, stirring until well blended. Add milk gradually, blending well and stirring over heat until thick and smooth. Add lemon juice, chives and parsley, then egg and whitebait. Line a 25 cm pie plate with flaky pastry. Pour in the mixture. Decorate with pastry pieces. Bake in hot oven 200 degrees C for 30 to 35 minutes. Serve hot with parsley garnish.

Whitebait pâté

125 g whitebait	1 teaspoon lemon juice
1 tablespoon olive oil	little black pepper
1 tablespoon melted butter	little grated lemon rind
generous pinch celery salt	mace or nutmeg, if desired

Sieve or mash raw whitebait. Add remainder of ingredients, except lemon juice. Simmer very gently until whitebait is cooked. Stir in lemon juice. Use as a sandwich filling or on canapes. Will keep in refrigerator for a week.

CRAB

Largest of edible crustaceans in the sea, found mostly in coastal waters in Australia, where a few specialized forms are represented in fresh waters inland. Most are crawlers and burrowers in the littoral region, some have invaded the sea by an adaptation of the last pair of legs, claws of which are flattened and used as paddles for swimming. These swimming crabs roam the sea without returning to their birthplace. The white flesh of crabs is delicious, but a meal of crabs takes time, for they have to be removed from the tough, bony sheathing in which they live.

Australian anglers do a lot of crabbing. In Western Australia, there is a long-standing tradition for whole families to catch their suppers on summer nights by wading in the Swan River and in Leschenault estuary to catch blue manna crabs in scoop nets. Australia has an important commercial industry in crabs caught by trapping and spearing.

Australia has a wide variety of crabs, including sponge crabs, box and dawn crabs, pebble crabs, robber crabs, swimmer crabs, ghost and soldier crabs, pea crabs, sand and mud crabs, sharp-snouted crabs, frog crabs, spider crabs and the deepwater giant Tasmanian crab. Many of these are top quality table fare, but only sand crabs, known also as blue manna or blue swimmer crabs, and the larger mud or mangrove crabs appear regularly on the angler's menu. These are the only crabs sold commercially.

Crabbing techniques

Crabbing can be done from piers but a boat gives the angler a better chance to find likely spots. Crabs do not bite well if the boat is drifting past in winds or currents, however, so the boat needs to be kellicked. If there is so little movement in the water that it is possible to drift gently the angler has the advantage of covering more ground. The best places are usually in from the channels or on the deeper sandflats.

Boat owners can effectively berley crabs to their moorings by dropping down meat bones, fish heads or similar fare 2 or 3 days before they go crabbing. By the time they have cleaned these bones the crabs are ready for whatever bait is put down. All fish baits work well on crabs, but the best crab baits are tough. A bait from which a crab can tear a big piece and disappear with it is completely ineffective. The size of the bait is important as the crab must be able to get a good grip on it. A piece about the size of a large pencil rubber gives the crab something to concentrate on. The bait should be firmly set on a strong 5/0 or 6/0 hook as periodically big flathead come along and grab it.

The bait should be kept on the bottom with a sinker or a piece of sheet lead, and when the flathead, bream and other fish begin to attack the large bait, several lines should be put over. Crabs usually take a bait by making off with it. As the angler tries to haul the crab in, it drags like a dead weight and occasionally kicks as it tries to tug the bait off the hook. The angler should pull the crab up slowly, with the same pressure on the line throughout, working slowly and rhythmically.

A good landing net is essential and the net should have a handle to meet the prevailing conditions. If a skiff is being used, the handle does not have to be as long as in a boat of high coaming. The recommended net is of nylon monofilament mesh, and crabs do not become as badly entangled in this as in prawn netting or cotton mesh. It is wise for inexperienced anglers to work in pairs, with one concentrating on a smooth retrieve, the other on lowering the net and guiding it under the crab as it surfaces.

Crabs are easy enough to tip out of the net, but they are difficult to get into a bag. This is why experts use a fish box as the crabs cannot be left to roam the boat. Crabs can be picked up safely enough by the rear of their shells or by their broad hind flippers. But care must be taken to keep the fingers clear of their big nippers as these can inflict a sharp if not dangerous bite.

Western Australians in seeking blue mannas wade into the water with their scoop nets, each crabber wearing sandshoes to protect his feet from broken glass on the bottom. In vintage seasons the 19 km of the Swan between Fremantle and Perth is studded with the yellow lights of the crabbers' pressure lamps. Many use a baby's bath to carry the crabs they catch, towing it behind them on a rope. When they have enough to feed everyone in the crabbing party they leave the river and cook the crabs in kerosene tins.

In most States veteran anglers have had experience with a variety of crab traps but there have been steady moves against many of them by the authorities and it is always wise to check with Fisheries Department inspectors on the legality of the traps to be used.

Mangrove or mud crab

Scylla serrata: One of the best-known swimming crabs of the family Portunidae. Large tropical crabs which are plentiful on the Queensland and northern New South Wales coasts. They can measure 20 cm across the shell and weigh more than 2 kg. They vary in colour from green, shortly after moulting, to brownish-green. Some specimens are marked with purple or have a tint of blue in their shells. They live in the mud of mangrove-lined shores and are not found south of Sydney.

Mud crabs have exceptionally long and powerful claws which they can move with surprising speed to inflict nasty bites on the unwary. These large meaty claws help make the mud crab Australia's most important commercial variety as

Mud crab

the claws contain a fine-flavoured meat considered more succulent than the body meat. They can deliberately cast a claw with a powerful contraction of the muscle. The new claw gradually grows with successive moults. Such is the high regard in which the claw meat is held that one-clawed mud crabs bring a markedly lower market price.

They favour the mud of estuaries and foreshores, emerging at night to feed when the tide is low. They are caught commercially by spearing, by dragging them from their holes with special crab hooks or by trapping them in baited hoop nets or crab pots. Many professionals do not kill them, but tie them up and keep them for sale in the markets while still alive.

Sand or blue manna crab

Portunus pelagicus: A delicious crab of the bays, estuaries and open seas which is among the world's most sought after swimming crabs. A fast-moving crab of exceptional manoeuvrability which reaches a width of 20 cm across the shell but does not approach the weight of the mud crab. The legs and body are mottled in blue, purple and white. Females have brownish casts and thicker, smaller claws than the males.

Blue manna crabs are widely distributed through the Indian and Pacific oceans and range through tropical and temperate waters along the Australian coasts. Adults are frequently found in numbers in the shallows of bays and estuaries. Big catches are made in summer months with seine nets. They are cooked before marketing. Grant reports that Moreton Bay anglers use baited hoop-nets or crab-dillies on them from jetties and anchored dinghies or catch them with lines baited with fish, sometimes held in a nylon stocking, gently bringing the crabs alongside and scooping them aboard with landing nets.

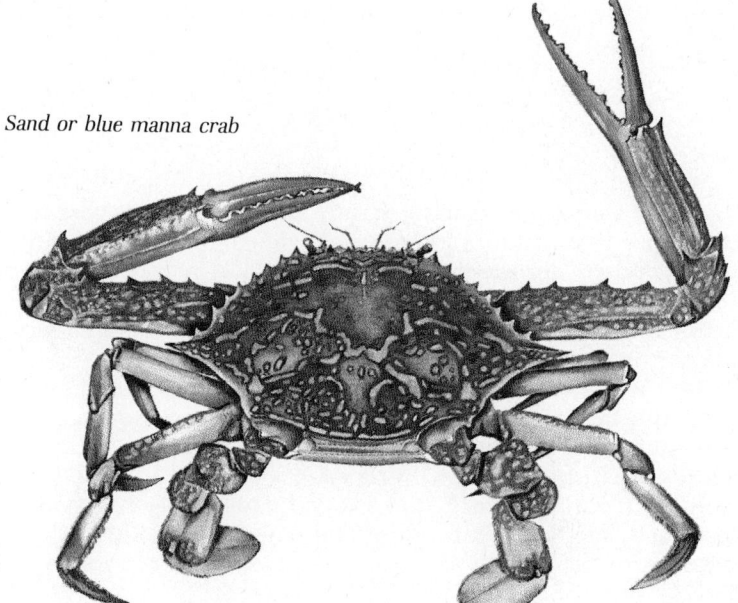

Sand or blue manna crab

Ghost crab Ocypode ceratophthalmus: Also known as the swift crab. An amphibious shore crab with an extremely wide distribution in Australia, frequently occurring in numbers on tropical and sub-tropical beaches. They are greyish-white to greenish-cream in colour and this helps camouflage them at night as they move across the sand scavenging for food. They run with a distinctive high body position and are particularly elusive in dodging anglers unwise enough to leave their bait exposed at night on the sand.

Fully-grown ghost crabs span 18 cm, leg-tip to leg-tip, inhabiting shoreline burrows. Many Queensland anglers consider it is worth the time and effort of digging out ghost crabs as they are such outstanding bait (which see) for flathead, parrot-fish, and other species. They spend a considerable time out of the water but will scurry swiftly back to it when chased, and burrow so quickly into water-covered sand that it is easy to see how they acquired their name. They have been known to tear off the flesh of freshly caught fish at night.

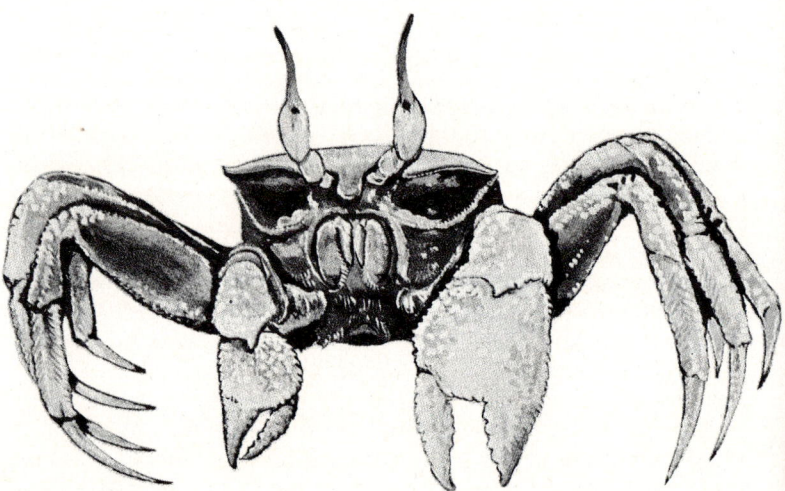

Ghost crab

Soldier crab Mictyris longicarpus: Notable sand dwellers, which grow to a little more than 2.5 cm across but congregate in large armies which swarm across the beaches feeding at low tide and disappear at high tide. Frequently vast numbers of them are exposed when sandbars subside or sudden changes in shoreline sands occur.

They are especially prevalent in south Queensland and along the temperate Western Australian coast, moving with a characteristic singlemindedness across sandflats, as if taking confidence from their own numbers. When they finish feeding each crab burrows back into the sand with what has been described as the action of an animated centre-bit. Soldier crabs are excellent bait for species such as whiting and bream

Soldier crab

but there is a trick in placing them on the hook. Some are as wide across as the hook, the points of which should protrude from the eyes to exploit the bream's habit of killing soldier crabs by biting away the eyes. Very small soldier crabs set three or four at a time on the hook take heavy toll of whiting.

Spanner crab

Ranina ranina: Also known as frog crab. Delicious eating when the frog-like cast is split lengthwise, enabling the angler to pick out the meat. Takes its name from the spanner-shaped main claws, which like the body contain splendid meat.

Spanner crabs have a vivid red to scarlet colouring that has perturbed many anglers while they were standing in knee-deep water along Australia's temperate coastline. This concern is only temporary, however, as spanner crabs are timid sand-burrowers which scuttle around for a few metres before digging back into the sand. When it is offered a bait, the spanner crab will close its claws on it and hang on so tightly they can be swung clear of the water. They use these same claws to catch small whiting. Adults reach a shell width of 14 cm and 1 kg in weight.

Hermit crab

Of the family Paguridae, are 10-limbed crustaceans well represented along the Australian coast; they use the empty shells of molluscs to protect their own soft abdomens. Their hind bodies are spirally twisted to fit in the interiors of shells, and one of the nippers, invariably bigger than the others, is used to close the shell opening after the rest of the body is inside. They move to larger shells as they grow, making the swap at speed, and never before the new shell has already been chosen. They can take such a tenacious grip on the inside of a shell they are seldom dragged out alive.

The largest Australian hermit crabs reach 25 cm, including body and limbs. Two of the largest, *Trizopagurus strigimanus*, and *Dardanus arrosor*, are frequently caught by off-shore trawlers in deep waters. Several other varieties of hermit crab frequent tropical reefs and are brilliantly coloured, including the porcelain-spotted hermit crab *Dardanus megistos* which has a scarlet body vividly sprinkled with white spots. Another striking hermit crab is the miner *Cancellus typus*, which does not live in shells but in a burrow which it cuts in soft stones by using the hard, bony plates on its tail.

Giant Tasmanian crab *Pseudocarcinus gigas:* Largest of all Australian crabs and second in size only to Japan's giant king crab. They measure up to 35 cm across the back, have pincer arms more than 45 cm long, and the biggest specimens weigh 14 kg. They are bulkier but not as big overall as the Japanese crabs.

Tasmanian giant crabs have been shown in trawling surveys to be reasonably plentiful at between 90 and 150 m off Bass Strait and the eastern coast of Tasmania. Occasional strays are found as far north as the New South Wales central coast. They have not yet been exploited commercially although their flesh is plentiful and delicious, mainly because of the costs involved in taking them in quantity.

These crabs are formidable specimens when alive, with pincers that could snap a man's arm. Their white shells and pincers are splotched in scarlet and the legs are covered in a reticulated pattern of brown hair. When hauled aboard trawlers they can be handled without concern as the sudden reduction in water pressure virtually paralyzes them.

Spider crab Of the family Majidae, are well represented in Australian waters, usually in harbours around the growths that accumulate on the piles of jetties and wharves. They camouflage themselves in a variety of marine growths which they keep attached to the carapace with numerous hooked hairs, and the covering is so complete it often obscures the spines and joints of the legs. Australian seaweed spider crabs lift pieces of weed into position with pincer limbs, and renew their camouflage each time they cast shells in the ageing process.

Robber crab *Birgus latro:* A prominent member of the hermit crab family, often called coconut crab. They are very well known all over the Indo-Pacific region, feeding on fallen coconuts and climbing coconut trees to knock the nuts to the ground. They grow to 45 cm in length and have a very powerful pair of nippers that are capable of slicing off a human finger.

Robber crabs are highly destructive in copra plantations since they climb the coconut palms to great heights to tear away the husk around the nuts and gouge out eyes to get at the flesh. Robber crabs are considered excellent food.

Of the family Potamonidae, are widely distributed in Australian rivers, and in inland Australia frequently occur some distance from rivers. They can withstand severe drought conditions, burrowing deeply into sand in search of moisture. There are six known species in Australia but five appear to be restricted to the Cape York area. The sixth, *Holthuisana transversa*, is found in all the northern parts of Australia.

Freshwater crabs seldom exceed 5 cm across the body. They are olive-brown in colour and have convex backs. Their burrows often add to seepage problems in bore drains and inland dams. Aborigines are especially adept at catching them with crab hooks.

R. J. STREET

Freshwater crab

The sand or blue manna crab is often found in bays and estuaries.

CRAYFISH

A crustacean of the family Palinuridae, which is a gastronome's delight all over the world. Found from the Mediterranean to the South Pacific, and from the Caribbean to South Africa. In Australia, the confusion of names which appears to afflict all our sea creatures probably is at its worst when crayfish are discussed. It is known here as sea-crayfish, spiny lobster or rock-lobster, but the truth is that we have no Australian lobsters.

The French call it langouste, South Africans call it crawfish, and the Americans decline to buy it unless it is called lobster. So our sea-crayfish becomes Australian lobster for the export market. But the true lobsters of the northern hemisphere belong to the genera *Homarus* or *Nephrops* and have far larger claws. Ironically, they are claimed to be better eating than our crayfish, which nevertheless find a ready market both locally and overseas.

The numerous species of Australian marine crayfish are matched by the variety of freshwater crayfish distributed across the whole Australian continent. There is hardly a river, lake, creek, pond, dam or swamp that one or other of the freshwater species of crayfish does not inhabit.

Here the problem of accurate names arises again. In south-eastern Australia, freshwater crayfish are generally known as yabbies, but various other Aboriginal names are used for it in Western Australia. In Queensland and northern New South Wales, what are elsewhere called yabbies are known as lobbies, and yabbies are the ghost nippers or burrowing shrimps, *Callianassa australiensis*.

The western crayfish or rock lobster

Most plentiful of all Australian crayfish is *Panulirus cygnus*, a succulent crayfish marketed as rock lobster; it is a saltwater variety found along the south-west coast of Western Australia. Averaging half a kilogram in weight, it is the main reason Australia now has a $100 million-a-year crayfish industry. This crayfish brings an average of $10 a kilogram, sometimes as much as $17. Perhaps the biggest advantage of this variety is that the eggs float in a planktonic state, returning to the shore after about a year. Scientists can accurately forecast the size of the annual catch up to three years in advance by studying the eggs.

Western Australian production is more than 60 per cent of the total annual Australian catch of more than 100,000 tonnes. Three-quarters of the catch is exported, mainly in the form of frozen tails to the United States though a market for whole cooked crayfish has developed in Europe, and a whole live crayfish market to Japan is growing fast. The catch comes from an area of 20,000 square kilometres of sea, extending from Bunbury to Shark Bay, including the reefs of the Houtman Abrolhos Islands, off Geraldton. These last-named are shallow waters worked by small boats of 5 to 8 m in length. Fewer than 15 per cent of all the boats used are longer than 15 m. Most

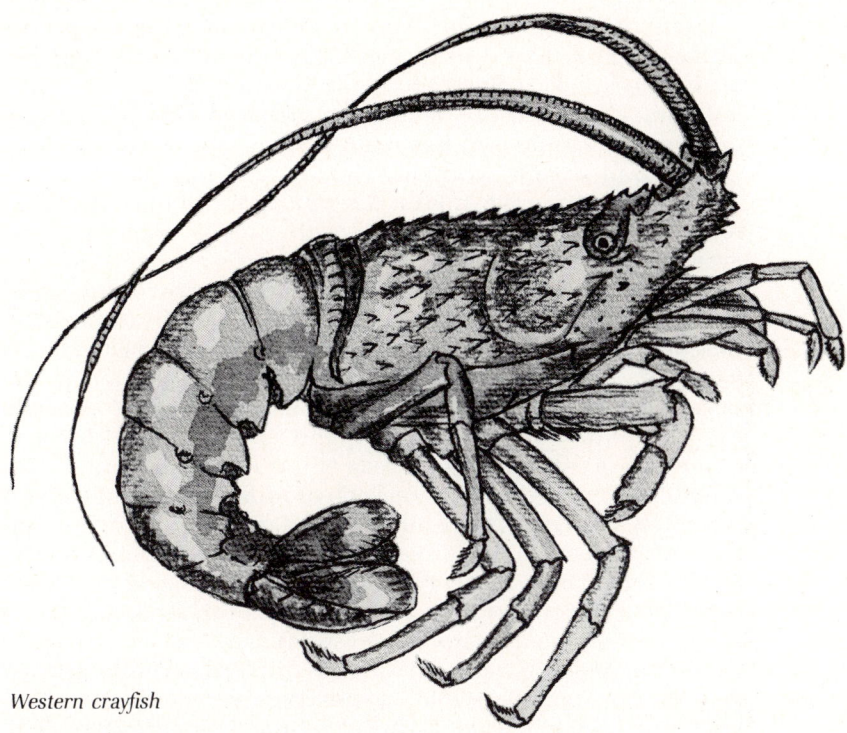

Western crayfish

of the boats use echo sounders and the larger ones have two-way radio.

Fishing goes on the year round, being divided into the white season (November to January) and the red season (January to August). The white season refers to moulted crayfish which are light pink in colour. After moulting they leave the coastal reefs for deeper water where their normal red colour returns.

Crayfishing became a big industry in Western Australia during World War II when canned crayfish were supplied to American soldiers in the Pacific. Before that only a few small sailing cutters had caught crayfish with hand-hauled pots.

Once the trade in frozen tails began in 1947 the catch rose steadily to a peak of almost 10 million kilograms in 1963. Thereafter the catch fell, apparently due to overfishing. Since then legislation and strict enforcement of size limit regulations have checked the decline. But the smaller catches have been offset by rising prices on the United States market.

The southern crayfish

The main species caught by fishermen of South Australia, Victoria and Tasmania is the southern crayfish, *Jasus novaehollandiae* which grows to a larger size than the Western Australian species. It is closely related to the New Zealand crayfish, *Jasus edwardsii* and it has been suggested that it may be the same species due to larvae having spread across the Tasman Sea. As its name implies, this crayfish frequents the southern coasts and was once abundant around Tasmania.

Jasus verreauxi is the other major species of eastern Australia which is found from southern Queensland to Victoria and fished at Port Stephens, Port Hacking, Broken Bay and Bateman's Bay. Various shades of green in colour, it is the giant of the family and has been known to grow 90 cm long and 8 kg in weight. Normally they range from 2 to 7 kg.

The southern crayfish is brighter in colour than its northern relative, being mainly reddish, with purple markings. The average weight is between 0.5 and 1.5 kg.

The total crayfish production of the four eastern States does not exceed 5.5 million kilograms and is worth around $10 million a year. Fishing on the New South Wales coast extends from July to December but further south is restricted to the period from October to March. The fishery has existed since the last century but it did not expand until after World War II. Extension of fishing to new areas of the Tasmanian and South Australian coasts has increased production. Biological research by the C.S.I.R.O. resulted in the minimum size limit on female crayfish being raised in Victoria and Tasmania. The legal limit in New South Wales is 25 cm measured along the body from the rostrum (beak) to the tip of the tail. Bag limits apply in Tasmania, Victoria and N.S.W.

The range of the southern crayfish extends to the southwest of Western Australia while various highly-decorated species are found in tropic waters. These include the painted crayfish, *Panulirus ornatus* and *Panulirus versicolor* of the Great Barrier Reef and Western Australian respectively, both of which are good eating but not easily caught in lobster pots.

Australian fishing methods

Sea-crayfish are caught in baited traps, either beehive-shaped or square, made of cane or tea-tree, woven on a heavy wire frame or of metal and heavy-gauge mesh. These pots, which can be as big as 120 cm in diameter, have an incurved entrance which makes it easy for the crayfish to enter but difficult for it to get out. The bait is any type of offal.

Most commercial fishing boats are fitted with pot-hauling gear and tippers. Crayfish do not keep well in refrigerators and many boats, therefore, are fitted with wet wells or tanks through which sea water is pumped and in which the catch can be carried alive.

Crayfish need to be handled carefully for their shells are often rough and spiky. A flip of their powerful tails is enough to cause a badly lacerated hand. Fishery regulations vary from State to State, but the taking of female crayfish with eggs attached is generally forbidden.

The Balmain bug The second family of Australian marine crayfish is the Scyllaridae, whose antennae are modified into plate-like shapes. These plates, projecting at either side of the head, are used like a shovel to burrow into the sea floor.

CRAYFISH ■ C

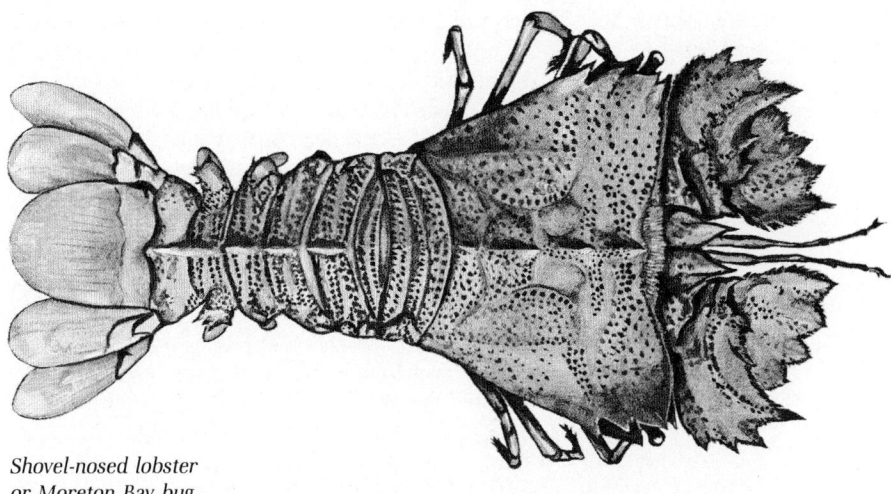

Shovel-nosed lobster or Moreton Bay bug

Largest of the tribe is the broad-fronted crayfish *Scyllarides sculptus*, deep red in colour and about 30 cm in length. More common is the flapjack *Ibacus peronii*, growing about 20 cm long and a brighter red. This curiously-shaped crayfish, very flattened and compressed, is also known as the Balmain bug from the days before pollution drove it out of Sydney Harbour. Occasional specimens are now brought up by the prawn trawlers, whose crews call this strange crustacean a prawn-killer.

A close relative is the so-called shovel-nosed lobster *Thenus orientalis*, slightly larger and more drab in colour. Queensland prawners often trawl up this crayfish in Moreton Bay. Both it and the Balmain bug are edible, indeed epicureans claim the morsels from their tails are more tasty than the flesh of the larger species, but their appearance is against them.

Many quaint species of small crayfish representing links with the hermit crabs are found on sandy or muddy coasts where they live in burrows. Most of these display a wide tail-fan and prominent nippers. The largest species, *Thalassina squamifera*, growing to 22 cm long, inhabits the mangrove swamps of northern Australian and was regarded as a delicacy by the Aborigines. Another is the delicate white or pink ghost-nipper *Callianassa australiensis*, which buries itself up to 30 cm below ground in tidal estuaries. Both are esteemed as bait.

Freshwater crayfish

All the many species of Australian freshwater crayfish, from the largest to the least, have large and fierce-looking claws similar to those of the European lobster. The two remaining pairs of front legs also carry smaller nippers. These inland crustaceans all belong to the family Parastacidae, of which large specimens of the genera *Astacopsis*, *Euastacus* and *Cherax* are found in both eastern and western Australia.

C ■ CRAYFISH

Potentially the largest is *Astacopsis gouldi*, of Tasmania, which has been observed growing to 40 cm long and weighing to 6 kg. Its colour is dark green to black. The Murray River crayfish *Euastacus armatus* is easily identified by its white claws and the white spines on the tail. It grows to about 35 cm. Equally large is the Western Australian marron *Cherax tenuimanus*. Being longer and thinner than the others, a good specimen weighs 1.8 kg. The name is Aboriginal, like that of the smaller Western Australian species called jilgies.

Large coastal freshwater crayfish, growing to about 30 cm, are found in rivers and streams all down the coast from Queensland to the Bass Strait. Their colour is dark olive green to grey with deep red markings. Their claws are big and serrated, protected with spines, while the lesser nippers are picked out in orange-red.

The so-called black and white yabbies (*which see*) of the inland are also *Cherax* species. Black yabbies, green-black in colour, are the larger, growing 20 to 25 cm long, and are often caught for food. The light-coloured (white) yabbies commonly growing to 12.5 cm in length, are in demand as bait. A 3 m length of prawn net, weighted at the bottom and drawn through the water with ropes is an effective outfit for catching yabbies. Dip or hoop nets about 60 cm in diameter, with bait tied in the middle or suspended above, are preferred by some fishermen.

Usually children have great success with a fragment of meat or fish tied on the end of a length of string. When the yabby can be felt biting at the bait, it is drawn to the surface slowly. The little crayfish is then smartly jerked ashore or caught in a scoop net.

A good way to prepare the yabby for cooking is to pull off its tail, first giving the fan a slight twist to free the interior organs. If this is done carefully, nothing is left in the shell but clean meat. The advantage of this method is that any mud or rotting matter in the yabby is removed and cannot be cooked in the meat to spoil the taste.

All freshwater crayfish, large and small, have a bad name for burrowing and cause a great deal of damage to farm dams, riverbanks and irrigation channels. By this means they survive droughts, reposing in the moist earth in a comatose state. They also move from one waterhole to another, crawling through the dew-wet grass at night. They can accomplish these feats because their gills are adapted to be used as lungs for breathing air. As a result they can be kept out of water alive for as long as a week provided they are in a damp bag placed in the shade. One proviso is that they should not be too crowded, otherwise they are liable to start eating each other.

See Cookery.

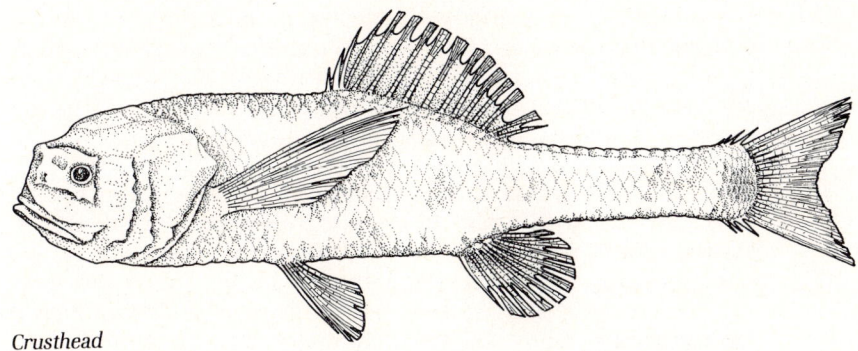

Crusthead

CRUSTHEADS

Very small blue-black or brownish-black deepwater fish of the family Melamphaeidae, which according to Whitley have been found in two species off Tasmania and New South Wales. They are highly interesting because they are transitional fish, between soft-finned and spiny-finned fish. They look like tadpoles that have been given a head like an aircraft cabin. Crustheads, also known as midnight fish, grow to 8 cm and occur to depths of 1500 m.

CUCUMBER fish

Chlorophthalmus nigripinnis: A small marine species which like freshwater smelts and the dragonets smells strongly of cucumber. Closely related to lizard fish but with far larger eyes, a dorsal fin originating below the level of the ventral fins and smaller teeth. Cucumber fish are green on top, silvery-yellow underneath and grow to around 30 cm. They are frequently caught by trawlers at depths between 90 and 180 m. They are distributed in New Zealand, Tasmania, Victoria and New South Wales.

Cucumber fish

CURING A method of preserving jaw bones of large fish, usually shark. The technique recommended by famous Australian shark fisherman Alf Dean is to start by cutting off the shark's head then clean off as much meat as possible and lower it to the bottom of the bay on a line. The sea lice will clean off the remainder. Use crossed sticks to hold jaws open securing with ties, and place the jaws in a solution of 10 parts water to one part formalin with a pint of peroxide for bleaching purposes. With the jaws thoroughly covered, allow to set for four or five days, remove and allow to dry in the shade (not in the sun). After thoroughly drying, coat with a good clear lacquer for a beautiful finish.

CURRENTS Constant bodies of water in motion, usually in one direction. The greatest movements of the oceans are due, not to the tides, but to the heat of the sun, the cold of the polar regions and the spin of the earth. These are the basic factors responsible for the winds, the weather and the great ocean currents which influence seasonal appearances and migrations of fish. A knowledge of currents and experience of when they can be expected can take a lot of the gamble out of angling.

Air and water heated in the tropics move out towards the polar regions while cold air and water from the poles return to the equator. In the atmosphere this process creates the north and south-easterly trade winds on each side of the equator and the north and south-westerlies of the cooler latitudes. In the latitudes of the southern hemisphere between 35 and 60 degrees, the north-westerlies blow at gale force to give the name to the Roaring Forties.

On each side of the equator, the trade winds and the westerlies produce vast figures of eight in the atmosphere as warm air rises and cooled air sinks. In a similar way the warm water of the tropics moves through the surface layers of the ocean while the polar water sinks to the bottom.

Friction between the moving air and the water surface propels the upper layer of the ocean in the same general direction as that in which the wind is blowing—westerly in the tropics and easterly in the latitudes of the westerlies. The direction of these drift currents is given as that towards which the wind is blowing. This is the opposite practice to that used in describing the movement of the wind.

Currents usually average a speed which is around 2 per cent of that of the wind. In the oceans Coriolis force diverts the current to the right or left respectively according to whether it is flowing across the northern or southern hemisphere.

Ocean currents therefore generally move in circular orbits clockwise to the north of the equator and anti-clockwise south of it, the shape and size of the orbit being defined by the continental land masses. South of the continents in the southern hemisphere, the currents move from west to east but this flow is reversed nearer Antarctica.

Flowing like huge rivers through the oceans, currents carry huge quantities of water for thousands of kilometres across the earth's surface. The majestic Gulf Stream whose warmth tempers winter in the British Isles moves some 50,000 tonnes of water a second along the eastern shores of the United States. The Pacific equivalent of the Gulf Stream is the Kuro Shio, a warm current that sweeps right across the ocean from Japan to the western coast of North America and is cooled by another current, the Oya Shio, on the way.

The mightiest of all these rivers of the oceans is the current that circles Antarctica. This is known as the Southern Ocean current and it carries more than 100,000,000 tonnes of water every second—roughly 100 times as much as all the rivers of the world put together.

An offshoot of this current flows northward along the west coast of Australia to join the Equatorial current of the southern Indian Ocean. The northern part of this ocean is remarkable in that the flow of its currents is completely reversed twice each year. This is due to the monsoonal diversion of the trade winds created by the extremes of summer heat and winter cold in the land mass of Asia. A similar monsoon in the tropical north of Australia brings heavy rain at times between December and February.

Because the seas retain heat better than the land, the warm-surface currents are the world's great climate conditioners. But it is the cold currents drawn to the surface by the off shore winds along the western coasts of the continents that are of most significance to fishermen.

This water, rising from maybe 360 m, brings up supplies of nutrient salts from the storehouse of the ocean depths. As a result the surrounding sea is soon rich in every sort of marine life. This is the situation that arises when the Humboldt current of the South Pacific reaches the coast of Peru. As long as prevailing southerly winds blow, upwelling of nutrient waters takes place along many hundreds of kilometres of the Peru and Chile coastline. Fish and seabirds flourish. But soon after Christmas each year a change takes place. A warm current known as El Nino, named from the Spanish title of the Infant Christ, is diverted southwards. In some years El Nino is strong enough to cut off the supply of nutrient salts. The plankton, the fish and even the seabirds are destroyed. In a short time all that is left on that fruitful coast is the stench of death.

D

DAPPING The lowering of a fly, natural or artificial, on a hook at the end of a line so that it touches or hangs just above the water. The line should not touch the water, and neither the rod nor the angler should be visible to the fish. In these circumstances the fly has all the appearance of a living one, and many species of freshwater fish that normally feed on insects are readily caught. This method was originally developed to catch trout centuries ago, and there is a written record of this technique being used by anglers in Macedonia in the second century A.D.

Dapping is used extensively on lochs and lakes in Ireland and Scotland, where the anglers have specialized equipment, and it is used occasionally in Australia by anglers with normal fly fishing tackle. Dapping has an advantage in that the line is kept clear of the water, and so the distorting optical effect that makes even the finest leader visible as it lies on the surface of the water is avoided. The fly can be manoeuvred in the air to imitate a natural insect in a way that is impossible with normal methods, and without disturbing the surface of the water as happens when a fly that is attached to a floating leader is moved.

Dapping tackle for use on lochs consists of a very long but light rod, and a blow-line of light silk floss that is designed to catch the lightest breeze. Flies may be the normal artificials, though many localities have their own special dapping flies. These are often palmer (all hackle) tyings that sometimes have small double hooks attached to hand just below the main hook to make the hooking of jumping fish more certain. In some areas natural flies are regarded as more effective than artificials and often two are impaled on the one hook.

Mayflies are one of the main items in a trout's diet, and when these insects hatch from the water and also dip down onto it to lay their eggs, the trout often jump up to take them out of the air. Trout are remarkably clever at this, and even young fish rarely miss their mark. This is the time when dapping is most effective, although a properly dapped fly will almost invariably take fish that are close enough to the surface to see it, whether the fish are surface-feeding or not.

On lakes, dapping is usually conducted from small open boats which are rowed to a favourable position and allowed to drift with the breeze. The angler holds his rod high so that the blow-line catches the breeze and carries the fly as far as possible downwind of the boat. By manipulating the rod and the amount of line he has out, the angler causes the fly to dip and hover just above the surface of the water, in just the same way that the natural flies do. Trout either take the fly just as it touches the water, or leap out of the water to take it in the air, which is thrilling and spectacular.

Stream fishermen who are aware of the effectiveness of dapping sometimes dap a fly from the concealment of a high bank, or from behind rocks or streamside bushes. Normal fly tackle is sometimes modified on the stream to take advantage of a breeze by adding a few yards of fine nylon to the leader so that it will 'blow'. Great care has to be taken with concealment, for such modified tackle cannot achieve the distance of the long rods and blow-lines.

The time for dapping

Fishermen take fish by dapping in the early evening, when approaching darkness aids concealment, and the angler can get closer to feeding fish. At this time many insects conduct their mating flights, and lay their eggs on the water, and many species of sedges and mayflies, which between them form the bulk of trout food, hatch. Consequently, insect-feeding fish are very much on the alert for flies dipping down to touch or skitter across the surface, and the angler who can imitate this action with his fly should have exciting sport.

To fish with most advantage at this time the angler should approach the water from the eastern side. From this side the pearlescent afterglow of the setting sun is reflected off the water, and the angler can see the rises of feeding fish long after darkness otherwise makes them invisible. Large flies fished across weeds in the darkness have been responsible for some very large trout. The trout apparently take them for frogs—a conclusion based on an examination of stomach contents. Both bass and Macquarie perch also may be taken in this way, and doubtless other species, too.

Many coastal streams of New South Wales and Victoria contain sprats of freshwater herrings. These fish unfortunately are small, rarely being caught over 20 cm long, although they do grow to 30 cm. Their reaction to a dapped fly is fast and furious, little concealment being necessary, and 20 or more are often taken in 30 minutes. As they make delicious eating, they provide the fly fisherman with some fun on ultra-light tackle when the trout season is closed.

DART or swallowtail

Swift, graceful swimmers of the family Carangidae prominent in the surf and around beaches in tropical Australia. They grow to 1.2 m and around 22 kg, though there are several

D ■ DART

species of 60 cm and 75 cm. A dart of 8.5 kg or more is rated exceptional. They are similar to leatherskin but deeper in form and lacking dorsal or anal finlets. There are powerful pads of teeth in the throat for crushing shells of oysters, pipis and other molluscs. They are such fast, lively swimmers they sometimes become stranded in the shallowest water.

Snub-nosed dart *Trachinotus blochi:* A brilliantly silver, deep-bodied species with a blunt, rounded snout. They are splendid food fish and pugnacious fighters. They are found in coastal and ocean waters off north and central Queensland, with a few stragglers as far south as Moreton Bay. The breast is faintly tinged in yellow, the sickle-shaped dorsal fin edged in black.

Black-spotted dart *Trachinotus bailloni:* Another vividly silver species, greenish above, with two to five prominent black spots along the torso. They shoal in hundreds in clear coastal and reef waters off Queensland, with their dark-tipped dorsal and upper caudal fins above the surface. Black-spotted dart grow to 56 cm and are good table fish, if somewhat dry. Grant recommends filleting and skinning them before cooking. They should not be confused with the related swallowtail *Trachinotus russelli*, or the deep-bodied leatherskin *Scomberoides tala*.

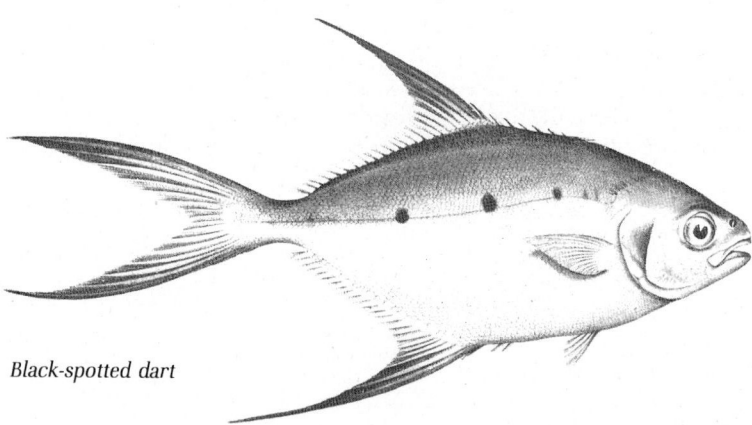

Black-spotted dart

The oyster-eater *Trachinotus anak:* A blunt-nosed heavy-bodied dart that reaches 1.6 m and is believed to cause damage to many oyster leases. One fish can consume three dozen oysters in a single meal, crushing the shells in the bony structures at the bottom of the gullet. Very similar to snub-nosed dart.

Dart *Trachinotus russelli:* An outstanding quarry for beach fishermen who bait with peeled prawns, yabbies or cut fish. They are common in coastal waters from Gladstone to northern New South Wales, shoaling in numbers, and vigorously attacking baits. Catches of 30 dart in a day are common.

DEEP-SEA fishing

Most Australian fishermen who put to sea do not hope to catch marlin, sailfish or any of the other game fishes. Helped by the boating boom which began in the 1960s and has continued on into the 1980s, their main aim is to get out among the big fish denied to them close to shore. Fast aluminium and fibreglass boats enable them to try several locations during an outing, and with echo-sounders they have invaluable assistance in finding the best spots. A sport that was limited to the wealthy before 1950 has become an activity most can afford. If you can't afford your own deep sea boat, it is comparatively simple to join one of the many clubs that regularly venture into deep seas. Boat builders these days will incorporate special features for deep sea fishermen such as bait tanks and fish boxes and such is the high standard of the available navigation equipment no fisherman need worry about returning home in the dark.

Although the major proportion of the world's ocean space is at a depth below 180 m, food for fish is scarce out beyond the continental shelf, where there are two basic groups of fish. These are the bottom-dwelling or benthic fishes, and the free-swimming or pelagic fishes. When they cannot find large reefs across which they can drift while fishing for pelagic fishes such as tuna and bonito, deep-sea fishermen try to get their lines down on to the bottom with heavy sinkers of at least 450 g in weight, with two or three lines adjusted above it on short traces. Lines are lighter today than they were 20 years ago but different types of sea floors yield different varieties of fish. Flathead, gurnard, flounder, and morwong are found over sandy bottoms. Recent research has shown that a lot of species live in deep seas as well as in shallow waters, including the dories, cod, eels, sharks, and the flatfishes. Nannygai or redfish, gemfish and ling are far more plentiful in deep seas than close to shore.

Deep sea tackle

Most deep-sea fishing boats are well equipped with heavy handlines, but these have the disadvantage of requiring heavy sinkers to reach the bottom. Lines with breaking strains of 40 kg do not lose many big fish but they lack the 'feel' of lighter lines. Handlines tend to tangle and for this reason rod fishing is increasing off shore. Using a rod of around 2 m with a stiff butt, anglers can reach the bottom with lighter lines and smaller sinkers. Large centrepin reels with a long line capacity and a quick retrieve, will handle even the fastest currents. Special deep sea hooks should be used. Short traces or leaders are advisable. A big selection of metal lures for deep sea fishing have produced fine catches but the lures can be expensive and their loss clearly upsets an angler more than the loss of a yellowtail, prawn, or piece of squid. Small, reasonably priced 27 mg radios are recommended, for they provide a sensible link to shore stations. More and more off shore boats these

D ■ DEEP-SEA fishing

days are fitted with centre consoles that enable fishermen to move freely around the boat to play big fish.

Deep sea locations

This type of fishing is extremely popular right along the coast of Western Australia, where there are far fewer game boats than on the east coast. The Indian Ocean yields a wide variety of exciting species and it's little wonder that with 6800 km of coastline at their disposal boat registrations are soaring in the west. In the south catches of Western Australian jewfish, pink snapper, blue groper, morwong and samson fish predominate all the way round to Bunbury, a noted base for deep sea anglers. Cockburn Sound is the State's busiest waterway, with its channels dredged to a minimum of 18 m. Esperance has reported Westralian jewfish to 25 kg being regularly taken off shore. Each winter more and more boat owners are trailer-hauling boats to Exmouth, Dampier, Port Hedland and other tropical spots.

South Australian deep sea fishermen have recently become excited over the sighting of southern bluefin tuna in excess of 226 kg off the southern side of Kangaroo Island, about 20 km from the southern tip of the State. Several record tuna have been landed there and 135 kg breaking-strain lines have been broken by big tuna. Tuna in excess of 90.6 kg have also been reported in the south-east of the State and Robe and Port Macdonnell. Add all this to the known presence of 15 kg snapper (all the year round) in St Vincent Gulf, the big sharks in Streaky Bay, and yellowtail kingfish off Rapid Head and it becomes clear South Australia is abundant in deep sea fishes.

Victorian off shore anglers have big problems with bad weather and the big seas of Bass Strait, but they still land occasional small marlin, yellowfin tuna to 35 kg, and outstanding snapper, flathead and school sharks. One of the best spots is Lady Julia Percy Island near Port Fairy, home of a big seal colony and a variety of big sharks. Yellowtail kingfish are taken as far west as Port Phillip Heads. In the Lakes Entrance region up to Mallacoota, mako sharks, bluefin tuna, and yellowtail kingfish are taken regularly. There is plenty of exciting fishing in Port Phillip and Westernport Bay, which is why sportsmen dislike leaving these safe waters.

Although Bermagui has declined as a deep sea port, there is still plenty of action right up the New South Wales coast to Sydney Harbour. Broken Bay, Cape Three Points, Hole-in-the-Wall, Regs Ground and the Patches all have yielded splendid catches of jewfish, morwong, flathead, snapper, teraglin and albacore. The waters of southern Queensland and northern New South Wales offer exciting prospects for anglers who get away from the shore, with yellowtail kingfish, sweetlip, red emperor, and pearl perch. To the north Barrier Reef fishing has become world famous, but apart from the marlin off Cairns most of it is undertaken from charter boats. It is undoubtedly true that the presence of so many holidaymakers has prevented Barrier Reef fishing for non-game species developing as it should have done for amateurs. Professional boatmen worry about the tides and the sharp rise and fall in currents, they find the fish and supply tackle and bait. It is not until they get out alone beyond the outer reef that sportsmen anglers can try their skills.

See Game fishing.

DIRKFISH Of the family Notographtidae, are small eel-like fish around 15 cm long which inhabit tropical waters in Queensland, Northern Territory and Western Australia. They have spines, scales and fins and slender ventral fins near the throat which, according to Whitley, are never found in eels.

DOGFISH A group of small, harmless sharks found mostly in deep water but occasionally in shallow coastal waters. They have a superficial resemblance to sharks but have several different features which suggest that they are of independent origin. Dogfish are edible but are not sold under their own name as food because of public prejudice. But a certain amount finds its way on to the market as 'flake' and 'sea fillets' despite the fact that misrepresentation is now illegal. Dogfishes lack an anal fin, have five gill openings on each side, and two dorsal fins. They are found mainly in the colder waters of southern Australia. They seldom grow beyond 1.6 m in length. Perhaps the most interesting of them is the prickly dogfish *Oxynotus bruniensis*, a blunt-nosed, heavily-scaled character found in New South Wales, Victoria, Tasmania, South Australia and southern Western Australia. They are frequently trawled on the continental slope between 150 and 450 m.

DOLPHIN fish *Coryphaena hippurus:* A truly international blue-water fish with an extensive distribution throughout the oceans of the world. It usually is described as dolphin fish in order to distinguish it from the intelligent sea-mammal of the same name. They appear on international game fishing record lists as mahi-mahi, the Hawaiian name for them.

Dolphin fish

D ■ DOLPHIN fish

The dolphin is a streamlined, fleet-finned swimmer, fast enough to run down flying fish and other speedy pelagics.

On a line, it is a fast and bold fighting fish, dashing about wildly on the surface and usually putting up some amazing leaps. In common with other very fast fish, such as the tunas, some of its fins can be folded into recesses in the body to give improved streamlining. In this case the rather large ventral fins, which are unusually close together, fold away into an abdominal groove.

In its form it presents a number of unusual features. It has a tightly compressed, deep body, and its steep frontal slope and surmounting bony crest give it a high front elevation which becomes more pronounced with age. Its unusually long dorsal fin, which runs from the top of the head back to the butt of the tail, contains no hard spines. Its very wide tail fin is so deeply forked as to leave the lobes extraordinarily long and narrow.

Its colours, and the colour changes it undergoes when removed from the water, are more remarkable still. The eyes are emerald green with black pupils. The head is olive green, the dorsal fin dark purplish-blue, the back and upper body brilliant green-blue merging to yellow or silver on the belly and the tail fin greenish-olive gold. There are yellow areas under the throat and jaws and numerous blue-green spots on the head and body. The whole is overshot with varying tones of gold and purple. On removal from the water its colours fade and brighten again repeatedly as it extends and folds its big dorsal fin and flushes of gold and pink come and go on its skin. On death the superb colours fade away to a dull leaden-grey.

Dolphins are found sparsely on the east and west coasts of Australia, but they favour warmer waters and are more plentiful in the north. But for Japanese longline fishing, they probably would be found in their greatest numbers on the outer margins of the Barrier Reef. An overseas catch was weighed in at 36 kg, but the biggest so far landed in Australia is 18.5 kg for a fish taken off Sydney. The very large fish often travel alone, or sometimes two or three may be seen together. More often shoals are met where there are a number of juniors from 1.5 to 4 kg in company with a much lesser number of adults of average size.

Technique for dolphin fish

They usually are taken by trolling at a fast rate with garfish, mullet or fish strip, or with artificial lures such as the large reb-2, feather jigs, plastic squid, plastic octopus, chromed plugs, or spoons. When these fish are met in company, some almost invariably follow up and tail one that is hooked and in play. With quick work, by which other lures are out again before each fish is boated, it may be possible to take a number before the school breaks away.

The methods of fishing for dolphin are straightforward, except for the trouble of landing the fish. They will take a trolled bait of mullet or garfish quite freely, or almost any trolled lure. One Queensland sportsman used a bauble from a Christmas tree. Dolphin often show, travelling down the face of a swell behind a boat, as opalescent chips of colour only slightly different from the blue deeps around them. They can also be located by watching a solitary bird, which first finds a dolphin or two and then follows them around. As the dolphin chases flying fish, the sea-bird takes sporting shots as the small fish glide across the waves. Alternatively any large piece of flotsam on the sea will have a number of small forage fish around it and is worth prospecting. Sometimes anglers find a floating box with fish inside it and the luminescent dolphin underneath waiting for one to make a mistake. Under such conditions lures trolled or cast to the waiting dolphin are almost certain to provoke a strike.

Some anglers use tough paper in large sheets as dolphin attractors. On a known ground, a boat can drop the sheets off while going out and fish around them coming home, and so provide more predictable fishing. Baits or lures such as a drone 3½ spoon, feather jig or squid at a speed of 6 to 8 knots seem to get great results. Tackle for sport fishing should be a light game outfit, such as a 9 kg game rod, 4/0 game reel and 8 kg line. With this kind of equipment, a reasonably big dolphin has a good chance to show a newcomer why it is treated with such respect by experienced anglers.

Dolphin flesh commands good prices on American markets. It is considered to be the superior of coral trout and barramundi by game fishermen on the Barrier Reef, but as it is a relatively unfamiliar species is not sought by the general public. The flesh cooks greyish-white but is of excellent flavour.

DORY

Dories found in our waters include: the silver dory *Cyttus australis*, which reaches 60 cm; the mirror dory *Zenopsis nebulosus*, which grows to a little over 30 cm and has striking silvery, translucent colouring, with a faded dark blotch and hangover-type dorsal; the warty dory *Allocyttus verruscosus*, which has an enormous dark eye and two rows of enlarged bony scales on the lower sides; the spiky dory *Neocyttus rhombhoidalis*, which again has an enormous black eye larger than its snout, no black body spot and a deeply compressed body; and the ox-eyed dory *Cyttosoma boops*, which has a very large mouth for this species that forms a kind of tube, and an eye twice as big as the snout.

John dory

Zeus faber: A member of the family Zeidae, of which there are at least 10 species in Australian and New Zealand waters. Also known as St Peter's fish. The john dory, largest of the dories, is among the finest of all table fish and has firm, white, tender flesh of outstanding flavour. They are also one of the ugliest of our fish. In Queensland, an entirely unrelated fish, the southern butterfish, *Selenotoca multifasciata*, is sometimes called john dory, to the embarrassment of fisheries biologists trying to untangle that State's muddled fish names.

John dory are not fast swimmers and have to rely on stealth and a curious mouth-action to capture their prey. Often only the dorsal fin moves as they move quietly about searching for food, but when they get within range of the food their jaws move faster than the eye can follow to grasp it. They feed mainly on young fish and this is by far the best bait for anglers eager to catch a good meal of them. Baits need to be well displayed, whether they are dead fish, yellowtail or mackerel.

Mirror dory

Silver dory

John dory

John dory are thin, flat fish with prominent black spots the size of a ten cent piece on their sides. They are greenish or brown in colour and the characteristic black spot is rimmed in yellow. The mouth is very soft, probably because it is so extensible. They grow to 60 cm, but average between 0.5 and 1 kg. They are most at home around offshore reefs. They sometimes swim into deeper channels in harbours and bays and occasionally can be seen moving quietly along under moored boats. There is a strange sluggishness in all their movements.

The distribution of john dory extends from Western Australia to South Australia, Tasmania and Victoria, up the New South Wales coast and as far as Bundaberg in Queensland, and in New Zealand in both islands. They are surface and bottom fish found between 25 and 150 m.

See Cookery.

DRAGONET

See Thornfish or dragonet.

DRAGON FLY

See Aquatic Insects.

DRAINAGE divisions

Australia's rivers have been grouped into 12 drainage divisions and scientists such as the late John Lake use these divisions to show the approximate distribution of our inland fishes. This method cannot precisely pinpoint the areas of distribution because even when a species is widespread in a division it is unusual for it to occur in every river in that division. 'Water velocity, type of river bed, cover, and other physical and biological conditions vary along the length of a river as well as between adjacent rivers,' said Lake. 'Even minor changes, let alone major ones such as dams and weirs and clearing stream banks, can change fish abundance quite dramatically and usually adversely.' Lake gave the distribution of bass in Australia, for example, as Drainage Divisions 1 (as far north as Fraser Island and the Mary River), 2, 3 and 4 (near the mouth of the Murray River only). Enlarged maps of the 12 drainage divisions are provided in the *Atlas Of Australian Resources* published by the Commonwealth Government Printer in 1975.

DRUMMER

A group of large, deep-bodied, weed-eating fish of the family Kyphosidae that are of growing importance to anglers, especially in New South Wales where the bulk of our drummer fishing is done by rock fishermen. Generally, drummer are not regarded as good food fish, and they are rarely seen at the markets, but they are rated highly by sportsmen because of their outstanding fighting qualities. The Queensland varieties of silver drummer appear to be much better eating than the darker varieties in the south.

D ■ DRUMMER

Drummer are very powerful fish and run with dramatic speed when hooked. They are exciting fish to play as some species grow to 90 cm and around 13 kg, and they have broken many lines. They bite warily but rush for sanctuary among the rocks immediately they are hooked. Fighting a big one demands high angling skill.

They feed largely on algae and have a fondness for deep water close to rocks where there is plenty of wash and ample supplies of seaweed and cunje. They can be effectively berleyed to the angler's bait as they are renowned scroungers for food, however much the surf may pound. The ideal spot for them is below broken water.

Queenslanders have learned that the drummer's edible qualities improve if they are bled immediately they are caught, and then gutted and filleted. They place the skinned fillets in a bucket of seawater and wash them vigorously until a thick froth disperses. They then cook them for the next meal. There is a strong feeling in the south, however, that even this procedure cannot improve the larger drummers.

Silver drummer

Kyphosus sydneyanus: This is the species which gives New South Wales anglers so much good sport, often appearing in numbers around ocean rocks where there is plenty of movement in the water. They are mainly weed-eaters, and can be caught on handlines and by spearing. They grow to 75 cm and around 10 kg but average fish are between 3.5 and 4.5 kg.

They are a compressed, deep-bodied fish with short heads, smooth mouths and bodies covered in prominent longitudinal bands. The scale pattern is strong. The fins, too, are very scaly and the gape of the mouth does not reach the front border of the eye. The colouring is dark silver on the upper body, varying to greenish-grey. They are caught on the same tackle used for the closely related rock blackfish.

Silver drummer are very common in South Australia and Western Australia, where they are mostly known as buffalo

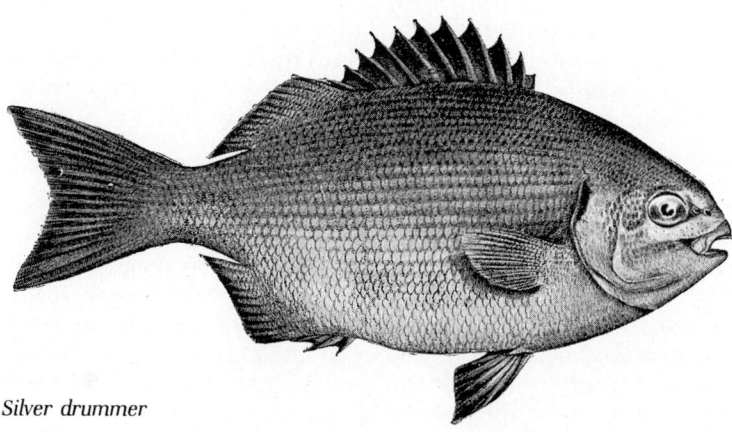

Silver drummer

bream and grow to a bigger size than those in the eastern States. Over there they are real tackle-busters. But South Australians and Western Australians do not fish them as much as anglers in New South Wales and Queensland as they have so many large fish that are better table fare. Indeed there seems to be little doubt that the bigger the silver drummer the more their edible qualities deteriorate.

The related buffalo bream of Western Australia reaches 95 cm and 12.5 kg. Another related species from Lord Howe Island and Norfolk Island, the dream fish *Kyphosus fuscus*, sometimes causes nightmares in those who eat it, according to Whitley. This species is known as narnwai.

Low-finned drummer

Kyphosus vaigiensis: A Queensland species of tropical waters frequently taken by spear fishermen who find a ready target in such deep-bodied fish. They are splendidly marked fish, growing to 55 cm, with dull blue bodies that are tinged with grey above and are lighter below the body. Golden lines or bands run lengthwise along the rows of scales. There are sometimes dull patches of yellow just behind the mouth.

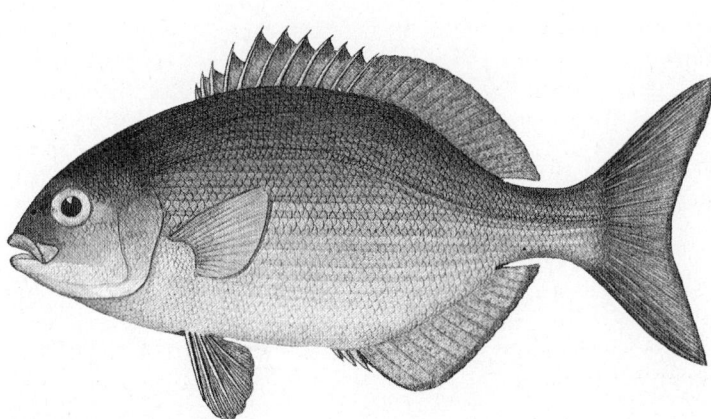

Low-finned drummer

Topsail drummer

Kyphosus cinerascens: Another prevalent Queensland species slightly smaller than the low-finned drummer, growing to between 30 and 40 cm. They are readily identified by their high dorsal fin. They are grey in colour with vivid golden bands running along the sides, and they are mostly found in Queensland's northern coastal waters.

Southern drummer

Kyphosus gibsoni: A common variety in south Queensland and northern New South Wales waters, inhabiting rocky headlands and reefs. They are dark on top, lighter beneath and the dull golden bands which run along the sides are narrower than the bands in topsail and low-finned drummer. The soft dorsal fin is violet-grey and they grow to 60 cm.

D ■ DRUMMER

Angling techniques for drummer

Drummer, like the closely related rock blackfish with which it is often confused, will take a variety of baits, including weed, prawns, crayfish, cunje, shellfish and crabs. They bite during the day and night and are mostly caught by rock-hoppers using rods or, occasionally, handlines. They are often attracted by a berley of bread crumbs.

They have small mouths so that hooks should range from No. 4 to 1/0 strong. The rock crevices and kelp in which they seek refuge when hooked take a heavy toll on lines for they are very strong swimmers. Stout tackle is essential whatever the rigs selected, usually 10 to 13 kg nylon line or a 15 cm reel fitted to a strong rangoon rod. Some anglers prefer to fish a weed or cunje bait under a float about 30 to 20 cm above the bottom. Others like to fish with a sinker on the bottom and rig the hook on a cast tied 60 to 90 cm above the sinker, and this technique probably accounts for more of the bigger fish.

E

EEL

Slippery, snake-like fish of the order Anguilliformes, which includes eels, congers, morays and similar forms. More than 70 members of the family occur in Australia, the majority of them in tropical waters. Many are excellent table quality but those Australians prepared to eat them try only freshwater eels. At one time some of the freshwater eels were hung in fish shops but this is now a fairly uncommon spectacle. Several of the northern saltwater eels are notable for their colouring and weird markings, and a few for the viciousness with which they will attack.

Most anglers regard eels as a nuisance and it is rare for attempts to be made to catch them on fishing gear. They are fished on the bottom with a tough combination of rod, reel, line and hooks and unless the angler turns them in the first 4.5 to 6 m they attach themselves to submerged trees, branches, snags, weeds, and other underwater objects by biting into them with strong teeth and hanging on. In position a 1.5 m long 9 kg eel is immensely difficult to dislodge. Barrier Reef species have been caught up to almost 4 m long.

Anglers frequently call reef eels *Gymnothorax*, sea snakes, a practice that is understandable considering this eel's ability to inflict serious wounds with their large, powerful teeth. Spear fishermen operating in the tropics quickly learn to be wary of species such as the pike eel *Muraenesox cinereus*, which will attack savagely and tenaciously with its long, conical teeth. These species, quick to resent trespassers on their territory, will not hesitate to attack those who disturb them.

Freshwater eel

Australia has two groups of freshwater eels, which are distinguished solely by the length of their dorsal fins. The long-finned eel *Anguilla reinhardtii*, is confined to one species, has a dorsal fin that extends along almost two-thirds of its length, and is found in eastern Australia from Queensland down to Tasmania. The short-finned eel has two species: *Anguilla bicolor*, which is found only in the north-west of Western Australia; and *Anguilla australis*, found in Queensland, New South Wales, Victoria, Tasmania and South Australia.

Australia has a small but growing commercial fishery for short-finned eels. Until recently this was confined to Victoria, where the main production areas were Lake Colac, Glenaire, Sale, Lake Purrumbete, and the Maffra Lagoon, but Tasmania is now contributing an increasing weight to the annual Australian catch, all of which is exported.

Short-finned eels are caught in conically-shaped fyke nets which resemble airport windsocks made of cotton or synthetic material of 2 to 2.5 cm mesh. Nets are divided into compartments of varying diameter with cane hoops which act as a frame. The entrance to each compartment is controlled by a conical valve of netting which prevents the eels from escaping.

There are several colour variations in the short-finned eels, and eating quality varies according to their colour. Choice short-finned eels generally are silver in colour, while golden eels are poorer in quality, and browns are inferior again. The colour is associated with their sexual condition. Silver eels are mature, while brown and golden members of the species are juveniles.

The breeding habits of these eels are a phenomenon of nature. They live all their lives in rivers and lakes and when their sexual instincts stir they descend to the ocean, usually when the stream they inhabit is in flood. They go out into the sea to a depth of 350 to 550 m, where the adults spawn and die. They migrate to the sea solely to breed, travelling incredible distances overland at night wriggling through damp grass in dozens of short stages, always moving with an unfailing instinct towards the place where they will spawn. They rest around rocks and other cover by day and at night continue their migration from one waterhole to another until they reach the sea.

The young emerge from their eggs and gradually float to the surface of the sea, drifting about for a time in a larval stage which sees them as slender, transparent creatures often mistaken for fish. When they are about 7 cm long, and have passed through their metamorphosis, they head for the nearest land, floating down the coast seeking an estuary or harbour that is fed by fresh water. They move upstream right to the source of the river and then spread out to even the most remote waterholes and billabongs. As in their parents' migration to the sea, the young elvers overcome apparently insurmountable obstacles on their journey inland, climbing steep rocks, waterfalls and cataracts, working their way into reservoirs and weirs that stop other fish. How they know when they leave one waterhole and wriggle across country during rain or heavy dew that there is more water a kilometre or so away remains unexplained.

These inland migrations of elvers or 'eel fare' expose them in large numbers, and overseas during these periods they are taken in surprisingly large quantities, particularly in English

Moray eels are large and often vividly coloured. Voracious and predatory, they may attack trespassers that disturb them..

rivers. They are then pounded into a paste and fried in butter, emerging as appetising cakes. Those that escape this fate, which in Australia means the entire eel population, live for many years in their chosen lagoons and headwaters.

Little research has been done on Australian eels, but it is believed the eastern variety breed near New Caledonia and those of north-western Australia near Sumatra. In Europe fully investigated life histories of freshwater eels have shown that they breed in the Sargasso Sea. The eels take two years to travel from their breeding place across the Atlantic almost 5000 km to where they enter the rivers of Europe.

The story of how European eels breed took 20 years to uncover. Just after the turn of the century when the eel supply of Denmark dwindled alarmingly the Danish Government gave Johannes Schmidt the task of discovering the reason. Schmidt was equipped with a special research vessel and skilled staff and for the next two decades he roamed the Atlantic, often picking up the floating leaf-like fish that were the baby eels floating from their birthplace in the Sargasso Sea to their freshwater homes in Europe and America. Schmidt tracked the developing elvers step-by-step in one of the great feats of piscatorial research. Schmidt came to Australia in 1929 as part of a two-year voyage around the world and it was he who found evidence that the breeding place of Australia's freshwater eels was in deep water north of Australia, possibly in New Caledonia.

Schmidt found larvae floating south, developing into elvers at places along the east coast, at which point they moved into rivers. This explained why, when large quantities of larvae appear off a certain river mouth, there can be a sudden eel plague. In 1939 in the Clarence River of New South Wales, for instance, they appeared in such numbers they fouled the nets of fishermen, attacked fish caught in the nets, and became such a threat to the fishermen's livelihood, fisheries experts had to be called in to help. They disappeared almost overnight.

The conger eel *Leptocephalus wilsoni:* A mighty fish that attains 45 kg, but is mainly a southern species, seldom found in Queensland. Adult specimens average around 15 kg. They are powerful eels of vicious disposition that grow to at least 1.5 m, brownish-yellow in colour on top, with purple tinges, and white or yellow below. The edges of their vertical fins are dark.

Marine eel The rocky shores and off-shore reefs of our coastline carry a wide variety of marine eels, most of them a pest to fishermen whose fish they eat, and numbers of them dangerous to spearmen. They invariably have fang-like teeth but their bites are not poisonous. Some reach 3.5 to 4 m in length, while the smaller varieties are about 60 cm long. The bigger ones are as much as 15 cm across. Some are beautifully coloured.

The feeding habits of these eels have intrigued scientists and fishermen alike for decades. The eels first bite viciously into their victim's body. Then they tie a knot in their own tails, slipping it around the victim and gradually tightening it until by the time it reaches the victim's head enough pressure is exerted to rip the head loose, and with it mouthfuls of flesh. The eels use this same method to escape when they are caught on anglers' hooks, tying knot after knot in the lines attached to the hooks.

Moray or reef eel Family Muraenidae: There are at least 16 species of morays in our waters, several of them notable for their vivid colouring. They are almost invariably large, and one variety, the long-tailed eel *Thyrsoidea macrura*, is the world's largest reef eel. It has reached a world record of 3.8 m in Australian waters. This was a long-tailed eel taken in the Maroochy River, Queensland. Another caught in a crab-pot in south Queensland's Coomera River was 3.7 m long. These are a uniform dark brown above, lighter below, with dusky black fins and tails twice as long as their bodies. They will move deep into fresh waters. They are voracious and predatory and quite fearless about attacking a man who disturbs them.

Other less dangerous but attractive reef eels include the clouded reef eel or starry reef eel *Echidna nebulosa*, a Barrier Reef coral-dweller that grows to 75 cm and is vivid yellow to whitish in colour, rows of black blotches that are broken up

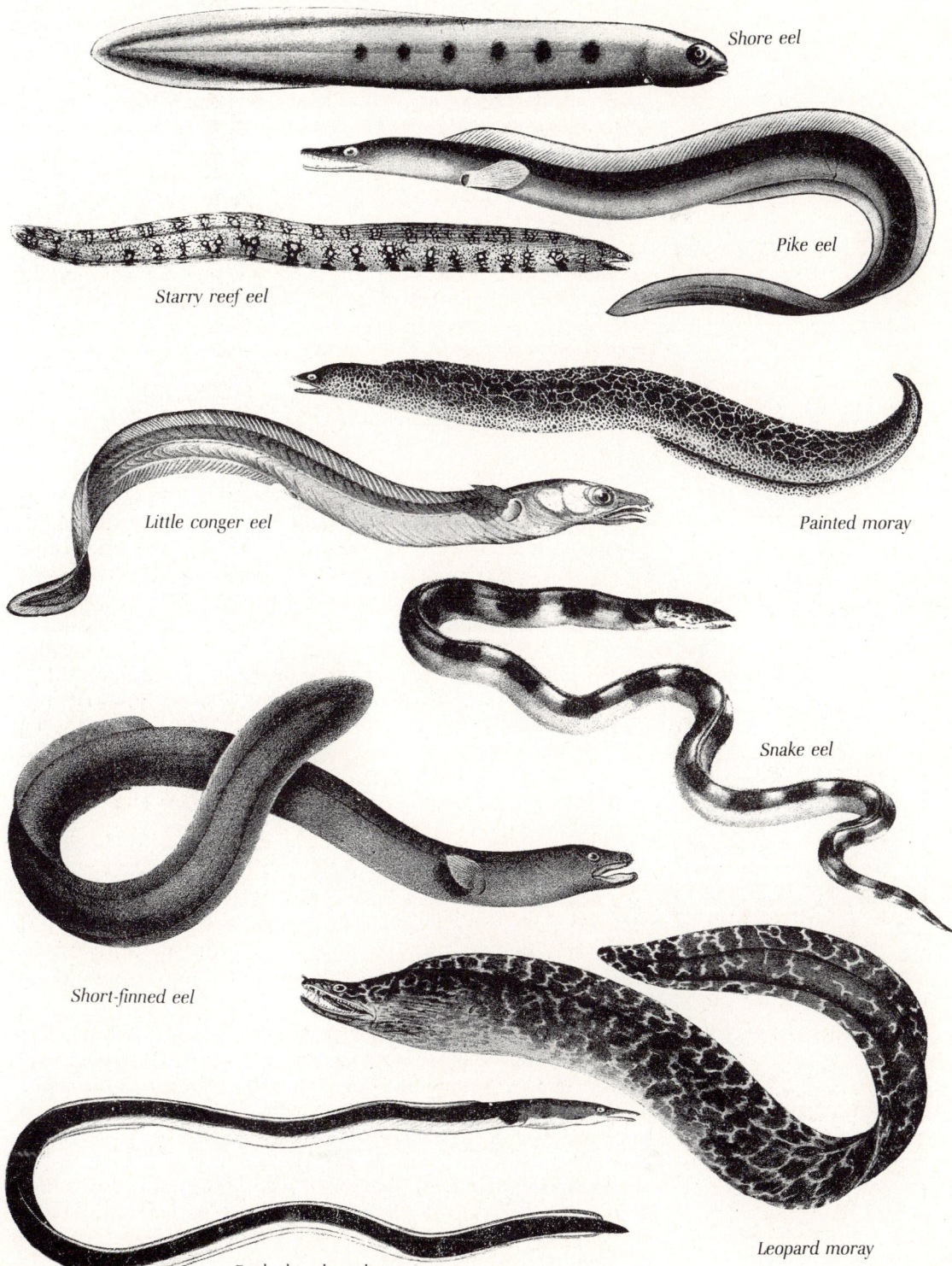

into star-shaped spots along its sides. The painted reef eel *Gymnothorax pictus*, is a beautiful eel with highly variable colouring. The young are a golden colour with round black spots about the eye and three longitudinal stripes. Adults are brown or grey, and have tiny black spots. The tesselated reef eel *Gymnothorax favagineus*, is a striking carpet-like eel of bluish-black, covered in white lines. The lines are more prominent in the young than in adults. It reaches 1.2 m.

Pike eel *Muraenesox cinereus:* Is widely known among anglers for the damage it sometimes does to their tackle and to their catches. It has vicious, long teeth that can inflict appalling bites and it will frequently attack when it is taken aboard a boat. Although it is mostly found in the sea, it will venture into freshwater streams, where it can be found in brackish backwaters. Pike eels are grey on top, silvery along the sides and their fins have a broad black margin. They grow to 1.6 m.

Shore eel Not true eels, now grouped with clingfishes, family Gobiesocidae. Common southern pygmy eels. The most plentiful are the red-banded shore eels, *Alabes dorsalis*, which seldom grow beyond 10 cm and are found just below the tide mark. They are green on top, with dark spots that fade quickly after death. They change to red when placed in preservative and it is from this that they used to be given the specific name *rufus*.

Snake eel Of the family Ophichthidae: Are among the most attractive of all the eels in Australian waters, with a characteristic habit of back-pedalling into the coral when danger threatens. The half-banded snake eel, for example, is a bright yellow-brown with contrasting black bands across the narrow body. They reach 55 cm.

Worm eel Of the family Ophichthidae: Are small eels not very often seen by Australian anglers, but present in fair numbers around estuaries and reefs. Perhaps the best known is the short-headed worm eel *Muraenichthys breviceps*, which grows to an average of 20 cm. They are brown along the sides, darker on top, with several black markings. Common in Tasmania.

ELEPHANT fish Probably only one species of this oddity appears in Australian waters, *Callorhynchus milii*, which also is known as the ghost shark. They are really a form of shark and have cartilaginous skeletons. Their striking feature, however, is the prominent proboscis or snout which has a fleshy lobe with a flap hanging from the end downwards in front of the mouth. They are common in Tasmanian waters and along the southern Australian coast, and in the waters of New Zealand's South Island. They swim like skates, undulating their pectoral fins, and while they sometimes appear in seine nets they rarely take the hook. Elephant fish reach 1.1 m and 8.5 kg.

EMPEROR

Bream-like fish with slightly pointed heads and scaleless cheeks belonging to the family Lethrinidae, found almost entirely in the warmer waters of Queensland, Northern Territory and Western Australia. There are at least 12 species along the Australian coast and around 40 of the family Lutjanidae, with which they are closely allied. Very few of them stray out of tropical water and several of those that are fat-lipped are confused with the sweetlips, which, as Whitley points out, more properly belong to Plectorhinchidae. Almost all of the species are good sporting fish and some are splendid table fish.

Red emperor

Lutjanus sebae: A vividly coloured fish that fights strongly when hooked and has become a favourite fish among anglers visiting Barrier Reef waters. They grow to 1.2 m and almost 22 kg, and are one of the few Queensland fish in which adults are just as appetizing as juveniles. They are also known as government bream, queenfish, red kelp and king snapper.

They mainly inhabit coastal waters, where they are taken on lines with a variety of baits. They are most abundant in Queensland waters from Gladstone northwards but have been taken as far south as Moreton Bay. Few fish can match their brilliant colouring: the salmon-pink body which mostly carries three pronounced dark bands in the shape of a government arrow. The bands disappear with maturity and the fish change to a rich red colour and later still, to a vivid pink.

Red emperor

Red-finned emperor

Lethrinus fletus: A good food fish common along the Queensland coast, where they are the quarry of hundreds of line fishermen. A fish of many aliases, including snapper bream, squire, sweetlip, brown kelp fish, brown morwong, coral bream, grey sweetlip, piggy, grass sweetlip and red throat. Grant classifies it as grass sweetlip.

Marshall says they are usually fawnish-orange above, lighter below, with pale pink horizontal lines along scale-rows, and blue lines and spots on the head. The body is heavily blotched and the inside of the mouth is scarlet. They grow to 45 cm, and average around 30 cm. They take their correct name from the pale pink and oblique dark-pink bands running across the dorsal, anal and caudal fins. Young specimens frequent mangrove swamps and feed on sea grass *Zostera*, but they move to the reefs as they mature.

Spangled emperor *Lethrinus nebulosus:* A very beautiful reef-dwelling fish also known by the local names of sand bream, yellow sweetlip, green snapper, and even morwong. They are common in off-shore waters north of Gladstone, but Grant says strays sometimes move as far south as Moreton Bay. They are mostly taken by handlining, particularly after dark, and they fight pugnaciously.

The body colouring is fawnish or olive-green, lighter beneath and each scale has a pearly-blue central spot and a smaller basal spot. The inside of the mouth is pink to reddish, the cheeks have blue bands and spots, and the fins and pink tails are littered with pale spots. They reach 80 cm. Large numbers are often taken by mesh netting at night.

Spangled emperor

Sweetlip emperor *Lethrinus chrysostomus:* The most abundant of the Queensland emperors, and one of that State's outstanding table fish. Many a southern angler has returned from a trip north still stunned by the performance of these fish, which, when they are encountered in large numbers, can tax the fisherman's ability to keep pulling them in. They bite freely and they fight powerfully, taking small fish baits, molluscs, squids and crustaceans. They often can be berleyed up from a coral bottom to within a few metres of the surface.

Sweetlip emperor

Sweetlip emperors are olive green on top, silvery below, and their bodies are slashed with dark vertical bands. Their heads vary from salmon pink to vivid red and the dorsal fin, bright crimson. They reach 9 kg and 90 cm but average around 1.5 to 2.5 kg.

Emperors in Western Australia
To overcome the problem of selling chinaman fish, a species of doubtful reputation known to cause ciguatera poisoning, professional fishermen in north-western Australia have renamed the chinaman fish 'red emperor'. And to overcome any further problems from this they have labelled the true red emperor *Lutjanus sebae*, or government bream, 'ladyfish'.

The true red emperor or ladyfish is caught to enormous sizes off Onslow, among the archipelago known as Mackerel Islands. Ladyfish up to 12 kg are not uncommon. These Western Australian fish start life with the characteristic red arrow above the flank, and at full growth they are a glorious tomato red, with thick lips and great oval bodies. Ironically, there is no known case of chinaman fish causing ciguatera poisoning in Western Australia.

ENGLISH perch

See Perch, English.

ESTUARINE perch

Macquaria colonorum: Fine sporting fish now separated from bass, which they closely resemble. They have been recorded up to 10 kg, with the males maturing at 22 cm, females at 28 cm, whereas bass mature at far smaller sizes. Their elongated bodies are deeper than bass and their snouts markedly longer. They are dark grey and silvery on top, lighter below and their overall colour is noticeably paler than bass. They follow a more restricted diet than bass and feed closer to the bottom on shrimps, prawns and small fishes.

E ■ ESTUARY fishing

Estuarine perch are common in most estuaries under tidal influence from the Richmond River in northern New South Wales south and west to the mouth of the Murray in South Australia. They have been reported in Tasmania but this depends on a few sightings in Ansons Bay from which it has since disappeared. However, Last, Scott and Talbot in their book, *Fishes Of Tasmania*, accepted its presence on the island, adding that illegal activities of gill-net fishermen may have endangered it. Estuarine perch are fine fighting fish that have recently been considered for fish farming. But they do not handle well and usually die immediately after capture. They have a high tolerance to salinity and breed in salt water during July and August. They are taken by the same methods as bass (*which see*), but in deeper water.

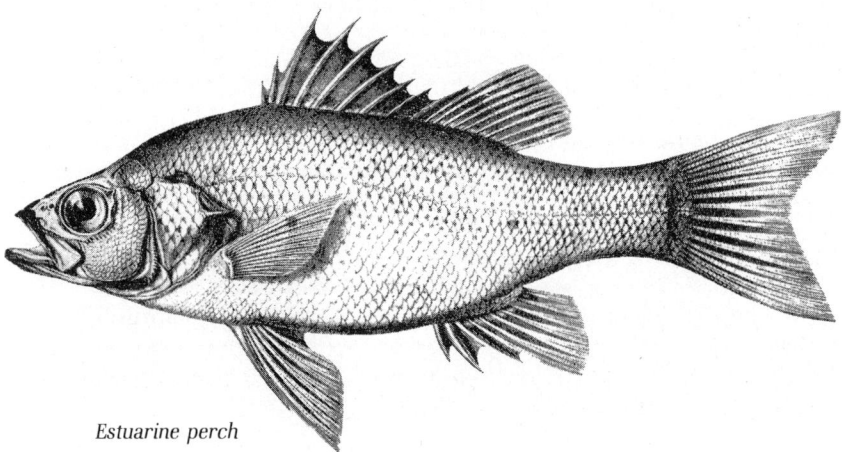

Estuarine perch

ESTUARY fishing This comprises not only fishing river mouths, but all water up to the tidal limit in conditions that vary enormously according to rainfall and tides. Heavy rains can produce an acidic run-off that influences both the presence and survival of estuary species. Strong downstream currents flow at a different rate to the heavier saltwater, which forms a wedge down on the bottom. High, inflowing tides bring with them food on which many species feed and many fish that are conditioned to choosing their own degrees of salinity. The remarkable truth is that the same species can flourish in both saltwater and freshwater and in the brackish combination of the two. Australia has some fascinating rises and falls in tides, ranging from barely visible changes of a few centimetres to changes of as much as 15 m. We also endure a lot of violent storms in which waters surge down rivers into estuaries, bringing with them debris and silt that make the estuaries disaster areas for fish. The wise estuary fisherman learns to avoid the periods immediately after storms, reserving his energies for quieter periods when fish can consume the crustaceans, yabbies, prawns and the small organisms that come in on the tide.

When and where to fish estuaries

Night-time fishing is usually the best, for this is when most species of fish move in from the sea or down from the higher reaches of the rivers. Many fishermen prefer to work by moonlight, hugging the shores, whereas those who fish by day move to the deeper channels. All of this is worth studying, for by far the highest percentage of Australia's edible coastal species depend on estuary environment. Sole, mullet, trevally, mulloway, barramundi, flathead, luderick and trumpeter are all at times adversely affected by bad conditions in estuaries, but they all instinctively return when normal conditions again prevail. Bream spawn in the brackish waters of estuaries, as do bass and salmon. Whiting thrive on river sandflats.

When an estuary becomes extremely muddy from floodwaters most of the adult fish move out to sea. This is the time when bream and whiting can be caught along adjacent beaches, the dusky flathead on shallow off shore flats and snapper on the reefs. But when the water clears, the fish waste little time in returning. Spring tides are always more difficult to fish than the neaps because they produce much stronger currents. Those who regularly fish in estuaries like to move out in boats at sunrise, anchor in a fancied spot, and fish the oncoming tide. At the flood they move to other locations to fish the runout or drift with the current across the sandbars. The river mouth is often the best place to fish at high tide when hungry fish enter from the sea, just as it is an ideal spot when heavy rains carry fish out of the estuary into the sea. In prolonged dry spells, it pays to move up river well away from the mouth, for that is what the fish do.

EVOLUTION of fish

Three kinds of fish have come down to us from prehistoric times. They are the cyclosomes or jawless fish, now represented by the hagfish and the lampreys; the cartilaginous fish, which are mainly sharks and rays; and the teleosts or fish with bony skeletons. The teleosts make up by far the greater part of the 30,000 or so species of fish in the world, of which fewer than 600 are cartilaginous species. Other creatures such as jellyfish, starfish, crayfish and cuttlefish are not fish at all, but belong to the other great families of sea-dwellers, coelenterates, echinoderms, molluscs and crustaceans.

A link between the starfish and fish is the lancelet, a small sea animal, like a worm, found in shallow waters around Australia. About 5 cm long and almost transparent, the lancelet is starting to be a fish, with the first stages of a backbone, a nervous system and gills. Lampreys, a couple of species of which inhabit Australian rivers, have a more complicated anatomy, with seven gill pouches on either side of their serpentine bodies. Because of their appearance, they are sometimes confused with eels, which are true fish. As well as being without jaws, the lamprey lacks paired fins and scales,

E ■ EVOLUTION of fish

while its gills and sense organs are primitive. Its mouth is a mere sucker by which the lamprey attaches itself to another fish in order to draw all the blood and other juices from the body.

Some 140 species of sharks and rays swim in Australian seas. One species, the Leichhardt's sawfish, a type of ray, is found in rivers of our northern tropics. Unlike true fish, the skeletons of both sharks and rays are composed of gristle or cartilage; the gill slits, usually five in number, have no cover and the scales are toothlike, the harsh skin of sharks causing severe injuries to the human body.

Most cartilaginous fish have a second set of nostrils, known as spiracles, set behind the eyes in sharks and on top of the head in rays. In sharks, the backbone extends to the upper tip of the tail-fin and in both species the fins are equipped with horny outer sections.

Reproduction of the cartilaginous fish is achieved by bodily contact between the sexes and in most species the young are born alive. Dog fish and skates lay eggs, however, and so does the whale shark, whose eggs are almost 30 cm in length. This difference is by no means absolutely clear cut, for some of the teleosts are also viviparous.

One of Australia's living fossils, the Queensland lungfish, representative of a family of fish that almost died out 200 million years ago, has an anatomical link with the cartilaginous fish through their gristly skeleton. These fish get their name from the lung which permits them to breathe air directly from the surface when the river or billabong in which they live becomes foul. The lung is a modified air-bladder containing numerous blood vessels, but these fish also possess gills which they normally use.

Both the lungfish and the burramundi, another primitive Australian fish related to fossils of more than 50 million years ago, have large scales and rather clumsy fins, the lungfish's pointed tail-fin somewhat resembling that of a catfish. However, the burramundi, whose name is commonly mispronounced as 'barramundi' is a bony fish, the head being covered with large flat plates.

After the female has laid her eggs, the male burramundi carries them in his mouth until the young hatch and does not eat for this period. However, this self-sacrifice is not unique. It is also practised by the marine catfish, the male of one species carrying up to 55 eggs in his mouth for nearly 70 days, as well as some freshwater species.

Form and movement

The fantastic variety of shapes seen in fish is proof of the way in which evolution has tailored each species to its environment. Built for speed, like a rocket, a torpedo or a dart; snake-like, flattened vertically or horizontally, rounded, stretched like a needle or a ribbon—every kind of shape you can imagine as well as shapes that defeat the imagination completely. What dictates the shape is where and when and how the fish picks up a living.

Most fish base their power on their tails. Strong muscles flick the tail to and fro, propelling the body through the water at a speed determined by the manner in which the fish's body is streamlined. The fastest fish in the oceans is accepted as being the tuna, whose smooth, fusiform body and well-forked tail streak through the water at speeds in excess of 60 km/h.

This is a shape refined by many long journeys through the oceans, a shape shared by the humble herring, the mackerel, the salmon and many other distant voyagers. The tapering body and forked tail are sure signs of a strong swimmer. In contrast, the flatter shapes of the coral reef fish indicate that they depend more on the ability to manoeuvre than on speed.

Heads and mouths are shaped by feeding habits. Big ugly heads and heavy jaws mark the bottom-feeders who crunch shellfish. Chunky bodies and wide fins balance the head. Then there are the fish of the sea bottom, eels that wriggle through the water and the halibuts, flounders and soles who flipped over from a vertical existence to life on the horizontal.

The greater the depth and pressure, the more bizarre are the forms that arise from it. The fantastic angler fish, camouflaged with barbels and carrying a luminous bait on its fishing-rod; the disc-shaped deep sea batfish that creeps about the decks of fishing boats for hours after capture and the oarfish, often 6 m long, whose flattened sinuous bodies gave rise to sailors' stories of sea serpents.

Just as strange as the monsters of the deep are the pipefish, razorfish, sea horses and sea dragons of the weedy shallows. The razorfish, thin as their name implies, swim with heads pointing down and tails up. Like the pipefish, the sea horses and sea dragons are encased in rings of bone; the sea dragons, which are only found in Australia, being camouflaged with weedy growths of skin.

Evolution has gone a stage further with the flying fish and the mudskippers by equipping them respectively to fly in the air and hop about on the land. Pectoral fins enlarged to wings allow the flying fish to leap out of the water and glide for varying distances—the longest recorded is 360 m with a maximum height of 10 m.

The mudskippers and those of the blennies known as saltlickers of tropical Australia use their pectoral fins as limbs to move about ashore: the mudskippers move among mangrove roots which they even manage to climb, while the saltlickers skip over the rocks with the aid of their strong tails. Although both species breathe with gills, they can survive out of water for relatively long periods.

BILL MYATT

F

FISH farming The cultivation and breeding of freshwater fish to provide fish for sport or for sale to restaurants is a comparatively new exercise in Australia. But the artificial propagation of fish is far from a new science and was practised in China at the start of recorded history. Ancient Chinese collected the eggs of fish by placing mats in streams or ponds. After fish spawned on them they sold the mats with fertilized eggs to the owners of rice fields who with careful watering hatched the eggs. The Romans also practised fish culture and General Lucullus in the first century B.C. built canals from his fish ponds to the sea. Marine species that bred in fresh water moved up the canals to his ponds and stocked them with their young. Australian fishing clubs keen to augment fish supplies for members face bigger problems.

Selecting a pond site

This is perhaps the most vital factor in the operation, for the location has to be on ground free of silt or industrial debris where the fish can be protected from birds and predators. Spring water is best but the flow should not be too fast or it will lower the temperature and remove natural food. It's worth the expense of a qualified engineer who can lay out plans for the pond according to specifications provided by law. In most States obtaining brood stock is no problem and can be arranged through the various State fisheries. The New South Wales Fisheries Division has a list of around 20 commercial warm water fish hatcheries that readily supply golden perch, silver perch, catfish, Murray cod, bass, goldfish and trout to farmers and fishing clubs. Arranging the ideal water supply is more difficult. The main thing is not to be too ambitious and keep the area under water small and deep enough to provide oxygen for the fish. The ideal setup is to build several ponds that can be drained in turn independently of the other ponds.

Selecting the right species

Trout are the glamour fish of Australian inland waters, but sportsmen need not necessarily restrict their pond culture to just this species. Some very good ponds in which Murray cod are bred have been built in the Riverina. Here bore water is preferred to river water. One fish farm has 34 ha under pondage, with a large reservoir surrounded by 85 ponds of varying shapes, depths and volumes for various species, of which the Murray cod is the preferred variety because of its high table quality. Whatever species are introduced, they should only be released into waters in which they occur naturally.

Trout propagation is the only form of fish culture that has so far had any impact on the public, however, with clear evidence of its success showing up on the menus of dozens of big city restaurants. Trout hatcheries with a strong supply of clean water of the right temperature that include well-built hatchhouses and raceways are here to stay. Good strains of brood trout are available from departments eager to promote the sale of fish in our markets. Fishing clubs wishing to enquire about the practicality of pond culture in their region should write to the fisheries department in their State.

In stocking an inland fish farm, the main problems are predatory birds such as cormorants, removing cannibal fish such as mosquito fish, avoiding excessive plant growth and supplying enough oxygen. But by following guidelines laid down by fisheries departments, fish suitable for the table can be available within two years of stocking.

See Stream improvement.

A farmer releasing fish fry into a dam.

FLATFISH

FLATFISH Delicious eating fish comprising the flounder, sole and Queensland halibut families in Australia, where flatfish belong to four families that include around eighty species. They are among the world's most edible fish but in Australia they are becoming increasingly scarce and never have grown to anything like the size of the flatfish of Europe. Considerable quantities of one New Zealand flounder, the yellowbelly, have been sold in frozen form in Australia.

There are a few areas in Australia which produce flounder for the angler drifting a bait over mud or sand flats or for the angler casting and retrieving a bait over the sand and mud of the beach or estuary. But most of our flounders and soles these days are taken by fishermen with handspears.

Flatfish begin life in the same symmetrical form as other fish, with eyes on each side of their heads. They swim close to the surface in a vertical position until they are about 12 mm long. Then one eye moves across their heads to the same side and adjacent to the other eye. The fish then heads for the bottom where it moves over the sand, both eyes on the upper surface, which in some species is on the right, others on the left side. Sole may be distinguished from flounder by the preoperculum, the bone in front of the gill cover. On a flounder the preoperculum is separated from the operculum or gill cover; on the sole the preoperculum is joined to the gill cover.

Outstanding European flatfish such as the plaice *Pleuronectes platessa*, the turbot *Rhombus maximus*, and the halibut *Hippoglossus vulgaris*, which grow to 270 kg and 2.5 m, are not present in Australian waters. Our biggest flatfish, the Queensland halibut, grows to at least 10 kg.

Queensland halibut *Psettodes erumei:* Largest of Australia's flatfish, growing to 60 cm and at least 10 kg, but fish seldom caught by anglers. They are mostly taken by trawlers in the far north fishing to a depth of 45 m. As in many other flatfish, the eyes may be on either the right or left side of the head. Juveniles are darkish brown in colour, sometimes black, and have wide transverse bands

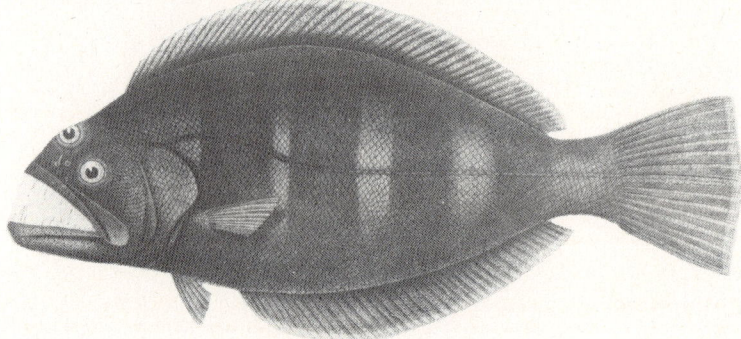

Queensland halibut

across each side. They are one of the few flatfish in which the colouring of the lower side closely follows that of the upper side. Adults, according to Grant, are a uniform dusky brown. Curiously, they bring poor prices at the markets, for they have outstanding edible qualities. Some trawlermen, aware of the public's ignorance about the fish, do not consider them worth sending to market. But among ichthyologists there remains a strong feeling that these fish have yet to get a chance to show their market potential.

Sole

Flatfish of the family Soleidae frequently confused with their relatives, the flounders. Both fish are haphazardly given the other's name in Australia, varying even from one State to the next. Like flounders, soles have strikingly flattened bodies and both eyes are close together on one side of the head. Like flounders, they are ground fish, living and feeding on the bottom, and seldom venturing near the surface.

The eyes and colouring of soles appear on either side of the head in a few species, but in the majority of soles the right side is uppermost and contains the eyes. Adults generally show coloured patterns only on the upper side. In contrast to flounders, the lower jaws are not prominent, the cheek-bones or preoperculums are not free, and the sides of the cheeks are covered with scales. They move with the same undulating motion as flounders, which is markedly different to the vibratory undulations by which the other flatfish, skates and rays, progress.

Some soles prefer estuaries, others are purely oceanic, and at least two species inhabit fresh water. Queensland has a unique freshwater sole, which because of waterfalls and other obstacles has been unable to return to the sea and has adapted to new surroundings and developed fresh instincts. This sole was discovered in a mountain stream of York Peninsula many years ago by the Rev. J. E. Tennison-Wood, and was labelled *Brachirus selheimi* by Sir William Macleay. One astounding aspect of this sole's development has been that the ova have gradually altered from pelagic to demersal, or ova that sink to the bottom instead of floating on the surface.

Large numbers of sole occur in Australian waters, but few are common enough these days for them to reach the markets in profitable numbers. They mostly remain gourmet fare which occasionally find their way on to the tables of the best restaurants and onto the dining tables of discriminating anglers.

All soles are carnivorous, existing on smaller fish, molluscs, crustaceans and sand worms. Soon after birth many of them push their way up rivers for kilometres beyond the influence of salt water and there attain maturity in reasonable safety, returning to the sea only when fully grown adults ready to reproduce.

F ■ FLATFISH

Black sole   *Achlyopa nigra:* A superb table fish that grows to 40 cm. They were once plentiful around the Australian east coast but are not often seen now in numbers, though prawn trawlers and seine nets frequently take them in Moreton Bay, Queensland. Periodically large numbers are sighted in Port Phillip Bay, Victoria.

Black sole are olive-brown to black in colour, with numerous dusky blotches rather like smudged thumb prints on the upper surface. Their tails taper off to what Grant describes as a terminal point.

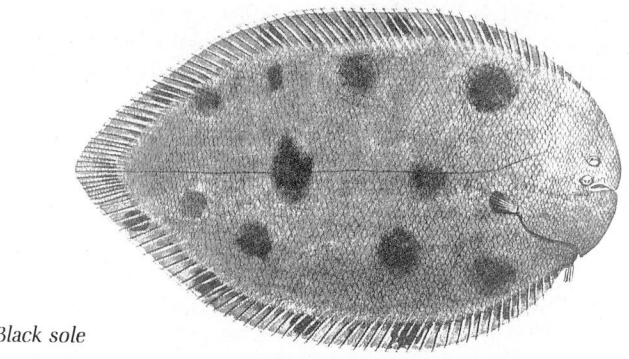

Black sole

Peacock sole   *Achirus pavoninis:* A north Queensland species that grows to 20 cm and, like the black sole, has its eyes on the right side. The tail fin is rounded and clearly separated from the side fins. This is a prettily marked sole, with an array of dots or spots that are paler than the rest of the fish scattered across a reddish-brown background.

Tongue sole   Easily distinguished from the true oval-shaped soles by their elongated bodies, which represent an animal's tongue. Their eyes are on the left side of their bodies and like true soles they are excellent eating.

Probably the best known of the tongue soles are the two-lined tongue sole *Cynoglossus bilineatus*. They grow to 40 cm and are dull silvery-white on the blind side, with all their markings on top. There are two clear lines running lengthwise down the both sides of the body, and they vary from sandy to brown in colour.

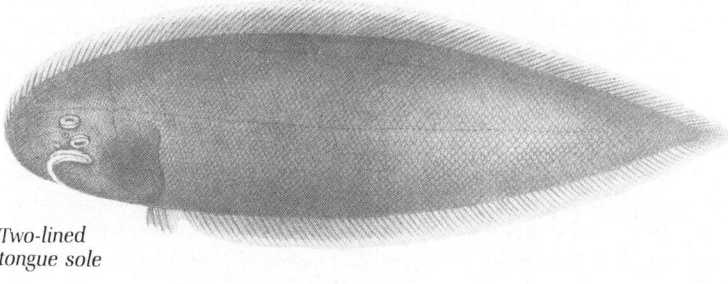

Two-lined tongue sole

Flounder

Numerous species of this highly appetizing flatfish family exist in Australian waters, though anglers seldom take big catches of them. They are mainly taken in nets or by spearmen as they cling fairly close to sandy bottoms and muddy inshore areas, where they feed on small sea worms, crustaceans, and small shellfish. New Zealand probably has the best of them as sport fish in the southern part of the world, and has at least three species which provide good sport on a light rod with small hooks baited with earthworms slung below the sinker and fished on the bottom on rising tides.

All flounders have the characteristic of being able to change colour quickly to suit their background. Grant suggests putting this to the test by moving one from a white-painted floorboard to the surface of a damp, dark sack and watching the changes in colour that occur in only a few minutes. They are often prettily patterned on top, and the bottom side is usually silvery or yellowish.

Flounders swim, both eyes upwards, with a wavy motion of their bodies and tails which, Whitley says, compares with the propulsive motion of flying carpets in the *Arabian Nights*. In some species the eye moves through the head to almost join the other eye, but in most species the eye moves around or across the head. They invariably have more prominent lower jaws than soles and the preoperculum or edge of the cheekbone is free. Albinos or piebalds are more common than in many other fish.

Australian flounders seldom exceed a length of 40 cm. Flounders produce millions of eggs that float. Most flounders succumb easily to spotlight spearing at night.

Black flounder

Rhombosolea retiaria: Also known as mud flounder, river flounder, estuary flounder, this species is thicker through and more bluntly pointed in the snout than most flounders. The body is dark green to black above, sandy and muddy below. Darkish red markings are splashed across the tail and upper surface and the spinal column is frequently green. They are easily spotted by their balanced oval outline, the spots on top and by their fondness for estuaries.

Greenback or yellowbelly flounder

Rhombosolea tapirina: is a much valued food fish and not enough are caught in Australia to meet the demand. New Zealand, which prefers the name yellowbelly to greenback, has for years sold sizeable quantities of this fine table fish in frozen form to Australia. For marketing purposes they are commonly known in Australia as New Zealand flounder. They grow to 38 cm.

Under the name greenback flounder, they are fairly common in Victorian and Tasmanian waters, inhabiting muddy and sandy inshore areas and often entering tidal rivers. They often disappear suddenly after appearing in numbers for some weeks. There seems to be a difference between the fish

F ■ FLATFISH

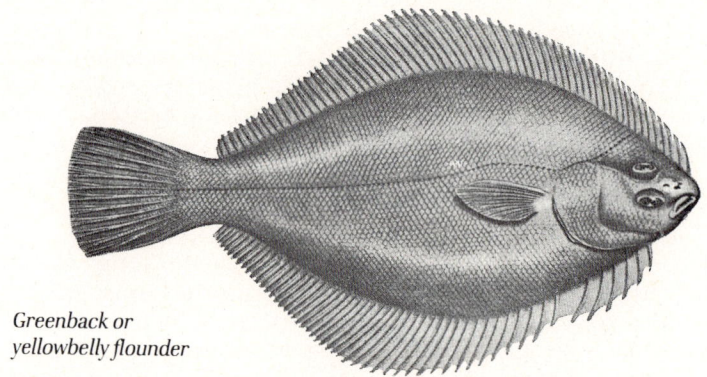

Greenback or yellowbelly flounder

of this species that prefer warmer waters to the north and a very similar flounder that is apparently confined to southern waters and has a rounder outline with a fleshy snout.

Large-toothed flounder

Pseudorhombus arsius: Perhaps the commonest flounder on the Australian eastern seaboard. They are brown in colour, with or without dark blotches and rings. The fins have brown spots and there are two clear ringed blotches on the lateral line of their bodies. They average a little over 30 cm, but have reached 40 cm. They get their name from the exceptionally large teeth on both jaws. Found in Western Australia, South Australia, New South Wales, Queensland and the Northern Territory, but also in South Africa, India and China. They take prawn or flesh baits fished over shallow estuary banks. Offshore they get down as deep as 55 m.

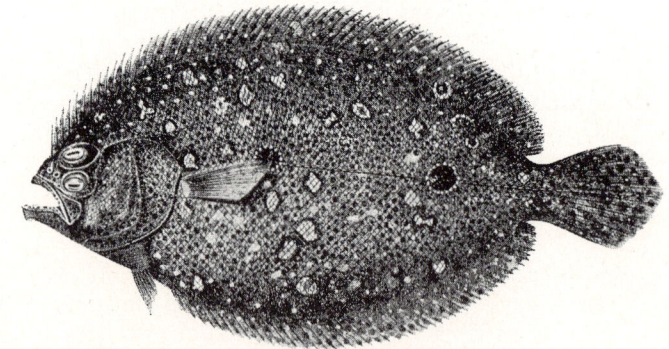

Large-toothed flounder

Long-snouted flounder

Ammotretis rostratus: A delicious eating species, dark to light brown in colour, with or without small dark spots. The right pectoral fins are blackish. They grow to around 30 cm, and are found in all Australian States. One of the commonest of the flatfishes, sometimes incorrectly labelled sole in both Tasmania and Victoria. They inhabit muddy and sandy bottoms to a depth of 80 m. Juveniles enter fresh water.

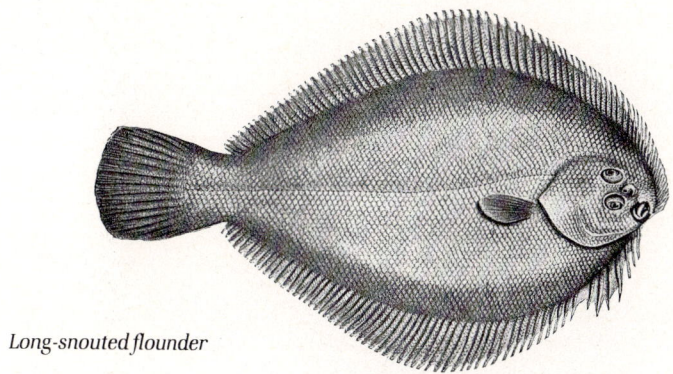

Long-snouted flounder

Sand flounder

Rhombosolea plebeia: Diamond-shaped and thinner than other *Rhombosolea*, and found in sand or mud not far below the surface. Also known erroneously as dab, tinplate, square, patiki (Maori) and diamond. They are blackish-green on the upper surface and white underneath.

Bass Strait flounder

Arnoglossus bassensis: A greyish brown variety, with several conspicuous blotches and spots. One of the left-eyed flounders noted for their excellent taste. The Bass Strait flounder is distributed in Tasmania and South Australia, and lives on sandy bottoms in depths of 90 m. Juveniles occasionally enter estuaries and seem tolerant of low salinities. They reach 24 cm in length.

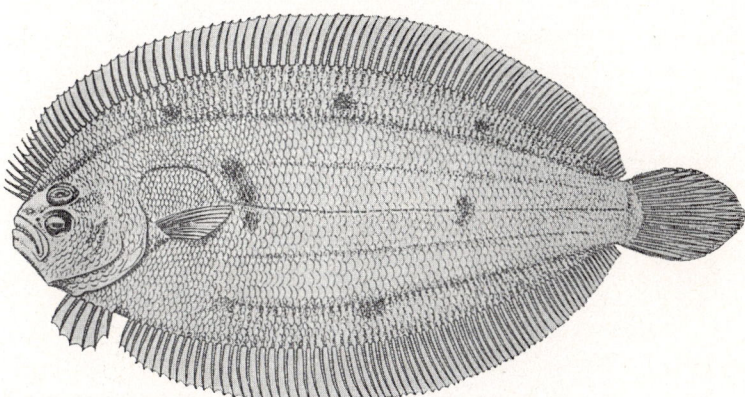

Bass Strait flounder

Crested flounder

Lophonectes gallus: The most abundant flounder in Tasmanian waters, where it occurs on muddy bottoms and frequently is taken in scallop dredges. The scales are large for a flounder and are present only on the ocular side. Crested flounder are light tan to dark brown in colour, with darker markings on the dorsal surface. They reach 20 cm in length and are found in all States.

F ■ FLATFISH

Crested flounder

Small-toothed flounder

Pseudorhombus jenynsii: A fine table fish, brown or grey in colour, with darker spots and markings. Five large ocelli or blotches are most prominent, and these ocelli have a number of white dots on them and are surrounded by a dark ring. The fins are spotted, and the teeth markedly smaller than in near relatives. They grow to 35 cm.

Small-toothed flounders are found in all Australian States, but are mostly taken in Queensland and around beaches of Bass Strait Islands. They are frequently caught in numbers in the Derwent River, Tasmania, and in Western Australian waters.

Small-toothed flounder

Spotted flounder

Ammotretis lituratus: A southern species taken in South Australia, Victoria and Tasmania. They are light grey in colour, with small, evenly spread black spots. They grow to 25 cm, and both juveniles and adults occur off surf beaches, rarely in estuaries.

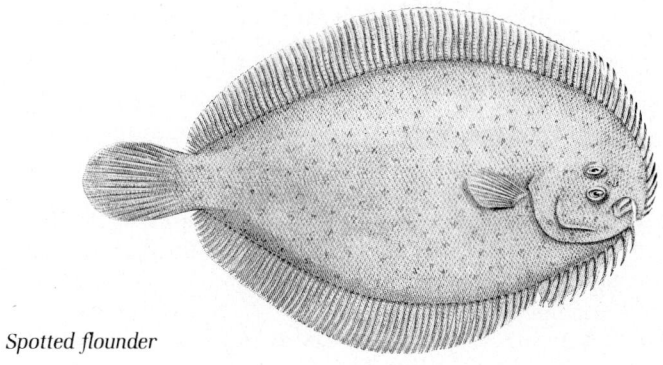
Spotted flounder

Catching flounder
The boat angler should drift his boat slowly over the sand and mud, the same as he would in drifting for flathead. An ordinary boat rod and reel are used with a 6.5 kg line. A 90 cm nylon leader, 4 to 5 kg, is rigged below a running sinker.

At one time hooks of about 1/0 were used but nowadays with so few big flounder about a much smaller hook is called for. A No. 1 hook is big enough, and in some spots a No. 4 or 6 is better. Sandworms, the best flounder bait, are more easily baited on a No. 4 or 6 hook than the larger sizes. The moment a bite is felt the angler sets the hook and the fish is retrieved with little or no trouble.

In a few areas where flounder or sole are found along the beaches or on the sand and mud flats of the estuaries, the angler uses a long beach rod, a casting reel and a 5 kg line. The terminal tackle is rigged so that the No. 4 or 6 hook is on the end of a 45 to 60 cm nylon leader, attached below a running sinker. As for boat fishing, the sandworm is the best bait. Flounder will also take pieces of prawn, marine worm or craytail.

Spearing flounder or sole
Flounder spearers use a single-pronged spear with a light attached. To prevent loose wires from dangling around the spearer's feet, the spear handle is hollowed and the wires from the globe to the battery are run through it. If only a night or two's spearing is contemplated the fisherman uses a dry cell battery which he usually carries in his left pocket. The serious spearer uses a wet cell battery (6 to 8 volt) which is either carried in a haversack at his side or floated beside him on a special float-board.

The best spots for spearing are shallow-water sand flats found along the shores of the bays and inlets or along ocean beaches. The spearer wades quietly through the shallows at night, probing the sand ahead with his light beam. When a flounder or sole is seen the light beam is kept on it until the spear is thrust home. Flathead are often speared on these flounder-spearing trips.

FLATHEAD

FLATHEAD Elongate, bottom-dwelling fish with flattened, depressed heads, familiar even to those Australians who never dangle a fishing line. Flathead, represented by at least 40 species in Australian waters, are not outstanding sport-fish. Their popularity depends entirely on their delicious table qualities. They inhabit shallow to deep water and change colour to suit their environment. Flathead are not found in America or Europe, ranging from China south to the tropics, through Indonesia and down Western Australia and Queensland to the southern Australian States.

Flathead are taken in large numbers by line, trawlers, and hauling nets, and are frequently hooked by fishermen bottom fishing for other species. They are caught from jetties, rocks, seawalls, sandbars, and by flathead specialists who drift for them in boats. They burrow into the seafloor, gathering their food by stealth, exposing only their upturned eyes as they lie in the sand waiting for crustaceans and small fish. They are not as plentiful on Australia's west coast as they are on the east, nor do they grow as large there, but Swan River flathead (duskies) reach 2 kg and receive special attention from jetties and rocks.

The most frequently caught species belong to the family Platycephalidae, which are the cooler-water variety. This group includes fringe-eyed flathead, sand flathead, dusky or mud flathead, dwarf flathead, red-spotted flathead, Harris's flathead, and bar-tailed flathead. The dusky flathead is the largest Australian flathead, growing to around 1.2 m and 14 kg, though fish from 7 kg upwards are considered first-rate catches.

The spiny flatheads belong to the family Hoplichthyidae, a deep-water variety distinguished by the absence of scales and the row of bony bucklers along the lateral line. The eyes are large, set prominently in a flattened, expanded head. This family are abundant in depths around 275 m, especially in the Great Australian Bight.

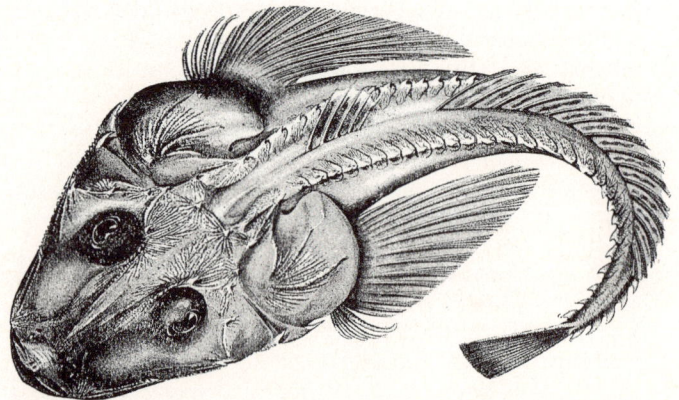

Spiny flathead

Another family, Suggrundus, are a tropical variety found from Japan to the China coast and through the East Indies down to northern Queensland and north-west Australia. This group can be identified by the ridges in the head and by the form of their teeth. All the flathead families have in common exceptional table qualities despite their sometimes grotesque appearance.

Dusky or mud flathead

Platycephalus fuscus: An estuarine species common to all Australian States. They have an elongated, depressed body, with bony ridges along the upper surface of the head. The mouth is large, the teeth small but needle-sharp, and they feed on small fish, molluscs, worms and crustaceans. Most anglers seeking dusky flathead use cut baits such as yellowtail fillets, with chained hooks or a wire trace as a precaution against the ability of big duskies to bite through lines. They reach 1.2 m.

They are greyish-brown to olive-brown on top and along the sides, white below in some areas, and the sides carry darker, irregular mottling. The head is dusky, and like the ventral and dorsal fins, it is brown-spotted. But the distinguishing features in dusky flathead are the large dark blotches on their tails.

Although the name mud flathead is in common use in Queensland for this species it is a misleading label, for these fish are caught from clean sandy beaches as well as from muddy bottoms. However, Grant says the duskies caught from sandy bottoms are generally much paler in colouring, ranging from fawn to mid-brown, than those caught on muddy bottoms.

Dusky flathead are most plentiful in summer, especially from January to March, when they move out of upstream creeks and flats towards the mouths of estuaries to spawn. These fish are much larger than most of those taken in winter. They are inclined to hang woodenly on the line without fighting after they are hooked. The preopercular spine on each side of the head can be dangerous when they are landed and most veterans stab them through the head with a knife or clamp a boot over their heads to avoid a painful sting as they remove the hook.

Dusky or mud flathead

Bar-tailed flathead *Platycephalus indicus:* A large flathead of estuarine waters of the north-west of Western Australian, Northern Territory, and northern Queensland, seldom seen south of Capricorn. These fish reach 1 m, but at that size lack flavour. Juveniles are splendid eating. They are caught on a variety of fish baits, including yellowtail, sea pike and trumpeter.

The upper surfaces of their bodies are liberally spotted with brown. The main body colour is sandy brown, white below, and there are ill-defined black blotches across the back. The caudal fin is brown, and in Coates' illustrations is splashed with orange-yellow and carries dark blotches.

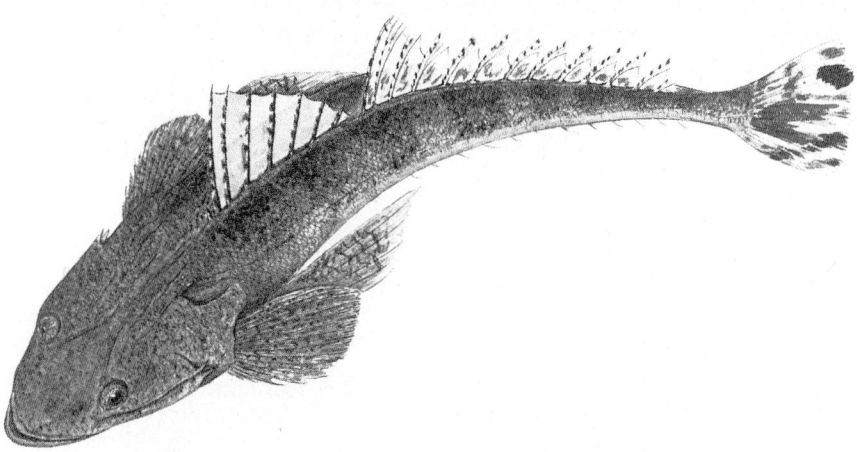

Bar-tailed flathead

Sand flathead *Platycephalus arenarius:* Found around the mouths of estuaries and on off-shore sandflats. They are a lighter brown, sometimes with a green tinge, and are marked with light blue spots. There are chestnut bands on the spines and rays of Queensland species. The tails are white with black stripes. They are easily recognised by the 'flag' set in the caudal fin.

Sand flathead are not a large variety, seldom exceeding 45 cm, and averaging 30 to 35 cm, but they bite eagerly on small cut fish baits and will take peeled prawns and yabbies. Interesting experiments with artificial lures have shown they will take them as readily as any bait provided the lures are presented properly.

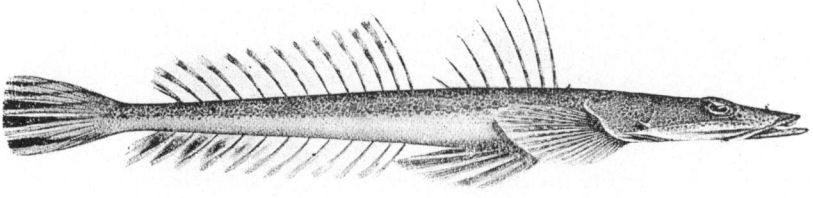

Sand flathead

Tiger flathead

Platycephalus richardsoni: For years the main species of flathead caught off New South Wales, but now sadly depleted by over-fishing. They grow to 65 cm, and around 1.3 kg. Roughley rated it second only to the john dory among fish caught by trawlers off the south-eastern Australian coast. The flesh is white, tender and flavoursome and tiger flathead do not grow so big they become unappetizing as other flathead species sometimes do. They remain highly edible for long periods of storage.

They usually are found in deeper waters on sandflats off-shore. The teeth are large and prominent. Their body colouring is brown with darker bands or blotched and they are mostly decorated with creamy spots or markings. They are not found in Queensland and are uncommon off the New South Wales north coast. They are only found in quantity in Victoria along the east coast around Cape Everard and only a few reach the eastern Tasmanian coastline. But the annual commercial catch in Tasmania still reaches 100 tonnes.

Tiger flathead

Fringe-eyed flathead

Cymbacephalus nematophthalmus: A very common fish in Queensland waters, where they are also known as rock flathead and sammy dong. Frequently taken in trawlers' nets usually in coastal waters and estuaries close to rocky outcrops and weedbeds. They are easily recognized by the large deep pit or eyebrow above the eyes. The body is usually dark brown with a series of dark crosses along the side which run into a series of speckles and blotches. They grow to between 35 and 40 cm, but are excellent eating. They produce a series of squeaky grunts on capture.

Long-spined flathead

Platycephalus longispinis: Another small variety which does not grow much beyond 30 cm in length but yields splendid fillets. This one takes its name from the large, sharp pre-opercular spines on the sides of the head, and is sometimes known as spiky flathead. They are yellow to sandy in colour with small, distinct pink specks.

Grassy flathead — *Platycephalus laevigatus:* A southern species known in Victoria as black or rock flathead, with a far more rounded body than any of our other flatheads. They inhabit grassy *Zostera* flats and sometimes are exposed to commercial net fishermen in places where the tide falls sharply. They are found in New South Wales along the south coast, in Victorian bays such as Western Port, in South Australia, and along the south coast of Western Australia, where they often take baits set for other fish.

Long-headed flathead — *Platycephalus haackei:* A deepwater South Australian and Western Australian species notable for the head which is at least a third the length of the body. They are light brown above, silvery to white below, with dark, irregular spots and fins speckled with brown. They reach 43 cm.

Deep-sea flathead — *Neoplatycephalus speculator:* Deep-water flatheads of compressed, elongate appearance and excellent table value. They have ridged, broad heads, flattened snouts, and tough, bony bucklers on the lateral line along the sides. They go down to 1500 m but are mostly caught between 275 and 450 m by trawlers. Distributed in Western Australia, South Australia and New South Wales, they grow to 55 cm.

Red-spotted flathead — *Platycephalus caeruleopunctatus:* Another species seldom sighted by anglers but which often finds its way to the table. They are largely confined to southern Queensland and are identified by the clusters of thick red spots all over the body. They provide fine white meat fillets, and are known in the fish trade for their continued good flavour after long periods of storing.

Rock flathead — Several species are known as rock flathead, but the main ones are *Platycephalus laevigatus*, a common variety in South Australian and Western Australian waters, *Thysanophrys cirronasus*, a weedeater which occurs in Queensland, New South Wales, Western and South Australia, and *Cymbacephalus nematophthalmus* which is confined to northern Australia but does occasionally get down into northern New South Wales. Rock flatheads are richly decorated fish and they come in brighter colours than other flatheads, often being splashed with reds.

Rock flathead
Platycephalus laevigatus

FLATHEAD DRIFTING RIG

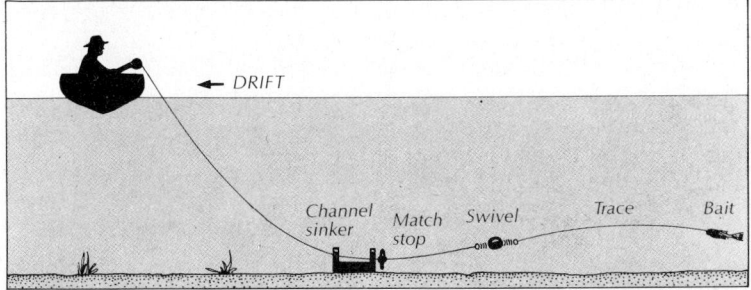

Drift-fishing for flathead
A highly successful flathead technique in all States in which one or more lines are offered the fish either from spool casters or short rods. The motion of the boat drifting with the tide or wind is just enough for the bait to attract the attention of the fish. Care should be taken, however, to prevent the boat fouling the lines. The wisest practice is to go out with companions who can take turns in paddling to keep the boat away from the lines. The chained hook rig (Ron) is frequently used when drifting as the top hook holds the bait clear of the bottom while the rig itself is dragged along the bottom. Fish taken by drifting mostly are big enough to warrant 6/0 hooks.

Spinning for flathead
More and more Australian anglers are discovering the joys of spinning for flathead, although only a decade ago veteran anglers scoffed when Vic McCristal, the well-known angling writer, advocated this method of fishing for them in a magazine article. For the truth is that flathead spend a lot of time around weed beds in tidal lakes and estuaries and by retrieving the lures across the top of the weed big flathead can frequently be enticed to take the lures.

Spinning for flathead requires a strong 2 m spinning rod, strong reel and an awareness by the angler that a vigorous, erratic retrieve is essential if the lure is to catch the eye of the fish. The Abu range of lures, especially the shiner and killer, spoons and swaybacks are all highly effective. The rod has to be worked energetically from side to side to get plenty of action on the lures.

Flathead angling from piers and wharves
This has always proved a rewarding form of fishing for Australians as flathead bite all the year round. They are caught on live bait, fresh prawns, squid, beach worms, octopus, mussels, and mullet gut and can be lured to the fishing spot by berley. But flathead have big mouths and can easily pick loose any bait which is too soft or not firmly attached to the hook. Live baits such as yellowtail, pilchards and mullet should be hooked through the back, behind the dorsal fin. Usually the weight of the bait is sufficient to take the hook

F ■ FLOATER

down where it will move about near the bottom. Too big a sinker merely anchors it on one spot and lessens the prospects of it attracting a sizeable flathead.

FLOATER *Schindleria praematura:* A coastal fish shaped like garfish that can only be caught in fine gauze and which has the distinction of being Australia's lightest fish. They weigh only a few milligrams and are only 2.5 cm long when fully grown. Floater are related to mackerels and blennies and are a classic example of a condition known as neoteny, which delays growth throughout their lives. They are found, says Whitley, in New South Wales, New Guinea, and across the Pacific to Hawaii.

FLOATS The use of floats to convey the bait to the fish, hang the bait at a predetermined depth, and to indicate a bite, is as old as angling itself. The diversity of modern angling has created floats made from a wide range of materials in a multitude of shapes and sizes, each with its own special application.

Floats have always had rare fascination for anglers, many of whom have more floats than they will ever use. An English writer summed up by saying that floats catch more anglers than fish, and suggested that the float's major role in angling was to give pleasure to the angler.

Anglers who become 'float happy' seldom realize that floats can often handicap efficient fishing, because they inevitably exert some resistance to a fish taking the bait. The guiding principle in selecting the right float is that it should be as light as is consistent with the distance it has to be cast, the weight of the bait and nature of the water being fished.

Quill and pencil floats Always popular for luderick fishing from boats in the estuaries. They permit the use of a minimum of lead to weight the float almost to neutral buoyancy. This low buoyancy is essential in seeking the timid luderick. The quills and lead are so light that they are only used from boats moored over the 'nigger' ground, or from shore or jetty locations where only a very short cast is needed. Pencil floats are virtually large quills made from wood. Cedar is the usual material. They offer the least possible drag in the water consistent with reasonable casting distance. Used in preference to the quill where the shore-based angler needs to cast a little further out for the fish. Also useful when a strong wind upsets the very light quill rig. Both quill and pencil types may be used as fixed or running floats. Apart from luderick, these floats are very useful for bream, and in the smaller sizes for garfish. Excellent for bait fishing for yellowtail.

Weighted casting floats Used mainly nowadays as luderick floats by rock fishermen. The rough conditions and stronger winds encountered when

FLOATS FOR LUDERICK

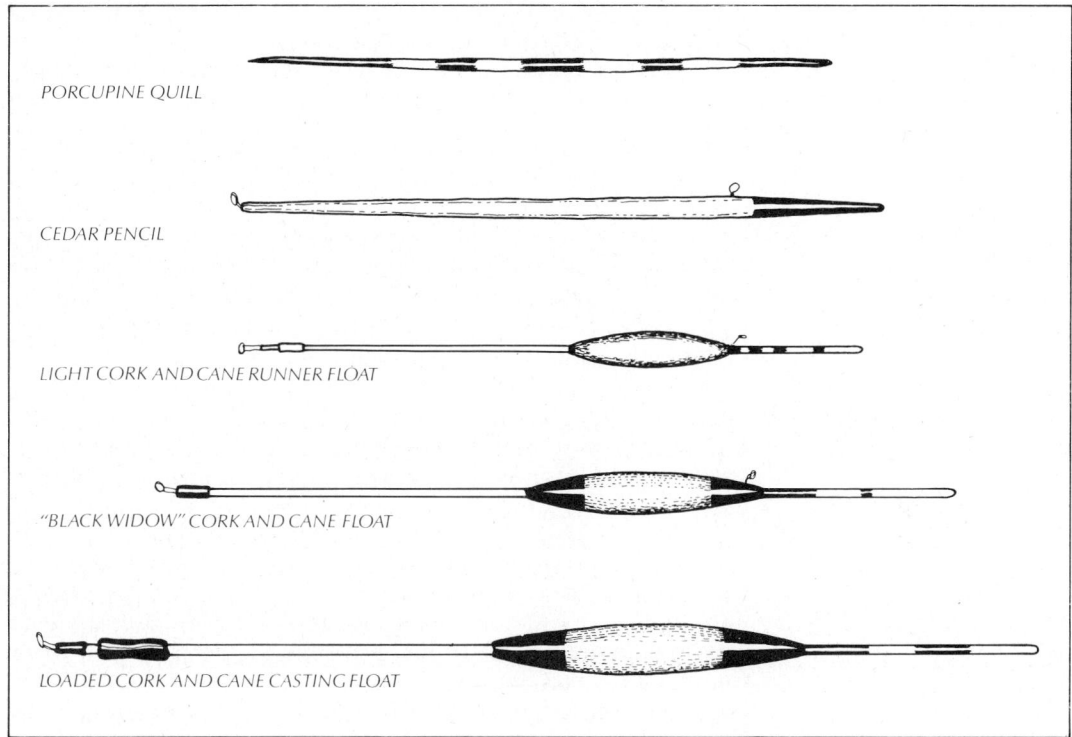

surf fishing enforce a larger float. Rock fishermen usually need to cast a greater distance than his colleagues in the estuary, so they need a heavier float on this score, too. These floats need to be weighted to a very low buoyancy, and must be streamlined to offer the least possible drag in the water when the bait is taken.

These stemless floats have two applications. Mostly they are used in rock fishing for all types of fish except luderick. They are very efficient in estuary fishing when drifting baits from the shore for flathead. Live baits are most effective. Small bobbies, not much larger than an ordinary bottle cork, are sufficient for estuary work unless the wind dictates otherwise. The bait should be set barely clear of the bottom. The angler casts the float into a deep channel, then walks with the drift.

In rock fishing, bobby corks are used from small sizes described above to floats big enough to be visible from a great height when cliff top fishing. The bobby cork has almost completely displaced bottom rigs for close-in rock fishing. Bobby corks supporting as much as 55 g of lead may be cast up to 65 m from the rocks with geared or side-cast reels. Within reason, there is no limit to the depth which may be fished with a running bobby cork. Their effectiveness and

Bobby corks

F ■ FLOATS

versatility have made them very popular with the rock fishermen. The smaller bobby corks, usually fixed floats, are used for fishing the white wash close in around the rocks for bream early in the morning or late evening. The shallow depth, usually no more than 3 m, renders a running rig unnecessary. The line is weighted with a minimum of lead so that the bait will swirl about in the wash in a natural manner.

Bobby corks carrying from 15 to 55 g of sinker are used when it is necessary to cast any distance, and to get that bait down in deep water. The traditional 'bottom' fish will rise to a moving bait set just clear of the bottom. Bobby corking is a much more pleasant form of fishing the rocks than bottom rigs with their attendant evils of snagging and loss of terminal tackle. The bobby cork technique is more fruitful usually than bottom fishing, as the moving bait attracts more fish. Use of live bait, such as yellowtail, or mullet, under a bobby cork is one of the best ways to seek such deep water species as mulloway and snapper. Where deep water occurs within casting range, live bait bobby corking can be very productive with tailor, salmon, bonito, kingfish and occasionally with tuna. At least one tuna over 45 kg weight has been taken from the rocks by this method. Bobby corks are particularly valuable in high winds. A bobby capable of supporting a sinker and bait of 100 g may allow a reasonably straight line to be maintained even in a gale, and often enables experienced anglers to carry on fishing in conditions which send others home.

Balloon floats Used in game fishing to support big shark baits at the required depth. Yellow is a popular colour, being readily visible under most lighting conditions at sea. Usually the balloon is attached to the line by light thread, which snaps when the shark pulls the bait down.

Plastic bottle floats These have been put to use in a unique manner by deep sea fishermen. They are used to set baits, usually live yellowtail, deep down. The float is attached by jamming the line into the mouth of the plastic bottle with a moderately tight cork. The strike straightens the line, pulls out the cork and releases the bottle. Some magnificent tuna and kingfish have been taken with rod and reel from deep-sea fishing boats with this method.

Freshwater floats At one time these consisted of smaller versions of quill, pencil, egg or shafted floats. These have been superseded to a large extent by the clear plastic bubble. This float is the least conspicuous type of all, an important factor in streams and lakes where the angler often fishes in clear, relatively shallow water. Some plastic bubbles may be filled with water to give casting weight and the required buoyancy with very little lead, or even no lead at all. The plastic cigar is an alternative form which has never met with general acceptance.

SPECIAL PURPOSE FLOATS

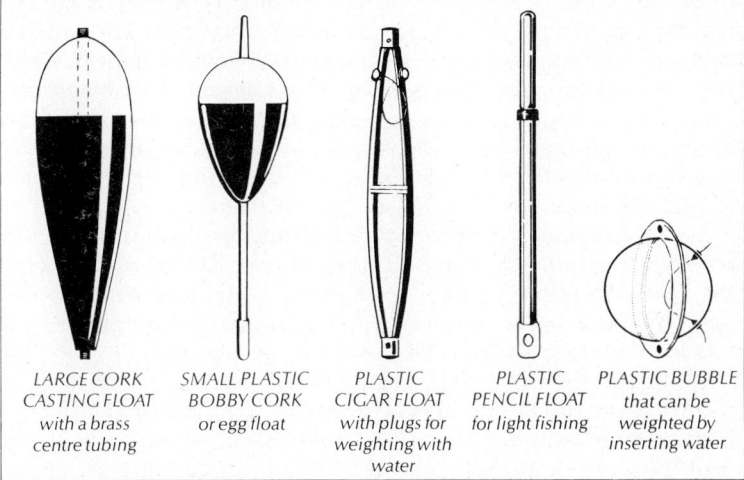

LARGE CORK CASTING FLOAT with a brass centre tubing

SMALL PLASTIC BOBBY CORK or egg float

PLASTIC CIGAR FLOAT with plugs for weighting with water

PLASTIC PENCIL FLOAT for light fishing

PLASTIC BUBBLE that can be weighted by inserting water

Float fishing tackle

In fresh water the plastic bubble may be used with baits or wet flies. Spinning rods are best used in this type of fishing, as the weight of a bubble rig, especially if the float has been loaded with water, is too great for a fly rod.

The outstanding tackle for bobby cork fishing from the rocks is the sidecast reel with matching long, light rod. This will be found suitable for fish from bream to heavy drummer and the smaller tunas and kingfish. The swivel is obligatory with sidecast reels. Overhead geared reels also fish nicely with the bobby cork. Threadline reels tend to give casting trouble through the line catching on the stopper knot. They are only suitable for shallow depths with fixed floats.

The secret of success in bobby corking is to use a light line, no more than 6.5 kg b/s. A matching light rod tip will stand considerable strain and it takes strength to break it. Light line offers less wind resistance, and does not sag so deeply between rod and float if the latter is riding well out. The reel most favoured for luderick fishing, at least in New South Wales where these fish are sought extensively, is still the time-honoured centrepin, usually the all-metal, 10 cm diameter models such as the Rapidex or Avon Royal.

For deep-sea fishing for tuna, or kingfish, light game tackle is the most successful gear. Boat rods with side cast and large capacity surf reels have put up some outstanding performances, and are satisfactory for light gamefishing when cost has to be considered. However, many of the best fish hooked with this gear have been lost through reel failure or more commonly through the lines overheating due to friction at the rod tip. Game tackle, with its larger capacity reel and roller runner at the tip, gives the angler a better chance to handle his fish and is imperative with the really big ones.

Float material

Weighted casting floats for luderick, beautifully constructed and finished, are usually made from cork and cane. Float stems are of cane or aluminium rod, which usually have a cap of red or orange fluorescent lacquer or bright plastic sleeving to render the thin stem more visible in the water. The dead flower spikes from blackboy trees, *Xanthorrea*, provide suitable material for home-made floats and the small bobby corks which are used by a larger section of the populace.

Bobby corks are provided in a variety of sizes in both cork and polystyrene foam plastic. Polystyrene is better than cork for use with large sinkers for long-distance casting. The polystyrene is lighter than cork, permitting a smaller float with less air resistance for a given weight of sinker. Cork is better for fishing close in rough water which subjects the float to battering on the rocks. Bobby corks should be finished in red or orange luminescent paint for maximum visibility in all conditions of light and water. This also applies to cane stems on weighted casting floats.

Running bobby corks should be bushed with a fine plastic tube. Excellent foam plastic bobbies moulded onto the bushing are available. The home float builder can use the PVC tubing from scrap lengths of household wiring, or the quills from empty ball point pens. The bushes will need to be glued if the float is of polystyrene. 'Aquadhere' glue is used as most of the quicksetting glues and resins dissolve the polystyrene. With luminescent paint, the polystyrene bobby cork can be given a couple of coats of 'Aquadhere' and allowed to set hard before painting. Homemade cork bobby floats should be painted white before use.

FLOUNDER See Flatfish.

FLOWER of the wave *Iso rhothophilus:* A species of the family Atherinidae found from New South Wales to Western Australia that is common in the 'soup' of the breaking surf for most of the year. They appear in what Whitley calls thin grey lines in the white foam and in silvery streaks as they turn in a school. The Japanese gave them their name which is far more poetic than their appearance deserves. They have a brown to silver belly with a fleshy bottom that fits strangely onto a compact little tail. Parasites sometimes attach themselves to the tiny (up to 6.5 cm) flower of the wave until they can find larger fish or hosts. Allied species have been discovered recently in the Hawaiian islands.

FLY fishing The technique of 'presenting' an artificial fly to feeding fish so that it imitates a natural insect. Fly fishing appears to have originated for catching trout in Europe about 2,000 years ago. The first historical reference which has come down to us is found in the writings of the Roman historian Aurelius during the second century A.D. But it is likely that flies were in use long before that, because trout, one of the most common and sought after freshwater fish throughout the Northern Hemisphere, often feed exclusively on small insects. Over the centuries the system has developed into an exciting, challenging and delightful way of fishing, its pleasures enhanced by the beauty of the waters which fly-taking sportfish generally inhabit. Modern anglers now use it to catch virtually any kind of fish, from freshwater herring, trout, bass and barramundi to saltwater mullet, bream, salmon, tailor, tuna and even large species such as sharks and bill fish.

The techniques—some simple and some extremely subtle, some ancient and some modern—which are used for fooling wary fish into accepting the angler's mimic fly, and the great fighting qualities of traditional species fished in this way, such as trout and bass, make fly fishing an intriguing and rewarding art.

The generic term 'fly fishing' today covers many kinds of fishing with fly-casting tackle. Since there are no insects in saltwater, the 'fly' used there is actually a small feathered lure, which is usually cast and retrieved to imitate small baitfish. The modern saltwater branch of this ancient art is called 'saltwater fly rodding' to distinguish it from fly fishing proper. Distinctions blur, however, when lures are cast with fly-casting tackle for freshwater fish. This is usually done in areas where the trout or other fish commonly pursue small baitfish, or are responsive enough to lures (because of territoriality, aggressiveness and curiosity) to take them readily. Bass fishing with fly rods, where the lure is often the small floating type called a 'bug', is known as bass-bugging, not to be confused with 'plugging' or 'plug casting', for which entirely different tackle is used.

Other specific kinds of fly fishing are nymph fishing, dry fly fishing, wet fly fishing, dapping and salmon fly fishing (with two-handed rods). Many anglers also make a distinction between stream fly fishing and stillwater (lake and reservoir) fly fishing, not only because of the aesthetic and environmental differences, but because subtly different styles of tackle and fly presentation are required.

There is a clear demarcation between the flies and lures designed for fly casting (which are too light to be cast any other way), and the larger, heavier ones which can be cast with spinning or plug-casting tackle. The lightest bait used with spinning or plug-casting tackle weighs about 3 g, yet some of the smallest flies and lures, weighing only a fraction of a gram, are much more successful, in some circumstances, than larger ones. This is often true even for very large fish, and it was for this reason that the equipment and techniques of fly casting were developed.

From the purely physical point of view, the greatest difference between fly casting and other kinds of fishing is that because the flies are so light, a heavy line is needed to make the rod 'work'—flex and unflex—during the casting action.

Other differences are due to the nature of the fish themselves. The brown trout of Europe, for which fly fishing developed, are an extraordinarily wary species which feed by sight rather than by scent. They are fast learners, and in heavily fished waters develop a wide knowledge of standard angling techniques, becoming very difficult even to observe, let alone catch. Being sight feeders, they prefer very clear waters in which they can not only easily find their food, but also see intruders approaching. Thus fly fishers must cultivate the art of careful, silent stalking if they wish to be successful.

Brown trout grow very large, some strains reaching about 50 kg (though few Australian specimens have been caught exceeding 10 kg), yet they can often be found in small streams, surviving only because of their extreme wariness. This and their preference for cold water makes them an ideal species for stocking mountain streams.

Fly-tying

WINGED WET FLY

NYMPH WET FLY

STREAMER WET FLY

HACKLED WET FLY

Many of the insects trout eat are too fragile and delicate to be placed on a hook, but it is possible to create hardy imitation insects by tying various materials onto tiny hooks with fine thread. Many good fly fishers are also expert fly-tyers, capable of creating in a few minutes a completely new artificial fly, closely resembling a 'natural', from feathers, silks and fur.

Untold thousands of recipes or patterns for artificial flies have been developed, and hundreds are well known and in common usage around the world. Some have remained unchanged for centuries, which is not surprising since neither the trout nor the insects they eat have altered much for millions of years. Many anglers who tie their own flies prefer slight variations on standard patterns. On rare occasions one of these, or even an entirely new design, proves so successful that it may become widely established.

Despite the great number of artificial flies, most anglers rarely fish with more than a few dozen different patterns in their entire lifetime, and about a dozen are enough to cover virtually all the fishing situations one is likely to meet in a single season. Despite the thousands of different species of both aquatic and terrestrial insects which trout eat, many are closely related, and similar enough to be well imitated by a single pattern. There are for instance 100-odd species of mayfly in Australian waters, each varying slightly in size and colouring, but all with the same basic shape, so that no more than about half a dozen artificial patterns are needed.

Expert fly-tyers attempt to imitate natural insects according to three basic criteria—size, shape and colour—as seen by the fish from underneath when the fly is floating on the water and outlined against the translucent sky. Thus artificial flies sometimes look quite different to natural ones when viewed in what seems the usual way, looking downwards on the fly against an opaque background.

It should also be realized that a fish's brain and eyes are different from those of a human's, and that fish do not 'see' things exactly the same way that we do. The physical properties of water, particularly the refractive qualities of the air-water interface, distort the appearance of insects as seen in the air from below. How well fish see colours or how well they delineate detail is still not known, though it is apparent that species such as trout and bass are extraordinarily sensitive to tiny movements, and to details which do not at first seem important to humans.

It has been found that trout sometimes distinguish between tiny hatching mayflies and the various similarly sized pieces of flotsam drifting along on the current because of the way the upright mayflies' wings appear when seen from beneath against the sky. An angler who does not have an imitation mayfly which will float with its wings 'cocked', or does not know how to cast it so that it will sit correctly on the water, will not catch any fish.

In general, dry flies which imitate ephemeral insects such as mayflies and diptera should be tied from light, translucent materials so they will float easily and appear as delicate as the natural when viewed by the fish from below. Wet flies and lure flies, on the other hand, are tied from denser, heavier, more opaque materials so they will sink easily, and be more easily seen by the fish against the opaque background of stream sides or bottoms.

See Fly-tying.

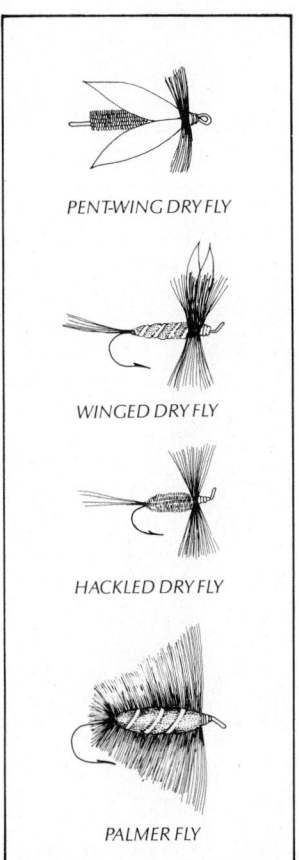

PENT-WING DRY FLY

WINGED DRY FLY

HACKLED DRY FLY

PALMER FLY

Fly lines

Early fly fishers used fine lines made from horsehair, and when it later became available, silk, tied to the end of a rod, to dangle the fly over the water so that it appeared to be flying or dipping down to lay its eggs the way a live, mature aquatic insect does. A breeze would sometimes carry these flies some distance away from the angler, and even today fishing with such 'blowlines' is popular in parts of the British Isles.

The other common way of getting the fly to the fish, in the days before the development of more advanced tackle made casting possible, was to allow the current to carry it along. This meant that fishing could only be done in a downstream direction. Since trout always face upstream when holding in a current, the angler was in plain view of the quarry, unless great care was taken to remain hidden behind bushes and other cover.

The development of fly-casting tackle and technique, however, brought with it the use of silken lines waterproofed with various oil emulsions. The standard line for stream use was 30 m long and 'double-tapered' over a length of about 5 m at each end to a slimmer tip. To one of these tips the tapered leader was tied, with the fly on its end. The reason for the tapered end was so that the line would uncurl properly at the end of the cast, and fall gently onto the water the way a natural insect does, without disturbing the fish.

Leader lengths varied from about 2 m up to as much as 6 m. The butt of a leader was only slightly thinner than the tip of the fly line, and the tippet of the leader was usually as fine as possible, considering the size of the fish being sought. The leader gradually tapered from its butt to its tip to form an invisible link between the heavy casting line and the fly, as well as enabling the fly to land more delicately on the water. The greatest wear on a fly line occurs near the tip, so when one end was worn out, the line could be reversed on the reel.

Modern fly lines closely follow the long-established character of the old silken lines, but are made of synthetics, and so require little maintenance, whereas silk lines had to be dried, carefully stored and regularly aired for good performance. Today's leaders also closely follow the old recipes, except that they are made from nylon monofilament instead of gut, and are stronger for a given diameter.

Line sizes

Silk lines were coded by size with letters, the most common size used for ordinary stream fishing being classified as an HCH, indicating that the belly of the line was of a certain standard diameter, and the tips were half this diameter. Today's lines are numbered according to weight as determined by the American Fishing Tackle Manufacturers' Association (A.F.T.M.A.). This is because every rod casts best with a line of a certain weight. The number indicates the weight of the first 10 m of the line, exclusive of the tapered tip section.

A.F.T.M.A. FLY LINE STANDARD

Weight in g	100	120	140	160	185	210	240	280	330	380
Line number		3	4	5	6	7	8	9	10	11	12

Many rod makers mark the line size most suitable for each rod on the butt just above the handle.

Lines are formulated either to float or to sink (and a few have floating mid sections but sinking tips), depending on whether they are for use with dry or wet flies. All dry fly and most nymph fishing is done with floating lines, which can be easily lifted off the water and re-cast, and so are the easiest to use for continuous casting.

Fly rods The idea of using a long, flexible rod to swing or swish the line upstream seems to have been well established by the 1600s, though much fishing was still downstream with flies which were either held on the surface or dangled above it. Since flies were difficult to keep afloat, they were also allowed to sink below the surface as the current carried them to feeding fish.

During the mid-1800s, however, it was discovered that rods made from tempered split-cane had the springiness to hurl waterproofed silken fly lines as far as 20 m. The line was swished through the air in much the same way as a stockwhip, but not allowed to crack at the end of the forward extension. Thus the new art of upstream fly casting was born.

Casting upstream had great advantages, enabling the angler to sneak up behind the fish, getting close enough to spot each feeding trout. The fly could be cast so it would alight delicately on the surface just upstream of the quarry, float downstream into the fish's 'window' of vision, and, if everything had been done correctly, be taken.

Tempered split-cane rods, lovingly handcrafted by extremely skilled tradesmen, consequently became the basis of fly fishing for about a century, until in the late 1950s a new material, fibreglass, appeared. By the 1960s, cheaper but quite serviceable hollow, tubular fly rods were being made from this material, and cane rods became rarer. Today's fly rods are made from carbon fibre, boron fibre and kevlar, often in esoteric mixes with fibreglass.

These are superior to either cane or glass for most fly-casting purposes, although split cane is still available from a few specialist rod makers. The best split-cane rods are usually impregnated with synthetic resins for waterproofing and for greater strength than the old cane rods had. Fibreglass retains considerable popularity because of its relative cheapness and toughness, and some makers say that the limits of glass technology have not yet been reached. Future improvements are likely to be made in the bonding resins and the methods of laying the fibres, which will keep these rods viable well into the future.

The modern fly rod for stream use is from 2.4 to 2.6 m long, weighs about 1 kg, has its reel seat at the butt just below the cork handle, and carries from seven to nine very fine line guides. It breaks down into two or three pieces for easy transport, and the better models come complete with protective bag and rod case.

Rods for lake and saltwater use are stiffer, because heavier lines are needed to cast the greater distances. The leaders used for saltwater fly rodding are also considerably thicker than those for freshwater fishing. Some modern fly rods, especially those with a high ratio of carbon fibre in their construction, are so versatile that they can be used with several line sizes, so that a single rod may be used for a multiplicity of purposes.

Fly reels

Fly reels have changed little during the past half century, except in the case of saltwater models, which feature much greater line capacity than freshwater reels, as well as brake systems. Until this century, fly reels were considered merely storage places for the line when it was not actually being cast, but the discovery that fly-casting tackle could play very large and powerful fish led to the development of techniques for playing them directly off the reel, as in other forms of fishing. The result has been an increase in the sophistication of fly reels.

Some models now feature geared retrieve systems, so that a single turn of the handle may result in several rotations of the spool. Many have an exposed braking rim, on which pressure with the palm of the line hand can be used to brake a running fish. Saltwater models intended for larger gamefish usually feature multi-disc star-drag systems as used on other reels.

Popular in the U.S.A., but little used in Australia, are automatic reels, with clockwork type springs, which rewind the line when a lever or button is pressed. Since the amount of line which can be rewound this way is limited, they are not suitable for use against the generally larger trout found in this country.

Many older reels were too heavy to balance properly with the extremely light rods made from graphite, boron and kevlar. This has led to the manufacture of light reels made from substances such as magnesium and carbon fibre.

Dry fly fishing

During the late 1800s, F. M. Halford, recognized as one of the greatest fly fishing masters of all time, developed a set of 36 floating flies. They were intended to represent all the important insects which trout ate on the surface of the extremely rich chalk streams in the south of England, long famous for their huge brown trout. (Australia's brown trout are the direct progeny of these trout, which is why they have the potential to grow so big in waters where they have an adequate food supply.)

This great master's understanding of what trout ate and how they behaved was so complete that most of his original patterns are still used all round the world. Halford's fry flies were intended to be cast upstream to feeding trout which had been sighted and stalked by the angler, the method which has remained the epitome of the art ever since. It is still considered to be a demonstration of the highest skill for an angler to catch successive trout with only one cast per fish.

There are also sound practical reasons for always trying to catch a trout (and other fish) with a single cast, for each cast involves fast physical movements which may alarm the fish either by the falling of the line on the water or by the movement of the rod and line in the air. There is also the danger of accidentally casting the line close to fish which have not been observed, causing them to flee, and so alarming other nearby fish. Thus experienced fly-casters always try to stalk into a position where they are not only well hidden, but from

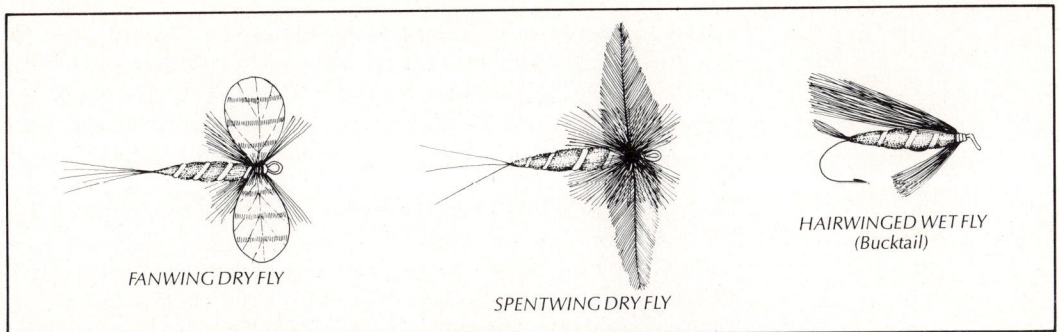

FANWING DRY FLY

SPENTWING DRY FLY

HAIRWINGED WET FLY (Bucktail)

which they can place the fly so accurately and delicately in front of a feeding trout that it is taken without hesitation.

Masters of fly-casting also try to select only the largest trout in a pool, ignoring smaller fish in the knowledge that once a trout has been hooked, its frantic attempts to escape will alarm other fish, making it impossible to catch them. This is particularly important during a rise when all the fish in a river 'up', presenting a rare chance for any lucky angler on the scene to catch larger-than-usual trout.

The dry fly is traditionally fished with a floating fly line and a floating leader, but on many occasions a sunken leader is used, especially in extremely clear, still waters where a floating leader appears as an anomolous distortion of the surface when seen from below, casting an enlarged shadow on the bottom and alarming the fish. The classic dry fly is made to float downstream at precisely the same speed as the current, although some are subtly articulated to imitate the movement of creatures such as terrestrial beetles or grasshoppers which have fallen onto the water and are trying to escape.

Dry fly fishing largely revolves around the aquatic insects which are the main component of trout's diet, and the most important of these around the world are the mayflies (Ephemeroptera) and sedges or caddis flies (Trichoptera). There are altogether some 400 species of these two orders in Australia, and our trout dine on them at all the various stages of their life cycles.

Nymph fishing

Early in the 1900s another legendary fly fisherman, G. E. M. Skues, realized that there were times, especially in spring, when trout fed exclusively on nymphs, the immature underwater stage of various aquatic insects. Skues' experiments with new kinds of artificial flies, and the best means of presenting them to feeding trout, led to his development of the art of nymph fishing. This involves casting a small fly made from hydrophilic materials upstream of a feeding trout so that it drifts down to it beneath the surface, and is accepted as a natural nymph. Most artificial nymphs represent the larvae of either mayfly or caddis, which together form about three-quarters of the diet of trout in most streams they inhabit.

Study of the way in which nymphs behave, and of what it is that attracts them to the trout's attention, causing a fish to eat a particular nymph out of the myriads inhabiting a particular section of stream, eventually revealed that different species of nymph swim with particular kinds of movements. This led to the art of articulating an artificial nymph so it appeared to swim like the natural. Some masters, such as English angling author Frank Sawyer, developed the ability to make an artificial nymph swim like the natural insect to such a high degree that they were able to catch trout with bare hooks! This proved that in some cases at least it was not so much the size, shape and colour of the fly which attracted the trout, but its behaviour.

See Nymph fishing.

Lures Although artificial flies have been tied from ancient times to imitate as closely as possible the natural insects which trout ate, it has also long been known that trout (and some other fish) often attack 'flies' which look nothing at all like real insects. Some lures either look like, or are made to swim like, small aquatic creatures such as frogs, tadpoles and small baitfish, while others appear to tease, enrage or otherwise arouse the fish into striking at them.

Perhaps these lures work so well in some circumstances because fish, not having hands with which to examine strange objects, must take them into their mouths. There is also the matter of territoriality. Some fish, especially brown trout, establish specific territories which they guard against intruders, so that lures may at times be seen as a threat to the fish's personal aquatic kingdom. In clear waters, trout and bass can often be observed pursuing and striking lures with their shoulders or slapping them with their tails, as a result of which they are sometimes hooked in various parts of their bodies. Quite obviously they are not trying to eat such lures, and long observation has convinced many (including this writer) that such fish are curious or angry rather than hungry.

On those occasions when fish are constantly 'biting short' and failing to hook up solidly, the fly or lure is usually not a good representation of anything the fish wants to eat. In such cases it is generally productive to experiment with flies more like the natural food which can be observed in the locality.

Wet fly fishing The artificial flies used in traditional wet fly fishing are often almost identical to dry flies of the same name, but are tied of materials designed to allow the fly to sink rather than float. Thus the well-known Coachman dry fly, which represents a white-winged caddis, is tied with stiff cock's hackle legs which support it on the water's surface, whereas the wet version of the same fly is tied with absorbent hen's hackle which enables it to sink. From this it can be seen that traditional wet fly fishing and nymph fishing are closely allied.

When is the wet fly most useful? Obviously not when the fish are feeding on the surface, but rather on those windy days when the flies are blown away from the surface, so that the fish tend to dine near the bottom on 'drowned' flies, nymphs or larvae. There are also many streams where the water is made so rough by rapids and small waterfalls that any insects landing on the surface are soon drowned. In such locations the trout may very rarely take flies on the surface, for all their food is at lower depths.

Lake fishing is often not really wet fly fishing in the traditional sense, but lure fishing. The lure may represent small baitfish, or nothing in particular, attracting the trout or other fish for the reasons outlined earlier. But since fishing with small feathered lures has been in use for many centuries around the world, by anglers in Europe, Indians in North America and islanders in the Pacific, it was inevitable that when fly-casting tackle was developed in the 1800s, it would soon be used for casting and retrieving small lure-flies.

Reservoir fishing also tends towards lure fishing rather than true fly fishing, because the constantly varying water levels prevent the establishment of a stable littoral zone with shallow water weed-beds in which a complex ecological system can develop. The result is a smaller and less consistent population of aquatic insects than in a similarly sized lake or lagoon. Nevertheless, many highland reservoirs from time to time have dense populations of insects such as dragonflies, craneflies, midges and sedges, resulting in not only good wet fly fishing, but occasionally excellent dry fly and nymph fishing.

Saltwater fly rodding

There are no insects in saltwater, so strictly speaking there can be no true fly fishing there. Yet small feather lures are so successful in many situations that a school of saltwater fly rodding has developed. There are records of both English and American fly rodders catching large saltwater fish in the late 1800s, but the sport did not really get under way until the latter half of this century, for here, too, the development of new techniques had to await the arrival of new materials from which improved tackle could be made. It was principally the development of fly rods made from that extremely tough and versatile material, fibreglass, with the simultaneous invention of non-rotting synthetic lines, which resulted in saltwater fly rodding becoming popular. Popularity has led in turn to the manufacture of specialized fly reels designed to carry the larger fly lines and hundreds of metres of backing needed for playing very large fish. Many such reels also have anti-reverse and free-spool mechanisms combined with sophisticated star-drag systems.

The great advantage of saltwater fly rodding over other fishing methods, in certain circumstances, is that fish take the little feathered lures much more readily than any other kind.

Fish also tend to hold onto saltwater flies and not reject them the way they reject metal and plastic ones, and thus to be more often and more solidly hooked. In test situations where schooling fish can be cast to, so that virtually every cast produces strikes, a saltwater fly will usually hook, hold and land two to four times as many fish as metal, plastic or wooden lures, even though the solid lures attract as many hits.

Fly rodding's great disadvantage is that its casting range is limited. Few fly rodders can consistently cast more than 25 to 30 m, and on windy days, or while casting in the surf, this distance may be considerably reduced. On the other hand, once a fly has been cast with a floating line (the most common type), it can be instantly picked up into a backcast and then thrown directly forward to another target without any need to retrieve line onto the reel between casts. Thus a skilled fly rodder may actually make many more aimed casts per hour than an equally skilled spincaster or plugcaster. This can be a great advantage in certain fishing situations, such as wading shallow saltwater flats, or casting to mangroves from a drifting boat in an estuary.

The difficulties involved in controlling a long, heavy fly line in the air, or in the water when there is wave action which tangles the slack line at the angler's feet, plus the generally high level of casting skill needed to accurately present flies at long distances, means that saltwater fly rodding will probably never have a large following. But anyone who has experienced the heart-stopping strike, the powerful runs and acrobatic leaps of a good gamefish on fly-rodding tackle will attest that no other kind of fishing can be quite so exciting or challenging. For the fact is that the long, powerful but delicate fly rod provides a better 'feel' as the fish is played than any other kind of rod, so that the fly rodder is actually in more sensitive and personal touch with his fish than anglers using other tackle.

Fly fishing entomology

A complete understanding of fly fishing requires detailed knowledge of how fish such as trout and bass behave in their natural surroundings, and particularly what, and how, they eat. Both are predatory species at the top of the food chain in their freshwater habitats, and both are largely insectivorous, living principally on the thousands of insect species available to them.

The most important orders of aquatic insects (*which see*) for fly fishers are the Ephemeroptera (mayflies) and the Trichoptera (caddis flies or sedges), followed by Odonata (dragonflies and damselflies), Plecoptera (stoneflies) and Diptera (two-winged flies). This last order is one of the largest insect orders, its species, many still unclassified, probably totalling about 150,000 and including mosquitoes, midges and craneflies. Midges (very small mosquito-like insects) and craneflies (large mosquito-like insects) tend to hatch en masse, creating very exciting rises of trout.

Aquatic insects typically lay myriads of tiny eggs in the water. The eggs hatch into larvae or nymphs, an immature stage which closely resembles the adult. A mayfly nymph, for example, is very similar in shape to the adult mayfly, except that it lacks wings. At this stage, the insects are completely aquatic, but most go through a winged terrestrial stage during which they disperse from the water, mate, and lay their eggs, starting the cycle all over again. Most have an annual life cycle, though a few have several generations each year, and some have two-yearly generations.

Mayflies, the classic trout fly, begin their life cycle as tiny eggs, hatching into very small nymphs. Some prefer the fast water of rapids, others the still sediments on pool bottoms, while many are specific to the beds of water weeds adorning the pools of fertile streams. They are herbivores and scavengers, playing a vital role in the ecology of the inland waters by converting vegetable matter to animal tissue, which then can be utilized by creatures further up the food chain, such as fish and birds.

They grow towards adulthood in stages marked by the shedding of outgrown husks or skins. As maturity approaches their wing pads develop, until finally they swim to the surface and struggle through it. Sitting on the surface, they shed a final husk, unfold their damp wings, and after a brief period of flapping to dry them, rise in unsteady flight to seek shelter in the grasses and streamside shrubs.

Mayflies are unique in that they have two adult stages—the one already described as hatching from the water, known as the 'sub-imago' by entomologists and the 'dun' by anglers (due to its dull colouring), and the fully mature (sexually capable) adult, called the 'imago' by entomologists, and the 'spinner' by anglers because of the way it flies. In the case of the smallest mayflies, *Caenis*, duns change into spinners only a few minutes after leaving the water, but for most species the process takes 12 to 24 hours.

On shedding the final husk, the imago, now a shining and active insect (some are highly coloured, though most Australian species are black or reddish-brown), seeks mating partners in the swarms which gather near the water. After copulation, the impregnated females dip down onto the water to lay their eggs, finally falling 'spent' on the surface. This activity typically occurs on warm, still summer afternoons, reaching a peak during the period between sunset and darkness, and producing what is called the 'evening rise'—the trout's daily feeding spree.

The other occasion when massed rises of trout commonly occur is during a hatch, when large numbers of mayflies (or other insects) hatch from the water simultaneously. Since it is very easy for fish to see even tiny insects sitting on the surface silhouetted against the sky, most fish prefer to take their food from the surface whenever it is available there, which is why dry fly fishing is so effective.

Anglers who wish to master fly fishing are well advised to begin by practising with the dry fly on small clear streams, where it is easiest to observe the fish as they inspect and either take or refuse the fly. Such observation enables the angler to hone his presentation until his casts begin to win regular acceptance.

Spring is the time of the largest hatches, and thus of the most regular rises to duns, sedges, stoneflies and so on, and summer evenings are the best times to find trout feeding at the surface. There are, however, many other occasions when trout feed exclusively on the surface. Mid-summer evenings, just as darkness draws its shroud across the water, often bring massed hatches of beetles, and on windy summer days large numbers of grasshoppers are blown onto the water—large succulent insects particularly beloved by trout and bass. Spring thunderstorms can produce large hatches of flying ants and termites, resulting in spectacular rises.

Although classic fly fishing hinges principally on the way trout dine upon aquatic insects, there are also many species of terrestrial insects which regularly fall on the water, sometimes figuring prominently in the diet of freshwater fish. The most important of these are the Coleoptera (beetles), Lepidoptera (moths and butterflies), Isoptera (termites), Orthoptera (grasshoppers) and Hymenoptera (wasps, bees and ants).

Precisely which insects trout eat at any particular time depends mainly on availability, which in turn depends on the nature of the stream and its environment. Slow-flowing, fertile, weedy streams have immense numbers of aquatic insects; fast-flowing, stony streams have relatively small populations and the fish are necessarily more dependent upon the terrestrials which accidentally fall in. Streams with many overhanging trees and bushes have a regular rain of tree-dwelling beetles, ants and bugs, especially on windy days, and sudden rainstorms wash myriads of insects off leaves and branches, producing sudden feasts for the fish and resulting in excellent fly fishing.

From this outline it may be seen that fly fishing involves the gradual discovery of such a vast, interrelated chain of natural events (encompassing climatology, ecology, entomology and many other fields), that it can involve a lifetime of interesting and rewarding activity for its devotees. It requires not only practical expertise in matters such as casting, but also has a philosophical and intellectual side. Because of these deeper dimensions of what is generally regarded as merely a quiet recreation, it is no accident that more has been written about fly fishing than about any other sport, or that classics such as Izaak Walton's *The Compleat Angler* have become hallmarks in the history of English literature.

JOHN TURNBULL

FLY fishing in lakes and reservoirs

The river angler who turns to the lakes and reservoirs for his trout fishing will not find the fish lying in some selected feeding position, as they do in the river. When lake trout are feeding they fossick among weed beds along the shoreline or work a regular beat a little farther out. Thus on most occasions the fly man looks for some movement before casting, rather than casting blind in the hope of the trout seeing the fly. If there is no movement the angler resorts to blind casting or stops fishing.

Lakes and reservoirs present a number of problems for trout. In a stream trout can lie in the current and by merely opening their mouths allow the pressure of water to fill them. The trout will then close their mouths allowing the oxygenous water to flow over the gill filaments and out through the gill slits. In a lake, however, the trout must keep on the move to keep the required amount of water flowing over the gill filaments. In some lakes at certain periods of the year there may be areas of water holding a particularly high oxygen content which enable the trout to lie in the one spot and gulp in the water. The Australian sun, however, soon robs much of the water of its oxygen.

Most man-made lakes and reservoirs offer few opportunities for spawning, and this can be disastrous for the trout. Some trout are able to absorb most or all of the eggs during the spring months following their production but many trout become egg bound and die.

A quiet spot on the shores of Lake Burley Griffin, A.C.T.

Trout have one advantage in living in a lake or reservoir: they can swim in any direction. In a fast-water stream the trout can only swim upstream at certain speeds or downstream faster than the current. All swimming in fast water is arduous work. The still waters of a lake are easier.

If the waters of a lake are not too hot or too cold, about 20 degrees C, the trout feed wherever food is found. In hot weather they feed deeper to get away from the warm water above as well as the bright sunlight. In cold weather they move closer to the surface, although they are not likely to feed near the surface on days when cold air and water inhibit the activity of the insects there.

Most trout in lakes, particularly brown trout, are essentially shallow-water feeders. They spend most of their feeding time working through the half-submerged grasses and underwater weedbeds along the shallow margins of the lake. In lakes where there are no shallows and consequently no weedbeds, the fishing is invariably poor. Extreme heat or cold or bright sunshine will force the trout out of the shallows into the deeper waters off shore. Large numbers of anglers along a lake shore will achieve the same result.

Dry fly fishing on Australian lakes is limited to those days when sufficient numbers of damsel flies, dragon flies, caenis flies and other insects are above or on the water to induce the trout to feed there. Long fine leaders are necessary and the fly line may be degreased if the angler finds that the floating line frightens the fish.

On lakes where there are large weedbeds or areas of half submerged tussocks along the shoreline, good dry fly fishing can sometimes be found at night. A grey sedge or cinnamon fished on a dead drift alongside the weed and grasses will often take big browns. A large white moth or medium size muddler minnow is also good when the skies are overcast. Most serious fly fishers, however, go to Australian lakes and reservoirs prepared to fish nymphs, longtails and wet flies.

FLY fishing streamers or longtails

Streamer or longtail flies are tied to imitate those small fish on which the larger trout feed, which include such species as galaxias minnows, smelt and gudgeon. Judging by their colours, some patterns are imitations of the game fish themselves. The red and black longtail represents a small red-bellied blackfish; the red and yellow longtail represents a small trout under certain clear water conditions; the olive longtail represents a small bass or estuary perch. And the redfin longtail is a deliberate attempt to imitate in feathers and silk an English perch or redfin.

The fact that large wet flies tied in a particular way to imitate small fish are known by three different names causes a lot of confusion. In America, England and elsewhere they are called streamer flies; in New Zealand they are called matukas;

in Australia, longtails. As patterns from all three countries are used here, the confusion can be understood. If the angler remembers why each name is used, the confusion disappears. On American patterns, the large feather is tied in only at the hook eye and the feather 'streams' when the fly is retrieved or held in the current. On Australian patterns, the feather is tied all the full length of the hook shank and only the 'tail' is free to move. The word 'matuka,' as used for the New Zealand patterns, is the name of the bird (now protected) whose feathers were first used to tie this kind of wet fly in that country.

Knowing that the longtail or streamer is so effective, the fly man may well ask why the trout will refuse, let us say, a silver wobbler but take a longtail, when the wobbler acts and looks so much like a small fish. There are probably three reasons for this: firstly, under different conditions of light and water a spinning or wobbling lure may look like something good to eat or to steer clear of; secondly, a metal lure is not only seen but 'felt' and there are days when a game fish does not react the way we wish to the vibrations and thirdly, a longtail, despite what it's been tied to represent, quite often resembles some insect, particularly if it is left to drift around in the current. There are days when game fish may not like feeding on small fish (spinners or wobblers) and may be searching earnestly for moths, grasshoppers, dragonflies, damsel flies and other large insects, all of which various small longtails imitate very well.

There are two main ways in which a longtail can be fished in a stream: upstream on a tight or a slack line, or downstream on a tight line. The downstream method includes a certain amount of slack line fishing but it is exceptionally difficult to become skilful enough to hook a trout on so large a fly with a slack line. The two upstream methods enable the fly fisherman to stand behind the trout, a big advantage for the inexperienced. Although it is often easier to cast from a wading position in the stream, big trout can still be caught by the angler casting from the bank.

In fishing the longtail upstream with the tight-line method, the fly is cast upstream and retrieved down again at a pace slightly faster than the current. The line is kept taut throughout the retrieve, and any trout that strikes hooks itself. This technique is successful in those stretches of water where the trout lie close to the banks or to the river bed, waiting for any small fish that may come downstream. When minnows or small fish swim downstream they have a tendency to work towards the surface, giving the angler an opportunity to see the swirl of a big, feeding trout.

In fishing the longtail on a slack line, the fly is cast upstream and allowed to drift back on a slack line. Some fish will be lost on the strike in this method as the angler is not in direct contact with the fly, but it is very effective below weir walls where numbers of small fish are injured coming through the outlet valves. This method also takes many big fish feeding on drowned insects, as was mentioned earlier in regard to longtails being taken for creatures other than small fish.

Fishing a longtail downstream is far easier for the beginner than fishing it upstream. There is one major disadvantage in that the angler, being upstream from the trout, must kneel to fish or hide behind some cover.

In downstream fishing the longtail is cast towards the far bank and then allowed to tumble downstream until it reaches a likely spot. The line is tightened and the fly swung back across the stream. It is then retrieved back upstream to the angler's feet. Retrieving the fly in short jerks is the most effective method, although when this fails a slow retrieve may be successful. Another successful method is to retrieve the fly about a metre and then to let it tumble back downstream again. This action is repeated until a trout strikes the fly or it reaches the angler's feet.

Longtail fishing in lakes

In clear water, under a bright sun, the bodies of minnows and some other small fish appear translucent. Longtails for this kind of fishing should be light in colour. White floss-silk ribbed with silver tinsel is good, but the best imitation of all is the one with the clear plastic body and greenish-yellow feather. Fly action is important when bright light and clear water combine to make perfect visibility. The longtail should be worked in short jerks in imitation of the minnows darting about in the shallows. The leader must be long and fine: 2.7 m tapered to 1.7 mm.

In clear water with no sun, in the early morning and late afternoon and evening, the minnows no longer appear translucent. At these periods, longtails with dark bodies are the most effective. Black or red is the most popular, and there is no need to use expensive fly-body materials, as ordinary darning wool is as good as any.

Exciting fishing can result from casting longtails to surface-feeding trout. When the angler can see the trout chasing minnows or smelt, the fly must be worked fast to interest these actively feeding fish. To prevent the tell-tale burr on the water, an old silk fly line should be degreased so that it sinks quickly or the purpose may be served by one of the modern sinking plastic lines. The angler will certainly get many follow-ups when the fly is worked slowly, but very few trout will take it. Perhaps the best method is to retrieve the fly so fast that it skims across the surface. But only the fly, and not the leader or line, should leave a wake.

Casting longtails to deep-feeding trout in lakes is essentially 'blind' casting. When no trout can be seen feeding, choose a spot where the lake bed shelves off into about 3 m of water some distance from the shore. Degrease the silk line or use one of the fast-sinking lines and cast out, letting the line, leader and fly sink almost to the lake bed. Retrieve the line slowly with the left hand, using the handtwist retrieve, and at the same time lift the rod tip in a series of short jerks. If this fails, try retrieving fast, shuttling the line in with the left hand. When this method is used, the trout will usually hook itself. One of the best longtail patterns for this deep water fishing is a red and black matuka. In waters where there are still large numbers of smelt, the green matuka is an effective pattern.

Best Australian longtails and streamers
Clear water matuka, early in the season matuka, red peril, yellow peril, green matuka, red and black matuka, black matuka, silver garland marabou, yellow and black marabou, redfin matuka, black and white marabou.

FLY fishing the stream

The beginner's best approach to fly fishing is to forget all the thousand and one rules that have grown up around the art and concentrate on basic principles. There will be time later to tackle the more complex problems and to study those diagrams showing how to cast a fly quartering upstream.

To some so-called experts it sounds apocryphal to tell an angler that no two spots he fishes will ever be exactly alike, but the sensible thing for the novice fly fisher is to approach each as a separate problem. He will need some experience to do this, but he is the only one who can do the experiencing. He will have to learn to cast properly, but fly fishing is so simple that a few hours of practice will put the fly fisher in business. The angler does not have to be a tournament caster to be a really good fly man. There are fly fishers whose every cast makes a tournament caster wince. These men, however, catch many good trout and some from waters where one would think that long, accurate casting was essential.

The trouts' food is brought to them by the current along certain paths or placed in certain spots though the average trout stream contains a given amount of food in every cubic foot of water. On wide, deep stretches where the current is slow a given amount of food will take a long time to pass within eyesight of a fish lying in a particular spot. But in every stream there are places where the river narrows and races over stones, or where it is constricted between a rock or a half submerged log and the bank and here the food is concentrated and is more easily seen as it is quickly washed past. That is where the trout are when they are hungry, and that is where they will hit the artificial fly.

Thus when the angler wants to know where the trout are feeding he walks along the bank of the stream until he finds a spot where a lot of water passes by possible trout shelter in a short time. As big trout do not want to wear themselves out by battling against the press of the current they lie in the quiet waters of an eddy behind the snags or logs or close to the bank where they can dart out quickly to intercept food that is passing. If the stream is a hard-fished water the trout will want a deep hole to dodge into when danger approaches. A hole with a submerged log in it is ideal, as the larger a trout grows the more it appreciates a protective covering over its head. A red and black longtail jiggled around these 'bolt-holes' will occasionally tempt a big trout into striking.

Exploiting deep holes

In waters where there are a few deep holes or submerged logs the most likely spot to find the bigger trout is under the undercut banks. These spots are both resting as well as feeding places. A yellow and black marabou streamer drifted slowly past these undercut banks is often effective. The deep hole that is often found at the end of a fast, shallow run is one of the best spots for the beginner to fish. He can stand above the pool and let the current carry his nymph or longtail into it. By pointing his rod tip towards the spot where the fly is moving, and by holding the line taut between his left forefinger and thumb, the angler can feel the slightest touch.

The normal reaction to a touch or sudden tug on the line is to whip up the rod tip, and so beginners rarely have to be taught how to hook a trout, unless it is to impress on them not to strike too hard when using fine leaders.

One of the main reasons why so many inexperienced fly fishers fail to catch trout is that they cannot get it into their minds that the fish are easily frightened. They seldom take into account that the trout are sensitive to vibrations caused by an angler clumping along the river bank or clinking stones together as he wades. And they do not understand that the trout can see them just as easily as they can see the trout, and mostly the trout sees them first. A fly man does not sit down quietly among the bankside scrub with little or no movement as does the bait fisher. The fly man stands up, waving his arm and rod around.

So the wise angler stalks his fish as if he were stalking a deer. He uses all available cover and dark backgrounds. He should certainly not wear a white shirt on a fly fishing trip. In some shallow water stretches it may be necessary to crouch or even kneel to cast or work the fly. Under conditions like this, ripples created by wading will frighten a big trout, and the mud stirred up by a careless wader spooks big fish.

On almost every good trout water there is an ideal spot that cannot be approached by wading or by casting from the bank without the angler showing himself to the feeding trout. Such spots often hold one or two medium to large size trout. The average angler cannot fool these fish so they grow to a large size. Here there may be some tree stump or bush behind which the angler can hide. He should walk quietly up to this, recognizing that the trout will see him. He should sit quietly behind the available cover and wait for 15 to 20 minutes or until he feels that the trout have overcome their fright. Using the bow-and-arrow cast, the angler flicks out a wet fly across the water. By carefully manipulating the rod tip from his sitting position the angler can imitate many of the small creatures found darting about the quieter waters close to the river bank. This method has accounted for many big trout taken from spots passed over by the majority of anglers.

Trout fly fallacies

There has been a lot said about precise imitations, and no doubt most serious fly men hope that the fly they choose is a close imitation of the fly on the water. But the truth is that there is no fly that is an exact imitation of anything living. At least no fly made of fur, feathers and silk, and they are the only flies worth a place in the fly box. At best an imitation of an insect is as much like the real thing as a tailor's dummy is like the real man. Hence the answer is to offer the trout something of the same size, colour and shape as the insect on the water and by a lot of fly rod magic try to make the artificial come to life. If a small cockchafer beetle is being blown on the water try any one of a score of similar size flies with peacock herl bodies, any one of which could pass as a rough copy of the real thing. It is better to do this than to spend valuable time searching through the fly box trying to find something that does not exist—the perfect imitation.

Another common fallacy is that the fly fisherman must wade. There certainly are streams and lakes where wading helps to fill the creel, but there are also many more places where getting into the water is neither desirable nor necessary. Even along some of those streams that have come to be accepted as 'wading waters' there are ways of fishing them without having to wade.

Techniques for big trout

Obviously as a trout grows it will tend to feed on larger items of food. A trout of 225 g or less is quite satisfied to feed exclusively on the wide variety of insects found in or on the stream, adding to this an occasional feast of earthworms and other terrestrial creatures washed in by floodwaters. A big trout will spend a part of its time feeding on these items too, but if and when larger items like freshwater crayfish, large frogs or small fish are available these are likely to become the main food for the big fish. With this in mind, the angler sets out on his big trout trips armed with a range of large wet flies which he knows can be worked to imitate large creatures of the trout stream.

Unfortunately, many fly men never progress beyond casting a big wet fly or streamer across the stream, letting it run down and then bringing it back upstream against the current. Occasionally, this simple method works, but this 'down and up' technique limits the fly man to certain waters on certain days. As big trout lie on the bottom of the pools and runs during the day it is essential to get the fly down deep. For many years fly men used very large wet flies. A lot of material can be added to a fly to make it bulkier but it is rarely heavier and is definitely harder to sink, and what is perhaps more important, the bulky fly never looks attractive to a big trout.

F ■ FLY fishing the stream

The secret is to wind strips of lead wire to the hook shank before the fly is tied and to keep all fly materials to a minimum. The finished pattern sinks quickly, stays deep where the big fish feed, and reacts much more effectively to the twitching of the rod tip and the movements of the current. If the fly fisher does not tie his own flies he can add a couple of split shot a few inches above the hook eye of a standard pattern.

For early stream fishing when the waters are running fast and discoloured, a large yellow and black marabou or red and black palmer is cast upstream and allowed to sink deep. The fly is then allowed to work downstream with the current to a spot about 13 to 18 m downstream. Next it is worked back upstream in short jerks so that it darts along the bottom like a minnow. If the waters are badly discoloured the angler can try a large silver garland marabou, an excellent fly for discoloured waters. The same method can be used with a standard unweighted fly, as long as the current is not so strong as to prevent the fly working deep. Unweighted wet flies, streamers and longtails are easier to work with and catch more fish, but it takes a lot of experience to get them down deep in fast water.

A good pattern for those streams that are only slightly discoloured is a white-bodied streamer with two long black feathers tied to extend well beyond the bend of the hook. In clear water a silver tinsel body and a yellow feather is effective. Try placing a single split shot right against the hook eye instead of two split shot a few centimetres from it. When the fly is weighted close to the hook eye it will nose dive each time the rod action is stopped. This darting forward followed by a sudden nose dive is extremely attractive to trout.

A large wet fly should rarely be cast straight into a spot alongside a log or undercut bank. It should always be cast beyond the hot spot and worked past it. A big trout can be easily scared by something that drops on top of it, but is attracted to those things that move towards or past it.

Fly fishing at night

Those anglers who are allergic to the bite of mosquitoes or whose eyesight is poor may not like it but today much of our best trout fishing is done during the approach of darkness or at night. This is particularly so in streams within 150 km of the big cities.

Despite the years of research done on the habits of trout very little is known about the effect of darkness on these species. Some fish do not feed freely through the day because of predators. Other cold-water fish like the salmon and trout prefer night feeding because the water temperature is more to their liking. There is the possibility also that in many streams trout are forced to feed at night because of the increasing number of anglers moving about the banks. The fact that big trout feed extensively on creatures like small eels, freshwater crayfish and yabbies may be a reason for night feeding, as these creatures are sensitive to light and are most active during the dark of night.

The best time for night fishing is in summer and autumn when there is increased activity in a trout stream, the waters are generally clear, and as far as the angler is concerned it is a more pleasant period for night fishing. In summer the hot, bright sun drives the trout into the pockets of shadows where they remain until sundown. As the first shadows stretch out across the stream, insect activity increases, as anyone knows who has taken a stroll through the bush at dusk on a summer evening. The first creatures to be noticed are the black crickets which scramble out from beneath stones or out of cracks in the ground. They come out in hundreds to drink at the nearest water. Many finish down the throats of the bank-feeding trout. Any medium-size black beetle dry fly will do as a black cricket imitation.

The fly should be cast on the quiet water near the river bank and allowed to drift. There is no need to give much action to the fly to imitate the black cricket, only an occasional jiggle to attract the trout's attention. The next insect to appear is the shiny-bodied black beetle. This beetle hides under stones or behind the bark of trees and it, too, finds its way down to the water's edge. Trout feed extensively on black beetles as can be seen by inspecting the stomachs of trout caught some hours after a thunderstorm. A dry or wet pattern fly can be used but it is important to choose one of the beetles tied with material that gives that shiny black body.

The black beetle fly can be fished in the quiet waters along the margins of the stream or it can be cast farther out to the faster water. The trout seem prepared to take this insect anywhere in the stream. Again, little action of the fly is needed, except to attract attention. This pattern is also effective in lakes at sundown and after dark. In the rivers a No. 2 or No. 10 is about right; in the lakes it may be advisable to use a hook as large as a No. 8.

A large dry fly cast onto a pool during the day may do one of two things: it may bring up some big trout the angler did not know was there, or it may scare the scales off every fish in the pool. But the same fly cast on the same pool at night has an excellent chance of bringing a big trout up if the angler has been careful about his approach. The trout that comes up to look at the fly may not take it—it all depends on the skill of the angler and the whim of the fish.

Some of the big flies used after dark are the muddler minnow, white moth, grey sedge and red and black palmer. If the angler has tried these without success, he should quickly try one of the same patterns on a small hook. This often induces a strike.

It could be that one of the secrets of bringing a big trout to the surface at night is not so much the fly itself but the ripples it sends out when it alights. The most popular technique seems to bear this out. The dry fly is cast onto the water and then left for at least five minutes. Then it is jiggled enough to send out tiny ripples. If this does not bring any response after three or four tries, a tiny black seal's fur nymph drifted around the pool may induce the trout to strike. When this fails after 10 or 15 minutes, the angler should move on to the next pool.

At night, particularly if there is no moonlight or starlight the angler must rely on his hearing rather than his eyesight to judge when to strike. After a few trips he develops a sensitive ear to that sudden slurp, or splash and slurp that indicates his dry fly has been taken. With practice he develops his timing so that he neither strikes too soon and whips the fly away from the trout, nor strikes too late and finds that the trout has ejected the fly.

FLY-TYING The art of decorating a hook with feathers, fur and tinsel to resemble an insect. Anglers, most of whom begin as spin and bait fishermen, are constantly surprised by the ease with which they take trout when they turn to fly fishing. Tying artificial flies is a hobby in itself within the greater hobby of fly fishing. A few anglers tie their own flies, while others buy flies ready made from the tackle shop or have them made to their own requirements by fly-dressers. But anyone who possesses patience, an ability to concentrate, deftness of hand and a good eye for colour and form can learn to tie flies. The abilities of a good needlewoman are the basic skills of fly-dressing although it helps to know what the artificial fly is supposed to imitate and what it is expected to do.

Artificial flies are classed as either wet or dry. These descriptions indicate whether the fly should sink under the water or float on top of it. A dry may represent any one of a variety of insects found either naturally or accidentally on the surface of ponds or rivers. The wet fly imitates the immature forms of several aquatic insects or even small fish.

Thus the materials of which a wet fly is made are those that will absorb water, such as cotton and wool, whereas silk and the oily feathers of water-birds are chiefly used for dry flies. While wet flies are made with hen feathers, dry flies require hackles of stiffer and more buoyant cock feathers.

Hackles are the long narrow neck feathers of the cock bird and one of the most important raw materials of the fly-dresser. They are usually obtained as cured necks which offer a variety of feathers for flies of various sizes. The quality of the neck can be judged by pulling out a sample feather and testing it for stiffness by passing it between the fingers against the grain.

The stiffest feathers are usually from the necks of older birds. Hackle feathers come in a considerable variety, one of the best-known among fly-dressers being the Coch-y-Bondhu, the web of which is dark at the edges and against the quill and reddish in the centre.

PARTS OF A FLY

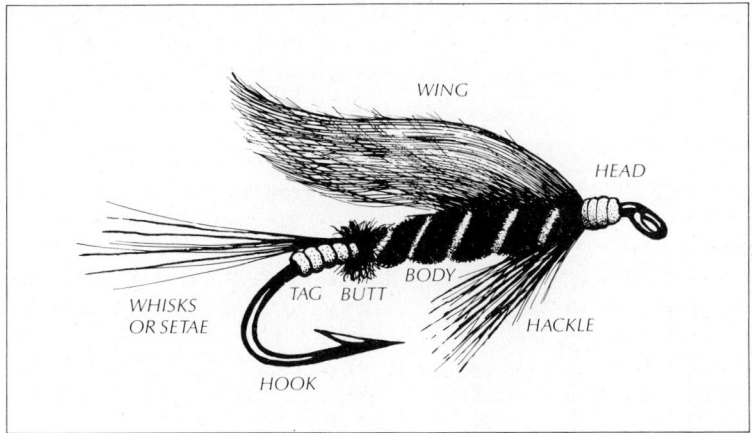

Some good quality hackles are expensive and many of the old fly patterns call for exotic plumage and other materials now difficult to obtain. Almost always, however, an adequate but less costly substitute can be found or a similar feather dyed to the shade required.

Sometimes a special texture or quality is necessary and only the genuine material can be used. The fur from hare's ears, for instance, produces a unique fluorescent effect when it touches water. Peacock herl (the long barb from the bird's tail feather) is another that is hard to replace.

Seal's fur provides dubbing (body material) for several types of wet fly. One of these, the matuka, a New Zealand fly much favoured early in the Tasmanian trout season, is made with the long hackle feathers of the Indian jungle cock. These feathers are worth about five cents each when they can be obtained. When tied in like beetle's wings, they create a distinctive click as the fly is drawn through the water.

Therefore the use of these expensive feathers is considered essential to the matuka's success. Quantity and quality of dressing have a lot to do with the way an artificial fly moves over or through the water. More hackle creates greater buoyancy. Sparse dressing allows smoother and swifter underwater movement.

Patterns of artificial flies are available which cover the entire life cycle of aquatic insects through the immature stages to the fully-fledged adult. When the fish are feeding on a hatch of fly, the angler is able to use an artificial bait that imitates the natural food.

Colour and texture play equal parts in this imitation. Feathers, furs and even quills can be dyed easily to match natural colours. The dye or mixed dyes are dissolved in boiling water which must be kept simmering after the feathers have been added. Then add 15 g of vinegar and continue to simmer until the feathers show the desired colour. Place the

F ■ FLY-TYING

FLY-TYING TOOLS

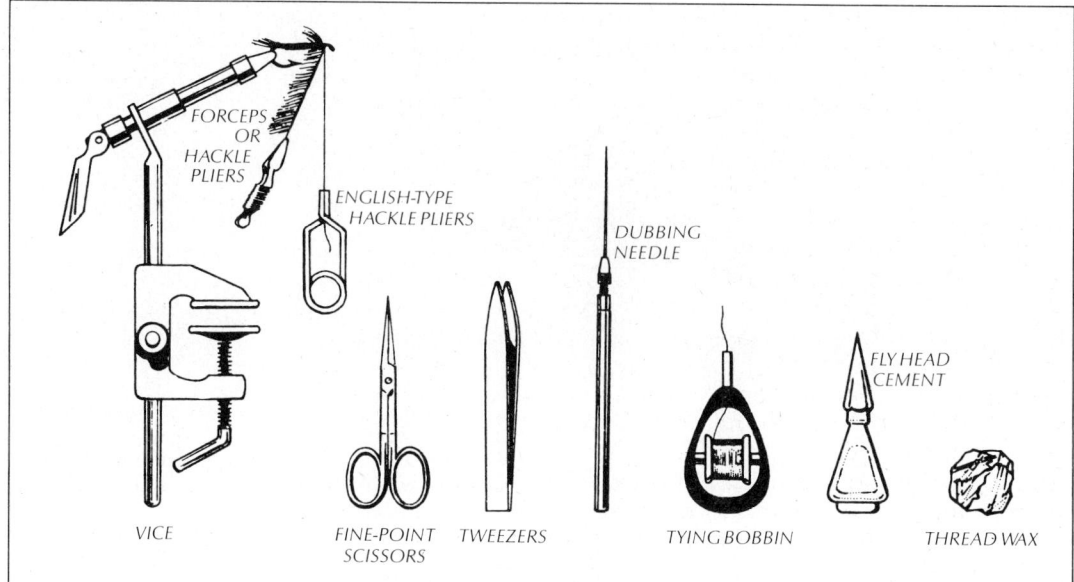

FORCEPS OR HACKLE PLIERS
ENGLISH-TYPE HACKLE PLIERS
DUBBING NEEDLE
FLY HEAD CEMENT
VICE
FINE-POINT SCISSORS
TWEEZERS
TYING BOBBIN
THREAD WAX

feathers in a paper bag and dry quickly in a hot oven to retain the natural lustre.

The most important tool in the fly-dresser's kit is the vice which holds the hook while the fly is being tied. The vice is mounted on the edge of the work bench or table and it is a good idea to fit it up with a gadget called a third hand. This is a kind of clip which holds the thread taut when it is not in use.

Other essentials are hackle pliers, which are a specialized type of spring forceps, tweezers and a couple of pairs of scissors of different sizes. One of these should be a pair of curved manicure scissors and both pairs must be kept very sharp. A device called a whip finisher is also very useful for securing threads and a pair of wirecutters help if you have any thick quills to handle. Endless permutations and combinations can be achieved with these tools.

How to tie a fly   To tie a fly, the hook is mounted in the vice, barb downwards, with the eye slanted to the right. No. 10 is the usual hook size for trout in Australia. Take some lengths (each about 45 cm) of gossamer silk or Tyrolean thread of the required colour and wax them with cobbler's wax. Wind a length of this silk evenly along the shank of the hook, starting slightly to the left of the eye and continuing almost to the bend of the hook.

If the fly you are attempting has whisks or setae, now is the time to tie them in. Whisks are made from a couple of fibres of a pheasant tippet (neck feather) similar in colour to the hackle being used. Hold the fibres in place with the tweezers or a finger and thumb and secure them with a turn or two of silk so that the long ends project beyond the bend of the hook. A half-hitch of silk will anchor the whisks in place.

Body material such as fur can now be tied in, winding back towards the eye of the hook. The tweezers will be needed to lay the fur in position so that it can be caught against the shank by the silk. If peacock herl is required, it can be wound just like the thread, using three strands together. It is first secured to the shank with a couple of half-hitches of silk. Wound bodies, of whatever materials, should be evenly tapered from whisks to hackle.

The barbs of the hackle feather should be no longer than the shank of the hook being used. Strip off all down from the quill and tie it securely to the shank with the dull side of the feather towards you. Clip off the projecting quill end.

Wind the feather around the shank, keeping it taut at all times with the tip held in the hackle pliers and the feather at right angles to the hook. When the fly is dressed with the appropriate amount of hackle, fasten with a couple of half-hitches, making sure that the windings are kept very tight.

Some hackle flies are said to be tied palmer style. This means that a second hackle feather is tied in close to the whisks and wound around the shank until it combines with the normal hackle. This feather is tied in a reverse manner, that is, the tip is tied to the shank and the end of the quill taken in the pliers.

Finally, the thread is secured with a strong knot at the head of the fly. The recommended knot is the whip finish which fastens the end of the thread against the shank inside the windings. The whip finisher has a loop of wire at the end and this loop is bound to the shank with half-a-dozen turns of silk. Holding these windings firmly in place with finger and thumb, thread the end of the silk through the loop of the whip finisher and draw it back through the windings.

A similar knot can be tied with a little more difficulty without the aid of the tool by substituting a loop of strong thread for the wire loop of the whip finisher. The head of the fly is completed with a dab of clear nail varnish.

The fly described is one of the many wingless varieties. Wings are attached after the whisks and before the hackle. They vary according to the insect it is wished to imitate. The wings can be double or single. They may be buzz wings made from the matched breast feathers, or fan wings of tiny breast feathers.

The wings of dry flies are usually tied erect and must be carefully matched in order to balance correctly. Conversely, the wings of wet flies are tied flat against the hook. A pair of matched wing quill feathers, one from a left and the other from a right wing, are needed to make double wings. Two pieces of approximately similar size are nipped from the web of each feather with the finger and thumb. One left and right pair of these pieces is laid dull side up and the other pair

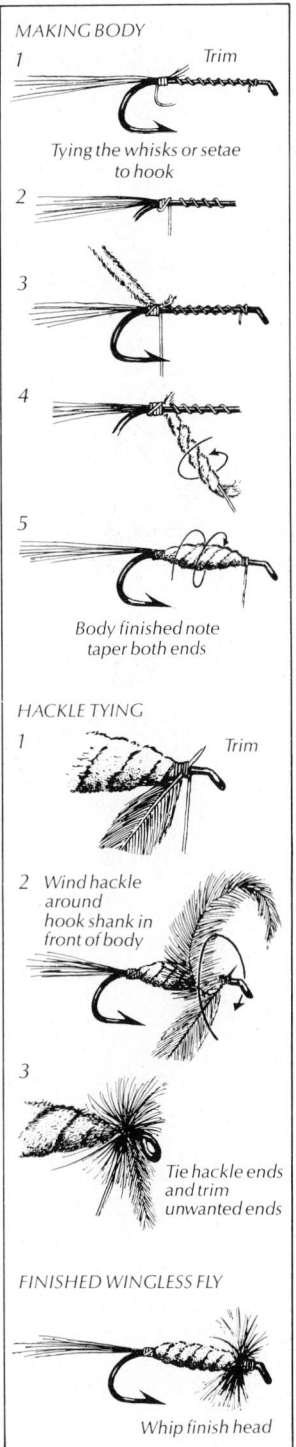

TYING A FLY

MAKING BODY
1 Trim
Tying the whisks or setae to hook
2
3
4
5
Body finished note taper both ends

HACKLE TYING
1 Trim
2 Wind hackle around hook shank in front of body
3 Tie hackle ends and trim unwanted ends

FINISHED WINGLESS FLY
Whip finish head

ATTACHING WINGS

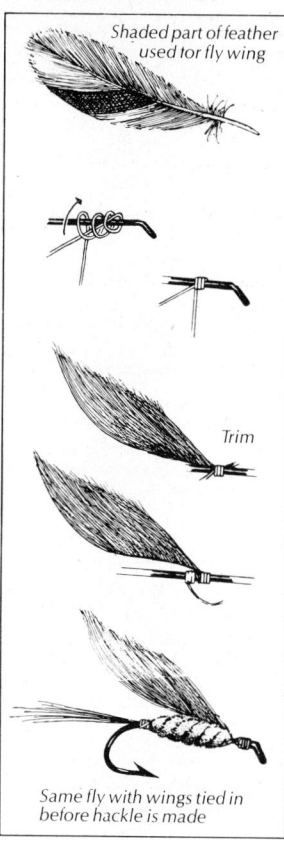

Shaded part of feather used for fly wing

Trim

Same fly with wings tied in before hackle is made

bright side up. The feathers will be seen to curl away from each other.

One side of each piece of web must be drawn together so that the barbs come to a point. The four pieces of web are then laid on the shank of the hook, two on each side, and the points secured with turns of silk before and behind. Protruding ends are clipped off. A couple of turns of hackle are wound in front of the wings and the remainder behind so that the hackle barbs hold the wings upright.

Single wings are secured by stripping the lower part of the web from the rachis (the solid part of the quill) and securing these ends to the shank before and behind. The bare ends of rachis are then clipped off.

Peacock quill is sometimes used as body material. The quill is stripped of fibre with the thumbnail and the root end of the quill clipped off with a slanting cut. This cut end is then secured to the hook with one or two half-hitches of silk. The quill is then wound evenly and tightly around the shank of the hook.

All the foregoing instructions are basic to the making of the majority of wet or dry flies, although colours and materials vary greatly according to the individual patterns. Raffia, tinsel, horsehair and wires of various metals all have a part to play as tying materials as well as silk, wool and cotton. Occasionally flies are tied in reverse (with the head towards the eye of the hook) to simulate an insect in upstream flight.

Many of the famous fly patterns are named after the insects they imitate (march brown, whirling dun, black spinner); others such as the red tag or hare's ears, get their name from the materials of which they are made. Some, like greenwell's glory or hardy's favourite, are named for the flydresser who invented the fly or the angler who made it famous.

Now and then a fly dresser is asked to tie a fly to match some particular insect specimen. In this way a repertoire of Australian flies has been built up. The bogong moth, the green or red and black matukas, the tea-tree beetle and the burrinjuck wonder are a few well-known local examples.

FLYING fish Among the world's most difficult fish to identify, these fascinating fish are much sought by museums. They fly at speeds up to 65 km/h for up to half a minute, the distances and heights covered varying according to whether they are in the trough or crest of a wave on take-off. Flights up to 45 m are common and 180 m is not beyond them. They are fish of the open seas which fly simply to avoid enemies such as the dolphin fish and bonito (see Tunas). There are at least six species in Australian waters, most of them in the tropics, but some reach Tasmania. New Zealand has at least three species, including *Cypselurus lineatus*, the world's largest flying fish, which grows to 45 cm, a warm water variety that ranges south to Cook Strait but is more plentiful north of East Cape.

Flying fish

They are more frequently sighted than taken, though some are captured in dip nets or fly on to light vessels at night.

Flying fish do not flap their wings like birds or bats but they do vibrate their pectorals sometimes as they fly. The pectorals are extended as the fish flash up from deep water, move along the surface by propelling the powerful tail from side to side, and spread their wings. They actually glide rather than fly.

The best known Australian species are *Cypselurus melanocercus*, the great flying fish, commonly seen in southern Queensland waters, and *Exocoetus volitans*, the common flying fish, which replaces the great flying fish in central and northern Queensland waters. The great flying fish grows to 42 cm and has a 45 cm wing span. The common flying fish seldom grows longer than 25 cm.

FRESHWATER ecology

The study of freshwater organisms in relation to their environment. The suitability or fitness of the environment determines the types of organism which occur therein. Some freshwater organisms can survive under one set of physical, biological and chemical conditions and not under another. Other organisms may survive under a wide range of conditions. By measuring and analysing the physical and chemical characteristics of a lake or stream biologists can now predict with reasonable accuracy the species that can exist in this water.

Thus, the first step in understanding the ecology of fresh water is to define the physical and chemical characteristics of such an environment and relate these to the organisms present. Australia, by virtue of its large size and varied climate and structure, encompasses freshwater habitats of widely differing character. Such varied habitats naturally contain a bewildering variety of inhabitants.

A given environment normally harbours more than a single species, and several populations may exist. This assemblage of populations is referred to as a community. The different species making up a community usually exhibit a wide variety of shapes and sizes. Each species occupies a particular place within the community and this place, the organism's relations to its habitat and other organisms, is referred to as a niche. A species typically possesses evolutionary adaptations suiting it for the particular niche that it occupies. Thus herbivores typically possess non-biting mouth parts whereas carnivores possess structures suited for biting and seizing their prey. Trout, for example, are well equipped with numerous teeth whereas the more sedentary, omnivorous, carp has few teeth. The inhabitants of fast-flowing streams typically possess streamlined bodies, holdfasts or other devices to prevent being swept downstream. Such modifications are often in sharp contrast to those of lake-dwellers. Here again, the biological conditions of a community are a factor influencing the distribution and occurrence of species. An aquatic animal, with a highly specialized diet can only live in waters where its food occurs. The high occurrence of certain predators will eliminate some species of prey from the habitat. For example the introduction of trout into Australian waters has resulted in the disappearance of the smaller, indigenous galaxiids from many streams.

In a large community the number of inter-relationships between individuals, populations and species is extremely high. The members of the community react with the environment to form an ecosystem. Within this system plants capture solar energy and produce energy-containing matter which serves as the foundation for food chains of varying complexity. The herbivores graze on the plants and are preyed upon by carnivores which are in turn preyed upon by larger, secondary, carnivores. There is a constant flow of energy through the community, by the consumption of organic material at various levels. Large numbers of food chains are usually present, which interlock with each other in such a manner as to form, as it were, a complex lattice-work.

No one food chain can be separated from another. For example, a water-beetle may be eaten by a fish, frog, or even a bird, all of which may in turn be eaten by various predators. Following a particular channel of this energy-flow through the community is an exceptionally difficult task. Scientists studying such an energy-flow must select a small community with few species. Some of the brackish-water lakes to be found in Victoria contain few species, because of the relatively high concentrations of salts dissolved and are well suited to such studies.

If one examines a food chain it becomes apparent that the organisms within can be arranged into what is called a pyramid of numbers. At the bottom of the pyramid are multitudes of energy-producing plants, then a smaller number of herbivores which feed upon them, then a still smaller number of primary carnivores, followed by an even smaller number of secondary carnivores. The animals at the top of the pyramid are usually the largest organisms in the community and those at the bottom the smallest, but most abundant organisms. The predators do not normally eat themselves out of their food supplies as they can rarely increase in numbers as rapidly as their prey.

There is a substantial loss in mass from the bottom to the top of the pyramid. Only a small amount of food (approximately 10 per cent) consumed by an organism is used in the formation of more living tissue (that is growth), the majority being used to supply the energy needed for the organism to fulfil its metabolic requirements. Thus 100 kilograms of phytoplankton produces approximately 10 kg of herbivorous zooplankters which in turn produce 1 kg of carnivorous zooplankters. If the food chains resulting in fish production have a large number of links, or trophic levels, then a great amount of primary production is needed to cause an appreciable increase in fish production. Similarly, a food chain with relatively few links is a more efficient secondary producer. Fish culturists in the U.S.A. have produced 1 to 2 kg of fish for every 2 kg of specially prepared fish food. This is an extremely high conversion ratio.

The fundamental roles which organisms perform at different nutritional levels can be defined thus:
1. Producer—Organisms capable of using solar radiation and inorganic materials to synthesize energy-containing organic substance. Such organisms include large green plants, smaller phytoplankton and minute photosynthetic bacteria.
2. Consumers—Organisms, typically animal, that are incapable of using solar energy to synthesize matter and thus depend directly or indirectly upon the producers. Such organisms are divided into herbivores and carnivores.
3. Decomposers—The bacteria and fungi which break down organic substance to the elemental state, thereby returning nutrients into the cycle for use by the producers.

Only a few of the factors and principles involved in freshwater ecology have been mentioned but already the complex interrelationships between any organism and its physical and biological environment can be seen. When considering other factors, such as the differing lifestages of each organism, the overall picture becomes increasingly complex. The number of differing ecosystems to be found in Australian freshwaters is immense. It is beyond the scope of this article to even attempt to describe the various types.

As trout are probably the most fished-for freshwater fish in Australia, let us consider a few aspects of the ecology of a typical trout water. Trout are able to survive and do well in both running and still waters, even though the physical characteristics of each habitat differ greatly. Nevertheless both types of habitat must possess water which does not rise above 25 degrees C for any lengthy period of time during the summer. Should this be the case then the fish will be unable to fulfil their oxygen requirements and will perish. Temperature is by no means the only environmental factor influencing the amount of dissolved oxygen in the water. In a stream the rate of flow, number of rapids, amount of organic detritus and numerous other facts must be taken into consideration. In a lake the depth, steepness of sides, rates of inflow and outflow must be considered along with other facts. The geographical location and climate of both types of water must also be considered.

Obviously waters carrying a stock of trout must fall into the same loose category when considering the closely related physical and chemical characteristics of temperature and dissolved oxygen. However other characteristics may differ markedly. Primary production is strongly influenced by two main factors other than temperature, namely light and the availability of dissolved nutrients. Temperature together with light availability largely determine the seasonal pattern of production. Increasing day length and rising temperatures result in greatly increased primary production during the spring and summer, providing the latter parameter does not become too high.

The climate of the locality in which the water is situated will naturally exert a strong influence on this annual rhythm but, by and large, all Australian trout waters show a seasonal pattern of production rising to a peak in the early summer. However, the magnitude of this production is greatly influenced by the amount of dissolved nutrients in the water concerned. Waters occurring in limestone country are richer in dissolved chemicals than those occurring in granite country and exhibit a proportionately greater production. The seasonal pattern of production may differ in large deep lakes as thermal stratification may affect the distribution of dissolved nutrients.

Thus physical relationships determine the amount of primary production in a trout water. As mentioned previously such parameters also determine the types of organisms that occur, certain species of phytoplankton being found in one water and not in another. Differing species have differing optimums of temperature, light-intensity, and nutrient quality and availability. Primary plant production is closely followed by secondary animal production. If the physical inter-relationships are said to be complex the biological inter-relationships in a productive trout water can be said to be of immense complexity. For example if only 100 species occurred and each species had some sort of relationship with every other single species the number of individual relationships involving two species only would be nearly 10,000.

The situation is further complicated when one realizes that every species is invariably connected with more than one other species. The food chains are not separate from one another. They interlock, cross over and are closely inter-related. For example some mosquito larvae feed on zooplankton and some on phytoplankton. These larvae are preyed upon by trout, frogs, water-bugs and beetles, or dragonfly larvae, all of which are preyed upon by trout. However, dragonfly larvae and larger water-bugs may prey upon young trout and small frogs and thus become part of a higher link in the chain, as well as reversing the predator-prey relationship between the trout and these in the above example. Juvenile dragonfly larvae and water-bugs may prey directly upon the zooplankton and thus become part of a lower link in the sequence.

In a productive water large numbers of species are invariably present and the number of inter-specific relationships is very high indeed. The species composition of running-water and still-water communities differ to a large extent and the respective ecosystems vary accordingly. Nevertheless a much simplified food chain can be constructed for both types of water and indeed is applicable to any aquatic habitat. Such an illustration shows only the major trophic levels and may impart a false sense of simplicity. If we take such a schematic diagram a step further and show a few of the major invertebrate groups occurring in a lake such as Eucumbene the following inter-relationships become apparent (*see diagram*).

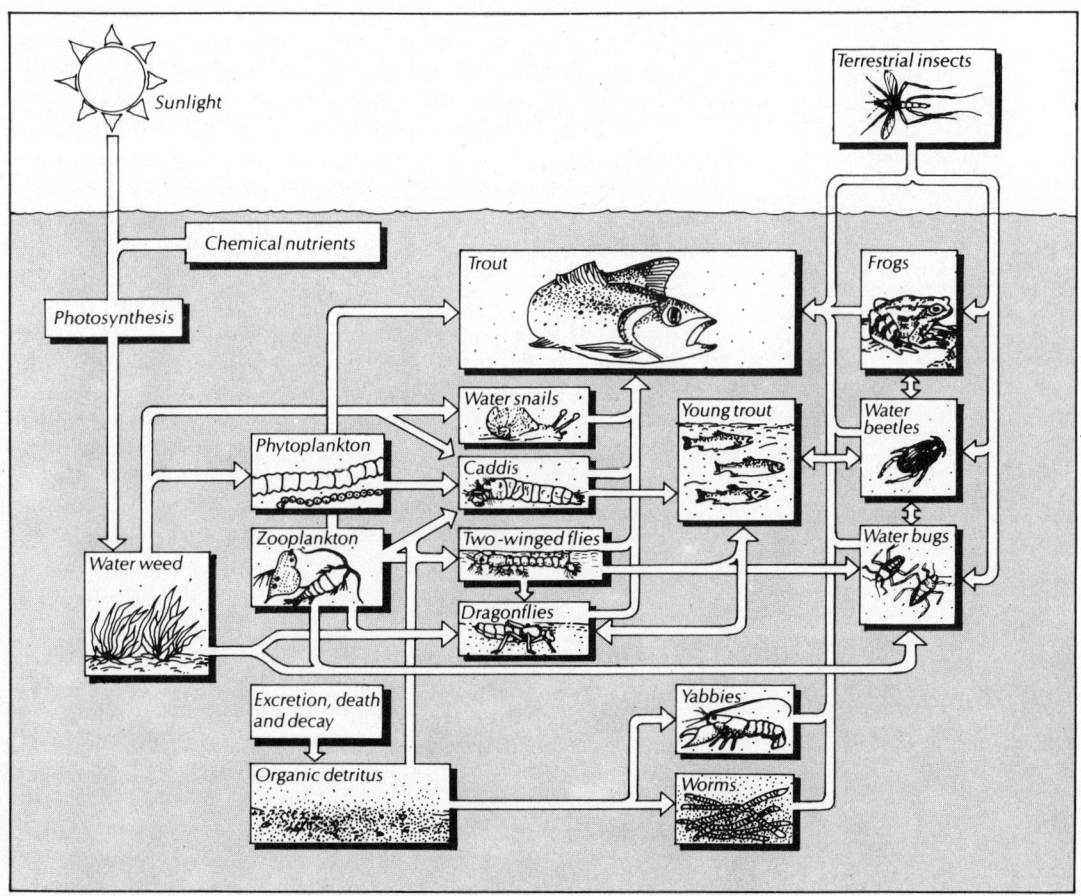

A simplified diagram of a food chain for a still-water habitat such as Lake Eucumbene, showing the complex predator–prey relationship between some of the species present.

It must be stressed that some of the main predatory relationships only are shown. Many flies and stoneflies are not included as they do not occur in appreciable quantities in Lake Eucumbene. If a similar diagram was constructed for a stream these two groups would feature prominently. The direction of the arrows indicates the flow of food, or energy, through the eco-system. One should note that one organism may be used differently by various stages of development of another organism. For example, yabbies will, on occasion, catch and feed on young trout fingerlings, especially in the feeder streams running into the lake. As the trout increase in size this relationship is reversed and larger trout will feed on yabbies. The trout-dragonfly larvae relationship mentioned earlier is another example.

Diets vary within a group. Some species of caddis, for example, have carnivorous larvae, others herbivorous larvae and some phytophagous (feeding on organic detritus) larvae. Note that one intraspecific relationship, cannibalism in trout, is shown.

If the above groups were broken down into separate species the picture would become immensely more complex. The excretory products, together with the products of death are broken down by bacteria and fungi present in the water and substratum and the chemical nutrients are released for re-use by the primary producers. No parasites are shown although some do occur.

Food availability is only one of the factors influencing trout production. Intraspecific relationships play a major role in the ecology of such fish. Numerous such relationships exist; the total number of fish comprising a water's population, annual mortality, competition for spawning space, the annual recruitment of young fish and many other factors are of importance. Here again, physical, interspecific and intraspecific relationships are all inseparable.

Too many fish in a given area of water will result in a smaller amount of food being made available to each individual and increasing competition for spawning space. However, competition for spawning space is as much a consequence of the limiting physical factor of an insufficient spawning habitat as it is of the biological factor of over-population; and so on.

Although the organisms touched on above do not, by and large, occur in salt water the ecological principles remain the same. It must be stressed that the subject has only been touched on.

How will a knowledge of ecology benefit the angler? Such a knowledge is essential to the formulation of beneficial fishery management policies. Fisheries biologists can only predict when, where and what to expect of a fishery when in possession of the necessary ecological data. Any ecosystem, by virtue of its myriad interlocking relationships, can be easily thrown off balance. The removal or addition of a single species could start a chain reaction which results in the ecosystem being severely disrupted. Snap decisions cannot be made.

A fuller understanding of what goes on below the surface will certainly improve one's catches. Knowing just when to present what bait and where the fish are likely to be are obvious advantages. The serious fisherman will be much more of a 'complete angler' when in possession of pertinent ecological knowledge. He will also begin to comprehend the need for conservation and look to the future of Australian fishing. He will learn that the obvious solution is not necessarily the correct one and consider the facts carefully before advocating re-stocking, before carrying fish from one water to another, and before making any decision to alter the habitat concerned.

RICHARD TILZEY

FRESHWATER fishing

Inland fishing in Australia has known dramatic changes but in the 1980s remains a satisfying and rewarding medium for well-equipped sportsmen prepared to study the problems involved. The erection of new dams, prolonged drought, the influence of the Murray River irrigation scheme and the Snowy Mountains development, are just a few of the factors that have revolutionized the freshwater fishing set-up enjoyed by our grandfathers. The marvel of it all is that the banks of our inland rivers and lakes remain studded with amateur fishermen eager to match their skills against the man-made handicaps and the wiles of the fish themselves.

Frogs

Witchetty grub

Plastic imitation lures may be used with or without a trace.

F ■ FRESHWATER fishing

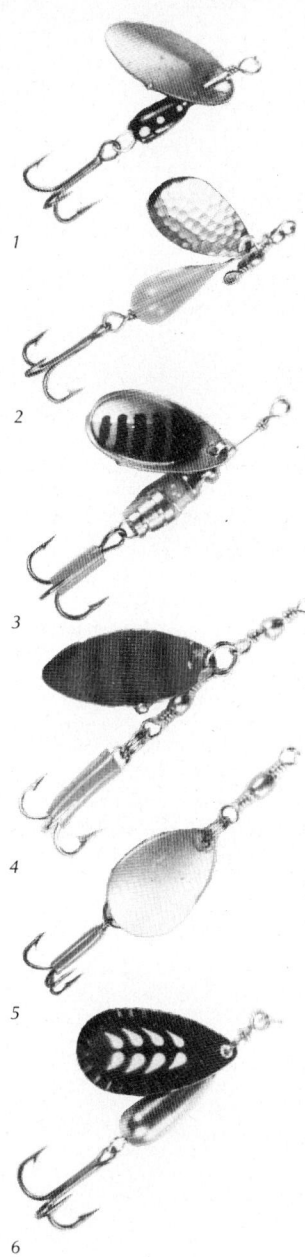

A selection of freshwater lures:
1 Dickson's Model 339;
2 Gillies' Tear Drop;
3 Dickson's Model 1037;
4 Halco Perch Strike;
5 Gillies' Small Colorado;
6 Abu Dropper.

The first essential is to pick out the gear that will do the job and for this the inland angler can do no better than to select an all-purpose spinning rod 1.75 m to 2.5 m long, fitted with a threadline spinning reel with an open or closed face, and 200 m of 2 kg to 3 kg breaking strain nylon line. This, plus a dozen split shot, sizes 1, 2 and 3, half-a-dozen running shot, sizes 1, 2 and 3, a selection of spinners, spoons, wobblers or wrigglers, a couple of anti-twist keels, two plastic bubble floats, half-a-dozen French hooks, sizes 5, 3 and 1, half-a-dozen flatted sneck hooks, size 1, half-a-dozen Kendal Kirby long shank hooks, size 4, and a landing net, comprise the ideal outfit with which to start freshwater fishing. Later on, when the freshwater fisherman has learned to cast and retrieve and generally master this spinning gear in among trees and other hazards, he can go on to fly fishing.

Apart from his basic tackle, the inland angler needs to study the species of fish available in particular locations and find a reliable spot or two. It is not easy. Experienced inland anglers guard information about productive locations as if they were protecting the crown jewels. More and more properties in the outback are erecting 'No Fishing' signs in the 1980s and with the exception of stock routes fishermen usually require permission for access to angling spots.

The big challenge for freshwater fishing lies in the unfished waters of the north, where new roads and facilities provide the chance to test conclusions with fish that seldom encounter sophisticated equipment. The sight of a Queensland or Northern Territory barramundi attacking a modern lure can be awesome. Sooty grunter, jungle perch and saratoga are not backward either when presented with a worm or shrimp bait or a well-chosen fly. As the fisherman travels north, he encounters new fishing spots on all the smaller rivers and ponds. Overfishing has already brought a closed season on barramundi fishing, but out in the wilderness the challenges remain.

Bass fishing is notorious for the fact that good bass spots are difficult of access—but no fisherman who has ever tangled with Australian bass ever moans about the hardship of getting in and out. There are fighting bass in Tasmania in places like the Blackman River and Ansons River, in Victoria near the coast as far as the Glenelg River, and in the freshwater reaches of New South Wales coastal rivers. New South Wales rivers mostly only fish well when the water is clear and low, but Lake Eucumbene is always worth a try thanks to continual government re-stocking and the basic truth that it holds nine times as much water as Sydney Harbour.

Recommended baits and technique for catching all inland fishes are given in the entries on the fishes themselves.

See Fly fishing; see also Trout.

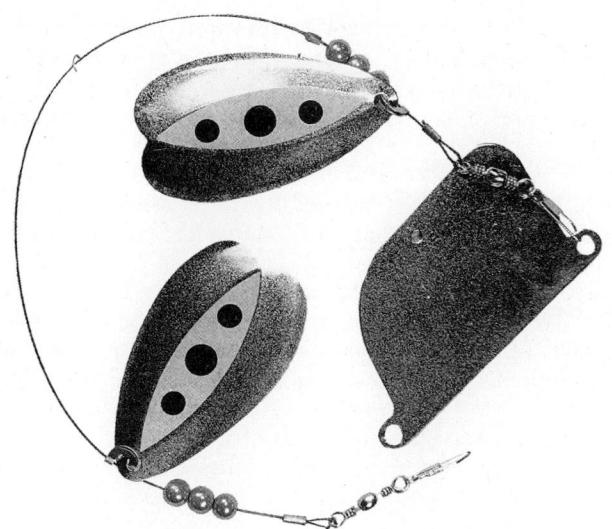

The Flex-I-Troll is an effective trolling jig, ideal for large inland waters.

FROSTFISH

Lepidopus caudatus: Its Maori name Para means 'to spring' or 'to leap' and refers to the last moments of the average specimen when it seems to leave its own element to spring to its death. *Lepidopus* means 'small scales' and *caudatus* refers to the small tail.

This very narrow, ribbon-like fish is related to the New Zealand barracouta or snoek, to which it bears some superficial resemblances. It is without scales; the name *Lepidopus* refers to the ventral fins, tiny degenerate limbs which resemble scales. The body is strap-like, with a dorsal fin running the entire length from the head to the small, deeply forked, well-shaped tail. Colour is bluish-silver, shading to a darker blue at the root of the dorsal fin. As in the barracouta the lower jaw is long. The upper jaw has about 40 sharp teeth, with long fangs at the point.

Frostfish have been taken, though rarely, and apparently by accident, on set-lines in deep water when small fish—pilchards or minnows—have been used for bait. On autumn nights one is sometimes caught in a seine—an unusual occurrence. They are predator fish, found in N.S.W., Victoria, Tasmania, and South Australia, where they are grouped as cutlass fishes; also in the northern hemisphere where they are known as scabbard fish. Both the European and the Maori names are derived from its suicidal habit of casting itself ashore, always on beaches with a gentle slope where the line of surf begins some distance out, and nearly always on frosty nights in autumn. The fish is nearly always in good condition on these occasions; has not recently spawned, displays no evidence of illness or damage. On its passage to the sand it has

F ■ FROSTFISH

been observed to swim in a regular fashion. Moonlit nights are the best for finding this fish, which is reckoned a great delicacy and brings a high price.

In early mornings, a gallop along level beaches on a good horse just at break of dawn is the best method of 'frost-fishing'. When the fish is discovered the tail may be looped through the gills for easy carriage, bandoliered over the rider's head or the horse's. The hunter has to be early to beat the sea-birds, which like humans find the fish the best of eating. A 120 cm fish will weigh no more than 2 kg, about half or less the comparative weight of a barracouta. A coating of what looks like fine aluminium dust rubs off with too much handling.

They are occasionally taken by trawlers at depths between 200 and 600 m. The flesh carries a high proportion of fat in the autumn and winter seasons in which it is found, and there is very little bone.

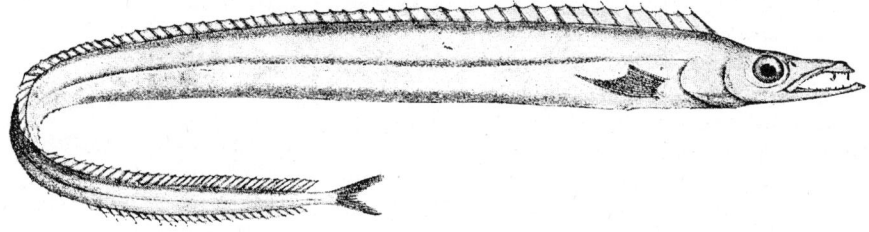

Frostfish

G

GALAXIAS

There are at least 18 members of the tiny Galaxiidae family in Australia. The name *Galaxias* means the Milky Way and was apparently given to these minnows because of their coloration, which often is milky and strewn with dots like tiny stars. The species is confined to the southern hemisphere and ranges from southern Queensland to New South Wales, Victoria, south-west Australia and Tasmania, where they are the dominant family among Tasmania's freshwater fauna. Country people often confuse them with baby trout, but the galaxias all lack scales or an adipose fin.

Among the best known galaxias are the jollytail *Galaxias maculatus*, mountain trout *Galaxias truttaceus*, the mud galaxias *Galaxias cleaveri*, the Clarence galaxias *Galaxias johnstoni*, and the Shannon galaxias *Paragalaxias dissimilis*. They vary in length from 5 cm to 17.5 cm, depending on age and the species. Several of them are confined to fresh water and most of them cannot stand long periods in sea water. They are excellent destroyers of mosquito 'wrigglers', and will leap from the water to catch flies. In aquaria they can be trained to take chopped meat from attendants' fingers. The climbing galaxias *Galaxias brevipinnis*, can negotiate moist rock faces and weirs by using pectoral fins which project laterally and horizontally from low on the body. The jollytail is believed to be the most abundant galaxias and in some regions is known as whitebait. In Queensland, the jollytail was responsible for reports that trout were present in the streams of the Tamborine and Lamington Plateau districts.

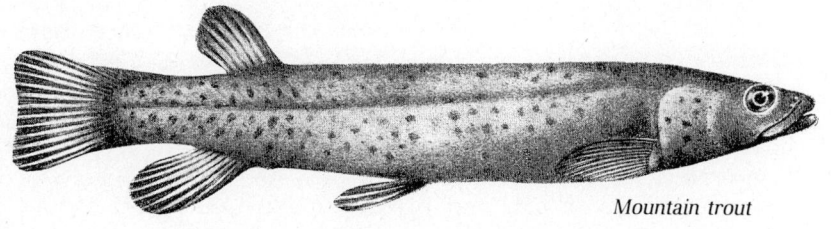
Mountain trout

GAME fishing

Angling, usually by trolling, in deep offshore waters for big fish that fight tenaciously when hooked, has been popular off every Australian State since 1933. Game fishermen and properly equipped game fishing boats have multiplied steadily since then, but the fishing at some of the grounds where the sport began has just as steadily declined and new centres from which game fish could be taken have had to be found. In New Zealand, as in Australia, marlin have been taken since early in this century, but the sport did not really flourish until 1926 when the former dentist-turned-western-writer Zane Grey fished the Bay of Islands. In several thrilling weeks, using gear New Zealanders envied, Grey landed fish in numbers and sizes that brought world-wide publicity to New Zealand's game fishing grounds. A decade later he did the same for Australia. By the 1980s the sporting ethics Grey advocated were strong enough in Cairns, Australia's main game fishing centre, to return 90 per cent of the fish caught to the ocean (*see Tagging*).

The first confirmed capture of a marlin in Australian waters was a black marlin of 54 kg landed on a twenty-one thread line by Dr Mark Lidwill in 1914. This catch was confirmed by Lidwill's fishing companion Dr D. L. Maitland, who with Dr Lidwill pioneered Australian game fishing in the waters off Port Stephens between 1910 and 1914. There is another report that Dr Lidwill caught a 39 kg marlin off Port Stephens in 1910. The significance of these catches was that they were recorded many years before Roy Smith, fishing off Montague Island on the far south coast of New South Wales, landed a black marlin of 118 kg in what has often been mistakenly reported as Australia's first marlin catch.

Smith's marlin catch did in fact cause more anglers to follow suit than Lidwill's had done about 16 years earlier. Smith made his catch in February 1933 and in February 1934 a group of anglers set up camp at Bermagui, near Montague Island. W. C. Wentworth caught a striped marlin and a party of Victorians had 17 marlin strikes in a fortnight, their catches including a 145 kg black marlin. In March 1935, W. J. Wallis and R. Michaelis made a world record catch of one mako shark and 14 marlin, nine of them striped marlin.

These catches in turn inspired Zane Grey's Australian visit in 1936, when fishing off Bateman's Bay, he caught numerous marlin, blue pointer, mako, hammerhead, grey nurse, tiger, thresher and whaler sharks. The thresher shark was the first taken in Australian waters. From January that year until March around 100 marlin were caught in Australian waters, many of them off Bermagui. These fish were landed by a handful of pioneers who included Errol Bullen, a close friend of Grey, and they helped establish game fishing in Australia. When he returned to America, Grey wrote the book *An American Angler in Australia* in which he wrote glowingly of Australian game fish and predicted that our waters would

A huge marlin broaching as it fights for survival.

yield fish of a size and variety unmatched anywhere in the world. Since World War II Bermagui has not lived up to this forecast but other centres such as Cairns have done so.

Following Grey's praise other game fishermen of world distinction visited Australia, most of them heading for Bermagui. These included Dr Richard Sutton in 1937, singer Harry Lauder in 1937, Michael and Mrs Lerner in 1938 and Kip and Mrs Farrington in 1949. All of them landed outstanding fish. On Lerner's visit discussions were held with the Game Fishing Association of Australia which led to the formation in 1939 of the International Game Fishing Association, the ruling body for the sport which confirms world record claims. This gave game fishing standards, particularly in the landing of fish, which it had previously lacked and undoubtedly attracted many sportsmen.

Ten years before he helped establish Australian game fishing as a sport, Grey had done the same for New Zealand. In 1926, at the invitation of the New Zealand Government, he set up camp on Urupukapuka Island at Otehei Bay, and in a few weeks landed 17 mako sharks, one black marlin, 41 striped marlin, including a world record fish of 204 kg (450 lb)*, and six kingfish. Grey's paid fishing companion, Captain Laurie Mitchell, caught 20 striped marlin, six makos, three large kingfish and two black marlin, one of them weighing 442 kg (976 lb), a world record that lasted until 1952.

Grey took with him to New Zealand a secretary who worked with him on the book *The Angler's El Dorado*, photographers

* World records are still judged in imperial measures.

G ■ GAME fishing

and reporters from newspapers and magazines. He fished from the local charter boat *Alma G*, which is still in the Bay of Islands. Mitchell fished from the *Marlin*, a boat Grey felt was more suitable for taking film for the movie on his trip. Between catching fish, writing his book and filming, Grey produced articles for the *New Zealand Herald* which, after a lot of argument from indignant locals, helped lay the foundations of today's game fishing techniques.

Zane Grey was highly critical of the failure of New Zealand game anglers to try to stop big fish and fight them. The locals claimed Grey could do this only because he had long lines and tackle far superior to that with which they fought fish. Grey said playing a fish until it drowned, starved or choked to death was unsporting. New Zealanders said their tackle called for infinite skill. The upshot of the rather heated debate was that Grey gave up writing the articles in annoyance at all the protests, and New Zealanders paid closer attention to the methods Grey showed them.

The veteran boatmen of New Zealand, including Francis Arlidge, skipper of the *Alma G*, agree today's techniques on game fish are still basically what Grey advocated in 1926, trolling with a short, stiff rod, a single hook instead of treble hooks and teasers to lift fish to the bait. The only changes since then have been in the method of baiting and in the appearance of outriggers that permit baits to be trolled further astern of the boat and make it skim invitingly over the water. Nobody doubts that the publicity Grey gave to both New Zealand and Australian game fishing not only established the sport here by enthusing local anglers but focused world attention on our fishing for the first time.

The Game Fishing Association of Australia, founded in 1937, originally ruled only on records of sea-going game fish, but it now includes freshwater species such as rainbow trout, Murray cod and Australian bass among the fish recognized for records. The G.F.A.A. in 1985 comprised 58 clubs, plus an office in each State and a headquarters in Sydney, where it controls the Australian Fishing Museum.

Control of game fishing

Under the rules of all clubs affiliated with the Game Fishing Association of Australia—which is affiliated with the International Game Fishing Association in America—all fish must be caught from a boat at sea on 'prescribed tackle'. Fish must be fought, gaffed and secured from the boat from which it was originally hooked by the angler, who must hook, fight and bring the trace to hand unaided by any other person. Until the fish is secured, no person other than the angler may touch the rod, reel or line. The angler may be assisted in adjusting or changing the harness. There is no restriction on the use of one or more gaffers in addition to the person holding the trace. No part of the rod or reel may be rested on the boat whilst the fish is being fought and until the trace comes to hand. Should, however, the person handling the trace lose hold of it before the fish is gaffed, the angler must at once pick up the rod and continue the fight in accordance with the Rules.

Disqualifications
The following will disqualify a catch:
(a) Failure to comply with the rules and tackle specifications of G.F.A.A.
(b) A broken rod, that is, a rod which has been broken into separate pieces. *Note:* Any lesser damage which might be defined by I.G.F.A. as 'a broken rod' should be reported when a claim is being submitted for a World Record.
(c) Changing of rod or reel, joining the line, or removal or addition thereto, during the playing of a fish.
(d) Handling or using a hand line or rope attached in any manner to the line or trace for the purposes of holding, lifting or bringing a fish to the boat.
(e) Shooting, harpooning or lancing any fish, including sharks, at any stage of the catch.
(f) Mutilated fish will not be eligible for recording. Small superficial cuts, scratches or small cuts made by the trace or line, old healed scars and regeneration deformities shall not be considered mutilations.
(g) Beaching or driving into shallow water any fish hooked from a boat in order to deprive the said fish of its normal ability to swim.

Weighing and recording
The following procedure is to be followed when weighing and recording a fish.
(a) The fish must be weighed on land by an Official Weight Recorder appointed by a State Branch or Club which is affliated thereto.
(b) The scales must be approved by the State Branch, must have been checked for accuracy and must be in conformity with the Act governing Weights and Measures.
(c) The actual tackle used in the capture of the fish must be exhibited to the Official Weight Recorder at the time of weighing. A committee of the Club at the centre at which the fish has been weighed may demand this tackle for inspection, should such action be deemed necessary.
(d) The Official Weight Recorder shall certify to the correctness of the information on the official 'Capture and Weight Recording Certificate' issued by the Secretary of the Club.

This certificate shall state:
(i) Name and address of the angler.
(ii) Date and approximate location of the capture.
(iii) Species of fish.
(iv) Gross weight of fish and sling; net weight of fish.
(v) Length of the fish (measured from the point of the lower jaw to the crotch of the tail), and the maximum girth measurement (at the thickest part of the body, usually behind the pectoral fin).

(vi) Line class, length of double line, length of trace, number of hooks and type of hook rig.
(vii) It must also bear the signature of the boatman or fishing companion, as witness that the fish was caught by the angler unaided, on the tackle described in the Certificate and strictly in accordance with the Rules of G.F.A.A.
(viii) Where it is impossible to bring a fish to an Official Weight Recorder, a Statutory Declaration by an angler, setting forth weight as ascertained on tested scales, together with details of tackle used.

Protests

Any protest relative to the weight of or manner of weighing a fish must be made to the Official Weight Recorder before the fish is removed from the weighing stage. Any such protest shall be decided by the Committee of the Club at the centre at which the fish has been weighted. Any such decision shall be final and binding on all concerned.

Any protest relative to tackle used, or alleged manner in which a fish was killed or landed, must be lodged in writing within fourteen days of the weighing of such fish with the Secretary of the Club at the centre at which the fish was weighed. Any such protest, together with all relevant evidence obtainable by the aforementioned Secretary, shall be immediately forwarded to the State Branch of the Game Fishing Association of Australia in whose waters the capture was made and whose decision in all such cases of protest and/or dispute shall be final and binding on all concerned. No protest shall subsequently be recognized unless lodged as set out above.

Claims for an Australian record

Any application claiming an Australian Record must be forwarded through a State Branch to the Secretary of the G.F.A.A. and be accompanied by:
1. A Capture and Weight Recording Certificate supporting any such application which must be countersigned by an independent witness, whose full postal address shall be given, certifying to the correctness of the weight and measurements set out in such certificate.
2. A Statutory Declaration by the angler stating that all the Rules of the G.F.A.A. were strictly observed.
3. The entire leader, the double line, and at least 15.24 m (50 ft) of the single line closest to the double line, leader, or hook. All line samples and the leader (if one is used) must be submitted in one piece.

G.F.A.A. records for men, women and juniors are kept in the following line classes:

1 kg (2.20 lb)	8 kg (17.63 lb)	37 kg (81.57 lb)
2 kg (4.40 lb)	10 kg (22.04 lb)	60 kg (132.27 lb)
4 kg (8.81 lb)	15 kg (33.06 lb)	
6 kg (13.22 lb)	24 kg (52.91 lb)	

All lines submitted with record claims are uniformly tested in a nationally recognized laboratory. To replace a record for a fish weighing less than 10 kg, the replacement must weigh at least 250 g more than the existing record. To replace a record for a fish weighing between 10 and 50 kg, the replacement must weigh at least 500 g more than the existing record. Above the 50 kg weight, the replacement record must weigh at least 1 kg more than the existing record.

Line testing
All lines will be tested by an authority approved by G.F.A.A. executive in accordance with Rule 6.

Racking
If the angler used two or more lines of different strength joined together to capture a fish, the line shall be classified under the heaviest of the such lines. A sample of all lines must be submitted.

Photograph
If possible a full length photograph of the fish, showing dorsal and pectoral fins, should accompany the claim. In the case of a shark, a second photograph should be submitted showing the teeth. In photographing the catch, do not stand in front of the fish. Do not hold the tip of the dorsal fin, thus concealing its height. All fins, tip of the jaws, sword or spear, must show clearly. For identification purposes, a fish lying on its side is far preferable to one that is hanging or held. The surface beneath the fish should be smooth and a ruler or marked tape should be placed beside the fish if possible. Shark photographs should show the full length of the fish and the nature of the front teeth.

All claims on two hook tackle must be accompanied by a photograph or sketch of the hook arrangement indicating the necessary measurements. Recognition of the capture of an Australian Record will not be granted by the G.F.A.A. until after two months from the date of capture of the fish. Any claim received by G.F.A.A. more than two months after the date of capture will be recognized only in extenuating circumstances to the satisfaction of G.F.A.A. executive.

Claim for a world record
The claim should be forwarded to the Secretary of the G.F.A.A. who will forward it to I.G.F.A. The claim should include the following:

1. An affidavit attested by a Notary Public or a Justice of the Peace.
2. An official Claim Form of the I.G.F.A. correctly filled in.
3. All details and certificates required for an Australian Record Claim.
4. Photographs as for a G.F.A.A. record.

Record size fish

G.F.A.A. will record all game fish and sharks which are eligible for a 'Merit Pin' Award as well as those which are Australian Records. The State Branches may make their own minimum weights for recording fish. For both Australian and world records, a new record will be accepted only if it is heavier than the existing record by:
(a) 0.5 kg or more if 45 kg weight or over.
(b) 0.25 kg or more if under 45 kg weight. Lesser differences will be treated as a tie.

Certificates will be issued by G.F.A.A. for captures which are Australian Records. Certificates will be issued also for a tie.

All Clubs affiliated with G.F.A.A. must adopt G.F.A.A. Rules as part of their Constitution. Each Club affiliated with the State branch of G.F.A.A. shall keep a list of game fish and sharks captured, showing the name of the angler, weight of the fish, tackle used, approximate locality and date of capture. The Club shall forward this list to the State branch at the close of every season. The State Branch shall then forward these particulars to the Secretary of G.F.A.A. who will advise State branches of captures made. Where a non-member angler captures a fish which obviously approaches a world record, affiliated clubs are asked to co-operate to see that the fish is properly weighed, measured, witnessed, photographed and registered according to the requirements of I.G.F.A.

Game fishing harness traces, hooks and gaffs

These are essential parts of the game fisherman's kit, but they have altered little over the years.

Harness is used on heavy fish with heavier gear and is used when fighting a fish from the game chair in the boat, but owing to the enormous popularity of light game fishing much of the fishing is done standing up either in the stern or at the bow. For a heavy harness you have the choice of a kidney harness which fits around the waist and clips on to the two reel plates, or the more conventional shoulder harness which fits over the shoulders and also clips onto the reel. The shoulder harness gives more leverage but the kidney harness is less tiring.

The great advantage of the kidney harness is that there are no straps to cut into the shoulders. The shoulder harness is usually made from strong but flexible leather, padded with either felt or foam rubber. The two leather straps fastening onto the reel with clips should be adjustable to suit the user. Noted game fishing writer the late Athel D'Ombrain had long and satisfactory service from a harness made from an old vest or waistcoat with a strong piece of canvas sewn around the back and fairly high up. It had the great advantage of being easily put on in a matter of seconds and there were no straps to cut the back or shoulders.

Quick-snap-on brass clips are essential for fastening the harness to the reel and nothing has yet been produced to better the 'piston hanks' used in sailing boats for this job. For standing up fishing with light gear, a well-padded rod bucket with a movable socket that straps around the waist is all that is required. A supporting strap from the rod can be added if necessary.

The use of a double line is not required, but if one is used the double line must consist of the actual line used to catch the fish. In salt water, the double line for line classes 1 kg to 10 kg inclusive should be limited to 4.57 m (15 ft). The combined length of the double line and leader should not exceed 6.1 m (20 ft). The double line on all classes above 10 kg should be limited to 9.14 m (30 ft). The combined length of the double line and leader should not exceed 12.19 m (40 ft). The double line must be connected to the leader, if one is used, with a knot, splice, snap, swivel or other device. In fresh water, the double line for all classes of tackle should not exceed 1.82 m (6 ft). The combined length of the double line and the leader should not exceed 3.04 m in fresh water.

The use of a leader is not required, but if one is used, the leader should be limited to 4.57 m (15 ft) inclusive for line classes from 1 kg to 10 kg. On all classes above 10 kg the leader should be restricted to 9.14 m. There are no rules on the material or strength of the leader and there are no minimum lengths. In fresh water the length of the leader should be restricted to 1.82 m (6 ft) on all classes of tackle.

The single strand piano type wire in use in Hawaii is now popular at Cairns for big black marlin, but it has the disadvantage of kinking at times and it is wise not to use it more than a few times before discarding it. However, it is easy to rig, can be quickly cut from a roll, and either shortened or thrown away when considered risky from possible kinks or rusting. Nylon covered wire was used for a time but did not prove very popular.

Mustad hooks are still the best game fishing hooks and are in general use throughout Australia and New Zealand. For very large fish size 14/0 and 12/0 are recommended but size 10/0 is a good average size for marlin. If the marlin are small No. 8/0 is quite satisfactory.

Points and edges of hooks should always be kept sharp and clean and for this a small file is essential. Always make sure the tip is not damaged at this is the most important part of a hook. When trolling lures, it is better to have hooks with a straight set such as Limerick or O'Shaughnessy rather than an offset bend which tends to make the lure spin.

Many boatowners make the mistake of having only one gaff on board. This is a dangerous practice as it is quite possible to lose one or two on a fish. Shark gaffs must be much larger and stronger than those used for marlin, but both should be of the detachable head type and can be made from either stainless or non-stainless steel. Make sure they are made by an expert in metal working and that they are properly tempered. Two

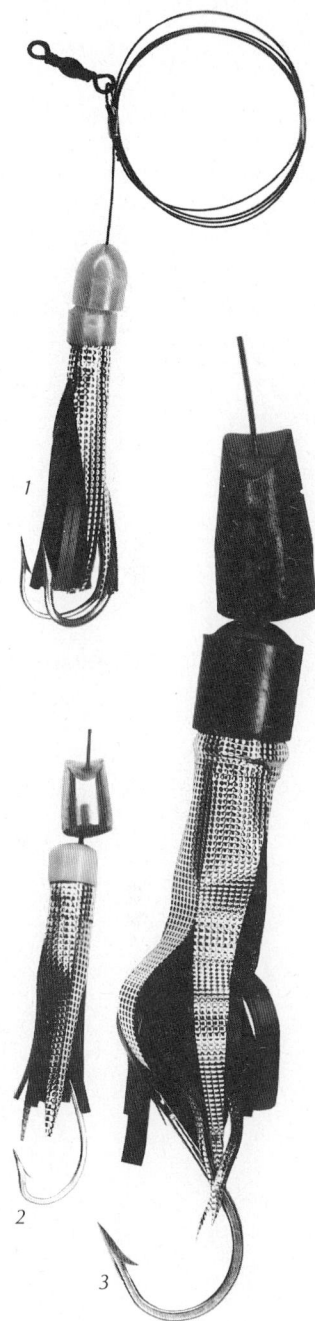

Some deep-sea game fish lures from Ssvenstrand:
1 Bullethead;
2 Small Knucklehead;
3 Large Knucklehead.

short hand gaffs, made with a ring in the centre for attaching the gaff rope to, should also be carried as these are often of more use than the detachable ones. The gaff rope must not exceed 9 m.

Game fish baits

A large range of baits can be used for marlin and game fish, depending on the locality being fished and the type of bait available. The bait most popular, from Sydney north to Port Stephens and beyond, is the common bonito, known by several names such as mackerel or skippy. They arrive in large schools but owing to their popularity as bait for many types of fishing they are at times difficult to obtain.

Many other types of fish can be used. Among these are small yellowtail kingfish, rainbow runners, frigate mackerel, mullet and the small common or blue mackerel, known to fishermen as 'slimies'. For smaller game fish yellowtail and garfish are excellent bait. Tailor can also be effective, although this fish is rather soft and does not last long when trolling. For drifting almost anything can be used, such as snapper, nannygai, morwong or flathead. For sharks, larger baits are best and these include striped tuna, yellowfin tuna and large bonito.

Game fishing lines

For light tackle game fishermen throughout Australia favour monofilament nylon. Multifilament, and lead core multifilament lines may be used. Wire lines are prohibited. Monofilament lines have the advantage of not fraying like linen and braided lines, though they have a remarkable capacity to stretch. Game anglers still sometimes talk about catching a fish on a three or nine thread line, but most of them have never used linen lines and this is simply a usage which has continued since the early days of game fishing when linen lines were standard equipment.

Earlier problems of reel stresses with monofilament have been overcome by the use of heavy metal spools. Some remarkable captures have been recorded with the mono lines and they certainly have helped anglers set new records in the lighter classes.

Backing not attached to the fishing line is permissible, with no restrictions as to size or material. The backing must not exceed the 60 kg (130 lb) line class and must be of a type of line approved for use under G.F.A.A. rules.

Australian game anglers, almost to a man, follow the standards set in line strengths by the International Game Fish Association in America. These are designed to coincide with rods and reels which can be said to balance the lines. Theoretically, sporting ethics determine which combination may be used. For the largest white sharks and fish of 450 kg to 900 kg, heavy gear and lines with a breaking strain of 60 kg would normally be used. Anglers fishing for very light fish would use the 5 kg breaking strain line with an equivalent rod and reel to balance the line.

Unfortunately the widespread use of points for club competitions, with most points allotted to fish caught on extra light gear, has led to what has been termed 'stunt fishing'. For example marlin of 90 kg can sometimes be caught on 5 kg b/s line, but it is not the correct type of gear for fish of this size. If it was not for the lure of points, fishermen would use much heavier lines for powerful fish of this type.

Game fishing rods and reels

Just as monofilament lines have superseded linen lines, fibreglass rods have taken over from split cane rods in game fishing. This is almost entirely due to the strength, flexibility and maintenance-free construction of the fibreglass rods, which are available in a huge range of balanced weights. Anglers can have fibreglass rods made to suit their personal physiques and fishing styles.

The first fibreglass rods were far from a success, but they have been improved a lot over the years and every season the number of anglers using split cane decreases further. Rods are available in all sports stores, but some anglers buy rod blanks and make up their own rods. Several local makers have installed manufacturing facilities to turn out blanks to their own specifications instead of relying on glass blanks from overseas.

Any rod giving the angler an unfair advantage will disqualify the catch. They must be made in accordance with sporting ethics and while no definite rules are laid down the rod tip must be made to balance the tackle used.

They are usually near these weights:

For 60 kg test 400 to 475 g tip   15 kg test 150 g tip
    35 kg test 300 to 400 g tip   10 kg test 100 g tip
    20 kg test 200 g tip   5 kg test   85 g tip

The use of very light lines with heavy rod tips, apart from being unsporting, is impractical also, as a very light line would break before the rod tip could flex properly.

Make sure a hole is bored in the metal butt cap so that the rod can be pinned to the rod socket in the chair; this can save many a rod and reel from going overboard and is essential if you wish to gaff your own fish.

Reels, too, are manufactured to suit each type of line and it would be senseless as well as impractical to use a very large reel on a small rod.

The most popular reels in use now are of the lever action, disc brake style such as the Fin Nor, Everol, Policansky and Penn International brands. These reels are probably high priced by post-war standards for they are beautifully engineered and as they are designed for monofilament nylon use they should be practically indestructible. Star drag reels are still used and they catch a lot of fish, but the control of the drag does not give the speed and efficiency of the lever action reels mentioned above.

A considerable number of new designs are appearing on the market. While they may be good, there is only one way to find out and that is to try the clutch and see that it has a nice soft action and to make sure the reel is made from good material and will not seize up on a very vast run. If they cannot stand up to this test without heating up, the reel is useless. Beware of home made reels no matter who makes them. Also make sure the reel will withstand the pressure of nylon, as this can expand the drum and end up in the reel seizing and the line breaking.

Game fishing in New Zealand Began almost by accident, after years of big fish breaking primitive gear. On 12 February 1915, Major A. D. Campbell, of Scotland, boated a 105.5 kg striped marlin in the Bay of Islands, the first caught on a rod in New Zealand. Since that time New Zealand waters have been fished consistently and have won a world-wide reputation. But game fishing was looked upon as a sport only for millionaires until it began to boom in the 1920s. The late Zane Grey's visit in 1926 and his subsequent book *The Angler's El Dorado*, popularized New Zealand waters around the world and since then the sport has never looked back. When fishing recommenced after World War II, the numbers of New Zealanders from all walks of life eager to go game fishing grew so fast it became almost impossible to book a charter boat at peak periods of the season without booking years in advance.

The coastal waters of New Zealand teem with fish of all descriptions, but those regarded locally as game fish are the broadbill swordfish, blue, black and striped marlin, mako, thresher and hammerhead sharks, yellowtail (kingfish) and tuna. The New Zealand marlin provide thrills equal to any obtained elsewhere in the world and celebrated anglers from many countries gather there to enjoy the sport. The game fishing waters are on the east coast of the North Island. Varying in width, they stretch 480 km from Manganui in the far north to the easternmost sweep of the Bay of Plenty. Here the coastline is indented with numerous bays, inlets, coves and harbours, with a protecting screen of islets at varying distances from the mainland. The northern harbours are strikingly beautiful and some are almost landlocked. Australian anglers who contemplate sport among the game fish of these coastal waters can therefore depend upon sheltered and pleasant bases from which to make their excursions.

Main New Zealand game fishing localities

The six main bases for deep-sea anglers are Whangaroa, the Bay of Islands, Tutukaka (near Whangarei), Kawau Island, Mercury Bay and Tauranga, where the game fishing centre at Mayor Island is 35 km out by boat. All the fishing grounds are less than 300 km or four hours' drive from Auckland, the main tourist entry port of the North Island. For tourists in a hurry the fishing bases may be reached in an hour or less by amphibian aircraft, allowing visitors with only a day to spare a full day's fishing.

In February 1958, when an American sportsman, Philip Tabers of Buffalo, arrived in Auckland on the liner *Monterey*, he had a one-day stopover in Auckland and an urge to try game fishing. After an early breakfast he stepped from the ship into a taxi, was driven a kilometre or so to board an amphibian which took an hour to reach Otehei Bay, in the Bay of Islands. Tabers caught a mako shark of 145 kg, returned to Otehei Bay at 5 p.m. and was back on board the liner at 6 p.m. telling fellow passengers about his battle with the fish.

There is a vast difference between Tabers' mode of travel, launch and tackle and the facilities Zane Grey used 30 years earlier. Grey, of course, designed his own rods and reels, bearing no relation to today's streamlined marvels. The deep-sea launches now in use make those Grey used look like rowing skiffs. Launches vary from 9 to 15 m, but many more amateur anglers are pursuing the fish in their smaller private boats. Anglers usually become members of the fishing club at the port they use, and as members they are eligible for cash prizes and trophies in contests conducted each season. Charter launches, all licensed to carry up to four fishermen and skippered by men expert in the art of game fishing, are available for hire at all the fishing centres. All of them are equipped with first-class fishing tackle, the use of which is included in the daily charter rate. Most of the launches have radio telephones, invaluable as a safety measure and also as a means of finding out where the best strikes are being made. The majority are twin chair boats towing two or three marlin baits and a tuna lure or two, but there are boats with flying bridges and four chairs that can tow four or five baits and a couple of lures as well.

New Zealand game fishing regulations

There are few game fishing restrictions—there are no closed waters, and no licence fees. The only regulations an angler need concern himself with are those that say that swordfish and marlin may be taken on a rod and line, the line no heavier than 39 thread or 60 kg and no more than four swordfish or marlin may be taken from one boat in one day. The season extends from 1 November to 30 June. Early every morning through this period fast modern launches leave each centre to hunt in the open ocean and around the reefs and islands for game fish. The best months for fishing are February, March and April, although fish, more particularly sharks, may be caught at any time of the year.

Main New Zealand game angling species

The most commonly encountered large game fish is the striped marlin. In New Zealand waters this species averages around 110 kg, but every season a number of the heavier fish run to 180 kg or more. Since the broadbill swordfish is rare, the black marlin is the premier game fish in that part of the world. They have mostly been taken at from 180 to 270 kg, but every season one or more big specimens have been weighed in at more than 360 kg. The 442 kg black marlin which Captain Laurie Mitchell captured in the Bay of Islands in 1926 was a world record until 1952. Small black marlin are extremely rare and one of 52.5 kg taken at the Bay of Islands in 1955 created quite a lot of interest in game fishing circles. Pacific blue marlin, positively identified as such in New Zealand only 10 years ago, range in weight from about 135 to 270 kg.

The true swordfish, the broadbill, is relatively scarce and very few have been taken. The four which were caught in the Bay of Islands during the 1964–65 season were the first taken since 1928. Some are seen from time to time, usually at long intervals, and any such sighting makes headline news.

The mako shark holds second place for numbers caught each season and its speed and fighting ability are assessed by New Zealanders as almost equal to those of the striped marlin. They should know, for their waters hold the world's most prolific supply of these speedy blue pointers. They average around 110 kg, but every season several of more than twice this weight are brought in. A world record mako, weighing 481 kg (1061 lb), was caught at Mayor Island in 1970 by J. B. Penwarden.

Although it can be said to prefer somewhat warmer waters, the hammerhead shark is frequently captured off New Zealand. This species takes a trolled bait and gives a very good account of itself, but cannot be compared with the mako as a fighting fish.

Thresher sharks are much more rare in these waters but specimens from 135 to 225 kg keep occurring in the lists of catches. Larger specimens have been taken on occasions and New Zealand held the 1984 world record with a thresher of 364 kg (802 lb) taken at Tutukaka south of the Bay of Islands in 1981 by Dianne North.

Among the smaller game, the yellowtail kingfish and the yellowfin tuna predominate. The yellowfin does not average as large as those taken on some Australian fishing grounds but the yellowtail have been running somewhat heavier than their Australian counterparts.

Plentiful light tackle fish

Most popular light game fish in New Zealand is the yellowfin tuna, caught in vast numbers only in recent years. Numbers have increased spectacularly and their average weight has increased from about 20 kg to 30 kg, with many over 45 kg. Bluefin tuna are rarely caught in New Zealand waters. Also high on the New Zealand light tackle list are yellowtail, which grow up to 45 kg and more, but any fish over 10 or 15 kg will give the fisherman all he can ask for in the way of thrills. A most sporting fish for its size is the kahawai, used almost

Two large yellowfin tuna caught off Narooma, on the New South Wales south coast.

GAME fishing ■ G

universally as bait for bigger fish. Kahawai do not run large, a 3 kg specimen is a good fish, but they have all the verve and fire of a well-conditioned rainbow trout and catching them on ultra light gear can be an exciting prelude to bigger things. Kahawai weighing between 1 and 2 kg are used almost exclusively in New Zealand as bait for big game fishing. They are plentiful and easy to catch.

Favoured game fish techniques in New Zealand

As all major game fish in New Zealand will take a trolled bait or lure, most fishing is carried out by this method. In trolling, the kahawai bait is trolled about 15 to 24 m astern of the launch at a speed varying between four and six knots. For drifting, one bait is set deep and the other shallow. The shallow bait is held at the desired distances below the surface by a float. All sorts of fancy gadgets have been used as floats, including plastic bottles, from 2 litres to 500 ml. The deep bait is allowed to lie from the end of the rod. In both cases, the fish swallows the bait and the angler is in business.

Trolling has an advantage over drifting that many fishermen would be reluctant to forgo—the thrill of seeing the strike. There are other reasons for its popularity. Fishermen are more comfortable with the launch moving and they feel they are getting value for their money. And this way, too, the fisherman feels he is actively fishing instead of passively resigning himself to waiting until a fish happens to come along. Mayor Island is the only centre in New Zealand where drifting is still practised extensively. More and more fishing is being done on light tackle. The average New Zealand marlin or mako can be slaughtered on 60 kg line, landed comfortably on 35 kg line and gives great sport on 20 kg line. As the experience of New Zealand amateur fishermen grows, so does their skill, and they are turning to lighter tackle.

Game fishing in Tasmania

The predominant gamefish taken in Tasmanian waters is the southern bluefin tuna *Thunnus maccoyii*, which occur in large numbers on the eastern seaboard from February to June. Indeed, the history of tuna fishing in Tasmania goes back 100 years, as there is a record of a large 'tunny' having been brought ashore at Triabunna in 1869 weighing 180 kg. In February 1954, an incomplete fish was washed ashore at Cloudy Bay in Bruny Island. From measurements taken of it, C.S.I.R.O. experts estimated it to weigh 385 kg.

For many years bluefin tuna were regarded as a curiosity and were occasionally used as crayfish bait, but no effort was made to exploit them commercially. Then, in 1938, pioneer game fisherman Reg Lynne, having heard tales of large tuna on the east coast, chartered and equipped a boat to operate from St Helens, where he and his party captured several school bluefin to 18 kg, but failed to take a large fish.

At the same time, Bern Cuthbertson, who operated *Weerutta II* from Fortescue Bay on the south-east coast of Tasmania, and his friend Bill Ritchie, decided to catch a large tuna, the presence of which they had observed for some time. They caught several fish over 45 kg on crash lines made from heavy cord with a wire trace, using a bicycle tube as a shock absorber. As there was little demand for tuna, the fishermen indulged their sporting instincts against the large fish and proved them to be present in large numbers in the Fortescue Bay area. The heaviest was a fish taken by Bill Ritchie in 1953, which weighed 100 kg. But it was not until 1951 that the late Dr George Robbie and some friends in his vessel *Sea Flyer* decided to catch bluefin with rod and reel.

In the following three years their captures were so impressive that mainland game anglers became interested and following a visit from Tom Bell, then President of the Game Fishing Association of Australia, the Tasmanian Game Fishing Association was formed. The first fish fell to the rod of its secretary, Ian Cutler, in June 1956. It weighed 70 kg.

The 1957 season saw some serious angling as prominent game fishermen descended on Tasmania to test the field. One of the first to visit the new ground was George C. Thomas III, of California, a former captain of the United States Tuna Cup team. Thomas was fishing with George Miedecke, the local Club President, when a double strike occurred. Miedecke boated his fish first, to be followed a quarter of an hour later by Thomas' bluefin. Both were using 35 kg lines and when the fish were weighed the first turned the scales at 68 kg and the second at 75 kg. Thus the Australian 35 kg line class record was broken twice in 15 minutes.

Eighteen days later, Tom Mitchell raised the 20 kg line class record with a fish of 63 kg and four days later A. W. Stewart raised Thomas' record with a fish of 86 kg. The following day Ian Cutler lifted the 35 kg record with a fish of 96 kg. At the end of May, Tom Bell and Ian Cutler, fishing from Bob Young's boat *Niree*, had a momentous week during which they captured 21 fish over 45 kg, including an Australian record at 96 kg. Tom Bell had the distinction of taking six of these fish in three hours while fishing alone at Cape Pillar.

The 1958 season commenced with bad weather conditions which persisted throughout. The first large fish went to Dolly Dyer which, at 67 kg on 20 kg gear, set the line class record for both men and women. The following day when he boated a 71 kg specimen the men's record was lifted by her husband Bob.

The Dyers' example in the use of lighter tackle was followed by N. Oliver and Tom Mitchell, each of whom took a 72 kg bluefin a fortnight later on 20 kg lines. Tom Mitchell raised this mark to 83 kg on the same gear the day after his 72 kg capture. The season closed a fortnight later with the 20 kg Australian record in the hands of George Miedeke with a magnificent fish of 90 kg.

These were exciting days, when in two seasons 10 Australian records were created. The recollection of the 1869 180 kg fish from Triabunna, together with the estimated 385 kg specimen from Cloudy Bay, made all anglers wonder what 1959 held in store. But records had fallen at too fast a rate to continue forever and 1959 saw only one record broken. This was the meritorious capture by Ian Cutler of a 78 kg (172 lb) bluefin tuna on 15 kg line, which stood for many years as the world record bluefin capture for that line class. The line tested at 12.6 kg.

In 1960, there was another outstanding catch, when Bill Stewart, of Victoria, took a bluefin of 110 kg on a 20 kg line and established an all tackle Australian record for a bluefin until George Park lifted it with a fish of different species, *Thunnus orientalis*, weighing 282.59 kg on a 60 kg line at The Peak in 1965, thus relegating Bill Stewart's fish to the present 20 kg line class Australian record. Like Dolly Dyer's women's 20 kg line national record of 79 kg set on a return visit in 1963, these catches set high standards.

With the then common use of heavy tackle, short fights went with multiple captures. These often occurred within a narrow locality, which strongly suggested that the large fish, like their smaller counterparts, travelled in schools, a habit that could be exploited if no time was lost in bringing the fish to gaff. In only one instance where lighter gear was used (Cutler 7/5/1959), were two large fish taken by one angler in one day.

From the early days, a convention was established for the angler who caught a '45 kg plus' fish to present a bottle of whisky to his skipper and as the fish became scarcer and the angler more delighted, one bottle per 45 kg was donated. As a result bluefin caught in Tasmania are referred to as bottle fish. Every year several two-bottlers are landed. Three-bottlers, between 135 and 180 kg, have been hooked and lost and at least one eight-bottler has been sighted.

While the spectacular part of Tasmania's fishing began and continued with the capture of these big bluefin, they were not the only tuna taken, for interspersed with the 50 to 100 kg, fish from 15 to 25 kg were taken in far greater quantity. As heavy tackle was the rule when big fish were present, the smaller ones presented no problem to bring to gaff and therefore deserved little mention as an angling feat.

Migratory habits of tuna

Tasmanian game fishing depends on the fact that the bluefin stick to their established pattern of movement each year. They are thought to breed in the Indian Ocean, south-west of Sumatra, where they begin a migration which takes them round the western tip of Western Australia, across the Great Australian Bight to the waters south of Port Lincoln in South Australia, then round the southern tip of Tasmania, up the east coast, across eastern Bass Strait and up the coast of New South Wales to the vicinity of Eden.

At Eden, commercial pole fishing begins in September and October and continues on until December, when the fish migrate southwards and reverse the migration to the Port Lincoln area, where pole fishing begins shortly after it stops at Eden. It has been established that the fish pass through Bass Strait but it is this stream of fish which provides game fishermen in Tasmania with most of their sport.

The Tasmanian season begins in the Fortescue Bay area usually in February and continues to the end of June, when the fish rapidly diminish in numbers. Big fish apparently do not follow the same migratory habits as smaller fish, but appear to be the fringe of a migratory pattern from the Tasman and Southern oceans, superimposing themselves on the smaller fish in a well-defined season beginning at about the first week in April and ending at the end of May.

Since June 1963 an increasing number of Japanese longliners have called at Hobart. These vessels have fished the south-eastern Tasman and Southern oceans for big tuna, at first with considerable success, but lately in increasing numbers for diminishing returns. Since the longliners first appeared on the scene, the numbers of big tuna taken by game fishermen have shown a marked decrease. Thus it appears that bluefin from 25 kg plus to 100 kg plus migrate to the open ocean and that fish from 50 to 100 kg plus reappear on the Tasmanian south-east coast. But fish from 25 to 50 kg are now extremely rare in local waters and their path of movement intrigues as well as puzzles anglers.

Much of the Tasmanian coast is seldom fished. Gamefishing activities are extending up the east coast, but the south-west and west coasts have not been touched, although they are known to contain bluefin. They are inhospitable areas for gamefishing vessels, as they are in the path of the Roaring Forties and shelter is widely spaced, yet these waters undoubtedly will present a challenge in the years to come.

Tuna hotspots
To date more fish have been taken in the area from Pirates' Bay to Tasman Island and bounded by the Hippolite Rocks to seaward, than at any other part of the east coast, though the areas adjacent to Maria and Schouten Islands have been proved to contain good fish. The southern area is one of great beauty, with perpendicular dolomite cliffs rising for hundreds of feet from the water's edge and there is shelter from all weather except a hard easterly in Fortescue Bay.

Pirates' Bay, the usual point of departure and return, is an all-weather port for small ships, as is historical Port Arthur, further southwards. Pirates' Bay is a little over an hour's drive from Hobart on a well-laid bitumen road. The area is sheltered from the prevailing winds which swing from N.W. to S.W., but occasional blows from the N.E. to S.E. make gamefishing a proposition for only the stoutest of enthusiasts. Happily, such weather is infrequent and very few days are lost to the angler by bad weather.

While southern bluefin are taken in greatest numbers, other species of tuna provide variation during the season. In February and March, a number of albacore are taken and in March and April striped tuna appear in reasonable numbers. Occasionally, a rare slender tuna also known as Falla's tuna, *Allothunnus fallai*, is taken. Few are captured outside Tasmanian waters. Slender tuna grow to 1 m and 14 kg.

As tuna predominate, the lures used usually are artificial ones, with the 50 and 70 g red and white featherjig predominating. Large tuna will strike on natural baits, but the waters are full of barracouta, which chop them to pieces and have discouraged the use of this method. This is unfortunate, as the almost total use of artificial lures strictly limits a thorough assay of the waters fished.

Sharks are constantly being taken around Tasmania by commercial fishermen, including some large whites, but not many are taken by game fishermen. The best catches to date were a 21.5 kg blue shark on 2 kg line by Allen Ziebel in January 1984 at Yellow Bluff, and a 22.5 kg mako shark on an 8 kg line by Joy Rowler in May 1983 at Pirates' Bay, both Australian records.

Over the last few years, a small number of yellowtail kingfish have been taken in the vicinity of Schouten Island, again on an artificial lure.

For decades high hopes have been held that marlin would be taken on the Tasmanian east coast. Numerous authenticated billfish sightings have been made over the years, all of them with the exception of a 540 kg black marlin washed ashore dead on the north-west coast in 1961 identified, mistakenly then, as broadbill swordfish. In 1972, a partly incapacitated blue marlin was caught in Storm Bay and was estimated to weigh 550 kg.

One broadbill was observed in a fight with a mako shark south of Tasman Island in 1958 and identified from photographs by Colonel Howard, of Miami. Another was observed in a fight with a mako in Munro Bight in 1961 and was taken headless aboard a gamefishing vessel. In both instances, the broadbill was killed by the mako.

A small broadbill was taken by a shore fisherman at Four Mile Creek, near Falmouth on the east coast, in April 1966 and another was taken by commercial fishermen wide of Bicheno in June 1967. This fish, presented to the Tuna Club by its captors, weighed 100 kg. Tuna Club member, Tom Jenkins, made a beautiful fibreglass model of it. A broadbill of 165 kg was taken by commercial fishermen north of Strahan on the west coast at the end of March 1969, the head and bill of which was donated to the Tuna Club.

Numerous other unauthenticated billfish sightings by commercial fishermen were probably broadbill swordfish and as the evidence of broadbill in Tasmanian waters has been more positive than that for any other part of the coast of Australia, local game fishermen hope that one of their number will be the first to place this elusive fish on the Australian record chart.

Tasmania's first marlin

Chances of taking a marlin appeared to be slender in Tasmania, as black and blue marlin like high temperatures and the striped marlin seldom ventures below waters of 21 degrees C. However, on 30 March 1969, the game fishing fraternity was astonished by the capture of a magnificent striped marlin by game fisherman Keith Jessup, from his vessel *Sea Rover II*, wide of Schouten Island. The weight of the fish exceeded the 135 kg capacity of the scales at Coles Bay on the day of its capture and the fish was brought to Hobart four days later, when it weighed 134.7 kg. It is not unlikely that this fish would have been near the Australian all tackle record of 144.5 kg had it been weighed on the day of capture.

The fish was taken on an artificial lure at 10 km/h in water temperatures of 20 degrees C, a high reading for that locality and it seems not unlikely that the east Australian current swung closer to Tasmania in 1969. It was the third marlin Keith had had on in three weeks. The first threw the hook and the second peeled off all the line from a 6/0 Penn. The third was not so lucky and earned the distinction of being the first marlin to be captured by a game fisherman in Tasmanian waters. The only Tasmanian marlin to make the Australian record charts, however, was the superb 154.67 kg striped marlin caught by Toby Lyall in February 1976.

As prospecting progresses northwards, it seems likely that more marlin will be taken. Here the waters east of Flinders Island should, at least theoretically, offer the best potential.

Game fishing in Tasmania developed with and largely because of the charter vessel. Although an increasing number of private vessels fish the waters, the charter vessels still produce the best captures because of the knowledge of their skippers, who are almost without exception, commercial fishermen with long experience of the waters they fish. The vessels are mainly commercial fishing ships, extremely seaworthy, and supply fishing tackle for the angler who does not have his own, usually up to the 37 kg (81.57 lb) line class.

The ready availability of charter vessels operating from Port Arthur and Eaglehawk Neck, Bicheno, St Helens, Pirates' Bay, Triabunna and Coles Bay, enables any angler who wishes to take game fish to do so, be he novice or veteran, club member or occasional angler and no angler's licence is required for game fishing.

It is difficult to compare game fishing in Tasmania with that of any other part of Australia. While Australian line class records for bluefin tuna have been taken in Tasmanian waters, the field has become a predominantly light tackle area, now that the chance of having one's reel denuded of line by a big fish has diminished and the fibreglass rod and monofilament nylon line have made the game less risky than it was in the days of linen thread. It is a great pity that fish in the 22 to 45 kg class do not appear in local waters to give a 5 kg line its ultimate test, but this is a lament on all waters where they fish for bluefin.

After 1960, the activities of the Tasmanian Game Fishing Association declined and in 1961 the Tuna Club of Tasmania was formed, which has its headquarters in Hobart (P.O. Box 507, Sandy Bay). The Tuna Club has been active from that date and ultimately incorporated the Tasmanian Game Fishing Association.

In 1968 the Game Fishing Club of Northern Tasmania was formed. Its headquarters are at 1 Arncliffe Road, Austins Ferry, Tasmania 7011.

The Game Fishing Club of Northern Tasmania will certainly make its contribution to the exploration of waters which the other bodies have been unable to touch and an exciting future is open to it.

The Tuna Club enjoys excellent relations with commercial fishermen, often well beyond its sphere of operations, as it does with Government authorities, and the Tasmanian Government and its appropriate Departments have shown active interest and assistance in the perpetuation of the sport.

GARFISH

Long, slender fish with needle-pointed beaks protruding from their lower jaws, which despite many bones are delicious food fish. There are at least 18 of the garfish family Hemirhamphidae in Australian waters, but only a few of these interest anglers. They are called half-beaks in America, where garfish are the species Australians call long-toms. Garfish are closely related to flying fish (Exocoetidae), long-toms (Belonidae) and billfish (Scomberesocidae).

Introduction of threadline reels, enabling anglers to cast light floats and light baits, created a boom in garfishing. Previously few fishermen had been able to do this with centrepin or baitcasting reels. Garfish provide good sport and are also outstanding bait for other fish. They are widely used as such in trolling, by rock fishermen and by anglers using sidecast reels from the top of cliffs with whole garfish on chained-hook rigs.

Fairly calm water is needed for good garfishing, as garfish like to congregate in shoals in shallow water when the sun is shining, but any winds strong enough to create choppy waves will send the shoals into deep water. The ideal spot is where the sun shines on *Zostera* (eel-grass) beds. The fish feed freely in this weed. Berley is used frequently when garfishing, usually bread crumbs, bran or pollard, and water sweeps this away.

Most worms and crustaceans found in the stomachs of garfish possibly got there by accident because the garfish is primarily an eater of weed and algae. It has been noticed that in some areas the garfish will feed either on eel-grass or seaweeds, but rarely the two together. The assumption is that the algae is eaten at low tide, the eel-grass at high tide. In some areas, Westernport Bay in Victoria, for example, large quantities of 'cropped' eel-grass being washed ashore is a good sign that large numbers of garfish are in the bay.

Garfish are difficult to see in shallow water and it is possible for an inexperienced angler to walk within a few metres of a shoal and not see it. The experienced angler will quietly watch for an occasional flash of silver as a fish turns, or he will pick a dark object on the sea bed and concentrate on it to see if anything moves across it.

Black-barred garfish

Hemirhamphus commersoni: A northern species with an extremely long lower jaw, which Grant describes as a beautiful fish. It is easily recognizable by the four to nine large vertical black blotches on its sides. It is bluish-green on top and silvery along the belly, with a vivid silver lateral band.

They grow to 50 cm and although they are occasionally caught on the New South Wales north coast are more abundant in north Queensland. They are robust fish which offer good sport and have the highly edible qualities common in garfish.

Queenslanders frequently use the smaller specimens for bait when trolling for Spanish mackerel.

Black-barred garfish

River garfish

Hemirhamphus ardelio: Found in all Australian waters except those of Tasmania, a long-beaked gar particularly common in south Queensland and New South Wales, where it feeds among beds of eel-grass *Zostera* in rivers, estuaries and lakes. Also known in Queensland as the splinter gar and needle gar. River garfish are more accessible to anglers than sea garfish and thus are more popular quarry. They can be caught all the year round but like the sea garfish prefer quiet water unruffled by boisterous winds.

River garfish grow to 35 cm and are pale green above, with narrow dark streaks running along the back. There is a faint

G ■ GARFISH

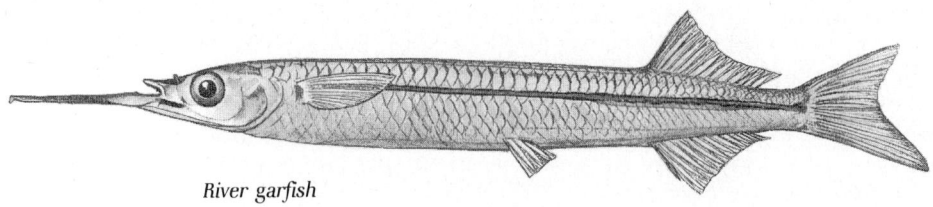

River garfish

black spot at the base of the pectoral fin. The upper part of the head is slightly darker than the rest, with golden reflections. They slowly swim close to the surface and will bite freely on any of the baits recommended for sea garfish, but maggots, sandworms, small pieces of prawn or small balls of dough rolled in cotton wool are the most popular baits.

Commercial fishermen take river garfish in seine nets known as beakie or garfish nets. Anglers mostly fish for them from boats, when the tide is rising, seeking them out in weedy flats. Best months for them in Australia are April and May. In New Zealand, where they are widely distributed from south to north, they are often known as pipers or by the Maori name, takeke. Moving in shoals they are a particular favourite of bigger pelagics such as kahawai.

The species found in Victoria, South Australia and Western Australia, *H. regularis ardelio* and *H. regularis regularis*, are close relatives. The long-jawed garfish or Georgii garfish *Rhynchorhamphus georgii*, common in Queensland tropical waters, also has a close resemblance to the river garfish, but the beak of the lower jaw is far longer, usually around one-third of the length of the fish.

Sea garfish *Hemirhamphus australis:* An oceanic species found in all States including Tasmania. It will enter estuaries but seldom penetrates far from the mouth. It is much lighter in colour than the river garfish, is longer and of more slender build, growing to 45 cm and 225 to 335 g. Its scales fall off like soap flakes when the fish is handled.

Sea garfish are bright green on the back, with three narrow dark-brown streaks and a silvery lateral band. The lower jaw has a long, spear-like projection and the teeth are very small and closely arranged throughout the jaw. The triangular upper jaw is longer than it is broad, which distinguishes it from the river garfish.

They are not found in north Queensland and those caught in coastal and ocean waters of south Queensland are apparently stragglers from New South Wales. In Victoria and South Australian waters most of the big garfish are taken at night from piers, but good catches can also be made by day. They are outstanding tailor bait and much used as whole baits when trolling for large pelagics.

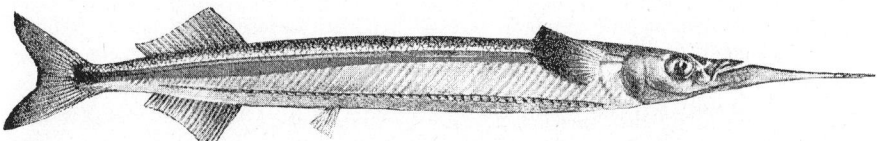

Sea garfish

Short-nosed garfish

Hemirhamphus quoyi: A north Western Australian and Queensland species similar to the snub-nosed garfish, but distinguished by a lower jaw that forms a beak, as long as its head, and by a striking silver band which runs right along its body and has a blue-black line above it. Along with the snub-nosed garfish it is common in Moreton Bay and the Brisbane River, where both species penetrate a long way upstream. It is an especially flavoursome fish with firm white flesh and sells quickly in the Brisbane markets, reaching 35 cm in length.

Snub-nosed garfish

Arrhamphus sclerolepis: A heavy bodied, short beaked species found along the north coast of New South Wales, the entire Queensland east coast and the north-west of Western Australia, penetrating deep into rivers and estuaries and into brackish and fresh water. Queenslanders berley shoals of them into the fishing area by dangling big chunks of bread enclosed in fine mesh netting.

Snub-nosed gars grow to around 40 cm and provide excellent sport for northern anglers, who sometimes call it the snubbie or short bill. It is particularly partial to bacon fat. It is sea green above and silvery below, frequently splashed with pink. Three black lines run from the dorsal fin to the head. The flesh is firm and white and delicately flavoured.

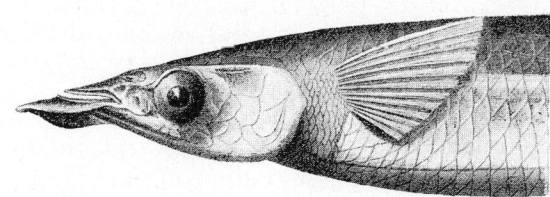

Snub-nosed garfish

Welsby's garfish or three by two

Hemirhamphus welsbyi: A flat-sided species well known to Queenslanders and prominent in that State's fish shops. It has an outstanding reputation as a table fish and because of the ease with which it fillets is highly popular among professionals. There is a prominent silvery lateral band narrowing at each end of its body and a conspicuous black blotch just below the dorsal fin on each side of the body. They grow to 42 cm, but anything over 25 cm is a first-rate specimen.

G ■ GOANNAFISH

Garfishing tackle and techniques

The best rod for boat fishing for garfish is a light fibreglass or cane rod of about 2 m. With this is used a threadline reel, or if the angler prefers, a 7.5 cm centre-pin or a 7.5 to 10 cm sidecast reel. Seventy metres of 3 kg nylon are sufficient, but as the threadline reel must be filled to within 3 mm of the edge of the spool a longer length of line, or backing, must be used for this type of reel.

Floats used for garfish must be light and all one needs is a porcupine quill that will buoy up the baited hooks and a single split shot. Long casting is seldom necessary in boat fishing for garfish and so a large float to buoy up a fairly large sinker is unnecessary. Some anglers prefer to use only two No. 8 or 10 hooks, each being placed on a leader a different length from the other. Twelve centimetres and 20 cm is a good combination when the fish are feeding near the surface.

The standard practice is to use a 90 to 120 cm leader when the garfish are feeding at or near the surface. On this 2 kg nylon leader three hooks are attached by 7.5 cm snoods; a single split shot at the end of the leader keeps it from tangling when cast.

When garfish are feeding below the surface a 2 m leader with three No. 10 hooks attached to 12.5 cm snoods is used. Two split shots may be used on this longer bottom, one at the extreme end and one halfway along the leader. Sea garfish will take a variety of baits including dough, maggots, kelp maggots, marine worms, prawn, tripe, bacon rind and boiled mutton flap. It should be kept in mind, however, that the fish's mouth is very small and only a piece of most baits is used, a piece a little smaller than a pea. It is wise not to strike too soon or too hard but to let the fish slide the float along a few centimetres and then to gently but firmly lift the rod tip. This applies particularly at night, when some of the best garfishing is to be found, because at night the tendency is to strike too hard and to tear the hook through the fish's delicate mouth. As with whiting fishing at night, a light-coloured bait is best for catching garfish. Tripe is a good night bait.

As a table fish the garfish ranks high. The flesh is white, flaky, tender and has a delicate flavour. Garfish can be fried, baked or boiled and are an ideal cold dish. Those anglers who do not like the bones should first roll the fish in flour and cook it well and then the whole backbone and finer bones can be removed in one piece. One end of the backbone is held firmly and the flesh carefully separated, first from one side of it, then the other.

GOANNAFISH *Halosaurus pectoralis:* A very rare and unique deep sea fish found in the Great Australian Bight. They grow to 60 cm, have no spines in front of the dorsal or anal fins and because of the shape of their heads and their slender bodies have attracted

Goannafish

the bemused attention of ichthyologists from McCulloch to Whitley. The depth at which they occur has been placed at between 650 to 800 m. No other fish have the same disposition of fins or the same shape of head.

GOATFISH

A group of vividly coloured marine fish with barbels on the lower jaws that resemble the beards of goats. They are sometimes caught by anglers in inshore waters, in bays and near reefs. They are found in all Australian States, but are most plentiful in the tropics and are also known as red mullet. They are excellent eating. Goatfish use their barbels to detect food, usually crustaceans. They are fish of warm seas and apart from the barbels are similar in outline to whiting.

Yellow goatfish

Upeneus sulphureus: Also known in northern Queensland as sunrise goatfish because of their bright colouring. Two prominent yellow lines run right along the body and the dorsal fin is barred in yellow. The body colour is bright pink on top and a lighter salmon-pink beneath. They grow to 18 cm. The tail is often red.

Mottled goatfish

Upeneus tragula: Grows to around 45 cm and is brown or yellow in body colouring, with brown mottling. There is a dark bar extending right along the body and the caudal fin carries darkish bands.

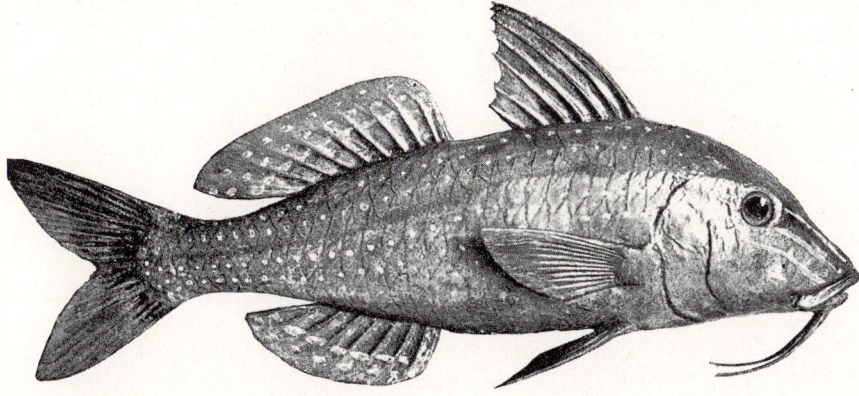

New Zealand red mullet

G ■ GOBBLEGUTS

New Zealand red mullet *Upeneichthys porosus:* A goatfish found around south-eastern Australia, identified from other species by their reddish colour and steep head profile. There is a clear separation or cleft in the dorsal fin. This species grows to 45 cm and is common in rocky areas. They are prized food fish.

GOBBLEGUTS Tastelessly named fish of the family Apogonidae, more politely but less commonly known as cardinal fish, big eyes or soldier fish. They are represented in Australia by many species, all of them small, carnivorous, large-scaled, big-eyed and with large, gaping mouths. They are fish of contrasting habits, some preferring to school, others moving about alone, some inhabiting reefs, others living in holes in sponges. They need that big mouth, for as Whitley and other experts have pointed out, the male carries the eggs in his mouth until they hatch, often incubating as many as 150 eggs.

Southern gobbleguts *Vincentiana novaehollandiae:* Found in New South Wales, Victoria, Tasmania and South Australia. Bright red in colour, with black blotches or spots across the head and upper body. They grow to 12.5 cm and inhabit rocky, shallow water.

Big-eyed cardinal fish *Epigonus lenimen:* A deepwater species of southern Australia with an enormous blue eye far out of proportion to its body. They have slender bodies, reaching 20 cm in length, and like others of the same family two dorsal fins.

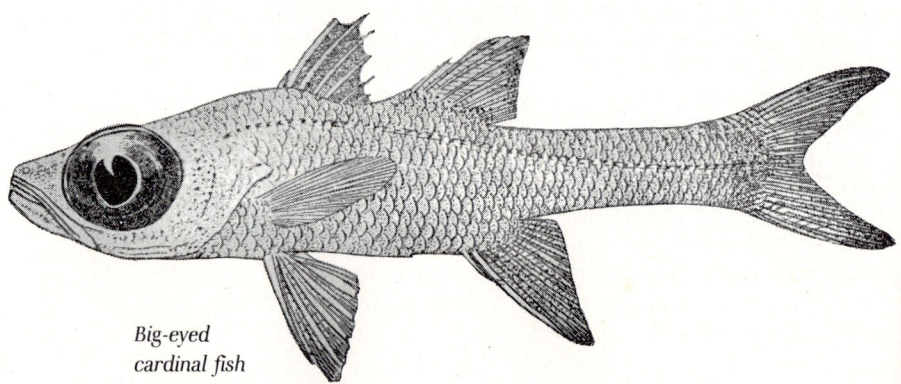

Big-eyed cardinal fish

Wood's siphon-fish *Siphamia cephalotes:* A coastal and estuarine gobbleguts found in all States except Queensland. This one grows to only 5 cm and is silvery in colour and speckled with black dots. Occurs in shallow water near seagrass beds.

GOBLINFISH Ugly marine fish of the family Scorpaenidae, a few of which are found in Australian waters, one of them in numbers. They are also known as saddlefish because of the shape of their heads.

Goblinfish

The family consists of fish with rough, ill-shaped heads and strong extended dorsal spines which often carry venom. The northern Australian stonefish is one of the family. They have small mouths, tiny teeth and large eyes which dominate their heads and they grow to around 22 cm. They are found in New South Wales, Victoria, Tasmania, South Australia and Western Australia as well as in northern waters, often in shallow water close to reefs where they apparently lie around for hours at a time waiting for food to turn up.

GOBY

A bewildering variety of tiny fishes mostly found in coastal waters. A few venture into fresh water. Gobies average between 15 and 30 mm when mature. There are 1800 species of goby in the world, and Australia has 400 of them. Gobies are sometimes found in shallow water attached to rocks by their ventral fins. They are mostly dullish brown to grey in colour, according to Whitley, with mottling that harmonises with sand and mud, but some have ornate markings. One is transparent and almost invisible. Most are slimy and scaleless and several species are taken in nets with prawns. They are similar to the related gudgeon. Tasmania alone has 14 species, including the abundant Tamar goby *Favonigobius tamarensis*, which flourishes in both salt and fresh water.

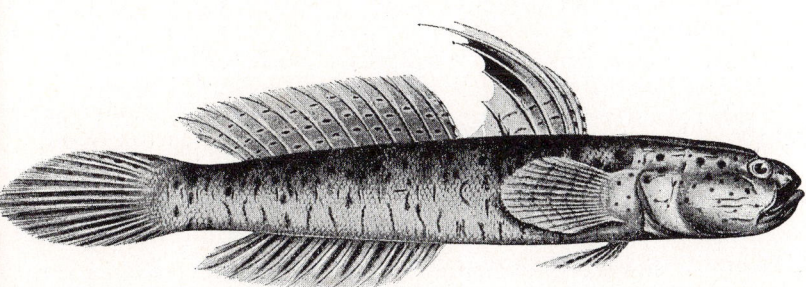

Crested goby

GOLDEN perch

Macquaria ambigua: A particularly handsome freshwater fish that is winning growing acceptance as a top-class sportfish. It is now widely fished for in eastern Australia by anglers using a variety of baits, including freshwater and saltwater mussels, shrimps, prawns, worms and yabbies on a rod or handline, and over the past decade has won respect as a dogged, vigorous opponent.

The colour varies from olive green, dark grey to silvery on the back and golden, cream or yellowish-white below. Purple or reddish tints on the head are common, with occasional reddening of fins before and after capture; the fins are yellow, sometimes with white margins on the median fins. Smaller specimens commonly have a spotted, brown or intense golden colour.

Older specimens have a conspicuous lower jaw, noticeable open pores on the lower jaw and a deep concavity between the nose and the shoulder. The caudal fin is distinctly rounded. The body is strong, deep and muscular in appearance. A strong, pointed anal spine and razor-sharp gill covers can inflict painful but not necessarily dangerous wounds on unwary handlers.

The generally accepted name among commercial fishermen and sporting anglers is golden perch, but yellowbelly is still in common usage in western New South Wales, Queensland and South Australia. They are also known as callop, Murray perch, white perch and freshwater bream.

Confusion with other species

Golden perch are sometimes confused with silver perch, Murray cod and Macquarie perch, with which they may co-exist naturally, and to a lesser extent with bass and estuary perch, with which they sometimes co-exist as a result of stocking, such as in the Clarence–Nymboida River system in New South Wales.

Silver perch are greyer in appearance, with smaller scales, a smaller mouth and a convex (slightly forked) caudal fin. Macquarie perch are darker, blacker or greyer in appearance, and have larger scales, prominent pores near the upper jaw, a distinctly rounded upper jaw, a larger eye with a distinct white margin, no protruding lower jaw and a less concave caudal fin.

Murray cod have a more cylindrical body and a softer belly. They are distinctly spotted or mottled, green above and cream below, and have distinct white margins to the fins which may fade soon after capture, large eyes and a large mouth. When viewed briefly in the water, however, during pursuit of a lure or bait, golden perch and Murray cod may show a remarkable similarity in colour, shape, general behaviour and particularly swimming and striking action.

Bass and estuary perch can be distinguished by their larger eyes, more silvery appearance, a convex caudal fin, a larger mouth and a less protruding lower jaw. They do not fight as strongly when hooked.

Distribution

Golden perch are distributed throughout the Murray–Darling, Bulloo–Bancannia and Lake Eyre drainage systems. Their northern limit is the Georgina River, almost half-way between Lake Eyre and the Gulf of Carpentaria. There are natural populations in a number of coastal streams, including the Fitzroy near Rockhampton in Queensland. Populations in other coastal rivers such as the Clarence–Nymboida are of more obscure origin as the species has become widely distributed throughout New South Wales, Victoria, Queensland and the A.C.T. as a result of deliberate introductions. They were even introduced to Western Australia for brief periods, as well as to the far north of Queensland and to the Northern Territory.

Golden perch may grow to a large size. Numerous fish taken from Queensland, New South Wales, Victoria and South Australia have exceeded 10 kg in weight and a 19 kg fish was taken from the lower Murrumbidgee River near Wagga. In 1938 a fisherman in Kow Swamp, Victoria, was reputed to have taken one which weighed 23.5 kg when cleaned. In the higher reaches of the Murrumbidgee River above Burrinjuck Reservoir several fish exceeding 8 kg were taken during 1980–82 and in stocked lakes and farm dams throughout eastern and southern Australia there are consistent records of fish in the 7 to 9 kg class. The maximum recorded length is 76 cm.

Growth varies depending on environmental conditions but is particularly influenced by temperature and food availability. In South Australia fish reached 16 cm in their first year, 37 cm in three years and 59 cm in nine years. In the colder but food-rich waters of Lake Burley Griffin, A.C.T. fish reached 35 cm in two years and weighed up to 1 kg. At four years of age they commonly weighed 2.5 to 3.5 kg.

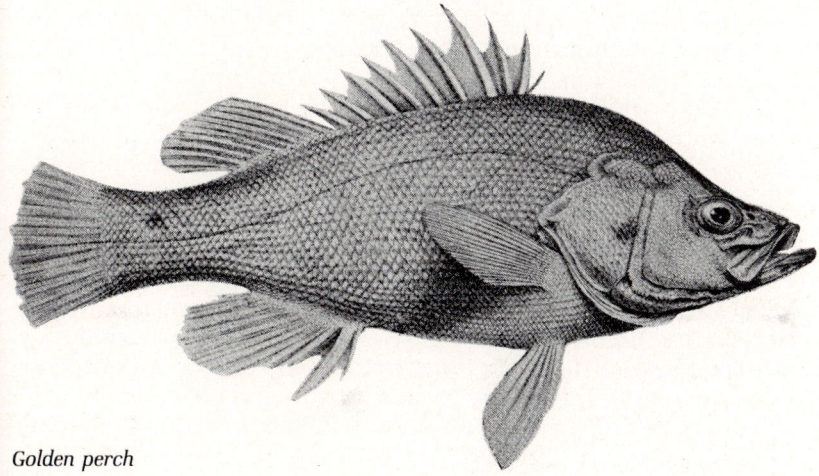

Golden perch

G ■ GOLDEN perch

A healthy golden perch, one of the dominant native fish in waters west of the Great Dividing Range.

Migratory habits

Golden perch are renowned for their capacity to undertake remarkable long-distance migrations. A 1.1 kg fish tagged and released below Euston on the Murray River was recovered 10 months later from the Murrumbidgee River near Leeton; it then weighed 2.1 kg and had travelled a possible 350 km. Another tagged and released in the Murray River in South Australia was recovered 2000 km upstream in Queensland in a tributary of the Darling River.

In New South Wales, fish in Burrinjuck Reservoir migrate each spring and summer up the Murrumbidgee River, through the A.C.T. to what is probably the upstream limit known for the species, between Canberra and Cooma. They return to the Reservoir in autumn. Large-scale upstream migrations and temporary gatherings at obstructions to their passage have been observed at numerous other locations. One of the more famous is a weir near Manilla on the Namoi River. Large numbers of fish migrating upstream gather temporarily at a low rock wall where they have to negotiate a small slot in the rock before proceeding. They are easy prey for anglers under such conditions.

The general tendency for the species is to migrate upstream wherever possible and this simple device helps to ensure adequate dispersal of the fish throughout the habitat range.

Less is known of the downstream movement but the return of fish to Burrinjuck Reservoir during autumn is presumably a response to lowered water temperatures and declining food supplies in the Murrumbidgee River upstream. Large numbers of golden perch have been observed moving downstream from Googong Reservoir on the Queanbeyan River and Lake Burley Griffin on the Molonglo River, particularly during autumn. The movement is apparently triggered by release of water through small gates set low in the dam wall in Lake Burley Griffin, or by overtopping of the wall in the case of Googong. In each instance some fish are killed by the fall or as a result of contact with concrete obstructions in the fast-flowing waters, but the majority appear to be unscathed.

Breeding and stocking programmes

Spawning in golden perch normally occurs at night and the fish commonly gather in pairs or small groups beforehand. It takes place during spring and summer and probably only when water temperatures exceed 23°C. Fish are thought to mature at between three and four years of age, possibly four to five years in colder waters, and females can hold eggs in a semi-advanced state for prolonged periods before rising water temperatures and possibly flooding stimulus triggers sudden maturation and release for fertilization. Resorption of eggs may occur if conditions are not suitable for spawning. A female may produce up to 650,000 eggs.

The eggs are 1.1 mm in diameter, spherical and amber in colour. They are buoyant and thus float downstream after fertilization, adding to the distribution of the species already partly achieved by migration of adults. The eggs hatch within 24 to 33 hours.

The larvae feed mainly on zooplankton. Older fish rapidly switch to crustaceans such as shrimps and yabbies, molluscs, insect larvae including mudeyes, and small fish including *Gambusia*, goldfish, Australian smelt, western carp gudgeon and European carp. While it is difficult to distinguish between males and females for much of the year, immediately prior to spawning the females are easily recognizable because of their heavily distended stomachs.

Golden perch will not breed in farm dams and other impoundments unless water levels and temperatures are accidentally or purposefully regulated. However, spawning can be induced artificially by injection of a pituitary extract from European carp or a synthetic hormone, notably one known commonly as gonadotrophin. The use of gonadotrophin is now commonplace in commercial private and government hatcheries and was even used successfully during 1984–85 by an amateur angling group at Bingara in northern New South Wales.

Fingerlings produced in commercial hatcheries are now widely used for stocking farm dams and larger impoundments and some streams throughout eastern and southern Australia. Golden perch fingerlings can be transported long distances with few problems and thus are well suited to use in stocking programmes; they are equally useful as an aquarium species, but eventually outgrow most tanks.

In tanks they rapidly become adjusted to their environment and readily take food such as yabbies, shrimps, *Gambusia*, goldfish, European carp, trout fingerlings, mudeyes and worms. They quickly show strong recognition of any individual who feeds them on a regular basis and will approach

G ■ GOLDEN perch

the surface to take hand-held food. In the A.C.T. tank-maintained fish show strong activity all through the summer but become torpid and largely inactive during winter.

Commercial usage Golden perch are grown for commercial sale as fingerlings in private and government hatcheries in Victoria, New South Wales and Queensland and the species is now Australia's most prolific and successful farm fish. Adults are taken commercially from specified rivers and lakes by the use of drum nets and gill nets and are a popular table fish. The flesh is white, firm and exceedingly palatable.

Prior to cooking it is essential to remove excess fat from the flesh, particularly along the back line and adjacent to the stomach. If it is not removed, it will contaminate the flesh during cooking, producing an undesirable 'earthy' or 'muddy' taste which has unfortunately given many freshwater fish in Australia an undeservedly poor reputation as table fish. Residual earthy tastes in the flesh can be removed simply by soaking the fillets in white or red wine for a few minutes or by a liberal sprinkling of lemon juice. Golden perch can be kept for long periods in the freezer, and is excellent for mornays, barbecues, smoking, grilling or frying, and sweet-and-sour dishes. Bones are easily removed, an advantage for small children.

Feeding behaviour

Several distinct patterns of feeding behaviour have been noted. In the first, fish remain in or near cover such as rocks, logs, stumps, shaded areas and overhanging trees and shrubs and move out quickly to take passing prey. This is common during warm weather and when light intensities are high.

In other instances the fish feed along sandbanks, weedbeds, rock and pebble areas, sometimes in or immediately below rapids, on prey which is already exposed or which they frighten into the open. Occasionally they will burrow into crevices and weedbeds in search of specific items. This behaviour is common during dull, overcast weather when light intensities are low, particularly during the late afternoon feeding period.

The fish feed actively at night. On rare occasions they have been observed during daylight, on the Murrumbidgee River, rising to take live grasshoppers from the surface.

In aquarium tanks the feeding behaviour is interesting. The fish swallow yabbies with a strong sucking motion from several centimetres away. The yabbie may be swallowed either head or tail first, but if taken head first it is commonly reversed in the gullet before being swallowed. Sometimes, especially with large yabbie, the prey is partially disgorged soon after ingestion and banged against a rock to kill the animal. It is then re-swallowed. Both claws are commonly spat out forcibly soon after final ingestion.

Golden perch take a wide variety of lures and flies. This one was caught on a lure in the Murrumbidgee River near Canberra.

G ■ GOLDEN perch

Environmental problems

Golden perch are well distributed throughout the warmer and more sluggish streams of inland Australia and appear well-adapted to the extreme fluctuations in temperature and flow conditions in these streams. Their adaptability is demonstrated by their capacity to survive and grow in such diverse locations as farm dams in all States and Territories, reservoirs and lakes of various types and temperature regimes varying from Menindee Lakes in far western New South Wales to the relatively cold waters of the Googong Reservoir on the Queanbeyan River. Whilst in many of these waters they represent only a stocked population with nil or limited capacity to breed, they are more tolerant of lower temperatures and flowing water than was previously realised. This should result in a significant re-evaluation of their potential for use in waters previously regarded as suitable only for introduced species such as trout, redfin perch and Atlantic salmon.

The main cause of decline in the natural range of the species since European settlement of Australia is environmental change associated with the construction of weirs, reservoirs and locks on the major river systems. These impede the natural migration of the fish and in some instances increase their vulnerability to fishermen and other predators. In addition, the regulation of rivers to reduce the incidence and intensity of flooding, and the lower temperature of water released from impoundments limit the capacity of the fish to breed and the survival of young.

Three protozoans, two flatworms and various nematodes, of unknown disease or parasitic significance, have been recovered from golden perch. *Lernaea cyprinacea*, commonly known as anchor worm, is a common parasite, especially under warm conditions.

Sudden fish kills have been noted in several locations. A large-scale kill of two- to three-year-old golden perch in Lake Burley Griffin in the late 1970s was tentatively ascribed to an overly sudden drop in water temperature to approximately 4°C. Minor fish kills of unknown cause are commonly seen in Lake Burley Griffin, Lake Ginninderra and Burrinjuck Reservoir in autumn and spring.

Angling technique

Once thought of as a 'touchy' or spasmodic biter, not usually fit for anything more than setline fishing in rivers and lagoons, golden perch have in recent years gained considerable respect amongst anglers who have adopted more appropriate sportfishing techniques such as lighter lines, lures and flies, and a hunter rather than a trapper approach.

Golden perch will take a great variety of lures and flies. Flies are useful only in relatively clear water and usually only in a mixed fishery where the main quarry is trout. Large flies such as Mrs Simpson, hamills killer, craigs nighttime and a variety of similar large flies tied with an array of orange materials have proved to be the most successful. Best results have been during late afternoon and immediately after dark. The take is clean, strong and purposeful and the fish fight vigorously.

The fish also take a great array of lures, particularly the deep-diving models which work at the depths where the fish most commonly feed or rest. Minnow and yabbie-type lures have proved to be extremely successful and there are more than 50 suitable lures on the market. Amongst the more popular are models produced by Shakespeare, Abu, Heddon, Cotton Cordell, Daiwa, Hot n' Tot, Helin, Gudebrod, Burke, Rapala, Rebel, Whopper Stopper, Storm and newly emerging cottage-industry lure makers in Australia.

A wide variety of spoons and spinning-vane type lures including Wonder Spoon, Gibbs spoons, Wonder Wobblers, Voblex and Celta also will take fish, particularly in shallow or flowing water. While it is possible in some areas to take fish all year round, lure fishing is most successful during the warmer months.

BRYAN PRATT

GRAYLING

Prototroctes maraena: Sometimes called 'cucumber herring', apparently because of a fancied resemblance of its odour to that of the fruit. The grayling is a very distant and somewhat diminutive relative of the trout, salmon and other notable Salmonidae but belongs to the family Prototroctidae. The Australian grayling has close relatives in New Zealand, South America and the associated Falkland Islands and is more distantly allied to the European grayling and the Arctic grayling, both of which are larger fish and more spectacular in the angling sense. Grayling are protected in Tasmania and should be regarded as an endangered species throughout their range.

Grayling are freshwater fish of the temperate zones and prefer cold, clear water but, like the trout, some move into the sea in those regions where temperatures are low. The Australian species is a small fish growing to a maximum of about 32 cm or 0.5 kg and appears to be confined to the coastal and mountain streams of southern New South Wales, Victoria and Tasmania. It is a well-rounded fish, with the single dorsal and small adipose fin common to the trout. The ventral fins are well back under the centre of the body, but somewhat further forward than those of the trouts. The head is small, after the style of that of a fat female trout, though the mouth is comparatively tiny, with but little gape. The tail fin is deeply forked.

It has a dark-grey narrow band running along the sides from the gill cover, behind the eye, to the butt of the tail. Above this band on the upper body, it is olive-brown. Below the band it is yellow. There is a dusky band across the middle of the light-blue dorsal fin and the small adipose fin is one of its

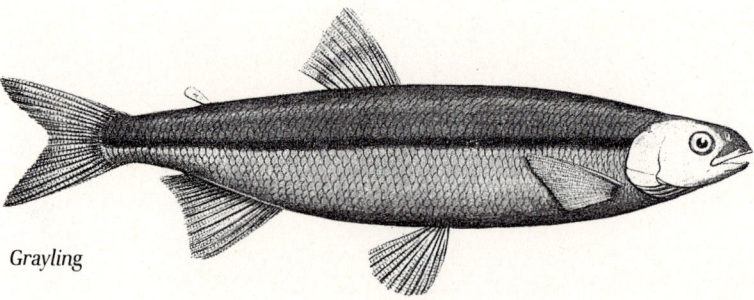

Grayling

distinguishing characteristics, for it is golden yellow edged with a white margin backed by a black band. The eyes are pale bluish-white.

The grayling is scarce in Australia, where it feeds almost exclusively on insects and is almost impossible to catch on anything other than small flies. Mainland anglers now are finding that it is present in patches at places like the Shoalhaven River, and some are promoting interest in it by taking it on small wet flies and tiny dry flies. It is an excellent sporting fish, leaping freely and waging a very fast and hard fight for its size. It is surprising how much line it can take out against the adjustable drag as it makes away from the angler with its short, sideways wriggles.

Allowing for its size, it is a good food fish, the flesh being firm, white and of a delicate flavour.

GROPER The common name of several species of large saltwater fish, including the giant Queensland groper, which is one of the largest fish in Australian waters, the blue groper, which is really a tusk fish of the wrasse family, the southern (Australian) groper, the New Zealand hapuku and the New Zealand bass groper. In the Persian Gulf, groper have been recorded up to 3.5 m long and well over 450 kg. The Queensland groper grows to 2.2 m and over 280 kg, at which size they are slow and vulnerable.

There is confusion in classifying groper, a fish frequently grouped with rock cod. Because of their size, however, they are highly prized by anglers, all of whom hope one day to catch a big one. All varieties of groper are fish of immense strength and tenacity with the wit to dash for a hole, ledge or crevice when hooked and there defy attempts by anglers to dislodge them.

Southern groper have been slaughtered for years by spearmen, and in New South Wales a ban on the taking of blue, brown or red groper was imposed for all fishermen from the start of 1969. This ban followed recommendations by the Amateur Fishermen's Association Advisory Council, which said sizeable blue, brown or red groper had become extremely rare and should be fully protected. The ban still applies to spearfishing, but groper may be taken with a line.

Queensland groper

Promicrops lanceolatus: Tropical groper achieve great toughness, but are curious fish always interested in taking a look at wrecks and caverns, where they sometimes take up residence. They have frightened many divers and spearmen, but there is no confirmed case of these huge fish deliberately attacking man.

They are considered excellent eating up to 25 kg, but above these weights the flesh becomes coarse and unpalatable. Juveniles are highly attractive fish of a bright golden yellow with darkish cross bars and as they mature the body colour turns a blackish-brown or purple and the tails and fins turn yellow.

These big warm groper are frequently confused with estuary rock cod, another big fish of the same regions also known as spotted river cod and greasy cod. Estuary rock cod grow to 225 kg and 2 m but have a sharper, more angular snout than the rounded shape of the groper's preoperculum. A great deal of this groper's weight is in the head and the mouth of a fully grown specimen is frighteningly large. The largest Queensland groper so far reported weighed 287 kg. Brisbane biologist Ernie Grant handlined and released one of 186 kg in 1967 at Heron Island.

Very old specimens are sometimes sighted in New South Wales when the water is warm, lurking around jetties and rocks but these are mostly slow-swimming fish. Generally their habitat is confined to Western Australia and Queensland. They mostly eat crabs and small fish, but will take eagerly to most baits, especially if they are trolled.

Queensland or northern groper are common in Barrier Reef waters, but are more abundant in the Gulf and in bays and estuaries of the Northern Territory and the north-west coast of Western Australia. They are sometimes seen swimming along the bank of an estuary with the big dorsal fin above the surface. They demand extremely strong tackle, mostly 90 kg nylon or cord tied to a springy mangrove tree, although in a boat lighter gear can be used because it is then possible to follow the big specimens when they are hooked. They have a

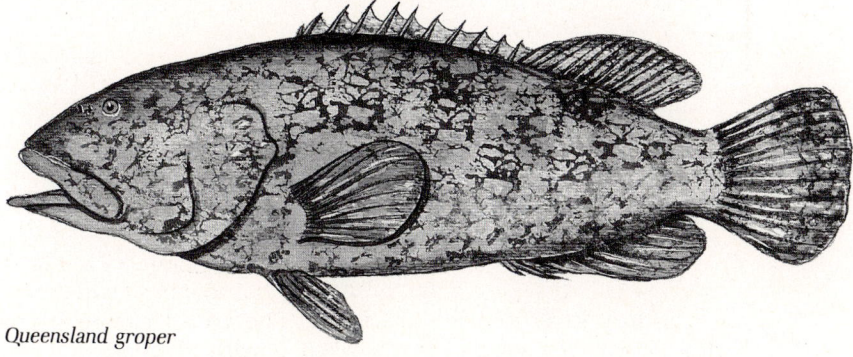

Queensland groper

formidable array of fine teeth which make a strong wire trace standard equipment. As they move in close to the shore and take fairly big baits, sinkers are unnecessary. They eat ravenously when hungry, but prefer salmon heads, ray flaps, sawfish and shark cuts, live catfish and live ray or any live whole fish.

Bass groper *Polyprion moeone:* The Maori name Moeone means 'sleep on the sand' and refers to the habit and habitat of this big fish. It is extremely like a Northern Hemisphere bass and at one time was thought to be a seasonal variant of the hapuku, to which it is related and which it greatly resembles, but it is closer to the bass. It is wider and deeper in the body than hapuku and has larger scales. It is also thought to have larger eyes, but it is difficult to tell for these expand in the process of being brought up from the depths it normally inhabits. The massive head is steel-blue, the body a vibrant blue to black above and an iridescent silver underneath.

This fish is infrequently caught because of the very great depths it inhabits in Tasmanian, New South Wales and New Zealand waters, generally below the 180 m mark. They are usually taken between July and December by commercial fishermen exploiting the commoner hapuku during the time of their annual offshore migration. They are caught on the same baits and with the same methods. Specimens have been weighed at up to 80 kg. The flesh is white and firm, with a delicate taste.

The depths make it difficult to gauge the feeding habits as the swift pressure changes during the reeling-in process cause the fish's stomach to be extruded from the mouth with the bursting of the pressure bladder, causing the loss of the contents. The fish has been identified with *Polyprion americanus*; also with the bass found in deep water off the coasts of Europe from Norway to the Mediterranean and also from the Cape of Good Hope and the Southern Indian Ocean.

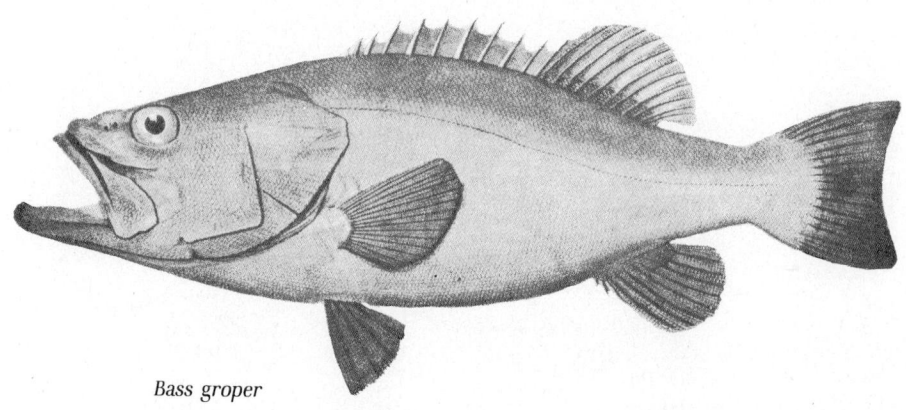

Bass groper

GROPER ■ G

New Zealand groper or hapuku

New Zealand groper (hapuku)

Polyprion oxygeneios: A popular, well-armoured New Zealand fish also taken in deep waters off Tasmania, Victoria, New South Wales, South Australia and Western Australia, a prized food fish, very deep and of large capacity, with big scales, sharp spines and a pointed underslung lower jaw. Its Maori name means 'big belly'; the generic name *Polyprion* is derived from the Greek, means 'many saws' and refers to the saw-like serrations on the head and spines. The specific *oxygeneios* means 'sharp jaws'. The common name 'groper' is a corruption of the Portuguese 'garupa' applied to fish belonging to the family Serranidae. In New Zealand the Maori name hapuku (sometimes distorted to hapuka, whapuka or habuka) is the North Island usage; 'groper' (sometimes grouper or gruper) is more common in the South.

It is light grey in colour as a rule, but the colour deepens according to the location where it is caught—darker colour in a rockier habitat. The head is large and may be nearly a third of the total weight. This splendid fish has been taken in weights of 63 to 67 kg, but it is more realistic to expect about a 6 kg average, the weight having been reduced over years of intensive fishing. Some of the larger fish seem to be more common in waters further south. In some years, from some fishing ports, average weight may have been below 4 kg. Little is known of its early years, as few if any specimens less than 1 kg weight have been caught.

It is caught in all depths to 240 m or more, but the incidence follows a pattern: the fish prefers the shallower waters in summer months and begins to head for the deeper about late April or early May. While it is believed to be a rock-haunting fish and is most easily caught in the vicinity of rock outcrops (particularly when these emerge from level, tide-swept, sandy underwater plains) some smaller specimens have been taken over sand in the otter trawl, especially in company with large schools of red cod *Physiculus bachus*, also known as hoka (Maori: to eat anything). This movement away from the shore anticipates the spawning season of July and August, after which the females especially are spent and in poor condition. As many are scarred on the jaws and the shoulder undersurfaces, it is thought that spawning may involve the trenching of the ocean bottom. The Murray cod of Australian inland waters *Maccullochella macquariensis*, a relative of this groper, follows just this method in establishing egg-beds.

Immediately before spawning the roes and milts may weigh as much as 3 to 4 kg. They are excellent eating, but a luxury from waters where the fish population is diminishing. Roe counts may be as high as several million a kilogram. The hapuku move inshore again in October and November, but they are then in poor condition. Rock fishing is best from about February and when the fish are in good trim almost any bait entices, heads of smaller fish being satisfactory. The angler, however, must be prepared to make a fast change of bait; the groper is a choosy fish and frequently, with no prior notice, all fish may refuse hitherto successful bait.

Baits and techniques for groper
The best bait is octopus or squid; swimming crabs *Nectocarcinus antarcticus* are excellent for rock fishing, and blue cod, when this is available. Groper will bite at slabs of red cod or butterfish; the snook or New Zealand barracouta is a sound standard bait; but groper preferences vary. In winter, in deep water, frozen snook is excellent; at other times they may prefer the fresh fish and, rarely, flesh that is on the turn.

Groper are predatory; they seem to eat anything and some have been caught with birds (of a deep-diving variety) in their stomachs. A favourite food is the crayfish or spiny lobster; sometimes a stomach will be found to contain a large specimen undamaged and groper have been caught from 50 m with the feelers of a large, undamaged lobster still protruding from the jaws. In fact groper swallow most of their food whole; a 50 kg groper can just about close his mouth on a household bucket without denting it; but the jaws are equipped, nevertheless, with rows of cardiform teeth excellently adapted for ripping smaller prey apart. The groper must be vulnerable to sharks; perhaps this is the reason they haunt the bottom rockpiles, but it is not at all uncommon to have a shark rip the body from the head at the surface, and this enjoins caution.

When caught in a significant depth, groper seem to be incapable of adjusting to swiftly changing pressures and almost inevitably the food is regurgitated and the air-bladder broken. The reversed stomach frequently protrudes from the mouth. After the fish is hooked it demonstrates for a short time its characteristic bite; a strong, persistent downward pull repeated at deliberate intervals; but as it is raised towards the surface it acquires its own buoyancy and comes to the top as fast as the fisherman can pull slack line. Professional fishermen using lines stretched from a heavy bottom grapnel will find their hauling work done for them soon after they break out the grapnel prongs. Hooks on such lines are usually a few metres apart or more; this arrangement permits boating fish with ease while others wait on the line. Also long lines are used, with baits on snoozings up to 2.5 m in length and 5 m apart on the line, which may lie along 300 m of bottom or sometimes much more.

School groper follow one another and may follow one another on to the hooks, for which reason a man fishing alone is recommended to use two lines to coddle the biting frenzy along. Even in the deepest water the use of berley has shown results; though it floats away while sinking slowly in a strong current the cruising fish will still trace it to its source when it hits bottom.

The fact that the numbers of large groper have diminished under heavy fishing seems to indicate they are capable of living to a great age.

Since groper is a fish that carries a good deal of fat it is ideal for grilling, baking, frying or steaming. It has an excellent flavour and is suitable for preparations of raw fish such as Tahiti salad. The larger specimens tend to be a little coarse; but even the coarsest are delicious. Perhaps the best cooking method is in the Maori oven (hangi) with fresh greens, preferably the puha or sow-thistle, afterwards eaten with the flesh. This of course is rarely practical but it is worthwhile experimenting with this cooking method.

Queensland gropers can grow to an immense size—the largest so far recorded weighed 287 kg.

As with most fish, the meat is least coarse near the head; the steaks are preferable to the (dearer) cutlets; the latter, from near the tail, are ringed with skin which improves the appearance and aids the cook, but they carry the most muscle and the least fat.

With any decent-sized fish the head itself provides an excellent meal. Two large slabs of flesh may be cut from the cheeks, one from the thorax and one from flesh between the gills at the underpart of the head. Professional fishermen call these the tongues and throats and frequently take them home while they send the body of the fish to market. The rest of the head is armoured but, especially in a fishing camp, the head boiled whole affords excellent pickings as well as a good soup stock.

Groper bodies are furnished with medium bone, of such quality, however, that it presents no difficulty to the diner.

A convention most fishermen have adopted from the Maori is that they prevent the fish from touching the gunwale as they boat it; the belief is that if this happens no more fish will be caught that day. This may have a basis in fact; striking the outer planks of a boat will produce far-carrying vibrations in the water and the average groper has a muscular tail that delivers a hearty slap.

In other superstitions the fish must not touch the anchor or any other iron in the boat, nor, later, should it be cooked in an iron vessel. Another Maori prohibition forbade the carrying of food on the boat or even mentioning the name of any.

For blue and red groper, see Wrasses.

GRUNTER An important group of freshwater terapon perch distributed over tropical and sub-tropical regions of north-western Australia, the Northern Territory, Central Australia, Queensland and New South Wales. They take their name from the peculiar internal noises they make when breathing and it is by this noise rather than by scientific reasoning that they are grouped. They have defied attempts to classify them. Most grunter are perch. They are fish of rare endurance, able to withstand arduous conditions in bore water and in sun-parched areas of the outback.

There are a number of grunter that have been identified by only single specimens, including the Barcoo grunter caught in Cooper Creek, Central Australia and Welch's perch or grunter. Others classified from fish sent to museums from remote regions of the outback include the Norman River grunter and leathery grunter. One grunter, the English wyandotte or yellowtail grunter resembles jungle perch and is found in Queensland, the Northern Territory, New Guinea and Western Australia, where anglers sometimes refer to it as yellowtail.

Grunters most frequently sought after are those of the genus *Hephaestus*, or sooty grunter of which there are at least four species in Australia. They are robust fish with the dorsal spines and rays of about equal length, growing to 28 cm. Clean fighters, they give satisfying rewards to anglers who treat them to a sporting approach by using lines down to 1.5 kg.

Coal or sooty grunter are found in all streams from tropical Western Australia, through the Northern Territory to the central coast of Queensland. Several varieties are known to exist in a single area in the Josephine Creek, north Queensland, and in longer rivers such as the Burdekin and Herbert. Where longer streams rise inland, for example on the Atherton Tableland, grunters are the dominant species well upstream of any incursions by jungle perch, mangrove jack or barramundi. They share their habitat in most cases with eel-tail catfish and eel when inland.

Recently there has been considerable interest in the transportation of this species for fish stocking. Mount Isa Mines retained the fisheries consultant Hamar Midgley to stock Lake Moondarra with grunter, following research by Midgley which proved the feasibility of transportation over long distances. Thousands of the fish were transported 300 km from the Gregory River system and released in the lake with less than 1 per cent mortality, a tribute to the success of the methods pioneered by this remarkable man.

Sooty grunter, lumped together as a species, are an ideal subject for family and light tackle angling. They take a wide variety of baits freely, including worms, insects, pieces of meat and shrimps, fished by conventional methods. The best bait rig appears to be a No. 2 suicide hook fished without a sinker, with the bait being cast and re-cast so that it sinks continually from the surface to the bed of the stream. The technique is not unlike fly fishing. A float can also be used if more casting distance is needed.

Lures are widely used for grunter on the Queensland coast, ranging from Bellbrook floaters to large streamer flies. A comparison of actual results between two experienced anglers, one using flies and the other surface lures, showed the larger lures were more successful by a ratio of 2 to 1. Techniques and tactics are identical to those listed for jungle perch, with which species grunter are in permanent competition.

As fighters, grunters from a good set of rapids are outstanding. Those from lagoons or still water are less active. Where rivers divide to long, deep pools separated by rapids, the lower end of each run provides superior fishing. Grunter will be found in the deeper pools but will not strike so freely as those in flowing water.

Some fascinating grunter fishing can be had when streams are high. Grunters appear to breed during wet seasons and can afterwards be seen trying to scale small waterfalls or moving up shallow rapids. Under these conditions they will still take baits or lures freely. One odd sidelight, unlikely to be explored fully, was noticed when unusually large and bulky lures were fished for barramundi and repeatedly caught sooty grunter, some little larger than the lure. Generally, lures and baits are slightly smaller than those fished for Australian bass, owing to the smaller mouth of the grunter.

As table fish, grunters are adequate rather than outstanding. They are bettered by jungle perch, mangrove jack, bass and golden perch. Size in a good stream runs from 225 g to 2 kg, though many are caught in pan sizes of 450 g or less in other locations. They are difficult to scale if allowed to dry out, but fillet easily. Flesh quality improves greatly if these are bled and cleaned quickly. Possibly the reason for a slightly lower flesh quality is diet; grunters are omnivorous, eating a wide range of vegetable and animal matter. In the tropics they are known widely as black bream although the need for better nomenclature is causing the growth of sooty grunter as a more suitable tag.

Silver perch or bidyan

Bidyanus bidyanus: A splendid table fish frequently caught in inland streams and waterholes, but which suffers from the prejudice of anglers who rate silver perch as inferior to other top inland species. Also known as bidyan grunter, black bream, grunter or Murray perch. Silver perch are ideal fish for smoking (*which see*).

Silver perch are common in Queensland, where they are regarded as a southern species. They are also found in New South Wales, Victoria, South Australia and Western Australia, where a variety, *Bidyanus elliptica*, are found in the headwaters of west coast rivers. They invariably penetrate further upstream than golden perch and are particularly plentiful in the Murray River.

Whitley credits silver perch with growing to a weight of 8 kg, but fish over 1.5 kg are outstanding specimens. They are exciting sportfish which will take flies, lures and baits of worms of prawns. They gather in schools in running water, biting eagerly, fighting strongly when hooked.

For Dr Bryan Pratt's scientific assessment of the fish, see Silver perch.

Spangled grunter

Leiopotherapon unicolor: Also known as jewel perch, bobby, nicky and simply as perch. They are a very common freshwater fish and one of the most prolific breeders. They have to be heavily fished when kept in ponds to prevent unmanageable populations developing. They grow to around 450 g, but are mostly caught at weights under 225 g.

Spangled grunter are handsome, slender, spotted fish, grey to blue in colour, sometimes silvery. Each scale has a darkish border. They are widely distributed throughout tropical and sub-tropical Australia, splendid pan-fish which fight dourly when hooked. Their main diet comprises freshwater insects and shrimps and they bite avidly on worms and prawns.

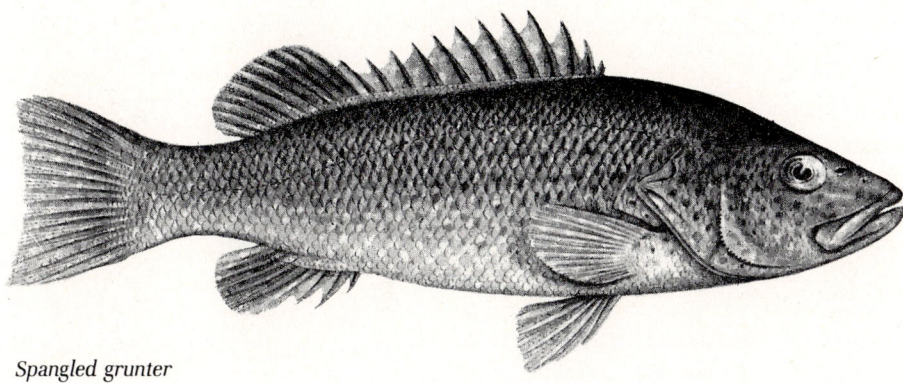

Spangled grunter

Bronze grunter

Mesopristes alligatoris: A north-western Australian variety that grows to 30 cm and has a more pointed snout than other grunter. The head is brown, the eyes yellowish and the body is deep and compressed.

Black-striped grunter

Amniataba percoides: A common variety of grunter easily recognized by the black stripes across the body. Found mainly in Central Australia, Western Australia and Queensland. They have a very small mouth, are greyish-blue in colour, silvery beneath, and grow to 20 cm. Abundant in Gulf of Carpentaria rivers.

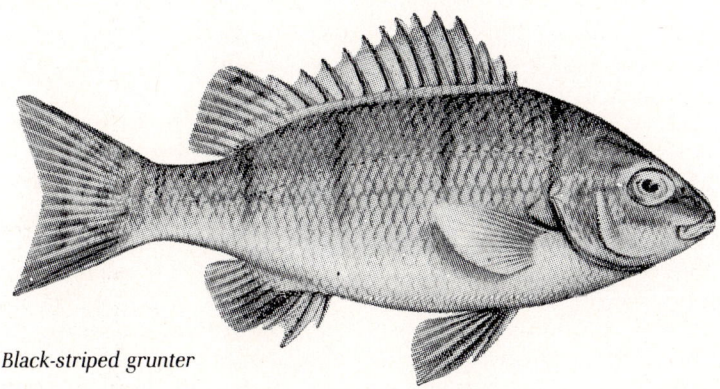

Black-striped grunter

GUDGEON

Small, pop-eyed marine, estuarine and freshwater fish which Whitley and Marshall grouped in the family Gobiomoridae but which have since been classified by McCulloch, Scott and others in the family Eleotridae. This difference of expert opinion hardly matters to anglers for gudgeons are dormant, sluggish fish, though they do arouse respect for their ability to stay alive in inland waterholes and dams during severe droughts.

Gudgeons mostly are only a few centimetres long. Some are brightly coloured and provide appealing aquarium displays.

G ■ GURNARD

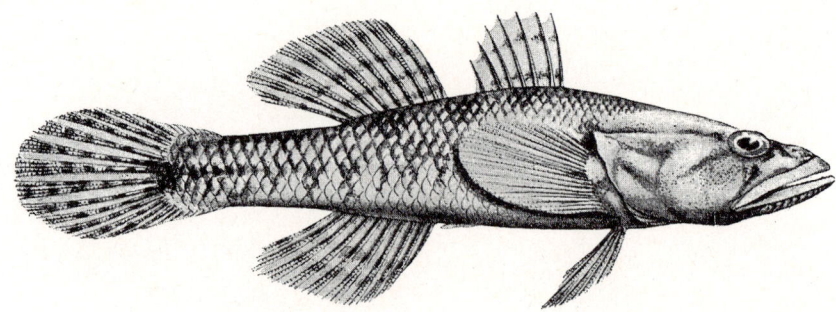

Flat-headed gudgeon
Philypnodon grandiceps

One or two are considered good table fare. But they are such light fish they could never be rated angling species and indeed some are lifted from shallow pools by willy-willies and carried across land for short distances before falling from the sky.

The wide selection of gudgeons in Australia includes the flat-headed gudgeon *Philypnodon grandiceps*, which grows to 12 cm and is found in all States except Western Australia and Tasmania, the Daly River gudgeon *Bunaka herewerdenii*, the checkered gudgeon *Mogurnda striata*, the western carp gudgeon *Hypseleotris klunzingeri*, the Cox's gudgeon *Gobiomorphus coxii*, and the firetail gudgeon *Hypseleotris galii*.

GURNARD Bottom-dwelling fish of the family Triglidae. All of group have their heads encased in protective bones and use the extended lower rays of the pectoral fin to creep about the bottom in search of food, turning over pebbles and shells in the hunt. The wing-like pectorals, in fact, are so large some gurnard are understandably mistaken for flying fish. They are fish of brilliant colouring, mainly of good table quality after skinning and some grunt or groan as they are lifted from the water.

Perhaps the most plentiful of the species is the red gurnard *Chelidonichthys kumu*, which is distributed in all Australian States, New Zealand and across to South Africa. They grow to 60 cm and 2 kg and prefer coastal waters down to around 150 m, where they can feed on small fish, crabs and shrimps. The body is more tapered than in other gurnard and they have large fanlike pectorals. In New Zealand, they are mainly brownish or olive above, whereas the same fish in South Australia is reddish above.

Butterfly gurnard *Paratrigla vanessa:* A species seen mostly by trawlermen because of the depths they inhabit. They are found in cooler waters in New South Wales, Victoria, Tasmania and South Australia, growing to around 30 cm. There is a distinguishing black blotch on the membrane of their dorsal fin. They are red above, silvery or white beneath.

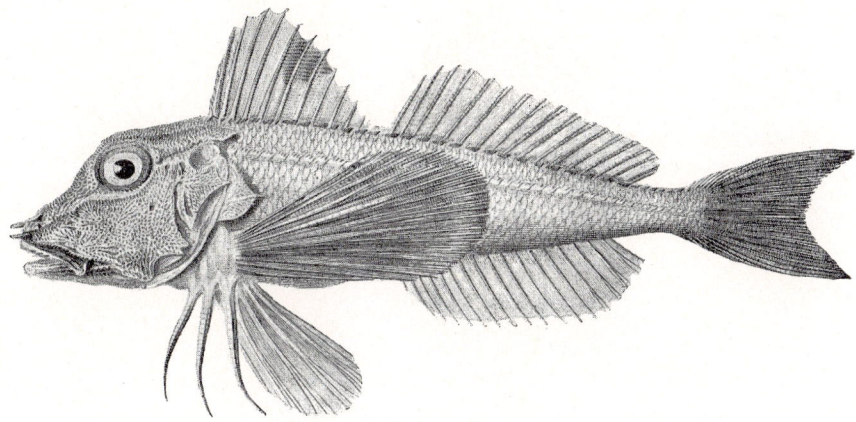

Butterfly gurnard

Flying gurnard

Or latchet, *Pterygotrigla polyommata:* A southern and southeastern Australian variety with large pectoral fins that look as if they could fly but cannot. Indeed their habitat is 75 to 180 m down. They are plentiful in trawler catches and are well known at fish markets, beautiful pink to reddish fish with silver bellies and olive-green edging on the pectoral fins. Their flesh is highly flavoursome. An important commercial species. Grows to 2.6 kg and over 50 cm.

Spiny gurnard

Paratrilga papilio: Highly attractive fish of vivid red body colouring, with an orange or golden band across the chest and throat. They are fed on by larger fish and do not themselves grow large enough to have any commercial significance. They have rows of spiny bucklers on each side and their pectorals are splashed in blues and greens. They are found in all Australian States, except Victoria. Averages 18 cm in length.

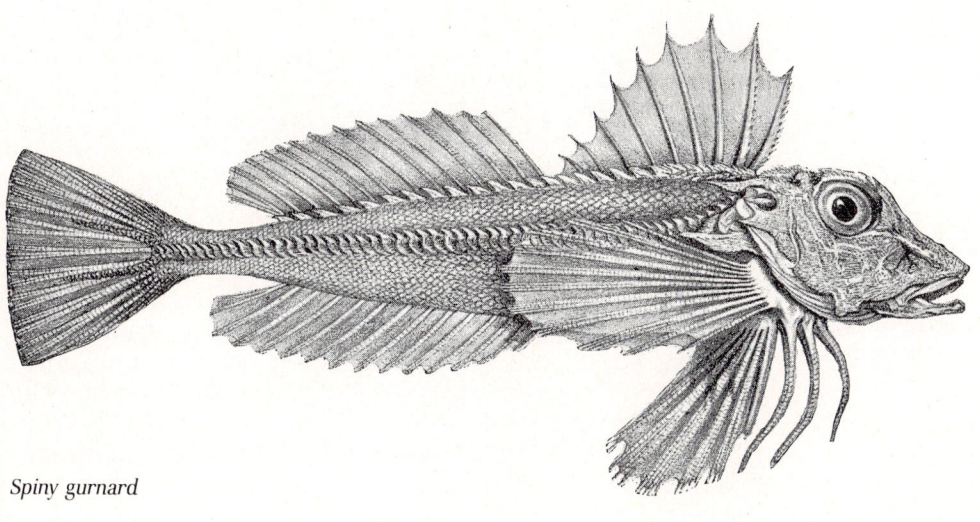

Spiny gurnard

H

HAIRTAIL A fascinating sportfish of the family Trichiuridei, related to the barracoutas and the frost fish, which it superficially resembles. The hairtail family appear to be represented in Australia by one genus and three species: the Australian hairtail *Trichiurus coxii* found in New South Wales and Western Australia; the northern hairtail *Trichiurus haemula* found in Queensland; and the spiny hairtail *Trichiurus savala*, occurring in Queensland, Northern Territory and Western Australia. Also known as cutlass fish, they are not peculiar to Australia, ranging from the seas of India through the East Indies and to Japan, where they are fished for in the deep waters of Tokyo Bay and in the Osaka area. Hairtail are first-rate food fish.

Hairtail grow to a length of 2.2 m and approximately 5 kg, but usually are from 90 cm to 1.5 m, averaging about 1 kg to each metre. The Australian hairtail is a very silvery fish with a highly compressed, scaleless body, tapering to a threadlike tail. The dorsal fin which is continuous from the back of the head contains 140 soft rays and has a black blotch between the first and fourth rays. The outer edge of the dorsal fin is dark grey. The pectoral fin is dark in colour, but ventral fins are absent.

The mouth contains a single series of razor-sharp compressed teeth in both jaws, the lower jaw being longer than the upper. The latter has two pairs of enlarged, barbed teeth in front and there are minute teeth on the palatines.

The hairtail swims in the normal way, that is, with its lateral line parallel to the surface of the water and not, as is sometimes thought, vertically, though it possibly assumes this position when resting or feeding. It tends to move in schools, this being obvious when a collection of fishing boats are grouped in a small bay. When the fish arrive the action transfers from one boat to the next as the school passes, invariably returning to the first boat as the bay is circled. This process continues until, as if by the turning of a switch, they all disappear. They are seldom caught or seen during daylight hours or at periods of low tide, though the author has occasionally located them at these times on the bottom in extremely deep water to where, he suspects, they retire when not feeding.

Very little is known about the growth rate or the breeding habits of the hairtail. The male of the species is, according to Gilbert Whitley, bigger than the female, a number of which, approximately 1 m, caught at Waratah Bay in the Hawkesbury River, New South Wales, in September, contained roe measuring approximately 0.7 mm in diameter.

Because of the small size of some hairtail taken by fishermen in New South Wales, it might not be unreasonable to assume that one of their breeding places is the waters of the drowned valleys that comprise the Hawkesbury River complex. Despite the vast numbers taken each year by the amateur fishermen, they continue to provide excellent sport and it would seem from this they are prolific breeders.

From the stomach of the carnivorous hairtail small, whole shrimps, prawns, yellowtail, and whitebait have been taken and there is no doubt it subsists on other marine creatures as well. It has a great liking for yellowtail which, as a consequence, has become a favourite bait of hairtail fishermen. A fierce predator, it has been seen to jump clear of the water when pursuing prawns—a fascinating sight.

A close-up of a hairtail's mouth showing the barbs on the upper fangs and further back, the peg-like teeth that mesh together.

H ■ HAIRTAIL

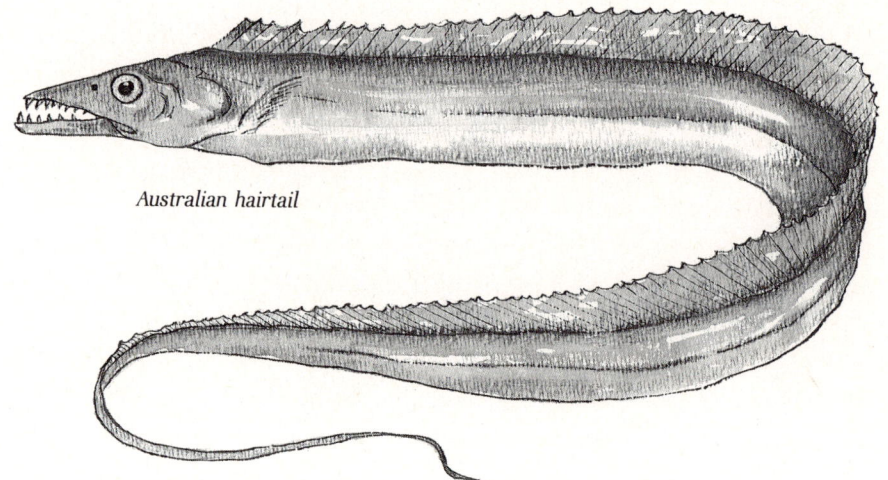

Australian hairtail

Angling techniques

In no other state of the Commonwealth is fishing for hairtail so specialized a sport as it is in the Cowan Creek arm of the Hawkesbury River. Here they are taken all the year round with the favoured months being February, March, April and May. A boat is almost a necessity, as easy access to most grounds is by water only. In recent years, hairtail have been taken in large numbers from Sydney Harbour and Botany Bay. No one knows the reason for their sudden appearance in these areas, but theories expounded have storms and/or deep-water dredging as the cause. They have also been caught in ocean waters over reefs off Sydney.

Various methods are used, but the most popular is handlining, though the light tackle rod and reel exponents are finding it a tough, determined antagonist. Whichever the method, terminal tackle is basic, comprising one 3/0 hook (or two, linked) attached to a minimum 20 cm of wire trace, in turn attached to a curtain ring with a diameter of at least 3 cm (*see Rigs, bay and estuary, 10 and 11*).

Line breaking strain varies but usually ranges from 7 to 9 kg. The bigger diameter of the heavier line minimises cut fingers which frequently occur when a hooked fish lunges to escape. Finger stalls or strips of adhesive tape are popular preventives for this hazard. Fine lines down to 2 kg are not unusual when rod and reel are used.

A sinker is unnecessary, though one or two split shot crimped above the wire trace will not deter the hairtail, and take the bait more quickly to the required depth. Finding the level at which the fish are feeding is deemed to be important, though variations of a metre or so have little effect. Five to 6 m can be taken as mean depth but, where three or four fishermen occupy the one boat, an accepted practice is for each to fish at different depths until one catches a fish. The others then adjust accordingly.

A live yellowtail is without equal as a bait and these little fish generally can be caught in the area fished. Almost as effective are fillets of yellowtail—one from each side of the fish—placed skin to skin and the hook passed through both. Such a rig rarely fails, as the oil or body juices from the cut flesh permeate the water and attract any hairtail in the vicinity.

A very timid biter, its attentions are first intimated by a light but steady pressure on the line. If the fisherman strikes the moment he becomes aware of this, he will most likely lose the fish. When, by feel, he knows it has the bait in its mouth, the experienced hairtail fisherman actually teases and excites the fish by very gently raising and lowering the bait a couple of times. This entices the hairtail to tighten its grip, whereupon the strike is made.

Reaction is instantaneous and quick reflexes are necessary. The long compressed body of the fish gives it great purchase upon the water and a large specimen requires considerable effort to bring it to the boat. The length of the fish precludes the use of a net, hence the curtain ring into which the finger is slipped to facilitate pulling it aboard. It is then grasped behind the head and the hook removed, care being taken to avoid the slashing teeth which can inflict serious injury. To kill them, knock them on the head or squeeze firmly behind the gills.

Time and tide are important considerations, the most productive conditions occurring when there is a high tide approximately an hour after dusk. If the evening is clear and the water so phosphorescent that the line glows, one's chances of catching them are improved, though exactly why this should be is another of nature's mysteries. Spin fishermen have been successful using whole garfish on a ganged hook rig and, though the use of artificial lures is patently practical, this aspect of hairtail fishing has largely been ignored.

DICK LEWERS

HARDYHEADS or silversides

Small, lively fishes of the family Atherinidae that are widespread in most temperate and warm coastal shallows. They often appear in great numbers near jetties and shorelines, leap-frogging over floating objects. About 22 of the world's estimated 150 species are found in Australian waters. Dense masses of them have been spotted from aircraft and hundreds

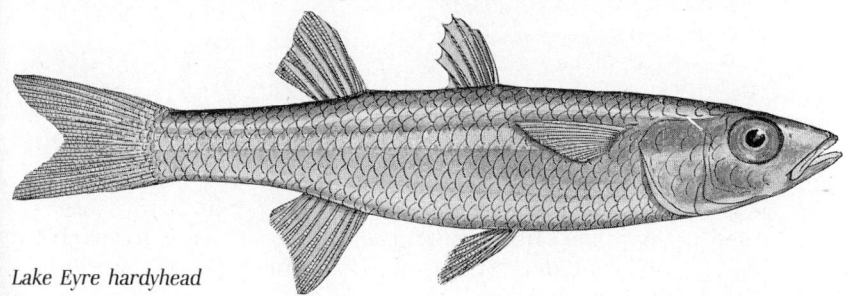

Lake Eyre hardyhead

of kilograms have been taken in a single haul of a net. They form a food supply for sharks, sea birds and larger fishes, and are used as live bait by tuna fishermen.

The most common species include the southern blue-eye *Pseudomugil signifer*, which occurs from Sydney, north to southern Queensland and has been recorded up to 26 cm; the flower of the wave *Iso rhothophilus*, a compressed variety with a scaleless head and thorax (*which see*); the smallmouthed hardyhead *Atherinosoma microstoma*, abundant on Australia's south-east coast; the Lake Eyre hardyhead *Crateroce- phalus eyresii*, which are found in both fresh and marine waters; and the Mitchellian freshwater hardyhead *Crateroce- phalus stercusmuscarum*, which are common in the northern waters of the Murray-Darling system and extend into northern South Australia.

HARLEQUIN fish Strikingly coloured fish of the family Anthiidae, also known as Chinese lantern, scarlet rock cod, tiger cod and Japanese lantern. They have an array of large teeth which are shown in a large, gaping mouth, and give them a frightening appearance. They are found in Western Australia and South Australia, where five members of the family have been recorded. They show up, too, in craypots, but are not often caught by anglers, except in King George's Sound. The family Anthiidae also includes the Western Australian breaksea cod, and the black-banded sea perch, and all members of the family are noted for their lavish colours. Black-banded sea perch venture into Victoria and southern New South Wales.

Harlequin fish are pugnacious fish, ready to fight viciously, equipped with two strong canine teeth in each jaw and rows of fine teeth. A strong trace and strong hooks are essential if the angler is to have any chance of landing them. They vary considerably in colour and are either reddish-brown or scarlet on top, with yellowish and pink blotches across the body. They have bluish-black spots on the top of the head, the fins are bright red and the spinous dorsal often is mottled in blue. Yellow and black blotches sometimes stretch right along the middle on each side of the body. They grow to 75 cm, but specimens of 50 cm or more are first-rate catches.

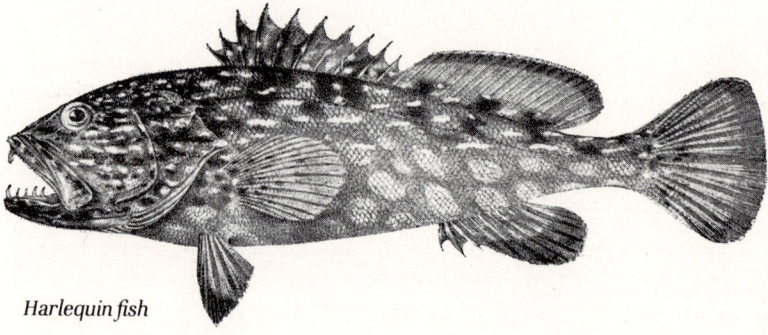

Harlequin fish

HERRING ■ H

HERRING, Ox-eye or tarpon

Megalops cyprinoides: The fast-swimming Australian tarpon or ox-eye herring is a relative of *Tarpon atlanticus*, a giant American sportfish which grows to 90 kg and which maintains a sport-fishing industry almost on its own in Florida. Unfortunately, there is no comparison in size with the Australian variety. Shoals of fish from 1.5 to 2.5 kg are common in many rivers of the northern half of Australia, south to Moreton Bay, where they are caught in summer, and in Papua. But the largest fish so far recorded by an amateur angler weighed 5.5 kg though they are known to grow to 1.8 m.

Reports of larger fish which 'would' weigh 9 kg should be treated with reserve, as a lateral view of the tarpon gives a misleading impression of size. Further, the tarpon's habit of 'rolling' on the surface, with the large and threadlike dorsal fin very much in evidence, can mislead an observer.

Tarpon are silvery along the sides with olive-green backs. The last ray of the dorsal fin is exceptionally long. The scales are large, the eyes fatty and the mouth has a bony throat plate. They often enter fresh water.

Tarpon are often easy to locate, as the gulping of air at the surface and the release of bubbles afterwards is necessary for the oxygenation of the gill system in this species. Like most of their relatives in the family of giant herring, tarpon are tremendously bony and so of no commercial interest. Anglers find them interesting primarily as a challenge fish. They may have to roll at the surface only once every 15 minutes, or may come up frequently, but anglers find they occur repeatedly in definite areas. In spring, it is often the first backwater inside a tidal estuary.

The tarpon's breeding habitat appears to be similar to that of the barramundi, with fingerling-size tarpon evident in small freshwater creeks, lagoons and rivers immediately after the wet season. The fish which live in fresh water are mainly immature, from 22 to 45 cm, with the larger sizes being taken in tidal estuaries and inlets. Tarpon as small as 7 cm kept in a fish tank often feed on small insects trapped on the surface, leaping up to 15 cm clear of the water after 'striking'.

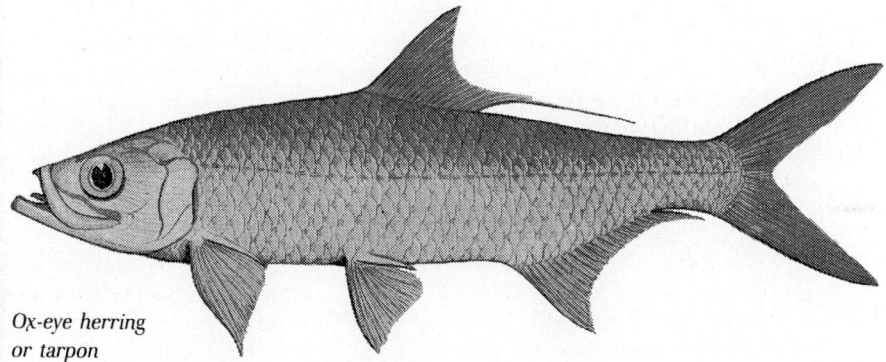

Ox-eye herring or tarpon

Fishing for tarpon is easy enough, but landing one is something else. A shoal of fish may be located and the best efforts of an angler fail to induce a strike at the lure. When a strike comes, the bony mouth offers little chance for a hook to hold, especially as the fish can leap and run wildly, thrashing the head at what some estimate at 10 beats to the second. On occasions, as many as 20 or 30 strikes may be taken without landing a fish. On others, one strike may hold.

Lighter lures with a very fast rod are not so easily thrown by the thrashing head as heavy ones. Another tactic which works well is a bait, usually prawn or yabby, fished on a single sharp 2/0 hook about a metre below a light float. This also is more difficult for the tarpon to throw. In theory an angler who leans forward and lowers the rod just as a fish clears the surface and then draws back, lifting the rod at the same time, will turn the average tarpon over in mid-air and take much of the steam out of it. It helps to have very sharp hooks.

Lures known to be successful include Killers, Reb 2's, chrome spoons and jigs. A sonette spinner, re-rigged with a saltwater fly on a single hook, proved successful insofar as the percentage of fish landed per strike was concerned. The best retrieve is fast but not irregular and no trace is necessary unless there is a risk of other species, which is mostly the case.

The best tackle is variable, but a fast-tipped tubular spinning outfit or baitcaster fits the casting distance most accurately. Broadly speaking, tarpon can be fished more successfully from a boat, with casting more rewarding than trolling.

HOOKS Lengths of metal wire curved back to form a point, usually barbed, on which to catch fish. There are hundreds of hook patterns and types of hooks and the skill with which the angler selects his hooks for various types of fishing has an important bearing on success or failure to catch good fish. The size and strength of the fish he is seeking, its feeding habits, the shape of the mouth and teeth, the water being fished, the bait used and the ability of the fish to run when hooked all have an influence on hook selection.

The parts of a hook, the point, the barb, the bend, shank, eye, gape and bite all should be considered before final selection is made. Hook design may appear simple enough but it has taken centuries for the hooks now in use to be perfected. Australians and New Zealanders are fortunate that they now have available in their tackle shops the best hooks obtainable in the world.

Development of modern hooks

The earliest information on fish hooks in English literature is in *The Treatise of Fishing with an Angle*, by Dame Juliana Berners, which was included in the Book of St Albans, a famous sporting book produced in that town in the year 1486.

Along with a lot of other information on angling, it gave detailed instructions on heating and cutting barbs on needles, forming them into hooks and heat-treating them for rigidity and toughness. Apparently this was still standard practice 167 years later, in 1653 when Izaak Walton published the first edition of *The Compleat Angler*.

But the history of fish hooks goes a long way farther back than that. We have no idea how far back in antiquity it was when the Australian Aborigines and the natives of Papua-New Guinea and the Pacific Islands first began to use pointed wood or bone gorges and fish hooks made from pearl shell. There are in existence old pearl-shell lures, with an action similar to that of a spoon and bearing a hooked spike, which Solomon Islanders claim have been trolled behind canoes from time immemorial.

Knowledge of the time of man's emergence from the wood, bone and shell age in other areas is more precise. There is evidence that copper was first worked in Egypt or nearby Asia Minor about 5000 B.C. and that copper fish hooks were one of the earliest uses for it. The use of bronze originated on the island of Crete about 4000 B.C. and this gave the fishermen of those primitive times a harder and more rigid hook.

It is thought that metallic iron was first produced in Egypt about 2000 B.C. It appears though that it did not come into use in Europe until about 1000 B.C. It is not known when or where carbon steel was developed but it is plain that steel hooks, both barbed and barbless, were in use some hundreds of years before the Christian era. However, manufacture of steel hooks on a commercial scale does not appear to have occurred in England until well after 1600 A.D. when some of the needle makers of London took it up as a side-line.

Despite the fact that Walton does not specifically mention it, there is evidence that one of these, Charles Kirby, invented and produced his famous Kirby pattern in 1651, and this is still the same pattern which is in extensive use throughout the world under that name today. But his activities and those of other needle manufacturers were soon cut short by the disastrous London fire of 1666.

Those who could reorganize soon established themselves again in other locations and then over the next 70 years the majority became centralized in the little town of Redditch, probably because they could obtain water power to suit their requirements. They developed new patterns and in time became the major source of supply, capturing most of the market throughout the world. Names such as Milward, Allcock, Willis, Sealey, James and others were known and respected.

Disaster again overtook the British fish hook industry during World War II. The town of Redditch was bombed almost out of existence, together with the nearby manufacturing complex of Coventry, which was a major source of

PARTS OF A HOOK

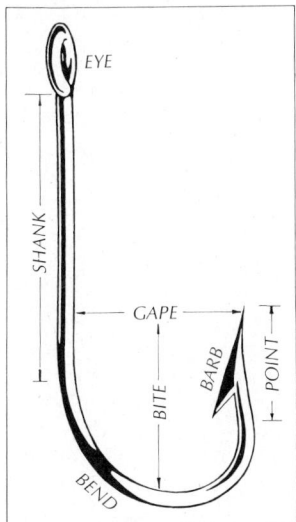

supply of electrical equipment and meters for the nation's air force and other services. As a matter of priority, Coventry was reconstructed speedily and the new plants absorbed most of the available labour-force from Redditch.

For almost 30 years there was little effort by the manufacturers to revive the industry and English hooks were hardly seen in Australian tackle shops. Recently there have been signs that a revival has taken place. Shakespeare-Allcock stainless-steel hooks came on the market and met with immediate approval among Australian anglers. Since then Sealey also has released a range of stainless-steel hooks.

The world's largest manufacturer of hooks in the past three decades has been the firm of O. Mustad & Son, established at Oslo, Norway, in 1832. This company does a tremendous worldwide trade in hooks and claims to make over 6000 patterns. Allowing for eye types and different sizes, it manufactures more than a million items. No wholesaler or dealer could ever carry the entire range, so in the various countries they stock only those types which are in popular demand in their areas.

The designation of hooks

Hook pattern or design varies according to the form of fishing or the characteristics of the species being fished for. Anglers often are confused when they come to order hooks, because of the antiquated systems of specification still in use. These have been handed down from the pioneer hook makers, who seem to have had a penchant for starting at the middle and then working both ways. For instance, in designating the graduated sizes they chose a hook near the middle of the range and specified it as size No. 1. As the smaller hooks below it in the range decreased in size they were specified as No. 2, 3, 4, 5 and so on, even down to the minutely tiny No. 24 in some patterns. As the larger hooks above it increased in size they were specified as 1/0, 2/0, or 3/0, even up to 18/0 in some heavy patterns. In most patterns the manufacturers make the less used sizes in the even number only. Sizes for the same identical number, such as 6/0, are not always the same in different patterns, nor for identical numbers in the same pattern when made by different firms.

Ordinary hooks are made from special gauges of high quality carbon-steel wire. This has to have special qualities which enable it to be worked satisfactorily in the machines and give a brittle-free, strong, rigidly tough hook after heat treatment. Each size in a series is made from its own standard gauge, but for special purposes it may be made in a number of other gauges. If a packet of hooks of a specific size is marked 'X Strong' it means that they are made in the heavier gauge of wire usually prescribed for the next larger hook in the series. '2X Strong' or '2X Stout' would indicate the gauge used in the same pattern of hook two sizes larger and so on up to 4X. In the same way, a packet marked 'X Fine' would indicate that

BAITING A HOOK

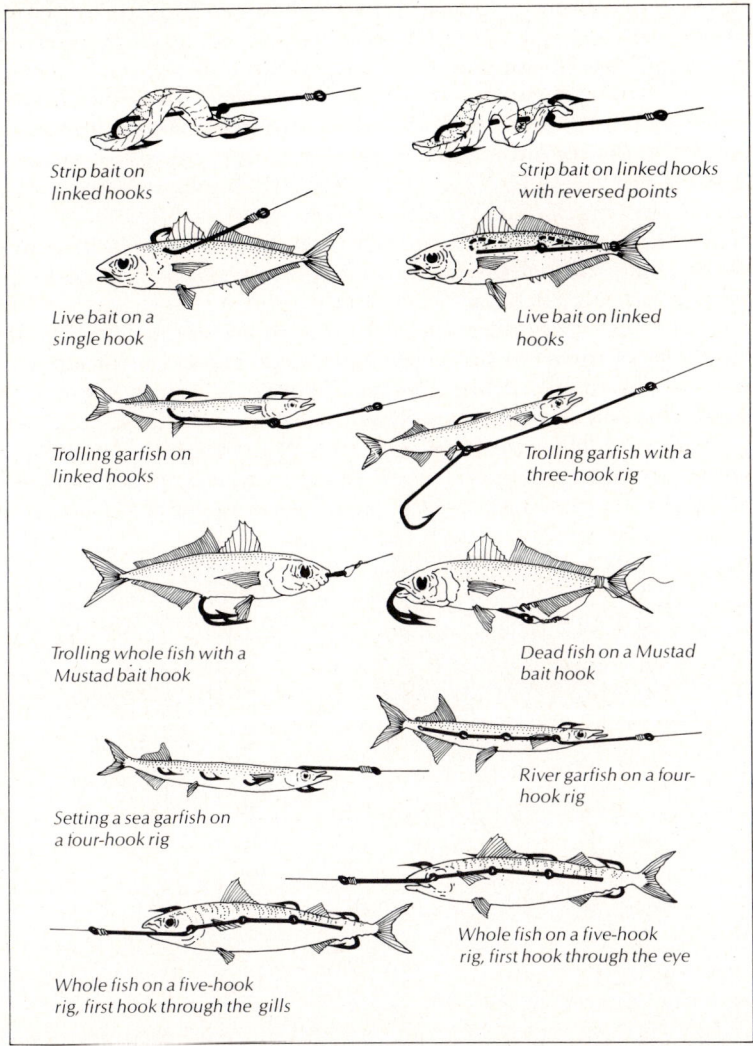

Strip bait on linked hooks
Strip bait on linked hooks with reversed points
Live bait on a single hook
Live bait on linked hooks
Trolling garfish on linked hooks
Trolling garfish with a three-hook rig
Trolling whole fish with a Mustad bait hook
Dead fish on a Mustad bait hook
Setting a sea garfish on a four-hook rig
River garfish on a four-hook rig
Whole fish on a five-hook rig, first hook through the gills
Whole fish on a five-hook rig, first hook through the eye

the contents were made from wire of a gauge normally used for hooks one size smaller, and so on down to '4X Fine'.

The traditional unknown quantity 'X' was also used to indicate variations in the length of the shank. A label of 'X Long' or 'XL' would indicate that the shank of the hook was the same length as that of the next larger size in that pattern. '2X Long' or '2XL' would indicate a shank as long as that of a hook two sizes larger and so on up to 6XL. In similar manner, 'X Short' or '2X Short' would indicate that the shank was only as long as that of a hook one size smaller or two sizes smaller, respectively. Nowadays some manufacturers have adopted a more sane policy of marking their hooks '¼ inch extra long', '½ inch extra long', '¼ inch extra short' etc., but they are mostly European firms, who stick to imperial measures.

How hooks are made

Fish hooks are made from carbon-steel, rustless nickel alloy and stainless steel. Stainless steel suitable for hook manufacture has been developed since World War II and the quality of some of the products is very high. Stainless steel has a big advantage in that it does not rust and require replacement of the hook after a short period of storage. Neither does it stain and rot the line where it is snooded to the hook. Stainless steel hooks are particularly advantageous on lures. They do not rust and become blunted from corrosion of the point and often a pair of brightly flashing hooks is one of the attractions which induce fish to strike at it.

Steel hooks usually are finished blued, japanned black, lacquered bronze or electroplated in cadmium, nickel or tin. In the cheaper finishes bronze lacquer is the one mostly preferred in Australia. Cadmium and the thin nickel plating stand up well in fresh water but are unsatisfactory after a short period of use in salt. Tin plating remains bright longest and is most resistant to salt.

Selecting a hook

In the same way that there is no universal rod, there is no all-purpose hook. Choice usually is a matter of compromise between various factors, such as the requirements of the bait, size and nature of the fish's mouth, its weight, speed and method of resisting. For instance, fine wire hooks do less damage to soft baits, are less easy for fish to detect in them and less lethal or incapacitating to live bait. They penetrate a soft mouth more easily but are more prone to cut their way out under pressure. Light, fine-wire hooks of special patterns are used for tying trout flies because they need less hackle to keep them buoyant.

Heavy wire hooks have greater strength and rigidity. They do not penetrate as readily as a fine hook, but they are more suitable for fish with hard, bony mouths because they resist bending and crushing. Those with a short spear (distance between the point and the tip of the barb) are more easy to sink beyond the barb, but they pull out more easily than those with a long spear. A hook with a short shank is more easily hidden in a bait, but one with a long shank is more easily held in baiting it, easier to handle in extracting it from the fish's mouth and may prevent sharp teeth from cutting through the line.

Important considerations influencing the choice of type and size of hooks for various angling purposes may be gathered from the following discussion of the popular patterns shown in the accompanying hook chart.

(1) Kirby

This is the original pattern introduced by Charles Kirby, of London, in 1651. Old as it is, it still is in common use today. It is a moderately stout hook, with a fairly long shank and a small ring eye. The bend is well rounded to put the pull on a fish well down in the bottom of the curve. There is a wide gape but only a moderately deep throat. The needle-pointed spear is straight and of moderate length, with the point set approximately parallel to the shank.

One of the innovations which Kirby introduced in this pattern was the kirb or sideways bend which is now so familiar to anglers. A hook is said to be kirbed when it is seen to be offset to the right, when the point is viewed from above with the eye pointed toward the viewer. If it is offset to the left it is said to be reversed. Kirbed or reversed hooks are favoured because it would seem that they are less likely to pull out of a fish's mouth without catching, but in actual use the straight hook seems hardly inferior in this regard.

(2) Kendal Kirby
This is a later modification incorporating a hollow point. This is achieved by forming the spear with a concave curve between the point and the barb, whereby the point is fined down for easy penetration. In the days before the introduction of automatic machines such hooks used to be hand filed and usually were a work of perfection. This pattern still has a very big sale today.

(3) French
There probably is more of this pattern sold in Australia than any other. It is a moderately short shanked, kirbed hook with a deep throat and long, hollow pointed spear. The emphasis is on rigidity and holding power. The shank and the rounded bend are forged (flatted on the sides) for greater strength. The shank is turned down into a ball eye. This is an improvement in that it allows the line to be passed through the eye and snooded onto the shank so that the link and shank lie in a straight line. It also permits the hook to be linked onto the end of a loop tied in a line as a cast, so that the hook projects straight out in line with the nylon.

The French hook is extensively used in fishing for snapper, morwong or nannygai on the offshore reefs and in drifting for sand flathead. It is frequently used in angling for bream with cubes of fish flesh or with hard-shelled crabs. The larger sizes are very suitable for fishing for the lighter Barrier Reef species, such as sweetlip emperor and coral cod. The pattern is also favoured by most anglers in fishing the big inland rivers for yellowbelly, silver perch or eel-tail catfish. Some anglers use the smaller sizes, such as 8 and 10, in fishing with green weed or sea lettuce for luderick. Others take the kirb out with a pair of pliers and link size 4/0 or 5/0 to form the four-hook chain rig used in fishing with whole garfish, though we believe there are other hooks more suited to this purpose.

(4) Viking
A Mustad modification of the French hook. It is of lighter construction, with a longer shank, wide gape and a long barb flared out behind a long hollow point. The kirbed bend and

shank are forged and the shank is tapered down to a small turned-down ball eye. The wide gape of this hook allows the point and barb to stand clear when used with a thick bait or a live fish.

It is an excellent pattern for angling for soft-mouthed fish, such as mulloway, for it is not an easy hook to throw once it is embedded. Its lighter construction and long, tapered shank make it liable to spring sideways, so it cannot be recommended for bony-jawed species. With size 5/0, the small eye makes it possible to run a big beach worm up the hook, head first over the snood onto the line, as in baiting for big mulloway.

(5) Beak

A shorter-shanked version of the Viking hook, with the same wide gape, forged shank and bend and small turned-down eye, but without the same degree of taper. The long, hollow pointed spear has a decidedly turned-in point. In theory this should give shallower penetration in hooking a fish but make the hook somewhat harder to throw. In actual use, it hooks fish just as deeply as straight-pointed models of similar size and it certainly is not an easy hook for a fish to get rid of.

The standard type is of light construction and very suited to breaming or similar angling purposes but, of course, it may be had in heavier gauges, up to 4X, if a dealer could be located with stocks of the required size. The model shown in the chart has two slices in the back of the shank to help prevent strip bait from slipping down into the bend and shrouding the point and the barb.

(6) Sneck, ringed

In Australia sneck hooks are much used in New South Wales but are not very popular in other States. They mainly are used in fine-line breaming and in angling for luderick. The sneck pattern has a very square bend and the usual kirb or reverse to the point. Its chief virtue is that it will accommodate a thick bait without having to squeeze it in the bottom of the bend and thus it is particularly suited for use with fish cubes and other similar bait. It is particularly effective in hooking fish, but the shallow throat and short spear make it somewhat easy to throw. The long-shanked, ringed pattern shown under this number on the chart is mainly used by luderick anglers in fishing with green-weed bait. The square bend takes the weed without squeezing it into a waist and the ringed eye helps to hold it at the top of the hook.

Sizes 12 to 8 are used with weed in the estuaries and 10 to 6 when luderick angling with weed or sea-lettuce from the ocean rocks. Sizes 14 to 10 are very useful in fishing for garfish with bread, dough, peeled prawn or other soft baits and sizes 12 to 8 are very useful for hooking mullet.

(7) Sneck, flatted

This is the same pattern as above but with a flat on the end of the shank to hold the snood of the line, instead of an eye. It is

GAME HOOKS

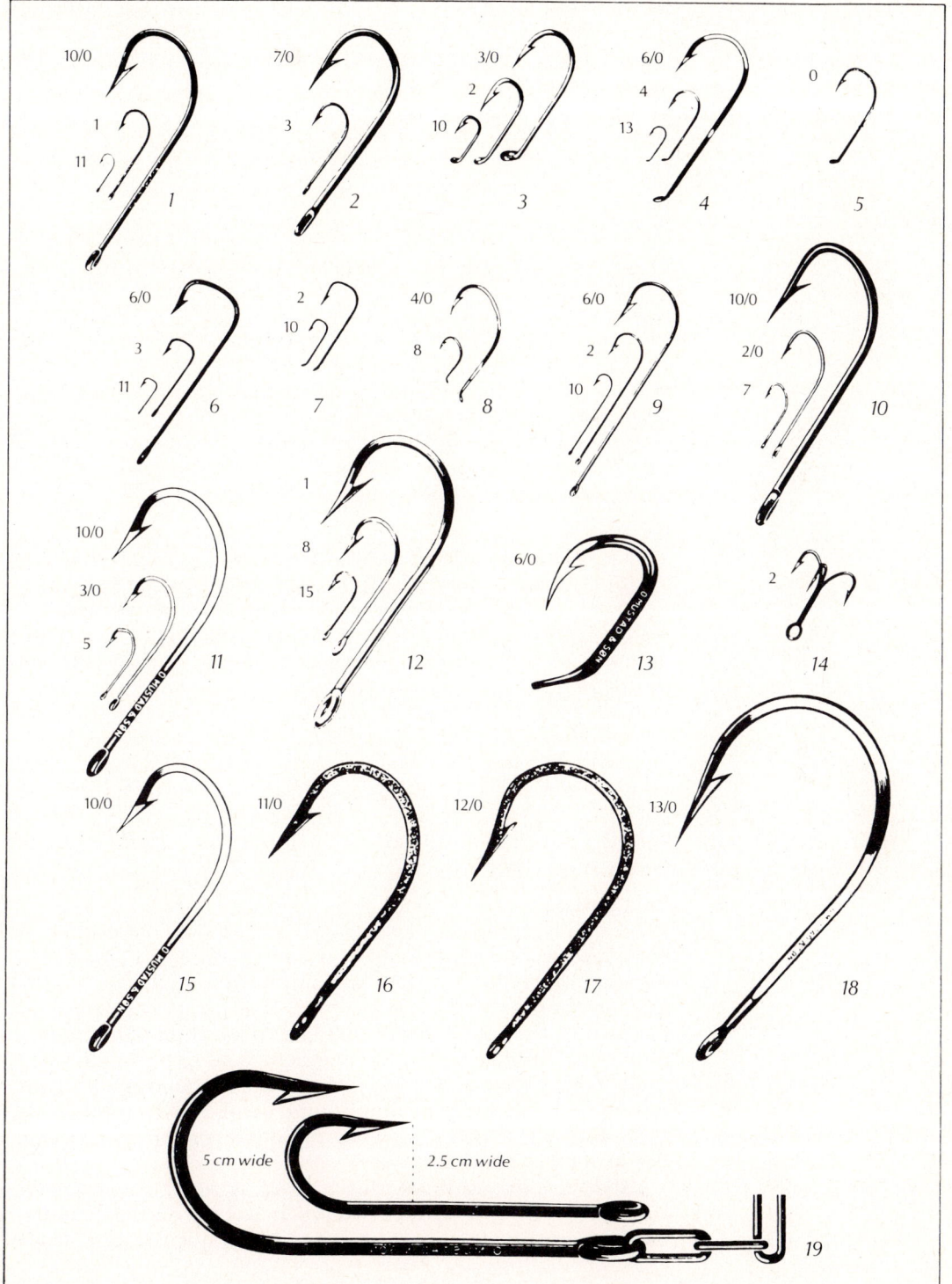

treated separately because anglers regard it as a particular pattern which cannot very well be replaced by any other. It has a relatively short shank and usually is available in fine and stout gauges. Fine wire sneck hooks are considered to be the best for use with soft baits such as pipi, mussel, yabby or small beach worm in fine-line angling for bream. They are easily hidden in the bait, are not easily detected by the fish and they hook well. But, with a bony-mouthed fish like the bream, they may be crushed and break at the rather square corners of the bend.

They are extensively used for breaming in the estuaries and in surf angling from the beaches, in sizes No. 2 to 2/0. Some anglers fancy the fine gauges for drifting down rivers where they can cast into rocks or oyster beds with bait such as live prawns. If a fish does not pick up the bait, the hook usually snags. Fine hooks may be broken to save the line, or they bend, and to save time they may be straightened up with strong fingers or pliers for further use. As noted above, the smaller sizes of flatted sneck may be used for luderick, but it then is usual to half hitch the line around the weed or cabbage, just above the hook, to hold it up.

(8) Suicide

The original suicide hook was produced by Sealey in the 'Octopus' brand. Mustad market a modified suicide pattern in the 'beak' series. This has a moderately short forged shank, a particularly wide gape, short throat and parabolic bend, with a turned-in point and well flared barb. This is a highly effective model in hooking fish, but owing to its short shank, wide gape and shallow throat, it pulls out more easily or is more easily thrown than some other patterns. It is not suited for use with large tough bait or hard shelled crabs; for these fill the shallow bend and leave little of the point available to penetrate the fish.

This pattern is supplied with a moderately tapered shank and a turned-up ball eye.

(9) Carlisle

This pattern has long been noted as an inexpensive hook of good quality and many uses. It is a long-shanked hook with a parabolic bend and a needle point with a well flared barb. Mustad Quality 9920, in sizes 3/0 to 8/0, is particularly popular for fishing for tailor, dusky flathead, pike, threadfin salmon, queenfish and many other species which chop line freely with their teeth. Owing to their convenient construction it is possible to chain two or more of the same size by forcing the barb of one through the eye of the other and then re-flaring the slightly depressed barb.

Used as a single hook, this pattern is much favoured for sand flathead, nannygai and others. In smaller sizes it is much used for leatherjackets and in sizes 5 to 3 it is the ideal hook for sand whiting.

(10) Limerick
This is a straight hook, which means that it has no kirb or reverse. It has a moderately long shank, a ring eye, a parabolic bend and a long spear with a modified hollow point. The parabolic bend puts the pull on the fish well in under the barb and it is not an easy hook for a fish to throw.

It is in general use throughout the world for various forms of fishing but in Australia it is most used for swinging in pairs behind lures trolled or used in spinning for pelagics such as tailor. For this purpose it usually is procured 2X strong, in tinned finish. Flat hooks swing past each other without locking the kirbs and shrouding the points in the bends. Kirbed hooks are not suitable to swing behind lures, since the kirbs cause them to spin.

Limerick hooks with eyes of various sizes to suit lure manufacturers' requirements, are available. Double limericks also are supplied for rigid attachment to jigs, spoons and similar lures. A double limerick with a safety pin attachment also is provided to pin and clip the bait so that it trolls between the two barbs.

(11) O'Shaughnessy
This is another straight hook of high quality, generally used in fishing for the smaller game fish. It is similar in construction to the limerick, but the shank is forged for great strength and it has a straight needle-sharp point which is slightly turned out for deeper penetration. It has a more shallow back to the parabolic bend, which brings the pull on the fish in under the point and barb.

It is usually supplied in tinned or nickel finish, or may be procured in rustless nickel alloy. This hook is supplied on many of the larger lures, such as big 'knuckles' and the 'drone spoons' so much used on the Great Barrier Reef.

(12) Sea hooks
A strong, rugged pattern much used by commercial fishermen in bottom fishing on the Great Barrier Reef. It also is used on long-line equipment for tuna, or with wire leaders for school shark and other saurian species.

This type is characterized by a moderately long but stout shank, a large ringed eye, a bend that is more round than parabolic, with a heavily barbed straight needle point slightly turned out for deep penetration. It usually is seen blued or black japanned.

Anglers find it a good hook in fishing northern waters for big flowery cod, slimy cod, groper, wrasse, barracuda, shark, sawfish and others. In southern waters it is used a good deal for school shark and in New Zealand it is used for hapuku and bass groper.

To add to the muddle, the graduated sizes are specified in ascending numerical order as we proceed from the largest down to the smallest. No. 1 is about equivalent in size to a 12/0

Kendal Kirby and No. 20 is about small enough for yellowtail or luderick.

(13) Tuna
A somewhat unusual pattern which is chiefly notable for its curved re-entrant point. It has a heavily forged shank for greater strength, with a flatted end pierced with a hole for attachment of the wire trace or leader. The bend is in the nature of a reversed parabola, to bring the pull on the fish into the axis of the line. The incurved point has a deep hollow running back along the long spear to a strong barb.

It is much used in trolling and fishing for tuna around some of the Pacific islands, particularly Nauru and some parts of New Britain, but has not been employed extensively for such purpose in Australia.

(14) Trebles
These three-tang hooks are used almost exclusively in Australia on the spinners, spoons, plugs, wobblers, wrigglers and poppers used in angling for trout, bass, redfin, yellowbelly, Macquarie perch, barramundi, mangrove jack, javelin fish, flathead or jungle perch. Sizes in general range from 8 to 5.

In some of the trout districts in New Zealand, such as Taupo, the use of trebles on trout lures is prohibited and anglers are obliged to use a single hook only. A good range of spinners, spoons, flatfish and other lures with single hooks are available in the local tackle shops and anglers' catches seem to suffer little from the restriction.

Paired Limerick or O'Shaughnessy hooks almost invariably are preferred in trolling for big, powerful fish. When a fish is hooked only by one tang of a treble, the shallow throat often allows it to pull out or the relatively thin wire may allow it to straighten out or break. If a big fish with a bony mouth takes a treble into its mouth it may crush it. And a well hooked treble is too difficult to remove from a big fish that is snapping with a vicious set of teeth and wastes too much fishing time.

Hooks for game fishing

Many hook patterns and hook modifications have been devised for catching big fish, but at the ultimate it is those which demonstrate their ability to hook most fish and hold them until they are boated, that the manufacturers find worth persevering with in this more limited market. Therefore, there are not many types available in Australia, but those offering are tried and trusted patterns which have proved themselves over long periods.

(15) O'Shaughnessy
See (11).

(16) Bay king
This usually is procurable in short shank, 2X strong form, as shown in the chart. It is a heavily forged hook with a tapered, brazed ring eye. The bend is parabolic and the particularly

strong point is straight with a decidedly flared barb. The point is knife edged, that is, it is diamond shaped in cross-section and the edges at the sides are sharpened so that it may cut its way in for easy penetration. Usually supplied tinned.

(17) Southern and tuna
Very much used for marlin and tuna. Heavily forged with the shank tapering to a brazed, ringed eye. The bend is more round, with the point drawn in towards the shank to give straight penetration and bring the grip on the fish more in under the barb. The point is strong, knife-edged and heavily barbed.

(18) Sea master
Considered by many to be the best game hook ever made, and much used for big marlin, swordfish and mako sharks. It is heavily forged, with the shank tapering to a brazed, ringed eye. The bend is a blending of parabolic and rounded, with a decidedly re-entrant point which makes it difficult to throw. The point is slightly hollowed and sharply knife-edged, with a broad, strong barb which is well flared. The extra long point is kirbed and needs a good strike to drive it home, but it is seldom dislodged once it is well in. Supplied in several strengths; tinned finish.

(19) Shark hooks
These may be obtained with or without chain and swivel, which is approximately 75 cm long. Shark hooks are made in a big range of sizes which are specified as the measurement, in inches, across the width of the gape. Thus, they range, in 12 mm steps, from 2.5 cm wide to 12 cm wide.

This big brown trout was caught using a treble hook and a plug. The fly and broken line in the corner of the jaw are evidence of an earlier escape.

I

INTRODUCED fishes

Australia has had 11 species of fish introduced into its waters, all of them in fresh water and all of them highly controversial. Even the three species of trout that have provided excellent sport for thousands of fishermen—and regularly appear on restaurant menus—have not escaped the wrath of experts who claim we should not have upset our native fish by introducing aliens which challenge them for food and habitat.

Eight of the 11 aliens are self-maintaining, which means they can look after themselves and reproduce in our waters, but the other three have not shown they can spawn here and only survive because their stocks are regularly replenished from government hatcheries. They are the Atlantic salmon, quinnat salmon and brook trout. Periodically, accidental introductions are made but they are isolated, numbers unknown. There are Japanese fish in Sydney Harbour, which biologists say probably arrived in ships' water tanks that were flushed on arrival.

The introduced fishes are brook, brown and rainbow trout, Atlantic salmon, quinnat salmon, English perch or redfin, European carp, goldfish or golden carp, tench, roach and mosquito fish. Only the trout have improved the sport available to Australian inland fishermen, although South Australians have enjoyed redfin fishing. Carp, tench, roach and mosquito fish have proved a nuisance, which was why the late Gilbert Whitley, an outstanding authority on Australian fishes, wrote: 'The modern attitude to acclimatization and pisciculture is that it is unwise to liberate foreign or even Australian fish in our waters without preceding such introductions with biological and hydrographical surveys.'

J

JACKASS fish

See Morwong.

JAVELIN fish

A small family of fish from our semi-tropical waters which rate very high with anglers on account of their truly excellent eating qualities and their ability to put up a strong fight when hooked. They take their name from the long, powerful spine in the anal fin. They are mainly found in the closer coastal reaches, bays, harbours, rivers and tidal creeks. They are frequently caught on lures and in bait fishing are taken on small live fish such as mullet, herrings, pilchards and on dead baits such as prawns, yabbies, garfish, worms or fish strip. They are most fished for in the rivers and estuaries, around the mouths of the saltarms, around inshore reefs and along by the rocks of the foreshores.

The largest of the family, the spotted javelin *Pomadasys hasta*, has been known to grow to 65 cm and 5.4 kg, but most of the big fish caught range from 2 to 3.5 kg. The small-spotted javelin *Pomadasys opercularis* grows to 50 cm but is mostly 1 to 1.5 kg. A smaller species growing to 45 cm is the blotched javelin *Pomadasys maculatus*. The silver javelin *Pomadasys argyreus* is a small but not plentiful species seen only in far northern waters. It grows to about 40 cm and is distinguished by its silvery-grey body.

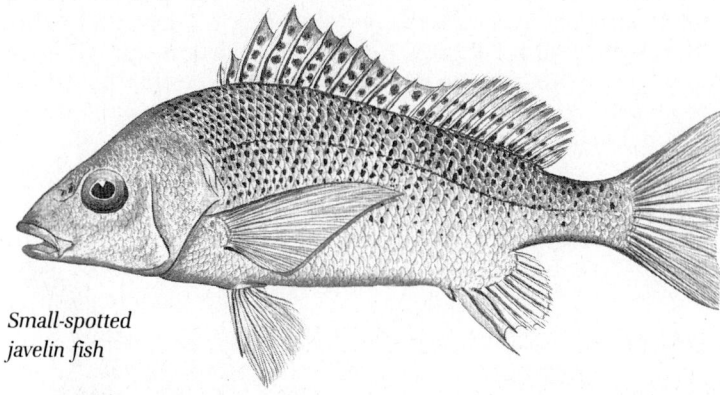

Small-spotted javelin fish

JEWFISH

See Mulloway.

JOHN dory

See Dory.

K

KINGFISH, Black or cobia

Rachycentron canadus: Sometimes known as a sergeant-fish or even as a black ling, the cobia is a renowned game fish which has been mastered by relatively few Australian anglers. Difficulty stems from the wandering habits of the fish. A few areas which have consistently produced good fish include Flat Rock, in Queensland, the Whitsunday Islands and the outer reefs off Cairns. Cobia have a solitary nature and are rarely seen in groups. They appear to be a non-specialized species which can feed on everything from bottom crustacea, crabs and crayfish, to surface fish.

Although fairly regularly caught by mackerel fishermen in smaller sizes around 18 kg, cobia are known to grow to 1.8 m and 67 kg and have been landed by Australian amateurs up to 49 kg. They are fairly well known to Australian game anglers on the Barrier Reef, but have been caught as far south as Port Stephens in New South Wales. The young cobia appear to inhabit inshore and estuary waters. One of the smallest cobia caught was a 1 kg fish taken in a deep coastal inlet. They have been taken on surf tackle after long fights and could always be possible to a mulloway angler. They are primarily fast, powerful and stubborn fighters well able to use their wide tail and symmetrical dorsal and anal fins.

Black kingfish will take a wide variety of bait and lures. Whole crabs are a delicacy they will not bypass, but live or trolled fish are also taken. Feather jigs appear to be their prime choice in lures, though they have been taken on drone spoons and konaheads as well. Perhaps their most common form of capture is by handline amateurs bottom fishing for reef fish, a case of accident rather than design.

Black kingfish or cobia

Oddly, for such a powerful sporting fish, cobia seen on the surface have an ugly and almost cumbersome appearance. The blunt head and brown body often resemble a wobbegong shark and at first sight the fish seems darker from above than it appears on capture.

The preferred habitat of the fish is generally over deep reefs and bomboras, though they can be caught at the surface and have been seen over the edge of the continental shelf. Obviously any species which can hold its own in the speedy company of pelagic fish is no slouch.

Much remains to be discovered about our cobia. They are an interesting sporting species which will attract increasing attention as anglers discover their habits more accurately. Meantime they are usually taken as an interesting, hard-fighting bonus fish—not always looked for but always welcomed. The biggest black kingfish on the Game Fishing Association of Australia's record charts in 1985 was George Walsh's 49.66 kg specimen taken in November 1971 at Southport, Queensland, on a 24 kg line. But for skilful fishing, Eric McElwaine's 30.39 kg cobia on a 6 kg line at Port Stephens, N.S.W., in March 1970 takes some beating.

KNOTS for anglers

Nylon fishing line is a difficult material to tie securely, so the complete angler has to learn to form and close some highly specialized knots.

Nylon is a plastic formed mainly from coal, air and water. In the final stages of production it polymerizes, during which process it is possible to form a number of apparently similar substances with slightly different molecular distributions, which give it somewhat divergent properties.

Anglers are always looking for the ideal line for their form of fishing and in most cases this entails a good deal of suppleness and freedom from taking a set when deformed, particularly where it is to be cast from reels. This calls for a supple line, which entails some degree of softness in the material. The original nylon 66 was far too hard and springy, so today most manufacturers use an alternative polymer known as capralactum. Some manufacturers, particularly Playtyl, are currently producing line made by blending a number of polymers in an effort to arrive at an ideal compromise between strength, elasticity, suppleness and knotting strength. Nylon line has a smooth surface and is very prone to slip out of a knot unless it is of such a nature as to produce a very tight jam. Its elasticity and softness also make the tying of safe knots difficult. When a knot is tied tightly, or when a heavy strain is placed on it, some of the turns pull tightly on each other and are placed under strain, which may remain even after the pull on the line is released. Due to its softness and elasticity, the line may neck down where pressure of cross turns bear on it, thus reducing the cross-sectional area and the strength at that point. A line that easily reacts in this way is said to have poor knot strength.

Good knots usually are so because the strain on the line is carried well back into the body of the knot and evenly distributed so that there is no serious necking down where the line enters. A knot has to be carefully formed by seeing that the turns and pass-throughs are correct and then it has to be carefully watched to ensure that they do not slip out of place, become tangled or wrongly crossed over each other in pulling it down or closing it. A knot usually sets more evenly and results in better strength if the nylon is moistened by placing it in the mouth for a few seconds before pulling it closed. In closing most knots the free end is required to be pulled tight, as well as the two sections of the line.

Knots in nylon should be pulled down tightly to close them and preclude possibility of later slip. But they never should be placed under excessive strain, such as would be produced by pulling with pliers. If turns in the knot are left under excessive strain it has to be relieved somewhere. Usually the squeeze on the line gradually necks it down until the cross-sectional area and the breaking strain are both reduced.

A knot that is tied and then placed under heavy strain may test satisfactorily immediately after tying but be found to fail at relatively low breaking strain a little later. Any line containing knots that is placed under excessive strain in playing a big fish or breaking away from a snag should be cut at the knots and retied before further use, if the maximum breaking strain is to be expected of it.

Joining lines The blood knot is by far the best knot ever devised for joining nylon lines. Fine line, say under 6 kg breaking strain, should be tied with four turns each side. Heavier line may be safely tied with only three turns each side. If the diameters of the two lines being joined differ by more than 15 per cent, three turns should be taken in the coarse line and four in the finer line. Where coarse line is being joined to very fine line, as in attaching leaders for competition casting, a double overhand knot is formed in the end of the leader and the fine line then passed through it and tied in a four or five turn half blood knot behind it.

Considerable care may be required to tie a really safe knot in some of the modern soft nylons. The turns should be laid carefully, with the ends projecting well through and then moistened by placing in the mouth. The two lines and the ends should then be pulled up evenly until the knot is firmly locked. If the operation has been successful the ends may then be cut off quite flush with the knot without fear of them slipping through. This is an important matter with line on threadline reels, where the turns in the spool tend to catch on a knot and stop the outward flow of line.

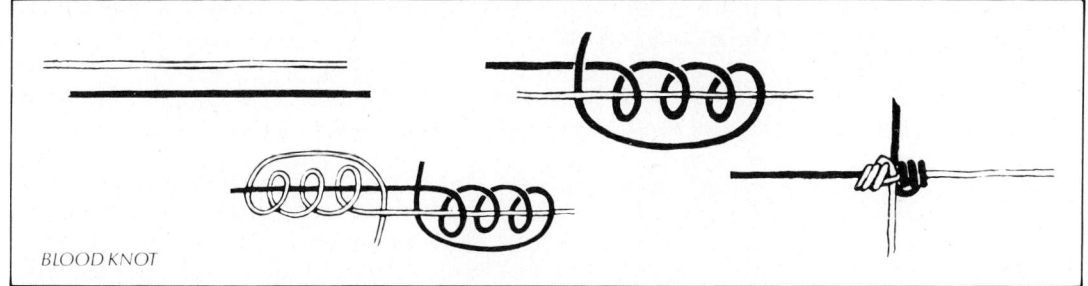

BLOOD KNOT

Tying to a ring or swivel

The three-turn half blood knot is regarded as the strongest and best for tying nylon line to a wire ring. There is some tendency to slip with the fine gauges and here the seemingly obvious course would be to take four turns, but this then becomes a difficult knot to pull down evenly. It is much better to take three turns and clinch the free end by passing it back through the last loop formed, as shown in the second sketch below. Any half blood knot is made safer by clinching it.

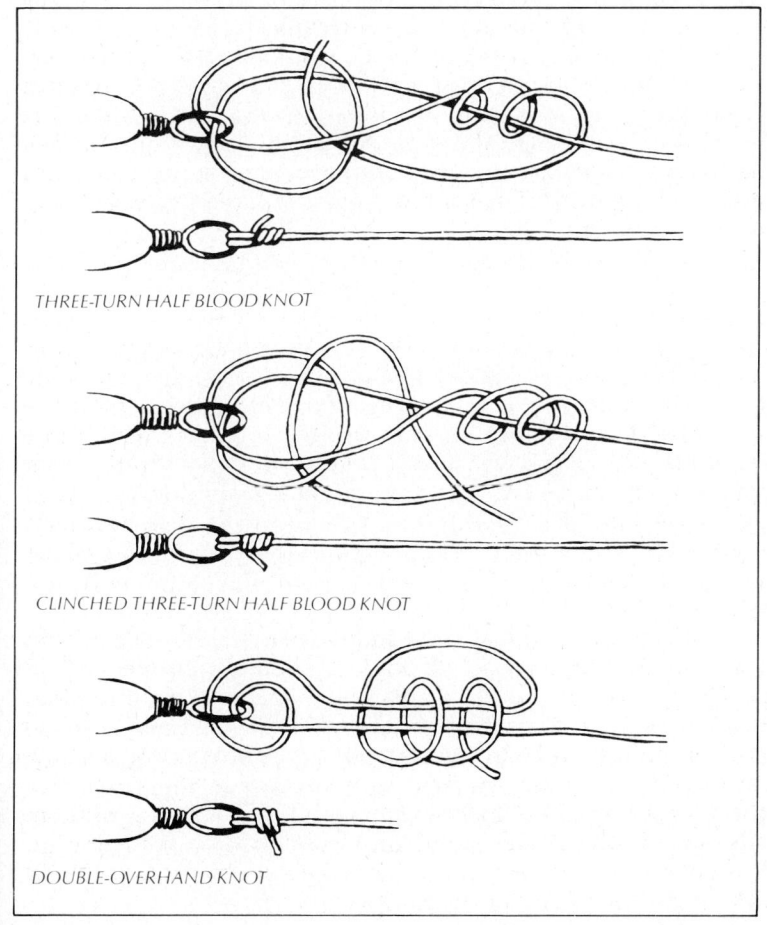

THREE-TURN HALF BLOOD KNOT

CLINCHED THREE-TURN HALF BLOOD KNOT

DOUBLE-OVERHAND KNOT

K ■ KNOTS for anglers

DOUBLE-OVERHAND LOOP KNOT

FRENCH HOOK TO LOOP CAST

REEF FIGURE OF EIGHT KNOT

TUCKED SHEET BEND

One of the disadvantages of this knot is that it is difficult to tie, particularly in regard to passing the end back through the two turns made around the ring. This makes it prohibitive for anglers with defective sight or for tying in poor light. The double-overhand knot is not quite so strong under test, but it is a very reliable tie and with a little practice it may be contrived in the dark. The free end is passed twice through the ring and then laid along the bight of the line. It is then doubled back in a big loop and the free end is passed around the two strands and through the loop twice, after which the whole may be pulled tight.

Tying loops

There are several ways of tying end loops in a line or leader, but tests show that the strongest of these is the double-overhand loop knot. It is made by doubling the end of the line back on itself and tying a double-overhand knot in the two strands, as shown in the sketch at left.

This tie has a particular application which is of some importance. It may be used to quickly make a very satisfactory rig for snapper fishing or drifting for sand flathead. A long loop is tied in the bottom end of the line so that it may be passed through the eye of a snapper sinker and then down over the end to link it on. Then, by doubling the line, two more loops, about 11.5 to 12.5 cm long, may be tied at short distances above. French hooks are then linked on to these in the manner shown in the second sketch at left. Owing to the turned-down eye, the French hooks stand straight out in line with the loop, which forms a stiff cast with little tendency to twist back around the line.

An end loop in a fly line is best made by binding and cementing, but there comes a time on the stream or lake when one has to be tied. The double-overhand is rather too bulky for the purpose. The perfection leader loop is also bulky, but in the thin tip of a tapered line is preferable. Where a leader is looped on the end of such a line the perfection loop is very safe when properly tied and it does keep the bulk down at that point. The sketch (above right) shows how the looped leader is linked through the bound or whipped loop on the fly line.

Where the free end of a heavy leader has to be tied into a loop the reef figure-eight knot is commonly used. With fine leaders this may show a tendency to slip, particularly if the strand of the loop is of larger diameter and smooth surface. The tucked sheet bend is another form of the figure-eight knot, but is more reliable. If the leader is of fine gauge it always is possible to guard against slip by tying a single-overhand knot in the free end, close down against the main knot.

KNOTS for anglers ■ K

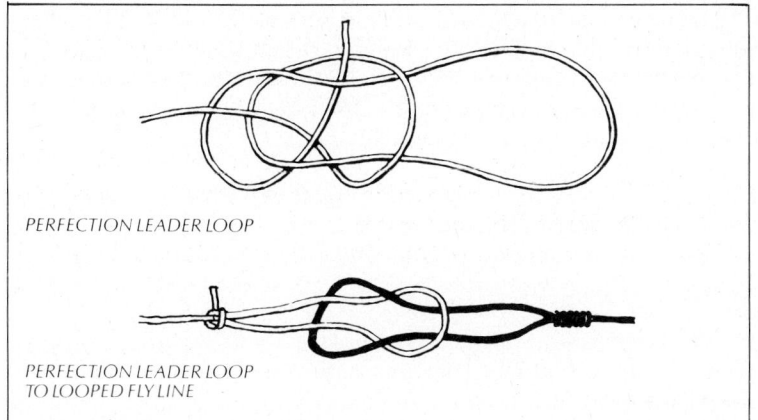

PERFECTION LEADER LOOP

PERFECTION LEADER LOOP TO LOOPED FLY LINE

Tying line to a reel
It is not every angler that has a big fish take his line out until everything depends on the final knot that ties it into the spool, but it may be just as well as to know how to prepare most effectively for such a contingency. When tied around a spool spindle of average diameter, the two strands behind the knot are pulling in opposite directions, almost at right-angles to the straining line. This tends to pull the knot apart and the popular double-overhand is hardly adequate for the purpose. That shown in the sketch is much more preferable, though a careful angler may choose to pass the line around the metal twice before tying back onto it.

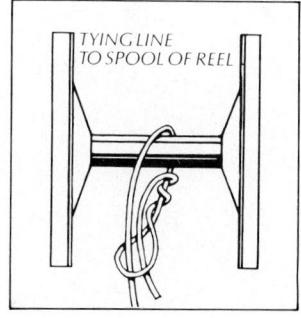

TYING LINE TO SPOOL OF REEL

Tying line to a hook
The best and safest method of attaching a hook to a line is to snood it on in the traditional manner. But, although it may not be so satisfactory, there are times when a more simple knot is useful, such as when a casual angler has not mastered the intricacies of tying a snood or where some extension of the rig from the hook makes it impractical to pass the loop over it.

Undoubtedly, the strongest fix for tying directly into the ringed eye of a hook is the clinched half blood knot, as illustrated, for tying to rings or swivels. However, this often is unsatisfactory in that the hook can become set at any angle to the line, even to the extent of doubling back and becoming twisted with it. It also is unsatisfactory for tying to a flatted hook because it sets the line at a right-angle to the shank.

The return knot, as shown in the sketches, is much more useful in this regard, particularly when used with hooks having turned-up or turned-down eyes or flatted shanks. It is easy to tie and sets the hook out as an extension of the line.

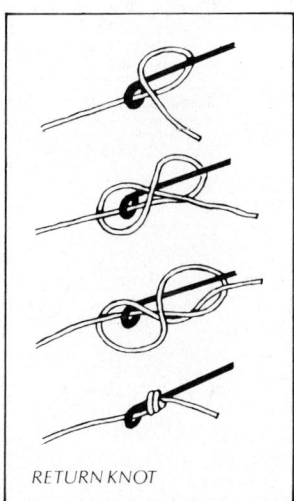

RETURN KNOT

Snooding a hook to a line or cast

This is a simple procedure and many fine-line breaming enthusiasts are capable of carrying it out again and again in the dark without error. But it is a little tedious to explain and some beginners do not have the patience to stay with it until they master it. There are several methods of tying it but the one shown in the accompanying diagrams is the quickest and most satisfactory. It also is the easiest once the procedure is understood and practised.

Taking it step by step, and paying close attention to the diagrams, the procedure may be explained in the following stages:

1. The end is laid along the shank of the hook and a loop is formed in the bight of the line, as shown. Although it is not made plain in the sketch, this loop should be about half as long again as the hook, so that it may be slipped over it a number of times, allowing for the length taken up each time in making a turn around the shank.

The thumb and forefinger of the left hand grips the hook, line and sharply curved back end of the loop, at the flat on the shank.

2. The lower strand of the loop is now picked up and carried up and over the shank, the bend of the hook passing through it in the process. This is most easily and quickly done by placing the first two fingers of the right hand (palm down) in the loop and then bringing it up and over, so that the hook goes through it. Care should be taken to see that the turn so formed goes around both the free end of the line and the shank and not between them.

3. Snooding now has reached the stage where there is one turn over the shank and the right hand is now palm up, with the fingers still in the loop. A little analysis of the position should show that the loop has to be turned over, as shown in step 3, before the manoeuvre can be repeated to wind the same strand in another turn around the shank. This is done by turning the hand over in a clockwise direction and swinging the fingers around in the loop until the hand is back in the original palm-down position.

4. The same strand may now be carried up and over to make another complete turn around the shank and the other two strands, taking the same care to see that the bend of the hook goes through the loop and that the turn goes over the free end and not between it and the shank.

The hand now may be turned over again to bring the winding strand into position to make the next turn. Four, five, six or more turns may be wound on in this manner, depending on whether the line is coarse or fine. As each turn is made, the second finger of the left hand (the holding hand) clamps down onto it to hold it from springing, as the right hand pulls it in under it.

5. When the required number of turns has been made, the snood is closed by first pulling back the standing line to take

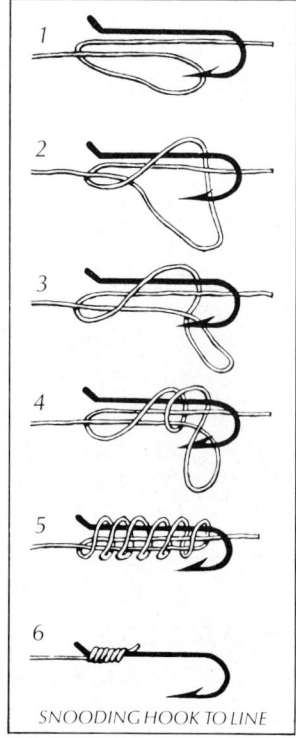

SNOODING HOOK TO LINE

up the loop. Some twist should be seen being carried back through as the loop closes. Care should be taken to see that in the final stage the loop does not slip in under the free end of the line, to get between it and the shank.

Without releasing the grip on the flat of the hook, the free end is now pulled out to take up back end of the original loop.
6. Before the snood is finally pulled quite tight, it should be worked back into its proper position against the flat on the shank. It should be twisted around until the flat kinks away from the line and not towards it, for this possibly may save the line from being chafed through on the edges of the flat in a long-drawn-out battle with a big fish. Where a turned-up or turned-down eye is involved, the snood should be turned until the line is pulling directly through it. These precautions are necessary, for once the snood is closed tightly it may be most difficult to shift it, particularly if the shank is showing signs of rust.

In snooding to a ringed hook, it is necessary to bypass the eye and treat it as a flat, if the hook is required to stand straight out on the end of the line. On the other hand, some anglers prefer to carry the line through the eye, from the back or opposite side to the bend, in order to cock it over on the end of the line, in the belief that it may hook a fish more readily in that way.

Tying to a fly

Tying a fine cast to a fly often is regarded as a precarious business, but mainly because so much has been written about it and so many alternative knots have been suggested. One or two of those reproduced here have been taken from line or tackle manufacturers' literature and included as a warning. A number of points have to be considered in tying to a fly. Some flies allow exceedingly little room behind the turned-up or turned-down eye to accommodate any form of knot, let alone a bulky one. Is the fly or nymph required to project straight out in line with the cast or should it set at an angle or even upright in the water? Does the free end lie back along the belly or back of the fly, or does it project forward or sideways where it causes a flare in the water or presents a false whisker which warns the trout that all is not just what it seems? It takes a good deal of experience to sort out the best knots for various fly-fishing purposes.

The single knot is yet another form of the figure eight. Some manufacturers' literature recommends it, but forget it! It is a hangover from the days of gut and with fine, polished nylon it has a wretched tendency to slip.

The double knot is tied by running the fly up the line, making an overhand knot around two turns of cast and bringing the fly back through them. It appears to be popular in Europe, but is not considered as one of the best in Australia. Where a cast has to be attached to the straight ringed eye of a streamer fly or matuka, the clinched half blood knot provides

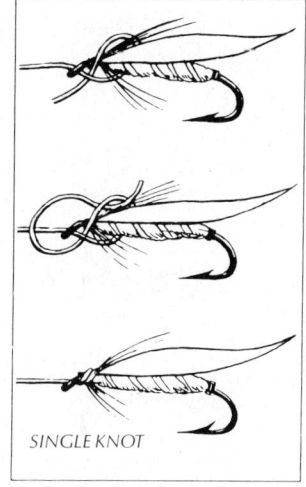

SINGLE KNOT

the maximum strength obtainable, providing that sufficient turns have been taken around the cast. The lure knot is much less difficult to tie but does not have the same strength. With both of these knots the lure may be shoved round sideways to the cast, but it is of little import with streamers, since they are drawn through the water and tend to right themselves.

Hardy's favourite is a veteran tie which is still popular today. It is a double-entry knot, in that the end of the cast is passed through the eye of the hook twice. This may be a difficulty on some of the tiny hooks on gnats, duns and other midget flies. It is absolutely non-slip with nylon and vies with the two-circle turle for superiority in strength and safety. The free end of the cast lies along the belly of the fly.

The turle knot is very simple to tie, is safe with nylon and takes up little space on the neck of the fly. It is made by

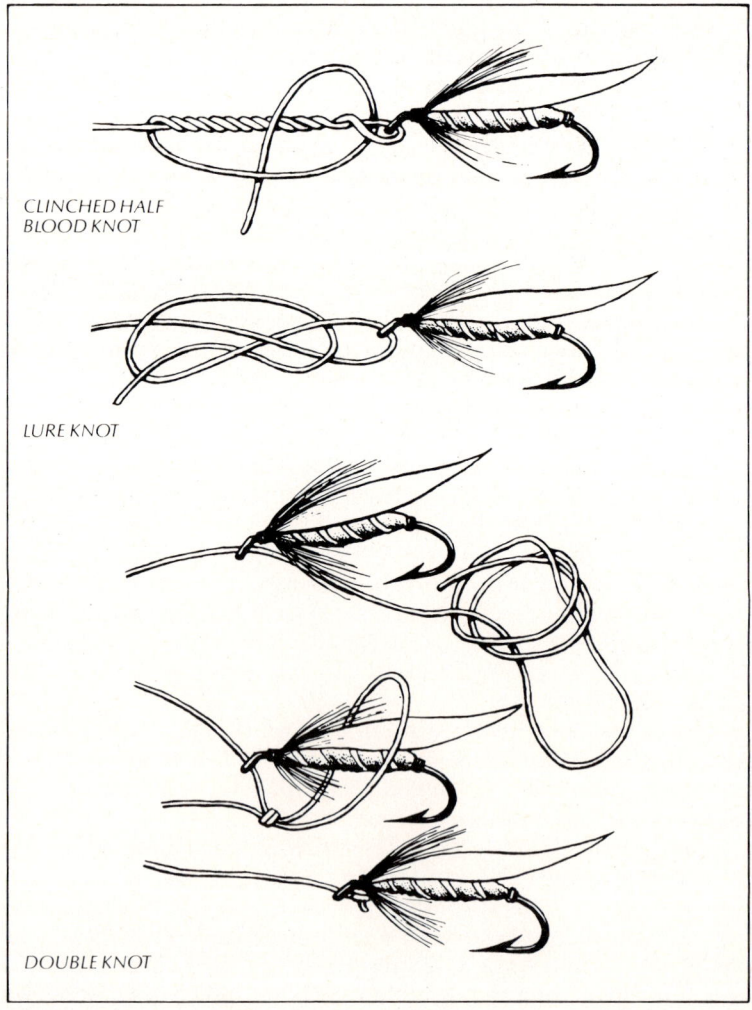

CLINCHED HALF BLOOD KNOT

LURE KNOT

DOUBLE KNOT

running the fly up the cast, throwing a loop in the end and tying it in with a single overhand knot. The fly is then run back down and it and the free end of the cast are pulled back through the loop. The loop is then pulled down tightly onto the neck of the fly. Some slight slip may occur when first pull is made on it after being in the water, so the free end should be left a little long. This is of no consequence, for it lies along the back of the fly. The double turle is made by tying a double-overhand knot in the end of the cast to hold the loop. It is not so elegant on very tiny flies as the plain turle, since it presents more bulk. The end should be left long and it lies along the back of the fly in the same manner. It presents somewhat better knot strength than its lighter counterpart.

The two-circle turle knot is more tedious to tie and is bulky, but in point of strength it surpasses Hardy's favourite by a small margin. It is made by forming a double loop (two strands), tying with an overhand knot and then bringing the fly and free end back through so that the two loops may be drawn down on the neck of the fly, as before. It is best to pull gently on the standing line to partly close the first loop and then to pull on this loop to tightly close the second one. The first may then be closed down by again pulling on the line, taking care to see that the turns lie side by side and are not crossed.

The end may be cut flush, for there is no tendency to slip here, but if it is left long it lies back between the wings of the fly. It is a particularly good knot to use with large fly hooks, such as those employed in angling for large salmon, or in saltwater fly fishing for yellowtail kingfish. It is less conspicuous and appears to lend least bulk when tied to a fly hook with an upturned eye.

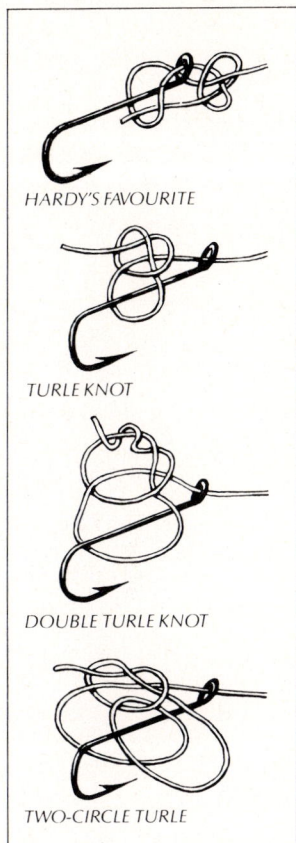

HARDY'S FAVOURITE

TURLE KNOT

DOUBLE TURLE KNOT

TWO-CIRCLE TURLE

L

LAMPREY Primitive parasitic fish of the families Geotriidae and Mordaciidae, frequently confused with eels. Lamprey have no scales, lower jaws or paired fins. Their jawless mouths are lined with thorny teeth that form a sucking disc. With the teeth, they rub away a patch of flesh on the bodies of other fish, enabling the sucking disc to be attached to the host fish. Lamprey spend much of their lives in the sea but are believed to move into fresh water to spawn. Two species of lamprey have been identified in Australian waters. These are the pouched or wide-mouthed lamprey *Geotria australis* and the short-headed lamprey *Mordacia mordax* (synonymous with the narrow-mouthed lamprey *Yarra singularis*). Overseas, lamprey are often regarded as a table delicacy, but they have no angling or commercial value in Australia. One or other of the three species named above are found in all Australian States.

LEATHERJACKET Small, drab-looking fish with long, spiky dorsal spines, of the family Aluteridae (Last, Scott and Talbot classify them in the family Monacanthidae). They are also known as file fish, trigger fish and leather johnnies. Only in recent years and in areas where other fish are scarce have anglers set out to catch leatherjackets. To snapper fishermen anchored over an underwater reef, the leatherjacket are a curse and cause them to soon up-anchor when the leatherjacket start to steal baits or bite through lines. There are about 50 species in Australia, one of the few countries where they are eaten. Elsewhere in the Pacific they are sometimes poisonous.

Leatherjacket give quite good sport when anglers are not trying to catch something else, and when skinned soon after capture their flesh is white and firm and of pleasing flavour. They require skilled preparation and cooking but their bones are less troublesome than in other small fish.

Leatherjacket have exceptional manoeuvrability, swimming very fast, hovering and swimming backwards at will. This explains their exasperating habit of suddenly disappearing and re-appearing. Some anglers claim that they are never there when wanted and always there when not. Small specimens were once used as bait for craypots but there does not seem to be a sufficient number of them about these days for this purpose. They belong to the family of trigger fish, so named because of the large trigger-like spine on the back. This spine when not erected lies in a groove along the fish's back. The large incisor teeth are strong and adapted for biting hard calcareous growths like coral and tube worms. These teeth, as most anglers know, can bite through fine wire hooks.

Beaked leatherjacket

Oxymonacanthus longirostris: A strikingly coloured little leatherjacket frequently spotted swimming among coral and around the edges of reefs close to deep water on the Great Barrier Reef. They grow to 10 cm. They have a light green body, sprinkled with heavy yellow to golden blotches, a bright yellow snout and are often edged in pinks.

Fan-bellied leatherjacket

Monacanthus chinensis: A widely distributed variety occurring in New South Wales, Queensland, Western Australia, Japan, Malaya and New Guinea and regarded as the pig-fish of pier anglers everywhere it turns up. It is characterized by a deep body and a pelvic spine that cannot be moved. It is green all over the body, paler on the belly and has a prominent drooping of the skin near the ventral spine. Grows to 30 cm and should not be eaten, as flesh from this family has caused death. Large shoals of fan-bellied leatherjackets are sometimes found among sub-tropical weed belts.

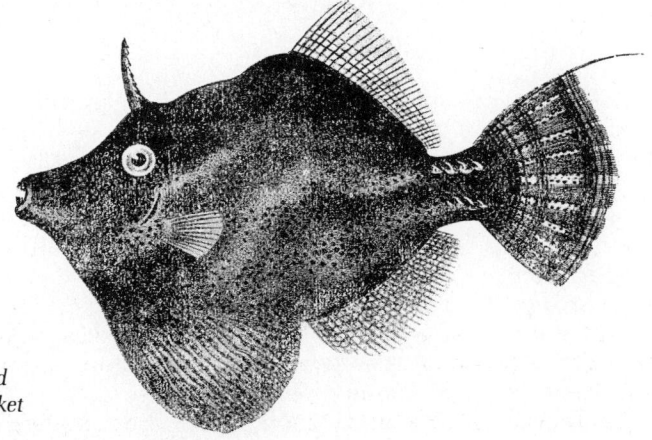

Fan-bellied leatherjacket

Figured leatherjacket

Osbeckia scripta: A big, attractive-looking species so far found only north of Townsville and apparently favours warmer seas. The body is a mottled olive-green with light-blue markings and yellow or yellow-blue fins. They grow to 90 cm and are far more slender than other leatherjackets and have a less pronounced spiky dorsal fin.

L ■ LEATHERJACKET

Horseshoe leatherjacket *Meuschenia hippocrepis:* Good-looking fish of brilliant hues that seldom reach the markets. They compete in colouring with wrasses and parrot fish and some of the trevallies or Barrier Reef exotics. The colour of the body is olive-green above, lighter below, and they are named because of the horseshoe markings on the side of the body behind the pectoral fin. They are found in all States except Queensland. Horseshoes are one of the most numerous of our leatherjackets and grow to 50 cm and 2 kg.

Prickly leatherjacket *Chaetoderma penicilligera:* Plentiful along the Queensland coast and abundant in the north. The flesh is probably poisonous. They grow to 22 cm and the greyish body has its own camouflage in the form of brown fern-like growths that hang like lank pieces of seaweed, out of which yellow eyes peer.

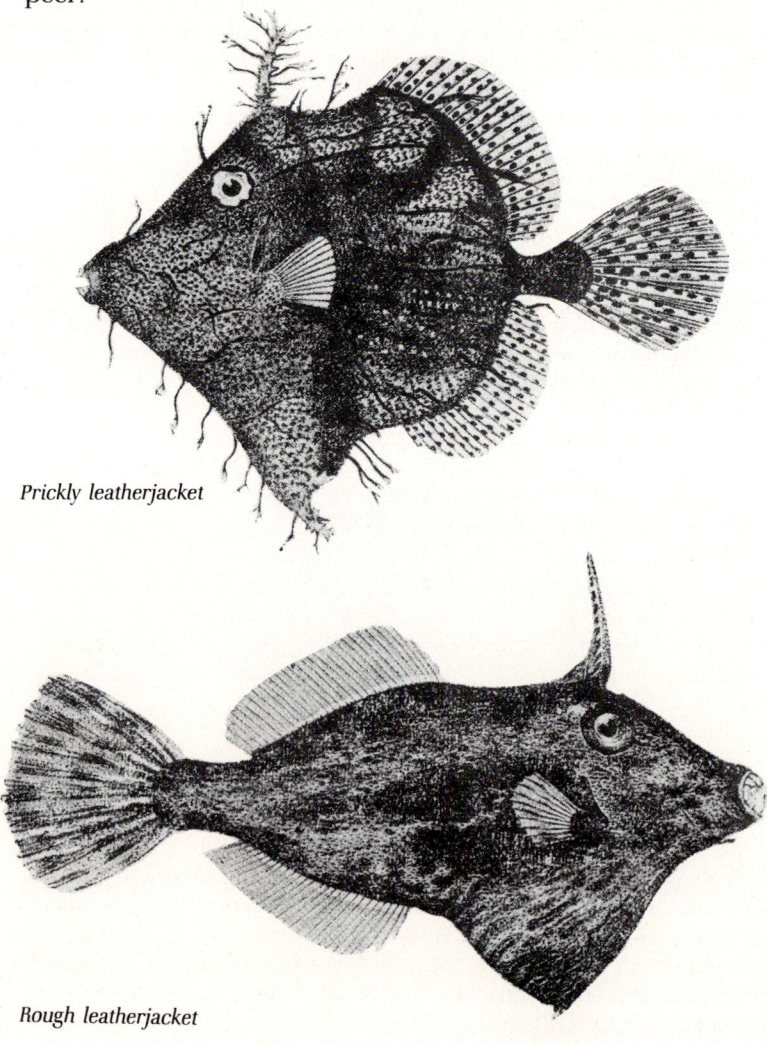

Prickly leatherjacket

Rough leatherjacket

Rough leatherjacket

Scobinichthys granulatus: One of three leatherjackets found in New Zealand where many youngsters acquire their first taste of angling's pleasures by catching them. They bite very hard and will take almost every bait presented to them. New Zealanders specialize in catching them on ultra-light tackle with wire traces attached to the hooks, sinkers on the bottom and the first hook 60 cm above it to avoid underwater vegetation. They grow to 25 cm.

The first spine of two dorsal fins that are set in a shallow groove usually has fine hooks behind. They live in weedy, rocky areas, feeding on crabs, shellfish and marine eggs down to 55 m. Schoolboys lock the dorsal fin in dead fish by raising the second spine with their fingers.

Toothbrush leatherjacket

Penicipelta vittiger: This species has a large and elongated band of stiff hairs on each side above the anal fin. It is found in New South Wales, Victoria, South Australia and Tasmania, reaching 500 g and 32 cm.

Toothbrush leatherjacket

Unicorn leatherjacket

Aluterus monoceros: A very rare specimen was taken off Caloundra and caused Marshall to include this variety in his collection of Barrier Reef exotics. They are believed to reach 75 cm and are found in all warm ocean waters. The colour is brownish, sometimes black and the fins are yellow.

Velvet leatherjacket

Navodon australis: Greenish with darker markings. Grows to a length of 27 cm. Found in South Australia and New South Wales. Caught in comparatively shallow waters and is quite common near reefs. It has a greenish body, with darker spots.

Yellow-finned leatherjacket

Meuschenia trachylepis (Grant classified it as *Cantherines trachylepis*): This species is mainly caught in the estuaries, but is a difficult fish for anglers to land because of its small mouth and strong, sharp teeth. It grows to about 40 cm and is found in New South Wales, Victoria and Tasmania, but is most plentiful in sub-tropical waters. Netted in large quantities in the south for marketing. An attractive fish of expert hovering skill, with an olive-green body and dark longitudinal bands. It has a very strong spine sprinkled with small barbs.

Yellow leatherjacket *Navodon ayraud:* Also known as the Chinaman leatherjacket. Yellow leatherjackets are olive yellow with bright yellow fins and blue-tinged heads and grow to 60 cm, averaging 45 to 50 cm. They are the largest of our leatherjackets, found around the southern half of Australia from southern Queensland to Western Australia, sometimes wandering into north Queensland. Their skin is so rough it is advisable to wear gloves in cleaning them. Yellow leatherjackets are voracious fish who often dispute among themselves for an appetizing bait. They have been caught by hand as they lost perspective in seeking surface bait. Traps containing baits sometimes only have to be lowered a metre over the side before returning them to the boat with several yellow leatherjackets. Despite this eagerness to eat, many anglers move on when leatherjackets appear in these numbers.

Catching leatherjackets
They prefer rocky-bottom areas along the beaches, in the bays and in the estuaries. Large numbers are sometimes caught over reefs and rubble grounds while anglers are fishing for snapper and these deep water specimens are much larger than those caught in the estuaries. Big specimens are also caught along the rocky shorelines in the bays.

Standard boat, surf or rock tackle can be used to catch leatherjackets, depending upon where the angler intends to fish. There is one item that is very important in fishing for leatherjackets: a short wire snood or an extra-long shank hook must be used or the angler will lose a lot of hooks. This prevents the leatherjackets' powerful front teeth from biting through the line.

Leatherjackets will take almost any saltwater bait, but pieces of craytail, prawn or mussel are easily the best. The trouble with mussel, however, is that traces of it are likely to adhere to the line and wherever it does the fish will bite through it. In the estuaries a No. 4 to No. 1 hook is big enough for the small and medium-sized leatherjackets to be caught there, but in the bays and along the rocky beaches a No. 1/0 hook is more suitable for the larger ones.

LEATHERSKIN *See Queenfish.*

LINES Metrication probably has had less success in fishing than in any other Australian pastime in which it has been introduced. For Australia's millions of amateur fishermen have simply ignored the new measures and it obviously is going to take a generation or two for these to become practicable. Rod lengths, sinker weights, sizes of the fish, and reel sizes all continue to be marketed and discussed in imperial measures, mainly because—with a few exceptions—the manufacturers are based in countries still using imperial standards. Worst of all, though, has been the refusal of Australian fishermen to recognize the term 'newton' when referring to their lines.

A newton is 'the force required to accelerate a mass of one kilogram to one metre per second squared'. In other words, the newton has officially replaced the term 'breaking strain', which Australians have used for generations. The Metric Conversion Board, in making the newton law, issued the following conversion for anglers: 1 lb b/s equals 4.44 N and 1 kg b/s equals 9.80 N. Thus a spool of line carrying the markings 200 m 45 N contains 200 m of line that has a breaking strain under the old standards of 10 lb.

Newtons proved unacceptable to so many fishermen the Australian Sporting Fishing Association decided to assess national records in kilogram line strengths, despite the fact that the kilogram force unit has been illegal in all Common Market countries since December 31, 1971, when newtons became law. It has been far simpler for fishermen to understand that a line with a 1 kg b/s has a 2.20 lb b/s under the old scale, 10 kg has 22.04 lb b/s and 60 kg 123.27 lb b/s. But the vast majority of them still ask for lines using pounds not newtons. The test of an outstanding fisherman remains the catching of a 2000 lb fish on a 130 lb b/s line.

BREAKING STRAINS OF AVERAGE HIGH QUALITY MONOFILAMENT NYLON LINES

Diameter		Breaking strain	
mm	in	kg	lb
0.10	0.004	0.6	1.5
0.15	0.006	1.5	3.0
0.20	0.008	2.4	5.0
0.25	0.010	3.4	7.0
0.30	0.012	4.9	10.5
0.35	0.014	6.4	14.0
0.40	0.016	7.7	17.0
0.45	0.018	9.1	20.0
0.50	0.020	11.3	25.0
0.55	0.022	13.6	30.0
0.60	0.024	15.8	35.0
0.65	0.026	18.1	40.0
0.70	0.028	20.4	45.0
0.75	0.029	23.1	51.0
0.80	0.031	25.8	57.0
0.90	0.035	31.7	70.0
1.00	0.039	37.2	82.0
1.10	0.043	45.3	100.0
1.20	0.047	54.4	120.0
1.30	0.051	63.5	140.0

LONG-TOM Family Belonidae: There are about 16 species of this family in Australia. They are also known as skippers, needle-fish and garfish in some countries. In fact, they are closely related to the garfish and flying fish families. Long-tom are long, slender fish that can skip over the water for long distances and have been known to leap-frog turtles and other floating objects. They can inflict a nasty wound with their sharp snouts, and are pugnacious when aroused and will swim towards wading anglers.

Long-toms are best distinguished from garfish by their jaws. Whereas the garfish has a long projecting lower jaw lacking in teeth, the long-tom has two long jaws and many sharp teeth. The long-tom's upper jaw is longer than the lower. Some species of long-tom grow to 1.8 m. Despite their bony bodies—the green or blue bones often cause concern about their freshness—they are splendid fish to eat, especially before they age.

Long-tom are fish of the open sea and of the estuaries, where they apparently spawn. They prefer tropical waters but some species come south in summertime. They are far more plentiful in northern waters than in the south and very rare around Tasmania and South Australia. In the north-west of Western Australia, they have grown to 4 kg or more, though most of those caught on a line are 0.5 to 1.5 kg.

They are difficult fish to hook on a lure because of their double beak of alligator teeth and narrow throat, and are best caught on small strips of fish bait on a single flight of 1 to 4/0 hooks. They are sometimes caught in numbers at the mouths of estuaries or in tidal creeks. They are fine sport because of their habit of leaping through the surface, although they do not become as fully airborne as their relative the flying fish.

Barred long-tom

Slender long-tom *Lewinichthys ciconia:* The species found mostly in our southern waters, though it has periods when it is plentiful in the north. They grow to 90 cm and are caught by professionals using seine nets, usually over a weedy bottom. They bite best on prawns or strips of squid and will snap at lures without taking them.

LUDERICK ■ L

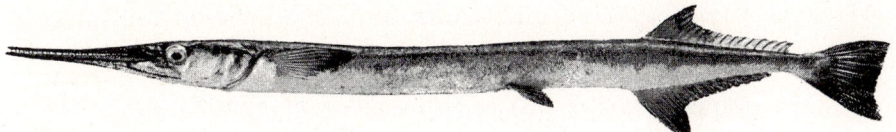

Stout long-tom

Stout long-tom

Tylosurus macleayanus: Found only off Queensland and New South Wales, where they reach 3 kg and 1.2 m. They have the same general characteristics as the slender long-tom but are noticeably plumper around the belly. Stout long-toms are among the most common of all fish in Moreton Bay, Queensland. They are green above, with silvery sides. Several species are plentiful in northern Queensland but they do not attract commercial fishermen like the slender varieties.

Freshwater long-tom

Stenocaulus kreffti: A shorter species, with a deeper, flat body, at times heavily stocked in northern Australian rivers. They are the only member of the family which extends into fresh water. They grow to 65 cm and are quite tasty.

Black-finned long-tom

Tylosurus melanotus: One of the species most common in northern waters. They have teeth that incline backwards and they are very facile in catching small fish such as anchovies, sprats, herrings and hardyheads. They are easily recognized by the black margined anal fin and the black pectoral fin. They grow to 60 cm and are good table fish.

LUDERICK

Girella tricuspidata: Fighting vegetarian, estuarine fish of many aliases, found mostly around reefs, piers, rocks and other places where weed grows. They are known in New Zealand by the Maori name parore and in Australia as niggers, darkies, black bream, rock perch and other local names. Whatever they are called, however, they have a big following among anglers who regard them as one of the gamest fish in Australian waters. Some anglers have such an affection for luderick they seldom fish for anything else.

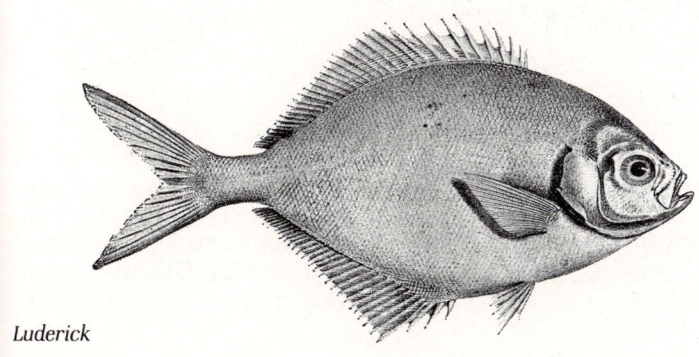

Luderick

LUDERICK

Luderick have a brownish or dark grey body, fully scaled, with between five and eight vertical bands slashed across the sides, which fade quickly after death. The dorsal of up to 16 spines is characteristic of the fish. The head and mouth are small, with teeth in front arranged in rows of three or more, with a flat edge on the female's teeth and three points on each of the male's teeth. Their colour may vary according to habitat; those found off Maroubra, near Sydney, are sometimes completely yellow or even albino white with silvery grey spots. Further north in New South Wales, Queensland and in the warmer waters of New Zealand's North Island, they are dark brown above and lighter below.

According to Grant, luderick have grown to 70 cm and 5 kg but they are most frequently taken at around 35 cm and 0.5 kg. They range from the southern and south-western waters of Western Australia to South Australia, Victoria, Tasmania and up the New South Wales coast to around Maryborough in Queensland. They are extensively hunted by commercial fishermen, who keep them alive as long as possible after netting because the flesh deteriorates rapidly at death. Anglers should bleed them on capture, skinning and filleting them as soon as is practicable and washing the fillets vigorously in salt water.

Weed is the sole bait of a vast majority of Australian luderick anglers, although they will take pipis, squirt worms, cunje, peeled prawns and beach worms. In New Zealand little parore angling is done with weed and baits of shellfish held on the bottom are used with a variety of hook patterns. They are fished for exclusively with rod and reel in both countries and with an extensive use of berley comprising chopped weed and sand or stale breadcrumbs. They have even responded to a berley that included finely chopped lawn clippings. The berley must be heavy enough to take it down where the fish feed.

Luderick require small hooks because of their small mouths, usually No. 12, 10 or 8, with flatted snecks, but some favour French hooks because they consider the ringed eye helps keep the bait in place better. They suck the bait in through their close array of teeth and the angler's hopes of success depend on allowing the fish a few seconds to take the weed and hook. Luderick rods are 2 to 3 m, fitted with a threadline or a 7 cm centrepin reel and most favoured line is an ungreased 1 to 2 kg monofilament.

In Victoria split cane rods and crouch reels are popular for luderick. In Queensland a school of luderick anglers has developed which dispenses with floats and fishes the bottom, but most others use a light pencil type float. They provide particularly good fishing off the training walls of the New South Wales north coast. They are often about in numbers under jetties.

Luderick in the estuaries

In rivers, tidal waters or estuaries the boat should be positioned carefully so that it is across the current. Split shot should be attached to the float to keep it hanging vertically when the current is strong, and thus the size of the float itself depends on the speed of the current. Berleying is essential if the fish are to be drawn and kept near to the boat, but the berley must not run off too fast with the current and lead the fish away. The secret is to berley a section of water and keep the berley there while one tempts the fish with appetizing baits.

As Wal Hardy stressed in his book, *The Saltwater Angler*, luderick are not always found on the bottom despite the fact that they do most of their feeding there. If they do not bite on the bottom, Hardy recommended raising the level of the bait about 30 cm at a time until the fish respond or the angler decides to move elsewhere. He said that most experienced anglers consider the luderick will rise to a bait more readily than they will go down to it.

Luderick fishing in a current can be both richly satisfying and exasperating. It demands a delicate balance of tackle to the current and experience in finding the lightest float that will do the job effectively.

Luderick from the rocks

Rock-hoppers catch many of the best and biggest luderick. They seldom run to less than half a kilogram from the ocean rocks and the average fish approach 1 kg in most such localities. Fish of over 1 kg excite admiration but are by no means unusual. Rock fishing for luderick is a very different proposition from fishing for them in a peaceful estuary. For of all the facets of rock-hopping, luderick fishing is perhaps the most dangerous.

The fine trace needed to outwit the shy, suspicious luderick makes it necessary to fish from low down, near the water, so that spent fish may be taken out in a long-handled landing net or drawn up a shallowly sloping rock. Concentration needed in watching the float often diverts the angler from keeping proper watch upon the sea. Despite these hazards, the numbers, size and fighting prowess of the fish make rock-hopping for luderick one of the most popular sports indulged in by Australian anglers. But the major attraction for the devotees is the luderick's fighting ability and dash when hooked. Few fish, weight for weight, offer such a tenacious and thrilling battle as the luderick hooked in the surge around the ocean rocks.

Theoretically, the tackle used is the same as that for the estuaries, but there are significant practical differences. Rock fishermen favour longer rods, up to 4 m. These rods allow the angler to use longer traces below the floats and to fish over bad foregrounds or to move back from a menacing wave without getting the line hung up. While the fine trace and matching fine tip are as necessary on the rocks as in the estuary, rock rods usually are a trifle heavier in the butt. This gives power for casting the heavier floats needed for the purpose. The Sportex 663 is one of the most popular blanks used today and is a well-proven rod when rock-hopping for 'niggers'. For those who prefer a shorter stick, the Grizzly 1081 is another good choice. Choice of reels lies between centrepin, sidecast and threadline types.

Preparing for luderick angling

The luderick fisherman's prospects frequently depend on his preparations as he must fish with a liberal supply of the right berley and with weed that is preferably gathered from the locality in which he intends to fish. The weed may be found on sticks, rocks or pieces of shell. There should be plenty of it. The novice is wise to experiment before he goes out in the tricky art of baiting a luderick hook. Do not use too much weed; a piece 10 cm long of the fibrous, dark green weed, rather than the leaf variety, is adequate. The middle of the strand is passed over the line about 12 mm above the hook and the two ends plaited in opposite directions down the hook. The weed is not wound too tightly around the hook as it needs to fluff out around it when dropped into the water.

The centrepin reel

Do not be fooled by a plain Nottingham reel labelled centrepin. The true centrepin has a spindle with a groove or flange just below its tip. A stirrup spring in the spool engages this groove to position the spool on the spindle. This makes for a very free-running spool with a long life. As wear occurs, the spool simply sits down a little more on the spindle. Reels of 10 to 12 cm in diameter are best on the rocks. They do not have to be expensive, but the spools must be light to cast well. The inexpensive capstan and steelite models have accounted for thousands of luderick. For the angler able to pay for quality, the imported Avon Royal 3 and Trudex reels offer luxury fishing.

The sidecast reel

Any small sidecast reel can be used for niggers. Recommended in this field is the Alvey blackfish reel, designed by champion New South Wales angler Ken Appel. The sidecast reel requires to have its spool turned so that its axis is parallel to that of the rod before casting and to have it returned to the fishing position afterwards, but it allows very good casting distance when needed to fish an outlying reef.

The threadline reel

These are the simplest reels for a beginner to learn to cast with and have become popular for this reason. But it is not easy in using a threadline to feed line precisely to match the current when fishing a 'draw'. The bail-wire and drag mechanism inescapable with this type of reel takes a lot of the finesse from nigger fishing. The main drawback is the inability to quickly release line while playing a fish in the rise and fall of the wash around the rocks. Too often, rock blackfish (black drummer) take the bait. With a plain reel, the angler can ease tension immediately and let the fish run. Though there is little hope of landing a big drummer on luderick tackle, it occasionally is done. Any form of reel with a drag set near the breaking strain of the trace will result in a smash-up if a drummer takes the hook. Good luderick anglers learn to use both centrepin and sidecast reels, even if they start on a threadline.

The choice of centrepin or sidecast is a matter for the individual. The centrepin is quicker to get into action where the fish are close in, as they usually are. There is delay when using a sidecast in that the spool needs to be turned to casting position to cast, then brought back into fishing position. On the other hand, the sidecast reel will cast a light float rig a greater distance with little skill needed on the angler's part. The locality concerned is the decisive factor but if the reel is to double as a light beach or bobby corking reel, the sidecast wins hands down.

Recommended rigs

Larger floats are needed to swim in the broken water around the rocks. Down currents will take light estuary gear down and keep it down for long periods and the rock-hopper usually needs greater casting distance. Accordingly, weighted, long-shafted casting floats, from 35 to 45 cm long, are used from the rocks. These floats have the tip of the stems painted with red or yellow fluorescent lacquer, or the angler adorns them with fluorescent plastic tube or fluorescent plastic golf tees, so that they may be more easily seen in the broken water. The shy, timid luderick will seldom look at a bait on line heavier than 2.7 kg breaking strain and 1.8 kg is wiser. This can be used straight through or as a light trace below a heavier main line, which is preferable, since rock blackfish and snagging on cunje-infested reefs can cause loss of floats with a straight-through rig. A good combination is 2.7 kg line and 1.8 kg trace. The trace needs to be from 1 to 4 m long, according to the depth of water and other conditions.

The float may be either fixed or running. Running floats give the advantage of having only a short tail hanging below the float when casting, but usually need a little more weight in the form of split shot or sheet lead at the terminal end to draw the line down after the rig enters the water. It is a good plan to buy, or make, all floats as running floats. A running float can be used as a fixed float, but not vice versa. A running float may be mounted in a fixed position by winding the line several times around the lower stem, then passing it two or three times through the lower runner. Most anglers prefer to use a fixed float to simplify the rig and make sure the bait actually drops down to where the fish are feeding.

The float should be ballasted with lead at the bottom of the tail so that a minimum weight is used on the line itself. The float should swim with only a few centimetres of stem showing above the water. The ballast needed is governed by conditions; in very rough water less ballast is needed than in calmer conditions.

Hooks, lead and bait
The best hooks are sneck or suicide patterns, from No. 10 to No. 7. Of the two, the sneck are made of finer wire and it is easier to slip a bait over the fine flat when baiting up.

The row of split shot, tapering in size from the float down, is seldom seen in use from the rocks nowadays. A short length of sheet lead pinched on the line makes a much less conspicuous sinker. A strip of lead 6 mm wide is only 3 mm wide when doubled and pinched on to the line. It should be mounted at least 30 cm above the hook, or higher in clear water. Many luderick anglers favour a two-hook rig, with the top hook attached by a short cast so that it hangs about 75 cm above the lower one.

The long-stranded green weed of the estuary angler is used as bait at times along the rocks, but the favoured bait is cabbage or lettuce *Ulva lactuca*, a pretty green weed found in pools and wherever there is a heavy wash over the rocks. This may be used in three ways:

(1) Most rock fishermen favour mounting an entire plant as a bait. Select a young, bright, fresh-looking plant, no bigger than a 10 cent piece. Pluck it carefully from the rock. Pass the hook carefully through the holdfast (root) down into the centre of the rosette. Anchor by throwing a half-hitch of trace around the holdfast and drawing tight. A variation of this is to strip the outer leaves from the plant and use only the young, tender inner leaves as the bait.

(2) Often lettuce throws out a long, narrow leaf. Take one of these longer strips, pass the hook through the centre and double the leaf over the hook. Anchor with two half-hitches around the ends, ABOVE the hook.

(3) The single leaf. This is the most difficult bait of all to present and dexterity comes only after considerable practice. Take a single leaf of cabbage. Pass the hook through it twice, then work the upper end of the leaf up over the flat of the hook until the leaf is held between the line and the flat, with the hook lying flat along the leaf. This bait is often deadly when the fish are shy and picky with the larger baits.

The sidecast rig
Sidecast reels twist the line during casting, so the line must be free to untwist itself after the cast has been made. This is achieved by mounting a swivel between the rod and the float. Since the fine line used in luderick fishing develops very little

torque, only the smallest and finest swivels will work. Large swivels have too much internal friction to work with fine line. The swivel has a better chance to operate properly if used with a running float. It is expecting too much for a fine line to rotate a heavy casting float.

Fishing technique

In the estuaries, luderick usually swim deep, feeding along the bottom. In the open sea, they feed where the water boiling back from the rocks carries scraps of weed and other food. Usually the best fishing is where there is choppy, broken water, especially near gutters with a long trail of milky water running out in the draw. In the swirl, food fragments are churned about or drift at all depths. Accordingly, the angler's bait needs to drift as naturally as possible. Some weight is needed on the trace, but the less there is, the better. A heavily weighted, inert bait will attract few, if any, luderick. It is possible to fish too deeply, where the majority of the strikes will be from rock blackfish and the useless cocky (rock kale). Depth of bait usually varies from 2 to 4 m, depending on the depth of water and very seldom exceeds 3.5 to 4 m. A good suggestion is to start at 2 or 3 m and to then vary the depth until bites are being obtained or the bait is catching on the reefs and pulling the float down.

The luderick's bite usually brings a gentle drawing down of the float. Only with the single leaf presentation does the angler set the hook immediately. With the more usual baits he gives the fish time to take the hook. Anglers give arbitrary figures, such as a slow count of one, two, three, but it is something which is only learned from experience. The spectacular sweeping strike with the rod is not necessary and is more likely to snap the cast than hook the fish. To set the tiny hook it is only necessary to lift the tip sufficiently to straighten the line.

If wind and wave conditions form a belly in the line floating on the water, a smart sweep of the rod is necessary to whip up the slack, but this should not cause a heavy strike at the hook. Judgment is needed. With a correctly weighted rig, the float should sink into each wave crest, emerging from the water again as the crest rolls over the float. This 'water down' often assists the timid pull of a luderick at the bait. If the float remains submerged after the wave rolls past, there is very likely a fish on the hook.

The vital line float
With such a timid fish, it is obvious that the line should not sink between the rod and the float. Should it be allowed to sink, the instant the angler moves the rod to set the hook the submerged line will pull the float over on its side. This does not give a clean lift, but transmits a warning down the line and allows the wary luderick to spit the bait out and flee.

In the old days, silk twist was the favourite luderick line.

L ■ LUNGFISH

This holds grease for an appreciable time and floats beautifully on the surface, even in rough water. Despite all its other desirable properties, nylon monofilament is not as effective in this respect. Many different line floats have been offered the angler, but none is better with nylon than plain old Vaseline. Fortunately, nylon is only just heavier than neutral buoyancy even when soaked and occasional re-greasing will keep it afloat.

Nets are unnecessary
Few rock-hoppers carry landing nets for luderick. Usually, fishing is carried out from very low rocks, with the angler pitting his safety upon his own alertness. After the often protracted battle, the beaten fish is stranded with a suitable wave or slid up a smoothly sloping rock.

Locating luderick
In a strange locality, anglers look for luderick where there is lively shallow water not more than 4.5 m deep—the fish are seldom found in deeper water. There should be some growth of cabbage in the vicinity, not necessarily a heavy growth. Sand or rock bottom is immaterial. Indented shorelines with gutters running into the rock creating swirl and white water are almost always luderick grounds. The luderick is one fish which seems to be adapting to civilization and it still fishes well at times around the ends of our polluted metropolitan beaches. This makes it a particularly valuable fish. Luderick may be caught all the year round, but on our east coast the best period usually is from January to June. Low rocks, awash at high tide, often carry a growth of cabbage. In some localities this growth is obviously cropped by luderick, rock blackfish and rock kale feeding at high tide. Look for such a cropped area around the gutters when exploring new territory.

Berley on the rocks
The rock-hopper does not carry the heavy bag of sand-mixed berley so necessary in the estuaries. It would be a physical impossibility to get such a burden to most of the luderick spots along the rocks. The rock-hopper berleys a wash by scraping weed from the surface of the rocks and allowing the surge to distribute it in the sea. Since most luderick grounds are slippery underfoot, the angler usually wears shoe plates. These serve a double purpose at the luderick grounds as berley scrapers and safety grips. The angler simply scrapes off the berley with his feet from time to time as he fishes and lets the backwash from the waves carry it down to the fish.

LUNGFISH

Neoceratodus forsteri: Fully protected freshwater fossil fish which many claim should not be called a fish at all. Lungfish have attracted world attention as survivors of fish that disappeared 200 million years ago. They are natives of the Burnett and Mary Rivers of Queensland, but since 1895 have

Lungfish

been introduced to some south Queensland waters, including Enoggera Reservoir, the North and South Pine Rivers, the Stanley River and the Condamine River. Large lungfish have been seen downstream from Somerset Dam. They have been sent to aquariums in other parts of the world, but these areas remain the only area in the world where they are free. Lungfish are also found in Africa and South America, but these are in no way related to the Australian Ceratodus.

Lungfish have characteristics of amphibians but die if they are taken from the water. But they can take in oxygen both through the gills underwater and when the water fouls by rising to gulp it in through a lung-type sac. Despite their notoriety they are far from being a fading species, breeding well in their own corner of Australia. They spawn in winter, producing grape-like eggs. Their bodies are too cumbersome for them to move on land and unlike the lungfish of Africa and South America they cannot survive long if they are trapped in pools that dry up. But they are surprisingly hardy fish, able to outlive other fish in waters that become polluted.

Australian lungfish grow to a maximum of 1.8 m and 45 kg, by which time they are thought to be as much as 100 years old. Whitley says they have survived in captivity for 33 years. They eat anything from apple slices, pieces of beef and liver, to corn and lettuce. They were eaten in numbers by Aborigines and the early settlers who, because of their pink flesh, thought they were a type of salmon. They are shy but inquisitive, hiding behind weeds from visitors, but unable to resist taking a peek when your back is turned.

Magazine feature writers, biologists and others have taken them in nets in the Burnett and Mary Rivers, returning them to these mostly turgid waters after brief inspections. All have remarked on the extreme sliminess of the Ceratodus and of the 'unreal' feeling of their bodies, indicating that although they have large scales lungfish felt like outsized slugs or snails. The more expert students of this remarkable fish have learned to expect the thick slime body covering.

They are an olive-green in body colouring, sometimes dark brown on the tails and fins and a dull golden colour on the lower jaw. The exceptionally small eyes are brown and there are touches of red on some of the over-lapping scales. They swim by moving the paddle-like tail and working paired flippers or fins. Their teeth, crushing plates shaped like a comb, have excited every ichthyologist who has ever examined one.

Not the least of the lungfish's achievements has been that they have several times been artificially bred. Indeed, they have thrived in museum aquariums where they have shown a particular fondness for chopped liver. Roughley suggests, however, that they locate their food by smell rather than by sighting, for they often swim into aquarium walls and are more at home lazing on the bottom of their pools or buried under sand. There is a theory that they do better in water that is too murky to permit the observation required in museum pools.

LURES *See Tackle.*

M

MACKEREL

Beautiful, graceful fishes of the family Scombridae, swift and powerful swimmers closely related to albacore, bonito and tunas of the Thunnidae family. Despite the speed and grace of their movement, they are not considered good table fish because of their soft flesh. They frequently move in vast schools. Peron saw some of these schools in south-western Australia in the 19th century and more recently scientists have followed the progress of shoals several kilometres long from aircraft. They are sometimes known as slimies because of their mucous skin. They have rich potential as canning fish but are mainly used for bait by amateur fishermen.

Blue or common mackerel

Scomber australasicus: Also known as slimy mackerel and spotted chubb mackerel, is an iridescent green fish with irregular dark green or bluish oblique or blotchy markings. They are silver below, with yellowish-green or bluish fins, some edged in black, and grow to 50 cm, although their average size is around 37 cm. They mature at 1.5 kg when nine to 10 years old. Mackerel have large mouths, with the gape reaching to below the front border of the eye. They are migratory fish of the open seas that sometimes enter coastal waters. They are immediately recognizable from jack mackerel by the absence of bony scutes along the lateral line. They are frequenty taken on medium spinning gear in southern Queensland and the other Australian States, and also occur off Hawaii, New Zealand, China and Japan.

See Spanish mackerel; see also Tuna.

Blue or common mackerel

MACQUARIE perch *Macquaria australasica:* Although the Macquarie perch are not considered game fish they do provide good sport for anglers and are an excellent table fish. They are found in the Murray-Darling River System and in the Yarra and Barwon Rivers, Victoria, in which streams they have been acclimatized.

Macquarie perch are dark, silvery grey on top and lighter in colour on the ventral surface. They grow to about 3.5 kg and 38 cm and the size of those caught today averages just below 1 kg. Specimens up to 1.8 kg are, however, fairly common in the Eildon district in Victoria, although the famous run of Macquarie perch up the Jamieson River seems to be a thing of the past.

Macquarie perch feed on worms, crustaceans and insects and while they are occasionally caught on a spinner or a small, dark wet fly, they are primarily bait fish. They can be caught in most places where perch congregate: alongside weed beds, close to or among underwater snags or alongside the main current in the stream. But the best spot is alongside sandbanks, particularly those spots where the water swirls around the sloping sand to form back eddies. In these sandy-bottomed areas where the banks slope down to the deeper waters, earthworms and shrimps are usually successful, but there is one bait that is very effective in these areas—that is the blowfly larva or maggot. These 'gentles' are possibly taken freely because they show up well over the sand and they are similar to the small grubs in the stream upon which the fish feed.

Sloping sandbanks are the usual places for the cattle to come down to drink, or the sandbank could well have been formed by the cattle themselves, but the Macquarie perch take no notice of the cattle.

Macquarie perch of the Murray River can be caught more easily than those transplanted into southern streams, but they can become very shy of man in the more heavily fished areas. If the angler tramps noisily along the bank or shows himself on the skyline he will lessen considerably his chances of catching a big fish. Provided the angler keeps out of sight of the fish in the shallows and does not thump around the bank the big fish will feed practically under his feet.

Macquarie perch

They have a frustrating habit of playing with the bait and not taking it properly. If they persist in doing this and refuse to pick up the bait and run a few yards with it in the normal fashion, the angler should change from a No. 4 hook to a No. 10 and should replace the small sinker with a single split shot. The best rig is to use a 2.7 kg line, a 90 cm leader and a No. 4 model perfect or sproat hook. If fishing in the current, a small round sinker can be placed on the line above the leader, but it should be rigged so that the line can run freely through it. To prevent it running down on to the leader, place a single split shot where the line joins it.

Always allow a Macquarie perch to run a few metres before attempting to set the hook, in fact the best technique is to let the line run out and then set the hook the moment it stops. When hooked, big Macquarie perch will often run into the current and turn side-on to it, thus making it almost impossible for the light-line angler to retrieve his fish. Only by easing off the pressure a little, without giving the fish enough slack to throw the hook, can it be induced to move. From that point on, the angler will have to 'play it by ear'.

For the best sport a 2.7 m, fairly whippy trout rod is used and quite often this is used with a threadline reel, but if a fly rod is chosen, the reel seat will have to be moved up to take this type of reel.

There seem to be no particular times for fishing for Macquarie perch, except that they bite best in the evening or during that lull preceding a thunderstorm when the thunder can be heard in the distance. Like most fish, Macquarie perch dislike sunlit waters on a hot summer's day and are more likely to be caught near patches of shade. They are also known as black bream, silvereye, white-eye, and mountain perch.

Macquarie perch techniques

MANGROVE jack

Lutjanus argentimaculatus: The *Lutjanus* group of sea perch or 'Pacific snappers' is a large and varied one containing at least 19 members, most of which have several aliases, so it adds to the confusion that the mangrove jack is also known by a variety of names, including creek red bream, red snapper, rock barramundi, dog bream, purple sea perch. In northern waters the name 'red bream' usually refers to immature mangrove jack of just under 1 kg weight. Much confusion is caused by the fact that in southern Queensland and northern New South Wales this fish often is erroneously called red bass. In the Northern Territory it is generally known as mangrove snapper, possibly the best and most accurately descriptive name yet applied to it.

The use of the name red bass is regrettable and should be discouraged, for it may be applied correctly only to a Barrier Reef fish, *Lutjanus bohar*, which is of the same family but is a quite distinct species. It is easy to see where the confusion arose, for the two fish are so alike in appearance that it takes

M ■ MANGROVE jack

close and well-informed inspection to tell them apart. The confusion is all the more regrettable because the mangrove jack is a splendid food fish and the red bass is known to have been such frequent cause of the ciguatera form of fish poisoning that it is not accepted for sale in the fish markets.

There are several features which enable clear distinction between the two species:

MANGROVE JACK	RED BASS
Eye pit: No pit before the eye.	A deep fossa or pit before the eye, between the eye and nostril.
Teeth in upper jaw: Two small canines at the front, followed on either side by bands of small, needle-like teeth of which the outer row is enlarged.	Two small curved canines at the front, followed on either side by a larger canine, a short gap and then a single row of short strong, needle-sharp teeth.
Teeth in lower jaw: Four big, sharp canines on either side of gap in front, followed by bands of sharp villiform teeth as in upper jaw.	Canine-like teeth at the front, followed on either side by two larger canines and a single row of strong, sharp-pointed teeth.
Scales: Easily dislodged, sometimes come away in handling.	Very tightly set and difficult to dislodge.

It is now considered that the mangrove jack lives in the estuaries, rivers or tidal creeks until it reaches sexual maturity, at a weight of 3 to 3.5 kg and then moves out to the offshore reefs, where some have been known to grow to as much as 90 cm and at least 10 kg.

It mainly is fished for along by the mangroves, logs or other cover in the estuaries, rivers and creeks. Sometimes it is found well up in the freshwater reaches of rivers. It occurs throughout all north Australian waters and is found as far south as

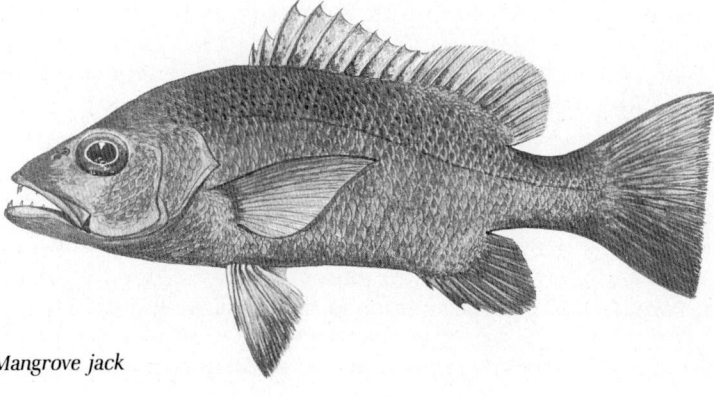

Mangrove jack

MANGROVE jack ■ M

A superb mangrove jack, often erroneously called red bass, caught at Ballina on the New South Wales north coast.

Nambucca Heads, on the New South Wales coast. It prefers dense cover and the strike at bait or lure is invariably followed by a dive back to the same cover. This can result in frequent snagging or cutting of lines on shell-encrusted mangrove roots. For a short distance the fish is a powerful fighter and the struggle to keep it out from snags or mangrove roots is always a drama. In open water the fish is still powerful but is much less trouble.

As it is well equipped with teeth, damage to tackle and even fingers is frequent. Wire trace is necessary. The habitat and feeding pattern of the fish has resulted in a wide range of 'answers' from anglers, but it is safe to say that the nature of the fish allows the angler little room for finesse. Either he turns a jack straight away or he loses the encounter.

Lure fishing for jack

This is an excellent species for lure fishing, since the fish appear to have territorial feelings about their living quarters. Thus they strike at an intruding lure just on principle, whether they are hungry or not. The same applies to a drifting bait of almost any kind, with prawn and crab high on the list of preferences.

Angling writer Vic McCristal conducted tank tests on a captured mangrove jack which clearly showed its preference for a prawn diet. One most notable trait of the fish (for a fish, that is) was intelligence. When new to the tank, it would lie on its side under the lip of an earthenware pipe to stay out of sight. Later it became tamer but the striking characteristic of the instant return to cover was apparent whenever it was fed. Tested for preference with fish flesh and live prawn, the prawn invariably was snapped up first. Therefore, a typical bait fishing method is to drift beside a patch of sunken logs or a deep corner of mangrove roots, using a big float, live bait and no slack line. Thus, the fish can be struck hard and instantly checked from dashing back to cover.

Alternatively, when using lures, anglers develop the knack of casting so the lure does not lie close to cover for long. This technique involves a retrieve which starts in the same split second as the lure strikes the surface, so that a jack has to chase out a few feet from cover. This margin often means the difference between success and failure. Occasionally a fish will follow right out and only strike as the lure is being lifted from the water or as it enters the shallows of a sandbank. These are the easy ones on which an angler stands an excellent chance. A further method which has had good results is the use of a sidecast outfit with linked hooks and gar baits cast close to cover and then retrieved, using an erratic retrieve with a side-swaying rod action.

The average size of creek fish appears to be about 1 kg. Larger specimens up to 2 kg are not uncommon, but fish of over 3 kg are rare. Occasionally runs of large fish, averaging 2 to 2.5 kg, are taken. It seems likely that sea run specimens of more than 10 kg return to the estuary mouths to spawn, but little actual research has been done to verify this. On one point anglers agree—the mangrove jack is not merely a capable opponent, it is a delicious table fish widely approved wherever it is taken. Comparison of the table qualities of grilled mangrove jack beside the highly regarded barramundi resulted in a unanimous vote of five experienced anglers in favour of *Lutjanus*.

Tackle and hooks for mangrove jack
The tackle chosen must be strong and durable. A strong spinning rod, a saltwater model reel able to cast up to 8 kg test monofilament, durable lures fitted with heavy duty rings and hooks—in fact, the same general approach recommended for barramundi—is the answer. Much of the fishing done in waters favoured for this species will result in unintended catches of cod, trevally and others even less wanted, such as fork-tail catfish.

Baits should be live prawns or mullet, the black fiddler crabs found in mangrove country or garfish on a linked-hook rig. The choice between bait and lures is for the angler. Depending how he uses it, bait will result in a greater variety of fish, including ordinary bream (*Mylio* spp.) and grunter. Or it may result in unwanted species such as catfish, sharks or mangrove eels, none of which take lures as freely as more desirable fish such as mangrove jacks, barramundi, estuary cod or flathead.

MARINE ecology

Ecology is the scientific study of the relationship between living creatures and their environment or conditions affecting the existence, growth and welfare of the creature in question. In the sea, these conditions include factors such as the chemical composition of the water, temperature, pressure and currents, depth, availability of food supplies and the shape and substance of the coastline and sea-bottom.

Oceans cover nearly 71 per cent of the earth's surface. More than three-quarters of the dry land is situated north of the equator. Eight-tenths of the southern hemisphere containing the larger part of the Pacific, the South Atlantic and Indian oceans, is covered by water. Two of these oceans—the Pacific and Indian—enclose Australia in a vast expanse of water.

Depth of the sea

If the earth was a perfect sphere and its solid surface was quite smooth, the entire globe would be covered by water nearly 3 km deep. But the bottom of the sea possesses even more impressive hills and valleys than those on land. The greatest sea depth so far measured is approximately 11 km, off the Mariana Islands in the western Pacific. This compares to the 8.7 km of Mount Everest, the highest point on land.

The Mariana Trench, as it is known to oceanographers, is situated in the centre of a chain of deep furrows or chasms, several of which exceed 9.5 km in depth, extending from the Aleutian Islands south to Tonga and roughly following the outline of the Asian continent. Similar chasms are found southwest of Sumatra and Java in the Indian Ocean, off the Pacific coast of South America and in the Atlantic.

More significant to marine ecology and to anglers, however, are the areas of raised seabed bordering the major land masses, known as the continental shelves and the underwater hills and valleys making up the great ocean basins.

The width of the continental shelves varies from around 1200 km to no more than a few metres, with around 60 km as an average. The average depth works out at 126 m compared to depths of from 4 km to more than 5 km in the ocean basins. Continental shelves take up about 7 per cent of the total surface area of the sea and this figure rises to nearly 20 per cent when the slopes leading to the ocean floor are added. These slopes descend in places as much as 9000 m to what scientists call the abyssal floor. The continental shelf and slope to the depth of around 180 m is known as the neritic zone, from *nerita*, the Latin name for the shellfish we call a mussel. This is the spawning ground of many varieties of fish and the most important part of the sea to fishermen.

The average depth of the oceans is around 3600 m, more than four times the average height of the land above sea level. More than three-quarters of the entire sea bottom lies between 3000 and 6000 m in depth. This area is crossed by a number of ridges dividing the deeper parts of the oceans into a series of basins. An example of this is the Macquarie Ridge, extending from Tasmania to the Antarctic. The significance of these ridges is that they impede the flow of deep currents. The Macquarie Ridge acts in this way as a barrier between the Pacific and Indian Oceans.

The position of these underwater ridges and rises, together with the coastal shape of the land masses and their continental shelves largely dictates the manner in which water moves around the oceans. These ridges and currents are associated with other factors such as climate and the chemical composition of the water in distributing the food on which all sea creatures depend.

Composition of sea water

The water of the seas is a mineral brew containing more than half the 90 or so elements found in nature, either in solution or as colloidal particles held in suspension. Most of this material has been eroded from the land by winds, rain or glaciers, or produced by chemical action or the action of living organisms in the sea itself.

Nine salts make up the greater part of all the dissolved solids in sea water. The chief of these is sodium chloride or common salt, of which the sea contains twice as much as all the other eight put together. An average sample of ocean water contains 35 parts of the combined salts by weight in every thousand parts. Of the 35 nearly 24 parts will be of sodium chloride, five of magnesium chloride, four of sodium sulphate and about one and one-eighth of calcium chloride. The one remaining part is made up of 66 per cent potassium chloride, 19 per cent potassium bromide, 3 per cent boric acid and 2 per cent strontium chloride.

Oxygen and hydrogen locked together in molecules of water are, of course, by far the most common elements found in the sea. But there are also large quantities of free oxygen in sea water, mainly taken in from the atmosphere, but also produced by marine plants. This oxygen, with nitrogen and carbon dioxide and other gases of the atmosphere, saturates the upper layers of the sea. In fact, the percentage of oxygen found in these surface waters is commonly 50 per cent higher than in the atmosphere, owing to the varying solubility of the gases which make it up.

Nitrogen is utilised in the form of nitrates, some of the most important of the nutrient salts which are the basic nourishment of all life in the sea. Carbon dioxide is taken up by the plants of the upper waters and turned into carbohydrate, releasing oxygen.

It is the oxygen in the sea, as on land, that is the key to life itself. Not only does it sustain all animals and plants, from the smallest to the largest, but also the bacteria of the seabed which break down the refuse of dead plants and animals and return the nutrient salts back to the sea.

These salts, which are compounds of calcium and iron, and

silicates and phosphates, as well as nitrates, are present only in very small amounts in sea water. They are thousands and even hundreds of thousands of times more scarce than chlorine, sodium, sulphur and magnesium. Strangely, although these are the chief mineral constituents of the sea they play only a minor part in maintaining life in it.

Among the many substances which the sea possesses in minute quantities is gold. Every tonne of sea water contains a grain of the precious metal, so that the oceans hold by far the world's richest gold deposit.

Salinity
The saltiness of the sea varies considerably. The Red Sea, for instance, contains 40 parts of dissolved salts to every thousand parts of water, compared to 20 parts in the Black Sea and no more than eight in the Baltic. Even in the open oceans salinity varies in places between the limits of 33 to 37 parts per thousand. Yet despite this variation, the relative proportions of the dissolved salts discussed previously remain the same. This means that the amounts of all the chief constituents of a sample of sea water can be calculated by the simple process of measuring one of them. In practice the constituent usually chosen is chlorine, the sample being said to have a chlorinity of so many parts in a thousand.

Factors causing this variation in salinity include rainfall, melting ice, evaporation and the number and size of rivers flowing into the area. Belts of high salinity occur in the tropics where hot sunshine combines with strong dry winds. In between, along the line of the equator, the salinity decreases owing to the cloudy skies and higher rainfall of the doldrums. But the lowest salinity occurs in the polar seas of the Arctic and Antarctic, owing to falls of rain and snow plus the effects of melting ice and the low rate of evaporation.

Salinity increases the density of sea water. As a consequence water of high salinity tends to sink and be replaced by water of lower salinity. But temperature also plays a part in the process, density increasing as the water becomes colder. In the polar seas these factors combine. When the surface freezes, the water below the ice becomes more salty. This high density water sinks, spreading out into the depths of the great ocean basins.

Less salty or warmer layers form above the polar water, sealing it from the surface. This water of the abyss maintains a temperature of around 1.6 degrees C, just above saltwater freezing point. On the ocean floor the water temperature is slightly raised by the enormous pressures, which average around 420 kg to the square centimetre compared to the familiar 1 kg we know at sea level. Pressure also increases density.

Scientific tests disclose that deep water held captive in this way by the forces of temperature, salinity and pressure may not have had contact with the surface for many hundreds of years. In land-locked seas, such deep waters become stagnant, as all their dissolved oxygen is used up.

In the open ocean, however, the deeps exist as a vast reservoir of nutrient salts moving slowly towards the warmer seas and awaiting release to the surface so that the amazing cycle of life in the seas can continue. That release is obtained through the mighty forces of movement engendered by winds and waves.

Waves The rush and tumble of the waves is the breath of the sea. Wind, tide and occasional severe undersea shocks all create waves, but the most significant of these factors is the wind. The waves that break on a beach in calm weather result from swells which may have been created by winds blowing many hundreds, or even thousands, of miles away over the ocean. Waves continue long after the wind that caused them has died down. This is because waves move more slowly than the wind.

Waves begin as ripples. If the wind continues to blow, the ripples become waves, which grow larger as the wind grows stronger. Three main factors combine in shaping an ocean wave: the speed of the wind; the length of time for which it has been blowing and the fetch, a word which describes the distance over which the wind has blown on the water.

A wind of 20 knots, for instance, has to blow for 10 hours over a distance of 8 km before it exerts its full effect. The wave then produced will have an average height of almost 1.5 m measured between crest and trough. The average period is a trifle over 5½ seconds and the wavelength 33 m. The period is the time taken for a single wave to pass a fixed point and the wavelength is the distance between successive crests.

However, wave action is more complex than this. Some waves are smaller, some larger than the average. Many waves produced by a 20 knot wind will reach a height of 2.4 m and one wave in ten will rise to 3 m. This may be due to two or more wave-crests running together. In this way the violent storms of the Pacific can whip up single waves more than 30 m high.

As a rule waves cannot rise higher than one-seventh of their length without collapsing into white caps. This is due to the basic way in which waves are formed. The action of the wind creates a circular motion in the body of the surface water as it lifts. As the wind blows more strongly this motion causes it to be stretched and distorted until the wave front becomes hollow and breaks up.

The motion that creates the wave and the way in which it works can be seen by watching an object floating in the sea. It will move forward with the crest of a wave but turns back in the trough. When the wave has passed the object will have hardly changed its position at all. Similarly, although the wave motion travels forward, often with great speed and force, hardly any water is carried with it.

When a wave moves inshore the shallower waters decrease its length and increase its height, causing it to break.

Coastlines bear witness to the violence of the waves. They are the hands of the ocean that over millenniums have carved and moulded the frontiers of the land. Every cliff and headland is a fortress to be assaulted. Sometimes the attack is brutal, the waves hurling rock fragments with shattering force against the cliff face. Sometimes it is stealthy as the salts in the sea water rot and corrode the rocks. Always the waves are grinding, dissolving and restlessly transporting the materials of the shore.

As waves sweep shorewards the shallower water decreases their length and increases their height. Eventually the drag of the seabed causes the collapse of the wave into breakers and surf. The manner in which waves dissipate their energy depends to some extent on the configuration of the shore and the direction from which the waves approach it. Bays and gradually shallowing shores are best protected from the violence of the sea.

Material scoured from the shore is washed out to sea and deposited in deeper water, decreasing the slope of the beach. In calmer periods this material may be washed shorewards again. Often the situation arises where silt and sand are washed to and fro with the seasons, according to tide and climate.

On many coasts profound geological forces are at work raising or lowering the seabed. On a submerging coastline the forces of erosion are hard at work, with bold headlands and river mouths opened up into wide estuaries. On the emerging coast the river mouths are narrow and the sea strives to swell the land by building off-shore bars. But in either case, the waves are busy at their task of changing the face of the world.

Tides

Twice every day the oceans rise and fall like the beat of a giant clock. A pull of gravity stronger than any force we can imagine swills around some 1,300,000,000,000,000,000 tonnes of water like slops in a basin. The muscles creating this stupendous movement are the attraction of the masses of the sun and the moon and the spin of the earth.

The effect of these forces is to create two tidal bulges, one directly beneath the moon as it revolves around the earth and the other on the opposite side of the globe. The first of these bulges is known as the direct high tide and the second as the opposite high tide. Between the high tides are two low tides at right angles to the lunar pull.

As the earth rotates, every point upon its surface except the poles becomes subject to these influences. On the open ocean the surface of the water rises no more than a metre but the shape of the coastline and the strength and direction of prevailing winds often magnify this effect.

This is the basic explanation of the ebb and flood of the tides. It would be a complete explanation if the wave motion was not interrupted by the variously shaped continents and islands and the moon was the sole agency at work.

A further complication is the earth's rotation, which applies what is known as Coriolis force—named after its discoverer, a French mathematician—upon the movements of the ocean. Coriolis force deflects tides or currents to the right in the northern hemisphere and to the left in the southern hemisphere.

The twice a day high-low pattern of tides is described as being semi-diurnal. The tides of the North Atlantic are of this type, but some parts of the Pacific experience diurnal tides—one high, one low each day. Other places, of which the junction of the Pacific and Indian oceans is one, have mixed tides of both characters.

The varied orbits of the earth, moon and sun and their different combinations have considerable effect on the tides. The sun exerts a similar influence to that of the moon but possesses less than half the force. The solar tide is most significant during the four periods in each month when it acts either with or against the pull of the moon. At new moon and full moon, the earth, moon and sun are lined up to produce spring tides—spring in this instance not referring to the season but coming from the Old English word *springan*, meaning to swell. When the moon moves to the first and last quarter the sun is at right angles, creating an opposing force that results in the abnormally low neap tides, named from the Old English word *nep*, meaning scanty.

Variations in the moon's orbit cause high perigee and low apogee tides, owing to increased or decreased gravitational pull. Similar inequalities arise from perihelion and aphelion in the earth's orbit around the sun. From time to time these events coincide, increasing the effects.

The rise and fall of the tide exerts a familiar to and fro motion in the shallower waters of the continental shelf. This movement is intensified in narrow channels, bays and river mouths and in some places creates sensational tidal bores. But every tide produces currents whose speed and size are conditioned by the lie of the shore.

Since the creation of the oceans, tides have played a part in carving, eroding and breaking down the coasts of the world, grinding rocks to sand and leaching away minerals of every kind into the oceans. The kingdom of the tides is that stretch of the shore between high and low water. It is here that life first crawled ashore to dry land and here many plants and animals continue to lead precarious lives, at times underwater and at other times high and dry. Seaweeds and shellfish anchor themselves to the rocks against the danger of the waves. Crabs burrow in the sand until the sea returns.

The tide is the fisherman's friend, too. As it rises fish follow the surging waters inshore to feast on food churned up by the surf. Usually the best catches are made in the hour before high tide and the hour after it. As the tide ebbs, the fish return to deeper water.

See Currents.

The Twelve Apostles at Port Campbell National Park, Victoria, are made of a hard rock left standing as the softer surrounding rock was eroded away by wind and wave action.

MARINE ecology

Colour The reflection and scattering of light by water molecules tends to make the oceans appear blue. This is a sign that the water is deficient in the microscopic organisms that are the basis of marine life. The minute plant life of the surface layers called phytoplankton contributes a yellow pigment to the water causing it to take on various shades of green.

The presence of other microscopic life may be detected by the colour of sea water. Diatoms sometimes make the polar seas look olive-green and the Red Sea gains its name from the hosts of tawny dinoflagellates that infest its waters at certain times. Clouds make the sea appear grey. Coastal waters, especially near a river mouth, may look brown or yellow through muddy sediments.

Plankton Life exists at all depths in the ocean, but the most important level for the fisherman is the depth to which sunlight can penetrate. This is the photic zone, the layer of the sea in which there is sufficient light for photosynthesis to take place. Photosynthesis is the process by which plants can use chlorophyll to convert the carbon dioxide in the water into carbohydrate.

In murky coastal waters the photic zone may go down no lower than 10 to 20 m, whereas in the clear ocean waters of the tropics it can extend to 300 m. The photic zone may include all the neritic area of the continental shelf and it will certainly mark the limit to which plants growing on the seabed can survive.

The animal and plant life of the seabed is known to the scientist as benthic from the Greek word *benthos*, meaning deep. Benthic algae, for instance, is seaweed clinging to the bottom by its root-like holdfast. The large group of fish and other sea creatures, such as whales and seals, that can swim freely in the oceans are called nekton, from *nektos*, another Greek word meaning swimming.

The remaining scientific classification for sea life is plankton, from a Greek word and this time meaning drifting. Plankton are the tiny creatures of the sea, plant and animal, which are too weak and helpless to do anything except drift with the current. They are the most important of the sea creatures in that, without them, none of the others could exist. Fishing, both as a livelihood and a hobby, depends on the existence of large quantities of plankton. The plankton, as we have already noted, depend on supplies of nitrates, silicates and phosphates, as well as the oxygen in the sea water.

A variety of living organisms, most of them microscopic in size and numbered in millions of millions, make up plankton. Plants are represented by the free-floating algae or phytoplankton. The most numerous of these are the diatoms, microscopic single-celled green algae growing in bivalves of silica. Other plant plankton are the dinoflagellates and naked flagellates, which propel themselves through the water by means of whiplike growths.

These tiny morsels provide food for many kinds of animal plankton, some of which are infant fish and crustaceans. Apart from these, most animal plankton are varieties of single-celled protozoa. Among these are the radiolaria and foraminifera, both of which construct minute shells. Most abundant of the animal plankton are the tiny crustacea such as copepods and pteropods, mysids and euphausids.

In turn the animal plankton provide food for many fish, including the huge whale shark, which grows to 15 to 18 m in length, and other creatures such as the blue whale, which rates as the world's largest animal. The whale strains plankton from the sea by means of a sieve of whalebone in its mouth while the whale shark has thousands of small teeth for a similar purpose. Blue whales are known to carry more than a tonne of plankton in their stomachs. All these varied forms of life rely in the end on the growth of phytoplankton, which is the grass of the oceans, and this growth is strictly controlled by the supply of nutrient salts.

In the temperate regions of the oceans the cycle of life begins much as it does on land. Winter turbulence has stirred up and mixed the deeper water with the surface layers, ensuring supplies of plant food. Phytoplankton grows quickly in the sunlight and by summer the nutrient salts are about used up. Unless further supplies arise by chance, growth ends until the next spring. Soon the grazing of phytoplankton by animal plankton and fish also falls off and winter comes to the ocean again.

In the tropics, phytoplankton can go deeper because of the greater penetration of light. But the supplies of plant foods are more limited because there is less opportunity for mixing of surface and deeper waters to take place. Therefore the phytoplankton, animal plankton and fish are scanty in comparison with the summer life of the cooler regions.

The animals in plankton are not confined to the surface layers of the sea by the need for light. Therefore during the day they sink to deeper waters, rising to the surface to graze at night. Creatures of the deeper waters which do not visit the surface rely for food upon the remains of dead plants and animals sinking from above.

Most varied assortments of fish are to be found on the continental shelf. These are chiefly demersal or bottom-feeding fish such as snapper, flathead or leatherjacket in Australia. But it is the vast shoals of pelagic fish such as anchovies, pilchards and herrings that follow the plankton drifting in the currents around Australia. Following them are the predators, such as the mackerel, the tuna, the marlin and the sharks. At all levels of the sea, small eats smaller, large eats small and largest eats all.

M ■ MARINE ecology

Estuaries, reefs and rocks

The activity of the waves and tides provides many of the favourite haunts of fish in coastal waters. Providing the sea is at a suitable temperature and salinity, wherever the continental shelf is raised sufficiently to create waters shallow enough for light to penetrate, a varied marine community of plants, crustaceans and fish is likely to be found.

Factors such as prevailing currents and the nature of the sea bottom vary the inhabitants of these communities. Sole and flounder lie on the sand and mudflats, luderick browse through the clumps of weed, teraglin prefer gravel, many species spend their lives poking about among the rocks.

Some names indicate these preferences—kelpfish, weedfish, sand whiting, rock flathead, or rock cod. Often the community relationship is that of prey and hunter. The snapper and colourful nannygai hang around the reefs snapping up the little fish, and in turn are snapped up by various species of sharks.

The keen fisherman studies the ecology and habits of the fish he plans to catch. He discovers that some fish, like the mullet, live in quiet inlets and estuaries but in the autumn and winter get the urge to travel up the coast in their annual migration to spawn in some distant river mouth. On the other hand some of the freshwater fish, such as the Australian *galaxias* minnows cannot resist the call of an equally perilous journey to the sea. And freshwater eels will travel overland from dams and lakes far out into the ocean depths to spawn and die there.

In this way the estuaries, river mouths and sometimes the surf on the beaches become thronged thoroughfares of fish. The young of many species, as well as the seasonal procession of migrants, ensure rich pickings for predators along the inshore shallows.

In the warm tropic seas of moderate salinity grow the most specialized communities of all. Wherever the sea floor rises to within 45 m of the surface, a relative of the sea anemone known as the coral polyp will be found at work busily manufacturing beautiful forms of calcium carbonate from the sea water. Many islands have been formed by sand washed up and vegetation developed on the foundations built by the endless industry of these creatures, whose masterpiece is the 2000 km long Great Barrier Reef, an account of which is given elsewhere in this book.

The polyps are plankton eaters, building their reefs to catch the food on the equatorial current. Around the reef arises a strange exotic community of coelenterates, molluscs, echinoids, crustaceans and fish. Strange partnerships develop between crab and mollusc, sea anemone and fish.

In the sunlit water all nature wears a party dress—brilliant butterfly-fish, humbugs, parrot fish with beaks strong enough to crush the coral to sand and weird coral fish equipped with long snouts for feeding in nooks and crannies. Amid all the wonders of the sea there is no area more like a garden.

MARINE ecology ■ M

The bed of the ocean

The abyssal floor, as the scientists call it, was the last abode of legends. Sea-serpents and monsters lived there, so the old salts said. As it turns out, the creatures leading strange lives in the huge darkness of the ocean depths are monstrous enough in shape, but they are mainly monsters in miniature. Compressed and contorted by huge pressures, strangely branched and spined, these fish light their way with photophores, luminous organs that shine in the dark.

The true giants of the depths are the squid which can grow to more than 15 m in length and 272 kg in weight. These huge molluscs are the food of the sperm whale, which reaches more than 18 m in size; the deep oceans must have witnessed many gargantuan combats between mollusc and mammal.

The ocean bed bears the scars of the earth's story in the shape of submarine volcanoes and eroded mountains. The mid-Pacific range, whose peaks still show at Wake Island and in the Hawaiian group, were a chain of coral islands more than 100 million years ago. They are estimated to represent the oldest mountains on earth.

A feature of the ocean floor that puzzles the geologists is the submarine canyons often found on the continental slope below past or present river mouths. A canyon of this type exists south of Kangaroo Island, South Australia. From the canyon a river of mud oozes down to the ocean floor.

Muds of various colours cover the ocean floor along the margins of the continental shelves. The greater part of the Pacific floor is covered with red clay of volcanic origin but a large part of all the ocean beds is covered with globigerina and radiolarian oozes composed of the shells of long-dead plankton. Millions of square kilometres are covered in this way, often hundreds of metres deep.

Masthead Reef, Queensland, was created, like all coral reefs, by coral polyps in warm tropical waters where the sea floor rises to within 45 m of the surface.

MARLIN   *See Billfish.*

MAYFLY   *See Aquatic insects.*

MIDGE   *See Aquatic insects.*

MIDWATER fish   The average angler encounters the fascinating fish of the oceanic midwaters only occasionally, when one washes up on a beach or he sights one entangled in the nets of commercial fishermen. But they form an important part of the angler's understanding of the seas and the fish in them.

The common names of midwater fish—scaly dragon fish, fang tooth, long-tailed snipe eel, pearly lanternfish, whipnose angler fish—are indicative of the bizarre forms of life in the deep sea. The fish themselves have a number of striking anatomical features or morphological specializations that suggest the midwater environment is vastly different from the more hospitable coral reefs or forest streams.

The midwater environment

The midwaters are those areas below the well-lit surface waters of the world ocean. In the open ocean, down to 100 or 150 m, enough sunlight penetrates to allow photosynthesis to take place; microscopic phytoplankton live and produce food in this region to support all life in the waters below. The waters are very dimly lit below 150 m, fading to complete darkness at about 1000 m, since sunlight is rapidly absorbed and scattered by sea water. The midwater region extends to just above the ocean floor; it is therefore a few kilometres in vertical extent in the deepest parts of the ocean. Midwater fish are only those fish below 150 m which are free swimming and not associated with the bottom. Deep-sea fish are all fish below 150 m, including those forms associated with the bottom, such as flat fish, rays and the like.

Within the midwaters, various environmental parameters or characteristics change with increasing depth. Most noticeable is the decrease in light. Since the red, yellow and violet portions of the light spectrum are those most rapidly absorbed by sea water, the light between 150 and 1000 m is predominantly blue-green. Pressure increases with depth and temperature decreases. Pressure increases at the rate of about 1 kg per square centimetre every 10 m. Below 1000 m, the temperature is usually 4 degrees C or below; at great depths the temperatures approach freezing. The amount of dissolved oxygen in the water rapidly decreases with depth to about 1000 m; below this depth oxygen increases slightly. Slight changes in salinity are not correlated with depth.

The waters of the world oceans can be classified into various water masses. Each water mass is identifiable according to its particular temperature and salinity characteristics.

These two characteristics are often plotted together as a temperature-salinity curve for any given vertical column of water. The temperature-salinity envelope for each water mass includes all the curves found therein. Low temperature and oxygen, minimal light and high pressure have all affected the fish of the midwaters, through the forces of natural selection.

Morphological specializations of midwater fish
Only a few of the general features and structural modifications of midwater fish can be described in this short article. A large number of midwater fish possess luminescent organs on various parts of the head and body. The light organs, or photophores, display a variety of shapes and structures and many include a lens, reflecting layer and pigment screen; the similarity to the basic structure of a vertebrate eye is striking. Light is produced either by luminescent bacteria which live in the photophore or by luminescent tissue in the photophore. Light is formed through a series of chemical reactions involving phosphorus and the enzyme luciferase. Those photophores with light-producing bacteria usually have a small opening to the outside. The relationship of fish and bacteria is mutually beneficial to both; the bacteria receive protection and probably nutrition from the fish, while the fish gains the advantage of light in the dark environment. Fish with their own luminescent material usually have photophores without a pore to the outside. The shape of individual photophores varies considerably, but the light produced is usually blue-green, much the same colour as the remaining sunlight below 150 m. The eyes of midwater fish are probably most sensitive to this colour.

Photophores are an obvious adaptation to life in a lightless or poorly lit environment. Many of other specializations of midwater fish are directly or indirectly correlated with the lack of light. The amount of food organisms, both phytoplankton and the larger planktonic organisms such as shrimp and other crustaceans, is much greater in the well-lit surface layers. The amount of food is proportionally less in deeper water, and a number of modifications involving feeding are apparent in midwater fish. Some fish have a light organ on the end of a filament or barbel, which originates under the mouth or on the top of the head; the light organ hangs just in front of the mouth and acts as a lure for food organisms. In most such fish, the mouth is extremely large and the dentition well developed. In the deepest living species, the musculature, skeletal system, scales, swimbladder, and kidneys may be very poorly developed. This is apparently a mechanism to conserve energy in an environment where food is very scarce. In these forms the stomach is often extremely distendable, an obvious adaptation for taking a rare, large meal. Some midwater fish have been captured which have another fish, larger than themselves, in the stomach. The eyes of midwater fish show great variation. Many species living below 1000 m have small or degenerate eyes. These same forms may have a highly developed lateral line system, which detects pressure waves. Fish of the upper midwaters often have well developed eyes, particularly those species with photophores. Others have developed tubular, or 'telescopic', eyes, which point either forward or upward. This specialization probably widens the field of vision and permits some binocular vision. The upturned eyes are probably an adaptation to predation from below the prey, utilizing the silhouette of the prey against the down-coming surface light. The body colours of midwater fish particularly the deepest species, are often black, dark brown, or deep red. In the midwaters where the only light is a dim blue-green, reds and browns will appear black. The dark coloration is doubtless a means of protective coloration, concealing an individual from either predator or prey.

The effect of low temperature on midwater fish is difficult to assess; although no morphological specialization can be correlated directly with low temperature, various biochemical reactions with the fish are probably changed, at least in rate, by low temperature. High pressure will only affect the air-filled or gas-filled spaces within the fish, and this is normally found only within the swimbladder. In a number of midwater forms the swimbladder is either completely absent or is secondarily filled with fat and the air space is obliterated; thus the effect of extreme pressure in these species is negated. In the zones of lowest oxygen concentration, the gill structures, which play the important role in fish respiration, are often highly developed.

Midwater trawling
Due to the great living depths of midwater fish, the capture of these interesting creatures is a difficult task. Some of the first midwater fish seen were from regions where strong upwelling brought them to the surface, as in the Straits of Messina. Occasionally midwater fish are washed up on beaches; a few such specimens have been found on Lord Howe Island. But the main instrument of collection is with deep-sea nets. The first such nets were small, conical plankton nets with round mouths and fine netting. In 1949, marine biologists at Scripps Institution of Oceanography in California developed a very effective midwater fish collector, the Isaacs-Kidd Midwater Trawl. This trawl alleviates most of the disadvantages of small plankton nets in fish collection. The large size, some 12 m long with about a 10-square-metre mouth and the restriction of the fine mesh to the last metre or so of the trawl, allow for fast trawling. The incorporation of a diving vane at the front makes the trawl dive as it is towed; at a speed of 4 to 6 knots, only three times as much wire as fishing depth is required. Although the high-speed trawl has revolutionized the capture of midwater fish, not all problems have been solved. The size and

complexity of the trawl require a large ship with a winch capable of holding thousands of metres of heavy trawling cable. The most serious disadvantage of the Isaacs-Kidd trawl is the lack of an opening-closing device. Fish are caught in the open mouth when the net is lowered and retrieved. The determination of the upper and lower limits of the vertical distribution for a given species therefore requires a large series of trawls at different depths. Development of an opening-closing device is under study; one experimental model utilizes electrical trawling cable and a series of electrical signals to open and close the trawl at depth.

Little midwater trawling with large nets has been accomplished in the waters around Australia and the midwater fish from the Australian region are poorly known.

Ecology of midwater fish

While the identification of species and the descriptions of morphological structure of midwater fish are important areas of study, research on the ecology and life-histories of these fish is equally fascinating. As a number of midwater species are used as food by commercially valuable species, knowledge of their biology is important. Aspects of feeding, reproduction, schooling behaviour, and patterns of migration and distribution are all profoundly influenced by various parameters of the midwater environment.

One characteristic feature of much of the life in the upper midwaters is the phenomenon of vertical migration. During the day, many fish and invertebrates live a few hundred metres below the surface; at night they migrate to the upper 100 m and some even reach the surface, where they can be dip-netted under a light. During the Second World War, ship sonar, operated for the detection of submarines, found a sound-reflecting layer in the ocean that was far below the surface, yet not associated with the bottom. This Deep Scattering Layer, as it is now called, rose to near the surface during the early evening hours and descended to greater depths at dawn, much as some forms of midwater life were known to do. Research has now confirmed that the Deep Scattering Layer is composed of midwater animals—fish, crustaceans and siphonophores—that daily migrate between the surface waters and about 500 m. The latest evidence comes from recent bathyscape observations made at the level of the Deep Scattering Layer. The gas-filled swimbladders of some midwater fish, the floats of siphonophores and the hard outer skeletons of shrimps are excellent sound reflectors that bounce back the sound produced by the sonar gear. While the composition of the scattering layer is now fairly well-known, other questions remain to be answered. Recent studies have shown that certain populations of lantern fish migrate from about 750 m to 50 m and return every day. The energy expended is considerable; fish averaging 5 cm in length are swimming almost 1.5 km every 24 hours. In addition, some of the migration forms have functional, gas-filled swimbladders. To keep a constant pressure in the swimbladder during the migration, an enormous amount of gas in relation to the size of the fish must be absorbed or secreted. How this is accomplished by the small fish is not clear.

A number of hypotheses have been advanced to explain the migration. The most plausible explanation is that the migration is a feeding migration to the food-rich surface waters; however, the feeding habits of midwater fish are little studied. The correlation of migration patterns with light intensity is striking and light may act as a triggering mechanism for the movement. However, this would restrict migration to the upper 1000 m and limited data indicate that deeper species migrate at night to levels above 1000 m. Hypotheses other than a feeding migration have been proposed. Reproductive potential may be increased by a concentration in the upper waters or the vertical migration may significantly influence the patterns of horizontal distribution. A countershading effect of ventrally placed photophores against downcoming light has been suggested; vertical migration into waters of the same light intensity during sunset and sunrise would influence the light balance of such a scheme. Many questions concerning vertical migration remain unanswered, questions that also involve other aspects of the life of midwater fish.

Many midwater fish possess photophores, the functions of which are not fully understood. The function of some can be inferred from their structure and position. For instance, the light organ on the barbel of some fish presumably acts as a lure for food organisms, for it hangs right in front of the mouth and often is adorned with small tassels or fringes. But the majority of photophores occur on the body of the fish, often in patterns, and their function is obscure. In some fish, such as the lantern fish, almost every species has a different pattern of body photophores.

In the vast midwater environment, there are special problems in the reproduction of midwater fish. The larval life of many species is spent in the surface waters, where food is most plentiful. Of particular importance is the finding of a mate during the breeding season. For certain species, like lantern fish, populations in a given area may number in the millions. Other species are much less numerous, particularly inhabitants of the deep midwaters. For these fish, the problem of finding a mate during the reproductive season is acute. Certain species of angler fish have solved this problem in a spectacular way. Large female angler fish often have one or two small males attached as parasites to them. The mouth of the male becomes fused to the body skin of the female and the blood vessels of the two become closely associated in this region. The male retains a small size, the eyes degenerate and no angling device develops. Nourishment for the male is entirely from the female and only the gonads of the male become fully developed. The males apparently become attached any time a female is encountered after larval transformation and the two sexes are assured of being together during the breeding season. Other forms of midwater fish are hermaphroditic; presumably, if a mate is not encountered in the breeding season, self-fertilization will take place. However, for many midwater species, the reproductive biology is unknown. A number of problems in midwater ecology are discussed in detail in *Aspects of Deep Sea Biology*, by N. B. Marshall, published in 1954 by Hutchinson, London.

Many of the unanswered questions outlined above are due to the inability to study midwater fish alive. Most fish brought up by deep trawl are either dead or near death, probably due to the changes in temperature and pressure, as well as the damage done in the net. Even migrating species that have been surface netted at night have quickly succumbed in shipboard aquariums. It is to be hoped that the difficulties in maintaining midwater fish alive can soon be overcome, for experimentation on living fish will help to solve many problems. Direct observations from bathyscapes can supply only some of the answers. Controlled experiments are necessary for the rest.

DR JOHN R. PAXTON

MILKFISH

Chanos chanos: A powerful swimmer along foreshores and mangrove covered estuaries that has recently won prominence as a light game fish right along the coast of tropical Australia and in Papuan seas. They grow to 1.2 m and often reach 13.5 kg, moving with great speed with a characteristic sweep of their heavily forked tails. They are burleyed inshore with stale bread and then will attack balloon-floated lines baited with bread crusts. Their swift strikes followed by dazzlingly fast runs provide outstanding sport.

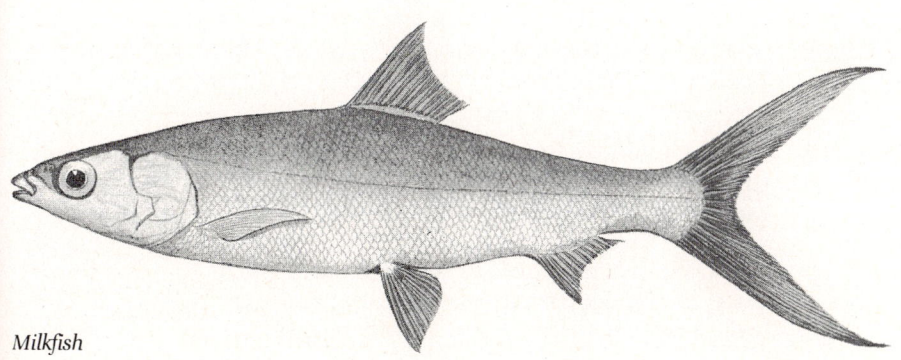

Milkfish

M ■ MINIMUM lengths

Grant records instances of milkfish stripping the gears of game reels. He does not rate milkfish as good table fare, but suggests that they can be made more palatable by overnight soaking in vinegar followed by pressure cooking. Milkfish are bred in ponds in the Philippines, growing very quickly and supplying a lot of protein for highly-spiced diets. Milkfish are members of the mullet family, feeding on detritus on the bottom of muddy estuaries. They are bluish along the back, silvery-yellow and iridescent on the sides. Their fins are yellowish, the tail with a dusky margin. They have very small, horseshoe-shaped mouths and are toothless. Whitley said their roe may include more than three million eggs.

MINIMUM lengths Every Australian State has set a minimum length for the capture of all significant commercial species. Fish which fall short of these minimums should be returned to the water, according to law. The minimum lengths were originally fixed so that every fish had a chance to spawn at least once before it was captured. Since the minimum lengths were set scientists have agreed that there is no longer any need for this type of protection in species which produce a large number of eggs. But because of the slaughter of vast numbers of small fish by anglers disdainful of the future most States have energetically enforced regulations.

Fines against fishermen found with under-sized fish are common in every State and many responsible sports fishermen believe these fines are nowhere near severe enough. Professionals are the worst culprits but this kind of larrikinism among amateurs will drastically affect our fishing heritage. There is always a wave of disgust among eastern State conservationists when South Australia's action in permitting fish of any length to be taken from jetties is raised. South Australian fisheries authorities either believe policing under-sized captures is unworkable or are prepared to let adolescents enjoy taking tiny fish. Easterners with the good of the fishing future at heart believe that on either count South Australia has taken a shortsighted way out of an admittedly difficult problem.

MOLLUSCS See *Abalone; Bait; Cephalopods; Mussels; Oysters; Pippis; and Scallops*.

MORWONG Fish of many confusing aliases which belong to the family Cheilodactylidae, noted for their outstanding table qualities. Morwong are found off the coasts of New South Wales, Victoria, Tasmania, South Australia, south-western Australia, and from the far north of New Zealand south to Cook Strait. They are important to our trawling industry, which in Australia has had to give them an official pseudonym, sea bream,

A record-sized grey morwong showing the huge mouth that is a feature of the species.

to coax the public to buy the big quantities marketed. They are not rated as top sporting fish, but actually fight almost as well as snapper and as they grow to considerable size they can offer strong resistance.

On the northern Queensland coast a number of species, including the yellow-tailed emperor, red-finned emperor, spangled emperor, painted sweetlips, netted sweetlips and others are often erroneously called 'morwong' of one type or another.

An accurate list of morwongs would include morwong, jackass fish or tarakihi, blue morwong or queenfish, brown-banded morwong, two magpie morwongs, red-banded morwong, dusky morwong and queens snapper. The red morwong is actually a sea carp. It is caught very occasionally by anglers fishing from the rocks with prawn bait but large numbers are taken by spearfishermen.

There is a magpie morwong caught along the north coast of New South Wales and southern Queensland which has yellow and black bands; the magpie morwong caught along the coasts of Tasmania, Victoria and South Australia has black and white bands. The blue morwong is the queenfish of Western Australia, where it is rated a good sporting fish of fair edible quality. It is common in South Australia and on the southern and south-western coasts of Western Australia.

M ■ MORWONG

As far as angling is concerned, more morwong are caught when the angler is fishing for something else, usually snapper, which frequent the same underwater reefs and rocky ground.

Grey morwong *Nemadactylus douglasii:* These are the porae of New Zealand, true morwong which are readily identified by the elongated fifth ray from the bottom on their pectoral fin, the almost oblong anal fin, and the branching soft rays in the upper half of the pectoral fins.

Morwong are greenish-grey to olive on top, usually with some purplish tints, greenish-yellow on the sides and silvery below. The membrane of the spinous dorsal fin is canary yellow and the membranes of the soft dorsal and anal fins are dotted with the same colour. They are mainly caught over, or in the vicinity of offshore reefs, although they will at times come in to feed over inshore reefs in shallower waters. They feed on the same kind of food as snapper: crustaceans, molluscs, marine worms, and small fish. When they are feeding ravenously they will take prawns, whitebait, squid, octopus, and any good fish bait such as mackerel, bonito, mullet, yellowtail, garfish, pilchards etc.

They are caught commercially off New South Wales. The quantities caught decrease as one moves south and relatively few are caught in cooler waters. Spring, summer and autumn seem to produce the best morwong fishing in the southern Australian States but this is probably because this is the period when most snapper men are out over the reefs. New South Wales anglers say that summer is the best time on the south and mid-coasts, and autumn and early winter on their far north coast.

Regular snapper tackle is used to catch morwong, excepting that this fish has a smaller mouth than the snapper and therefore requires smaller hooks. The same size hook that is used for the smaller inshore snapper, 2/0, is preferred for morwong. For boat fishing, an ordinary snapper rod and reel and a 9 kg line are quite suitable for all morwong. Sinkers that are heavy enough to hold the bait on the bottom are needed. When fishing from the rocks, a 3 to 3.5 m rangoon cane rod and a casting reel with at least 180 m of 7 to 9 kg line are used. Spoon sinkers are an ideal choice because they are less likely to get caught in the rocks than some of the other shapes.

Blue morwong *Nemadactylus valenciennesi:* Bright blue above and lighter below, with bright yellow lines on the snout and radiating out from around the eyes. The membrane of the soft dorsal fin is spotted. This species grows to 75 cm but average size is 25 to 40 cm. It is common in South Australia and fairly common in Western Australia. It is a common catch of underwater spear-fishermen and in South Australia is said to be reluctant to take a hook. In Western Australia, it is known as queenfish and rated as a good sporting fish of reasonable edible qualities.

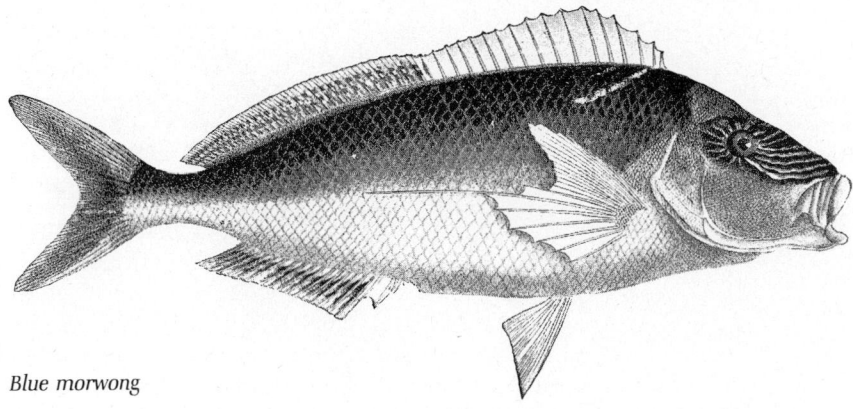

Blue morwong

Cheilodactylus spectabalis: Reddish-brown in colour, darker along the back, with five dark bars. The caudal fin is greyish-black. They grow to 1 m and 15 kg, but the average caught is around 60 cm. They do not have such a markedly elongated ray on the pectoral fin. They occur in southern Queensland, New South Wales, possibly in Victoria, and in New Zealand.

Brown-banded morwong

Nemadactylus macropterus: Silvery in colour with a reddish-purple tint along the back. A blackish band crosses the back in front of the dorsal fin to behind the gill cover and this makes it easily distinguishable from the morwong which do not have such a band. The seventh ray of the jackass fish's pectoral fin is greatly elongated, as is the morwong's.

The jackass fish have a wider distribution than the morwong and are found in all States except Queensland and the Northern Territory. But unlike the morwong, the jackass fish are not found over inshore reefs—they prefer the deep waters. The same tackle, baits and methods are used to catch jackass fish as are used for morwong.

Jackass fish

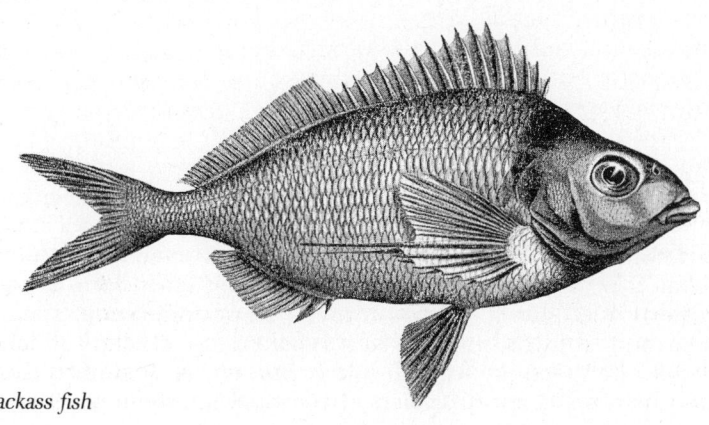

Jackass fish

M ■ MORWONG

Magpie morwong

Magpie morwong *Cheilodactylus nigripes:* A black-striped morwong ranging among jetty piles and shallow reefs in southern Queensland, New South Wales, and around southern Australia to Western Australia. They reach 40 cm and up to 2 kg in weight. Worms and shellfish form most of its diet but it takes a hook. A graceful fish, with silvery and whitish fins dominated by the oblique dark bands across the face, body and fins. Their yellow-to-orange lips are ringed with chocolate-brown. Decreases in numbers south of Bass Strait, where it is abundant. A frequent target for skindivers, but a far more difficult challenge for hook and line fishermen.

Tarakihi *Dactylopagrus macropterus:* A valuable New Zealand food fish and an excellent sporting fish, known in Australia as jackass fish, silver perch and squeaker perch. The Maori name means 'sharp spines and singing noise'; the singing noise is evident when a net full of these fish is brought to the surface and they rapidly release air to adjust to surface pressures. If a quantity is brought from the depth the water seems to boil, so crowded are the air bubbles that precede them. The 'sharp spine' is a single ray of the pectoral fin which extends much beyond the others. The scientific name, from *daktylos* meaning a finger and *pagrus*, a genus of fish, refers to the same circumstance. *Macropterus* means 'large-finned'. Another identification of this fish is a reddish-purple band along the back crossed at right angles by another which borders the nape, in much the same arrangement as the black stripes on a donkey.

Because of these marks fishermen, with a sublime indifference to latitude, have made this the Southern Hemisphere version of 'St Peter's fish', the fish caught by St Peter with a shekel in its mouth, the marks being fingermarks indicating where he held the fish while he extracted the coin (*Matthew XVII: 27*). The haddock has also been nominated and in Europe the john dory, though of course none of these fish could have survived in the fresh waters of the Lake of Gennesaret where this incident occurred. In another version this is the fish that Jesus fed to the multitude in the miracle of the loaves and fishes, but the St Peter story is the more common. St Peter is the patron saint of fishermen, being a fisherman himself and, additional to the keys, a sword and a book, another of his symbols is a fish.

Tarakihi is extremely valuable as a food fish, caloric value being so high it ranks far above beef or eggs and fat content is shown by analysis to be in excess of that of any other New Zealand fish. These fish are found on all types of bottom, but seem to prefer to travel. Outstanding specimens may weigh 4.5 kg and measure 75 cm in length; these would be well below the record but about double the average. They are best caught at or before the dawn, just before the groper begin to bite. The usual experience in deepwater grounds is that as the tarakihi stop biting the groper begin. Another circumstance is that they bite best before the tide starts running too strongly; as most of the east and south of New Zealand coasts are exposed to the Antarctic drift current, the flood tide runs more strongly than the ebb.

Wherever they are, tarakihi give excellent sport while it is their feeding time. In places where no groper are known to be present they may take a hook at any time of the day, but it is their practice to finish feeding before the larger fish begin. They are mostly caught on a bottom hook, set close to the sea-floor.

Tarakihi are also taken in quantities in an otter-trawl specially rigged to tow a little above the sea-floor. Such trawled school tarakihi are usually smaller than those fished with the line. The best bait is frozen snoek, but they will take this fish fresh, and sometimes red cod. Quality baits like squid and octopus are regarded as the best.

Stomach contents rarely if ever include swimming fish. They feed on crabs, including swimming crabs and krill or whalefeed in season. This krill includes surface-swimming forms, so the tarakihi has the ability to change depths and pressures with some facility. Other small swimming crustaceans and varieties similar to sandhoppers are favoured food.

Tarakihi are excellent eating and the fat content also ensures a fine flavour when the fish is smoked. The flesh is firm, white, palatable and never coarse. The flavour seems best when the fish has been taken in colder water. The fish is an important food-fish in Australia, common in Bass Strait and off other southern Australian shores.

MOSQUITO fish

Gambusia affinis: One of the most discussed of all Australian fishes, although few fishermen ever catch one. The reason is that mosquito fish were originally introduced to control mosquito plagues, a task that many ichthyologists believe our native fishes can handle more effectively. The fish has become controversial among freshwater sports fishermen because it is believed to have caused a reduction of native fishes, whose fins it habitually nibbles. Native fishes are certainly scarce in waters where gambusia are plentiful.

Mosquito fish belong to the family Poeciliidae and are noted for their fertility. The anterior rays of the male's anal fin form an intromittent organ known as the gonoposium. Fertilization occurs when this is inserted in the female. The young develop in the female and are expelled alive. They are a few millimetres long at birth but grow quickly. They breed in batches of between 50 and 80 several times a year. Guppies and mollies are now said to belong to the same family but only *Gambusia* have been introduced in Australia. First liberations took place in 1925 at Brisbane, and in New South Wales from 1926. In Western Australia, the first liberation occurred in 1934. It is now widely distributed in the eastern States and Western Australia and because of its high reproductive rate has an obvious advantage over more edible native sporting fish.

MOSQUITOES See *Aquatic insects*.

MOUNTAIN perch See *Macquarie perch*.

MOUTH almighty *Glossamia aprion aprion:* A freshwater gobbleguts or cardinal fish which like others of the family Apogonidae incubates the eggs in the large mouth of the male, which does not eat until the young are hatched. Grant rates mouth almighty highly as a panfish, although they grow to only 15 cm. He also reports that the mouth almighty has for some years been the subject of transplantation activities into dams and streams by the Atherton Tablelands acclimatization societies. They are a tropical variety, whitish-brown in body colouring.

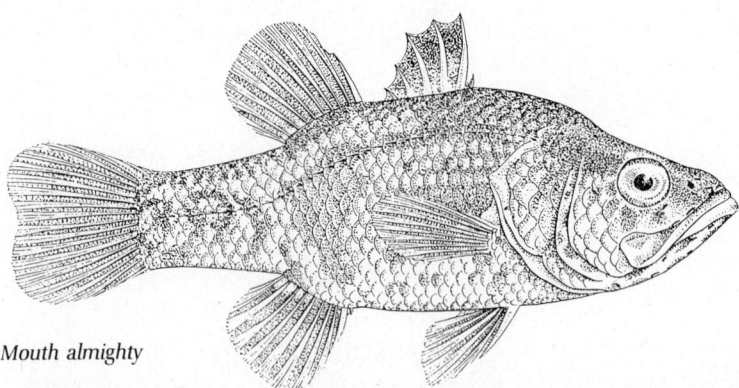

Mouth almighty

MUDSKIPPER Periophthalminae: Small (10 to 25 cm) amphibious marine fish that skip freely about mud-flats in search of small crustaceans and insects. Also known as johnny jumper, kangaroo fish, goggle-eyed mangrove fish, climbing fish and (wrongly) as

Mudskipper

lungfish. Five species are found in tropical Australia—Queensland, Northern Territory and north-western Australia. They can live for long periods out of water. The enlarged cavity that contains the gills encloses air as well as water and the surrounding tissue absorbs oxygen from the air, thus carrying out the functions of a primitive lung.

In 1770, Captain Cook's crew saw mudskippers hopping from stone to stone as nimbly as frogs in a Queensland mangrove-fringed mudflat. They enjoy the sun and the freedom of the mudflats at low tide. When disturbed they move about with a sculling motion of the pectoral fins. If they are scared these fins form arm-like limbs which enable mudskippers to hop quickly over the mud and even climb rocks and roots and trunks of mangroves. Noted ichthyologist T. C. Roughley called the mudskipper a piscatorial paradox—the fish which will drown if kept for too long underwater.

MULLET

Acrobatic pelagic fish of the family Mugilidae which skitter around our bays, lagoons and estuaries and are present in huge schools during migration periods. Mullet are an important commercial fish in Australia but most anglers are indifferent to them either as food fish or as sport fish. They are rich in minerals and American experts have calculated that they contain 900 times more iodine than the highest quality beef. They feed in the mud on microscopic vegetation and most of the 100-odd species found around the world are virtually toothless.

Mullet do not often strike at baits or lures but some Australian anglers float-fish them with flour dough mixed with cotton wool. In fresh water they sometimes take earthworms, bread, spaghetti or maggots. Overseas they are taken on fly rods and cane poles and are regarded as important bait fish for tarpon, kingfish, sailfish and snoek. New Zealand anglers generally have the same poor opinion of mullet as sport fish and table fare as Australians. The name herring is frequently used in New Zealand for their yellow-eye mullet which is not a true herring.

Of around 30 species of mullet in Australian waters, only about half a dozen species are of interest to the angler. Considerable confusion exists among anglers regarding names of different mullet species, mainly because of the close similarity of the many species. All species of mullet are essentially river fish, although some of them move from fresh water to salt water. The sea mullet migrates to the sea to spawn and other species move freely in the waters of the bays, inlets or surf and enter the rivers only during the flood tide.

Many of the mullet caught from piers, breakwaters and jetties are juvenile sea mullet, the larger sea mullet rarely take a bait. One species, the freshwater mullet *Myxus petardi*, is found in the headwaters of streams along the coast north of Sydney, extending to the south coast of Queensland. The so-called freshwater mullet of South Australia is actually the yellow-eye mullet, *Aldrichetta forsteri*.

Blue-tailed mullet

Valamugil seheli: Also known as black-spot mullet, blue-spot mullet, long-finned mullet, long-armed mullet and sand mullet. Largest of the Queensland mullets reaches 10 kg, the smallest 3.5 to 4.5 kg. Grant says they are common in estuaries north of Cairns, though stragglers are found as far south as Rockhampton. They are especially plentiful in Princess Charlotte Bay. Frequently taken in traps set for threadfins, mangrove jacks and barramundi, they are easily identified by their bright blue caudal fins and blue soft dorsal fins. The yellow pectorals have a prominent blue or black spot at the base.

Diamond-scaled mullet

Liza vaigiensis: One of the heaviest of our mullets, growing to 4.5 kg, found more in the waters north of Bundaberg, Queensland, than in northern New South Wales or in north Western Australia. Experts rate it a good food fish but it is unpopular as table fish in areas where more acceptable fish abound. The smaller specimens are used frequently for bait. They have a far broader head and much larger scales than other Australian mullet and are quickly identified by the six broken brown streaks running along a body that is olive green above, silvery along the sides and dull yellow beneath. The pectorals are very dark, the fins golden in colour. Even 30 cm specimens of this thick-shouldered fish yield good fillets.

Diamond-scaled mullet

MULTI ■ M

Fantail mullet

Mugil georgii: Also known as flickers, silver mullet, tychuree and small fantail mullet. They grow to 30 cm but are seldom seen beyond 25 cm as they are the smallest of all the Australian species of mullet. They are plentiful in shallow sand-flats in southern Queensland and large quantities reach the fried fish shops there. They are a vivid silver in colour, have a thick upper lip and almost straight caudal fin. They have a habit of flicking at the surface in large shoals.

Flat-tail mullet

Liza dussumieri: Steel blue above, silvery on the sides and white below, with no fleshy eyelid. There is a small black spot at the root of the pectoral fin preceded by a golden blotch. Although flat-tail mullet have been caught in all States except Tasmania, they occur rarely along the Victorian coast, and increase in numbers along the New South Wales and Queensland coasts. They grow to 45 cm and up to 1 kg, but most specimens average 28 cm. They are mostly used for bait.

Flat-tail can be caught throughout the year and are found in the greatest numbers in the lower parts of rivers. They are not good biters and only odd catches are taken on dough baits or bread. Standard mullet tackle is used on them in rivers and large schools are taken in seine nets.

Freshwater mullet

Myxus petardi: Found only in the coastal rivers of south Queensland and the eastern rivers of New South Wales. The Australian Museum has a specimen 48.7 cm long and there is a record of another reaching 80 cm but most of those caught are around 30 cm. Whitley says outback farmers cultivate them in dams and pools 'in unconscious imitation of the Romans of old'. They vary considerably in edible quality according to the conditions in which they are caught. They are remarkable in that they have fine teeth in both lips and larger teeth in the upper mouth.

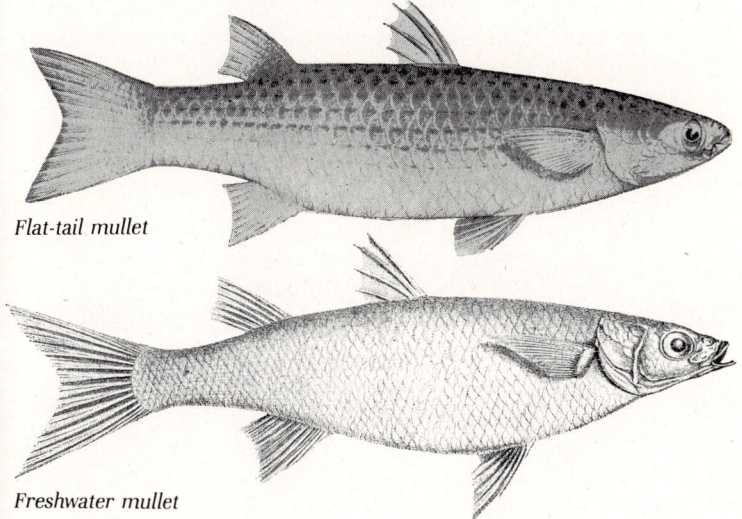

Flat-tail mullet

Freshwater mullet

M ■ MULLET

Long-finned mullet *Liza strongylocephalus:* A small mullet with an exceptionally long pectoral fin, blotched golden cheeks. Found in the far north of Queensland, where they are sometimes present in such numbers the night time flashing of a light from a dinghy can cause a protracted roar as hordes of long-finned mullet surface together. They grow to 25 cm and have a liking for mud flats.

Ord River mullet *Liza diadema:* Found in the Northern Territory, north Western Australia and parts of Queensland, where they grow to 50 cm. Whitley, who identified them as a separate species in 1945, reports that they are common most of the year in those areas but decline in numbers after the wet. They will move from salt to fresh water. They have a flash of bright orange above the eyes and there are no teeth on the palate and no fatty eyelids. They are greyish above, silvery beneath and each scale has a horizontal white streak.

Sand mullet *Myxus elongatus:* Known in some parts of Queensland as tallegalane and in others as Wide Bay mullet and in some areas of New South Wales as lano. They are one of the few mullet that make good pan fish, particularly when the fillets are skinned before cooking.

They are dark olive-green above and silvery below and have no fleshy eyelid as has the sea mullet. There is a prominent black spot in the axil of the pectoral fin. The sand mullet grows to 40 cm but average catches are around 25 cm.

Sand mullet are found in all States except Tasmania and are mainly caught over the shallow sandy flats near the river mouths and along the ocean beaches. They bite freely enough to provide good sport on light tackle.

The same tackle and methods used for the yellow-eye can be used for sand mullet, but the lines can be lighter. Some young anglers prefer to use a light rod, a small float and a No. 6 to 8 hook up to 45 cm below it. Sand mullet will take the same baits as do the yellow-eye, but marine worms, prawns and dough seem to be the most successful.

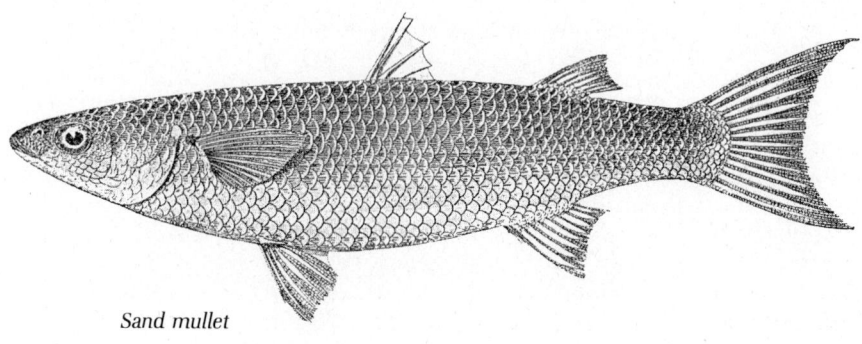

Sand mullet

MULLET ■ M

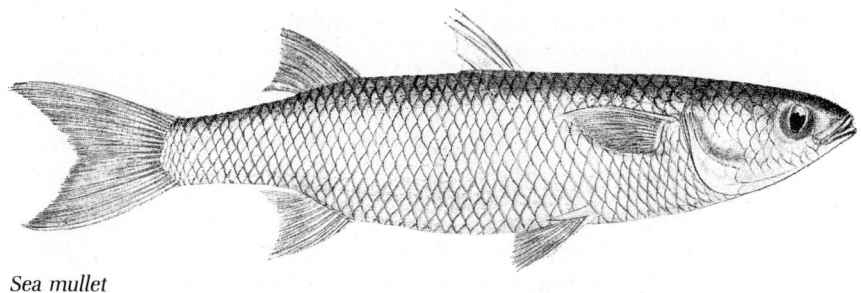

Sea mullet

Sea mullet

Mugil cephalus: One of the main commercial fishes of Queensland. They are olive-green above and silvery below in ocean waters but tend to become darker on entering an estuary or river. They have a small black spot at the base of the pectoral fin. They grow to 75 cm, or more, and to a weight of about 8 kg. Sea mullet range from Cairns in Queensland, along the New South Wales and Victorian coasts to Fowlers Bay on the South Australian coast. They are found too in Western Australia from Albany to Shark Bay and in Tasmania along the north-eastern coast.

They are also known as bully mullet, hardgut mullet, river mullet and mangrove mullet, and in New Zealand as kanae (Maori). New Zealand species are greyer and stouter than those of Australia and they find the southern part of the South Island too cold. Individual catches of 25 tonnes of this fertile fish have been taken in Queensland.

Fly fishing for mullet

Sea mullet feed on decaying sea weeds and grasses and diatoms. They also feed extensively on oyster eggs when these are obtainable. Big sea mullet rarely take a bait although an occasional one is caught when the angler is fishing a dough bait for other species. Victorian anglers have been fishing for sea mullet for the past 40 years with tiny black floating flies and while it is possible that not all mullet taken on a fly have been this species, it is the sea mullet the saltwater fly man goes after.

There are many misconceptions about fly fishing for mullet. In the first place the mullet probably do not take the fly always because they are hungry. Like the salmon running up to spawn, the mullet do not feed when preparing for their spawning run and the fly on the water is merely taken out of curiosity, annoyance or because of some complex conditioned reflex. The drawback to fishing a fly in saltwater areas is that the salt plays havoc with rods, reels and lines. Anglers today have partly overcome this problem by using fibreglass rods with stainless steel snake rings, saltwater proofed reels and plastic fly lines.

Tackle and techniques on sea mullet

To catch a sea mullet on a fly the angler needs a fairly heavy fly rod of about 2.5 to 3 m long, a tapered line and a 2.5 to 3.5 m nylon leader, tapered to 2X or 3X. There is plenty of room for experimenting with fly patterns but the most successful found to date is a black spider-pattern dry fly tied on a No. 10 or 12 hook.

Another misconception is to believe that the sea mullet strikes at the floating artificial as would a brown trout under certain conditions, but mullet have 'browsing' mouths and merely nibble at or suck in their food. What actually happens when an angler thinks he has a strike is that he has been fishing with a tight line and the big sea mullet moving forward suddenly jars the rod tip when he sucks in the fly.

To fish the fly, the angler takes up a position on the bank of the river where he can cast out to the main current where the sea mullet are congregating and maybe jumping. The fly is cast on to the current and allowed to drift and every now and again the angler twitches the rod tip to give the fly just enough movement to make it look like something swimming near the surface or struggling on the surface.

The sea mullet takes the fly quietly but deliberately and the moment the fly disappears or the leader acts strangely the angler lifts the rod tip. As most of the sea mullet caught on a fly average about 3.5 to 5 kg care must be taken on the strike, otherwise the 2X or 3X leader will snap like cotton. So far, heavier leaders have not been very successful, as they drag the fly and do not allow it to look like a natural insect.

What the sea mullet takes the fly as an imitation of is anyone's guess. Some believe that it is taken for a shrimp or other small crustacean, others believe that the mullet take winged insects, like mosquitoes, on the surface. But we must accept that the mullet merely takes the quivering insect because it is small and helpless; they may want to kill it just for these reasons rather than because the fish themselves are hungry.

Yellow-eye mullet

Aldrichetta forsteri: The main cool water species and the principal mullet marketed in South Australia and Victoria. Their range extends from the New South Wales south coast to Tasmania and across to the south-west of Western Australia. They are prevalent off both the North and South islands of New Zealand.

Yellow-eye mullet are an olive-brown above and silver to light yellow below. They have bright yellow eyes. The fins have a brownish margin. They grow to about 40 cm, are more slender than warm water species and take bait more readily.

Yellow-eye mullet are shoal fish and congregate over sand and gravel as well as mud flats. They also enter fresh water and have a fondness for brackish water. Swimming in shoals, they usually keep near the surface and they can be detected

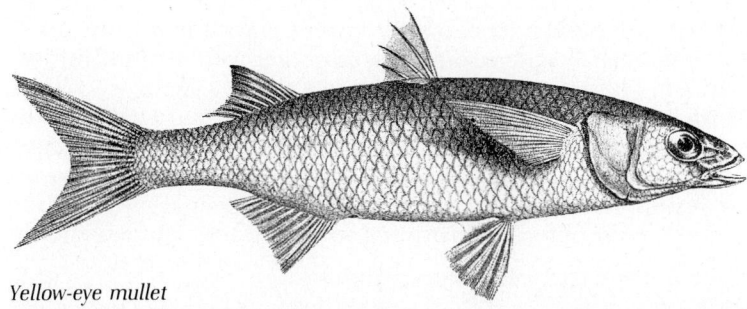

Yellow-eye mullet

by a ripple on the surface and the blue reflection that the shoals give to the sea. Before spawning they are quite plump, but immediately after are in poor condition.

There are probably more yellow-eye mullet caught on rod and line than any other species of mullet and when they are really on the bite can be caught three and four at a time. They are a fish that require plenty of berleying to keep them in numbers close to the angling location.

Pier fishing methods for yellow-eye mullet
The southern Australian pier angler usually uses a long, pliant rod, but not so whippy that it will not lift two good-sized mullet up to the pier. Threadline reels make casting easier, but almost any kind of reel will do. A 2.5 to 3.5 kg line is strong enough for any of the mullet likely to be caught. A small bean or round sinker is placed at the end of the line and two or three No. 8 or 10 hooks tied on 10 cm snoods above it. The hooks are baited with sandworm, dough or boiled mutton flap. In mullet fishing it is wise to keep a tight line and to keep the baits on the move. The moment a strike is felt the rod tip should be raised firmly.

One popular method in Victoria these days for yellow-eye mullet was introduced by an angler known for the catches of up to 100 mullet at a time from the bayside piers. He uses a rod of 3 to 4 m rangoon cane, with a whippy tip. To the end of the cane he attaches a length of 2.5 kg nylon line, the length being determined by the depth of water to be fished and the height of the pier above the water. No reel is used. A small medicine bottle cork is painted white and slit down one side with a razor blade. The line is then slid into the slit in the cork. To the end of the 2.5 kg line two short nylon leaders are attached, one about 15 cm long, the other about 20 cm. A single No. 12 dry fly hook is then attached to the end of each of the short leaders.

After a small piece of sandworm is placed on each hook, the baits are swung out across the water. The line beneath the cork can be lengthened so that the two baits fish close to the river bed, if that is where the fish are feeding. As soon as the cork makes a forward or downward movement the angler swings up the rod tip and in one movement lifts the hooked mullet on to the pier.

There is a knack in catching mullet with this rig but once this has been learned this technique will catch more mullet than any other yet devised. To keep the shoals of mullet around the pier or to attract them to the spot he is fishing, the angler scatters a handful or two of damp bread-crumbs in the water. If there is a slight current it may be necessary to mix the damp bread with wet sand so that it sinks and is not washed away before descending to where the fish can see it.

River fishing for yellow-eye mullet

Mullet are easier to catch in a river, perhaps because they have entered it with the sole purpose of feeding. The shoal is more compact and less scattered than in open waters and this concentration forces individual fish to take anything that looks edible.

Mullet have very small mouths for feeding over the weed beds and mud flats. Feeding mullet do not bite at the item of food but more often than not merely suck it in. Sometimes this feeding is sufficiently forceful to overcome any resistance of the bait, caused by a heavy line or a sinker. On other occasions the mullet feed so timidly that any bait that cannot be sucked in easily is rejected. The angler using heavy gear under these conditions will not catch many mullet.

Experienced mullet fishermen use the lightest line they can handle, the lightest gauge hooks and baits so small and light that it is remarkable that they interest the fish. These light baits on light tackle drift around in a natural manner and are taken by the fastidious mullet. Of course, fishing in an estuary, when the tide is running strong, entails the use of a sinker. When a sinker is used it should be attached to the end of the line and the No. 8 or 10 hooks attached to short nylon snoods above it.

During prolonged flooding in the river, fishing for mullet is not recommended if the angler intends to eat his catch, as the fish will taste muddy. In the smaller rivers and creeks the mullet usually run in after the tide has been rising for an hour or so. This run will continue until the top of the tide.

The best tackle for river fishing is a 3 m, fairly stiff rod, a threadline reel, 2 to 3 kg nylon line and No. 8 or 10 hooks. The best baits for fishing the river or estuary are shrimps, prawns, sandworms, pipis, dough, damp bread crusts, small pieces of fish, and perhaps most successful of all, boiled mutton flap.

Surf fishing for yellow-eye mullet

Numbers of yellow-eye and a few other species of mullet are caught in the surf each year. Some anglers do not bother to use surf tackle but manage with heavy spinning rods, salt-water threadline reels or even large trout reels, and 3.5 to 4.5 kg lines. When the surf is not too rough, and there's no loose weed or a side drift, and the mullet are feeding close to the beach, this tackle is reasonably successful. But there are many days when conditions are rough and a light surf rod, a saltwater threadline reel or a revolving drum surf reel, and a 4.5 to 5.5 kg line are more likely to give the surf man a trouble-free day.

No more than two hooks are used in the surf and these No. 8 hooks are attached to short snoods which are in turn attached to the line above a fixed sinker. Make sure when attaching the snoods to the line that the hooks cannot meet when the snoods are pointed towards each other. The weight of the sinker will depend upon the state of the tide, the wind and how far out the mullet are feeding. Sinkers as light as 20 g have been used, but one about 40 g is more likely to be used under normal conditions. Heavy sinkers are not recommended on lines as light as 4.5 or 5.5 kg.

On many days the mullet are not far out, and along such famous beaches as the Ninety Mile in Victoria, they may be found as close as 20 to 30 m from the beach. Fortunately, the mullet often feed over clean sand or light weed beds and the loss of terminal tackle is not nearly so heavy as it is for the angler casting way out for salmon.

Fishing for mullet in the surf the angler should again keep a reasonably tight line and should strike the moment the fish is felt. The best baits are sandworms, marine worms and mutton flap, and while a dozen or more other baits are good they are difficult to keep on the hooks when casting.

MULLOWAY or jewfish

Mulloway are a small group of large fish belonging to the family Sciaenidae and are closely related to the smaller teraglins. In the southern latitudes the jewfish *Sciaena antarctica* is the largest fish that anglers can expect to catch in the harbours, estuaries, tidal rivers or from the surf. It has been noted to grow to 1.8 m and 60 kg but the Australian record for an angler stands at 44 kg. Jewfish weighing around 35 kg are reported on rare occasions but fish up to 27 kg and slightly more, are fairly common. A big proportion of the large fish caught range around 15 kg.

The big mulloway is found along the coast from about Rockhampton around through the more temperate waters to Carnarvon. In the more northern latitudes it is replaced by two species: the spotted or blotched jewfish *Protonibea diacanthus*; and the silver jewfish *Nibea soldado*.

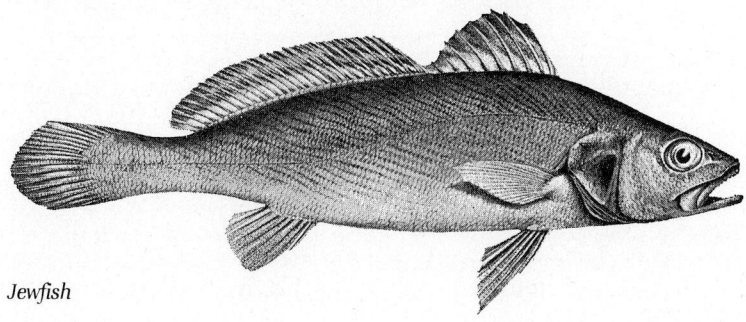

Jewfish

The spotted jewfish grows to a maximum of about 45 kg and, weight for weight, is probably the best sports fish of the family, for on a line it is fast and powerful with a good deal of endurance. All the mulloways are capable of making a drumming-croaking noise by vibrating their air bladders, but this species makes itself most audible and in northern waters may be heard under boats at night. It is easily distinguished from others of the family by the dark blotches or spots, on its back and dorsal fin, and the particularly strong second spine in the anal fin.

The silver jewfish, also known as grassy jew, banana jew and silver perch, is a smaller species, growing to a maximum of about 75 cm. It is common in the far north, particularly from the Gulf of Carpentaria to Darwin harbour. It is easily identified by its silvery-grey upper body, darkening to pinkish or greenish-grey along the back under its dusky dorsal fin and shading away to silvery white on the sides and below. The pectoral, anal and tail fins are yellow. It is often found in schools, bites well and is rated as a good eating fish, though not quite so choice as the other species.

Although some occasionally are taken in daylight, jewfish are nocturnal hunters and are mostly caught between late afternoon and early morning. In the estuaries and the surf the best time to fish is on a high tide between dusk and two hours after dark. Out on the offshore reefs a snapper fisherman may have the luck to hook a big one at any time of the night or day.

Jewfish usually rest and sleep during the day by holing up in caves or under ledges along the ocean rocks, or by lying up in potholes or crevices around the reefs. They penetrate away up the rivers, well beyond the limits of salt water, and spend the brighter part of the day in the deeper holes. Young fish, up to about 6.5 kg are known as school jew, and the very small specimens often are called 'soapies' on account of their soft, mushy flesh.

Some of the best places to fish for mulloway are in the surf, along the channels in and around the mouths of the estuaries, at tidal lake entrances, from seawalls and along the channels in the big tidal rivers. When properly fished, most success is had with live bait, such as yellowtail, tailor, whiting, mullet, luderick or big beach worm. Good dead baits are fresh whole fish as above, garfish, big pilchards or fillets of bonito, blue mackerel, salmon, mullet or trevally. Others are skinned tentacle of octopus and squid.

Fishing for big mulloway calls for a good deal of knowledge of the habits of the species and some skill in preparing and handling the tackle. They are fish which seize their prey with their front teeth and then turn it to swallow it whole. When one takes a bait it usually picks it up in its lips and carries it along a little way before deciding to swallow it. It must be given free line and no resistance until it has taken the bait well into its mouth. To hang onto a big jewfish when it is first

This 'old man' mulloway shows the fur-like texture that can develop on the skin.

hooked is a sure way of breaking a light line. It must be allowed to make its first run with a gradual build up of pressure until it is slewed around, after which it should be much easier to handle.

Jewfish are excellent eating. The larger ones become rather coarse in texture and lose some of their flavour but still sell readily in the fish shops.

MURRAY cod

Maccullochella peeli: Ranks with the golden perch (callop) as Australia's most important inland fish. They are a gourmet's delight and the most delicious of Australia's edible inland fish. Although reduced by heavy professional fishing, by changing environment and the introduction of foreign species with which it has to duel for food, they are still present in rewarding sizes and numbers.

Murray cod are the dominant fish in Australia's major inland system, the Murray-Darling and tributaries. But they are also taken in several east coast rivers, where they live in apparent amity with Australian bass and eels. Headwaters of the Orara, Nymboida and Richmond in New South Wales, and the Mary in Queensland, have produced Murray cod to 18 kg though the average is now smaller. The average length is 90 cm and some of 1.5 m have been caught. The biggest grow well over 45 kg. One caught in the Murray in South Australia in 1924 went 56 kg when gutted. Gilbert Whitley, former Curator of Fishes at the Australian Museum, Sydney, had a record of a 113 kg 1.8 m long Murray cod being caught in the Barwon

M ■ MURRAY cod

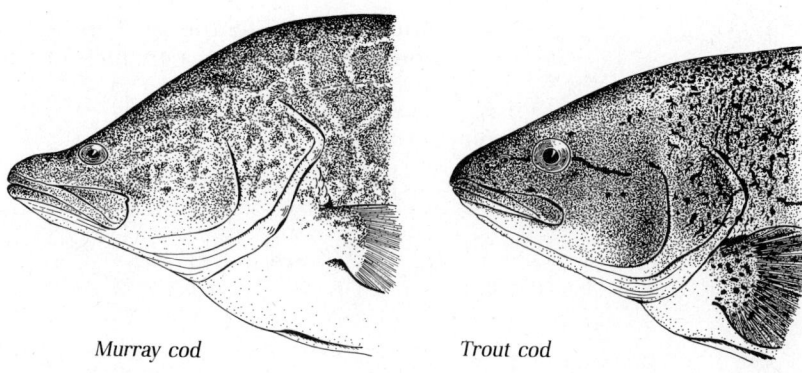

Murray cod

Trout cod

The Murray cod can be distinguished from the trout cod as there is no overhang to the jaw, the head slope is more slanted, the form is more elongate and the anal and ventral fins are almost translucent.

River near Walgett during the drought of 1902.

The Murray cod is green with a mottle pattern and not blue or white and spotted like the trout cod, which ichthyologists regard as a variety of the Murray cod and have given the name of *Maccullochella macquariensis*. Anglers generally agree that the trout cod is a superior sporting fish and is more often taken in fast moving water than the Murray cod, which prefers warm, stagnant pools. The Murray cod eats ravenously and as well as shrimps, crayfish and frogs, dead animals of many kinds small enough to be eaten have been found in their stomachs. They dote on grubs, worms and centipedes, which are thus often used by anglers.

Murray cod habitat shrinkage

A great deal of damage has occurred on the headwaters of streams on the western slopes of the Dividing Range, where rivers have shallowed with siltation. To the south, introduction of carp, English perch (redfin) and even trout has combined with the building of locks and weirs to deplete Murray cod. Native fish need natural rivers for survival and these waters are becoming scarcer.

Despite this, cod are still taken consistently in the Murray and its tributaries, the Edwards, Wakool, Murrumbidgee, and in Victoria the lower reaches of the Ovens and Goulburn. Improved fishing is found in the slow flowing Darling and tributaries. These rivers include the Macintyre, Gwydir, Namoi, Macquarie, Bogan, Castlereagh and the irregular Warrego and Culgoa, which drain from Queensland.

In Queensland the Condamine, Balonne, Weir and Moonie are well-known Murray cod waters, along with the Warrego and Culgoa. Cod are caught at times in Paroo waterholes, but not further inland in the Channel country streams which drain far western Queensland towards Lake Eyre. It is probable that a serious effort to stock permanent waterholes in the Lake Eyre system with cod would improve western fishing.

South Australia has the last 480 km of the Murray, which still appears to be well stocked. Efforts to transfer Murray cod to Western Australia earlier this century failed.

Angling pressure on cod is low and seasonal. To survive the drought and flood cycles of the driest continent on earth, native fish are specialized species which vary greatly in number. Breeding occurs during floods and under extreme drought conditions fish can become almost extinct. But the total length of the rivers runs to many thousands of kilometres of fishing water. Most of this is in New South Wales, for the Murray is legally New South Wales water though it is the Victorian border. The meandering inland streams are relatively small for their length. River kilometres between Wentworth and Moree are estimated at 3200—cod water all the way. Consequently, fish are able to re-establish themselves fairly fast in favourable seasons of high water level.

As a sporting fish, Murray cod are slow and heavy. Yet the nature of the fish is right in tune with the environment. In moderately clear water they are best fished with larger lures, though they will also take baits. In muddy water, they can be comfortably fished with large live baits. Because of sheer size, cod need heavier tackle than most freshwater fish. A fish of 50 cm can weigh 2 kg.

As the largest predator present, Murray cod rule the roost and take precedence for the best living quarters in any river. They are less active in daylight, so the primary job of the angler is to locate a large, deep pool well housed with snags, and with an abundant food supply close by. The two requirements—a good log for cover and a rich food supply—are easily seen, but many anglers fail to watch for the second essential. Food such as crayfish, mussels, forage fish and frogs are easily located. Crayfish leave holes in the banks, mussels are easily seen in clear water. Serious anglers will find them by feeling with bare feet along the edge of a sandbank. Forage fish are easily seen by torchlight at night.

Angling technique

Originally fishermen simply left many lines set, tied to roots and trees on the bank, and baited with a wide and wild assortment of bait, ranging from rabbit flesh to witchetty grubs (which see). As laws tightened on fishermen, the practice decreased but it did not disappear. Today more anglers are prepared to fish with a single rod or handline and pay closer attention to where fish are likely to be found.

As a territorial fish, given to controlling a definite area, Murray cod are adept at noticing any intrusion of food, especially vulnerable food, in their vicinity. For this reason, a live fish which has been hooked through the back with a strong 8/0 hook, so it can still swim in a restricted fashion, is bound to attract attention if it is placed beside the log under which a cod is domiciled. A large live crayfish or Murray lobster hooked carefully through the tail and suspended just clear of the river bed will struggle, and the flicking tail will call any fish in the vicinity. Live baits of this kind can be used to gently probe an entire area. If there are no bites within a few

M ■ MURRAY cod

minutes, move to the next likely place and try again. As a general rule, anglers can pick out cod from amongst other species—golden perch, silver perch, large catfish—simply by using large baits and lures. Fish of 0.5 kg weight, or crayfish 30 cm long, are not too large for cod.

Tethering the catch
When caught, cod can be kept alive on a strong tethering cord tied through the lower jaw, using enough length so the fish can lie comfortably out of sight at the river's edge. There is a definite process which gives maximum results in flesh quality. Murray cod are excellent eating even when not processed carefully, but best results are produced when the fish are treated with care. For optimum flesh quality, kill the fish by cutting the throat with a knife as soon as it is taken from the stream. Gut, clean and carefully remove all blood from the spine. Chill briefly, but do not freeze, in order to firm the flesh for filleting. Fillets should be thin, and care must be taken to trim any excess body fat around the fins and spine. Fat will be apparent on a prime fish, along the lateral line of the body, and this too should be trimmed. The fillets are white, clean and firm and can be cooked in the manner most favoured by an angler. This is a versatile cooking flesh of true quality. Smaller fish from 2 to 3.5 kg can be stuffed and baked with seasoned crayfish or even prawns.

Many anglers prefer lure fishing for Murray cod if rivers are sufficiently clear. The most effective method is to troll from a small boat, either with an outboard or behind oars. Trolling speed should be slow and has been measured at between 1.5 and 3 km/h. A stiff boat rod and strong spinning reel might be used, but many anglers prefer a handline for practical reasons. Only a short length of line is needed and among snags the breaking strain needs to be too high to be useful on a reel.

No wire trace is necessary. The line is tied direct to the lure. Originally, the popular lure was a large aeroplane spinner, with two blades on a wire shaft. A few anglers used large swayback bellbrooks, more so when either cod or golden perch were needed. About 1958 anglers on the Darling River had great success with the largest flopy lure, and by 1980 this lure had achieved wider recognition over most of the cod fishing country. Latest reports have told consistently of success with the deep running reb 2 lures in the largest size.

By a quaint anachronism, lures which spin were declared illegal in South Australia because cod took the spinners avidly when they refused to take baits. Worried about the effect this would have on Murray cod populations, the authorities banned spinners. However, wobbling lures are legal everywhere. Anglers will always argue over the worth of lures, but aeroplane spinners have been in constant use for 50 years and are an integral part of the river scene. They are an excellent lure which runs deep, can be bumped across most snags without fouling and still hook a striking fish cleanly. Few golden perch will go for a large aeroplane spinner; either cod or perch will take a wobbling lure. So either way the angler can hardly lose.

Rigs
Strong bait lines with extra strong hooks, or large 17.5 cm sidecast reel with short rod and 20 kg line. Troll lines can go as low as 9 kg test.

Baits
Live crayfish, fish, shrimp or frog, timber grubs or whole fish rigged on extra strong hook at least 5/0 and up to 10/0.

Lures
No. 3 or 4 aeroplane spinner, large flopy, large deep runner reb 2. Saltwater spinning reel, 9 kg line and strong casting rod, usually about 2 m in length.

Times
Early morning and late afternoon, close to cover in an area rich in fish food.

See Trout cod. See also Cookery.

MUSSELS

Mytilus planulatus: An edible bivalve found from New South Wales to the north-west corner of Western Australia and exploited commercially in Victoria. Although these mussels are eaten, and used for baits by anglers who recognize their high edible value to man and fish, the Victorians are the only ones who have got out of the backyard bottling stage and shown that our local mussels are as appetizing as those imported from overseas. Mussels are extremely fertile and in countries such as France and Italy where mussel culture is practised they show an extraordinary growth rate and give a flesh yield of more than 50 per cent of their weight. Australia's southern coast abounds in suitable areas where substrates of rock or wood are found in protected areas at a low littoral level and these waters could be enhanced as mussel grounds by the latest farming techniques.

There are many other species of the mussel family in Australia but only *Mytilus planulatus* can be considered for food or bait. The others are too small, or low in numbers or coarse in texture.

See Bait.

MAPS

The following fifteen pages of maps, arranged as shown on the key below, show major rivers, lakes and reservoirs, coastal features, towns, roads and railways. The sections covering arid central Australia are not included. Simplified sketchmaps of popular coastal fishing spots will be found in most of the articles on the States.

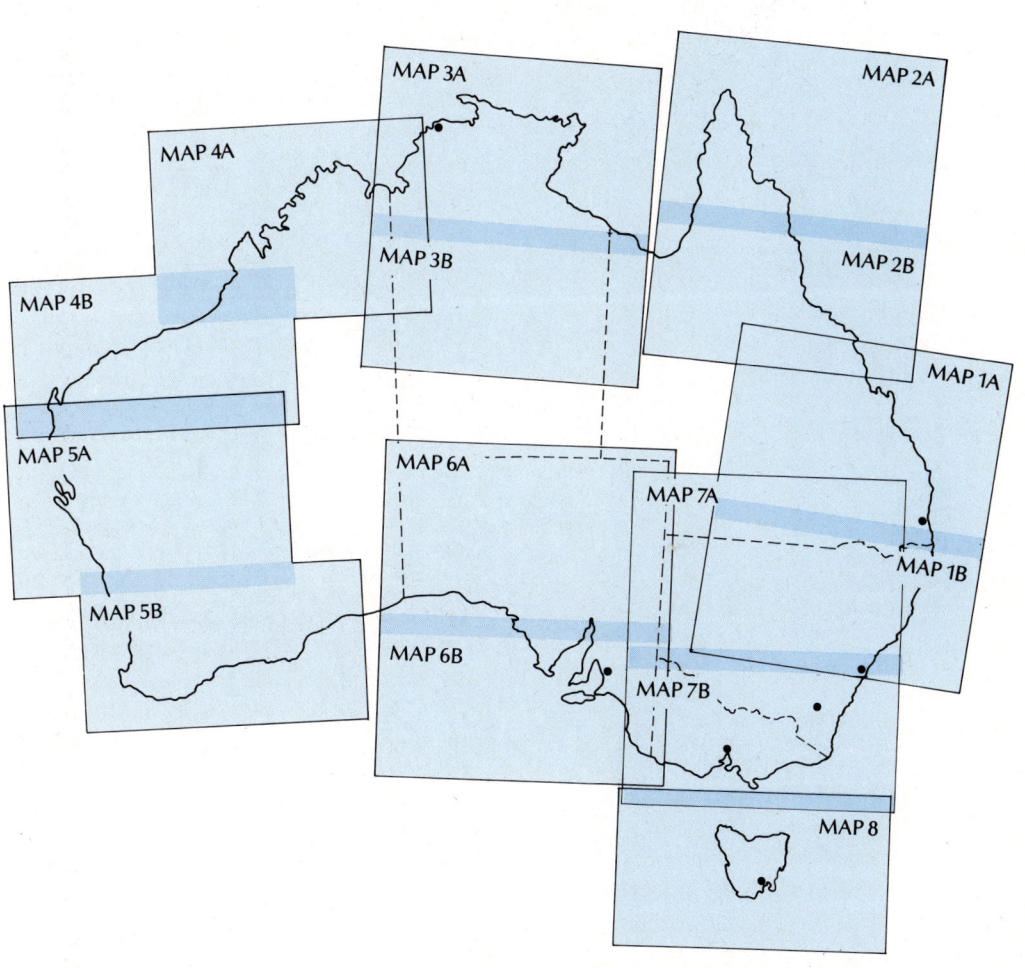

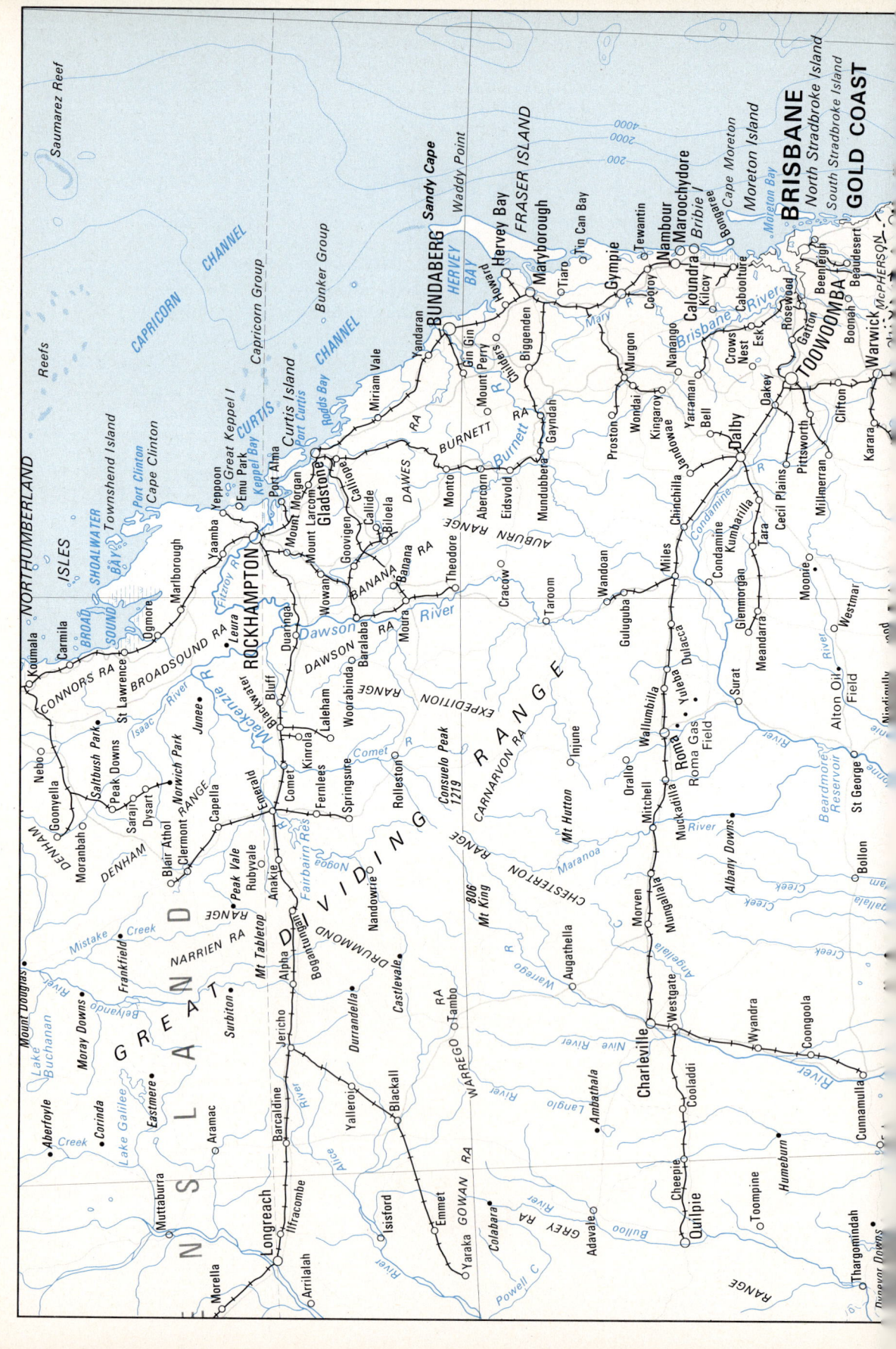

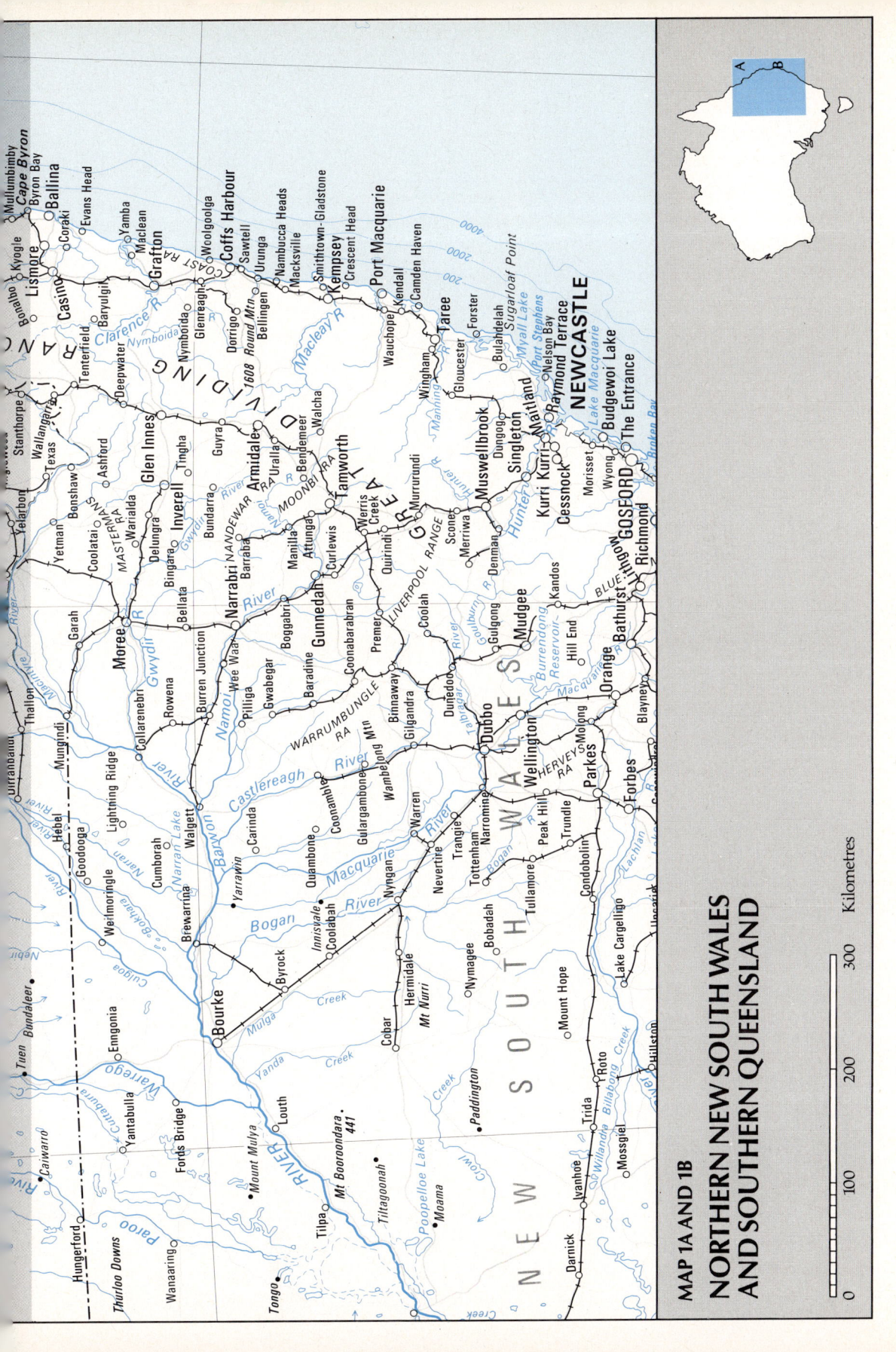

MAP 1A AND 1B
NORTHERN NEW SOUTH WALES
AND SOUTHERN QUEENSLAND

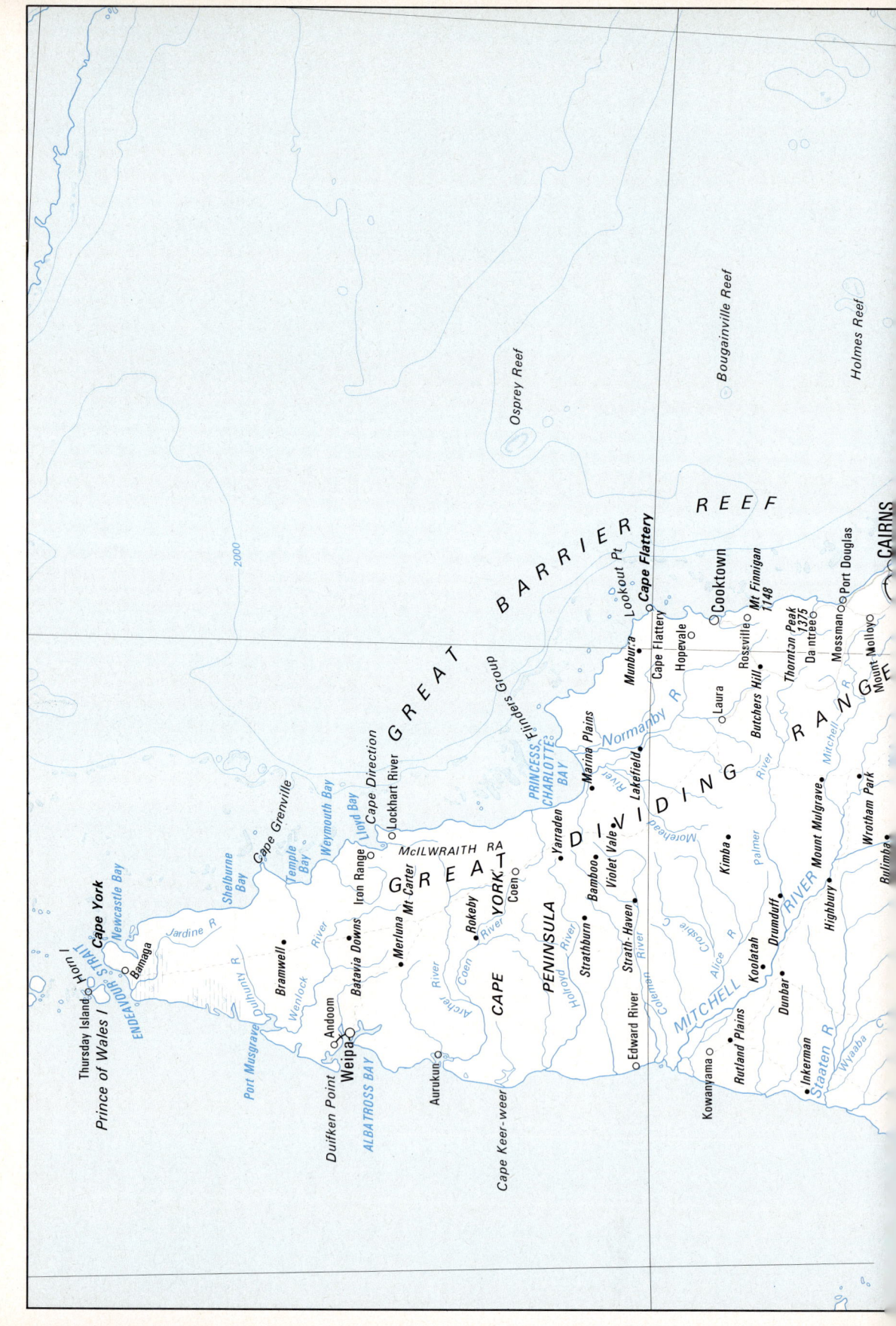

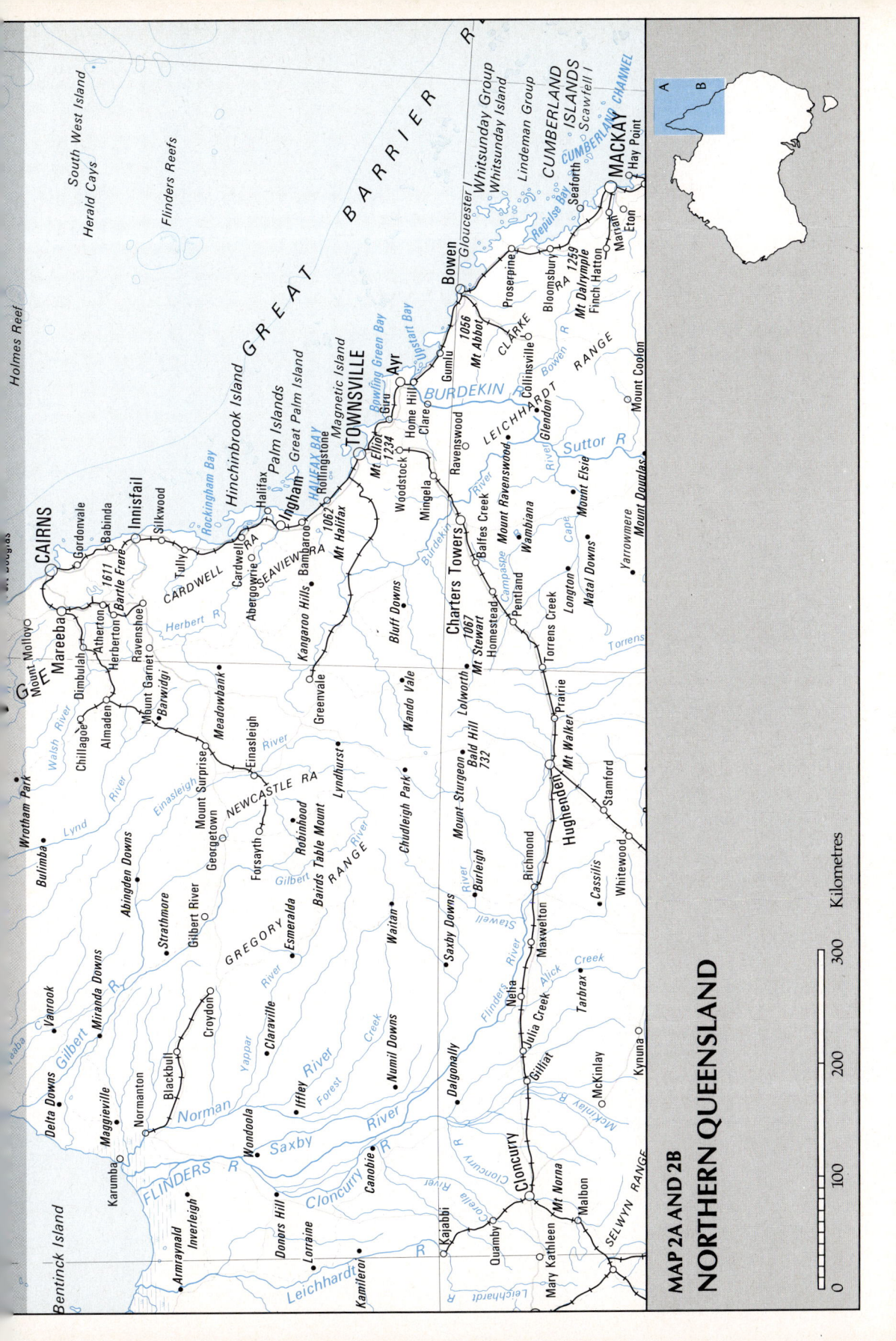

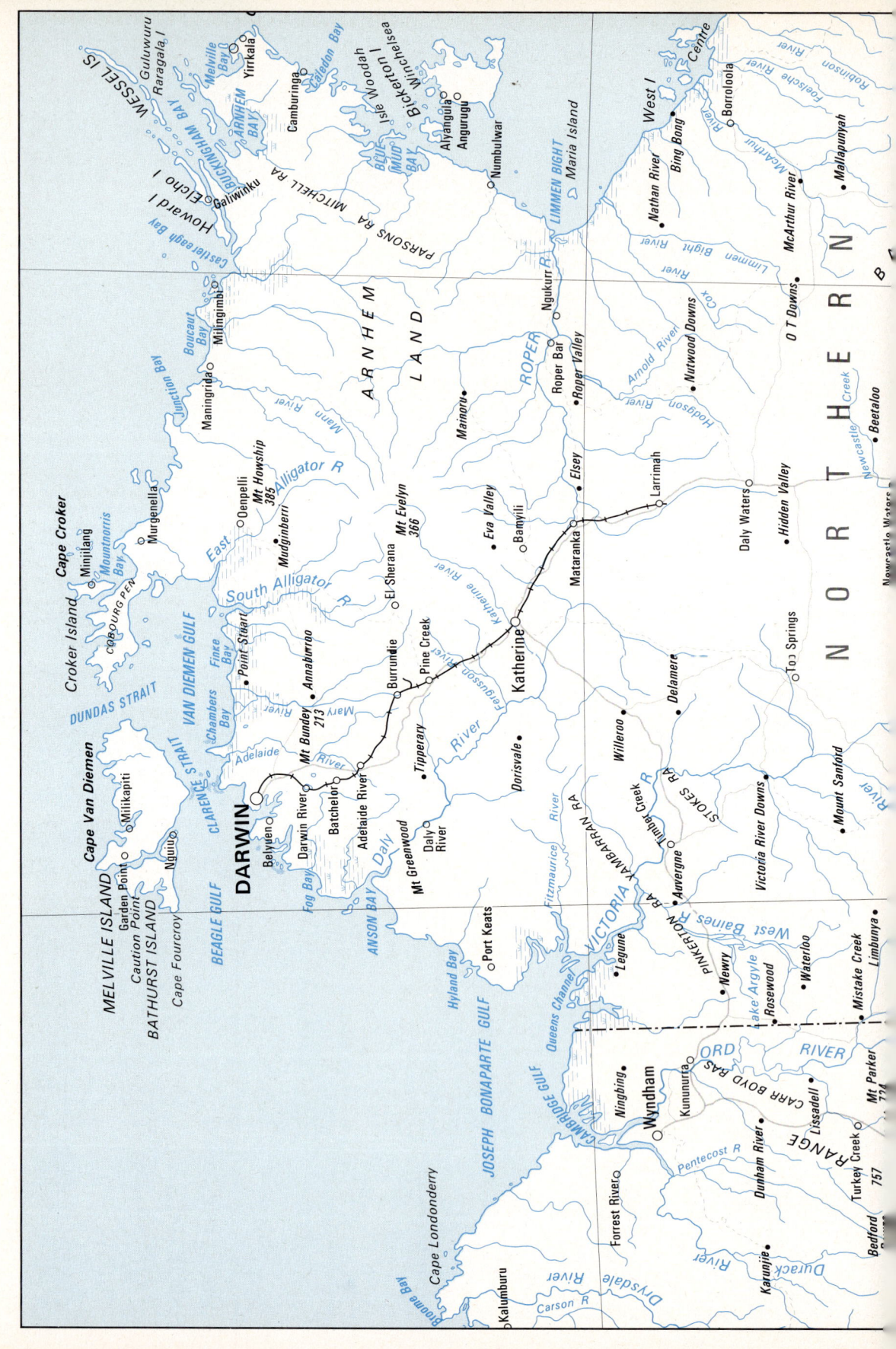

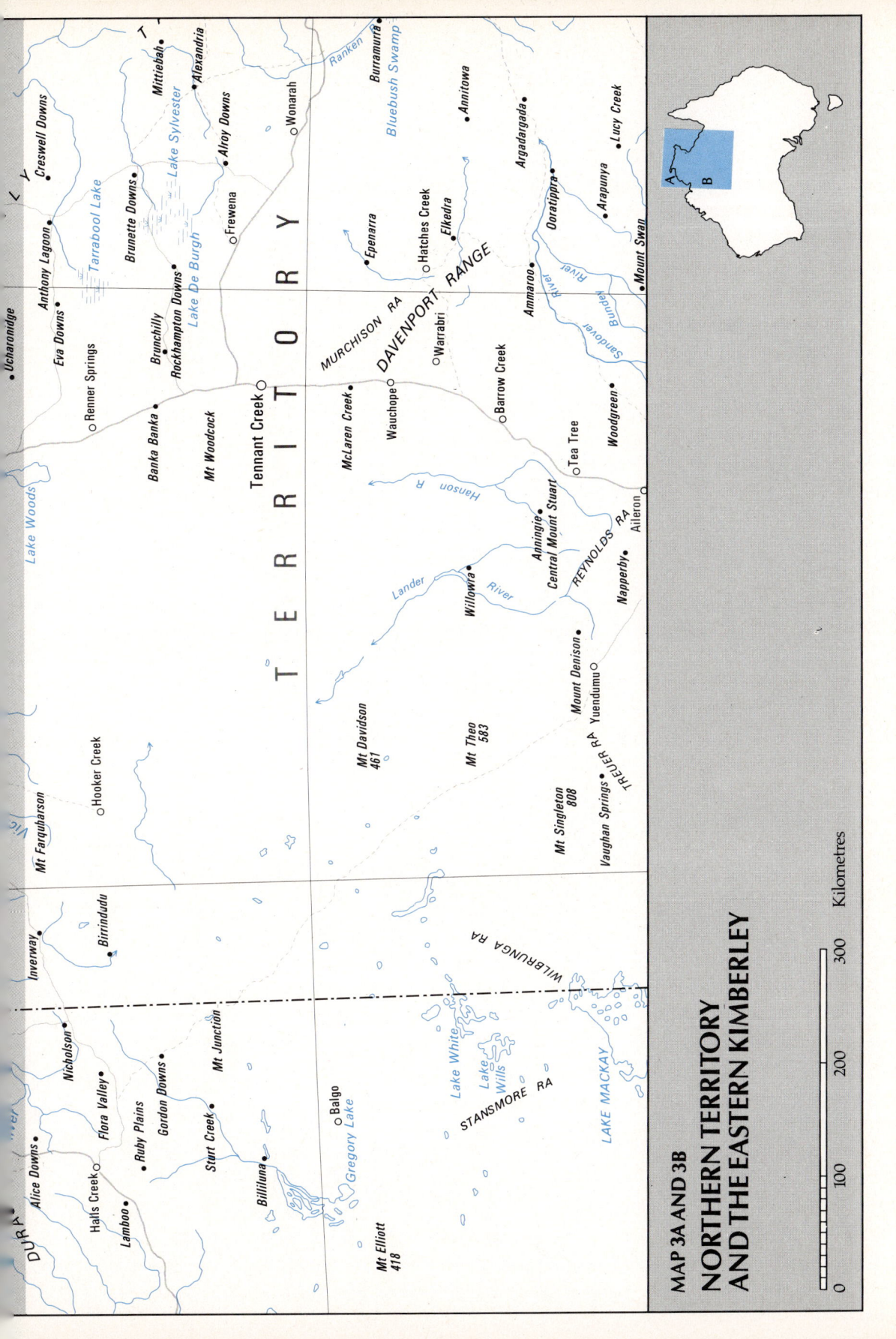

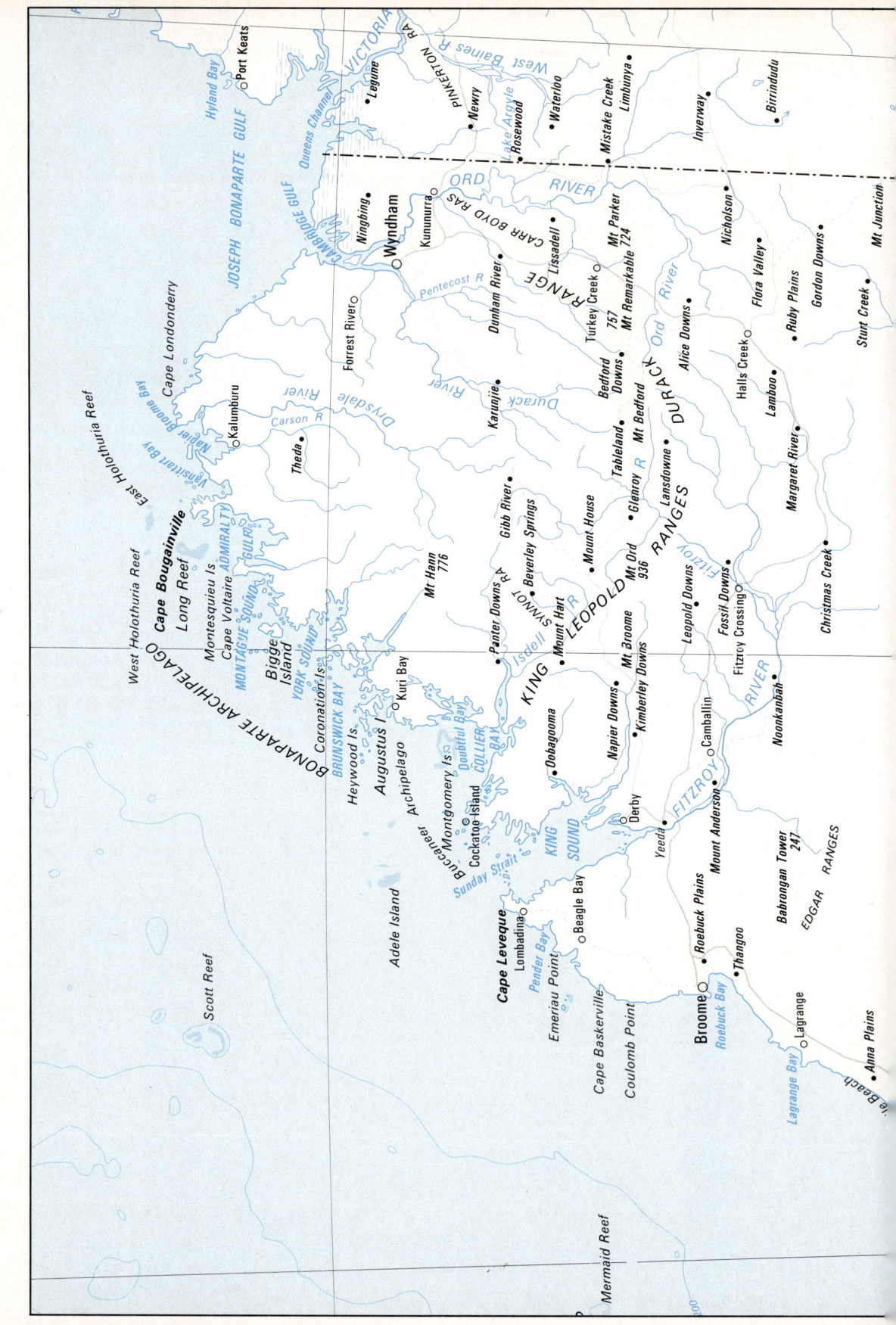

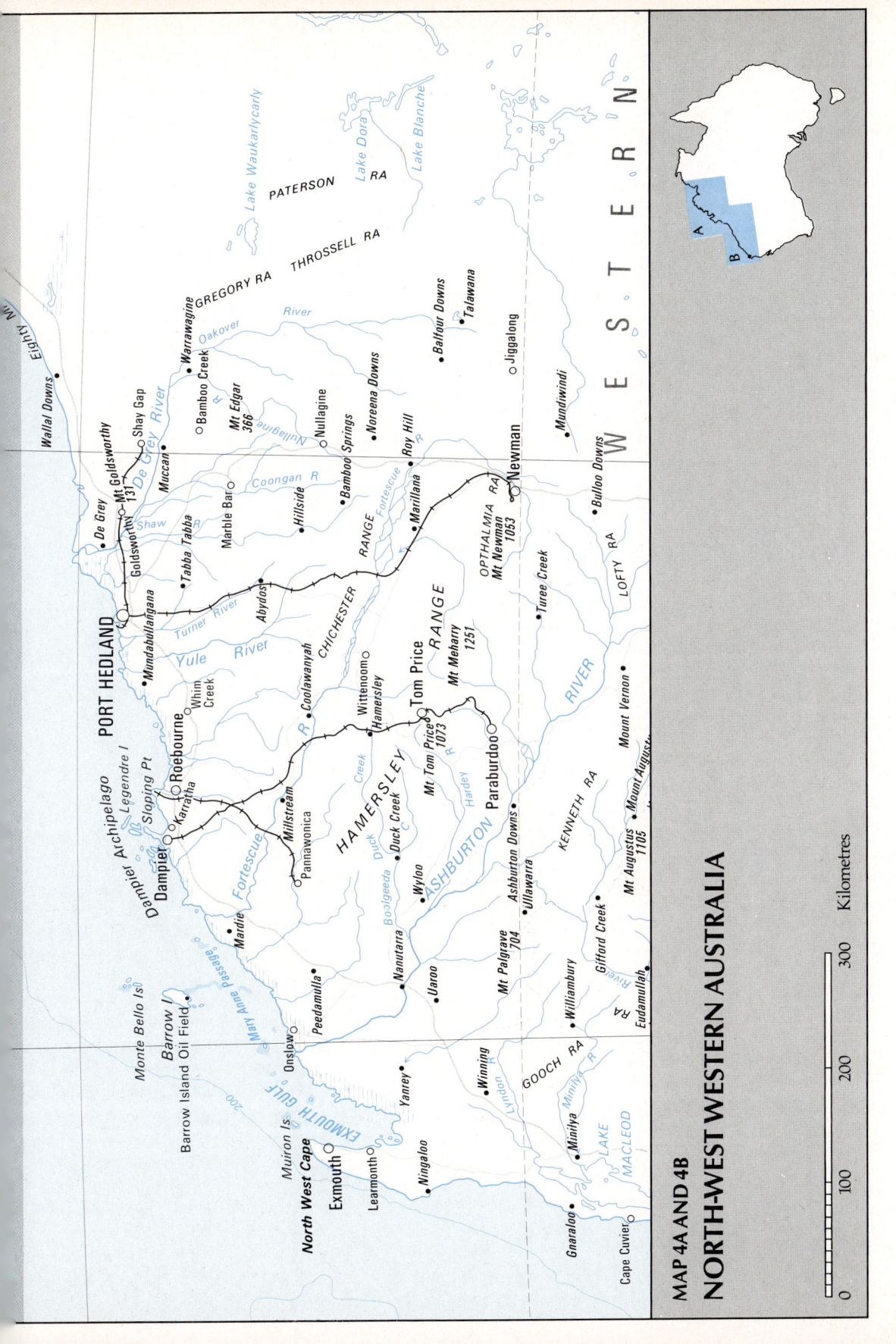

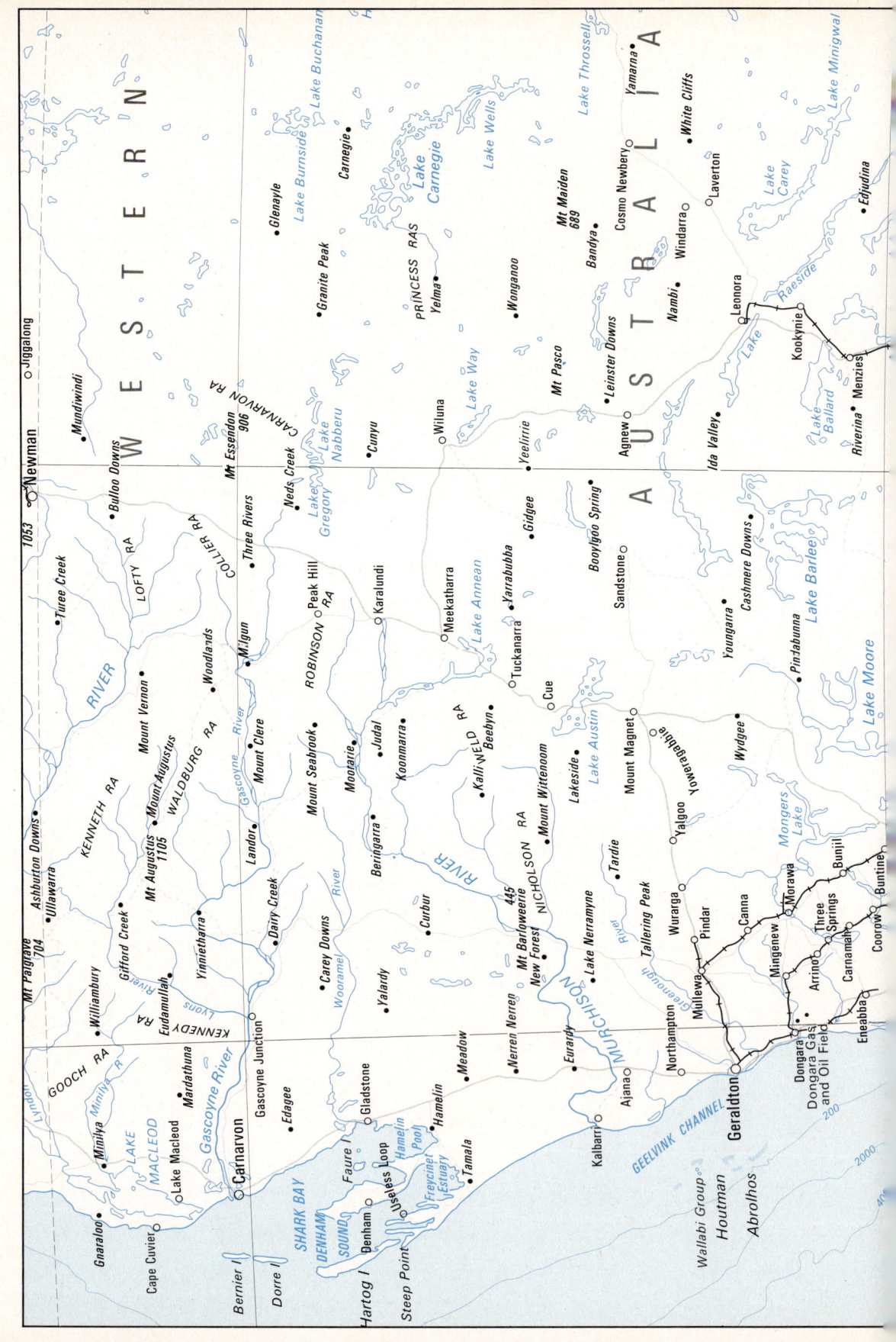

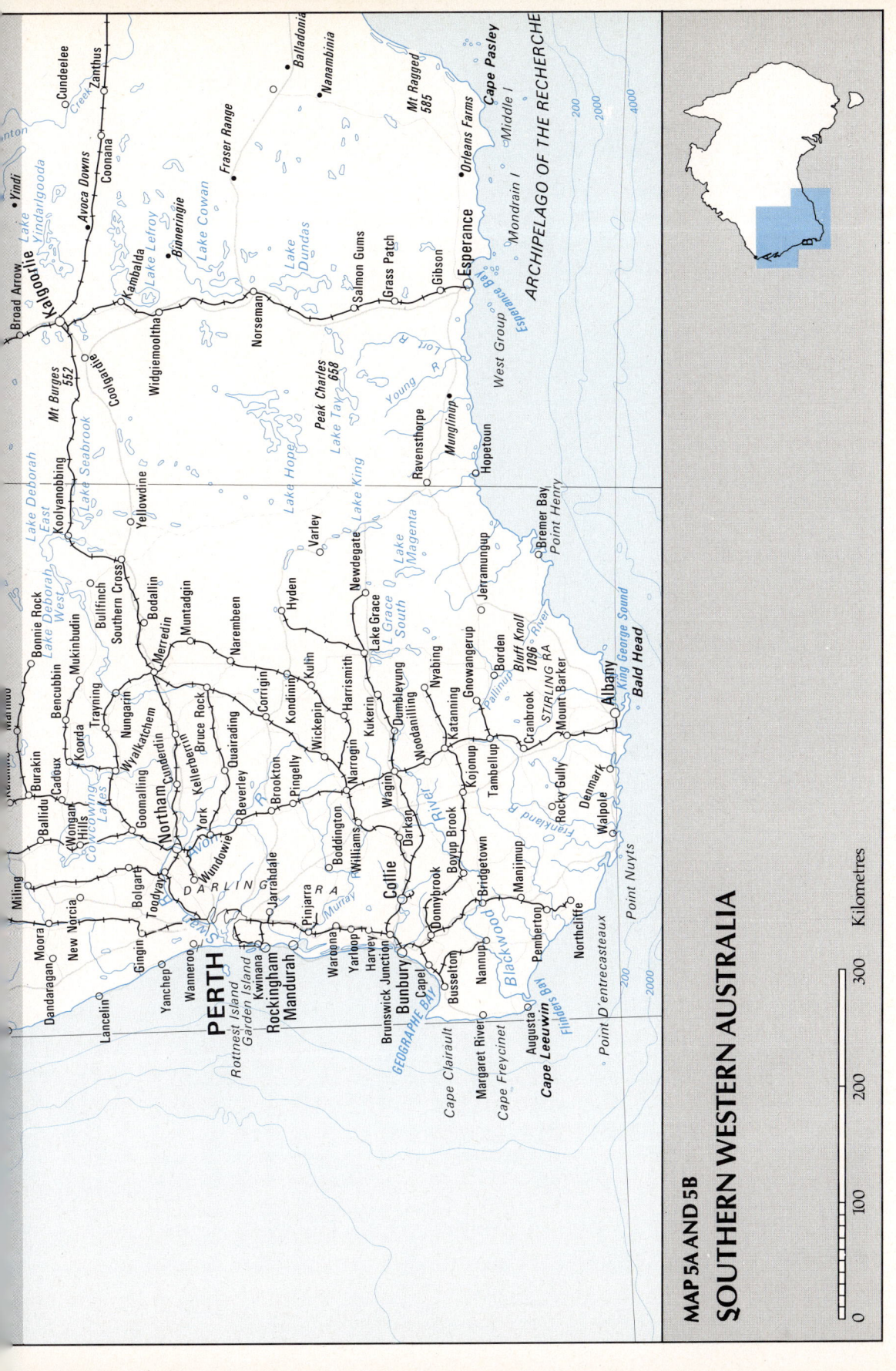

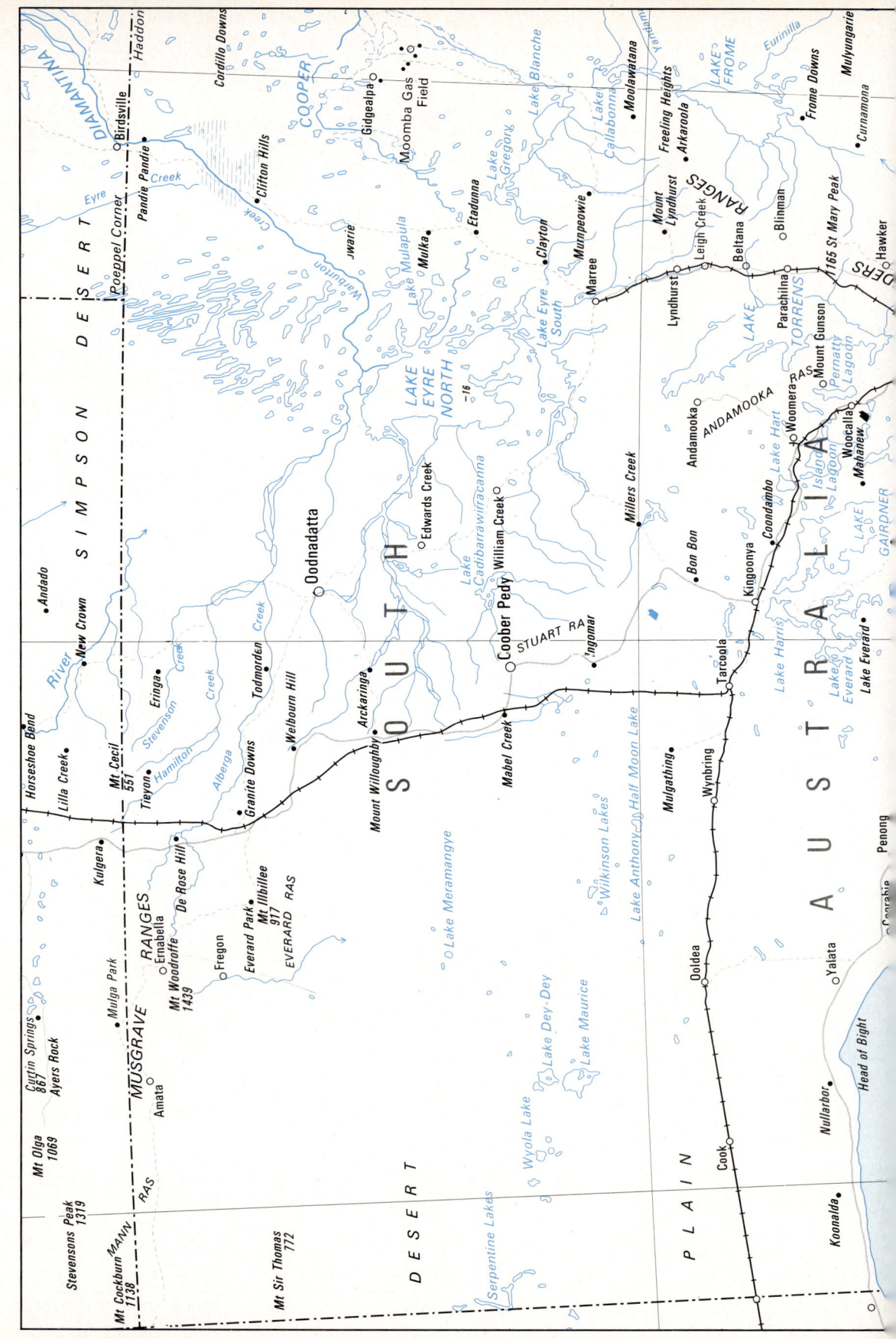

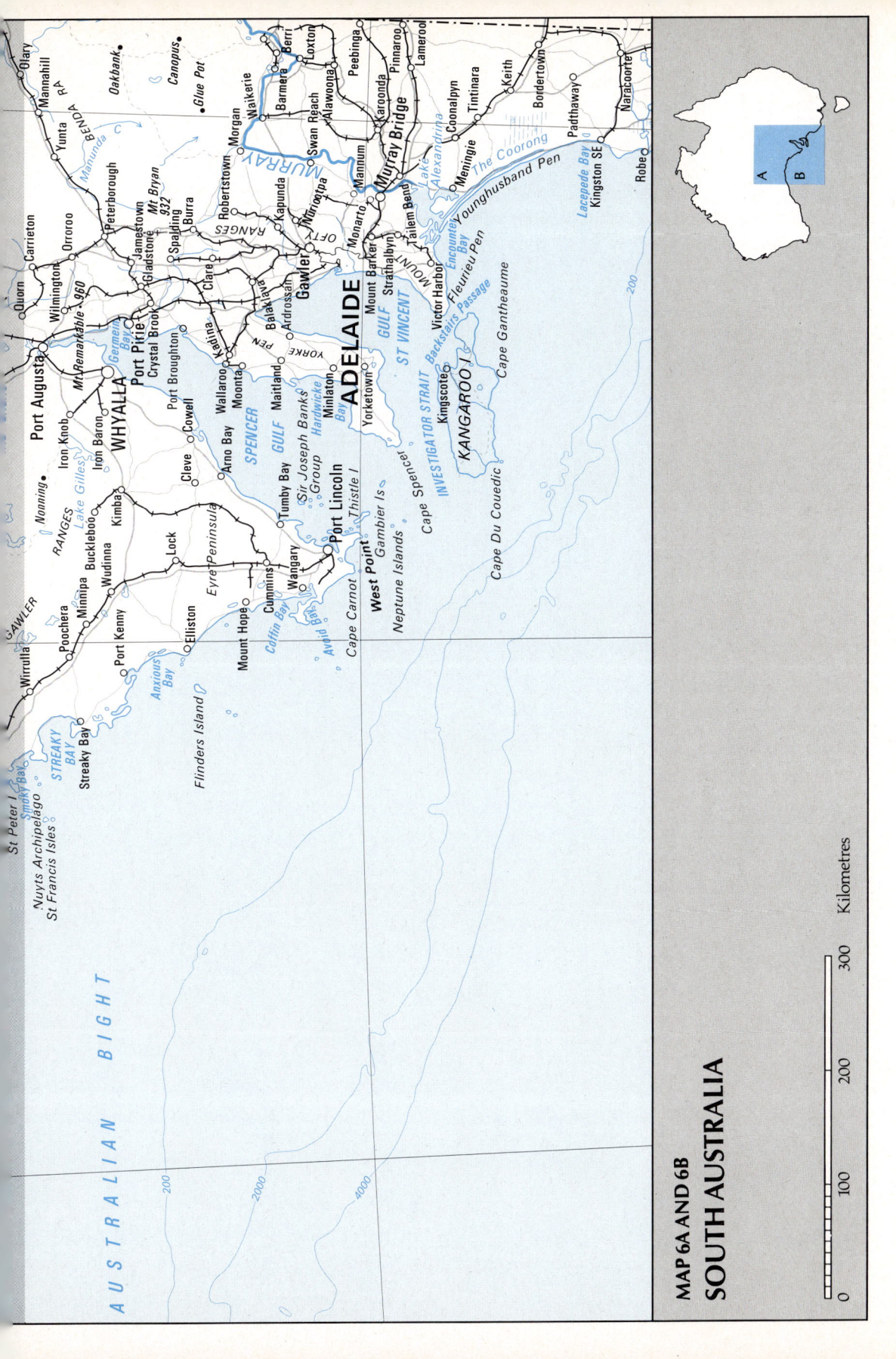

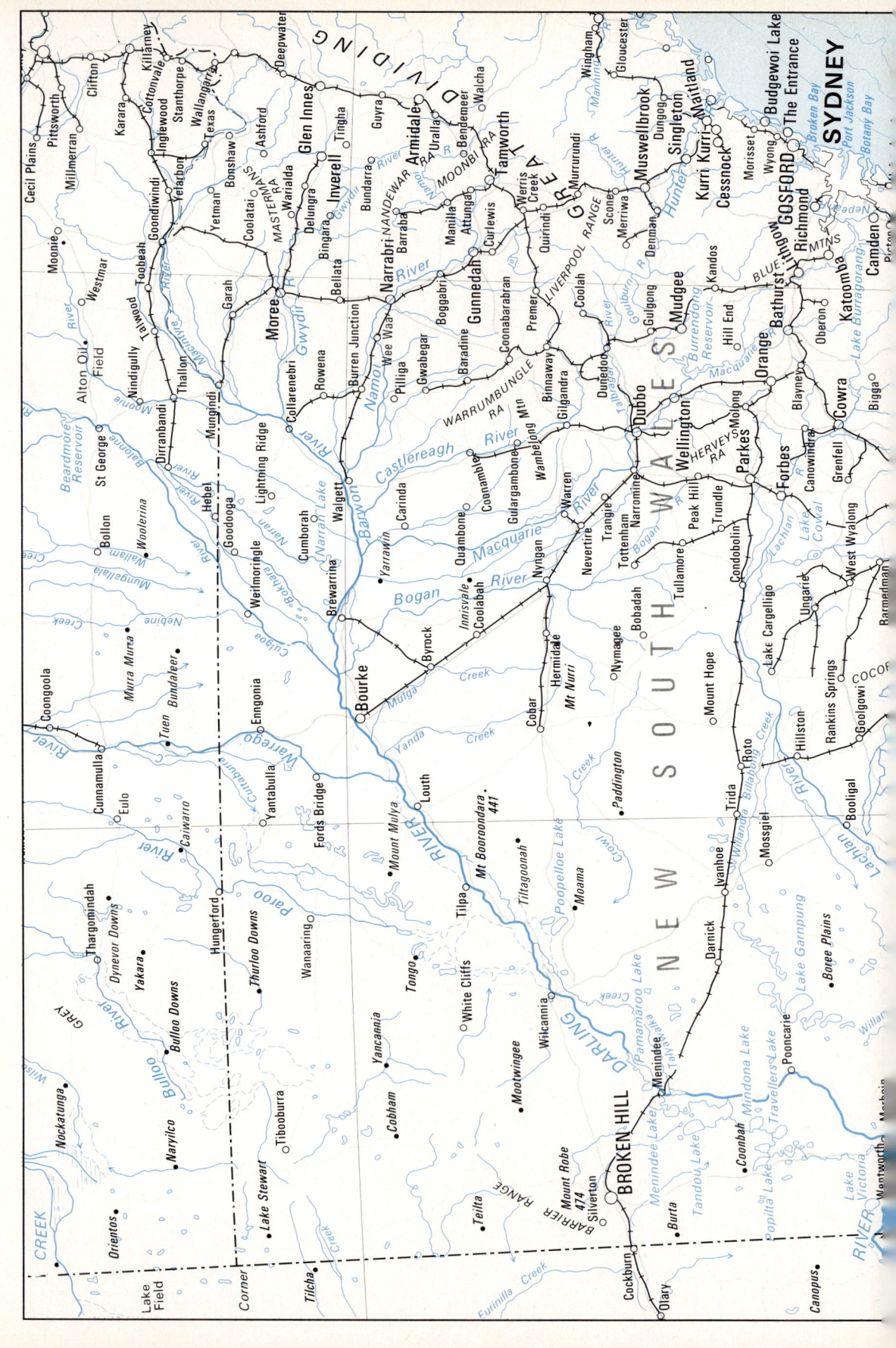

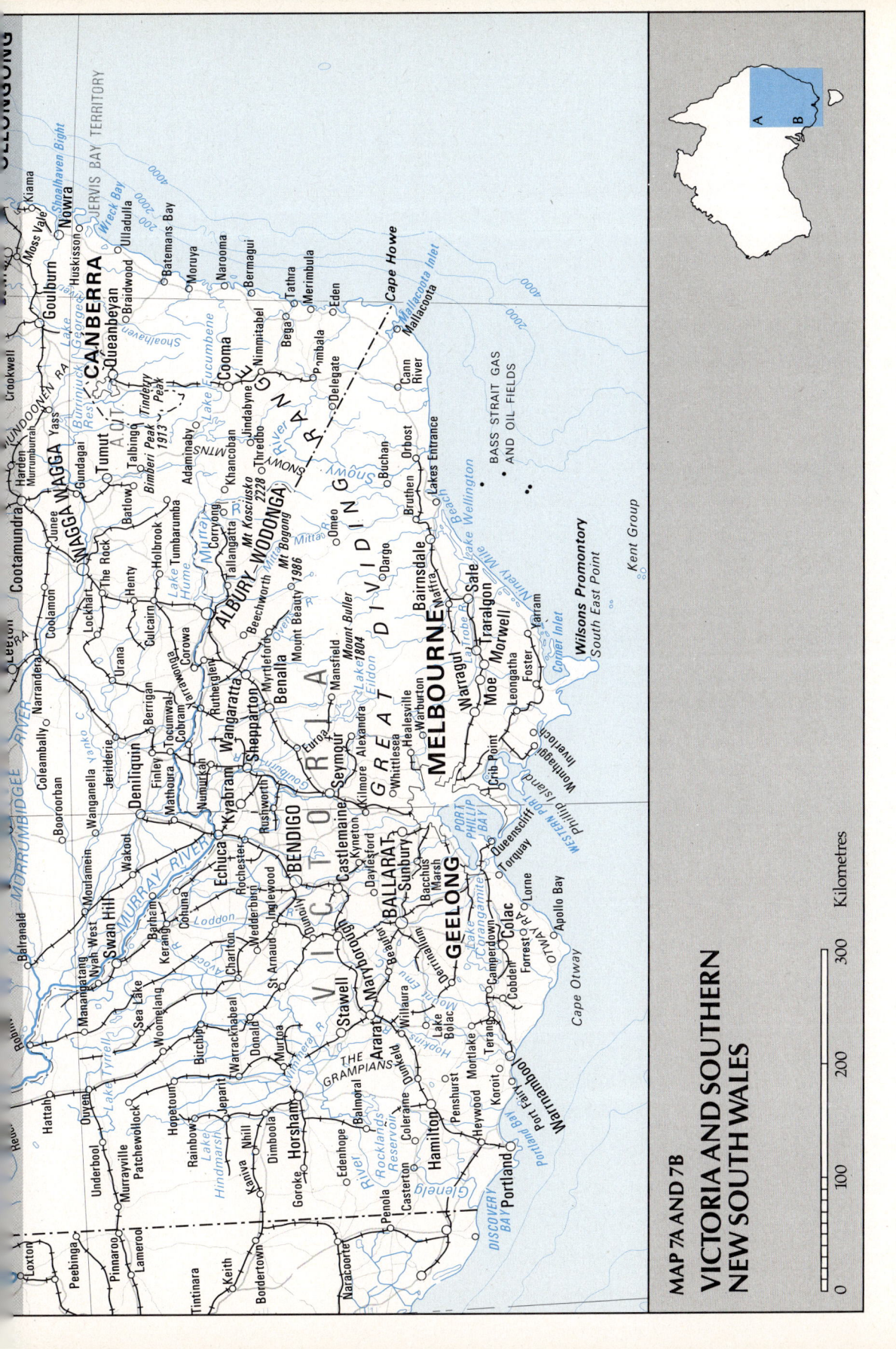

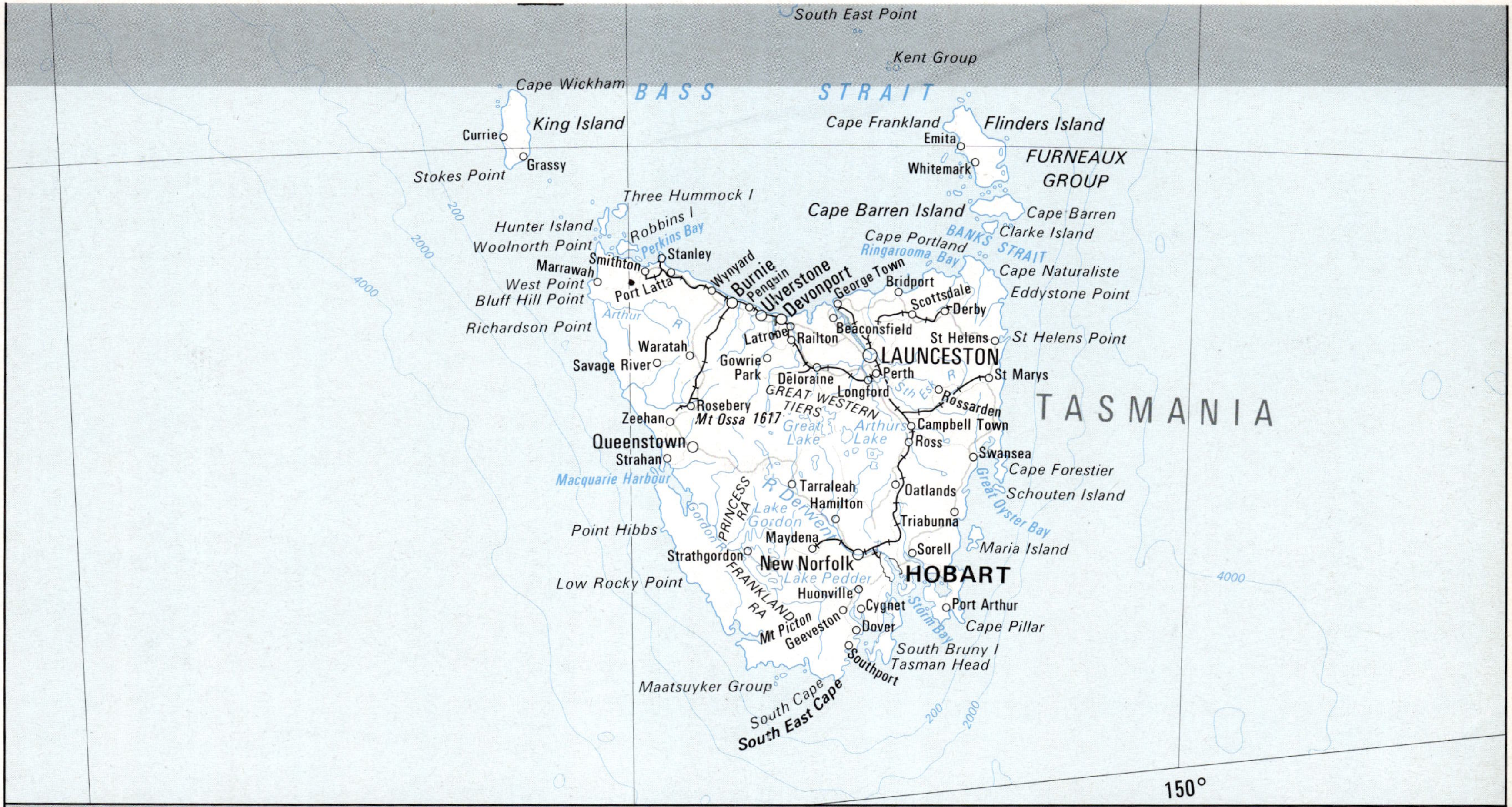

MAP 8
TASMANIA

N

NAMES of fish   Around 3000 species of fish have been identified in Australian waters, approximately 1600 in Queensland waters and on the Great Barrier Reef alone, but of these only a percentage are known by names recognized in all States. Government biologists and curators of fish at museums disagree over scientific names from one State to another and they in turn often disagree with authorities in New Zealand. Fishermen invariably use the colloquial name by which they recognize a fish, rather than the official name.

There may be some logic in the use of a colloquial name when it is applied to one particular species only, but in the past titles such as 'skipjack', 'horse mackerel' and 'swallowtail' were applied without discrimination to a number. We list various salmon, though none (even down to the little beaked salmon) is a true member of the *Salmo* genus. Our cod are almost legion, but the pitifully few members of the Gadidae, or true cod, found in our waters are of little significance, either to anglers or commercial fishermen.

Fish marketing authorities, with the tacit consent of their State Fisheries Departments, have renamed some species for sales purposes. For instance: in New South Wales the nannygai is sold as 'redfish' and the jackass morwong or tarakihi is marketed as 'sea bream' fillets. Anglers take no cognizance of commercial names and tend to stick to those which come down to them from their fathers. Traditional names, such as yellowbelly and blackfish, will die very hard, if ever, and probably should not be altered if they cause no confusion between species.

The biggest breakthrough in achieving uniform fish names came in September 1963, when a Commonwealth-State Fisheries Conference in Sydney issued uniform common names for 158 Australian commercial fish, crustaceans and molluscs. This represented the culmination of discussions which had continued intermittently since 1947. The conference concerned itself only with the main commercial fish leaving a vast number of sportfish and other species to the whims of the ichthyologists, museum curators, biologists, angling journalists, anglers, the fish markets and commercial fishermen.

Name changes of main interest to anglers were:
Blue mackerel replaced slimy mackerel or common mackerel.
Giant threadfin replaced Cooktown salmon or kingfish (Rockhampton).
Red-finned emperor replaced red throated sweetlip.
Red emperor replaced emperor.
Saucer scallop replaced Queensland scallop.

Since the 1963 Commonwealth-State Fisheries announcement, research has separated the trout cod from the Murray cod and it has been proved that two fish previously known as bass are separate species. These are now known as Australian bass *Macquaria novemaculeata*, and estuarine perch *Macquaria colonorum*. Considerable work has also been done on our large family of galaxiids, with about 20 species identified. Atlantic salmon *Salmo salar* were introduced into the Goodradigbee River, New South Wales, in 1963–64. The late John

An A.C.T. Conservation Service ranger weighs a European carp. The various fish marketing authorities, State Fisheries Departments and Fisheries Conservation groups are attempting to bring a greater uniformity to the common names given to different species of fish.

N ■ NAMES of fish

Uniform Names of Australian Fish

COMMON NAME	QUEENSLAND	N.S.W.	VICTORIA	TASMANIA	SOUTH AUSTRALIA	WESTERN AUSTRALIA
AUSTRALIAN SALMON *Arripis trutta*	Salmon	Salmon or Kahawai	Salmon	Native Salmon	Colonial Salmon	Salmon
BASS *Macquaria novemaculeata*	Freshwater Perch or Bass	Estuary Perch or Australian Bass or Perch	Gippsland Perch	Brackish Water Perch	Australian Perch or Taralgi	—
BLACK ROCK COD *Epinephelus damelii*	Saddletail Cod	Black Rock Cod	—	—	—	—
BREAM *Acanthopagrus australis*	Bream	Black or Silver Bream Surf Bream	Bream or Yellowfin Bream	Silver Bream	—	—
BREAM *Acanthopagrus butcheri*	—	Black bream	Greyfin Bream	Silver Bream	Black Bream	Black or Blue Nose Bream
CALLOP *Macquaria ambigua*	Murray or Golden Perch	Golden Perch or Yellowbelly	Golden Perch or Yellowbelly Freshwater Bream	—	Callop or Murray Perch, Tarki	Murray Perch
ESTUARINE PERCH *Macquaria colonorum*	—	Bass	Bass	—	Bass	—
GARFISH, RIVER *Hemirhamphus ardelio*	River Garfish	River Garfish	Garfish	—	Garfish	River Garfish
GARFISH, SEA *Hemirhamphus australis*	Sea Garfish	Sea Garfish or Beakie	Garfish	Sea Garfish	Garfish	Sea Garfish
GARFISH, SNUB-NOSED *Arrhamphus sclerolepis*	Snubnosed Garfish or Nobill	Snub Garfish	—	—	—	Shortbeak Garfish
LUDERICK *Girella tricuspidata*	Blackfish or Black Bream	Blackfish or Niggers	Luderick, Black or Rock Perch	Blackfish and Black Bream or Sweep	Blackfish	—
MACQUARIE PERCH *Macquaria australasica*	—	Macquarie or Mountain Perch	Macquarie Perch	—	Macquarie Perch	Murray Perch
MORWONG *Nemadactylus* spp.	—	Morwong or Sea Bream, Jackass Fish	Morwong or Teraki	Black or Silver Perch	Jackass Fish	Queenfish Queen Snapper
MULLET FLAT-TAIL *Liza dussumieri*	Tiger or Flat-tail Mullet	Flat-tail Mullet	Flat-tail Mullet	—	Jumping Mullet or Wankari	Brown-back Mullet

NAMES of fish ■ N

COMMON NAME	QUEENSLAND	N.S.W.	VICTORIA	TASMANIA	SOUTH AUSTRALIA	WESTERN AUSTRALIA
MULLET, SAND *Myxus elongatus*	Wide Bay Mullet	Sand Mullet, Tallegalane	Mullet	Sand Mullet	Sand Mullet	Sand Mullet
MULLET, SEA *Mugil cephalus*	Hardgut and Sea Mullet	Hardgut and Sea Mullet	Sand Mullet or Poddy	—	Mullet	River or Sea Mullet
MULLET, YELLOW-EYE *Aldrichetta forsteri*	—	Yelloweye Mullet	Yelloweye Mullet	Estuary or Sea Mullet	Freshwater Mullet	Yelloweye or Pilchard
MULLOWAY *Sciaena antarctica*	Jewfish or Dewfish	Jewfish or Silver Jew	Kingfish	—	Mulloway or Butterfish	River Kingfish
MURRAY COD *Maccullochella peeli*	Murray Cod	Murray Cod	Murray Cod	—	Murray Cod or Pondi	Cod
PIKE, LONGFIN *Dinolestes lewini*	—	Longfinned Pike	Longfinned Pike or Skipjack	Longfinned Pike or Jack	Snook	—
PIKE, SHORTFINNED OR STRIPED *Sphyraena obtusata*	Pike or Dingo Fish	Striped or Sea Pike	—	—	Pike	Pike or confused with Snook
RED ROCK COD *Ruboralga cardinalis*	Red Rock Cod	Red Rock Cod	—	Gurnet Perch	Red Rock Cod	Red Rock Cod
ROCK COD *Physiculus barbatus*	—	Victorian Rock Cod	Rock Cod	Rock Cod	Rock Cod	—
RUFF *Arripis georgianus*	—	—	Rough or Roughy	—	Wakaldi, Kaldi or Tommy Rough	Sea Herring or Roughy
SAMSON FISH *Seriola hippos*	Samson Fish	Samson Fish	—	—	—	Sea Kingfish
SCAD *Trachurus novaezelandiae*	Jack Mackerel	Cowanyoung	Scad	Horse Mackerel	Horse Mackerel	Jack Mackerel
SHARK, GUMMY *Mustelus antarcticus*	Gummy	Gummy	Gummy	Gummy	Sweet William or Gummy	Gummy
SHARK, SCHOOL *Galeorhinus australis*	School Shark or Tope	School Shark	Sharp Tooth Shark	Pegtooth Shark	School Shark	School Shark
SILVER PERCH *Bidyanus bidyanus*	Silver Perch	Grunter or Silver Perch	Silver Perch	—	Silver Perch	—
SNAPPER *Chrysophrys auratus*	Snapper	Snapper, Redfish	Snapper	Snapper	Snapper	Snapper
SNOOK *Sphyraena novaehollandia*	—	Sea Pike	Pike	Shortfinned Pike	Shortfinned Pike or Snook	Snook or confused with Pike

N ■ NAMES of fish

Uniform Names of Australian Fish

COMMON NAME	QUEENSLAND	N.S.W.	VICTORIA	TASMANIA	SOUTH AUSTRALIA	WESTERN AUSTRALIA
TAILOR *Pomatomus saltatrix*	Tailor or Pombah	Tailor or Tailer	Skipjack	Skipjack	Skipjack	Tailor
TARWHINE *Rhabdosargus sarba*	Tarwhine	Tarwhine	—	—	—	Silver Bream
TERAGLIN *Attractoscion aequidens*	Teraglin Jew	Teraglin or Silver Teraglin	—	—	—	—
TREVALLY, SILVER *Caranx nobilis*	White Trevally	Silver Trevally or Giant Trevally	Giant Trevally	Giant Trevally	Skipjack	Silver Fish or Trevally
TROUT COD *Maccullochella macquariensis*	—	Murray Cod, Blue Nose or Trout Cod	Trout Cod	—	Trout Cod	—
WHITING, SAND OR SILVER *Sillago ciliata* and allies	Winter Whiting	Sand Whiting	Whiting	Whiting	Whiting	Sand Whiting
WHITING, SPOTTED OR KING GEORGE *Sillaginodes punctatus*	—	Spotted Whiting	Whiting	—	Whiting	King George or Spotted Whiting
WHITING, TRUMPETER *Sillago maculata*	River or Summer Whiting	Trumpeter Whiting	Whiting	Trumpeter Whiting	—	Trumpeter Whiting
YELLOWTAIL KINGFISH *Seriola lalandi*	Kingfish	Kingfish	Yellowtail	Tasmanian Yellowtail	Yellowtail	Yellowtail Kingfish

Lake published two valuable books on freshwater fishes in 1971 and 1978. G. F. Mees showed in a paper published in 1977 that mosquito fish *Gambusia affinis* have been established in Western Australia for many years. Gerald Allen, of the Western Australian Museum, published a paper in 1980 formally identifying a group of approximately 45 rainbow fishes, of the family Melanotaeniidae. Seventeen scientists professionally active in research on Australian fishes published a book on *Freshwater Fishes Of South-Eastern Australia* under the editorship of R. M. McDowell. All of these works influenced the now accepted names of Australian fishes and the known distribution of those fishes.

NANNYGAI

Centroberyx affinis: Short, deep-bodied fish of the order Berycidae, bright red in colour with violet and silvery reflections, red fins and golden eyes tinged in red. They belong to the sawbelly or squirrel-fish family and are marketed as redfish or red snapper. Bottom-dwelling fish found in inshore waters, they are common around the southern half of Australia, from south Queensland to Tasmania and across South Australia to Western Australia.

Nannygai, according to Whitley, derived their name from the Aboriginal name "Mother Na di" or "Moora nennigai". They are an ancient form of fish similar to fossil deposits over 100 million years old. The development of spines in front of the fins is an approach to higher types, yet the nannygai and its relatives retain some primitive skeletal features. They grow to 60 cm in length but are more frequently taken around 46 cm.

Offered commercially as a substitute for flathead they were not successful in New South Wales under the name nannygai, but there was a big boost in sales when the State Fisheries Department condoned the use of the name "redfish". They are carnivorous fish that produce tasty small fillets, and are commonly trawled close to shore or hooked by sports fishermen on a variety of baits near rocky reefs. All members of the family have distinctive swallow tails. They are closely related to the king snapper of the Great Australian Bight and to the roughy.

Nannygai

NEW South Wales

This State has the greatest number of anglers and by far the largest turnover in fishing tackle. In saltwater fishing it offers a wide scope in good angling waters, both open and sheltered, inhabited by a fine range of species, though in the big metropolitan areas the potential has waned and is still deteriorating owing to over-fishing and pollution. In the freshwater division it has the widest range of trout waters and, thanks to the Snowy Mountains hydro-electric scheme, it boasts the best trout angling to be found on the mainland. In its coastal streams it provides the best range of bass waters in Australia and in the Murray-Darling-Barwon and the main tributaries it offers the best fishing to be had for native warm-water species.

Saltwater fishing from boats

From border to border, the New South Wales coast is flanked by 1450 km of good highway and the shoreline, if we include the major inlets, amounts to some thousands of kilometres. Over this length the climatic conditions vary from cool-temperate to verging on semi-tropical, with resulting changes in the more dominant species as one goes from one end to the other. With the exception of Jervis Bay, it lacks large, deep, wide-mouthed inlets and is not well endowed with offshore islands of size to provide ample contingent reefs and sheltered offshore waters. The prevalent heavy Pacific swell coupled with the prevailing strong south-west and north-east winds reduces the number of days in the year when one is able to enjoy open-sea angling in comfort, and for a lot of the time restricts the smaller powerboats to enclosed waters.

This is compensated for to some extent by the number of large estuaries, which not only provide good angling in sheltered areas but function as great breeding grounds and fish nurseries. It also is unique for the numerous tidal lakes which are well distributed throughout its entire length. These afford good angling for a number of species and are tremendous breeding grounds for fish, as well as nurseries for prawns. Some are of considerable size and many go through recurrent cycles in which their shallow entrances are sealed with sand and they become landlocked for long periods during dry times, until the occurrence of heavy rains causes an overflow which cuts the channels out afresh or brings down floods which sweep their heavy contents of young fish and rich fish food into the ocean.

The geological make-up of the coastal country contributes another important feature. From end to end, the high proportion of erosive sandstone has resulted in the formation of a great series of magnificent ocean beaches, which with their attendant species provide Australia's best surf angling. But this predominance of sand has been to some disadvantage in that an over-large proportion of the bottom to our offshore waters is in the nature of sandflats rather than the more productive reefs. The New South Wales coast sadly lacks the rugged volcanic reefs and the volcanic-ash mud bottoms of New Zealand. It is also the poorer in that lower water temperatures have precluded the formation of prolific coral reefs such as those that enrich Queensland, although a permanent warm current has fostered the growth of the Pacific's southernmost coral formations of this type around Lord Howe Island, some 480 km east of Port Macquarie on the New South Wales north coast.

Anglers and commercial fishermen alike are sadly handicapped by the lack of good harbours and safe embarkation points along the coast. It is possible to count the safe harbours on one's fingers and still have a few knuckles to spare. Four of these, Port Hacking, Botany Bay, Port Jackson and Broken Bay, are almost side by side near Sydney which favours Sydneysiders but leaves a good deal of the rest of the State exceedingly short of such resources. The few man-made harbours are mostly dangerous of approach in rough weather and risky as anchorages. Almost without exception, the rivers and big tidal lakes enter the ocean through shallow bars which are safe to negotiate only on a high tide in calm weather. This is one of the reasons why outside the Sydney metropolitan area there is little to be found in the way of charter-boat and party-boat services such as exist at most of the centres along the Queensland coast. This also is contributed to by the fact that most of the larger coastal towns such as Bega, Nowra, Taree, Kempsey, Grafton, Lismore and Murwillumbah are situated some distance inland from the sea.

This has been compensated for to a large extent by the enthusiastic way in which many boat-minded anglers have taken to trailer-boats. These range from small outboard-powered john-boats and 3.5 m open aluminium craft to big fibreglass runabouts driven by powerful dual outboard motors or a massive 110 h.p. Mercury. The smaller craft are used mainly in fishing the enclosed waters of the bays, estuaries, tidal lakes and rivers. The New South Wales coast is extremely well endowed with sheltered waters suited to fishing with this type of highly mobile craft.

The larger runabouts are largely used in fishing the offshore reefs and sandflats, sometimes even in moderately rough weather. They make some wet trips when spray is whipped in by a crosswind but they confer a big advantage in enabling the anglers to get out to the reefs quickly and to return speedily at the approach of bad weather. In calm weather many are launched directly into the sea from small coves, corners of beaches or other convenient spots, to avoid difficult bar crossings or to give more direct access to selected fishing grounds. In many of the deep-sea fishing clubs the members are almost entirely equipped with outboard craft. At most New South Wales Deep-sea Angling Championships, almost every boat entered is powered with an outboard motor.

In inshore waters boats are used in drifting for flathead, angling with weed bait for luderick, fine-lining for bream, working channels and sandflats for whiting, fishing the channels of the estuaries and rivers for mulloway and to some extent in trolling for tailor, salmon or kingfish. At the appropriate times some water-borne anglers concentrate on less-fished-for species such as garfish, mullet or hairtail. Blue-swimmer crabs get a lot of attention when they come into the estuaries and rivers. In the deeper inlets it is possible to fish reefs and holes for red bream, snapper, john dory, red rock cod and other reef fish. A pursuit which recently has gained popularity is trolling just outside the surf on the ocean rocks at early morning in moderately calm weather for pelagics, such as tailor, salmon, bonito, kingfish, striped tuna, mackerel tuna, samson fish etc.

The deep-sea boatmen fish the offshore reefs for snapper, morwong, jackass-fish, nannygai, sergeant baker, red rock cod, cowanyoung (jack mackerel), chinaman leatherjacket, kingfish etc. Big mulloway occasionally are taken on the outside reefs, but mostly at night. The teraglin also is taken mostly at night, though mainly over a gravel bottom. The shallower sandflats are fished extensively by drifting for sand flathead, flounder and sole. Common accompaniments to these are shovelnose rays, fiddler rays and gummy sharks. Big dusky flathead always are a possibility outside the surf on the beaches and along the inshore sandflats. On the deeper flats, particularly those toward the edge of the continental shelf, the sand flathead is replaced by the much sought tiger flathead. Occasionally these waters yield small catches of the somewhat scarce rose-red bullseye or the rare and mysterious tile fish.

Some power-boat equipped anglers are now getting a lot of excitement out of fishing for heavier and more lively species with light game tackle. They kellick or drift over the offshore reefs and berley to attract yellowfin tuna, bluefin tuna, or yellowtail kingfish. These are then tempted with live baits of small yellowtail, trumpeter, hardyhead, or with choice strip baits drifted in the berley. Yellowfin up to 55 kg and many kingfish ranging up to more than 13 kg recently have been taken in this manner.

Another development, at present only of commercial significance but with possible future implications for party-boat anglers, is fishing out off the edge of the continental shelf, at 700 to 1200 m, for big deep-sea species. They seem to be in good supply out there and big hapuku, two species of deep-sea bass to 65 kg and trevally to 22 kg have been taken. These are good food fish and although the flesh of the larger specimens may be coarse, it is of good flavour.

Far north coast

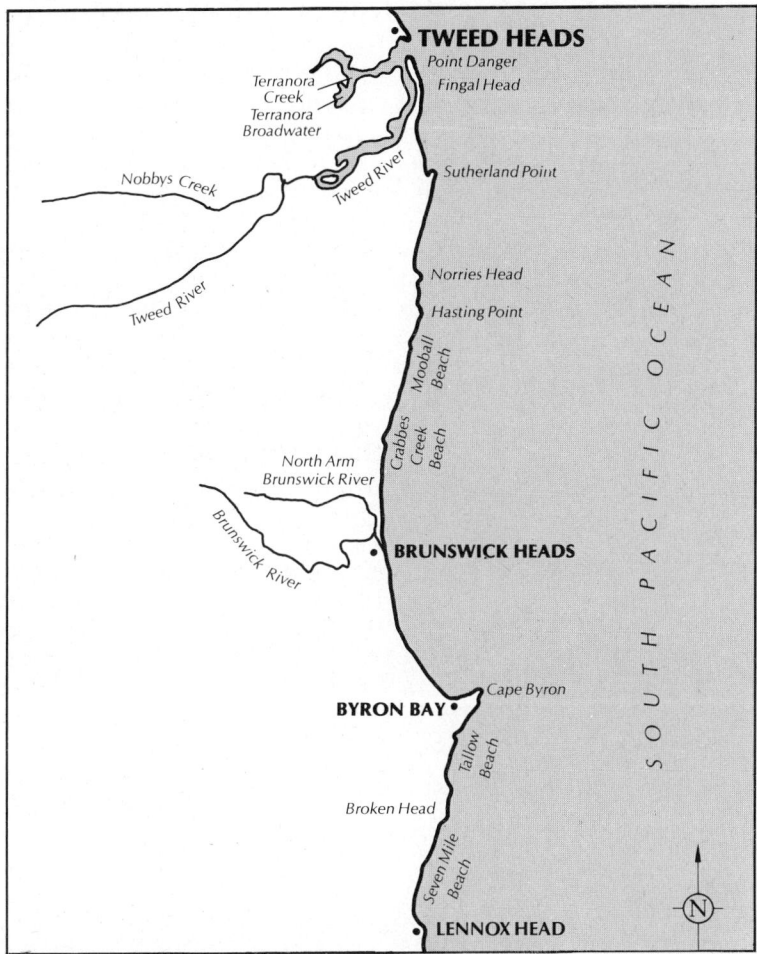

The far north coast of New South Wales offers sheltered camp sites, guest houses and motels from which a wide variety of fishing is within easy reach. There is good river fishing, ocean beach and headland angling, plus some productive off-shore reefs as far south as Lennox Head and Seven Mile Beach. Tweed Heads is a prolific fishing ground. Open beaches such as Duranbah, South Beach, Boganbar, Wommin Bay and Kingscliff offer tailor, bream, mulloway, nannygai and teraglin. Inside the Tweed, fishing from retaining walls, there are jewfish, luderick and bream. Brunswick Heads is one of the prettiest spots on the coast. Crabs and yabbies are plentiful on the river flats, there are safe inside or ocean beaches and flathead fishing from boats in the river. The northern side of the river entrance, where rocks attract jewfish, tailor, bream and a few drummer, is a favoured spot.

Forster – Tuncurry

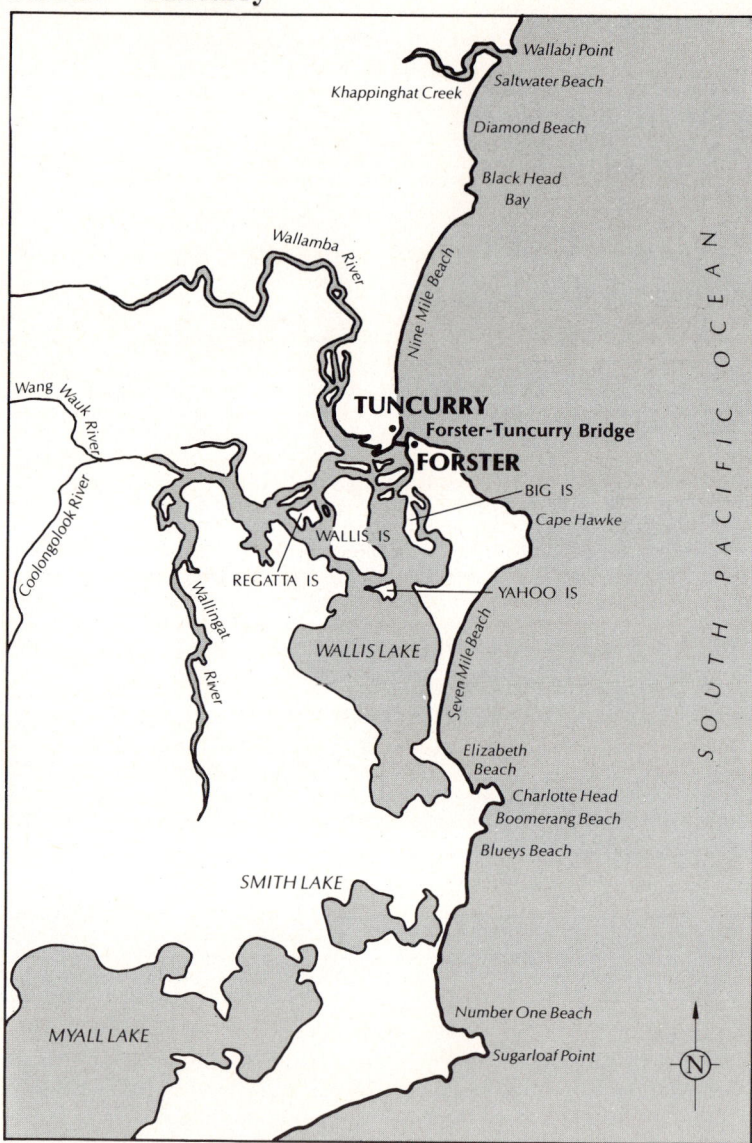

Forster is about 350 kilometres north of Sydney at the ocean entrance to Wallis Lake, which stretches south for 24 kilometres and is up to 10 kilometres wide. The lake is dotted with islands and surrounded by picturesque, wooded hills. Flathead, bream, whiting, blackfish and flounder are taken in the lake, and jewfish, snapper, whiting and tailor from neighbouring beaches and headlands south to Sugarloaf Point. Crayfish are taken from July to February, prawns from September to April. North of Tuncurry there is good fishing at Nine Mile, Black Head Bay and Wallabi Point.

Lake Macquarie – Myall Lake

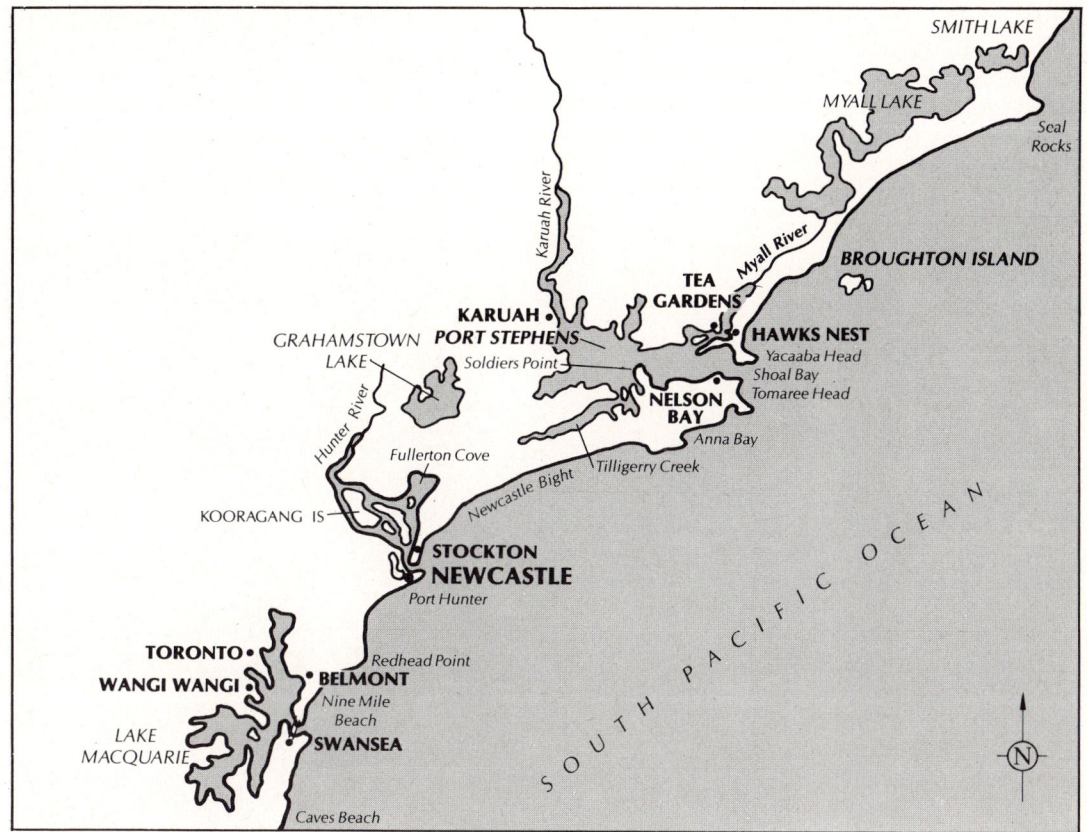

Overfishing has caused the angling quality of Lake Macquarie to deteriorate in recent years, but there is still splendid beach fishing at Nine Mile Beach and Redhead Point north of Swansea. Similarly, Shoal Bay, Nelsons Bay and the waters inside Port Stephens often disappoint, although locals treasure highly productive spots as far west as Soldiers Point and Karuah. Hawks Nest, Tea Gardens and the Myall River area remain some of the most reliable regions in the State; tailor, jewfish, kingfish, mackerel, snapper, drummer, whiting and trevally are taken most of the year. Ocean beaches south of Tomaree Head, such as Fingal Bay, Anna Bay Boat Harbour and Morna Point provide excellent catches for knowledgeable locals. To the north, the Myall Lake offers fine sand whiting in season, but the real jewel of this area is Seal Rocks, one of the finest fishing locations in Australia. No. 1 Beach, Boat Beach and the Blow Hole are outstanding flathead and bream spots, while the Isle of Capri and Cunji Island offer splendid snapper, salmon and drummer. The best spot is The Gap, where tuna, kingfish up to 27 kg, tailor and bonito move through the space between Cunji and the mainland.

Central coast

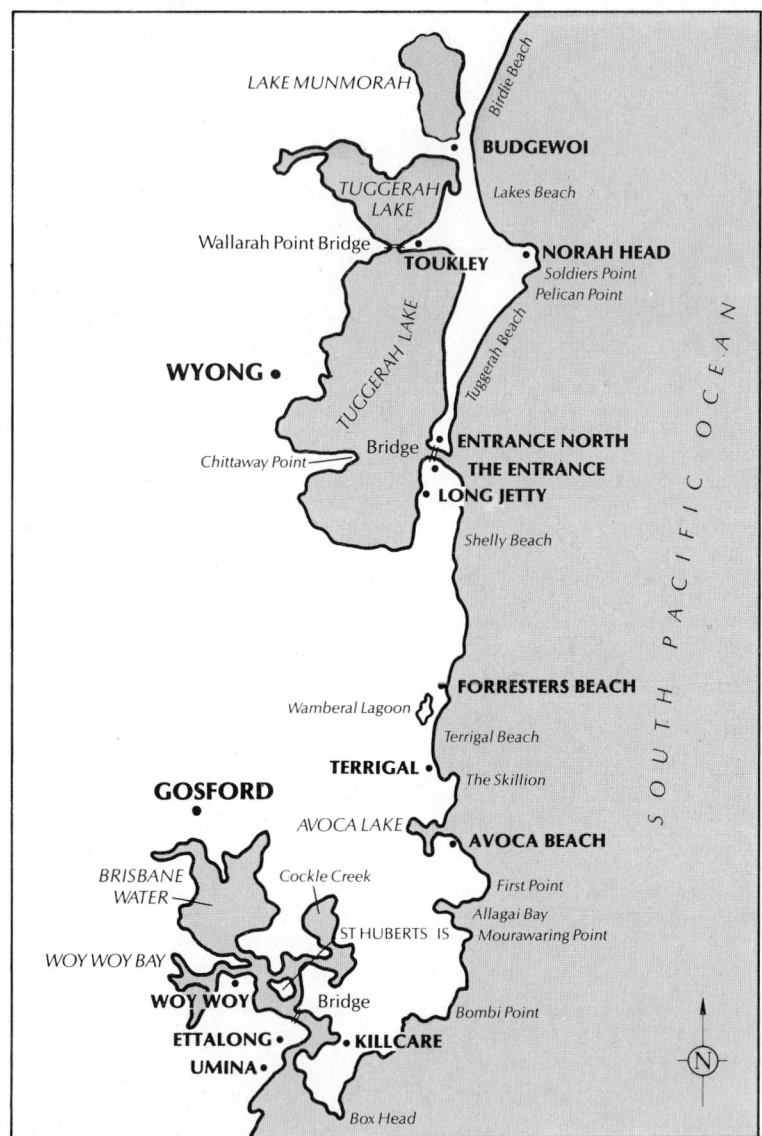

The central coast of New South Wales is one of the most heavily fished regions in Australia, but ocean beaches from Box Head to Budgewoi continue to provide good catches. Enclosed waters at Woy Woy and Brisbane Water are not what they were, but Forresters Beach (where there is a reef 200 m offshore), Shelly Beach and the coast up to Soldiers Point and Norah Head yield big snapper, jewfish, tailor and bream. Tuggerah Lakes are a maze of channels, shallows, weed and sandy and pebbly holes that keep bait shops busy virtually all year round.

Broken Bay

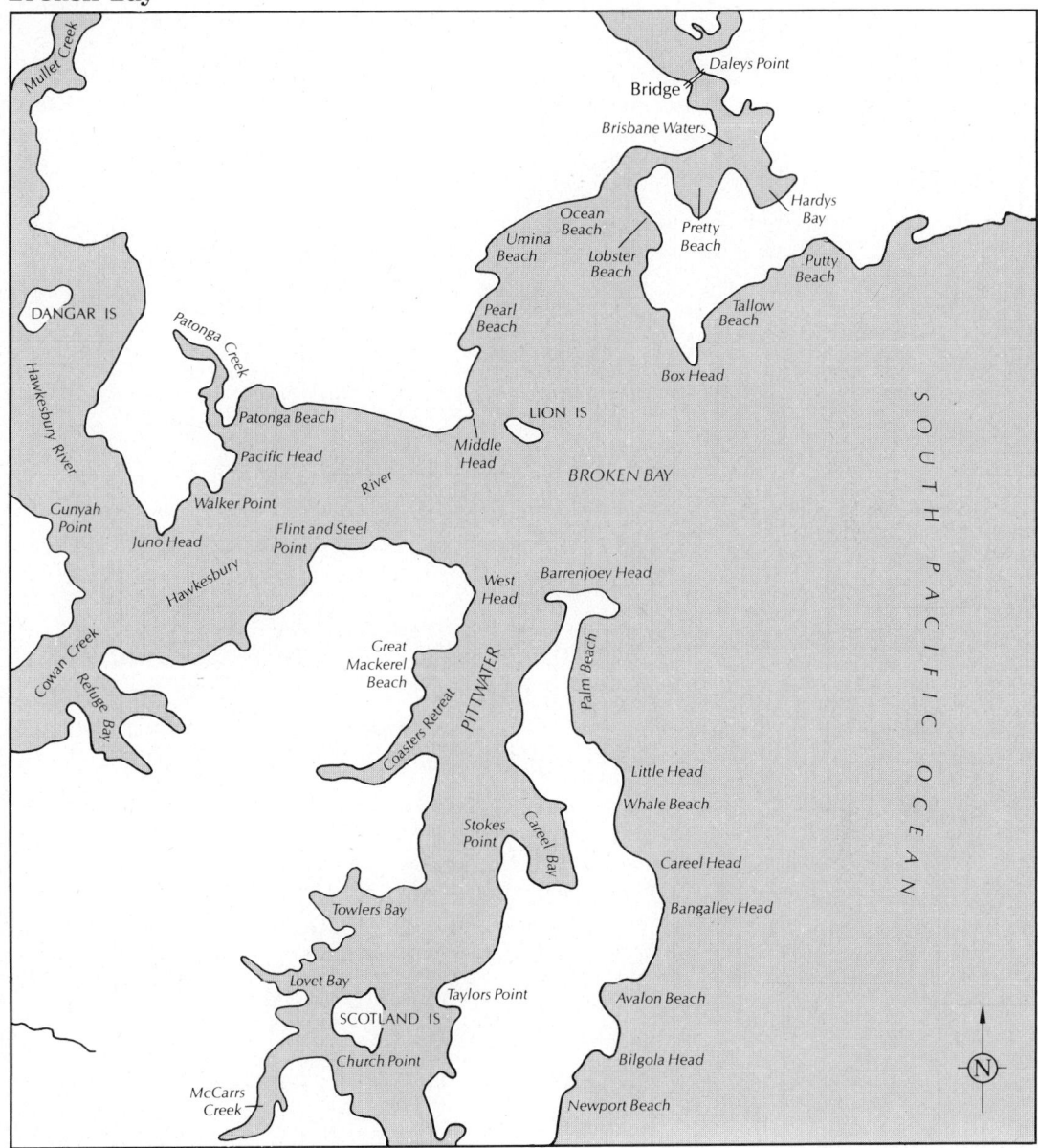

The junction of the Hawkesbury River, Pittwater and Brisbane Water make Broken Bay a prolific fishing ground where all the popular species for amateur fishermen are plentiful. Pearl Beach is renowed for its large jewfish, Pittwater for bream and snapper, while inside the Hawkesbury, Dangar Island and Coal and Candle Creek are reliable locations. Ocean beaches from Newport to Palm Beach are popular at sundown, particularly for those who can cast well out.

NEW South Wales

Sydney Harbour

Botany Bay

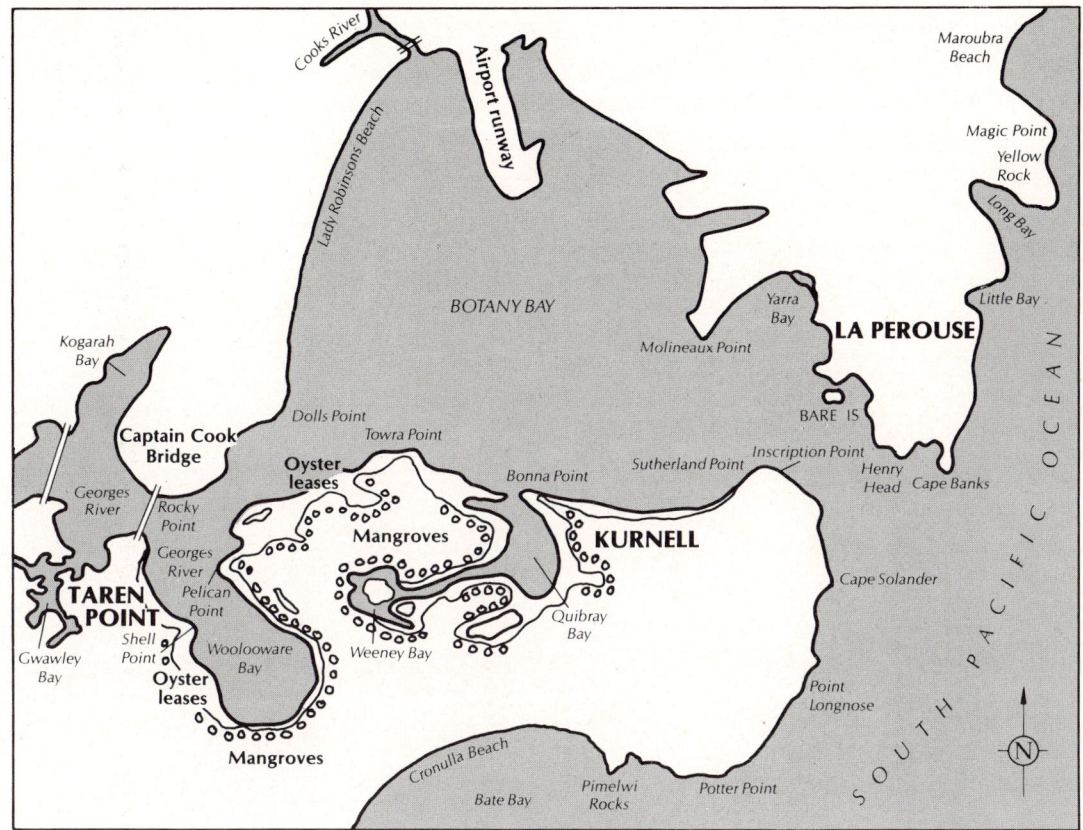

Within easy reach of the entire population of Sydney, the waters of Sydney Harbour and Botany Bay contain a wide variety of species, which attract a legion of amateur anglers. Fishing in the many arms of Sydney Harbour has improved since the 1960s, due to efforts by conservationists to halt the destruction of mangroves and swamps, and stricter controls on industrial pollution. In spite of the heavy traffic of commercial and pleasure boats, the Harbour itself provides bream, flathead, tailor, trevally, john dory, leatherjacket, luderick and others. Prime spots are the many wharves and the foreshores of points such as Balls Head, Blues Point and Bradleys Head. For boat anglers, there are good holes around Cockatoo and Goat Islands, Fort Denison and well up the Parramatta and Lane Cove Rivers and Middle Harbour.

Kurnell is still one of the best spots in Botany Bay and the airport runway extension remains popular. But oil spills continue to cause extensive damage, and there is concern over pollution levels in the Georges River and the destruction of sea grass beds and mangroves.

South coast

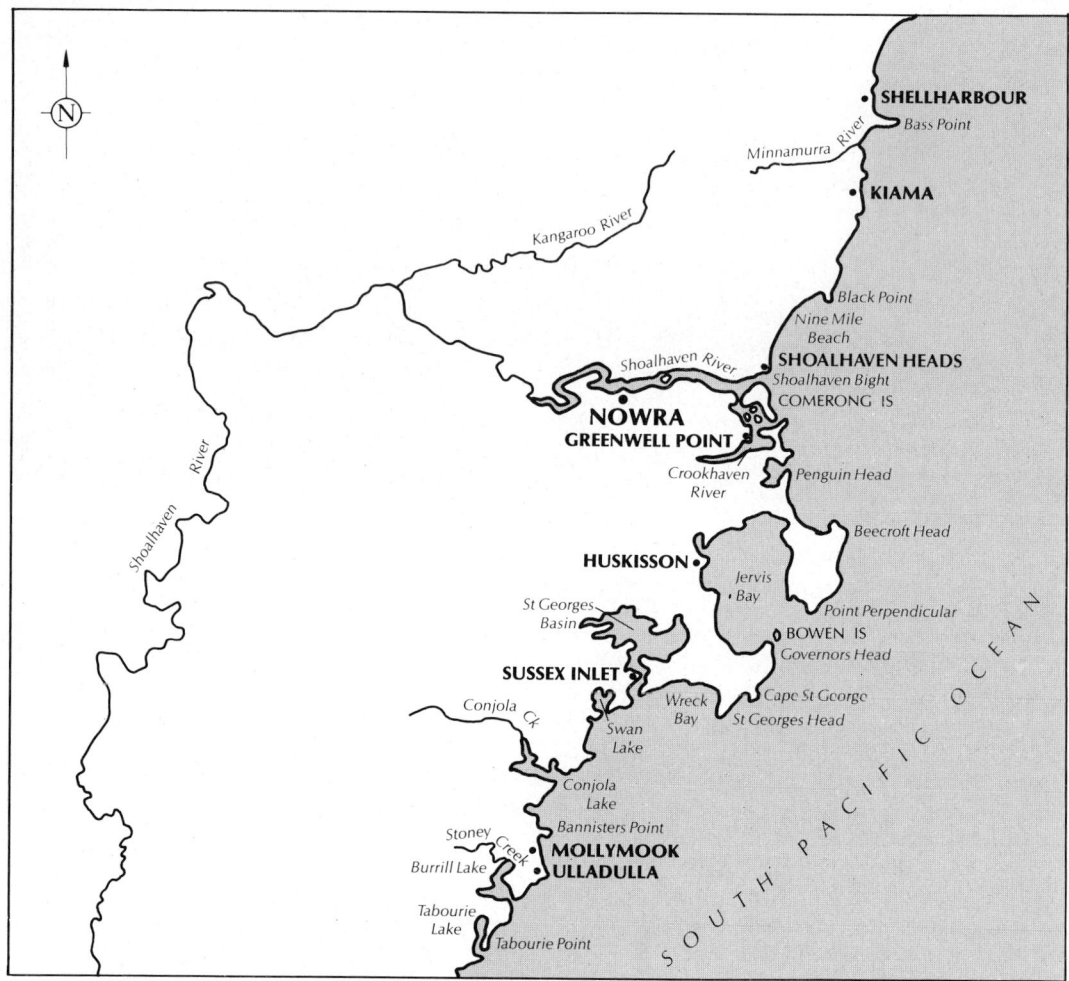

The south coast from Shellharbour to Ulladulla, within easy driving distance of Sydney, provides splendid fishing amid superb scenery. The Minnamurra River, 112 km from Sydney, is a reliable source of luderick, flathead and whiting. The stone wall on the south side of Comerong Island, at the mouth of the Shoalhaven, is another luderick hotspot. From Huskisson, a good boat enables anglers to reach even the remotest corners of Jervis Bay, a magnificent stretch of water where trolling with feathered lures has become popular. A close study of the strong tides that flow along Sussex Inlet will help provide good catches of red bream, garfish and mullet. The beach is a rod fisherman's delight, with big catches taken at dusk. Mollymook has deteriorated in recent years.

Land-based anglers are legion in New South Wales, fishing from jetties, beaches, banks and coastal rocks, such as those shown here at Jervis Bay.

Land-based anglers

In New South Wales they are legion. On fine week-ends they crowd the jetties, throng the seawalls and breakwaters, clamber over the rocks or line the beaches. Outside the metropolitan area, wherever the coast is flanked by good roads it is difficult to find a spot where a group cannot be seen fishing either from the rocks or a beach. Nobody knows how many they number, but they would be counted in terms of hundreds of thousands.

When national development interferes with feeding and breeding grounds, the pressure of commercial and amateur fishing begins to deplete fish stocks, anglers find that they need more efficient tackle, together with a thorough knowledge of species and where to find them. In the time available to them, few men could become expert in angling for all species. This probably is the main reason why saltwater anglers in New South Wales specialize more than most.

Some concentrate almost entirely on one form of angling, while others may specialize in two or three. Many consistently angle for luderick in the estuaries and from the ocean rocks almost throughout the year, with little thought to other species. Others spend all their angling time in surf-fishing and spinning from the rocks and then lay off in the summer months when conditions are not good. Bobby-corking from the rocks, fineline breaming, baiting with whole garfish on side-cast gear, berleying for drummer and even fishing the sewer outlets for trevally are other forms of angling which now are subject to specialization.

New South Wales is not as well provided with fishable seaside jetties as Victoria, most of the docking being done well up narrow harbours where pollution and heavy traffic have made the angling unattractive. Some of the best wharves went with the decline of the coastal shipping trade.

With the exception of Nobby's, at Stockton, there is little in the way of good fishable seawalls or breakwaters between Wollongong and Newcastle. Outside that area there are notable rockworks at the Shoalhaven Entrance, Forster, Harrington, North Haven, Port Macquarie, South West Rocks, Coffs Harbour, Yamba, Ballina, Brunswick Heads and Tweed Heads. Perhaps it should be mentioned that the outer end of the seawall at Harrington was miscalculated, with the result that sometimes a long length of it is buried under sand and some of it looks out onto dry sand instead of water, though the length of it along the river commands some very good fishing.

Some of the best angling from man-made structures is to be had wholly within the big estuaries. The seawalls in the Clarence, between Yamba and Iluka, are a notable example, particularly the Middle Wall which is famous for big catches of bream, luderick and mulloway. A couple of breaks in this wall where the tide flows through provide excellent tailor fishing. The seawalls in the Tweed also are heavily fished. But the fact remains that the big majority of the more experienced land-based saltwater anglers in New South Wales fish from the ocean rocks or the beaches, although a big section fishes the sandflats and channels of the tidal lakes or works from the rocks or beaches in bays, estuaries and rivers for whiting, bream, flathead, luderick, tailor or mulloway.

Distribution of species
Many of the more widely distributed species occur along the whole of the New South Wales coastline. Snapper are most sought on the offshore reefs but are still reasonably plentiful, excepting over the section between Port Kembla and Newcastle, where heavy fishing and trapping keep them decidedly scarce most of the time. Where they are plentiful, these fish begin to move inshore about August, probably in connection with spawning, and for a few weeks may be caught from the rocks or by kellicking a boat along under the cliffs. At this time big snapper may be taken around the bomboras, or from the reefs and holes in the bays. In this part of the world this species is definitely a fish of the reefs and they are found in their greatest numbers in the more reefy waters around Montague Island, Broughton Island and amongst the Solitaries north of Coffs Harbour.

Of other bottom-dwelling offshore fish that are taken in quantities, the teraglin and sergeant baker are well distributed right along the coast. Morwong and nannygai are plentiful on the southern and central sections but become scarce in the north where they mix with other more tropical species. Sand flathead and dusky flathead are distributed over the full length, but the deeper-dwelling tiger flathead becomes progressively scarce north of Port Macquarie and peters out south of the Queensland border.

Big mulloway roam the whole of the coast but are in their greatest numbers in and along the large northern estuaries, including the Clarence, Richmond and Tweed. Blue and brown groper, of the inshore reefs and kelp beds, occur throughout the range, but owing to depletion of stocks caused by spearfishing this species now is scarce, so its capture was prohibited for a period of five years, ending early 1974. In 1986 amateur fishermen were limited to two blue or brown groper per day and could take them only on a rod and line or on a handline.

A wide range of pelagics runs the coast each year. The seamullet, bream and luderick begin to come out of the estuaries about February and begin to gather for their spawning migration to the north. Huge quantities are taken in seine nets on the ocean beaches and in the mouths of the estuaries. The bream and the luderick present good angling until the migrations peter out about July. The tailor are moving for more than half the year.

Schools of small 'choppers' may be met on occasions early in January but the larger fish do not appear in numbers until later. They gather on the South Coast in February-March and then the process seems to slowly move north. They usually are at their best around Sydney from March to May, at Forster-Port Macquarie from April to June, South West Rocks-Coffs Harbour from May to July and Yamba-Tweed Heads from June to August. They mostly are scarce after August but often moderately big schools of large tailor appear briefly again about mid-October, particularly along the big estuaries on the north coast.

Luderick are one of the pelagic species that may be found along the entire New South Wales coastline.

The salmon begin to move out from Bass Strait and Victorian waters to appear on the far South Coast late in January. During February and March fishing for them can be most rewarding at Disaster Bay, but commercial fishing for the cannery breaks up the shoals before they proceed far past there. Spotter planes and highly mobile boats harry them all the way. They used to travel at least two-thirds of the New South Wales coast but for 15 years or more, so few ever got as far north as Sydney that anglers used to tell each other when they caught one. In pre-cannery days they used to appear off Sydney late in February in big shoals attended by a plague of sharks. For years the sharks continued to come without the salmon and then they, too, began to drop away.

Apparently the cannery fishermen now are becoming more preoccupied with tuna; in the 1980s small schools of salmon once again made their way up the coast past Narooma and Sydney, much to the gratification of surf anglers.

Kingfish appear in schools in late autumn and winter. The smaller fish, ranging from about 1 to 5 kg, are mostly taken by trolling around the estuary mouths and along by the surf on the ocean rocks early in the mornings. The larger fish, averaging around 13 kg, mostly are taken out over the offshore reefs while berleying for yellowfin and bluefin tuna. The big yellowtails, getting up towards 40 kg, seem to travel singly or in twos and threes.

Bonito by trolling

Bonito appear in schools about October and in most years are gone before June, although, occasionally, they are still around in fair quantities until September. They are trolled by anglers for bait and are heavily exploited by commercial fishermen for the bait shops. The smaller blue mackerel (common or slimy mackerel) appear at about the same time as the bonito. They appear in numerous shoals and often may be seen breaking water as they travel fast while feeding. They present little in the way of sport for the angler, as they mostly are taken on bait while fishing for other species, but while fresh they are about the best bait obtainable for most of the carnivorous fish.

Striped tuna and mackerel tuna also begin to appear about October. Early in the season they usually are not easy to interest in lures but later they provide thrilling sport on light tackle. They mostly are taken by trolling along by the rocky shore or over reefs early in the morning, or by running a boat up alongside a school where they are feeding and casting lures in amongst them on light spinning gear. Yellowfin and bluefin tuna appear in the late spring, although they have been rather erratic some years. Most success with them is achieved by berleying over the reefs and fishing with live yellowtail as bait, though in recent times some big tuna have been landed by anglers fishing from the ocean rocks. Most species have left the inner coastal waters by the end of May.

Flathead provide a good deal of the good eating fish on the eastern coast. There are some about at all times but there are very definite peak periods when the various species are taken in greatest numbers. Tiger flathead are most plentiful off the central coast from the end of September until mid-December, but these are solely for the deepwater fishermen. The sand flathead move in about February and usually are in good supply until May. Dusky flathead move down out of the creeks and rivers to gather at the mouths of the estuaries for spawning in December. A little later a lot of the larger fish move out to roam the surf on the beaches or to mix with the sand flathead in the shallower offshore waters.

Yellowfin tuna, such as this one caught near Bermagui, begin to appear in late spring and can be successfully caught by trolling.

NEW South Wales

Whiting for Christmas

Sand whiting are found all along the coast, though there is no doubt that the whiting fishing is much better in the far north than in the far south. They are a great boon to anglers in that they are at their best in mid-summer when other species are scarce. From Port Macquarie to the Queensland border they are at their peak around Christmas, at which time it is possible, at places like Brunswick Heads, to see long lines of holidaying anglers standing almost elbow to elbow as they fish for them. The far south has some slight compensation in that very occasionally one of the larger spotted whiting, more common to Bass Strait, is taken there.

Other species restricted to the southern section include the barracouta. At times a few stray away as far north as Port Macquarie, but they are essentially coldwater fish and only occasionally are they seen in quantities north of Bermagui. The king barracouta or barraconda once could be taken in considerable quantities between Eden and Gabo but very few are seen these days. A few Tasmanian or striped trumpeter and silver or bastard trumpeter appear from time to time and their northern limit appears to be Trumpeter Reef, off Bermagui. The edible gummy shark is much more prevalent in the south than it is in the central or northern sections.

One interesting rarity is the long, somewhat eel-like hairtail with its set of vicious-looking barbed teeth. As far as New South Wales is concerned, it is restricted to the Cowan Creek and Newport arms of Broken Bay, though on rare occasions odd ones have been taken from the open sea nearby and even as far afield as Port Hacking. Another that has become really rare is the bluefish. This carnivorous relative of the luderick once was encountered in schools on the New South Wales coast but has been missing for so long now that it could be considered extinct. It still is found around Lord Howe Island and on the coast of the North Island of New Zealand.

The most interesting area to fish is the north coast, for there one finds a great blending of the temperate-zone and subtropical species. Off South West Rocks the spotted Spanish mackerel is trolled by commercial fishermen and marketed as 'snook'.

On the offshore reefs, from Coffs Harbour to the border at Tweed Heads, it is common to see southern species such as snapper, morwong, sergeant baker, teraglin and mulloway brought up along with northern fish such as fusilier, sweetlips (red-finned emperor), Venus tusk fish, pearl perch, Maori cod, groper, greasy cod, black cod, magpie morwong and others. Amongst the more mobile pelagics, such as tailor, kingfish, bonito, samson and the lesser tunas, there is a smattering of big narrow-barred Spanish mackerel, school mackerel and turrum. The big spanner crab, with its nippers set at right angles, comes up orange-red, as if already cooked. A purplish-brown flathead, with white margins to its pectoral fins, is found with the 'sandies' and the 'duskies'.

Hairtail are generally restricted on the New South Wales coast to the Cowan Creek and Newport arms of Broken Bay.

Inshore, the sea gars and the river garfish are mixed with the short-nosed, flat-sided and snub-nosed species. Big mud crabs are more plentiful among the mangroves. Sometimes the ox-eye herring or tarpon is seen in the creeks. A few of the northern mangrove jacks (generally wrongly called red bass in the area) breed in the creeks where anglers make big catches of the southern bream and ludericks.

Crayfish hotspots

The New South Wales coast was prolific in marine crayfish before heavy fishing for the rich American market and the spearfishermen thinned them out. The big eastern crayfish *Jasus verreauxi* may be found all along the rocky and reefy sections of the coast. For commercial purposes it mainly is taken in the big lobster pots of traditional design, though where abalone has been giving out some of the divers have adapted hookah outfits to enable them to work the deeper reefs for crays. The southern crayfish *Jasus lalandei* is a smaller, reddish, coldwater species which is found, along with its larger relative, on the South Coast. It is in good demand in the markets, probably because of its smaller size and lower cost at today's inflated prices.

It is not generally known that the smaller seaside freshwater streams on the east coast often contain a big spiky-tailed freshwater crayfish. Coloured dull orange-red and blue-grey, this thorny crustacean grows to 25 cm or more. Experts coax them out from banks, logs or other cover with pieces of fish or liver on strings and scoop them out in landing nets.

The Aborigines had a neat method of capturing them. They would cut a stout green stick and split it at one end. The split was propped open with another small stick just strong enough to stand the strain. When a cray was seen, the open split was jammed down over its spiky tail. The prop stick either was broken or pushed out of place and the split closed tightly on the spikes and the creature was held until it could be lifted out of the water.

The Murray River lobster is another spiky-tailed freshwater crayfish of similar form and size, which may be identified immediately by its big white nippers. It is found chiefly in the Murray and Murrumbidgee Rivers and their tributaries. When the streams are running clear it often is possible to discern them on the rocky bottom because of their white nippers. They, too, may be coaxed up with fish or meat and taken in a landing net, though the more usual method of capturing them is by means of wire mesh cray traps. The form of trap, its dimensions and method of placement is specified in the Fisheries Department regulations. Only one trap can be used at a time.

Yabbies on a string

Yabbies (no connection with the saltwater yabby, which is a sand shrimp) are found in prolific numbers in rivers and waterholes west of the Great Dividing Range. They are found particularly in farm dams, creek waterholes, irrigation canals, artesian-bore drains, swamps and billabongs. Children capture them with meat on a piece of string for sport and eating. Anglers prize them as bait for cod and yellowbelly and usually take them with a 'yabby rake', which is a bird mesh scrape-net on a long handle. Where they are required in quantity at frequent intervals it is more usual to make up a throwing net. A 3.6 m length of prawn net is fitted with a discarded trace-chain along the bottom edge and light, long ropes are attached at the corners. Two persons each take the ropes by an end, the net is swung between them and then thrown out into the water. It is drawn in slowly, taking care to drag the chain on the bottom, so that the crayfish are gathered up and drawn out to where they may be taken from the net.

Freshwater yabbies are quite good eating, though they are somewhat sweet and should be well salted. There are about 90 species. Those in the southern inland districts are rather light in colour, varying from whitish to greenish-grey with bluish-grey nippers. In the north and north-west of the State they grow somewhat larger and are mostly coloured bright steel-blue with red nippers.

Notable prawn runs Owing to its numerous tidal lakes and estuaries the New South Wales coast is rich in prawns. With the exception of the greasy-back or greentail, they spawn in the open sea and after hatching the young make their way into the inlets to live there until about half-grown, when they begin to reach sexual maturity and feel the urge to go to sea in preparation for spawning. (For life history and species, *see Prawns*.) They move out in their greatest numbers from about mid-December to the end of February, on calm nights, in the dark of the moon, when there is a high tide a little after dark. They school up and swim down with the outgoing tide in great prawn runs.

Places like Myall Lakes, Toukley, Tuggerah Entrance, Lake Illawarra, Sussex Inlet, Durras Water, Corunna Lake and Pambula are famous for their big prawn runs. Anglers get out in boats or wade in with pressure lamps to dazzle them as they swim down, so that they may gather them in hoop nets. In other waters where there is no pronounced prawn run they are taken by dragging pole nets through the weed beds in daylight or over the shallow sandflats at night. The school prawn mostly constitutes the bulk of the catch and there usually is a good proportion of the big pinkish king prawns. Tiger prawns are not nearly as plentiful as they are in northern waters and are seen only on occasions. The greasy-back or greentail is the one species which can spawn and complete its life cycle in enclosed waters, even in tidal lakes that are closed for long periods, so it is taken more by pole-netting than in the prawn runs.

The coastal bass

The Australian bass has long been regarded as the outstanding sporting fish of New South Wales' coastal rivers, a tough, pugnacious fish that can be reared in hatcheries for supply to the public for stocking dams. They are good table fish, caught on artificial plugs and lures or by using crickets, grasshoppers, moths, green frogs, freshwater prawns and worms as bait. They are more tolerant to freshwater than estuarine perch, moving well up coastal streams.

Almost without exception, the sizable streams on the coastal watershed of New South Wales contain bass. Of course, some yield to anglers a great deal better than others. Bass fishing requires a good knowledge of the ways of the fish and some skill in the use of suitable tackle, since the fish mostly are taken on wriggling, wobbling, spluttering or popping plugs. Electric outboard motors, working from a 12 volt storage battery, with their silent approach to the fish's hiding places, have given a big fillip to bass angling for those enthusiasts who consider that the improvement in the sport compensates for the cost.

Any good coastal stream is worth trying for bass, anywhere from its estuary to the higher tributaries. Waters that have proved productive over the years include the middle stretches and upper sections of the Richmond and Clarence Rivers and the Macleay River up along by Bellbrook. The Hastings and the Manning usually have provided sport for those who know where and how to fish them. The Myall and Karuah are smaller streams but have yielded some good fish. The Hawkesbury or Nepean above Wiseman's Ferry and its tributaries, the Colo, MacDonald and Grose, are all good, though they are heavily fished and boat traffic is heavy in places.

South of Sydney, the middle reaches of the Shoalhaven and its tributaries, of which the best is the Kangaroo River, contain some nice bass. The Clyde River, in the region of and below Shallow Crossing, is another hot spot. The Moruya River is capable of providing good sport along most of its length where it is paralleled by the Braidwood road. The Tuross, up in the region of Eurobodalla and the Wagonga above Narooma are well worth fishing. The Bega and the smaller Pambula River also provide bass for those who know where to fish them, while the Towamba, south of Twofold Bay and the little Womboyn River down near the Victorian border on occasions have given bass fishermen some excellent sport. But bass experts emphasize that often more and better fish may be obtained from the small streams than from the large ones.

Lake Eucumbene

Australia's major mainland trout fishery was created by damming the Eucumbene River in 1957 and constitutes the largest impoundment in the Snowy Mountains, having a total surface area of 14,564 hectares and a volume, at full supply level, seven times that of Sydney Harbour. The initial inundation of the reservoir basin was accompanied by a great increase in trout production and spectacular catches caused anglers to flock to the lake.

Eucumbene's popularity with anglers remains undiminished, although the trout are not as large as in earlier years and little has been effected in the way of management. Nevertheless, every year a few brown trout exceeding 5 kg in weight are caught and the average length of this species in the angling catch appears to have stabilized at around 40 cm. Rainbow trout catches and average size fluctuate markedly from year to year as a result of irregular juvenile recruitment, but are usually somewhat smaller than those for browns.

Some idea of Eucumbene's popularity can be gleaned from a survey conducted in the 1970–71 season which found that anglers spent 578,781 man-hours fishing. The total catch included 100,000 brown trout and 114,000 rainbow trout with mean weights of 1.028 and 0.763 kg respectively, a total weight of 190 tonnes.

Open to fishing the whole year round, the lake is within easy reach of both New South Wales and Victoria. In the past decade or so there have been many improvements to major access roads, particularly the Snowy Mountains Highway between Tumut and Kiandra and the Hume and Federal Highways between Sydney and Canberra. Cooma airport is only a few kilometres from the southern arms of the lake. Winter anglers from Victoria can experience access difficulties during times of heavy snowfall, although these are usually of short duration.

Fishing is only one of the tourist attractions of the Snowy Mountains area and the visiting angler has a wide choice of camping sites, hotels and motels. Adaminaby, Berridale and Cooma all lie within an easy hour's drive to various parts of the lake, but serious anglers are advised to stay at one of the several accommodation complexes on the lake's foreshores. These are located at Braemar, Buckenderra, Frying-pan, Cooloowye (Old Adaminaby), Anglers Reach and Providence Portal. All have boat-hire facilities, tackle shops and other angler amenities. The proprietors of such establishments are usually a good source of up-to-the-minute fishing tips and some, such as Ron Berry of Anglers Reach and Norm Johansen of Braemar, are skilled anglers and a veritable mine of information. Tariffs and additional details can be obtained by writing direct to them or to the Snowy Mountains Tourist Association, Sharp Street, Cooma.

How to fish Lake Eucumbene
The lake is now almost thirty years old and both the trout fishery and fishing techniques have experienced many changes over this period. Gone are the days when a mass of trout was feeding around the edges of the rising waters. Eucumbene finally attained full supply level in 1974–75, submerging the last of the 'virgin' ground. The level of the lake

Lake Eucumbene, created in 1957, is the largest body of water in the Snowy Mountains region. When full it holds seven times the volume of Sydney Harbour.

is, of course, constantly fluctuating as a consequence of hydro-electricity demand and climatic factors, not the least of which being rainfall. Long-term forecasts predict full supply level being reached once in every 50 years, so it may well be many years before it is attained again. Thus there will be occasional instances when rising waters submerge ground that has had adequate time to become repopulated with earthworms, insect larvae and the like, which formed the bulk of the trout's diet during the initial inundation phase. During such periods fishing will again be excellent, but never will the trout reach the large average size resulting from the successive years of inundation during the lake's formation. Old news to Eucumbene regulars.

The normal fluctuations in the lake's level have resulted in the disappearance of topsoil from all but the most sheltered foreshore zones. As these fine particles retreat to greater depths, so do many of the nutrients and some of the accompanying aquatic fauna. The marked reduction in mudeyes (or dragonfly larvae) is probably attributable to organic substrate withdrawal and the advent of the yabby *Cherax destructor*, the juveniles of which often inhabit the crevices in submerged timber typically favoured by mudeyes, and the adults of which often prey on mudeyes. *Cherax destructor* was uncommon in Eucumbene before 1969–70 but has since become abundant and is now a major component of the brown trout diet. Decreasing numbers of mudeyes and increasingly abundant yabbies have contributed to a change in brown trout feeding behaviour. Eucumbene browns are now largely bottom feeders and are not as free 'rising' as in earlier years.

These are just a few of the changes that have occurred over the past twenty years or so. As in any ecosystem, one change invariably leads to another. Nothing is static. Long-term changes in the trout populations will be discussed later. Anglers who have regularly fished Eucumbene over many years have had to change their tactics and evolve along with the fishery. Angling success is still dependent upon where, when and how to fish.

Where to fish

At first sight Eucumbene is a little overwhelming to the visiting angler. The lake's shoreline extends for over 300 km when full and many reaches of foreshore present a uniform appearance to the uninitiated. Although the trout are evenly distributed around the lake for much of the year, certain physical features usually attract a greater concentration of fish. Irrespective of where the angler might be on the lake, it is well worth his time to seek such features out.

What are the features to look for? In general the angler should avoid flat, uniform reaches of shore, devoid of trees, rocks and gullies and search for a more irregular shoreline. Trout much prefer to frequent submerged trees, rocks and the like, a preference dictated largely by the fact that such structures harbour more food. The splits and cracks in timber and rock are usually inhabited by mudeyes and yabbies which when they venture forth to feed are often pounced upon by the waiting trout. Similarly, submerged bushes and trees provide good habitat for other invertebrate foods. Trout also prefer to lie in small gullies or crevices surrounded by an otherwise featureless bottom and probably seek cover in such locations.

The angler must learn to deduce the character of the bottom from the features exhibited by the immediate shoreline. A rocky headland will probably indicate that the rocks extend for some distance out under the water. Submerged trees reveal their presence by their uppermost branches protruding from the water. A small inlet in an otherwise level shoreline usually indicates the presence of a small channel or gully in the bottom. These and other features must be looked for.

Fly fishermen, by virtue of the fact that they usually only fish during the morning and evening 'rises', when the fish are actively cruising in search of food, can enjoy success on any region of open shore. Nevertheless, should they be seeking trout during the day or in the absence of a rise, they too must fish in areas having those features described above.

What to look for can be illustrated by a simple line diagram of an imaginary piece of shore.

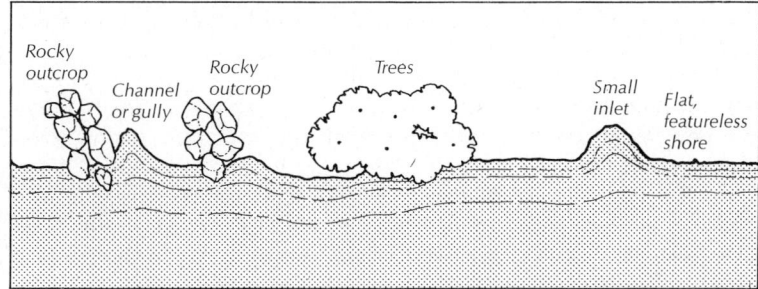

Flat, featureless shore is not very good for bait fishing, or trolling. Fly fishermen might enjoy good sport during a rise. A small inlet indicates the presence of a channel or gully and is a good place to fish. Bait fishermen should fish between half submerged trees and over the tops of totally submerged trees. Lures should be trolled as close as possible to the group. Fly fishing is generally impossible near trees. Rocky outcrops provide good fishing, and a channel or gully between outcrops is an excellent fishing spot.

The majority of bays in Lake Eucumbene possess the above features to some extent. However some bays are more featureless than others. A brief resume of the principal features of each area is listed here, starting at the dam wall and proceeding in a clockwise direction around the lake:

Addicumbene Reach: This area includes Wandella Inlet, Sanctuary Inlet, Hallstrom Island, Tolbar Inlet (Eucumbene Portal) and Benefield Inlet. The shoreline is heavily forested throughout. Good trolling can be had at certain times of the year but snags are plentiful and one must expect to lose lures. Good bait fishing exists in the many inlets. A boat is essential. Fly fishing impossible except for a small area at the Eucumbene Portal.

Seymour Bay: (North from Teal Island and west from Grace Lea Island). Well sheltered from wind. Relatively featureless but good gullies exist in numerous places. All types of fishing good.

Providence Reach: This area includes the Providence Portal, the Narrows, Illawong, Wangrabelle Bay and numerous inlets. Large stretches of shoreline are heavily forested and impossible to fish from the bank. Many rocky outcrops exist. During spring and autumn the trolling here is the best to be had on the lake. Snags are plentiful and one must expect to lose a few lures. The many inlets and irregularities afford excellent bait fishing although anglers wishing to bottom-fish have a limited choice of sites. Fly fishing is largely confined to the Providence Portal area. The junction of the Eucumbene River and the backed-up waters of the lake provide excellent fly fishing, especially in the autumn.

Grace Lea Island: Mostly timbered. Good trolling and bait fishing around its shores. Fly fishing is possible around the eastern shore but it is exposed to the wind.

Cooloowye and Adaminaby Bay: Numerous trees. Some rocky outcrops and gullies. Very exposed to the wind. Trolling good. Bait fishing average. Fly fishing poor except to the east of Merino Island.

Springwood Bay: Featureless. Trolling and bait fishing below average. Occasional good rises can provide excellent fly fishing.

White Rocks Bay: Once again featureless. No trees but a few rocky outcrops. Trolling slightly better than in Springwood but otherwise much the same.

Frying-pan Arm: Numerous rocky outcrops exist around its shores. Few trees on the northern shores but far more on the southern side. Very popular spot with fishermen owing to the numerous access points. Trolling and bait fishing good. Fly fishing good especially in O'Neill's Bay and the upper reaches of the arm.

Buckenderra Arm: This area includes Brookwood Bay, Rushy Plains Bay, Middlingbank, Wainui Bay and numerous inlets. Once again a very popular spot with anglers owing to easy access. Shoreline possesses all those features necessary for successful fishing. Brookwood Bay and Rushy Plains Bay give excellent trolling, bait fishing and fly fishing. Middlingbank and Wainui Bay give good trolling, average bait fishing and, at times excellent fly fishing, although Wainui is a little exposed to the wind.

Cobrabald Bay: Possesses many rocky outcrops, gullies and trees. All types of fishing good, sometimes excellent.

Middlingbank Broads: Shores largely featureless. Very exposed to the wind. Fishing generally poor although good bait fishing can sometimes be had near to the site of 'Eucumbene' homestead and in Maurellan Inlet.

Collingwood Bay: A few rocky outcrops but no trees. Trolling and bait fishing average. Fly fishing good when conditions are suitable.

Coppermine Bay: Numerous rocky outcrops and several large patches of trees. Trolling and bait fishing good, becoming excellent at times. Fly fishing very good except for the fact that the bay is somewhat exposed to the wind.

Braemar Bay: Shores mostly wooded. Good trolling is to be had but numerous snags exist. Bait fishing good but bottom-fishers will find their choice of venue limited. Good fly fishing, but in the south-west corner of the bay only.

The above summary should give the visiting angler some indication of the type of shoreline he can expect in various localities. Having chosen a bay in which to fish, the angler should then attempt to familiarize himself with its topography. A note-book comes in very handy. Local knowledge should be sought. The more intimate the knowledge that an angler has about his chosen fishing area the better his chances of success.

A concise knowledge of the physical features of the lake's bottom and shores is by no means the only factor influencing angling success. Climatic conditions, the time of year and several other factors greatly influence the way in which fish feed. It is no good for the angler to fish an area with which he is perfectly familiar if the fish therein are not feeding. His choice of venue should, therefore, also be influenced by the following factors—

Study the wind
The high altitude of Lake Eucumbene, together with its position among many surrounding hills and valleys, results in it being subjected to almost continual winds. The direction and force of the wind must be noted before choosing a fishing spot. In fact, the wind is the most critical climatic factor influencing the choice of a fishing spot. Most types of fishing have to be carried out on the lee side of the lake, especially if the wind is high.

Trolling or bait fishing from a boat cannot be carried out successfully in excessively choppy water. At the slow speeds needed for efficient trolling, a boat becomes difficult to control and strong gusts will cause it to slip sideways or even backwards. This inevitably results in snagged and lost lures. Bait fishing is extremely uncomfortable when carried out from a rolling boat, although the movement imparted to the bait often proves attractive to the trout.

The fly fisherman and mudeye fisherman should both have the wind at their backs and the choice of a bay on the lee side of the lake is a must. Both types of fishing are dependent upon having a relatively straight line between rod and bait and cross winds must be avoided. Casting is also much easier.

Trout feeding on or near the surface tend to align themselves into the wind and feed on insects and the like carried along in the surface drift. Trout also exhibit a tendency to swim upwind towards the food source; in every case the lee shore. Should an angler be fishing the lee side of a bay and the wind suddenly switches completely about (as often happens on Eucumbene), he should immediately make for the other side of the bay even if much fishing time is lost in proceeding there. He can be assured that the majority of fish in that bay are making the same journey as himself.

Should the wind be from the north, localities such as Seymour Bay, Providence Portal, Adaminaby Bay and the Frying-pan Arm should be fished. From the east: Providence Reach, Springwood Bay, White Rocks Bay, Upper Frying-pan, Rushy Plain Bay and Middlingbank should be fished. From the south; Middlingbank, Wainui Bay, Upper Frying-pan, Collingwood Bay, Coppermine Bay and Braemar Bay should be fished. From the west: Eucumbene Dam, Wandella Inlet, Sanctuary Inlet, Tolbar Inlet, Providence Reach, Cobrabald Bay and Wainui Bay. On those rare evenings with no wind whatsoever the lake usually fishes well wherever one might be.

Anglers fishing bait on the bottom are not so limited by the wind. Indeed, a slight advantage exists in fishing the windward side of the lake as the wave action washes out food organisms from underneath stones and the soil, thus causing the trout to feed more actively. However, this advantage is somewhat outweighed by the discomfort of being exposed to the wind, especially in winter months.

Boat anglers should exercise discretion *at all times*. Strong winds will spring up with little warning, and with such a large expanse of water, waves in excess of one metre in height are not uncommon. Lives have already been lost on the lake. Should anglers be caught in an exposed position, they should beach the boat and wait for the wind to die down or change direction, rather than run the risk of being swamped.

Time of year
An examination of the trout's life-history will reveal certain seasonal behaviour patterns, a knowledge of which can be used to the angler's advantage. One such example is the annual spawning migration. Trout must spawn in running water to ensure the successful development of their eggs. In autumn and winter there is a widespread movement towards the feeder streams entering the northern side of the lake. The main stream entering the lake is the Eucumbene River, the water from which flows into the northern tip of Providence Reach. The Eucumbene River has several tributaries which provide additional spawning facilities to those in the main stream and each year sees a large number of trout using these waters for spawning purposes. Smaller creeks enter the lake via Wandella Inlet, Sanctuary Inlet and Tolbar Inlet. These bays can only be reached by boat during winter months.

The brown trout spawning 'run' commences in late May

and continues through to early August. The great majority of brown trout use the spawning facilities provided by the Eucumbene River and its tributaries and large numbers of trout collect in the Providence Reach in April and May, prior to entering running water. Excellent fishing is to be had in this area during these months and many bag-limit catches are recorded. Bait fishing and trolling are the methods more usually employed, although superb fly fishing can be had in the Providence Portal area during April. The cessation of the brown trout 'run' is accompanied by the start of the rainbow trout 'run' which then continues through until October. Thus the period April to October is a good time in which to fish the above-mentioned places, as the concentration of fish is much greater than at other times of the year.

In 1972 State Fisheries regulations concerning the closed season on running waters entering the lake were altered to allow anglers to catch spawning brown trout in May and June. Prior to 1972 the closed season extended over the period May to September, inclusive; it now extends from July to October, inclusive, the last month being added to protect late-spawning rainbow trout.

Lake Eucumbene is Australia's major mainland trout fishery, and anglers still flock there in hope of spectacular catches.

Bait fishing is not permitted in running waters within the catchment. Spinning and flyfishing are permitted in all waters except the Eucumbene River and its tributaries above the Snowy Mountains Highway road bridge below Kiandra, where fly fishing only is allowed. With both methods of fishing it is essential to sink the lure down to the bottom-hugging, spawning browns. The spawning 'run' is usually triggered by increased stream flow rates. Thus the best time to fish is when the river is in flood. Spin-fishermen must use heavy or deep-diving lures and fly-fishermen are advised to use sinking lines. Casting upstream and across and allowing the lure to swing downstream before retrieving is often a very effective method.

Spectacular catches of spawning browns were recorded in the first few years following the altered closed season. These have declined, not because of a reduction in the number of browns spawning each year, but because the browns now appear to spawn somewhat later. Mark and recapture experiments with spawning browns in Eucumbene found that as well as exhibiting the phenomenon of 'homing' to the same spawning stream each year, individual fish returned to spawn at the same time as in previous years, irrespective of fluctuations in stream flow. Thus fishing exploitation has probably removed a greater proportion of 'early' spawners than 'late' spawners, causing a shift towards late running fish. June is now a better month to fish than May.

There are still many large trout in Eucumbene and it is probable that most of these fish frequent the deeper waters, which few people find practicable to fish. It is interesting to note that a large percentage of fish weighing in excess of 4.5 kg are taken near the start and finish of the spawning season, as they enter the shallower waters of the lake prior to and after spawning.

Another example is the seasonal change in the trout's feeding behaviour with relation to the seasonal change in the density and composition of available food. It is only commonsense that surface feeding is more predominant during summer months because of the great increase in insect and crustacean life. The water temperatures become too cold for such organisms during the winter and they largely disappear. Trout then become predominantly bottom feeders. Fishermen must ensure that their baits, lures or flies are fished accordingly.

A great amount of catch data has been collected from Eucumbene and it is interesting to compare such data on a monthly basis to determine fluctuations throughout the fishing year. Data collected over a ten-year period, totalling 124,997 man-hours of fishing, are treated thus in the accompanying table. One can see that brown trout were more readily caught in winter months with the lowest catch-per-effort (C/E) occurring during February and March, the months during which surface water temperatures reach their maximum. Conversely, rainbow trout were more readily caught in summer months with the highest C/E occurring in January, February and March. Overall C/E was generally higher in summer than in winter, although fishing pressure was low in the cold winter months, with only the more dedicated and probably more skilled anglers venturing forth, a fact which possibly inflated winter C/E values. Such data also suggested fly-fishing to be the most effective fishing method with a mean C/E for both species of 0.60, as against 0.46 for bait fishing and 0.39 for trolling/spinning. This comparatively high C/E probably reflected the greater skill exhibited by fly-fishermen, many of whom adopt this technique after becoming proficient at other trout fishing methods and are therefore usually experienced anglers. Although bait fishermen had a lower overall C/E of 0.46, this category embraced a variety of fishing methods, some of which, such as 'mudeyeing', were far more successful than others. Trolling/spinning was the least effective method overall, although this category again embraced several techniques and fishermen of varying degrees of experience.

Mean monthly C/E values for seasons from 1967–68 to 1976–77

	BROWN				RAINBOW				TOTAL BOTH SPECIES
	MEAN	BAIT	TR/SP	FLY	MEAN	BAIT	TR/SP	FLY	
August	0.19	0.25	0.15	0.05*	0.13	0.12	0.13	0.25*	0.32
September	0.25	0.28	0.21	0.21*	0.12	0.13	0.09	0.47*	0.37
October	0.20	0.20	0.23	0.14*	0.16	0.17	0.13	0.22*	0.36
November	0.20	0.21	0.22	0.25*	0.17	0.18	0.08	0.15*	0.37
December	0.24	0.25	0.22	0.32	0.21	0.29	0.17	0.31	0.45
January	0.21	0.18	0.24	0.30	0.29	0.36	0.16	0.25	0.50
February	0.18	0.16	0.19	0.39	0.31	0.34	0.22	0.20	0.49
March	0.17	0.15	0.18	0.34	0.26	0.29	0.14	0.23	0.43
April	0.25	0.17	0.28	0.60*	0.19	0.26	0.12	0.33*	0.44
May	0.35	0.23	0.37	0.49*	0.13	0.21	0.11	0.15*	0.48
June	0.46	0.49*	0.45	0.02*	0.18	0.23*	0.16	0.23*	0.64
July	0.29	0.14*	0.30*	—	0.15	0.25*	0.14*	—	0.44
TOTAL/MEAN	0.23	0.20	0.25	0.35	0.21	0.26	0.14	0.25	0.44

* = Value derived from < 100 hours mean effort.
C/E = No. of fish per hour of effort.
TR/SP = Trolling/Spinning

It should be noted that tagging experiments showed rainbows to be twice as heavily exploited as browns, so the higher mean C/E (0.23) for browns than for rainbows (0.21) only reflects the comparative scarcity of rainbows in the lake. As rainbows are now even scarcer than when these data were collected, overall trolling/spinning is now probably as effective as that for baitfishing as it is more effective (0.25) than bait fishing (0.20) for catching browns.

Water temperature: The vertical distribution of trout is often influenced by the high water temperatures that occur during the summer. Winter anglers can disregard water temperature as a limiting factor as such temperatures are relatively constant throughout the lake. However, during summer months there is a marked difference between temperatures at various depths and the vertical distribution of trout varies accordingly.

Both brown and rainbow trout prefer water temperatures between 11 degrees and 20 degrees C. Trout are cold-blooded animals and do not feel 'warm' or 'cold' in the human sense of the words. Their temperature preference is prompted more by the point of view of oxygen availability than from the actual water temperature. The amount of oxygen that can be dissolved in a given quantity of water is inversely proportional to the temperature of that water. The colder the water, the more oxygen it can dissolve and vice versa. Warm water in excess of 22 degrees C is not preferred by trout as it does not contain the desirable amount of dissolved oxygen and renders respiration difficult. As the water temperature increases so does the trout's body temperature. This causes an acceleration in the physiological reactions accompanying respiratory activity and creates the need for increased oxygen intake. Thus, the higher the water temperature the less the amount of dissolved oxygen available and the greater the amount of such oxygen needed. Rising water temperatures will therefore place an increasing strain on the trout's respiratory abilities and cause it great discomfort.

In Lake Eucumbene the water temperatures do not rise above 16 degrees C in the eight months from April to November. However, during the period December to March, the surface waters become warmer and the phenomenon known as thermal stratification takes place. This state of affairs is characterized by the formation of a thermocline (*which see*).

Boat anglers fishing a moving lure must ensure that their lures are fishing at the right depth and the most suitable place to fish is where the thermocline meets the bottom. Shore-based anglers must therefore pick a steeply sloping bank to ensure that the required depth is not beyond their casting range. It should be stressed that the above only applies to fishing between 8 a.m. and 5 p.m. during the months December to March. In the evening the fish will move into shallower water and feed actively to just after dawn. This is obviously a more suitable time in which to fish.

During April and May the surface waters cool, become denser and sink to become mixed with the deeper waters. The thermocline ceases to exist and the trout's vertical distribution becomes more even.

Wind will also have an effect on the position of the thermocline. Several days of strong winds prevailing from the same direction will cause the thermocline to tilt as the warmer surface water is driven over to one side of the lake. Thus the thermocline will be at a lesser depth on the lee side of the lake. Wave action will also oxygenate the surface waters and after several days of strong winds trout will often begin to feed at the surface during the day.

Sunlight: Trout dislike being exposed to bright light and anglers fishing the lake on a sunny day must ensure that their baits are fished down and away from such strong light. This rule is especially applicable when the water is clear and when there is no ripple. A pronounced ripple will break up the light rays and prevent them from penetrating as deeply as would be the case in still water. This rule should be observed throughout the year. A cloudy, overcast day inevitably results in better catches being made.

Winter (June–September): Baits, lures and flies best fished close to bottom. Mid-water fishing will often prove successful in those areas frequented by spawning fish.

Spring (October–November) and autumn (late March–May): Fish distributed evenly throughout depths. If the spring follows a severe winter many brown trout will remain close to the bottom. Good fishing at all levels (very few people fish at depths greater than 20 m, and thus the fishing at these depths has a predominantly unknown quality).

Summer (December–mid March): Fish just above the thermocline between 8 a.m. and 5 p.m. and a little deeper if the sun is bright and the water is clear. Shaded spots can be fished near the surface during late afternoon. Fish close to and on the surface during the evening, night and before sunrise.

These facts are by no means infallible. The feeding behaviour of trout is a complex matter and is not yet fully understood by fisheries scientists, let alone the angler. There is no set pattern of behaviour and a corresponding absence of definite, concise rules on where and when to fish. Often fishing conditions will appear to be perfect. A still summer's evening with no moon, yet not a sign of a rising fish. Why? Nobody is yet in a position to say. The angler must search for feeding fish. If the trout are not feeding in one bay they may be feeding in another, even though both bays are subjected to the same prevailing conditions.

Here again, an intimate knowledge of one particular area is a great advantage. Should an angler fish a chosen locality throughout the year he will become familiar with the habits and contrariness of the fish within that area. If the fish are not feeding in 'number one spot' he will immediately head for 'number two spot' and failing that move on again, until the fish have been located. Visiting anglers should seek local advice when it is available.

Access

The boat angler is not concerned with this problem as he is free to travel to any part of the lake. However it is obviously no good for the bank angler to decide to fish a certain bay if he cannot reach there. Eucumbene is fortunate in having numerous sealed and unsealed roads leading to most of its bays. The only sites that cannot be reached by car are Wandella Inlet, Sanctuary Inlet, the western side of Providence Reach, Coppermine Bay, Collingwood Bay and Rushy Plain Bay. Even then the angler can often travel to within a reasonable walking distance of these places.

Should the angler wish to cross private property he must seek permission to do so from the owner concerned. The irresponsible actions of a few anglers have in the past led to much ill feeling amongst local land owners. Nevertheless, anglers possessing the correct courtesies are usually allowed to cross such properties.

Hallstrom Island and Grace Lea Island are wildlife sanctuaries and should not be landed upon. Boat fishing around their shores is, of course, quite permissible. Anglers who also like to indulge in a spot of shooting should remember that the entire lake is a wildlife sanctuary. Duck shooting and the like is strictly forbidden.

The severe winter conditions can present problems. The Tolbar road is usually closed from June to October and is often still impassable in early November. Dirt roads and tracks can become very treacherous and a four-wheel-drive vehicle is desirable and in many places necessary.

Fishing pressure
At first glance this would not appear to be a decisive limiting factor. The lake could well withstand the onslaught of a much higher number of anglers without suffering damage to its fishery. Nevertheless, during the summer months heavy fishing pressure, whilst not appreciably reducing the number of available fish, will tend to put the fish off their feed in certain areas. The fish become increasingly wary and are not as ready to accept a bait or lure or to rise close inshore as they were in earlier months. A bay that is fishing well will often take up to a week to 'recover' from the sudden influx of anglers typically invading Eucumbene on such occasions as the Christmas holidays and the long weekend in January.

If large numbers of anglers are fishing the lake at the time, a visiting angler is well advised to seek a quiet spot. The number of fresh footprints on the bank, fire-sites, etc. should be examined in order to determine the number of anglers that have recently fished the site in question. The areas close to the boat-hire sites and main access roads are all heavily fished in summer, and an angler using these facilities will find the extra half-an-hour used in walking several kilometres away from such places time well spent.

All the above information, excepting that about access, provides a brief guide to where the trout are likely to be feeding under certain conditions. Water temperature, sunlight and seasonal food availability all have an effect in determining the depth at which trout are likely to feed and from the above a rudimentary key can be constructed showing the most suitable depths at which to fish during certain times of the year.

Fishing methods
The fishing methods employed in lake fishing differ greatly from those used by stream anglers. In many ways it is positively a disadvantage for a trout angler to have had extensive experience in stream fishing, as he will be reluctant to disregard known techniques and adopt new ones.

Three principal techniques are used on Lake Eucumbene: bait fishing, spinning or trolling and fly fishing. All three methods enjoy success and have a devoted following of anglers. The optimum conditions for one type of fishing are not necessarily those for another and the angler who is proficient in all methods is the person who will consistently catch fish the year round. For example, fly fishermen would do well to change to another technique during winter months, even though an adept fly fisher can catch fish throughout the year.

The information below provides a resume of the basic techniques needed for angling success in Lake Eucumbene:

Bait fishing in Lake Eucumbene: This is the most commonly used method of fishing the lake. Two principal baits, worms and mudeyes, are used by the majority of anglers. The traditional worm has to many people long been the symbol of a fisherman and must be employed as bait in every Australian inland water. Eucumbene is no exception and worm fishermen are many. This method meets with varying success in the lake, being influenced by the time of the year, and the type of bottom fished. The winter and spring months are undoubtedly the most suitable time for worm fishing.

Much of the terrain surrounding Eucumbene is rocky and dry for most of the year. Scrubworms and the like are never plentiful and the visiting angler is advised to bring his own supply in order to avoid hard spade work. A rod in excess of 2.5 m in length is advisable when fishing from the shore as this will facilitate effortless distance-casting with the minimum of weight. A fixed spool reel should be used for all types of bait fishing. The line need not have a breaking strain of more than 2.5 to 3 kg, provided a good light rod is used. Heavier line will inhibit the trout and also reduce one's casting distance. A smallish hook of about size 7 or 8 should be used, depending on the size of the worm. The hook should be passed through the worm at a point about one-third of the distance along its length, the worm threaded up the line and the hook passed through again at the same distance from the other end.

The majority of worm anglers fish on the bottom using a

running sinker rig. A sinker of 5–10 g in weight is sufficiently heavy to facilitate long casts. Rounded, ball or bean sinkers are preferable as they are not as inclined to snag on the bottom as are square shapes. A small split shot should be pinched onto the line about 50 cm from the hook and care taken to ensure that the line runs smoothly through the sinker, as the trout must not feel any resistance when it picks up the bait.

After the cast has been made, slack line should be taken up until the weight is felt. The angler should then pay out a metre of line and sit back to await a bite. The rod should be held at an angle almost parallel to the surface and the line should be lightly held between the finger and thumb. If the angler wishes to place the rod in a rest he is advised to stick a matchstick into the ground at an angle away from the water and tightly coil two turns of line around it. This will serve as an efficient bite indicator without causing sufficient resistance to make the trout drop the bait. The trout should be allowed to run for three or four metres before striking.

This method is employed to little effect by many anglers who simply throw their lines in anywhere, grab a can of beer or similar beverage, and lie back to await results. Such anglers usually return home fishless. Care should be taken to select a suitable site, as described above. The sinker should be retrieved for 60 to 90 cm at 10 minute intervals as the worm will otherwise burrow into the mud or under a stone, thus rendering itself invisible to the passing fish.

A bait lying on the bottom is less likely to be noticed by a fish than one just above it. Float fishing will provide better catches, as long as care is taken to ensure that the worm is at the right depth. Bubble floats are commonly used as their weight, when part filled with water, makes for easy casting. The angler must estimate the depth of the water and attempt to fish his worm within 30 to 60 cm of the bottom. A matchstick stop is tied into the line at the required depth and the line is allowed to run freely through the float. The weight of the worm is usually sufficient to ensure that it sinks to the required depth, but two to three split shot should be pinched on the line 30 cm from the hook during windy conditions as a drifting float will cause an unweighted worm to rise.

The depth of water that can be fished is limited by the length of line between float and hook that can be cast without difficulty. Deeper waters can be fished by using a small sliding float and placing the matchstick stop at the required depth *above* the float. The float should be correctly weighted so as to just show above the water. The trout will not detect such a small resistance when taking the bait. A boat angler does not need any type of float as he has only to lower the worm until feeling it strike the bottom, then reel in 30 to 60 cm of line. The addition of a small 'flasher' rig to the line when fishing in this manner will often improve catches, especially if the rod tip is continually raised and lowered.

Another excellent way of worm fishing is to cast an unweighted worm into the gaps between half and totally submerged trees and rocks. The worm is allowed to slowly sink to the bottom and remain there for a couple of minutes. The rod top is then sharply raised and lowered, taking up slack line with the reel. This process is repeated at one to two minute intervals until all the line has been recovered. The bait is then again cast out into a different gap. Added casting distance can be obtained by tying a small piece of cork on the line, using three half hitches (two will slip), about 30 cm from the hook and pinching on one or two split shot just under the cork. The combined weight of worm and split shot must be just sufficient to cause the cork to slowly sink.

Another successful fishing method employed on the lake is that using 'mudeyes' as bait. Mudeye is the name commonly used to describe the larvae of the dragonfly. Numerous species of dragonfly occur in Australia and there is a corresponding diversity in the number of types of mudeye. Two sorts of mudeye are used for bait on Lake Eucumbene, the Lake mudeye and the Coota mudeye. The Lake mudeyes, as their name suggests, occur in Eucumbene and are the larvae of dragonflies belonging to the Corduliidae family. The Coota mudeye rarely occurs in Lake Eucumbene.

All mudeyes are carnivorous and possess suitably adapted mouthparts, some of which can be extended at great speed to grasp other insects, small worms and similar invertebrates which constitute food. They are not active animals and rely more on stealth than active hunting prowess to seize their prey. There are several stages in the larval life, the final one of which clambers out of the water and completes the metamorphosis to form the adult dragonfly.

Lake mudeyes are to be found amongst submerged timber and the like, especially that covered in slime and similar detritus. Anglers can collect mudeyes by dragging out pieces of timber from the lake's shallows, and examining the surface and the cracks and crevices in the wood. A small axe is a handy tool to carry as it can be used to split open hollow logs and the like, which are much favoured by mudeyes. Collecting mudeyes is often tedious work, especially when they are in short supply. The angler who regularly fishes the lake or who is enjoying a lengthy fishing trip is advised to attach an old sack or sugar bag to a length of cord and lower it to the bottom in 3 to 4 m of water. The sack can be raised at daily intervals and a few mudeyes are usually found to be clinging to it.

Coota mudeyes occur in the small swamps and bogs found in close proximity to the lake. Should the search for mudeyes in Lake Eucumbene prove fruitless these swamps are good places to turn to. Coota mudeyes are easily distinguished from the Lake variety by their more slender, elongated shape.

Mudeyes are best kept in a tin containing damp straw and a

little water in the bottom. They will remain alive for several days, provided the temperature in the tin is not allowed to become too high.

Several techniques can be used in mudeye fishing. A small hook between sizes 5 to 3 is essential for all methods. Likewise, a light line is a must. Mr Ron Berry, one of the most knowledgeable of local mudeye fishermen, kept accurate records of his catch when using lines of differing breaking strain and found the number of fish caught to be inversely proportional to the strength of the line. Whereas a 3.5 kg breaking strain line would catch four fish, a 2.5 kg line would catch six, a 1.5 kg line eight, and so on. The use of a light, whippy rod will minimize the number of fish lost through the line being broken. Care should be taken to avoid tainting the mudeye with an unnatural scent before putting it on the hook. Heavy smokers must avoid using nicotine-tainted fingers. Anglers using hair-cream must not wipe their hands on their heads. Trout have an extremely well developed sense of smell and are suspicious of any unusual odour.

The mudeye can be fished on the bottom by using an identical running sinker rig to that described for worm fishing. Likewise, boat anglers can fish a mudeye just off the bottom by attaching a split shot to the line 30 cm above the hook, lowering the bait until the bottom is reached and then taking up 60 to 90 cm of line. However, these methods are not very productive as little movement is imparted to the mudeye. They are best used during the winter months and on bright, sunny days when the fish are lying deep.

The majority of mudeye anglers use a bubble-float rig. The bubble-float is threaded up the line and a match stick stop is tied on 45 to 90 cm away from the hook. A small split shot is attached to the line 30 cm from the hook. The mudeye is attached by pushing the hook through the thorax and bringing the point back through the abdomen. This gives the mudeye the appearance of clinging on to the end of the line. The bubble-float is three-quarters filled with water and serves the functions of acting as a casting weight and suspending the bait in midwater. It is not meant to act as a bite indicator.

The bait should be cast in between half-submerged rocks and trees and fished over the tops of such structures when they are totally submerged. A smooth cast is preferable as the mudeyes are easily jerked off the hook. Anglers should avoid using the mudeyes found crawling up rocks and trees just prior to hatching, as their exoskeletons are softening in readiness for this final act. Such mudeyes will not remain on the hook. The fish should be allowed to run with the bait for two to three metres before striking. A few loose coils of line can be drawn off the reel, placed on the water and watched carefully. In darkness the bail-arm of the reel is left in the open position and the line is lightly held between thumb and forefinger.

The summer and autumn months are the most suitable for this type of fishing. The last hour of daylight and the hour before dawn are the most successful times, although good fishing can also be had during the night and heavy, overcast days.

Mr Ron Berry has developed a technique that is a substantial improvement on the above method. A bubble-float is again an essential part of the rig but is attached by means of a snap swivel, the line being threaded through the eye of the swivel. This allows the float to revolve freely around the line and eliminates the twisting that so frequently occurs in casting. A small piece of cork acts as a stop and is tied into the line using three half-hitches. The distance between the cork-stop and hook should be as long as possible and is dependent upon the individual angler's ability to cast without jerking the mudeye off. The line between cork and hook is then greased, using mucilin or a similar compound. Avoid using a strong-smelling grease. The bubble-float is four-fifths filled with water so that it just floats.

The mudeye is attached by passing the hook through the centre of the abdomen and then bringing the point through the thorax. The mudeye is thus pointing down the line. The longer Coota mudeye should have the hook passed through the abdomen twice.

The rig is smoothly cast out making sure that the mudeye hits the surface beyond the bubble-float. The unweighted mudeye will then slowly begin to sink, drawing the greased line under the surface. The greased line, together with the way in which the bait is mounted on the hook, causes the mudeye to zig-zag downwards in an extremely natural manner. This slow motion often proves irresistible to trout. The line between the float and rod tip must be kept absolutely straight and free of resistance. A following (offshore) wind is almost an essential. Once again a few coils of line are placed on the surface and watched carefully, the trout being allowed to run with the bait before being checked. When the mudeye has completed its downward motion and is suspended under the float, the rod tip is slowly raised, bringing the float towards the angler and the mudeye to the surface, to start yet another attractive descent. Excess slack is taken up on the reel. Should a cross-wind spring up and put a bow in the line between rod and float, it can be straightened by raising the rod and flicking the line into the wind. This will also have the effect of bringing the mudeye to the surface again. A short rod, not more than 2 m in length, gives the best results using this method.

The bait should be fished around rock-covered spurs and in rocky gullies. Both boat and shore anglers can use this technique with equal success. Boat anglers are also advised to fish over the tops of submerged trees. The summer and autumn months are once again the most suitable times in which to fish, the periods from half an hour before sunset up until dark being the most successful. When fishing before sunset it is essential to cast into the sun. This method of fishing catches predominantly rainbow trout.

Mr Berry also uses the following technique with much success. The bubble-float is dispensed with and the small piece of cork is sited 45 to 60 cm from the hook. The remaining rig is the same as above.

This method is used from the shore. Stealth must be exercised when approaching the fishing spot as the absence of a bubble-float renders long casting impossible. Small gullies or gutters are the most suitable sites for such fishing. A typical stretch of shoreline contains several such spots. The chosen gutter is cautiously approached and the bait is cast out so as to land in the centre, being an equal distance from the sides of the gutter and the shore. If the gutter is 9 m wide, the bait should land in the centre 4.5 m out from the shore. The angler then stands motionless and watches the piece of cork. When a fish takes the bait the cork will disappear and the angler should wait until it is at least 30 cm under the surface before driving home the hook with a flick of his wrist. This technique catches predominantly brown trout as this species usually occupies such localities. During summer months, when this type of fishing is at its best, one gutter usually only contains one brown trout. The angler should spent no more than 15 minutes at each gutter and should move on immediately if he catches a fish. The same gutters can be fished during the following day as other fish have usually moved in to replace those caught previously.

Mudeyes can also be used with fly-fishing tackle. A special hook, with an attached clip to hold the mudeye, must be employed to enable the bait to withstand the rigours of casting. A slow-sinking line and a moderate jerky retrieve give the best results.

Although these mudeye techniques still meet with success on summer evenings, the increased emphasis on bottom feeding by brown trout and the decline in abundance of surface-feeding rainbow trout, have led many anglers to fish their mudeyes at greater depths. An excellent method of doing this is to use a bubble float with a tube through its centre, rather than the 'eyed' bubble float described earlier. Into this tube insert an equivalent length of valve rubber. The line is then threaded through the valve rubber and the hook attached, together with a medium sized split shot approximately 40–50 cm up the line. A 'stop' is then whipped onto the line above the float in such a way as to enable it to be slid up and down. A piece of monofilament nail-knotted onto the line is excellent in this regard, as it does not interfere with casting off the reel and is sufficiently tight to hold its position after adjustment. Thus the depth at which the mudeye is to be fished is selected by sliding the 'stop' up the line before casting. The 'stop' can be wound onto a fixed-spool reel without affecting the subsequent cast. After casting, line is slowly paid out until the 'stop' is checked by the valve rubber. The float is filled with sufficient water to be just buoyant and must be watched carefully, the rod-tip being sharply raised when its disappearance signals a bite.

This method is best employed from a moored boat but can be used off very steep banks. It is particularly effective amongst, and around the edges of, submerged, standing timber. When fishing at depths greater than 4 m, catches can be made throughout the day and not just during dawn and dusk.

Yabbies are now a major dietary item for Eucumbene browns, yet surprisingly few anglers use them as bait. Yabbies are easily obtainable by pulling submerged logs or branches from the water and splitting them open in exactly the same fashion as when searching for mudeyes. Only when lake level is rising rapidly are yabbies hard to find in this fashion, as they become temporarily stranded in deeper water. The yabbies found in such logs usually vary widely in size. Small yabbies, up to 3 cm in length, are best fished using techniques identical to those for mudeyes. Larger yabbies from 3 to 15 cm in length can be used in several ways similar to those used for worm fishing, but are best fished using a single hook with no weight of any kind. Hook size depends on the size of the yabby. It should be large enough to extend approximately one-third of the way along the tail section, at which point it is inserted through the ventral surface and brought out through the back, so that the yabby is facing down the line. The weight of the yabby is usually sufficient to ensure long and accurate casting.

A variety of habitats can be fished in this manner; timbered foreshores can be very productive. After casting, the yabby is allowed to sink to the bottom and then slowly retrieved using a 'sink and draw' motion. When disturbed, yabbies swim rapidly backwards and the 'sink and draw' motion approximates this behaviour. The angler should keep on the move, continually searching likely looking spots. As yabbies are largely nocturnal feeders, trout have become accustomed to hunting them during darkness and this is the best time to fish.

With all methods of bait fishing the earlier comments on line strength, made when describing mudeye fishing, should be heeded. Most anglers use line that is far too heavy. The sophisticated drag systems of today's fixed-spool reels are of such efficiency that lines of between 2 and 3 kg breaking strength are more than adequate. It is better to hook three times the number of fish than would have been the case with heavier line, even if a few are lost through line breakage. Trout have excellent eyesight and are often quick to assess poor bait presentation. Anglers should also remember that trout often venture into shallow water, particularly during darkness and in spring when lake level is rising, and should continually exercise stealth when fishing from the bank.

Fly fishing on Lake Eucumbene: The experience acquired by anglers fly fishing on rivers, creeks and other flowing waters, can prove to be a disadvantage when turning to lake fishing. The typical river fisherman approaches the lake with a comparatively small rod and the usual 20 to 25 m of double-tapered fly line. Such equipment, whilst being perfectly adequate for stream fishing, is not entirely suited to the lake. Given good conditions, any competent fly fisher will catch fish using the lightest of outfits. Nevertheless, good rises do not occur frequently in big waters and the angler must prepare himself to face the prevailing conditions.

The lake fisherman should possess a powerful fibreglass or carbon fibre rod from 2.4 to 2.8 metres in length. The usual double-tapered fly line should be discarded in favour of a forward taper or shooting head line of a weight matched to the rod. The reel should contain ample backing as the chance of hooking a large brown trout is always there, especially when fishing at night. Such equipment facilitates lengthy casting and also enables large, bushy flies to be cast with ease. Wet fly fishermen do not need to use tapered casts, although they are an aid to good casting and essential for dry fly fishing. Tippets of 2 kg breaking strain are adequate, but heavier leaders should be employed after dark.

The technique of fly casting is discussed elsewhere in this book and further reiteration is unnecessary. Nevertheless, the angler must familiarize himself with the 'double-haul' technique to fully develop the potential of the above equipment. The more traditional casting methods employed on streams and the like will certainly yield fish during the evening rise, as a 10 m cast will suffice. The fish move in towards the shore at dusk and are often to be found in less than 60 cm depth of water. However, during the daytime and on those nights when the fish are 'just out of reach', longer casting is essential.

Although Eucumbene rainbows are still predominantly surface/mid-water feeders, the browns are not as free rising as in earlier years. The decline in rainbow trout numbers has thus resulted in a decline in overall fly-fishing quality. Nevertheless, good rises still occur in Eucumbene, albeit more sporadic than before. Terrestrial and aquatic insects still comprise a significant proportion of the trout's diet during summer months.

The period November to April is the most favourable in which to fly fish Eucumbene, although experienced anglers can catch trout throughout the winter. The best sport is enjoyed during the autumn months of March and April, as the surface waters start to cool. During late December to mid-February the relatively high temperatures of the surface layers cause the majority of fish to swim to cooler, deeper waters. Fewer fish come in to feed around the shoreline at night and the fly fishing during this period is not as good as in other warm months. November and early December will provide good sport, especially if the preceding winter was mild or the lake level is rising. The evenings and early mornings are naturally the best hours to fish.

The fly fisherman should select his fishing site with as much care as that required for other techniques. Shallow bays, with numerous rocky outcrops, are the most suitable. The choice of location should be greatly influenced by the direction of the wind. As mentioned previously, the angler should fish the lee shore for the greatest chance of success. If the trout are rising freely within casting range the angler can largely ignore the structure of the bottom and simply proceed to fish. However, if few or no fish are rising the angler must ensure that he is casting over submerged rocks, stumps and the like, around which trout are likely to be feeding on nymphs and similar organisms.

The river angler is accustomed to moving from pool to pool, continually searching for fish. On the lake he has the choice of either selecting a site and remaining there, casting and retrieving methodically, or actively searching for fish along the shoreline. In general, the latter method is best employed during daylight and at dusk, or when no surface fish movement is discernible, and the former method during darkness when the fish are often cruising in search of food.

The stream angler has also to understand that now he will have to impart movement to the fly (except when dry fly fishing) as there is no running water to do this for him. The type and rate of retrieve varies with the mode of fishing. A deeply fished nymph has to be retrieved slowly with the line being coiled in one's hand, whereas a long-tailed fly is retrieved rapidly in short, sharp jerks, with the line being held in loose coils. The former movement imitates that of an insect nymph and the latter that of a young fish or tadpole. The angler must also comprehend the three-dimensional aspect of lake fishing. The fly can be fished over a wide depth-range. The choice should be influenced by those factors described beforehand; namely, light, temperature and time of year.

Wet fly fishing in Lake Eucumbene: This is undoubtedly the most effective mode of fly fishing the lake. A wide range of techniques is used. The wet fly fisherman seeks to imitate submerged food organisms and not those floating on the surface. His flies should be chosen and fished according to the aquatic fauna present at the time. The most successful fly fisherman is one who knows what to expect in the way of insect life in the water he is fishing. This statement is applicable to both wet and dry fly fishing, but whereas the dry fly man has only to look at the flies on and about the surface, the wet fly man has no such advantage. He must know what to expect as he cannot easily look beneath the surface.

Summarizing the principal groups of aquatic organisms

present in Eucumbene during summer months (*see also Aquatic insects*):

Caddis flies are not as common as in earlier years but still show up in the trout's diet. Small black, green or brown nymphs and any lightly dressed fly may prove good imitations. Dragonflies and damsel flies feature very prominently in the trout's diet, especially their larvae. A wide variety of mudeye patterns are now available. Mayflies and stoneflies are uncommon as such insects mostly prefer to complete their life-cycle in running water.

Many of the common two-winged flies, such as the mosquito, breed in freshwater and their larvae and pupae are avidly devoured by the trout. Small green or white nymphs and sparsely dressed flies of the same size and colour will suffice. Water bugs also feature prominently in the trout's diet. Their typically sharp, jerky movements and appearance can be imitated by fishing relatively small brown, bushy flies such as the red tag and coch-y-bondhu in a similar manner. Some members of the beetle group are also aquatic. Similar flies should be used to those described for the 'bugs'.

A few common carp *Carassius auratus*, and the occasional galaxiid are present in the lake. Such species are not plentiful and even though a certain amount of cannibalism takes place, fish do not feature prominently in the trout's diet. Tadpoles are much commoner. However, the successful catches obtained by trolling clearly indicate that the trout behaves according to its carnivorous instincts and strikes at anything resembling a small fish. The large matuka-like flies do not imitate anything other than small fish. Such flies are successful throughout the year and should be retrieved in a jerky, fish-like manner. Numerous patterns exist, the most popular of which include the Mrs Simpson, black phantom, red and black matuka, fuzzy wuzzy and hamill's killer among others. The black phantom is a particularly successful pattern. Tadpole nymphs also prove productive in December and January.

The angler should examine the stomach contents of the first fish caught and determine if he is using a fly of the correct pattern. The relatively short time involved in making such an examination is well spent. The fish need not necessarily have been feeding on an aquatic organism. For example, the first fish could well be caught on a Mrs Simpson, yet an examination of its stomach contents will show it to have been feeding on drowned black ants. A switch to a smaller pattern, representing this insect, should then be made, even though the fish was taken on a completely different fly. Large streamer flies are probably used too frequently on the lake by the majority of anglers. Big fish will take the tiniest of flies. One has only to examine the stomach contents of a few Eucumbene trout to realize that the great proportion of insect food organisms are less than 10 mm in length. Nevertheless large flies should be used during the darkness.

The choosing of a correct fly pattern is by no means as important as fishing the chosen pattern in the correct manner. Indeed, a non-radical fly pattern such as a red tag or coch-y-bondhu, in two or three sizes, will consistently catch fish throughout the year when used by a competent angler. Here again, a knowledge of the behaviour of those aquatic food organisms that one is endeavouring to imitate is more than useful. The chosen fly can then be made to behave accordingly. If the fish are feeding on caddis larvae the fly is slowly retrieved along the bottom. If tadpoles constitute the main diet, the fly is fished jerkily and rapidly, just below the surface; and so on.

A wide range of fly lines is now available. The angler wishing to fish just below the surface should use the more traditional floating line together with a leaded fly. The fly will sink quickly and prevent the cast from dragging on the surface. Mid-water fishers should use a slow sinking line. The fly can be either weighted or unweighted. The large matuka-type flies are best fished with such a line. Dry fly patterns are often very successful when fished in such a manner, as the stiff hackles, which normally provide flotation, move in an extremely attractive manner when underwater. Bottom-fishers should use a fast sinking line with an unweighted fly. When fishing a rocky bottom it is often advisable to grease the fly. This will cause the fly to float just off the bottom and will prevent it from becoming snagged. A general rule in the summer is to fish deep during the day and near the surface during the evening and night.

Fishing off steep banks with a sinking line can be very productive at times, as depths of up to 15 m can be reached. A few local fly fishermen have devised yabby patterns, but as yet these have met with mixed success. Freshwater shrimp appear to be increasing in abundance in Eucumbene and fly patterns matching this crustacean could well prove effective.

Dry fly fishing in Lake Eucumbene: Whereas the technique of correctly presenting a dry fly on a stream demands more skill than is required when fishing wet, this is not the case on the lake. Dry fly fishing is essentially a much simpler technique than that required for wet fly, the main skill being the selection of a correct fly pattern. The very nature of dry fly fishing largely precludes deluding the fish by imparting an attractive motion to the fly and the fish must be deceived mainly by the resemblance of the artificial to the natural. Trout are usually very selective when taking surface food and a good artificial imitation is an essential. Some movement can be imparted to a floating fly by tapping the rod butt or by twitching the rod. Large flies can be dragged across the surface. These methods often succeed.

It is useless to employ such a technique in the absence of rising fish and the dry-fly angler on Eucumbene is more limited in his fishing times than those using other methods. The evenings provide the best sport, with the occasional morning proving productive. The trout often rise freely on dark nights but the absence of light makes dry fly fishing extremely difficult, the angler having to rely upon the noise made by the rising fish as an indication of his fly being taken. The angler should look for cruising fish, anticipate the position of the next rise and cast accordingly, rather than work by simply 'chucking and chancing'.

Myriad patterns of dry flies exist and no purpose is served by describing them. The predominantly terrestrial insects drifting on the lake are flying ants, midges, mosquitoes and beetles. A few grasshoppers and moths appear in the diet but not in any great quantity. Mayflies and stoneflies are not plentiful. Large hatches of caddis occur at infrequent intervals.

A good dry fly fisherman will thus carry numerous patterns to ensure that he can correctly match the fly on the water.

There is particular satisfaction in taking fish on the dry fly, though there is little doubt that the wet fly fisherman will consistently take more.

On dark summer nights large browns will often move into the shallows and it is well worth searching along the shoreline using a large, bushy fly such as a black muddler minnow. This should be retrieved in short, sharp jerks, and taking fish are usually felt rather than seen.

Changes in the trout populations

The most pronounced change in the composition of Eucumbene's trout populations is undoubtedly the decreasing abundance of rainbow trout. Whereas rainbows once comprised the bulk of the angling catch, this is no longer the case. In 1961–62 rainbows formed 80.6 per cent of the catch. By 1970–71 rainbow representation had fallen to 52.1 per cent and had decreased further to 32.1 per cent in 1980–81. The last population estimates conducted for browns were in 1968 and 1970 when respective standing crops of 355,000 and 712,000 fish aged three years or more were estimated to be present. The large difference in these estimates is principally attributable to the marked difference in lake level between these two years, and demonstrates the ability of the brown trout population to expand (or contract) in response to prevailing conditions. In 1968 the lake was at a very low level following a lengthy drought, and its mean surface area of 8,008 hectares for the 1968–69 season was considerably less than that of 11,535 hectares in the 1970–71 season, which also saw new ground being inundated.

Although no further population estimates have since been conducted, it is highly probable that the existing brown trout population lies somewhere between the two estimates above, depending on lake level. Furthermore, the fact that the mean size of browns in the angling catch has remained at 39 to 40 cm in length throughout the 1978–79 to 1982–83 seasons, suggests a relatively stable population composition. Only one estimate of rainbow population has been made. In 1968 the standing crop of rainbows aged three years or more was calculated to be 218,000. Although catch data suggested that rainbow numbers also expanded as the lake rose in 1969 and 1970, there is little doubt that the existing population is far below that of 1968. As tagging experiments showed rainbows to be twice as liable to capture as browns, the percentage species composition in the angling catch suggests that in 1980–81, browns outnumbered rainbows by over four to one.

Thus, whereas brown catch-per-effort (C/E) has remained relatively stable, rainbow C/E has declined sharply. This has brought about a fall in overall C/E for both species, particularly in the summer months of January to March, the peak tourist-angler period. The catch in these months used to be dominated by rainbows.

In 1981, a chance event demonstrated the importance of rainbows to the Eucumbene fishery. The large commercial trout farm near Tumut was declared bankrupt and N.S.W. State Fisheries was able to purchase 300,000 rainbows approximately 20 cm in length from the receivers, at the bargain-basement price of ten cents each. These fish were placed into Eucumbene and the following 1982–83 season saw catch rates rise markedly, overall C/E being the best since 1970–71. Rainbows comprised an astonishing 82.5 per cent of the catch. Moreover, the growth rate of the stocked rainbows was excellent and demonstrated that Eucumbene contains ample food supplies for this species.

It is important to realise that with the increased shift towards bottom-feeding by browns there is now comparatively little dietary overlap with the surface/midwater-feeding rainbows. Thus the lake can, and should, support sizeable populations of both species if the standing crop of fish is to be near the theoretical maximum.

The success of this stocking has prompted many anglers and local businessmen to push for it to be repeated annually. However, it should be remembered that at normal fish-farm prices, each equivalent stocking would cost in the vicinity of $200,000. Such ongoing expenditure is prohibitive.

The major reason for declining rainbow numbers is competition between browns and rainbows in the lake's spawning streams. Without going into research details, such competition is having an adverse effect upon rainbow recruitment into the rod-fishery. Management strategies aimed at controlling the spawning runs and boosting rainbow recruitment have been devised, but N.S.W. State Fisheries have as yet done nothing to implement them. An economic appraisal of the fishery in 1977–78 found that it generated an annual turnover of $8 million, over half of which came from interstate anglers. Despite being a recreational resource of considerable economic value, it is at present neglected and its future as a quality trout fishery remains in the balance.

RICHARD TILZEY

Snowy Mountains An outstanding freshwater fishing region of great beauty in south-eastern New South Wales, containing all the continent's mountains exceeding 2000 m elevation, and the nation's most extensive snowfields.

About 2500 square kilometres of the region is snow-covered several months of each year, and about 100 square kilometres of the Main Range is so deeply covered for about six months each year that snow patches sometimes remain throughout the summer.

The eastern side of the Main Range forms the upper catchment of the famed Snowy River, once the nation's largest and best trout river, but now less productive because its flow has been greatly reduced by the reservoirs built on it and its tributaries for the Snowy Mountains Scheme.

The vast snowfields of the region are the source of three great river systems, the Murray River, the Snowy River and the Murrumbidgee River. Into these flow many other rivers and smaller streams, all of them stocked with both rainbow and brown trout in their upper reaches, and many also containing native species such as Murray cod, Macquarie perch, silver perch and golden perch in their lower reaches.

In general there are only trout in the cooler highlands above about 1000 m, and only native species where the rivers warm as they leave the mountains to begin their journeys across the plains. In between, a mixed population of warmwater and coldwater species exists.

The Snowy Mountains form one of the last great wilderness areas on the continent. Much of the region is accessible only on foot, and its good fishing, lovely streams, high mountains and superb views make it one of the most popular tourist attractions in the country. The National Parks and Wildlife Service, which administers Kosciusko National Park, estimates that about three million visitor-days are spent in the region each year by anglers, skiers, bushwalkers and others enjoying outdoor pursuits.

Much of the Main Range is above 1800 m elevation, and at this altitude is found the tree-line above which very few trees can grow because of the snow and intense cold. In this truly alpine area there is considerable evidence of past ice ages to interest visitors — glacial lakes, cirques and huge moraines where long-gone glaciers dumped the rocks they had carved from the range's core.

In the crest of the Main Range are most of Australia's highest mountains, including Mount Kosciusko (2228 m), Mount Townsend (2210 m) and Mount Twynam (2196 m).

Some 200 species of alpine plants flourish on these high

alpine meadows and in the sub-alpine frost-hollow valleys, of which about 60 species are unique. Many bloom profusely during the brief summer, so that the angler who fishes the valley floors may find him or herself treading amongst some of the rarest blooms on earth.

The Snowy Mountains region includes (and is often confused with) the Monaro (after *Maneroo*, the name the Aborigines gave to the rich, fertile, rolling foothills and meadows on the eastern side of the ranges). Whereas the higher, faster, rocky, eroding streams of the ranges produce mainly smaller trout rarely averaging more than half a kilogram, the slower, weedy, richer, depositing streams of the Monaro produce trout averaging more than a kilogram each. These streams have some of the fastest rates of growth for trout in the world, but are mostly small and subject to fish-kills in times of drought because of their low altitude. Many are also on private property along most of their lengths, where permission is needed for fishing.

Best known are the Mowamba River, the Maclaughlin River, the Bombala River, the Delegate River and their tributaries, all of which flow into the Snowy River. Also home of excellent trout fishing is the Umeralla River and several other smaller tributaries of the Murrumbidgee on the north-eastern side of the Monaro.

The streams of the Monaro are found on the eastern side of the Snowy Mountains. The slower, weedy streams of the region are rich in trout.

An important aspect of Snowy Mountains fishing today is the 'lakes', which are actually reservoirs formed by the Snowy Mountains Scheme to store the meltwater from the spring thaw of the snowfields for hydro-electricity and for irrigation during summer. This scheme traps the waters of the mighty Snowy River and its main tributary, the Eucumbene River, where they leave the mountains on the eastern side of the alps, as well as water from some of the smaller western rivers, channelling it through a system of underground tunnels into huge dams, from which it is eventually redistributed into the Murray River. Thus the snowmelt water which once was lost to sea down the Snowy River is now saved for use in the fertile but arid plains of the Riverina.

Many older anglers bemoan the deprivation of water from once-famous streams below these dams, but the dams themselves have become one of the region's main attractions for anglers because of the many large trout they produce. The result has been the creation of a tourist industry based on reservoir trout fishing, especially around Lake Eucumbene and Lake Jindabyne, where fishing centres now provide accommodation, boat-hire and other services.

Biological studies by K. C. McKeown in 1936 and A. D. Butcher in 1945 showed that the region's trout fed almost exclusively on insects, a fact which had previously been doubted as it was felt that the high growth rate of these fish could not be due to insect feeding alone. The region is extremely rich in aquatic insects, however. Mayflies and sedges (caddis-flies), the principal food of trout all round the world, sometimes hatch so profusely here that they cover the streams like carpets, and on some summer evenings their mating swarms form clouds across the pools.

Most streams are reasonably well stocked with either brown or rainbow trout or both. Continuous efforts have also been made to introduce brook trout to the Monaro streams but with little success, since they seem better suited to the higher, colder streams. Efforts have also been made to introduce Atlantic salmon to Lake Jindabyne and a few other waters. Some of these fish have been noted running into the Thredbo River during the autumn spawning season, but there is so far no evidence that they have formed a self-supporting population, though many which have been released directly from the nearby Gaden Hatchery have been caught in the lake in good condition, so it is obviously suited to them. Those originally introduced are believed to have been a sea-run variety that will not prosper in landlocked waters.

In general, the higher streams hold mainly rainbow trout, the lower streams mainly brown trout. Brown trout are more tolerant of high temperatures than rainbows, and so are more drought resistant. It also appears that a century of acclimatization has produced in some Monaro streams a high-temperature tolerant strain of browns which are much more suited to Australian conditions than the parent stock.

Fishing area access and accommodation
There is road, rail and air access to the region. An airport at Cooma has regular interstate flights, and road access from northern areas leads through Cooma directly to the Monaro and the Snowy Mountains, while access from Victoria is either via Albury or Khancoban. The Khancoban road may be closed during winter by snow, however, as may the road through Kiandra, and chains should be carried on both these roads in winter because of icy patches.

Cooma is the gateway to the Snowy Mountains for anyone coming from the north. The popularity of the snowfields in winter and the trout streams and reservoirs in summer has resulted in the establishment of a great deal of tourist accommodation in the area, ranging from caravan parks and motels to the more expensive chalets and lodges at the ski villages.

The Snowy River and its tributaries
The best known river in the region, the Snowy River is famed in film, stories and poetry. Although the dams have robbed it of much of its water, it still holds some excellent trout fishing, and its lower reaches are well suited to canoeing and rafting. The most popular area today is around Jindabyne, the new township on the shore of Lake Jindabyne, built to replace the old town which disappeared under the rising waters of the lake.

The lake was built just below the junction of the Thredbo, Eucumbene and Snowy Rivers, and so has better spawning facilities for trout than most other such lakes, and thus more fish. Its lower altitude makes its waters more fertile, and it tends to produce larger fish than the other impoundments. As well as good populations of brown and rainbow trout, it has numbers of Atlantic salmon and brook trout, though the future of these species is in doubt since they do not seem able to form self-reproducing populations.

When Lake Jindabyne is stable, as it occasionally is when water is not being drawn off for hydro-electricity, it produces rich weedbeds which shelter schools of small common carp on which the trout prey, a situation which produces excellent fishing. Like Lake Eucumbene, it also has large numbers of crayfish which help produce high growth rates in its fish.

The Snowy River is reached downstream from Jindabyne by taking the road from Berridale to Dalgety, where some pools are so large they require careful wading or a small boat to be properly fished. From Dalgety the road leads to Bombala, giving access to the Snowy River at several places, and crossing first Bobundra Creek and then the Maclaughlin River, both of which grow extremely large and very wary brown trout. Both are subject to drought however, and may be poorly stocked in dry years, but tend to recover quickly. The Bombala and Delegate Rivers may also be reached by this road.

At the southern limits of Jindabyne a road turns west and about 10 km later crosses the Mowamba River, a small meadow-type stream which is a declared fly fishing only water. Once very popular, it is now badly silted, and little fished because of the proximity of the large stocks of trout in nearby Lake Jindabyne. It does, however, hold one of the best populations of brook trout on mainland Australia, which the local fishing club is nurturing and hoping will become well established.

The road south through Jindabyne skirts the shores of the lake, and about 2 km from the town it forks. The left branch is the Alpine Way, leading around the south-eastern end of the Main Range, past Thredbo Village, the region's principal ski village near the source of the Thredbo River, and then through Dead Horse Gap and over the range to Khancoban on the way to Victoria. This road provides access to the pretty Thredbo River at several points before crossing it near Thredbo Village, and on the southern side of the range to the Geehi River, the Swampy Plains River and the upper Murray River, as well as to Khancoban Pondage, a reservoir with excellent trout fishing.

The right branch leads to Charlotte Pass within sight of Mount Kosciusko, passing through the ski villages of Smiggin Holes and Perisher Valley during its long climb up from Jindabyne. About 5 km out of Jindabyne it crosses the lower Thredbo River.

A turn-off at Sponnars Inn and another at Smiggin Holes lead to Guthega on the upper Snowy River. There are several access points to the river along this road where there is excellent fishing at times, though the water level can vary rapidly below Guthega Dam, so that considerable care is needed. Above the dam the fish are mainly small rainbows.

About 5 km out of Jindabyne, a turn-off leads to the Government-owned Gaden hatchery, one of the nation's oldest, largest and most productive trout hatcheries, which is usually open for public inspection, with large brood fish on display. Two other commercial trout farms can be found in the region, one on the Alpine Way not far out of Jindabyne, and the other at Rocky Plains near Lake Eucumbene. Anglers may fish at both of these for a fee.

The Kosciusko road formerly ran all the way to the summit of Mount Kosciusko, but is now closed at Charlotte Pass, about 8 km from the summit, in the interests of conservation. At the pass a platform provides magnificent views of the Main Range and most of the nation's highest peaks. Various walking tracks lead to the higher peaks and several glacial lakes, besides giving access to the alpine section of the Snowy River, which holds numbers of smallish trout, mostly rainbows. Not far below Charlotte Pass this road crosses Spencers Creek which has a good stock of smallish fish, but is sometimes polluted by the village at the pass, and so is unsafe to drink.

The Upper Murrumbidgee and Eucumbene Rivers (Kiandra and Adaminaby area)

Six kilometres south of Cooma the Snowy Mountains Highway branches off to the right, giving access to Lake Eucumbene, Tantangara Dam, Adaminaby and Kiandra. Eucumbene may also be reached from Berridale by roads which lead directly to Buckenderra and Braemar Bay, angling resorts on the lake's shores. The road to Braemar also leads to the huge wall of this immense dam, where there is a tourist centre.

The Snowy Mountains Highway leads through Adaminaby and Kiandra to Tumut, providing access to various fishing centres along the eastern edge of the lake. Adaminaby is about 50 km from Cooma, and here a road turns off the highway, leading to Old Adaminaby, Anglers Reach and several popular fishing spots. Another turn-off leads to the fishing centre at Providence Portal, near the upper limit of the lake, from which the lower end of the Eucumbene River can be reached.

At Adaminaby a turn-off leads to Yaouk on the Murrumbidgee River at the foot of the mountains. Downstream from Yaouk the river spreads into large, slow pools inhabited mainly by brown trout, while upstream it flows much more quickly over rugged terrain and holds mainly rainbows.

Eighteen kilometres from Adaminaby and not far from Providence Portal, a turn-off leads to Tantangara Dam, the oldest of the Snowy Mountains Scheme reservoirs, which often fishes well when Lake Eucumbene is unproductive because it is more sheltered from the wind.

The highway crosses several small tributaries of the Eucumbene River on the way to Kiandra. The river itself can be reached at several points, but can only be fished with artificial baits below the bridge at Kiandra, and with artificial flies from this point upstream. The tributaries of Lake Eucumbene are subject to different fishing seasons from the rest of New South Wales trout streams, and this varies from time to time, so it is wise to check with local tackle shops or with the Fisheries Branch of the N.S.W. Department of Agriculture.

The river is accessible for several kilometres around Kiandra, and at Rules Point, some 15 km from Kiandra, though some walking is required to get to the best of it. About 4 km past the Rules Point turn-off, another road leads to Yarrangobilly Caves on the Yarrangobilly River. The caves and a small swimming pool fed by a hot spring combine with this pretty stream's generally small trout to provide an interesting attraction for visiting anglers.

Continuing north along the highway brings one to the Yarrangobilly River near its source, and soon afterwards the road begins to descend into the Tumut Valley near Talbingo.

The Tumut River

The Tumut River rises at the northern end of the Snowy Mountains proper near famed Mount Jagungal in the Jagungal

Wilderness Area, but its waters are trapped in several dams before it reaches the plains, and although sections of it contain excellent fishing at times, the fishing is variable and difficult to predict. The upstream dams are too steep-sided to fish except from boats, and since boating access is difficult, they are little fished compared to more accessible dams such as Tantangara, Eucumbene and Jindabyne. Blowering Dam, the lowest of the dams on the Tumut River, is the most accessible and the best stocked.

The lower end of the Tumut River produces excellent fishing at times, but it is variable due to the changing water levels as water is released from Blowering Dam. A tributary of the Tumut River, the Goobragandra River, provides good trout fishing despite its population of redfin.

From Tumut, the Tumut River flows north to join the Murrumbidgee near Gundagai.

Fishing pressure
The Snowy Mountains region contains a wide variety of water, ranging from small, winding meadow streams of the high plateaux through the fast precipitous waters of the mountain gorges to the large-spreading rivers of the foothills and the vast expanses of the lakes. Although angling tourism tends to concentrate on the lakes, the more accessible streams, especially those of the Monaro, are also subject to high fishing pressure during holiday periods, but are for the most part not heavily fished during the rest of the year.

Fishing pressure, however, tends to concentrate on those sections of streams within some two hours walk from roads. Since most of the lengths of the majority of the streams are not accessible by road, there still remains much wilderness-type trout fishing for anyone prepared to backpack off the beaten track, especially on the more rugged western side of the Divide.

The plentiful insect life of the region makes fly fishing a popular and productive method of angling in both streams and lakes, although spinning, bait fishing and especially trolling are also extremely popular in the lakes.

A local angling body, the Monaro Acclimatisation Society, is very active in all fishing matters, and visitors will find it helpful. An inland fishing licence is necessary for fishing all these waters, and although fishing regulations are in general the same as those for the rest of New South Wales, some variations occur from year to year, so it is advisable to check with local authorities, such as the fishery inspectors stationed at Cooma and Jindabyne.

Visitors should remember that many of the streams and lakes are at high altitudes where nights can be extremely cold even in mid-summer, and where sunburn is a problem because of the increased ultra-violet light.

There are many caravan parks and camping areas at the lakes and towns. Many property owners will permit fishing and camping if approached courteously, though all outdoor fires may be banned during dry summers, when landowners become understandably nervous about allowing strangers on their properties because of the bushfire danger. Visitors are therefore requested to obtain permission before entering private property.

JOHN TURNBULL

New England

The vast upland area of the Northern Tablelands of New South Wales (New England) stretches from the Queensland border in the north to the Moonbis, north of Tamworth, in the south and from the rain-forested escarpments looming over the Pacific coastal flats in the east to the western slopes of the Great Dividing Range in the west. It is rolling sheep and cattle country, a land of wide vistas crossed by rugged ranges such as the Doughboys, the Ben Lomonds and the New England Snowys, where peaks rise to over 1500 m. To the east, in the eastern falls area, the plateau is studded by huge gorges into which creeks fall for hundreds of feet to form the headwaters of rivers like the Hastings, the Clarence and the Macleay. Barring droughts, New England enjoys adequate rainfall, especially in the east and is laced by several rivers and creeks. These streams, the altitude (generally over 900 m) and the hard work of the New England Trout Acclimatization Society and its affiliated clubs have combined to make New England the northernmost outpost of good trout fishing in Australia.

Organizations (clubs and hatchery)

There are records of trout ova from Tasmania being reared by the New England Trout Acclimatization Society as far back as 1885, but probably its first success was in 1902 when brown Loch Leven trout from New Zealand were released east of Armidale in Rockvale Creek, still one of the most notable trout waters in the region. These flourished in such spectacular fashion that soon other landowners were liberating brown and rainbow fry into their creeks. Local angling clubs were formed, all affiliated to N.E.T.A.S., and at present there are about 18 member clubs in such towns as Armidale, Guyra, Inverell, Walcha and Glen Innes.

The hatchery founded by L. P. Dutton eventually arrived at its present base on the Serpentine near Ebor. It is quickly becoming one of the best known in Australia, visited by thousands of touring anglers and visitors to the neighbouring New England National Park, who call to inspect the brood ponds and trough and gaze in awe at the massive old rainbows pensioned off in an angler-free section of the Serpentine. In recent years between 200,000 and 300,000 young trout, mainly rainbows, have been liberated annually by club members in public streams within roughly a 320 km radius of the hatchery. Some are sold to landowners for private fishing in farm dams where they can reach just under 1 kg in a year and some are air-freighted as far afield as Wagga and Parkes. The Dutton Hatchery, which is maintained by the Department of Fisheries and a good deal of voluntary effort by N.E.T.A.S., was chosen to rear ova of the Atlantic salmon sent from Canada. The experiment was a success and young salmon have been released further south in big water impoundments like Burrinjuck Dam: at present New England does not have large enough bodies of water for salmon. In 1967, American brook trout were hatched successfully at the hatchery. They have grown well and have spawned when only a year old—in contrast to rainbows which are two or three years old before they spawn.

New England trout problems
Although they have been widely established in New England for several decades, brown and rainbow trout are an exotic luxury which survive only through careful tending. By now probably all the streams capable of carrying trout have been stocked and these are often limited to headwaters in the highlands. New England has a border-line climate for trout. Even in normal summers, water temperatures in the lower creeks fluctuate between 25 and 27 degrees C, which test the trout's powers of survival. At the other extreme, storm rain often causes severe flooding which can play havoc with the trout population. Some of the fish are swept over the towering falls into the gorges.

The terrible drought of the mid-1960s devastated many of the best trout streams. Some were reduced to a series of stagnant, weed-choked pools with the rotting corpses of big trout floating belly up on the surface. Two droughts in the early 1980s again frustrated anglers, but by 1986 New England streams had fully recovered.

Other menaces to New England trout are over-fishing and heavy spraying with weedicides and insecticides (over 45,000 ha were sprayed with malathion in 1966 to control a grasshopper plague and many fish were poisoned). The over-generous bag limit of 10 fish per rod per day is often ignored, as is the minimum length of 25 cm. Thousands of young fish are 'skulldragged' from the creeks bleeding to death on great spinners or wormhooks. Such abuses become more common as increasing numbers of fishermen—many of them sea anglers who see no reason to change their technique for trout—visit the region. Finally, there are those characters who observe no sporting code at all, who peg baited handlines round a pool and relax with a box of beer, and the ruffians who explode gelignite in remote stretches, killing everything in the water as well as the fish.

All this is said to stress the point that no visiting angler to New England should expect a paradise of full creeks and pools a-boil with rising fish. Veteran trout men in the region talk of the legendary 1930s and 1940s, when the fishing was

Dutton's Trout Hatchery on the Serpentine at Ebor, N.S.W., releases between 200,000 and 300,000 trout fry a year into streams and dams in the New England area.

really magnificent. The rainbows, in particular, had reached a high peak of abundance then as, in virgin streams where they had no rivals and few human predators, they feasted on the rich feed of yabbies and freshwater shrimps. Photographs and plaster casts are retained of 6 kg rainbows caught on fly by that prince of New England fishermen, the late Geoff Godfrey, in the Moredon Creek dams near Tingha. Those days have gone, probably forever. Feed is no longer as plentiful, there are far more anglers about and the droughts have done their worst. New England no longer rivals the Southern Tablelands, with their vast water impoundments, in the consistency of its trout fishing.

Of course, much the same thing could be said of any trout area in Australia. The Monaro, too, had its crop of net-bulging legends about the days when only a few lucky men took the trouble to go into the bush after trout. New England's trout waters still have many attractions for the connoisseur. Indeed, if the Southern Tablelands have the abundance and the glamour, New England has the subtlety and the charm. Certainly, it is now usually much more difficult to catch the bag limit of legal-sized fish in a hard day by the water, but difficulty is half the allure of trout fishing, otherwise one is better advised to go to the fishmonger.

The best New England creeks

Most New England anglers would probably agree that the more reliable trout waters include the following streams—westward-flowing creeks, headwaters of the Murray-Darling system, like the sandy Macdonald River and its tributaries in the mountainous Walcha region, the Deepwater River north of Glen Innes and tributaries of the Gwydir in the rough country west of Guyra, such as the Booralong, Sandy, Ollera and George and Moredon Creeks, all harbour noble rainbows in their pools. The Beardy, which flows east, has its moments, but redfin are on the increase there. In general, the larger fish are found in the slower western streams like the Booralong. Here there is usually a better supply of feed and a larger body of water than in the east—but these streams, too, take longer to recover from floods and are more subject to drought and excessive heat. Men after specimen fish would be advised to concentrate on the west but they would need patience and luck as well as talent. Even during the droughts there were a few taciturn men in Armidale who regularly brought home rainbows between 1.5 and 2.5 kg. But these are men who know the water and keep their secrets to themselves.

There is more variety and adventure to be had by the eastward flowing creeks that plunge over the eastern falls to the Pacific. Most notable here is that splendid trout stream near Armidale, Rockvale Creek, which flows through lush pastoral country before pitching over Wollomombi Falls into the Macleay gorges. The Rockvale is excellent trout water along its entire length, as is its tributary, Boundary Creek. Eighty kilometres or so east of Armidale and Glen Innes, where the rolling grasslands buckle up into the stony, heavily timbered ridges of the New England Snowys and the undulating dairy country of the Dorrigo Plateau, there is a host of fine trout streams such as the Styx, Serpentine, Oaky, Guy Fawkes, Major's, Jock's Water, Little Nymboida and Little Murray and creeks have recently been stocked on the Carrai Plateau back of Kempsey. These are lovely crystalline streams cascading through forests and pasture to the gorges. They clear quickly after freshes and if their trout are often small they are always game and, usually, plentiful. A man in the eastern falls country feels like a pioneer angler and if he risks his neck by going down into the gorges he may fill his creel by some solitary pool in the wilderness.

Suggested New England lures
Recommendations on what flies to use for any region can often bring nothing but frustration to the visiting angler who faithfully does what the book pundits tell him. By New England waters, as by any others, the fisherman should follow the ancient precept of studying 'the fly on the water' before he makes his selection. There are times in New England when white moths are active, or mayflies, ants, grasshoppers or nymphs and the trout are feasting on these to the exclusion of other fare. Conditions vary from season to season and even from stream to stream. Trout are fastidious gourmets and may prefer different flies at different times of the day. And, of

There are many fine, secluded trout streams amongst the gorges of New England. This angler is landing a trout in a stream near Ebor.

course, the most successful fly men in New England, like their brethren the world over, often concoct flies and nymphs of their own. These modest, whimsical or bizarre creations are unknown to the fishing books but they can be lethal on the Rockvale or the Deepwater when flies of famous pedigree fail. One local expert, for instance, can be deadly by the western creeks with his own ragged, self-tied nymphs which consist mainly of yellow wool.

All these qualifications being duly stated, I suspect that most New England fly fishermen would agree that good results can be had in the region with these flies:

Wet flies: Marabou, longtail, matuka (black and red), coch-y-bondhu, grasshopper, jungle cock, black gnat, silver doctor, coachman, greenwell's glory and alexandra.

Dry flies: White moth, brown moth, greenwell's glory, may fly, bivisible, coachman.

Nymphs: Can be very effective; indeed, some of the best New England anglers use nymphs more than any other lures. Variations of mainly green, brown and black nymphs can be potent at different times. Perhaps the most popular type in New England is a small, black-bodied nymph with a red head.

As in all forms of fishing, imagination and on the spot invention often bring a tight line. For example, on one of those superb New England evenings when clouds of white moths were drifting over the Booralong and the trout were going mad for them, one angler, lacking anything like a white moth in his flybox, caught a real one, impaled it on a small hook and soon connected with a rainbow. The same man does wonderful things with a small worm on the end of his nymph. You can never tell what a trout may snap at, whether in hunger or irritation, which is an element of his fascination.

New England creeks are ideal for what the British call upstream worming. Creep up the bank of the stream and, with a small red worm as bait on a flyrod with a long trace or a light spinning rod, cast upstream to the head of a pool or a cascade so that the worm tumbles back to you over the pebbles. Do this properly and the trout will often furrow the water to get at the bait. Such delicate gear rarely fatally wounds an undersized fish. All in all, I found that upstream worming was the most reliable way of taking fish, particularly on those long, hot summer days when the trout brood under the bank and refuse to rise to any insect. You can fish the same way with shrimps or crayfish or any other creature you may think will be appetizing to a trout and which you find in or near the creek.

Worms are the staple live bait, but some locals swear by the witchetty grub and even take an axe with them to prise them out of dead trees, all fresh and lively, by the water's edge. In 1966, a man took a 2 kg rainbow out of the Styx with a witchetty and this at a time when the fishing was poor. If you have the stomach for it, maggots from a sheep carcass can be delectable to trout. (Do not despise the maggot. In England, where there is a maggot-breeding industry for anglers, maggots are banned from trout streams as the fish go for them so recklessly.) Grubs and grasshoppers, which can assume plague proportions in New England, are also good live bait.

Many sophisticated anglers consider spinners a butcher's way of taking trout. The brown trout usually ignore them anyway, but rainbows will bite at indianas, halcyons and spoon flashes. Young fish are especially prone to go for a spinner and are almost always so badly mangled by the hooks that they die soon after release.

When to fish in New England
Early morning or from late afternoon to dusk in normal weather are usually the best times for fishing, whatever your method. Bait and spinner fishing can be rewarding on wet days, especially with a fresh in the creeks while the water is reasonably clear-flowing, as is often the case in the eastern falls country. There is not much fly life on the water in New England until October, so most of the fly fishermen rely upon nymphs until then. Rainbow trout are at their best during October and November, becoming generally inactive during the hot summer months, then enjoying a burst of energy in March and April when the best specimens, fat after a season's feeding, are usually caught.

Brown trout are definitely at their best in the spring. Indeed, many of the New England fly fishermen maintain that the best sport of all is to be had at dusk in late October, after brown trout with a dry fly on the Serpentine. Brown trout are generally more sluggish in these warm northern waters than elsewhere and declined in popularity and consequently in distribution when the more glamorous rainbow was introduced. The rainbow is now by far the more prevalent throughout the Northern Tablelands, but in his strongholds, such as Oaky and Tia creeks in the eastern ranges, the 'brownie' is probably the favourite quarry of the fly men. They claim that, at his best, the brown trout is a more subtle opponent than the rainbow and even that he is better to eat. Spinner fanciers will waste their time and their costly lumps of metal if they go after browns in the quiet, snaggy pools they like, although these trout will respond to upstream worming if it is delicately done. Brown trout appear to better endure the hard conditions in New England. They came through the drought better than the rainbows and as they are hard to catch anyway and have their keen supporters, may soon be receiving more reinforcements from the hatchery.

Other backwater fish
When the trout are lying low, whether from a whim or from the heat, or if you would like a change, there are other kinds of fish well worth your attention in New England. In the larger creeks and rivers beyond the Dividing Range, such as the Gwydir and the Macintyre, are eel-tail catfish, yellowbelly (golden perch) and that ubiquitous English immigrant, the redfin. This perch has not thus far proved such a menace as it was feared it might be in those trout streams to which it has penetrated, such as Beardy Waters. It is doubtful whether it would ever do well in the rapid creeks of the eastern falls. Below Bundarra on the Gwydir, out of New England proper, you soon reach Murray cod water. Throughout New England there are plenty of eels to fish for, there are carp in a few creeks such as Salisbury Waters and an interesting little native to go after with light bait gear is the mountain trout or 'slimy',

regarded as a delicacy by the old hands. A 15 kg trout cod was taken from a pool at Buccarumbi, 30 kilometres south of Grafton, in 1985.

In the network of gorges below the great waterfalls and in such rivers as the Bellinger and George's Creek that splendid sporting fish the eastern bass flashes at spinners and moving bait at dusk or in the very early morning. To reach its retreats, however, you need to know your bushcraft and be a fair athlete. Bass numbers are declining in New England, as everywhere else, which is a pity for they are every bit as good to fish for as the immigrant trout. Many hope that eventually State Fisheries Departments will see the wisdom of bolstering the bass population with hatchery-reared fish, not only because bass prefer water unsuitable for trout but also because they give excellent sport in their own right. Ask any New England anglers who, lathered with sweat, emerge from a gorge with a sugar bag full of prime bass. Another native fish worth attention in these tumultuous waters below the eastern falls is the pink-eyed mullet, which fights like a rainbow on light bait gear.

Enjoying New England fishing
All the usual amenities can be had at such centres as Armidale, the heart of New England and the best central location, and at Glen Innes, Walcha, Guyra, Inverell, Dorrigo and Tenterfield. For those who wish to concentrate on the spectacular eastern falls country, Dorrigo is ideal and Ebor even better if you have a tent or caravan. The town offices of the New England Tourist Board will give you useful information; in fact, the Armidale tourist booklet is full of facts and advice on the trout fishing.

Write to the secretaries of the local fishing clubs in advance and do them the courtesy of joining their clubs. Your aim, after all, is to catch fish that club members have liberated in their spare time. Moreover you can often get good advice from club members. Each town has its notable fishermen who are usually pleased to advise the visitor and, if he is lucky, go fishing with him. Sports-shop owners, of course, can help on the best lures and the more profitable water at the time. New England landowners are usually generous in giving permission to fishermen to enter their properties, but such permission should always be asked. When given, it is often coupled with excellent advice about the creek. Such points, like the elementary one of treating landowners' stock and property with care, derive from simple commonsense and decency, yet it is astonishing how often they are ignored by those few hooligans who can give all anglers a bad name.

If you are after big, rare, fish and more placid angling, focus on the western creeks and the Rockvale; if you want vigorous exercise, more consistent sport and communion with the wilderness, then haunt the eastern falls country. You will probably do best of all if you climb down into the gorges, but this is murderous country. Only go into them well-prepared with food and sleeping equipment and a companion, preferably a local. Among primaeval scrub and boulders as big as houses you need to be intelligently prepared for getting lost, injury and snakebite. (Snakes are plentiful throughout New England and you will often see them by the creeks. Leave well alone and do not adopt the attitude of one man I know who, when his spinner latched on to a big black snake in Jock's Water, tried to land it.)

If the trout just will not respond, there are many compensations. There are other types of fish, mentioned above, and there is grand country to explore for all interested in the bush. New England has a colourful local history and its relics such as the old gold-mining town of Hillgrove and the story of the famous bushranger, Captain Thunderbolt, can be studied on the spot. Then there are attractions in the region for the naturalist (three national parks, the New England, Dorrigo and Gilbraltar Range), the geologist, the fossicker and for city men who just want to get away from it all.

And given reasonable luck and application, a black gnat or small worm should be dropped one evening at the head of an amber New England pool to witness the buccaneering slash that characterizes the strike of the rainbow—see crimson, white and gold as he leaps and feel a rod buck and throb to a fighting fish.

DEREK WHITELOCK

Trout angling in New South Wales

As elsewhere on the Australian mainland, many of the trout streams in New South Wales are borderline waters in which trout may thrive and breed only when the climatic conditions are favourable and this happy state of affairs is never permanent. Good and bad seasons come in rather regular cycles of a few years' duration and in the borderline streams the droughts inevitably wipe out the progress made during the good years and revert trout acclimatization in those waters to somewhere near its starting point.

The policy on trout acclimatization generally accepted is that it is only worthwhile introducing them where they may thrive and maintain stocks by the process of natural breeding. Unfortunately, a great deal of the New South Wales terrain does not favour trout breeding. Cool, clear water running over gravel beds is a prime requisite and in this regard we are a long way behind New Zealand, where most of its fast-flowing streams emerge cool and clear from dense forest or are continuously fed from permanent snows or glaciers. Most of our high country has been heavily denuded of timber for grazing purposes and now many streams contain more silt than gravel. Fresh or flood results in water heavily charged with brown mud which penetrates the gravel to smother trout eggs or recently hatched young.

In the absence of suitable dense forests we have to look for our cool, clear streams in the granite-sands country of the highlands, where altitude ensures low temperatures and sand promotes clarity. Most of the high country is of granite sands, merely because granite is one of the most durable of rocks and during bygone ages it has not weathered away in these areas to the same extent as the surrounding formations which were of different compositions. The State is fortunate in having some good high-country trout streams and in the Monaro district some of these are fed from snowfields for a substantial part of the year.

But the big dams are the bulwark of trout angling in New South Wales. Before they were constructed, trout stocks mainly were the result of fingerlings released from hatcheries controlled by the acclimatization societies and as a consequence trout angling was somewhat regarded as the preserve of the fly fishermen. The dams gave a new aspect to trout stocking. Their great size presented bodies of water of sufficient bulk and depth to form thermoclynes (which see) and maintain lower layers of cool water to harbour trout in hot, dry periods. They formed reservoirs from which fish could emerge to stock the tributary streams when they were in good condition. If the brown trout could not run to spawn in the late autumn, the rainbows probably would in the early spring.

Thus the dams became self-supporting and bred stocks of fish which could be angled for by spinning, trolling from boats and baitfishing, as well as by use of the fly. In themselves, Hume, Burrinjuck, Chifley and Wyangala have provided a great deal of good sport over recent years. These four, of which Chifley is decidedly the smaller, are open to anglers throughout the year and may be fished from boats. In addition, when climatic conditions have been reasonable, during the general open season, they provide some good angling in the streams above them and for some distance in the runs of cool water below their walls.

Oberon Dam, only comparable in size with Chifley, is under different regulations. It is well stocked, particularly with brown trout, but may be fished only during the general open season and anglers are not permitted to use boats. The beautiful big Burrendong Dam has good stocks of English perch and native fishes and fortunately, no carp. The Clarence Dam, Lake Lyell Dam and Wallerawang — all three near Lithgow — offer good trout fishing in season.

With the establishment of self-supporting stocks of trout in the dams and the better highland rivers the main purpose of the hatcheries has been to restock borderline streams and assist in research. The two main hatcheries, the Gaden, on the Thredbo, near Jindabyne, and the Dutton, on the Serpentine, near Ebor, were taken over by the New South Wales Fisheries Department. Attempts made to acclimatize Atlantic salmon in Burrinjuck Dam failed, apparently because the introduced

The big dams, such as Wyangala, play an important part in New South Wales' trout fishery, being large enough to maintain self-supporting trout stocks.

strain were a sea-run variety, but an odd Atlantic salmon still turns up at places like Jindabyne.

The greatest boost to trout angling in New South Wales was provided by the Snowy Mountains Hydro-electric Scheme (which see). Lake Eucumbene (which see) has had some marvellous years despite occasional falling-off in the numbers caught and average sizes, in accordance with the usual course of events following the establishment of such big dams. Allowing for this, it still provides satisfying angling at peak periods. And it is open to anglers all the year through.

After the major drought broke early in 1974 Lake Eucumbene filled to within 6 to 8 m of its capacity and this brought the fish with it. Good fishing has continued and the wide range of facilities at reasonable prices attract thousands of anglers annually, most of them catching two rainbow trout to one brown trout. Vigilant inspectors intensified their war against poachers using scoop nets at night in places like Swampy Creek and Gang Gang Creek and 1985 proved a boom year. The big dam at Blowering, with road access to 75 per cent of the wall, has proved a fishing bonanza, with rainbow and brown trout, Murray cod, redfin and yellowbelly up to 4.5 kg frequently taken in large numbers. So far no carp have penetrated Blowering Dam, which is frequently restocked with surplus fry from the Snowy Mountains trout hatchery, a commercial venture at the base of the dam. Five hours drive from Sydney, Blowering offers splendid fishing in a wide choice of scenic settings.

New South Wales is rich in what may be regarded as permanent trout waters, but drought is still a bugbear. The prime purpose of the dams is conservation of water for irrigation purposes and for generation of hydro-electric power, rather than the provision of trout. It is in the nature of things that the demand always will be equal to the supply and that in periods of drought it will exceed it. The exceptionally dry periods experienced in the 1960s and 1980s set the trout population back badly indeed. The Hume, Burrinjuck and Wyangala dams were drained down to a fraction of their capacity, with consequent great fish mortality. They have now all recovered from this setback. Wyangala offers trout as well as native fishing.

Even Lake Eucumbene suffered from the dry spell. As a result of the great demand for water it was emptied down to its lowest levels since it first filled. This had some adverse effect on the angling, but surprisingly not so much as the big influx of cold snow waters consequent upon the extra heavy falls during the winter of 1968. During the following summer the fishing was extraordinarily poor for Eucumbene and there was little activity on the part of trout until April 1969. It may be a long time before such a sustained dry period is experienced again over practically all the State but, nevertheless, it seems evident that big setbacks will continue at fairly regular cyclic intervals. The droughts of the early 1980s were not as severe as in 1969, but were still damaging to fishing.

The New South Wales trout streams are spread over a wide area and it is not possible to evaluate all of them herein. They may be roughly divided into the following districts: New England, Barrington Tops, Western, South-western and Southern.

New England is treated as a separate entry herein (*which see*). The Barrington Tops area is not extensive, a lot of it is served by rough roads and it is of more interest to local inhabitants than anglers in general. Erection of a road from Nowendoc to Wingham has made access a lot easier and some very good fishing for trout of moderate size may be had in streams such as Wild Cattle Creek, Barnard, Nowendoc or Pigna Barney.

The Western District includes the Oberon, Chifley, Wyangala and Burrendong dams, with their tributaries and run-offs. Below Oberon the little Duckmaloi and Fish Rivers suffer from successive droughts. Above and below Chifley the Campbell River fishes well. The Lachlan River, below the dam wall at Wyangala, usually provides sport all the way down to Cowra.

Some big trout are taken in the few kilometres immediately below the dam every year, but mostly the fishing is best there early in the season. Above the dam, the Lachlan and Abercrombie Rivers and tributaries such as Grove Creek show good spawning runs from the reservoir and fish well when conditions are good. Above the range of boats on the dam they are not fished very heavily owing to lack of access other than over rough roads through private property. Some anglers who know the country do well up in the region of Tuena, Bigga and Reid's Flat.

Out at Orange, trout angling is restricted to fly fishing only. A few nice trout always could be found in Lake Canobolas, Molong Creek and the headwaters of the Bell River. Consequent upon some irresponsible persons introducing redfin, a lot of these waters had to be poisoned and a fresh start made at stocking with trout. Angling in this area received a big boost with the construction of a new dam on the Belubela River, near Blayney, known as Carcoar Dam, which with redfin and trout is now comparable with Chifley.

The South-western District includes the headwaters of the Lachlan River in the Crookwell area. Here, small streams such as the Crookwell, Little and Isabella Rivers and Grabben Gullen and Wheo Creeks have been of more interest to local people than to anglers in general but with the recent increase in the capacity of Wyangala Dam there are signs that trout are becoming more plentiful. Better fishing is to be found in and adjacent to the Australian Capital Territory (*which see*), around Canberra.

The best angling in that region usually is to be found in the streams associated with Burrinjuck Dam. The spawning runs in the Goodradigbee and above Wee Jasper attract anglers from both New South Wales and Victoria. Access may be had to the river at the old hut just beyond Wee Jasper Creek at the suspension bridge and again at about 7 km above the village, below the beautiful camping ground on Micalong Creek. From there the river may be followed up some 8 km to its junction with Limestone Creek, where many big trout have been taken in the past. A higher reach of the Goodradigbee also is accessible at Brindabella, 55 km out from Canberra.

Some good fishing is to be had in the Murrumbidgee below the dam, though angling immediately below the wall is prohibited. Above the dam, at and beyond the big Taemas Bridge, the river is sluggish and the water is backed up for a long way. This section is fished more for cod, silver perch and Macquarie perch than trout. Farther up it is joined by the Yass River and this stream at times fishes very well.

At Albury, on the Victorian border, good angling may be had in the Murray River, below the Hume Dam, where big trout are taken along with redfin. The reaches of the Murray above the dam are accessible through Wymah, Talmalmo, Jingellic and Walerengang.

New South Wales inland rivers

One of the most important of the Australian fisheries is that provided by the native warm-water species of the inland rivers. It mainly is confined to the waters of the very extensive Murray-Darling basin, where over a huge area it provides sport, recreation and an occasional change of diet for the country people.

Of late years there has been a tendency to decry the Murray cod, yellowbelly, silver perch (black bream), Macquarie perch and eel-tail catfish (jewfish) as sporting fish. Since their habitat is in sluggish streams and big waterholes they cannot be expected to show the speed and dash of some of the fast-water fish. But it mainly is a matter of selection of tackle and angling methods. They mostly are fished for with natural bait on set lines and heavy handlines and a fish hooked in the gut or gills on such tackle puts up a very poor fight. Caught in similar circumstances, even a trout could not be expected to offer very exciting resistance.

In reality, a big cod hooked on a line in a snaggy bend of a river with steep banks of greasy mud can be difficult enough and sufficiently exciting for anyone. The yellowbelly, silver perch and Macquarie perch dash about and offer vigorous resistance when caught on a spinner or hooked in the mouth on light tackle. Fishing for inland fish demands as much knowledge of the habits and peculiarities of species and technical know-how, as almost any other form of angling. And if elusiveness is one of the attributes of a sporting fish, then there are times when they qualify in no uncertain manner.

In the early days of settlement the supply of native fish in the inland rivers at most times was prolific, although records and accounts leave no doubt that there were good and bad breeding seasons and lean as well as lush periods. For many years they sustained heavy pressure of fishing by amateurs with set lines and commercial fishermen with crosslines and drum nets. In those days one of the great features of this fishery was the remarkable ability of the native species to breed and renew their population after a setback from a prolonged dry period. One of the tragedies of angling in Australia has been man's alteration of water conditions in a major portion of the Murray-Darling system to such extent that these fish now are inhibited from breeding in it.

This is part of the price that has been paid for introduction of water conservation and development of the big irrigation areas. The big dams, such as the Hume on the Murray, Burrinjuck on the Murrumbidgee and Wyangala on the Lachlan, have greatly altered the water conditions in the rivers below them. In previous times in dry seasons they used to degenerate to a minimal flow and become, more or less, chains of waterholes which warmed up under the summer sun. Nowadays they are kept flowing at volume with cold water released from bulk storage at the dams.

The big dams have gone a long way in mitigating the floods

The extensive inland river system of the Murray-Darling basin is an important region for native warm-water species such as the Murray cod. Many anglers enjoy the calm of sluggish streams and waterholes.

which once used to occur in frequent cycles. Then the rivers would overflow their banks and the water would spread shallowly for miles over the plains, where it would be warmed under the rays of the sun. The floods filled the lagoons, swamps and big waterholes in the creeks and billabongs, leaving ample bodies of warm water where the fish could breed and the young thrive until the next flood came along to wash them out into the rivers. This kind of breeding still goes on prolifically in the Queensland and north-western New South Wales sections of the basin, but seems to have been greatly inhibited in the Riverina.

In the early stages of research at the Insland Fisheries Research Station at Narrandera, then under the direction of biologist-in-charge John Lake, it was established that after a period of ripening in a pond Murray cod could be induced to spawn when there was a rise in water level and the temperature rose from 17 to 21 degrees C. In a similar manner it was shown that yellowbelly could be induced to spawn when there was an influx of warm water to raise the temperature to not less than 24.6 degrees C. Silver perch were found to spawn after a slight rise in river or pond levels providing the temperature of water in the shallows was not less than 24 degrees C. Eel-tail catfish build a nest of gravel in a pond or river where there is a very moderate current. The fertilized eggs sink into the gravel of the nest and at Narrandera it was found that they hatched out in about seven days at water temperatures from 20 to 26 degrees C.

All these native inland species are particularly sensitive to temperature and water level variations. If suitable conditions do not present themselves they absorb their roe and there is no spawning. Even the catfish are critically affected by variation in water level. If a nest which they are building becomes exposed, even for a short period or if it merely appears to be in danger of becoming exposed, the pair will abandon it and go off to build elsewhere. Frequent variations may send them from spot to spot until they become discouraged and the female absorbs her roe. It appears that the frequent rise and fall in river levels incumbent on regulating and supplying water for irrigation purposes also works to deny the young fish some of the foods essential to their development.

At an early stage the young of the cod are largely dependent upon the young of the little western carp gudgeon for food. The female deposits her eggs on reeds and aquatic plants at the edge of the shallows, where under suitable conditions they hatch within 48 hours. During this time the male fish aggressively guards the eggs from small predatory water-creatures and shrimps which may be larger than himself. He may even stand on end in the water to direct a stream over them if he thinks it is needed. If there is a rise and cold water invades the shallows there is no hatch. If the level falls and the eggs are exposed and dry out they will be killed. Either way there is no hatch and the young cod miss out on an essential food.

Another big factor in limiting fish population has been the series of weirs on the rivers to regulate the water and distribute it to where it is required. These to a large extent have been bars to the movement of fish along the rivers and may be a big factor in preventing them from coming in from outside areas where they still breed freely.

As the result of all this stocks of native fish in the Riverina streams have dwindled sadly. For instance, catfish no longer are found in the Murrumbidgee above Wagga and both they and the yellowbelly are mighty scarce in the Murray above Corowa. Where large cod used to be commonplace in the lower reaches of these rivers, nowadays the capture of one is of such note that it usually figures in the local newspapers.

As the result of all this the bulwark of good fishing in inland New South Wales has shifted north to the Darling-Barwon River and its main tributaries between Wilcannia and Mungindi. The main tributaries with permanent flow are the Macquarie, Namoi, Gwydir and Severn. A big factor in populating these are the big fish nurseries to be found in the intermittently flowing rivers coming down over great distances from the dry country in central Queensland. They run only after heavy rains and during the major part of the year they are virtually chains of waterholes, several kilometres long, which heat up under the summer sun. Here the native fish breed prolifically and usually it is difficult to get a bait through the young to one of useful size. When these waterways run in their periodical floods most of the young fish are swept out into the main river and the waterholes left filled for the triggering off of the next spawning.

The extent of these fish nurseries is little realized. The Moonie comes down to enter the Barwon below Mungindi. Out from Walgett, through Lightning Ridge and its opal fields, one comes upon the Narran, which runs down into Lake Narran and this, in turn, empties out into the main river above Brewarrina. Just beyond Goodooga one comes upon the Bokhara, Ballandool and Culgoa Rivers, which join the Barwon below Brewarrina. Across the Mitchell Highway, beyond Enngonia, is the Warrego, which empties into the Darling about 32 km above Louth. And yet further west, coming in through the Queensland border at Hungerford, is the fantastically long Paroo, which runs away down past Wanaaring and through 96 km of swamps in the Paroo channel before joining the Darling at Wilcannia. All these represent some thousands of kilometres of rivers and creeks which are practically chains of waterholes raising fish and fish food under a hot sun.

These prolific breeding waters may be of great importance in the future. So far, the Darling-Barwon section has been free from the curse of altered water conditions which have bedevilled the Riverina. Keepit Dam, on the Namoi, is relatively small, is at low altitude and mostly has been well below capacity. Most of the water it releases is drawn off to meet the needs of the cotton growers around Wee Waa. Over the years it has been operating it would seem that the fishing in the river has improved rather than deteriorated.

In the past decade, conditions have changed rapidly. The really big dam on the Macquarie, at Burrendong, is now providing good fishing for English perch and natives, and contains a few yellowbelly. One of the largest dams in the State, at Copeton, has improved fishing on the Gwydir quite dramatically and provides good fishing for trout, cod, yellowbelly and perch.

Anglers fear that in due course the big flows of colder water and the constantly fluctuating levels may have the same effect on the Darling-Barwon and its tributaries as has been experienced in the south. Bearing in mind the probable periodical influxes of young fish from the dry-country waterways out to the north-west, the greatest handicap may be the weirs required to control and distribute the water in these rivers. If they should prove to work anything like the existing one on the Darling, at Bourke, they most certainly would bar the fish from migrating up the streams, as apparently they have been doing from time immemorial. The inland anglers are anxiously awaiting the result of future developmental work affecting the state of the rivers.

The Menindee Lakes present a gratifying example of where water conservation has reacted to the advantage of the inland anglers. These fill with warm water from the surrounding country and from overflows through anabranches of the Darling River. They are now the chief recreation grounds of the people of Broken Hill and anglers make catches of big cod, yellowbelly and other inland species.

Fishing regulations in New South Wales

All fishermen over 16 years of age must secure a licence to fish in fresh water in New South Wales. This costs $10 for 12 months from the date of issue in 1985 but a five-day licence was also available for $5. None of the fish caught by holders of these licences can be sold. Trout fishermen are restricted to one hand-held rod and line, bass fishermen to one rod or handline with no more than two hooks attached, and those fishing for other species to one rod or handline with no more than two hooks attached, or no more than four set lines. Trout bait must consist of natural flies or insects or the larvae thereof, or worms, frogs, shrimps, yabbies, mussels or artificial flies and lures. No restrictions on the type of bait apply to other inland species. Closed seasons on Lake Eucumbene are detailed earlier in this article; they apply at specified dates on other waters. A bag limit of 10 fish per day applies to trout, Atlantic salmon and bass on all inland waters except Lake Canobolas, where the bag limit is five. No licence is required to fish in salt water.

Minimum legal lengths in New South Wales

Any person found in possession of a fish below the minimum legal length is liable to a fine up to $500. Where the number caught represents only a small proportion of the population no minimum legal length is prescribed. All the principal fish species in New South Wales are under constant review.

Abalone	10.8 cm	Morwong, Red (Sea Carp)	25 cm
Blackfish, Rock (Drummer)	25 cm	Morwong, Rubberlip	28 cm
Bream, Black	25 cm	Mullet, Sea (including "Bully")	30 cm
Bream, Yellowfin	25 cm	Mulloway (Jewfish)	38 cm
Cod, Black Rock	33 cm	Shark, School	91 cm
Flathead, Common or Dusky	33 cm	Snapper	28 cm
		Tarwhine	20 cm
Flathead, Sand	33 cm	Teraglin	38 cm
Flathead, Tiger	33 cm	Whiting, Sand (Silver)	27 cm
Luderick (Blackfish)	25 cm	Whiting, School (Red-spotted)	20 cm
Morwong (Jackass Fish)	28 cm		

Minimum legal lengths of crustaceans

Fishes are measured overall under New South Wales regulations—from the point of the snout to the end of the tail. But crabs are measured along the body from the notch between the protruding frontal teeth to the centre of the posterior margin of the carapace or shell. Rock lobsters (crayfish) are measured along the length of the carapace or head, along a straight line from the point of the union of the second antennae to the centre of the posterior margin of the carapace or head, ignoring any hairs.

Crab, Blue Swimmer	6 cm	Rock Lobster (Crayfish), Eastern or Common	10.4 cm
Crab, Mud, Black or Mangrove	8.5 cm	Rock Lobster (Crayfish), Southern	11 cm

Bag limits for salt water
Amateur fishermen are restricted to the following bag limits in the marine waters of New South Wales:

Abalone   15 per person per day
Groper, Blue, Brown, Red   2 per person per day by rod or handline only
Morwong, Red   5 per person per day
Rock Lobster (Crayfish)   5 per person per day by lobster pot, trap or by hand

Prohibited species in New South Wales
The taking of the following species is totally prohibited from New South Wales tidal waters: black cod, *Epinephelus daemelii*; giant Queensland groper, *Promicrops lanceolatus*; estuary cod, *Ephinephelus tauvinia*; blue devil fish, *Paraplesiops bleekeri*; and elegant wrasse, *Anampses elegans*.

Angling methods
Angling for big cod usually is a waiting game and most are taken on set lines. Fishing mainly is done in the big snaggy holes by day and at the bottom of the runs at night. Yellowbelly tend to bite best in the deeper water at the bottom of the runs and silver perch in the current of the runs. Cod and yellowbelly often are found in the deeper backwaters and eddies, while catfish are distributed along the quiet bottoms.

The favoured baits for large cod are big yabbies (freshwater crayfish), small carp, bony bream or redfin, oak or kurrajong grubs, cormorant gut or galah. For smaller cod, yellowbelly and silver perch: yabbies, wood grubs, witchetty grubs, big milky blacksoil-plains worms, shrimps, frogs or river mussels. Yellowbelly often take freshwater shrimps or frogs when declining other lures. Silver perch and Macquarie perch prefer wriggling garden worms, live shrimps and black crickets. Catfish are taken almost solely on worms.

Shrimps are taken in traps made from sugar bags supported by wire hoops or kerosene tins punctured with numerous holes, baited with a sheep's head, meat or a cake of plain soap. Wood grubs are taken from infected oak trees (casuarinas) or split from fallen kurrajong logs. Witchetty grubs are obtained by shovelling the surface dirt off under the gum trees on the river flats and using a fine wire, corkscrew-like implement to extract them from their holes. Frogs are sought beneath logs and debris, beneath loose bark on the river gums and by pouring copious supplies of water into the big cracks in the dry mud along the river banks. Mussels are found in the underwater mud of the river bed. Bony bream are netted from the farm dams and artesian bore drains (*See Crayfish; Yabbies.*)

Cod, yellowbelly, silver perch and Macquarie perch may be taken on spinners and other artificial lures, but unfortunately they do not strike at them as readily as the bass of the eastern watershed and the inland rivers usually are so discoloured that the fish have a limited range of vision. The two species of perch may take small lures such as the imp spoon, celta spinner, wonder wobbler, voblex or streamer fly, usually worked in the narrow, deep runs.

Yellowbelly are taken on the small and moderate sizes of the flopy, Heddon river runt, aniseed prawn, Canadian wiggler, imp spoon, reb 2 No. 250, flatfish and others, all worked deep, near the bottom. Big cod are taken by trolling along the bottom behind boats with large lures such as the big flopy, flatfish No. 600, reb 2 deep runner No. 3000, big aeroplane spinners. Some provision should be made for getting snagged lures off logs or roots, either in the form of a long rangoon pole with split ring or spiral attachment, or a weight with similar attachment on a strong line.

Warm-water fisheries research

With the realization that fish stocks had deteriorated sadly in the Riverina, anglers and the New South Wales Fisheries Department began to perceive that there was need for investigation with a view to corrective or remedial measures. A biologist and assistants were allocated to the work and the Inland Fisheries Research Station was erected at Narrandera and officially opened in February 1962. An inland licence system—$10 per year in 1986—was to form the basis of the Inland Fisheries Development Fund which, assisted originally by a $60,000 interest-free advance from the State Treasury, was to make this first important research possible and, according to an official pronouncement, enable the department's scientists to begin searching for ways to improve fish stocks and provide better angling and bigger catches for sportsmen.

Over the three years following the opening of the Station a great deal of important work was done in determining the natural history of the native species. But, as far as anglers and the general public can tell, since then it has often bogged down.

Today, more than ever, there is urgent need for research in the inland rivers and a lot of it should be directed to the Darling-Barwon section with a view to averting damage to the fishery before it occurs, wherever that may be possible. But it needs to be researched with a firm purpose—carried out to an objective plan, with periodic checks on progress and with emphasis on practical application towards achieving the desired aims.

Introduced species in New South Wales
In the inland rivers most of the introduced species have been regarded as a curse, rather than a blessing. The three species of carp, goldfish, crucian and European or Bavarian in one form or another are widespread throughout the inland rivers and dams. They show little tendency to dominate the habitat in the running streams and big dams, but their habit of rooting in the bottom mud to sift it and search out digestible food muddies the water and destroys a lot of the bottom vegetation. Doubtless, they do disturb and eat some of the roe of native species. They are plentiful in some waters but provide little sport and are not generally fancied for eating.

The English perch or redfin is now widely distributed throughout all the rivers of south-western New South Wales. The extent to which it militates against the breeding of the native species has never been determined. No doubt it devours some of the roe and some of the young, but on the other hand its young are eaten by the cod. Its chief menace is that it breeds prolifically and eats up much of the available fish food. It does best in swamps and other large enclosed waters, often multiplying to the stage where the population outgrows the food supply and the average weight deteriorates.

It is important that it should not get into those northern waters which are still free of it, or into our good trout dams and streams. It is an offence to remove it from its habitat to other waters, but unfortunately there are those foolish, irresponsible people who will introduce it where it is least desirable. In this way it got into Lake Burley Griffin, at Canberra, from whence it must ultimately get into the Upper Murrumbidgee and Burrinjuck Dam. In similar manner it was introduced into the trout habitat at Orange and established in the Beardy at Glen Innes. And now, from the finding of dead specimens, it is feared that it has been introduced into Glenbawn Dam, on the Hunter River.

The English perch has provided a good deal of interesting angling in Lake George, a landlocked body of water from which it could not easily spread (see A.C.T.). It also provides a lot of angling in the Riverina, particularly in the big irrigation channels. But it cannot be classed as a high-grade sporting fish. It fights quite well when hooked on a spinner, but it only takes spinners freely on occasions and in the rivers these mostly are rare occasions. It has a poor, fiddling bite, is almost incapable of removing a bait from a hook, usually gets hooked deep in the gullet or gills and then pulls in with little struggle. It is only fair as a food fish and is best cooked as skinned fillets (see Perch, English).

Tench are slowly spreading in the Riverina and now occur extensively in the more sluggish parts of the Murray, Murrumbidgee and Lachlan Rivers, as well as in some swamps, dams and lagoons. They prefer a habitat where there is good growth of weed and their feeding habit of burrowing in the bottom muddies the water in which they live. In the past few years they have spread from Balranald up the Murrumbidgee to well above Narrandera and it looks as if ultimately they may fill the habitat formerly occupied by the English perch.

The tench is not a particularly good sporting fish and mainly is taken by fishing worms on the bottom. In shallow swamps they have been taken by muddying up the water to cause them to stand on their heads with their tails at the surface. Their flesh is white and of fair flavour but carries a lot of small bones (see Tench).

It is interesting to note that according to the findings of biologist John Lake the introduced species may begin to spawn at the following temperatures: redfin 12 degrees C, tench 16 degrees C, goldfish carp 15 degrees C and European carp 18 degrees C. Compare these with yellowbelly 23.5 degrees C, silver perch 23 degrees C and cod 20.5 degrees C, and we have a clue as to why the introduced species thrive in the altered water conditions in the Riverina while the native species now do not.

NORTHERN Territory

Despite its small population, the Northern Territory is an important fishing State with considerable potential for future growth. It differs from Queensland and tropical Western Australia in the relative populations of different fish. About 1800 km of its extensive coastline is largely inaccessible, locked up either in the Aboriginal sector (Arnhem Land and other tribal lands) or by sheer remoteness in the north-west coast.

The fishing picture is dominated by barramundi, which are now recognized for their economic role as a tourist resource. On a per head basis, amateur fishing pressures are only light. By contrast, Queensland is extremely decentralized and has a population about thirty times as large. One tropical city alone, Townsville, is twice the size of Darwin, while Cairns is about the same size.

The reason for the dominance of barramundi as a species contrasts with the picture along the coast of east Queensland, where to catch a barramundi or two in a day's fishing is really something to celebrate. The average angler in Queensland catches a higher proportion of mangrove jacks, estuary cod and other species. However, records show that barramundi on the east Queensland coast were originally dominant to the same extent as they currently are in the Northern Territory. If they are heavily fished, other species on which the barra normally preys have an easier time.

Most fishermen visit the Territory in pursuit of barramundi. Many are surprised to find the fishing more tightly controlled than they expected. The days of unrestricted open slather are long gone. Darwin is no longer a frontier town, but a sophisticated and well-run city.

Changes in attitude hinge on issues such as Aboriginal land

Barramundi, an exciting game fish, dominate as a species in the Northern Territory. This large female was caught in the Daly River.

rights, proclamation of National Parks, development of mining communities, and increased knowledge of fisheries management.

Amongst the changes are vastly improved access roads and highways. Twenty years ago, we floundered and fought our way through bulldust and boulders to reach the East Alligator. Today we drive out on a bitumen highway and camp where we are told. Fortunately, the fish are still there—especially early in the dry season.

Victoria River

The "Crossing" at Timber Creek, site of many pioneer adventures, is the upper limit of tidal influence. Rock bars and stony shallows provide shelter for an abundance of big prawns and baitfish, the most visible indicator of which is probably the popeye mullet. This is crocodile country, and no risks should be taken night or day. The safest way to gather live bait is undoubtedly by using a cast net, with which there is no need to enter the water. Otherwise, most anglers use lures.

Because of the extreme tidal range, it is possible to travel some distance down-river on a tide. A small boat here multiplies the fishing options, both above and below the Crossing. However, distances and times must be watched. It is a good idea to watch the timing of tidal movement for a day or two before attempting to use it.

Most of the Victoria here is fairly shallow so there is little need for deep-diving lures. Most of the action in recent times has centred around floating-diving lures and (when the water is clearer) on Vibrotails. Night fishing is also possible, using mainly surface lures with a strong action.

Daly River The Daly maintains a permanent flow right through the dry season, and can be canoed or drifted in a light punt from as far up as the town of Katherine. It is one of the most beautiful of Territory rivers, clear and natural for most of its length. Freshwater reaches provide a larger proportion of sooty grunter and forktail catfish, with barramundi increasing in numbers in the lower freshwater and tidal freshwater reaches (below Daly River Crossing).

The Crossing is a man-made barrier to the tidal rise and fall, and formerly was a regular hotspot for barra fishermen. However, the emphasis has shifted in recent years to trolling further downriver, a method so successful that it has become the choice of top local fishermen, such as the big-barra specialist Col Cordingley. It follows that small boats are the usual practice, and in fact there are few locations where boats are not used.

The Daly is a large river, and the tidal range pushes substantial fronts of muddy water upstream on a rising tide. Those trolling the tidal reaches usually study the water clarity with care, and use strong-action minnow lures. Some of the specialists favour extremely light line, which allows the lure to troll more deeply and with a free action.

Upstream from the Crossing, the river passes through rapids and rock bars, over weedbeds and under overhanging tea-tree and pandanus in a series of fish-rich pools.

One unique and useful inhabitant of this and the other Territory rivers is the giant prawn *Macrobrachium* spp, which can be located in the shallows at night with the aid of a strong torch. These make a top live bait and are so large that they are also eaten with relish by anglers. Prawns with a body length of 25 cm are common.

Although the Crossing itself can still provide barramundi on a rising tide, the best results come from ventures further downriver.

Darwin Harbour The pellucid tranquillity of Darwin Harbour, for all its appeal to anglers, can become dangerous at short notice. The tidal range is high, and fast rips can provide problems if the flow is against the wind. All tropical waters deserve respect in this regard.

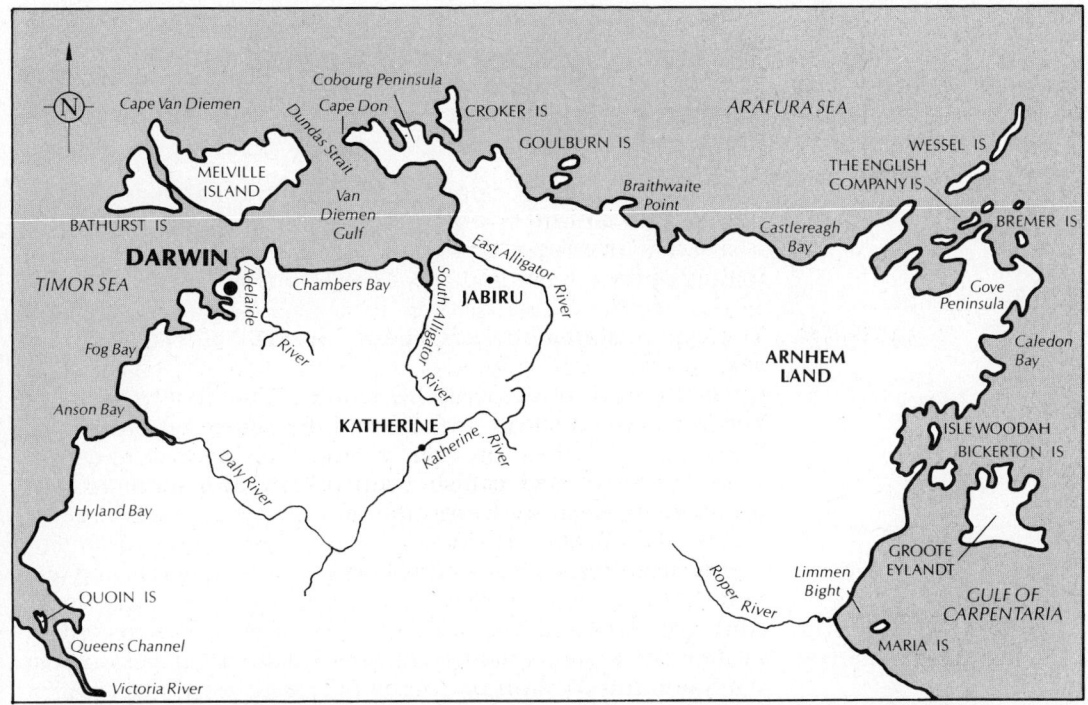

Darwin is very much a boating city, and the locals make full use of their wonderful harbour, especially on weekends. There can be occasional good results from spinning spots off the rocks around the Harbour, usually for queenfish and sometimes barramundi. Pikey bream are also freely available to anglers close to the rocks.

Boats remain the favoured way to reach major hotspots. A good echo sounder and land bearings can locate rough reef or sometimes a wreck (mostly from the cyclone or the war against the Japanese), over which a heavy handline and fresh or live bait will produce the fabulous black mulloway.

Queenfish are often easy to locate, feeding on bait under flocks of sea birds or causing bait to explode through the surface. Because the fish are often wary of approaching boats, it may be necessary to stop 50 m clear of the action and cast metal lures—Halco sliced lures and the like—past the school of bait, allowing the lure to sink well down and then retrieving it below the school.

Excellent creek and mangrove fishing can be had up the East Arm of the Harbour or by venturing a few kilometres further up Haycock Reach. The mangroves provide barramundi, golden snapper, mangrove jacks, estuary cod and javelin fish. Top period is the turn of the low tide for lure fishermen, with a switch to fresh or live bait fishing as the tide starts running. Species such as trevally and barracuda are likely at any time, running mostly with the tides.

Although much of the Northern Territory is inaccessible, the potential for fishing is enormous. Darwin is the centre for air and boat charter to island fishing camps and rivers such as the Daly, South Alligator, East Alligator and Roper.

Both Darwin Harbour and the nearby Adelaide River provide venues for crabbing. Mud crabs are a popular and regular fare with Darwin locals, and visitors may be lucky enough to organize a trip with locals either working crabs with a steel 'hook' at low tide or working crab traps.

The tourist industry has expanded to a very sophisticated level and Darwin is now the central point from which air charters to various fishing points are as common as charter boats. The Tourist Bureau can offer a tremendous range of fishing access, including the provision of professional barramundi guides. Sport fishing is available in several island camps, including the Aboriginal reserves of Bathurst and Melville Islands.

The level of fishing action is much wider than formerly, and excellent sports stores are able to offer advice on everything from fly fishing to blue-water. An increasing number of sportsmen are taking fly tackle north—and amongst the results have been items like milkfish on fly, queenfish on fly, barramundi—and Darwin is a comfortable and convenient centre from which to launch exploration.

Wildman and Mary Rivers

After the Adelaide, these two rivers provide an interlocked system of lagoons for barramundi fishermen. The most famous of these, the Corroboree Billabong, now is accessible by good road from the bitumen highway, and is the central point for a lot of barra fishermen. The standard method is by trolling from punts or small aluminium boats.

The extent of the change in Territory fishing is shown by the sheer number of boats now seen. It is not rare for over a hundred boats to be fishing Corroboree on a holiday weekend. Although traffic jams are possible, there are enough other lagoons available to ensure that good fishing is still the rule, especially for those who have obtained permission from landholders. Bird life is still prolific, but buffalo are now under tight control and fewer of them are seen.

Professional safaris fly and drive to a number of air strips, typical of which is the Wimray safari operation on the Mary. Accommodation is available at a number of these locations, and fishing is but one of the options available. Wildlife tours, photography, bird-watching and fishing now attract a strong market of tourists, at least through the dry season (May to November.)

The fishing in this area differs from that further west in that the flood-plain lagoons also contain saratoga, the rare and beautiful sportfish which attracts those looking for something completely different. It will take live baits, flies, lures and surface poppers, and is mostly found in the thick tangles of pandanus which shelter the edges of the lagoons.

In recent years, the introduced mimosa plant has gone wild along the edges of many Territory waterways. These tough and thorny shrubs are tall and have no natural enemies.

Water buffalo have adversely affected Northern Territory fishing as they muddy the water and destroy lily pads and foliage. Their numbers are now under stricter control.

Consequently, access has often been made difficult for fishermen. The extent and pattern of mimosa spread is specially clear from the air. Each wet season sees a further expansion of the plant, a problem which is of major concern to the Territory's primary industry authorities as well as the tourist trade.

As with all the lagoons from here east to Arnhem Land (East Alligator), lure trolling is the method most used, providing special value for visitors with less local knowledge. Crocodiles are still present in small numbers but sometimes in real size, and caution is always necessary.

South Alligator and East Alligator Rivers

These famous rivers of the Territory's coastal flood plain have felt the impact of mining development, through the uranium province centred around the new mining town of Jabiluka. Population growth and development have had to be balanced with Aboriginal ownership and the need for national parks. Because of these pressures, visitors find that fishing is becoming increasingly controlled. National parks officers and wildlife rangers are relatively numerous, and access to the various areas should be pre-checked in Darwin as well as with rangers on arrival, say within the bounds of Kakadu National Park.

The East Alligator forms the western boundary of Arnhem Land, and the causeway at Cahill's Crossing marks the normal limit of fishing access. A permit is required to visit the community at Oenpelli. Most tourists fish around the Crossing, upstream or down depending on the height of the tides and the corresponding muddiness of the water. Primary fishing is for barramundi, though forktail catfish are common and river sharks are often seen at the Crossing. Those fishing dead baits may also encounter saw sharks, shovelnose sharks and various forms of stingray in the tidal water.

The clarity of the water varies largely, in tune with the height and speed of the tides. On neap tides it is sometimes possible to find water downstream clear enough for lure fishing, and the locals always watch for signs of clear water—especially around the early months of the dry season when fishing is at its best. The prime barra fishing months have altered since the fishing pressure increased so greatly: fishermen try to get out as early as possible, and it is not unusual for some to be in action around April and May if seasonal conditions allow access. Lagoons adjacent to the Alligator River systems also provide good early season fishing, mostly for trollers. As well as barra, the catch includes saratoga (not a good table fish, and mostly put back), plus catfish, freshwater longtoms and archer fish.

On the South Alligator, a steady tourist industry has developed around the hotel/motel at Cooinda, in the vicinity of what was formerly the Jim Jim Crossing.

The Daly River crossing, like other such river crossings in the Territory, is a prime fishing site.

McArthur River

Things have changed on the McArthur, not so much through development as through the increase in the number and popularity of four-wheel drives. There has not been any aggressive tourist development here and the area remains best suited to those independent and self-sufficient souls prepared to explore off their own bat. The freshwater upstream reaches of the McArthur include areas of great scenic appeal and all the usual freshwater fish of the tropics. Downstream, one needs a small boat for best results in the mangrove estuaries inside the Sir Edward Pellew Group of islands.

The mining development once expected has not eventuated. Fishermen who have explored the area and some of the adjacent coastal creeks have discovered wonderful barramundi in the clearer tidal waters, but access is by courtesy of local cattlemen and landholders. The use of a cartop boat is strongly advised. The area cannot be rated as safe tourist country, as the remoteness and lack of facilities raise costs to unrealistic levels.

Roper River

This is a clear and beautiful small river on the southern boundary of Arnhem Land, with relatively scarce sites for camping at the rock crossing near the Roper Bar police station.

The rock wall provides a barrier below which about 20 km of fresh water rises and falls with the tides from the Gulf. For the exploring angler, it is possible to travel in an outboard boat downstream as far as the junction with the Wilton River, which comes in from the northern side.

Arnhem Land is closed to visitors without permits, and visitors are advised against unauthorized travel downstream to the Roper River Aboriginal community. While fishing is excellent, the limits within which it may be done are sharply drawn owing to the proximity of the Aboriginal lands. Legal limits may be checked first in Darwin and then on the spot at the police station.

One useful suggestion. Over recent years, several 4WD parties from Newcastle and Sydney have enjoyed wonderful fishing results from cartop boats taken to the Towns River and Limmen Bight after hiring an Aboriginal guide. This is still country for explorer-fishermen!

Tackle for Northern Territory fishing

Advances in the last decade have been so great that almost all tackle is now used and accepted in different areas in the Top End. The common method for barra fishing is trolling behind a small outboard boat, using minnow lures by Rapala, Nilsmaster, Golden Eye. Occasionally the traveller will notice areas tailor-made for casting, so the obvious choice is a single-handed rod (either baitcaster or spin reel) fitted with a reel of good quality such as Shimano, Daiwa, ABU, Mitchell or Shakespeare, and line from 6 to 10 kg test. Some sportfishermen use lighter lines with great success, but this practice is best suited to those with experience in fine-line fishing.

Increased expertise has made a difference to the quantity and variety of catches. Many Territory anglers go looking for species other than barramundi, and the shift towards threadfin salmon, queenfish, mackerel, snapper (actually a misnomer—the 'golden snapper' is a regional name for the large-scaled sea perch of the Lutjanid family), mangrove jack, estuary cod and the abundant trevallies is gathering force. Bait fishing for the black mulloway of Darwin Harbour and other locales calls for heavy lines, and it can make sense for the traveller to include a large handspool and some 30 kg line. Many locals use heavier.

Most lures are saltwater quality, using hooks of 2X strength or heavier. The quality of local sports stores today is a far cry from the distant past, and advice and information on tackle choice is freely given. It will be found that certain areas favour different lure colours and tactics, and the local methods should always be tested. At the same time there's no reason not to check out ideas of your own. There are places where fly fishing is magnificent, even off the banks, and much remains to be learnt as we develop advances in technique with poppers and streamers. Fishermen are no longer prepared to accept the traditional limits.

Choice of tackle falls into two broad categories for visitors. Those who fly north for a brief stay will need light, portable gear and are best served by using local safaris and guides. Those with their own cars—people on long service or retirement leave—can take more time. The boom in 4WDs has opened up many options, including a caravan or tent and a cartop boat or canoe of some kind. In this case, the visitor more closely resembles the local resident and can carry a greater range of gear, including spare lines, lures and tackle.

There are not a lot of people in the Northern Territory. But they are amongst Australia's most avid fishermen, and fishing is vital to the area because it is known to generate so much local travel business.

One final tip. Land maps of the areas you wish to fish can be bought in Darwin, and they are a great help in understanding the country and the fishing.

Vic McCristal

NYMPH fishing A specialized method of fishing with flies tied to imitate ephemerid nymphs. The word nymph strictly refers to insects that live for only a day but in angling it is frequently used more broadly to cover insects that may live two or three years and to describe a particular fishing technique.

Overseas a large proportion of nymph fishing is related to the mayfly family. In Australia more than 100 of the world's 500 species of mayflies have been identified (see McKeown's

Australian Insects). Nymphs comprise about 80 per cent of what trout eat, but the range of our mayflies obviously restricts the range of mayfly patterns that can be used, if we insist that our flies shall be more or less exact imitations.

As the life of each individual mayfly may be as long as three years, the comparative scarcity of Ephemeroptera species does not give the trout the number of opportunities of feeding on the nymphs, nor of rising to the large hatches created by these flies. However, the species of mayflies that do inhabit Australian waters are present in much larger numbers than the casual observer is aware. On some waters there are quite large hatches of river or lake march browns as well as those tiny slate-grey duns so common in the fly waters of the Snowy Mountains.

And what the trout miss where mayfly nymphs are concerned they readily make up through the prodigious numbers of caddis larvae they eat—grubs hidden in bundles of tiny stalks of grass, encased within a house of cemented pebbles, or curled up within snail-like shells constructed of cemented sand grains. One particularly interesting species of caddis weaves a tiny silk net whose conical shape brings food to the grub. A 2.2 kg rainbow examined at Lake Eucumbene had no less than 300 caddis grubs in its stomach and another trout taken from a Gippsland stream contained 36 large stick-caddis. The stick-caddis were easily seen because of the grass stalks. Some trout are so full of caddis grubs with their pebble houses that the fish almost rattle when handled.

For the mayfly, the process of hatching from a nymph to a winged dun is a hazardous business. The first part of the journey from river bed to the water surface is bad enough, but the three to 10 seconds it takes the nymph to free itself from the shuck or discarded body case, in full sight of hungry trout, is the most dangerous part of all. To speed up the process the nymph uses the underside of the surface film to literally peel itself out of the old skin. Some nymphs are probably not ready for the hatch because, having reached the surface, they turn downwards and swim back to the river bed. In this period of the hatch, the trout may feed on the nymphs rising to the surface, gulp down those in the process of hatching, or even leave it to the last second and feed on those nymphs about to launch themselves from their floating shucks.

When the trout are feeding on nymphs rising to the surface, a seal's-fur nymph fished on a 3 m leader, greased to within 30 cm of the fly, is the best method of interesting the fish. There is usually no need to work the nymph, although if the trout ignore it, inching it towards the surface should attract their attention. If, however, the trout are feeding at the surface—and the broken surface film will reveal this—a 'floating' nymph will be more effective. A gold-ribbed hare's ear or a hatching nymph is the pattern generally used for nymphs at the surface. A small, rather scraggy-looking seal's-fur nymph that is still dry is a good standby for hatching nymphs. Very rarely is this pattern refused if the trout are actually feeding.

Nymph presentation

Most successful nymph patterns must sink fast and this is one of the reasons why fine copper wire is used as ribbing instead of silk or other materials. The seal's-fur nymph that floats so well when thoroughly dry will sink readily when moistened in the mouth or the stream. A fur-bodied nymph that has been soaked in the stream is therefore of little use for fishing in the surface film as a hatching nymph.

Some nymphs when hatching pose an almost insurmountable problem to the fly fisher by going through a series of violent struggles before getting free from the shuck. These nymphal struggles are not often seen by the angler even if he goes to the trouble of lying flat on the bank with his face close to the water. But the feeding trout see them if we can judge by the exuberance of their feeding.

To imitate these struggles by gently agitating the rod tip is one way of trying to solve the problem, but it is not very effective. Another way is to use a nymph that has a small piece of fluffy feather attached to its sides by the gold or copper ribbing, as suggested by Dick Wigram for his summer brown nymph. The slightest movement in the water will cause these fluffy feather fibres to simulate the struggles of the nymph and, the angler hopes, deceive the trout.

Suggested nymphs for Australian waters

Brown, seal's-fur nymph, stick caddis nymph, caddis nymph, black nymph, red nymph, green nymph, hatching nymph.

O

See Game fishing

OFFSHORE fishing

Enoplosus armatus: Fish found in all Australian States around wharf piles, jetties and busy harbours, swimming, according to Whitley, like a fleet of gay little yachts, fins erect. They grind their teeth and grumble, he says, when they are caught and the grumbling resembles that of an old woman. The Australian species is unrelated to the old wives given their label by the naturalist Moufet, who was thinking of the close resemblance of another species (filefish and leatherjackets) to old ladies of sour countenance. Occasionally found in fresh water, they reach 50 cm and 4.5 kg. The spines are venomous.

OLD wife

Old wife

Lampris guttatus: A rare, large deep-sea fish known almost solely in Australia from specimens cast up on beaches in south-western Australia and Victoria. The opah, also known as the mariposa or moonfish, has a reputation as the most gorgeously coloured and most delicious table fish of all. It is widely distributed in most seas, often taken by Japanese tuna

OPAH

boats. Its flesh is red and it has no teeth. The opah is a full bodied fish rich in silver, lilac and rose colours and covered with silver spots, 1.8 m and up to 70 kg when matured. They inhabit deep seas and are rarely found in coastal waters, but have been reported off Western Australia, South Australia, Victoria and Tasmania.

OYSTERS *Crassostrea commercialis*: Edible marine mollusc of the family Ostreidae. The cultivated species occurs in abundance on Australia's east coast, from Mallacoota, on Victoria's south-east tip, to about 160 km north of the New South Wales–Queensland border, where it peters out and is replaced by other species.

The main areas of cultivation are inlets and estuaries all along the New South Wales coast, notably the Sydney-Port Stephens region where oyster farming is a major marine industry catering to the demands of a large market.

Because of the difficulty of retaining the soft body on a hook the oyster is practically useless as bait, except as an ingredient in 'dope', or special mixture. But the oyster is of particular interest to the angler inasmuch as oyster beds always attract black bream. The bream cracks open the shell of the young with its powerful front teeth and sucks out the oyster. Oyster beds also are breeding grounds for or give shelter to a variety of marine creatures which fish esteem as food. Thus the area around an oyster bed usually is a good place to look for black bream. Stingray, octopus and toadfish also prey on the oyster in the early stages of its life, before it has developed a sufficiently hard protective shell. In northern areas the big snub-nosed dart or 'oyster eater' *Trachinotus blochi* is very destructive.

In some oyster-farming areas and particularly at the mouths of estuaries, a thorny starfish occasionally poses a threat to growers. This creature feeds by extruding its stomach and it exudes a poisonous secretion over the oyster's inhalant syphon. When this is taken into the system it weakens the oyster and debilitates the adductor muscle which holds the shell closed. The starfish then can protrude its stomach so as to insert it between the shells to digest the victim. It is claimed that one of these marauders can eat two or three big oysters or 20 to 25 spat per day.

Cultivation of the oyster to good marketing size (7.5 cm or more in shell size) may take up to three and a half years. But New South Wales oyster farmers have developed unique methods for the dual purpose of defeating the predatory attentions of the black bream and other thieves and expediting growth. Cultivation of a crop begins with the setting out of bundles of sticks called cultch, almost always near the mouth of a river or inlet, to catch microscopic oyster larvae known as 'spat'. The sticks, 1.8 m lengths of 2.5 cm × 2.5 cm softwood,

The phase of most rapid growth occurs when the cultivated oysters are placed on horizontal trays. These racks are on an oyster farm on the Wagonga River near Narooma, N.S.W.

usually brush box, are wired together 10 cm apart, then bundled in layers to form an interwoven pattern, with openings narrow enough to admit the larvae to inner sticks but not sufficiently wide to allow bream or other predators to enter.

For some reason scientists cannot understand a majority of spat adhere to the underside of the stick, only a small percentage attaching themselves to the side and even fewer to the outer surface. Thus while predators can nibble the spat on the bundles' outermost layers, outer surfaces and sides, those on the sticks' undersides and on inner layers are fully protected. The spat feed on microscopic planktonic animals and plants washed in on the tide.

Oyster growth

Oysters grow to approximately 1 cm size in about six months. The oyster farmer then moves his bundles of sticks to a section of his waters where no spat occur. This is called a depot area. The farmer does this to avoid collecting more spat and thus ensuring uniformity of growth in his crop. When the oysters are about 15 months old and have reached an average size of 4 cm the farmer lays the battens on racks and turns them to the light, causing their growth rate to increase tremendously. The rate of growth can be expedited by continually 'working' the oyster battens, spreading them so that the oysters have more room in which to thrive in their continuing competition for space and food.

Where funds permit the farmer at this stage encloses the cultivation area in chicken wire, from the bottom to the limit of the king tide (1.8 m), to keep out predators, even though the oyster has then developed a shell hard enough probably to withstand the attacks of bream. In these enclosed areas the battens are spaced, 20 cm to 25 cm apart, horizontally on trays at a water level at which the oysters are exposed twice daily through tidal movement. This is the phase of most rapid growth. Oyster farmers staked their battens vertically until they found that another predator, the polydora worm, was attacking them. This tiny creature bores its way into the oyster shell and, once inside, excites and distresses the oyster, which tries to seal the intruder by spreading a film of mother of pearl over it. But the worm busily bores through the film to retain an opening to the outer side of the shell. The contest continues, the oyster spreading new film and the worm boring through it. Sometimes the oyster wins, effectively sealing the worm to its doom. But frequently the worm is victorious. The oyster, expending all its energy in vain efforts to resist the intruder, withers from starvation.

Observant oyster farmers who staked their battens vertically noted that the only oysters the worm attacked were those exposed only briefly by the tide. They reasoned correctly that this must indicate that the worm could not long survive out of water. So they changed the position of their battens to the horizontal, on trays, so that all the oysters on each batten were exposed by the tide for the same period—much too long for the worm to survive out of water. This effectively reduced polydora infestation to a minimum.

Sex life of the oyster
The oyster is a true hermaphrodite and it undergoes a continuing cycle of sex change. It may spawn when in either cycle, that is to say when either male or female. Spawning occurs only in suitable conditions: correct temperature (22 degrees C), correct salinity of the water and on the outgoing tide. The oyster releases with its eggs or sperm a hormone which the opposite sex sucks in, inducing it to spawn. This sets up a sort of chain reaction so that countless oysters spawn almost simultaneously. The spawn, in a milky cloud, washes away in the outgoing tide, attracting myriads of fish to feed upon it. This is just as well for each oyster releases so many millions of eggs that someone has calculated that if only one in 10,000 of the spawn survived, an area as big as Sydney Harbour would become a solid oyster bed. The surviving fertilized eggs become trochophore larvae within a few hours and swim for 14 to 24 hours by means of rapid movement of hairs on the body.

Like all sessile animals the larva is mobile for a brief time to ensure distribution of the species. Even though only about one-hundredth of a millimetre in size the larva already has a tiny shell within its body. When ready to attach itself to a surface the larva seeks a clean object, free of slime, marine growth, algae or mud. Marine biologists have found oysters on old car tyres, tea kettles, bedsteads, boxes, stones, sticks and similar objects discarded into the water. Thus the oyster farmer's spatcatching bundles provide an inviting surface for attachment of the young shellfish.

Ostrea angasi: A non-commercial species of oyster, frequently called the mud oyster, attaches itself to shells, stones, rocks, pier piles and so on. This species develops a very thick shell and does not normally occur in clusters. The big, irregularly shaped shells may be seen on the beaches in many of our bays and harbours.

The mud oyster

See Cookery.

P

PARROT fish *See Wrasses.*

PERCH, English (Redfin) *Perca fluviatilis:* A controversial, durable sport fish found in six Australian States and known as redfin in all of them. Introduced from England into Tasmania in 1862, into Victoria in 1868 and into New South Wales in 1888, it can now be caught in South Australia, Queensland and Western Australia as well. Some anglers regret they were ever brought to Australia, claiming they clear good waters of trout by taking all their food. Biologists have proved them to be in direct competition with Murray cod and other native species. A few anglers rate redfin a fish that provides sport when other species are scarce.

Redfin have a dark, humped back and brassy flanks and these are barred with five to six bands of olive green. On very small specimens there may be seven bands. The pectoral, ventral and anal fins are orange, sometimes bright red. The dorsal fins are sharply spined, as anglers soon learn if they try to land redfin without a landing net. Redfin have the ability to assume the colours of their immediate environment and for this reason some are dark with indistinct colouring while others are brilliantly coloured. When redfin are frightened they pale quickly and this helps them to 'melt' into their surroundings.

Redfin are found in the greatest numbers in the Murray River system and in many lakes and reservoirs in Victoria. In fact, the redfin have infiltrated into almost every water in Victoria except those streams in the far eastern part of the State. They have spread, too, in remarkable fashion through New South Wales inland waters. Catches weighing from 230 g to 1 kg are common. The biggest recorded from Victoria was 5 kg but John Lake in his book *The Freshwater Fishes of New South Wales* mentions one of 10 kg from that State. Redfin are particularly abundant in Tasmania.

Roughley records that the progenitors of the redfin now distributed so widely throughout Australian freshwater streams were a consignment of 10 fish received in 1868 by A. T. Bell, of Ballarat. They were placed in a wire-netting enclosure and nine weeks later the water level had to be lowered to carry out repairs and it was found then that seven fish had survived.

English perch or redfin

These seven were liberated into a body of water that later became known as Lake Wendouree. Tasmania's first redfin, 11 in number, arrived in 1862. Eggs and fry were taken from them for distribution in streams throughout the island.

There are many reasons for the redfin's fame as an angling fish: the wide variety of waters from which it can now be caught; its good eating qualities; its size in big waters; and the fact that it can be caught on baits, spinners and wet flies.

Although redfin can be caught throughout the whole year, they prefer sunny, fairly warm days and have a dislike of discoloured waters. In some lagoons they thrive long after the trout and the native fish have succumbed to high temperatures, but when caught from warm waters the flesh is apt to be soft and tasteless. Some anglers claim to have caught redfin after dark and there is no doubt that there are some exceptions in the perch family as there are in many other families of fish, but most anglers will agree that few redfin are taken at night.

The redfin's habitat
Most redfin waters carry a few big specimens, a number of medium sized ones and an even larger number of smaller ones. Strangely enough, very small specimens of a couple of centimetres in length are rarely seen even in waters like Eildon Lake where the redfin population is possibly in the millions. Small redfin tend to move around a lot and perhaps because of their numbers and the fact that they soon clean up an area of available food, never stay in the one spot for long. Medium size redfin feed more deliberately and will remain in the one spot if you keep throwing in breadcrumbs, bran or chopped-up worms. However, if you happen to lose a fish from that shoal after having hooked and played it the shoal soon follows the fast-disappearing fish.

The really big specimens are rarely seen swimming about the stream, as they prefer to travel alone or in pairs, but you may come across one or two or even more hiding among the roots of bankside trees or hidden among the submerged tussocks. In some streams and lakes, on days when there is no wind and little movement of water, you may see where the fish are by the movement of the grasses and tussocks above the water-line.

In hard fished water the bigger redfin often hide under the undercut banks, particularly when these are screened by tussocks or weeds. A small red and black matuka may sometimes tempt them from these hiding spots. Three or four lively earthworms baited on a No. 4 Model Perfect or Sproat hook are easily the best redfin bait of all, but the moment the bait has been mangled it must be changed. A big redfin will rarely take a mutilated bait. As redfin always travel in shoals, the size of each specimen in it being the same, the angler can quickly assess, after catching the first one, the size of the hook and bait to use. Providing, of course, that that particular shoal stops around.

Redfin baits and flies

No special tackle is used for redfin; most anglers use a trout rod, a 3 kg nylon line and a No. 4 to No. 1 hook, depending upon the size of the fish likely to be caught and the size of the bait to be used. A medium size yabby will hardly fit on a No. 4 hook and two or three freshwater shrimps would look out of place on a No. 1 hook.

In some big waters it is possible to catch most of the bigger redfin on longtail or matuka pattern flies and while these can be cast with spinning tackle and a few split shot for casting weight, the best sport is to be had with a flyfishing outfit. When the fish are biting well and the water is clear the sport with the wet fly can be fast and exciting. A leader tapered to 2X or 3X and about 2 or 3 m long works well with a 3 m fly rod and a longtail tied on a No. 6 hook. The best patterns are: red and black matuka, early in the season matuka, red peril, yellow peril, black and yellow marabou streamer. On most sunny days under clear water conditions the redfin prefer something with red in it. For ordinary wet fly fishing, a red tag or a zulu on a No. 10 hook is ideal.

Spinning accounts for many big and medium sized redfin. And probably every lure ever cast into Australian streams and lakes has taken a redfin at some time or another. But the most consistently successful redfin lures are those that combine plenty of action with plenty of vibration. Few of our freshwater fish react as quickly as redfin to vibrations in the water. One of the most successful redfin lures is a small propeller-type spinner with red wool at the rear. The ordinary silver or copper wobbler with a dash of red on it is also a good redfin catcher.

Bait fishing attracts most Australian anglers despite the growing popularity of fly and spinning outfits and most

PERCH ■ P

English perch or redfin are introduced freshwater fish that have rapidly increased to inhabit large areas of Australia's inland waterways.

baitmen prefer to fish on the bottom rather than to work their baits at other levels. When bait fishing in a reservoir or stream, the angler should allow the redfin time to take the bait well into its mouth and even run with it before he attempts to set the hook. As a general rule, a metre of slack line should be placed alongside the reel and only when this has moved out through the rod runners should the strike be made. A big redfin will drop a bait just as quickly as any trout if the resistance of the line or sinker is felt and for this reason all sinkers are rigged running with a 1 m leader below them. This ability to compete for food is probably the reason for the recent decline in trout numbers.

PERCH, Jungle

Kuhlia rupestris: A fighting tropical perch known as mountain perch in some areas of eastern Queensland. Recently recorded from the Maroochy River in Queensland, the range of jungle perch includes Queensland, Papua New Guinea and many Pacific islands. They belong to the group often referred to as flagtails. Three species have now been identified in Queensland, where they are sometimes known as mountain trout: *K. taenuira*, silver flagtail; *K. munda*; and the more abundant rock flagtail, *K. rupestris*.

In most respects they closely resemble the Australian bass

P ■ PERCH

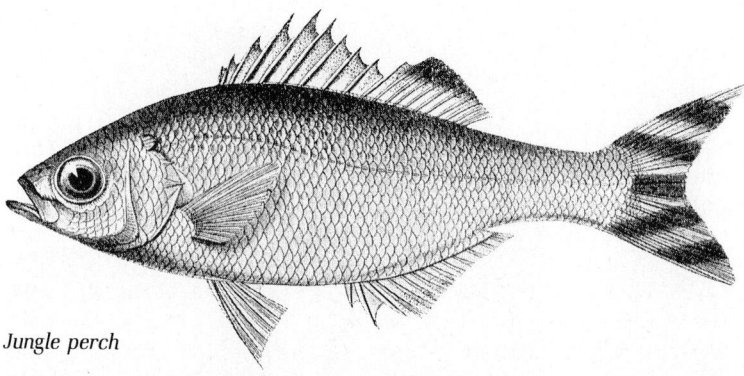

Jungle perch

and may be fished in exactly the same way with the same tackle. The preferred habitat is a natural stream among hills or mountains often surprisingly well up the sides of rainforest mountains. The only barrier to their upward movement appears to be an impassable waterfall. On some of the higher mountains in eastern Queensland such as Bartle Frere (1600 m) and Bellenden Ker (1590 m), these perch are found in exceedingly cold water in the foothills, having worked their way up numerous rapids and low falls. In these conditions, in crystal-clear streams flowing over granite, they are a much more wary fish than in slower, more turbid water.

Jungle perch usually are dark brown on top, lighter beneath, with dark spots on the head and body. There is a characteristic flag or blotch on the tail fin. A good-sized jungle perch ranges from 1 kg to 1.5 kg though they have been taken up to 3 kg. They grow to 45 cm. Their habitat is shared with several sub-species of the grunter, *Hephaestus* genus and in places with mangrove jack, *Lutjanus*. Competition for the ecological niche has resulted in population variations from stream to stream. In the Tully River, perch share the river with grunter but are in a minority. In Meunga Creek, perch are dominant and grunter are absent. In the Herbert River, perch are absent from the principal streams but are found in several mountain tributaries. All these streams are in one area, so it seems apparent that direct competition for food results in variable fish populations.

These are ideal subjects for light spinning tackle and perform well against lines of about 3 kg test. They are taken on fly tackle, using actively worked black streamers and longtails, but are generally difficult for trout fly fishers to master owing to the difference in habit and habitat. Very small flies, such as dries and nymphs, result only in small fish. Those of table size will take a bulky streamer or a large Muddler Minnow worked as a dry fly or a light popper.

Top baits on a 1/0 French hook, fished in the tail of rapids without weight, or shallow beneath a float, include crayfish and freshwater shrimps. Large surface insects, such as grasshoppers, also produce first-class results.

Lure fishermen get results from a wide variety of lures. Trout spinners, such as the Indiana, are useful in clearer conditions. Modern lures such as the smallest killer, midget bellbrook, small turbler, flopy and spicky are tops among sub-surface lures, but more entertainment can be had from surface poppers. These can be fished at mid-day for fair results and towards dusk for excellent ones. Proven lures include the lucky 13 tiny torpedo, small jitterbugs, spooks, top dogs, crazy crawlers and hula poppers. Shallow, running lures worked at the surface, by holding the rod tip high so that the retrieve creates a bow wave around the lure, are also deadly.

Jungle perch are rather difficult to scale, but have excellent table qualities, comparing with bream or Australian bass. Their wary nature, lovely mountain stream habitat and fighting ability make them a highly regarded light tackle fish. Taken on light line fished from a very light baitcaster with something like a Pfleuger skilcast reel, these come very close to the nature of wild trout in a good mountain stream. They are a magnificent sportfish and are found in greatest numbers in streams north from Mackay.

PERCH, Pearl

Glaucosoma scapulare: A highly prized fish which is limited to the relatively short stretch of the eastern coast between Rockhampton and Port Macquarie and is not very plentiful at any point in those waters. Its scarcity is all the more regrettable because of its excellent eating qualities. The late T. C. Roughley, in discussing the best table fish, described the pearl perch as the finest that he had ever tasted from Australian waters. It is scarce in the markets, so few people other than anglers who visit its home grounds have much chance of assessing its excellence.

In colour it is pearlish-greenish-silvery-grey with small golden-brown specks on the scales. It has extra-large black eyes and a small black patch on the outer side of the pectoral

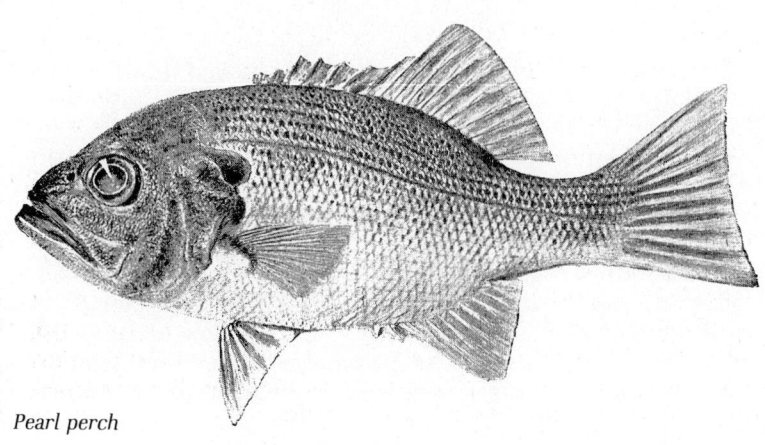

Pearl perch

P ■ PIGMY perch

fin near its junction with the body. Immediately behind the gill covers there is a large pearly white button, or outer end of the 'shoulder blade', covered by a thin dark membrane which usually rubs off easily after capture. This feature has earned it the alternative name of epaulette fish.

It is usually taken on the offshore reefs when fishing for snapper. Best catches mostly are made just before dark when it is fished for at 6 to 9 m above the bottom. Baits used are squid, prawn, octopus, small live fish or any good fish bait. The pearl perch grows from 4.5 to just over 5 kg but most specimens seen weigh from 1 to 2 kg. Its flesh is tender and of good texture, quite white and of excellent flavour. It has an important relative in the Westralian jewfish (*which see*).

PIGMY perch

Two species of the family Kuhliidae are found in Australian waters, attractive little fish that have been bred in captivity and are popular for aquariums. They are particularly common in the Murray-Darling system. *Nannoperca australis*, pigmy perch, occur in New South Wales, South Australia and the Northern Territory to a length of 7.5 cm. *Edelia obscura*, Yarra pigmy perch, are confined to South Australia and Victoria, and can be distinguished from *N. australis* by a distinct concavity in the nape immediately behind the eye. Pigmy perch make outstanding bait fish for larger species. Both our species are olive-green in colour, with dark bars along the body.

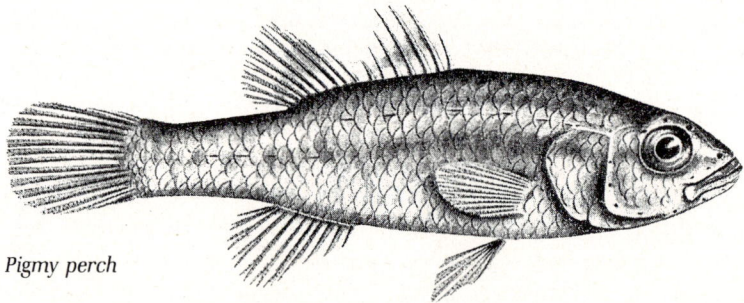

Pigmy perch

PHOTOGRAPHING the catch

Although photographic equipment has improved dramatically in recent years, there are still many anglers in Australia who cannot take quality photographs of the good fish they catch. This failure not only leaves a gap in the family album but can disqualify a genuine record claim. From the International Game Fishing Association, which decides on world record game fishing catches, to organizations that rule on State records, clear photographs of the catch have become obligatory. In Australia, with more than 3000 different species of fish already identified and many others likely to turn up, especially in the Barrier Reef, photographs for identification by ichthyologists at our museums have also become important to fishing knowledge.

The usual popular method of taking a family album type photograph is to have the fish held by the proud captor. If this is the way the angler wants it, he should beware of backgrounds which usually consist of a light pole, wire fence or backyard with washing flapping about. He must always try to get a plain light coloured background if it is a dark fish and a dark background if it is a very light coloured fish. A wide section of fibro plaster or masonite or even the sky are examples of contrasting backgrounds.

The angler holds the fish horizontally in front with both hands, making sure the fingers do not cover any important parts. He should forget the old trick of holding it out at arms' length to make it look bigger than it is. The cameraman should move in close with the camera and take the picture from the person's waist up, to ensure he gets the proud fisherman's delighted smile.

Most cameras these days either have a range-finder or are twin lens reflexes. Focusing is easy but the focus has to be exactly right. One can get away with a rather poor exposure if the fish is in focus, but the best exposed negative is useless if the fish is blurred.

Set the shutter on 1/125 of a second and this should ensure that there will not be any camera movement if the cameraman is not too steady with the shutter release. Anglers who recall the good old faithful box camera will remember the models that had a close-up lens built in—many models have—and this allows them to get within a metre or two. If it lacked a close-up lens they needed to make sure they did not get too close. Ideally they held the camera steady in both hands and gently but firmly pressed the shutter release lever. They never pushed it suddenly or the camera shook and the result was a disappointing, blurred picture. It was training modern photographers could use.

It is always wisest to take the fish where it is caught, out at sea, in the boat, on the surf beach or, with trout, down near the water's edge with natural surroundings and backgrounds. The subject should avoid standing up with the rod in one hand, a fishing bag over his back and draping the trout down alongside one trouser leg where nobody can see it and where it has to compete with all the other paraphernalia. Hold it up near the face level and look at the fish (with justifiable pride) NOT at the camera; it is the fish that should dominate the picture, not the angler even if he did catch a record. The angler who has a set of scales on which the weight can be seen should hang his fish from them, but not if the weight cannot be seen as this defeats the purpose.

Those who want the rod in the picture should lean it against one shoulder or somewhere where it will not obscure the fish. Big game fishermen mostly have no choice as they have to stand alongside a marlin or a shark which is hanging head downwards from a weighing station. A far better shot can be had—and here the angler does not lose any prestige either—if he can get his shark or marlin flat on a beach or wharf and squat alongside it with his rod and reel and show the fish at least in a more natural alignment.

Mass captures, say a good haul of snapper or bream or a few nice trout, are best taken spread out horizontally on a beach, or in the case of trout, on a ferny bank alongside the river. It is better to pick out the best fish rather than throw in everything. Avoid taking members of the party with this shot. Anglers will find that they have to move away a bit to include all the party and this spoils the record shot of their fish. Leave a knife or some other small object nearby to give a comparison of the size.

A good haul of medium-sized game fish can be well displayed if a framework of wood is made with nails driven into it halfway, the heads cut off the nails and the fish impaled on this from the back. Spanish mackerel, tuna, kingfish and this type of fish can be lined up well this way. Many angling bases in America have such frames at the fishing resort for this purpose.

Those who happen to catch a big mulloway or any sort of fish at night and want to photograph it when they get back to camp but have no flashlight equipment, can take a good picture by hanging the fish up on a door or some handy place and placing the camera on a table or box. They should get the picture lined up for view-finder and focus. Then get someone to hold a pressure lamp either side of the camera but not in front of the lens. Then they open the shutter on time exposure and give it two or three seconds. In this time, they lift the lamps up and down slowly to illuminate the fish evenly. With a fast film they can probably get quite a good shot at full aperture with 1/5 or 1/10 sec. However these days it is rare to find that someone nearby has not got a flash outfit with him. Most cameras these days are fitted with electronic flash units, and are seldom sold without flashlights.

Identification pictures

The angler who catches an unusual or unknown fish that needs to be photographed should remember that it is essential that the fish be shown lying full length with all fins showing and no other object of any sort alongside it. Here again backgrounds are most important. They must be absolutely plain and the right shade for the particular fish—dark for a light fish and light for a dark shaded fish. It is better to take all measurements and write them down rather than just place a ruler alongside the fish. Take a meter reading, being careful not to get a shadow where the meter picks up the light. Take at least two shots of different exposures. Do not photograph the fish head first or the tail end will more than likely be out of focus and in any case the fish will appear distorted. Wherever possible take close-up shots of any outstanding characteristics such as teeth or scale markings.

The angler must keep records of the weight of the fish and on no account clean the fish, as scientists are very interested in the contents of the stomach and other organs. Cleaning it may often damage the fish and in any case it spoils it for photographing or making a cast from it if this should be necessary.

When it is impossible to photograph the fish for a time, anglers should place it in a cool room but not freeze it unless it is to be kept for some days, as the fish needs to be soft and pliable. They can then arrange to do the photographing at a time that is suitable. Colour shots should be taken as soon as possible after a fish is caught.

Record claim photographs

Any fish which has to be sent to the International Game Fish Association with a claim as a record must be photographed showing all the fins and a clear outline of the fish and in the case of sharks, with a close-up of the jaws showing the shape of the teeth very clearly. For reproduction in magazines and newspapers a good clear enlargement of at least 20 cm x 15 cm on glossy paper is best. Smaller prints may be used but are not very popular and matte prints are bad as it is not always possible to make good reproductions from them. Photographs taken on a bright day, but with clouds over the sun, often produce the best pictures as you do not get hard shadows from fins or the tail and even if the picture may be a bit flat in lighting it mostly reproduces well and shows all the outline and characteristics of the fish.

Still a good technique is described by Randall (*Copeia*, 1961s No. 2, p. 251): 'The fish is brought to the laboratory as soon as possible after capture, laid in a wax-bottomed pan and the fins are pinned erect with slender non-corrosive insect pins. Formalin is applied with a fine brush to the fins, including the inside surface of the pectoral fin. Within a few minutes, depending on the size of the specimen, the pins can be removed and the fins will remain in the desired position. Excess mucus is carefully washed from the specimen, and the fish is placed in a water-tight glass-bottomed box, located over a cut-out section of a plywood table.

'The fish is then covered with about 10 cm of water, thus eliminating the surface reflections which result when a wet fish is photographed in air (admittedly fish can be dried before photographing them, but their life-like qualities may be lost). If the fish tends to float, a slit in the air bladder on the far side and application of pressure to the abdomen will usually expel the gas. It is advisable to perform this in a separate container of water to avoid fouling the water in the photographic tank. A brush is used to sweep dirt particles that do find their way into the tank out of the photographic field. Photo floodlights are directed on the specimen from the sides of the tank. The camera is placed on a stand built vertically from the table behind the tank.'

This method of photographing fish by Professor John E. Randall is mainly aimed at colour photography but could also be used quite well for black and white photographs.

Having outlaid quite a bit of money to ensure their catches are well photographed, the sensible anglers store all their fish negatives in suitable envelopes, with all data which may be valuable, such as where fish was caught, by whom, all measurements and weight, date of capture and, for future reference, any records of lighting and exposure and type of film.

ATHEL D'OMBRAIN

PIGFISH *See Wrasses.*

PIKE The name used in Australia for members of the family Sphyraenidae. These are not true pike, which are freshwater fish of the family Esocidae. The Australian pike have the same pointed heads and big teeth as European pike but there the similarity ends for their fins and other characteristics are quite different. There are about five species of Sphyraenidae in Australia. Shortfinned sea-pike are relatives of the West Indian barracuda but are not related in any way to the barracouta.

Short-finned sea-pike *Sphyraena novaehollandia*: Better known as 'snook' it is green above, silvery below, with four pairs of recurved canine teeth in the upper jaw and is found along the coasts of Bass Strait, the Great Australian Bight and Tasmania. Other than the striped sea-pike, it appears to be the only member of the family seen in those waters. Grows to 90 cm.

Snook are among the outstanding angling fish in the northern part of their environment, leaping through the surface when hooked and making dash after dash. They are abundant in eel-grass and around reefs and jetties. They bite eagerly on baits of strip fish, peeled prawns, squid and pieces of striped sea pike. They are mostly caught by trolling but some are taken in jiggled strip bait. Strong wire traces, 4/0 to 6/0 hooks and light to medium gear are required. They are taken in commercial quantities in South Australia, where they are caught by trailing a line from a boat. They have a habit of snapping at trailing objects.

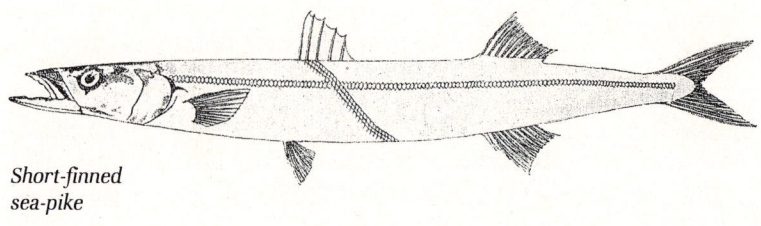

Short-finned sea-pike

PIKE ■ P

Striped sea-pike

Sphyraena obtusata: Also known as 'striped barracuda', 'sennit' and 'yellow-tail'. It is found all around Australia, though it is by far most plentiful in Queensland and north Australian waters. It rates highly with anglers on account of its speed and leaping ability when hooked. It is one of our best foodfish and is highly esteemed as bait for other species.

North of the Brisbane line these fish often school in considerable numbers and anglers have been known to take them at more than one a minute for over an hour. The young are often found in quantities in the rivers and estuaries and are prized as bait. They bite at small lures, small whole fish, squid, peeled prawn, or fish strip. One of the best baits is a belly-strip of striped sea-pike 'jiggled' by pulling it through the water with a jerky movement by using one hand after the other in a sideways movement to retrieve it.

Due to confusion with other species the striped sea-pike has been credited by some authorities with growing to a large size but in fact it seldom exceeds 55 cm. It is yellowish-green to greyish-green on the upper body and silvery-white on the lower sides and belly. Some specimens show one and others two yellowish stripes running from the snout through the eye to the butt of the tail. When first removed from the water these stripes often are overlaid with purplish tones. It may be distinguished from other Sphyraenidae by the rather square corners on its outer gill covers.

Striped sea-pike, which are often confused with barracuda, usually inhabit northern waters and are popular with anglers because of their speed and leaping ability.

Striped sea-pike

Sea pike will often leap clear of the water when taken on light tackle. They are caught on peeled prawns, hardyheads, strips of squid and fish, with the bait flicked vigorously through the water to give the appearance of a disabled fish. Anglers who can time their strike well can catch them at a rate of one a minute. Ernie Grant, the Queensland Government biologist, once took 97 in 60 minutes.

See Barracuda.

PILOT fish   *See Trevallies.*

PIPEFISHES   Long, narrow fishes of the family Syngnathidae with tube-like snouts, small mouths and jaws, and bodies encased in rings of stiff-jointed armour. They are in the same family as sea horses, and more than 40 pipefishes have been recorded around Australia, including 30 in South Australia and 22 in Tasmania. They are bottom-dwellers widely distributed in shallow marine areas, but a few species occur in fresh water and some are pelagic in the open ocean where they are mostly sighted by fishermen. The female lays her eggs under the body or tail of the male who 'mothers' them in a special area of skin there, protected by folds or a pouch, until they hatch. They consume mosquito wrigglers and most live among sea grasses.

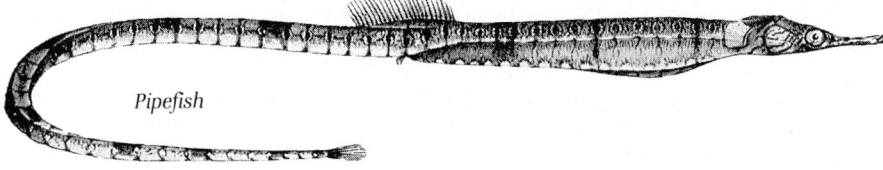

Pipefish

PIPI   *Donax deltoides:* Large bivalves of the cockle family known in South Australia as the Goolwa cockle. They were once harvested commercially in southern New South Wales with mechanical diggers and either canned whole, or used in chowder or soup. Throughout the rest of its range from southern Queensland to the south coast of Western Australia pipis are dug from the sand under the surf in considerable quantities by anglers who regard them as outstanding bait. Some gourmets take them for pickling in a brine of salt and vinegar.

The best hauls of pipis are made on isolated beaches where they have escaped the harvesting and over-fishing that depletes their numbers. In some places where they are extremely plentiful, the pipis lure considerable quantities of fish close inshore for anglers. But in spots where they have been harvested commercially there is clear evidence of the need for control to sustain their numbers.

Most Australian anglers take their pipis by hand, feeling for their holes with bare feet and then plunging in a hand to haul them out. They dig in quickly elsewhere when a wave catches the angler unawares and splashes up into the holes. The experts can detect them by searching the wet sand for the pipis' feeding tubes. They can only dig in with the aid of water and if waves leave them exposed on the sand they are at the mercy of the angler.

Pipis can be stored alive for short periods or frozen. Salmon, bream, trevally, whiting, flathead and mulloway are among the popular species that dote on pipis. But they are soft bait which the fish must be given time to swallow. Their great value on so many Australian beaches is that they are plentiful enough for several to be used in what becomes a highly appealing morsel to the fish.

See Bait.

POISONING

A number of known forms of poisoning may result from eating certain species of fish. These are quite distinct from food poisoning resulting from development of spoilage bacteria in fish which has been wrongly handled, poorly stored or improperly processed. They can be regarded as chemical, rather than bacterial and may be listed as ciguatera, tetraodontoxin, hallucinatory, gymnothoraxial, scombroidal, elasmobranchial and clupeoideal.

The porcupine fish is one of the species that cause the lethal form of poisoning tetraodontoxin if the flesh is eaten.

P ■ POISONING

Ciguatera

This is the most common form of fish poisoning in tropical and semi-tropical areas and the majority of illnesses caused by fish toxins in Australia are of this nature. It was first noted by the famous navigator, Magellan and later mentioned in 1606 by the Spaniard, Fernandez de Quiros and in 1774 by Captain James Cook, when the two last-mentioned had members of their crews poisoned in the New Hebrides.

The name ciguatera was applied to it by the Spanish who first settled in the Caribbean. More than 300 species of fish have been suspected of causing this poisoning at one time or another but only a proportion of these are known to have caused it from time to time with sufficient frequency to confirm that they definitely are suspect. Basically, the trouble is a matter of geographical distribution rather than species, though some are known as particularly dangerous carriers of the toxin. The unsafe waters are mainly around the West Indies, off the adjacent South American coast, around Japan, among the islands of the central and south Pacific Ocean and along the north-east coast of Australia. So far as is known, no case has been recorded south of Brisbane, but on rare occasions an offending fish has been taken from Moreton Bay. In recent years cases, often several at a time, have been reported in Brisbane suburbs and in 1968 a small epidemic occurred in the Sherwood-Corinda area when at least 16 people were affected. It has been claimed that most of the suspect fish reaching Brisbane come from the Gladstone area, which is at the southern end of the Great Barrier Reef.

In recent years there have been numerous cases of such fish poisoning in north Queensland, along the Great Barrier Reef waters. Some of the reef species are regarded as particularly dangerous, notably the chinaman *Symphorus nematophorus*; the red bass *Lutjanus bohar* and the paddle-tail *Lutjanus gibbus*. These are not accepted for sale in the fisheries co-operatives. There are a number of others which are not generally regarded as so dangerous, but which cause considerably more trouble because they are taken in much greater numbers and usually are not regarded with the same degree of suspicion. These include the coral trout, mackerel, reef cod, barracuda, emperor, groper (*Promicrops*), surgeon-fish and yankee whiting. Very occasional cases have been caused by the Maori wrasse and one only is recorded against barramundi.

It seems that almost any large fish in the danger zone may be regarded with suspicion. Among the edible species the incidence of poisoning is greatest in those which live close on the reefs, such as coral trout and the reef cod, while more mobile species, such as the sweetlip emperor, are less affected and the pelagic school-fish least of all.

In southern Queensland the majority of cases have been caused through eating mackerel, while in the north the chief offenders appear to have been the coral trout and cod. In the

Brisbane-Gladstone area the trouble mainly has occurred in September and October, while in the north it has had its greatest incidence in the autumn and winter.

Not every fish on a reef or in a school is affected, in fact the proportion may be extremely low. When it is traced, it usually is found to be in a rather large specimen of the species, for instance, in coral trout of over 3.5 kg. It is not usual to become poisoned by eating a normal amount of a contaminated fish at a single meal (not of the marketable species, at any rate).

The trouble mostly occurs among anglers and their families or friends, where a large fish is cut up, stored in the refrigerator and used for a series of meals. A northern city doctor, who is one of the two leading authorities on the treatment of this form of poisoning, says that a large proportion of the cases which he treats have a history along these lines: An angler catches a big fish at the weekend; it is served up at meals several times during the week and then the symptoms are severely aggravated by ingestion of beer or other alcohol on the Friday or Saturday.

The proportion of incidence among fish of various species has been much debated. Some incline to the idea that it is possible to get it from any big specimen of the very suspect species when the trouble is rife if one eats enough of it. But this does not seem to be the case. Marshall records that out of five big chinamen taken at the same time only one was found to be poisonous. The red bass *Lutjanus bohar*, which is very similar to the chinaman and is found around Noumea and is said to be the most poisonous fish at Tonga, has been estimated to be toxic to the extent of 5 per cent of its population. In some species incidence is rare and in others it would be very exceptional.

The cause is not known with any certainty, but it is evident that it mainly occurs in the presence of coral reefs or under conditions where the coral polyp flourishes. Some authorities consider that it is ingested when the fish eat certain algae produced in reef waters, or when they consume smaller species that have eaten it. Others are of the opinion that the chain starts with fish or marine creatures eating blue coral polyps. The natives of the Torres Straits islands know the trouble well and believe that it is caused through the fish eating certain seaweed berries when they are ripe.

Ciguatera can be serious and has caused deaths, particularly in the West Indies and the central Pacific islands. The exact nature of the toxin is not known, so there is no antidote and such cases of poisoning have to be treated symptomatically. The symptoms may vary widely, even among members of a family poisoned from the same fish. The first symptoms may be noted from three to 24 hours after ingestion of an effective amount of the toxin, or they may be accentuated and brought to notice somewhat later by consumption of alcohol. The first signs usually are general lassitude and a dull ache in the limbs, particularly in the knees. More distinctive symptoms which may occur include:

(a) Tingling in the hands, feet, lips and mouth.
(b) Weird sensitivity to heat or cold. Chilled beer may seem to scald the throat.
(c) Skin itch, particularly at the palms of the hands or soles of the feet. May be dramatically aggravated by consumption of alcohol.
(d) Dull frontal pain and headache. May involve aching of sound teeth.
(e) Vomiting, abdominal pains and diarrhoea.
(f) Tight chest pains with occasional heart irregularity.
(g) Sometimes blood is present in the urine.
(h) Shock, convulsions, blurring of vision, loss of muscular co-ordination or paralysis are other possibilities.

In a comparatively mild attack the more troublesome symptoms may pass off in 24 to 36 hours, but some degree of muscular weakness, numbness and tingling may persist for a week or more. In more severe cases the recovery period may be long and may involve a prolonged stay in hospital. Once a person becomes affected the symptoms may persist for a period of from several weeks up to many years and could be aggravated by eating unlikely things and particularly certain species of fish, canned tuna or anchovy paste. An attack does not impart immunity; on the contrary the sufferer becomes much more sensitive to suspect fish.

At the onset of ciguatera medical assistance should be obtained. If it is not available, early treatment may be to induce vomiting and to administer a purgative. Further medication may be determined by the symptoms.

Deaths in the central Pacific have been associated with eating fish livers and investigators believe that in a suspect fish the poison is more concentrated in the liver and intestines.

A considerable amount of research has been carried out under the direction of Professor Banner at the Hawaiian Marine Laboratory and by North Queensland doctors in conjunction with the late Dr Jack Barnes, of Cairns, and the Australian Institute of Marine Science at Townsville and Innisfail. An urgent requirement is some cheap and simple method of testing fish for presence of the toxin. Some authorities are of the opinion that the incidence of affected fish is increased by disturbance of the formations of the coral reefs. Others believe that there is greater incidence in the vicinity of those reefs threatened with devastation by the crown-of-thorns starfish. Certainly the toxicity in some species varies considerably from area to area. In the Yeppoon-Gladstone region anglers generally eat red bass, and rarely with any ill effects, while in other areas they have proved very dangerous. For many years big chinaman fish caught on the Arlington Reef near Cairns were served to guests at a local resort, apparently with no ill-effects, though this species has so often proved to be deservedly suspect elsewhere.

There are some problems here of great scientific and national interest which should present great scope for research.

Tetraodontoxin
A different form of poisoning brought on by eating fish of the order Tetraodontiformes, which includes the toadfish, porcupine fish, boxfish, cowfish, filefish, trigger-fish, triplespine, leatherjacket and sunfish. Here matters are rather complicated by the fact that in our more temperate waters one family of the order, the leatherjacket, ranks high among our choice eating fish. But the rest of this order must be regarded as ranging from extremely poisonous to gravely suspect. In contrast to ciguatera, the toxin is not something which is contracted by an occasional fish, but is inherent in them and can be expected to be present in somewhat similar consistency in all of the same species.

The poisonous reagent is *tetraodontoxin*, which when isolated is regarded as more deadly than strychnine, since less than one grain could provide a lethal dose. Like the ciguatera toxin, it is not destroyed by cooking and there is no known antidote. It is found in its greatest concentration in the liver, roe, entrails, skin and probably the visceral slime. It is an alkaloid very similar to muscarine, which is the poisonous reagent in some mushrooms and other fungi. As extracted in the pure state, it is odourless, tasteless and extremely poisonous.

Symptoms may include tingling of the lips, tongue and fingertips, weakness, nausea, headache, sweating, vomiting, sub-normal temperature, hypersalivation, progressive numbness, difficulty in swallowing, impairment of voice, cramps, difficulty in breathing or paralysis of the respiratory system. In a severe case deterioration may be rapid and death may result. Treatment is symptomatic and emetics and warmth are recommended while calling a doctor. If the patient survives for twenty-four hours the chances of recovery are good. Unlike ciguatera, the malady usually does not leave serious after-effects.

The most dangerous species are the toad fish, toadies, toadoes, tobies, puffer or globefish, as they are variously called. There are approximately 30 species in Australian waters, a large proportion of which are restricted to semi-tropical areas. It is possible to eat at least some of the flesh of this fish if it is free of skin, congealed blood or viscera.

In Japan a gourmet cult specializes in the epicurean preparation of the strips of flesh from their backs, but these species have caused numerous deaths there among the general public. Their lethal nature is well understood in the Philippines. Nevertheless they are extensively eaten there and a number of people die from them each year. Captain Cook suffered severely from eating part of one of these fish on his voyages of discovery to the Pacific. No comprehensive record has been kept of such deaths in Australia, but a man died near Sydney in 1821, a family was poisoned at Hobart in 1931 and there was another fatality when a family was affected at Sydney in 1951. Perhaps the most tragic case since then was when a young couple were fatally poisoned at Eden.

There are two families of boxfish and all species should be regarded as highly poisonous. A few years ago a man died as the result of eating part of one taken from Botany Bay. The somewhat similar cowfish probably are poisonous also, but they are rather too small to be considered for eating. The triplespines of northern waters have been eaten with impunity, but it may be as well to regard them with suspicion and there is little flesh on them, anyhow. The several species of porcupine fish are deadly, though they are of such unsavoury appearance that few would ever consider eating one.

The dozen or so species of trigger-fish found in north Australian waters must be regarded as highly poisonous. The redlined trigger-fish so often taken off Townsville has an evil reputation. One authority, writing of similar species at Mauritius, considered that their poisonous flesh acted primarily on the nerves of the stomach, causing violent spasms of that organ and shortly afterwards of the muscles of the body. The patient became racked with spasms, the tongue thickened, the eyes became fixed, breathing laborious and death occurred in a paroxysm of extreme suffering. The file-fish and some of the leatherjackets found in our northern waters mostly have flesh of bitter and disagreeable taste and usually possess poisonous properties. There appears to be no record of anyone having eaten any of our two species of sunfish but in view of their close relationship to the others they should be treated with suspicion.

Hallucinatory

There seems to be little, if any, incidence of this trouble within Australia, but it is remarkable because it occurs so close at hand in the Pacific Islands and is mainly caused by the sea mullet *Mugil cephalus*, which occur in great quantities on our coasts and are marketed here on a large scale. It usually occurs during the months of June, July and August and it appears to be mild and non-fatal, mostly taking from a few hours to a couple of days to pass off. Symptoms include dizziness, loss of equilibrium, lack of co-ordination, hallucinations and mental depression.

In the South Sea Islands the natives used to claim that the head of the sunrise goat-fish *Upeneus sulphureus* was poisonous and that eating the brain caused delirium. This species is commonly found along the north Queensland coast. At Norfolk and Lord Howe Islands a relative of the silver drummer, the narnwai or dream fish *Kyphosus fuscus*, sometimes produces vivid nightmares for those who eat it.

Gymnothoraxial
Mainly results from eating the moray eel. It is much in the nature of ciguatera, but the onset is more rapid and the symptoms more dramatically striking. In addition to those of ciguatera they may include production of excessive mucus, lockjaw, high fever or paralysis of the respiratory system.

The common green eel of the southern kelp beds is a member of the moray family. The five genera found in Queensland waters include the world's largest species, the long-tailed eel *Thyrsoidea macrura*, which has been known to grow to over 4 m. But since the flesh of reef eel is very oily and indigestible it is not eaten by Australians and there is no incidence of this form of poisoning.

Scombroidal
This is a malady caused by eating tuna which has become toxic only due to improper handling. Faulty storage of any of the tuna, bonito or albacore can cause the production of a histamine-like substance in the flesh. This cannot be detected by sight or smell and the fish appears to be quite good.

Symptoms may include headache, intensely itching spots, swelling of the lips, tongue and throat, abdominal pains and giddiness. The acute symptoms usually last only from eight to 12 hours and recovery is rapid and complete. This trouble does not appear to be met with in Australia where tuna is eaten from cans or heavily cooked. It is not unusual in Japan and some other countries and could appear in Australia and New Zealand with the establishment of restaurants where food is served in the Japanese style.

Elasmobranchial
Of rare occurrence and thought to be caused by eating the liver of the black-tipped sand shark, hammerhead or grey nurse. Eating the flesh of the two last-named Australian species is known to have caused mild gastric upsets. Ingestion of the liver may cause more serious troubles such as headache, nausea, vomiting, diarrhoea, aching joints, perspiration, pains in the chest, tingling of the lips and fingers, burning sensation on the tongue and in the throat, twitching of the eyelids and itching and reddening of the skin.

Clupeoideal
An ailment contracted through eating herring and some other species. It appears to be unknown in Australia and its chief interest here is that its incidence seems to be associated with the rising of the palolo worm, which in itself is non-toxic.

Other forms
There are a number of species of stinkfish in Australian waters which are considered to be highly poisonous, probably from a toxin of alkaloid form. However, their odoriferous nature and

the unpalatably bitter taste of the flesh would preclude most people from eating them. Some persons find that the flesh of the king barracouta or barraconda *Rexea solandri* has strong purgative properties.

WAL HARDY

POLLUTION Deterioration of water quality until it adversely affects aquatic life. For anglers the main outcome of pollution is the fouling of fresh water or salt water by industrial and agricultural effluent or sewerage outfall to an extent that it attacks or kills fish, destroys their food or ruins their normal habitat. But pollution has serious effects on the entire community: jeopardizing health, reducing food production, increasing the cost of manufactured goods, menacing aquatic flora and destroying tourist attractions.

Pollution is a world-wide problem. It is at its worst in rapidly developing countries such as Australia, where dramatic agricultural and industrial expansion is occurring. Indeed there is justification in Australia for strong measures to control waste disposal because fresh water is so limited and of such high economic and recreational value. There has been lethargy in the government departments which could move to check pollution and a lack of understanding among the public of the immensity of the problem.

The slowness of State and Federal governments in combating pollution has already caused extensive damage in every Australian State. Pollution research has hardly begun in some States. In a climate in which States duel to have major development ventures located within their own borders, there has been a tragic failure of governments to make agricultural and industrial enterprises responsible for the carelessness that causes pollution. Overseas it has become almost standard practice in many countries to compensate State or provincial fisheries when pollution kills fish.

Water pollution

Water pollution may be defined in various ways, depending on what aspects of the water and its value are considered. From the viewpoint of amateur angling, it is any change in water quality, brought about by human agency, which is detrimental to normal aquatic life.

For management purposes, pollution is usually categorized as being derived from either point sources or diffuse sources. Point source pollution includes sewage effluents, industrial waste discharges, accidental spillages and irrigation tailwaters. Diffuse sources include urban and rural stormwater runoff and groundwater infiltration.

Point sources are easier to manage, and most anti-pollution legislation is aimed at these. In New South Wales, for example, all discharges to natural waters must be licensed under the

A jet boat disperses foam from an oil containment boom near Kurnell, N.S.W.

provisions of the Clean Waters Act, and heavy fines may be imposed for non-compliance with the conditions set in each licence, or for effluent discharge without a licence. This management does not, however, eliminate pollution, as the links between water quality and the welfare of the total aquatic community are many, complex, and not well understood.

Diffuse sources must be controlled indirectly, and hence their management is more difficult than that of point sources. They are also highly time-variable, as they are usually linked with rainfall. They are increasingly becoming a focus of attention as point source management approaches a more satisfactory level. Reduction of pesticide and fertilizer usage, and soil conservation practices, are steps that can be and, in some cases, are being taken to reduce the pollution potential of rural runoff. Urban runoff, with its great diversity of pollutants, remains largely unchecked, and some form of stormwater retention and treatment may soon become necessary to reduce its polluting influence.

Some effects of water pollution on aquatic life are well known. For example, all biodegradable organic matter, which includes most pollutant material in sewage and industrial wastes, removes dissolved oxygen from water as it is metabolized by micro-organisms. If the oxygen is not restored, by diffusion, turbulent air entrainment or photosynthesis of aquatic plants, then its concentration falls to a level which will not support animals and mortality results. If this happens suddenly, as in the event of a large sewage overflow, the results may be dramatic, with river banks covered in dead fish.

More often, the effects are insidious, with perhaps only a small proportion of the more sensitive species being killed. However, if the total biotic community has been disturbed by stress, the secondary effects can be far-reaching. For example, the main food item for a fish species might be a small bottom-dwelling invertebrate. Populations of this invertebrate in a river or estuary could be decimated locally by deoxygenation of near-bottom water, while the remaining water remains well oxygenated. Under these conditions, the fish must either go elsewhere looking for food, or die from lack of food.

Acute toxicity from specific poisons, while not as important as deoxygenation, is still an important effect of certain pollutants. Some of the more common toxic chemicals discharged into water are chlorine, ammonia, phenols, so-called 'heavy' metals (this term covers all metals not normally found in water—all except sodium, potassium, magnesium and calcium—especially mercury, cadmium, lead, zinc, chromium and copper), and all compounds covered by the term 'pesticides'. Some of the organochlorine pesticides, dieldrin and endrin for example, are among the most toxic compounds to fish, endrin being lethal to some species in levels of less than one part per thousand million.

Organochlorine pesticides, and certain other organochlorine compounds, notably polychlorinated biphenyls (PCBs) are also well known for bio-accumulation. They are highly soluble in fat, so they become concentrated in adipose (fatty) tissues of fish, and this can be harmful to animals, including other fish, birds and man, that eat the fish. Pesticide residues in fish may also harm the fish itself if food is scarce and the fatty tissue is metabolized. Much effort is now being directed at the replacement of bio-accumulative pesticides by other types such as organophosphate, carbamate and pyrethroid compounds. These are also generally less acutely toxic to fish.

Much laboratory work has been carried out to determine the degree of toxicity of individual chemicals to fish. However, this is of limited predictive value for natural conditions, as it fails to account for the combination of toxic chemicals and environmental variables, or for the synergistic effects of two or more toxicants. In setting water quality objectives, therefore, most authorities include a safety factor, hopefully to allow for these effects. But no entry of any substance unnatural in an aquatic environment could be considered completely harmless.

In addition to the primary effects of pollution—deoxygenation by the biological breakdown of organic compounds and acute toxicity—there are several important secondary effects which can harm fish and other aquatic life. The best known of these is caused by abnormally high concentrations of plant nutrients, particularly forms of nitrogen and phosphorus, and is termed eutrophication. Its symptoms are the rapid, prolific growth of aquatic plants, usually microscopic algae (phytoplankton). These 'blooms' are unsightly and may produce objectionable smells. Certain species of, for example, *Microcystis*, *Nodularia* and *Glenodinium*, can secrete substances toxic to fish. The 'red tide' associated with fish kills in estuaries is a species of *Glenodinium*.

When the algae have used up all the nutrient which is in least supply, their populations collapse, that is they die in large numbers, and the resulting mass of organic matter decomposes, with a consequent large drop in dissolved oxygen level. Even during the height of the bloom, dissolved oxygen, which is high by day due to photosynthesis, falls at night when the plants respire but do not photosynthesize. The rapid changes in dissolved oxygen during blooms place stress on fish and other aquatic animals, and the oxygen drop during the decay phase can kill them. It has been recognized, for many water bodies, that controls must be placed on the quantities of plant nutrients entering them.

Levels of plant nutrients are high in sewage effluent, urban runoff and runoff from farmland or pasture which has been heavily fertilized. Sewage effluent can be treated to remove nutrients, but the cost is high. Urban runoff could possibly be treated, if the benefit were seen to be great enough, but the only satisfactory means of control over nutrient input from rural runoff is by adequate land management practices and this, in the first instance, means education of those that work the land.

No matter how much management control is placed on pollution sources, accidental spillages will always occur, although their harmful effects can be minimized by sensible procedures. The best known type of accidental spill is of oil, some spills of which have had devastating effects on marine life. Most refineries now in Australia were built without serious consideration for the effects of repeated oil spills on local ecosystems. The oil itself does not penetrate below the water surface, but it can cover intertidal areas, killing mangroves, oysters and other animals and plants living there. If chemical dispersants are used to break up and disperse a slick of spilled oil, however, fish and other sub-tidal organisms can be adversely affected.

Bacterial contamination of water, from sewage or urban runoff, may not have a harmful effect on aquatic life, but it can make the water potentially harmful for drinking or contact recreation. Fish caught in bacterially polluted waters, such as adjacent to major sewage outfalls, are safe to eat, provided they are cleaned and washed well with uncontaminated water. But filter feeders such as oysters and mussels accumulate bacteria and viruses and when taken from contaminated waters, should not be eaten (particularly if uncooked) unless subject to some form of purification such as is now standard for cultivated Sydney rock oysters.

Certain petrochemicals in low concentrations can, while

not apparently harming fish, induce objectionable flavours in the flesh. This is in some instances termed 'kerosene taint'. Apart from wasting anglers' time in catching fish which cannot be eaten, it costs the fishing industry heavily as tainted fish are obviously unsaleable.

In addition to detrimental changes to water quality, the welfare of fish and other aquatic life is under threat in many places from physical changes to habitats, such as dredging and reclamation works associated with urban development around estuaries. Destruction of important fish breeding, feeding and nursery areas can have profound influences on the welfare of the most important angling fish, many of which spend their juvenile stages in estuaries. It is therefore desirable, from the amateur angling and conservation viewpoint, that pollution and habitat damage be managed with care by close co-ordination between the relevant authorities. With the increasing public awareness of the value of natural environments and the need for conservation, the control of pollution will hopefully continue to improve. There is, however, still room for considerable improvement.

E. A. SCRIBNER

Habitat pollution

Perhaps the worst pollution damage has occurred in Australian estuaries, highly fertile areas where many sporting fish and prawns feed. Reclamation, unplanned dredging and the zoning of waterfront land as industrial has brought with it pollution which has killed the weed zone and stripped countless estuaries of sea grasses in which many marine creatures found their food.

D. T. Dunstan, marine biologist to the Division of Fisheries of the New South Wales Department of Agriculture, gives the decline of the Gippsland Lakes, in Victoria, bream fishery as an outstanding example of the importance of the weed zone to fish life. In 1919, the bream catch in these lakes totalled approximately 453,000 kg. By 1940, the catch had dropped to 19,500 kg, a fall of 95 per cent. This decline was attributed directly to the loss of vast beds of productive sea grass *Zostera* spp. which now occurs only in isolated backwaters.

Mr Dunstan says the importance of estuarine nursery areas for sea mullet has been amply demonstrated. This applies also to such commercial and sporting fish as bream, whiting and luderick, all of which are spawned at sea. Most of the marine sporting fish, in fact, inhabit estuaries at some time in their lives. The oyster, commercially the most important fishery in New South Wales, spends all its life in estuarine waters to complete its life cycle.

Despite this, waterfront development, bringing with it housing lots, marinas, launching sites for boats, parking lots and bridges, has resulted in destruction of irreplaceable marshland and mudflats. Curbs are needed on real estate

Water pollution has reduced the extent of mangrove regions in coastal and river areas, which in turn adversely affects the coastal ecosystems.

developers who turn to dredging and filling operations to create more waterfront lots that bring top prices.

In the estuaries of New South Wales there are some 107 sq km of mangroves, 155 sq km of sea grass beds and 58 sq km of salt marsh. However, due partly to natural causes (upland runoff, erosion), but mainly to man's activities (deforestation, land clearing, agricultural practices and urbanization), these figures are not static. Salt marshes, in areas where they are not protected by adequate zoning, will continue to be reclaimed by an expanding population. But mangrove swamps, which up until the late 1960s were viewed by local councils as the ideal locality for the disposal of embarrassing garbage and were being destroyed at an alarming rate, are now protected and are increasing in area and abundance.

Unfortunately this increase is occurring at the expense of the most productive component of the estuaries—the sea grass beds. Increased siltation is smothering these beds and increased water turbidity is reducing the substrate areas available for colonization but producing conditions favourable for mangrove establishment and propagation. If allowed to continue there will be a gradual increase in herbivorous fish species (mullet, luderick) and a decrease in carnivores (bream, whiting). A good example is the Georges River where the once prolific and highly productive weed beds have practically disappeared (only 0.268 sq km remain) whereas there are now

P ■ POLLUTION

2.038 sq km of mangrove which are increasing at the rate of 2 ha per year. Unless controlled dredging is undertaken, the silted backwaters of bays and inlets will be rapidly colonized by mangroves and open, useable, productive waters will be lost. The trapping of sediments by the aerial roots will accelerate accretion resulting in dieback and eventual salt marsh establishment, and in the long term, replacement with playing fields, parks and parking areas. If restricted to a depth of 2 m, dredging will be beneficial in restoring useable water and assisting in the re-establishment of sea grasses.

Every Australian State has striking examples of the pollution problem. In Queensland sugar mills have rendered long stretches of fine rivers almost barren by running their waste effluents into them as the easiest means of disposal. Professional fishermen around Brisbane have complained that their catches of mullet from Moreton Bay cannot be sold because of their strong kerosene flavour, resulting from the operations of local oil refineries.

For years fishermen in Sydney have been aware that fish caught around the hot-water outlet near the Kurnell oil refinery and elsewhere in Botany Bay usually have a strong kerosene flavour. The St George and Sutherland Angling clubs have complained that tailor and luderick taken from Boat Harbour around Tobagai, on the outer side of Cape Solander, are so strongly tainted they are inedible. Oil-tainted tailor are being taken as far north as Newcastle and Port Stephens. Victorian anglers who fish Westernport Bay have periodically had oil from big oil tankers kill most of their fish and give the survivors a strong oil flavour. Apart from menacing fish life, many thousands of Australian birds have been destroyed by oil leaks.

Oil is, of course, only one of the many causes of pollution. Floating solids that blanket out light penetration, waste that depletes oxygen content in the water and the run-off from heavily fertilized paddocks are just a few forms lethal to fish. One big sign on the banks of the Hunter River, New South Wales, reads: 'Acid Sludge Only To Be Dumped In This Area.'

Detection of the causes of chronic pollution is not difficult provided trained biologists, backed by the appropriate authorities, are given the task. Within a brief period, the chemical and biological characteristics of water at any point in a stream become constant. Through biological and chemical checks at selected points along a waterway, the causes and effects of pollution can be accurately pinned down, and thankfully the courts have accepted this by heavily fining guilty companies.

In Tasmania, where the Sea Fisheries Division controls saltwater angling and the Inland Fisheries Commission administers freshwater fishing, contamination of fish environments has become a constant problem in which the authorities have had only limited success. Investigation of pollution and effluents from industry and weed spraying takes more of the two administrative bodies' time each year.

In Western Australia, the Swan River Conservation Board has proved to be an alert watchdog against pollution of Perth's river front. Formed by act of parliament to keep the Swan River a pleasant place to swim, sail, play or fish, the board has vigorously hunted out sources of pollution and channelled them elsewhere. Hundreds of tonnes of dangerous snags have been removed from the upper Swan to make the river navigable as far upstream as Middle Swan.

Outside the Swan River little work is done to prevent water pollution. This State has as yet no worries from industrial pollution in its rivers, but pollution is occurring in serious proportions along the coast. Cockburn Sound, a big small-boat fishing area south of Fremantle, is becoming contaminated with alumina dust fallout, refinery oil spillage and sewage. Many Cockburn fish are flavoured by petroleum waste, in the same manner as those found in the vicinity of the refineries in Victoria, New South Wales and Queensland. Offshore oil exploration off the metropolitan coast has raised grave fears of future pollution of beaches and offshore fishing grounds.

The areas most vulnerable to pollution are on the north-west coast where industrial expansion is going ahead at breakneck speed, with little consideration being given to the conservation of natural assets involved there. Port Hedland is an example of what future developers should avoid. In the past decade a port that was once well known for its fishing has been so badly soiled by ore dust and harbour dredging that it is now one of the poorest fishing spots in the north-west. In a few short years man will have largely ruined a great national asset which has taken nature millions of years to evolve and develop. There is urgent need of an enlightened conservation policy, with the means and the will to vigorously pursue it.

Many experienced and responsible anglers believe that with the precise causes of pollution so readily obtainable State governments should take a far sterner attitude towards the culprits. Two interesting overseas cases demonstrate possible penalties. In England the Anglers' Co-operative Association succeeded in securing injunctions against Derby Corporation, the British Electricity Authority and British Celanese when pollution turned the River Derwent into 'an overheated sewer'. The A.C.A. took this action on behalf of a small workingmen's angling club, the Pride of Derby A.C. Renovations and alterations to plant treating effluents cost more than $4 million. In America a sporting fishing institute's bulletin described how the Hooker Chemical Corporation paid $25,000 compensation to the State of Ohio after pollution with phenol killed large numbers of fish in the Scioto River. One or two cases like those would serve to create deterrents and a public awareness of the pollution menace in Australia.

P ■ PORCUPINE fish

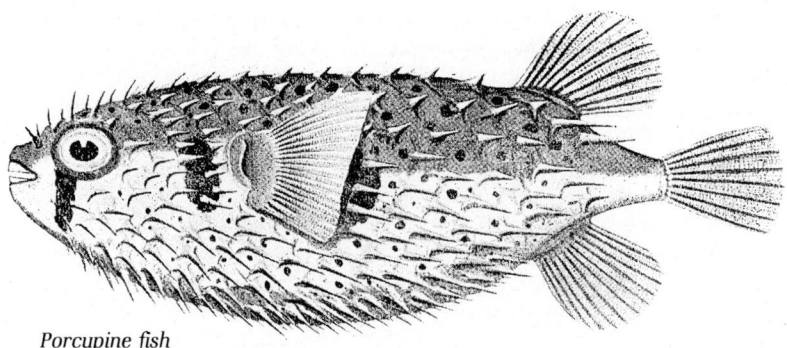

Porcupine fish

PORCUPINE fish Gruesome, spiny fish which blow themselves into well-armoured globes by filling their air bladders. They belong to the family Diodontidae and are poisonous to eat. They are found in all Australian States, can drift large distances when inflated, and vary in length from 30 cm to 90 cm. One species, the globefish *Diodon nichthemerus* is very common in South Australia, the spines becoming erect when it inflates. They present a difficult problem for predators. Whitley records that one species, *Atopomycterus nichthemerus*, gnawed its way out of a shark that had swallowed it. Whitley said Aborigines believed the fish was smooth until it swallowed a spiny anteater.

PORTUGUESE man-o'-war See Bluebottle or Portuguese man-o'-war

PRAWNS and shrimps Swimming crustaceans with five pairs of walking legs under the 'head' and five pairs of swimming legs under the 'tail' (abdomen). Prawns and shrimps are biologically complex animals with rather sophisticated nervous, circulatory (blood) and breeding systems. Hundreds of species have been discovered around Australia but only about a dozen are of importance to commercial or amateur fishermen.

Prawns may be separated into two major groups, penaeid and carid. The penaeids shed their eggs into the sea whereas the carids carry their eggs under the tail like crabs and crayfish. All the major Australian commercial species are penaeids and most of the world's prawn trade consists of penaeid prawns. The long-armed prawns *Macrobrachium* are common examples of carid prawns.

The commercial prawns of Australia are the shrimp of the United States, while the British have both prawns and shrimp in their waters. But what is a prawn and what is a shrimp? Regrettably there is no zoological definition. Nor is the problem solved by dictionaries such as Oxford and Websters which describe a shrimp as a small prawn or a prawn as a large shrimp. Consequently both names, shrimp and prawn, are commonly used, frequently interchanged and equally valid;

however, the Australian terminology and the word prawn will be used here for the penaeid species and carid species only will be referred to as shrimp.

There are commercial fisheries for various species in the estuaries or coastal waters of all mainland states of Australia. The eastern king prawn *Penaeus plebejus*, is sometimes taken in estuaries in north-east Tasmania but it is never plentiful in these southern waters. Since the early 1970s a pink deepwater prawn known as the royal red prawn has been trawled in commercial quantities from depths of 150 to 300 fathoms off the New South Wales coast.

Life cycles

Most of Australia's commercial species are found as adults at sea, the juveniles growing up in an estuarine environment. Penaeid prawns are normally bisexual, that is with separate sexes, and the female of most species grows much larger than the male. After mating, the female sheds the fertilized eggs into the sea and these soon hatch into tiny larvae which bear no resemblance to a prawn. The larvae moult frequently over the next two to three weeks, while drifting about with the ocean currents, until they resemble tiny prawns. At this postlarval stage they enter the coastal rivers, lakes and bays and adopt a bottom-living life like their parents. These juvenile prawns spend several months to almost a year in the estuary before they move back to the sea to breed and complete the life cycle.

The seaward migration or 'prawn run' takes place, usually at night, during the warmer half of the year but it can vary considerably depending on the rainfall and moon cycle. The run is strongest during the dark period of the lunar month and this is the time when amateur and commercial fishermen get the best catches as the prawns crowd into the channels leading out of the lakes and rivers to the sea. Heavy rainfall and flooding enhance the usual seaward migration of the prawns at any time.

Contrary to popular opinion prawns are not attracted to lights. In fact strong lights act as a repellent to prawns, and are only needed to help spot prawns on the surface when fishing with a scoop or dip net; when using large nets such as a drag net lights are unnecessary until it is time to sort the catch ashore.

The life cycle of some species can be quite unusual. The greasyback or greentail prawn *Metapenaeus bennettae*, for example, has a totally estuarine life cycle, a life span of up to a year, and normally does not go to sea. The school prawn *Metapenaeus macleayi* moves out to sea when mature and undertakes a short northerly migration along the New South Wales coast, whereas the eastern king prawn may move 1000 km along the coast to spawn off Queensland at two or even three years of age. Other species, particularly the deepwater ones, spend all of their life in the ocean.

The life cycle of the carid species is highly varied although all shed the fertilized eggs onto the swimming legs under their tail and are then referred to as being 'in berry'. Some carid shrimp are long lived and are hermaphrodites, one individual being either male or female at different times. The shrimp is usually a male for a year or two, then develops into a female and remains so for the last year or so of its life. The edible roe (ovaries) can often be seen through the shell over the head and tail of both penaeid and carid species as a conspicuous band of soft-looking, yellow-green or blue-green tissue.

Eastern king prawn *Penaeus plebejus:* One of the biggest and best-known species in Australia, growing to 30 cm. The colour of this, and most other species, is highly variable depending on the type of sea bottom and several other factors. It is usually light brown to reddish brown with bright yellow tips to the swimming and walking legs and a bright blue edge on the tail fan. Juveniles caught in estuaries where *Zostera* (eel grass) grows over the bottom are usually dark green in colour, while adults taken in deep oceanic waters are bright red.

This species is commonly caught along the east coast of Australia between Bundaberg in Queensland and Lakes Entrance in Victoria, and is a world champion swimmer, recording speeds of 6 km per day and breeding migration of almost 1200 km. It is very popular with amateur fishermen because it is plentiful in coastal lakes and swims near the surface when moving out of the estuaries to the sea and therefore is readily caught with a scoop net and lamp. The picture created by thousands of amateur fishermen armed with lamps and nets of all sorts around the Tuggerah Lakes on a warm summer's night is spectacular.

Sydney's famous harbour prawns consist predominantly of juvenile king prawns taken from both Sydney Harbour and Botany Bay, while in Brisbane the juvenile king prawns caught in Moreton Bay are sold as bay kings.

Western king prawn *Penaeus latisulcatus:* The western king or blue-legged king prawn differs from its eastern relative in having conspicuous blue coloration around the walking legs, but is otherwise indistinguishable from the eastern species except by prawn fishermen and prawn biologists. It is found in South Australia, where it is fished commercially in Spencer Gulf and Gulf St Vincent. It is abundant in Shark Bay and Exmouth Gulf in Western Australia and is also found in commercial quantities in Queensland. Occasional specimens are taken in New South Wales. *P. latisulcatus* also inhabit the waters of New Guinea, Malaysia and Japan.

Red spot king prawn *Penaeus longistylus:* Known to exist in Australian waters for many years but only began contributing significantly to commercial catches, particularly in northern Queensland, in the

1980s. It has a strikingly obvious red spot on each side of the tail above the third pair of swimming legs. The red spot king is usually found in the reef regions of northern Australia but is also known in Malaysia and the South China Sea.

Tiger prawn

Penaeus esculentes: The brown tiger prawn is found in northern oceanic waters from Shark Bay in Western Australia to central New South Wales. This tiger prawn, and other species, gets its name from the obvious crossbands over the head and tail. It grows to about 28 cm and is one of Australia's major commercial species.

Another tropical species, the giant tiger prawn or leader prawn *P. monodon*, has the honour of being the world's largest prawn, growing to more than 30 cm. It is noticeably darker than its relative, sometimes almost black in appearance. Although it is normally an inhabitant of northern waters in Australia, and elsewhere, specimens are occasionally collected in estuaries along the east coast as far south as Sydney Harbour.

Banana prawn

Penaeus merguiensis: Probably gets its Australian name because it resembles a banana in general colour and size; it is speckled golden-yellow in colour and grows to a length of about 23 cm. Banana prawns are found around the northern half of Australia and are one of the principal commercial species. In the Gulf of Carpentaria spotter aircraft look for a characteristic mud boil at sea produced by large schools of banana prawns, particularly at neap tides. Queensland anglers sometimes catch them with cast nets in coastal rivers as they are good bait as well as good eating.

School prawn

Metapenaeus macleayi: The most common species in the rivers of New South Wales and southern Queensland. School prawns are tolerant of very low salinity and small juveniles may be 60 km upriver from the sea. Their abundance is very closely related to rainfall cycles; they are more commonly taken after flooding when they form large schools while moving out to sea and along the coast. The name comes from this pronounced schooling behaviour. School prawns have a grey spotted appearance when they come from estuaries but attain a golden or sandy colour when found at sea. They grow to 15 cm. Their small size, relative abundance and comparative cheapness has made them the most common bait prawn in New South Wales and Victoria.

Endeavour prawn

Metapenaeus endeavouri: Also known as the brown prawn or bay prawn in Queensland. A light brown prawn with a blue tail fan, it grows to about 20 cm. Found only in Australia, from Shark Bay in Western Australia around northern Australia and down to Bundaberg in Queensland. It has grown steadily in importance to the Australian fishing industry over the past decade.

P ■ PRAWNS and shrimps

Greasyback prawn *Metapenaeus bennettae:* The famous greasyback or greentail prawn of New South Wales and eastern Queensland is usually abundant in Tuggerah Lakes, in central New South Wales, where it is eagerly sought by amateur and commercial fishermen; in Queensland greasies are probably even more highly regarded as food and bait. The shell over the head and tail is covered with numerous tiny, mat-like hairs which produce the unusually hard, rough surface responsible for their common name. This is Australia's smallest commercial species; males mature at only 7.6 cm while females mature at 7.6 to 10 cm and rarely reach 15 cm.

A closely related species, *Metapenaeus dalli* the western school prawn or greasyback prawn, is found along the Western Australian coast from Mandurah to Broome and is keenly sought by fishermen in the Swan River estuary in the summer months.

Coral prawn *Parapenaeopsis sculptilis:* A brightly coloured tropical species caught commercially in the Gulf of Carpentaria and found along the Queensland coast south to Gladstone. It has four pale crossbands evenly spaced along the head and tail, and a yellow patch along the lower edge of the head. It grows to about 15 cm and is a popular bait with anglers in central Queensland.

Banded coral shrimp *Stenopus hispidus:* A colourful shrimp found throughout the tropical waters of the Pacific and Indian Oceans. Interestingly, this shrimp is neither a penaeid nor a carid but belongs to a group with the characteristics of both. It is only a small species, growing to 10 cm, with flowing white feelers (antennae) and a large pair of third legs ('long arms'). The spiny body and arms are banded with scarlet on a white background.

Banded coral shrimp have the unusual habit of cleaning fish which are attracted to their waving feelers protruding from coral crevices. The fish remain still while the shrimp pick at parasites, damaged tissue or fungi on their body and fins with its claws. The shrimp do not leave their crevice to clean the fish, because fish naturally congregate around the shrimps' 'cleaning stations'.

Banded coral shrimp form long-lasting pair associations and perform courtship dances; in one pair the small male was reported to spend long periods 'saddle riding' on the back of the larger female.

Mantis shrimp There are more than 30 species of mantis shrimp around the Australian coast, ranging in size from 2.5 cm to 30 cm but all with the same shape. They are shrimp in name only because the body has a flattened cross-section and the second pair of limbs under the head are toothed raptorial claws resembling the front legs of the praying mantis insect—hence their name.

PRAWNS and shrimps ■ P

Brown tiger prawn

Eastern king prawn

Red spot king prawn

Greasyback prawn

School prawn

Mantis shrimp

Burrowing shrimp (yabby)

P ■ PRAWNS and shrimps

These claws function like the blades of a clasp-knife and are efficient in holding small fishes and other animals. Mantis shrimp are frequently taken in prawn trawl nets by commercial fishermen, sometimes with a penaeid prawn clutched in the great claw. However, the prawn was mostly likely caught by the shrimp while they were both inside the trawl net and the shrimp's common name of 'prawn killer' may be unjust. One scientist has described these shrimp as 'the thugs of Crustaceandom'.

A tropical species *Lysiosquilla maculata* has a tiger-like pattern with bold yellow and black bands, while the *Gonodactylus* species which live in crevices amongst coral reefs are brownish green with red and purple claws. The most common species found in southern waters is *Alima laevis*, now sold in the Sydney markets and eagerly sought by Europeans who recognize its similarity to the shrimps eaten in their homelands.

Bait shrimp   Keen fishermen are often seen on tidal mudflats in estuaries searching for the shrimps known as yabbies. These carid shrimp, belonging to the genus *Alpheus*, are easily recognized by their appearance and by the sounds they make. The first pair of legs is modified into heavy nippers, one of which is invariably much larger than the other. A peg-like projection on the movable part of this nipper fits into a socket on the fixed part. The sudden closing of the peg into the socket under strong muscular tension produces a sharp cracking or snapping sound not unlike that of a pistol. A volley of these sharp sounds makes the presence of *Alpheus* spp. obvious to those who are familiar with these creatures. These sounds and the associated jet of water produced by the peg slamming into the socket are believed to be used for defence and offence.

Alpheus spp. are found all around Australia, on coral reefs in the north as well as rocky shores and tidal flats in the south. The tropical species are mostly brightly spotted and barred, while those of the south are duller shades of green and red. The common species *Alpheus edwardsi* and *A. andouini* are greenish, while *A. strenuus* is rose red with darker markings.

Another saltwater yabby with a massive claw is the burrowing shrimp or ghost nipper *Callianassa australiensis*. This pinkish-white creature, which is well known to estuarine fishermen, is in fact more closely related to hermit crabs than prawns or shrimp. It is found on intertidal sand banks or mudflats from northern Queensland to Victoria, in burrows which go down as far as 76 cm. The burrows are essentially for one-way traffic only, each individual having up to three surface openings. Counts of up to 800 openings per square metre attest to the abundance of this popular bait shrimp. Amateur fishermen usually catch them with a manually operated commercial yabby pump while the professional bait fishermen use a powered sand-pump.

Prawn habitat

Penaeid prawns are typically inhabitants of the warmer seas and estuaries, although some species live at great depths where cold water is the rule all year round. They feed on whatever organic material is most readily available, be it animal or vegetable, and are most efficient in picking small food particles from the bottom. Contrary to popular opinion in some parts of Australia, they do not prefer rotting animals and these cannot be recommended as bait for salt or freshwater species. Surprisingly, old-fashioned kitchen soap is an excellent bait for trapping freshwater shrimp in an old stocking or kerosene tin.

Many species of carid shrimp are found in Australia's freshwater streams and lakes; they belong to the families Atyidae or Palaemonidae. The atyid shrimp are easily distinguished by their small size, about 2.5 to 3.5 cm in length, and the tufts of fine hairs on the tips of the walking legs. The palaemonid shrimp, which are also found in estuaries, are more robust and grow to about 15 cm. They are recognizable by the second pair of walking legs which are conspicuously larger than those adjacent.

Small prolific shrimp *Paratya australiensis* are commonly found in the rivers and lakes of eastern Australia, while other members of the family live only in cave pools and deep wells. The mountain shrimp *Atya striolata* grows to 3.7 cm and is found in the clear running water of mountain streams in south-east Australia.

The palaemonid shrimp, like the atyids, live in a wide variety of habitats but not in underground waters. The family has many genera in Australia but the dominant one is *Macrobrachium*, the long-armed shrimps of fresh and salt water. Various species of *Macrobrachium* are found in the estuaries and inland waters around Australia and they provide a welcome treat of fresh seafood for people living away from the coast; they also make good live bait for native fish species.

In northern Queensland rivers some estuarine species of *Macrobrachium* reach more than 15 cm in length and have an equivalent arm span. These large species are highly regarded as food while the smaller ones are more valuable as bait. In New South Wales estuaries *M. novaehollandiae* is common along the shores of lakes and rivers and these shrimp with their thick, long arms are commonly seen in commercial catches of river prawns. Small species such as *M. intermedium* are often seen darting around the pools and shores of New South Wales estuaries, particularly where weed beds abound.

See Bait.

NICK V. RUELLO

Q

QUEENFISH *Scomberoides lysan:* A tropical sporting fish of the family Scombridae, several of which are found in Australia. Aptly described as a large-mouthed leatherskin and also known as charlia, giant dart, skinny fish and white fish, they have few peers as light tackle opponents. They have power, speed and courage, and will leap repeatedly in the effort to throw the lure. Like the dolphin fish, they have sufficient body depth to grip water against the lateral pull of a fishing line.

Queenfish are species which look larger than life and because of the spectacular fight anglers often over-estimate their size. Their only drawback as a species is that their dry flesh, while quite edible, is not outstanding, but their flesh does make outstanding bait for other fish, particularly mackerel and flathead.

In 1985 the biggest queenfish on the Game Fishing Association of Australia's record list was a 14 kg specimen taken at Townsville on a 4 kg line by Andrew Mead in July 1983.

The common size caught by anglers is about 4.5 to 5.5 kg but they reach 14 kg and 1 m. A school fish, they are often found in greater numbers and smaller sizes in estuaries and inlets, with larger specimens being taken at sea, usually near reefs and headlands. One smaller sub-species appears to be oceanic, but this has not yet been substantiated by research.

Specimens of 8 to 9 kg are taken on light game tackle and baitcasters, for these are an ideal light gamefish. They extend as far south as Moreton Bay but are mainly reserved for anglers in waters from Gladstone north. Their speed is enough

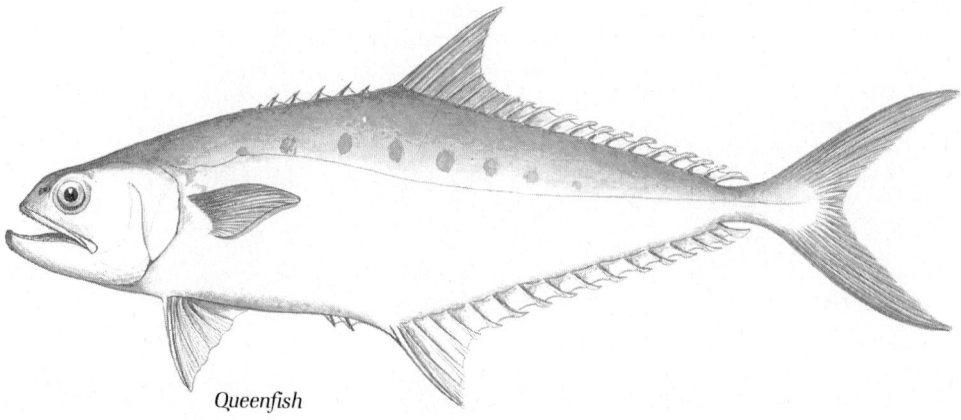

Queenfish

to put a decided curl in even a light line, especially since the average fight is within 90 m. Much of the leaping may take place within 25 m of the boat and this allows the angler an eye-to-eye contest each time the fish leaps, which is often.

Although the lines used by anglers are mostly in the 5.5 to 9 kg classes, queenfish are best fought on lines of 2.7 to 4 kg test. This gives both fish and angler a sporting chance, though the problem here becomes one of hooking the fish as the queenfish's mouth is fairly hard and hooks may not penetrate well on a light line. Tactics during a fight are generally governed by the fish, with scorching runs of up to 90 m and frequent changes of course. The principal aim is to keep a queenfish spending energy as rapidly as possible and it takes little encouragement. Newcomers to queenfish are often demoralised by the sheer speed, but since this is a fish of surface waters, there is little risk of being cut off. The fish's own speed is the thing which will exhaust it.

Queenfish have been taken at night in shallow water on dead baits and beside wharves on floating ones. The best sport comes from trolling or casting. Garfish again is an excellent troll bait, but lures are both easier to rig and just as acceptable to queenfish. Chromed spoons about 7.5 to 10 cm length, such as the Pfleuger, dam and drone are ideal. Plastic or feather squids, dartabouts and killer type plastic wobblers are freely taken. Even more spectacular, and increasingly being used, are surface popping lures such as the speed king and small konaheads. A wire trace is necessary, usually about 2 m in length for trolling. Shorter traces are necessary when casting.

In trolling around headlands seeking queenfish, mackerel and similar sport fish, anglers often go within 10 m of the rocks, weather permitting, and encounter big fish in surprisingly shallow water. The risk in this type of trolling is meeting rock-dwellers such as cod and coral trout, which will quickly cut a light line. This can be circumvented by trolling at a faster speed, about 6 to 7 knots, which is fast enough to make things awkward for slower fish. Queenfish will not be fazed by a few knots extra speed, for they have plenty of speed to spare.

QUEENSLAND

Queensland is favoured by circumstances which provide a wonderful range of species in both fresh and salt water. The sequence is obvious—a long coastline, a larger number of major rivers and volume of fresh water than any other State, a low population density for its 1.5 million citizens, topped off by 2000 km of Great Barrier Reef. The northern State is more decentralized than any other, so facilities are reasonably good except in the remote Cape York and Gulf of Carpentaria.

Official surveys have reflected the discovery that Queensland, with a warm climate ranging from sub-tropical to tropical and a strong regional angling tradition, has a higher proportion than other States of active fishermen. It also has a strong and thriving tackle industry, which includes the traditional sidecast firm of Chas Alvey & Sons, and major rod manufacturers such as Butterworths. There are now active sportfishing clubs everywhere between the Gold Coast and Thursday Island, and bill fishing for sailfish and marlin has expanded hugely along the entire coast after the original boom at Cairns.

In such a benign climate, fishing is possible all year round. Although there is some yellowbelly and Murray cod fishing in the inland systems, most freshwater fishing is in coastal watershed and streams. The coastal currents inside the Barrier Reef usually set with the prevailing winds, but the overall movement is to the south, bringing an equalizing effect to coastal temperatures.

The popular surf fishing is mostly for tailor, bream and sometimes mulloway, on beaches as far north as Bundaberg. There is no exact point at which surf fishing ceases but less is done north of Fraser Island than south of it. Spanish mackerel are largely seasonal throughout their range, which covers the entire coast. They are caught in Barrier Reef waters at any time of year, with catches peaking each spring. Around southern Queensland headlands such as Double Island Point, mackerel are more numerous in summer (apparently travelling from further north), an obvious favourite for Christmas fishing.

Queensland is lucky in the quality of freshwater fishing for native species. Water temperatures are consistently too high for any of the trout family, which are only rarely caught in Queensland—there are some in small streams near Killarney, in the high country along the New South Wales border. This lack is compensated by the richness and diversity of native species, all of which can be taken on fly as well as by more conventional tactics with bait or lures. Recent years have seen an upswing in fly fishing, and it is no surprise to meet fly fishers in pursuit of barramundi, bass, the different varieties of sooty grunter, archer fish, freshwater long toms and tarpon. It is now necessary to check for closed seasons, as there has been a closed season on barramundi (from November to January) for some years, and closures are likely to be introduced for bass.

Visitors to Queensland usually prefer winter to summer. There is a 'wet' or at least a wetter season between January and June, but it is only a problem in remote areas such as Cape York, where roads are still poor. Summer maximums along the coast are normally in the mid-thirties, though a hot summer day might run into the forties. Late winter is cool and dry and suits southern visitors who wish to avoid their own winters. Unless one has a specific target such as giant black marlin (spring) or barramundi (avoiding the closed season), the season for a visit to Queensland is not critically important, as general fishing is available all year.

Sunshine Coast

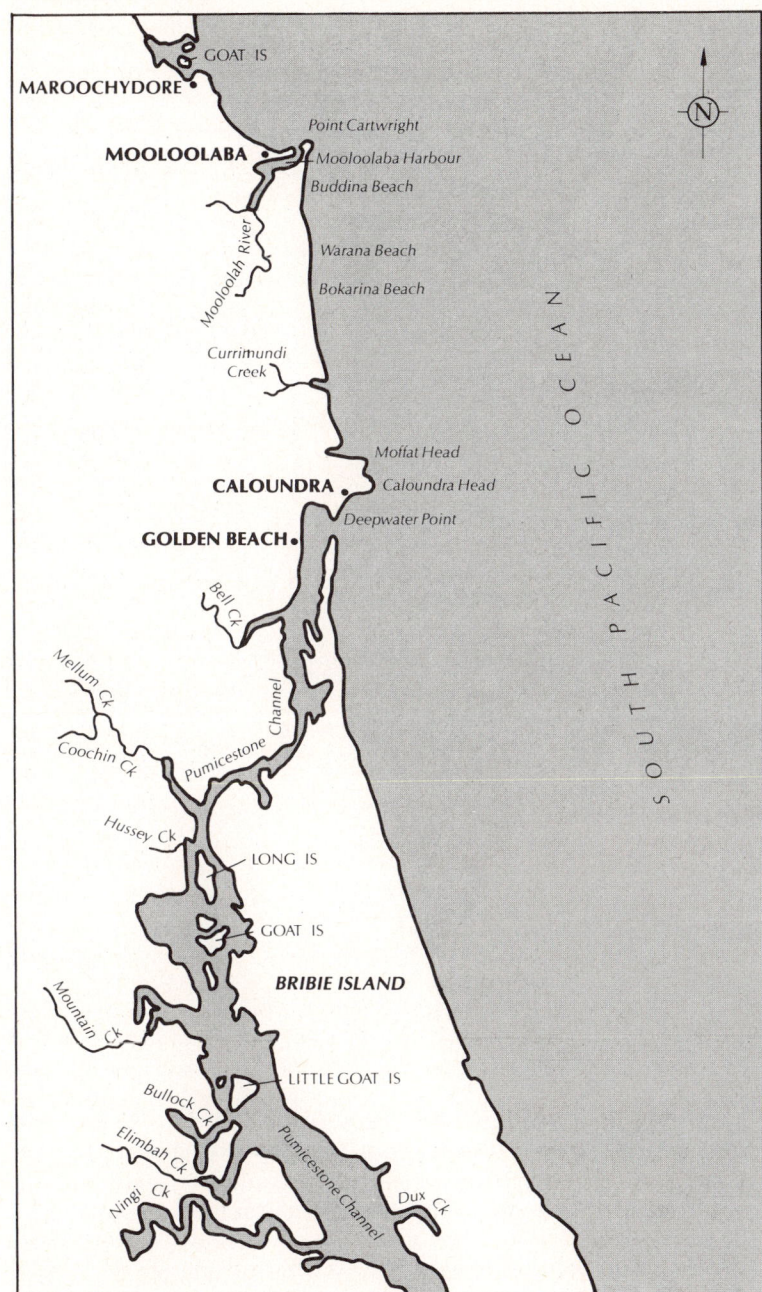

The Sunshine Coast from spots like Caloundra, Mooloolaba and Noosa Heads in the north to Bribie Island in the south is ideal for estuary and lake fishing and abounds with good beaches. Surf anglers must remember that 25 kg lines are regarded here as light.

Moreton Bay

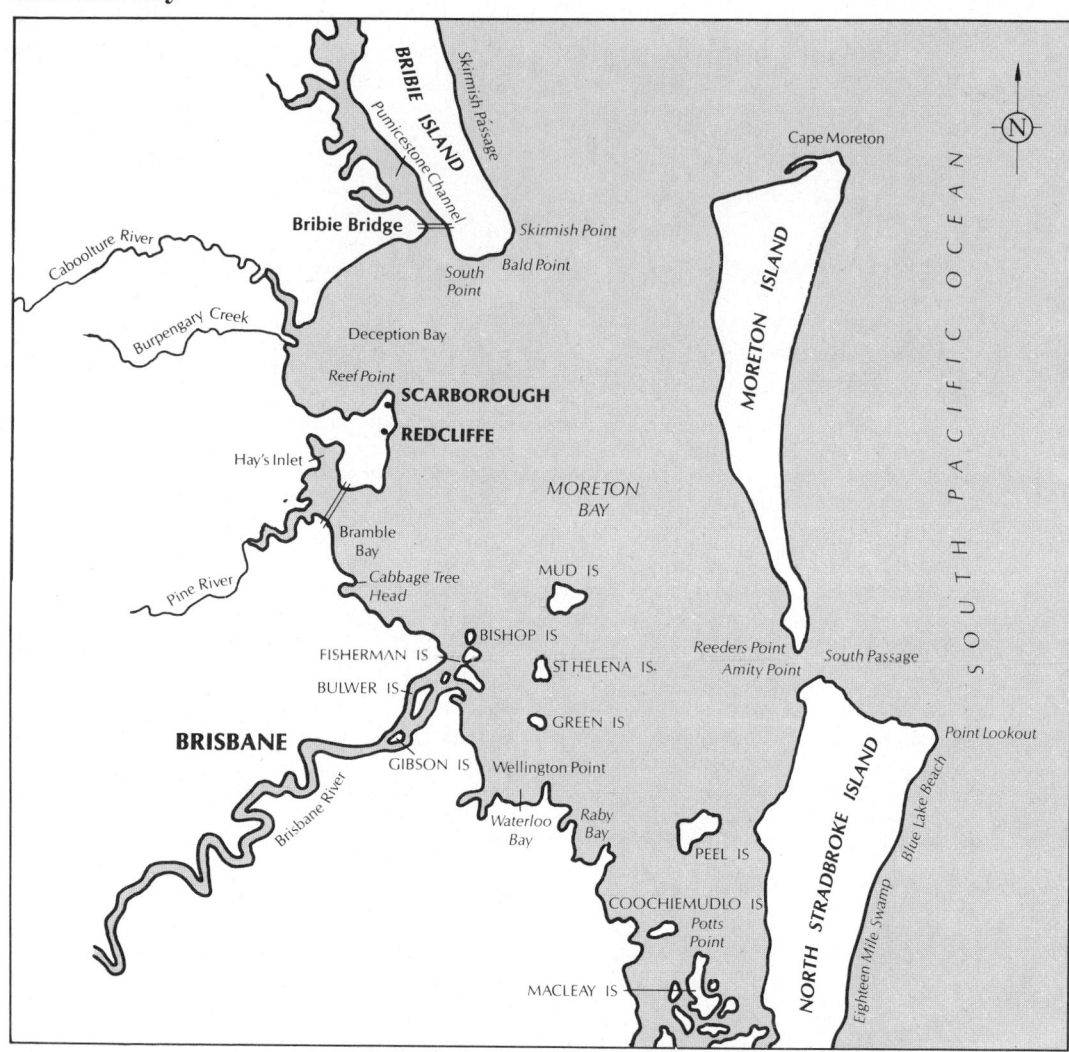

Most Brisbane residents have at some time fished in Moreton Bay, a large stretch of water bounded by Bribie and Moreton Islands to the north and east and Stradbroke Island to the south-east. A large part of the bay is encumbered by shoals and at the southern end there are dozens of small islands. Small craft use the South Passage or Rous Channel, larger vessels the channel between Bribie and Moreton Islands.

Tidal influence provides outstanding spawning grounds for a wide variety of fish and the delicious mud crab and Moreton Bay bug. Garfish, jewfish and bream are abundant and snappering with light tackle from the eastern or seaward side of the three islands is popular.

Southport Broadwater

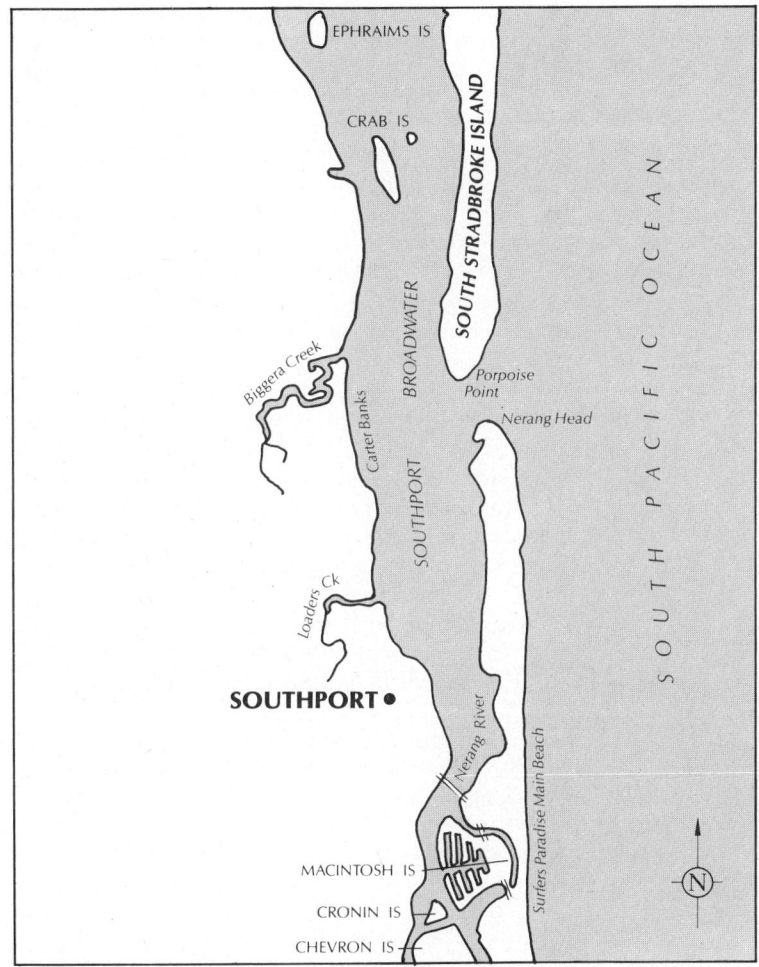

The beaches of the Southport Broadwater district attract a large number of anglers from Brisbane, only 80 kilometres away, as well as holidaymakers from the Gold Coast. A wide variety of small species enter the enclosed waters of the Broadwater through the channel between Nerang Head and Porpoise Point, but probably the best fishing is found on the eastern side of South Stradbroke Island and at Jumpinpin where it is separated from the larger North Stradbroke Island. Mining for beach sand minerals has destroyed many of the favoured old beach locations, but the popularity of fishing in the area can be seen by the large number of small boats that stand offshore to fish for bream, tailor, mullet and flathead.

Despite population pressure, the Southport Broadwater is an ideal spot for the angler whose stomach cannot cope with rough seas.

How Queensland compares

The Queenslander is an independent all-Australian who operates at a very practical level, with scant regard for the traditions of older lands. Increasing movement amongst fishermen means there is now much more harmony in the attitudes of anglers from different regions. A South Australian or a Victorian can take his or her home tackle north with complete confidence, although it is true there are regional preferences in the kinds of tackle chosen.

Perhaps the biggest difference the visitor will encounter is in the surf fishing of southern Queensland, which is dominated by the Alvey sidecast reel made in Brisbane. Amongst its devotees, the sidecast is not merely one kind of reel but a whole fishing method, so successful as to dominate beach fishing contests.

Most sidecasts are direct drive reels which can be turned sideways on a turntable to release line with minimal friction. One geared model of sidecast has been released for those who need greater retrieval speeds. The rod is usually longer than those used for geared reels. Although the sidecast system seems cumbersome, it is in fact highly efficient and allows an unweighted bait to be cast further, the sidecast success hinging largely on this factor and the robust nature of the reel. The use of linked hooks with pilchard and garfish baits is a large part of the system. The Alvey name has long been synonymous with practical, well-made products.

The former materialist attitude of Queensland fishing has changed greatly in the last decade, the result of a declining fishery resource and advances in the sportfishing outlook. Despite the reputation of the State, visitors do encounter problems and find they still need to know the tides, seasons and places to fish. Overall, there is a greater likelihood that a wire trace will be needed, or heavier line used—especially amongst the coral of the Great Barrier Reef. Along the east coast, the barramundi decline has been halted by tighter management measures, including closed seasons, but the best barra fishing is available in upper Cape York and the Gulf country. The settled country of Queensland has been fished for over a century and results are often little different from what might be found in New South Wales or Victorian estuaries. A heavily fished estuary is a heavily fished estuary, wherever one goes.

The situation improves greatly when species such as javelin fish, threadfin salmon, mangrove jack, estuary cod and trevally are encountered. The best estuary bait in Queensland is probably a whole fresh prawn. Bream, whiting, mulloway and flathead are found throughout the tropics, not necessarily in the same quantities or the same species as those of the south. Generally speaking, the variety of table and sporting fish, especially those likely to take lures, is greater.

Freshwater fishing comparisons include the absence of trout, the presence of bass in streams from the New South Wales border north to the Noosa River, saratoga in the Gulf country, barramundi north of the Mary River, and various kinds of grunter from the Fitzroy north.

Queensland's fishing laws

Although laws are liberal, they now include closed seasons for barramundi, and bag limits for barramundi, spanner or frog crabs and Australian bass. The use of nets, other than bait nets of stipulated size and design, is prohibited to all anglers. Certain areas close to weirs are closed to fishing. Fishing is likewise restricted or forbidden in certain lakes under the control of water supply authorities. Spearfishing is allowed in defined areas of salt water, but forbidden around jetties and in fresh water of any kind. In tidal waters, up to six hooks are allowed on a single line; in fresh water, one hook. Triple hooks are classed as a single hook.

Garfish are often taken in bait nets up to 16 m in length, with the legal mesh size between 12 and 28 mm. A cast net is also popularly used for catching bait such as herring, hardyheads, mullet and prawns. Cast nets are also subject to legal size limits.

Oysters other than those on commercial leases may be taken freely if eaten on the spot, a regulation more often observed in the breach than reality. Only male crabs (mainly mud and sand crabs) may be kept, and these should have a minimum carapace width of 15 cm.

Increased management measures have made the picture complex, when viewed right across the massive northern State.

MINIMUM LEGAL LENGTHS IN QUEENSLAND

Barramundi	50 cm	Luderick	23 cm
Bass, Australian	30 cm	Mackerel, Broad-barred,	
Bream, Pikey,		Narrow-barred,	
Yellow-finned etc.	23 cm	Queensland School,	
Cod, Estuary Rock	35 cm	Spotted	45 cm
Cod, Murray	50 cm	Mullet, Sea	30 cm
Crab (carapace)		Mulloway	30 cm
Mud, Sand	15 cm	Perch, Golden	30 cm
Spanner	10 cm	Saratoga	35 cm
Emperor, Red	35 cm	Snapper	25 cm
Emperor, Red-finned,		Tarwhine	23 cm
Sweetlips	30 cm	Teraglin, Jew, Silver	30 cm
Flathead, Bar-tailed,		Trout, Coral	35 cm
Mud, Sand	30 cm	Salmon, Burnett,	
Groper, Queensland	35 cm	Cooktown	40 cm
Javelin Fish, Small-Spotted,		Salmon, Dawson River	35 cm
Spotted	30 cm	Whiting, Gold-lined,	
Jewfish, Silver, Spotted	30 cm	Sand	23 cm

A system of habitat reserves, fish sanctuaries, wetland reserves and public oyster areas is detailed in the *Tide Book* put out annually by the Queensland Department of Harbours and Marine. This book is freely available in numerous outlets along the coast, primarily newsagents, and should be checked for changes to the regulations. More information on restricted areas, net sizes, bag limits and minimum legal lengths can be found in the pamphlet 'Recreational Fishing in Queensland' which can be obtained from the Queensland Fish Management Authority.

Fishing facilities
It is only during peak holiday periods that visitors might find accommodation scarce in resort areas. The coast to the immediate south and north of Brisbane (Gold Coast and Sunshine Coast) is thick with every variety and permutation of holiday accommodation, from caravans and camping grounds to luxury home units. The Sunshine Coast suits most anglers better than the surf-oriented Gold Coast, as there are more estuary areas such as the Noosa and Maroochy. The area within 150 km of Brisbane is famed for fishing country such as Bribie Island, the Jumpinpin area, and some beaches. Areas such as Moreton Bay and Tangalooma are now renowned for great fishing, ranging from whiting up to blue-water sport fishing, especially for sailfish and marlin. World records are now being set regularly in this area.

The quality of beach, estuary and sea fishing within 150 km of Brisbane accounts for the growth of the sportfishing scene in particular. It is a region where visiting anglers are well catered for, with bait, boats and a local population involved in fishing, which knows the importance of helping visitors.

Further afield, coastal Queensland as far north as Cooktown has ample accommodation in every community, including the smaller ones. Bait is available and boats of good quality are on hire everywhere, and a few inquiries are all that is needed to answer all a visitor's needs.

Queenslanders are generally free with fishing information, and the abundant sportfishing clubs are able to offer advice. As well, land maps and marine charts can be bought at newsagents in all towns. These are valued aids, as much of Highway 1 (Bruce Highway) runs inland away from the sea. Access to estuaries and seaside resorts often requires leaving the highway. Most roads are bitumen and are clearly marked.

Differences between tropical angling techniques are not so great as formerly, and all major coastal towns feature well-informed tackle outlets, some of them (such as Bransfords of Cairns) being world famous.

One vital point is the need for boats in most coastal fishing. While surf fishermen might not need a dinghy, the estuary, river or sea angler will need an appropriate small craft. It might be anything from a car-topper to a boat hired locally, but some means of getting out on the water is essential.

Cairns

With a population of only 50,000, the northern city happily proclaims itself the 'Sportfishing Capital of Australia'. The fishing potential of the Barrier Reef, known for so long, came to reality at Cairns for very logical reasons. The scenic coastline is an important advantage, as is the fact that the coral reefs come closer to the land mass in the far north. Further down the coast, fishermen may have to travel 200 km to sea to reach similar reefs. Off Cairns, some of the major reefs are within 20 km of the coast, and while these areas are naturally heavily fished, they cater to skindivers and tourists in a very positive way.

The sportfishing picture at Cairns has matured and gone through an obvious cycle since the giant billfish were first discovered by Captain George Bransford in the 1960s. Hundreds of marlin weighing over the status figure of 1000 lb (450 kg—the imperial system still applies with marlin) have been caught. Fullscale charter fleets developed over the years, and competition for charter work and escalating costs forced many changes. Today the peak season for giant marlin is October and November, and much greater emphasis is now placed on the expanding giant of light tackle fishing. It has turned out that smaller marlin and sailfish, as well as bluewater specials such as wahoo, Spanish mackerel, dolphin fish, cobia and others are available all year round.

There are useful lessons in the decline of the giant marlin business at Cairns. Originally, the season was thought to be of four months' duration, from September to December. However, all the large fish are females, and the peak breeding season which brings them together and makes them vulnerable to game fishermen is centred around the shorter period in October and November. Relatively few game fishermen can afford the charter rates, with total costs now often in excess of $1000 a day, and cheaper fishing of more or less equal quality has been located in other regions. Since it is impossible to earn a year's living in such a short period, alternative fishing of various kinds is usually the lot of the charter fleet for the rest of the year. Sometimes it is commercial fishing, including handlining, at others more use is made of light tackle opportunities, with superb anglers such as Jack Erskine and Jim Dalling catching world record marlin on lines as light as 2 kg.

It remains true that the world all-time record for black marlin is as likely to be broken out of Cairns as anywhere else in the world, and the marlin appear not to have suffered from the fishing. In recent years there has been a marked increase in the numbers of juvenile marlin to 50 kg, right along the Queensland coast.

In the wake of a gameboat a black marlin is towed back to port at Cairns. This area is still producing very exciting game fishing.

Facilities for tourists

Cairns has grown tremendously as a tourist destination, with no sign of any slowdown. Land reclamation and the building of its own international airport have increased the potential. At the height of the tourist season in winter (June to October) resources are heavily taxed.

Cairns has not always responded happily to the growth rate. Some of the more crowded van parks fill and overflow and become less than attractive. Visitors find the parking policies a real barrier to a happy visit. A useful improvement in a tourist town could well be to take heed of the Gold Coast policy with 'meter maids' helping out on expired parking meters. Parking is often crowded and difficult, with regulations that are restrictive rather than helpful. Petrol prices have always been higher, for some reason, than those of nearby towns and cities. However, street lighting has improved greatly, a new open mall has been built, and nightlife has expanded. Some excellent restaurants cater to discerning visitors. With the sole exception of the primitive attitudes on parking, tourism at Cairns is off and running.

The region has great tourism potential and is starting to attract increasing numbers of wealthy Asians. Even the frontal mudflat is widely used by visiting birdwatchers, as it provides a convenient and comfortable site for observation of seabirds and waders at low tide. When the tide is high, the city is picturesquely situated on Trinity Bay, with Mount Murray Prior and the Malbon Thompson range jutting into the skyline to the east and the Great Dividing Range (the Atherton Tableland) to the west. The harbour faces north along Cape York.

There are daily airline services to southern cities, and Qantas runs regular international flights to Singapore, New Zealand and other destinations. The modern international airport is also used by the national airlines of Papua New Guinea and other countries. Bus and train services run at least daily and usually more often.

The region makes a logical departure point for fishermen embarking for the Great Barrier Reef. There are regular departures in fast, modern reef fishing boats, and all varieties of fishing taste are catered to by a diverse fleet of craft. Cairns is base for hundreds of prawn trawlers and mackerel boats, so it is a natural region for connoisseurs of fresh seafood.

There is a wide choice of fast tourist day-trips to places such as Green Island, with its glass-bottomed boats and underwater observatory, and Fitzroy Island. The nesting colonies of seabirds on Michaelmas and Upolu sand cays are another popular day jaunt within easy reach. In recent times there has been an increasing demand for day trips to destinations such as the Bloomfield Fishing Lodge (north of Daintree) and to Cooktown and the luxury tourist resort at Lizard Island, by light plane. Destinations further afield include Karumba, Gove, Thursday Island and fishing camps at Burketown and the tip of Cape York.

Members of the local sportfishing clubs are friendly and helpful. The Australian National Sportfishing Association (A.N.S.A.) had its genesis at Cairns, and its code remains strong in the region. Those who trail or car-top small boats north find typical and varied fishing in the safe mangrove confines of Trinity Inlet, with maps available in local sports stores. The happy alternative for windy days, when boats might not go to sea, is an inland journey to sample the freshwater fishing of Tinaroo Dam on the Atherton Tableland. Several native species have been stocked experimentally in the dam. North from Cairns, the coast road runs beside the sea and opens up a wonderland of headlands, beaches and small estuaries all the way to Cooktown. This is a region of lush tropical beauty with many clear rainforest streams.

Daintree River

This is a beautiful rainforest stream about 100 km north of Cairns on the coast road. The headwaters rise in the forests of the Great Dividing Range inland from the village of Daintree. The river and its numerous tributaries, including Stewart

Rainforest rivers like the Russell offer diverse fishing for species such as sooty grunter, archer fish and mangrove jack.

Creek and Alexandra Creek, are renowned for their sooty grunter fishing. The area has been settled for about 100 years, and as the result of inevitable erosion, siltation has occurred and the river is mostly relatively shallow. There are said to be a few small crocodiles still evident in the river, and these are sometimes seen by tourists.

The river is tidal for about 10 km, and is fished by locals and visitors alike for barramundi, tarpon, javelin fish and queenfish. Trevally and flathead are more abundant around the sandbars of the river bar, which although shallow is safe in calm water for boat access to Snapper Island and the reefs outside. Snapper Island is a convenient location for sheltered trolling for mackerel and other pelagics such as barracuda and queenfish.

The lower reaches of the Daintree are mangrove-lined, providing all the usual potential for estuary cod, grunter, mangrove jack, bream, threadfin salmon, small barracuda and sometimes barramundi. Access across the river is by barge, but the condition of the road north to Cooktown is variable and even debatable. It is not always safe for family cars and may be seasonally closed north of Cape Tribulation. This is beautiful but mountainous country best left to independent fishermen with four-wheel-drive vehicles.

Facilities at the attractive and quiet village of Daintree are excellent, with stores and van parks. Charter power-boat trips out to the Reef can be arranged, either here or further south at Mossman or Port Douglas. Although most tourism centres on winter months, fishing is great during the rains in summer—

the time when locals enjoy some of their best fishing.

It should be noted that the wet season in this area is only rarely flood weather. Runoff is fast and the summer picture is one of healthy streams and lush scenery, as opposed to the low-water conditions of the 'dry'. Floods cause no more problems in the north than they do in New South Wales or Victoria.

Gregory River

Two of the most beautiful Gulf country rivers in North Queensland are the Gregory and O'Shannassey, which enter the sea through mangrove deltas near Burketown. They intrigue anglers since the headwaters are remarkably close to those of the Georgina, a south-flowing stream which carries only inland fish such as yellowbelly and silver perch as it wanders slowly through the Cooper Channel country towards Lake Eyre.

The northern watershed is completely tropical, with the upper reaches containing sooty grunter (*Hephaestus* spp.) plus catfish, tarpon, archer fish, freshwater long toms, banded perch and others. Some of the creeks also hold saratoga but these are now less common. Closer to the sea, the picture is improved by the presence of barramundi, for which the Escott Lodge on the Nicholson delta is famed.

As with many inland rivers, the country away from the rivers is harsh and arid, providing a spectacular contrast to the lush beauty of the river itself. Upstream reaches carry freshwater crocodiles, and saltwater crocs are still present in the lower and tidal reaches, so care should always be exercised. A variety of freshwater whaler shark is present, as are saw sharks and rays, but these rarely give anglers any problems.

The Gulf is cattle country, and permission should be asked from landholders before it is fished. Most cattlemen have no serious objection to sporting anglers willing to leave a clean campsite.

Fly fishing has proved a surprisingly successful method here, largely pioneered by the fishery consultant Hamar Midgley. Ordinary trout tackle is ideal, with small black wet flies favoured. The most popular gear is usually light spinning tackle or baitcasters, but small trout spinners also work well. Larger minnow lures such as the Nilsmasters, Rapalas and others are the method of choice in the barramundi country.

Bait fishing in the freshwater Gulf rivers is simplicity itself, using small cubes of corned beef impaled on a No. 1 suicide hook and fished without a sinker, or else under a float, preferably under overhanging trees.

This part of the Gulf is vast, flat and isolated. It is *not* suited to wet season visits and is safest for family cars from June to November. Although roads have improved, there is little bitumen and much black soil. Visitors should seek advice on local road conditions from nearby centres, or from Burketown or Karumba, before tackling the Gulf. The nature of the

Mitchell River

country is such that visitors should be self-sufficient for supplies, fuel, and especially water. The usual visitor is independently organized, and four-wheel-drive vehicles are standard equipment.

Cape York's Mitchell River has one of the largest tributary areas in Australia, with wet season run-off causing extensive and regular flooding. Should irrigation ever eventuate, this area will feature large dams of extensive surface area. Relatively few anglers visit the Mitchell. Upper tributary rivers such as the Lynd, Walsh, Palmer and Alice are fished by anglers from Cairns and the Atherton Tablelands for sooty grunter and catfish, but barramundi only occur within about 150 km of the sea. In the dry season, these rivers are reduced to chains of deep holes, which hold the surviving fish population.

If anglers could obtain permission from the Aboriginal community, using paid guides, there is scope for wonderful fishing in the Mitchell delta.

Port Douglas

This is an important tourist embarkation point for Reef trips, about 55 km north of Cairns. The little town has boomed in recent years, with a strongly developed tourist industry. The film entrepreneur Ben Cropp has his headquarters here, and other renowned charter-boat skippers include Manny Sims, one of the most enduring and popular charter operators in the country. The standard of accommodation and restaurants is high, without the crowding and parking problems which have come to be associated with Cairns. Party and charter boats take fishermen and skindivers to locations such as Low Isles and the accessible reefs. These include Tongue, Batt, Pickersgill, Chinaman, Escape and the long string of famous marlin reefs, the Ribbons.

Local charter and boat-hire of all kinds is available from Port Douglas, and car-top enthusiasts can reach the local inlet, the port itself, the Mowbray River or the Daintree estuary. Port Douglas is an excellent base for access to the crystal rainforest streams, including the North and South Mossman, Stewarts Creek and Baileys Creek (the area north of the Daintree).

Shute Harbour

This has been a major tourist area for many years, tourism being the major focus and fishing generally taking second place. A huge number of boats and charter services, including bareboating, are available for the busy resorts of the Whitsundays—Hayman, South Molle, Lindeman, Dent, Daydream and Long Island. Although on this section of coast, the Reef is about 80 km out to sea, there is excellent blue-water fishing amongst the rips and currents of the islands.

Everything from bonefish to sailfish have been caught amongst these islands and, apart from cyclones, the waters are fairly sheltered. However, they can be dangerous waters

Useful bait prawns can be found in pannikin grass, which surrounds many small streams in Queensland.

during high winds, partly because the area is one of greater tidal range. Wind-against-tide situations can cause surprisingly rough water, so despite the splendid scenery of sheltering islands, visitors should treat the area with respect.

Strong sportfishing clubs have developed in this area (primarily at Proserpine on the mainland), and fishing advice is freely available. The fact that the tourist boom has made fishermen less visible does not mean they are not present. This is one of the State's top fishing areas.

Tinaroo Dam

This large dam on the Atherton Tableland is mainly fed by the upper Barron River, which ultimately passes over spectacular falls into the Barron Gorge, just outside Cairns, from whence it enters the sea. The Tablelands country is popular with coastal dwellers, being cooler and drier. There are excellent caravan parks, hotels, motels and other accommodation.

The dam has contained freshwater fish since it was constructed, the major edible species being sleepy cod (to 3 kg) plus smaller species such as archer fish, banded perch and mouth almighty—none of which are exactly the stuff of angling dreams. In more recent times, the Walkamin Fisheries Research team, headed by biologist Mal McKinnon, has stocked sooty grunter, saratoga, silver perch and hairback herring in the dam, hoping to establish a viable fishery. Eeltail catfish are known to be breeding, but results to date have not been spectacular in angling terms. The most reliable capture, and

Q ■ QUEENSLAND

The Barron River Gorge provides exciting fishing for jungle perch and, further downstream in the tidal waters, barramundi.

excellent eating, is the sleepy cod, which is sometimes caught around the shoreline. Favoured locations for the sleepy cod are amongst snags and weedbeds, but they are a very sedentary fish and action is often slow.

Great Barrier Reef

The Reef is one of the world's great fishing attractions, and is the backbone of Queensland's tourist industry, now a mammoth, rivalling primary industries in cash flow. The Barrier Reef picture necessarily includes the enclosed waters and coastline adjacent to it. There is some difficulty in comprehending the scale of a natural wonder which reaches north for 2000 km and includes an area of 160,000 sq km. The southernmost end is in the Bunker Group south-east of Gladstone, from whence it extends up the Australian coast and across Torres Strait to Papua New Guinea.

This is not an unbroken barrier, but one composed of thousands of separate coral reefs ranging from tiny coral bomboras to massive areas of coral and sand. Some reefs, such as the Ribbons south of Lizard Island, are relatively narrow but provide a protective wall against the open ocean. The Swain and Saumarez Reefs, from 200 to 450 km east of Mackay, cover a huge area. In general, the major reefs are separated by channels from 50 to 70 m deep, and some of these are dangerously studded with niggerheads and bomboras—which however are magnetic attractors for fish and fishermen. Some are intersected by waterways resembling rivers, negotiable at high tide. Others provide sheltered lagoons for relatively secure anchorage.

The unfortunate truth about the Barrier Reef is that it is

further out to sea than suits tourists or fishermen. It is only from about Innisfail (100 km south of Cairns) that the reefs encroach within about 30 km of the mainland.

From this point south, the Reef is increasingly further out to sea, and fishermen from Townsville south routinely travel 100 km and more out to sea to fish.

At its natural best the Barrier Reef is among the best fishing grounds in the world, and good fishing is not confined to reef areas alone. Inshore waters include rocky continental islands surrounded by coral, occasional small reefs, regions of dead coral bottom, not to mention areas between the reefs where pelagics, including sailfish and small marlin, are common.

The entire Great Barrier Reef is now under the control of the Great Barrier Reef Marine Park Authority (G.B.R.M.P.A.) which has subdivided the massive complex into zones. Fishing is allowed in most of these areas, but there are some areas of restricted used, including total protection on areas of major scientific interest.

For the average visitor, there are three options on fishing the Reef. You might stay on one of the island resorts; tour the coast and join party boats going out from major towns; or trail your own boat north behind your vehicle for total independence.

Of the Barrier Reef resorts, only Heron Island and Green Island are on true sand cays, both vegetated. All other resorts are on continental islands, mostly within a short distance of the coast. All are within reach of great fishing, and run boat trips for visitors.

Selecting a base

In choosing an island resort it must be understood that they attract a clientele with varied interests, of which fishing is but one. Many do not cater significantly for fishing, other than occasional blue-water trolling or handlining for reef fish. Experience has shown that it is wise to double check with any resort before accepting the blandishments of travel agents that Barrier Reef fishing is part of the deal. And all fishing arrangements are conditional on weather being suitable—the southeast tradewinds prevail along the coast for much of the year.

The main offshore resorts and their embarkation points include Heron (Gladstone), Keppel Island (Yeppoon), Brampton Island (Mackay), all the Whitsunday island resorts (Shute Harbour), Magnetic Island (Townsville), Orpheus Island (Dungeness), Hinchinbrook Island (Cardwell), Bedarra and Dunk Island (Mission Beach), Double Island, Fitzroy Island, Green Island (Cairns) and Lizard Island (plane only, from Cairns). Visiting fishermen are advised again—double check about available fishing first and do not hesitate to complain loud and clear if you suffer from misleading information.

Those who tour the coast by car, joining party boats at suitable centres, get a better look at the fishing. But touring should be done at the right time. Summer months are often wet, or if sunny extremely hot and humid. Rain is likely in March and April, with south-easters developing during the winter months from May through to September. The peak tourist period is from June to August. September and October can be unsettled, but the humid weather of November often provides a series of calms (and occasional violent thunderstorms) and is a prime blue-water fishing month.

Despite the great distances, the coast is easily toured by car. The further north one goes, the better the fishing and the more numerous the tourist attractions. More boats are available and it is easier to see the true Barrier Reef from centres like Cairns and Port Douglas. Unless equipped with a caravan or tent, it is necessary to book well ahead for the prime tourist season.

Reconstructed and new roads have altered the travel conditions for motorists, with roads being widened, bridges rebuilt and roadside camping and accommodation vastly improved. Of importance to fishermen towing boats or vans is the happy fact that few if any steep grades are negotiated, unless one wishes to drive inland over the mountains.

Fishing clubs

A wide variety of fishing clubs operate in Queensland, and members of the appropriate organizations are welcome guests in every town during fishing trips. It is usual for visitors to pay their own way or their share of expenses.

The Australian National Sportfishing Association has clubs in every large and most small coastal towns. A.N.S.A. members usually have their own small boats and run family-oriented excursions, sometimes more than once a month.

Other centres such as Townsville and Cairns have deep-sea angling clubs, which either hire charter boats or buy their own from the proceeds of club outings. It is necessary to fish in the same way as the club members on these deep-sea trips, which are sometimes open to visitors. In some areas, the use of rods on these boats is still prohibited, with the result that some humorous confrontations have occurred.

Party boat angling

This is usually bottom fishing over extremely rugged coral country, in depths from 20 to 60 m. A suitable list of equipment would include handlines on large plastic spools, each with several hundred metres of 20 to 30 kg nylon line, a few dozen large hooks from 4/0 to 8/0, and the same quantity of heavy sinkers. Some plebeian types simply use heavy rusted nuts, picked up around industrial workshops. A lot of tackle is lost on the bottom.

For rough bottom fishing it often helps to rig the sinker on the bottom of the line, with the two hooks set 50 cm and 1 m up the line.

The best baits are tough and fresh. Squid is a magnificent reef bait, and when small sharks are caught, they are generally cut up as bait. Belly flaps from tuna and mackerel provide top baits, and small whole fish such as garfish and herring are often used.

At night, the desirable coral trout largely go off the bite and fishing is often for red emperor, a prime table fish. An oddity of reef fishing is that fish seem to prefer the same top quality flesh which anglers prize, and it is not unusual for prime baits to be cut from desirable fish caught during the day.

Along such a great distance of coast, it is natural that fishing varies from place to place. Gladstone fishermen can take a very mixed catch. Specialist boats from Cairns or Townsville often focus on red emperor and coral trout.

Mackay is a prime base for some of the larger charter boat operations. Cruises of a week or more are available here, as elsewhere along the coast, both to the Reef and among the islands. Shute Harbour is ideal for those seeking shorter day trips, as fishing is available over rough bottom within the confines of the island groups. Shute Harbour itself is perfectly sheltered and makes a fitting base for those with their own trailer boats. It opens out through the scenic islands of the Whitsundays. Trolling has become popular, providing mackerel of several kinds, trevally of various kinds, cobia, queenfish, and always barracuda.

Excellent concrete ramps are provided into calm water at Shute Harbour, Airlie Beach and Cannonvale. The fishing is made safer through the operation of the coastguard system—visitors can fill out trip sheets before leaving and report on their return, availing themselves of the protection available to all boats. Two-way radios are extensively used, although in this area the islands sometimes impede reception.

Bowen is a thriving seaport with an active sportfishing club and excellent launching ramps, giving easy access to inshore fishing and the islands north of the Whitsundays. Gloucester Island and the smaller islands near it are popular destinations.

Townsville is now a thriving city with a population over 100,000. The discovery of inshore sportfishing grounds, including sailfish and small marlin, has helped this area tremendously, and a wide range of charter boats for bluewater sport and reef fishing work out from Townsville. The former bugbear of great distances to the Reef was largely removed when Jim and Ann Dalling and other game fishermen put the finger on fabulous billfish country close to shore. The fish are not gigantic, fitting light tackle and smaller boats, and this has worked to reduce charter costs to much more bearable levels.

There are three sportfishing clubs active in Townsville, plus the game fishing and reef fishing organizations. Traditionally, charter reef trips leave early Saturday morning or sometimes Friday night. The range of species and tactics are similar to those north and south, though the fishermen themselves stress that they have better local methods and variations—

normal in fishermen everywhere! Large craft tend to return on Sunday night from weekend trips, but Townsville sportfishermen in their own smaller boats might fish the Palm group further north and return early Sunday morning to take advantage of the calmer seas. Wind governs the whole scene.

Although over-fishing of the closer reefs has caused something of a decline, overall reef fishing catches have held up fairly well. Some take the view that this is partly the result of improved technology in both navigation and echo sounders, but it is hardly rational to expect improved technology to increase actual catches.

The Townsville area is monitored by the Great Barrier Reef Marine Park Authority and by the Australian Institute of Marine Science, based just outside Townsville. Both these organizations are happy to advise visitors, and visits for groups of interested people can be arranged with both G.B.R.M.P.A. and A.I.M.S. Of course, this does not extend to the casual visitor who drops in without warning.

Dungeness, near Lucinda at the southern end of Hinchinbrook Channel, is virtually the fishing port for the sugar district of Ingham. Charter fishing can be arranged here, with shorter trips to the Reef than are available from Townsville, or to the Palm Island Group. This last is famed as an area for big trevally, queenfish and mackerel.

Cardwell, at the northern end of Hinchinbrook Channel, gives access to the major islands of Hinchinbrook, Goold and the Brooks. The beachfront is exposed to the sea, with one boat ramp which is often difficult to handle. At low tide, the mud flat is exposed and boats have to wait for high water. If a wind springs up, the sea becomes rough enough to make launching or retrieving of boats difficult or dangerous. Locals are good judges of the right time to come or go. Hinchinbrook Island itself is magnificent, with spectacular mountains rising over 1000 m high, and a huge area of complex mangrove channels and bays. Most of the waters are shallow and summer visitors should always be wary of the lethal box jellyfish, which often occurs in the muddy inshore waters.

Innisfail is another of those universal 'sugar towns' with its quota of fishing clubs. Ramps in the area are good, usually sheltered, and include locations at Flying Fish Point, right in Innisfail near the town wharf, and at the miniature shipping port of Mourilyan, 11 km south. A number of islands provide magnificent options, including the Barnards and, further south, the Family Group. The game-boat skipper Peter Bristow was primarily responsible for locating the sailfish and marlin grounds out from here, mostly along the 40 m line inside Beaver Cay. The reefs are fairly close and are large in number and variety.

Visitors who bring their own boats north should obtain local advice first, and compare it with the essential marine charts of the reef areas they wish to visit. Even the locals usually go to

Chains of small islands, such as Masthead Island, and their surrounding reefs form part of the Great Barrier Reef along the coast of Queensland.

sea in company or using the radio umbrella provided by the coastguard, which provides a worthwhile advisory source for visitors as well as locals.

The distances are infinitely greater than those marine fishermen are used to in the southern States. It is not necessarily smart to take a small outboard boat 80 km or more to sea. Barrier Reef waters can be as rough and dangerous as seas anywhere.

Effects of the tides

Since most of the Great Barrier Reef is on a continental shelf with depths rarely exceeding 60 m, the large tides have a major impact on fish movement. The Reef is worth a visit in particular during the bigger tidal periods at full and new moons so long as weather is calm. Reefs vary amazingly in form and structure, ranging from large areas of flat sand cay to tangles of bomboras and niggerheads among which navigation is at best precarious. At low tide, the higher reefs often have massive areas exposed, or provide access to sheltered pools ablaze with every colour and form of coral and water life, including fish. The golden rule for safety is simple and blunt—look, don't touch. There are a great many dangers—moray eels, stonefish, stinging corals, several varieties of stinging jellyfish, lethally poisonous cone shells, sharp razor clams, and so on. However, the suitably dressed visitors is safe enough in protective shoes. Something better than sandshoes, too. Even sea urchin spikes will penetrate light footwear.

A reef which seems almost colourless, even drab, from above the surface comes to life suddenly when one enters the water with mask and snorkel.

The more obvious aspects of tidal fall include the appearance of the shallower corals above the surface. Some individual reefs feature winding channels almost like creeks and rivers, in which crystal marine water ebbs and flows. Others are so shallow that at low tide, water spills over the edges in miniature falls. Some locations have deep but narrow channels, with the slope of the continental shelf outside and the shallower, sheltered waters of the reef platform inside. On big tides, dangerous rips form between these openings and a wind-against-tide situation can be impressively rough, something like a deep river running out through a mouth into a storm-tossed sea. Obviously, fishermen are bound to watch such areas closely. All else aside, these same places are among the best fishing areas. Marlin fishing north of Cairns is usually along the tidelines outside the reef openings. Spanish mackerel and other pelagics are often found on the up current side. The larger billfish are often handy to shoals of rainbow runners, scad and other small pelagics near the outlets through the reefs.

Fishermen trolling through new country often work their way through fields of coral niggerheads where coral trout, jobfish and always trevally are likely to slam off into cover after striking the lure or trolled garfish. It is an unfortunate truth that the best times to troll are early morning or late afternoon, preferably when the tide is low. Spanish mackerel, dogtooth tuna and wahoo are usually wider out, clear of the corals or in the drop-off country where depths change suddenly. On the outer barrier, falling tides present the switched-on fisherman with the sight of colour changes and temperature changes in the water—the sun-warmed water of the shallows being some degrees hotter than the oceanic water.

Many of these changes are imperceptible to an untrained eye. Professional marlin crews wear good quality polaroid glasses and use echo sounders to pick up every possible piece of information.

It is quite possible for a novice to enter what is the world's top fishing arena and not see any sign of a fish. You still need to watch keenly, to read the ocean for every possible clue, and, above all, to be ever alert.

Lures and tackle
The range of tackle used is incredible. In the 1980s, specialist sportfishermen such as Jack Erskine blazed new trails catching world record marlin on *2 kg line*. That does not imply that 2 kg line is ideal for the Barrier Reef, just that some fishermen are capable enough to do it in certain circumstances.

However, the range of techniques and skills has exploded to a point where Australian fishermen are matching the rest of the world. Sportfishermen are using lure casting as well as trolling, fly fishing as well as bait. Many commercial mackerel fishermen have discovered the advantage of a troll rod and reel and can be seen trolling with 25 kg line as well as their conventional cord handlines.

If we look at it from the average point of view, a short boat rod with a geared reel—Penn, Daiwa, Shimano—with a capacity of 300 m of 15 kg line will handle a great deal of reef fishing. Such an outfit will cope with mackerel, all the various trevally, barracuda, dolphin fish, jobfish, cobia, and can still fish a reasonably flat coral bottom for reef fish such as sweetlip, emperor and coral trout. In rougher country, it is a simple matter to include a couple of heavier handlines for bottom fishing with bait.

The common troll lures should be capable of working well at effective troll speeds without any line twisting. Twenty years ago, it was rare to see much more than a feather jig or a Drone spoon. Today, high speed troll lures, home-made surface poppers, top-line high speed minnows by Bomber or Rapala and a huge range of either original Knuckleheads (American) or their subsequent copies are likely to be about. Firetail jigs rigged over the heads of trolled garfish are basic to mackerel fishing, taking other species as well. Townsville's well-known authority Mal Florence had much to do with innovations including front-weighted, high speed troll lures, and these are still being made by a number of Queensland's custom lure makers. Most major towns, especially in the north, have one or more professional lure crafters whose work is keenly sought. The lure business is a volatile and active one subject to frequent change, and visitors should check with any of the major northern sports stores for recent developments.

Lures have to face tremendous crushing forces and pressures. Many of the fish have spectacular teeth—Spanish mackerel, for example, have been known to cut through high density plastic lures. The great trevally has been seen to buckle stainless steel spoons. It is quite possible to confront a long fight with any one of dozens of great fish from 15 kg upwards, so all tackle and especially lures must be adequate for the action. Heavy gauge hooks are standard equipment.

Sportfishermen refer frequently to the 'razor gang', those species whose razor teeth cut lines so easily. Thus a wire leader is often needed when trolling, but is much more seldom used when bottom fishing. It is a fairly simple matter, should some protection be needed, to use two or more linked hooks when fishing with bait. It is up to individual choice and fishing circumstance whether wire is used. However, it should always be available for use if necessary. Length of wire is variable according to cases. A typical choice might be an 80 cm leader when trolling for mackerel, or a 50 cm leader when casting lures.

A number of northern sportsmen have swung towards using two-handed spin rods and high quality spin reels such as the Penn 550SS. Rod length in this case is often 2.3 m or longer.

If boats are trailed behind cars for a northern expedition, the visitor should understand the limitations of boat size. It is theoretically possible to fish 60 km to sea in a small aluminium outboard boat, but it is certainly not safe. Northern locals usually fish the Reef with larger craft, often in pairs or in association with a larger boat. Smaller boats (the traditional '14-footer') should stay within easy range of the coast, as there is plenty of magnificent and often sheltered fishing around the inshore islands.

Reef fish
The pattern of fish movement is a complicated mosaic. Where fishing pressures are low, as on the less accessible reefs, catches are likely to be much more mixed. Boats or groups which consistently fish in one area and one style are more likely to come up with predictable species and proportions. Club fishermen at Cairns, for example, seem to catch more red emperor than do club fishermen from Townsville.

In more remote country, coral trout are certainly much more numerous. Biologists have recorded that heavily fished reefs near Cairns contain only 6 per cent of the natural abundance of coral trout, put down to angling pressure on this very desirable species. Around Lizard Island (120 km north of Cairns) coral trout are often 16 times as numerous as around Cairns. Around islands on the extreme northern sector of the Great Barrier Reef Marine Park, this writer has seen large numbers of coral trout in shallow water only waist deep, quite close to the coast. Along the settled country further south, they no longer occur in significant numbers in such locations.

The situation is similar with prime table fish such as the Maori wrasse. These giants can be seen over the shallows along the outer reefs, heavy fish over a metre long.

Regional names often cause confusion, and some textbooks have done less than they might have towards decreasing the confusion. When the I.G.F.A. opened record categories for various trevally, major errors and omissions in the textbooks quickly became evident. Three or four different large trevallies were often called 'turrum'. It was evident some authorities had not bothered to check details.

Identification of species is not an easy job, and taxonomic studies lag a long way behind fishing exploration. Many of the more cautious authorities will go only so far as nominal identification of a doubtful fish, such as *Lutjanus* spp. The trouble lies mainly with the incredible diversity of fish species, with all their potential for regional variants.

Many of the so-called 'cod' family, for example Queensland groper, greasy cod, estuary cod, coral cod, honeycomb cod, passionfruit cod, black-tipped cod, lunar-tailed cod, white-lined rock cod, barramundi cod, purple cod, tomato cod, blue spotted cod, Maori cod and others are not necessarily of the

One of the most plentiful fish in Queensland waters is the coral trout. They are beautifully coloured and can be caught using hand lines as well as rods.

same family. The coral trout family is known to include up to five colour variations which may or may not be of species level.

The perch family is at least equally confused and confusing, with ample evidence of dispute and indecision amongst the taxonomists who know most about them.

Reef tackle busters

Barrier Reef fish are hard on gear and fishermen. The Queensland groper grows to over 300 kg, the greasy cod over 100 kg. Coral trout and others sometimes exceed 25 kg. Since their habitat often includes coral caverns laced with sharp corals, nylon line stands only a chance. Many coral species feed by inhaling prey from ambush, the huge bucket mouths engulfing vast quantities of water as they rush their prey. Groper sometimes do not even need to move.

When in trouble, these and other fish usually head for cover in the coral. Coral trout are known to jam their open gill covers under coral clumps to avoid being pulled out.

Where things become radical is through the habit of big fish eating little fish when the little fish is in trouble. On the Barrier Reef, the 'little' fish that has been hooked may weigh several kilograms and be swallowed before it can be landed by something weighing a hundred kilograms. The process is known to fishermen as being 'monstered'.

The largest fish which are eaten by others can extend even to black marlin and sharks. It is a humbling experience for an angler to discover that the marlin he can hardly handle is being eaten by something much larger, usually a tiger shark. Many such episodes have put the thought of swimming right out of the minds of fishermen.

Virgin fishing waters

Developments in the last decade have pushed the definition of virgin fishing much further north. Hundreds of trawlers and fishing boats are licensed to operate from bases at Cairns, Townsville and Karumba. A flock of game fishing boats work from Lizard Island in season. Roads have improved to formerly remote areas such as Cooktown. So while the fishing is still good along most of the accessible coast, it is no longer virgin in the sense of having seen few fishermen.

The most accessible of the pristine fishing is probably now along the outer Barrier, where few sportsmen venture. Some forms of angling are in better shape than others, and the swing to fly fishing has recently opened up many new options, involving things which have not been done before, over the spreading sand cays of the hundreds of major reefs.

The sole remaining sector of the Reef which justifies the word 'virgin' is north of Lizard Island. This is a tradewind belt, and relentless winds make this a fairly secure preserve of untouched fishing, a stretch of about 600 km of little known water, still marked on the charts as 'dangerous to navigation'.

Of course, the whole area is new to first-time visitors, and an increasing army of discoverers is venturing into the action-packed fields of fishing for mangrove jacks, cod, barramundi. Those with their own boats, or able to afford charter boats, take it much further into those incredible marine arenas where the fisherman is left stunned, awed, and aware of the first goose pimples he has felt for years.

Not everything written about the Barrier Reef is true. But much of it is, and the observant angler can still see great dramas and experience fishing stranger than any fiction. In recent times this writer has met whales, killer whales, false killer whales, manta rays, great groper and giant sharks...

The Reef is still there.

Vic McCristal

QUEENSLAND halibut

See *Flatfish*.

R

RAINBOW fish

Melanotaeniidae: A group of small, colourful freshwater fishes represented by four species in Australia, where they have proved useful destroyers of mosquito larvae. They are also known as jewel fish, freshwater sunfish, rainbow fish or pink ear and come in a wide variety of colours and fin shapes. They frequent tropical pools and lagoons, particularly on Moreton, Stradbroke and Fraser Islands. They are in many aquariums, where fishermen are often asked to identify them for small boys. The southern rainbow fish *Rhadinocentrus ornatus* attains 6 cm and is usually yellowish-brown in colour with the dark margins of the scales a prominent lattice-work. It has two dark lines running along the sides. The northern rainbow fish *Melanotaenia splendida* has opalescent spots along the body and scarlet flecks in the caudal and dorsal fins. It reaches 9 cm and is distributed from the Burdekin area to Charters Towers and Cairns. The crimson-spotted rainbow fish *Melanotaenia fluviatilis* has a bright pink spot on the gill cover which glows during the breeding season. Light green on top, silver below, with pink streaks towards the tail, it grows to 9 cm.

See also Sunfish; Wrasses.

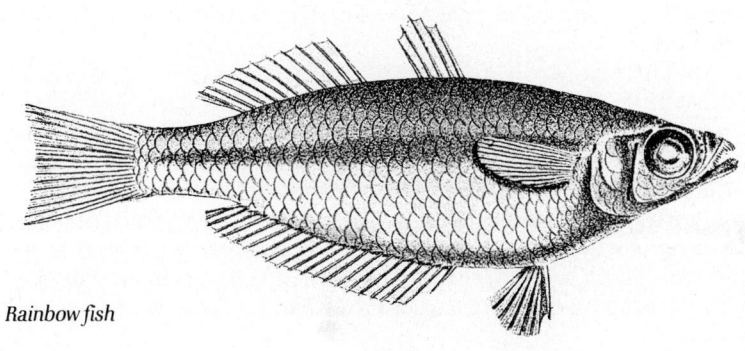

Rainbow fish

RAYS Fish-like animals which at one time were considered true fish but which are now regarded as a separate class, forming with sharks and sawfish a group that has wholly cartilaginous skeletons. Australian waters are rich in rays and sharks (*which see*), though there is a long-standing prejudice in this country against eating the flesh of sharks or rays. This attitude to eating rays or sharks probably stems from the unsound notion that they do not feed as cleanly as fish.

Part of the problem in enjoying their table qualities is the removal of the tough skin. The flaps, the most edible parts, are cut off and immersed in hot, salty water. This removes the skin to reveal white meat which should then be soaked in cold water and vinegar for 20 minutes. The fillets are then ready for cooking. In some Australian cities ray meat is marketed as skate.

There are at least 50 species of rays that can be caught by anglers in Australian waters and many of these range widely over the Pacific and Indian Oceans. Few of them are dangerous, though some grow to enormous sizes and cause plenty of excitement among the unknowing when they are sighted. The devil or manta ray, for example, grows to a width of 4 m and a weight of 747 kg.

Rays have no gill covers and five slits open from the gill chamber. Like sharks they usually produce their young alive, though some members of the group such as skates, family Rajidae, deposit eggs that are protected by tough, horny envelopes. Male rays have large external organs attached to the ventral fins known as claspers that serve as what McCulloch called conduits for the sperm cells. There are frequently marked differences between the sexes of one family. The male may have a large spine, but not the female; the teeth may vary in males and females of one family.

Cowtail ray *Dasyatis sephen:* Also known as the fantail ray. An abundant ray in warmer latitudes. It occurs along the north coast of Australia, Queensland and New South Wales, where it is seen on shallow flats. It carries a long, sharp, venomous spine and the tail back to the base of this barb is heavy and powerful enough to pierce an arm or leg if it is not very carefully handled.

Cowtail rays grow to a width of at least 2 m in tropical waters but only to around 60 cm across the flaps along the New South Wales north coast. They are dark greyish to black in colour on the upper surface, white below. The tail is very long and much heavier back to the sting than in the whiptail ray and tapers down to a whip with a deep fold of skin running along beneath it for half the length from the sting to the tip. They are potentially dangerous to anglers, for the spine is well back along the tail and can be used well forward of the eyes.

The cowtail ray has a wide distribution outside Australia

GENERALISED EXTERNAL FEATURES OF A RAY

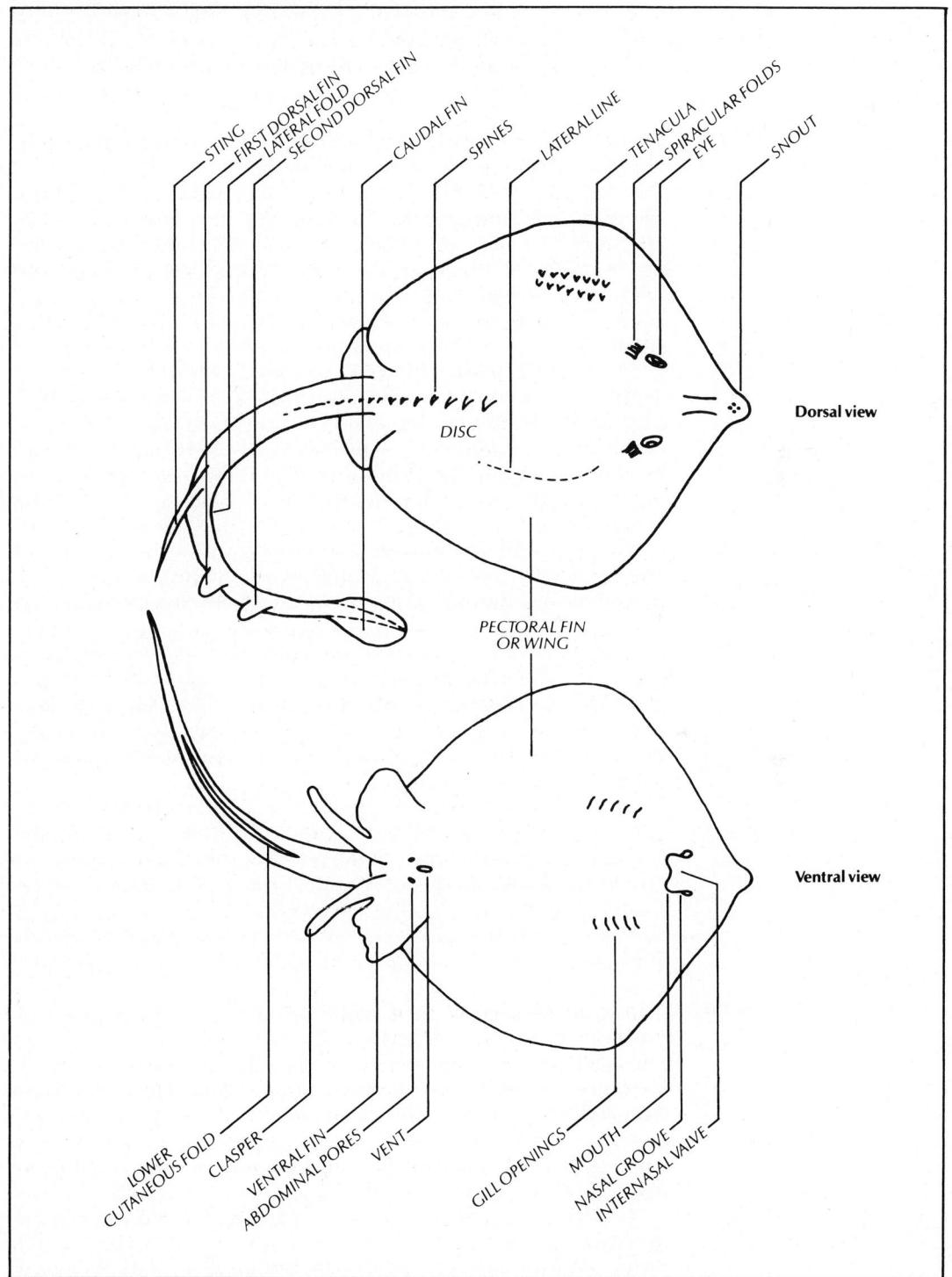

and is found in the waters of Indonesia, Malaya, Ceylon, India and across to the Red Sea. It is also common in Indo-China and the Philippines and is found away out in the Pacific through the Melanesian Islands and over towards the American Pacific coast.

Devil ray *Manta alfredi:* Also known as manta rays, devil-fish or diamond fish. Members of the family Mobulidae, some of which are the largest known rays, reaching a width of 6 m. Sometimes in northern waters they leap through the surface and descend in a vivid splash of foam and they have been known to swamp and smash boats carrying men trying to harpoon them.

Devil rays will travel in schools of 10 or 12, which surround small fish, raise the ends of their pointed pectoral fins and beat the water, frightening the fish into a huddle so that they can then be swept into the devil ray's vast mouth with their protruding head fins. These fins or horns, set on either side of the mouth, are said to have provided this ray's name. They are so wide across that frequently when they swim close to the surface with each wing-tip out of the water, they delude anglers into thinking two sharks are swimming side by side.

They are found along the coast of Queensland, in north and north-western Australian waters, and stragglers have been sighted as far south as Port Jackson. Despite their size they are harmless to man except when they have turned on tormentors trying to harpoon them and thrown themselves clear of the water into boats. The whip or tail has no spike. But they have strength enough to tow small boats behind them at high speed when they are harpooned. Sometimes they get caught up in the anchor lines of launches and cause plenty of fuss until they are dislodged.

Devil rays are blue-black or grey-black on top and whitish grey underneath. The diamond-shaped disc is wider than it is long and the flaps are pointed and wing-like. There are numerous teeth in the lower jaw and when small fish are swept into the mouth they are sieved out by the gill rakers. The devil ray's young are up to 1.5 m across at birth and up to 9 kg. The young are born alive.

Eagle ray Family Myliobatidae: Frequently known in Australia as the bull ray or mill ray. In New Zealand it is sometimes called whip ray or cowfish. The three species in Australian waters are not as prevalent as some of our other rays, although in southern Queensland they show up in sufficient numbers to have become a pest on oyster-banks, crushing the shells with remarkably powerful teeth. A graceful swimmer capable of high speeds.

The largest eagle rays grow to about 2 m across the flaps, but the average are from 38 cm to 60 cm across and weigh under 45 kg. Most of those taken are hooked accidentally in

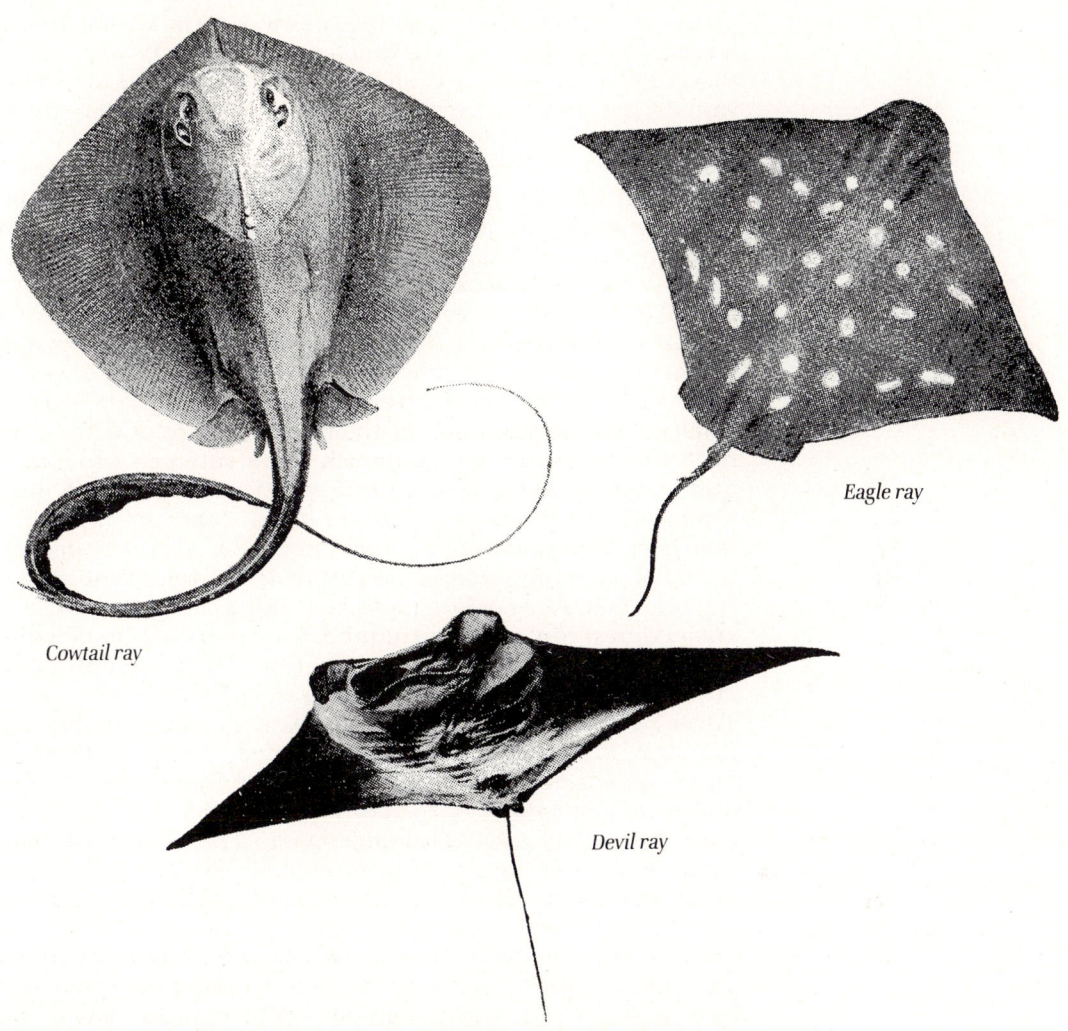

Cowtail ray

Eagle ray

Devil ray

the surf. They are particularly vulnerable to spearfishermen despite their swimming ability and when pressed adopt the customary ray tactics of dropping their flaps into the sand to anchor themselves. They are perhaps the most edible of our rays as their flesh cooks firm and is not as gelatinous as other species. The juvenile specimens taste rather like crab.

Eagle rays have raised heads which give them a bat-like appearance and their long tails have serrated spines. They are heavier than most other rays of their size because of their deeper bodies and thicker flaps. The common variety, *Myliobatis australis*, is usually brown to olive green on the upper surface with obscure bluish blotches or markings. In north Australian waters, there is a spotted species, *Aetobatis narinari*, which is slate-brown to dirty grey on the upper surface with many large white dots. This variety has a very long whip-like tail up to four times as long as the body.

R ■ RAYS

Fiddler ray   *Trygonorrhina fasciata:* A harmless variety of the family Rhinobatidae, without barbs or serrations which takes its name from the pattern on its back which resembles the markings on a violin. They grow to 1 m and are poor fighters when hooked. They use their cobblestone-like teeth to crush shells.

The brown fiddler or banjo ray occurs along the Australian east coast from south Queensland to Tasmania and is common down the coast of New South Wales. The southern or green fiddler ray is found from Port Phillip along the shores of South Australia and Western Australia to well north of Perth.

Numbfish   Also known as electric rays or torpedoes, classified by McCulloch as members of the family Narcobatidae and by Marshall as of the family Torpedinidae. This family includes a number of species which are armed with organs for producing electric discharges or shocks and some can inflict quite a severe shock when touched. The shocks come from inbuilt electric cells and are used to scare off would-be attackers and to stun or disable prey.

The most common species, numbfish *Hypnarce subnigra*, are only taken by anglers on rare occasions. They are distinguished by a very short tail and have terminal tail fins set very closely behind two posterior dorsal fins. They are dark brown above, white below and grow to 60 cm.

They are fairly plentiful in shallow waters on coasts south of the tropics and are repeatedly turned up in trawls. McCulloch once observed one variety to deliver 50 successive shocks within 10 minutes, intense discharges at first but gradually weakening until they were almost imperceptible. There are two members of the family which are nearly always found in deeper waters.

Stingarees   A large group of rays of the family Dasyatidae, which have a tail armed on the upper surface with one or more serrated spines that can inflict painful wounds. The spines vary in length up to 30 cm, and can cause blood-poisoning or death. Stingarees are common in shallow water. There are many species, but only a few are of interest to anglers. The larger stingrays that are sometimes hooked by anglers in the surf, in the estuaries and out on the offshore sandflats are heavy and stubborn and are seldom landed. There are numerous records of people being injured by big rays. A young woman swimming off a beach in New Zealand and a young man in a pool in Australia were killed with stab wounds near their hearts.

Smooth stingaree   *Dasyatis brevicaudatus:* The largest in the world and grows to 4.2 m long by 2 m across the flaps. It is dirty-grey-to-brown on the upper surface and the skin on the back and fore part of the tail is smooth and almost free from tubercles. Its favoured food is the nannygai. Cook, who recorded the capture of one of these in his journal for 5 and 6 May 1770, was so impressed by

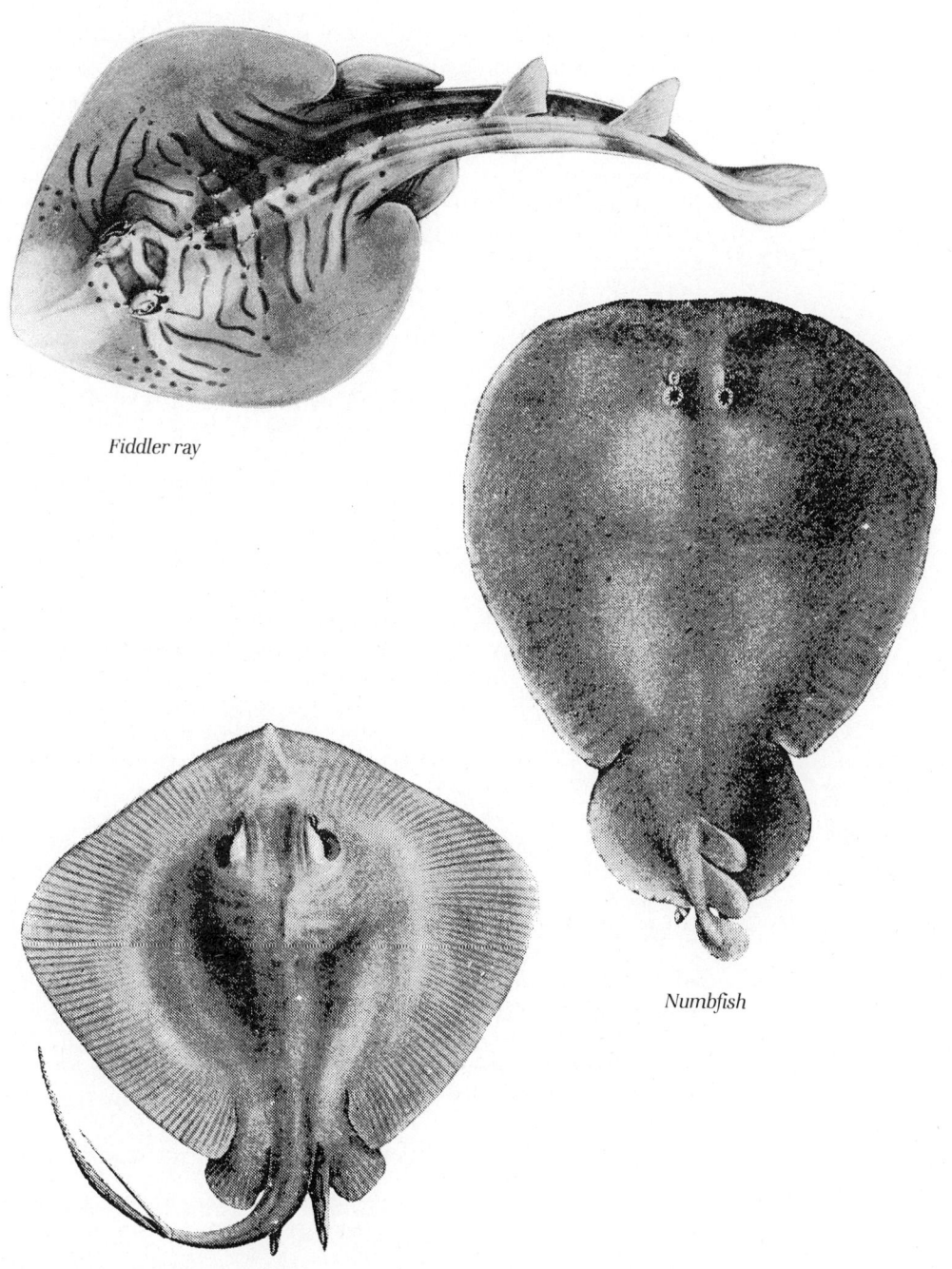

Fiddler ray

Numbfish

Smooth stingaree

the 110 kg ray he named the locality Stingray Harbour. But later Banks and Solander gathered so many plants around the foreshores he altered the name to Botany Bay.

Black stingaree *Dasyatis thetidis:* Also known as the thorntail, was taken on rod and line by Dr Watkins off Newcastle and it was 3.3 m long by 1.7 m across the flaps and weighed 154 kg. This species is dirty-grey to black, with a smooth skin that carries some small spines around the eyes and along the back. The tail is long and very rough with spines, particularly towards its extremity. This is the big ray most commonly hooked in the surf along our east coast, but it is also found on the sandflats, in the bays and harbours and away up the tidal rivers.

Estuary or brown stingaree *Dasyatis fluviorum:* Also grows to as much as 1 m across the flaps. Olive-brown on the back, lightening toward the edges of the flaps, having clusters of tubercles on the back and numerous small spines along the dorsal line. The tail is particularly long and has small flanges of skin running along the top and bottom behind the venomous spine or spines. Probably the best eating of the big stingrays, for flaps are often seen in the markets. Very common in Queensland bays and estuaries. Reaches a width of 1.2 m.

Blue-spotted stingaree *Dasyatis kuhlia:* Is a small variety with a kite-like disc wider than it is long. The brown body is scattered with prominent blue spots and the tail tip is banded. Frequently seen half-buried in sand or on coral reefs. Plentiful in the Arafura Sea.

Common stingaree *Urolophus testaceous:* This smaller species, also known as a sand ray, grows only to about 75 cm and most specimens caught measure from 30 to 40 cm in length. It occurs on muddy and sandy flats from mid-Queensland down the eastern coast and through Bass Strait to South Australia. This species is most commonly caught in the surf along big ocean beaches.

They frequent the shallow offshore sandflats and to a lesser extent are found in the bays and estuaries. Distinguished by their short tails which end in flat, paddle-like terminal fins close behind the venomous spines which have a small residual posterior dorsal fin set just in front of them. Sandy to light brown on the upper surface. They also enter deep water.

Whiptail ray *Dasyatis warnak:* Also known as coachwhip ray and leopard ray. Most plentiful of all rays in north Australian waters. Found from around Geraldton right around the north and down the Queensland coast to northern New South Wales. Particularly plentiful in the Gulf and on the Barrier Reef north of Cairns. It grows to 1.5 m across the flap, and its long, thin, tapering tail is several times the length of its body and usually white with a great number of broad blue rings around it. There

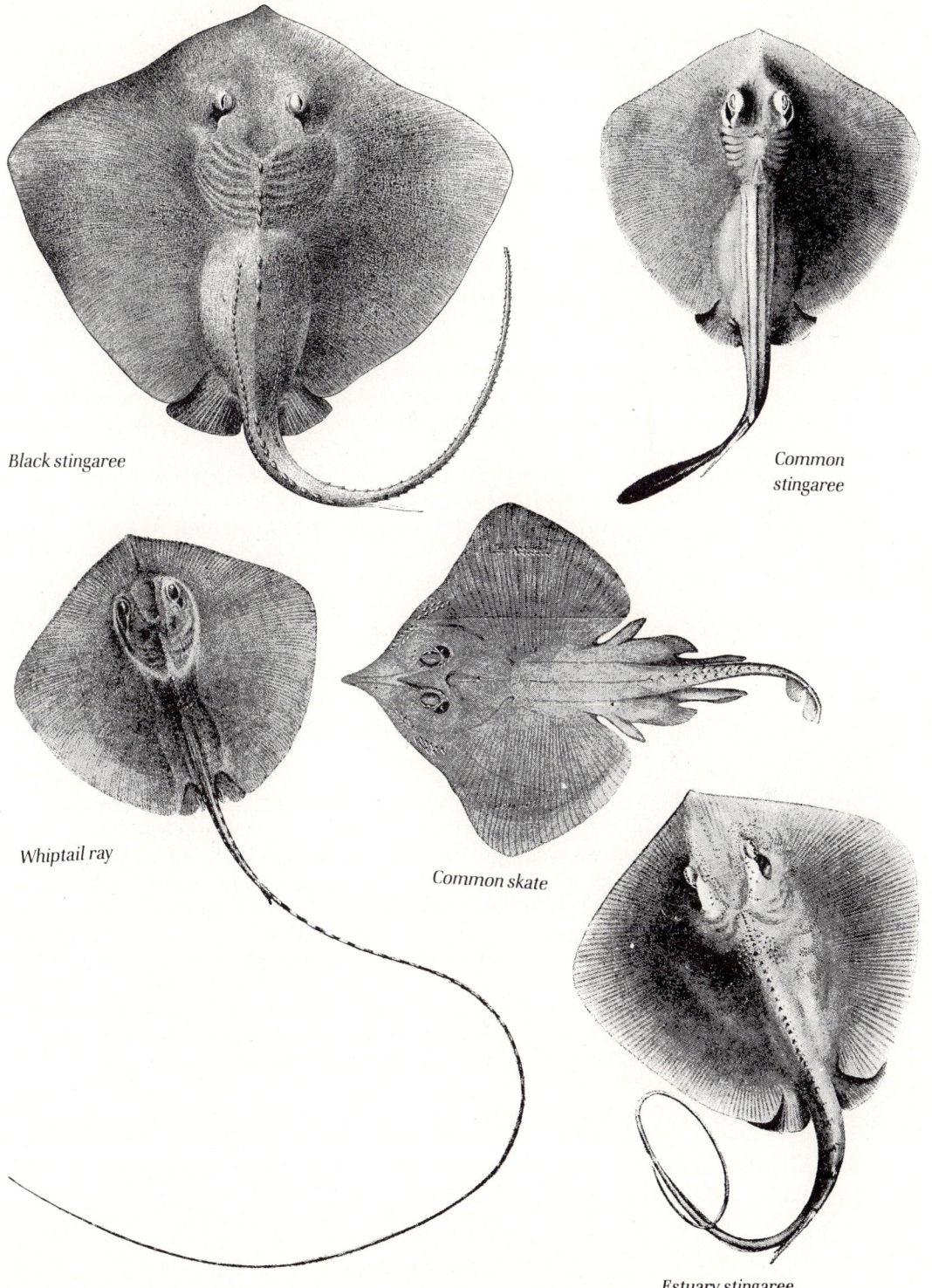

Black stingaree

Common stingaree

Whiptail ray

Common skate

Estuary stingaree

is at least one serrated spine. They are variable in colour, often very pretty. Mostly they are light brown with many dark-blue spots. Some are brown with a reticulated pattern of cream lines and spots. Others are light blue with dark-blue markings. The whiptail ray's sting is well back on its long tail and therefore it is not safe to handle with the thumb and finger in the eye sockets as is done with common stingaree. It is sometimes classified in a separate genus, *Himantura*.

Skate Family Rajidae: Also known as thorn-back rays. They are flat fish very similar in appearance to rays and are mainly found in temperate waters. They swim by undulating their disc flaps. Skates are distinguished from the rays by the tail, which has no sting and ends in a blunt tip without a terminal fin, but has two posterior dorsal fins well back towards its end. In our waters there are 12 species most of which are good eating, but skate has never won the popularity here that it has in Europe as a table fish.

They prefer the colder waters of the southern coasts and skate flaps are a market commodity in southern Australian cities. Largest is the great skate found along the south coast from New South Wales to South Australia. It has been known to grow to over 1.8 m in length by 1.3 m across the flaps.

The small common skate makes its way north as far as south Queensland. The Melbourne skate and denticulated skate are common in Port Phillip and along the Victorian coast. The big New Zealand skate, thornback skate and white spotted skate are the main species around Tasmania. The Bight skate is found along the southern shores of Western Australia.

Shovelnose ray Members of the family Rhinobatidae, also known as guitar fish. The group includes the fiddler ray. All of this variety have snouts that are flattened and broadly triangular in shape. Their tails are powerful and shark-like. Several species are found around our shores. They have no venomous spines and are quite harmless. In northern waters some species grow to a considerable size, but they average 1.3 m.

Banks's shovelnose ray *Aptychotrema rostrata:* A species commonly caught on south Queensland and New South Wales coasts. Grows to 1 m, and sandy to light brown on upper surface. This is the common shovelnose of Moreton Bay where it is found around sandy beaches.

Southern shovelnose is mainly caught in South Australia and along the south and south-west coast of Western Australia. Similar in colour and appearance to Banks's but the snout is shorter and broader.

In North Australian and Barrier Reef waters the white-spotted shovelnose *Rhynchobatus djiddensis* grows to 2.7 m and 190 kg. Up there another species, *Rhinobatos batillum*,

Common shovelnose ray

grows to 2.4 m. It is olive-green or brown on the upper surface with denticles around the eyes and along the dorsal line on the back. There are two dark blotches on the shoulders and distinctive white spots splashed across the body. They sometimes bury into the sand on the shallow flats. Front portion of snout creamy white and almost transparent.

Sawfish

Largest of the Australian rays, growing to 7.2 m. Members of the family Pristidae, sawfish are frequently confused with the saw-shark family, Pristiophoridae. They are remarkable for their rostral blade or saw, a sword-like snout equipped with up to 25 or more needle-sharp teeth or spikes. The saw is used to thrash around in a school of fish to disable their prey and in a struggle at close quarters sawfish can inflict nasty wounds with it. Sawfish are found mainly on the Barrier Reef and in north Australian waters but they have been known to wander as far south as Sydney. They are common in the Gulf of Carpentaria and in Northern Territory estuaries. A tropical species found in 1845 by the explorer Leichhardt lives in the freshwater Lynd River, Queensland.

Green sawfish

Pristis zijsron: Also known as the narrow-snouted sawfish. The saw in this variety, up to 1.8 m in length, causes extensive damage to nets in Queensland and Northern Territory estuaries and there is a serious risk of injury to the commercial fishermen as they attempt to free the fish from their nets.

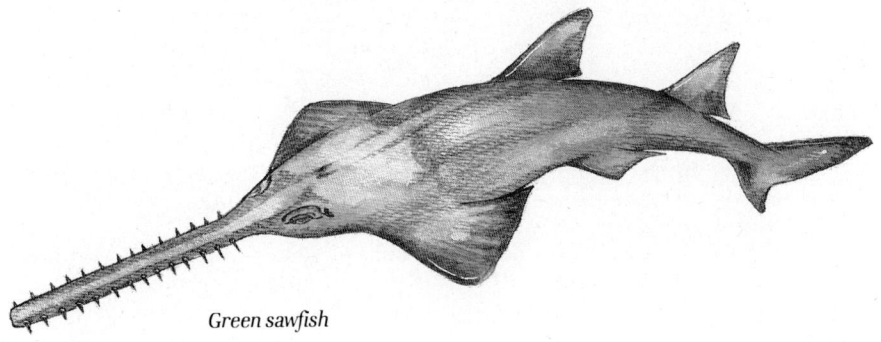

Green sawfish

Grant records that it is common to find some of the larger saws badly scored and gashed, presumably caused by warding off blows from one another in mating battles between adult males. The teeth of this sawfish are extremely hard. The young are born alive and their tiny saws have a gelatinous edging to them at birth which protects the mother from injury.

Like the Queensland sawfish *Pristis clavata*, which is a smaller species with only 18 to 25 teeth on each side, the green sawfish will enter fresh water. Grant reports that the green sawfish has been found more than 240 km from the sea in the Gilbert and Walsh Rivers of north Queensland.

They are greenish-grey in colour, yellow on the sides and white beneath, and they feed on small sea creatures, using the heavy, flattened saw to disable prey. There is no record of them having deliberately attacked humans, though they have inflicted injuries accidentally by striking people with the saw. Green sawfish grow to a length of 7.5 m. A 5 m specimen was taken from Sydney's Manly Beach.

In Leichhardt's sawfish *Pristiopsis leichhardti*, the first dorsal fin is set well in front of where the ventral fin begins. The saw has less teeth than the other species, about 18 on each side. This species inhabits the freshwater rivers that flow into the Gulf of Carpentaria.

REDFIN *See Perch, English.*

RED indian *Pataecus fronto:* A scarlet coloured fish with long dorsal fins which extend unbroken from head to tail and resemble the head-dress of North American Indian chiefs. They are very thin fish that grow to around 22 cm and are found in Queensland, New South Wales, South Australia and south-western Australia. They belong to the family Pataecidae, commonly known as prow fish.

Red indian

Red Indian fish, sometimes called forehead fish, have minute teeth in rather gaping jaws and apparently live on small crustaceans and small sea animals. They are closely related to the whiskered prow fish *Neopataecus waterhousi* and the smooth prow fish *Pataecus vincenti*, which are confined to South Australia and Western Australia.

RED morwong

Cheilodactylus fuscus: A rich copper colour, with a pair of prominent blunt protuberances growing in front of the eyes. They grow to about 45 cm and are found along the southern coast of Queensland and New South Wales, inhabiting rocky and weedy areas. Red morwong also frequent the snapper reefs. Despite their name, red morwong are not a morwong and their other label, 'sea carp', would be a better choice of name to avoid confusion. They are first-rate table fish often taken by line fishermen. Red morwong are fairly numerous around the New South Wales coast but only comparatively few are caught. They seem most plentiful from October until April. Channels running through kelp and weed-covered rocks, and spots where there are patches of white water where the waters run off into deeper waters are good spots to catch red morwong. They will bite freely on green prawns or crabs. A No. 2 hook is the best size.

Red morwong

REELS

See *Tackle*.

RIGS

Methods of arranging one or more hooks, sinkers, rings, swivels, floats, anti-twist keels, and lengths of line or twine at the business end of the line to fool the fish and overcome difficult conditions. A remarkable variety of rigs are used by anglers in New Zealand and Australia, but when examined closely most of them turn out to be variations of a few basic methods.

R ■ RIGS

Rigs are an integral part of fishing lore and many of them have been handed down through families of ardent anglers. Others have survived as a matter of custom. Some have originated because of better tackle. All the sound, practical rigs take into account both the behaviour of the fish they are meant to catch and the prevailing conditions.

The rigs that follow have been grouped for easy reference. When preparing these rigs, considerable care was taken to ensure that only the most popular rigs, tested in the field and proven efficient, were included. Methods used in each Australian State have been carefully considered to provide functional rigs that are basic for each category. This should not deter the angler from experimenting with variations of his own design. Indeed, experimentation is urged and, certainly, variations will be required where conditions and locales warrant them.

Where figures are quoted, they should be regarded as the mean for the quarry sought. For example, it has been proved that Trolling Rig 1, suggesting an 8 kg line in combination with 4/0 ganged hooks, is an appropriate rig when using a rod in trolling for kingfish. The light tackle enthusiast may choose the 4/0 ganged hook arrangement, but prefer a lighter line, e.g. 3 kg, whereas the competition fisherman may use a 9 kg line. Either choice is the correct one, for if there is one axiom that holds good in all fishing, it is that 'no man or his methods can be held infallible'.

Wherever possible, swivels have been used as the link between trace and main line; they serve to keep line twist to a minimum. It is emphasized that, for optimum efficiency, swivel sizes must be kept as small as possible commensurate with line sizes. As a guide, the following should be noted:

Lines kg	to 5	5–7	7–9	9–11	11–13	13–18	18–27
Swivels no.	12	10	8	6	3	1	2/0

The nylon trace, or 'leader' as it is also called, should preferably be of a lighter breaking strain than the main line. Thus any force exerted by either fish or fisherman will, if greater than that required to break the main line, break the trace and preserve the line intact. Exceptions to this rule occur when wire is used, or when the various light tackle rigs with ultra light lines are used to catch comparatively large fish, the bodies or teeth of which could chafe or cut the finer gauge. Then the reverse applies, i.e. heavier trace than the main line.

The sinker sketches are intended to be symbolic only. Many anglers prefer a helmet sinker when fishing from the beach, whilst others believe the ball sinker has greater holding potential. The choice is up to the individual.

Sinkers are of two kinds, fixed and running. The word 'fixed', as it should, implies that the sinker is not free to move along the line. For example, split shot crimped to the line when float fishing, can be called 'fixed sinkers', as can the lead fastened to the end of the line in some of the deep sea, rock, and other rigs. A running sinker, i.e. one that is free to travel along the line, allows the fish to mouth, swallow, and swim off with the bait without its natural wile cautioning it against any weight attached. This tends to be more of a problem with small fish than with large ones which are less apt to notice the slight addition in weight. Notwithstanding this latter observation, the use of a running sinker is generally to be preferred.

Accuracy and effectiveness of bait or lure presentation can be affected by bad rig design. For example, Rig 3 (rigs for stream fishing) would be unwieldy if the sinker were placed above the swivel, whilst if we were to replace the 15 cm traces shown in Rig 14 of the section on saltwater lake fishing, with 33 cm traces, the hooks would in all probability catch in the brass rings and be practically useless.

RIGGING A RUNNING SINKER

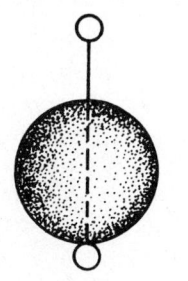

Tie brass rings to each end of a length of nylon passed through a ball sinker

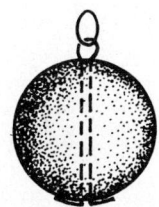

Push a bobby pin or a split pin, with a brass ring or swivel in its eye, through a ball sinker and turn protruding ends back to secure

Rigs for beach fishing

Rarely, if ever, is a fixed sinker justified when beach fishing, the running sinker being preferred. Sinker weights and styles will vary with water conditions, and weight will certainly be influenced by the breaking strain of the line used. Distance will be sacrificed if the line is too heavy for the sinker, whilst line will be lost through breakage if the sinker is too heavy for it. Weights shown in the illustrations can be regarded as the optimum for the lines shown.

A careful study of the methods used in the different states indicates that whilst styles of sinker may vary from state to state, the running ball and the running helmet are held in the highest regard. Contrary to popular belief, the ball sinker tends to bury into the bottom rather than roll across the top of the sand: it is usually the effect of current on bait and line that causes a rig to be swept along a beach.

When sand crabs are troublesome, the use of a cork or piece of foam plastic of appropriate size will help foil their attacks on the bait. Rig 8 illustrates the method used. Whilst the use of cork in this fashion inhibits casting, it does so only to a minor extent, and should not give cause for concern.

It is important when using a rod, that the first two metres of the main line (as opposed to the trace or leader) be inspected frequently for wear caused by its bearing against the tip guide during the initial stages of the cast. The occasional removal of 0.5–1 m of the main line will save many a fish that might otherwise be lost. (For rigs to use when spinning from the beach, *see rigs for spinning*.)

Rock fishing rigs

With the tremendous improvement in current day rods, the necessity for very heavy lines when rock fishing is no longer as vital as it used to be. Few fish caught from the rocks will break lines of 7 kg breaking strain when matching rod and reel are used. The main cause of broken line is abrasion from rocks

R ■ RIGS

RUNNING BOBBY CORK RIGS FOR SIDECAST REELS

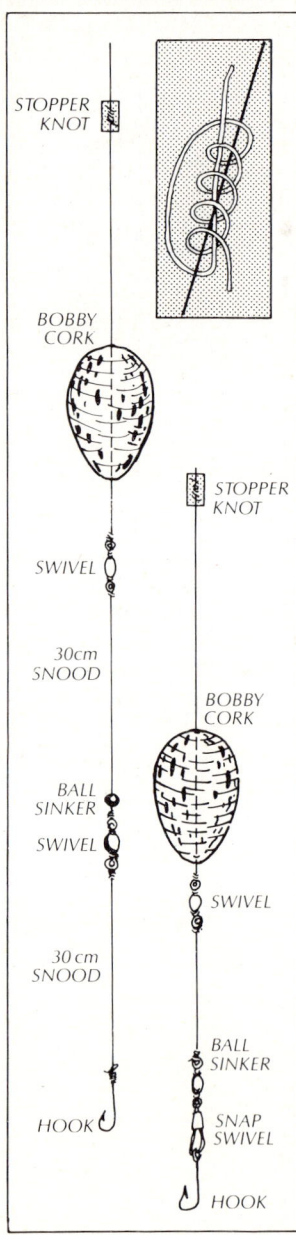

Inset: Wrap short length of line four times around line, pass end through and pull up slowly. The stopper will hold depth, but may be slid to any position on line.

and barnacles, etc., but even this can be considerably reduced by careful handling of equipment.

The breaking strains shown should be regarded as the safest minimum for the species listed. They are deliberately quoted thus for the challenge they offer the light tackle exponent. As mentioned earlier, the competition fisherman may find it expedient to double them.

One of the most productive forms of rock fishing is 'bobby corking' (Rigs 6–9), especially if live bait is used. The running float rig facilitates distance casting, and permits greater accuracy which is essential when fishing confined areas. When using the tennis ball float (Rig 9), the line should be threaded through the ball walls with a needle. The rubber of the ball will then contract on the line and obviate the need for a stopper. Adjustments for depth remain simple. (For suitable rigs for spinning from the rocks, *see rigs for spinning*.)

Rigs for bay and estuary

Whilst tidal ebb and flow can create powerful currents in estuarine waters, generally conditions differ markedly from those found, for example, in places pounded by the ocean swell. In the calmer waters of bay and estuary, where wharves, jetties, and bridges open up areas otherwise inaccessible to many anglers, the use of lighter tackle becomes a practicality.

The small fish species predominate, e.g. bream, garfish, mullet, luderick, ruff, flounder, bass, whiting, etc., and rigs must be changed to suit. Rig 1, the simplest of all rigs, is also the most deadly for the timid estuarine bream, whose counterpart in the surf is less hesitant about taking a bait. Float fishing is popular because it is not accompanied by the dangers inherent in bobby corking from the rocks.

The opportunities to practise saltwater fly fishing are greater and, though this sport is as yet in its infancy, it is nonetheless a lusty infant with an increasing number of followers. Related rigs warrant inclusion in this section. Where waters are relatively still or the current slow-moving, berley can be used to advantage. Distribution methods vary from handfuls into the water to the refinements of berley holders which release the scraps of food over a period. Rig 9 shows such a set-up; variations are limited only by the imagination of the angler. (For suitable rigs for spinning and trolling in these waters *see rigs for spinning* and *rigs for trolling*.)

Rigs for saltwater lakes

These are vast areas of salt water which, for the great part of the year, and even for year after year, are cut off from the ocean. Most abound with the smaller fish species that are found in bays and estuaries, and tackle used can and should be as light as commonsense will allow.

Fly fishing for surface fish such as mullet and tailor is quite feasible, whilst flathead definitely will take a fly worked carefully across the bottom. Rig 8 illustrates the rig for mullet and tailor but, when fishing for flathead, a lead core line, or split shot attached 30 cm in front of a fly tied to a tapered leader, should be used.

Berleying to attract and hold fish in an area should be resorted to whenever possible. The lack of current facilitates this. Rig 13 has proved very effective for mullet and garfish and, if the depth fished is varied, bream and other species will respond accordingly. (For spinning and trolling rigs in these waters, see rigs for spinning and rigs for trolling.)

Rigs for deep sea fishing

In rigging for deep sea fishing, the angler has to contend with both depth and water current, and frequently a combination of these. Where strong currents prevail, heavy sinkers, e.g. 224 g to 453 g, are often used.

Where a number of anglers fish from the same boat, it is of benefit to all if individual line size and sinker weights are collectively identical. In 110 m, with a strong current running, (either surface or bottom) a heavy line, weighted with a 224 g sinker may be swept along to tangle with a neighbour's lighter line and heavier 453 g sinker. In these circumstances uniformity pays off, and fishing remains the pleasure it should be. Traces, both hook and sinker, should be of lighter breaking strain than the main line, particularly when fishing over reefs. Then, if either becomes fouled, necessitating break-off, the main line will remain intact.

Where leatherjacket are prevalent, great care must be taken to avoid pieces of bait adhering to the line, for the sharp teeth of these creatures will bite through 14 kg nylon with the greatest of ease. Unexplained 'break-offs' can often be attributed to the voracity of these fish.

Rigs for stream fishing

The rigs in this section have been carefully chosen and represent the most popular bait and fly rigs of a selection used by stream anglers throughout Australia. Spinning and trolling rigs for stream conditions can be found in the appropriate sections. Where a float is shown, the sketch is symbolic only; the type of float can vary from area to area. For example, the tennis ball rig shown in the rock fishing section, is used for barramundi fishing in Queensland, whilst the bubble float rigs in the freshwater lake and dam section are often used when stream fishing for trout, roach, and tench, etc. Regardless of rig choice, the haphazard placement of bait or lure can cancel its effectiveness. Stream lore should be learned and that learning judiciously applied.

Rigs for freshwater lake or dam

Though lakes and dams invariably hold their share of sunken logs and submerged trees, the normally placid waters

SMALL FIXED BOBBY CORK

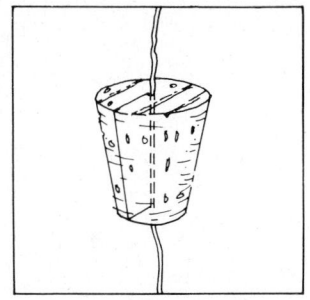

LOADED BOBBY CORK

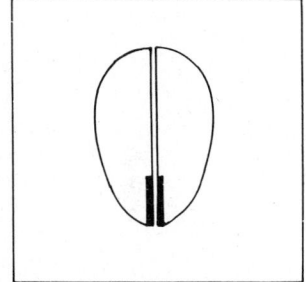

Cork (top) is slit vertically to the centre with a sharp knife and the line forced into the slit; for light rigs with or without lead in shallow water. A lead tube glued into a bobby cork (bottom) will give casting weight with a smaller sinker.

encountered allow the angler to use the lightest of tackle whether he be fishing from a boat or the shore. Rigs may differ slightly from those used in saltwater lakes, but the fundamentals are the same. Where trout live, the bubble float rigs (Nos. 6–7) when used with bait such as mudeyes and shrimps will prove extremely effective. Offshore winds, i.e. winds blowing from the water to the angler, can quickly negate the effectiveness of float fishing by blowing the rig into shallow water. Rig 10 shows a simple way of overcoming this problem. Fly fishing is very popular. Rig 5 depicts the terminal rig, but details of line, leader, and flies, should not be regarded as the optimum for all conditions. They are, however, suitable for the average fisherman, and the best for the beginner in the early stages of his learning. Where sinkers must be used, they should be as light as possible. Modern day threadline reels greatly assist the angler in this regard, for sufficient distance can often be achieved with only the weight of the bait on the end. (For other appropriate rigs, see *rigs for spinning* and *rigs for trolling*.)

Rigs for spinning
The term 'spinning' is often confused with the word 'trolling'. Whereas trolling can only be associated with boats, the former can be practised from a boat, beach, rock, bank of a stream, or shore of a lake or dam, and it is this major difference, together with the repetitive practice of casting and retrieval, that distinguishes between the two. Either baits or lures can be used as the rigs illustrate. Various depths can be reached by the judicious use of sinkers, but paravanes are not recommended because of their bulk.

As with trolling, an important factor is the rate the lure travels through the water, and this can influence one in the choice of a reel. Reels with a fast rate of retrieve, i.e. with high gear ratio of, for example, 5:1 are excellent for spinning from the rocks for striped tuna which seem to demand speed from their quarry. Whilst a low ratio, say 2:1 (slow rate of retrieve) will be quite suitable for fish such as the bass, flathead, pike, or mangrove jack and others. The correct reel drag setting is again (as with trolling and, indeed, whenever a reel so fitted is used) of great importance, and careful attention to this aspect will separate the successful angler from the not-so-successful.

Rigs for trolling
When trolling, i.e. towing a lure or bait behind a moving boat, the problem of line twist is frequently encountered. Of the rigs illustrated, only Rig 1 does not attempt to overcome this by making use of either a keel, a swivel, or both. If the ganged hooks are correctly placed along the bait—usually a garfish with the beak either snapped off or tied to the shank of the leading hook, then even this rig will keep the line relatively free of twist.

Sinkers may be added to take the bait or lure down to where it is thought the fish are; the use of a paravane as shown in Rig 8 will accomplish the same thing and act as a keel as well. When using a rod and reel, pay careful attention to the drag setting. This should be adjusted to the point where the combination of boat speed and water pressure just fails to pull line from the spool. A correctly set drag, together with the shock absorbing qualities of the rod, will allow a striking fish to take the bait or lure without breaking the line or incurring the loss of terminal tackle. Note with the line breaking strains the disparity between rod and handline fishing. The heavier hand line compensates for the lack of assistance given by both rod, and reel drag.

The illustrations show various lure styles. They are symbolic rather than actual depictions, and should be so regarded, for what suits in the north may be quite unattractive in the south. Trolling speeds will vary with the species sought, but rarely is it necessary to exceed a speed of 7 to 8 knots. It would be reasonable to regard 4 knots as an average for all species.

DICK LEWERS

A shark mackerel taken with a cast, not trolled, lure on medium spinning gear.

R ■ RIGS

RIGS FOR BEACH FISHING

	LINE		TRACE		HOOKS	SINKER
	Rod	Hand	Rod	Hand		Running
	kg	kg	kg	kg		g
Bream	6.8	6.8	5.5	5.5	1/0 to 3/0	56–85
Dart	6.8	6.8	5.5	5.5	1 to 2/0	56–85
Flathead	6.8	6.8	5.5	5.5	3/0 to 6/0	56–85
Salmon	6.8	6.8	5.5	5.5	3/0 to 6/0	56–85
Mulloway	7.7	11.5	6.8	9.0	3/0 to 8/0	56–85
Whiting	6.8	6.8	2.3	2.3	4 to 1	56–85
Mulloway	7.7	11.5	6.8	9.0	3/0 to 8/0	56–85
Flathead	6.8	6.8	5.5	5.5	3/0 to 6/0	56–85
Mulloway	7.7	11.5	6.8	9.0	3/0 to 8/0	56–85
Tailor	6.8	6.8	Nylon 5.5 plus wire	5.5	3/0 to 5/0	56–85
Tailor	6.8	6.8	5.5	5.5	3/0 ganged	56–85
Bream	6.8	6.8	5.5	5.5	3/0	56–85
Tailor	6.8	6.8	5.5	5.5	3/0 ganged	56–85
Bream	6.8	6.8	5.5	5.5	3/0	56–85
Tailor	6.8	6.8	5.5	5.5	3/0 ganged	56–85
Bream	6.8	6.8	5.5	5.5	1/0 to 3/0	56–85
						Fixed
Whiting	6.8	6.8	5.5	5.5	4 to 1	56–85
Ruff	6.8	6.8	5.5	5.5	6 to 1/0	56–85

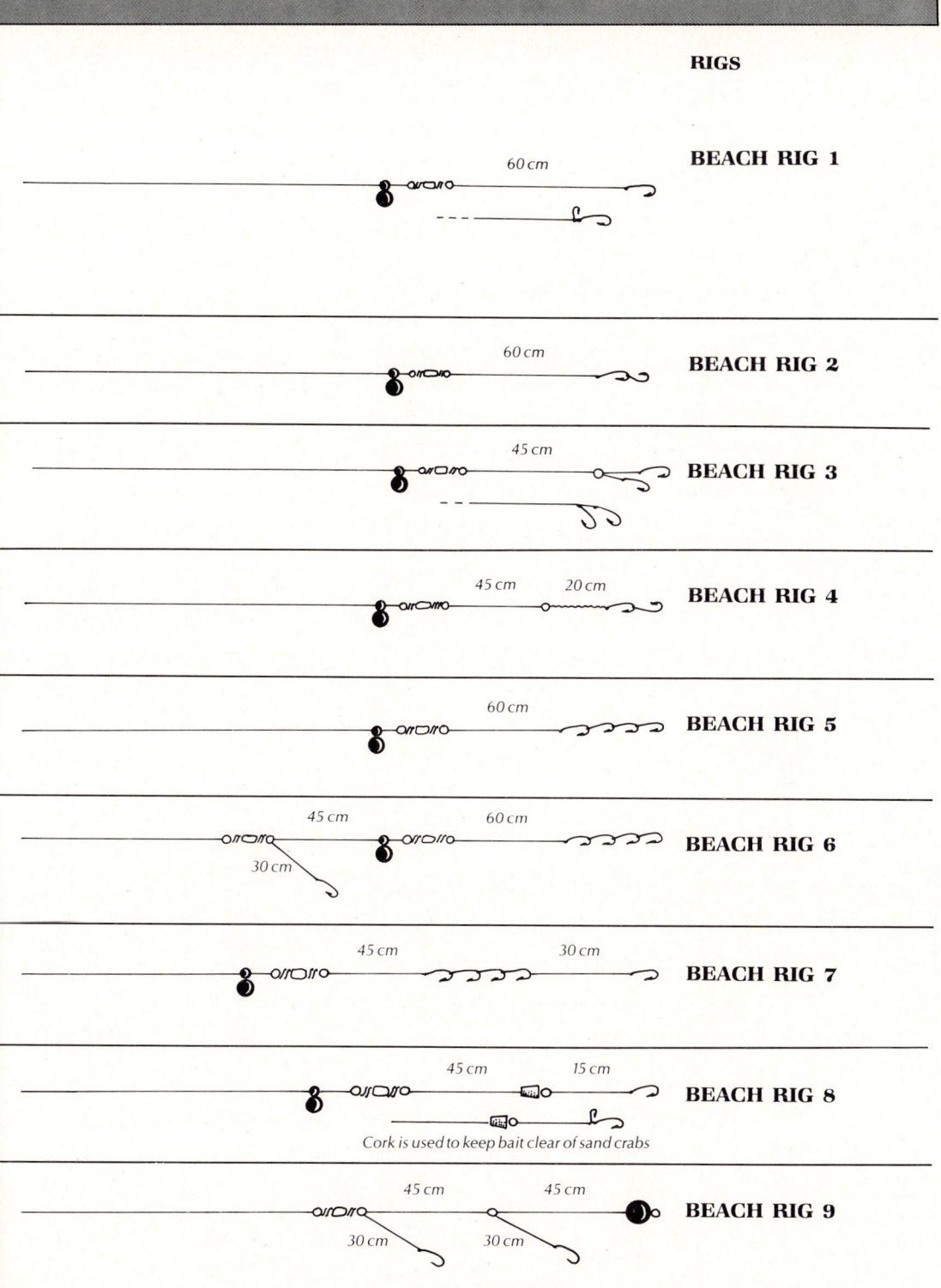

R ■ RIGS

	LINE		TRACE		HOOKS	SINKER
	Rod	Hand	Rod	Hand		Running
	kg	kg	kg	kg		g
Shark	9.0–22.5		Wire		8/0 to 12/0	113
Shark	9.0–22.5		Wire		8/0 to 12/0	113

RIGS FOR ROCK FISHING

Bream	6.8	5.5	1/0 to 3/0	28–56
Morwong	6.8	5.5	1/0 to 4/0	28–56
Rock cod	6.8	5.5	3/0 to 6/0	28–56
Rock flathead	6.8	5.5	3/0 to 6/0	28–56
Groper	11.5	9.0	3/0 to 8/0	28–56
Ling	6.8	5.5	1 to 3/0	28–56
Mulloway	11.5	9.0	3/0 to 8/0	28–56
Parrot fish	6.8	5.5	1/0 to 3/0	28–56
Snapper	9.0	7.7	3/0 to 6/0	28–56

				Fixed
Rock cod	6.8	5.5	3/0 to 6/0	28–56
Groper	11.5	9.0	3/0 to 8/0	28–56
Parrot fish	6.8	5.5	1/0 to 3/0	28–56
Ling	6.8	5.5	1/0 to 3/0	28–56
Drummer	6.8	5.5	4 to 1/0	28–56
Bream	6.8	5.5	1/0 to 3/0	28–56
Morwong	6.8	5.5	1/0 to 4/0	28–56
Rock cod	6.8	5.5	3/0 to 6/0	28–56
Rock flathead	6.8	5.5	3/0 to 6/0	28–56
Groper	11.5	9.0	3/0 to 8/0	28–56
Ling	6.8	5.5	1 to 3/0	28–56
Mulloway	11.5	9.0	3/0 to 8/0	28–56
Parrot fish	6.8	5.5	1/0 to 3/0	28–56
Snapper	9.0	7.7	3/0 to 6/0	28–56
Pike	6.8	5.5	2/0 to 5/0	28–56
Drummer	6.8	5.5	4 to 1/0	28–56

RIGS ■ R

RIGS

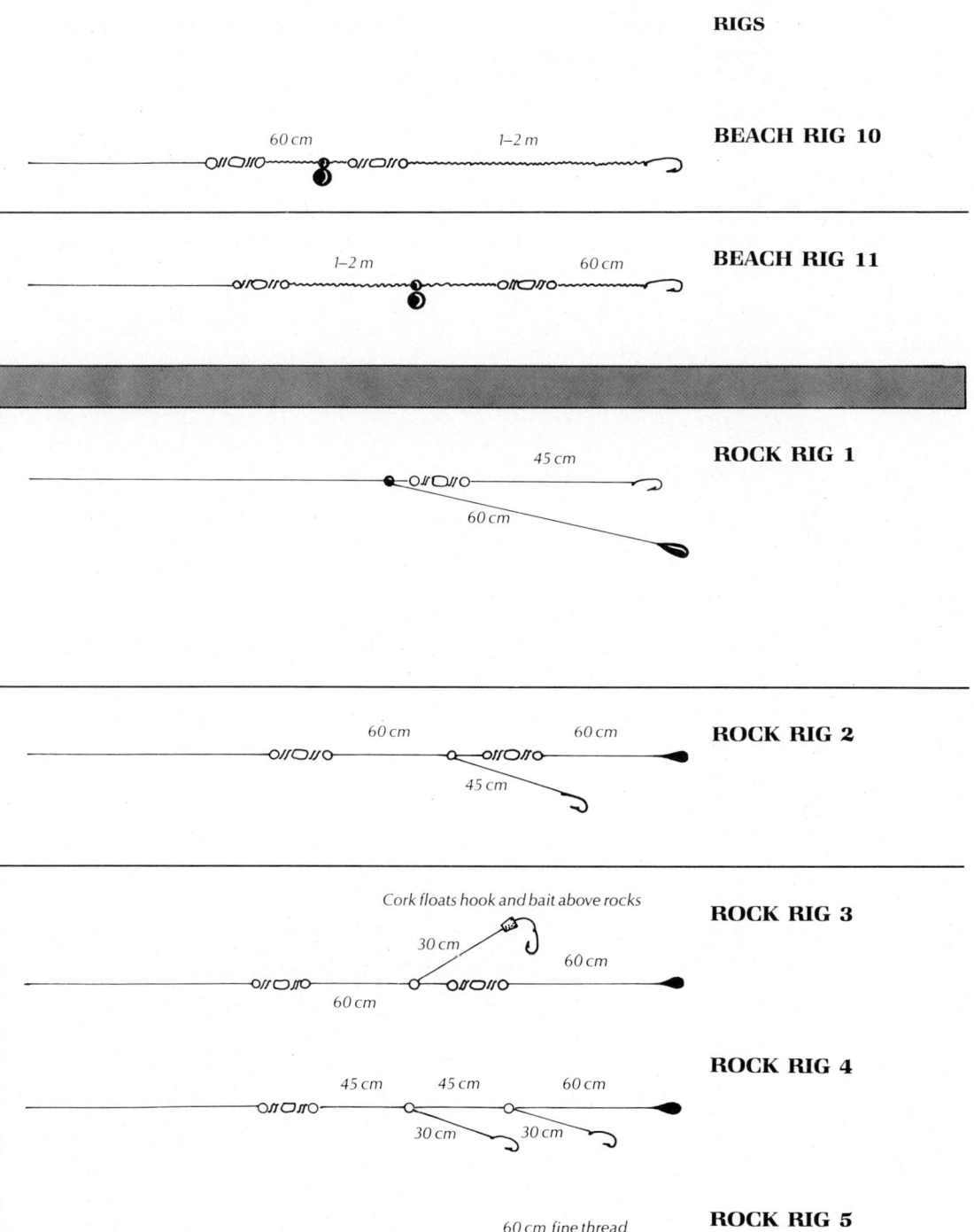

BEACH RIG 10

BEACH RIG 11

ROCK RIG 1

ROCK RIG 2

ROCK RIG 3

ROCK RIG 4

ROCK RIG 5

R ■ RIGS

	LINE		TRACE		HOOKS	SINKER
	Rod	Hand	Rod	Hand		Running
	kg	kg	kg	kg		g
Bream	6.8		5.5		1/0 to 3/0	7–14
Morwong	6.8		5.5		1/0 to 4/0	7–14
Rock cod	6.8		5.5		3/0 to 6/0	7–14
Rock flathead	6.8		5.5		3/0 to 6/0	7–14
Groper	11.5		9.0		3/0 to 8/0	7–14
Ling	6.8		5.5		1 to 3/0	7–14
Mulloway	11.5		9.0		3/0 to 8/0	7–14
Parrot fish	6.8		5.5		1/0 to 3/0	7–14
Snapper	9.0		7.7		3/0 to 6/0	7–14
Pike	6.8		5.5		2/0 to 5/0	7–14
Salmon	6.8		5.5		3/0 to 5/0	7–14
Bonito	6.8		5.5		3/0 to 5/0	7–14
Striped tuna	9.0		7.7		3/0 to 5/0	7–14
Drummer	6.8		5.5		4 to 1/0	7–14
Trevally	6.8		5.5		1 to 3/0	7–14
Tailor	6.8		Wire		3/0 to 5/0	7–14
Kingfish	11.5		Wire		3/0 to 5/0	7–14
						Fixed
Drummer	6.8				4 to 1/0	Split shot
Luderick	6.8				10 to 6	Split shot
Sweep	6.8				5 to 1	Split shot
Ruff	6.8				6 to 1/0	Split shot
						Running
Bream	6.8		5.5		1/0 to 3/0	7–14
Morwong	6.8		5.5		1/0 to 4/0	7–14
Rock cod	6.8		5.5		3/0 to 6/0	7–14
Rock flathead	6.8		5.5		3/0 to 6/0	7–14
Groper	11.5		9.0		3/0 to 8/0	7–14
Ling	6.8		5.5		1 to 3/0	7–14
Mulloway	11.5		9.0		3/0 to 8/0	7–14
Parrot fish	6.8		5.5		1/0 to 3/0	7–14
Snapper	9.0		7.7		3/0 to 6/0	7–14
Pike	6.8		5.5		2/0 to 5/0	7–14
Salmon	6.8		5.5		3/0 to 5/0	7–14
Bonito	6.8		5.5		3/0 to 5/0	7–14
Striped tuna	9.0		7.7		3/0 to 5/0	7–14
Drummer	6.8		5.5		4 to 1/0	7–14
Trevally	6.8		5.5		1 to 3/0	7–14
Tailor	6.8		Wire		3/0 to 5/0	7–14
Kingfish	11.5		Wire		3/0 to 5/0	7–14

RIGS

ROCK RIG 6

ROCK RIG 6a

ROCK RIG 7

ROCK RIG 8

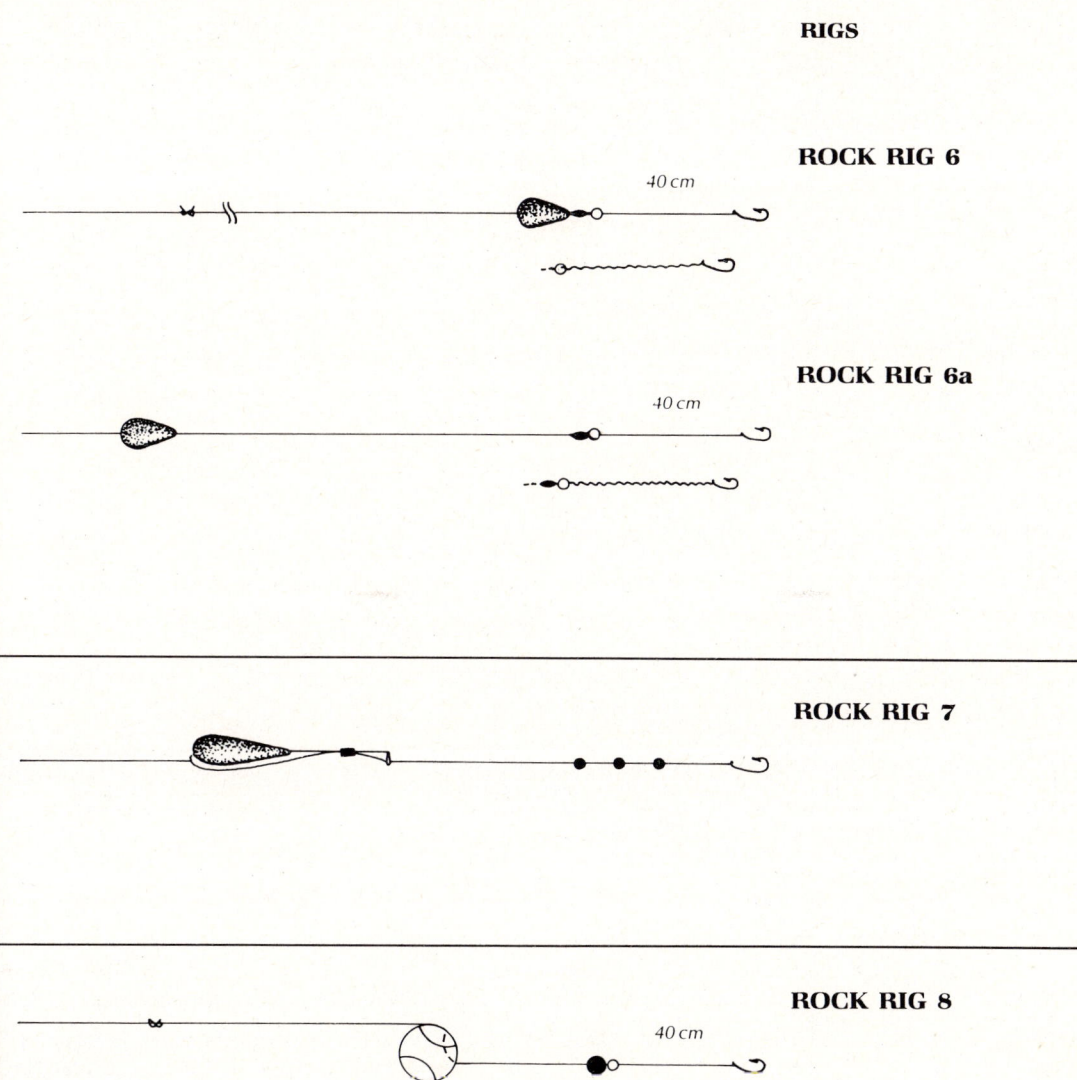

R ■ RIGS

	LINE		TRACE		HOOKS	SINKER
	Rod	Hand	Rod	Hand		Running
	kg	kg	kg	kg		g
Bream	6.8		5.5		1/0 to 3/0	7–14
Morwong	6.8		5.5		1/0 to 4/0	7–14
Rock cod	6.8		5.5		3/0 to 6/0	7–14
Rock flathead	6.8		5.5		3/0 to 6/0	7–14
Groper	11.5		9.0		3/0 to 8/0	7–14
Ling	6.8		5.5		1 to 3/0	7–14
Mulloway	11.5		9.0		3/0 to 8/0	7–14
Parrot fish	6.8		5.5		1/0 to 3/0	7–14
Snapper	9.0		7.7		3/0 to 6/0	7–14
Pike	6.8		5.5		2/0 to 5/0	7–14
Salmon	6.8		5.5		3/0 to 5/0	7–14
Bonito	6.8		5.5		3/0 to 5/0	7–14
Striped tuna	9.0		7.7		3/0 to 5/0	7–14
Drummer	6.8		5.5		4 to 1/0	7–14
Trevally	6.8		5.5		1 to 3/0	7–14
Tailor	6.8		Wire		3/0 to 5/0	7–14
Kingfish	11.5		Wire		3/0 to 5/0	7–14

RIGS FOR BAY AND ESTUARY FISHING

	Rod	Hand	Rod	Hand	Hooks	Sinker
Bream	3.0	2.2–4.5			6 to 1/0	
Bream	3.0	2.2–4.5			6 to 1/0	3–7
Tailor	4.5	6.8	Wire	Wire	1/0 to 5/0	14–56
Bream	3.0	4.5	2.2	3.0	6 to 1/0	14–56
Flounder	3.0	4.5	2.2	3.0	6 to 1/0	14–56
Sole	3.0	4.5	2.2	3.0	6 to 1/0	14–56
Flathead	4.5	6.8	3.0	5.5	1/0 to 5/0	14–56
Threadfin	6.8	9.0	Wire		1/0 to 5/0	14–56
Tarwhine	3.0	4.5	2.2	3.0	6 to 1/0	14–56
Bass	3.0	4.5	2.2	3.0	4 to 1/0	14–56
Mulloway	6.8	13.6	5.5	11.5	3/0 to 8/0	14–56
Whiting	2.2	3.0	2.2	3.0	6 to 1	14–56
						Fixed
Bream	3.0	4.5	2.2	3.0	6 to 1/0	Split shot
Flounder	3.0	4.5	2.2	3.0	6 to 1	Split shot
Whiting	2.2	3.0	2.2	3.0	6 to 1	Split shot
Bass	3.0	4.5	2.2	3.0	6 to 1/0	Split shot

RIGS

ROCK RIG 9

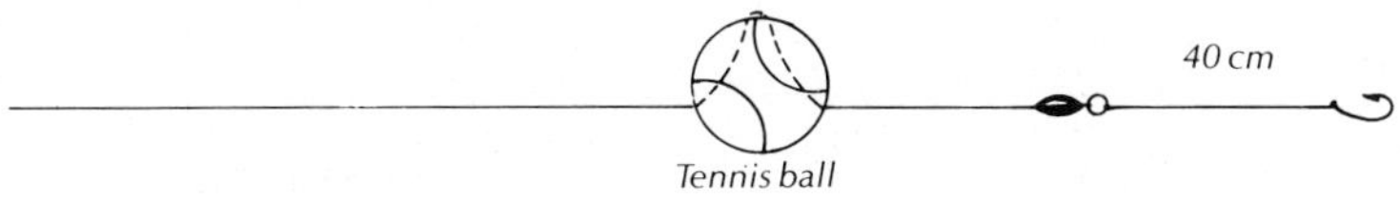

Tennis ball — 40 cm

BAY AND ESTUARY RIG 1

BAY AND ESTUARY RIG 2

BAY AND ESTUARY RIG 3
60 cm

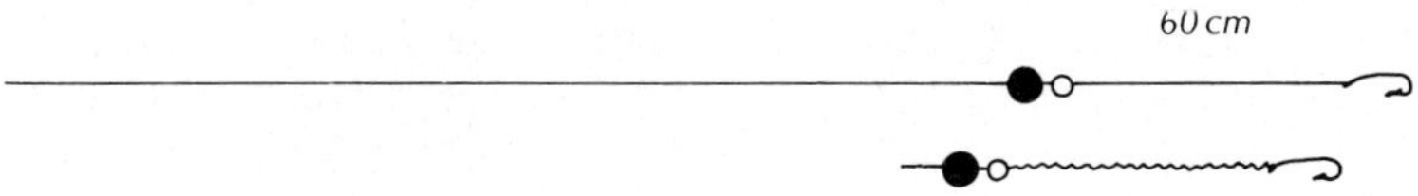

BAY AND ESTUARY RIG 4
40 cm   20 cm

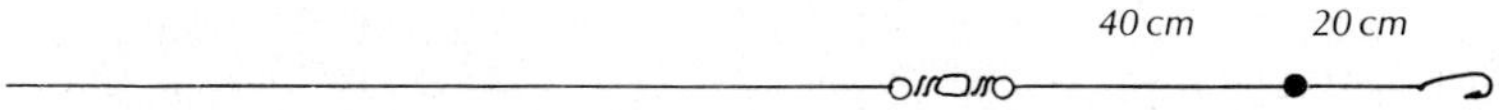

R ■ RIGS

	LINE		TRACE		HOOKS	SINKER
	Rod	**Hand**	**Rod**	**Hand**		**Running**
	kg	kg	kg	kg		g
Bream	3.0	4.5	2.2	3.0	6 to 1/0	
Whiting	3.0	4.5	2.2	3.0	6 to 1	
Bass	3.0	4.5	2.2	3.0	4 to 1/0	
Flathead	4.5	6.8	3.0	5.5	1/0 to 5/0	14–56
Bream	3.0	4.5	2.2	3.0	6 to 1/0	14–56
			Double nylon			
Flathead	4.5	6.8	3.0	5.5	1/0 to 5/0	14–56
Tailor	4.5	6.8	3.0	5.5	1/0 to 5/0	14–56
Bream	3.0	4.5	2.2	3.0	6 to 1/0	14–56
Flounder	3.0	4.5	2.2	3.0	6 to 1	14–56
Sole	3.0	4.5	2.2	3.0	6 to 1	14–56
Flathead	4.5	6.8	3.0	5.5	1/0 to 5/0	14–56
Tarwhine	3.0	4.5	2.2	3.0	6 to 1/0	14–56
Bass	3.0	4.5	2.2	3.0	4 to 1/0	14–56
Mulloway	6.8	13.6	5.5	11.5	3/0 to 8/0	14–56
Whiting	2.2	3.0	2.2	2.2	6 to 1	14–56
						Fixed
Bream	3.0	4.5	2.2	3.0	6 to 1/0	14–56
Flounder	3.0	4.5	2.2	3.0	6 to 1	14–56
Sole	3.0	4.5	2.2	3.0	6 to 1	14–56
Flathead	4.5	6.8	3.0	5.5	1/0 to 5/0	14–56
Tarwhine	3.0	4.5	2.2	3.0	6 to 1/0	14–56
Bass	3.0	4.5	2.2	3.0	4 to 1/0	14–56
Mulloway	6.8	13.6	5.5	11.5	3/0 to 8/0	14–56
Whiting	2.2	3.0	2.2	2.2	6 to 1	14–56
Hairtail	4.5	7.7	Wire	Wire	1/0 to 4/0	
						Running
Hairtail	4.5	7.7	Wire	Wire	1/0 to 4/0	3.0

RIGS

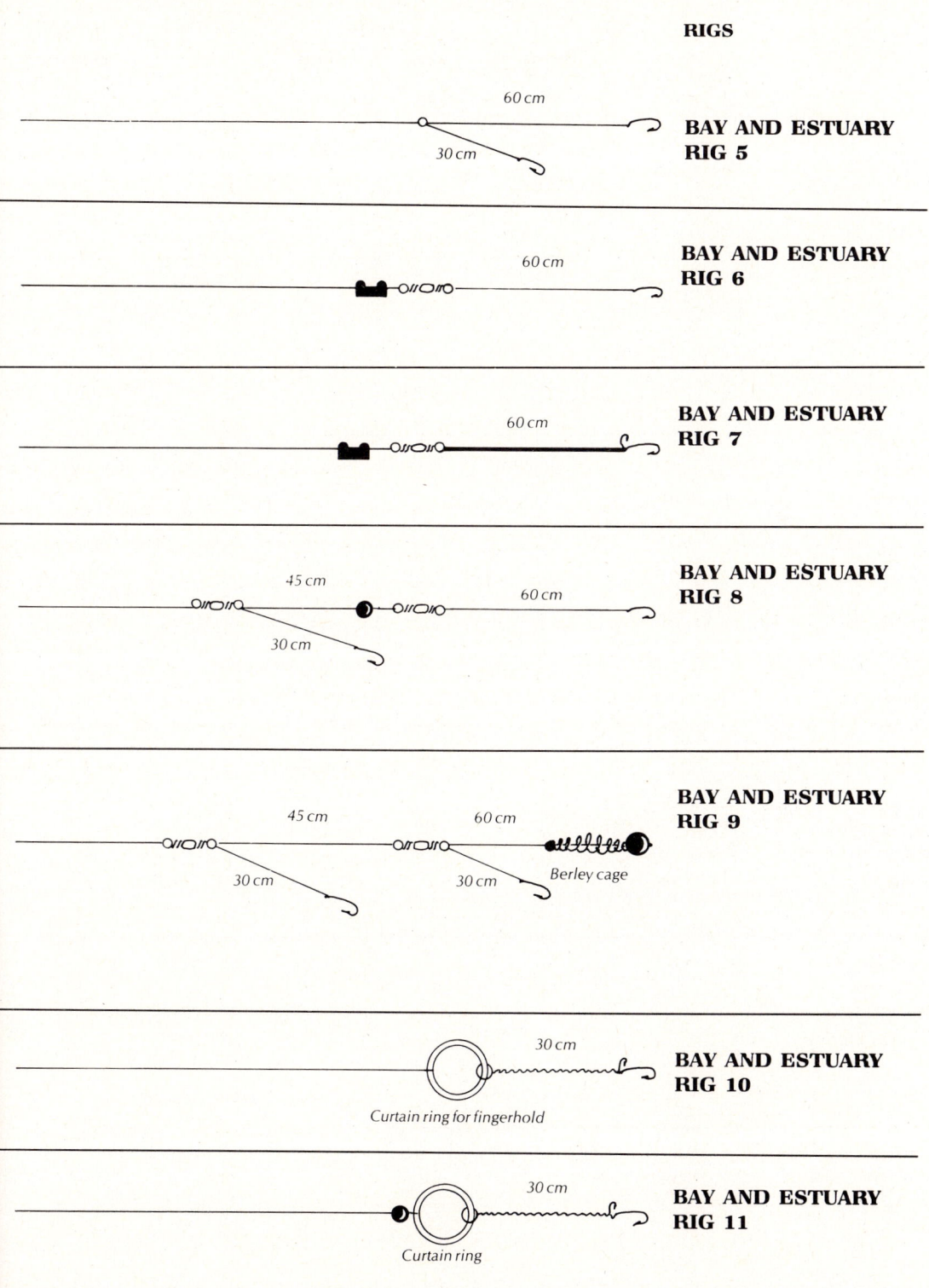

BAY AND ESTUARY RIG 5

BAY AND ESTUARY RIG 6

BAY AND ESTUARY RIG 7

BAY AND ESTUARY RIG 8

BAY AND ESTUARY RIG 9

BAY AND ESTUARY RIG 10

BAY AND ESTUARY RIG 11

R ■ RIGS

| | LINE | | TRACE | | HOOKS | SINKER |
| | Rod | Hand | Rod | Hand | | Running |
	kg	kg	kg	kg		g
Tailor	4.5	6.8	Wire	Wire	1/0 to 5/0	
Barramundi	6.8	18.0	Wire	Wire	3/0 to 9/0	
Squid	2.2	4.5			3/0 single No. 1 treble	
						Fixed
Luderick	3.0				10 to 8	Split shot
			Tapered rod			
Tailor	WF8F or S		3.0		4 to 3/0 fly	
Striped tuna	WF8F or S		3.0		4 to 3/0 fly	
Bonefish	WF8F or S		3.0		6 to 1/0 fly	
Tarpon	WF8F or S		3.0		4 to 2/0 fly	
Long tom	3.0				4 to 1	
Mullet	3.0		2.2		12 to 8	
Garfish	3.0		2.2		12 to 8	
Trevally	4.0		3.0		2 to 2/0	

RIGS

RIGS

BAY AND ESTUARY RIG 12

20 cm

BAY AND ESTUARY RIG 13

Single hook only is baited; do not bait treble hook

BAY AND ESTUARY RIG 14

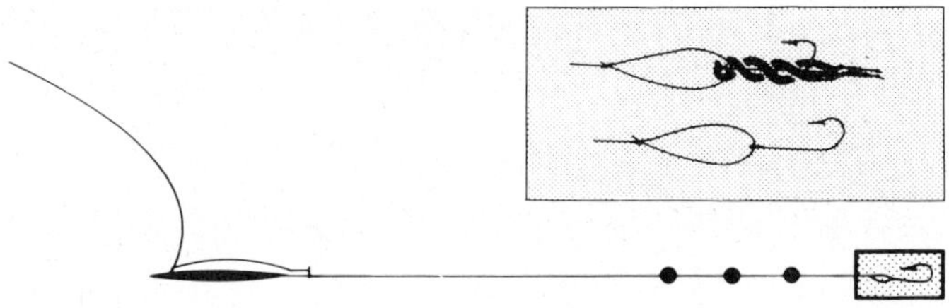

BAY AND ESTUARY RIG 15

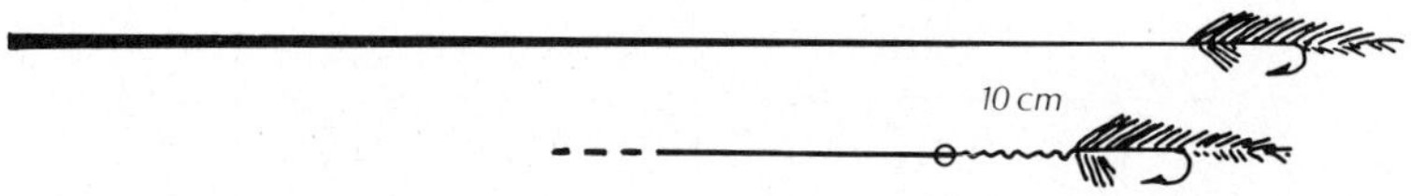

10 cm

BAY AND ESTUARY RIG 16

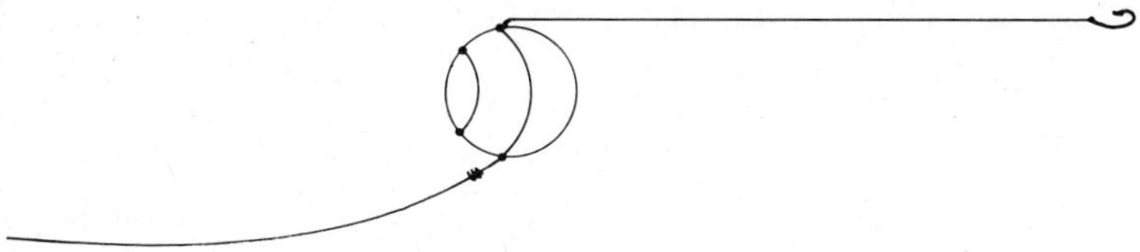

60 cm

BAY AND ESTUARY RIG 17

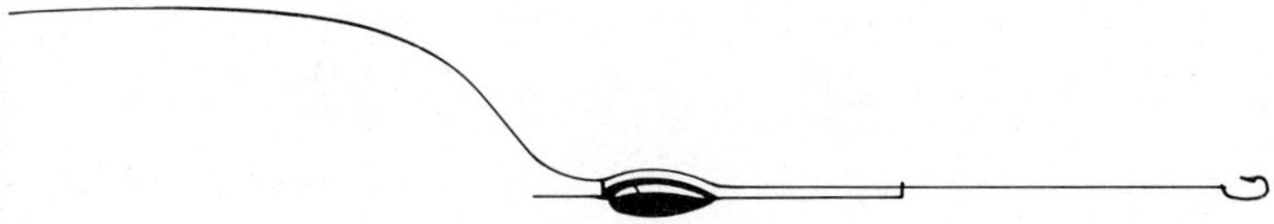

R ■ RIGS

| | LINE | | TRACE | | HOOKS | SINKER |
| | Rod | Hand | Rod | Hand | | Running |
	kg	kg	kg	kg		g
Tailor	4.5		Wire		1/0 to 5/0	
Mullet	3.0		2.2		12 to 8	
Garfish	3.0		2.2		12 to 8	
Tailor	4.5		Wire		1/0 to 5/0	

RIGS FOR SALTWATER LAKES

	Rod kg	Hand kg	Rod kg	Hand kg	Hooks	Running g
Bream	3.0	4.5			6 to 1/0	
Leatherjacket	3.0	3.0			10 to 8	
Bream	3.0	4.5	2.2	3.0	6 to 1/0	3–7
Whiting	3.0	4.5	2.2	3.0	6 to 1	3–7
Bream	3.0	4.5	2.2	3.0	6 to 1/0	3–7
Flathead	4.5	6.8	3.0	5.5	1/0 to 5/0	3–28
						Fixed
Whiting	3.0	3.0	2.2	2.2	6 to 1	7 to 14
Flathead	4.5	6.8	3.0	5.5	1/0 to 5/0	
Tailor	4.5	6.8	3.0	5.5	1/0 to 5/0	

RIGS ■ R

RIGS

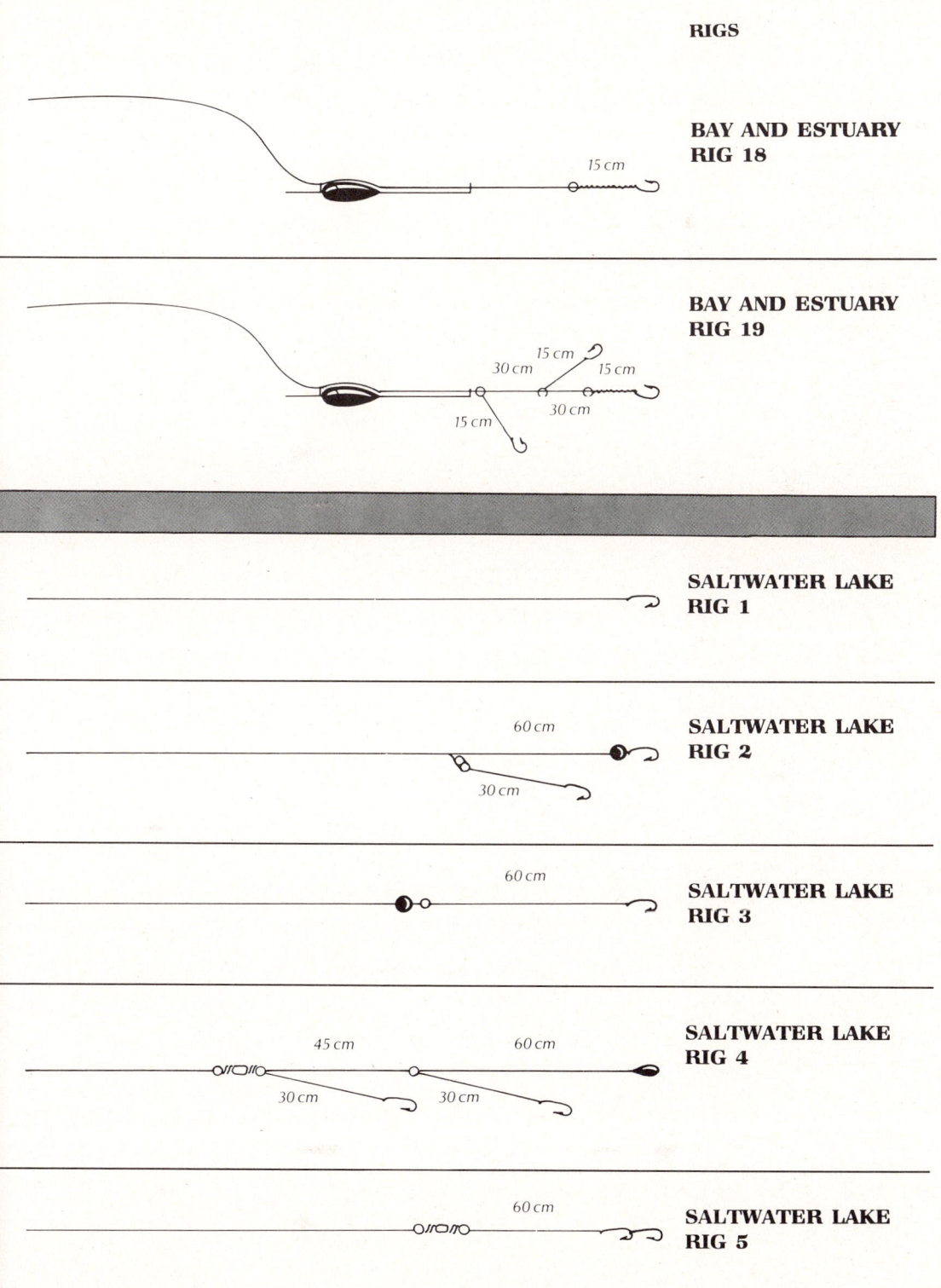

BAY AND ESTUARY RIG 18

BAY AND ESTUARY RIG 19

SALTWATER LAKE RIG 1

SALTWATER LAKE RIG 2

SALTWATER LAKE RIG 3

SALTWATER LAKE RIG 4

SALTWATER LAKE RIG 5

R ■ RIGS

	LINE		TRACE		HOOKS	SINKER
	Rod	**Hand**	**Rod**	**Hand**		**Running**
	kg	kg	kg	kg		g
Flathead	4.5	6.8	Wire	Wire	1/0 to 5/0	7–28
Tailor	4.5	6.8	Wire	Wire	1/0 to 5/0	7–28
Tailor	4.5	6.8	3.0	5.5	3/0 ganged	28–56
Flathead	4.5	6.8	3.0	5.5	3/0 ganged	28–56
			Tapered leader			
Mullet	⎧ Tapered		1.4		20 to 16 fly	
Tailor	⎩ fly line		3.0		1 to 3/0 saltwater fly	
Flathead	Lead core or tapered line		3.0		1 to 3/0 saltwater fly with split shot leading	
Mullet	3.0		2.2		12 to 8	
Garfish	3.0		2.2		12 to 8	

RIGS

SALTWATER LAKE RIG 6

SALTWATER LAKE RIG 7

SALTWATER LAKE RIG 8

SALTWATER LAKE RIG 9

SALTWATER LAKE RIG 10

SALTWATER LAKE RIG 11

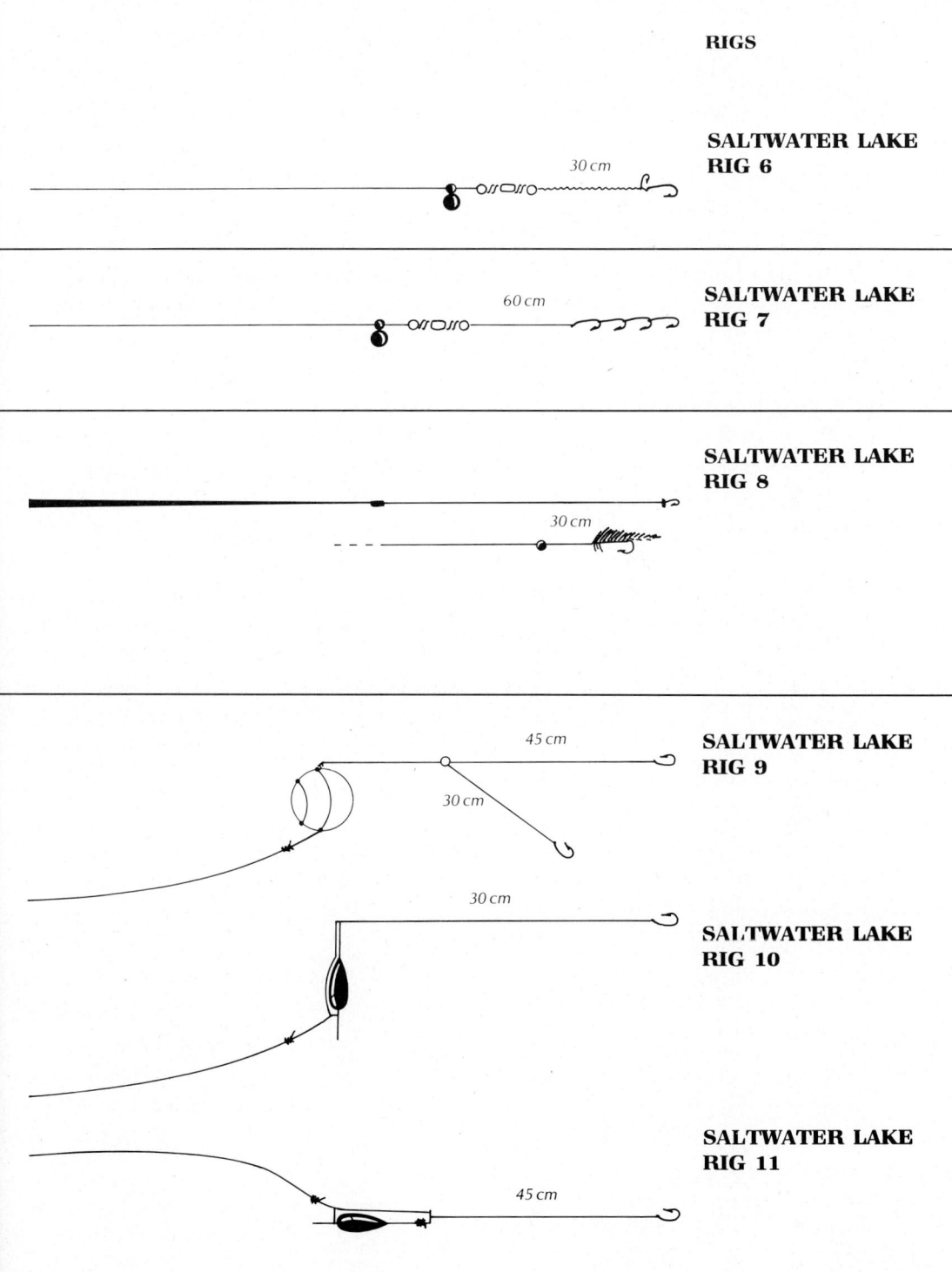

R ■ RIGS

	LINE		TRACE		HOOKS	SINKER
	Rod	Hand	Rod	Hand		Fixed
	kg	kg	kg	kg		g
Luderick	3.0				12 to 8	Split shot
Mullet	3.0		2.2		12 to 8	
Garfish	3.0		2.2		12 to 8	
Mullet	3.0		2.2		12 to 8	2–4
Garfish	3.0		2.2		12 to 8	2–4
Leatherjacket	3.0		2.2		12 to 8	2–4

RIGS FOR DEEP SEA FISHING

				Running
Leatherjacket	6.8	Wire	4 to 1/0	28–56
				Fixed
Bluefish	11.5–15.8	9–13.6	1/0 to 3/0	113–226
Snapper	11.5–15.8	9–13.6	3/0 to 7/0	113–226
Morwong	11.5–15.8	9–13.6	1/0 to 3/0	113–226
Gurnard	11.5–15.8	9–13.6	3/0 to 7/0	113–226
Flathead	11.5–15.8	9–13.6	3/0 to 7/0	113–226
Nannygai	11.5–15.8	9–13.6	1 to 2/0	113–226
Sergeant baker	11.5–15.8	9–13.6	1/0 to 5/0	113–226
Jackass fish	11.5–15.8	9–13.6	1/0 to 3/0	113–226
Red emperor	11.5–15.8	9–13.6	3/0 to 6/0	113–226
Teraglin	11.5–15.8	9–13.6	3/0 to 7/0	113–226
Sweetlip	11.5–15.8	9–13.6	3/0 to 6/0	113–226
Mulloway	11.5–15.8	9–13.6	3/0 to 7/0	113–226

RIGS

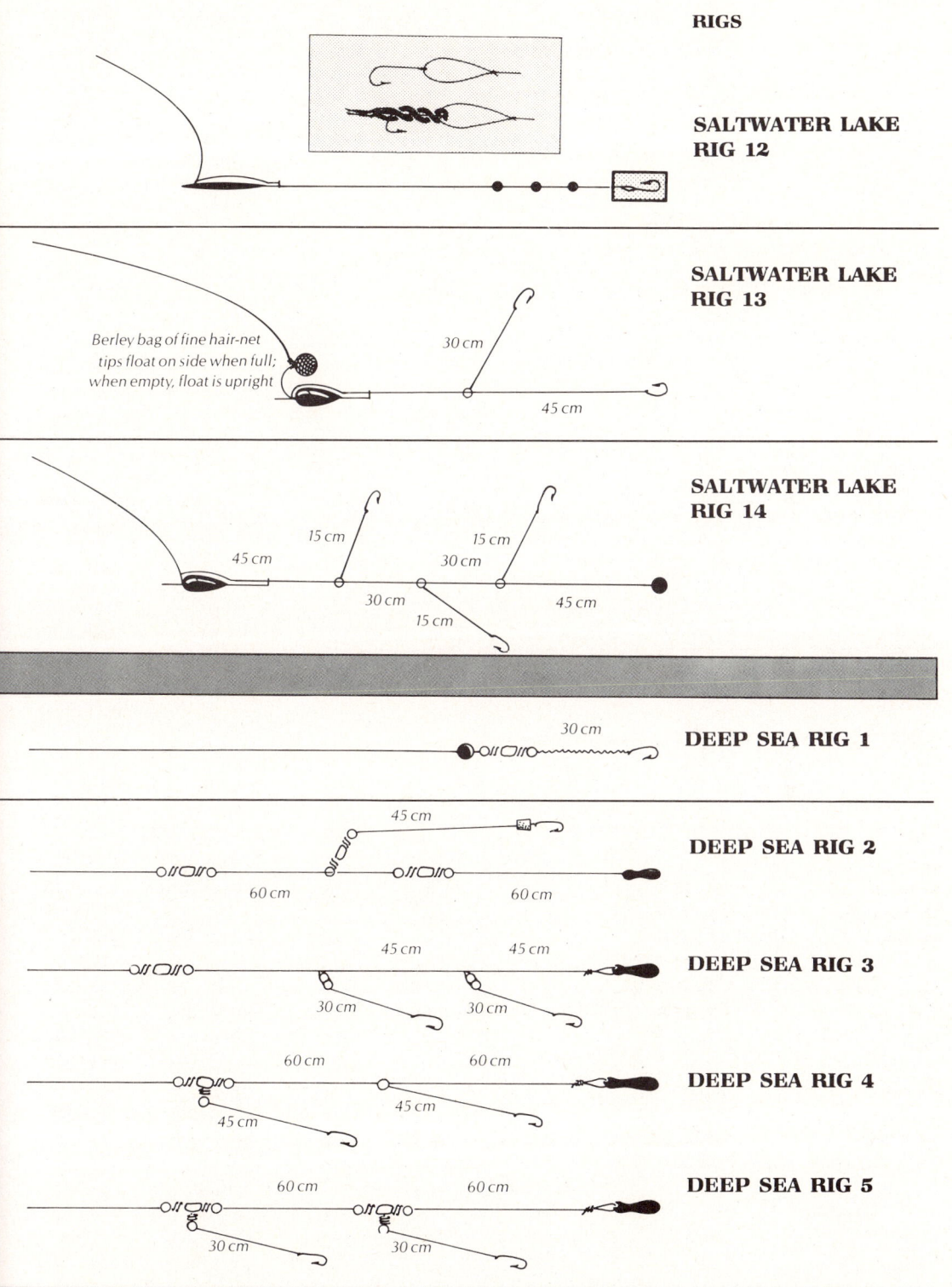

SALTWATER LAKE RIG 12

SALTWATER LAKE RIG 13

Berley bag of fine hair-net tips float on side when full; when empty, float is upright

30 cm
45 cm

SALTWATER LAKE RIG 14

45 cm
15 cm
30 cm
15 cm
30 cm
15 cm
45 cm

DEEP SEA RIG 1

30 cm

DEEP SEA RIG 2

45 cm
60 cm
60 cm

DEEP SEA RIG 3

45 cm
45 cm
30 cm
30 cm

DEEP SEA RIG 4

60 cm
60 cm
45 cm
45 cm

DEEP SEA RIG 5

60 cm
60 cm
30 cm
30 cm

R ■ RIGS

	LINE		TRACE		HOOKS	SINKER
	Rod	Hand	Rod	Hand		Running
	kg	kg	kg	kg		g length of chain
Bluefish	11.5–15.8		9–13.6		1/0 to 3/0	113–226
Snapper	11.5–15.8		9–13.6		3/0 to 7/0	113–226
Morwong	11.5–15.8		9–13.6		1/0 to 3/0	113–226
Gurnard	11.5–15.8		9–13.6		3/0 to 7/0	113–226
Flathead	11.5–15.8		9–13.6		3/0 to 7/0	113–226
Nannygai	11.5–15.8		9–13.6		1 to 2/0	113–226
Sergeant baker	11.5–15.8		9–13.6		1/0 to 5/0	113–226
Jackass fish	11.5–15.8		9–13.6		1/0 to 3/0	113–226
Red emperor	11.5–15.8		9–13.6		3/0 to 6/0	113–226
Teraglin	11.5–15.8		9–13.6		3/0 to 7/0	113–226
Sweetlip	11.5–15.8		9–13.6		3/0 to 6/0	113–226
Mulloway	11.5–15.8		9–13.6		3/0 to 7/0	113–226

RIGS FOR STREAM FISHING

	Rod kg	Hand kg	Rod kg	Hand kg		Fixed
Bass	3.0	4.5			4 to 1/0	Split shot
Trout	3.0	4.5			10 to 1	Split shot
Redfin	3.0	4.5			1/0 to 5/0	Split shot
Tench	3.0	4.5			6 to 4	Split shot
Roach	3.0	4.5			12 to 8	Split shot
Blackfish	3.0	4.5			6 to 1	Split shot
Carp	3.0	4.5			1 to 3/0	Split shot
Catfish	4.0	5.5			1 to 2/0	Split shot
Silver perch	3.0	4.5			4 to 1/0	Split shot
						Running
Murray cod	9.0	13.6	6.8	11.5	1/0 to 8/0	28–56
Callop	4.5	6.8	3.0	5.5	1/0 to 3/0	28–56
Redfin	4.0	5.5	3.0	4.5	1 to 3/0	28–56
Catfish	4.0	5.5	3.0	4.5	1 to 2/0	28–56
Bass	3.0	4.5	2.2	3.0	4 to 1/0	28–56
Trout	3.0		2.2		10 to 1	28–56
Redfin	3.0	4.5	2.2	3.0	1/0 to 6/0	28–56
Tench	3.0	4.5	2.2	3.0	6 to 4	28–56
Roach	3.0	4.5	2.2	3.0	12 to 8	28–56
Blackfish	3.0	4.5	2.2	3.0	6 to 1	28–56
Carp	3.0	4.5	2.2	3.0	1 to 3/0	28–56
Catfish	4.0	5.5	3.0	4.5	1 to 2/0	28–56
Silver perch	3.0	4.5	2.2	3.0	4 to 1/0	28–56
Murray cod	9.0	13.6	6.8	11.5	1/0 to 8/0	28–56
Callop	4.5	6.8	3.0	5.5	1/0 to 3/0	28–56

RIGS

DEEP SEA RIG 6

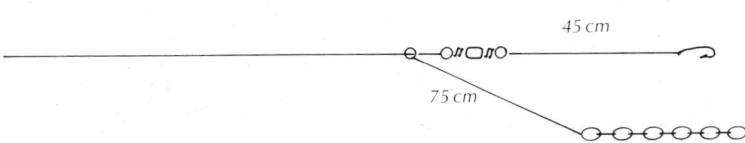

45 cm
75 cm

STREAM RIG 1

30 cm

STREAM RIG 2

60 cm

STREAM RIG 3

45 cm   60 cm
30 cm

R ■ RIGS

	LINE		TRACE		HOOKS	SINKER
	Rod	Hand	Rod	Hand		Running
	kg	kg	kg	kg		g
Trout	Tapered fly line		Tapered leader		20 to 8 flies	
Macquarie perch					20 to 8 flies	
Barramundi					1 to 3/0 flies	
Trout	Tapered fly line		Tapered leader		20 to 8 flies	
Macquarie perch					20 to 8 flies	
						Fixed
Roach	3.0				12 to 8	Split shot
Tench	3.0				6 to 4	Split shot
Redfish	3.0				1/0 to 3/0	Split shot
Mangrove jack	5.5				1/0 to 5/0	Split shot
Mullet	3.0				12 to 10	Split shot
Barramundi	9.0				3/0 to 9/0	Split shot
Forktail catfish	9.0				2/0 to 5/0	Split shot
Forktail catfish	7.7				4/0 ganged	

RIGS FOR FRESHWATER LAKE OR DAM FISHING

	Rod kg	Hand kg	Rod kg	Hand kg		Running g
Trout	2.7				10 to 1	
Redfin	2.7	4.5			1 to 4/0	
						Running
Trout	3.0		2.2		6 to 1	7–28
Redfin	3.0	4.5	2.2	3.0	1 to 3/0	7–28
Callop	3.0	4.5	2.2	3.0	1/0 to 3/0	7–28
Murray cod	9.0	13.6	6.8	11.5	1/0 to 8/0	7–28
Silver perch	3.0	4.5	2.2	3.0	4 to 6	7–28
Tench	3.0	4.5	2.2	3.0	4 to 6	7–28
Carp	3.0	4.5	2.2	3.0	4 to 1/0	7–28

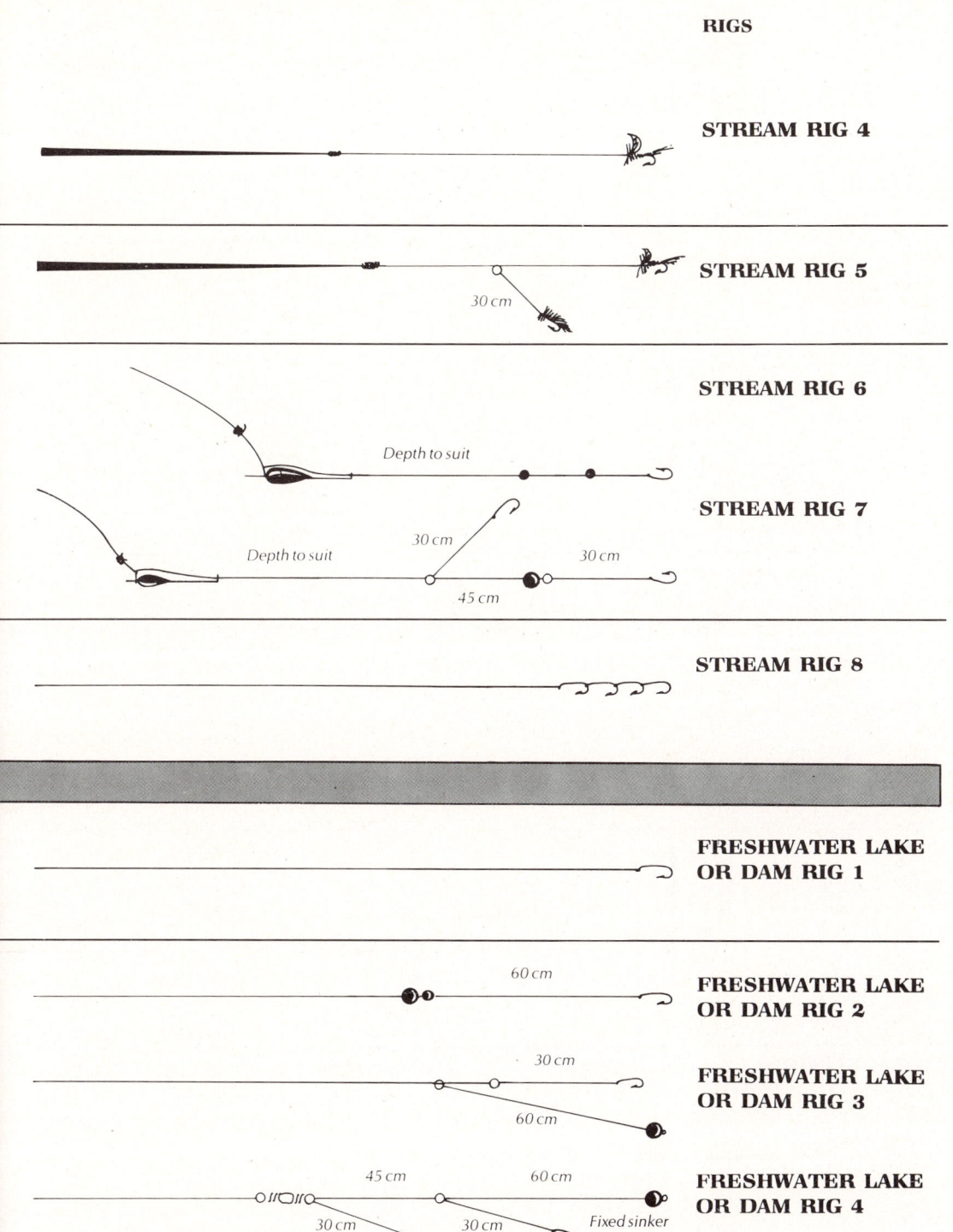

R ■ RIGS

| | LINE | | TRACE | | HOOKS | SINKER |
| | Rod | Hand | Rod | Hand | | Running |
	kg	kg	kg	kg		g
Trout	DT7F		Tapered 4X		20 to 6 flies	

						Fixed
Trout	3.0				6 to 1	Split shot
Redfin	3.0				1 to 3/0	Split shot
Bony bream	2.2				6 to 8	Split shot
Carp	3.0				1 to 3/0	Split shot

Trout	3.0				6 to 1	Split shot
Redfin	3.0				1 to 3/0	Split shot
Bony bream	2.2				6 to 8	Split shot
Carp	3.0				1 to 3/0	Split shot

Trout	3.0		2.2		20 to 6 flies	

Trout	3.0				6 to 1	3–14
Redfin	3.0				1 to 3/0	3–14
Bony bream	2.2				6 to 8	3–14
Carp	3.0				1 to 3/0	3–14

RIGS FOR SPINNING

Tailor	6.8
Kingfish	8.0
Bonito	6.8
Striped tuna	6.8
Pike	6.8
Salmon	6.8
Mangrove jack	6.8
Forktail catfish	8.0

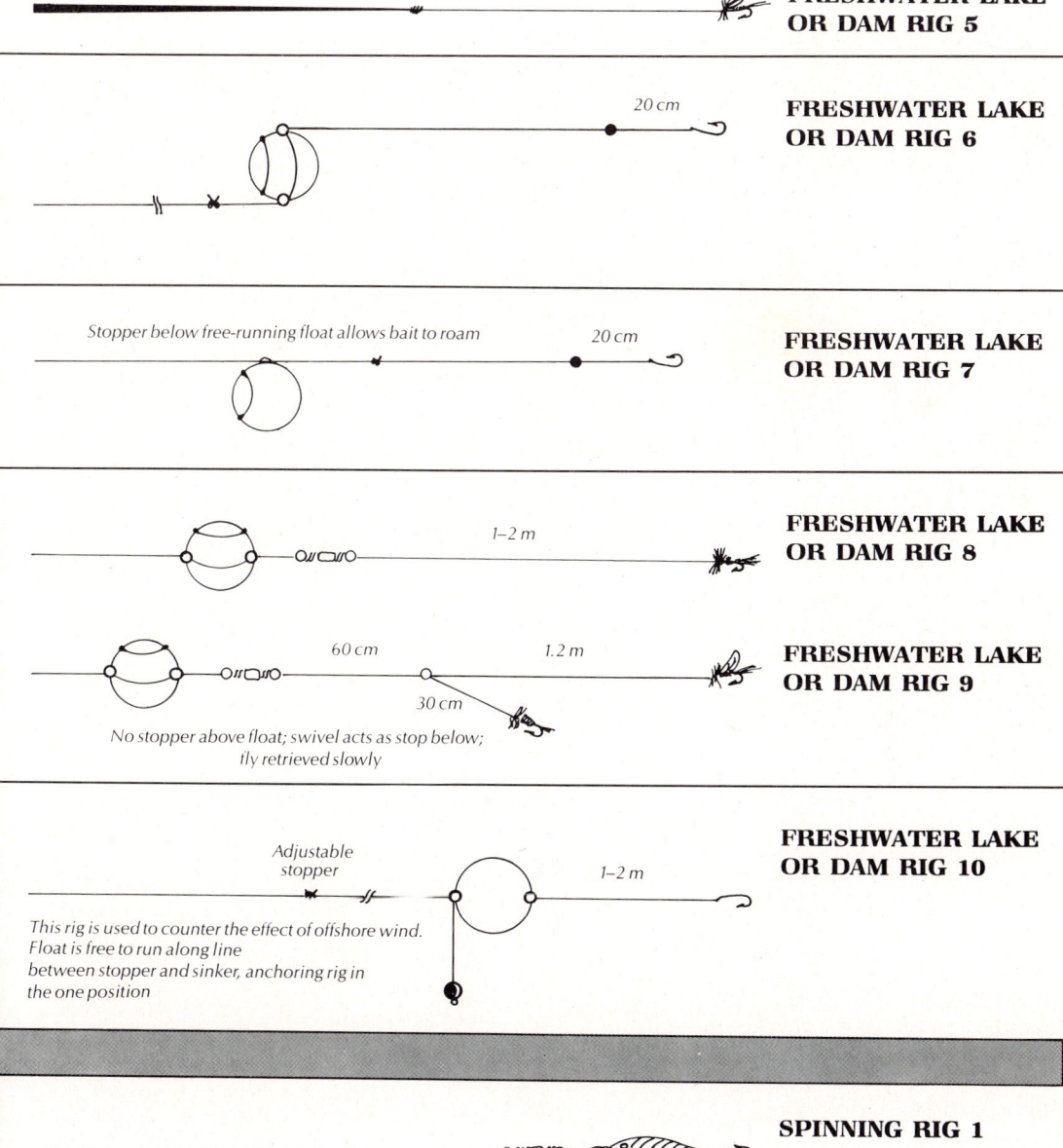

R ■ RIGS

	LINE		TRACE		HOOKS	SINKER
	Rod	**Hand**	**Rod**	**Hand**		**Running**
	kg	kg	kg	kg		g
Tailor	6.8		Wire			
Kingfish	8.0		6.8 nylon			
Bonito	6.8		4.5 nylon			
Striped tuna	6.8		4.5 nylon			
Pike	6.8		4.5 nylon			
Salmon	6.8		4.5 nylon			
Mangrove jack	6.8		4.5 nylon			
Forktail catfish	8.0		6.8 nylon			
Dart	6.8		4.5 nylon			
Tailor	6.8		Wire			
Kingfish	8.0		6.8 nylon			
Bonito	6.8		4.5 nylon			
Striped tuna	6.8		4.5 nylon			
Pike	6.8		4.5 nylon			
Salmon	6.8		4.5 nylon			
Mangrove jack	6.8		4.5 nylon			
Forktail catfish	8.0		6.8 nylon			
Dart	6.8		4.5 nylon			
Mulloway	7.7		6.8 nylon			
Tailor	6.8				4/0 ganged	
Kingfish	8.0				4/0 ganged	
Bonito	6.8				4/0 ganged	
Striped tuna	6.8				4/0 ganged	
Pike	6.8				4/0 ganged	
Salmon	6.8				4/0 ganged	
Mangrove jack	6.8				4/0 ganged	
Forktail catfish	8.0				4/0 ganged	
Flathead	6.8				4/0 ganged	
Bream	4.0				4/0 ganged	
Tailor	6.8		Wire		4/0 ganged	28–56
Kingfish	8.0		6.8 nylon		4/0 ganged	28–56
Bonito	6.8		4.5 nylon		4/0 ganged	28–56
Striped tuna	6.8		4.5 nylon		4/0 ganged	28–56
Pike	6.8		4.5 nylon		4/0 ganged	28–56
Salmon	6.8		4.5 nylon		4/0 ganged	28–56
Mangrove jack	6.8		4.5 nylon		4/0 ganged	28–56
Forktail catfish	8.0		6.8 nylon		4/0 ganged	28–56
Kingfish	7.7		Wire		3/0 to 5/0	

RIGS

SPINNING RIG 2

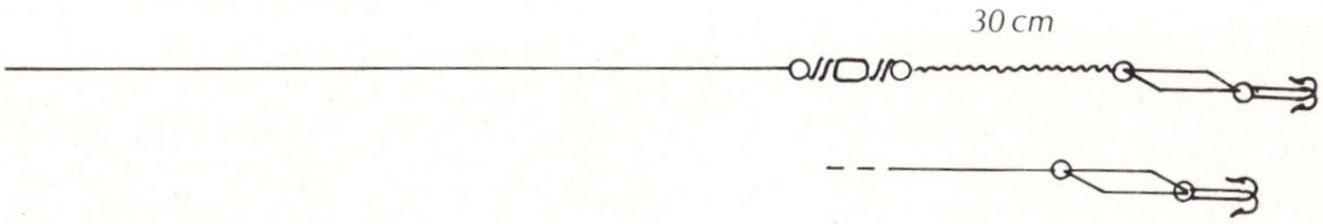

30 cm

SPINNING RIG 3

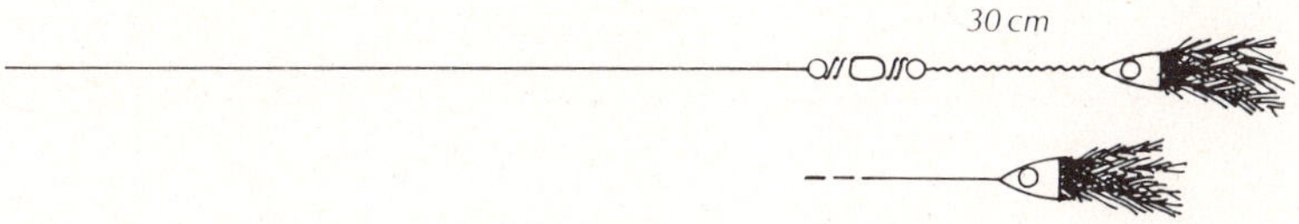

30 cm

SPINNING RIG 4

SPINNING RIG 5

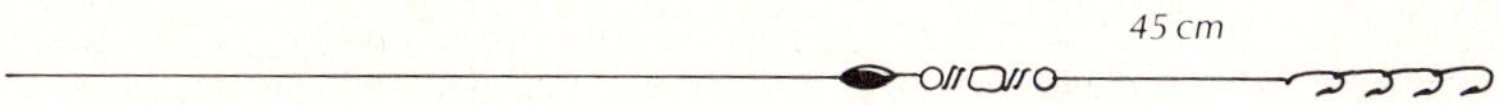

45 cm

SPINNING RIG 6

Flasher   1.2–2 m

R ■ RIGS

	LINE		TRACE		HOOKS	SINKER
	Rod	Hand	Rod	Hand		Running
	kg	kg	kg	kg		g
Flathead	5.5		4.5			14–28
Bream	4.0		3.0			
Redfin	4.5		4.0			
Murray cod	8.0		6.8			
Callop	5.5		4.5			
Redfin	4.5					
Murray cod	8.0					
Callop	5.5					
Trout	2.7					
Bass	2.7					
Trout	2.7				Fly hook 10	
Tailor	5.5				1/0	
Bonito	5.5				1/0	
Striped tuna	5.5				1/0	
Murray cod	8.0				1/0	
Redfin	5.5				6	
Trout	3.0					
Murray cod	8.0					
Redfin	5.5					
Callop	5.5					

RIGS FOR TROLLING

Tailor	5.5		9–13.6	4/0 ganged
Kingfish	7.7	13.6–22.6		4/0 ganged
Striped tuna	5.5	13.6–22.6		4/0 ganged
Bonito	5.5	9–13.6		4/0 ganged
Pike	5.5	9–13.6		4/0 ganged
Queenfish	8.6	13.6–22.6		4/0 ganged

RIGS

SPINNING RIG 7

60 cm

SPINNING RIG 8

60 cm

SPINNING RIG 9

SPINNING RIG 10

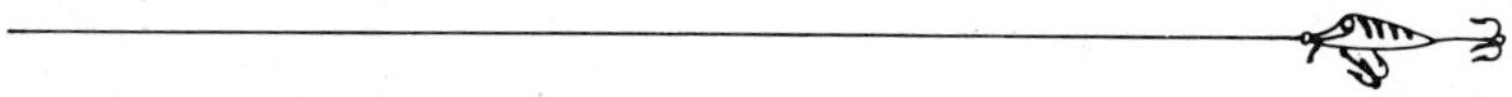

SPINNING RIG 11

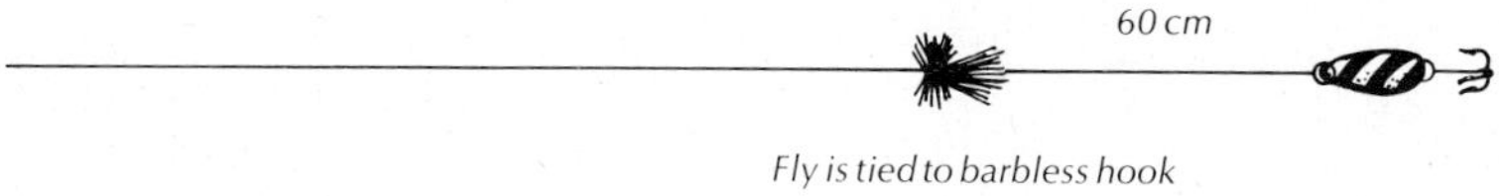

60 cm

Fly is tied to barbless hook

SPINNING RIG 12

TROLLING RIG 1

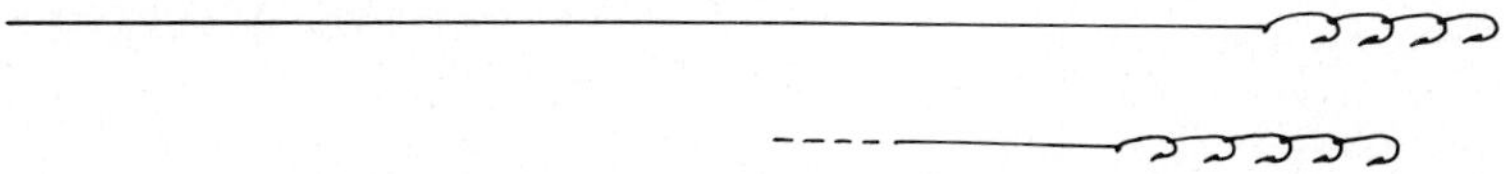

R ■ RIGS

| | LINE | | TRACE | | HOOKS | SINKER |
| | Rod | Hand | Rod | Hand | | Running |
	kg	kg	kg	kg		g
Tailor	5.5	9–13.6	4.5	7.7–12.2	4/0 ganged	28–56
Kingfish	7.7	13.6–22.6	6.8	11.5–20.5	4/0 ganged	28–56
Striped tuna	5.5	13.6–22.6	5.5	11.5–20.5	4/0 ganged	28–56
Bonito	5.5	9–13.6	4.5	7.7–12.2	4/0 ganged	28–56
Pike	5.5	9–13.6	4.5	7.7–12.2	4/0 ganged	28–56
Queenfish	8.6	13.6–22.6	6.8	11.5–20.5	4/0 ganged	28–56
Tailor	5.5	9–13.6	4.5	7.7–12.2		
Kingfish	7.7	13.6–22.6	6.8	11.5–20.5		
Striped tuna	5.5	13.6–22.6	5.5	11.5–20.5		
Bonito	5.5	9–13.6	4.5	7.7–12.2		
Pike	5.5	9–13.6	4.5	7.7–12.2		
Queenfish	8.6	13.6–22.6	6.8	11.5–20.5		
Striped tuna	5.5	13.6–22.6	Double nylon 4.5	Double nylon 11.5–20.5		
Tailor	5.5	9–13.6	Wire			
Barracouta	6.8	13.6–22.6	Wire			
Striped tuna	6.8	13.6–22.6	5.5	11.5–20.5		
Bonito	5.5	9–13.6	4.5	7.7–12.2		
Striped tuna	6.8	13.6–22.6	5.5	11.5–20.5		28–56
Bonito	5.5	9–13.6	4.5	7.7–12.2		28–56
Striped tuna	8.6	13.6–22.6	5.5	11.5–20.5		
Bonito	8.6	9–13.6	4.5	7.7–12.2		

RIGS

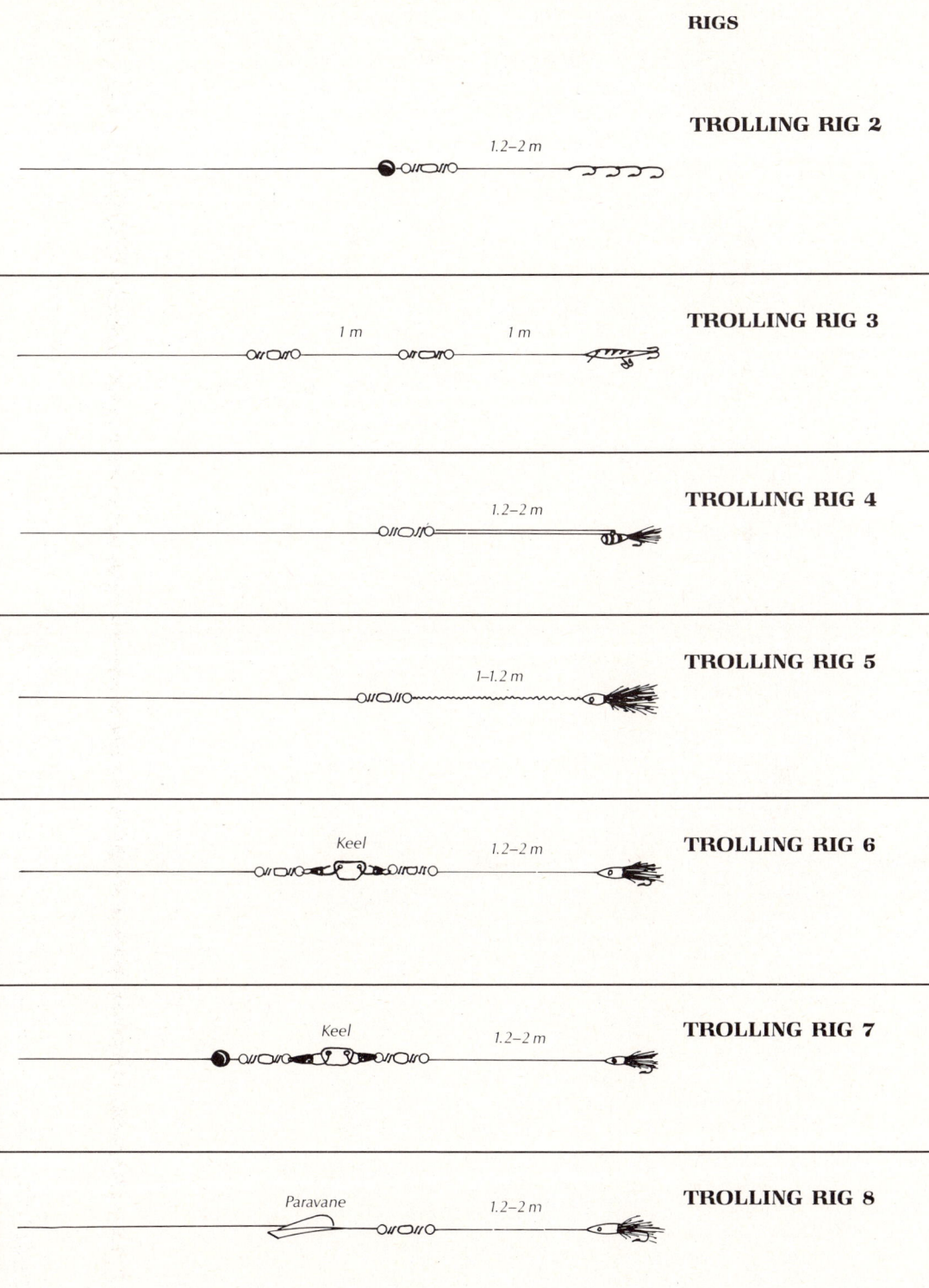

TROLLING RIG 2

TROLLING RIG 3

TROLLING RIG 4

TROLLING RIG 5

TROLLING RIG 6

TROLLING RIG 7

TROLLING RIG 8

R ■ RIGS

	LINE		TRACE		HOOKS	SINKER
	Rod	**Hand**	**Rod**	**Hand**		**Fixed**
	kg	kg	kg	kg		g
Tailor	5.5	9–13.6	Wire			2 × 14–56
Barracouta	6.8	13.6–22.6	Wire			
Barracouta	6.8	13.6–22.6	5.5	11.5–20.5	4/0 ganged	4 × 14
Murray cod	13.6	22.6–27.2	11.5	20.5–25		
Trout	11.5	22.6–27.2	9.0	20.5–25		
Murray cod	11.5	22.6–27.2	9.0	20.5–25		
Kingfish	7.7	13.6–22.6	Wire	Wire	3/0 to 5/0	

RIGS

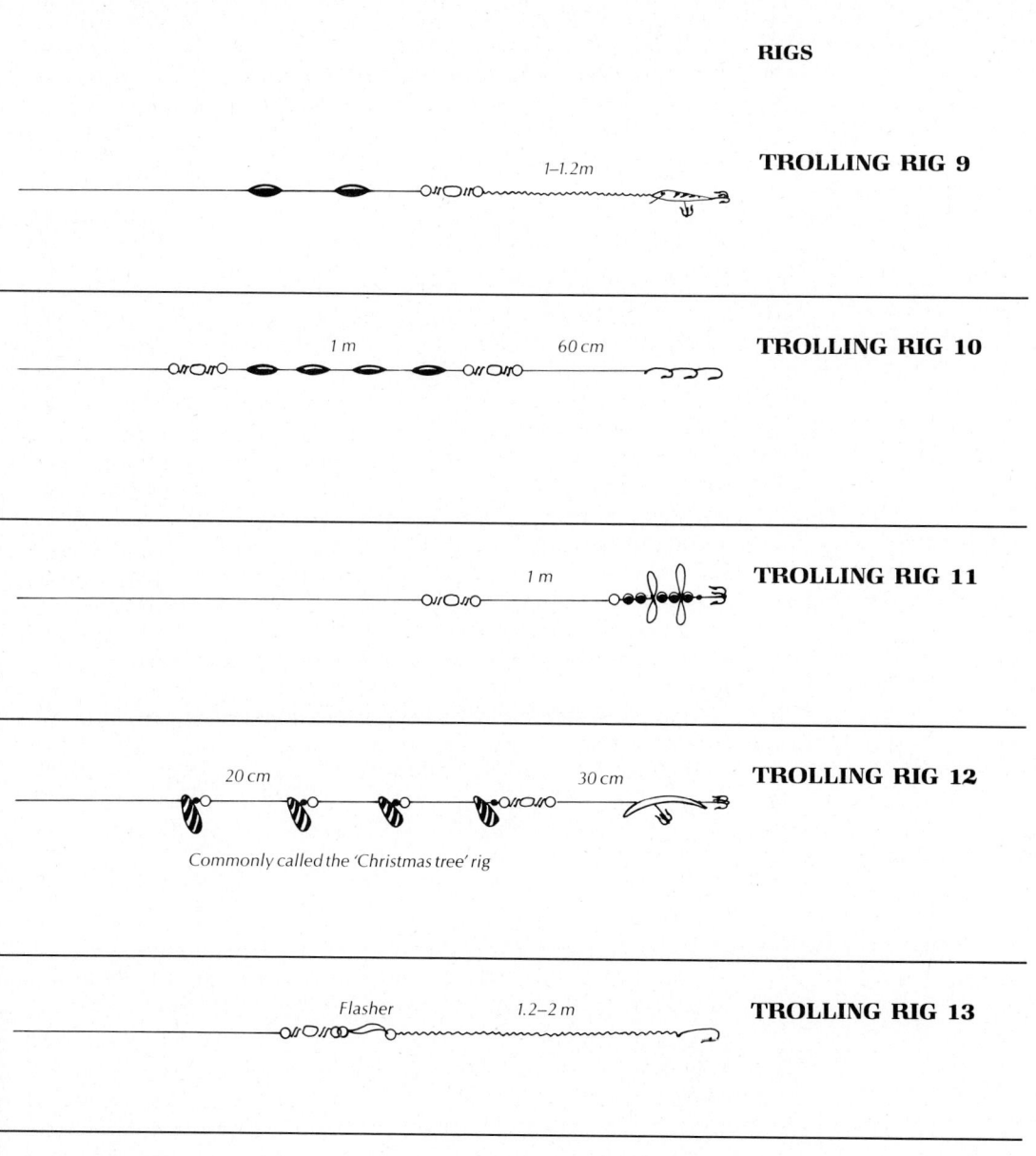

ROCK fishing

Rock fishing occupies its own niche in angling. While people fish from the rocks in South Africa, New Zealand, Norfolk in England and in Japan, only in Australia is the sport big time—and at that the real home of rock fishing lies mainly along the eastern coast. Nowhere else is the sport pursued so intensively as along the strip from Double Island Point, adjacent to Fraser Island in Queensland, to the New South Wales–Victorian border. This is because in most localities along this lengthy shoreline wave-cut, more or less level platforms have been formed at convenient heights for fishing ocean waters. These unique stances are due to geological accident.

The coastline embraces a variety of climate from sub-tropical to cool temperate, an infinite variety of sea floor from sand to reefs and heavy weed growth, and in places very deep water right beneath the angler's toes. It would be impossible to enumerate the species sought from the rocks—every species sought in deep sea, estuary and beach fishing plus some, groper and rock blackfish are examples, found only in the close-in reefs. The full spectrum runs from bream and luderick to marlin.

So the sport offers a wider variety of species than any other form of angling, and the potential danger inherent in the terrain provides a spice of adventure.

The danger is subjective—responsible, sensible rock-hoppers live to a ripe old age and negotiating difficult terrain keeps them fit. But the foolhardy can pay a high price. During the nine months from 1 July 1983 to 1 April 1984 eight rock-hoppers were swept to their death. Whenever the writer has been on the coast at the time of a fatality there has been a heavy sea running, the danger obvious. (*See Safety in angling.*)

Fishing techniques

There are four methods used in rock fishing, each of which breaks down into a number of applications. These are floating bait, float fishing, bottom fishing, and fishing with lures.

Floating bait

The simplest rig of all. Simply a hook on the end of the line, or a flight of three ganged hooks. A small sinker may be mounted on the hook if enforced by wind or water conditions. The single hook rig is effective for a wide range of quarry from light fishing for bream to sterner work with appropriate tackle for groper, rock blackfish, etc. The most widely used application is fishing whole pilchards for tailor and salmon. The pilchards, imported from Western Australia, have superseded garfish for this type of fishing. A soft, oily fish, the pilchard leaves a berley trail in the water.

Good tackle or bait shops offer snap-frozen pilchards in blocks. It is best to thaw them out and thoroughly dry-salt them to toughen them, then re-freeze. Unsalted pilchards soon fly to pieces when casting. The hook flight is made up of

Rock fishing is a big sport in Australia, where it is pursued intensively along the wave-cut platforms of the eastern coast.

three 5/0 hooks linked together. The best pattern is the Mustad 4200. Open the eye with a pair of wire cutters sufficiently to pass the barb of the next hook through the eye. Bend the eye inward about 15–20 degrees. Link up and close the eyes again with pliers. Mustad offer the 4202 pattern with eyes opened and bent, but the writer has found these hooks brittle at the eye and unreliable in use.

While intended primarily for tailor and salmon, the whole pilchard attracts other species—the writer has taken large bream, snapper, one mulloway, one black rock cod, striped tuna, bonito, trevally and barracouta with this bait and rig. Fixed spool reels—sidecast or threadline—are needed to cast the unweighted bait. The pilchard is cast out and slowly retrieved through the water. Bait or lure fishing? It's a borderline case. To mount the pilchard, measure the bait against the hook flight with the eye of the bait against the bend in the uppermost hook. This gives the position for the bottom hook to be passed through the bait, then the other hooks in turn, with the uppermost hook passing through the eyes of the baitfish. Properly presented, the pilchard swims naturally through the water during retrieve.

In the north, a similar rig with larger hooks and baits such as whole 'chopper' tailor, etc., is used to take big Spanish mackerel from the rocks in season.

The best way for a beginner to start his rock fishing career is fishing for tailor and salmon with the three-hook rig. Early morning and after sunset are prime times for these fish.

Float fishing

Almost completely trouble-free and often very prolific fishing. There are two specialized forms of float fishing—luderick and live bait fishing for game fish. Floats may be stemmed, or simple unstemmed 'bobby corks'. Cork is old hat nowadays, and most serious rockhoppers make their own floats and bobby corks from foam plastic. This is freely available as offcuts from surfboard makers. Rough out the float body with a keen knife, pierce the centre with a knitting needle to take the bush or stem as the case may be, then spin it on a mandrel in an electric drill to sand to the finished shape. Paint with fluorescent red Glowmaster paint. Other makes with strong solvents have a ruinous effect on plastic. Bobby corks should be bushed; quills from empty ballpoint pens make excellent bushing and are fixed in the bore with Araldite. Stemmed floats may be stemmed with cane or aluminium welding rod.

Bobby corks range from tiny floats about the size of a ten cent piece for bream and luderick to monsters the size of a large orange for visibility when cliff-top fishing from a great height. Average bobby corks should support a sinker of about 50 g for casting. Bobby corking has accounted for about every species taken from the rocks.

Luderick are dealt with elsewhere in this book. The other specialized application is game fishing with live baits in suitable deepwater habitats. A live yellowtail under the bobby cork has accounted for a range of game fish from salmon to marlin, the latter taken from the old torpedo tubes at Jervis Bay. When using I.G.F.A. regulation tackle, which is unsuitable for casting, live bait anglers often replace the bobby cork with a balloon, if the wind is favourable, to take the rig out to sea.

Bottom fishing

More beginners have broken their hearts starting off with bottom fishing than we will ever know. Short casting distances in an unsuitable locality can mean a frustrating day snapping off rigs fast in the bottom and re-rigging. Yet most snapper are caught with bottom rigs—in the hands of skilled anglers who have studied the art and perfected their casting technique. No matter how zany it may look, the beginner who wishes to emulate the successful bottom-fishing angler should practise his casting on the beach, or on dry land, until he can cast 70 m every time without thinking about it. In some south coast snapper grounds even 70 m is not far enough to keep out of trouble. A few really top hands can cast 100 m or better with a 113 g snapper sinker and bait. A fast retrieve is needed to recover the rig without dragging it into a snag. Sidecast reels should be Alvey 650 or 700 models; in fact Alvey do not recognize any of their smaller models as a 'surf' reel. Multipliers should have a gear ratio of 4:1, as should a large threadline reel if such is your choice. Both multipliers and threadlines should be strongly made with robust gears; rock fishing will sort out the shoddy models.

A running rig is always preferable for bottom fishing. Many fish, snapper and morwong in particular, run before taking the bait down; the jerk as the line straightens against the big sinker has lost many a fish. On a clean sand or gravel bottom a conventional beach rig is all that is needed; but a rock or weedy bottom requires a modified rig. Use spoon sinkers or snapper leads on a trace from 60 cm to 1 m in length. The line passes through a large beach ring at the end of the sinker trace, and the short hook trace is tied to another beach ring which acts as a stopper for the running rig. If using a sidecast reel mount a No. 12 swivel above the hook trace. Old hands will raise their eyebrows, but swivels are stronger than many realise. I have snapped many rigs caught up in the bottom, but only broken one swivel. Use a hard line, Angler or Tortue, and the tiny swivel, and you can bottom fish all day with a sidecast without developing line twist. Most important of all, the little swivel will run through the beach ring freely should a big 'red' take off with the bait. Beach rings come in two sizes; use the larger size on the rocks.

Casting heavy sinkers way out over the foreground reefs imposes a heavy strain on the line at the rod tip, and abrasion from the rough bottom must be allowed for. There is no need to use heavy line and lose casting distance because of these factors—use a shock leader. It takes an exceptionally powerful surf rod to pull 9 kg through the rod. I use 8 or 9 kg line in this class of fishing with a shock leader of 14 or 15 kg about two rod lengths in length. This looks after casting shock and abrasion on the bottom. Using one of the super fine lines—Platil Strong, Damyl Steelpower or Stud Plus, increases spool capacity and reduces resistance from wind and currents, but they are not suitable for sidecast reels. Use normal line for the shock leader. Using lighter line for hook and sinker traces averts line loss if forced to snap off when snagged on the bottom.

Lure fishing
Lure fishing from the rocks reached its zenith with the high speed spinning boom which lasted for about a decade with the Australian Seascape 621 reel—in its day, the world's fastest surf reel. Alas, the Seascape, like many Australian multipliers, is no more. Nor do hordes of anglers travel the coast with high speed reels seeking tuna. High speed spinning has given way to live bait fishing. But it was an exciting period. Nowadays most rockhoppers carry spinning gear as a second string while awaiting a strike on game fish or snapper line. Fortunately, overseas manufacturers now offer some fast—5:1 ratio—multipliers, and that excellent high-speed sturdy threadline, the Mitchell 499, is still with us. Alvey also offer a geared sidecast which has an enormous retrieve rate, but my long experience with sidecasts suggests that such a reel is suitable only where you can safely let the lure rest on the bottom to untwist the line before commencing retrieve. A good technique, really. Many a good snapper has taken a spinner jigged

A selection of big floating and deep diving minnow lures by Rapala are commonly used by rock fishing enthusiasts.

on the bottom. In deepwater localities many a game fish has been taken close in, and the sidecast reel is excellent for fishing big floating and deep diving minnows, which can be cast as far as a pilchard. Use a drag model sidecast—your next strike could be a tuna!

There is an enormous range of metal casting lures—misnamed 'spinners' by rockhoppers—and minnows available. They will all take fish. An excellent high speed lure is a simple torpedo shape moulded in lead and finished with iridescent adhesive tape available in good tackle shops. But you will need to mould your own. A big bean sinker prettied up with the iridescent tape is also a good high speed lure.

Baits

Pilchards apart, the best baits are found around the rocks. As they are gathered at low tide, and necessitate venturing into the inter-tidal zone, always have a mate watching the water for you when bait gathering.

Cunjevoi: A universal bait, the disadvantage is that everything goes for it—including all the rubbish fish. Best fished as floating bait or with a bobby cork to keep it clear of the bottom where all the eels and other nasties dwell. Excellent for rock blackfish in particular. Most just cut off the tough muscular top of the animal, as the soft abdominal parts fly off the hook when casting. This is a mistake. Cut the cunje straight across the 'teats'—the inhalant and exhalant apertures—right through, and use the complete half. Pass the hook first through the soft parts, finally anchoring the bait in place by the hard muscular part. It's the soft bits which attract the fish.

Pilchards: As well as using them as a lure for pelagic fish, half a pilchard makes a good bream and snapper bait.

Crab: In most places the best bait of all. Red bait crab can be caught by hand in the hard coralline red weed beds. This crab has taken a hammering and is getting scarce in many areas. Don't take more than you are likely to use, and return gravid females with the egg mass under the operculum. *Any crab is good bait*, and I am just as happy with the plentiful black rock crabs. Usually you need a crab spear to get them out of their crevices. The best method is to search the rocks at night with a powerful torch; the crabs feeding out in the open will freeze when a bright light strikes them. Crabs are fished whole (groper), or cut (groper, snapper, bream, trevally, etc.). Be very careful on the rocks at night.

Large shell fish: Tritons, turban shells, etc. Excellent bait for groper, rock blackfish, snapper and bream. Likewise octopus—when you find one.

Rods and reels

The angler has never had it better. The choice is absolutely bewildering. The most popular rods around the rocks today are fibreglass, which is low-priced, light and seemingly everlasting. While the latest in technology is carbon fibre, few surf rods are offered in this material and it is prohibitively expensive. We'll stick to tubular glass but hope prices for carbon fibre will come down.

Nobody offers better surf blanks than the Australian makers, Butterworth and Gatorglass. There are so many blanks, and so many very similar, that it is useless to name individual models. You must be guided by your needs.

Surf rods range from 335 to 396 cm in length, with the most popular length about 366 cm. Modern rods are fast taper, or multi taper, with light tips and powerful butts. This makes them very versatile—I have caught groper with 11.5 kg line, and fished the beach with 3.6 kg line—*with the same rod*! For most rock work a rod which pulls from 3 to 5 kg when the tip is at right angles to the butt will serve you well.

When choosing a ready-built rod you need the winch fitting at the butt, right against the sand spike, if you are intending to use a sidecast reel. If the rod is to be used with a multiplier or

R ■ ROCK fishing

threadline reel, the winch fitting should give you a good hand spread for casting power—at least 60 cm from the butt. 'Intermediate' rods with the winch fitting about 45 cm from the butt are an abomination—they suit no reel ever devised. I don't know why people build them. They are top-heavy when casting with a multiplier, and endanger your sex life with a sidecast.

If your interest is strictly light fishing there is one outstanding blank for the sidecast or threadline—the Butterworth 7162L multi taper. This long rod—427 cm—will cast a maximum 60 g weight. It is so light that I have caught luderick with it. I also landed a striped tuna with it!

Don't try to cast heavy sinkers with it, or use it with a multiplier, which imposes heavier casting stresses than fixed spool reels. 'Multi taper' means that the wall thickness of the blank is also tapered. The Butterworth designations give the number of wraps of fibreglass in the blank—in a multi-taper this only applies to the butt section—then the length in inches and finally whether the blank has been rolled with heavy or light glass. Thus MT 7162 L is a multi-taper blank with seven wraps of glass, 162 in. long and built of lightweight glass cloth. FT denotes fast taper, with the same wall thickness throughout.

This Alvey 650 E5 was designed specifically for rock fishing. The reel features handles mounted on the robust fibreglass spool for direct, powerful wind, and a strong, smooth drag action with optional anti reverse.

The most versatile reel for general rock fishing is the sidecast, with an Alvey model for every purpose. Wooden spools have long since departed the scene, the spools now being phenolic resin in the lower-priced model, and more robust compressed fibreglass in the better models. Nothing wrong with the phenolic—I have one about 25 years old and still catching fish. There is a choice of plain or drag models. A rod bucket is needed with a sidecast surf outfit.

There is a wide choice of multipliers and threadlines, very sophisticated, and beautifully engineered. For rock work, any good quality big threadline by one of the leading makers will do the job. Multipliers are easier now for the beginner with centrifugal or magnetic spool control, but once you've got the hang of casting with the multiplier, learn to cast without the training wheels. Anti-backlash devices lessen casting distance. With all types of reel, the spool must be correctly filled for maximum casting ease.

One final word on the sidecast reel—you can fish from a height in heavy seas and winch up your fish—something no geared reel can do. No rock fisherman should be without a sidecast outfit. It removes dangerous temptation.

GEORGE BROWN

ROD design and construction

Rod building is well within the capabilities of the average fisherman who, if he is prepared to forsake a few hours' fishing time, can make one equal to, and probably better than, any found in the racks of most fishing tackle shops. And he can save money by doing so. How good the final product will be depends on the care taken during assembly, an understanding of what is required of the rod, a working knowledge of the tools and materials used in its construction, and the quality of the blank and other fittings chosen. Remembering that you invariably get what you pay for, always choose the best fittings you can afford, for you will want your rod not only to be worthy of its maker, but capable of handling the biggest of whatever species it is intended to be used upon.

Basic tools and materials
Tools: hacksaw, file, surgeon's scalpel or very sharp penknife, small sharp scissors with fine points.
Materials: sandpaper; two-part epoxy resin, 24-hour kind (Araldite or Resiweld are excellent); nylon binding thread; binding filler; rod lacquer; Hypalon tubing for handgrips; reel seat; line guides; sand spike and/or butt cap (if rod type demands them); masking tape (*not* transparent sticky tape or electrician's tape); rod blank; methylated spirits; white Chinagraph pencil.

Rod blanks
Today's rod blanks are usually made from hollowglass, carbon fibre (also called graphite), boron, or a combination of these.

Hollowglass is slowly losing way to a composition blank comprising a mixture of hollowglass and carbon fibre, with boron composites trying, not successfully so far, to edge the others out of the main sales stream. Solid glass blanks are rare; they are heavy and lack the versatility of the other materials, though some highly respected blanks are made with a tip section of 15 to 30 cm of solid glass.

Most blanks are made by wrapping glass or composite cloth, cut to a predetermined shape and size and impregnated with resins, under considerable pressure around a steel mandrel. The cloth is secured in place by spirally binding it with adhesive tape, and the cloth-wrapped mandrel then baked in an oven. The mandrel is subsequently removed, and the finished blank either surfaced by grinding smooth, or left with the impression of the adhesive wrapping (which is stripped from the blank after the baking process) in its surface. The latter surface is said to give the blank an additional 25 per cent strength over the sanded blank. Sanded blanks are still strong enough for their purpose, whatever it might be, and certainly easier to bind runners to than the ridged, unsanded kind.

Carbon fibre blanks are dearer, lighter, stronger and stiffer, with a faster action than hollowglass blanks of similar design. They usually have a series of graphite fibres running in one direction from butt to tip, although one brand is constructed with radial fibres intertwined with the longitudinal fibres to give additional strength.

Carbon fibre blanks are also more versatile, being able to handle a greater range of lure and line weights than similar blanks in glass. They are said to conduct electricity, so the user must be careful to avoid using them in an electrical storm or wherever there is a likelihood of the rod touching power lines (remote, but possible). Glass/carbon fibre composite blanks are an excellent compromise, being less expensive but with much the same attributes as the all-carbon-fibre kind. Some are made with an inner spiral of carbon fibres overlaid by fibreglass, while others are made of a cloth with a carbon fibre/glass weave.

Manufacturers tend to claim that their new blanks are 'more sensitive' or 'super sensitive', but fail to tell us than what! By sensitivity they mean the ability to transmit more quickly the signal of a bite or fish interest or general feel. At the risk of 'expert' backlash, I think that this is more a sales pitch than a viable practical attribute; I find it hard to believe that the average, honest human being is capable of recognizing, or reacting positively to, such fine distinctions normally measurable in fractions of a second only. My reflexes are as sharp as anyone's, and I cannot pick the difference.

At time of writing, boron/glass blanks are even more expensive than the carbon fibre, with little (in general practical terms) to justify their higher cost.

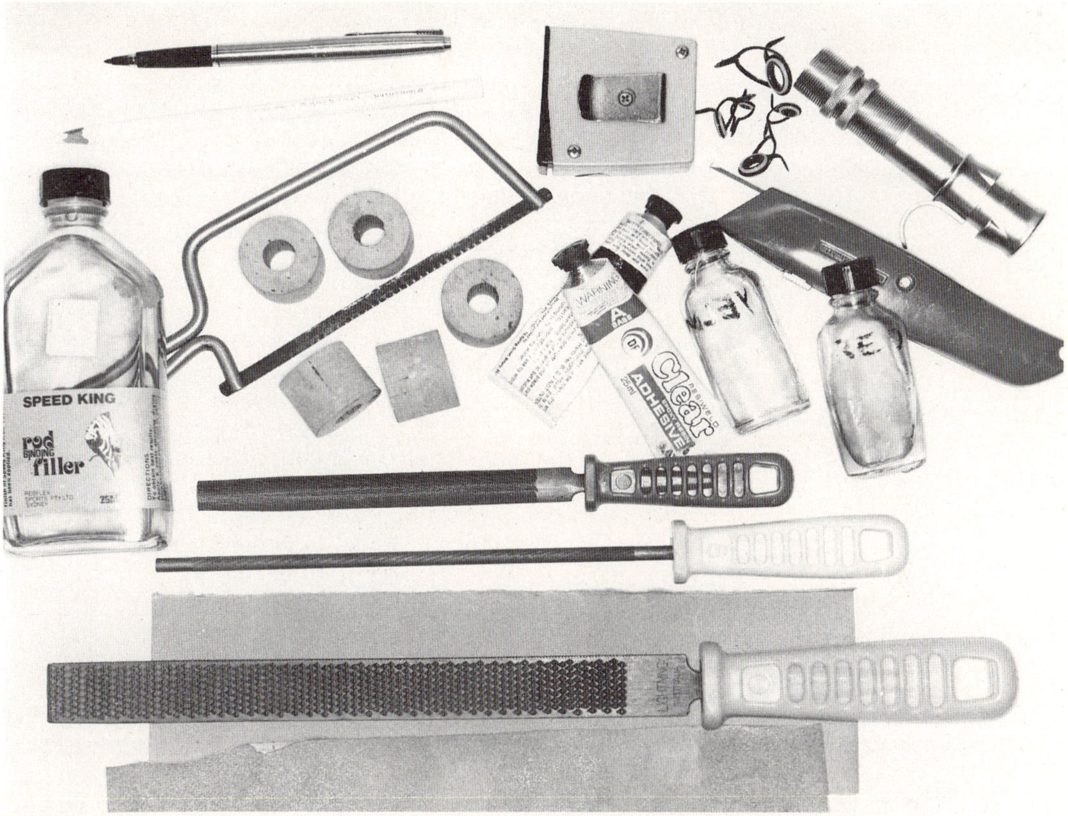

ROD design and construction ■ R

Rod actions

When we speak of rod 'action' we are referring to those qualities that allow it to bend, recover from that bend, and act as a cushion against the fighting lunges of a hooked fish. There are three basic actions for a rod—fast, medium and slow—with manufacturers' modifications that allow in between actions for the very fussy or for specialist purposes. These actions are built into the blank by the cut of the cloth, the length of the blank, the number of wraps of cloth around the mandrel, and the diameter of the mandrel. Minor variations, such as a 'medium-to-fast' taper, can be built in by altering any of these.

A fast action blank is one that has a fine tip and, by comparison, a large diameter butt. It flexes most along the top 20 to 25 per cent, that is it has a 'tippy or fast action'. The medium action blank of the same length might have the same size tip, but a smaller butt diameter; it flexes from the tip to about 30 to 40 per cent of the blank, whereas a slow action blank would have an even smaller diameter butt, and bend from the tip right through to the butt. Each of these actions, and the degree to which they are effective, can largely be controlled by the cut of the cloth.

Most fishermen are quite capable of building their own rods provided they have a few hours to spare and the right equipment.

R ■ ROD design and construction

The security of your reel depends on the reel seat. Note positions of reel seat for different reels.

A rod's action has an important bearing on the type of reel to use with it, especially if the reel is the overhead or free-spool kind. For this reel, where backlash is often the result of badly matched tackle, the medium to slow action blank is better suited, while the threadline (alias spinning, eggbeater or fixed spool) and sidecast reels, which lack backlash problems, are more easily managed when married to the medium, or fast action blank. Yesterday's fly rods were nearly all built on slow action blanks, but today are tending more to the medium-to-slow action style.

Better control over the comings and goings of a hooked fish is possible with the slow action rod which tends to absorb the frantic and often powerful lunges it makes. The faster action rod with its flexible tip and powerful butt is more likely to snap the line if the angler is inexperienced. Powerful butts, however, are necessary where big fish are encountered in order that lifting power be more positively applied.

Carbon fibre rods have an action that seems to be a combination of all three. At first feel they seem too stiff to be of any use for light lure casting, despite their relatively slim profile. The fisherman soon becomes accustomed to this change, however, and finds that such a rod can handle a greater range of lure weights than its fibreglass counterpart.

Earlier I made mention of a rod's ability to recover from the bend placed in it when casting. This recovery is very important where accuracy is necessary, as in the case of the fly fisherman delivering his fly to the nose of a trout. If the rod tip does not return to its normal position quickly, the consequent oscillating of the tip will throw curves into the line thereby reducing the chance of accurate presentation of the lure. Carbon fibre rods recover rapidly, and are popular with many fly fishermen for this reason.

Rod guides

Rod line guides of the 1980s are a far cry from those used twenty years earlier. The stainless steel, chrome-on-brass, porcelain, and tungsten carbide guides of that era have been replaced by aluminium oxide, ceramic and silicon carbide, materials that are lighter and harder wearing. Of today's materials, silicon carbide is the best, but also the dearest.

Things to look for in guides are light weight, strength, rust-proof frames, correct size, durability, and low coefficient of friction. The last attribute is important in today's age of nylon line which friction can rapidly destroy as the line is pulled against the sides of the tip guide when a large fish makes a run for it. Today's extra tough and durable materials also eliminate the possibility of the tip and first guide being grooved by the nylon line rubbing against it. This grooving increases the area of line subject to friction, and break-offs become commonplace. A common problem in the days of metal guides (with the exception of tungsten carbide, which was too brittle, anyway), grooving is unheard of with aluminium oxide or silicon carbide guides, although it can still occur with the cheaper ceramics.

Most rods used for game fishing are fitted with either a full set of roller guides, or conventional guides and a roller tip. Roller guides have an axle around which rotates a line bearing, and the degree of friction created is, for all practicable purposes, negligible. They are expensive, however, and require frequent maintenance to prevent jamming through the effects of dirt and salt build-up. Silicon carbide guides are almost as good, requiring no maintenance other than a rinse under the tap.

Snake guides, so named because of their shape, are still a popular choice with fly fishermen. Merely a twisted length of stainless steel wire forming a rough half circle, even they are being replaced with ring guides, some with sapphire inserts.

Reel seats or winch fittings

Choose your reel seat carefully, for the security of your reel depends on it. Avoid cheap ones. The best are still those made of brass and heavily chromed, but a carbon fibre/glass composition type is excellent if the better quality model is purchased. The latter type can be snug-fitted to the rod blank, but those with an inside diameter about 3 mm larger than the outside diameter of the blank are better, especially if they are of chrome-on-brass. The constant flexing of the blank, albeit slight at the reel seat position, can nevertheless wear the blank at that point where the inner edge of the reel seat opening

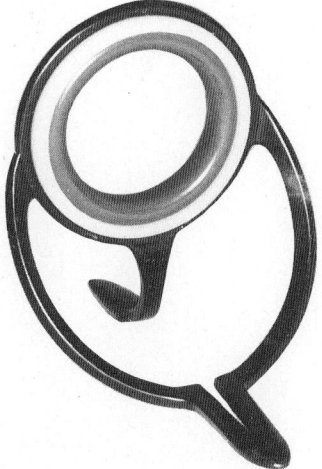

Today's line guides are lightweight, durable and have a low friction coefficient, which helps reduce the wear on the line. This model is a Fuji aluminium oxide line guide.

R ■ ROD design and construction

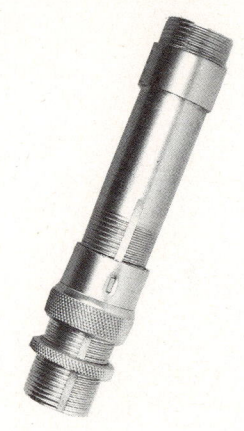

This chrome-on-brass reel seat features an extra locking ring that prevents the first ring from working loose in the field.

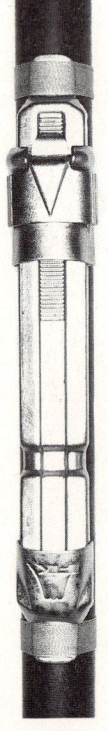

A very effective Fuji reel seat which can be bound to the blank.

bears against the blank.

An extra locking screw is recommended on the chrome-on-brass reel seat, the second one preventing the first from working loose in the field. It is not necessary with the composition type because of their design.

Versatile snap-lock reel seats are also available. These are usually bound to the blank, allowing for quick location changes, or permitting two or more to be attached to a rod thereby making it suitable for use with different kinds of reel.

Rod grips and extensions

Once upon a time (and even today with many fly rods) hand and butt grips were made from cork, generally by glueing bored cork rings together. Today, most rods have grips of Hypalon or other synthetic material. These grips, which are soft yet close grained enough to be long wearing, come in various lengths that are easily pushed down the rod blank to a predetermined permanent position. The ease with which the Hypalon grips can be mounted has virtually seen the demise of cork, neo-cork and neoprene, once claimed as wonder materials for rod construction. Many of the top quality game rods such as those made by Jack Erskine of Cairns, have decorative leather grips like those on tennis racquets or golf sticks, or grips made of flocked material that is easy to handle and kind to the hands.

Where a blank has a preferred action but lacks the length desired, glass or composition extensions are frequently added by the rod builder. Aluminium tubing once featured prominently for this purpose and is still used, but glass extensions can be bought for just that purpose and are to be preferred because of their better bonding qualities. Such extensions are almost invariably inflexible, and are best kept as short as possible.

Ferrules

Where a rod consists of two or more pieces, a ferrule is used to join the different lengths together. The trend today is to produce multi-piece blanks with piece-to-piece joins moulded during manufacture. These are called 'glass-to-glass' or 'built-in' ferrules, and they are usually superior to the metal kind. The latter, which may be made of chromed brass, German nickel silver, or bronze, are becoming less popular because of their inability to fit the faster taper blanks without action-damaging blank cutting being required. They are also becoming increasingly more difficult to buy, most tackle shops carrying but a token stock which is invariably 'not the size I want'!

No attempt should ever be made to reduce the diameter of the blank in order to fit the ferrule. Such reduction will seriously damage the blank, weakening it to a point where breakage is certain to occur within a short time. If a metal ferrule is too big for a blank, then the blank should be built up

ROD design and construction ∎ R

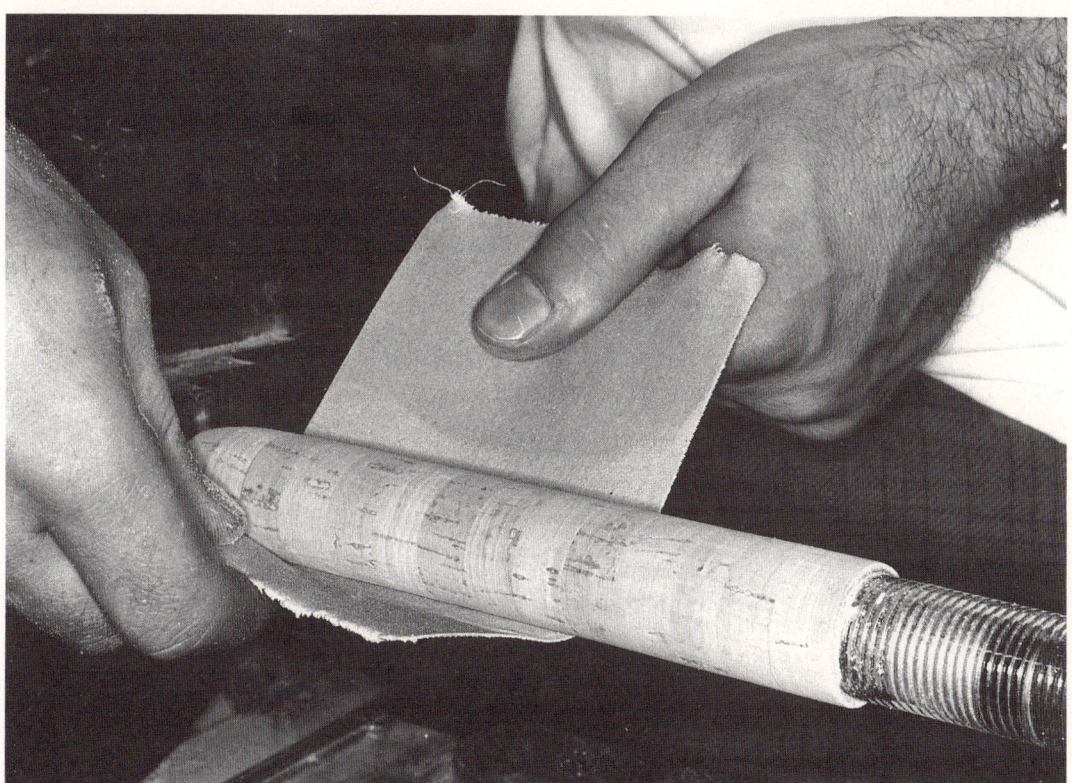

When the glue has set, a cork grip can be shaped using a rasp, and then finished with coarse and fine sandpaper.

to suit. Because of the small tolerances involved (inside diameters are measured in fractions of a millimetre), this is normally done by applying a layer of rod binding thread to the blank before sliding the ferrule into place.

Binding, filler, and rod lacquers

With the exception of the tip guide, line guides (or rod runners) are always bound to a rod blank and *never* glued. If glued, serious damage to the blank can occur if ever the guide has to be removed. The best bindings are those made of nylon or terylene. Silk or cotton should be avoided because their durability can be affected by moisture, causing them to rot and break. Nylon thread comes in different diameters, the two most popular being sizes A (fine) and C (thicker). While the first inclination might be to choose the thicker thread for security purposes, I prefer the finer thread because the additional turns required to cover a given length give greater strength, and the final result is a much neater appearance. There are other sizes, but these are universally popular.

Many rod builders underwrap their guides. They first put down a layer of binding to cover the area to which the guide is to be bound. The guide is then bound to the underbinding. This method protects sensitive, thin-walled blanks from abrasion, by the guide feet, that can actually fracture the blank

SPECIALIST ROD HANDLES

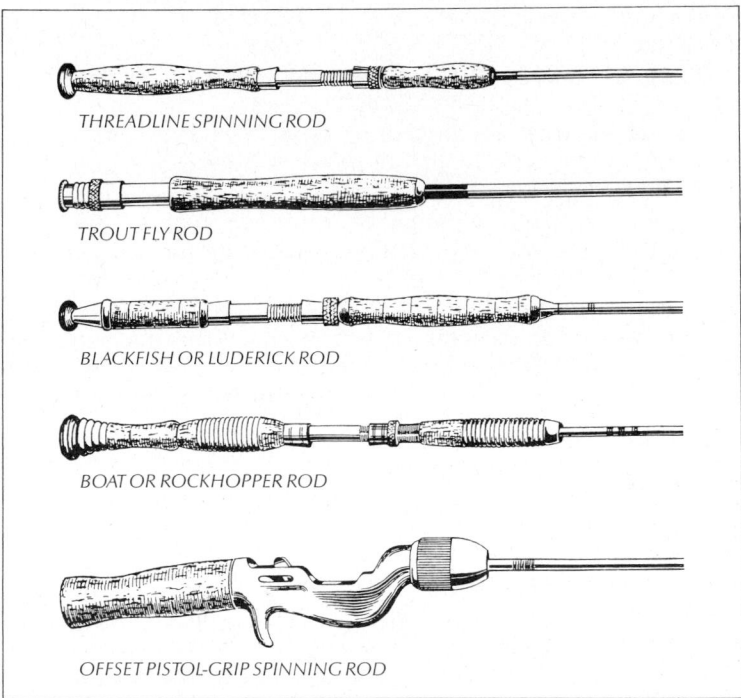

THREADLINE SPINNING ROD

TROUT FLY ROD

BLACKFISH OR LUDERICK ROD

BOAT OR ROCKHOPPER ROD

OFFSET PISTOL-GRIP SPINNING ROD

wall. By using contrasting colours, very attractive bindings can be produced. Some rod builders double wrap the guides, binding them down with two layers of thread. This gives much greater strength to the guide binding, but is rarely essential and is more in the nature of a sales gimmick. In all my many years of rod building, I have never found it necessary to double wrap a guide.

When binding a guide to a blank, always start your binding 5 to 10 cm from the end of the guide foot, and bind up to the ring, not vice versa. This will eliminate any unsightly gap where the thread starts to climb up over the foot. Begin by binding each guide to the blank by one foot only. This will enable you to sight along the guides and make minor adjustments to alignment before the other foot is bound down. When all are straight and true, then complete the binding of the other foot.

If underbinding is carried out, make sure that it is given a couple of coats of filler before the guides are bound over it. Binding filler prepares the bindings for the coats of lacquer to come. It is not applied to the entire blank, only to the bindings. It tends to tighten the thread, gets rid of trapped air bubbles that can find their way into the lacquer and spoil the finish, and has an adhesive effect on adjacent turns. You could liken it to an undercoat of paint. A minimum of three coats is usually required on the underbinding, and a further three or four coats on the guide binding. It must be left to dry thoroughly (usually only about 30 minutes) before applying rod lacquer.

Two-part epoxy resin rod lacquers seem to be the most popular finishes used at this time. A good rod lacquer must dry crystal clear, remain flexible and bond well with the blank, and the quality epoxy lacquers meet these requirements. Their initial high cost is more than compensated for by the professional finish they impart and the protection they give the bindings. Always give at least two coats for a deep rich finish, and allow a minimum of 12 hours between coats. Each coat preceding the last should, when dry, be lightly sanded to remove any dust particles or fluff that will be obvious as a raised projection in the finish. The final coat should be given in a dust-free environment if a perfect finish is to be achieved.

Rod building glues
The only parts of a rod that require glue to secure them are the tip guide, ferrule, foregrip, reel seat, butt grip and sandspike. The most popular adhesives are the two-part epoxy glues such as Araldite and Resiweld. Of these there are the 5-minute kind or the 24-hour kind. The only time the 5-minute glue should be used is when glueing the tip guide to the blank, and then it is preferable to use the longer setting glue. An alternative is the type known as Super Glue, but that sometimes fails to work and cannot be relied upon for long life. For all other purposes the 24-hour glues are the best, because they remain workable for longer periods, thereby allowing you reasonable time to reposition components should that be required.

Simple steps to rod building
Let's assume that you have all the components necessary to build your rod—blank, line guides, ferrule (if needed), reel seat, fore and butt grips and sandspike, together with the materials listed at the beginning of this section.
1. Any dirt on the outside of the blank will prevent proper bonding of glue and rod lacquer, so make sure that it is thoroughly cleaned using methylated spirits.
2. Line guides should be aligned along the 'spine' of the blank. To find the spine, hold the tip of the rod in your left hand, and balance the blank, about 40 cm from the tip on the first finger of the right hand. Now rotate the blank by rolling it along your first finger. At a certain point you will feel the blank jump into a position in which it wants to stay. The spine lies along the top of the blank in that position. Mark its position, at several places along the blank, with the Chinagraph pencil. If you are building a rod for a threadline or sidecast reel, the guides should be mounted on the underside of that spine. If it is an overhead or baitcaster reel, the guides will be positioned along the top of the rod (along the spine).

Decorative binding can be built up near the foregrip and when underbinding giving both aesthetic appeal and a professional appearance to the rod.

R ■ ROD design and construction

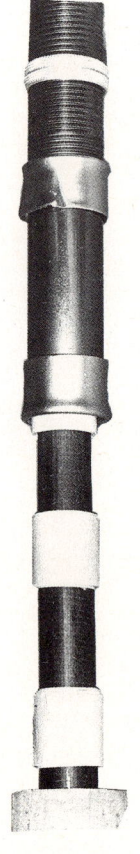

The reel seat is pushed over wraps of masking tape and then glued into position.

3. If you are fitting a sandspike, glue it into position and set the blank aside for at least 12 hours until the glue has set.
4. Having decided on the length of the butt grip, take an appropriate length of Hypalon tubing, and thoroughly wet the inside of the tube by pouring some methylated spirits into it, using the palms of your hands as stoppers to prevent it from running out.
5. Push the Hypalon tube down over the blank, allowing the methylated spirits to thoroughly wet the outside near the butt. Some force will be necessary to push the Hypalon into position, but it will slide easily along the blank because of the wet, slippery surface. No glue is necessary if the bore of the Hypalon is of smaller diameter than the outside diameter of the blank at that point where it is to finish, but a thin smear of Araldite can be used if there is any doubt about the security of the grip. The Araldite will also act as a lubricant to the positioning of the Hypalon tubing. Wipe away any surplus glue with a rag soaked in methylated spirits.
6. Take the reel seat and, with the sharp tang of a file, score the inside surface in numerous places. This scoring provides a key for the glue. Because the reel seat is a loose fit on the blank, it will be necessary to pack the blank at that point. This is done by winding masking tape around the blank, at three points within the reel seat area, until the reel seat is a tight slide-on fit.
7. Using plenty of Araldite or Resiweld, coat the masking tape packing, and partially fill the space between the three different layers. Slide the reel seat into position, making sure that the hood aligns with the spine on the correct side for the type of reel to be used. Set the rod aside for at least 12 hours until the glue has set.
8. The next step is to fit the foregrip which is done in exactly the same manner as described in step 5. Once again set the blank aside for 12 hours if glue has been used.
9. Glue the tip in position using 5-minute Araldite or Resiweld, making sure that the ring is accurately aligned with the hood of the reel seat. Note that it pays to check the alignment and positioning of these different components about an hour into the setting period just to make sure that nothing has been accidentally touched or knocked. You will then have time to readjust them before the glue finally sets.
10. If you want to shape the Hypalon grips once the glue has set, do so before the line guides are bound in position. They can be shaped by hand using coarse, then fine sandpaper or, if you are lucky enough to have a lathe, quickly finished using the same abrasives. Unless you are very fussy about your rod's appearance, the Hypalon can be left without shaping.
11. Before binding on the guides, clean the blank once more, making sure that all surplus glue has been completely

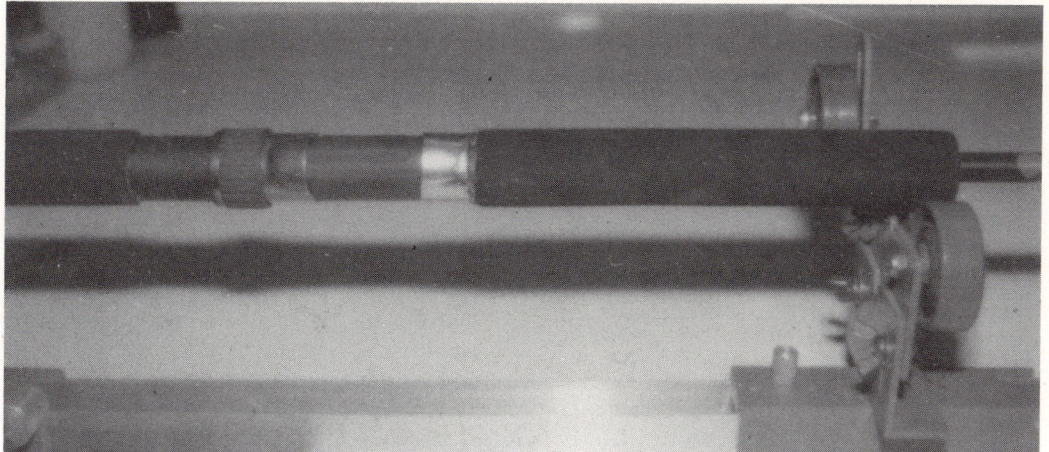

Today most grips are made of Hypalon, which is easily mounted onto the blank. Ensure the foregrip is of a comfortable length.

removed. It is much easier to remove in the pre-setting stage using the rag and methylated spirits.

12. The positioning of the guides along the blank is important. For threadline and sidecast reels, a good general rule is to have the bottom guide (the one closest to the reel) located midway along the blank. For overhead reels, this bottom guide can be brought several centimetres closer to the reel. Use a minimum of five guides for any rod, and preferably six or seven. Space these remaining guides along the blank so that the inter-guide spacings decrease as they near the tip. The progression should be gradual and have a balanced look about it.

13. When their positions have been determined, tape them to the blank, mount the reel on the rod, and run the line through the guides and tie it to some object, a nail in the wall for example. Put a good bend in the rod, and note the lay of the line around the blank. It may be necessary to move a guide backwards or forwards in order to have the line follow the bend of the rod as closely as possible—any obvious departure from a smooth flow can be corrected by changing the location of a nearby guide.

14. Wash your hands well before starting to bind if you do not want your bindings to have a grubby appearance. Having marked the final locations of the different guides (with the Chinagraph pencil), decide on the length of your under-bindings (if you want one) and do these first. They should extend about 1 cm beyond either foot of the guide.

15. When the underbindings are finished, tape the guides to the rod, centring them over the underbinding. Only tape one foot; you will be binding over the other one. Commence your binding about 5 mm away from the foot, and bind up towards the ring, locking the thread under the last six or seven turns. Wrap each foot separately. Do not carry the

binding thread from one foot to the other; a break in the thread would necessitate a rebinding of both feet instead of just one.

16. Bind all guides in place, but only bind one foot of each. Sight along them to ensure accurate alignment, gently move any that have to be re-positioned, then bind the other foot of each. Give them a final check for alignment, and prepare to fill and lacquer them.
17. Before using a binding filler, take the handle of a teaspoon and gently rub the bindings with it. This will close up any unsightly gaps. Then apply three or four coats of filler, allowing each coat to dry thoroughly before applying the next. Use your forefinger or a fine brush to apply the filler.
18. Mix the two-part lacquer carefully, taking care to avoid any air bubbles in the mix. If too many bubbles are trapped, they will not have time to rise to the surface before the lacquer has set, and will be visible within the finish. Apply the lacquer with a stiff-bristled brush and set aside to dry.

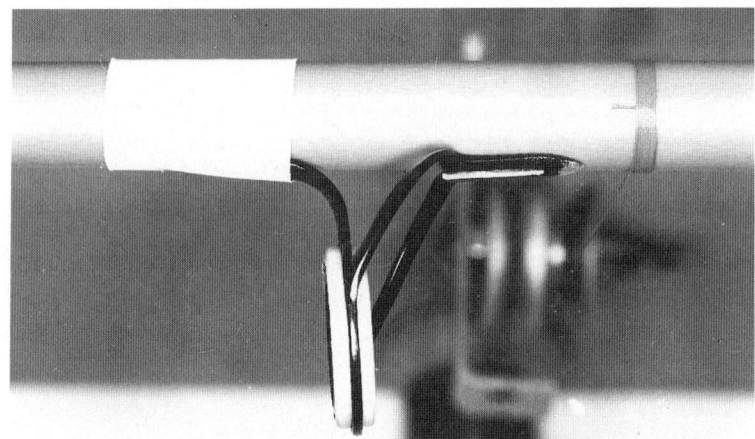

Commence binding by locking the binding thread under itself. Always bind up to the line guide.

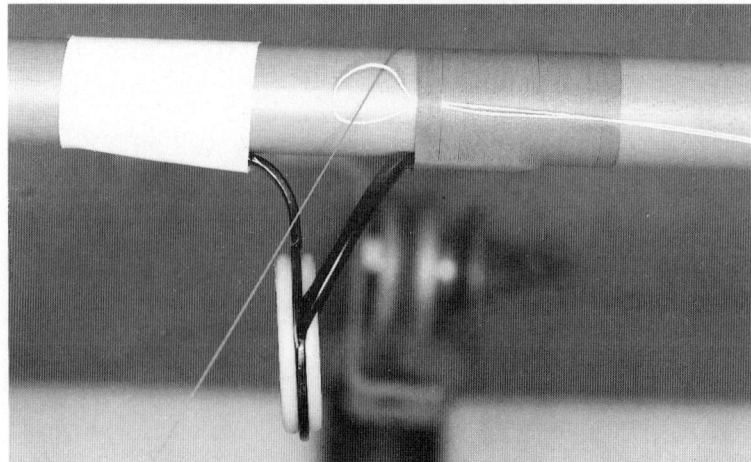

About 10 turns from the end of the binding, insert a pull-through loop, bind over it, and pass the binding thread through the loop.

Unless you have a rotating rod holder, you will need to turn the rod every fifteen minutes for at least four hours. If you do not do this, the setting lacquer will sag beneath the rod and you will finish up with an unsightly uneven finish to each runner.
19. When the first coat has dried (usually at least 12 hours), check to see if there are any dust particles embedded in the lacquer; if there are, lightly sand them away using a very fine (1200 grit) abrasive paper. Apply a second coat of lacquer, taking care to see that it is done in as dust free an atmosphere as possible. A third coat can be given if needed.
20. When the lacquer has dried thoroughly, apply a polish (such as Mr Sheen) to the entire rod, and buff up well. The finished product will be as good, and probably better than, any rod you can buy off the rack in any tackle shop. Happy fishing with it!

DICK LEWERS

Pull the loop under the binding together with the end of the binding thread. Cut the binding thread flush with the binding with a sharp blade.

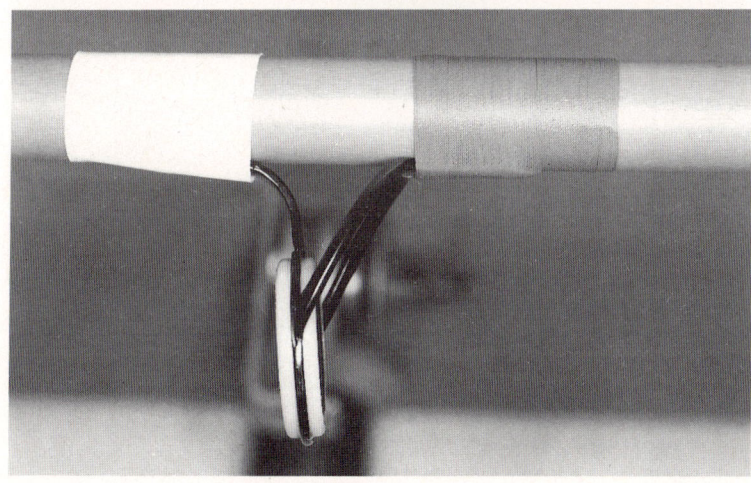

Any gaps in the binding can be pushed together using the back of a spoon or some other smooth tool.

RUNNER, Rainbow

Elagatis bipinnulatus: Splendid vividly coloured fighting fish closely resembling their relatives the kingfish. Runners are widely distributed fish of both tropical and temperate seas, apparently travelling widely. They are taken off New South Wales in summer months, but appear to disappear northwards in winter. They are frequently caught at Lord Howe Island and in New Guinea.

They are normally numerous over sunken reefs well offshore and are consistently taken there by marlin anglers interested in a top bait. They vary in size from about half a metre to 1.5 m in length and up to 10 kg. They often travel in large shoals. Movement appears to be regulated by current and tidal changes and runners which are over a reef one day may not be there the next.

Rainbow runners have at times been located off the edge of the continental shelf in up to 180 m of water and schools are often found well down below the surface. They take trolled feather jigs and strips. One caught on a baitcaster exhibited strength about equal to a mackerel of the same size.

The brilliant colours which give the fish its name, longitudinal bands of dark blue, light blue and green shading into yellow, make it an attractive little fish. They can be distinguished quickly from kingfish by the small, two-rayed finlet behind the anal and dorsal fins. Those not interested in using it for marlin bait will find it an excellent white-fleshed table fish, again about equal to mackerel.

Runners are relatively soft in the mouth and quite a few are lost after being hooked. For this reason they should not be handled in a jerky fashion, but rather with firm and continuous pressure. They are normally caught on squid lures or feather jigs, but will take a wide variety of artificial lures including flies. The average or common size appears to be about 60 cm and at this size a 6/0 hook is sufficient. If handled carefully, runners live well in live bait wells and can be kept alive overnight.

Rainbow runner

S

SAFETY in angling

There are numerous accidents and some loss of life annually in most forms of angling practised by Australians. Injuries can be sustained unexpectedly through momentary carelessness with hooks, knives, spearguns etc. Accidents can be caused by the fisherman himself through mistakes in judgment, such as to the state of the sea, safety of a fishing position, the stability of boats or the risks attendant upon handling big fish etc. Apart from snakes on land, there are also several forms of dangerous, poisonous or injurious aquatic life which the angler should guard against.

The most dangerous form of fishing is spearfishing and, in addition to those drowned or accidentally shot with spears, every year people are killed, shockingly mauled by sharks or painfully stung by rays. Veteran skindivers insist, however, that sharks affect spear-fishermen more psychologically than physically. They claim that waters inhabited by man-eaters are well known, and that attacks are rare considering the frequency with which skindivers swim among sharks.

Boating accidents

Boat handling, which is dealt with separately in this book, sometimes is at fault and has caused fatalities, even in calm water. There should always be one competent person totally responsible for the handling and safety of the boat. It then is his responsibility to keep it in safe waters and to avoid collision, swamping, capsize, running on the rocks, holing or other serious mishap.

The most common troubles on angling outings and fishing boats are broken bones, seasickness and severe sunburn. If the boat has a well-equipped first-aid kit, a splint can be applied to the broken limb. Seasickness comes to most boat anglers at some time in their lives, but some of the several brands of pills now on the market can help lessen the nausea it causes, if not eliminate the sickness altogether. The best treatment is to take one tablet, such as Qwell, with tea of coffee before going down to the boat, another may be taken after lunch, if needed. Too many seasickness tablets can cause worse nausea than the malady itself.

S ■ SAFETY in angling

Every year sunburn causes many anglers great discomfort and virtually wrecks their enjoyment. Sunburn can be quite serious. Children, in particular, need to be protected from it and to be treated effectively for it if their parents are so heedless as to let them become badly burned.

This is one case where the little care and trouble entailed in prevention is decidedly preferable to the discomfort and pain that may result from heedless exposure. A white skin which has not been exposed for some time is very vulnerable. Suitable clothing, particularly in regard to headgear, is essential. Sunscreen creams are freely available and up to a point some are remarkably effective. A lipscreen stick helps to protect the lips from blistering or chapping. Oil never should be applied to the skin, either before or after exposure. It is worth noting that at the higher altitudes heat and ultraviolet rays are not filtered by the atmosphere to the same extent as on the lowlands. A combination of this circumstance and strong reflections from the surface of the water can cause severe burning to the face and lips of anglers fishing the high-country lakes.

Severe sunburn can cause nausea, attacks of cold-shivers and even prostration. In the absence of medical advice, suitable treatment may consist of prolonged warm showers, plenty of warm beverages such as tea or coffee, application of a good sunburn cream (a remedial cream, not a sunscreen cream) and warm covering.

Boats should have buoyancy tanks or coolite secured to strategic parts of the boat to ensure they still float buoyantly if they should capsize. Until the angler has learned to handle a new boat and knows its capability he should stick to places he knows are safe and localities with which he is familiar. Fishing boats should be carefully loaded and extra passengers taken only if the owner is certain the boat will remain safe if rough water is encountered.

Parents who pile an entire family into a holiday fishing dinghy with only a few centimetres of freeboard are asking for trouble. Even in reasonably sheltered water the overloaded boat is seldom far from danger. If there are children or non-swimmers aboard, the skipper should ensure that lifejackets not only are available but are being worn. When the skipper is unfamiliar with the engine of a boat, he should make a short run to check the controls and to see how the engine and the boat answer to them before attempting to leave the pier with a load.

The pumps or bailing facilities should be adequate and should be well checked before making a trip and there should always be a long line aboard, however effective the anchor. For trips out of harbour into the open sea, flares and distress signals are a wise precaution. It is unwise to venture into the open sea until a boat has been tested in all conditions and has acquitted itself well inside the harbour.

SAFETY in angling ■ S

Rucksacks are the safest and most comfortable way to carry fishing gear whilst rockhopping.

Fire is one of the biggest hazards of the sea but usually it can be effectively countered with extinguishers of the right type. These are the chemical extinguishers which cover the flames with a blanket of foam and they are by far the most dependable in confined spaces. Never depend on water to extinguish a fire and beware of petrol or oil leaking into the bilges. There it will evaporate to create a highly explosive gas in the bottom of the boat which could blow it to pieces.

Rockhopping accidents

Mishaps to rockhoppers and missing boats make more headlines in the newspapers than all other Australian angling misadventures. Rockhoppers, in fact, lose their lives too frequently in Australia, but there are no statistics available on annual fatalities in any of the States nor of what proportion they form of the large angling fraternity which engages in this branch of the sport. Freak waves repeatedly are blamed by newspapers for these deaths. Veteran rockhoppers deny that these are the main contributing cause. They say the pattern

S ■ SAFETY in angling

and rhythm of the sea is predictable and that one always has to be prepared for the fact that some waves mount considerably higher than others. It is clear, however, that the rockhopper's heedless independence often carries with it a lack of responsibility in regard to his own welfare. Senior anglers should very fully advise juniors on the risks they run and should carefully watch over the safety of any inexperienced persons who may accompany them.

Many rock fishing hotspots now have stakes or rings cemented into adjacent rock to assist the angler, who can tie himself there while fishing or hang on to the stake. It is debatable, however, whether such spots are not best avoided altogether. The sight of an ardent rockhopper swinging down a flying fox rig from the headland at Bondi Beach, Sydney, to reach a fishing position off Ben Buckler has thrilled many spectators, but they cannot be blamed for wondering if it is worth the risks involved.

Through the Easter Holiday of 1964 a heavy ground swell pounded the coast near Sydney, causing severe damage to the waterfront and sending sheets of spray over South Head Lighthouse. That same weekend two anglers died while trying to fish from a rock platform 3 m above the sea. They were warned by local fishermen but said they had come to fish and that was what they intended to do. Records of rock fishing fatalities show that at least thirty rockhoppers have been killed at the same spot.

The rockhopper's best defence is his own good sense. A low shelf with a rock face behind it is the worst possible position. A heavy sea sweeping in across the shelf piles up against the wall and returns with more height than it started with, a type of backwash that has taken toll in many places. Thus the rockhopper should be very certain of mild conditions before committing himself to a position with a poor line of retreat.

Every rock fisherman faces the possibility of being washed off. Accordingly the clothes worn should be chosen with this unpleasant fact in mind. Far too many rock fishermen, especially in winter, wear clothing which would drown an Olympic swimmer. Boiler suits, army greatcoats and heavy boots are not intended for swimming. They have no place on the rocks. A good warm pullover, or better, two light sweaters worn under the shirt, will keep you warm and will do the same if you go for a swim.

Footwear is essential but it must be light and easily removed. Plastic sandals are ideal in most localities, cling to the rock well, and are long wearing. Choose sandals with a good pattern inside the sole as well as a good deep tread to grip the rock. Some makes allow a bare foot to slide about inside the sandal when wet and can throw the angler off balance on steep ground.

For those who intend to fish locations where the rocks are slippery, shoe plates are essential. The best plates are of spring steel. But as the plates themselves can be dangerous on steep, hard rock such as granite and basalt, it may be necessary to wear other footgear on the walk in and change to the plated shoes to fish.

Shorts are the only sensible pants. Cut-down woollen trousers are very warm, and experienced rock fishermen recommend a skin diver's wet suit in winter. A featherweight proofed nylon windcheater of the anorak type will keep off rain and spray, and provide a lot of warmth.

If they were truthful, most rockhoppers would agree that the hazard and challenge inherent in the sport provokes them to accept rockhopping rather than other forms of angling. When personal risk is taken into account, no other form of angling compares with rock fishing. But 20 to 30 m of polypropylene rope in the rucksack, with one or two net corks, can make it safer, giving the angler a floating line which is no weight to carry. But the sensible man uses a lot of discretion and keeps out of trouble.

Dangerous aquatic life

One of the most alarming features of recent angling experience in Australia has been the appearance in numbers of the deadly box jellyfish or sea wasp. The prevalence of this menace in Queensland, where it has taken a number of lives, has not only worried anglers but made many parents chary of allowing their offspring to swim in the sea.

The very small blue-ringed octopus, seldom exceeding 15 cm across its tentacles when fully extended and measuring around 4 cm across the body proper, also has caused some fatalities and temporarily paralysed a number of people. When disturbed, the rings, with a diameter of about that of a five cent piece, flash bright blue. The octopus usually is well marked with these rings.

Some shells while still alive are also dangerous. All live cone shells should be handled with care, for people have died after being stung and cone shells have caused some very painful and dangerous wounds with a stiletto-like sting which is ejected through one end of the shell. A rare sea urchin, once thought to be found only in semi-tropical waters, has been known to kill when its sharp, brittle spine penetrates the skin, breaks off in the flesh and injects venom into the body. Some of these killers were found at Watson's Bay in Sydney Harbour. The northern stonefish has caused agonising pain and some deaths and the sea snakes are recognized as some of the most deadly of the serpents.

Encounters with these creatures are rare, however, and a far greater number of injuries to fishermen are caused by their own lapses in concentration. Fish hook wounds in the scalp, back or fingers, punctures and lacerations through carelessness in handling fish with sharp gills or spines and burns sustained while cooking the catch are more common.

First-aid kit

Ideally, the angler's fishing equipment should include the following list of items, which will fit easily into a tackle box or special emergency kit. But it must be stressed that such an outfit always should be assembled with due regard to circumstances and conditions under which it is to be used. A trip of prolonged duration or a journey into isolated or rough and difficult country would call for larger quantities of some items and a more extensive range than would be required on a simple visit to the seaside. Some areas present different hazards to others and the commonsense course of inquiring into the conditions in an unknown area before going there warns the angler to avoid possible unpleasant experiences, as well as allowing him to have remedial measures on hand. Some distinction also has to be made between emergency kits carried on the person and a basic outfit held in camp or on a vehicle.

List of First-aid Requirements

Triangular bandage
Rolled gauze bandages 2 cm and 5 cm
Surgical gauze
Roll of sticking plaster
Band-Aids, preferably assorted shapes on plastic, in tin
Antiseptic swabs
Antiseptic cream
Tweezers
Large sharp needle or splinter probe
Small scissors
Sharp, clean knife
Snake bite kit, including crepe pressure bandage
Headache tablets
Seasickness tablets
Anti-diarrhoea tablets
Tube of Tannifax
Glycerine and tannin
Plastic forceps

In addition there are certain precautionary items, which in some circumstances certainly should not be overlooked:

Insect repellent
Lip screen stick
Sun screen cream
Sunburn treatment cream
Indigestion tablets

SAILFISH See Billfish.

SALMON, Atlantic *Salmo salar:* A prized sporting fish also known as landlocked salmon which will leap high and often when hooked and ranks among the most tenacious of freshwater fish. Atlantic salmon bred in their native habitat have been reported up to 45 kg—the world record for a specimen caught with rod and reel is a fraction short of 36 kg—but the average runs to between 7 and 10 kg in those areas of the world where they flourish. They have been introduced to both New Zealand and

Atlantic salmon

Australia with disappointing results and it seems certain they will not prosper in either country as they do in Canada and Greenland, in Europe from Russia to Portugal and in the American State of Maine. The average size of those caught in Australia is probably no more than 2–3 kg.

Overseas it has been found that the chief sporting value of Atlantic salmon is in fly fishing, but the turbulence of the water in which they have to be fished for often interferes with efficient use of flies. In North America, Norway, Sweden and Spain, the high premium placed on access to water permitting enjoyment of the angling potential provided by this fish has made salmon fishing with the fly both expensive and exclusive. It is a fish which will leap 2 m into a powerful waterfall and literally swim upwards through a torrential flow.

Salmon are mostly more silvery in colour than trout, with a lot of irregular dark spots, some shaped like an X. They are slender and rounder in the body, particularly at the butt of the tail, than trout and the back edge of the tail is markedly forked in young fish and moderately forked in mature specimens. There are no spots on the tail. Unlike Pacific salmon, Atlantic salmon spawn more than once and with few exceptions they return to their parent rivers for this purpose.

Introduction to Australia
In Australia, where water temperatures of inland streams have become colder with the completion of so many irrigation schemes, the New South Wales Department of Fisheries began a notable effort to establish Atlantic salmon as a landlocked fish. Earlier introductions into Tasmania and Victoria (in 1864–70) had failed. The New South Wales Director of Fisheries, Dr Don Francois, arranged for the Canadian Department of Fisheries to supply free of charge from its Nova Scotia hatcheries 100,000 salmon eggs a year for three years. The eggs went initially to the government hatchery at Jindabyne, New South Wales, and later to Ebor, New England. In October, 1963, 9000 fingerlings were introduced in Micalong Creek, a tributary of the Goodradigbee River, a few kilometres from where it flows into Burrinjuck Dam. A release of 25,000 fingerlings were introduced into the Goodradigbee in 1964 and other releases were later made in Lake Jindabyne.

From the time these releases began the Burrinjuck area went through one of the worst droughts in its history and failure of the fish to become acclimatized cannot be considered a fair test. It is now present only in Lake Jindabyne and at two New South Wales hatcheries.

The chance of hooking such a superb fighting fish has undoubtedly added spice to fishing in Lake Jindabyne, but few have had success though it is possible salmon were caught there by anglers who did not recognize them. The first authentic report of a salmon being taken came in 1966 when an American, on holiday in Australia, caught one. A number of small fish from 38 to 43 cm were later caught, some of them in roe. The largest fish taken was just over 1 kg and 48 cm long.

The attempt to introduce Atlantic salmon at Burrinjuck was conducted under such adverse conditions the delivery of the third 100,000 eggs from Nova Scotia was delayed until conditions improved. At Burrinjuck and in surrounding rivers water was at record low levels and in New England the Ebor hatchery stream remained at a low level even after the breaking of the drought. Meanwhile fisheries officials are constantly seeking information from anglers about catches of Atlantic salmon, which strongly resembles brown trout.

Technique for Atlantic salmon
The Atlantic salmon strikes flies in a conditioned reflex rather than through a desire to eat, striking best in stale water when the sun is strong. It does not have to be stalked by anglers remaining out of sight, as is required for trout, for it is disdainful of someone flailing the air. Unlike the trout, which instantly rejects a fly, Atlantic salmon mouth the fly or splash at it before taking it with a heavy, dead pull. The chance of taking a trout declines with each cast, whereas on salmon the fish becomes more interested with each cast and is gradually enticed to bite. It strikes well at bright spoons, wobblers, plugs and live baits, especially soon after returning from the sea, but it is on wet and dry flies that it excels as a sporting fish. Its survival in Australia probably depends on liberation of hatchery-reared fish.

SALMON, Australian

Arripis trutta: A great sporting fish but not a true member of the salmon family. It belongs to the perch family Arripidae, which contains only two members, the ruff *Arripis georgianus*, and the Australian salmon. It was probably named by Australian pioneers who saw in it a resemblance to the northern hemisphere salmon. In New Zealand it is known by the Maori name kahawai, in Tasmania large specimens are called black backs and the young newfish. In Victoria and South Australia half-grown fish are called salmon trout or bay trout and on the east and west coasts the big specimens are labelled buck salmon. Under these varying labels it is the main fish sought from the beaches and along the ocean rocks in

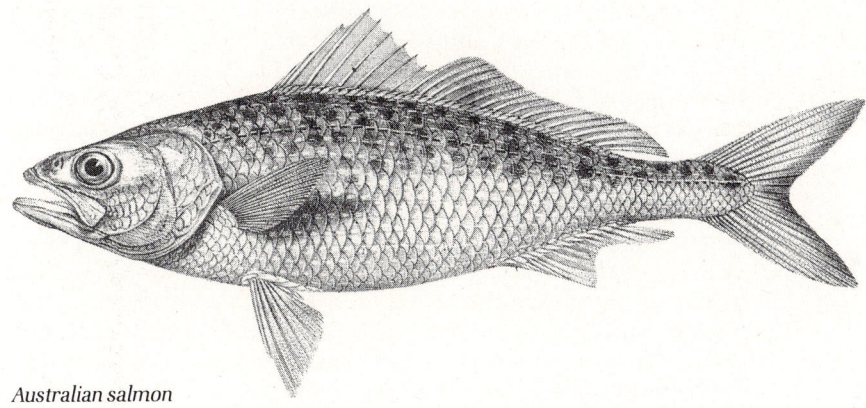

Australian salmon

Victoria and South Australia for a major part of every summer. West from Port Lincoln, South Australia, the salmon fishing is perhaps the best available anywhere.

It is an abundant fish, it fights with great dash and stamina, frequently leaping above the surface and when it is present in numbers provides exciting sport. Canning activities have curtailed salmon angling on parts of the Australian east coast, but off South Australia and the Western Australian south coast the adult salmon is the best known of all sporting fish. In Tasmania, it is much fished for in tidal rivers on light tackle.

In Western Australia salmon schools gather on the south coast at the beginning of each year before making a migration to the west coast. In the western State, canning has not seriously depleted salmon numbers as it has on some parts of the east coast. The west coast salmon runs from 2.5 to 5.5 kg and though identical in outward appearance with the east coast salmon, nevertheless belongs to a separate sub-species. The difference lies in the gill rakers. The east coast salmon, to some extent a plankton feeder, has fine hairlike extensions of the inner gill rakers, whereas the west coast sub-species, a hunter of small fishes, has developed hard, tooth-like extensions on its gills to help grasp and swallow a freshly grabbed morsel.

Few fish take bait as readily as the Australian salmon. Its bite is not slashing like the chop of a tailor, but deceptively fumbling. When a salmon is hooked it becomes an exciting acrobat. Because of its partiality to small fish it can be induced to take artificial lures and large numbers are taken by spinning in the surf or from the rocks, or by trolling from boats.

Western Australian south coast salmon feed principally on immense schools of mulies or blue pilchard which mass in the Great Australian Bight each autumn. Salmon landed by anglers at Bremer Bay often disgorge masses of freshly swallowed mulies—which can then be used again for bait. Sometimes as many as 30 baits may be retrieved from a single salmon. Bait casting with ganged hooks and mulie bait is the favourite method of catching salmon in Western Australia. Professional bait fishermen catch the mulies in Albany Harbour and snap freeze them into packets of six. The mulie weighs a little under 56 g and is best cast in still conditions or with a following breeze. In windy conditions a surf sinker is used. The salmon, though it prefers a mulie to most other baits, is far from being a fussy feeder.

The Australian salmon is not a popular eating fish. Its flesh, unless treated properly, is strongly flavoured and stringy, but it improves vastly when canned. Western Australian country anglers take home large quantities of salmon to preserve in domestic bottling outfits. This way they are delicious. With such fine fighting fish so plentiful off the south and south-west coasts, some of Western Australia's keen sporting anglers have tried in recent years to catch them from the shore on 1 kg line, which would give five-to-one advantage to a 5 kg salmon. So far the salmon have won, but many have been caught on a line as light as 2 kg.

Favoured Western Australian south coast spots for salmon are at Bremer Bay, Two People Bay, Albany, Denmark, Walpole, the Warren River mouth and Augusta. Around the south-west corner salmon gather at places like Cowaramup, Canal Rocks and Yallingup, before taking off across Geographe Bay for beaches 80 km on either side of Fremantle. This seems to be their last northern haunt, though occasionally salmon have been caught as far north as the Murchison River mouth. Amateurs at Canal Rocks, in March and April, often count their salmon catches in dozens. When salmon schools hit the Fremantle moles there are traffic jams of fishermen and sightseers on the breakwater roads. The rocks bristle with bending rods and swinging gaff-handles.

In the east, starting from February, the salmon formerly made spectacular migrations north up the coast, travelling in huge shoals past Sydney going as far as Port Macquarie and Coffs Harbour. But the intensive fishing by canneries ended this, and for years Sydney anglers have had to go as far south as Narooma to catch a salmon. A switch by the canneries to tuna could revive the big migrations, but apparently too many fishermen are still using equipment better suited to salmon fishing than following the tuna.

The salmon spawns at sea and the eggs are pelagic. Bass Strait apparently is the major spawning ground in eastern Australia. Nowadays on the east coast they are largely restricted to the areas south of Sydney, with numbers increasing as anglers move down the coast. Large quantities are taken off the beaches adjacent to the Gippsland Lakes. They are very plentiful in Bass Strait and all around the Tasmanian coast. They also occur around Lord Howe Island where they are of better flavour and far more edible than those caught off the New South Wales coast.

Tackle for eastern salmon

In the east, where salmon usually average from 2 to 2.5 kg and seldom weigh more than 5 kg they are fished for on standard surf gear, with sidecast, threadline or geared reels. Vast numbers are caught on metal lures such as the rigglejig and tailor ticer or modern equivalents by anglers trolling from boats or spinning from rocks and beaches. Some fishermen make good catches from jetties using a casting float. In shallow spots, such as inshore reefs and sand flats standard bottom rigs are effective. In New Zealand salmon frequently are taken by snapper fishermen from deeper water than they are found in Australia.

The best bait for the eastern variety is fresh beach worms, but they bite eagerly at mackerel, bonito, pipis, yellowtail, mullet, squid, prawns and almost all fish baits, though they sometimes prefer the lighter coloured baits. Cuttlefish, whiting, garfish, octopus and squid are all effective at these times. They sometimes saw through a fine nylon cast, so linked carlisle hooks are used. This means that the top hook holds the strip bait up away from the lower barb so that the point is not shrouded and the fish have difficulty removing the bait without becoming hooked.

SALMON, Quinnat

Oncorhynchus tshawytscha: Generally known on the American east coast as chinook. Largest of six species of Pacific salmon, it has defied attempts to introduce it on a large scale into Victorian and Tasmanian waters but has flourished in the South Island of New Zealand. Quinnat salmon up to 18 kg have been taken in the South Island, where the salmon runs cause intense activity among anglers. The average catch during these runs varies from 5 to 7 kg.

Salmon fishing is thrilling, but it is also arduous as it often involves walking a kilometre or more over loose shingle to reach clear pools that are fishable. New Zealanders use aircraft extensively to reach out-of-the-way stretches, but even then the trudge back to the plane carrying two or three heavy salmon—there is a bag limit of six a day in the main areas—can be wearing on both waders and tempers.

All species spawn in gravel in fresh water and die soon afterwards. As the fish mature in the sea and reach spawning time, their silvery appearance and blue backs change to a variety of shades, including pink, red or black. The young alevins remain in the gravel until the yolk-sac is used up and when they emerge linger in fresh water for periods up to a year. Their ocean life varies up to three years and when they return to fresh water to spawn at three or four years they have enough reserves never to have to eat again during the short life left to them.

Understandably, the attempts to introduce them in Victoria and Tasmania were made in waters with access to the sea. Sir

Samuel Wilson arranged the first shipment to Victoria in 1874 but the fish hatched in transit and were lost. Another importation was tried in 1877, when some 50,000 eggs hatched successfully and the fry were widely distributed in Victorian streams. In 1936, a further attempt was made with a shipment of eggs from New Zealand and shipments continued until 1946. Salmon flourish in Lakes Purrumbete and Bullen Merri, Victoria, from which fish between 8 and 9 kg are taken. They were seen to 'run' and were recovered fully mature but failed to spawn. The lakes are restocked yearly. Similar efforts to introduce quinnat salmon into the Great Lake in Tasmania failed. Fish in spawning condition died.

The breeding process
The female deposits from 3000 to 5000 ova on the redds and these are immediately fertilised by the milt of the jack fish. It is considered that less than 3 per cent of these eventually reach the sea as smolts a year or less later. It has been noticed in recent years that many of the young fish migrate downstream as fry, but even if only two reach adult stage the population is thus in balance. In the early stages the young fish are subject to considerable predation on their way to the sea and after and even mature fish have numerous marine enemies for which they must be constantly on the alert if they are to reach the rivers to spawn.

The female selects suitable shingle to build her redds or nests as they are sometimes called. Spawning takes place in the tributaries of the snow rivers where the shingle is clean and free from silt or mud. This can be up to 130 km or more from the sea, but many do spawn in the upper reaches of the main river. The redd is excavated to approximately 30 cm in depth by the vigorous action of her powerful tail and in the process sizable rocks are often moved. At this time she is partnered by a virile jack which remains close behind her awaiting the completion of the redd and the convulsive movement when the female moves to the top of the redd. She then turns on her side and with a shuddering movement she sheds her eggs which fall to the bottom of the redd. The jack at this moment is caressing her side with his body and at the precise moment the eggs are shed he ejects milt over them. This fertilizes the ova and gives them life.

There is considerable competition among the jacks for the right to serve the female, so to speak. It is a question of the survival of the fittest or the best fighter. The commotion in the shallow waters is spectacular as jack fights jack and spray can rise to 2 m or more on occasion. The hen fish may prepare and use more than one redd until all her 4000 to 5000 ova are shed and fertilized. The shingle from each new excavation covers the eggs in the preceding redd, otherwise the eggs are covered by the hen farming shingle from just above and in either case the eggs are cushioned among the crevices in the stones and out of sight. When the last redd is covered the tail of the fish is

SALMON

A splendid Quinnat salmon taken near the mouth of the Waitaki River in New Zealand. Quinnat have not fared well in Australian waters, where they have failed to spawn.

usually worn to a mere stump. Both sexes then drift downstream slowly with the current and die and the bodies are soon covered in shingle or silt. When the ova hatch two months later as alevins and later when the yolk sac is absorbed they remain in the area as fry for a time and it is thought that the dead bodies of the parent fish, now almost disintegrated, are used by the small fish as food before they begin their migration down to the sea as smolts.

Fishing methods for quinnat

As a rule the quinnat angler uses a rod from 2.5 to 3 m in length, in fibreglass, either in tubular or solid; split cane or Rangoon cane, many being one piece. Monofilament of up to 270 m with breaking strain of 8.5 to 10 kg is used on either fixed or revolving spool reels, but in general the former are favoured most because of their efficiency in casting light lines over long distances.

S ■ SALTWATER bass

The popular lure is the silver ticer which is a solid wedge type metal unit averaging 56 to 84 g, on which a single treble 2/0 hook is mounted. This is cast across the river slightly upstream, then wound back and another cast made. This procedure can go on for hours without result, or a strike can occur at the first cast. It is all a matter of luck.

The fish are from 3 to 11 kg with a general average of 7 kg. The sale of quinnat to the public is prohibited, although it was legal up to the 1950s, but this was controlled by regulation.

New Zealand lakes contain varying populations of land-locked quinnat, the chief one being Lake Coleridge in the Canterbury area. These are fished for mainly during November, the first month of the season for the back-country lakes, and are captured on small ticers and baits from 7 to 14 g. They also take the streamer fly, and on many occasions they accept the dry fly. Their size is, of course, limited through being land-locked and few are caught in excess of 1 kg.

GEORGE FERRIS

SALTWATER bass

Apart from the outstanding freshwater bass *Macquaria novemaculeata*, which provides exciting sport in coastal rivers and lakes of the eastern States, Australia boasts some intriguing seagoing basses which regularly crop up on offshore outings.

Red bass

Lutjanus bohar: Repeatedly confused even by experienced anglers with the mangrove jack but quite definitely a separate species. Also known in some areas as kelp bream and kelp sea perch. These robust, handsome fishes are a confirmed cause of the form of food poisoning known as ciguatera (*see Poisoning*), though some fishermen still insist they are safe if they are gutted immediately they are caught.

Red bass are found in shoals in northern Queensland, where they are particularly plentiful on the Outer Barrier Reef.

Red bass

They have a very dark red body, stretching from the tip of the snout along the back and top of the head, are salmon pink on the sides and whitish pink beneath. Below the lateral line and parallel to it, a series of faint pink bands run back to the tail. The gill covers, cheeks and throat are yellow and the head is splashed in dark lavender. The spiny dorsal fin is dark scarlet, black at the edges. They are immediately recognized from the related mangrove jack by the conspicuous pit on the head in front of each eye, says Grant, who points out that this pit is absent in the mangrove jack (*which see*). Red bass grow to 12 kg and 90 cm.

Sand bass

Psammoperca waigiensis: Closely related to barramundi or giant perch, a species with which they are often confused. Also known as dwarf palmer, sand perch, glass-eyed perch, jewel-eye and reef barramundi. They are found in reefs and rocky areas along the north Queensland coast.

Sand bass can be distinguished from barramundi by colour. They are dull brown fish; barramundi are greenish-grey. They also have granular teeth on the tongue, says Grant, which barramundi lack. The dull brownish body may have horizontal streaks along the side. Grant also says they are good eating but lack the popular appeal of their larger relation, the barramundi.

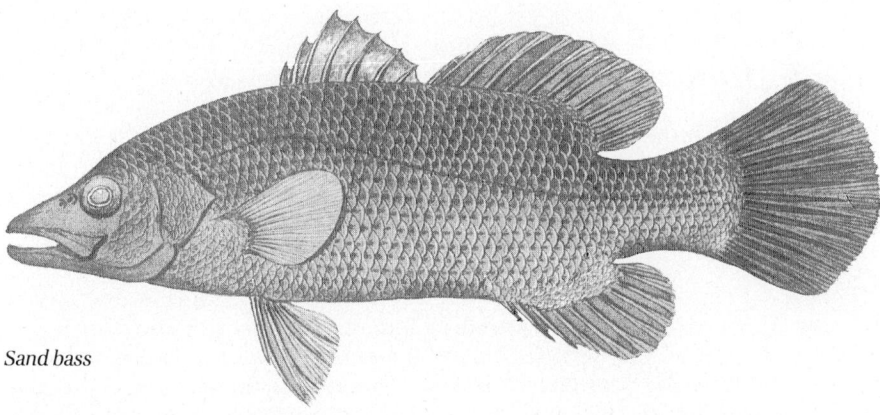

Sand bass

SAMSON fish

Seriola hippos: A fast game fish closely related to the yellow-tail kingfish, but its shape, with deep body and humped head, is more suggestive of the turrum or other big trevallies. However, it lacks their long, sickle-shaped pectoral fins and the tail. Samson fish are related to the amberjack, which they closely resemble.

It is found from around Moreton Bay and along the New South Wales coast to Gabo. Only very occasional specimens are taken through Bass Strait, but it is of frequent occurrence on the west coast of Western Australia, particularly around

S ■ SARATOGA

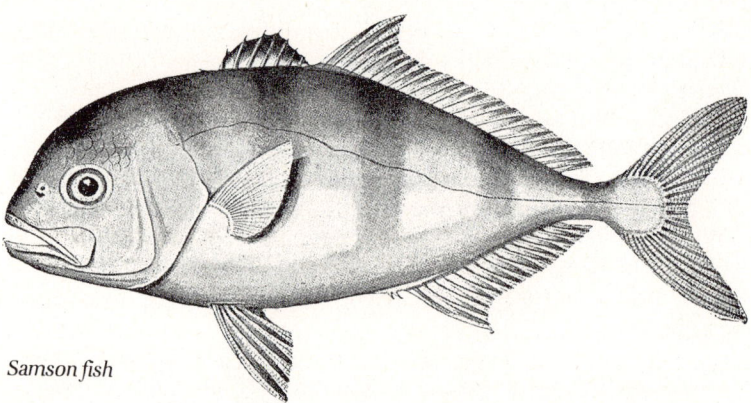

Samson fish

Rottnest and the Abrolhos Islands. It is somewhat erratic in its appearances over the area of its distribution. It was relatively scarce on the New South Wales coast for close on 20 years but has been more in evidence in recent seasons.

The samson is bluish-green on the upper body, merging to golden-yellow on the lower sides and white beneath. The first or smaller dorsal fin is dark blue and others a blending of green and yellow. The younger fish show about five blotchy, dark vertical bands on the sides, but these fade out with age. Usually samson are distinguishable from similar species by their reddish teeth.

On the New South Wales coast this species appears to grow to a maximum of 75 cm. Scott credits it with growing to 1.5 m and 50 kg, but these figures very probably have arisen from confusion between the samson and amberjack on the Western Australian coast. As an edible fish it can only be classed as fair, the larger specimens becoming tough and dry. The biggest samson on the Game Fishing Association of Australia's record list in 1985 was one of 27.5 kg caught on a 15 kg line by Roger Madden at Tweed Heads in October 1978.

SARATOGA *Scleropages leichardti:* Although only one general species is recognized, this fascinating fish may yet prove to be present in several varieties in North Australian waters. There is great diversity in range, from the Dawson River in southern Queensland to the top end of the Northern Territory. The saratoga is a comparatively primitive species, with relatives scattered widely across the earth. There is the giant arapaima of the Amazon, the aruana of South America, the belie in the upper Nile and other species in Sumatra.

The identification of this fish has been made difficult by confusion over common names. It was the original 'barramundi', an Aboriginal name for fish with large scales, but popular custom permanently transferred that name to the then more prevalent giant perch *Lates calcarifer*. The species is known as saratoga or saratota in all North Australia, with local exceptions on the Jardine and Dawson River.

The saratoga does not appear to stand up to competition from other species and prefers a still-water habitat that includes swamps and lagoons. It is a voracious feeder on surface insects, prawns, fish and other water life and grows to at least 90 cm and a weight of 11 kg. In areas where perch-like fish such as barramundi-perch or sooty grunter are numerous, saratoga become scarce or disappear completely. They seem happiest in the clear lagoons of such areas as the coastal plains of the Northern Territory. Saratoga to 15 cm are good eating but larger fish become coarse and flavourless.

Saratoga baits, lures
In daylight the fish lie in the shelter provided by logs, water-lilies or shoreline pandanus, and fishing is simply a matter of casting towards this cover with lure or bait. The saratoga is not fussy over baits. One method is to cast towards a visible, surface-cruising fish with a float and a meat bait set to hang about 1 m beneath it. The saratoga may be seen to move towards the splash, investigate first the float and then the bait, which it swallows. As the float sinks, the angler strikes. Any kind of wobbling or spinning lure can attract saratoga. Those lying under cover can often be seen by painstaking observation from the bank, and on occasion these will strike instantly at a popping lure which lands near their home.

Fly fishermen also may have good sport with this species, using either bulky dry flies such as the Muddler Minnow, or streamers of various kinds. Fish seem to strike after smelling, if that is the word, the feathers and hair in the smaller lures. One veteran angler prefers a combination of fly and spinner, which seems to work on both sight and scent and which certainly catches fish. There is often a deliberate and leisurely air to the saratoga's strike, totally unlike the faster reaction of other species. Far from deliberate is the frenzied fight which follows the hooking. Saratoga go for the sky and their bronze, pink-spotted scales make a spectacular display. Being deep-bodied, they can offer strong resistance in the water and tackle needs to be reliable to take them.

The fish are somewhat bony, with closely placed ribs reminiscent of a rainbow trout. They are quite edible, but not of outstanding quality. The large scales are difficult to remove, so complete filleting is the usual answer. Fish of 3.5 to 4 kg are

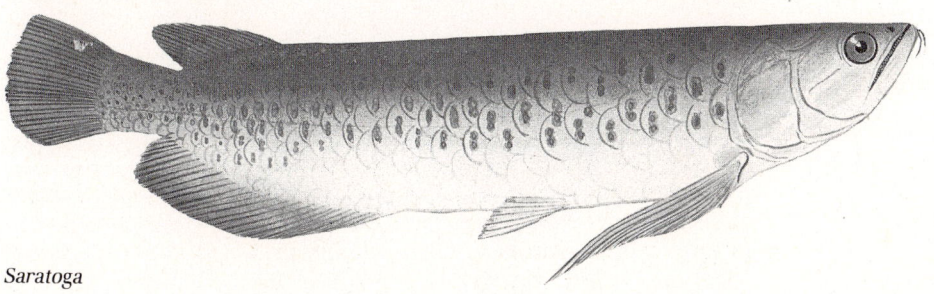

Saratoga

recognized as bigger than average. Rods and reels need to be the usual spinning or bait outfits, but longer rods are required if bait fishing is preferred. A line of 7 kg test is adequate to deal with them, and the large and upward-sloping mouth can take a strong 3/0 hook. For colour, action and a distinctly unique personality, the saratoga is an intriguing and interesting quarry for Australian light tackle anglers.

SAWFISH *See Rays.*

SCALLOP Bivalve molluscs of the families Pectinidae and Amusiidae. They are found in Queensland and in the Shark Bay area of Western Australia, but have been exploited so far commercially only in Tasmania and Victoria, where scallop fisheries developed rapidly and, through over-production, have since declined. Tasmania, which dominated the scallop industry until 1963, has seen the collapse of its scallop fishery. Efforts to save Victoria's Port Phillip Bay scallops by banning professional exploitation led to clashes between fishermen and authorities in 1985.

Scallops are found in beds and strips and the tidal pattern plays an important part in their distribution. They are lightly distributed in areas where there are strong currents and eddy systems but in these same conditions they grow faster, produce higher quality meats and have stronger shells than in areas where currents are weak. They feed by filtering plankton and other minute food from the water. They can see, and they swim up to 5 m by ejecting water in two streams from the rear end of their shells. The edge of the mantle carries numerous eyes which enable them to avoid predators such as starfish.

Pecten alba of the family Pectinidae are the saucer scallops found in New South Wales and on the east coast, while the Amusidae are the family found in Western Australia and Victoria. Scallop fishery is notoriously variable. In the ten years to 1980–81 Australia's annual scallop harvest varied between 5,000 and 17,000 tonnes, with a value of $800,000 in 1970 and $5.7 million in 1980. Victoria dominates the scallop market, with Bass Strait the most productive field. A Bass Strait Authority had to be set up largely because Tasmania and Victoria could not agree on who owned the scallops the Strait yielded.

Scallop

SHARKS

Most anglers regard sharks as fish but scientifically they are not fish but are grouped in the same class as rays. About 90 different sharks are found in Australian waters, many of them feared because of their insensitivity to pain and the viciousness and persistence with which they attack. Even the so-called harmless sharks take heavy toll of the nervous system of any angler caught in the water with them.

Sharks are the biggest creatures taken by man on rod and reel, but they differ from all other bony fish in several important respects. Unlike animals and fish, sharks and rays do not have a bony skeleton. The framework of their bodies consists of hard cartilage or gristle. They do not bear scales, but are clothed in a tough skin which in most cases is covered with a vast number of closely massed bone-like particles or denticles. In some sharks these make the skin so rough they shred tightly held nylon line as they brush past it. Shark skin is known as shagreen. Sharks' teeth are a development of the denticles seen on the skin.

Unlike fish, sharks have no air bladder to give them hydrostatic stability. They have difficulty adjusting themselves to float at a certain depth and have to remain in constant motion to retain their balance or stability by swimming. This is why sharks in aquariums swim constantly round and round their prison pools. It was estimated that Skipper IV in six years of captivity in Sydney's Taronga Park Zoo swam 320,000 km or eight times around the world.

GENERALISED EXTERNAL FEATURES OF A SHARK

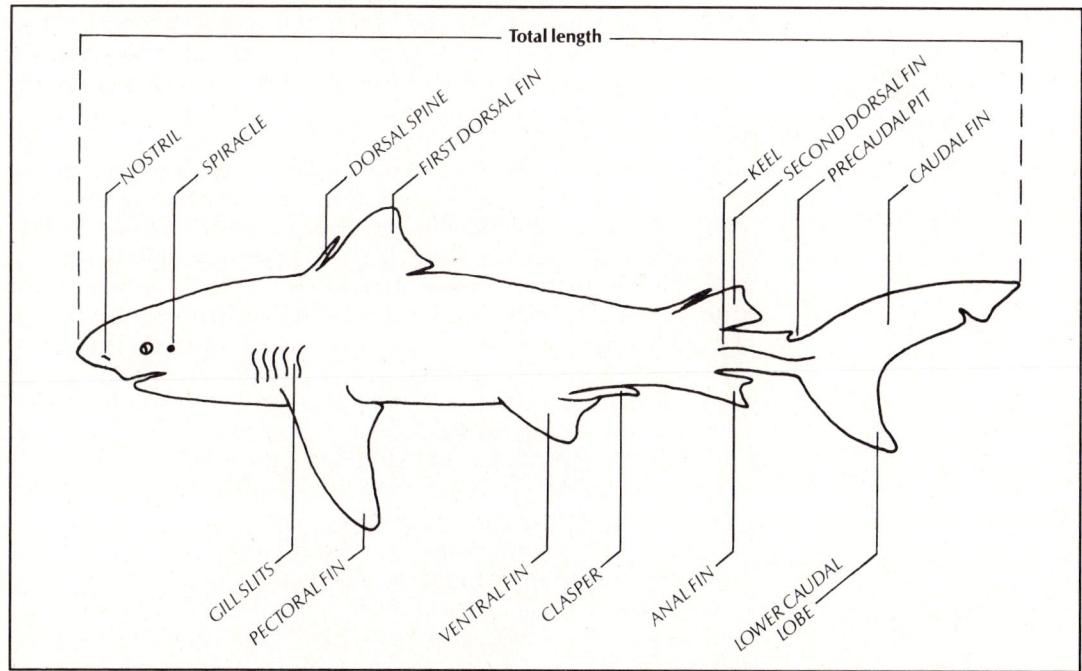

Sharks also are completely different from bony fish in their method of breeding. With the exception of the huge Greenland shark, they produce their young alive and developed sufficiently to take care of themselves. Tiger sharks that have been cut open have contained 56 well-developed embryos. Whaler sharks produce as many as 18 offspring at a time. Female wobbegongs or carpet sharks have been dissected to disclose 37 well-formed young. This sharply contrasts to the bony fish which eject their ova into the water where it is fertilized. Sharks produce eggs but these are fertilized internally by copulation.

The Greenland shark and a few of the smaller sharks, especially the primitives, lay eggs and leave them to hatch. Often these eggs have tendrils or hooks on them for the purpose of attaching the eggs to rocks or kelp. The brown spiral egg-case of the Port Jackson shark is frequently found on our ocean beaches and the somewhat cylindrical egg-case of the spotted cat shark is commonly thrown up on the New South Wales south coast. The minority of sharks that do lay eggs produce only two eggs at a time and these may take up to five months in the water to hatch so in shark terms they are comparatively barren.

Not the least of the shark's extraordinarily well organized equipment is his streamlined form. They are almost the perfect shape for speedy swimming, easily pushed through the water, able to follow the scavenger role for which they have been shaped by 200 million years of evolution. They move continuously, but seemingly without effort, for they never appear to tire.

Sharks rarely breathe through their nostrils. They take in water for this purpose through spiracles, small holes behind the eyes, or through the mouth, and the water passes over the oxygen absorbing membranes of the gills before it is discharged through the gill slits. Fish have only one gill slit at each side but sharks have one for each gill. The majority of sharks have five slits at each side, but some have six or seven.

However, sharks in their present form probably are far smaller than they were in primitive days. Scientists who have found their remains in geological deposits 200 million years old discovered large teeth, some in fossil form and some of later origin, which prove that in the distant past they were of colossal size. The same adaptability that has preserved them for so long is apparent when they move into fresh-water for long periods. This same adaptability is one reason why it is never safe to believe that some waters are safe from shark attacks. There have been cases of water, such as Narrabeen Lakes near Sydney that has been closed to the sea for months, suddenly revealing dangerous sharks.

The eyes of most sharks have a rare ability to cope with whatever conditions in which they live and hunt. Some have a nictitating membrane or third eyelid which slides over the eye to protect them in encounters at close quarters. Others just roll their eyes forward until the pupil is covered and only the white shows. The eye has marked sensitivity for seeing in the depths, since it is equipped with a number of seeing rods or light sensitive nerves. To heighten the sensitivity, any light that penetrates through these nerves is reflected back on to them by a set of mirror-like discs behind the retina. To control this sensitivity when swimming at or near the surface the pupil is closed down to a flattened slit in the form of the figure eight.

But sharks hunt more by scent and sound than by sight. Water is taken in through the nostrils, near the front of the snout, passed through the sinus and exhausted through the gills. Their sense of smell is very keen, for in some sharks as much as two-thirds of the brain is olfactory lobes. The broad-headed hammerhead has grooves right along the leading edge of its broad snout to lead water into the orifices of its nostrils.

Spearfishermen have learned how very sensitive sharks are to underwater sounds. Vibrations appear to tell them from a long way off that a fish is in trouble. Frequently when there are apparently none in sight several sharks turn up almost as soon as a good fish is speared. When crayfish are caught underwater, the clicking of their tails is enough to bring sharks to the scene from considerable distances. And nobody can doubt the shark's facility in detecting moving schools of fish and other sharks feeding once they have seen the speed with which big sharks arrive at such a scene and the voracity with which they immediately attack the school.

Shark attacks

The first recorded fatal attack in Australia was in 1791 when an Aboriginal boy was taken in New South Wales. In 1803 a M. Lefevre was taken at Hamelin Harbour, Faure Island, Western Australia, and in 1837 a boy, Alfred Howe, was killed by a shark in the Macleay River 80 km from the harbour. Between 1791 and 1958 about 300 attacks, 100 of them fatal, were made on swimmers and others in Australian waters. Forty-nine of these were on ocean beaches, the rest in the open sea, in lakes, estuaries, creeks and harbours. Attacks were recorded from Cape York right down the eastern coastline of Queensland, New South Wales and Victoria, to South Australia and Western Australia.

Ideas suggested as protection against sharks included electric barriers, air bubbles, shooting, loud hooters and strong-smelling repellents. All have been tried and turned down, but the one method that has proved successful since its inception in 1937 is the use of mesh nets stretched in 450 m lengths in front of beaches. The success of this scheme off Sydney and Newcastle beaches has been remarkable.

The nets are made of heavy manila rope with a 30 cm mesh and are anchored in pairs with glass floats attached to hold them upright. They are laid parallel to the beach in a spot chosen by the contractor. When a shark pushes into the net its struggles entangle it more and escape is impossible. The nets are lifted daily and re-set usually in different positions. Since the introduction of meshing there have been no attacks on the Sydney beaches and only two at Newcastle, both at Merewether, one of which was fatal. Sydney Harbour is still a problem, however, as was shown in early 1985 when two dogs were taken by sharks in water off Rozelle.

Oddly enough the two largest sharks, the whale shark and the basking shark, are completely harmless, and experts regard only seven species as potentially dangerous to swimmers. Of these, four species—the mako, hammerhead, grey nurse and thresher—are unlikely to be dangerous. This leaves the whaler, the white shark and the tiger shark.

There are a number of species of whaler sharks, but they all have the same behaviour pattern and method of feeding. The common or black whaler is the species widely met with on most beaches. They are savage and determined, often travelling in quite large schools, and they will swim many kilometres up rivers and harbours in search of food. Even the smaller 2 to 2.5 m whaler is quite capable of killing a bather.

When a shark attack occurs, it is very difficult even for an experienced fisherman to be sure what species of shark is responsible and it is here that wildly imaginative statements come freely. The most exaggerated usually is on the size of the shark, some attaining fantastic lengths. Frequently blamed is the grey nurse, the most unlikely of any of the seven possible attackers, a well-known sea-bed-haunting fish-eater which spends a great deal of its time on the bottom near reefs. Contrastingly, the whaler will tackle anything in the water.

The great white shark must undoubtedly be considered as a potential danger, but it lives mainly on dolphins, seals, other sharks and large fish and on the eastern coast mostly keeps to the deeper waters. White sharks do appear along the surfing beaches and have been taken in the mesh nets, but they are not taken in any numbers and are usually smaller specimens of 100 kg or so.

The tiger shark is one of the few sharks identified as the killer after a fatal attack in the surf.

On 27th October 1937, a shark killed Norman Girvan and possibly Jack Brinkley, 70 m from the shore in 6 m of water off Coolangatta, Queensland. It was later caught and contained an identifiable part of the victim in its stomach. The shark measured 3.6 m and weighed 385 kg.

The tiger shark is a scavenger and will pick up extraordinary items while hunting for food. Apart from fish and other sea creatures, lumps of coal, bottles (full of beer), old boots, petrol tins, mutton birds, penguins, a bag of potatoes, hens, roosters, and the brass case of an 18-pounder shell have been found in their stomachs.

Of the other species, the mako and the thresher shark are

essentially fish eaters and keep out in the deeper waters. The hammerhead is by far the commonest shark along our coastline, and more of these are caught in the mesh nets than any other species. They spend a lot of time on the surface and are at home in the surf where they hunt small fish and the big dorsal fin of this shark has probably been responsible for more shark alarms than any other species. But only a very large hammerhead could be considered dangerous to man and attacks from this species are very uncommon in the surf.

Sharks do not have to turn on their sides to attack, as any game fisherman can verify. They will swim right up to captured fish and chop great pieces from the body, the top of the broad head frequently protruding clear of the water as they do so. Tiger sharks will swim about on the surface after trawlers have thrown over the rubbish such as stingrays and other small fish, and will lift their heads clear of the water as they swallow the fish.

The theory that sharks attack more on dull days is false; although a number of attacks have occurred on such days, just as many have taken place on fine sunny days, in clear and muddy water and at high and low tides. But a majority of attacks have occurred between 2 p.m. and 6 p.m.

Game fishermen have helped combat the shark menace over the years by catching many large sharks, to such an extent that many are complaining now of the absence of large tiger sharks and the falling-off in the number of whalers. Fisheries inspectors who go out with contractors setting the nets off Sydney beaches believe the sharks know the nets are there and move well out to sea to avoid them. Dangerous sharks are seldom caught in the nets, and it is rare for the nets to yield more than a few sharks.

There is a great deal still to be learned about the natural history, peculiarities and characteristic behaviour of sharks, particularly in regard to shark attacks. Anglers who fish a lot for them soon come to realize that generally they do not esteem surfers or surf-board riders as food; for if they did, there could be a hundred fatalities a day along quite short sections of the Australian coast. But the fact remains that an occasional shark will make an attack, either deliberately or through mistaking a bather for fish or other known food.

The procedure of protecting against shark attacks by netting the surf beaches would appear to be inadequate and illogical. Each beach is netted only intermittently and never is fully protected. A large proportion of the sharks follow shoals of fish as they migrate along the coast, so it would seem impossible to keep a particular section clear of them by this method. Illogical as it seems, the fact remains that over the past few decades it has proved remarkably effective on the Sydney metropolitan beaches and more recently in other areas.

As a result, today it generally is recognized that in the shark season it is much more dangerous to bathe along the foreshores in the estuaries, bays and harbours and even away up the coastal rivers, than on a surfing beach in a regularly netted zone. By 1985 Sydney's metropolitan beaches had been free of shark attacks for 48 years, a remarkable testimony to the effectiveness of meshing.

Freshwater sharks
Sharks in fresh water seem a scary phenomenon, yet they are far from rare. Many cases of shark attack have been recorded from freshwater rivers in Australia. Fortunately, sharks living in fresh water or moving into it from tidal water are generally less than 2 m in length. They are not often caught because anglers do not use large enough baits on them. A whole fish of 1 kg weight fished in tidal fresh water can yield some astounding results, but most anglers keep their 1 kg fish for something better.

In tropical Australian waters, sharks, stingrays and saw sharks are regularly recorded in fresh water. Travel writer Vic McCristal recorded encounters with saw sharks on the Ord River, Western Australia and with whaler sharks in the Daly and East Alligator Rivers. In Papua, he saw a 6 m saw shark taken in a net in Lake Murray by natives from the Mission at Pangoa and one of 5 m. The larger of these was estimated to weigh over a tonne and its 2 m saw was preserved at the Mission.

Generally, a river environment lacks the conditions which suit the larger sharks. Lake Murray is an exception, since it is a spreading body of shallow water not more than 6 m in depth, some hundreds of kilometres from the sea. However, it contains numerous fish and a large variety of freshwater turtle.

Adaptability of saltwater fish to a freshwater habitat is variable. Some estuarine species such as Australian bass and barramundi live in a tidal environment which changes in salinity with the tides. Fish adapted to this environment, and this includes species such as whiting, flathead, bream and blackfish, can easily adjust to upstream conditions. They are regularly caught well above tidal influence and far from any brackish water. An odd facet of this is that they also adapt to a changed diet and flathead have even been caught on insect baits being fished for bass.

The chances are that any fish entering on a habitat which is theoretically wrong for it is likely to be hungry. Freshwater sharks in the tropics, for example, have probably been accustomed over the years to feeding on remnants left by estuarine crocodiles and wallabies and kangaroos bogged in bankside mud during the dry season and an occasional fish.

Shark attacks are possible in an environment where crocodiles and wallabies are becoming scarcer.

Dangers from other species depend on conditions. Very muddy water may cause an unwitting angler to step on a freshwater stingray, with risk of a badly stabbed leg.

Of course, the risks to Australian anglers from freshwater sharks are much slighter than on open beaches or river bars, but the risks increase in major tropical rivers. An angler needs to be observant wherever he fishes and anything large enough to cause trouble is easily seen in most cases.

Shark fishing techniques
There is probably more fishing carried out for sharks by fishermen in Australia than in any other part of the world. In America the shark is not considered much of a fighter but anyone who has played a big tiger, white or whaler shark in Australian waters has been very thankful when the contest is over. Our sharks are extremely powerful and appear to be possessed of unusual cunning. Many a long fight has been terminated at the boat when the victim rolled itself up in the heavy steel trace and cut the line with one sweep of its big tail.

Although some fishermen now use light tackle for shark fishing, this is often only to score more points for a competition. Frequently it results in the loss of the shark after a long and tedious struggle. Advent of light tackle may also be partly due to the weight of captures having declined in size and weight since the introduction of netting along the beaches. In the past sharks were fished for with nothing under 60 kg line and a correspondingly heavy rod. Some used a 36 kg test line which in many respects was reasonable enough, but even this was not strong enough for really big sharks of a tonne or more in weight.

The game fisherman usually drifts for sharks or drops anchor over a known reefy bottom to try for them. Hammerhead sharks and makos are often taken while trolling as both will take a moving bait and hammerheads are better taken on the troll than at anchor, as they swallow the bait better as a rule. The bait, usually a large tuna with one side filleted off, is hooked near the tail with a 16/0 Mustad hook and often tied to the body as well. This is attached to a 9 m trace with a breaking strain up to 230 kg and is then let out from the boat to be floated with a football bladder, balloon or cork, or kept at a desired depth. Sometimes the bait is dropped down directly under the boat 30 m or more.

Usually two rods are used. One bait is floated out 45 or 55 m from the boat, and set for little more than trace depth. This is known as the floating bait. The other bait is fed down to near the bottom and is known as the deep bait.

Berley in the form of chopped up scraps of fish is placed in a metal basket over the stern and this imparts an oily slick which drifts for hundreds of metres down with the current. The Australian Game Fishing Association has banned the use of any mammal for bait or berley. This resulted from the widespread killing of porpoises for bait and berley.

When the float commences to bob under the water, the fisherman immediately retrieves the other line in such a way that it will not be fouled up if a shark is hooked. When the shark takes the bait it will often swim a short distance and drop it and no attempt to strike the hook home is made until a long and definite run is made. The float, which is tied on with very light string, breaks off under pressure of the water and comes to the top, and as the launch is started and the fisherman has made several hard strikes to set the hook, it is often picked up with a landing net for future use. A brightly coloured detergent bottle may be used for a float by pushing the line into the bottle with a cork. When the shark dives, the cork pulls out and the bottle is left to float away or sink.

Mako sharks will often swim to the surface after taking the bait and attack the float. Fights with sharks usually last many hours and are not spectacular like those with the leaping marlin—unless the shark is a mako, which often make several leaps.

Weather conditions off the Australian coast in summer are usually rough from the prevailing north-easters which may blow at from 15 to 25 knots, making the fight difficult, especially if there is an ocean swell running. In these conditions the shark mostly keeps deep down and it is often advisable to play it from a fair way off, perhaps 90 m to 140 m. It is hard work fighting a big shark straight down under the boat. The idea is to try to bring it to the surface by playing it away from the boat, a position that enables the fisherman to do the job with much less strain.

When the shark is brought alongside, the trace is taken and as it is pulled in, the slack portion is paid over into the water so that in the event of the shark making a breakaway, the trace will not endanger the gaffman or anyone in the boat. Immediately after gaffing, the shark may roll and thrash about. At times a second gaff must be driven in, especially if the first one is in danger of pulling out. Then the tail rope is put over the tail and the shark tied to a bollard for towing home.

Small sharks can be taken on board if the boat is large enough but to do this they must be beaten on the tip of the snout with a heavy waddy or baseball bat. Hammerhead sharks can be looped over the head as they mostly come alongside with very little life in them if properly played out. A mako should never be taken aboard as they are hard to kill and may come to life if not tied down, endangering all on board.

It is not uncommon for a shark tied alongside to be attacked by other sharks and if this happens and the captive is mutilated, the shark is disqualified. Shooting or lancing sharks brought alongside will also disqualify the catch.

Sharks' teeth
The nature and characteristic shape of a shark's teeth and the number and formation in each jaw can be an invaluable aid to identification of the species. In some cases the distinction between varieties is wide and remarkable; for instance, the contrast of the blunt, pavement-like teeth of gummy shark

with the curved, awl-like fangs of the mako, or the finely serrated big triangular teeth of the great white shark. Mostly distinction may be made even between closely allied species; for example, the cobble-stone-like teeth at the back of the scroll-shaped jaws of the common Port Jackson shark are smoothly rounded, while those of its cousin, the crested Port Jackson shark, have a keel across their tops which bears a small cusp at each side.

But often teeth-charts are more useful as an aid to identification at a post-mortem than they are at the kill, for it can be an exceedingly risky business to closely examine a shark's teeth, establish the pattern and count the rows, even when it supposedly is dead. It is recorded that a fisherman once had a hand bitten off by a shark which previously had been disembowelled. Data on the dental equipment of some species are still incomplete, but its value as an aid to identification has been demonstrated on a number of occasions when it was possible to make positive determination of the species by examination of a tooth, or fragments of teeth, dug from boat planking or other material which had been subjected to attack.

A close-up of the mouth of a 5.5 metre great white shark shows the huge serrated triangular teeth for which it is notorious.

SHARKS

The black tip shark is brown on the body, whiter below and has black tips on the fins. It has been recorded as growing up to 3 metres in length, but is usually smaller.

It could be said that a shark has teeth all over its body. The rough shagreen of the skin is a growth of placoid or plate-like scales which are actually dermal teeth growing from the hide. They are coated with dentine and each has an interior pulpy canal carrying a nerve and blood vessels. In some species they may be microscopically small and rounded so as to present a smooth surface, but no matter how small, they still are teeth. These denticles of the shagreen are of distinctive shape in each species and could be an aid to identification, though little information is available and they are known to change shape with their position on the body. They usually bear little, if any, resemblance to the teeth in the shark's mouth.

As with scales, the set of the shagreen denticles is back towards the tail, or they lie with the flow of the water as the creature swims. Nevertheless, many species present very rough hides due to spikes with spear points, plates with knife-edges, or studs with sharp keels. That is why a shark may shred a heavy line in two with a single flick of its tail. The abrasive nature of a shark's hide was demonstrated some years ago when a young woman walked into the edge of deep water at Karumba (Gulf of Carpentaria) to wash mud from her legs. A big shark charged at her but missed. In passing, its side came into contact with her legs and the shagreen abraded away a good deal of skin and surface flesh.

In the course of evolution, some of the skin denticles of sharks and their close relatives, the rays, have undergone remarkable development and change to fit them for specific purposes. Their teeth in all their diverse forms, the dorsal spines of the Port Jackson sharks, dogsharks and others, the venomous spines of the stingrays and the big needle-sharp spikes which fringe the long snouts of the sawfishes, are all specialized developments of the shagreen.

Land animals and the mammals of the sea have bony skeletons and their teeth are anchored in sockets in the bone of their jaws. Sharks and rays have no bones and no skeletons comparable with those of the animals. Rigidity of the body and other skeletal functions is provided by a framework or system of gristly cartilage which becomes almost as rigid as bone. Sharks' teeth are not bedded in the jaws—they are set in the skin. Over the jaws, the skin that forms the gums is thick and beneath it there is a heavy pad of cartilage in which the teeth take rise. This cartilage is not rigidly attached to the jaw, but to some extent may roll over it. This may be illustrated by lifting the snout to open the mouth of a freshly killed mako. As the mouth opens and the skin pulls on the gums, those rows of horrid, long, recurving and irregularly slanting fangs roll forward until the front rows project outside the lips, as if reaching forward for the prey.

The mako's jaw
As well as varying so greatly in the form of their teeth, sharks differ greatly in the number with which they are equipped. Some species may have around a hundred in each jaw, whereas others may be equipped with several thousands. In the larger, sharp toothed sharks the teeth are arranged in rows in each jaw. The mako has 24 rows of teeth in the upper part of its mouth and 22 in the lower. By counting the number of teeth in the front rows of the upper and lower jaws a dental formula for the particular species may be arrived at. For example: Dental formula conveys that the shark has 11 teeth on each side of the median gap in the upper jaw, and 15 on one side and 14 on the other in the lower jaw, which has two central teeth at the mesial slit where the jaws junction behind the lower lip. But the formulae find little application, probably because there is little such data available for the various species.

There is still a great deal that is not known for certain about sharks and their teeth. It once was supposed that some of the many rows in the mouths of these selachians were in the nature of a reserve, and that when a front row wore out, or was damaged, it was shed and the second row moved forward to take its place. But this theory is now going into the discard. Sharks' teeth are very durable and in the normal course of their lives they suffer very little damage to them. More than the front rows function when the shark goes into action but it is difficult to see what function some of the back rows perform, for they are covered with a fold of membrane from the back of the mouth. Perhaps they are an emergency supply which enables a line to move up and thus fill a gap at the front, but no one yet has photographed a shark's jaw to show teeth between rows on their way forward.

A study of the teeth of the numerous species provides some striking examples of how nature has supplied them with dental equipment suited to do the work required of it. The pavement-like teeth of the gummy are especially suited to crushing crabs and shellfish; the recurving fangs of the mako are strikingly adapted to the seizing and holding of prey of swallowable size; the closely meshed, saw-edge teeth of the school shark enable it to chop a fish in two with the angler feeling almost no pull on his line; while the jagged incisors of the tiger and the big finely serrated triangular blades of the great white shark are functionally patterned for slicing up big carcasses.

Those sharks (mostly of the whaler family) which more commonly are seen to attack large food, such as wounded or dead sharks, towed gamefish or whales, usually operate by nosing in to grab a big mouthful and wriggle or lunge vigorously until it is torn away. Where the food is of smaller size and not rigidly attached, they shake it until the mouthful is sheared off. A great white shark could take a man and, with one chop and a shake, bite him in half.

Some huge teeth of the white shark type have been dredged up from the Pacific Ocean. These were not fossilized, but appeared to be of fairly recent origin. Large fossilized teeth of this nature have been unearthed in many places, notably in Malta and Australia. A particularly well-preserved specimen unearthed at Sharkstooth Hill, in California, was almost 15 cm long. Using the present-day white shark for comparison it seems that the giant which possessed that tooth probably was more than 24 m in length.

The dredging of those big teeth in a relatively fresh state raises the question of whether these giant selachians are extinct or still in existence in the ocean depths. David G. Stead, in *Sharks and Rays of Australian Seas*, gives credibility to their continued existence in a vividly descriptive account of the appearance of a huge white shark off Port Stephens in the year 1918. It was so monstrous that sight of it deterred seasoned fishermen, well used to sharks, from going to sea again during the few days it was in the area. Their estimates, perhaps somewhat astray in the excitement of the moment, credited it with a minimum length of 30 m and sometimes a good deal more. It lifted their crayfish traps, 1 m in diameter, pot after pot, taking trap, crayfish, mooring ropes and all. The men who saw it were unanimous that it was a white shark of such size as they had never heard or dreamed of before. Stead and the local fisheries authorities could only come to the conclusion that it must have been really gigantic to so intimidate men with long experience of the sea. So perhaps out there in the Pacific Ocean there still may be leviathan sharks equipped with and ready to use such monstrous teeth.

Basking shark

Cetorhinus maximus: The second biggest fish in the sea, exceeded in size only by the whale shark. A giant with the streamlined shape of a mako or white pointer, like the whale shark it is harmless and it eats by sifting minute living things through numerous comb-like projections of the gill arches. The gill openings, which stretch completely around the neck, distinguish it from all other sharks.

The basking shark's gill arches resemble very long teeth and appear to act in the same way that whalebone does in the whale. The water is strained through and the food collected by the combs. The gill-slits are very wide, but the head is pointed. The mouth is huge and in the young the snout is particularly long and rather bizarre in shape.

The name basking shark comes from their habit of drifting along with the currents on the surface of the sea, apparently basking in the sun. Their colour above is blackish-brown and lighter below. In old-time whaling days, basking sharks were hunted for the oil in their livers. They have also inspired sea-serpent yarns by authors haunted by the ghastly spectacle of their carcasses or skeletons.

The European species, *Cetorhinus maximus*, is said to weigh up to 3500 kg and two specimens taken in California weighed 2980 kg and 3895 kg. They were 11.4 m and 9 m long respectively. Examinations of skeletons in America show that some grow to 12 to 15 m, but they also have an oddity in a specimen which swims far more freely than its giant relation and grows to around 2 m.

The South Pacific variety is distributed in New South Wales, Victoria, South Australia, Tasmania and New Zealand, where one caught in a net off Paraparaumu measured 8.5 m.

Bronze whaler

Carcharhinus brachyurus: A shark that grows to 3 m and gets its name from the bright bronze colour of the whole of the top portion of the body, which has been described as 'like a new penny'. Similar in some respects to the common whaler, but the body is more rounded than in the common whaler and the teeth differ slightly. They are broad at the base on both upper and lower jaws, serrated in both jaws, the cusps very narrow in the lower jaw and much broader in the upper jaw, but considerably narrower than in the common whaler. They have 32 teeth in a row in each jaw compared with the 30 or less in the common whaler.

A grey or creamy strip appears along the sides from the eyes and the lower colouring of the body is also creamy white. While the bronze whaler is reasonably plentiful along the eastern Australian coastline, it is not nearly as common as the true or black whaler and its name is given to the black whaler far too often. This has been encouraged by newspapers who seem to think that every whaler seen or caught must be a bronze whaler.

It is more plentiful off the Queensland coast than off New

South Wales. It is a smaller shark than the common whaler. The average weight is about 90 kg. But its fighting qualities are no different from the common whaler and if anything, it may be a slightly tougher fighter. Like the common whaler it is a shark of the open seas, but it has no hesitation in entering harbours and inlets and should be regarded as just as much a menace to swimmers as the common whaler.

Blue whaler *Prionace glauca:* An uncommon species also known as blue shark, rarely taken by game fishermen. Grows to about 3 m in Australasian waters and possibly larger. A closely allied species in Europe reaches a length of 4 m.

This shark is a brilliant blue above, changing abruptly to white below and is essentially a cold water shark. It has been recorded off Lord Howe Island, off New South Wales, South Australia, New Zealand and Tasmania where it is relatively common.

The teeth, which are broader in the upper jaw, are serrated in both upper and lower jaws. The dorsal fin is nearer the ventrals than the pectorals and the pectorals are long and narrow.

Only a few have been caught by Australian game fishermen and none of these have been in excess of 3 m or 90 kg. It is capable of being a dangerous shark to bathers but owing to its rareness is not one to be greatly worried about.

Grey nurse shark *Odontaspis arenarius:* A slow-moving creature of sleepy habits, often erroneously described as a devastating man-eater. There is no evidence that it shows the ferocity with which it is credited in some newspapers. This misconception may have resulted from the fearsome teeth of the grey nurse, which can be protruded to grasp their prey. But only the teeth are frightening in this sluggish creature.

The grey nurse shark is easily identified by the two dorsal fins, both large, the first slightly in advance of the ventral fins, and by the long pointed, awl-like teeth, with two small spine-like cusps on either side. The third eyelid is not present in this shark and it has five gill slits in front of the pectoral fin.

The grey nurse's colour is variable, either a dull grey or a pale brownish above, turning to a greyish white below. The

Grey nurse shark

average size is 2 to 3 m. Stories of 4 to 5 m sharks have not been substantiated. Their weight averages between 90 to 160 kg.

They are essentially fish-eaters and follow up the large schools of fish, such as salmon and mullet. Mostly they are found lazing on the bottom around reefy areas often in quite large numbers. They live a long time in captivity, aimlessly circling aquariums, without molesting small fish or skindivers.

This is an extremely docile shark when hooked, putting up the worst effort of any species. It is easily pulled to the surface on a handline, though sometimes when hooked it will move a few metres ahead and rest on the bed of the ocean and then become very hard to shift if the fisherman is using light gear.

Grey nurse sharks, when not following school fish along the shoreline, gather about reefy grounds in deeper water, where they may be caught during most months of the year but particularly in late summer and early autumn. They are common to Queensland, New South Wales, Victoria and South Australia.

Sphyrnidae: A family of sharks with an oddly-shaped head and a reputation for attacking humans. The hammerhead gives an unpredictable performance when hooked, sometimes fighting tenaciously, sometimes sulking on the line. It is a comic creature as it cocks its head from side to side, focusing first with one eye and then the other on a trailing bait. Four of the world's nine species of hammerheads are found in Australian waters.

The name hammerhead is an obvious one for this shark because of the curious shape of the head, with the eyes placed

Hammerhead shark

Hammerhead shark

on the lateral extensions of the 'hammer'. The colour is an ashy-grey above, fading to pale yellowish below, but when it is following a moving bait it looks light brown. It has five gill openings and two dorsal fins, the first dorsal tall and sickle-like, the second dorsal very small.

The hammerhead grows to a very large size and specimens of 6 m have been recorded, but the average size of those captured by game fishermen is usually 3 to 3.5 m. They do not weigh as much as some of the other species caught because of their slight build and a 230 kg hammerhead is above average in weight. The hammerhead is common to the open seas and has a very wide distribution. It has been captured in Western Australia, Northern Territory, New South Wales, Queensland and Tasmania.

Although the hammerhead has a relatively small mouth and small teeth, it is a surface-loving shark, always on the move, and will enter harbours and estuaries. At times it has been found many kilometres up inland rivers, where against all behaviour patterns it will attack man. They are believed to detect and home-in on prey through sensory organs in their hammer-shaped heads.

Hammerheads are extremely inquisitive sharks which take trolled bait readily and seem to depend on a very keen sense of smell more than on sight. If they are following a trolled bait, the boat should be taken in circles or figure eights at a fast speed. The hammerheads will follow the same course as that taken by the boat, apparently following the smell of the bait. They have an incredible turn of speed when first hooked and at times race several hundred metres along the surface before diving deep to keep up the fight at a rapid pace. They are viviparous and may give birth to 30 or 40 young, even after capture while being brought in by a game fishing boat.

Drifting for hammerheads with a floating bait often results in the shark making several runs with the bait before taking it. Very frequently they appear to hold it in their teeth rather than swallow the bait and it is not uncommon to lose a shark after five or 10 minutes when it apparently just drops the bait, the hook not having penetrated the hard jaws. Young hammerheads are a considerable nuisance to game fishermen as they mutilate marlin baits and are too small to be hooked.

Hammerhead species can be separated by differences in their heads such as variations in the nasal groove and the position of mucous pores. Their food consists mainly of school fish and they often travel in parties of 10 and 15 following closely on a large school of pilchards. One or two sporadically cut in through the pilchards, capture what they want and then drop back and swim along with the rest. These are the small hammerheads of about 2 m.

They are one of the commonest sharks and frequently cause shark alarms on surfing beaches. But the chances of an attack by one in the surf are remote.

Mako shark or blue pointer

Isurus oxyrinchus: The only shark Americans regard as a game fish, an honour due to its high-leaping fighting qualities and great speed, known for many years in Australian waters as the blue pointer or snapper shark. The name mako, a Maori word, has been generally adopted since the beginning of game fishing in Australia. The teeth of this shark were greatly prized by the Maoris who wore them in their ears.

The mako is a shark of the open seas, preferring the colder waters to the warmer tropical seas. Its fighting qualities are legendary. One of the best examples occurred on 18 February 1950, when famous American game angler Alfred Glassell landed a 140 kg mako shark, fishing around Bird Island in the Bay of Islands. Twice the mako was hit by a big whale spade which almost severed its head. Then it was towed for two hours back to the dock and hoisted for weighing. When it was lowered to the dock, the mako came to life, cleared the dock of people and with its head almost off wriggled desperately back to the water. Only Glassell's photographic record remains to show he caught and weighed that fish, for it got away.

The mako's general colour above is a dark gun barrel blue changing abruptly to white below. Five moderately large gill slits are present, a large first dorsal fin and very small second dorsal. The teeth are large, slender and awl-like similar to the grey nurse shark, but lacking the two cusps on either side of the base. It grows to a length of 4 m and a 3.6 m specimen caught by Aircraftsman B. D. H. Ross at Mayor Island, New Zealand, weighed 453 kg. It probably weighed more but the scales used did not register over that weight.

The mako's distribution
This extends from southern Queensland where it is not common, down the New South Wales coast to Victoria, Tasmania and South Australia to New Zealand where many are captured by game fishermen and it is highly regarded as a fine sporting shark. On a number of occasions it has been known to attack boats and even jump aboard, causing panic amongst

Mako shark

the crew. One leapt aboard a game fishing boat off Sydney, the fisherman and the crew deserting the cockpit while the shark crashed about taking chunks out of the coaming before eventually leaping overboard to freedom. Sometimes the mako will come straight up to the boat after being hooked, offering no resistance until alongside. Then anything may happen and it is a dangerous practice to allow it to do this before being played out.

Mako will take a moving bait readily. For years it was considered the only shark to do this, but this is not correct as the hammerhead shark will also readily take a trolled bait and both the common whaler and the tiger shark have been known to do so. As a shark of the open seas, it is not a potential danger to surfers although it does swim along the surf beaches at times. Its food consists mainly of pelagic fish, such as mackerel, kahawai, trevally and maomao, but it will take the usual baits used by game fishermen for marlin and other sharks.

The great twisting leaps of a hooked mako are one of the most enthralling sights a game fisherman sees, and they may be repeated several times in quick succession. The mako shoots clear of the water by several metres, twisting in midleap and landing back with a mighty splash sometimes upside down, head first or tail first.

Similar species occur in South Africa, California, Hawaii, Japan, Europe and the East Indies. In Sydney and Port Stephens, New South Wales, they appear in early October and they may be taken through the summer months to February or March.

If a shark can be beautiful, there is no doubt the mako deserves that description, for the body is symmetrical and its movements graceful. But it is very solidly built, particularly at the tail joint which broadens out like the tail of the swordfish and it is here that it gets the great power for its spectacular twisting leaps that carry it high into the air. The glistening blue body and the large round dark eyes add to the general attractive appearance.

Extra heavy tackle is required for the biggest makos, heavy trace wire being essential. Long-shafted 14/0 to 16/0 hooks are preferred by veteran game anglers. They take a feathered lure but are mostly caught by fishermen trolling for marlin with live bait.

Porbeagle shark

Lamna nasus: A swift-swimming shark similar in appearance to the mako, but not rated highly by game fishermen as it lacks the mako's superb fighting qualities. Also known as Beaumaris shark and mackerel shark, prominent in New Zealand, particularly in Cook Strait. If taken by Australian anglers it may be mistaken for the mako.

The porbeagle has a streamlined body like the mako but it is stouter, with its length compressed. Its general colour differs from the mako and is a slaty grey on the upper part, sides and body, changing to a yellowish or white underside. The teeth are the main identifying feature of this shark, however, as they are much smaller than the mako's and far broader, with two small cusps at the base. The eyes are deep green while those of the mako are darker, almost black.

The average size of New Zealand specimens is just short of 2 m but it grows to 3 m and occasional 4 m sharks have been recorded in Europe and America. Heaviest porbeagle recorded weighed 317 kg but anything up to 180 kg is an outstanding specimen. They are distributed in Western Australia, Tasmania and Victoria and are plentiful in the Atlantic and at the eastern end of the Mediterranean.

Porbeagles feed on schooling fish and because of their fondness for school mackerel have, like the mako, been labelled mackerel shark. Off Wales they are given the Welsh name Beaumaris. The name porbeagle is of Cornish origin.

There is no record of porbeagles being caught by Australian game fishermen unless they were wrongly identified, but in New Zealand it is captured regularly in 90 to 180 m. It is a shark that disappoints when hooked and is usually taken when drifting with live bait.

School shark, snapper shark, or tope

Galeorhinus australis: A small, harmless gummy shark which normally grows from 1 to 2 m and is rarely taken over 2 m. Most of those taken by anglers are just over 1 m. A great pest to deep sea fishermen, especially when snapper are running. They rush the snapper as they are pulled in on a line and sever them neatly just behind the head.

They often enter harbours where they cause trouble to fishermen. They are frequently named as the young of nearly every kind of shark, such as whaler, grey nurse or tiger shark, but the characteristic double-tailed appearance of the caudal fin makes it quite easy to separate from the young of any of the other types. The general colour is a slaty purple to a light bluish-grey and white underneath. Common off Queensland, New South Wales, Victoria, Tasmania and South Australia.

The shark is viviparous and from 15 to 35 young may be born. The teeth are small. They can eat snapper, jewfish and other commercial types of fish, but they are quite harmless to man. School shark are an important edible fish in Tasmania, where they are caught on long lines to 550 m. Tagging records indicate they live for 40 years.

Seven-gilled shark

Notorhynchus cepedianus: Not regarded as harmful to man in New Zealand, but any shark of 3 m in length could be. Its Maori name, tuatini, comes from the strangely shaped teeth, with which weapons were made. It is also known as Tasmanian tiger shark and broadsnout.

The seven-gilled shark has been recorded in New South Wales, Victoria and South Australia, but is more common in

Tasmania and New Zealand. The seven gill slits and the single dorsal fin set well back near the tail make this shark easy to identify. It has a broad, round head and snout and the teeth differ in the upper jaw to the lower. Those of the upper jaw are jagged and have cusps, while those in the lower jaw are comb-shaped. There is a single median tooth in the upper jaw.

The general colour above is a sandy-grey, marked with black and white spots and the lower portion is white. Adults grow to over 3 m but the average size taken off Tasmania and South Australia is 3 m. They are common in bays and deeper estuaries.

Thresher shark *Alopias caudatus:* Members of the family Alopiidae, known as thresher sharks, are a coastal oceanic group easily recognized by their huge upper caudal lobe, which is at least as long as their total length. There appear to be two distinct forms in the world, and many variations of these. One form, characterized by *A. caudatus*, has relatively small, round eyes and is a surface or midwater dweller. The other form, typified by *A. superciliosus*, is a deep-water dweller with very large, oval eyes. Both are found in Australian waters.

They are distributed off all coasts of Australia, Tasmania and New Zealand, where visiting anglers catch more of them than Australians. New Zealand holds the present world record, a thresher of 417 kg (922 lb) caught in the Bay of Islands in 1937 by W. W. Dowding on a 59 kg b/s line. A shark that lives on school fish, mackerel, snapper, morwong and the like, which averages between 135 and 180 kg when landed by Australian anglers. The general colour above is bluish-grey and white below. Its teeth are slender and pointed but the bases are hard-rooted and broad.

The thresher uses its distinctive tail to drive a school of fish into a crowded mass and sometimes swishes the tail to stun them, quickly picking up the disabled fish. But there appears little foundation for the story that the thresher feuds with whales, as the thresher lives on small school fish.

Thresher shark

Tiger shark

Galeocerdo cuvieri: A big, dangerous shark with a broad, evenly rounded snout, making almost a semi-circle. It fights stubbornly and because of its size tests the angler's stamina, but it does not fight as long as the mako, nor does it produce the mako's spectacular leaps. The tiger shark probably got its name from the dark bars that cross its body vertically. In Australian waters these bands disappear with age.

The distinctive teeth are rather coarsely saw-edged and lean sideways, with a prominent notch facing inwards. The colour is a dark grey, sometimes with a tinge of brown. The dark bars are irregular in shape but fairly uniform in spacing. The tiger shark has five gill openings, the last one or two above the junction of the pectoral fin. The eyes are fixed and staring and cannot be shut. The nictitating membrane (Marshall calls it a 'third eye') is transparent and works from below the eye like a screen wiper.

Tiger sharks grow to a length of from 4.5 to 6 m and are regularly taken at 450 to 600 kg. They are scavengers eating almost anything they can pick up and stomach contents have included whole dogs, tin cans, turtles, car tyres, dolphin, lobsters, squid, birds and even parts of crocodiles. They are cannibals and will eat other sharks. They are found from tropical North Australian waters all round Australia to the southern States and beyond to New Zealand. Tiger sharks, mainly of a closely allied species, are widely found in all the world's seas. They are keenly sought by anglers because of their size and strength and many very long battles have taken place with these large sharks off Sydney Heads and along the coastline to Brisbane and beyond.

While the general tendency now is to fish with lighter gear, this and other large sharks are best fished for with lines of 59 kg b/s and 9 m traces, allowable under I.G.F.A. rules. This is because tiger sharks when brought to gaff have the habit of rolling in the trace, and breaking free. Good bait is large bonito, tuna or similar fish on a 16/0 hook. Fish from a boat at anchor or drifting, lowering the line to between 15 and 30 m with float attached.

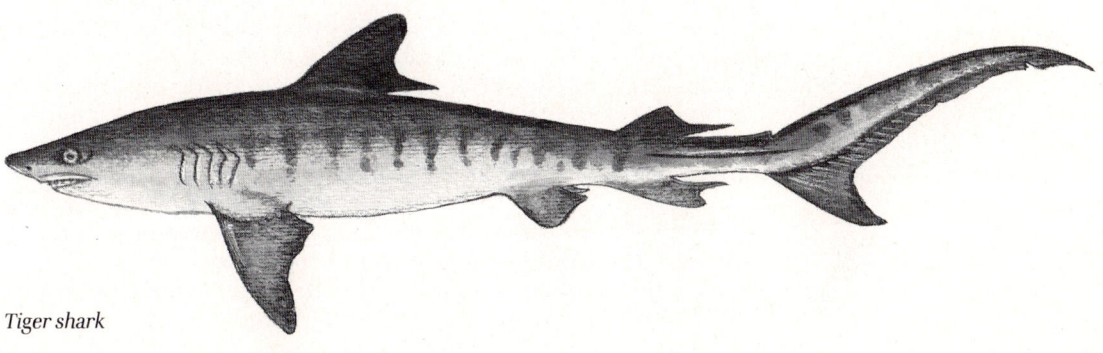

Tiger shark

Tiger sharks frequent deep waters off the coast but also move about the surfing beaches and at times enter harbours and estuaries. They are not at all reluctant to enter shallow water, where their efficient teeth are a menace to skindivers and surfers. Food can remain undigested for long periods in their stomachs. The famous Australian Shark Arm Case is one instance in which a human arm was found after having been in the shark for at least eight days and possibly 18 days.

Tiger sharks average from 220 kg to 300 kg and a 5 m specimen of 1500 kg was netted at Newcastle by Nick Gorshennen. They will attack people in the water, especially where shipwrecks have taken place, and it is probable that they have been responsible for surfing tragedies along the Australian east coastline. Many captures were made off Moreton Island, Queensland, when the whaling station was in operation there, but these have fallen off considerably since it ceased operation. Netting has also depleted the numbers of tiger sharks around Sydney and Newcastle and large tiger sharks have become increasingly hard to capture at both these places.

Whale shark *Rhincodon typus:* The largest shark in the sea, and oddly enough, completely harmless and docile. Indeed it is so sluggish skindivers can romp all over it without arousing the slightest irritation. Growing to a length of 21 m, this beautifully marked monster with two tiny eyes has a world-wide distribution, mainly in the tropics. One 12 m shark weighed 14 tonnes when landed. It was first identified in 1828 in Table Bay at Cape Town, South Africa, but the first Australian recording was by Nelson and Alf Mitchell off Broughton Island, Port Stephens, in 1936. Since then they have been frequently washed up on Australian beaches often sparking barbaric behaviour among sightseers who carve souvenir hunks from the carcasses.

Noted skindiver Ron Taylor and his wife Valerie took some wonderful film of one with which they swam, hitch-hiking a ride by holding onto the enormous dorsal fin. Nothing could have as emphatically underlined the extreme docility of the whale shark.

On first sighting whale sharks underwater it is difficult to make out any shape and all you are aware of is a number of white spots moving along. Once you have made out the shape of the shark the three or four ridges running the full length of the body become evident and then the great tail fluke swinging in a slow 5 to 6 m arc.

The eyes are so tiny that they are hard to locate and the large dorsal fin is located well back from the head beyond half the length of the body. The mouth terminal is at the front of the head and not located underneath as in most sharks and in one of the two washed up at Birubi Point, Port Stephens, New South Wales, the mouth measured 1 m across. Set in a wide mass like coarse carborundum paper, the tiny pointed teeth number 6000 in each jaw.

Like so many huge ocean creatures, the whale shark lives on food strained through comb-like gill-rakers though they have been seen to stand vertically in the water, when ravenous, to feed on small fish, crabs, plankton and jellyfish. It is considered to be a warm water fish, but its wide distribution suggests that it may turn up anywhere. Its appearance off the Australian coastline as far down as Jervis Bay adds to this theory.

Whaler shark

Carcharhinus obscurus: The common or black whaler shark grows to at least 4 m and 450 kg but the average weight of most of those caught by game fishermen ranges between 110 to 200 kg. Among the same species there is a smaller bronze whaler (*C. ahenea*) and the cocktail shark of South Australia, known in Western Australia as the Swan River whaler.

The colour is a sooty grey above, whitish below, similar to most species of sharks, with the area between the dorsal fin and the head frequently tinged in bronze. This is why the species is frequently misnamed the grey nurse.

The teeth in both jaws are serrated. Those of the upper jaw are broad at the base and notched on the outer edges, or oblique and swollen at the base. In the lower jaw they are smaller and erect. Five gill slits are present. There are two dorsal fins, the second dorsal being very small and there is a pit at the root of the caudal fin. The nostrils are nearer the mouth than the tip of the snout.

The name whaler appears to go back to the days of the old whalers at Twofold Bay, on the New South Wales south coast, where they were among the most common species seen around the whales. The common whaler is found from Queensland to New South Wales, Victoria and New Zealand.

This shark probably makes the greater percentage of attacks on humans along the eastern coastline. Fearless and savage, it is to be found both in the outer seas and along the coastline, frequenting the surfing beaches in large numbers. They particularly like to move about the entrances to harbours and swim long distances up estuaries and rivers. As a fighting shark it is one of the toughest of any encountered and when hooked usually goes deep and swims in circles.

The whaler's main food seems to be school fish but they will eat almost anything and when one shark has been caught and tied alongside a game fishing boat, it is not uncommon for others to come and tear hunks out of the shark already captured. When partly grown, about 2 to 2.5 m, they swim just below the surface in large schools, often in company with tiger sharks.

When the mullet are 'running' and fishermen are netting them along the beaches the whalers come right up into the first few centimetres of water to capture any of the injured mullet which have escaped the nets. Whalers have been on beaches feeding on the carcass of a stranded whale and one was left momentarily stranded on the beach as the waves went back and had to await the next big wave before it was able to wriggle back into the surf.

A whaler captured by Bob Grunsel at Newcastle, New South Wales, in his shark mesh net was just under 450 kg. It was a female with 15 young sharks of about 1 m inside it, which were removed from its stomach on the deck of the shark boat.

There is a colour phase in whalers which has black tips to the extremities of the fins and tails and is known as a black-tipped whaler to game fishermen. This should not be confused with the small 1.5 m black tip whaler found in North Western Australia, Northern Territory and Queensland, *Carcharhinus melanopterus*.

Specimens taken in the Hawkesbury River at Jerusalem Bay, New South Wales, and at sea off Port Stephens, New South Wales, have leapt from the sea, revolving rapidly in mid-air to crash back on their sides in a smother of spray. Black tip whalers are known by fishermen as spinning sharks. Specimens like this up to 135 kg and 3 m in length have been caught off Port Stephens.

White shark *Carcharodon carcharias* (White Pointer): Largest of the man-eating sharks grows to a length of 12 m and sometimes more. The general build of this shark resembles the mako, with much the same shaped tail and the straight back. They lack the elongated tail of other sharks and this gives them far more speed in the water. The distinguishing feature of the white shark is the large triangular and serrated teeth in both jaws.

White shark is a misleading name as its general colour above is greyish to black and it is white below. It has a marked keel on each side of the tail as in the mako shark and like that shark the tail joint is very broad and powerful.

The white shark ranges from southern Queensland, New South Wales, Victoria, South Australia and Western Australia, but not in Tasmania. South Australia has become world famous for the huge white sharks captured there by game fishermen off Port Lincoln and Streaky Bay. Market gardener Alf Dean has captured six of these monsters all over 1 tonne in weight. The largest, 1207 kg (2664 lb) and 5 m long, he caught 2.5 km out of Ceduna on a line with a breaking strain of 59 kg. This was the largest fish ever taken on a rod and reel anywhere in the world. Dean has set seven world records with white shark catches. The only other angler to land a fish over a tonne was Bob Dyer, also with a white shark. Dyer's wife Dolly holds the women's world record with a 477 kg (1052 lb) shark caught on a 59 kg b/s line.

The largest of Dean's white sharks measured 5 m but he and other anglers have seen much larger specimens in Streaky Bay. Dean has lost white sharks much larger than those he has captured. In 1954, he played one he estimated at 1800 kg for five and half hours before losing it. The shark pulled his 10.9 m cutter 20 km in the struggle.

Huge white sharks were common off Moreton Island in Queensland during the whaling station's operations there, and some very large ones have been seen and captured off Sydney Heads and Port Stephens, New South Wales. One sighted off Broughton Island, Port Stephens, was estimated at 7 m. This same fish was sighted there some years later and was estimated to be over 9 m and to weigh in the vicinity of 2270 kg. Roughley tells of white sharks' teeth dredged from the ocean floor that must have come from a fish computed at 27 m in length.

White sharks are fished for in South Australian waters between October and May and much the same season applies on the Australian east coast. Dean believes these sharks live in the same area most of their lives. Proof of this theory is that he lost a 680 kg white shark off Ceduna in 1958 and in December 1960 landed the same shark with his own hook and trace still in its jaw—within less than 2 km of where he originally lost it.

White sharks will eat almost anything, and will eat seals, dolphins, other sharks, including their own kind, if they are hungry enough. They have often rammed fishing boats as they took berley bags. They will follow ships in mid-ocean for days feeding on garbage.

The use of dolphins or other mammals both as bait and for berley has been banned by the I.G.F.A. This rule is intended to prevent anglers increasing the weight of sharks before they catch them, by feeding them well.

By reason of its great weight, the white shark is a mighty adversary for game fishermen and is considered the top prize amongst all sharks. Although it is mostly found in the deeper oceans it frequently haunts the shorelines and has the sinister name of white death or man-eater for that reason. No doubt it has been responsible for some deaths among surfers, and it has been the proven cause of death to several skindivers.

White shark

S ■ SHARKS

Gummy shark — *Mustelus antarcticus:* These harmless members of the shark family Triakidae live on smooth sea bottoms feeding on crabs, shrimps and shellfish which they crush with smooth, flattened teeth. They are slenderly built and have a fairly smooth skin, and have good edible qualities. Also known as sweet william shark, spotted dogfish, gummy and by the Maori name mango. They are found in all Australian States and in both islands of New Zealand. They are closely related to the whiskery shark *Furgaleus ventralis*, found only in South Australia and south-eastern Australia, which has a thicker body. They average around 1 m.

Spotted catshark — *Asymbolus analis:* Slender, harmless members of the family Scyliorhinidae, light brown in colour, with numerous dark tan spots along the body and fins. They grow to 1 m and are found in Tasmania, Victoria, southern New South Wales, South Australia and south Western Australia. Trawlers catch them to a depth of 180 m.

Wobbegong shark — *Orectolobus maculatus:* The mottled wobbegong or carpet shark is common along all the eastern coastline of New South Wales, Southern Queensland, Victoria, South Australia, Western Australia and Tasmania. They have a beautifully patterned skin, marked with symmetrical designs in varying shades of brown and grey, but a repellent mouth fringed with stringy growths. The name wobbegong is an Aboriginal name which apparently was widely used by many tribes.

Wobbegongs live among the rocky weed-covered areas along the coast and lie on the bottom most of the time picking up their food from whatever passes by. Their skin patterns no doubt act as a camouflage. When a fish comes within range they can dart forward with surprising speed and snap it up. They usually grow to around 2 m, but one of 3.18 m was netted at Jibbon, New South Wales. Their teeth are long and sharp.

They sometimes attack the feet of fishermen while working on the nets, but unless the foot is lifted from the bottom they seldom take hold. For this reason many net fishermen move along by shuffling their feet if they think a wobbegong is nearby. One man, bitten by a wobbegong, lost his foot at the ankle and crayfish hunters have had hands and arms severely injured. There are several species, none of which were regarded by the Aborigines as edible.

Wobbegong

SHARKS ■ S

Port Jackson shark

Pork Jackson shark

Heterodontus portusjacksoni: Perhaps the oldest of all sharks, sometimes said to be living fossils. They closely resemble fossils from the Carboniferous age, around 200 to 250 million years ago. They are a harmless species found in fairly shallow water among reefs and rocks in southern Australia, growing to 1.5 m. Also known as bullhead sharks or oyster crushers.

Port Jackson sharks have a subdued disposition and lack the savagery of some other sharks. They loll on the sea bottom one on top of the other, refusing to prowl and scavenge for food, living on crustaceans and sea urchins and whatever comes their way.

The two dorsal fins each have a fixed spine. The head is blunt, bullshaped and there are both grinding teeth and grasping teeth. The body colour is tan to pale brown, with prominent dark marks on the snout and below the eyes. The upper lobe of the tail is short and blunt, the lower lobe short and rounded. They are too inactive to appeal either to spearmen or anglers.

Zebra shark

Stegostoma fasciatum: Also known as leopard shark. Harmless, narrow-bodied shark with remarkably extended caudal fins and prominent ridges along the full length of the back. They laze on the bottom unless they are disturbed and this sedentary disposition and their small mouth makes them interesting mainly for underwater cameramen. When zebra sharks are young, they are covered in pale stripes across dark-brown bodies, but as they grow the stripes disappear and are replaced by numerous dark spots and the body colour turns to a dusky yellow. They average 2 m in length but have been recorded up to 3 m.

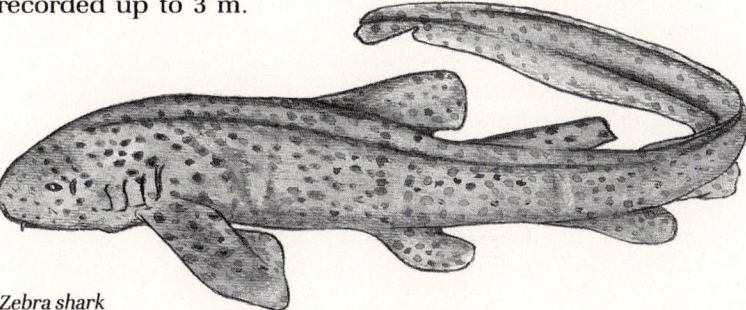

Zebra shark

SHRIMPS See Prawns and shrimps.

SILVERBELLY Small fish (up to 23 cm) of the family Gerridae found on tropical Australian coasts, usually in shallow water. They are nuisance fish trapped in large numbers in trawling nets and generally resembling the related pony fish. They are also known as silver biddy, soapy, roach and pip. They are sometimes confused with tailor, a much more admirable fish of fighting qualities lacking in Gerridae. The common silverbelly *Gerres ovatus* is found in New South Wales as well as Queensland and is highly regarded among anglers as a bait fish. They average around 12 cm but reach 23 cm. The lowfin silverbelly *Parequula melbournensis* is a solitary member of the family seldom sighted in schools, but abundant in the shallow waters of Victoria, South Australia and Western Australia early in the year. They have short, deep, compressed bodies and grow to 20 cm. The Darnley Island silverbelly *Gerres argyreus* is common in Queensland where it swims into shallow bays in vast schools. There are five distinctive vertical bars made up of reddish-brown spots beneath the lateral line. Queenslanders net them for bait. They reach 23 cm.

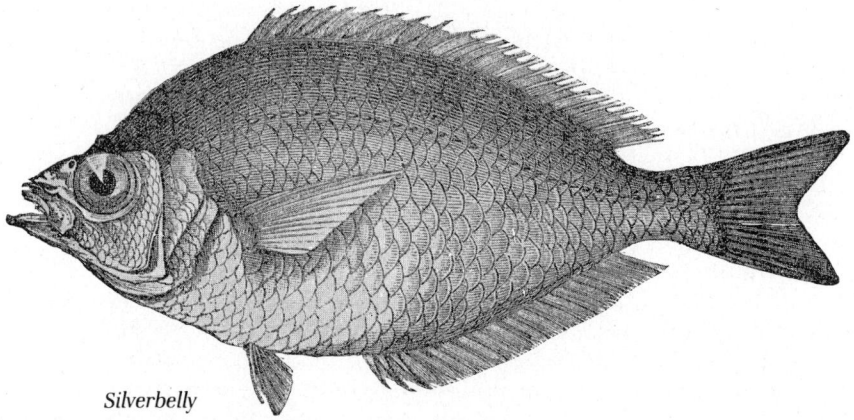

Silverbelly

SILVEREYE See Macquarie perch.

SILVER perch *Bidyanus bidyanus:* The third most important native freshwater fish in Australia, ranking only behind Murray cod and golden perch. They are variously known as bream, black bream, Murray bream, grunter, bidyan, tcheri, Murray perch, sooty grunter and bidyan grunter, depending on locality. They have a peculiar habit of emitting a sound resembling a grunt, produced by vibration of the swim bladder, when captured.

In appearance they are typically perch-like, with an uneven outline above the head caused by a depression or concavity, giving the impression that the head is too small for the rest of the body. This becomes more pronounced in very old fish.

SILVER perch ■ S

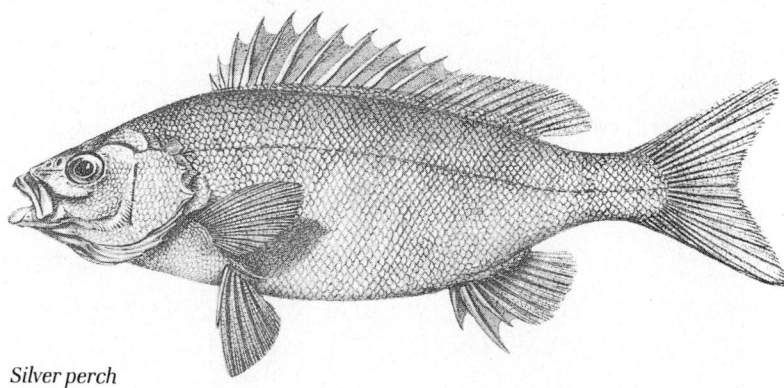

Silver perch

The fish are silvery in colour, darker above and sometimes develop a bronze tinge. The mouth is small, the dorsal and anal fins have strong spines and the body is covered with small scales. The gill covers are exceedingly sharp and can inflict a painful wound, well-known by all fishermen who seek Australian native fish.

Silver perch are common in the entire Murray-Darling River system except at the higher altitudes. Generally their range covers that of the Murray cod and golden perch but extends further upstream than the golden perch and they are present in immense numbers in dams such as the Burrinjuck on the Murrumbidgee River. These fish often school in large numbers and are some of the few larger native fish which are sometimes seen near the surface. They are common in the inland streams and waterholes west of the Great Dividing Range in Queensland and have been introduced to numerous dams, waterholes, lagoons, irrigation canals, farm ponds and creeks throughout Australia. The related species of silver perch *Bidyanus elliptica*, are found in the headwaters of a number of streams flowing to the north-west coast of Western Australia. Another member of the family, spangled perch *Leiopotherapon unicolor*, is discussed with other grunters (which see).

Silver perch in the range 226 g to 2 kg are caught frequently by anglers while bait fishing, but fish of up to 3 kg are not uncommon. They are known to have reached 8 kg. Detailed information on growth rates is not available but preliminary studies have shown that silver perch can grow faster than golden perch during the first two years when kept under similar conditions and at the Inland Fisheries Research Station at Narrandera fish were grown to 27 cm in one year.

Spawning conditions and processes have been investigated also by John Lake at Narrandera. Spawning may occur after slight rises in river or pond levels provided temperatures in the shallows reach 23 degrees C and fish were typically ready for spawning with mature gonads some time before the actual spawning period. Males are mature at two years of age and females at three years. Spawning may occur in October or

November but if no rise in water level occurs this may be delayed until conditions are more favourable. Silver perch in the Murrumbidgee River near Canberra were seen to delay spawning until the second week in March.

Fecundity is high and a 2 kg fish may yield up to 500,000 eggs. Males are difficult to pick from females by external examination but females are typically a larger and more rotund fish at spawning. At spawning two or three male fish follow the female near the surface of the water and activity and speed increase this time when fish may actually thrash the water surface. Eggs are spherical, amber-coloured at first but colourless and transparent later, approximately 3 mm in diameter, nonadhesive and pelagic, but will come to rest on the bottom in still water. Hatching is rapid and takes approximately 30 hours at temperatures between 22 and 31 degrees C. Young fish begin to feed at about six days after fertilization Larvae feed on both phytoplankton and zooplankton (that is, both plant and animal plankton). Adult fish are omnivores and at times may feed extensively on zooplankton, shrimps, filamentous algae and aquatic plants.

Silver perch are a welcome and valuable addition to Australia's meagre crop of native freshwater sportfish. Vast numbers of them are taken each year by bait fishermen using worms, yabbies and shrimps and a single school of fish may provide continued sport for a number of anglers for a whole day. Many anglers have now become aware that silver perch, despite their small mouths, will take an artificial lure avidly and fight strongly on light tackle. Fish can be taken from the larger and deeper waters using lures such as medium-sized flopy, tiger minnow, salamander, abu hi-lo, abu killer, heddon deep six, swayback, bellbrook wobbler and redeye.

Frequently after freshes or rises in river levels silver perch move out of the deeper water well up into rapids and smaller stretches of water. Here they can provide delightful sport on small celta, Hardy's imp and hot shot on light spinning tackle and will sometimes take trout flies of the larger type such as taihape tickler, Mrs Simpson, fuzzy wuzzy and Hamill killer. In Queensland silver perch are renowned for their occasional gathering at the heads of waterholes and flowing reaches and are gaining reputation as a sportfish when taken on light tackle from these locations.

Silver perch are excellent to eat, the flesh being whiter, firmer and drier than that of callop and Murray cod. They are taken extensively in commercial drum nets and gill nets and the annual yield varies between 20,000 and 45,000 kg.

Silver perch have the typical Australian native freshwater fish's tolerance to high water temperatures although they cannot stand prolonged handling during experimental work or during stocking and transporting operations. There have been several instances of large-scale mortalities of silver perch in Burrinjuck Dam in recent years that have not been explained. They are ideal fish for farm dams because they eat both plant and animal material, but will not spawn as they need flood water of set temperature to stimulate breeding.

A number of private individuals and some angling associations and acclimatization societies have succeeded in breeding large numbers of silver perch in captivity for the stocking of dams and lakes. Silver perch have been bred for stocking of Lake Burley Griffin in Canberra, A.C.T. It is generally acknowledged that silver perch show the best possibilities to date for lake stocking with native fish. They are well suited to smoking.

BRYAN PRATT

SILVERSIDES
See Hardyheads or silversides.

SKATES
See Rays.

SMILER
Highly ornamented fish of the family Opisthognathidae, which are represented by several species in Australian waters, most of them between 30 and 45 cm in length and all of them varying considerably in colouring and marking. They are strange fish of coral reefs and rocky areas which Whitley says appear to signal to each other by lowering the dorsal fin. They are also known as harlequins, grinners, jaw fish, monkey fish, pugs and missing links and are believed to incubate their eggs in the mouth. The vividly coloured, figured species are found only in New South Wales and Queensland, others in Western Australia and the Northern Territory.

SMOKING of fish
This may be carried out by either of two processes: hot smoking or cold smoking. Both processes have come into much more general use in Australia in recent years and nowadays most anglers are aware of the palate-appeal of expertly smoked fish and realize that it is not outside their ability or resources to produce it.

Hot smoking
This is quite distinct from cold smoking. It is a method of quickly cooking fish while imparting to it a desirable smoke flavour. Any edible fish may be cooked in this manner and in most cases the flavour is considerably improved by it. It is a popular method of handling the somewhat flavourless fish such as trout, redfin, eel-tail catfish, blue fork-tail catfish, silver trevally and others. It also is very applicable to the more oily and strongly flavoured species such as tailor, mullet, half-grown salmon, barracouta or kingfish.

This process, known in Australia since early times, came into popular use with the introduction of the locally made 'Sportsman' smoker-cooker. There are now several varieties of smoker-cooker on the market. All are easy to use.

The fish is scaled, cleaned and filleted and cut to convenient sizes. An exception to this is trout, which is filleted without scaling, for the scales do not come loose in cooking and the flesh may be lifted cleanly out of the skin. Some species with thick skin, such as redfin, salmon, tropical groper or northern cod are best filleted and then skinned by running a knife through between the skin and the flesh. Weed-eating fish, such as luderick and drummer, also are best skinned.

The grid is set on a sheet of paper and the fillets arranged on it, skin side down, so that they may be heavily salted by sprinkling with fine salt. A little pepper assists in rounding off the flavour, and some gourmet cooks prefer to add a sprinkling of brown sugar. A small measure (about a tablespoon) of selected sawdust is then sprinkled on the bottom of the cooker. The grid and its load of fish are placed in it and the slide-on lid is closed.

The cooking time is regulated by the amount of methylated spirit put into the burner. With light fillets the open container should be a little more than half-filled, so that it burns for 12 to 13 minutes. With thick pieces it should be three-quarters filled, to burn from 16 to 18 minutes. The burner is then set in the centre of the stand, lit with a match and the cooker placed over it. When the spirit is burned out it is allowed to stand for a couple of minutes before removing the lid to reveal beautifully browned smoked fish, ready for immediate eating.

This process may be used to smoke oysters, peeled prawns, mussels or scallops, in fact almost anything that can be rested on the grid. The art of cooking with it lies in applying the heat for just long enough to cook the fish thoroughly. It produces a moist, flaky product with a good smoke flavour, which to some extent depends on the type of sawdust used. It should be free from resins or undesirable gums. Suitable dust may be obtained in small bags from most tackle dealers. In an emergency it is possible to rasp some from dry oak (casuarina), well dried heart wood of long-dead snow gum, gidyea, myall, belah and others.

Cold smoking

This is a much longer process, whereby the fish is cured but not cooked. Cold-smoked fish which has been suitably processed may be stored at room temperature for several weeks or kept in a refrigerator for months. But its chief attraction is the delectable 'smoked-fish' flavour which it imparts.

The angler with a catch to smoke may process it according to his requirements. If he merely wants to convert it to smoked fish to be cooked and eaten in the next few days he may cure it only mildly by cutting down the smoking time. If he wishes to carry it in the refrigerator for a few days longer, the treatment must be more thorough. If it is to be stored at room temperature and kept for some weeks, the curing must be adequate for that purpose. The heavier the salting and smoking the less the original flavour of the fish will predominate.

Almost all of the edible fish may be smoked to good advantage, but perhaps it is a tedious gilding of the lily to smoke highly delectable species such as whiting, bream, mulloway, snapper, flounder, threadfin salmon, coral trout, sweetlips and the other emperors, barramundi and those species which are high-grade table fish in their own right, unless it becomes a matter of necessity in preserving a big catch. Since cold smoking involves more time, it is therefore more economical in man-hours when applied to quantities. Some fish, such as trout, redfin, eel-tail catfish, marine goat fish and others not often taken in big quantities may be more conveniently handled by hot smoking.

Species particularly suitable for cold smoking by the brining process are tailor, blue fork-tail catfish, barracouta, silver trevally, tommy ruff, mullet, the smaller salmon, eels, luderick and fish roes.

Larger species may be adapted to brining by filleting them to strips of appropriate size, but often it is more convenient to treat them in larger pieces by dry salting. Fish of this class include school mackerel, Spanish mackerel, tropical groper, estuary cod, flowery cod, the various rock cods, gummy shark, school shark, Taylor's shark and elephant fish.

A basic fact to keep in mind while cold smoking is that blood and viscera will not cure. Therefore, the cleaning of the fish must be thorough. The head is discarded and all sign of gills and entrails must be removed. All congealed blood from along the backbone and in the region of the gills must be carefully cleared away. It is then thoroughly washed to remove surface blood and visceral slime. Small fish, say up to 340 g may be smoked in the round but somewhat larger specimens are best opened up. This is best done at cleaning, by running the knife along either side of the backbone and removing it along with the dorsal and tail fins. This leaves two fillets still connected along the belly line. Larger fish are filleted in the normal manner.

The fish or fillets then are placed in a leaching bath for 30 minutes to draw blood out of the flesh. This is made up of one cupful of salt to 4.5 L of water. The fillets are briefly rinsed in fresh water to clear away any blood in the solution still clinging to them. Then they are transferred to the brine.

Experience has shown that time of immersion in the brine is more important than its strength, so it is not possible to halve the time by doubling the quantity of salt, for in a given time fish does not take much more from a concentrated solution than it does from one of moderate strength. A good working solution of brine may be made up of 450 g salt, 225 g brown sugar and 14 g saltpetre to each 4.5 L of water. Some experts, particularly when the fish is to be kept only for a short period, omit the saltpetre and add a little more salt.

It should be kept in mind that the fish in the brine takes up a considerable amount of salt, so if a quantity is being treated it should be immersed in an adequate amount of brine to supply the required salt. Within reason, the brine may be used for a small number of batches by adding more salt and brown sugar to maintain effective strength. If it becomes too heavily charged with blood and slime or too exhausted of salt, it will not cure. If there is any doubt as to its quality, it is best to replace it with a new freshly made solution.

Time of immersion in the brine depends upon the size of the fillets and the period of time the product is to keep before cooking. For very light fillets which are to be cooked within three or four days the safe minimum seems to be one hour. For fillets from 340 to 680 g—1½ hours; from 680 to 900 g—2 hours; and fillets from tailor to 2.7 kg—2½ hours. When the product is required to be kept at room temperature for ten days, or more, the fillets should be brined for 12 hours.

During immersion in the brine the salt removes a lot of the body fluids from the flesh and so deprives harmful bacteria of the moisture without which they cannot survive and multiply. The fluids which are extracted from the flesh are partly replaced by salt, which has an inhibiting influence on spoilage bacteria. Most are effectively retarded in their development by a salt content or solution of 5 per cent or more.

According to C.S.I.R.O. research, the ideal condition is reached in brining where there has been an uptake of salt equal to 2 to 2.5 per cent of the weight of the fillet. Unfortunately the angler-smoker has no means of measuring salt content, so he must see that the brine is right and then work on a basis of time of immersion. Firms specializing in butcher's supplies usually can supply commercial preparations, such as 'Tartrazine' or 'Annatto', which may be added to the brine to produce better colouring of the product, but their use is optional.

The fillets will float on the surface of a brine of the correct strength, so a grid, clean board, a weighted plastic dish or some such means must be devised to keep them totally immersed. They should be repacked or stirred from time to time, to ensure that the brine has access to all parts of them.

When they are removed from the brine they are not rinsed, but are drained and then hung to dry. Proper drying is one of the most critical stages in the process. They should be hung by means of wire S hooks to a rail or line in a shady place where there is a good circulation of air. The salt in the brine breaks down a certain amount of muscle tissue and as the fillets dry this forms a glossy film or pellicle on their surfaces. At first it is wet and dripping, but as it dries it becomes tacky. The fish does not have to become bone dry, in fact it would not do so until it had been hung for quite a long time and it would not accept smoke and cure properly if it did. When it is quite tacky and there is no evidence of free or excessive moisture, the fish is ready to go into the smoker.

In warm weather when there is a breeze this setting of the pellicle may take less than two hours. If conditions are not good, say in very humid conditions or in still, cold weather, it may take six hours or even more. A good tacky pellicle helps to absorb the smoke and when it dries out in smoking it acts as a protective seal. If the fish were placed in the smoker while still too wet, it would steam and soften, rather than cure. Smoking would take a good deal more time and the colour and flavour would not be so good. If it were to go into the smoker with a bone dry surface it would not absorb smoke and would dry out instead of curing.

There is no great difficulty in telling when it is at the correct stage of dryness once one has had a little experience, but the beginner is required to use a little judgment. The fish must be tacky enough to stick lightly to the fingers, but there should be no wet brine left. This is emphasized for if it goes into the smoker too moist there is the temptation to counteract slow curing by increasing the heat, which may partly or wholly cook it. If the examination is only cursory, there may be the tendency to assume that it is cured because it has been in long enough, in which case it could come out moist and clammy—a condition which could lead to rapid deterioration or the early formation of mildew. Yes, it should dry to the stage where it is 'stiff tacky' rather than 'wet tacky'.

In drying, the fillets should be kept out of direct sunlight. They could be hung in an open shed, under a stretched canvas, or failing such facilities they could be placed under a shady tree. They should be hung so that they are well separated and air may circulate between them. This is a stage where flies could be a nuisance, so someone may have to swish them away with a leafy bush or arrange fly-proof cover.

A method of dry salting may be used instead of the brining. Some may find this less trouble and not so messy, but it is not so easily controlled, particularly in trying to achieve the lighter degrees of salting for short-time keeping and retention of natural flavour. It is, however, more applicable to the treatment of big fillets and large fish, such as Spanish mackerel, tropical groper, big cod or shark. Processing of large fish in this way calls for a generous supply of salt. Coarse salt may be used, but fine salt is more easily applied and dissolves in the juices more quickly.

The fish is cleaned, washed and leached, as in preparation for brining. A quantity of salt is then placed in a large container or on a plastic sheet and the fish or fillets are dredged in it, taking care to see that it adheres to it or is rubbed in well. Particular care should be taken to see that it is well salted throughout the abdominal cavity if the fish is being treated in the round. A water-tight container, preferably a large shallow one, is required for stacking the fish while they cure. If none is available, suitable accommodation may be contrived by lining a wooden box, or even a stout carton, with a plastic sheet.

The fish is picked up, with as much salt as will adhere, and placed in this container. As the salting continues they are packed in even layers and a moderate sprinkling of salt is spread on top of each layer. The final layer is given a heavier covering of salt.

The time required for salting depends on the nature of the fish, and the period for which it is likely to be kept. Small fish, or chunks from larger ones which have been split down into skinless fillets of moderate thickness, may require as little as six hours. Heavier fish whole, or thick fillets and chunky pieces, may require salt treatment for as long as 12 hours. In cutting skinless fillets from big fish it is advisable to keep them to no more than 2 cm thick. Heavy chunks or thick fillets from big fish, such as Spanish mackerel, should be scored deeply with a knife every couple of centimetres, on the skin side, to allow access of salt and smoke. They need the maximum time of treatment, both in salting and smoking.

When the fish is considered to have been sufficiently salted it is very briefly rinsed in fresh or salt water to remove free salt. It is hung to dry until the pellicle forms and reaches the desirable degree of 'tackiness', as described in connection with brining, then transferred to the smoker for smoke-curing.

Design of smoke-houses

In Australia ideas as to what constitutes a good fish-smoker have changed somewhat in recent years. But it must not be forgotten that the construction of one is often an emergency matter, or has to be carried out in some remote spot where materials are at a premium. Anglers are resourceful people and in emergencies batches of fish have been processed in smokers made entirely of stakes and bushes, but this is a haphazard business and certainly cannot be recommended as a normal procedure.

Where there is some degree of permanence, as in the angler's backyard or at a seaside shack, pains may be taken to build a highly efficient smoker from suitable materials. The old style of smoke-house, where the fish is smoked over the fire, is now ruled out, excepting for emergency purposes. It works at too high a temperature, the fire is too difficult to get at to replenish or control and the only practical fuel is sawdust. The structure with an external fire pit and smoke tunnel is more efficient, more convenient to operate, gives better control of the fire and the smoking temperature and allows the use of alternative fuels.

The nature of the structure, its size and the materials used may depend on the frequency with which it is operated, the size of the batches to be smoked and the resources available. For small quantities at infrequent intervals the drum smoker shown in the accompanying sketches would be hard to better. The top is removed from a suitable 220 L drum and a large hole cut in the bottom. It is set over a small pit, from which a smoke tunnel runs underground for 2 to 2.5 m to a fire pit,

SMOKING of fish

FISH SMOKERS

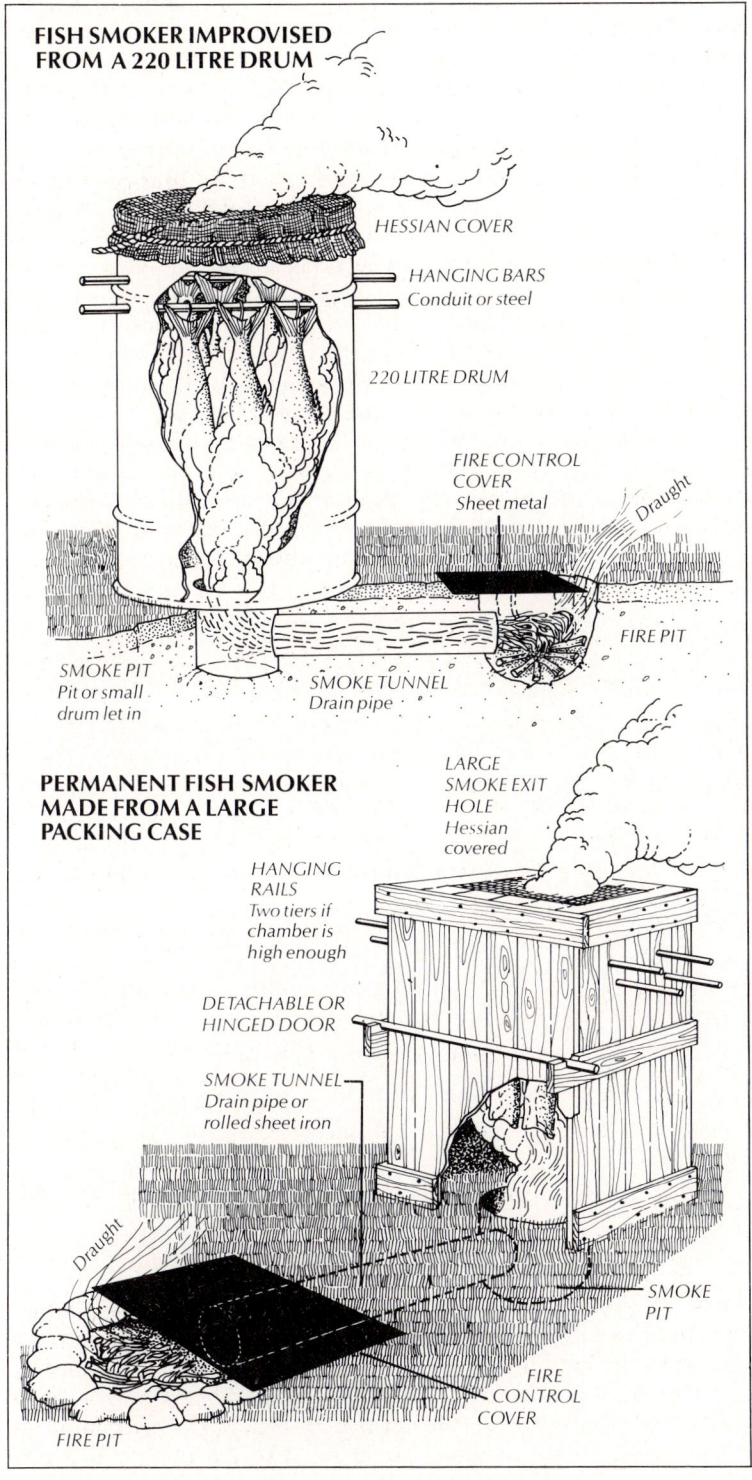

FISH SMOKER IMPROVISED FROM A 220 LITRE DRUM

HESSIAN COVER

HANGING BARS
Conduit or steel

220 LITRE DRUM

FIRE CONTROL COVER
Sheet metal

Draught

FIRE PIT

SMOKE PIT
Pit or small drum let in

SMOKE TUNNEL
Drain pipe

PERMANENT FISH SMOKER MADE FROM A LARGE PACKING CASE

LARGE SMOKE EXIT HOLE
Hessian covered

HANGING RAILS
Two tiers if chamber is high enough

DETACHABLE OR HINGED DOOR

SMOKE TUNNEL
Drain pipe or rolled sheet iron

Draught

SMOKE PIT

FIRE CONTROL COVER

FIRE PIT

which is dug deep enough to have its bed 7 to 10 cm below the underside of the tunnel. A flat metal sheet is used as a cover to control the fire.

Cross bars are inserted through holes in the sides to provide a means of hanging the fillets on S hooks. A hessian cover is tied over the open top to retain the smoke, yet to allow sufficient escape to provide a moderate draught through the tunnel. If the lie of the land allows it, there is some advantage to be gained from erecting it on a slope so that some moderate inclination assists in getting the tunnel to draw. It also is a good idea to have the tunnel run in the same direction as the prevailing wind. The tunnel may be contrived from earthen drain pipe or large diameter downpipe.

The drum should be clean and never should have contained any poisonous pesticide or other such substance. It is very important though to warn that the cutting should be done with a cold chisel and not an oxy-acetylene torch. Drums which have contained motor fuels may release enough vapour from the seams when heated, even after washing with warm water and detergent, to cause a serious explosion.

A similar smoke-house to take a larger load of fish is shown in the second sketch. Here the smoke chamber may be a large wooden case, made from a combination of timber and flat iron, or even corn bags tacked onto a frame. The smoke still enters from the tunnel through a large hole at the centre of the bottom. Hessian still is used at the top to allow egress of smoke. The door could be hinged or a sheet of detachable metal or a corn bag tacked in place. The tunnel may be contrived by rolling a discarded sheet of galvanised iron or similar material to a diameter of 20 to 25 cm.

Discarded kerosene refrigerators are sometimes found around seaside shacks. One of these may be converted to an excellent smoke-box if the works are removed and large holes are cut in the bottom and top for ingress and egress of smoke. The sliding racks provide a means of loading the fillets in, skin side down, though some smoker experts prefer to always hang them with the thick end down.

The old style, over-the-fire smoker is less efficient and more difficult to operate, but in emergency or with limited material it may be the obvious one to construct. At a pinch it may be erected from a few stakes, a roll of hessian or some canvas from a discarded tent and some clouts or nails. The sketch shows how the frame and fire pit should be arranged. If hessian is used for the walls it may be necessary to lean bushes against it or provide other cover on the windward side to prevent the wind blowing the smoke through before it reaches the fish.

With hessian or canvas the fire risk is high, for sparks could be blown up out of the fire pit. This is best made by sinking about one-third of the length of a 22 L drum into the earth at the centre of the smoker. Of course, if materials are available

Life history

Not a great deal is known of the snapper's biology although some research is being undertaken in New Zealand because of the species' importance in the commercial fish landings.

Snapper spawn in spring and early summer in moderately sheltered waters near the entrance to estuaries, bays and gulfs. The spherical eggs, about 1 mm in diameter, are externally fertilized and then float at or near the surface for one or two days before hatching.

The larvae and very young fish are presumably midwater or bottom-dwelling, since none have so far been taken in surface plankton hauls over known spawning grounds. The smallest snapper generally seen are about 2.5 cm long and probably a month or two old, at which size they are perfect miniatures of the adult fish, even to tiny blue spots along the back. Their general body colouring is similar, but with five vertical bands of darker pink. They are often taken in shallow water in small-mesh piper garfish or herring dragnets. Their favourite habitat seems to be in the channels and gutters dissecting mudbanks and sandbars in shallow tidal bays, particularly where a bed of eelgrass, a zone of seaweed or a mudstone or rocky reef provides a food supply and shelter from large, predatory fish.

The young-of-the-year fish (cockney bream in Australia) grow to about 10 cm by the end of their first summer. The arrival of cold winter weather drives them, together with most other small fish, out from the shallow water and they winter in the deeper channels near or outside the harbour mouths. The following spring they return inshore.

These seasonal inshore-offshore movements become more pronounced as the fish grow and when they mature at the end of their third or fourth year, at 20 to 30 cm, the movements are reinforced by the spawning migration. Large groups of adult school snapper congregate in certain areas at some time between late winter and early summer prior to and during spawning, depending on the locality and prevailing water temperatures. Fishermen believe that some of these schools of snapper may travel a considerable distance between the time they first assemble and when they actually spawn, but there is as yet no direct evidence of this. The spawning itself, the time when both male and female fish in the school have running ripe roes, may be over in a week or so at any one locality, but may vary in timing between different localities by several months. After spawning, the schools gradually disperse, the fish moving first to inshore feeding grounds in late summer and autumn and then out to deeper grounds in the winter. Large snapper, alternatively, may remain inshore during the winter.

A certain proportion of the snapper population, particularly those fish inhabiting rocky coastlines and reefs, is less migratory and may stay in the same area for several years. Tagging experiments on adult snapper in New Zealand have not revealed any long-distance migrations; most tagged fish were recaptured near their original tagging sites and the short distances travelled by the others were consistent with the theory of inshore spawning movements during summer.

Age and growth rates

Determining the age and growth of snapper is not merely an academic exercise. Scientists can use this information to work out the 'age-structure' of a population, that is, whether it is composed of young, middle-aged or old fish and then make predictions on the future abundance of snapper in that locality. A super-abundance of three-year-old juveniles, for example, should provide a good crop of sizeable adults in five to 10 years' time when they have grown to 40 or 60 cm in length.

The scales of a snapper, like those of most fish, show growth rings, which provide a considerable amount of valuable information on the growth history of the fish. Usually one ring is formed each year, marking the winter months when body growth virtually ceases. Eight rings would mean the fish had passed through eight winters; widely spaced rings would mean a fast-growing fish and so on. The scale rings can be seen with the naked eye, but are best studied under a lens or microscope, or by making an enlarged photographic print using the scale itself as a negative.

Present research indicates that the snapper is a relatively slow-growing fish. Growth rates vary considerably between localities and presumably depend on the water temperature and food supply. Individual fish vary; a five-year-old may be from 22 to 32 cm. From 30 cm onwards snapper grow about 12 mm per year, the amount decreasing annually. New Zealand west coast fish appear to grow faster than the above rate and they certainly grow bigger than on the east. Snapper take four to five years to reach 450 g in weight, and seven to 10 years to reach 1 kg. Weight gain in subsequent years is probably more rapid. These are conservative estimates from limited research data; in favourable localities the growth rate would undoubtedly be greater. Old man snapper from 10 to 13 kg may have 25 or more scale growth rings and are undoubtedly very old fish.

Snapper differ so much between localities that it is impossible to give an average or maximum size. The smaller school snapper range from 800 g to 2 kg, while reef snapper probably range from 2 to 4.5 kg. Whitley credits one fish with having grown to 1.3 m and 20 kg. Equally big fish, usually 'the one that got away', are reported by anglers from time to time.

Snapper feeding

As anybody who has cleaned a snapper will know, these fish feed on a wide variety of marine organisms. The very young fish feed mainly on small planktonic and bottom-dwelling

Snappers, distinguished by the large bulge on their heads when they reach maturity, are a marvellous food fish, growing to 1.3 m and reaching 20 kg.

crustaceans, while larger juveniles feed on similar but larger crustaceans, also brittlestars, various marine worms, gastropod and bivalve shellfish and small fish. Adult fish apparently feed on whatever is locally most abundant, from the soft salps or 'chain jelly' in the plankton to hard-shelled molluscs. Small herring-type fish are also eaten, particularly during summer when schools of these small fish are abundant inshore.

Sometimes a group of snapper will feed almost exclusively on one kind of animal, such as planktonic jellyfish and salps, chitons scraped off rocks, mud crabs taken in tidal creeks, juvenile flounder from a tidal mudflat, one particular type of shellfish from a sandy or muddy bottom, or anchovies or sprats from a shallow bay. Anglers can use this characteristic to their advantage by observing the gut contents of the first snapper caught and then baiting their hooks accordingly.

The commercial snapper fishery

In Australia, snapper form a relatively minor part of the overall commercial fish catch. Although the fishing grounds extend as far north as Fraser Island in Queensland and Shark Bay in Western Australia most of the catch is taken in New South Wales waters. In Western Australia (principally Shark Bay) and South Australia, snapper is an important commercial fish.

Most of the boats engaged in snapper fishing also take part in other fisheries, such as prawn, crayfish, snook, shark and whiting. They employ a variety of fishing methods: gill-netting, long-lining, handlining, beach seining, ring netting, trapping, Danish seining, and otter trawling. The last two methods are used on the south-east trawl grounds between Port Macquarie in New South Wales and Bass Strait. Steam trawlers operated from 1915 onwards, but became uneconomic after World War II; Danish seiners started in 1936 and there has been a recent revival of interest in motor-trawling with Vigneron-dahl gear. While the main species taken by trawling and Danish seining are morwong and tiger flathead, quantities of snapper are being caught. Overall, catches of snapper are made throughout the year, with the heaviest catches in the north during winter and in the south during summer.

Snapper angling
Snapper are sought by anglers in southern Australia and northern New Zealand, from Geraldton on the Western Australian coast and Bowen on the Queensland coast south to Cook Strait, New Zealand. They can be taken north and south of these limits, but with less regularity. In Australia there is a general distribution of big fish along the open, exposed coasts and smaller fish in the bays and estuaries, though there are many local exceptions. To be successful, a fisherman must get to know the movements and habits of snapper in his own area.

Eastern and southern Australia
In spring there is an inshore movement of snapper before they spawn. Big snapper start to appear around the ocean rocks along the mid-coast of New South Wales in August and are fairly plentiful until the end of October. From August to October the runs of snapper enter Port Phillip Bay. For a time they mill around and probably spawn on grounds off Ellwood before dispersing to numerous reefs in the bay. They usually take a few weeks to recover before they start taking baits again. A second run of smaller snapper occurs in December and together with the big fish they provide good sport until March and April when there is a general departure. A survey of snapper reports has shown that the majority of big snapper caught in southern Australia are taken in darkness or in the brief half light preceding or following it.

The young cockney bream, up to 12 cm, hungry little pink fish that frequently infest the bays and tidal lakes, particularly around the sand flats and in the inlets near shore, are usually foremost among the 'pickers' that strip the angler's hooks of baits intended for larger snapper, whiting, bream, and flathead. When the cockney bream exceed 12 cm they become known as red bream; during this phase of their development they still thrive in the deeper inlets as well as offshore, but are more likely to be found in the vicinity of deeper holes and channels. At about 30 cm in length they are called squire, and having reached a legally and domestically acceptable size they are a welcome addition to the angler's catch.

Western Australia
Cockburn Sound, the big natural harbour south of Fremantle, has many offshore lumps and coral patches where big snapper feed. But in the winter, during the roughest storms, these snapper come close to shore and are caught at Palm Beach, Naval Base, Woodmans and Robb Jetty. Most weigh between 5 and 10 kg though fish over 14 kg are occasionally landed. Early in 1969 a boat fisherman gaffed up the floating head-half of a big humpheaded old man pink. A curved shark bite mark told the story of the missing half. The top half weighed about 18 kg.

Western Australian big snapper fishermen on the shore use squid and octopus, half mullet or other small fish, usually on an 8/0 or 10/0 hook.

Pink snapper take deepwater baits from Esperance round to Onslow. They take a smaller hook than jewfish *Glaucosoma hebraicum* and most west coast deepsea rigs are baited paternoster style, with a big hook below for jewie and a smaller hook above, 2/0 to 5/0, for snapper. A snapper's tug-tug bite is easily distinguished from a jewfish's ponderous fumblings. Other fish which take the 'snapper' hook on a deepsea rig include baldchin groper, red rock cod, sweep and blue morwong. Average snapper caught 'outside' in Western Australia are between 5 and 10 kg but each autumn a run of squire occurs off Perth's northern coastline. These take smaller hooks and baits and are often caught so fast that four or five dozen 450 g to 2 kg fish may be boated.

Shark Bay is the home of west coast pink snapper. Immense schools which once used to provide a thriving industry have been depleted to the extent that professionals now find them hardly profitable. There is a curious theory about the disappearance of snapper from big areas of Shark Bay. The old Asian pearl-diver fishermen used to say that if one used snapper bait to catch snapper, one would catch fish all right, but snapper might never return to that spot. Of course, when snapper fishing became big business in Western Australia in the 1950s professionals were not fussy about what bait they used when the snapper were biting madly. They also used to clean and gut their catches over snapper grounds which, according to the theory, had the same effect on the snapper living below. A final blow came with the use of snapper traps. Huge cylindrical drums of wire netting, they were dropped onto snapper patches. Not only did they ruin the coral in which snapper fed, but they were occasionally mislaid, or left lie during a spell of bad weather. If this happened, snapper would continue to enter a trap to feed on the bodies of earlier prisoners. And this, according to the old story, also helped scare them away.

Today snapper boats still operate off Shark Bay every May and June, but they never use snapper bait and they always clean their catches miles away from snapper country. Amateur fishermen who trail boats 800 km from Perth for a weekend among the snapper often bring home huge quantities of fillets. The professionals say that amateurs are continuing to make the mistakes that frightened early schools away and are also catching too many undersize fish. Shark Bay's spawning grounds abound with snapper but a bag limit of 10 a day is in force.

Another fish often taken by Shark Bay snapper fishermen is the black snapper or painted sweetlips *Plectorhynchus pictus*. It is a northern species, more related to the sweetlips family than the southern pinks. They grow to about 8 kg and are just as good eating as the pinks, some say better. More significantly, the black snapper can be used as a bait for pink snapper without endangering future fishing.

Black snapper are not regular biters in areas outside Shark Bay. North of Carnarvon another type of snapper becomes common, the yellow sweetlips, spangled emperor or, as it is also known, the north-west snapper. The north-west snapper has a colourful coat of blue spangled with gold, which may become quite brown or silver, depending on the country he lives in. They are caught both in deep water and close to shore, are powerful fighters and like big baits.

Where, when and how to catch snapper
As the distribution and seasonal movements of the various size groups of snapper are quite complicated and as they vary somewhat in different areas, the angler must get to know his own fishing grounds. There are few simple rules to snapper fishing and only some general guidelines are given here. The rest must come with experience. The keenest and most experienced boat anglers get up before dawn to get out to favoured reefs by daylight, as snapper generally bite best from dawn until a little after sunrise. This is usually also the calmest period of the day, before the prevailing winds blow up between 8 and 9 a.m.

In Australia the best snapper fishing is had over reefs and gravelly bottom, but good catches are also taken over clear bottom. The larger runabouts and launches use modern echo-sounders to locate offshore reefs. The sounders show the depth as bleeps on a cathode ray tube, as flashing lights on a dial or as a tracing of the bottom contours on sensitized paper; with practice, the type of bottom—mud, sand or rock—can also be interpreted from the strength of the echoes.

Without sounders boat anglers must use known cross-bearings on coastal land-marks or drift-fish with the current until they find the snapper, anchoring or kellicking when they come to the best patches. Drifting over reefs or rough ground is a good way to locate snapper—as long as you can afford the occasional piece of gear which snags on the bottom. The speed of the drift is crucial, as it becomes impossible to get the bait down to the snapper and keep it there if the drift is too fast or the current too strong. This is one reason why it is important to get out to the chosen area at the right stage of the tide. The other reason the tide is important is that it controls much of the behaviour of the snapper.

In open water snapper generally bite best around the turn of the tide, particularly near eddies and the edges of tidal streams. There are many theories for this: the fish follow the moving current edge, the tidestream uncovering hidden food organisms, the brisker water stimulating feeding activity and so on, but these remain unproven. In inshore areas snapper tend to move into the shallows on a rising evening tide to feed, either among the seaweed and boulders or in the surf zone of a beach or on the mudflats and in the tidal creeks of an estuary.

Snapper are usually bottom feeders, but at certain times can be taken on baits fished in midwater or at the surface. When big snapper are in along the rocks some anglers throw garfish or other bait pieces from the tops of cliffs at daybreak and wait for snapper to take them as they float near the surface.

Schools of snapper sometimes work below surface kahawai schools, feeding on the pieces of herring and sprat which drift down. It is worthwhile drift-fishing through such an area, with lines set below the kahawai level (if set too high simultaneous kahawai strikes may cause a terrific tangle). The snapper school may follow its prey right up to the surface, feeding savagely and providing a treat for the angler who can work carefully into such a school without causing it to sound.

Snapper can be taken on almost any rig, but one of the most popular in Australia involves a running sinker or 'snapper boom'. This essentially allows the line to run freely through or past the sinker, so that the snapper is unencumbered by any weight during its first run, giving time for the bait to be swallowed and the hook set firmly by the angler's first strike. It also allows the bait to float naturally a short distance above the bottom, at a desired distance away from the shore or boat. Several such lines can be effectively fished by one or two anglers, but they tangle more easily than the simple bottom rigs if used by many fishermen in one boat. With a light sinker such a line is very effective as an unattended 'stray line' drifted back in the current well behind the boat; it will often catch as much or more snapper (with an occasional kahawai, trevally and barracouta) than three or four lines bottom-fished below the boat. The latter will, of course, take more bottom fish, so that two types of fishing can be carried on at the same time. In Australian waters almost all offshore snapper fishing is done by bottom-fishing reefs.

The relative success of an unattended line, whether it is a stray line over the stern or a temporarily slack bottom rig, is attributed by some fishermen to the absence of vibrations normally present in a tautly held line. The running-sinker rig is particularly effective for the plump, medium-sized school snapper which come inshore in summer.

Snapper hooks and bait
The mouth of a good snapper is hard and bony and can blunt, crush or break weak hooks. For the big fish of the species French and beak hooks are recommended and sometimes the O'Shaughnessy, up to 8/0 to 10/0 for the Australian old man snapper. For small to medium fish sizes 1/0 to 4/0 are appropriate. The strongly recurved rolling hooks, about size 2/0 with a short shank, used by the Japanese on their commercial longlines are very effective in holding medium-sized snapper. The weight of the sinker will depend on whether fishing is done from shore or a boat, on the strength of the current, the type of rig used and on the personal preferences of each angler; the normal weight range is 100 to 450 g.

Most snapper anglers use 4.5 to 9 kg monofilament nylon or slightly heavier if the bottom is rough, on a rod and reel. Heavier braided nylon or terylene handlines are used in some areas where larger species, such as groper, are sometimes caught and fishermen using these are often regarded as 'skull-draggers' or 'meat-fishermen' by those purists using rods and light tackle. The latter sometimes do not realise that the handline trace holding the snapper may be as frail as their own gear and that there is as much skill (and more finger-burning) involved in handlining a vigorous snapper as there is in pumping and winding a rod and reel.

Snapper will bite on almost any bait. Australian anglers have found that live yellowtail are very good bait for the big fish, as are small sea garfish, pilchards, mullet and other similar small fish. Small squid are good and fresh king prawns frequently are effective. Those who fish Westernport Bay contend that bonito is the best snapper bait in that bay, though the few who can procure it still use craytail. The smaller snapper are less selective and take readily to cuttlefish, squid, garfish strips, yellowtail, mullet cubes and fresh prawns. In Victoria and South Australia pilchards, whitebait, pipis, mussels, bay salmon, beach worms and a variety of cut-fish baits are used, such as jack mackerel (cowanyoung), sergeant baker, kingfish, blue mackerel and nannygai.

See Cookery.

SOLE *See Flatfish.*

SOUTH Australia The South Australian coastline measures 4038 km and this includes 651 km of coastline around twenty-three offshore islands. The main coastline stretches in a gentle curve from east to west and is washed by the same ocean. But there are distinct current changes at various points and a warmth in the water which banks up in the two large gulfs that dominate the coastline.

Until recently South Australia's prominence in angling stemmed from the world record white sharks taken around Dangerous Reef, Kangaroo Island and along the west coast at Ceduna and Streaky Bay. All the seven fish weighing more than an imperial ton (2240 lb — 1015 kg) that have so far been taken in the world on rod and reel were caught in these waters, six by the same man, Alf Dean, a farmer from Irymple, Victoria, and the seventh by the late television personality Bob Dyer.

Over the past few years, however, tuna have also placed South Australia on the world record charts and no fewer than four world record claims for tuna were made in May and June, 1980. Perhaps more significantly, broadbill swordfish have been sighted in South Australian waters. They are harpooned or netted each year in the month of August at the top of St Vincent Gulf, offshore from Port Wakefield. In 1985 one was even lassoed in the North Arm of the Port Adelaide river. This suggested that this prize gamefish might be caught off South Australia by game fishermen prepared to risk the unpleasant August weather.

According to the most recent figures published, there are 472 marine, brackish and freshwater fish in South Australian waters. This is not a large fish fauna compared with other Australian States and is dwarfed by the Barrier Reef area, but several species are so abundant they provide a valuable commercial fishery. The visitor soon discovers that the South Australian coastline runs through warmer latitudes than he imagines and because of this many outstanding species of first rate sporting and table quality are freely available. Huge catches of Australian salmon, bluefin tuna, snapper, whiting and sea mullet are made, but freshwater anglers are hampered by so many rivers drying up in summer.

Saltwater angling in South Australia
With a wide choice of fishing grounds with all their variety, it is understandable that saltwater angling is developing rapidly in South Australia. In 1960 one could count on two hands the number of surf rods in use along any stretch of beach and you would hardly ever see a rock fisherman. Today anglers stand like pickets on a fence, side by side for as far as the eye can see on South Australian beaches. A good example is Waitpinga Beach which is some 105 km south of Adelaide. On any Sunday between April and August the number of anglers on this stretch of beach is considerable.

Boat fishing as a sport in South Australia has boomed during the last few years. It started in Adelaide and spread in all directions. As each new area was discovered to be productive so the boats went further and further afield until it has reached a stage where trailer boat owners will travel 650 to 800 km for a week of whiting fishing.

Spotted or King George whiting in South Australia and Western Australian waters (not to be confused with the sand whiting of the eastern Australian coastline) have reached 4.5 kg. The bag limit of 30 per person per day is often reached, although they can only be retained if they are more than 28 cm in length.

In South Australia the fishing varies a good deal with the time of the year. In the south-east summer is best. In the gulfs, it is good all the year round, but from a comfort viewpoint summer and autumn are the more enjoyable times. These gulfs, whilst totally enclosed, can get mighty rough during the boisterous winter weather and many lives have been lost as a result of risking the elements. On the west coast there is a saying that it breeds storms and 'whoppers' and it is a rough, rugged coastline largely inaccessible to anything but four-wheel-drive vehicles, except around the main towns along the shore. Often a party will go to the west coast for a fortnight and not be able to fish from the rocks or beach at all due to inclement weather. On the other hand, should the weather clear for one or two days the week's wait for the break in the weather could be handsomely rewarded.

The offshore islands are at their best from November to mid-June and are probably the best all-around fishing grounds in the State, as seldom a day passes when it is not possible to fish from a lee shore. The Group Islands are now accessible by a charter service from Tumby Bay, and Wedge Island and Spilsby Island may be hired for short periods. Boats are provided along with amenities at reasonable rates.

South Australian saltwater angling falls conveniently into four zones and each can be treated as a separate entity:

The south-east coast

This section extends roughly from the Victorian border to Backstairs Passage, some 110 km south of Adelaide. This stretch of coastline is approximately 590 km long and is made up of long barren ocean beaches broken here and there by relatively low limestone cliffs and odd granite outcrops. The longest stretch of beach is aptly termed Long Beach and measures some 210 km from the Cape Jaffa region to the mouth of the Murray River. Rock fishing in this zone is reasonably good, with catches of salmon, snapper, mullet and garfish fairly common.

The beaches, however, present local anglers with a bonanza in the form of mulloway, salmon, bream, school shark, snapper, whiting and flathead. The whiting is, of course, the silver whiting and should not be confused with the King George or spotted whiting also found in abundance in South Australia. The south-eastern zone is most productive from an angler's viewpoint during the months of December through to May.

A splendid fishing area within this zone is the Coorong, a

South-east coast – Adelaide

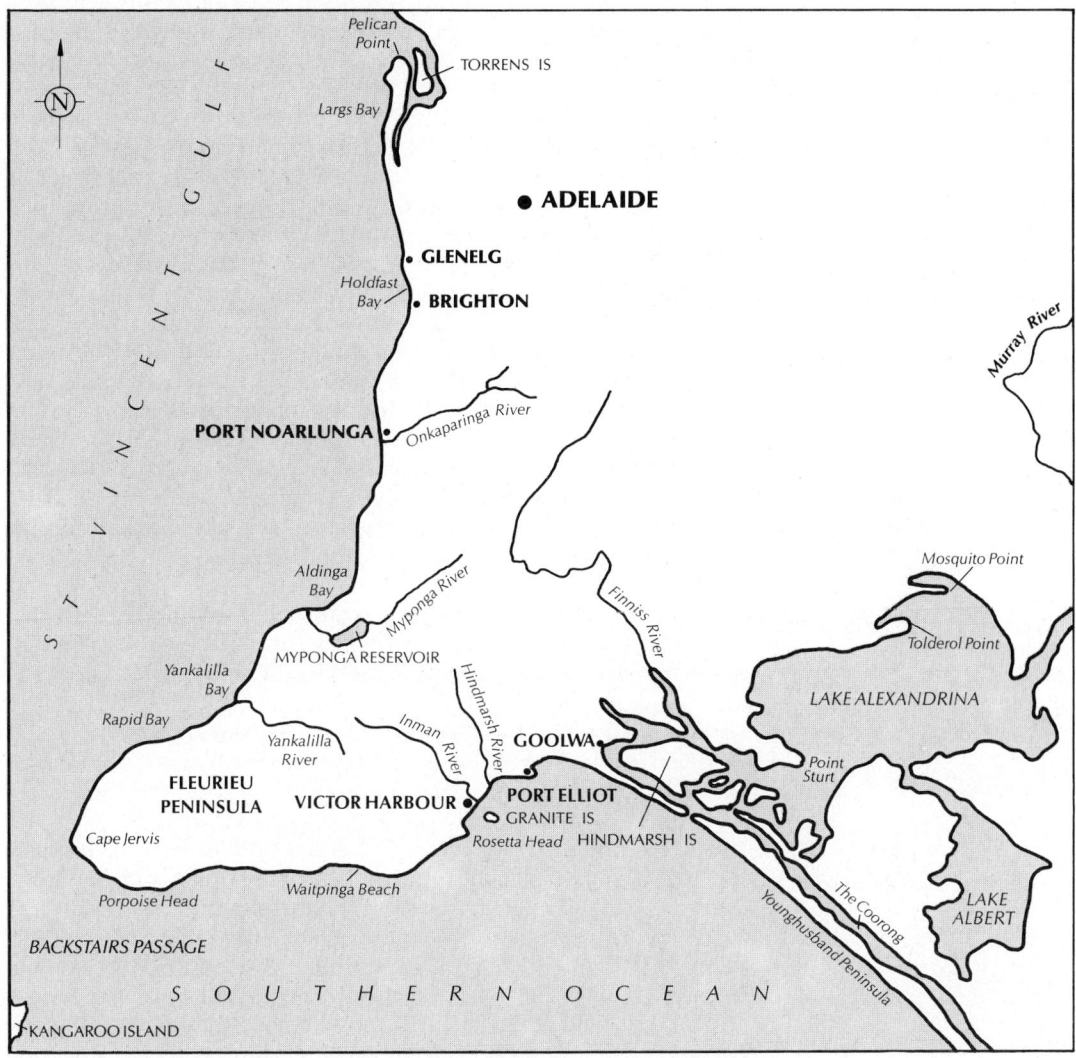

long, narrow body of salt water, some 130 km in length, which is productive all the year round and it literally teems with bream, mulloway, salmon trout and mullet. In the summer flounder are speared in large numbers in the Coorong.

Access to the seaward side of the Coorong for mulloway and school shark is difficult but can be achieved with local guides and a Land-Rover. Location of deeper gutters along the beach enables either salmon spinning—preferably in winter—or bottom fishing with bait and linked hooks for either mulloway or gummy shark. The wreck site at the 65 km section of Long Beach is considered a hotspot. Access signs are situated a few kilometres east of Salt Creek settlement.

S ■ SOUTH Australia

The south-east has a fishing atmosphere all its own. Travelling from Adelaide, a continuing series of small fishing villages behind sandhills and broken low cliffs offer a wide choice for visitors. Choosing between Kingston, Robe, Beachport, South End and Port MacDonnell depends mostly on where you come from—Port MacDonnell, Donnivans or Nelson (across the Victorian border) are the popular choice with people from Mt Gambier. The Donnivans section of the Glenelg River is within South Australia and here South Australian regulations apply. Progress behind the sandhills and around the lakes of this region is best made in a four-wheel-drive vehicle.

As well as the usual salmon, sweep, trevally, whiting and tommy ruff of the south, the reefs are rich with southern rock lobster and this is one region in Australia where amateurs often fish for crays in preference to fish. Deepsea fishing is excellent and the deeper lobster pots occasionally bring in the giant crabs which are mostly used as souvenirs. They are too imposing to eat and too large for anything up to a 55 L pot. Salmon spinning is probably the most popular sporting method locally. The rocks and beaches will provide salmon up to 5 kg, and the estuaries offer smaller ones.

The gulf waters This section of coast covers the waters of the Spencer Gulf and St Vincent Gulf, which are virtually seas in their own right. Spencer Gulf, for example, is roughly 320 km in length and 130 km wide at its widest point. St Vincent Gulf is somewhat smaller and is the most popular boat fishing area in the State. Virtually every known species of South Australian fish can be taken here throughout the year.

The gulf waters are always much warmer than those of the ocean immediately south and one has only to look at the map of the State to see that Kangaroo Island, Althorp Island, Wedge Island, Thistle Island, Pearson Island and Dangerous Reef form a natural barrier which restricts the bulk of the water leaving the gulfs during any tidal movement. The average depth of the gulf is 18 m, the average width is 64 km, the length is 320 km and this volume of water cannot force its way through the small gaps between the islands during any tide cycle. For this very reason the gulf waters do not change quickly enough to become cold and fish are inclined to linger in the warm water.

The west coast This piece of coastline, in excess of 1900 km, stretches from Port Lincoln to Eucla and comprises hundreds of small and large white sandy beaches, high, rugged cliffs which sometimes stretch for kilometres without a break, rugged granite outcrops, countless small offshore islands and snug sheltered bays and coves. Much of this area is still largely unexplored by even the most ardent professional or amateur angler. Groper, salmon, snapper, spotted whiting, trevally, tuna and many other sporting fish abound in this area. Several South

St Vincent Gulf – West coast

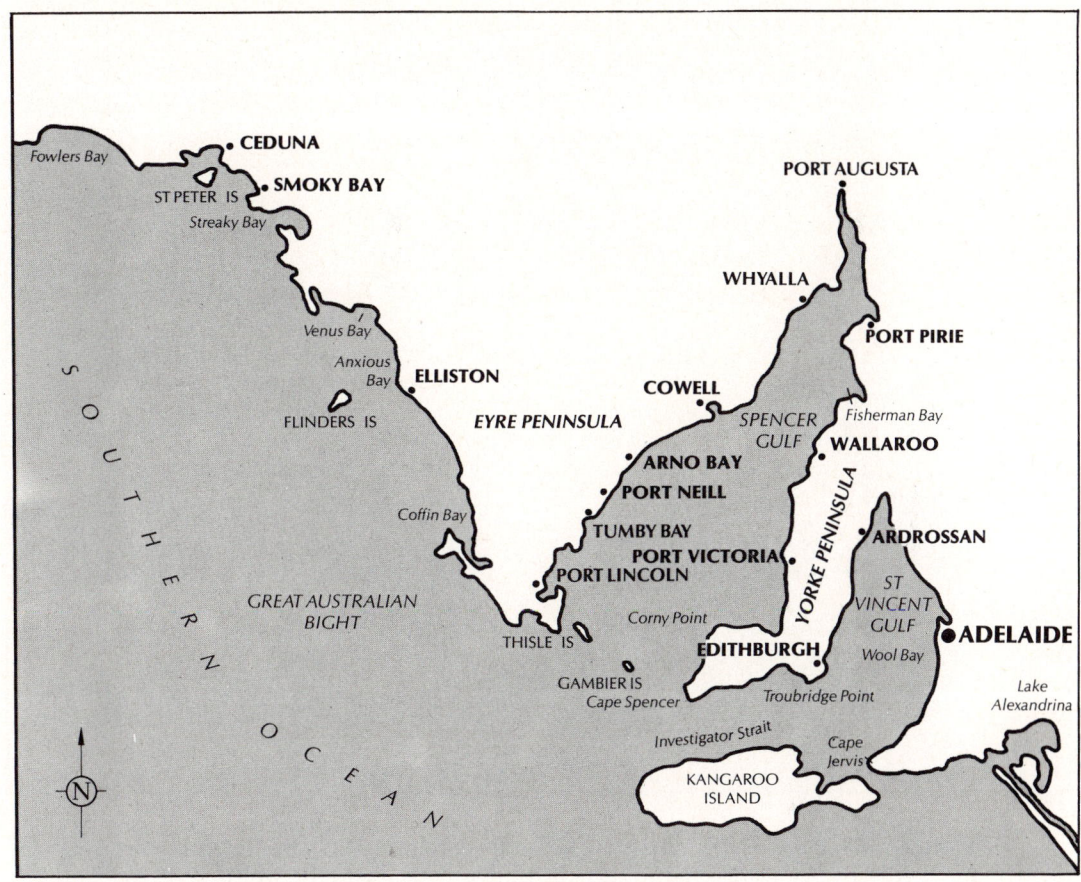

Australian anglers have devoted five years largely to this area and travelled 36,800 km in four-wheel-drive vehicles and have still not covered the whole coastline.

These islands are spread over an enormous area, although, in essence, they have little coastline length and the effective fishing grounds comprise the northern coastlines of each island. Kangaroo Island, Wedge Island, Thistle Island, Pearson Island, Flinders Island and Greenlee Island are but a few of these. Kangaroo Island, the second largest Australian island after Melville Island, Northern Territory, obviously predominates. These offshore islands are well south of the coastal main currents and as a result the same species of fish taken on the west coast are taken from these islands, but at completely different times of the year. Tailor and salmon, for example, are more prevalent on the west coast during October, November and December, whereas from the southern coastline of the offshore islands, March, April, May and June are preferable.

The offshore islands

Kangaroo Island

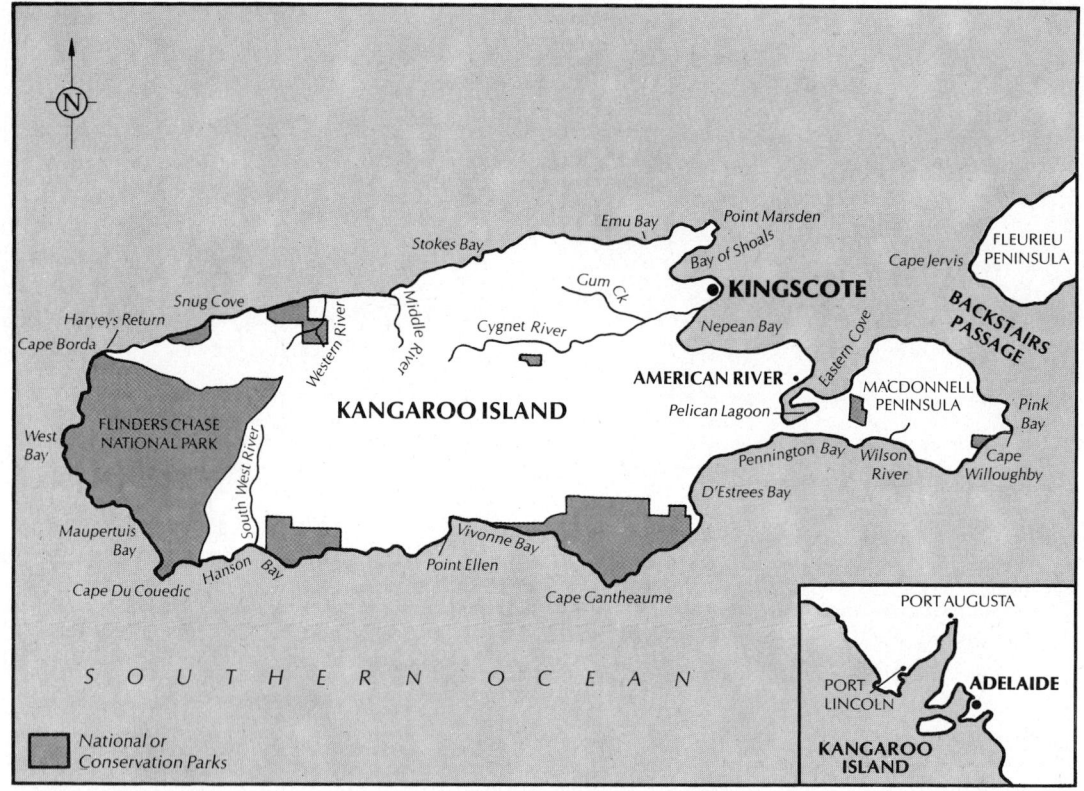

Kangaroo Island One of the best angling fishing trips easily available in South Australia can be had at surprisingly small cost by taking a motor ferry which carries tourists and their cars from Cape Jervis to the island, a farming area about 145 km long and up to 55 km wide. Most experts agree the sporting potential of this region has barely been touched. Most make a round trip via Kangaroo Island to Port Lincoln and return around the Gulf.

Several small streams on the island abound with bream for those who like quiet fishing with light tackle. The main bream streams are the Cygnet, Middle and Harriet. Several small creeks also yield good fish. Spinning for big blackback salmon usually reaches a peak in mid-winter, when huge shoals blacken the water under the cliffs. The main townships are Kingscote and Penneshaw and there are guest houses at American River. Accommodation includes hotels, camping grounds and guesthouses.

Game fishing boats use the island as a base and as well as the great white sharks notorious in southern waters there are shoals of tuna which have made Port Lincoln (west coast) among the best spots in Australia for commercial fishing.

The southern tip of Kangaroo Island is one of Australia's most remote fishing spots, but, as in the other waters of the Great Australian Bight, there is a wide variety of species.

The coastline of Kangaroo Island produces most species of southern sea fish and access is by good roads to most regions. The eastern end of the island is sufficiently rugged to produce sheltered water whatever the direction from which the wind is blowing.

The discovery in the early 1980s that the seas south of Kangaroo Island contained world-class bluefin tuna, excellent snapper, big sharks, barracouta and snook, triggered a rush to the area by fishermen despite well-known hazards. The area was noted for big seas, lacked mooring and fuelling facilities, and was a day's cruising from safe anchorages, but nobody doubted that anglers' enthusiasm would quickly result in exciting development. The venture out of the sheltered waters of St Vincent Gulf appeared certain to attract world attention to South Australian game fishing in waters further south.

Notable fish in South Australia

Surf fishermen from other States would revel among the hordes of Australian salmon which inhabit the beaches between April and August, while snapper, trevally and garfish are abundant.

Visitors to South Australia intent on a good fishing holiday should decide before their visit the type of fish they wish to concentrate on as in a limited time weather could make or break the trip. They should also carefully organize their itinerary, as facilities are best in areas such as Mt Gambier, Naracoorte, Adelaide, Victor Harbour, Wallaroo, Port Lincoln, Kangaroo Island, Streaky Bay and Ceduna, but deteriorate as the townships diminish in size. But it's hard to criticize a State that limits catches of its succulent whiting to 30 a day!

Game fishing in South Australia

Eastern States anglers will have trouble in South Australia in securing the services of charter boats during the game fishing season, as this coincides with the rock lobster season. Professionals who could earn big money every day from crayfishing are understandably loath to accept anything less for charter work. There are odd exceptions, namely, at Kingscote and American River on Kangaroo Island, and Port Lincoln and Coffin Bay. Arrangements should always be made well in advance if possible.

Recommended tackle in South Australia

Basic angling techniques differ little between South Australia and any other State when they relate to rock, beach and boat fishing. The same gear is standard in South Australia as it is in other States. Sidecast exponents hold their own, threadline reel enthusiasts find ample scope for their chosen type of tackle and overhead geared reel fans are well represented. In short, what is suitable for tailor in New South Wales is suitable for tailor, salmon and mulloway in South Australia. Tackle that is suitable for trout in the Snowy is suitable for the Torrens Gorge and the Finnis River. Victorians who prefer salmon will find their gear, suited to Victoria, also works in South Australia. Game fishermen, on the other hand, may need heavier tackle than they are accustomed to if they seek record white sharks, or bluefin or yellowfin tuna.

South Australia's fishing laws

Fishing regulations are strictly enforced and the penalties for law-breaking are severe—a fine of $1000 for a first offence. Fishing is totally prohibited in the American River (Kangaroo Island) upstream from Picnic Point; the Salt Fields area leased by ICI between Port Adelaide and St Kilda; and any waters within 135 metres of the locks on the Murray River.

All berried rock lobster (females carrying eggs) are protected at all times. Male rock lobsters may not be taken west of the Murray mouth from 31 May to 1 November, and south and east of the Murray mouth from 30 April to 1 October.

MINIMUM LEGAL LENGTHS IN SOUTH AUSTRALIA

Abalone, Black .... 13 cm	Salmon, Australian Sea ... 21 cm
Green .... 14.5 cm	Shark, Gummy (from fifth gill
Bream, Black .... 28 cm	slit to tail base) .... 45 cm
Callop or Golden Perch .. 33 cm	Shark, School or Snapper
Catfish (Freshwater) ..... 33 cm	(fifth gill slit, etc.) ...... 40 cm
Cockles (Goolwa) .... 3.5 cm	Silver Perch (River
Cockles (Sand and Mud) .. 3 cm	or Silver Bream, Tcheri) 33 cm
Flounder .... 23 cm	Snapper .... 28 cm
Garfish (from tip of upper jaw	Sweep .... 21 cm
to end of tail fin) ...... 21 cm	Trout, Brown,
Groper .... 60 cm	Rainbow .... 28 cm
Mullet (all species) ...... 21 cm	Whiting, Australian,
Mulloway or Butterfish .. 46 cm	King George, Spotted .. 28 cm
Murray Cod .... 46 cm	Whiting, Western Sand,
Rock Lobster, Southern	'Yellowfin' .... 24 cm
(total carapace) ..... 9.85 cm	Yellowtail Kingfish ...... 40 cm

Bag limits in South Australia

The following limits per person per day apply throughout the State:

King George whiting   30
Blue crabs   40
Razor fish   50
Black cowrie   1
Abalone   5
   Two or more persons using boat   total 10
Rock lobster   5

Freshwater fishing in South Australia

From a sport-fishing viewpoint this is of little consequence. Trout fishing, despite acclimatization efforts and wishful thinking, has not reached the standard of other States, largely due to the lack of suitable streams. South Australia's main freshwater species are indigenous, though several common species have been introduced, mainly redfin, tench and carp. It must be remembered that 650 km of Murray River flows through the State and never dries up! The weight of Murray cod, catfish, redfin and callop taken from this river by amateurs and professionals during any one year reaches impressive figures.

The Torrens Gorge within the City of Adelaide is one of the best trout fishing areas. The others include Finnis River which rises in the Adelaide Hills and empties into Lake Alexandrina, a little above the town of Goolwa, and the lower Onkaparinga River below Mount Bold, which produced a brown trout of 7.8 kg a few years ago. But there are 60 or 70 other streams which have been stocked by the Acclimatization Society in Adelaide, the South Australian Fly Fishers' Association. The Light River carries good rainbow and brown trout by local standards but seldom do they exceed 2 to 3 kg in weight. The Para River carries fish and so, too, does the Wakefield River.

A local legend has it that fish released in the Finnis were washed out by floodwaters into Lake Alexandrina where some have, in fact, reached astronomical proportions. Whether large fish are few and far between or whether South Australian trout anglers do not seek them determinedly enough is debatable. Some argue that South Australians do not know how to catch trout in a lake as large as Lake Alexandrina.

The River Murray

Within the borders of South Australia are 650 km of the River Murray. The river offers splendid fishing waters for big fish. Giant Murray cod are still taken, callop are still caught up to 5 to 6 kg, tcherie exceed 1.5 kg, catfish run to over 3 kg and these are just a few of the available species.

From Blanchetown up, there are locks or man-made barriers which control the rise and fall of the water. These are numbered from number one upwards and locks one to six inclusive are in South Australia. Fishing within 135 m of any of these locks is illegal. The river ranges from 60 to 90 m wide (below each lock) to almost half a kilometre wide in some of the long, straight stretches. The depth varies from 1.5 to about 30 m with all the deeper sections usually found beneath cliffs which mainly occur on the outside radius of each river bend.

An angler fishing the South Australian section of the river can fish from a boat or from the shore but, because some of the river is enclosed by private property, permission should be sought from property owners prior to entry being made along the banks. This is usually freely given on asking. Two-thirds of the river is open as declared fishing reserves.

An increasing number of anglers are hiring flat-bottomed houseboats which enable them to fish not only the deep water of the Murray River but the muddy flats as well.

The predominating species in the Murray are Murray cod, callop, redfin perch, Macquarie perch, catfish and brown trout. But amateurs fishing in the River Murray or in any South Australian freshwater stream or lake must observe the size limits listed above.

There are also special restrictions on fishing gear. At any one time you may use no more than two rods and lines or two handlines, or one rod and line and one handline.

From a tourist viewpoint, the river is well endowed with amenities for it passes by some of the largest cities and towns in South Australia. These include Tailem Bend, Waikerie, Loxton, Berri and Renmark. Barmera is just off the river but it is built on the banks of Lake Bonney. Barmera is accessible by water because the lake is connected to the river with a deep water creek. Each of these towns or cities provides everything that a holiday maker requires in the way of accommodation. There are other towns of lesser note, such as Swan Reach, Blanchetown, Overland Corner, New Residence, Cobdogla, etc., but they do not provide the same facilities as the larger centres. At Berri it is possible to hire catamaran house-boats. Ten-berth vessels can be hired by the week, day or month if bookings are made in advance.

GORDON HUME AND KEN JURY

SPANISH mackerel

These are the fish of the family Scombridae, four varieties of which are found in Australia. Dampier spotted one in Shark Bay, Western Australia, and the species has lived up to its reputation by providing fine sport for several generations of Australians. The Game Fishing Association of Australia lists them as tanguigue.

Narrow-banded or barred Spanish mackerel, *Scomberomorus commersoni*, is known by a variety of names, including Queensland kingfish and snook. In Queensland it is a valuable commercial fish, yielding clean, firm flesh with little or no waste and growing to 2 m and 63 kg. The young are common in the Gulf and Torres Strait, as the adults migrate north from the Barrier Reef to spawn. They are blue or grey on top, whitish beneath and their bodies carry between 25 and 50 narrow silvery bands or bars. The spinous dorsal fin is bright blue. Queenslanders rate it their top sportfish on light gear and highly appetising table fare.

Although it is present along the Queensland coast all year and provides 10 per cent of the yearly commercial catch, the principal season runs from July to December. It is taken in relatively short seasons around December and January on the New South Wales north coast as far south as the Macleay River.

The standard commercial technique is trolling with garfish baits, circling a school of feeding fish. Lures are sometimes used but are less successful than the fish baits. Strip baits of

S ■ SPANISH mackerel

Narrow-banded Spanish mackerel

bonito and feather jigs are also successful. Lines for commercial fishing are usually bulky linen or braided nylon with a 'piano-wire' or Bowden wire trace of at least 6 m. Fish are clubbed as they are caught, then held in large iceboxes.

Queensland anglers catch less fish but have more fun in the process. In season narrow banded Spanish mackerel can be caught from rocky headlands or harbour walls using surf tackle with lures, or fresh baits fished under a large styrox or similar float. To experienced anglers, they are not difficult to land, at least after the first run is turned. Fish up to 15 kg can be landed on ordinary spinning and baitcasting tackle without great difficulty.

Trolling and casting from outboard boats is a more likely method of taking larger mackerel. They will take almost any trolling lure, but the best may be something like a 3½ Drone spoon trolled at about 6 or 7 knots and held well beneath the surface by 225 g of lead near the top of the wire leader. Two metres of wire trace about twice the breaking test of the line is all that is necessary for amateur angling for these. A sharp gaff aids in control of a captured fish and a club is added insurance. Spanish mackerel have sharp teeth, and have inflicted serious bites on professional fishermen.

Spanish mackerel do not normally leap when hooked, though they often do so when feeding. One is credited with jumping right through a sailing boat's mainsail.

One method of feeding is a vertical rush from the bottom to strike garfish and flying fish at the surface. Fishermen frequently see them leap astounding distances into the air, in some cases estimated at 9 m.

Queensland sportfishermen have developed improved techniques for occasions when they refuse to respond to trolling. Moving in close to a school of fish, suddenly stopping the motor and then casting a lure or bait amongst the fish, a strike becomes much more certain. By watching from a distance to ascertain the direction the school is travelling, anglers can stop in its path. Surface popping lures are tremendous killers and often allow the angler to see his fish as it strikes.

Australia in 1985 held six world records for narrow-barred mackerel, including two caught on the same day (26 May, 1979) by Lady Joan Ansett off Queensland's Hayman Island. She landed one of 30.84 kg on a 15 kg line and one of 34 kg on a 24 kg line.

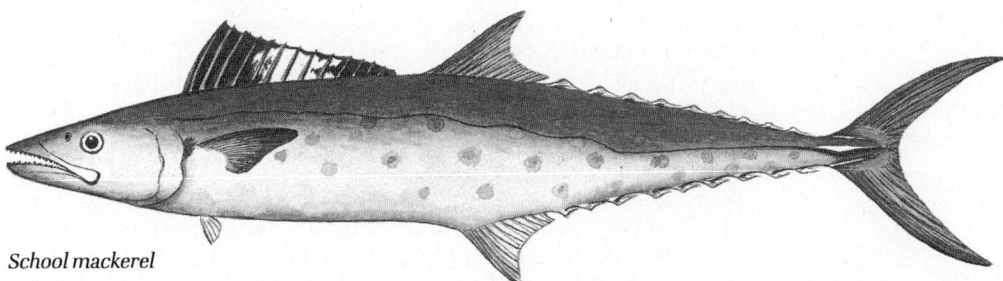

School mackerel

School or doggie mackerel

Scomberomorus queenslandicus: Sometimes known as blotched mackerel and spotted mackerel. A common fish in Queensland and Western Australian bays and estuaries, whereas the bigger narrow-banded Spanish mackerel prefers the open sea. Anglers around Townsville and other cities down to Brisbane know it well, for they have specialized in trolling for this splendid fish for many years. They are the smallest of the Scomberomoridae, growing to 80 cm and averaging around 2 kg. They have three irregular groups of bronze to silver blotches or circular spots on the back and right along the sides. They are excellent eating, usually served in 'steaks'.

Broad-barred or broad-banded Spanish mackerel

Scomberomorus semifasciatus: Very similar in profile to the narrow-barred Spanish mackerel, with the important difference that the bars on this fish are thicker and about half as many as on the narrow-banded variety. The thick bars on the younger specimens of this fish fade as they grow older and the body colour blends into a bronze colour. When it is killed, this striking colouring dwindles to a flat greyish tint immediately noticeable because of the change to dullness. They are found from around Broome in Western Australia, north around the top end to Queensland and down as far as Moreton Bay. They grow to 7.7 kg but average 1.3 to 2.7 kg.

Spanish mackerel in Western Australia
Flat reefs and rocks which plunge into deep blue water near the Murchison River mouth have contributed to another new brand of shore fishing for Spanish mackerel. Every March,

Broad-barred Spanish mackerel

April and May, anglers catch numbers of these sleek fighters, between 9 and 22 kg. Most Western Australian anglers use ordinary surfcasting rods and threadline or sidecast reels, with 7 to 11 kg line.

Shore fishing for mackerel at the Murchison was pioneered by two Perth anglers in 1957. Since then it has become a major sport. The river-mouth settlement of Kalbarri is booked out during these three months by anglers who want to catch a mackerel from the shore. And many of these include anglers who could easily go out and catch a mackerel in a boat. They arrive with their packets of frozen garfish and their big chained hooks with wire traces. The mackerel come through in bursts. Some anglers baitcast, some float out with balloons. When a mackerel hits, the technique that works in the west is to allow it to run as far and fast as it likes on the lightest possible drag. Given its head, a mackerel tires at about 180 m. It can then be brought ashore in about 15 to 20 minutes.

See Cookery.

SPINEFOOT A group of smooth-skinned coastal and reef fish whose strong dorsal spines are liable to inflict a painful wound. These fish of the family Siganidae are also known as stinging bream, rabbit fish, black trevally, mi mi and happy moments, an ironical expression of what the angler goes through if he is stung by one. The stings are venomous but not fatal. There are about 20 members of the family in Australian waters, mainly in Queensland and around and through the Northern Territory to Western Australia. Spinefoot grow to 33 cm and 1.7 kg.

Golden-lined spinefoot *Siganus guttatus:* A common Queensland variety abundant around northern Queensland reefs. They grow around 35 cm, a strikingly coloured fish, with slaty-blue bodies streaked with longitudinal lines. There is a prominent light yellow spot under the last dorsal ray. They are seldom taken by anglers because they are vegetarians, but spearfishermen take large numbers of them. They are not among our best table fish.

Golden-lined spinefoot

Black spinefoot

Siganus spinus: Another common Queensland fish found mostly in reef waters, although they do venture into estuaries and rivers. This spinefoot inflicts very painful stings with the first spine of the dorsal fin, which points directly forwards and hence the fish should be handled with extreme care. They are olive-brown in colour, sometimes chocolate-brown with lighter blotches and along the sides there is a series of close-set light blue blotches. They grow to around 35 cm. They often go through a remarkable series of colour changes after capture.

SPOTTY

See Butterfish.

STARGAZERS or stonelifters

Eleven species of the family Uranoscopidae are found in the southern half of Australia, including both the Queensland and Western Australian coasts. They are bottom-dwellers with upward-staring eyes that can be erected, and repulsive, bony heads. They bury in sand and some can stun their prey with an electric shock. They are also known as bulldogs or Winston Churchills. They can live a long time out of water and leap off the ground. Their nostrils communicate with the insides of their mouths, a remarkable feature in fishes. They often account for sport fishermen's snags on what appears to be a sandy bottom and can prove so obdurate that anglers are forced to break their lines. The best-known variety, *Ichthyscopus lebeck*, has a pale brown body over which are scattered pale yellow spots. There is a large brownish blotch on the cheek. They grow to 75 cm and 8.2 kg and are poor swimmers, usually taken by fishermen seeking bream or flathead.

Deepwater stargazer

STONEFLIES

See Aquatic insects.

STONELIFTERS

See Stargazers or stonelifters.

Herring cale

STRANGER Fish of the family Odacidae, also known as weedy whiting or rock whiting. The family includes Herring cale, *Olisthops cyanomelas*, which are found in Australian States in weed beds. The group have teeth that are fused to a cutting edge and dorsal fins with 14 or more spines and are invariably brilliant in colouring. Herring cale tend to dash at their prey and will take prawn bait. The long-rayed rock whiting *Neoodax radiatus* closely resemble parrot fish and are found only in South Australia and Western Australia. They are slender, elongated fish with a single dorsal spine, the first spine of which is about twice as long as the second spine. The outer rays of the ventral fin are similarly extended. Bridled rock whiting *Neoodax frenatus* are also confined to South Australia and Western Australia. They have a slightly more conical snout than others of the family.

STREAM improvement The art of making streams more suited to providing an optimal habitat for the fish species therein. Habitat improvement is probably a more suitable alternative title as the majority of the techniques employed are aimed at increasing fish production. The term 'stream improvement' has in the past been used by various governmental water 'conservation' authorities to describe the desnagging and canalization of rivers and creeks as part of flood mitigation schemes. Such so-called improvement has, in the great majority of cases, been to the marked detriment of fish populations as well as other members of the aquatic biota. An engineer's interpretation of stream improvement is often the complete reverse of an angler's interpretation.

Stream improvement has long been practised overseas, especially in Europe and North America, but little has been carried out in Australia. The absence of such a practice is at first sight somewhat perplexing, as Australian streams are relatively few in number to start with and cannot be expected to forever provide sport for an ever-increasing number of anglers. The great majority of Australian streams could be improved to some extent and many have a real need for improvement. Indeed, stream spoilation seems to be the rule rather than the exception, as flood mitigation schemes, together with increasing water abstraction, turn more and more rivers and creeks into open ditches with little or no flow.

One of the major factors mitigating against stream improvement in Australia is undoubtedly the virtual absence of riparian (or private) fishing rights on Australian streams. The Australian freshwater fisherman is indeed fortunate in comparison with his European and North American counterparts, as he has access to practically all fishable creeks and rivers. The purchase of an inexpensive inland fishing licence thus allows the angler to fish virtually anywhere within the State concerned (except when a closed season is in force upon a gazetted water). In Europe and the U.S.A. fees exceeding $50 per day are often required to fish a restricted section of some of the better waters. The owners of the fishing rights to such waters, however, are usually very active in protecting and improving the quality of the fishing in them. It is obviously in their own interest to do so: better fishing means more paying anglers. Although recreational freshwater fishing in Australia is a multi-million dollar industry, the fact that the responsibility for managing freshwater habitats lies with government bodies has meant that few habitat improvement programmes have been implemented. The importance of recreational fishing, both in terms of the industry it generates and the relaxation and enjoyment it affords to a major section of the Australian community, remains largely ignored by the governments of the day.

Effective catchment management

The greatest problem in Australia is undoubtedly the legacy of catchment mismanagement which began with the indiscriminate wielding of the first white settlers' axes. The trees on the fertile floodplains were typically the first to be felled. As early as 1803, Governor King issued a proclamation aimed at protecting trees along New South Wales streams. This read in part: 'From the improvident method taken by the first settlers ... in cutting down timber and cultivating banks many acres of ground have been removed, land inundated, houses, stacks of wheat and stock washed away by former floods which might have been prevented in some measure if the trees and other native plants had been suffered to remain...' Such a proclamation, although showing an awareness of the problems facing the stream environment, regrettably had little effect on what was to follow. Over-grazing, over-cropping, poor forestry practices, soil degradation, swamp drainage and reclamation, damming and water abstraction, gold dredging, organic and inorganic pollution, introduced animals such as the rabbit and European carp, and the increasing incidence of burning-off, are but some of the many factors which, when interwoven with the widely fluctuating natural cycles of drought and flood, swiftly led to the degradation of most Australian streams. European man has accelerated the normally slow erosion cycle at least a thousandfold and in some habitats one hundred thousandfold.

Although it can be said that some progress has been made

towards more effective catchment management over the past three decades or so, mainly through improved farming techniques and bushfire control and the successful introduction of myxomatosis, an enormous amount has yet to be done to return most stream environments to anything resembling their original levels of fish productivity. A multi-disciplinary approach to catchment management involving farmers, foresters, soil conservation authorities, water supply commissions, engineers, limnologists, fisheries and wildlife scientists and the like has been sadly lacking in the past. Some progress in this direction is now being made, particularly in Victoria where a Standing Consultative Committee on River Improvement was formed. In 1983 this committee produced an excellent review of the problems besetting Victorian streams, entitled *The State of the Rivers*. The many facts outlined in this report are, in virtually every case, equally applicable to rivers in all other States; it should be read by every concerned freshwater angler. An earlier booklet, *Revegetating Victorian Streams* (1982) also contains much valuable information. Both are obtainable from the State Rivers and Water Supply Commission, Victoria.

Other States are lagging somewhat behind Victoria in their river catchment management strategies, but the increasing public environmental awareness, together with accruing scientific evidence of the damage done, have resulted in tougher environmental laws being passed. In most cases, for example, an environmental impact statement now has to be prepared for scrutiny and debate before any development with the potential to disturb existing habitats, be they aquatic or terrestial, is allowed to proceed.

Promoting stream improvement
The members of angling clubs, acclimatization societies and so on, usually have an intimate knowledge of the streams in their particular area and are thus ideally placed to assist in improvements to these waters, as well as being in the best position to reap the immediate benefits from such improvements. Such people should thus be in the frontline of habitat improvement organizations and concerned anglers should become members of these groups. Although the problems facing many Australian streams are numerous, there is much that can be done at a practical 'grass-roots' level to alleviate existing and further damage.

Maintain a constant watch over the existing aquatic habitat. Potential sources of damage such as pollution, over-zealous abstraction or clearing, gravel mining and the like, can often be swiftly stopped by making representations to the appropriate local or state government authorities. Environmental legislation has been greatly strengthened in recent years, and any proposed development within the catchment of the stream in question should be thoroughly scrutinized by local anglers and vetoed accordingly.

Examine ways in which the existing habitat can be improved. Obviously, much will depend upon the character of the water concerned and the species of fish it contains. Australian streams encompass a wide variety of habitats, so it is extremely difficult to draft a set of generalized habitat improvement rules. What may be good for introduced trout species, for example, may well prove detrimental to desirable native species. A sound knowledge of the biology and life cycle of the fish species in question is an essential base from which to proceed. A recent survey of the coastal streams lying within the distribution range of the Australian bass found no fewer than 310 dams, weirs and other barriers across them, of which only 29 had functioning (or inoperative) fish ladders. The Australian bass spawns in estuarine waters during winter months and the success of its life cycle therefore depends upon unimpeded access between its freshwater river habitat and estuarine breeding grounds. For this species an obvious method of habitat improvement would be to either remove any barrier or install a fish ladder. In most cases, specific detailed information should be sought and the problems defined before proceeding with corrective action.

There is one problem common to many Australian streams that can be readily tackled by fishermen—declining streamside vegetation, which is particularly prevalent in grazing areas. Trees such as she-oaks and river gums are often the most important stabilizing component of the stream bank. Their disappearance usually results in bank erosion during floods and a consequent widening and shallowing of the stream. In grazing areas there are virtually no young trees growing to replace the existing adults and unless steps are taken to exclude stock from the river bank every tree will eventually disappear. Co-operative fencing ventures between anglers and landowners could do much to alleviate the problem. After specific stock-watering sites have been chosen, the rest of the river bank can be fenced off and allowed to revegetate. An environmentally aware landowner, once made to realise the long-term possibility of erosion, should readily agree to such a proposal. In addition, fisheries research both here and overseas has demonstrated that fish biomass in streams with overhanging vegetation is inevitably greater than in those with cleared banks—an added bonus.

The ways in which stream habitats can be improved are myriad and it is beyond the scope of this brief article to enumerate all of them. As stated earlier, each habitat must be treated on its own particular merits. A wealth of pertinent information can be obtained from soil conservation and fisheries and wildlife authorities and the like. An angler actively engaged in habitat improvement is contributing much to the future of his sport. In today's society the responsible angler is probably the only true friend that a freshwater fish has.

RICHARD TILZEY

SUCKER fish

SUCKER fish Family Echeneidae: Ancient fish, also known as remoras, which travel the oceans by attaching themselves to marlin, rays, turtles, sharks, other big fish and to sailing boats by means of a powerful sucker pad or suction disc. They are good swimmers but prefer to ride on other fishes' backs. There are at least 10 species of sucker fish in Australian waters. Fossils have proved remoras to be millions of years old. Australians take them freely in bays and coastal waters. They fight well and are good table fish.

The suction pad on the sucker fish is so powerful that the disc will tear loose from the fish's body before force detaches the object to which the sucker fish is attached. The pad has been formed by a modified spiny dorsal fin becoming flattened to form a series of ridges set inside a fleshy outer oval rim. When sucker fish attach themselves to a big fish they press the oval rim against the host's skin and turn up the ridges by muscular action to create suction chambers. They can detach themselves at will to feed on pieces of the host's food and for this reason have a reputation as complete parasites. But they can feed themselves when swimming free.

Aborigines used sucker fish to catch turtles, by tying a rope to the fish's tail and dropping it near a resting turtle. The fish attached itself to the turtle and then both were hauled into the canoe.

The action of the sucker fish's disc in no way harms the host fish. They often seem to be very friendly with the sharks on which they ride, but their remains have been found inside sharks often enough to indicate they are not completely tolerated. They are not the tell-tale proof of the presence of sharks in the vicinity which some anglers suggest.

Sucker fish are black, blue-grey, white or creamy and brown in colour, often with two white stripes stretching the length of the body, which is slender and elongated. The largest of the species reaches 1 m but 20 to 45 cm is the average size of the majority. They have pointed heads, with the suction disc extending from the snout tip to behind the head. Their tails are soft, with straight edges and well developed, and their scales are usually invisible. They prefer the open ocean, but are found inshore and in tropical and warm waters.

Of the common forms found in Australia, the short sucker fish *Remora remora* grows to around 45 cm. Short sucker fish have a rounded pectoral fin and are a dusky brown colour. The slender sucker fish *Echeneis naucrates* reaches 1 m and has a pointed pectoral fin.

Short sucker fish

A close-up of the sucking dish of the sucker fish showing the movable vanes set inside a fleshy ring.

SUNFISH

Huge pelagic fish of the family Molidae, which drift across vast expanses of ocean, carried more by the currents than their own propulsion. They are among the great oddities of the sea, increasing in size from birth to adult by 60 million times, according to Whitley, who believed this is probably the greatest growth rate in the entire animal kingdom.

Sunfish are particularly vulnerable to spearfishermen, but despite their great size they are no prize and most thoughtful anglers are annoyed when they see one carried triumphantly ashore by a beaming skindiver. The giant sunfish spearmen kill are sluggish fish, totally ill-equipped to resist attack.

All species of sunfish lack a distinct caudal fin or caudal peduncle. The opposite single dorsal and anal fins are both large and similar in shape. They go through remarkable changes as they grow, the larvae (one female was found to contain 300 million eggs) ultimately developing into fish almost 3 m long, with a fin-span of 3 m and a weight of up to 1 tonne. The teeth in the lower jaw of all species are fused into a single unit. They are related to the leatherjackets.

S ■ SUNFISH

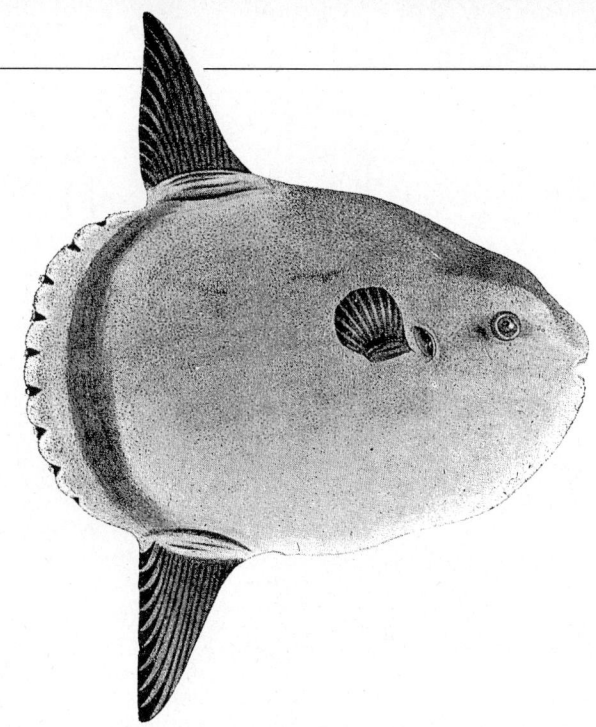

Sunfish

Short sunfish or ocean sunfish — *Mola ramsayi:* This member of the sunfish family is a uniform dull brown or yellow colour in life, turning silvery to white after death. They grow to more than 3 m and exceed a tonne in weight. They have been found in all Australian States and in New Zealand usually washed up on beaches or taken by spearmen. They have deep, greatly compressed bodies and rounded rear-ends.

Oblong or short sunfish — *Triurus laevis:* Also known as ranzania. These are probably the fastest swimmers in the sunfish family, moving in schools at high speed in sharp contrast to the indolent movements of their relatives. They are fairly rare and look like fish chopped in half except for the fin rays set down the bluntly truncate tail. There is a series of curved bands running down under the snout, eyes and upper body. The body colouring is vivid silver. They grow to around 90 cm and 9 kg and are found in Western Australia, South Australia, New South Wales and Queensland.

SUNFISH, Freshwater — See Rainbow fish.

SURF fishing — The southern half of the continent has the finest array of ocean beaches in the world and this, coupled with the excellent sport species that are found in the surf, has made Australians the world's leading exponents of surf angling.

This is a sport which varies considerably in character as one proceeds around the huge Australian coastline, for it has to be adapted to the nature of the seashores, water conditions, prevailing winds and species offering.

On the eastern coast the northern limit of really good surf angling may be said to be Sandy Cape, at the northern tip of Fraser Island. This big island of almost virgin forest presents some 145 km of excellent beaches, which in season yield great numbers of whiting, mainly of the sand, gold-lined and somewhat smaller northern species. Other catches include bream, tailor, flathead, mulloway, dart etc. More unique to the area are the occasional red-finned emperor (sweetlips), great trevally, young turrum, oyster crusher, beach salmon, school mackerel, crescent perch etc.

As one proceeds south there is some excellent surf fishing to be had on the Sunshine Coast, between Noosa Heads and Caloundra, but then the next stretch of approximately 160 km, from the mouth of Pumice Stone Channel to Southport, is sheltered by the offshore islands of Bribie, Moreton and North and South Stradbroke. Under normal conditions there is little surf in Moreton Bay and land-based angling is mostly for whiting and stray flathead. But excellent surf fishing may be had by those who can manage to get out to the big ocean beaches on the eastern shores of the above-mentioned islands.

Surf fishing in Queensland

Surf fishing in New South Wales

In Australia, modern methods of surf angling originated in New South Wales. Experienced anglers agree that the best results are to be had on the northern section of the coast, from Port Stephens to Tweed Heads. The main species taken along there are sand whiting, tailor, yellowfin bream, flathead, mulloway and dart. The game little dart is a warmwater species which is common on the north coast but seldom makes its way as far south as Sydney. Inedible species encountered include the prickly porcupine fish, the common sand stingray and the shovelnose, fiddler and eagle rays.

The larger brown estuary ray and the big black ray are often hooked but seldom landed. When they find themselves in trouble they dig their big flaps into the sand and defy efforts to shift them on the light line. The angler has the satisfaction of seeing a big tail breaking the surface in the surf as it is lashed about but he usually runs out of patience and strains the line to where it breaks. Around the corners of the beaches, or where there are kelp beds off-shore, it is not unusual to hook a wobbegong or carpet shark. Some of these grow to around 45 kg or more, and give the persistent angler a lot of hard work with rod and reel before being landed. The smaller Port Jackson shark also is occasionally met under similar circumstances, though it is more common south of Sydney.

The beaches between Port Stephens and the mouth of the Shoalhaven River nowadays do not fish nearly as well as they did 25 years ago. It seems that constant bait-gathering and heavy foot-traffic on the beaches at low tides has greatly denuded them of worms, pipis and other fish food. It is notable nowadays that as the tailor travel the coast near Sydney they frequent the surf on the ocean rocks but pay scant attention to the surf on the beaches. However, when conditions are right, many surf anglers manage to get some good sport and on occasions some big catches are made, though most who take their fishing seriously like to go further afield when the opportunity presents itself.

The tailor fishing generally is not so good on the south coast, but this is compensated to some extent by the presence of the Australian salmon. There was a time when shoals of these splendid sportfish travelled the coast up to Port Macquarie and beyond. But with the establishment of the canneries at Narooma and Eden the pressure of commercial fishing for them became so intense that for many years only a few ever managed to straggle as far north as Sydney. The canneries have now contracted to one big plant at Eden and commercial preoccupation with off-shore tuna often permits more salmon to elude the nets and get through to gladden the hearts of the surf fishermen. Beyond the zone of intense netting, at Disaster Bay and at Mallacoota Inlet (in Victoria) the salmon fishing at times can be dramatic.

On the south coast the gummy shark begins to become of significance in the surf. Some grow to as long as 1 m and a large one can give the angler a good tussle on light tackle as well as provide some good edible fillets. The silver trevally is often taken from the holes in the beaches, or by fishing from the rocks to cast just behind the surf at the corners of the beaches, preferably between sunset and dusk. Snapper are always a possibility where there is a bar of rock running out from a beach or where the surf may wash crabs or other food out of the rocks in the corners.

Surf fishing in Victoria

Surf angling is not so good in the colder waters of the Victorian coast, though some really good sport is to be had around the Gippsland Lakes Entrance and along the famous Ninety Mile Beach. The species taken are mainly small tailor, salmon, whiting, trevally and gummy shark. Bream are remarkably scarce, for the blue-nose bream of that region haunts the rivers and estuaries and is very rarely found in the surf, notwithstanding that every winter some of the larger ones migrate up the coast far enough to be caught under the cliffs around Sydney.

A large proportion of the tailor and salmon taken in Victoria are composed of immature fish. The tailor are usually classed as 'choppers' and the half-grown salmon are known as salmon trout or bay trout, which are decidedly better eating than the large 'buck' salmon. In and around Port Phillip Bay snapper are much more common and may be found to be a factor in surf angling in season.

Speaking generally, the surf fishing on the west Victorian coast is not particularly good, though it is very much brightened by the incidence of the big spotted whiting and the small tommy ruff. Good access to the coast is provided by the Great Ocean Road, which closely parallels it most of the way from Geelong to Warrnambool and then by the Prince's Highway as far as Portland.

Surf fishing in South Australia

From there the road deviates away inland through Heywood, to cross over into South Australia at Mount Gambier and then run on to make a total of more than 270 km before touching the sea again at Kingston. For the next 48 km there is access at various points through the sand dunes to the big beaches of the Coorong, which run in an almost unbroken chain for approximately 200 km, to the entrance to Lake Alexandrina, opposite Victor Harbour. The use of these magnificent beaches is largely denied to the surf angler because the highway is cut off from the surf by that unique narrow arm of the lake which parallels it for close to 130 km.

Adelaide, on the St Vincent Gulf, offers poor surf angling. At times some good sport may be had around Victor Harbour, 90 km south, and some excellent fishing may be enjoyed away out on the ocean beaches of massive Kangaroo Island, which shelters the mouth of the Gulf. The huge Spencer Gulf is similarly protected by the inturned headlands of Cape

Spencer and Cape Catastrophe, as well as by the screen of smaller islands across its mouth. A great deal of surf fishing is done in the gulfs, mainly for spotted or King George whiting and tommy ruff with a chance of taking small tailor, salmon or flathead for good measure. In the weak surf common in calm weather it is not unusual to see anglers wade out into the shallows to stand there and fish.

The best surf fishing in South Australia and possibly for the whole continent, is to be found along the Flinders Highway where it closely parallels the western coast of the Great Australian Bight from Port Lincoln to Ceduna, a distance of 416 km. Competent surf anglers who have fished this stretch speak in glowing terms of the sensational sport to be had with shoals of big salmon, large tailor, big spotted whiting, ruff and other species. A lot of this territory is still so little fished that in some places it is possible to stand among the local seals while casting.

Surf fishing in Western Australia

Beyond Ceduna the Eyre Highway skirts the Bight shore at varying distances for over 800 km before deviating off to Norseman. Very little is known of the angling possibilities along this section. It is almost unpopulated, so tourist anglers tend to treat it as a 'no man's land', hesitating to deviate from the highway for fear of a motor breakdown in a remote and waterless spot. But we do know that at Esperance, which is 200 km south of Norseman and off the usual tourist route, some of the local sportsmen find the surf angling very good. Fishing is also very good around Albany, away to the west, on King George Sound, but this is best reached by one of the several good highways from Perth.

The south-west coast of Western Australia, from Perth down to Yallingup and Augusta, approximately 320 km, is famed for its good surf fishing. Along there the western sub-species of the salmon averages about 1 kg heavier than that of the eastern coast and it is still found in quantity. The tailor are big and provide some sensational sport. The little tommy ruff, or 'herring' as it is called in the vernacular, moves in shoals and gives rise to a lot of light-tackle specialization. There are also some species that are unique to the west. Yallingup is on about the same latitude as Sydney and Perth is on a level with Taree.

The coast north of Perth is not easy for the tourist surf angler to fish, since the Geraldton Highway, 498 km long, deviates away inland and does not touch the seashore again until it reaches Dongara, about 65 km south of Geraldton. North of there, the road again runs inland for more than 240 km, to where it is possible to turn off through Coburn to go out on to either of the long peninsulas to Carrarang or Denham to fish Denham Sound, or to merely follow along the back of the massive Shark Bay. Carnarvon, 980 km north of Perth, is approximately on the same latitude as Bundaberg and Fraser Island on the east coast. Although conditions are different, we again may consider this the northern limit of good surf angling. Beyond there conditions become more tropical, species are more mixed, the fishing becomes rougher and tougher and the handline is the usual form of tackle used by local sportsmen.

Since we have specified these limits, some explanation of conditions beyond them may be in order. The central coast and north coast of Queensland are sheltered and shallowed by the Great Barrier Reef. The surf is in the nature of big choppy waves rather than ocean swell. A lot of the shoreline is mangrove mud flats interspersed with beaches and headlands. As a rule the beaches are shallow and lack those formations which in southern surfs attract the fish. Most contain an element of wind and run out into mud flats. A vigorous surf stirs it up and converts the water to the colour of milk-coffee.

In semi-tropical waters the yellow-fin bream, sand whiting and tailor of the south are sadly missed. The pikey bream is a good sports fish but it mostly is taken in estuaries and tidal creeks. The northern whiting is a small species and a lot of those found on the beaches are immature. Pickers and pests are legion but good edible sports fish are scarce on the beaches. Some of the most spectacularly beautiful beaches in the north, including Ellis Beach, are to be found north of Cairns, but fishing them usually produces only small whiting, little crescent perch that give poor sport and are worse eating, bony-framed triple-spines, fork-tailed catfish, rays, small Taylor's sharks, and so on.

Trying to surf fish the far-northern beaches, such as those in the Gulf of Carpentaria, is generally a futile business which results in frequent break-offs from big sharks, rays or sawfish. The angler probably lays a row of the smaller ones out along the sand, with a collection of forked-tail catfish of various sizes, but if there are any threadfin salmon, bream, steelback, mangrove jack or other good edible fish he has been in luck. There is an abundance of good fish in the north—in some places it is a super-abundance—but they usually are found in places other than the beaches. Most of the fishing is done on the offshore reefs, in the estuaries and along the rivers and tidal creeks. In the rivers and creeks and the greater part of most estuaries, mud and mangroves make it almost essential to use a boat.

Over on the north-west coast the huge tides (they rise almost 12 m at Broome), make fishing the surf difficult, and the previous remarks about mud, mangroves, pests, pickers and broken tackle still apply. And, of course, fishing in the far northern section is limited through the road turning inland at Broome and covering 2094 km before it emerges onto the sea again at Darwin.

Nevertheless, typical surf gear is never a dead loss in the

Surf fishing in northern Australia

north. It is one of the handiest forms of tackle for fishing the river mouths, delta channels, salt-arm entrances and more solid estuary banks for threadfin salmon, pikey bream, steelback, mangrove jack etc, or for tempting barramundi with live bait. It has a big edge on the single-handed spinning rod in handling big estuary cod and small groper. And it is ideal for casting garfish or the heavier lures from jetties or breakwaters for queenfish, school mackerel, great trevally etc.

Surf-fishing equipment

Present-day surf-casting tackle as used in Australia has been developed after a long period of trial and error. An outfit should be selected with care, for it is of little use if it is not carefully balanced or if any of the components are not suited to the purpose and quite adequate under all conditions. It should be kept in mind that on the beaches the best fish are usually found in the more active sections of the surf. When conditions get tough we still aim to go on fishing the rough surf until things get so bad that the fish are forced to move away out to deeper water.

Thus, the design of a good surf outfit is determined greatly by the need to cast a heavy bait and sinker over considerable distances. It takes a No. 8 ball sinker (74 g) to hold a good tailor bait out where the fish may be expected to find it in a vigorous surf. Contrary to what might be expected, the ball sinker does not roll on the average bottom but sinks into the loose sand and holds there. Where the surf is more vigorous or a sideways drift is scouring the sand down to a hard bottom, it may be necessary to use a No. 2 helmet (95 g). The oval flange on this tends to prevent rolling and it digs in to resist the shoreward pull of the surf on the line. The last resort to hold in a rough surf over a normal bottom is the dump (170 g). This is a compact, somewhat bullet-shaped sinker which readily sinks into the sand, but its weight precludes casting over other than moderate distances and could strain a light rod.

Surf-reel knowhow

Casting such weights well out into the surf demands the expenditure of considerable energy and this largely determines the length, strength and spring required in the rod, the characteristics of the reel and the strength or gauge of the line that should be used with it. Three types of surf-fishing outfit are in popular use today. These are the geared surf-casting reel, the threadline reel and the sidecast reel.

The geared surf-casting reel is the most versatile and in the hands of an expert it is the most convenient and effective in handling a large fish, but it may be the most difficult to learn to use. More discrimination is needed in selecting it than is called for with the other types. The smaller, 'cut-down' or foreshortened reels of good quality are best for long-distance, smooth, trouble-free casting. One Australian-made reel with ball-race bearings and neoprene washer damping on the end of the spindle works well with a fairly large line capacity.

Big line capacity results in a heavy load of nylon on the spool, which develops strong momentum at the high rotary speed entailed in casting. Thus it behaves as a flywheel and is most difficult to control. A reel of small capacity and light spool construction may be controlled by feathering it with the thumb. A heavier reel needs some inbuilt form of damping to assist in maintaining stability. External automatic anti-backlash controls have appeared in various forms, but usually they have been discarded in the end.

In using a geared reel the angler has to learn to use a thumb to distribute the line evenly over the length of the spool as it is wound in. This is important in avoiding springing of the line, with consequent jamming on the spool due to overlapped turns. Laying the line on the spool is not difficult and after a time it becomes automatic. There are a few models on the market with automatic layer-winding devices, but they never have been particularly popular. Geared surf reels are fitted with a brake, in the form of a 'star drag', usually a four-pointed star-nut situated under the handle bar. Screwing this clockwise increases the drag against the fish in taking line off the spool against winding pressure. This is a big help in avoiding straining the line to breaking point when a fish bucks, lunges or makes an unexpected dash.

Provision is made to throw the spool out of gear so that it will run more freely during a cast. Some have a small 'throw-over' lever switch on the outer edge of the front end-cap which may be tripped over with the thumb. This type needs tripping back to engage the gears again at the end of the cast. Others have a 'push-down' thumb pad in about the same position. This is pushed down to release the gears and it automatically springs up again as the handle is turned and the gears engage. One well-known Australian-made reel disengages gears when a plunger is pushed down and the handle is pulled axially outwards. They automatically engage again as the handle is turned and pressed inwards. Yet another has a toggle post which is stood up against spring pressure to free the spool. As soon as the handle is turned its crossbar knocks the toggle post down and automatically re-engages the gears. Geared reels are mounted above the rod. The geared reel does not put any twist in the line, neither in casting nor retrieving.

In selecting a threadline reel for surf angling there is only one type that is adequate and that is the large saltwater model. Those of the smaller intermediate size are not capable of making long casts with reasonably heavy line and do not have sufficient mechanical advantage for retrieving heavy sinkers through sand and surf, or in handling a big fish. Fortunately the heavier model, with larger spool, heavier gears and longer handle crank, outperforms them. Threadline reels are mounted below the rod.

The correct saltwater threadline reel for a right-handed angler is one that winds with the right hand. This is stressed because it is in direct opposition to the requirement with a single-handed spinning rod. Most American and a few other big reels of this type are made with left-hand winding, but in playing a big fish in the surf or in continuous spinning with a heavy lure they quickly give the angler a 'glass' left arm and greatly handicap him.

The line is guided onto the fixed spool of a threadline reel by a bail-wire which is fixed to the rotary drum. To cast, the bail-wire is swung back to where it automatically locks, thus freeing the line and allowing it to spring off over the end of the spool when the cast is made. Nearing the end of the cast, a turn of the handle releases the lock on the bail-wire and allows it to spring back into position to automatically pick up the line and layer wind it back onto the spool as the retrieve is made. Reels of this type have a drag which is adjusted by turning a control knob on the front end of the spool.

Threadline reels put a twist in the line of a full 360 degrees, or one complete turn, for every turn of line that springs off over the end of the spool, but they take it out as the line is wound back on again.

Sidecast reels are made with spools of large diameter to give free casting and a quick and strong retrieve without the use of gears. Those used in surf fishing range from about 12 to 18.5 cm diameter. Owing to their bulk, they are used near the butt of the rod handle to preserve the balance. They have large line capacity and with light line they are unrivalled for casting garfish or other unweighted baits over long distances. Usually they are fished with in a different manner from that used with the previously mentioned reel types.

In preparing to cast with a sidecast reel, the spool is turned around on its swivelling mount until its axis is parallel with that of the rod. When the line is released it runs out by springing over the side of the spool, much the same as with the threadline reel. On the completion of the cast the spool is turned back to the winding position and the left hand guides the line onto it as it is wound in. This type of reel puts a 360-degree twist in the line for each turn that springs off over the side of the reel in casting. Since it winds it back straight onto a rotary spool this twist is not removed. This makes it necessary to use a light swivel with any rig fitted to the line in order to give the twist a chance to work itself out. It has little chance to do so where a continuous heavy strain is kept on the line, as in fast spinning with heavy lures.

Selecting the right surf rod

Each of the above types of reel requires a somewhat different design in the surf-casting rod to work with it. With a geared reel the rod has to be rather more powerful than with the other types. In making long casts the angler has to put his shoulders into it and expend some energy to set the spool rotating at sufficiently high speed to keep line up to the heavy sinker as it flies away out. For this purpose the rod needs to have parabolic action rather than tip action, so that practically the whole length of it is used to store up energy as it bends on the heave and to impart it again as it straightens out.

With a threadline reel the spool does not have to be accelerated up to top speed, for it is fixed and the line springs off over the end of it. The same large initial expenditure of energy is not required, so this type of reel works best with a somewhat more springy rod which has a good deal of tip action. The same applies to the sidecast reel, but here the fine line flows even more freely over the end of the big spool and to make the most of that characteristic potential for throwing light weights it is usual to choose a quite long rod with a great deal of tip action.

Surf-casting rods for use with geared reels are mostly from 3 to 4 m in length and usually are made up from a suitable tubular fibreglass blank. Some of the better-class blanks are of good quality and are remarkably durable. The reel seat should be 70 to 80 cm above the butt of the handle, according to the length of the angler's arms. This is of prime importance in allowing ample separation of the hands to permit good leverage with the arms and some action from the shoulders in casting. It also allows much better control in retrieving or in playing a fish, for with the butt well down on the thigh or against the groin, the left hand has a lot better leverage in holding the rod while the other winds.

Good surf rods for use with threadline reels are of about the same length, but the reel seat is placed at from 67.5 to 75 cm from the butt. This is because in casting the right hand goes somewhat further forward, so that the index finger can hold the line against the stem of the reel. In retrieving, the left hand also grips somewhat further forward, to clear the rotary drum and the bail-wire. And, of course, there is not the same need to separate the hands so widely to get such powerful leverage in casting.

For use with a big threadline reel, a rod should have a very good forward handgrip, for since the reel is offset on a long stem, reel and rod wobble can become an annoying factor in winding in. A larger lower rod ring or line guide is advisable to reduce friction in gathering in the wide spiral throw of the line caused by its spiralling off over the lip of the spool.

With rods for geared or threadline reels it is essential that the handle butt be fitted with some form of tapered butt cap or durable rounded wooden end which may be easily driven into the sand. This is the only safeguard to keep sand out of the reel. When a fish is brought in to be unhooked it bucks about and kicks sand around freely. In fishing it is often a big convenience to be able to stand a rod up while cutting bait, preparing new rigs etc. And it is the best way to keep track of it and avoid stumbling over it in the dark. A rubber button has no place on the butt end of a surf rod.

Rods for use with sidecast reels vary from 4 to 5 m in length. Once they were almost exclusively of rangoon cane, but now good tubular fibreglass blanks 4.5 m long are readily available. With a 22.5 cm wooden butt, these make up to 4.7 m. The reel is placed under the rod and seated about 22 to 25 cm from the handle butt. Since the big spool throws wide spirals in casting, and the action is mainly in the tip, the lower line guide is usually placed about halfway up the rod. Some have an open guide bound on close down near the reel, so that the line may be slipped into it for winding in.

The choice of lines
For heavy-duty work with geared reels it is usual to employ 10/10.5 kg (0.50 mm) nylon line. This stands up to heavy work and gives less snap-off at the tip in casting heavy sinkers. Due to heavy forward pressure on the spool in casting, the spindle bearings on some reels soon wear at the front and cause wider clearance between the flanges of the spool and the frame at the back. This precludes the use of fine gauges of line, for it may slip in over the flange of the spool and be cut off.

Saltwater model threadline reels are mostly used with 7.5/8.5 kg (0.45 mm) nylon line. Since the strain of casting is less, it stands up well to prolonged fishing. The spool of a threadline reel should be filled to within 45 mm of the lip for good casting. Fine line runs off freely over the lip and places more turns in the top layers on the spool, from where it runs most freely in making long casts. And, of course, fine line offers less resistance to the surf and imposes less drag on the sinker. But there is a practical limit in regard to standing the strain of hefting those big sinkers.

Since the baits used with sidecast reels are mostly weighted only lightly with a small sinker, some anglers get down to very fine line for the smaller species and use 5.5/6 kg nylon (0.35 mm). Others prefer 6.5/7 kg (0.40 mm) and for heavy duty most use 7.5/8.5 kg (0.45 mm). Here, line gauge is a big factor in making long casts, for an unweighted garfish has high air resistance and little weight to carry a lot of heavy line behind it. Some newly imported sidecast reels now have interchangeable plastic spools by means of which it is possible to change from one gauge of line to another, or to reverse the spool so that by reversing the direction of winding twist may be fished out of the line.

Casting with a geared surf reel
It is a good idea to start by practising on the flat sand of a beach, where the sinker will lodge in the sand where it lands and may be wound back without catching on obstacles. There are two methods of casting but the old swing has mostly given way to the overhead cast as now taught in the casting clubs.

Grip and stance are important. The rod handle is gripped firmly by the right hand immediately behind the reel seat, so that the thumb may hold the spool from rotating by pressing

CASTING WITH A GEARED REEL

partly on the end flange of the spool and partly on the wound nylon line. The left hand grips the rod handle near the butt, so that the hands are well separated to obtain good leverage. The weight of the body is taken on the right foot with the left foot about 30 cm in front of it with the heel lightly down. The angler faces squarely in the direction of the point he is going to cast to, with his eyes directed about a metre above where the sinker is intended to land.

The spool is freed by operating whichever mechanism is used to disengage the gears and then the line is released until the sinker hangs about 75 cm below the tip of the rod, taking care to see that the line is not twisted around the tip ring. The rod is now brought back and the butt elevated until it is horizontal at a little higher than shoulder height, with tip extended out behind and the length of it in line with the target. The right hand, with the reel now under the rod, is level with or a little behind the point of the shoulder, about on a level with the ear. The left hand, gripping the butt, is extended out in front of and a little to the right of the face.

With the thumb jammed hard on the spool to hold it from rotating, the cast is started by the right arm's pushing the rod up and over, as the left arm begins to pull the butt down using the moving right hand as a fulcrum in applying leverage to the rod. A good deal of force is exerted at this stage, the right hand moving forward and downwards in unison with the left. As the rod comes over past the vertical, it and the trailing sinker have acquired considerable speed and momentum. The pressure of the arms has now eased, the swing of the rod begins to slow, with the result that the bend now springs over in the opposite direction to flick the spinner on its way. This is the point where pressure on the spool should be released to let it spin and give out line to keep pace with the flight of the sinker.

As the rod comes over, the body sways forward and the weight is progressively transferred from the right to the left foot. In making a powerful cast the muscles of the leg and back push against the arms and rod. As the sinker goes away the thumb is used to lightly (and that means lightly) feather the spool flange and winding to prevent the spool from over-running and causing a backlash. The hands continue to come down until the rod is brought to rest at about 45 degrees, with the left hand still gripping the rod butt beside the left hip. As the sinker hits the water the thumb is jammed hard onto the spool to prevent an overspin. In the meantime, the weight of the body has come over past the left foot and the right is brought forward 30 to 37 cm in front of it to retain balance.

The left hand now brings the butt round in front where it can rest against the thigh or come up against the groin. With the right hand supporting the rod, the left now takes a grip from underneath in front of the rod so that the thumb and forefinger may be used to guide the line onto the spool. The right hand then releases its grip and engages the gears, either by turning the handle or operating the appropriate shift control. The slack is then wound in until the weight of the sinker can just be sensed at the other end of the moderately taut line, after which the angler sets the star drag to give a moderate degree of braking, and then waits for a bite.

It is wise to begin by trying to cast only moderate distances and then to progressively reach out as one gets the feel of the gear and acquires some facility in controlling it. Good casting is largely a matter of practice. Freedom from trouble is achieved by developing a smooth swing, timing the release of the spool correctly and feathering the spool with just enough thumb friction (not pressure) to prevent over-running.

Accuracy in surf casting is chiefly a matter of aiming straight and swinging the rod over in a vertical plane along that line of aim. Body twist or side sway should be kept to a minimum for they ruin accuracy. In punching a bait out against a headwind a forceful cast with a low trajectory is used. To cast with a following wind the bait is thrown high so that the wind may help in carrying it out. In casting in a cross-wind a forceful cast and low trajectory are used, with a good allowance for wind deflection. After a little experience an angler should be able to fish through a long session in the dark without suffering a serious backlash.

Casting with a threadline reel
The angler using a big threadline reel quickly learns that as soon as the line is allowed to go slack there is a tendency for turns to loosen up on the spool and spring off over its lip. This type of reel is easier to cast with than any other but the secret of trouble-free angling with one is to always have the line under tension. The weight of the sinker hanging from the tip, when the rod is being handled or stood up in the sand, is sufficient to keep the line taut and avoid this trouble.

Casting is carried out in the manner detailed above for the overhead geared reel, but the difference in the equipment and the fact that the threadline reel mounts under the rod, make some further explanation and instruction desirable. To prepare for casting, the outfit is adjusted so that the sinker is hanging from 65 to 75 cm below the rod tip. The handle is then slightly turned to rotate the winding drum so that the bail-wire is on top. The right hand grips the rod handle immediately behind the stem of the reel, the index finger first having picked up the line to carry it back and hold it firmly against the front of the stem. The left hand is now used to swing the bail-wire forward and down, until it locks in the casting position with a click.

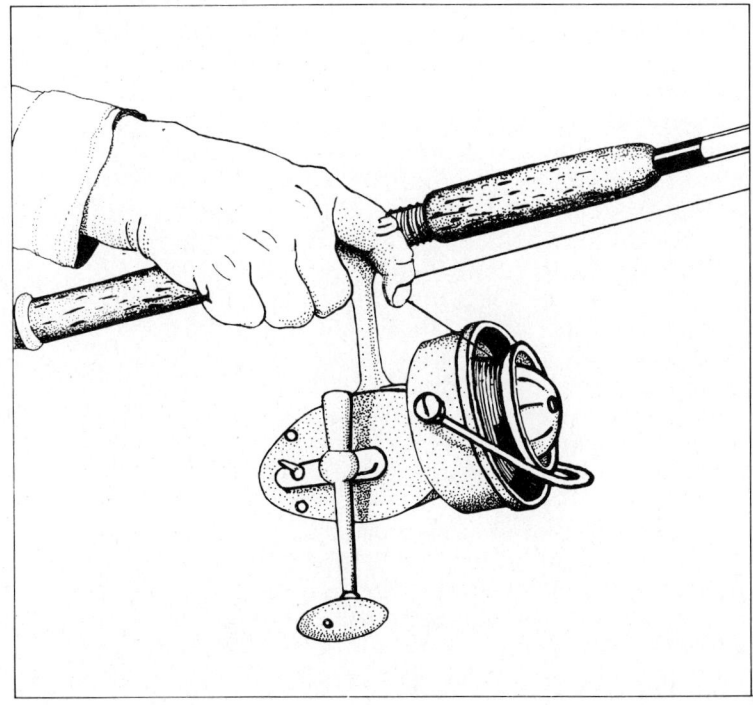

When casting with a big saltwater threadline reel, the line is held on the first joint of the index finger, preferably by pulling it back firmly against the stem of the reel.

When the left hand grips the butt and the rod goes back at shoulder height, preparatory to making the cast, the reel is on top. The heave need not be so strong, since there is no rotary spool to set spinning and bring up to speed. As the rod comes over, the index finger releases the line at precisely the right instant and the sinker goes speeding on its way. The sinker goes on its way so fast from a threadline outfit that it is difficult to follow it with the eye, but it slows up quickly towards the end of the cast through the line pulling tightly over the lip of the spool from deep down in the slot.

In fishing with a threadline reel it is necessary to smartly check the flow of the line at the end of a cast. As already indicated, toward the end of the cast the line is pulling tightly on the lip, but when the sinker descends onto the water the line begins to settle and slack is produced. As soon as the tension is eased the pull on the lip is released, with the result that the turns in the slot spring and gush out over the lip to create more slack. This makes it necessary to smartly change the hand grips at the end of the cast and use the right hand to turn the handle and release the bail-wire so that it swings over and picks up the line. At the same time the rod tip is raised to tense the loose turns in the spool as the unwanted slack is being wound in.

Casting with a sidecast outfit
The sidecast reel and rod are rather larger than other types of gear and a little more brute force may be needed in using such an outfit, though it is very easy to cast with once the angler understands its characteristics.

The reel is mounted beneath the rod, about 22 cm from the butt. In preparation for casting, the line is adjusted so that the sinker hangs from 1 to 1.5 m below the rod tip. The reel is then turned to the casting position by depressing the spring catch and turning the spool on its swivel mount until its axis is parallel with that of the rod. The left hand then takes the line at the spool and the thumb and index finger grip the outer edge of the reel, with the line held under the thumb at the front edge of the spool and the finger at the back. The remaining fingers grasp the rod handle behind the reel seat.

With the rod now held diagonally across the body, the right hand takes a grip on it, from underneath, so that the fingers will be on top at a comfortable distance, say 75 cm, above the reel. The rod is now swung back alongside the shoulder, the left hand going out and across level with the face. The cast is made in stepping forward off the left foot. Some active anglers make it on a run down the beach to the water's edge.

The casting movement is started by raising the right arm to its full extent and pulling the left hand down strongly on the butt as the body sways forward and the rod comes up. As it comes up and over the right arm is brought more behind it and the body is thrust forward on the right foot against the resistance of the rod. The right arm continues to push forward

SURF fishing

CASTING WITH A SIDECAST OUTFIT

and the left arm pulls down and back towards the body as the rod comes over through the vertical and reaches that point which involves the critical instant of release. There, the thumb is lifted to release the line and the sinker or bait flies on its way. The rod continues on its swing until it comes to rest at between 45 and 30 degrees, with the tip pointed at the target.

As the sinker hits the water, the thumb is clamped across the spool to stop the flow of the line and the rod tip is raised to take up slack. The reel is now turned back to the winding position and the lock clicks as the spring drops into place to hold it rigid. The left hand now takes a new grip on the rod, some 30 to 35 cm above the reel and the thumb and forefinger guide the line onto the reel as the unwanted slack is wound in. Owing to the short distance between the reel and the butt of the rod, the short handle can be uncomfortable against the lower abdomen, so a rod bucket hanging from the belt often is used with this type of equipment.

Sidecast gear is mainly used for casting unweighted or lightly weighted garfish. This usually involves casting at a higher trajectory than that used in throwing heavy sinkers with a geared reel. If the line on a sidecast reel becomes heavily twisted, through use of an inefficient swivel or from continuous spinning with heavy lures, it is possible to fish the twist out by doubling the line back on itself at the reel and winding in the opposite direction.

SURGEON fish A group of slab-sided reef-dwelling fish of the family Acanthuridae, often vividly coloured. Surgeon fish are frequently taken by spearfishermen but seldom by anglers. All of the family have a sharp, erectable spine on each side of the body at the butt of the tail. They are also known as tangs, doctor fish and spinetails. Surgeon fish inhabit the warmer waters of Queensland, the Northern Territory and Western Australia and only occasionally enter New South Wales. Herbivorous scavengers that can inflict nasty cuts.

The bristle-toothed surgeon fish *Ctenochaetus strigosus:* A Barrier Reef species. They are reddish-brown in body colouring with longitudinal wavy lines. The head and chest carry numerous small golden or light brown spots. Grows to around 30 cm.

The ring-tailed surgeon fish *Acanthurus xanthopterus:* A plentiful Barrier Reef fish with a prominent white bar across the butt of the tail. They are attractive fish, with greyish-green bodies and wavy grey lines across the body. The dorsal fin and anal fin are a bright salmon colour, with light blue stripes. Grows to 60 cm and is of good table quality.

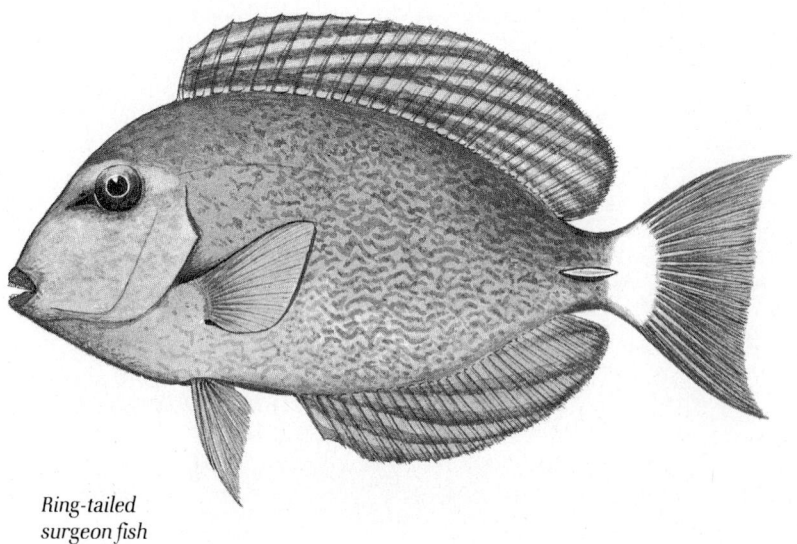

Ring-tailed surgeon fish

Convict surgeon fish

Acanthurus triostegus: A vividly coloured variety which is seen in large schools in Barrier Reef pools. The body colouring is greenish to olive, the jaw and throat white and there is a black line through the middle of the snout. The sides are marked with narrow black bands, which is where it gets its name, and it is also known as the five-banded surgeon fish.

SWALLOWTAIL

See Dart or swallowtail.

SWEEP

Full-bodied marine fish of a generally high edible quality that belong to the family Scorpidae. The young are frequently caught in the shallow waters near wharves, breakwaters and rocks and the mature fish in deep coastal waters. This co-operation with anglers has made them a highly popular angling fish in four Australian States and in New Zealand, where one member of the family, Mado, figures prominently in the catches of saltwater fishermen seeking snapper and the allied blue maomao.

Banded sweep

Scorpis georgianus: A plentiful coastal variety frequently caught by rock fishermen, but probably less highly rated as table fare than other members of the family. These are symmetrical fish with deep, compressed bodies and smoothly arched dorsal and ventral fins. They grow to 33 cm. There are three or four vertical bars across the brownish-black body. Popular with southern States rock fishermen.

Sea sweep

Scorpis aequipinnis: Common in South Australia, Tasmania and Western Australia, this member of the family inhabits more open water than other sweeps. They are also several centimetres longer, reaching 45 cm on average. They are a compact, deep-bodied fish, brownish-black in colour, paler beneath and completely devoid of the bars on the above species.

Sweep Scorpis lineolatus

Mado *Atypichthys mado:* This variety is plentiful off the piers of Queensland and New South Wales, a fork-tailed fish of yellow colouring with brown longitudinal bands or stripes. They grow to around 30 cm in Australia, where the closely related *Atypichthys strigatus* is distributed in Tasmania, Victoria, New South Wales, Queensland and Lord Howe Island. The longitudinal bands are darker in *strigatus* than in *mado*.

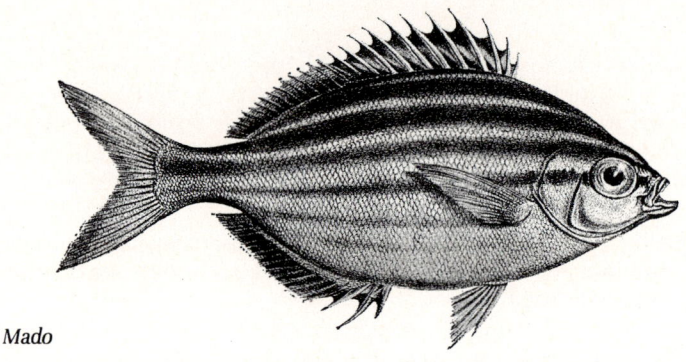

Mado

TACKLE

The equipment used in catching and landing fish. The angler's efficiency depends a lot on how he selects and uses his tackle from a bewildering array of items now available at sports stores and tackle shops, and his enjoyment of the sport is in direct ratio to the ethics with which he uses his tackle. Rigs, reels and lines for each fish are covered in this book under the species themselves and hooks are listed separately.

In the 1980s, amateur fishermen have witnessed a dramatic swing towards tackle that exploits graphite. Graphite rods or a mixture of graphite and plastic have proved lighter and stronger than fibreglass, and tackle shops have followed the trend evident with tennis rackets and swung over to graphite. Most shops these days report that 98 per cent of the fly rods they sell are made of graphite, which not only offers greater strength but produces easier and more accurate casting. Threadline reels with corrosion-free graphite spools are another important development in fishing tackle.

Other standard items of interest to all anglers include:

Beach rings
Small brass rings used mainly to provide a running sinker for sand or mud bottoms where an ordinary running sinker could bury and become clogged. Also allows the use of helmet sinkers as running sinkers on the beach to hold the line in strong currents or heavy surf.

Cliff gaff
A special gaff for bringing big fish up onto high cliffs. It consists of a heavy body with a gaff hook, or hooks, at the lower end and split rings at each end. A heavy cord, long enough to lower the gaff to the water from the cliff top, is attached to the head of the gaff. In use, the split rings are fitted around the fishing line and the gaff slid down the line to the fish. Its weight brings the hook(s) below the fish and these are sunk home with an upward strike on the gaff line. Cliff gaffs are not used widely, as too often the gaff rotates around the fishing line on its way down, twisting the gaff line around the fishing line. A perfected cliff gaff could make cliff top fishing an exciting sport along rocky coastlines.

T ■ TACKLE

NETS

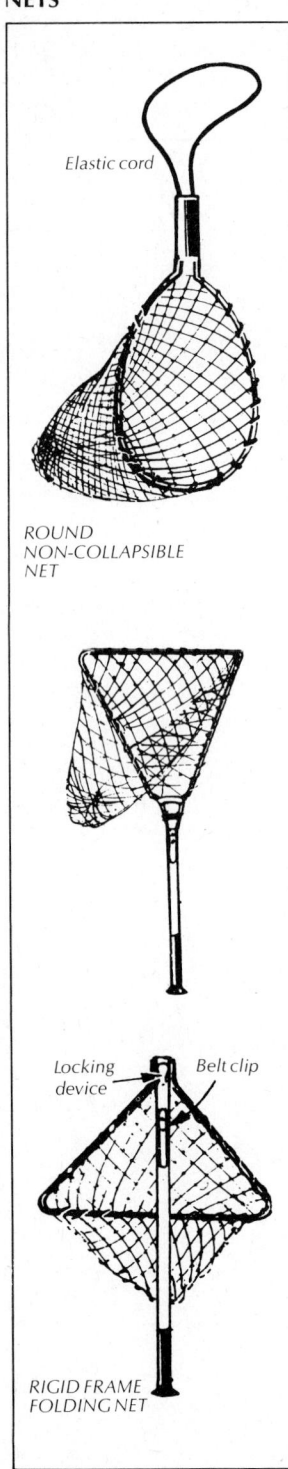

ROUND NON-COLLAPSIBLE NET

RIGID FRAME FOLDING NET

Gaffs and landing nets

Broadly, landing nets are preferable for fish which present too small a target to the gaff. Gaffs are better for fish which would require a large, unwieldy net. Nets are of two shapes in the main—round, for netting fish in open water and various forms of triangular nets. These, with a flat front, allow the net to cover an area of bottom in shallow water.

Gaffs are large, barbless hooks which are driven into the fish to land it. There are two main patterns: (1) Bent back shank, which angles the point outwards and permits easier penetration. (2) Parallel point, for fish with large, hard scales or tough hides such as large sharks. Game gaffs sometimes are fitted with detachable heads which can be released from the handle should the fish make an unexpected plunge.

Both gaffs and nets are fitted to handles of various lengths, from 45 cm or so for small boat fishing to handles up to 3 m long for landing large fish from high rock platforms. Telescopic models are available. These provide a compact tool to hang from the angler's belt and spring out to full length upon operating a trigger in the handle.

Handlines

While not used to a great extent by shore fishermen nowadays, the traditional handline is still favoured by many boating anglers. The traditional cork is being supplanted rapidly by large spools of wood or plastic. The spools have many advantages. Firstly, any line is easier to handle and less prone to kink if kept on a large diameter spool. The spools usually have a casting lip turned or moulded on them to permit smooth line flow from the spool. Anglers who can use a handline on a casting spool or hand-caster fish beaches and estuaries with considerable success. If using a hand-caster, a small swivel in the rig is essential to prevent build-up of line twist.

With nylon monofilament, anglers seeking sizeable fish with handlines need very heavy line. Otherwise, a fast fish can cause injury to the angler's hands with nylon's propensity for over-heating and cutting. This use of heavy handlines reduces the sporting content of handling a big fish.

In recent years line winders have become increasingly popular in deep-sea fishing. These are simply large reels fitted to the gunwale of the boat for line stowage and handling. Their first immediate advantage is to eliminate countless metres of line which would otherwise be coiled on the deck. They allow the deep-sea fisherman to use finer lines, with less trouble accordingly from wind and current and more sporting satisfaction in boating a large fish. The lighter lines allow lighter sinkers to be used, with less snagging and more strikes accordingly. The Brisbane firm of Alveys have played a big part in developing these aids for the deep-sea fisherman.

Keels and paravanes

Some trolling lures tend to spin and so twist the line. Some large spoons are particularly bad in this respect but are very

A good landing net is an important part of a fisherman's tackle. Without it this Snowy Mountains trout fisherman would have trouble landing the fish on the bank.

desirable lures from the fish-taking viewpoint. The most effective answer in popular use is the keel, which stabilizes the line. Ball-bearing swivels are advisable.

Paravanes are a miniature and simplified version of a navy device for cutting mine cables. When trolled, they dive deep, taking the lure with them. In recent years paravane and lure have been combined, giving a much simpler rig. The Reb 2 deep runner lures are a good example of this type of lure.

In the main, it is good practice to use lures free from spin and with them the need for keels. The less impediment on the line the better as a rule. However, some spinning lures are extremely effective, hence the keel.

Nylon traces

Traces of different diameter nylon to the line itself are used mainly in two applications: (1) When fishing over rough ground, especially in deep-sea and rock fishing, mounting the sinker on a lighter trace saves possible heavy line loss. If the sinker is snagged only the sinker is lost. (2) When distance casting with light sportfishing line. The shock load of casting quickly fatigues the line at the rod tip and loss of terminal tackle results. A.N.S.A. rules permit 1½ rod lengths of heavier leader to overcome this. The heavier leader also assists in landing or boating a heavy fish. When the fish comes to gaff, the leader is through the line guides with a few turns on the reel. Game fishing rules also permit heavier leaders to assist in boating a beaten fish.

DEEP-DIVING PARAVANE

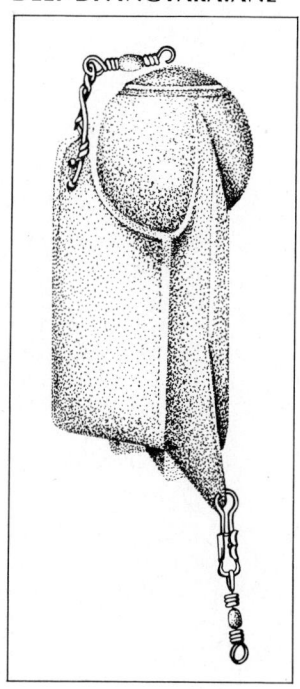

T ■ TACKLE

Leaders
Lengths of line between the hook and the main line, not to be confused with traces. Leaders usually are well below the breaking strain of the main line. They are invaluable when fishing from the rocks or over reefs where hooks are likely to be snagged as they break before the main line and thus preserve the main line for the angler. Leaders are also useful when long casts have to be made with heavy sinkers for fish that bite timidly or have small mouths. The leader allows the fish to nibble at the bait and provides the angler with a 'feel' denied by the heavy line. Similarly leaders that are heavier than the main line save the main line from breakage by taking a heavier load. Contrastingly, traces are usually short lengths of heavy line or wire aimed at negating the effects of sharp teeth such as those of a hairtail or barracuda.

Fishing bags or baskets
The type of conveyance used for bait, tackle items and storage of the catch depends on the type of fishing undertaken. Trout fishermen prefer a bag which can be strapped to their backs and enables them to move all over a stream without concern. Beach fishermen favour baskets in which they can store reels, sinkers, knives, bait and even a sweater or waterproof coat and still have room for the catch. Rock fishermen prefer bags with detachable linings that preserve the bags against slime but still provide them with manoeuvrability as they hop about the cliffs. Boat fishermen usually favour tackle boxes, with a bait bucket kept handy.

Lures
From a bewildering array, fishermen have to choose the lures that will suit their pocket book and do the job required of them. Lures fall into three basic categories—imitations, spinners and plugs. The imitations are copies, usually in plastic, of insects, squid, beetles, and other creatures fish are likely to encounter. Some of them are remarkably accurate replicas, but this form of lure lacks the popularity of plugs, spoons and spinners.

Spoons are mostly made of copper or stainless steel and are intended to imitate the action of a swimming fish without turning a full circle. Spoons are available in singles and doubles, with treble hooks, dressed with furs and feathers or enamelled in bright colours. Consideration should be given to the required rate of retrieve before you buy a spoon. Tailor fishermen require a slower retrieve than tuna fishermen, while trout fishermen probably need both fast and slow retrieving lures to match the moods of an unpredictable fish.

Spinners turn a full circle and mostly are blade-type lures, but again dressed with vivid colouring, feathers and fur, with a lot of holes and ridges on the blades. One of the most effective for Australian anglers has been the aeroplane spinner in which two blades mounted on a wire shaft and separated by a

A range of lures for fresh and saltwater, including imitations, spinners and plugs:

1 *Soft plastic worm*
2 *Soft plastic anchovy*
3 *J.M. Gillies' Imp*
4 *Halco Imp*
5 *Dickson Model 4736S*
6 *Sportland Beaded Spoon*
7 *Gillies' Red Eye*
8 *Shortland's Jointed Wobbler, Model 61*
9 *Gillies' Super Duper*
10 *Spinwell's Finney*
11 *Dickson's Model 4263*
12 *Halco Spinner*
13 *Gillies' Wonder Wobbler*

TACKLE ■ T

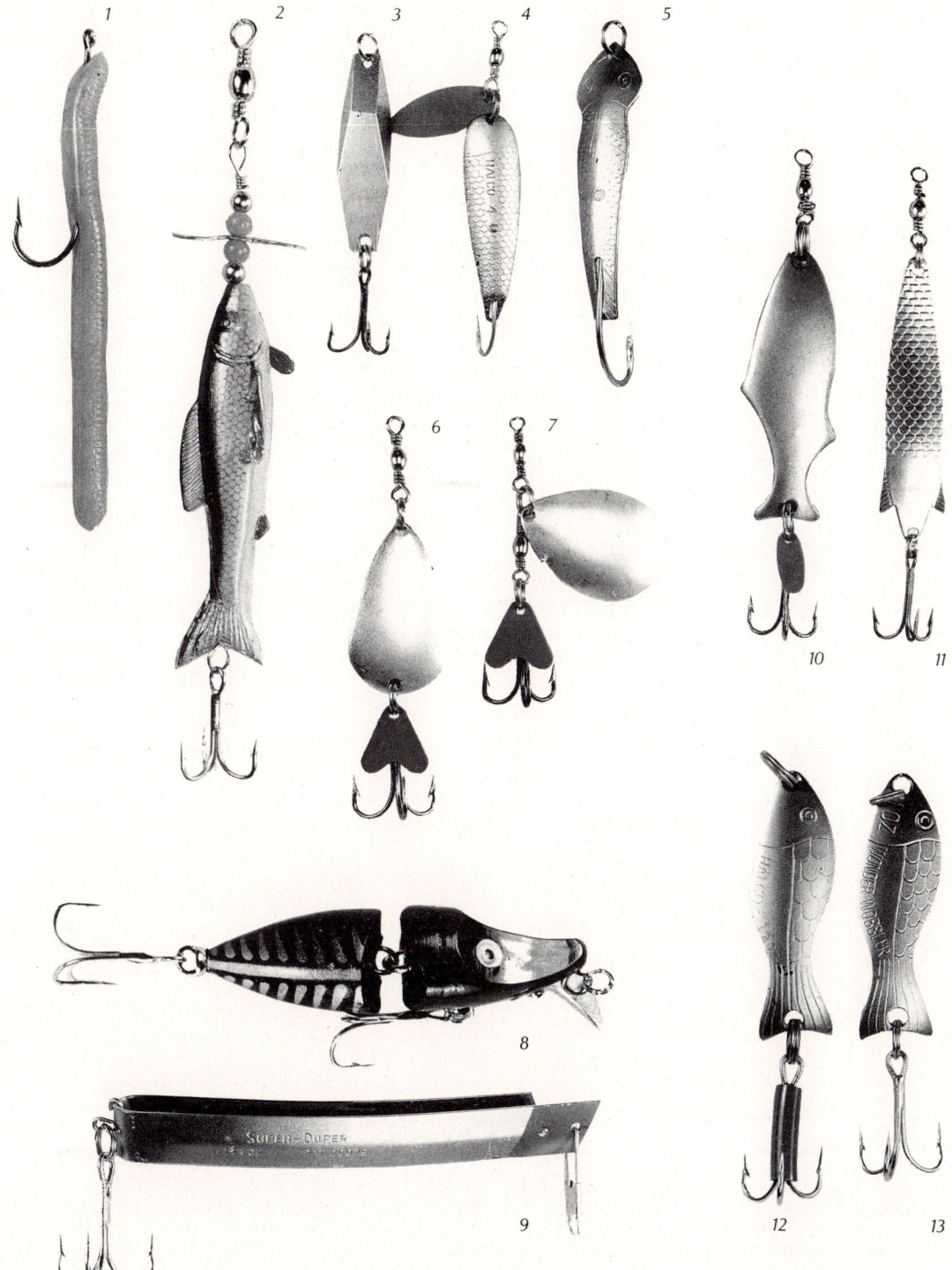

T ■ TACKLE

POPULAR OLD AND NEW REELS

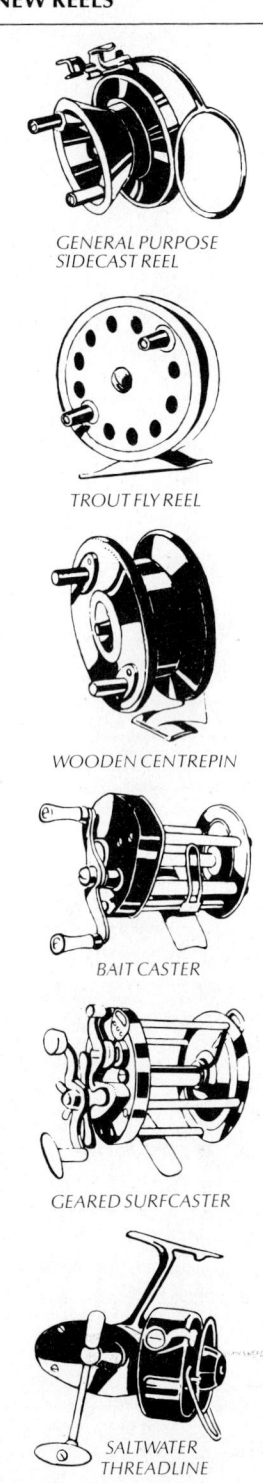

GENERAL PURPOSE SIDECAST REEL

TROUT FLY REEL

WOODEN CENTREPIN

BAIT CASTER

GEARED SURFCASTER

SALTWATER THREADLINE

collar or bead rotate like propellers in the water, just ahead of a set of treble hooks covered in feathers or some other camouflage. The size of the blades on aeroplane spinners varies and anglers need to consider the strength of the line they intend using before deciding on a size. The bigger the blades the heavier the line required to troll aeroplane spinners effectively.

Plug is a term adopted from Americans which is intended to describe lures of insects, minnows or small fish hunted by the angler's quarry. Some of them are designed to dive deep, others to run along the surface. One of the most successful of all time, the Flopy, is a diver and a floater. The action of most floaters depends on the retrieve, with the plug matching the antics of an insect or water creature as it is reeled in. Divers mostly come with adjustable bibs which anglers can set according to the depth they intend to fish. It is important to remember that lures are intended to attract fish, not kill them. A Christmas Tree rig to which is attached several coloured spinners may interest the fish, but the angler still has to get the fish to take the bait on the hook at the bottom of the rig.

Just as some fishing addicts make their own sinkers, enthusiastic lure specialists enjoy experimenting with home-made lures. The late Wal Hardy, a skilled metalworker, experimented long enough to produce the Tailor Ticer and the Rigglejig and put them on the market. James Heddon is said to have gone home and begun fashioning lures after a bass struck at a piece of wood he had been whittling and had thrown into a creek. Heddon lures became world famous.

Reels

Among Australian sportfishers, the most popular saltwater reels are the centrepin reel, the sidecast reel, the threadline or fixed spool reel, the closed face or push-button reel, and the baitcasting reel and its big brother, the multiplying surf reel. Trout fishing reels are discussed under fly fishing. All of these reels have their advantages, but the two that qualify as the closest to all-purpose reels are the threadline reel and the closed face reel.

The threadline reel is by far the best reel for novices. It is always mounted under the rod, and performs several complicated tasks simultaneously. After the bait has been cast and the fisherman wants to retrieve, he can simply turn the handle—not the spool—which is attached to the body. This in turn rotates a main gear in mesh with a pinion gear, which usually is a cuplike fitting that envelops the spool and revolves around it. As the rotating head revolves, it carries the line pick-up assembly with it, traps the line, and winds it around the spool, automatically cross-laying the line on the spool. The cross-laying is vital, yet is achieved simply and easily by the threadline mechanism.

The closed face reel is fitted on top of the rod and many consider it easier to use than the threadline reel. Both the spool and the mechanism are totally enclosed, apart from a

CASTING WITH A THREADLINE REEL

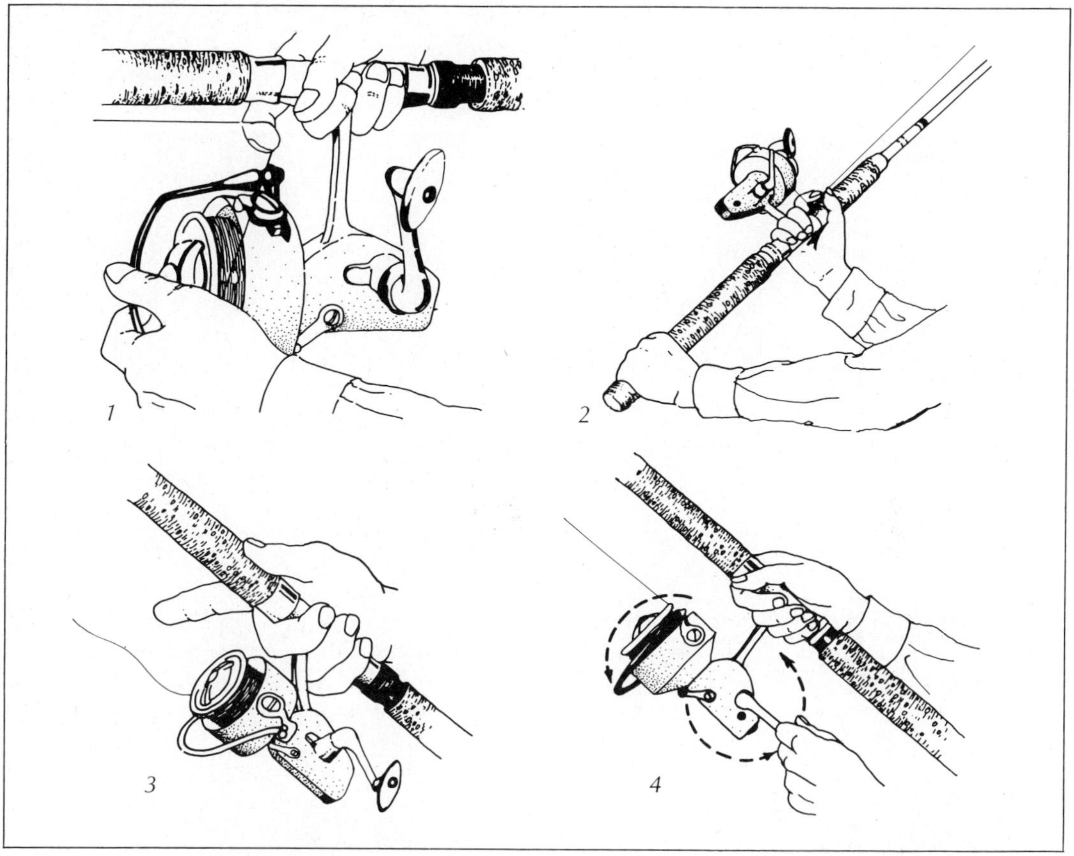

Threadline reel

1 Before casting, hold the rod as shown using the index finger to trap the line tightly against the rod. With the free hand move the bail-arm across the face of the spool until it locks in the open position.

2 To cast, raise the rod over the shoulder to the 1 o'clock position, keeping the free-running line trapped against the foregrip with the index finger.

3 Bring the rod forward with a snapping motion, halting abruptly at the 10 o'clock position and simultaneously releasing the line held by the index finger.

4 Retrieve line by winding the reel handle in an anti-clockwise direction. Do not use the reel to winch in the fish, which should be done with a pumping motion.

CASTING WITH A CLOSED-FACE REEL

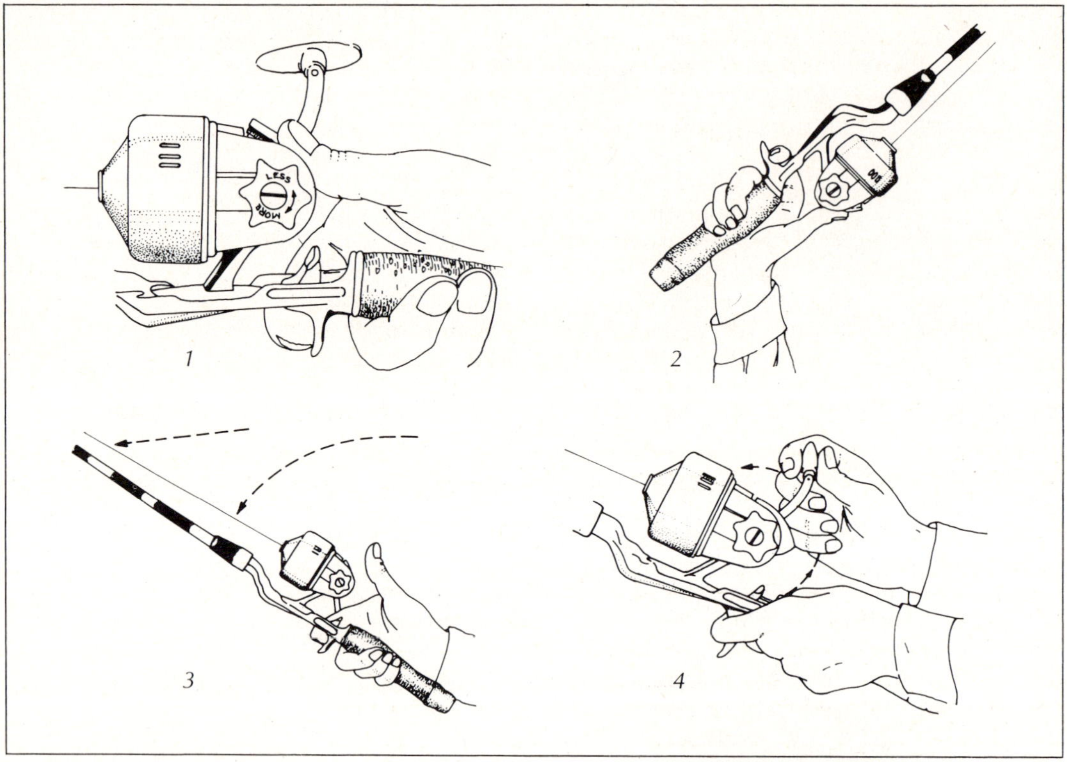

1 With a pistol-grip rod, the reel is mounted above the handle. To ready the line for casting, depress the thumb lever and hold it down.

2 To cast, raise the rod over the shoulder to the 1 o'clock position, keeping the thumb lever depressed to prevent release of line.

3 Bring the rod forward, halting abruptly at the 10 o'clock position and simultaneously lifting the thumb off the lever to release the line.

4 Retrieve line by winding the reel handle in an anti-clockwise direction. Do not use the reel to wind in the fish, which should be done by pumping the rod.

Closed-face reel

small circular hole in the centre of the cone covering the spool through which the line passes. By using a pistol grip, the push button on the closed face reel drops to a convenient height for the thumb. When the thumb button is held down, pins on the pick-up head trap the line against the lip of the winding cup until the angler chooses to release it. When the cast is finished, the fisherman turns the handle to re-engage or extend the pick-up pins which then trap and hold the line. The pins need to be checked regularly for wear.

Sinkers

These come in many shapes and sizes. The most important sinkers in Australia are as follows:—

1. Ball sinker. The most universal type, suitable for all applications except where it is desired to hold the line steady in a strong current. The smaller sizes are usually termed 'ball shot'.

2. Split shot. Small ball sinkers moulded with a split into which the line is pinched by closing the shot with pliers. They have the advantage of quick application, since the hook or swivel does not have to be removed to affix them. Their serious disadvantage is their tendency to damage and weaken the line with their sharp corners when pressed into position on the line. Most experienced anglers prefer small oblongs of sheet lead for this reason.

3. Snapper lead. This is the common sinker for deep-sea fishing on reefs, hence its name. Also favoured by rock fishermen when they need to cast great distances, because of its excellent casting balance.

4. Bean and barrel sinkers. Running sinkers for estuary fishing, slightly less conspicuous than the ball type.

5. Channel lead. The 'picker's doom' of the estuary bream fisherman. Mounted as a running sinker and used to overcome current or tide run. The bait is lowered or cast from the boat and allowed to drift to the desired spot. The channel sinker is then lowered into the water and runs down the line. This keeps the line deep with a long leader moving gently in the current. The line is free to run through the sinker when the bait is taken.

SINKERS

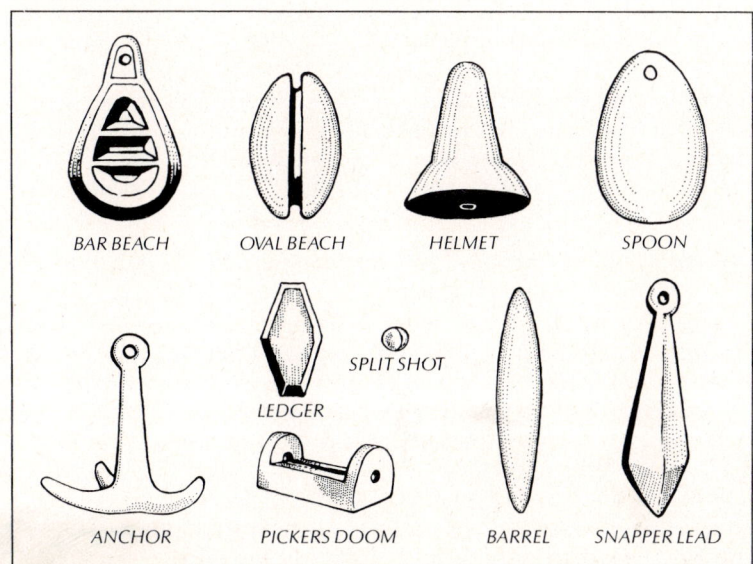

SWIVELS

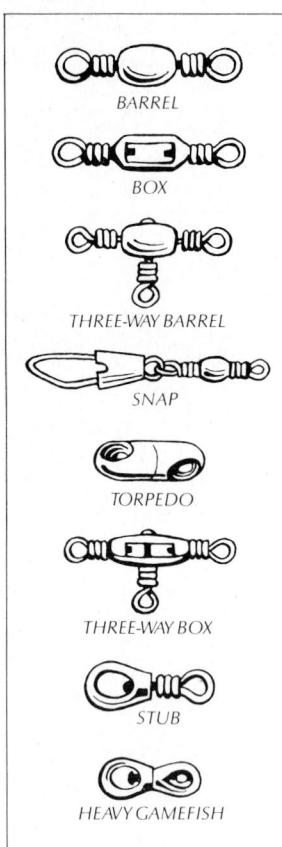

BARREL
BOX
THREE-WAY BARREL
SNAP
TORPEDO
THREE-WAY BOX
STUB
HEAVY GAMEFISH

Snap swivels
These are swivels fitted with a snap ring or safety pin arrangement for quick attachment to lures or ringed hooks. 'Crane' stainless steel swivel specially recommended.

Split rings
Split rings of various diameters are used to attach hooks to lures. Stainless steel rings are best, as copper and bronze finished rings rust quickly, necessitating frequent replacement.

Swivels
Widely used now with any rig and essential with sidecast reels. Their purpose is to prevent line twist, or in the case of the sidecast reel, to correct twist after casting. The most important factor when using swivels is to relate the swivel size to the line diameter. Fine lines cannot exert a strong torsional effort and will not overcome the friction in a big swivel, so the line remains twisted. Similarly, swivels seldom operate efficiently when under tension, due to the increased friction in the swivel bearings, unless ball bearing swivels are used. These are rather bulky and heavy for fine line fishing but excellent with heavier applications.

Recommended line and swivel sizes: Line up to 5.4 kg b/s, No. 12 to No. 10 swivel; from 5.4 to 8 kg b/s, No. 10 to No. 8; 8 to 11 kg b/s, No. 9 to No. 6, and so on. Swivels are much stronger than many anglers think. 'Crane' stainless steel swivels are tested to 20 kg in the smallest (No. 12) size. The smaller the swivel that can be used the better.

Traces
Steel wire traces are used in two applications: with fish whose sharp teeth are capable of severing the line; in game fishing for sharks whose rough hide (shagreen) can fray through the line while the fish is in play. Wire traces for flathead and tailor are not as popular as in former years. The security of the wire trace is achieved at the cost of many strikes. Modern nylon-covered fine wire traces are an improvement on the old twisted fine wire trace, which rusted quickly. They are also better than the single strand stainless steel trace, which kinks very readily.

See also Floats; Hooks; Lines; Rod design and construction.

TAGGING of fish

A wide array of techniques and methods which have been used for several hundred years to facilitate the study of fish migration, growth, mortality, behaviour and population structure. Invertebrate animals such as abalone and prawns are also tagged for similar reasons. Many species of fish, crustaceans and molluscs have been tagged in Australia since the 1930s, mainly by scientists, but more lately by amateur fishermen assisting in co-operative programmes.

Tagging helps to evaluate fish populations and proportions taken by user groups, and this can influence policies on bag limits, closed seasons, quotas and so on. Overseas and local tagging operations have shown some species to travel great distances while others seldom stray from their home grounds. Some species have been shown to grow remarkably quickly, and others slowly. Tagging could indicate the need for complete or partial bans on the catching of some species, both locally and internationally, or results could suggest the relaxation of restrictions on the capturing of others.

The first attempts at tagging were made in the seventeenth century, when English landowners tied coloured ribbons around the tails of trout to prove ownership. Few innovations were noted until the late 1800s when the Danish fisheries biologist, Petersen, tagged plaice by attaching numbered bone discs to them. Since then, there have been a great many types of tags developed for various purposes.

Types of tag at present in use in Australia

Most of the methods used to mark fish have been tried in Australia. These range from simple fin clipping (in certain combinations) to identify hatchery-reared fish, to the insertion of dart and internal tags made from a wide variety of plastics and metals. In freshwater, biologists usually capture fish by passing an electric shock through the water, stunning the fish. They can then be gently handled while the tag is applied. In salt water, the electric current spreads too quickly, so nets, traps or hook and line are used. For very large oceanic fishes such as marlin, dart tags with plastic or metal heads are used, both having a plastic streamer and message. The dart tag is fitted to the end of a tagging pole, and jabbed into the fish when it is played to the boat. The angler then cuts the trace and frees the fish.

Strap tag:

Also called the operculum tag, since it is usually attached to the gill cover. It consists of a shaped strip of monel metal, one end of which is clipped through the other with special pliers. At present used on tailor, bream, luderick and trout.

Streamer or dart tag:

This consists of a plastic, nylon or steel head to which is attached a piece of coloured plastic tubing bearing a message and number. The head is inserted into the dorsal muscles by means of a special applicator. This is a very popular tag and is manufactured commercially in different sizes. Presently being

T ■ TAGGING of fish

used on marlin, tuna and other gamefish, tiger flathead and jackass morwong, drummer, tailor, snapper, and freshwater fish such as golden perch and Murray cod. A small version has also been used on rock lobsters and mud crabs.

Loop tag:
This is a plastic tube which is inserted through the body near the dorsal fin and joined by means of a nylon ball-and-socket to form a loop. It has been used extensively in Queensland on tailor, bream, and reef fish such as coral trout. Its main disadvantage is that it causes considerable damage to the fish.

Internal tag:
This is usually a flat plastic rectangle bearing a message. It is inserted into the body cavity through an incision in the belly, and often has a plastic streamer protruding outside the fish. This tag stays in the fish for many years and has been used extensively on Australian salmon and school sharks. Its main disadvantage is in its difficulty of detection.

Other tags:
Specialized tags have been developed where the need arises. For example, many thousands of prawns have been tagged around Australia using a very light plastic strip which is threaded through the prawn's tail. These have been so successful that a modified version is being used on very small barramundi in the Northern Territory, and on small whiting in South Australia and New South Wales. Other tags developed overseas include various dyes and brands, micro-tags inserted into the skulls of very small fish and detected with magnets, and sonic tags which transmit a signal. These have been used on marlin and swordfish to track individuals' movements for days at a time.

Ideally, tags should possess the following features: They (1) should not damage the fish or cause its death; (2) should not alter the fishes' behaviour, making it more or less susceptible to capture; (3) should be retained by the fish for long periods; (4) should be easily seen; and (5) should possess a message which can be clearly understood by the finder.

Information derived from tagging

1. Migratory routes and speeds of travel of fish.

2. Fish population estimates. It is possible to estimate the total population of lakes and ponds from tagged fish (e.g., Eucumbene). The proportion of tagged to untagged fish is used as a basis for population estimates. The greater the number of fish marked and the greater the number of recoveries the more accurate the estimate.

3. Age and growth studies. With some fish it is impossible to determine the age from the scales. The tagging of these fish and their recapture after a known interval will yield information on the amount of growth that has taken place during the period of freedom. With fish which have 'readable'

scales the recapture after a known time period provides a valuable check on age-determination as interpreted from the scales.

4. Definition of stocks. Many marine fish cover vast distances, and it is important to know whether there is one large population or a number of separate populations before implementing conservation and management policies. The tagging in each area will show if the stocks are separate and determine the degree of intermingling, if any, between stocks.

5. Relative catch rate by user groups. Provided most recovered tags are returned, estimates of exploitation by foreign and local fisheries on stocks can be made.

Co-operative gamefish tagging
The concept of tagging large marine gamefish by means of dart tags was developed by Frank Mather, of the Woods Hole Institution, Massachusetts, U.S.A. He designed the dart tag as a miniature harpoon in 1954. After various field trials and modifications in design, he assisted the Floy Tag and Manufacturing Company, of Seattle, Washington, to make the first mass-produced tag suitable for marking fish which were too large to be handled. Mather than enlisted the help of sportfishermen, and in the late 1950s they tagged 3042 fish, consisting of sailfish, marlin and giant bluefin tuna. Fifteen recoveries had been received by 1961, and co-operative tagging programmes between scientists and anglers had begun.

The tagging of gamefish in Australian waters by volunteer anglers was first envisaged in the late 1930s by pioneer gamefisherman, Athel D'Ombrain. He tagged the first marlin off Port Stephens with a home-made tag and helped Frank Mather in the development of the modern marlin tag. In 1962, D'Ombrain obtained some of the mass-produced tags from the United States, and organized large-scale gamefish tagging in Australia—it had commenced in that year when the radio and TV personality Bob Dyer tagged the first Cairns black marlin.

The assistance of volunteer anglers in tagging programmes is now very widespread. A 1984 worldwide survey of these programmes showed that, in 78 of them, over half enlisted the help of sportfishermen. One such Australian operation, the New South Wales Fisheries Gamefish Tagging Programme, has grown to such an extent that it is now the largest of its kind in the world, in terms of numbers of fish tagged by anglers. This venture began in late 1973 in response to numerous requests from gamefishing and sportfishing associations. For a short time the programme was restricted to New South Wales, but the Game Fishing Association of Australia (G.F.A.A.) and the Australian National Sportfishing Association (A.N.S.A.) were keen to make it a national scheme. With the agreement of the

T ■ TAGGING of fish

FISH TAGS

1 Nylon barbed tuna tag with stainless steel needle applicator
2 Floy tag with steel head and clear plastic sheath with stainless steel slotted applicator

other State fishery departments, tags were soon being sent to clubs and individuals all around Australia, to Papua New Guinea, New Zealand, and even the Persian Gulf. In the ten years since, the project has flourished under the direction of senior biologist Dr Julian Pepperell, and more than 32,000 marine gamefish have been tagged.

Modelled on the successful American system developed by Mather, tags of two types (nylon barbed or steel-headed) are issued to active blue-water anglers. A tagging kit contains 5, 10 or 20 tags, each attached to an appropriately numbered postcard. A descriptive pamphlet is included together with a stainless steel applicator if required. The angler is requested to construct a tagging pole using the applicator supplied. Gamefish are played in the usual manner and brought to the boat where they are wired, but instead of a gaff, the tag pole is stretched out and a yellow plastic dart tag jabbed into the upper anterior part of the back, avoiding the head, spine or belly region. The tag ideally should incline back to reduce water friction, and the head should anchor below the spines of the dorsal fin. The bottom of the dorsal sheath on the hump of a marlin or a sailfish is an excellent place to strike the metal-headed tag designed for these species. For smaller gamefish such as tuna, mackerel, dolphin-fish and yellowtail kingfish, the fish is best brought on to the boat in a landing net and held upside down in a wet towel. This disorients the fish and stops it struggling. The tag can then be carefully inserted at the base of the second dorsal fin and the barb locked in place behind a fin ray. The fish can even be measured fairly accurately holding it in this way, before it is gently released. Because of the size of the tags used in this programme, it is recommended that only fish weighing more than 2 kg are tagged.

After tagging the fish, the angler fills in the postcard with information including the names of the skipper, boat and angler, species, length and weight (estimated or measured) of the fish, condition of the fish (usually the extent of injuries and so on), location of release, fighting time, angler's address, and club membership if any. Cards are returned to Fisheries Division, either directly or through club secretaries. The Division offers incentives for tagging, including handsome certificates and embroidered patches for jackets. Most game and sportfishing clubs present their own tagging trophies, and several prestigious national and State awards are made for tagging on an annual basis. Nearly all tournaments and conventions in Australia now have a hotly contested tagging section and, in fact, some gamefishing tournaments are almost entirely tag-and-release affairs these days.

The main species tagged on the programme are yellowtail kingfish (over 6000), black marlin (over 5000) and skipjack tuna (also 5000 plus), and in all, more than 40 species have been tagged. Since the scheme commenced 657 recaptures of tagged fish have been recorded, including 385 for yellowtail kingfish (6 per cent of those tagged). The great majority of kingfish recaptures have been of small fish under 5 kg, and most have been recovered very close to their points of release. As more kingfish are tagged, it is becoming apparent that adult fish are the ones that travel. The record to date for the species was for a 7 kg kingfish tagged off Sydney and recaptured off Rockhampton, 1200 km north, after only 1204 days.

Of all the species tagged, the black marlin has provided the most spectacular results, with many recaptures recorded over a wide area of the Pacific Ocean of fish tagged off the east Australian coast. Most of the black marlin are tagged each spring between Cairns and Lizard Island with usually between 500 and 800 being released. Some of these tagged fish have been recaptured off New Guinea, the Solomon Islands, New Zealand, southern New South Wales, Kiribati, in the Marshall Islands, and the fish that set the record was taken 7200 km to the east of Australia, north of Tahiti! A small black marlin, about 35 kg, was tagged off Cairns and swam over 800 km to the south in just 14 days—a speed of 57 km per day. In early 1985, a black marlin was tagged off southern California and recaptured off New Zealand.

These results and others indicate that the stock of black marlin in the Pacific Ocean probably mixes fairly freely, and that therefore future management of the species should be internationally organized. Many of the black marlin recaptures have been made by Japanese long-lining boats, and their co-operation in returning information indicates their willingness to assist such efforts.

If a tagged gamefish is recaptured, the following information should be collected:

1. The species and, if possible, the sex;
2. The tag number;
3. The location where the fish was caught and the method used;
4. The date of recapture;
5. The length of the fish from the tip of the nose, with the mouth closed, to the fork in the tail; in the case of marlin and sailfish, measure from the tip of the bottom jaw to the fork;
6. The whole weight.

If possible, the whole fish, with tag in place, should be frozen for examination by biologists if warranted.

All of this information with the tag should then be forwarded to:

>The Officer in Charge,
>Gamefish Tagging Programme,
>New South Wales Department of Agriculture,
>Fisheries Research Institute,
>202 Nicholson Parade,
>Cronulla, N.S.W. 2230.

T ■ TAGGING of fish

Information on the programme, and tagging equipment may also be obtained by writing to the same address.

Other Australian marine tagging operations
Many other scientific studies on marine fishes and invertebrates undertaken in Australia in recent years have stressed the importance of tagging.

Tailor were tagged, with the assistance of amateur anglers in both New South Wales and Queensland in the late 1970s. In New South Wales, over 3500 were tagged and 180 recaptured. Many of those were recovered in southern Queensland after journeys of between 500 km and 1000 km. The Queensland operation was centred on Fraser Island, and while 7 per cent of the 1500 tailor tagged were recaptured, very few made their way over the New South Wales border. The mystery then remains as to the return route of adult tailor south after they have spawned in southern Queensland.

A typical scientific tagging study of estuarine species was carried out by N.S.W. State Fisheries biologists in Lake Macquarie in the late 1970s. There, 3014 bream were tagged, of which 10 per cent were recaptured. One-tenth of these (30 fish) were recovered outside the lake, some as far away as Queensland. In the same study, 1260 luderick were tagged, with 6.5 per cent being recaptured. Only seven of those were recovered outside the lake.

The C.S.I.R.O. has studied southern bluefin tuna for over 20 years, and in that time has tagged tens of thousands throughout their territory in southern Australia. Because of intense commercial exploitation of this species by both local and Japanese fishermen, recapture rates are often very high, showing the amount of tuna fishing being done. These results have helped bring about the recent imposition of strict quotas on all boats involved in taking tuna within the C.S.I.R.O.'s range.

Other intensive tagging programmes have centred on jackass morwong in New South Wales and Victoria, whiting and snapper in South and Western Australia, sharks in the Northern Territory and Victoria, and prawns in most States.

Prawn tagging has also helped in the management of stocks, and has shown some remarkable movements of their schools. Several prawns tagged off Lakes Entrance in Victoria were recovered by prawn trawlers in Hervey Bay and Moreton Bay, Queensland.

Freshwater tagging in Australia
Tagging of freshwater fish in Australia has been most productive over the past two decades, with both natives and introduced species, especially trout, having been tagged in many areas.

In the late 1960s and early 1970s, many thousands of native freshwater fish were tagged in the Murray–Darling River system, mainly by South Australian biologists. Results showed that different species can have quite different movement patterns. For example, golden perch (also called yellowbelly or callop) often swam great distances when river conditions were right, some being recaptured thousands of kilometres from their points of release. In contrast, Murray cod tended to be territorial, often remaining in local parts of rivers for years and thereby confirming the suspicions of many experienced inland anglers. Golden perch have also been tagged recently in Keepit Dam, New South Wales, and anglers should be on the lookout for the small yellow dart tag placed high on the back of these fish.

Many thousands of trout have been tagged in Australia, the most intensive operation probably being on Lake Eucumbene, in the Snowy Mountains, during the 1970s. Over a ten-year period, brown and rainbow trout were labelled with opercular strap tags by the then resident biologist, Richard Tilzey. What came from this study was a clear picture of angler catch rates for both species, and it provided background material for various management plans for the lake. One interesting, if unexpected, sidelight was the demonstration of the repeated homing of brown trout to their parent streams, provided the streams still held resident brown trout populations.

Some freshwater species are the target of a co-operative tagging operation in Queensland. Here, jungle perch, sooty grunter and Australian bass are marked during club outings with equipment issued by the Queensland Fisheries Department.

A far bigger scheme is that launched by the C.S.I.R.O., together with the Queensland and Northern Territory Fisheries Departments, in the early 1980s. This is an intensive campaign to tag barramundi. This fish is usually marked with a medium sized dart tag (anglers co-operate here), while very small fish have a modified prawn streamer tag threaded through the body near the dorsal fin. It is hoped that the outcome of this important work will reveal barramundi catch rates of both amateur and commercial fishermen, although even with a good reward offered for the return of tags, illegally netted fish will always pose a problem.

JULIAN PEPPERELL

TAILOR

Pomatomus saltatrix: A highly popular game fish on all Australian coasts south of the Tropic of Capricorn. It is a voracious pelagic that probably provides more good sport for more anglers than any other species. One of the two members of the family Pomatomidae. The other is the American bluefish, also a noted fighter. The tailor does everything at speed, whether it is eating, hunting or merely swimming about in schools. Tailor grow to 1.4 m and up to 16 kg but average from 1 to 2 kg. Tailor over 4 kg are big catches. They can frequently be spotted by observing flocks of terns that flutter over a shoal,

T ■ TAILOR

diving for tit-bits the tailor leave in chopping up their prey.

Tailor are silvery white on the belly and pale green to greyish or bluish above. The lower jaw protrudes and it has a series of strong, needle-pointed, unevenly spaced teeth in both jaws, the upper one being additionally armed with an inner series of similar small teeth. These intermesh so closely when the fish bites that it is able to shear a garfish or a fine nylon line through with one chop. This shearing action of its teeth undoubtedly gave rise to the name of tailor, although there once was a tendency in some quarters to spell it as 'tailer'. It was known to Queensland Aborigines as pombah and to those further south as dially. The half-grown fish generally are spoken of by anglers as choppers.

A tailor just removed from the water is a beautiful, gleaming fish which kicks about vigorously and snaps viciously, so care should be used in placing fingers near its mouth. The larger ones always seem to have a decidedly pugnacious look about them. Its low first dorsal fin can be laid down in a groove, possibly to give improved streamlining and speedier turns when in pursuit of prey. The second dorsal fin and the anal fin are higher and considerably longer and almost counterbalance each other. The tail fin is moderately forked. Its scales are small and thin and are easily removed.

Tailor are found in all States, excepting the Northern Territory, though they are less common in Tasmania. The best tailor appear in the late autumn and early winter along the Australian eastern and south-western coasts and move north close to the shores of Western Australia and up the New South Wales coast. Fully roed tailor are found on the north coast of New South Wales in June and July. Those that escape commercial fishermen and anglers penetrate as far as Rockhampton on the east coast and Carnarvon on the west coast.

The south coast of Western Australia has produced some of the continent's biggest specimens. A 9.2 kg (21 lb 3 oz) tailor was caught at the Donnelly River mouth on the south coast. Bigger fish than this are known to exist in the area between Carnarvon and Shark Bay. But the average tailor caught within 80 km of Perth on a weekend weigh less than 450 g. In this area, average tailor sizes have been dropping rapidly in recent years. As Western Australian professionals seldom catch tailor, amateurs have only themselves to blame. However, despite the falling average size, average catch numbers have never been better. Perhaps the tailor is a fish which reproduces faster if fished heavily, or perhaps the average size declines if it breeds prolifically. Every summer a score or more spots on Western Australian metropolitan beaches are intensively fished with mulie (pilchard) and whitebait baits.

Bait-casting with a whole mulie bait is an idyllic sport when the land breeze is on the angler's back early on a summer's morning. The unweighted bait is allowed to sink about a metre, then retrieved slowly through the water. The popular

Tailor

bait-casting rig, until recent years, was a gang of two or three hooks with a treble at the end. These days there is a trend towards the use of the flight of four 3/0 kendall kirbys.

In between the chopper and the whopper tailor, on the west coast, there are many places where 1.5 to 3 kg fish are the order of the day, with the occasional 4 or 4.5 kg tailor thrown in. Big tailor are still caught in Western Australia at Lancelin, between Jurien and Dongara, at the Greenough reef, Murchison River mouth, Shark Bay and Carnarvon.

Off the Australian east coast, tailor travel north at the same time each year, but their origin is puzzling as those found in Bass Strait and around Tasmania are fairly small and seldom show up in quantity. From mid-summer they begin to appear around Gabo Island, moving up the coast in schools. They appear progressively rather than the same school travelling up the coast from top to bottom. They are at their best on the New South Wales north coast and the big specimens are seldom seen further south. Mostly the big fish turn up in winter, the smaller fish in late summer and autumn.

Often the first tailor appear off the mid-New South Wales coast just before Christmas and they become quite plentiful by February, with the average weight improving until May, June and July when fish of 2 to 3 kg are fairly common. The best tailor period from Port Stephens to South West Rocks is generally in May and further north into Queensland they are at their best in July and August. In all of these peak periods the best times to fish for them are from sunrise to 9 a.m. and from 4 p.m. to 8 p.m., particularly when there is a high tide at about dusk.

Tailor bite eagerly at the right baits, will take a spinner and can be caught by trolling from boats. They are mainly found along ocean beaches, above shallow offshore reefs, around the ocean rocks and in bays and estuaries. Their needle-sharp teeth cut so efficiently it is essential to use chained (gang) hooks, nylostrand casts or a wire trace. They prefer bonito, mackerel, dart, spikey, flathead, salmon, garfish, yellowtail and tailor baits, usually cut into strips 7 to 10 cm long and 2 to 4 cm wide and threaded on to linked carlyle hooks.

Tailor have soft mouths and should be handled carefully if they pull hard or leap or somersault in the air. They have two main approaches to bait. They either tear in and grab the bait and are off with it before the angler moves, or they pick up the bait, shake it, and drop it. If they adopt this nibbling and dropping stratagem they usually can be hooked by the angler who pulls the bait away a few centimetres at a time. They are quite capable of exploiting the fast-moving wash that runs up the beaches and thus should be played well out until most of the pep has been extracted from them.

Tailor respond best to the chromed plugs, plastic wriggling lures, plastic jigs, plastic squid, feather jigs and spoon lures. A lot of good catches are made with sidecast reels by anglers using pilchards, a whole garfish or similar small fish as bait. Beach fishermen usually resort to big running shot or heavy helmet sinkers to keep the bait well down on the sand and slow it down in being washed back onto the beach. Rock-hoppers prefer very light sinkers when spinning with garfish in order to keep the garfish washing around well out of the kelp.

TANGUIGUE   *See Mackerel, Spanish.*

TARAKIHI   *See Morwong.*

TARPON   *See Herring, Ox-eye or tarpon.*

TARWHINE   *See Bream.*

TASMANIA   The smallest and southernmost state in the Commonwealth of Australia, Tasmania, with its many small neighbouring islands, is some 68,000 square kilometres in area. It is bordered by two major oceans—the Southern and the South Pacific—and is separated from mainland Australia by Bass Strait. The coastline, approximately 5,500 kilometres in length, was formed by the effects of sea, wind and the long-ago movements of the land masses. It demonstrates many land forms, from steep, barren and bleak cliffs in the south and west, to the more gentle lagoons, bays and beaches of the northern and eastern shores.

Tasmania lies directly in the path of the strong westerly gales that roar in from the Indian and Southern Oceans, striking the western and southern coasts in all their fury. Fishing in these areas is controlled, to a great degree, by the prevailing weather conditions and it is only when the weather is kind that the natural harbours and inlets in the area may be entered from the seaward side. Along the northern and eastern shores, on the other hand, fishing is enhanced by the comparatively warm waters of the eastern Australian current,

The waters surrounding Tasman Island on Tasmania's rugged south-east coast, are an excellent area in which to fish for tuna and trumpeter.

which flows southwards from the New South Wales coast until it reaches the Furneaux Group of islands at the north-eastern tip of the State. Here it divides, a portion moving westward along Tasmania's north coast, while the bulk of the warm water flows south along the east coast, then westward past Tasman Peninsula and Bruny Island to Recherche Bay and South Cape, where its influence ends.

Being a mountainous state, with a cool, temperate climate and abundant rainfall, Tasmania sheds large volumes of cold, fresh water through many small streams and four major waterways. This State pioneered the introduction of trout and salmon to Australia and the rich tradition of trout fishing is maintained by thousands of wet and dry fly enthusiasts. The estuaries of the four major rivers—the Derwent, Tamar, Huon and Gordon Rivers—are the main meeting points of fresh and salt waters. The first three estuaries loom large in the Tasmanian fishing scene. They provide food and shelter for many juvenile fish species, which seek the quiet bays and shallow waters; they offer sanctuary to adult marine fishes; and they permit the movement of many fish between their normal freshwater and saltwater habitats. The Derwent, Tamar and Huon River estuaries also afford anglers a wide variety of fishing in a calm, satisfying environment beloved by many recreational fishermen. The estuary of the Gordon River is little fished, however, largely because of its remoteness.

From the Tasmanian shoreline, the continental shelf slopes gradually over a distance of 20 to 50 kilometres, parallel to the east, south and west coasts, to its limit at the depth of 200 m. This area is fished by a few hardy anglers in large, sea-going cruisers. On the east and south-east coasts there are large deep sea trevalla and striped trumpeter, while on the west coast, morwong, striped trumpeter and western salmon are taken. Many other varieties, such as deep water flathead, ling and shark, are moderately numerous. There are some poisonous and venomous sea creatures, including the blue-ringed octopus. Toadfish, and porcupine fish—the flesh of which is so strongly toxic that it has been fatal—live in coastal shallows, and there are dogfish, scorpion fish, rays and stargazers which can inflict painful wounds if carelessly handled.

Tasmanian waters hold a vast number and a wide variety of sporting fish, gamefish and fish prized for their edible qualities. Such variety caters well for some 100,000 Tasmanian anglers as well as the many visitors who take advantage of the changes in environment and fish species that can be found in comparatively small areas.

Saltwater species in Tasmania

The most numerous species in Tasmanian waters—gemfish, Australian salmon, trumpeter, morwong, flathead, trevalla and snapper, tuna, billfish and shark—provide sport for many thousands of Tasmanian and visiting anglers. Other species include bream, which are present in most creeks and rivers that flow into the sea; silver trevally, which visit shallow waters in large numbers; and flounder, whiting and rays, which frequent the sandy shallows. Some fish are localised, often depending upon the effects of warm currents. Some species of flathead, for example, are found only in Bass Strait, while luderick and yellow-tailed kingfish occur in warmer northern and north-eastern waters, john dory and snapper in isolated communities, and ling and cod in their special environment. Leatherjacket, mullet and garfish are ever-present. It should be noted that fish colouration, size and even body shape may vary considerably as may their location and the density of population.

Gemfish Two species of these small-scaled or scaleless predators with large, fang-like teeth are important in Tasmania. King barracouta, also called gemfish, hake or southern kingfish, are coloured blue and silver with a dark marking on the leading edge of the dorsal fin and reach 1 m in length and 8 kg in weight. Although trolling anglers sometimes catch them, they are uncommon in the shallow coastal waters, and are taken mainly by trawling in water up to 800 m in depth. They have been seen in all regions and are occasionally taken on lures. Barracouta, also known as 'couta' or 'snoek', are common in large schools in all Tasmanian regions during summer and autumn. They are blue-grey and silver in colour and grow up to 1.3 m long and 6 kg in weight. They are highly regarded as sporting fish, as they attack a moving lure or jig with fury.

The flesh of both fishes is of good quality, firm and tasty, and is highly regarded when smoked.

Australian salmon

Both sub-species of Australian salmon are present in Tasmanian waters. The western salmon, also known as buck salmon, is a large fish that breeds in waters to the south-west of Western Australia and is found on Tasmania's west coast. It is olive green on the back with faint spots, and silvery beneath. It is known to reach 91 cm in length and 9.5 kg in weight, but only juvenile fish are found in Tasmanian waters, where they are taken by trolling or spinning with lures.

The eastern salmon, known as the blackback or colonial salmon, breeds to the east of Victoria, from where it moves into Bass Strait and southwards along Tasmania's east coast, although a few find their way into the southern and western waters. Adults are dark olive green on the back, which gives them their popular name, while the juveniles (called cocky salmon) are lighter in colour with many black spots. They are popular sportfish sought by many recreational fishermen using a wide variety of spinning and trolling lures. A few anglers pursue salmon using saltwater flies.

Both salmon are popular for their fighting qualities, but their flesh is not highly regarded for the table.

Trumpeter

Three species of trumpeter are present in Tasmanian waters, all being highly regarded as table fish. The striped trumpeter, real trumpeter or Tasmanian trumpeter is pale greenish white in colour with three dark longitudinal stripes along the side. Large adults are taken in deep water on the continental shelf, by anglers using heavy tackle and droplines. Some juvenile fish, up to 2 kg in weight, inhabit inshore reefs on all coasts where they are taken in gill nets and on hand lines. Bastard trumpeter, or silver trumpeter, are common in shallow coastal waters, where they are taken mainly in gill nets and, very occasionally, on handlines. Real bastard trumpeter inhabit deep reefs on the east and south coasts, where they feed on plankton, and they are sometimes taken in trawls.

Morwong

Banded morwong, carp or red moki are large fish which inhabit exposed reefs in all areas, where they are taken in gill nets. The flesh is dry but tasty and is best when baked. Magpie perch or magpie morwong are known to reach 41 cm in length and 2 kg in weight. They are an excellent table fish, and are common on shallow reefs in Bass Strait where they are occasionally netted or speared.

Dusky morwong, also called strongfish or nunda, grow to 1.2 m in length and 14 kg in weight. They are uncommon, but are sometimes taken in nets, and the flesh smells of iodine and is of poor eating quality. Morwong, the popular perch or jackass fish, are greyish silver on the back with a broad black saddle on the shoulders. These fish, which grow to 4.5 kg in weight, inhabit inshore reefs and kelp beds, where they are taken in gill nets and on handlines. The flesh is excellent eating. Grey morwong or great perch are also excellent table fish, but are unfortunately scarce in most regions. Juvenile fish are sometimes trawled in water up to 100 m in depth on the north-east coast.

Another rare species, queen snapper or blue morwong, are beautifully coloured with a bright blue body and head, yellow markings around the eyes and yellow edges to the scales. They are sometimes taken in gill nets near King Island, at the north-west tip of the State. Table qualities are excellent.

Tuna The eastern Tasmanian coast is well known for magnificent game fishing, tunas providing anglers with much enjoyment, and some huge specimens. Southern bluefin tuna are the largest and most sought-after, and are known to reach 2.2 m in length and 208 kg in weight. From February through to July, dedicated anglers seek these fish from bases at Pirates Bay, Triabunna and St Helens. Large fish have also been found in the west and north-west, but few fishermen try for them because of the isolation and the variable weather conditions.

Albacore, dark greenish-blue fish with silver undersides, are easily distinguished by the very long pectoral fins. The average size of these fish in Tasmanian waters is approximately 3 kg. During the summer months juveniles are taken on trolled lures, while adults are found in offshore waters during winter. The white, tasty flesh is known as the 'chicken of the sea'.

Huge shoals of blue mackerel, also known as common or slimy mackerel, enter coastal waters in the north and east where they are netted and caught on lures. The flesh is quite tasty. Skipjack tuna, sometimes called stripey or aku, are the most abundant tuna found in this region, and readily take a wide variety of lures. The flesh is dark and is ideal for canning.

Four other members of this group of fishes are present in Tasmanian waters, but only in small numbers. Australian bonito and frigate mackerel are rare visitors of poor eating quality. Butterfly mackerel (or butterfly tuna) are sometimes caught on trolled lures, while slender or Fallas' tuna are occasionally caught on lures between the Tasman Peninsula and Ansons Bay. The flesh of this last fish is oily, but quite palatable.

Billfish Although billfish are not abundant in Tasmanian waters, game fishermen anxiously await the first sighting of these magnificent fish, usually in December. Broadbill swordfish, distinguished by a flat, sword-like snout, which is longer than the

From late summer to midwinter, the eastern coast of Tasmania provides magnificent tuna fishing. Southern bluefin tuna are the largest and most sought-after, but albacore, blue mackerel, skipjack, bonito and frigate mackerel can also be caught.

dorsal fin, are known to reach 6 m in length and 450 kg in weight. These solitary, carnivorous fish of the open ocean are caught occasionally by professional fishermen but have so far eluded amateurs. Blue marlin are very rare in Tasmanian waters, the last recorded specimen of approximately 550 kg being caught in Storm Bay in 1972, and although sightings of black marlin have been noted, they cannot be confirmed. Striped marlin, however, are moderately common in the east coast region during late summer and autumn and a few are caught each year.

Flathead

Although there are large numbers of flathead in Tasmanian waters, the varieties are few. The most abundant are sand flathead, sometimes called bay or slimy flathead, which are common in all regions. Caught on baits or lures, fished close to the bottom, they are good table fish. Tiger flathead, usually called the king flathead by Tasmanian anglers, are also common in all regions. They frequent sheltered bays and estuaries, where they may be caught on baits or lures, and are excellent table fish. Castelnau's flathead, or yank flathead, are large fish, which are moderately common in bays and large estuaries along the north coast where they grow to 90 cm and up to 8 kg. Small populations of rock flathead are found in

Bass Strait and in south-eastern waters. Spiny flathead, toothy flathead and deepwater flathead are also present, but are rare and of no interest to fishermen.

Trevalla Popular fish with anglers, warehou are common in shallow coastal bays and estuarine waters, where they school in large numbers and are taken in gill nets and on baits. They are also known as blue warehou, snotty trevally or snotty. The flesh is firm and tasty, but quickly deteriorates. Spotted trevalla, silver warehou or mackeral trevalla are common in shallow waters in all regions during summer and autumn. They are taken on baits and in gill nets and will occasionally take lures. The flesh is of good table quality. White trevalla or white warehou grow to 6 kg and are moderately common on the continental shelf, where they are trawled in depths of 500 to 800 m. The flesh is tasty. The largest of the family are deep sea trevalla, also known as blue eye or stony eye trevalla. Known to reach 36 kg in weight, they are caught on droplines over rocky bottoms in depths of 100 to 600 m. The flesh is excellent and is very popular in the restaurant trade. Rudderfish, New Zealand ruffe and Tasmanian rudderfish are also present, but rarely taken.

Sharks The most common species of shark in Tasmanian waters is the white pointer, which is dangerous to swimmers as it enters shallow waters, and has caused at least two deaths; the blue pointer, considered a good gamefish but also dangerous, as it will sometimes attack boats when hooked; bronze whalers, often found near beaches and in estuaries, which are also dangerous and good gamefish; the inquisitive thresher sharks, which have been known to attack boats; and school sharks and gummy sharks, harmless species taken by longlining and sold as 'flake'. Many other sharks, such as grey nurse, blue whaler, hammerhead and basking shark, are found in Tasmanian waters.

Coastal fishing

The north coast Stretching some 500 kilometres from Cape Portland in the north-east to Cape Grim in the west, the north coast includes King, Three Hummock, Hunter and Robbins Islands. From Cape Portland to Bridport, the coast road gives limited access to Ringarooma Bay and Anderson Bay, where flathead, whiting and flounder are found. Morwong, trumpeter and cod may be caught off Waterhouse Island. Population is sparse in this area, but Bridport provides limited accommodation including a caravan park, and boat launching facilities with parking space and picnic grounds nearby. Fuel for cars and boats is available and a landing ground for small aircraft serves the area.

Moving west, access to Noland Bay, Stony Head and Low Head is provided by unsealed roads that lead off the main

Bridport-to-George Town road. Fishing along this strip of coastline is limited to the customary flathead, flounder and whiting, but at Low Head some snapper and yellowtail kingfish inhabit the rocky reefs near the mouth of the Tamar River. Boat ramps are provided at Bellingham, Weymouth and Low Head, the last being the best. Fuel and the usual amenities of a large country town are available in George Town.

West of Low Head, the main population centres are Devonport, Ulverstone, Burnie, Wynyard and Stanley, all coastal towns providing a wide range of camping, boating and fishing facilities. The Bass Highway gives access to coastal areas from Devonport to Smithton. The most useful boat ramps are at Smithton, Stanley, Wynyard (where there are two), Burnie, Ulverstone, Devonport (where there are three) and Hawley Beach, which is about 15 km east of Devonport. Airports are located at Devonport, Wynyard and Smithton, and there is a landing ground for small aircraft at Currie on King Island.

Fishing along this coast centres on both species of Australian salmon, barracouta, flathead and whiting in the shallow waters, and striped trumpeter and trevalla in the deeper water of the continental shelf. In the west, tailor, luderick, yellowtail kingfish and Castelnau's flathead are common.

The west coast

The region from Cape Grim in the north to South West Cape is the wildest, least developed and least fished of all Tasmanian coastal waters. Small towns at Marrawah and Arthur River offer some amenities to visitors, while Strahan, within Macquarie Harbour, provides accommodation, food and fuel and a boat ramp, as well as a landing ground for small aircraft. Fishing is excellent at times at Green Beach, near Marrawah, at Arthur River and in Macquarie Harbour. Flathead, salmon and barracouta are plentiful, while warehou, morwong, trumpeter and the occasional snapper are also present.

The south coast

The short section of coastline from South West Cape eastwards to South East Cape is similar in most characteristics to the west coast. Both are affected by the often strong westerly and southerly winds, and recreational fishing is limited to a few large boats, which venture out from Hobart when fine weather permits.

The east coast

There is a great variety of fishing along the stretch of coast from South East Cape to Bruny Island, Tasman Peninsula, and north to Eddystone Point. Anglers can find accommodation, including caravan parks, and other facilities at Southport, South Bruny Island, Eaglehawk Neck, Orford, Triabunna, Swansea, Coles Bay and St Helens. Boats are available for hire in many places, particularly Eaglehawk Neck, Triabunna and St Helens.

Tuna and billfish arrive on this coast in January each year

and attract many game fishermen for the six-month season. Principal centres are Eaglehawk Neck, Triabunna and St Helens, the main fishing areas being on the seaward side of Tasman Peninsula, Main Island and Freycinet Peninsula, and offshore from St Helens.

Other fish are present in a wide variety of species and numbers. Warehou, morwong, flathead, whiting and cod are available in most areas, and john dory, ling and snapper are caught on the deeper reefs. There are bream in most creeks and rivers, the most popular areas being the Prosser River at Orford, the Little Swanport at Pontypool and the Swan River at Swansea. Australian salmon, barracouta and occasional tailor offer anglers some excitement when large schools are encountered. Best fishing spots are Cloudy Bay, Adventure Bay, Marion Bay, Maclean Bay and Anson Bay.

Estuary fishing
Four major rivers deliver water through large estuaries to the sea—the Huon and Derwent in the south, the Tamar in the north and the Gordon River, which discharges into Macquarie Harbour, in the west. The estuaries of some of the smaller rivers, such as the Prosser, the Little Swanport, the Mersey and the Arthur, also offer good fishing for flathead, salmon, barracouta and bream.

All estuaries contain both rainbow and brown trout which use these waters to reach the sea in spring, and to return to fresh water for spawning in autumn. These beautiful fish are frequently caught in gill nets and sometimes on lines by bait and spin fishermen. An Inland Waters licence, which may be purchased from most sports stores, is required by law if trout are sought in these waters or if they are to be kept when accidentally caught.

The Derwent and Huon Estuaries

Ideal for day trips from Hobart, both the Derwent and Huon Estuaries provide calm, sheltered waters which literally teem with a wide variety of fish. Flathead, whiting and cod are numerous and popular, while Australian salmon and barracouta invade the estuaries in considerable numbers, offering good fishing to those anglers who prefer spinning for sportfish. Silver trumpeter, morwong and warehou, which usually arrive in summer and autumn, may be netted or caught on lines. Each year many squid are caught by jigging from wharves and jetties, and bream fishing is a favourite pastime from early summer through to autumn. Boat ramps are located at Huonville, Cygnet and Garden Island Point in the Huon, and at New Norfolk, Bridgewater, Hobart (where there are six), Kingston and Taroona in the Derwent.

The Tamar Estuary

Some 65 kilometres in length from the city of Launceston to Low Head, the Tamar Estuary holds good flathead, whiting and cod. Barracouta, salmon and some occasional tailor also visit this water, providing exciting fishing for spin fisherman. A few yellowtail kingfish and large snapper are caught in the lower reaches of the river, while warehou and silver trumpeter seek shelter there in the autumn and are taken in gill nets or on lines.

The Gordon Estuary

On the west coast, the Gordon Estuary is the termination of a major river system with many feeder streams, which drain a large area of wet highlands. The Gordon discharges huge quantities of fresh water into Macquarie Harbour, and being isolated and remote from major centres of population, is fished only lightly.

Coastal lagoons
In many areas there are small coastal lagoons which often provide exciting fishing. Various species visit these waters seeking shelter and food while some appear to be permanently resident there. Those lagoons having access to the open sea—Cloudy Bay Lagoon on South Bruny Island, Moulting Lagoon near Swansea and Big Waterhouse Lake in the northeast, for example—hold sea mullet, salmon, flathead, silver trumpeter and bream, both the species and their numbers varying considerably during the year. Like the major estuaries, many of the lagoons are fed by small, trout-carrying streams. Licences are required if these fish are taken.

Control of the saltwater fishery is vested in the Tasmanian Fisheries Department whose headquarters are in Hobart. The department will supply detailed information and advice on all aspects of recreational or professional fishing from its head office or from branch offices in Launceston and Burnie.

JOE THUREAU

Trout fishing in Tasmania
Past records of trout catches in some Tasmanian waters are almost fantastic. Fish of more than 10 kg have been common. Tasmania's trout fishing today, because of the enormous variety and quantity of fishing waters available, is for connoisseurs Australia's best and likely to remain so. One of the biggest brown trout caught in Tasmanian waters was the 12.7 kg (28 lb) fish caught by Sir Robert Hamilton as early as 1887. Biologist Richard Tilzey considers that the brown trout fishing now available on Tasmania's Lake Pedder is the best in the world. Lake Pedder brown trout are free-rising fish that average 2 to 3 kg and offer sport which lifelong trout angler Tilzey ranks superior to that on Lake Eucumbene.

Tasmania will always be of major importance to the history of trout fishing in Australia and New Zealand, for the first brown trout spawned in the southern hemisphere was hatched in 1864 at Salmon Ponds, near Hobart, from ova transported by sea from England. From the small original stock to which this fish belonged, the waters of all Australia received their first liberations of brown trout and from these, thousands upon thousands were subsequently artificially reared in hatcheries all over Australia and New Zealand.

Rainbow trout first came to Tasmania in 1896 from California. Successfully released in Lake Leake in 1905 and then in 1910 in the extensive waters of Great Lake, the rainbow has since done well in almost every Tasmanian lake or reservoir into which it has been placed. The release of rainbows in Tasmanian rivers, however, has not been successful because they quickly move downstream to the sea. A few streams have small rainbows in their cold and swift upper reaches but otherwise Tasmanian rivers carry brown trout only. There appears to be no solution to this problem; in any case most Tasmanian anglers seem happy enough with the situation as it is. Several noted overseas authorities have applauded this confinement of the rainbow to lakes and reservoirs as the ideal arrangement, unaware perhaps that this is the only possible arrangement anyway in Tasmania.

Eastern brook trout are also present in some Tasmanian waters. The initial introduction of this species took place early in the century but self-maintaining populations failed to become established. In 1962 a further introduction was made after the consignment of 50,000 eyed ova arriving by air from Nova Scotia in February of that year. Since the brook trout spawns earlier than both the more aggressive brown trout and the rainbow trout, it is preferable to keep it separate if possible to allow the spawning grounds to remain undisturbed once the brook trout have used them. Further, this species, like the rainbow trout, would quickly migrate to the sea from Tasmanian rivers. Thus the Inland Fisheries Commission has found difficulty in finding suitable waters for brook trout stocking. However the Commission's policy to re-introduce this species must be commended, and a self-maintaining population has been established at Clarence Lagoon in the Central Highlands.

The 'brookie', as it is commonly called, is faster to grow than the other trouts, is a free biter, a good fighter and is considered by many as the best of the three for the table. Moreover, it provides just a little more variety for anglers. All in all there is much to be said for its reintroduction. Although it was introduced in the past in New South Wales, Tasmania is the only State at the moment where the brook trout is found.

An unsuccessful attempt was made between 1864 and 1889 to introduce the Atlantic salmon. This involved 1,000,000 eyed ova imported from Britain over the 25 year period. When it is remembered that it took about 29 years and something like 7,750,000 eyed ova to acclimatize quinnat salmon in New Zealand waters, it is easy to understand the optimistic attitude of those who favour further attempts being made to establish other species in Tasmanian waters, since there are an estimated 3000 lakes on the island.

The enormous variety and quantity of fishing waters in Tasmania provides some of the best trout fishing in Australia.

Licence fees, bag limits, guides

Tasmania, with its tremendous amount and variety of water, has indeed been bountifully blessed by nature. The relatively close proximity of all this wealth of fishing to the main centres of population is of tremendous significance. The cost of an all season all waters adult licence is $24, not a great price to pay for Australia's most abundant trout waters.

The bag limit in Tasmania is 12 fish per day. Twenty-four hour fishing is permitted and the legal minimum length is 22 cm. No special tackle is needed to fish successfully in Tasmania. It is, however, advisable for visitors to make enquiries from a Tasmanian tackle store where licences are obtainable, about prevailing conditions and successful baits, lures and flies at the time. Local knowledge is of tremendous assistance anywhere. This is readily available in Tasmania.

The visitor's main problem is in recognizing waters that are permanently closed, reserved for fly fishing only or reserved for angling with artificial lures, and in adhering to closed seasons on waters that are open for nine or twelve months. This is why it is wise to consult a member of the Tasmanian Professional Trout Fishing Guides Association, a body recognized by the Tasmanian government.

The Tasmanian climate is such that before December the weather can be very changeable and unpredictable. The hottest and driest month is February, the calmest and most settled March. But probably the best generally accepted period for fishing is during December and January. Like everywhere else, however, Tasmanian trout fishing has its ups and downs.

Tasmanian licence fees are:
Full season for adults over 17 years $24
Full season for anglers 16 to 17 years $4.00
Licence for two weeks for persons 17 years or older $16.00
Three day licence $8.00

A person under 16 years does not require a licence nor does anyone with a Pensioner Health Benefit Card. T.P.I. pensioners may apply for a complimentary licence.

Techniques for noted locations

By world standards the average size of Tasmania's trout may not be large, but this figure could certainly be increased in some places if their numbers were decreased. Lake Crescent at Interlaken, near Oatlands, is an exception. Brown trout of 7 to 9 kg or more are taken from this comparatively small lake regularly each season. The lake carries an enormous food supply and hence can support such monsters. Natural bait fishing and spinning are the most productive methods here.

A rather novel practice carried out by the Inland Fisheries Commission in Tasmania is the annual trapping and transfer of wild adult brown trout, chiefly from the spawning run up the Liaweenee canal, which flows into Great Lake. These fish, averaging 1.5 kg, are taken by oxygenated tanker to other waters. The main purpose of the programme is to lower, or at least keep in check, the number of brown trout in the Great Lake and to provide better fishing in other waters. Experiments have shown that the brown trout so transferred from Great Lake are more readily caught in some waters elsewhere and that brown trout aged four years and more improve their condition and growth rate in the new waters. Although fairly costly when calculated at cost-per-trout-per-kilometre, this is an excellent work and has the support of many leading anglers. The transfer has been reduced in recent years, but between 1,000 and 2,000 adult trout are still transported to other waters.

Apart from Lake Rowallan, Dee Lagoon and the Lagoon of Islands, the Tasmanian fishing season is open from August to April inclusive in most rivers and lakes. The exceptions above (which are classified as 'rainbow trout waters') open in early October and close in late May. Great Lake is a further exception, opening in August but closing in late May. Seasons and regulations change from time to time, so it is important to check the 'do's and don'ts'. An Angling Code available free of charge with each licence summarizes the rules.

All methods of fishing are productive in Tasmania. The use of live bait, in one way or another, is successful throughout the entire season. Hand-spinning is very popular, as there is no difficulty in operating the gear reasonably well. Trolling from boats, too, has quite a following in those lakes that are suitable, such as Great Lake, Lake Sorell and Arthurs Lake. Fly fishing, with its special skills, requirements and complications, is becoming very popular and those who master this branch of the sport are rewarded with some extremely good fishing.

Some Tasmanian lakes have around their margins good supplies of crustaceans commonly called 'shrimps'. The fish feed freely on these and Tasmanian fly fishermen have developed a high degree of skill in catching these trout. Indeed, the standard of fly fishing in Tasmania is very high. This is readily proved when the difficulties that visiting anglers frequently experience are compared to the relative ease with which most Tasmanian fly fishermen tackle the waters of the Australian mainland.

The Central Plateau

This area is the scene of extensive hydro-electric undertakings. Natural lakes have been raised in level, new lakes have been formed and there is considerable interconnection by canal, tunnel and pipeline. In addition there lies to the west of Great Lake the Western Lakes region, a vast chain of lakes, at an altitude of some 1050 m and ranging from mere tarns to some exceeding 400 hectares. The total number of these lakes, many of them un-named, has been estimated to be in the vicinity of 1000. Improved road access is now available as far as Lake Augusta and Lake Ada, but beyond these are only rugged four-wheel-drive and walking tracks.

Brown trout inhabit the entire system, ranging in weight up to 4.5 kg or more, with an average of between 1 and 1.5 kg in many lakes, slightly smaller in some and slightly larger, surprisingly enough, in some of the smaller ones. A four-wheel-drive vehicle is ideal transport here. Pack horses are sometimes used, while many anglers simply make their explorations on foot. But however anglers get there, the highland lakes, set in remote moorland, are a sight to behold. The further one goes into these lakes the less likely they are to have been fished heavily, if at all. Their rugged beauty cannot fail to impress the anglers and the chill air has a special freshness.

The readily accessible waters of the Central Plateau are many and, depending on prevailing conditions, can at times provide really good fishing for both brown and rainbow trout. There is, however, little or no river fishing compared to that to be found on the lowlands. Arthurs Lake is at present very popular, many shacks having been built on its western shore. Accommodation is available at Miena (Great Lake) or, perhaps more centrally, at Bronte, some 32 km further west. Although the maximum air temperature during the summer months is only about 16° C and the minimum little more than 5.5° C, camping under canvas is quite comfortable and pleasant. Caravans, of course, are very popular.

Most of the Central Plateau is rock country with sparse vegetation, the twisted snow gums predominating on the ridges while areas of white top are confined to the lower ground with occasional graceful white gums. For variety of lake fishing within easy reach of town this area is unequalled in the whole of Australia.

The north The northern half of Tasmania undoubtedly possesses better and more numerous fishing waters than the south. However, excluding those of the Central Plateau, the remainder is principally river fishing. This is of two distinct types: the rippling, bubbling, stony-bottomed kind of stream; and the slow, flat, deep, weed-lined river. Both are quite different yet both can be excellent. In the former case, for instance, provided big fish are not sought, the St Patrick's River, some 32 km north-east of Launceston, is an exceptionally beautiful little river with a charm all of its own and has captured the hearts of many visitors, especially dry fly enthusiasts. On the other hand the Macquarie River, about 48 km south-east of Launceston, has great beauty of a different kind and sometimes, in late October or November, provides wonderful mayfly fishing, when the red spinner hatch is at its best.

Launceston is an ideal centre for this area, half an hour by car in any direction whatever leading to fishing of one kind or another, while the nearer lakes of the Central Plateau are little more than an hour's drive away. Day trips therefore are common. Indeed it is not unusual for an angler to slip out on a summer's evening after dinner to fish the evening rise. The North Esk and South Esk rivers unite at Launceston to form the Tamar Estuary. The extensive waters of these rivers and their many tributaries provide something like 4000 km of river fishing within a 64 km radius of Launceston.

The south Southern Tasmania is far from devoid of fishing waters; it's just that the north has so many more. Even so, the tributaries of the Derwent, the Coal River, the Huon River and a few others are well worthy of attention. In addition the lower Derwent power development scheme has provided several new reservoirs of considerable size within easy reach of Hobart. A number of lagoons and ponds also have been stocked and these are sometimes productive. Hobart anglers are naturally regular visitors to the Central Plateau, a drive of 150-odd kilometres taking them well into the lake country where many have built weekend huts.

The west The west coast of Tasmania is the mountainous and forest-clad side, its southern portion to a large extent still to be

Lake Pedder, in Tasmania's mountainous west, was stocked with brown trout fry in 1972. The brown trout grow to trophy-winning sizes and provide challenging fishing.

opened up. Lake Pedder was stocked with brown trout fry in 1972 and soon produced monster brown trout averaging 5 kg. Numbers of trout have since increased and the average size has fallen to around 2 kg. However, trophy-sized brownies are still common and Lake Pedder provides challenging fishing.

Many new hydro-electric storages are being created on the west coast as part of the Pieman, King and Anthony–Henty power schemes. Lake Rosebery and Lake Mackintosh have already proved good trout waters. What manner of trout fishing may one day be found there is problematical, but there are indications that the west coast is fast becoming a major centre. In addition to the hydro-electric storages, the major rivers (the Gordon, Pieman and Henty) provide excellent fishing for large sea-run trout in very rugged but unspoilt surroundings.

The north-west

The north-western coast has many streams along its entire length, varying in size from respectable rivers to mere creeks. All of them hold trout. There are many small fish here—but also a few good ones. The Inglis and the Flowerdale, near

Wynyard, are typical of this kind of stream, flowing through beautiful flat country in their lower lengths after plunging down from the rugged foothills of the Western Tiers, where some of them hold small rainbows in their headwaters. When the whitebait enter the estuaries of various of these rivers in the spring, some exceptional sea-run brown trout are taken—up to 7 kg and over.

The Mersey-Forth hydro-electric power scheme provides the north-west coast area with a number of sizeable artificial lakes and waterways where excellent fishing is sure to be found. Lake Mackenzie and Lake Rowallan, for example, which always provide good fishing, have become the haunt of many local and visiting anglers. This area is only some 80 to 95 km south of Devonport, set in some of the most rugged and spectacular country on the island.

The east The eastern side of the island offers good trout fishing in both lakes and rivers. Lake Leake, near Campbell Town, provides consistent fishing. Certainly over the years this lake has been a wonderful fishery and an accommodation house was built nearby many years ago. A few kilometres south of Lake Leake lies Tooms Lake, which is rather similar in size and shape. This lake is reached from the township of Ross.

Fingal and Avoca are both good centres for river fishing in this section, the South Esk being common to both, while that lovely little dry fly stream, the Break-o'-Day, unites at the former township and the equally fascinating St Paul's comes in at Avoca.

On the eastern coastline itself fishing may be found in all coastal streams, such as the Scamander and George. On the north-east coast there are some very good lagoons, Blackmans Lagoon and two Waterhouse Lagoons. Some excellent fish, brown and rainbow trout, may be caught here.

Fly fishing, spinning and bait fishing are all productive on these rivers. In this area of Tasmania there are reasonable numbers of small grasshoppers to be seen after Christmas and anglers using them as bait often have great success.

DAVID SCHOLES AND R. D. SLOANE

MINIMUM LEGAL LENGTHS IN TASMANIA

Blackfish, Tasmanian	22 cm	Flounder	23 cm
Crayfish, giant freshwater (from rostrum to end of carapace)	13 cm	Trout, Brook, Brown or Rainbow	22 cm

Grayling are fully protected at all times. Possession of perch, tench, carp or goldfish is prohibited, whether alive or dead. Licence holders are restricted to one rod and reel except in specified bream waters, where two rods and lines may be used. Fishing from a boat within 100 m of an angler is illegal unless the boat is securely moored.

TENCH

Tinca tinca: These European fish are sluggish, bottom-dwelling members of the carp family originally introduced from England to Tasmania in the 1870s and thence to the mainland. They were widely distributed in Victorian streams by the Geelong and Western District Acclimatization Society in 1876 and further liberations were made in that State by the Ballarat Fish Acclimatization Society in 1877. Now reasonably abundant fish in Victoria and South Australia, they have rapidly increased in numbers in a variety of locations such as lakes, swamps and in the lower and more sluggish sections of the Murray River in South Australia. It is generally expected that tench will spread and eventually have the same distribution as that of the redfin perch.

Tench are not very attractive fish in appearance. They are solid in body shape, with small scales which are golden-yellow in colour. The body colour is darker above and lighter below, with a slight greenish tinge. There are two small barbels near the mouth and the iris of the eye is bright orange.

Tench have a preference for pools and sluggish water generally, with a muddy bed in which they can grope for worms and molluscs. In Europe they spend a protracted time in a torpid condition buried in the bottom mud, but in the Australian environment where winters are less severe the fish are commonly active throughout the year. As a result of the continued scavenging of these fish, all dead and decaying matter that would otherwise foul the pool is turned over and over and eventually eliminated. Thus tench may be highly useful to other fish. Tench have the typical carp ability to withstand low oxygen concentrations and may be useful for stocking ponds or canals not suitable for other fish.

Tench of between 1 and 1.5 kg are caught frequently by anglers, but fish may reach far greater size if sufficient food is available; a fish of 7.7 kg and 70 cm in length has been recorded. They are good fish to eat and, together with redfin perch, form the basis of the commercial freshwater fishing industry in Victoria. However, there is considerable badly informed opposition to these fish in South Australia and New South Wales markets, where they are usually sold well below their true market value. Part of this opposition probably arises because of the generally unfamiliar greenish-bronze body colour, the slight reddish tint to the fins and the slimy exterior which is objectionable to many people. In addition tench are commonly associated by many people with the non-edible carp, a member of the same family to which they bear a slight resemblance.

In England, tench is commonly known as the doctor fish because it is believed that its slimy skin exudes a fluid calculated to cure any sick fish that rubs against its sides. This fallacy may have raised some doubts as to the edibility of tench in this country. Surprisingly, tench are not widely sought by anglers in Australia. This is in direct contrast to the situation in Britain, where tench are eagerly fished for and in fact are known as the 'Opening Day' fish. This refers to the fact that some 90 out of every 100 anglers seek tench when the coarse fishing season opens in that country each June.

Best baits for tench are undoubtedly worms or bread pieces, but they will take almost any offering such as freshwater mussels, shrimps, a variety of insects and their larvae and small yabbies.

TERAGLIN Smaller members of the Sciaenidae family and closely related to the mulloways. The common teraglin *Attractoscion aequidens* is found only along the coasts of southern Queensland and New South Wales. It is an offshore species, usually found at from 27 to 90 m and unlike the mulloways it does not enter the harbours or estuaries.

Teraglin usually are found around reefs, and particularly where the bottom is in the form of gravel beds. For no apparent reason they often frequent a particular reef or area to the total exclusion of others nearby which seem to offer the same attractions. Snapper fishermen often take a few by day but the big catches are made by fishing for them specifically at night. Very often they are found to be feeding anywhere up to 9 m above the bottom, and the baits must then lie accordingly. Sometimes, when they are biting well, others will follow a hooked fish to the surface and then the sport becomes fast and furious. They may be berleyed up in a similar manner. Suitable baits are prawns, blue mackerel, bonito, yellowtail, mullet, garfish, salmon and squid.

The teraglin is often confused with the mulloway but may be conclusively identified by its much finer scales, the slightly concave back edge of the tail fin and the fact that the membranous lining of its mouth is deep yellow to pinkish yellow, instead of dull reddish-grey and orange as in the mulloway. One has been known to grow to 1.3 m and 9 kg but most range from 1 to just over 2 kg. Teraglin are excellent eating, rated higher than mulloway, and bring top prices in the markets.

The silver teraglin *Otolithes argenteus*, also known as yankee whiting and wire-tooth, occurs along the eastern coast of Queensland, north from about Fraser Island. At times it is

Silver teraglin

plentiful off Alligator Creek, just south of Townsville. It grows to about 80 cm and is a beautiful silvery fish which is in iridescent blue and pink shades when first removed from the water. It has a large, distinctive dark blotchy area behind the eyes, on the gill covers. It ventures into shallower water than its southern relative, but is fished for in a similar manner. It is an excellent food fish.

BRYAN PRATT

THERMOCLINE

A narrow zone or layer of water where water temperatures rapidly alter and thus affect fish activity. The radiant heat in the middle of summer penetrates only to a certain depth of water and thus only the surface water is warmed. This warmer water expands and becomes less dense than the cooler water below it. A sharp division between the surface water and that beneath it on which it is literally floating occurs. The thermocline is the layer of gradation between the warm and cold water. Temperature of the water between the top and the bottom of the thermocline drops sharply, theoretically at the rate of 0.01 degrees C per centimetre of depth.

As the densities of the warm and cold waters differ, no mixing occurs between them. The deeper, cold water, although initially having more oxygen, is depleted by the respiratory activities of bottom dwelling animals and the like, together with the processes of decay. Thus the thermocline presents the most favourable conditions of oxygen availability for trout in a lake such as Eucumbene and trout are frequently found in this zone during the day in summer. In Eucumbene the thermocline is usually at a depth of 4.5 to 9 m during the period December to January and at 7.5 to 12 m in February and March.

The depth of the thermocline is subject to fluctuations according to the prevailing climatic conditions. To find the precise depth of the thermocline, the angler attaches a thermometer to a piece of cord marked at metre intervals and drops it down to increasing depths, noting the temperature at each depth.

A thermometer of the maximum and minimum type should be used, as it is relatively inexpensive, will accurately record deeper temperatures and will eliminate the need for a sampling bottle to be used together with the thermometer. The reading on the maximum arm should be ignored and that on the minimum recorded. On finding the depth of the thermocline, the angler should fish in its upper half or just above it.

THORNFISH or dragonet

Bovichtus variegatus: A fairly common fish in rocky areas of South Australia, New South Wales and Tasmania. Their flesh is poor eating but they are caught on light lines and small hooks quite frequently in the colder waters where they live on

Thornfish

marine animals, crustaceans and small fish. Among the uninitiated thornfish arouse great speculation immediately they are caught and they are repeatedly sent to museums for identification. They grow to 28 cm and are bluish-grey or olive-brown in colouring with dark mottling on the head and body. All the fins are speckled in scarlet. The rather slender body bristles with bits and pieces. There are two separate dorsal fins, pectoral fins with five or six rays, ventral fins set in advance of the base of the pectorals and there is a prominent spine in the upper gill plate.

THREADFIN salmon

Polynemidae: These excellent sporting fish are extremely interesting and present a number of contradictions. They probably were named salmon by the early settlers because some possessed pink flesh, but they are not salmon at all. Later, ichthyologists recommended that they be known as threadfin, but the original name stuck and now they are popularly known as threadfin salmon.

They are most at home in the discoloured, muddy water of the deltas and estuaries and in the discoloured coastal waters at the close of the wet season. Perhaps this is related to the fact that the snout and eyes are encased in a thick gelatinous membrane or shield which has a perspex-like appearance. This is crystal-clear when the fish is removed from the water, but after death it soon clouds over and gives the impression that the creature must have been swimming blind. Despite its habitat of muddy water the flesh carries no taint of it when cooked and most anglers who fish for them rate threadfin salmon highly among our most choice eating fish.

Another of their physical peculiarities is the growth of a cluster of long, thread-like rays or filaments in front of each of the pectoral fins immediately below the lower edge of the gill cover. It is thought that, as in the case of the gurnards, or goat fish, these filaments possess a sense of taste or fulfil some other such function which may assist in the location or selection of food. The number of rays present is one of the distinguishing features which help to determine species. They also have caused the colloquial name of 'tassel-fish', but it is misapplied here and should be reserved for another fish.

There are a number of species, of which four are of interest to anglers in Queensland and other north Australian waters. The fish of this family once were a lot more plentiful than they are today and in favoured waters, such as Princess Charlotte Bay, they used to move into the estuaries in great shoals. In the early boom days of gold and tin mining in north Queensland, Chinese used to salt and dry them for sale on the fields. Since then, as with the barramundi, intensive fishing and pollution of the rivers have seriously depleted their numbers. In 1985 at Rockhampton anglers were thankful for 2 kg threadfin whereas 10 kg specimens were common a decade earlier.

The closely compressed body, with its wide but deeply forked tail and other large fins makes these fish fast and powerful fighters on a line. They have a peculiarity (somewhat in common with the chinaman leatherjacket) in that with age they develop large bony nodules on the vertebrae. This makes them difficult to carve up, so for cooking they usually end up as two fillets and a thick backbone strip.

Giant threadfin, Cooktown salmon

Eleutheronema tetradactylum: This is the most common of the group and in various areas has been given a number of names, including 'blue salmon'. It grows to considerable size in Indonesia and southern Asia and in India one is said to have been taken at 145 kg, but in Australian waters the name giant threadfin is a misnomer. Here it grows to a maximum of about 70 cm or 2.5 to 4 kg and is exceeded in size by Sheridan's threadfin. In view of the general acceptance of 'blue salmon' among anglers and commercial fishermen, it probably would be better to use the name 'blue threadfin salmon'.

It is well distributed along the coast and around northern Australia to the far north-west coast, but probably is to be found in greatest quantities on the east coast of Cape York and in the deltas and estuaries of the Gulf of Carpentaria. Those taken by anglers usually average 1.5 to 2 kg though the compressed body and broad fins give them considerable length and suggest they would weigh more. In the far north

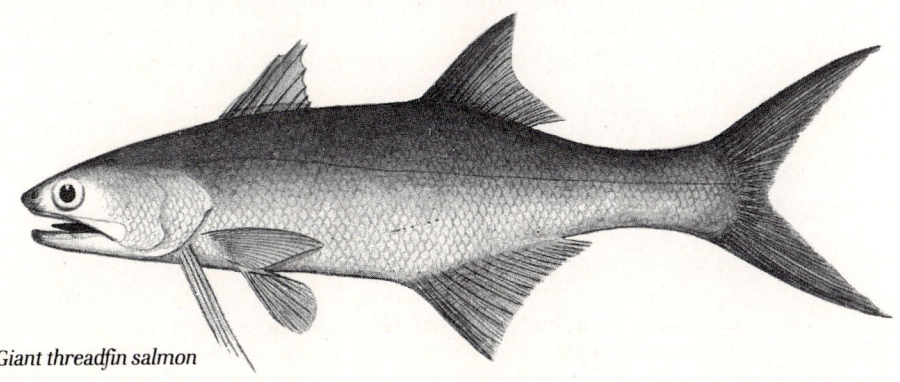

Giant threadfin salmon

T ■ THREADFIN salmon

they used to be taken in quantities by placing nets across the mouths of saltwater creeks at high tide and then gathering in the catch after the ebb.

The blue threadfin salmon is bluish-black to dusky greenish-black on the upper body, merging into white on the lower sides, usually with very faint pink tints on the belly. It has four (on very rare occasions only three) moderately long rays on each side which reach back only to about the rear edges of the pectoral fins. Its snout prominently projects beyond the lower jaw.

Flat threadfin salmon *Polydactylus multiradiatus:* A smaller member of the family which grows only to about 30 cm. It is commonly met with on the coast and in the rivers of Queensland occurring in greatest numbers in the north. It is greenish-golden on the head and back, sides bluish-silver to silver pink on the abdomen, with yellow tones in the region of the vent and the anal fin. The tail fin is greenish-yellow and the pectorals are yellowish with a considerable peppering of black specks. It has seven rays on each side.

Sheridan's threadfin salmon *Polydactylus sheridani:* Often known as Burnett salmon and king salmon. It has a more rounded body and possesses greater weight for length than the blue threadfin salmon. It has been recorded at 30 kg and specimens over 18 kg are not uncommon in some of the Queensland fish markets. It is commonly found along the whole of the Queensland coast, around into the Gulf of Carpentaria and across north Australia. It has always been in evidence around Maryborough and usually figures prominently there in the catches of the commercial fishermen and those anglers who have learned to troll for it.

It is light bluish-grey on the upper body, shading to silver-white on the lower sides and belly, where at certain times of the year it becomes golden-yellow. It is lighter in colour than the species previously described and shows a good deal more yellow in the fins. It has five (on occasions six) extra long rays at each side, the longest of which reach back past the vent. The snout projects only slightly beyond the tip of the lower jaw.

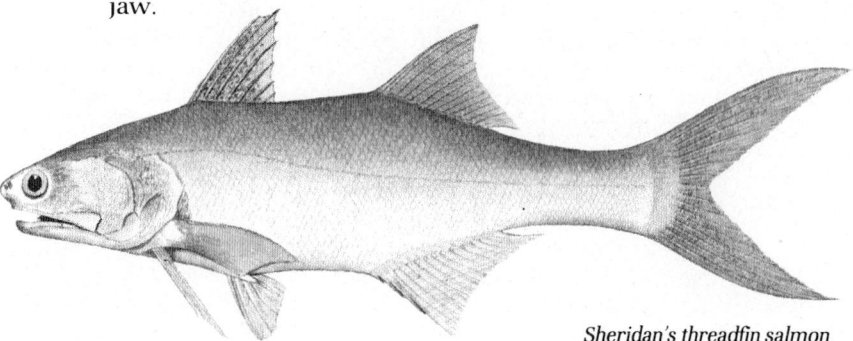

Sheridan's threadfin salmon

Striped threadfin salmon

Striped threadfin salmon

Polydactylus plebejus: Often known as puttynose or puttynose perch. A smaller threadfin salmon which grows to 48 cm but usually averages from 30 to 35 cm. It occurs only in moderate quantities in the rivers and estuaries on the central and southern coast of Queensland and some occasionally move down to northern New South Wales but from present knowledge its habitat does not seem to extend across north Australia.

It is golden-yellow, with darker greyish-yellow tones along the back. It has conspicuous (particularly in the larger specimens) dark-brown lines running longitudinally along its back and sides between the rows of scales. It has relatively larger eyes than the species discussed previously and the snout overshoots the lower jaw to the extent that the tip of the latter is immediately below the front margin of the eye. It has five long rays on each side which extend past the pectoral fins to the rear edges of the ventral fins but not nearly to the vent.

Fishing for threadfin

The habitat of these fish includes inshore sandflats, deltas, estuaries and the lower reaches of rivers, usually where the water is discoloured by mud raised by wind or tidal currents. Favoured fishing places are around the mouths of creeks or estuaries on a rising tide. A wide variety of gear is used in fishing for them with bait, although standard surf-angling tackle (with geared, sidecast or threadline reel) is best for casting out onto the flats. These fish have a deep gullet and an amazing facility for severing nylon line. The two larger species may confound the angler by repeatedly biting through a 9 kg line above a pair of large hooks linked together. When a bait is taken on an ordinary bottom rig the fish usually shoots to the surface, shows its two dorsal fins and quickly cuts itself free. Suitable bottom tackle is a 7/0 hook on a 30 cm wire trace or a pair of 6/0 or 7/0 Mustad 9920 carlisle hooks linked together and attached to a 23 cm wire trace and swivel.

The best lure is small live fish, usually in the form of mullet or northern school whiting. When live bait is not conveniently obtainable they are angled for with small whole fish, including the above and herrings, garfish, pilchards, yellowtail, striped barracuda and trumpeter. They may also take prawns, crabmeat or fishstrip baits. They take a dead bait with a rather hesitant, fumbling bite, whereas they grab at a live one.

Fishing for them with lures is often a very doubtful procedure, often because they cannot sight the bait in the muddy water, but it can be exciting at times. It requires a good strong threadline spinning or baitcasting outfit with a 5.4 kg line, which is about the heaviest which may be used with this type of tackle. Sidecast gear serves quite well. To be on the safe side it is best to work the lures on a short wire trace. Best times to spin are in the very early morning and at dusk, though good results sometimes are to be had by working the mouth of a creek or saltarm near the top of a rising tide in the afternoon. Best results usually are obtained by working the lures at a fast speed. A lot of threadfin, particularly Sheridans, are taken by trolling.

Most successful artificial baits seem to be surface lures such as the Reb 2 series, but a lot of fish have been taken on big chrome jigs, plastic squid, big spoons and trolled garfish.

The threadfin is a very speedy opponent and usually puts on an acrobatic display by leaping a lot. A big fish must be let run or it probably will break the line. They have a good deal of stamina and endurance, but a few long runs under pressure enable the angler to tire them and begin to lead them about, after which they can soon be brought aboard or to shore. The angler lucky enough to get among big biting threadfin will experience some angling thrills to treasure for a long time.

TILEFISH *Branchiostegus wardi:* A highly edible deepwater fish of the south Queensland and New South Wales coasts. Found at depths between 110 and 180 m. They are mostly light grey in body colouring, with grey vertical bars or reddish spots across the body. They have no angling importance but are fish of some fascination because of a legendary calamity in 1882 when more than 11,000 km^2 of the Atlantic were found to be covered in dead tilefish. The cause has never been discovered but it is generally believed that an estimated 1438 tilefish which died were the victims of a temporary flood of cold water through the warm water zone. The tragedy was thought to have eliminated the tilefish but gradually they began to reappear again and today more than 4,530,000 kg of tilefish are caught in America every year. They are found on the outer edge of the continental shelf and are ideal for smoking. They grow to 52 cm and 1.7 kg.

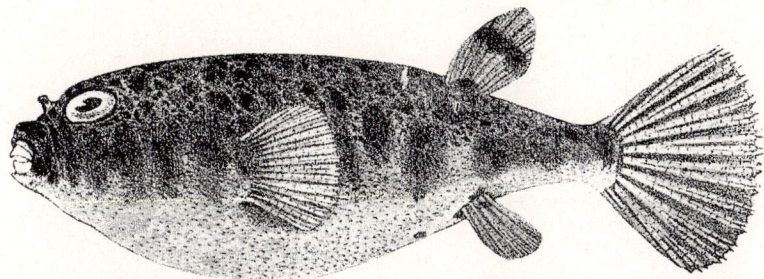
Common toadfish

TOADO or toadfish

Poisonous, self-inflating fish of the family Tetraodontidae with a facility for changing colour to suit their surroundings. They are common in all Australian States. They are also known as globefish or puffer fish. They are most abundant in warm water and most of Australia's thirty species occur in Queensland, including the banded toado, the common toado, the marbled toado, stars and stripes toado, the silver toado, and the weeping toado. Before inflating they are shaped like an avocado and whatever the body colouring are easily recognized by their uniform covering of small spines and by the large dark blotches on the upper surface. They are scavengers with strong fused teeth that form a beak in front. They have a great fondness for crabs whose legs they nip off around the sandflats. Grant points out that they are one of the few fish that allow themselves to be stranded by receding tides, scratching themselves a nest in the sand until the tide rises again. They are a fish which should never be eaten as they have been responsible for several confirmed deaths, including one in Sydney in 1951. They are sometimes found in fresh water.

TOMMY ruff

Arripidae: A splendid fish which is plentiful in South Australia and Western Australia. Also known as ruff, roughie, tommy rough and sea herring, it is a smaller relation of the Australian salmon and belongs to the same perch family. Unlike the salmon it is a good table fish, popular with jetty fishermen.

Many World War II servicemen have strong memories of this fish as it was often served to them interminably in cans as Perth herring. Western Australian anglers mostly call it herring and it is one of the staple fish taken by south-west anglers. Soon after the salmon start their autumn migration in the west, masses of these fish start moving along the same path with the same spawning urge. Between 20 and 25 cm long, the tommy ruff turn the sea dark over large areas. They stop to feed around the rotting weed banks along the south-west corner and there develop an unforgettable taste for maggots; a taste which Western Australian anglers cultivate by using hooked clusters of home-grown maggots or 'wogs' to catch herring almost the whole year round.

T ■ TREVALLA

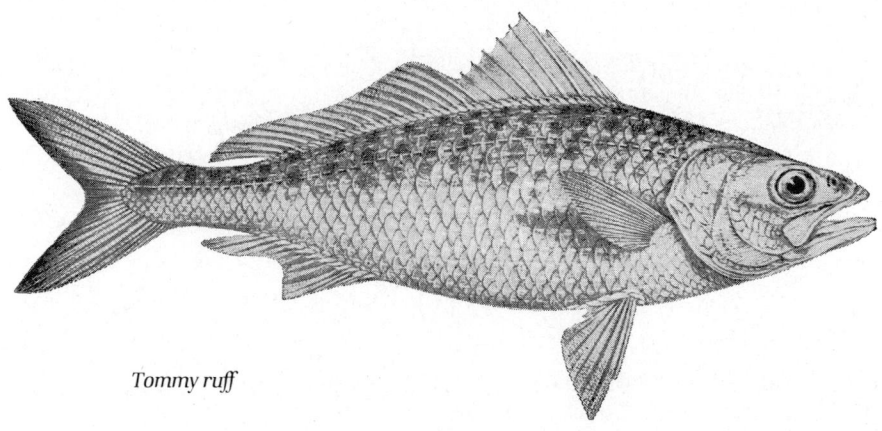

Tommy ruff

Herring are gutsy little scrappers with a zest for berley flavoured with sardine oil and such baits as whitebait, bran, crayfish, prawn and, of course, wogs. When they have just spawned off Rottnest Island they are so hungry they will take any bait—even a piece of white cloth dipped in oil. When they have returned to normal appetite, herring are a challenging little fish to catch. They penetrate the estuaries but are mostly caught from beaches and rocks. Western Australian herring experts at Grant St, City Beach or Mullaloo are often thrilled by catching two dozen or so in the early morning. Mostly they use an oval or conical wooden casting float which will get the line out 45 or 55 m.

In the float or 'blob', as Western Australians call it, a slot or groove is cut to contain a wad of pollard and sardine oil berley. Below the blob, which is free-running, is a 2 m trace of fine line with one or two No. 6 suicide hooks baited with, invariably, a bunch of wriggling yellow wogs. Herring fishermen at surf beaches may substitute for the blob a sinker and berley cage, floating the trace off the bottom with a small cork. Off jetties and groynes the favoured rig is a light berley cage of coiled wire and two or three baits on short traces. Next to the illustrious maggot, herring prefer whitebait. They will take the same three-hook gang meant for small tailor or trevally.

In South Australia tommy ruff are around in large numbers throughout the year, but the biggest catches are made in the winter months when they move close to shore. Tasmanian biologist Peter Last classifies *Arripis esper* as a separate species to *Arripis georgianus*, which is so prevalent in Western and South Australia.

TREVALLA Elongated, compressed fish of the family Centrolophidae, often taken by deep sea trawlers. They are fish of delicious flavour, with large eyes and mouths and steel-blue colouring. They grow to 1 m and are found in South Australia, Tasmania, Victoria and New South Wales in depths up to 825 m. The

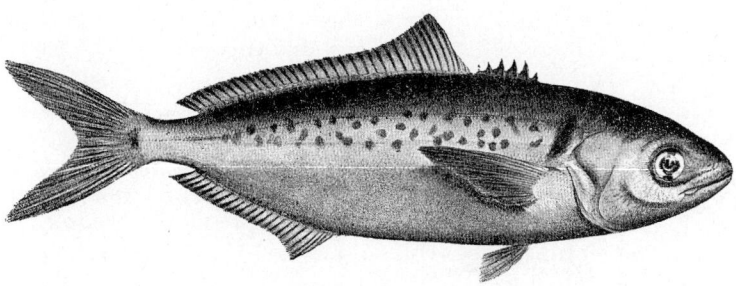

Mackerel trevalla

most common species is the deep-sea trevalla *Hyperoglyphe antarctica*. They are closely related to the warehou *Seriolella brama*, which is very common in New Zealand, inhabiting kelp beds to depths of 90 m. They feed on small marine animals, mostly crustaceans, seaweed and other fish, and are taken in deep trawls, by deep-sea handlining and on winched cable rigs. They are among the largest and best-eating scale fish found in Australia and have big commercial potential.

TREVALLIES

The magnificent family Carangidae comprises fast streamlined fish whose speed, size and hearty appetites invariably provide plenty of excitement for anglers. Apart from fish bearing the name trevally, other important fish such as turrum, yellowtail, pilot fish, runner, dart, queenfish, samson fish and kingfish belong to the family. Various members of the family are found in all Australian States and in the northern waters of New Zealand south to Cook Strait, in the surf, in estuaries and bays. They are important commercial fish, many of them splendid eating.

Young trevallies frequently hunt in big schools close to the surface, voraciously feeding on smaller fish. Older members of the family tend to go-it-alone more. There are at least 30 trevallies in our waters, which with other members of Carangidae probably takes the representation of the family in Australia and New Zealand to more than 50 species. They have a characteristically powerful body, compressed and built for a fight. The tails or caudal fins invariably are strong and deeply forked.

Off the ocean shoreline, the most consistent lure taker in north-western Australia is the trevally. In this corner of Australia three types of trevally provide the main sport close to shore: the black or great trevally, the yellow-finned or lowly trevally and the rubber-lip or golden trevally. Trevally schools of 1 to 1.5 kg hang around creek mouths and rocky outcrops and at that size they are excellent eating. The goldens seem to prefer living near the piles of north-west jetties. There fishermen catch them by jigging with silver spinners or home-made lures of string and tin foil. Occasionally lowly trevally are found in north-western Australian billabongs.

T ■ TREVALLIES

Yellowtail kingfish *Seriola lalandi:* Striking members of the family, renowned among Australian anglers for their fighting qualities. Mostly they are called kingfish and they should not be confused with the black kingfish of northern Australia, which should properly be called sergeant fish or cobia. They are related to the smaller yellowtail, so often used for bait and which children catch from wharves. For some reason many anglers imagine yellowtail are the young of a far more spectacular species.

To avoid conflict with the smaller fish of the same name, yellowtail kingfish was made the uniform name of this fish at the conference of States in 1947. Yellowtail have a prominent formation of scutes, raised scales along their lateral line which are high and hard towards the tail. The yellowtail kingfish has no scutes and no easily discerned lateral line. Yellowtail are small fish. Yellowtail kingfish grow to 2.4 m and 68 kg although those in the large schools so common off our coasts are far smaller than these limits, and a fish of 17 kg and 1 m is regarded as a good catch.

Yellowtail kingfish, in fact, count yellowtail among their normal diet of small fish, as well as pilchards, mullet herring, garfish etc. They also consume big meals of squid and octopus found in their customary habitat among reefs and rocky shores. Schools up to 10 to 12 km thick, although rare, have been reported off Australia.

They are usually most plentiful from October to December when other fish are in short supply and thus they sell well in the markets, despite a toughness of the flesh in mature fish. Their future may rest mainly in the canneries, where modern processes can improve their table appeal.

Yellowtail kingfish mostly feed in the early morning or late afternoon and this is the best time to fish for them. Baits comprising any of their favourite foods such as squid, cuttlefish and octopus work well and so do most small live fish. Hook sizes should be adjusted to suit the size of fish in a particular school, varying from 5/0 to 10/0, with hooks in between these sizes most common. They will take feathered and metal lures with relish.

Yellowtail kingfish are particularly abundant in South Australia, but unlike the eastern States, they are seldom seen there in the markets because in the periods that they are most plentiful many more palatable fish are available. But at places like Coffin Bay and Thevenard, they provide popular angling,

Yellowtail kingfish

TREVALLIES ■ T

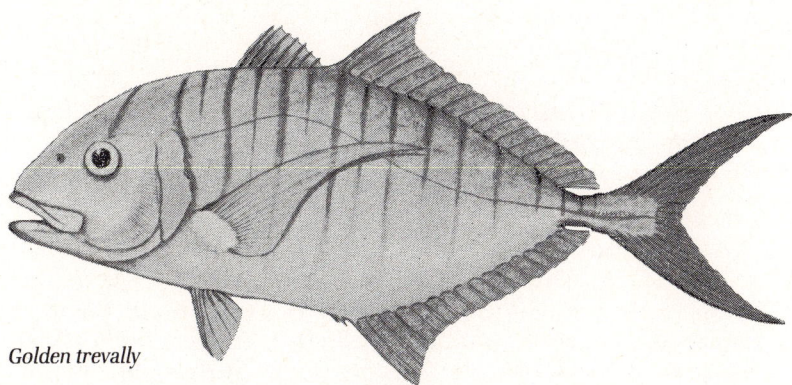

Golden trevally

just as in Geraldton Harbour and around Rottnest Island they thrill Western Australian fishermen.

Golden trevally

Gnathanodon speciosus: Also known as banded trevally and king trevally, these are a big, handsome variety frequently caught by line anglers in north Queensland around reefs. The young have attractive golden bodies, with thin vertical bands along the sides. As they mature the body colouring turns to silver and the bands fade, but on death the golden colours and bands vividly reappear for a few moments. All the fins are canary yellow to golden and the pectoral fin has a black smudge right at the base. They fight pugnaciously when hooked and are of a very high table quality. They grow to more than 38 kg and around 1 m.

Spotted trevally

Caranx melampygus: A fish of warm waters, commonly caught near the coast of Queensland, especially in the north, but not as big or as compressed as most trevallies. They reach 75 cm but the average sizes taken are around 35 to 45 cm. They are a vividly coloured silver fish with dense flecking of blue or black spots, the colours darkening as they mature. In life they have the striking sheen of blue and green tones which fade rapidly after death. They are firm-fleshed table fish, but are sometimes a little dry.

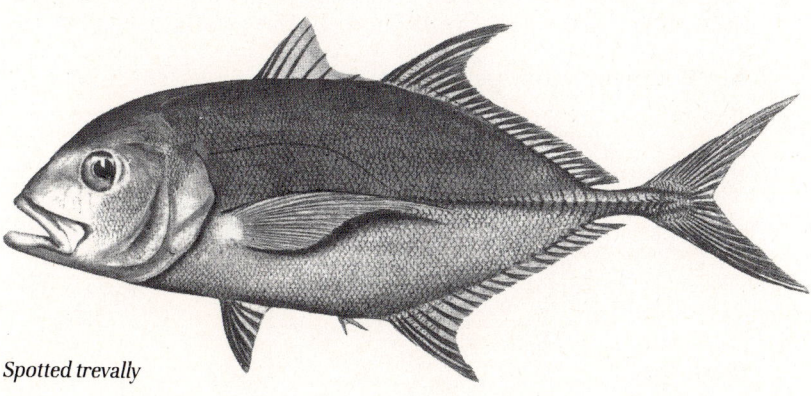

Spotted trevally

T ■ TREVALLIES

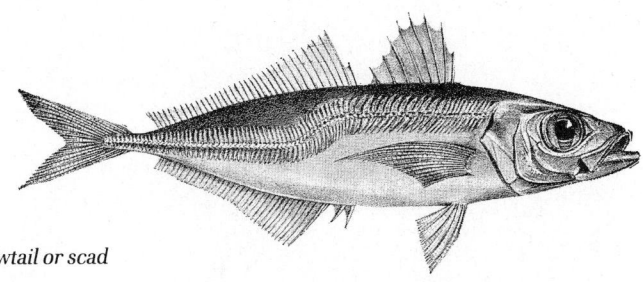

Yellowtail or scad

Yellowtail or scad *Trachurus novaezelandiae:* Sometimes known as bung. A small fish, usually 10 to 20 cm, found in numbers in bays, harbours and around estuary mouths. It provides great sport for juniors fishing from jetties and is highly prized as a bait fish. Greenish-yellow in colour and identifiable by the row of hard scutes along the lateral line, most plainly seen at the tail. Closely related and almost identical in appearance with the cowanyoung or jack mackerel *Trachurus declivis*, which is more commonly found out around the offshore reefs and in the big wide bays. Classified as horse mackerel in South Australia, where it reaches 45 cm.

Great trevally *Caranx sexfasciatus:* The biggest of all Australian trevallies, growing to more than 1.3 m and 39 kg. They are very similar in appearance to turrum. Grant advises that the best method of telling these fish apart is by a count of the soft dorsal fin, which he says has 21 rays on the great trevally and 29 to 31 rays on the turrum. There is a round black spot on the great trevally's gill-cover.

Great trevally prefer warm water and are caught right along the north Queensland coast by line anglers, often moving in big schools. They are attractive fish apart from their very dark eyes, the bright yellow body colouring of the young changing to bluish green in mature specimens. They are very challenging fish to hook as they fight savagely for life if not as spectacularly as turrum.

Diamond trevally *Alectis indica:* Also known as diamond fish, plumed trevally and mirror fish. Very similar, too, to the pennant fish *Alectis*

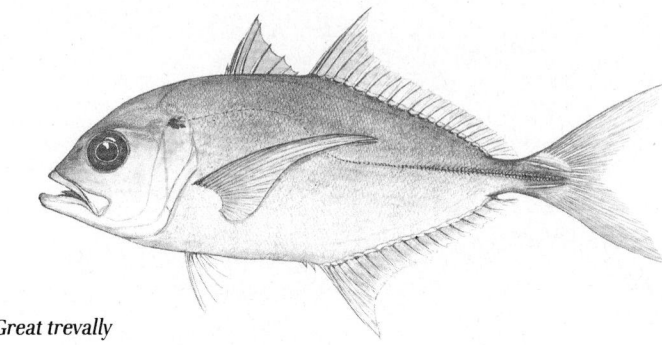

Great trevally

TREVALLIES ■ T

Diamond trevally

ciliaris, which has a shorter, more rounded snout than that of the diamond trevally, which is long and pointed. These fish take their name from their body shape. They are common around northern Australian reefs and wharves and have distinctive trailing rays of dark blue extending well beyond the tail.

Diamond trevally grow to more than 1.5 m and 12 kg. They are light green to canary yellow on top and dull silver beneath, with green fins and yellow caudal fin. They have thick, protruding lower jaws and remarkably clear bodies, which in the silvery colouring of the younger fish accounts for the name mirror fish.

Caranx nobilis: Also known as white trevally. This is the northern species of fish, which are also found in South Australia, and in Western Australia where they have been confused with *Caranx georgianus*, known as skipjack trevally or simply called trevally. They are very appetizing fish if they are bled soon after capture. The silver trevally have up to 27 rays on the soft dorsal, whereas skipjack trevally have a maximum of 24 rays. Grant says they grow to 1 m in his State (Queensland) and Scott says they reach 75 cm in his State (South Australia). Scott recommends them as a fish for smoking. Warren Cornelius caught a world record lowly trevally *Caranx ignobilis*, weighing 30.20 kg, on a 6 kg line off Monte Bello Island, Western Australia, in July 1981.

Silver trevally

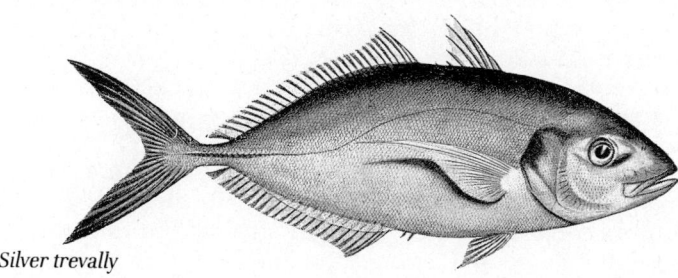

Silver trevally

T ■ TRIPLESPINE

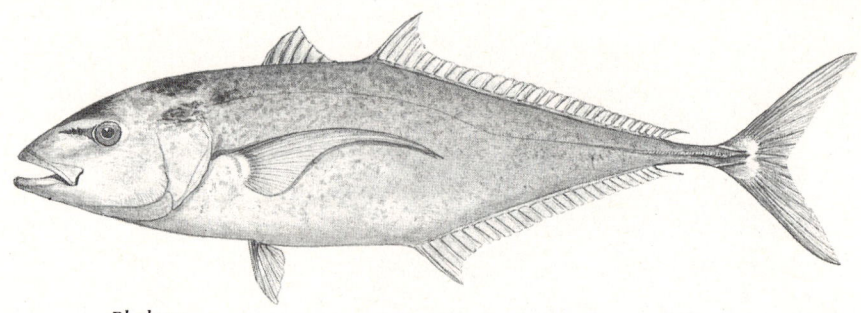

Bludger

Bludger *Carangoides gymnostethoides:* A true trevally of Northern Australian reef waters which anglers use almost entirely for bait. The flesh is dark, soft and oily but is edible. Bludgers are well proportioned streamlined speedsters but fishermen frequently feel cheated when they hook one when trolling for Spanish mackerel. They are green on top, silvery white beneath with dark spots on the gill covers. They grow to 85 cm and are of poor table quality.

Pilot fish *Naucrates ductor:* A nomad fish that ranges over vast areas of the ocean and has a habit of swimming with the larger marine animals such as sharks, feeding on scraps they leave. They were said to lead ships to safety in ancient times. They are heavy-bodied fish with smallish scales and gaping lower jaws. There are thick dark bars up and down their dark blue bodies. They reach 60 cm and are found in Queensland, New South Wales, Victoria, Tasmania, and South Australia.

Pilot fish

TRIPLESPINE *Triacanthus biaculeatus:* Also known as silver leatherjacket or tripod fish. A smallish fish, averaging a length of 20 cm, with some reaching 25 cm. The rough feel of the skin has caused them to be labelled leatherjackets, but they belong to the family Triacanthidae, which comprises certain horned fish. They are a very common fish along the Queensland coastline, but their flesh is unpalatable and could be harmful. Triplespine are pale green on top, silvery below and there is sometimes a prominent dark spot on the bottom of the dorsal fin. They have three extended spines, the dorsal and two ventrals.

Tripletail

TRIPLETAIL

Labotes surinamensis: Also known as jumping cod, flasher or dusky perch, these outstanding food fish are famous for their jumping prowess. Caught in a net they give quite remarkable performances of leaping and when caught by anglers they have jumped right out of boats. They reach 1 m and 14 kg but are seldom taken over 4 kg. They are warm water fish, plentiful in Queensland and down the New South Wales coast. A related species is found in the Indian Ocean. They eat small fish and most types of sea debris. Their flesh is highly flavoursome. Tripletail get their name from the formation of the dorsal, caudal and anal fins, which give it the appearance of having three tails. They are blackish across the body and head, paler beneath, where they sometimes are tinted yellow. The pectoral fins and the margin of the tail are a faint yellow.

TROLLING

A popular method of fishing large areas of salt and fresh water in boats, which by and large catches more sizeable fish than those caught by bait and fly fishing. The technique works best along certain types of coastline and off the shoreline of inland lakes, but is only effective if the boat moves at the correct trolling speed.

The tackle needed for trolling is somewhat specialized and differs from that used for other methods. A comparatively short rod not more than 1.8 m long is required. The rod should be flexible enough to absorb the shock of a large fish hitting the lure, yet stiff enough to set the hooks, especially if a large lure is being used. A variety of reels can be used for trolling as distance casting is not required. An ordinary centre-pin reel will suffice but has the disadvantages of a limited rate of retrieve and usually no adjustable drag. A fixed-spool reel will overcome these disadvantages but will put a twist in the line every time a fish takes line against the drag. This will eventually lead to the line having to be run out behind the moving boat to be untwisted or to be discarded.

The most suitable reel is one of the multiplying variety, with a smooth range of drag adjustment and a suitable gear ratio. A geared reel of the baitcasting type may be used for casting the large trolling lures and will not put a twist in the line.

A monofilament line of between 4 and 5.5 kg breaking strain should be used in conjunction with a lighter trace, having a breaking strain of half a kilogram less than the main line. This will ensure that only the lure is lost if it becomes snagged on submerged scrub and the like. Half-blood knots should be used throughout. A swivel is necessary with all types of lure and it is attached between line and trace.

When lures of the spinning, rather than wobbling type are used, an anti-twist vane is essential. These vanes are made either of lead or a clear plastic material and have an attached swivel. The type of vane used depends on the depth required, as the lead models will naturally fish much deeper than the plastic ones. Care must be taken to ensure that the trace and not the main line is attached to the swivel. The plastic vanes, because of their light weight, will exhibit a tendency to turn when trolled at high speeds. This can be prevented by drilling a small hole in the apex of the keel and pinching in a split shot of suitable size. A shiny lead vane should be avoided as trout will strike at this instead of the lure. The use of ball-bearing swivels greatly enhances the effectiveness of all types of rig. A small snap swivel should be attached to the end of the trace. This facilitates easy exchange of lures and provides additional insurance against the line becoming twisted.

Saltwater trolling
In the 1980s a lot of saltwater fish are taken by trolling. Some fishermen specialize in trolling, others simply do so on the way out to their game fishing spots. Some operate with heavy nylon on rubber shock absorbers, others with heavy lines tied to a cleat on the boat, but those who get most fun out of it are the anglers with rod and reel. Trolling with nylon fine enough to work on a reel is virtually impossible without some form of anti-twist device in front of the lure and trace. There are patented twist deflectors, lead keel-sinkers, and brass plates with swivels. Of these the lead keel-sinker works best because it can be used at a wide variety of boat speeds. Most of the custom-made paravanes and deflectors only operate at low speeds with the lures well down below the surface. Lead keel-sinkers of 250 g to 300 g in weight keep the lure only just below the surface, where it is more likely to attract pelagic species.

Saltwater trolling offers a wide choice of spinners, spoons, plugs, lures, whole fish and fish pieces. Tuna and bonito respond best to lures trolled at 5 to 7 knots, a speed which demands strong tackle and hooks that won't tear out of the mouths of these large fish. The best fun comes from using a strong spinning rod and stout sidecast or threadline reel that will drop lures close to fish that are feeding. Tailor are taken trolling close to shore and both salmon and yellowtail kingfish

Boat speed is a vital factor in successful trolling, producing just enough movement in the lure to tempt the fish, but still allowing them the chance to attack it.

usually are taken close in. Bonito move along the coast in big shoals and offer fine sport for those who troll the mouths of estuaries.

In selecting a lure from the big modern range of plastic wriggling, gliding and wobbling baits, some prefer those fitted with metal 'bibs' or deflector plates that control the depths to which the lure descends. Experience will show how far back from the boat to troll the lures or baits. Striped tuna and mackerel tuna, for example, stay well wide of the land and are fairly shy, but they will take baits trolled well back on thin lines. The Barrier Reef produces some of the world's best trolling, offering a wide choice of locations: estuaries, mudflats, coral reefs or open seas. Game boats in the north use a 'daisy chain' technique, offering a series of lines carrying four or six knuckleheads or feathered jigs, and it is not uncommon to see three or four fish being landed simultaneously.

Importance of boat speed

Not more than three anglers should troll from the one boat. One person should let his line out directly astern and the other two should hold their rods at right angles to their respective sides of the boat. Two anglers per boat is preferable. The use of three lines increases the chances of their becoming tangled with one another. When a fish strikes one lure the other line(s) should be immediately retrieved if they are likely to interfere with a catch.

For freshwater trolling a boat fitted with an outboard motor capable of cruising at low speeds is needed. Boats carrying a motor in excess of 40 h.p. should be fitted with a smaller motor for use when trolling, as the prolonged running of a large motor at low speeds will result in vibration and eventually harm the engine. The exact h.p. of a suitable motor depends on the size of the boat. Three people should *not* venture out on a lake such as Eucumbene in a boat less than 4 m long because of the contrary weather conditions. Anglers should also keep a constant lookout for floating debris, rocks and trees lying just beneath the surface. Rowing will result in good catches as the jerky progress of the boat imparts an attractive action to the lure. However, one has to work hard to catch fish and the lazier angler would do well to use a motor. Canoeing is also effective. Oarsmen and canoeists have better control over the speed and direction of their craft than an angler with an outboard motor.

Where to troll
Careful study should be made of the shoreline along which one is trolling. Flat, featureless areas of shoreline should be avoided. At sea look for signs of fish feeding. Inland the lure should pass as close as is possible to those submerged features which are attractive to trout. Risks must be taken and the angler should expect to lose a few lures when fishing in this manner. The lure should be fished close to the bottom when trolling in the proximity of the shore, except in summer months when the trout lie in deeper offshore waters during the day. The thermocline must then be fished and the angler will need either a heavy trolling weight or a lead core line. The majority of anglers do not fish their lures at depths exceeding 9 m and there is little doubt that they miss fish through their failure to do so, especially in summer months.

When the correct rig has been assembled and the boat is moving at the required speed, the lure is dropped overboard and the line is paid out. Multi-hook lures should not be cast out in fresh water as the trace will become entangled with the hooks. Although fish are often taken close to the boat, at least 45 m of line should be paid out to fish effectively and up to 90 m is used successfully by many anglers. The exact length of line to be paid out is determined by the type of lure, weight of lead, speed of boat and the depth required. Should anglers not be able to estimate the amount of line paid out by looking at the reel spool, they are advised to mark the line at 9 m intervals by tying in pieces of floss or the like. Most lures possess a characteristic action which can be felt through the rod. The absence of this vibration usually means that the lure is not fishing correctly and it should be retrieved and inspected for weed or fouled hooks.

Most anglers troll at a constant speed and direction. Should the fish be feeding well this will catch fish. However, if the fish are not 'on', as is usually the case, the angler should resort to other tactics. A good trick is to vary the speed of the boat, the amount of variation being determined by the range of speeds within which the chosen lure will perform correctly. Slowing the boat will cause the lure to fish deeper and increasing the speed will have the opposite effect. Likewise, a zig-zag path will cause the lure to fish at varying depths as it will slow down when the turns are being made and speed up during the straights. This variation in depth and direction will cause the light to strike the lure at different angles and thus ensure that it is fishing to its maximum effectiveness for at least some of the time. On a relatively narrow inlet it is advisable to proceed backwards and forwards across its width, the length of each turn being decided by the amount of line behind the boat. For example, if an angler has 90 m of line extending behind the boat he should make his turn 140 m wide.

Alternative manoeuvres
A successful method is to circle at the mouth of a river or inlet. Should no strikes be obtained the angler should cut across the centre of the circle, performing an 'S' shaped movement, and proceed in the opposite direction. All of these motions help make the light strike the lure at an effective angle of reflection. If an angler is proceeding in a set direction and receives several strikes, he should circle back and troll across the 'hot-spot' in the same manner. It is unwise to simply turn the boat around and go back across the area in a different direction, as the light will strike the lure in a manner dissimilar to that which proved successful. On a sunny day the angler must make sure that the sun is behind the boat. Should the boat head into the sun a fish will be dazzled if it is following the lure and usually will not take it. Further, the lure may be travelling in the shadow of the boat, another fact that will discourage the fish from taking it.

Snagged lures often can be recovered by reversing the engine and proceeding back over the obstruction. If this fails the line should be pulled at a variety of angles before breaking.

Selecting trolling lures

A lot of thought goes into the design of the majority of today's lures and nearly all will catch fish when correctly used under suitable conditions. But their hydro-dynamic qualities differ greatly and each design usually possesses a characteristic motion in the water. The success of a lure depends just as much on when and how it is fished as on its design. One lure will catch fish under a certain set of conditions but not under any other. The angler should carry a wide range of lures of varying colours and designs, to ensure that he has at least one suited to the conditions prevailing at the time. Here is a list of the main types of lure suitable for trolling and spinning.

Spinner
The name commonly given to lures which possess one or more moving parts revolving around a central axis. One of the most popular and least expensive lures is the 'Celta' which is

available in a large range of colours. Sizes 3 and 4 are the most popular but larger ones can be used with success. They can be trolled at high speeds provided a suitable anti-twist device is used. 'Mitchell' and 'Colorado' spinners are also successful. The Abu Company manufacture several spinning lures, such as the 'Sonnette', which are very good, as are Devon spinners.

Spoons
The name suggests these lures resemble the bowl of a spoon. They have no moving parts. The 'Eucumbene' spoon, 'Tantangara' spoon, Pegron 'Tiger-minnow', Wonder Wobbler and the Frog, Tiger and Red and White Wonder spoons are all suitable. Anglers wishing their lure to fish a little deeper will find the Wonder Flash and Wonder Snowy heavier than the above types. The attractiveness of these lures to trout can often be improved by removing the treble hook and replacing it with a longtailed fly.

Non-spinning lures
There are a few lures, other than spinners, spoons or wriggling plugs, which are popular with anglers who spin or troll in estuaries, lakes and big dams. Notable among these are the Super-duper, the Baltic Minnow and the Baltic Bobber.

Plugs
This term covers various lures, most of which are designed to give a great amount of movement in the water. Their relatively complex designs have proven to be of great effect and a number of them undoubtedly are highly successful. One of the most popular lures is the Helin Flatfish. This really belongs in a category by itself but can be loosely described as a plug. It is available in a large range of colours and sizes and the angler should have several in his tackle box. Yellow (YE), yellow-red and black (YB), perch scale (PS), fluorescent red (REL), orange (OR), orange-red and black (OB), light orange and red (LOR), and silver or gold reflectors (SIF) or (GOF) are some of the colours available. Sizes F7 to X5 are the most suitable, but larger sizes can be used when trolling deep. Flatfish have to be trolled relatively slowly, the speed depending on the size of the lure—small sizes can be trolled more rapidly than larger. Flatfish have a side to side wriggling motion very similar to that of a swimming fish and this often proves irresistible to the trout.

The Helin Company also manufactures a lure similar in style to the Flatfish called the Swimmerspoon. This lure possesses a similar action to that of the Flatfish but has a lead keel and can be fished faster and deeper. A plug with a similar action is the Canadian Wiggler, available in three sizes and a variety of colours. The largest two sizes with a background colour of orange, red or silver are the most suitable. This design fishes much deeper than the Flatfish and has to be worked at a higher speed.

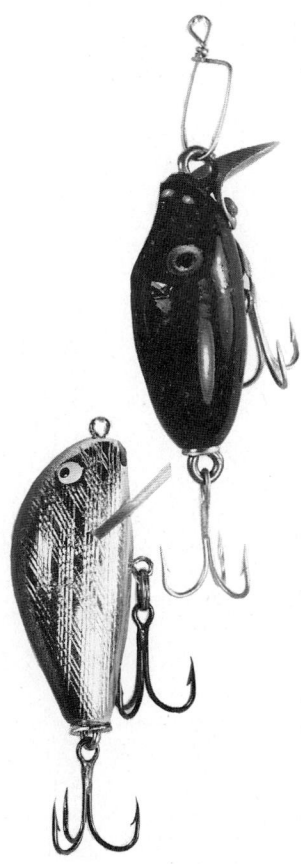

The Rebel Fast Back (left) is ideal for shallow water spinning and the Bellbrook Midget (right) is a highly successful freshwater trolling lure.

A highly successful range of lures with good fish-getting action is the Reb-2. The Quarter-back, No. 250, is a small fat wriggler always popular for trolling near the surface. The Half-back No. 350 is a somewhat larger bait of the same type which is attractive to the larger fish and particularly suited to deep trolling. No. 500 is a small wriggling smelt or minnow which looks particularly life-like in action. The No. 350 half-back deep runner has a broad metal bib which makes it particularly good for trolling deep down in the thermocline of a lake.

The French-designed Flopy is also an attractive lure, available in several sizes, the larger of which should be used. The flopy is made of a soft rubber compound and is a good 'hooker' as the pliable body will not act as a lever against the jaw of a hooked fish. One great advantage with this lure is that it possesses an adjustable paravane and can thus be fished at different depths.

There are many other plug type lures on the market, several of which can be trolled successfully. They include the Heddon Sonic, Deep-Diver and River-runt Spook, the Arbogaster, Jitterbug and the Bellbrook.

Saltwater trolling lures

Feathered lures used to be the overwhelming choice for saltwater trolling but then a wide range of plastic and metal lures became very popular, including blades such as the Teal Swinger Spinner, the Roto Spinner, and the six-sided Pencil Spinner which can rotate on the connecting trace between swivel and split ring. Gillies' Wonder Whizz, which skips along the surface, and a Huntington Drone called the Sea Ducer will take most surface feeders and small game fish. The silver-coloured Halco Barramundi is another ideal spoon for light game fish. The Werner Kossman Bristle Spinner and the Bristle Jig operate well from slow moving boats. In the Flexi-Troll series, the Giant Cowbell, which comprises a series of blades of vivid colours attached to a stainless steel wire with a plastic keel creates a choppy water effect. The Red Sea Chief, a hard plastic variety, red underneath and white on top; the Abu Egon, fitted with a plastic tube near the hooks; Sevenstrand's Konahead, available in a range of colours and feathers; and the Swayback type lure have all taken good fish when trolled. Heddon's Tiger Prowler, Zara Spook, and Magnum Tadpolly have the advantage of enticing larger species of both fresh and saltwater fish.

Flies

Large streamer-flies such as the Mrs Simpson, Hamill's killer, fuzzy wuzzy and matuka may be trolled effectively. However, these lures have little motion in the water and are best used when rowing or canoeing among trees and the like. If used with an outboard motor the rod tip must be constantly raised and lowered to give them a darting motion. A weighted line is required.

Which lure to use and when

The respective actions of each type of lure should be considered but the all-important influencing factors are light and colour. The way in which a lure reflects its colours is of prime importance in determining its attractiveness to trout.

A sound general rule is to use lures with bright colours during dull days and those with dull colours on bright days. For example during December and January a most successful lure is the Celta spinner. On overcast days a Silver Celta with green or black stripes should be used, but this should be changed for a darker Copper Celta with the same coloured stripes on bright days. Failure to do this will result in reduced catches. On days with alternate periods of cloud and sunlight the lures should be changed accordingly.

When to troll

Saltwater trolling is productive all the year round but April and May are the best months in which to troll most Australian lakes and dams while the trout are beginning to congregate prior to spawning. Cold, frosty mornings are particularly good. A typical routine followed by an expert would be to use a red fluorescent flatfish (RFL) Size No. F7 or X4 from daybreak until a quarter of an hour before sunrise, then change to an orange flatfish (OR) of the same size.

This would be fished until one and a half hours after sunrise and then exchanged for a Baltic minnow which in turn could be fished with until 10 or 11 a.m. If the day is bright and still, fishing would then be discontinued until 3 p.m. when the above procedure would be reversed, ending with a red fluorescent, gold or silver flatfish being fished during the hour before nightfall. If the day be overcast and windy, fishing could be continued between 11 a.m. and 3 p.m. using a red or orange Canadian wiggler or a deep-working spoon. Longtailed flies can be used during dull days in May but, as mentioned previously, a rowboat or canoe is preferable.

In the spawning months, April to August, many brown trout can be caught by pausing at the mouth of an inlet and casting a lure towards the bank. The Baltic minnow is especially suited to this purpose and should be retrieved at a normal rate. One should move on after having caught one fish as there are usually not more than two brown trout to each small inlet. This technique can be repeated during September and October, when shore-based anglers can also adopt this technique, if access is practicable.

Considerable success is possible in winter months by using a yellow flatfish (YE), Size No. X4 during the mornings and evenings, and a perch scale flatfish (PS) of the same size during the day. Canadian wiggler or a deep working spoon should be effective during sunny weather. If the day is windy with quick moving clouds passing across the sun, a Canadian wiggler with an orange background and black stripes could be a successful lure, especially in October. This lure is most productive when trolled in the shadows of trees, particularly those cast by the rising sun.

December and January are the months in which the Celta is most productive. Trolling a Canadian wiggler frog pattern during the first half of December also is often successful. In February and March the water starts to cool and trolling meets with more success. A variety of lures may be used throughout this period, with overcast days providing the best sport. Should the fish not respond to the lure used it should always be exchanged for another equally suited to the light conditions. There is a constant need for experimentation. There may be odd occasions when one does best by reversing the rules.

The use of a gang spinner, commonly known as a Christmas tree, will often improve catches, especially of rainbow trout. A trace of not more than 45 cm is required behind such a rig. This equipment is relatively expensive but will not be lost on snags provided a trace of the correct breaking strain is used. There is little doubt this rig will catch the eye of more trout than is normal with a single lure. Dull conditions are more suited to the use of a cowbell as the trout's field of vision is often limited by cloudy water and overcast conditions. Whereas a single lure passes unnoticed, a relatively large cowbell may get attention, but numerous fake strikes can be experienced with this rig as fish will often strike at the hookless blades instead of the actual lure.

On hot summer days when the fish are lying deep jigging frequently will give results. A heavy lure, such as the Baltic minnow, should be lowered down to the thermocline and rapidly jerked up and down while the boat is standing still.

TROUT

Sportfish of the family Salmonidae, none of which are indigenous to Australia or New Zealand. European and American members of the family have been introduced with marked success in New Zealand, Tasmania, New South Wales and Victoria and with limited success in South Australia and Western Australia. They have failed in Queensland despite 90 odd years of effort to find cool water for them. Trout are world famous for their guile and for the subtleties in tackle and techniques they demand of anglers. They are regarded as a big asset to tourism wherever they become established, luring anglers to streams and visitors to hatchery ponds.

Brown trout and rainbow trout have adapted well to our cooler streams. Other Salmonidae, including Loch Leven trout, Kern River or Gilbert's trout, migratory salmon, salmon trout, brook trout, sock-eye salmon and quinnat salmon have all been introduced, generally with disappointing results, but there are hopes for brook trout in Tasmania.

Unlike trout in other countries, Australian trout feed almost entirely on insects. This has been clearly shown in studies of trout food by scientists in New South Wales, Victoria and

Western Australia. American experts have expressed surprise at the size of Australian trout and have said they must be sea-fed to reach such sizes, but this is impossible in the majority of Australian streams.

The average brown trout caught these days in Australia is around half a kilogram in weight, but much bigger fish are taken from outstanding streams. In some years brown trout from hot spots such as the Thomson River, Victoria, average from 1.5 to 2 kg. The world's record brown trout was one of 18 kg (39.5 lb) caught in Loch Awe, Scotland, in 1866 by W. Muir. The biggest brown caught in Australia was 13 kg, taken in 1887 in the River Huon, Tasmania, by Sir Robert Hamilton, then Governor of Tasmania. The Huon also produced a brown trout of 10 kg in 1955.

The average rainbow trout in Australia is marginally heavier than the brown trout, but again outstanding waters produce big rainbow. For example, the average size of rainbow trout taken from Lake Eucumbene, New South Wales, was around 2 kg. In Lake Purrumbete, Victoria, rainbow trout have averaged 2.7 kg in past years and trout of 4.5 kg are common. The world's record for rainbow trout stands at 17 kg (37 lb), for a fish caught in 1947 by West Hamlet in Pend Oreille Lake, Idaho, U.S.A. The biggest Australian rainbow on record was one of 9 kg caught in Lake Purrumbete in 1938.

Until a decade ago, there was a tendency among biologists to split trout into a bewildering number of species. Fortunately for anglers, this trend has given way to a new one in which all trout are lumped together except when permanent differences can be seen in them. This is logical as trout are still undergoing evolutionary changes and judgement of permanent features is not always reliable.

How trout were introduced
French naturalist De Quatrefages first suggested that propagation to any extent desired was possible by artificial fertilization of fish ova, back in 1848. De Quatrefages's view was received sceptically until Joseph Remy, a fisherman of Bresse, demonstrated what basically remains the modern technique of stripping eggs from trout to the French Academy of Sciences. This was the beginning of fish culture, as the methods Remy had developed were taken up by scientists around the world and hatcheries were built in Britain, France, and America.

In 1852, an attempt was made to ship salmon ova to Tasmania by a Mr Boccius, but the shipment failed to survive. At this point James Youl, later Sir James, then Agent for Tasmania in England, became interested in the problem of transporting ova to Tasmania. Experiments began in England in 1854 on problems such as the period elapsing between fertilization and hatching, and the effect of temperature on the hatching period.

The work won the support of Edward Wilson, president of the Acclimatization Society of Victoria, who with other influential colonists raised £1200 to make another attempt in 1860, to ship ova from England. Despite elaborate efforts to keep the ova alive in an ice house, they all had died 68 days after leaving England. A third attempt failed in 1862 when, despite additional supplies of ice, 80,000 ova died. All the time experiments continued in England and it was found that it was not necessary to pass a continuous stream of water over the eggs or to ensure that light reached the ova.

In 1864, 25 tonnes of ice was taken on board the steamer *Norfolk*, together with 100,000 Atlantic salmon ova and 3000 brown trout ova. Unlike the previous attempts, this time the ova were not disturbed during the voyage and 74 days later the first successful shipment reached Melbourne. Four thousand salmon ova were left in Melbourne and 400 of these hatched. The rest of the salmon ova and all of the trout ova were sent on to Tasmania, where it was estimated that 30,000 ova, 300 of them brown trout ova, were alive.

On 4 May 1864, at the Plenty Hatchery, the first trout in the southern hemisphere hatched and the next day the first salmon. Six pairs of brown trout reached maturity in the Plenty Ponds and the progeny of these became the progenitors of brown trout in the whole of Australasia. It is generally agreed by scientists such as Victorian A. Dunbavin-Butcher, who have researched these early struggles to introduce foreign fish to Australia and New Zealand, that the turning point came when Sir James Youl conceived the idea of packing the ova with moss and ice, a procedure that is largely followed today.

When acclimatization began
New South Wales got its first trout in 1888 when John Gale secured 300 fingerlings from Ballarat, Victoria, which with Tasmania had pioneered introduction of the species. Further shipments from Victoria and New Zealand established trout in New South Wales but despite the erection of a hatchery at Prospect the State was dependent on shipments from New Zealand until the New South Wales Government built modern hatcheries at Jindabyne and on the Serpentine River, New England. South Australia received its first trout in 1910 and for years secured its trout from the Ballarat hatchery. Western Australia did not introduce trout until 1930.

Queensland began its long and so far unavailing struggle to introduce trout in 1887, when some Ballarat trout were released in the Gold Creek Reserve near Brisbane. In 1896, a hatchery was established at Killarney Creek, near Warwick, the headwaters of the Condamine River. From 1897 to 1900 Killarney trout were introduced into Queensland streams from Stanthorpe in the south to near Gympie. The only release that met with any reward was the first one at Spring Creek, where trout may still be taken in a stream bounded by waterfalls. Spring Creek trout reach 1 kg and an occasional one up to 1.5 kg. In the 1950s rainbow and brown trout were introduced in Lake Tinaroo, north Queensland, and in waters of the Atherton Tablelands, but without success. In 1965, 2000 trout were released into Paluma Dam by the Townsville City Council. The Ravenshoe and District Amateur Fishing Club has also conducted a trout stocking programme, releasing two-year-old brown trout into South Cedar Creek and the Tully River above Koombooloomba Dam.

The first trout to reach New Zealand came from Tasmania in 1867. They were brown trout from the stock carried to the Plenty Hatchery by the *Norfolk*. New Zealand's first rainbow trout were liberated in Lake Taupo in 1903.

Trout habitat
Trout require water with a high oxygen content and they do best in water with a minimum of sediment that clears quickly after flooding. Fast running water with a gravel or boulder bottom with temperatures between 14 and 19.5 degrees C, such as that common in New Zealand, enables them to flourish. Cover is particularly crucial to them in Australia, where the vast majority of trout waters are landlocked and the trout depend on insects for food. Streams with overhanging trees, logs, boulders, deep holes and water-edge brush are ideal.

Rainbow trout prefer colder water than brown trout, but brown trout like deeper water than rainbow trout. Browns do well in dams that are well covered provided they can get down to the depths that suit them. Rainbows are better suited to colder, swift-moving water. Both adapt well to changes in environment.

Brook trout *Salvelinus fontinalis:* One of the most attractive of all freshwater sportfish both in appearance and fighting qualities and the most edible of all trouts. Brook trout bite more freely than other trouts, grow faster and have had a prominent part in the development of fly fishing in the eastern United States of America. For this reason it is sometimes called eastern brook trout. It is a char and not a true member of the family Salmonidae which includes various trouts and salmons. Like other chars, it can be detected from the trouts by its smaller scales and more rounded body. It is easily distinguished by the heavy whitish, maze-like pattern of lines on its back, the wavy dark lines on the dorsal fin and the white margins on the leading edges of the pectoral, ventral and anal fins.

The brook trout is native to north-eastern America, from Georgia to the Arctic Circle, but it has been introduced with great success to most of the suitable waters in the rest of America. It reached England in 1865, Europe in 1884, New Zealand in 1890 and from there, but only temporarily, New South Wales. It was first introduced into Tasmanian waters early in the century but was not a success, as self-maintaining populations did not become established, apparently because

Brook trout grow faster, bite freely, display excellent fighting qualities when hooked and are the most edible of all trout. All in all an excellent sporting fish!

it cannot thrive in waters in which there are existing stocks of brown or rainbow trout. Since 1963, brook trout have been released in various specially chosen waters in Tasmania and in the 1980s recaptures of healthy fish in Clarence Lagoon have been confirmed. Since 1965 brook trout weighing over half a kilogram or more have been taken from time to time on the fly. The world record weight for brook trout is 6.6 kg (14.5 lb) for an 80 cm fish, taken in America, but a brook trout of more than 2 kg is an outstanding catch.

Brook trout are caught with live bait, spinning lures and by plug-casting and trolling. But they are considered to be pre-eminently a fish for fly fishermen, feeding on insects, crustaceans and molluscs. The biggest American catches of brook trout are on spoons and spinners but this is probably because a majority of Americans prefer these methods rather than the dry fly. It does best in very big areas of water where it has a chance to escape the challenge of other trout and of predators. Although large suitable expanses of water are diminishing all over the world, many American management schemes give the brook trout preferential treatment because of the pleasure it gives dedicated fly fishermen and because of its excellent flavour.

Brook trout are colourful fish but their array of colours diminishes when they are acclimatized away from their native wild habitat. They have distinctive red spots along the sides and down towards the belly, pink or reddish lower fins and patterns of black wavy lines on the dorsal and caudal fin. The

T ■ TROUT

HOOK ARRANGEMENTS FOR TROUT

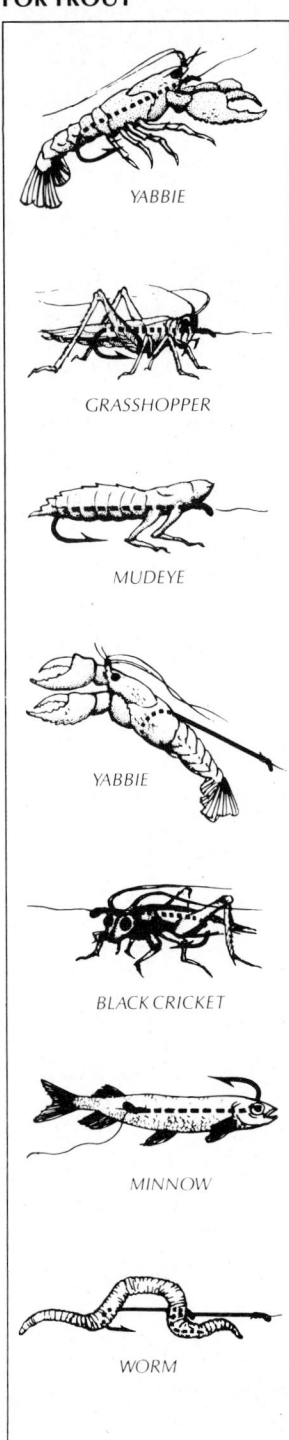

YABBIE

GRASSHOPPER

MUDEYE

YABBIE

BLACK CRICKET

MINNOW

WORM

caudal fin is only slightly forked, almost square and thus they are frequently referred to in America as 'squaretails'. American tests have shown that they prefer cold water, that the upper limit of their tolerance is 25 degrees C and that they are never abundant in water above 19 degrees C.

When wild brook trout dwindled in the United States of America because of loss of habitat, overfishing and other causes, a domestic strain more suited to life in hatcheries was developed. The domestic strain will nibble the fingers of hatchery visitors but wild brook trout are particularly timid and will scurry for cover. In domesticating the wild brook trout, and in trying to rear the species economically in hatcheries, the Americans sometimes undertook constant inbreeding which produced albino brook trout, washed-out versions of the wild and domestic strains that lack the pigmentation needed to protect them outside hatchery waters. Most albino brook trout are kept for the entertainment of hatchery visitors, genetic curiosities with black as well as the pink eyes common in animal albinos.

Brook trout were first introduced into Tasmania early in the century, with liberations in Snow Creek, which runs into Lake Leake. Fish up to 450 g were caught in the 1907–08 season. At the same time Lakes Crescent and Sorrel were stocked and several brook trout between 1 and 2 kg were taken. But they did not survive in waters that already contained good stocks of brown and rainbow trout. This experience was echoed in New Zealand, where brook trout liberated in a shallow alpine lagoon reached 1 to 2 kg but did not achieve self-sustaining populations. A few small specimens remain in the headwaters of some streams populated by other species.

In February 1962, a consignment of 50,000 eyed-ova of brook trout reached Hobart by air from the Canadian Department of Fisheries fish culture station at Collingwood, Nova Scotia. As they were cold-water fish and temperatures were then high, they were hatched out at Miena near Great Lake, at an altitude of 1050 m. Although mortality was still high because of the warm conditions, brook trout proved easy to cultivate, but provided a tricky problem for those deciding where they should be liberated. Water free of rainbow and brown trout was very scarce.

By May 1963, the brook trout were mature fish of 20 to 25 cm and fifteen months old and at this stage the decision was taken to keep half the stock in the Plenty Hatchery at Miena and introduce the other half into a farm dam at Dairy Plains, near Deloraine. But none of the fish released in the Dairy Plains dam survived and stripping of the Plenty stock met with only limited success.

Left with only 677 fingerlings from around 30,000 ova, the Tasmanian Inland Fisheries Commission released 600 fingerlings into Clarence Lagoon in December 1963. The following December two fish of around 450 g were caught there on the dry fly at the spot where the Clarence River joins Laughing Jack Lagoon. In April 1965, fish of 680 g were landed, clearly indicating a downstream migration from Clarence Lagoon.

Following its policy of providing more species of trout for anglers, the Commission made its biggest release of brook trout in July, 1966, when 9642 fish 15 to 20 cm long were put into Little Pine Lagoon on the Central Highlands. Simultaneously, 1000 fish of this size were liberated in Harvey's Lagoon, at an altitude of 450 m. Little Pine Lagoon, the major liberation point, is easily reached by anglers from Hobart and Launceston and it gives the brook trout ready access to a large network of other splendid waters.

Subsequently, fingerlings were introduced in Little Waterhouse Lagoon at sea 22 km east of Bridport, in October 1966, and at Derby, where 3200 fingerlings were released in the waterhole in 1966. The releases at Harvey's Lagoon, Little Waterhouse Lagoon, and at Bridport were in enclosed waters that prevented migration and in water free of brown trout which gave the less aggressive brook trout ideal growth prospects.

Lacking reports from anglers on the condition of the brook trout in Harvey's Lagoon, the Commission carried out test netting and found that the two-year-old brook trout were up to 37.5 cm long and 1 kg in June 1967. The Commission's prediction that Harvey's Lagoon would later provide excellent fishing soon was fulfilled. For brook trout to have doubled their length in a year in an enclosed water suggested that future liberations of the fish in Tasmania would be in enclosed waters. Anglers and fisheries biologists, aware that brook trout do not coexist well with other trout, are entitled to be thrilled that stock introduced into Clarence Lagoon in the 1970s have done well and have justified further releases.

Brown trout

Salmo trutta: Regarded as the aristocrat of freshwater sportfish and the most difficult to catch of all trouts. They are natives of Europe and have become favourites in all of the places where they have been introduced, the delight of sophisticated anglers in four continents.

They vary in colour patterns from brown to blackish-brown, with numerous red and black spots on the sides and dorsal area. These markings are bigger than those on rainbow trout but are more vivid on brown trout taken from some waters than those caught in others. The black spots are X-shaped and sometimes have a pale border. There are no spots on the caudal fin. There is often a yellowish margin in front of the dorsal, anal and outer edge of the ventral fins. In waters where the fish tend to be cannibals, feeding on their own or other fish species, the male often develops a hooked underjaw, similar to that on some male salmon.

The hardy brown trout may be caught in all kinds of waters, from tumbling mountain streams to placid rivers and lakes,

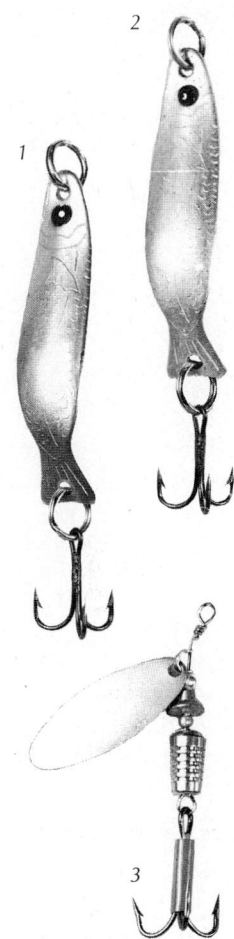

Three successful trout lures which come in a variety of colours:
1 Golden Minnow
2 Salmon Minnow
3 Burrinjuck Bug

T ■ TROUT

Brown trout

but it thrives best in the deeper, quieter waters of the weedy rivers and lakes. Trout authorities seem to have only recently become aware of what most serious trout men have known for a long time, that the brown trout is able to survive longer in heavily fished waters or waters close to cities than can other members of the salmon family.

The brown trout is a more cautious feeder than the rainbow trout or brook trout and while there are times when the waters are so discoloured that brown trout can be caught fairly easily, on most occasions it becomes a matter of stalking and trying to fool them. In waters which stock both rainbow and brown trout, tests have shown that four rainbows are taken for each brown.

From the fly fisherman's point of view the brown trout is a more selective feeder than the rainbow trout and the successful fly-man will often have to use dry flies that are almost a perfect imitation of the insect on which the brown trout are feeding. It is this caution by the brown trout plus its ability to survive in warmer waters that has enabled it to overcome to a certain extent the spilling over of the cities and towns into the trout country.

Rainbow trout *Salmo gairdneri:* A native American trout and like brown and brook trout a fine sport fish. Migratory rainbow trout are known in America as steelheads, those that do not migrate by an array of local names such as Kern River trout, Nelson trout and Kamloops.

The upper body is greenish blue, sometimes purple, the sides tending toward silver with small black spots and these are most numerous above the lateral line. The head and the dorsal, caudal and adipose fins are also black spotted. Sea-run rainbow are uniformly silver with no black spots. A broad crimson band can be clearly seen along the flanks and this becomes much brighter and tends to spread during the breeding season. The jaws of the males are larger than the females during the breeding but do not become distorted or hooked as do the jaws of some of the other members of the salmon family.

Rainbow trout thrive best in fast-flowing mountain streams. It has been found, in Victoria and elsewhere, that the best places to stock rainbows are those lakes and reservoirs that

Rainbow trout

have no outlet to the sea. It seems to be a waste of time placing rainbows in streams with easy access to the sea, as the fish quickly disappear. Large schools have sometimes migrated from Tasmanian streams to the sea, and are known as sea runners.

Rainbow trout feed on much the same food as do the brown trout and the bait fisherman does not use different baits for the two species. Likewise, the spinner man is content to use the same lures for both, except that in a fast-water mountain stream where the best rainbows are a slightly different lure may be used from the lure used in the slower streams or deep pools where the best browns are caught.

While the fly angler may be content to use similar flies for both species of trout, he may often find that the rainbows are far more partial to bright colour. Most rainbow trout flies tend to be gaudy and even in crystal clear waters are effective. Flashy flies like the kingfisher, the silver doctor and the Early in the Season Matuka are all good rainbow trout flies (*see Casting a fly; Dapping; Fly fishing*).

Hatcheries in Australia

Trout were first introduced into Australia just over a century ago. Their introduction has proved extremely successful and trout are now established in many freshwater streams and lakes in all States, excepting Queensland—and the Northern Territory. Such success would not have been possible without the development of efficient trout hatcheries within Australia.

Tasmania was the first of the Australian States to try to introduce salmon and trout and Australia's first hatchery was constructed near Hobart in 1841, in readiness for a shipment of eggs from Britain. This and three other subsequent shipments of eggs failed to reach Australia in a viable condition. The first successful shipment was made in 1864 when the steamer *Norfolk* brought a consignment of brown trout eggs to Melbourne as the result of a joint venture of the Salmon Commission of Tasmania and the Victorian Government.

From these eggs approximately 300 brown trout *Salmo trutta* were hatched at Hobart and of those reaching fingerling size 38 were released in the Plenty River and 135 retained in the hatchery ponds. From the progeny of these fish the remainder of Tasmania, most of the mainland of Australia and New Zealand were eventually supplied. Thus these 300 fish constitute the original stock from which developed all the brown trout to be found in Australasia. Three thousand Atlantic salmon *Salmo salar* eggs in this same consignment also hatched and were released as fry, but did not survive.

The pioneer hatchery, 'The Plenty', is still active. The original ponds and buildings, having been superseded by more modern facilities, now form the Youl Memorial Fish Hatchery Museum—named in honour of James Youl who supervised the initial shipments of eggs (*see Trout*). This museum was opened in 1964 to celebrate the centenary of the successful introduction of Brown Trout into Australia. Anglers passing near Hobart will find it well worth a visit.

The first mainland State to receive Brown Trout eggs from Tasmania was Victoria. Hatcheries were established in Geelong and Ballarat and the resultant trout fry were liberated in Victorian streams. Trout were not introduced into New South Wales until 1888, when the State Fisheries Commission released several thousand fry, obtained from the Ballarat Hatchery, into waters throughout the State. During the following year (1889) trout eggs were incubated for the first time in New South Wales, a makeshift hatchery-room being set up in Phillip St, Sydney. More modern hatcheries soon followed.

Rainbow Trout *Salmo gairdneri* were first introduced into Australia in 1894 when a consignment of 3000 eggs from New Zealand were laid down in New South Wales. The Rainbow Trout had previously been introduced into New Zealand from America. This species was introduced into Tasmania in 1898.

Successful establishment and distribution of both species of trout throughout suitable Australian waters have gone hand in hand with the increasing development of Australian hatcheries. State Fisheries authorities are now responsible for the running of most hatcheries, although valuable work is still carried out by hatcheries controlled by the acclimatization societies.

State hatcheries are now to be found in New South Wales, Tasmania, Victoria and Western Australia.

Locations of the hatcheries
New South Wales has the Gaden and Dutton hatcheries. The Gaden hatchery is near Jindabyne in the Snowy Mountains. It is beside the Thredbo River and is reached by taking the Kosciusko road and turning off to the left at a point 6 km past Jindabyne. The Dutton Hatchery is on the Serpentine River near where it is crossed by the New England National Park Road, close to Ebor, in the Armidale district. Both hatcheries are open to visitors. Victoria's Snob's Creek Hatchery, the largest of its kind in Australia (50 ha) is open to visitors and is 138 km north-east of Melbourne, close to the Eildon Weir, on the main road some 3 km on the Melbourne side of the Weir. Tasmania's Plenty Hatchery lies beside the Plenty River, north-

west from Hobart. The Corra Linn Hatchery is near Launceston. Western Australia's Pemberton Hatchery is in the cool temperate region of the south-west of the State.

Hatchery procedure

The work carried out by a typical trout hatchery stems from the cycle of events during the hatchery year. This starts with the collection and fertilization of eggs from mature fish. Under natural conditions a large proportion of brown and rainbow trout usually mature during their third year of life, and spawn at age three. Some male fish will mature during their second year, but this is unusual in female fish. At the age of four years, practically every trout will be mature and some will already have spawned once. Maturity is more a product of age, rather than size and consequently a slow-growing, stunted trout of 15 cm length from an overpopulated small creek may be mature, whereas a faster-growing lake trout of the same species may not be mature until it reaches 35 cm. An examination of each fish could show them both to be at least three years old.

When a trout is fully mature and ready to spawn it is said to be 'ripe'. In Australia brown trout ripen during the period May to August and rainbow trout during August to October, with the great majority of each species ripening near the middle of their respective time-ranges. Thus, if a hatchery is rearing brown trout its 'year' commences in May or June. In those hatcheries rearing rainbow trout only, the year commences two months later.

Trapping and stripping: A ripe female trout carries the eggs loose in the body-cavity and when spawning takes place these eggs are shed through a urino-genital pore directly behind the anus. By applying gentle pressure to the body of a ripe female the eggs can be squeezed out in a similar manner. This is commonly known as 'stripping' the fish. Milt (sperm) is obtained from a male trout by the same procedure. Thus the first duty of a hatchery worker is the catching and stripping of ripe fish.

Ripe trout are obtained either by trapping fish from natural spawning 'runs' in waters in the vicinity of the hatchery or by keeping a brood stock in selected hatchery enclosures. If a hatchery is sited in an area in which large numbers of wild fish run to spawn, the former procedure is usually adopted. At the Gaden Hatchery near Jindabyne, New South Wales, large numbers of trout run to spawn from nearby Lake Eucumbene every winter. These fish are trapped in selected tributaries, stripped and then have their eggs carried back to the hatchery.

Rearing: The incubation of the eggs is a relatively simple process. On reaching the hatchery, the green eggs are laid down in hatching devices. For a period of 36 hours after fertilization, the eggs may be handled in a relatively rough fashion, but after this time must be disturbed as little as possible. Nowadays, there is a variety of hatching devices, but all have the same function in common, namely, to ensure a flow of fresh, well-oxygenated water over the developing eggs.

The traditional hatching device consists simply of a trough through which is passed a constant flow of water. The trough is still most commonly used in Australia. The eggs are placed in wire-gauze trays situated just below the surface of the water. These troughs require a large amount of floor space and increasingly sophisticated equipment has been developed, more from a need to increase the number of eggs that can be hatched in a given space than from a need to improve the method of hatching. Densely populated countries like America have experienced an increasing demand for young trout to restock heavily fished waters. This demand resulted in the need to increase the production from hatcheries and a great deal of development work towards this end has been carried out overseas. Eggs can now be incubated in glass jars, drip-tray incubators, and similar equipment; all of which are more easily serviced and have a greater egg capacity than the traditional trough.

Glass jars (commonly known as Downing jars) are used in some Australian hatcheries. Their design is such that the eggs within are not disturbed by the flow of water passing over them. Drip-tray incubators consist of a vertical bank of trays containing eggs, down which a constant stream of water is allowed to drip.

At regular intervals the developing eggs are examined and dead eggs removed with a bulb or tweezers. This is known as 'picking' the eggs. Dead eggs are easily recognizable by their opaque-white appearance and must be removed from the healthy, orange-coloured eggs, before becoming infected with fungus, the filaments of which would soon spread throughout the whole tray or jar. These examinations are continued until the embryos reach the 'eyed' stage. The arrival of this stage is signalled by the appearance of two pigmented eyes, visible through the shell of the egg. Eyed eggs will withstand rough handling, and it is at this stage of development that eggs are exchanged between hatcheries or shipped over long distances, as the case may be. The eggs become eyed after about one third of their total development time has elapsed.

When introducing trout into 'virgin' waters it has been found practicable to place eyed eggs into containers known as Vibert boxes, which are then buried in the beds of the streams concerned. A Vibert box consists of a square glass receptacle with perforations, large enough to permit a newly hatched trout to escape, in its upper sides. Whilst the box will allow these trout to emerge, it protects the developing eggs from the predators occurring in such waters. The box must be buried in gravel coarse enough to allow a constant flow of water over the eggs. This practice has been largely discontinued in Australia as the emergent trout fry have been shown to have a relative mortality rate higher than that of hatchery-reared fish, especially in waters already containing trout.

The water temperature in the trays or jars has a direct effect on the length of the hatching period. The colder the water, the longer the eggs take to hatch. For example, a brown trout egg will take 118 days to hatch at a temperature of 4.7 degrees C and only 35 days at 12.2 degrees C. At the same temperatures a rainbow trout egg will take 100 days and 28 days, respectively. The newly hatched trout, or alevins, carry their own food supplies in the form of yolk-sacs and thus do not feed. The hatching period is a critical time of development and care must be taken to ensure that an excessive increase in water temperature does not occur, as the consequent drop in oxygen-availability will result in a high mortality.

An alevin absorbs its yolk-sac after two or three weeks, depending on temperature, and then begins to feed actively. At this stage they are only a few centimetres long, just beginning to resemble the fish that the angler so eagerly chases and are known as fry. The majority of eggs hatch in spring, by which time an ample supply of microscopic food is becoming available to the fry in the wild. Should spring be late in arriving, because of a severe winter, the low water temperature ensures that the eggs do not hatch prematurely.

When the fry are feeding actively they are transferred to a nursery tank and from there to an external pond or raceway. Many hatcheries do not have space available for covered nursery tanks and the fry are then transferred direct from the trough in which they are hatched to the open-air water enclosures. Overcrowding must be avoided, as this will result in reduced growth and increased mortality.

Feeding: A variety of diets has been used in hatcheries throughout the world, but as yet a universal artificial trout-food has not been adopted. It is most unlikely that such a standard food will ever be developed, as the correct feeding of trout is a highly complex problem. Many variables must be taken into account and what works well in one hatchery will not necessarily prove so in another. Raw meat usually comprises the main bulk of the diet. Substandard (i.e. unfit for human consumption) liver and spleen are commonly used in Australia because of their low price. However, an all-meat diet lacks certain ingredients necessary for the trout's correct development and this is always supplemented with dry-feed pellets similar to those used by chicken farmers and the like.

Trout fry are fed about five times daily. Small amounts of food should be made available at frequent intervals, rather than large amounts at infrequent intervals. A certain amount of food wastage is bound to occur and excess food must be removed before it fouls the water. Regular feeding with small amounts of food ensures that wastage is kept to a minimum and that food is made available for most of the time.

The frequency of feeding declines as the trout become older. As the fry become larger they are known as fingerlings. Small fingerlings are usually fed four times daily, medium to large fingerlings two or three times a day and adults once or twice daily. There are no fixed rules about the frequency of feeding and the broad rule-of-thumb can be said to be to give the fish food if they will eat it. Mechanical feeders which release a set amount of food at pre-determined intervals are now being manufactured but as yet few are in use in Australia.

The condition of the fish is closely watched to ensure that there is no deficiency in the diet. If this is so, the fish will develop characteristic symptoms the recognition of which will enable the nature of the deficiency to be pinpointed and checked. For example, an iodine deficiency will cause a condition known as goitre, similar to that occurring in humans for the same reason. Goitre can be easily recognized, its development halted and eventually cured by the regular addition of small amounts of iodine to the diet.

Ponds and raceways: A constant flow of well-oxygenated water is essential for the correct functioning of the ponds and raceways. The majority of Australian hatcheries rear the fingerlings in circular concrete ponds of about 6 m in diameter. Water is introduced through jets, so positioned as to cause a current to circulate around the pond. The central drain is always surrounded by a wire screen with a mesh size small enough to prevent the fish escaping. The circular current in such ponds causes excess food to collect at the centre, around the screen, from whence it is easily removed. Raceways can be simply described as being greatly enlarged troughs, as they possess similar hydraulic characteristics. The comparative efficiency of each type of water enclosure has been the subject of much discussion. Raceways have been found to be capable of carrying higher number of fish per unit volume of water, and to give a more rapid growth-rate, than circular ponds. However these advantages are offset by the fact that raceways must be supplied with a much greater volume of water than is the case with circular ponds: no small fact when considering the water requirements of a large hatchery with numerous ponds and/or raceways. Especially so when considering the periodic occurrence of drought in many of Australia's trout-fishing areas.

Grading: Thus, from November onwards, throughout the summer, the work to be done in the hatchery assumes a set routine. The fingerlings are fed regularly and at certain intervals are graded for size. The presence of relatively large fish in a pond has been shown to inhibit the growth of smaller fish in the same enclosure. Some fish hatch earlier than others and thus have the advantage of an increased growth period. Even fish which hatch at the same time do not necessarily have identical growth rates. Therefore, after a brief period of time a pond can contain trout extending over a relatively great size-range. The fish in each pond must be sorted and placed in other ponds containing fish of an identical size only. Towards the end of summer a distinct difference can be seen between the size of trout in specific ponds, the fast growers being up to twice the size of the slow growers. Many factors other than food-availability affect the growth-rate of trout and the occurrence of slow growing fish cannot be solved simply by increased feeding.

Commonly occurring hazards: The ponds and raceways must be kept clean at all times. Excess food, algae, or similar debris will increase the chances of bacterial or fungal diseases occurring. Owing to the presence of large numbers of fish in a relatively confined volume of water, disease, should it occur, spreads very rapidly. Whole stocks of fish have been lost as a result of a single, sharp outbreak. A variety of diseases have been recorded in overseas hatcheries, but fortunately few of these have been observed in Australia. The regular addition of precise amounts of suitable fungicides, or similar chemicals, to the water, will greatly lessen the chances of disease occurring. In addition to increasing the likelihood of disease, an excessive build-up of debris can harm fish by reducing the concentration of dissolved oxygen in the water. Fine particles of waste-matter can also cause gill-irritation, which leads to increased mortality, especially during the fry stage.

Liberation: The question of what is the most suitable size, or age, at which fish should be released, has been the subject of much research. Is it better to release a certain number of three-month-old trout, reared at a cost of x dollars, or to release half that number of six-month-old fish reared at the same cost? Success is measured in terms of the number of hatchery-reared trout which are eventually caught by the angler, or survive to breed.

For many years the practice has been to release trout as fingerlings. In hatcheries with limited pond space, one year's stock cannot be carried into the following year and this practice is still continued. However, it has now been found more effective to release fish as yearlings, by which time they are considerably larger and more able to cope with their new environment.

In the wild, trout experience an exceedingly high mortality during their first year of life. The young fish are at the mercy of numerous natural predators. Research has shown that only 2 to 3 per cent of the fry survive to be yearlings. In many waters the percentage is probably considerably lower than this. However, by the time the trout reaches yearling size it has outgrown many of its natural predators and becomes more adept at the art of survival. Approximately one half of the yearlings will reach the age of two years, and half again, the age of three years. Thus, the benefit of releasing yearlings instead of fingerlings becomes obvious. If 1000 fingerlings were released into a stream only 10 to 15 would reach the age of two years. A release of only 20 to 30 yearlings would achieve the same result, and at a lesser cost.

Cannibalism is one of the major causes of mortality. Fry and fingerlings can be released into 'virgin' waters with considerable success, as many will reach maturity. The cold-water streams of Australia do not carry many species of native fish. Only the eel and the river blackfish constitute a real threat to the fry. The fish belonging to the Galaxiid family are too small to feed on the fry, and they themselves are preyed upon when the trout become larger. It is unfortunate that the introduction of trout has resulted in the disappearance of *Galaxias* species from many waters in which they were once found.

The fingerlings or yearlings may have to be carried over a considerable distance before being released. During the journey they must be kept in cool, well-oxygenated water. A variety of live-fish containers are used in Australia. In New South Wales the fish are placed in strong polythene bags, half-filled with water. Oxygen is piped into the remaining half of the bag which is then sealed and placed into a stiff cardboard carton. The number of fish to each bag is governed by the following factors: average size of fish, length of journey, and water temperature. The latter is often regulated by the use of ice during long journeys. The cartons are then carried by road, rail, or air, to the desired destination. In Victoria and Tasmania the fish are carried in specially equipped trucks. The fish from Snob's Creek hatchery are carried in 200 L drums which are continually supplied with oxygen from cylinders on the truck. Up to 8000 small fingerlings can be carried in each drum. The fish are often anaesthetized to prevent them from becoming distressed. The Tasmanian trucks are equipped with even larger water containers.

Overseas hatcheries have constructed more sophisticated equipment. Specially designed water-tankers with built-in oxygenating and refrigeration units are often used. Up to 1360 kg of fish can be carried in one such tanker. More use is being made of aircraft when liberating fish over large areas of water. The fish are released from a height of 150 m and enter the water with no ill-effects. Such a mode of release involves little man-power and, under suitable conditions, is very economical. The fish are carried in water contained in a specially prepared 'hopper'. Eildon and Glenmaggie reservoirs, in Victoria, have been stocked by this method.

The distribution of fish is made in accordance with the requirements of the waters concerned. Many Australian waters present ideal conditions for natural reproduction and need never be stocked. But other waters in which trout are found present marginal conditions for survival and must be stocked at regular intervals. Drought, bushfires and similar phenomena can totally destroy such fisheries, and the need for re-stocking is often great. In New South Wales the majority of young fish are distributed to the acclimatization societies in various parts of the State, who then release the fish in their respective areas.

The contribution that hatchery-reared fish make to the fishery can be estimated by marking them prior to release, and then watching for their appearance in anglers' catches. Fin-clipping or tagging are two commonly used marking methods.

The release of fish usually continues throughout the summer. By the time that the last fish has been liberated, the spawning season has commenced once again and yet another hatchery 'year' is under way.

The role of hatcheries

Nowadays, hatcheries no longer have the prime function of introducing trout into new waters. Trout are now present in every lake and stream suited to their survival. Thus, there has been a shift from introduction, to the seasonal re-stocking of hard-fished waters, or those with a high natural mortality. Indeed, the brown trout has been so successful in Tasmania and New South Wales, that the practice of re-stocking them has been discontinued. Various waters, such as Lake Eucumbene in New South Wales, undoubtedly have been over-populated with brown trout, and it is feasible that efficient fishery-management policies will advocate their part-destruction—the complete reverse of re-stocking. Such steps have

Self-sustaining trout populations are now present in most suitable Australian waters, and hatcheries tend to rear fish to yearling rather than fingerling size.

long been effected in several New Zealand lakes, with considerable success. The supply of food in a given body of water will remain relatively constant from year to year. Should the trout population in such a water increase in number, there will be a lesser amount of food available to each fish, causing its growth to be retarded. Acute over-population will result in a population of stunted, under-sized fish of little use to the angler, and should be avoided at all costs.

Rainbow trout are more easily caught by the angler, and are more spectacular fighters than brown trout. They are an extremely popular fish with most anglers and are hard fished for. Such a high fishing pressure, and the correspondingly high angling mortality, mean that many waters have to be seasonally re-stocked with rainbow trout. The brown trout too has a large following of anglers, who prefer it to the rainbow trout because of its greater cunning and relatively larger size. However, because of such cunning fewer fish are caught and no re-stocking is needed. A good example of the higher catch-rate of rainbow trout is provided by Lake Eucumbene. Whereas there are probably three, or even four, brown trout to each rainbow trout in the lake, catch data compiled by State fisheries workers show that two rainbow trout are caught for every one brown trout. This state of affairs is resulting in too large a brown trout population, and the average size of the fish is declining.

Because of the presence of trout in all suitable waters, present-day hatcheries are beginning to rear fish to the yearling, rather than fingerling size prior to liberation.

Some hatcheries are once again being used to facilitate the introduction of new species of fish into Australia. In Tasmania Clarence Lagoon has been regularly re-stocked with brook trout since the 1970s. In New South Wales attempts are being made to introduce the eastern brook trout *Salvelinus fontinalis* from North America, and a land-locked strain of the Atlantic salmon from Europe.

An increasing amount of fisheries research is being carried out in many hatcheries. Various aspects of the trout's life-history are under study. The knowledge thus gained will be used to implement more effective fishery-management practices. Additional work is also being carried out in such fields as selective breeding and dietetics, and with some indigenous fish species. Snob's Creek Hatchery carries a large complement of scientific workers, and is typical of such development.

The future of trout hatcheries
Introduction of any species of fish into a new country can only be said to be successful when self-reproducing populations have been established in the wild. By this yardstick the introduction of trout into Australia can be said to have been extremely successful, as numerous wild populations exist in many areas of the country. As mentioned previously, brown

trout have proved so successful that the practice of rearing them is declining and has been completely discontinued in New South Wales and Tasmania. Could this not eventually be the case with rainbow trout, also? Will there be, in fact, a continuing need for trout hatcheries?

The answer is yes. Whereas many of Australia's lakes and streams are ideally suited for trout and need no re-stocking, many such waters present marginal conditions for survival, and therefore have unstable trout populations. Any change in the environment caused by phenomena such as periods of drought, or bushfires and the like, will result in a deterioration in the trout fishery provided by such waters, and a corresponding need for re-stocking.

Other waters, although at first seeming ideally suited for trout, may lack certain features necessary for the fish to successfully complete their life cycle. For example, large lakes may have inadequate spawning facilities. This will result in the numerical decline of the trout population therein. Such waters have to be regularly re-stocked. Several Tasmanian lakes fall into this category.

The Australian trout fisherman at present has access to large areas of lightly fished waters, but there is no doubt that as Australia's population increases, as it is bound to do, existing waters will be subjected to higher and higher fishing pressures. Trout have already been introduced into the great majority of suitable waters in Australia, and the unavailability of new waters, other than those created by hydro-electric schemes and the like, will inevitably lead to the necessity of increasing production from existing waters. Hatcheries will no doubt play a vital role in such matters.

Introduction of new species of fish will also continue to be a function of tomorrow's hatcheries. Unsuccessful attempts to introduce brook trout and Atlantic salmon into Australia have been made in the past, and it may well be that further attempts, at present in progress, will require many years of work before success is complete. Authorities are becoming concerned about the decline in indigenous fish populations and fish such as the Murray cod and golden and silver perch are now being reared at Narrandera hatchery to restock depleted areas.

See Cookery.

TROUT, Coral

Plectropomus leopardus: Together with red emperor and other members of the Lutjanidae family, coral trout are finely-fleshed Barrier Reef fish, forming a primary part of the Queensland fishery. Their range in territory extends widely to New Guinea waters, and across to Western Australia. Coral trout in larger sizes have been known to carry the poison ciguatera, the result of having eaten fish which in turn live on an organism which forms on damaged coral. As a general rule, coral trout can be eaten with complete safety.

T ■ TROUT

Coral trout

The methods of commercial fishing are similar to most kinds of reef handline fishing. Strong lines baited with squid or fish flesh are lowered to the bottom over sunken reefs, and jigged until taken. A fairly long wire trace and strong hook is used, as the fish tends to dive in among coral for shelter when in trouble.

At times large numbers of trout are caught in individual areas, but the fishing-out of accessible areas on the Barrier Reef has become apparent to commercial fishermen in recent times. It is becoming necessary to range wider out. Scientists believe there is a relatively slow growth rate. It is known that trout have a complex sex ratio system known as *protogynous hermaphroditism*, allowing recruitment of necessary males into the population by the sex reversal of functional females. Heavy fishing can upset the delicate balance of numbers sufficiently to make recovery slow. From a non-commercial viewpoint, coral trout numbers in fished-out areas are sufficient for sport and table.

Coral trout are regularly taken on lures trolled by mackerel fishermen close to rising coral reefs. The fish will often come well up off the bottom to take a lure or bait. It has also been shown that they can be taken on lighter tackle and cast lures, by anyone willing to risk a few tackle losses. The method is simply to drift in a boat beside the reef, and cast in between coral heads and bomboras with jigs or baits. The bait is retrieved fast in order to force the fish to chase it. After being hooked, the fish dives back for cover and must be held out by the angler. It makes for interesting fishing, and once the technique is mastered so the angler knows the limitations of the coral terrain, it can be extremely productive.

On rocky areas of the coast, such as at Cape Tribulation and Bowen, the inshore coastal waters are clear enough for coral growth and coral trout. The fish then can be caught from the mainland. Accessible areas where fish are heavily speared have shown that trout can learn about spearmen, and become extremely shy about skin-divers.

The handsome colouring, salmon pink with violet spots, leads to use of the name 'trout', a resemblance further

TROUT cod

expanded by tail shape. A strong fighter well equipped with teeth, the coral trout bears no other resemblance to his freshwater namesake. Their range extends wherever coral grows, and beyond it over the edge of the continental shelf in tropical seas, where they have been taken in depths to 180 m. In Western Australia, coral trout are among the most prized northern deep sea fish. They are incredibly strong fighters for their size, and beneath the gorgeous red coat, spotted with blue and gold of this variety, is a pinkish white flesh second to none. They take deep sea and shore baits and are often caught on lures trolled behind boats or cast from the shore.

TROUT cod

Maccullochella macquariensis: Only recently confirmed as a species separate from the Murray cod *Maccullochella peeli.* Both fish have similar diets and are of the same excellent table quality and respond to similar angling methods, but trout cod prefer cooler water. Trout cod grow to 80 cm and 16 kg, which is around half the maximum length and maximum weight of Murray cod. For many years it was thought that trout cod were merely the cold-water version of Murray cod but studies by American biologist Dr Tim Berra confirmed trout cod as a distinct species.

Trout cod have not benefited from achieving their own identity and they are scarce in waters where they once were common, probably through overfishing. They can be clearly distinguished from Murray cod by their blunter snout and deeper, rounder bodies. Murray cod appear almost elongate by comparison. In trout cod, the anal and ventral fins and tail are dark, whereas they are filmy, almost translucent in Murray cod. The upper jaw overhangs the lower jaw and the head slope is straight. They are distributed in the upper reaches of the Murray-Darling system and are currently known at Glenbawn Dam, Lake Sambell, Sevens Creek near Euroa, and in the

Trout cod

Murray cod

The trout cod and the Murray cod have only recently been confirmed as separate species.

Murrumbidgee River near Tharwa, A.C.T. The future of trout cod is viewed with misgiving by some biologists, and there appears an urgent need for more research on this fish. An 11 kg trout cod was taken in Lake Sambell near Beechworth, Victoria.

TRUMPETER

Beautiful, deeply-bronzed fishes of the family Latridae confined to southern Australia, New Zealand, Chile, St Paul and Amsterdam Islands. They are delicious food fishes, much sought by gourmets, but not to be confused with the small, striped fishes called trumpeters. There are at least three members of the family in Australian waters, including the bastard trumpeter *Latridopsis forsteri*, the striped trumpeter *Latris lineata*, and the real bastard trumpeter *Mendosoma allporti*, and they all rank among our finest table fare. The bastard trumpeter is rarely caught by anglers and feeds mainly on invertebrates, but the others occasionally are taken by amateur anglers.

The trumpeter may run to about 27 kg but is generally caught around 13 kg and is an excellent sportfish. Like the blue cod it must have clean water and will reject all baits if the bottom water it inhabits has been dirtied by storm. It prefers a coralled rock reef in water 18 to 130 m deep and is commoner in colder water; but in summer it comes into the shallows, leaving again in autumn as the surface gets colder. It lives on moving prey.

The best bait is barracouta, either fresh or taken in the summer months and deep-frozen, but the trumpeter will bite freely at squid, octopus, red or blue cod, sea-perch, spotties, tarakihi or even the flesh of its own kind. Early morning is the best time.

Trumpeter may be the first fish to be caught on a new or long-unused ground, but because they bite freely, experience seems to indicate they will also be the first variety to be fished out. It is in its best condition in May or June, immediately prior to spawning; in August, appearing again, it is usually thin. Spawning takes place in the deep water to which the trumpeter heads in its winter migration.

Bastard trumpeter

It is not unusual for the body cavity to contain large quantities of a fine white fat, like the fat that shawls the entrails of a well-conditioned lamb, and fat is also distributed throughout the flesh. It is an excellent fish for smoking, comparable to Scotland's finnan haddock and perhaps superior.

TUBEMOUTH

Remarkable finger-thick fish of the family Siphonognathidae, found in seaweed beds in South Australia and Western Australia. Only two species have been confirmed in Australia. *Siphonognathus argyrophanes* is the most common, a slender-bodied fish with a mouth at the end of a tube-like snout and a frail filament attached to the top jaw. They grow to 43 cm and are the grassy green colour of their habitat.

TUNAS

A group of fearless, streamlined fish from the families Scombridae and Thunnidae which Roughley estimated could swim at 48 km/h and placed them second only to marlin for speed. Whitley said tuna have been timed at 64 km/h and are highly regarded as a food fish and sporting fish. The tuna family, close relatives of the mackerel, includes albacore, bonito and frigate mackerel (*which see*). They are present in large numbers in Australia and several of the 11 species in Australian coastal waters have been exploited commercially.

Tuna were generally known in Australia as tunny until the discovery of a potentially big export market to America, where tuna is rated a luxury fish. The name was then changed to conform with that used in America. Since then southern bluefin tuna, yellowfin tuna and striped or skipjack tuna have been developed into important export fishes.

Tuna usually are an iridescent blue on top, yellow, black and white or blue on the fins, and silvery below. They are spotted, striped or plain according to species. A distinguishing feature of the tuna and the Spanish mackerel is the hard keel and usually two smaller flanking keels, on each side of the butt of the tail. This helps to distinguish them from the trevallies, which have only hard scutes. Tuna have distinctively forked tails and tuck their fins into grooves to improve their streamlining and increase their swimming speed. Their stomachs are relatively small and to sustain the energy expended by such fast movement they eat voraciously and digest their food rapidly, which keeps their body temperature several degrees higher than the water in which they swim.

Until 1936 tuna were considered an attractive sportfish of no commercial value in Australia. But an aerial survey of New South Wales and Tasmanian waters by Stanley Fowler of the C.S.I.R.O. revealed big schools of tuna and other pelagics. This led to the establishment of canneries at Narooma, New South Wales, and at Port Lincoln, South Australia. In 1941 the various species of tuna in Australian waters were clearly tabbed for the first time in an important C.S.I.R.O. report by Dr Serventy and in 1950 the Commonwealth Government chartered an American tuna clipper, *Senibua*, to demonstrate live bait pole fishing for tuna in Australian waters. The *Senibua* caught 117 tonnes of tuna in 70 days' fishing and this, together with a visit to South Australia in 1956 by two American skippers of pole fishing boats led to the introduction of the new method in New South Wales and South Australia.

Tuna production in Australia ebbs and flows despite help from spotter aircraft, and commercial boats concentrate almost exclusively on juvenile southern bluefin off the Eyre Peninsula of South Australia and off the southern coast of New South Wales. The fish are between two and a half and four years old and weigh 6.5 to 22.5 kg with occasional fish of more than 45 kg. Japanese longline fishermen hunt adult bluefin tuna six to eight years old further out in the Tasman Sea and in the Indian Ocean. Strangely, commercial tuna catches have had no marked effect on tuna as a sport-fish and they are taken in numbers every year, usually by trolling from game fishing boats.

Albacore *Thunnus alalunga:* The general colour and shape of this tuna is similar to the southern bluefin, but it has a yellowish tinge in the lower half of the body which is mainly silvery white marked by longitudinal streaks which merge into each other. The extremely long pectoral fin which extends back beyond the level of the anal fin is its main distinguishing characteristic. Seldom weighing more than 23 kg most Albacore taken by game fishermen are from 4.5 to 10 kg. It is not a commonly caught species although its range extends from southern Queensland to Tasmania, Victoria, South Australia and Western Australia.

This is the most prized tuna because of the white flesh. The name albacore was used for the southern bluefin in some places and for the Spanish mackerel at Geraldton. The turrum *Carangoides emburyi* is sometimes given this name, but with the capture of more albacore it is becoming more widely known. It takes a lure similar to those used for other species of tuna and will also take live bait.

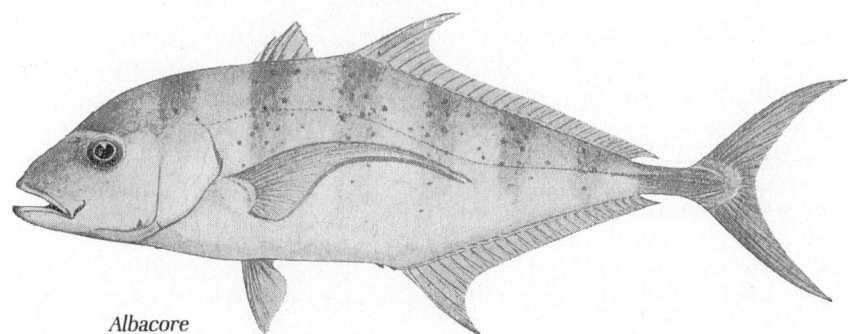

Albacore

Bonito

Sarda chiliensis australis: Although it is not recorded in Western Australia and only occasionally in Victorian waters, this is the most prolific bait fish along the Australian eastern coast. Offshore anglers use bonito fillets for snapper bait and for deep-sea anglers its dark red flesh seems to attract every sporting fish up to shark and marlin. It is also known as mackerel, horse mackerel, skippy, skipper and skipjack because of its habit of breaking the surface when feeding. The name 'skipjack' has also been applied to at least half-a-dozen other species.

Bonito are a bright blue-green or blue-black above and silvery below. The fins are dull grey, the body small and stout but beautifully streamlined. The first dorsal fin is relatively high. The New Zealand striped bonito or striped tuna *Katsuwonus pelamis* has only five stripes on each side, on the lower half of the body below the lateral line, whereas the Australian bonito has at least 10 stripes running along each side of the body, both above and below the lateral line, filling the space from the dorsal fin to the belly.

Bonito appear around headlands and shallow, reefy areas in summer. It is a speedy, tough, fighting little tuna that provides good sport on light tackle. However, it is mainly taken by trolling at speed and has been known to take a bait trolled at 28.8 km/h. They strike savagely or not at all and are caught on all kinds of lures such as white, red and green feathers, plastic jigs, plastic squids, streamer flies, metal tubes and teased rope.

They grow to 90 cm and 5.5 kg but the average taken are 40 to 45 cm and 450 g to 2 kg.

They feed on shoals of pilchards, anchovies and hardyheads and will respond to squid, shrimp and crab baits. Many game anglers in search of bait may put out four lines at a time and commercial fishermen use special trolling rigs with half-a-dozen or more hooks fitted with teased rope lures which they call 'wogs'. Bonito are fast and powerful for their size, so with a fish on each hook there is plenty of excitement.

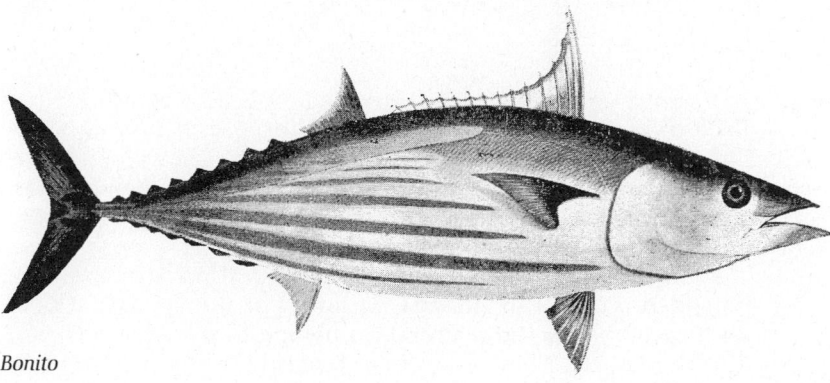

Bonito

Leaping bonito *Cybiosarda elegans:* A sub-tropical fish, also known as Watson's bonito, which frequents coastal waters and estuaries but is not very common along the Australian southern coastline. In Queensland in midwinter extensive shoals swim inshore to feed on sprats, anchovies and hardyheads. Like its close relative, the Australian or striped bonito, it is a fine bait fish. It seldom stays long in the one place.

The leaping bonito is a strikingly marked little fish, differing from the common bonito by having a combination of spots and broken bars above the lateral line and continuous longitudinal lines below. The dorsal fin is black in front and pearly white behind and is decidedly taller than in the bonito. They are often caught among common bonito and may go unobserved until the difference is pointed out. They average about 450 to 675 g. Excellent baits for marlin.

Dog-tooth tuna *Gymnosarda unicolor:* A big white-fleshed tuna of Northern Territory and outer Barrier Reef waters, sometimes caught by offshore mackerel trolling boats. Roughley credited it with growing to 90.6 kg or more, but Grant says its limit is 69 kg. Even so it is one of the biggest of the tunas, a powerful, tapering fish with distinctive curved teeth in both the upper and lower jaws. The body is bluish-black above and silvery below. In mature fish, the fins are grey, but in juveniles the finlets are yellow-tinted.

Australia held five world records for dog-tooth tuna in 1985, including one of 64.49 kg taken on a 15 kg line by John Johnston off Lizard Island, Queensland, in September 1975. A great piece of fishing!

Dog-tooth tuna

Mackerel tuna *Euthynnus alleteratus:* A sub-tropical species also known as little tuna and in America as false albacore. It is a striking-looking fish, easily recognized by the patch of wavy mackerel-like markings on the back, which extend from the dorsal fin to the tail and four or five rounded black spots on the belly between the pectoral and ventral fins.

Some have spots level with the pectoral fin and they are considered to be an Atlantic variation of the species. Those with spots below the pectoral fin belong to the Indian Ocean and the Pacific. They are robust, tapering fish which shoal in

Mackerel tuna

inshore coastal waters, where they feed on pilchards, blue sprats and herring. They were called mackerel tuna because they are so common on mackerel grounds where they are a constant nuisance to professional mackerel-trolling boats.

Mackerel tuna are a dark-fleshed fish usually caught at around 4.5 to 6.8 kg, but grow to 16 kg and 1 m. They fight hard when hooked. In the waters of the Barrier Reef they are fished to provide highly effective baits for emperors or sweetlips and for rock cod. Though they prefer the sub-tropics, they are sometimes caught as far south as Eden on the New South Wales coast and in Western Australia from Shark Bay northwards. Trolling is the most practical method of catching them.

Northern bluefin tuna

Thunnus tonggol: Similar in appearance and colour to the southern bluefin, but its distribution is in sub-tropical and tropical seas and in the East Indies, Japan and Ceylon. Although it occasionally strays down as far as Eden on the south coast of New South Wales, it is found mainly from Port Stephens to North Queensland waters. Numbers are taken in Western Australia as far south as Busselton.

Streamlined for speed like all the tunas, this fish is more tapering in the body than the southern bluefin and the number of gill rakers also differs from those in the southern bluefin. Another sure method of identifying it is by examining the liver which is plain in the northern bluefin but streaked on the outer surface with fine parallel black lines in the southern species. The livers also differ in colour; that of the southern is dark while the northern tuna's is pale brown.

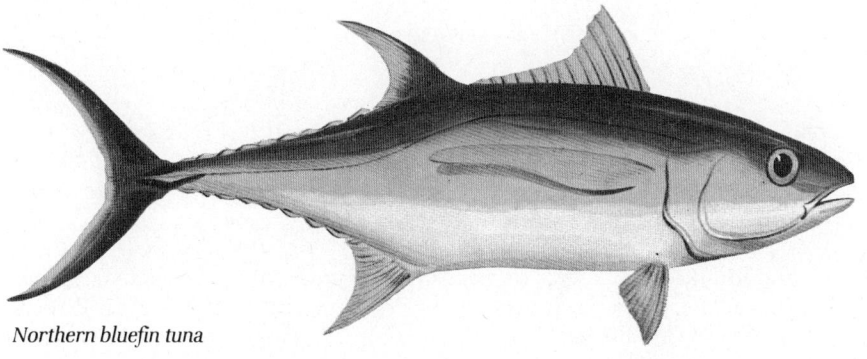

Northern bluefin tuna

These fish grow to about 38 kg but average from 11 to 16 kg. They are a fast-moving fish and feed on pilchards, anchovies, garfish and other small marine life. White or red feather lures are used mainly to catch them while trolling, but at times garfish are a very good bait to use for the purpose.

Australia held five world records for *Thunnus tonggol* in 1985, the biggest being Tim Simpson's 35.90 kg catch on a 15 kg line at Bermagui in April 1982.

Pacific big-eyed tuna

Thunnus obesus: Similar in appearance to the yellowfin tuna, this offshore fish has been taken in Australian waters by fisheries research teams, in quantity by Japanese longliners, and possibly unknowingly by game fishermen. Young specimens sometimes penetrate Queensland estuaries and coastal waters.

Big-eyed tuna are bluish-black above and silvery below and juveniles have longitudinal rows of pale spots on the flanks. The finlets are yellowish but seldom bright. They grow to 1.8 cm but are mostly caught at around 90 cm. They are distinguished from other tunas by their large eyes. They are classified as a white meat fish and are at a premium in the Japanese canning industry, but so far have not been exploited commercially in Australia.

Southern bluefin tuna

Thunnus maccoyii: A superbly shaped fish of uniform bluish-black colour above and silvery white below, which occurs in numbers from Sydney to Tasmania and west along the southern coast to Cape Leeuwin in Western Australia. They have become exciting fishing recently at Portland, Victoria, and off Port MacDonnell, South Australia, between April and July.

Along the Australian east coast, southern bluefin tuna are seldom seen north of Sydney and from there north their place is taken by the northern bluefin tuna. Southern bluefin range from 2 to 100 kg, but the average taken near our coasts are from 15 to 30 kg. They are carnivorous on all small fish and have a fondness for squid. The best lures are small to medium purple and pink squids on Christmas tree rigs.

Southern bluefin tuna

Port MacDonnell is proving the best tuna spot between Mallacoota and Adelaide, largely because the reef formed by the continental shelf is only 15 or 16 km south of the breakwater. There in a depth of around 180 m the main problems are the barracouta that attack tuna lures. Portland tuna average 14 kg but at Port MacDonnell tuna of 20 kg are common and Kevin Ossman took one of 93.2 kg on 24 kg trolling gear in 1981.

Australia held ten world records for southern bluefin tuna in 1985, eight of them caught in the waters off Tasmania, the world's hotspot for this species. Probably the best catch was Jim Allen's 106.50 kg southern bluefin on a 15 kg line off Tasman Island in May 1980, although Rodney Beard landed one of 116.50 kg on a 37 kg line off Tasman Peninsula in May 1979.

Striped tuna

Katsuwonus pelamis: Also known as skipjack tuna and oceanic bonito, this is a smaller fish than other tunas, rarely weighing more than 9 kg. The average size is 3 to 5 kg. Striped tuna is almost world-wide in distribution and has been recorded in all States of Australia, but has been exploited commercially only in Victoria where boats based on Lakes Entrance took them with gill nets until 1964 when they transferred their attentions to edible sharks.

It has longitudinal stripes along the lower part of the body which is a light silvery colour. The upper portion of the body is dark blue with a brighter rich blue patch towards the tail broken up by vertical bars, but this fades quickly after death to a dull grey colour.

The range of the fish is closely related to a warm current (17 degrees C and above) near the coast and this varies from year to year. It is most abundant during the summer months but strays may be caught any time of the year. A strong fighter, it takes almost any kind of trolled lure and is an excellent game fish on light tackle.

The striped tuna is used overseas for canning and is quite a good food fish when prepared in this way. Interest in the Victorian striped tuna commercial fishery declined when it was found that the same gill net method could be used for sharks that brought higher prices. So fishermen modified their nets to fish the sea bottom for sharks, leaving the striped tuna to anglers.

Yellowfin tuna

Thunnus albacares: A magnificent fighting fish with sweeping sickle-like pectoral fin. For many years only small specimens of this powerful fish were taken by game fishermen on the eastern coast of Australia, but during the last few years many large specimens have been taken from 65 to 90 kg. One caught off Wolf Rock, southern Queensland, in 1975 weighed 95 kg and measured 1.8 m.

The name yellowfin is misleading, for the bluefin tunas also

T ■ TUNAS

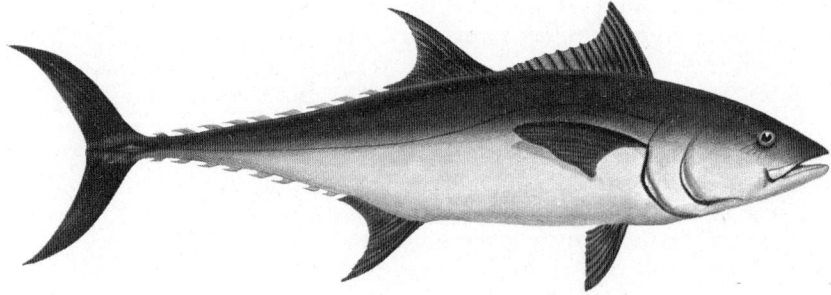

Yellowfin tuna

have yellow fins or finlets. The main means of identification apart from the brilliant blue and gold colouring of the fish is in the length of the pectoral fin. This is not as long as in the albacore but it extends considerably more than in the bluefins, reaching well beyond the level of the second dorsal to about the level of the anal fin. The second dorsal and anal fins are taller than the first dorsal and increase relatively as the fish grows older. In large fish they may extend back to the level of the tail flukes. The larger fish with very large second dorsals and anal fins are often called allison tunas, but it is considered that the two are identical and that the larger finned fish are a growth stage of the yellowfin.

Yellowfin tuna are caught regularly off Sydney and Port Stephens. Although taken on a trolled bait at fairly fast speeds, they are mainly caught on a whole live fishbait while drifting. They will follow hooked fish up to the surface and when scraps of bait are thrown overboard, will remain around the boat at a few feet below the surface taking the bait offered. However they are quite able to pick out a fish with a hook and line attached from a fish floating free, and are not easy at times to hook.

They range from Queensland, New South Wales, Lord Howe Island to Tasmania and Western Australia, and in these places are sometimes taken by reef fishermen using cut baits driftfished over the bottom. They are found in New Zealand's northern waters south to around East Cape in summer. They are such energetic fighters they cause plenty of excitement before they are boated. The flesh is highly edible when it is bleached in hot water and deep fried.

Frigate mackerel *Auxis thazard:* The smallest of the tunas in Australian waters, classified in the Katsuwonidae family in South Australia and in Scombridae in Tasmania. It grows to a maximum of 1.3 kg but most seen are under about 0.5 kg. It is reputed to be a semitropical species but it seems to be significant that it is found sparingly from the south coast of Western Australia around to Eden on the south coast of New South Wales and

Frigate mackerel

that captures outside these limits are very occasional. In the past it has been reported as common around north Australia but this may require checking, for the species observed probably was the maru frigate mackerel, which is now known to occur in that area.

In some accounts of New Zealand species it appears to have been confused with the common or blue mackerel, giving the impression that it occurs in shoals around the North Island whereas it is a comparative rarity there. It is, however, well distributed in the Indian and Pacific Oceans and is represented in the Atlantic by an almost identical relative, *Auxis rochei*.

Like the rest of the tuna, the frigate mackerel is a fish of the blue waters and is seldom seen in the estuaries and harbours. It usually is taken in trolling offshore for other species. Sometimes two or three may be taken in the one day and then no more seen for a long time. It is torpedo shaped, being of more rounded and deeper body than the common mackerel. Since it trolls very well as a bait, it is prized as a lure for game fish. It usually has eight small free finlets between the second dorsal fin and the tail and seven underneath between the anal fin and the tail. As it comes from the water, it is a dark blue on the upper body, shading away to silvery-white on the belly. It has broad, wavy dark lines forming mackerel-like vernicular markings on its back, somewhat more coarse than on the common mackerel but similar to those on the mackerel tuna, though less distinct on account of the dark background. On death it rapidly changes to a dull leaden colour, which has given rise to the vernacular name 'leadenall'.

Maru frigate mackerel

Auxis thynnoides: A small tuna, very similar to the frigate mackerel. This was known only in the East Indies and Japan until a large school entered Port Stephens and a number were obtained at Shoal Bay in January 1947. The Asian variety differs from the other species *A. thazard* in having a noticeable band of scales on each side of the lateral line. It has the same rounded body as the frigate mackerel but is slightly smaller. They turn up occasionally in catches of bonito that have been taken by trolling.

TUNNY See Tunas.

TURRUM *Carangoides emburyi:* A warm-water game fish of impressive fighting ability. They grow to 40 kg but even fish half that size are seldom landed without a twenty-minute or half-hour fight. They are members of the trevally family and are found in Queensland, Northern Territory and Western Australian waters, but are rarely seen south of Gladstone. Small fish are splendid table fare, but they become dry and rather unpalatable as they mature.

When turrum are hooked they make an initial run of at least 180 m, sound and swim broadside on, repeating the resistance again and again as they are brought to gaff. Large turrum strike without warning and usually are taken when trolling spoons, drones, or baits of cut fish or garfish. Many an angler fishing the bottom with a handline has been surprised by the turrum's fighting qualities, even on heavy gear.

Turrum often are confused with the great trevally, *Caranx sexfasciatus*, which is also a noted fighter, but according to Grant the two can easily be distinguished by the count of the soft dorsal fin, which has from 19 to 21 rays in the great trevally compared with 29 to 31 rays in the turrum. Young turrum inhabit inshore coastal waters while the larger specimens move out into deeper water.

They are opalescent blue above and silvery below, with yellow spots scattered over the upper body. There is a small dark blotch on the gill-cover and at the base of the pectoral fin. The fins are a smoky olive colour. Five or more darker bands may extend from the top of the body around to the middle of the sides. One outstanding catch was the 19.50 kg turrum on a 15 kg breaking strain line by Mrs S. Nathan at Keppel Bay, Queensland, a record which has remained on the Game Fishing Association of Australia's books since 1955.

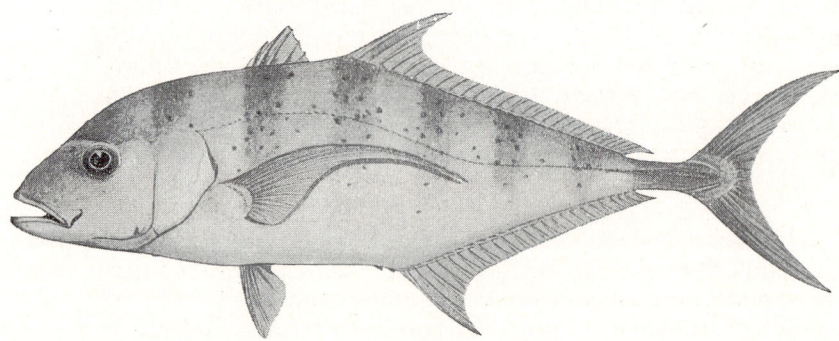

Turrum

V

VICTORIA

Few Victorian anglers have to travel far to find good fishing. Victoria has 29 river basins in which there are approximately 237 streams and 133 lakes, reservoirs and dams. Many of these hold large populations of trout, while some yield Murray cod, Macquarie perch, river blackfish, carp, redfin and eels. Two lakes, Purrumbete and Bullen Merri, are stocked with quinnat salmon. Along the coast there are scores of beaches, bays, estuaries, inlets and saltwater lakes, which provide every conceivable kind of saltwater fishing.

Saltwater angling in Victoria

Anglers visiting Victoria to fish for marine species will find that they will often have to change their methods to catch the same fish they have been catching in another State. For instance, Victorians pride themselves on having the best bream fishery in Australia. They may not be able to catch bream in their hundreds on one outing as in some of the hotspots up north, but they can catch them all the year around because the Victorian species of bream does not leave the estuaries.

The warm water current that feeds the New South Wales' shoreline does not follow the coast around southern Victoria, so there are fewer pelagics than in northern waters. The main beach fish is the salmon, with the occasional tailor. Worms in one shape or another are the main estuary baits, and whitebait and pilchards the major beach and offshore baits. The best fishing spots on the Victorian coast are listed from east to west.

Bemm River

Moving into the State from New South Wales along the east coast, the first popular angling spot for estuary fishing is at Bemm River. Some 433 km from Melbourne, this small estuary is about 20 km off the highway. Well-serviced with a hotel and a small store, as well as plenty of cabin-type accommodation and an excellent camping park, it has everything the keen angler needs. There is a launching ramp and a jetty, and smaller boats can be launched over the sand beside the jetty. Although it is not an offshore venue, it offers large numbers of fish in the estuary and also provides some of the best beach fishing in the State.

The one drawback is the lack of hire boats coupled with the fact that there is no shore fishing except in the bream spawning season in September and October. But as it is only a small water—about 650 hectares—it is very good for cartoppers. The little estuary is very shallow with lots of sea grasses and weed to provide food for a wide variety of fish. Species such as bream, estuarine perch, bass, mullet, luderick and flathead can be caught in numbers. The Victorian southern bream, which does not go to sea, is slightly thicker in the shoulders than the northern species but otherwise similar in appearance.

Most fishing is done in the lake, which is called Sydenham Inlet; this name is rarely used and the whole area is known as Bemm River. There is a bass fishery in the river, and at times both estuarine perch and bream can be caught. Between August and November fish are most likely to be caught in the river and bream and mullet can be taken from the bank.

The entrance to Bemm is often sanded over and it is usually opened by using explosives whenever the water reaches the height where it starts to flood the roads and farms upstream. The quality of the fishing is not dependent on whether the entrance is open or closed, but when closed it does affect the gathering of bait. As bream and perch do not go to sea the opening and closing of the sandbar does not affect them, but it does decide the quantity of migratory species such as mullet, luderick and flathead.

Sandworm is the top bait for all species in the estuary and can be pumped on the gravel beds just out from the river mouth and in the sand down the channel near the ocean. The worm beds move short distances from time to time so they are not always in the same spot. Worm is often hard to find when the water is high and the entrance is closed, so always have wave waders with you. The vast amount of seagrass and weeds means there is never any shortage of shrimps, which are excellent bait for the perch and bream. From Christmas to Easter there is usually a big run of green bait prawns in the lake, although occasionally, if the entrance is closed for too long in the spring, there will not be any. Prawns can be caught at night with a spotlight and a dip net, from a boat or by walking in the shallows. Kept in their natural water overnight, they will stay alive for the next day's fishing.

Because the estuary floor is mud in most places, the common way of anchoring a boat is to use mud poles—25 mm × 40 mm hardwood poles about 4.5 m long, which are pushed into the mud at each end of the boat. The boat is tied to the poles and so held in the one spot rather than yawing around on the end of an anchor. On particularly windy days it may be necessary to use an anchor as well. The mud poles will not work in sand.

The entrance to the Bemm River in north-eastern Victoria often sands over and has to be opened with explosives when the water level rises to flood roads and farms upstream.

For bream fishing, long, soft rods similar to the Jarvis Walker 'Port Hacking' rod are used to achieve good casting distance from the boat. This enables the fish to move off with the bait without realizing it is tied to something, and also gives good power for hooking and fighting the fish. It is not necessary to hold the rod in the hand all the time. Put it down in the boat with the tip at right angles to the bait and the fish will usually hook themselves.

The biggest problem at Bemm River is to find the fish; that requires some patience while moving around until the right spot is located. Big flathead are usually caught down the channel on live mullet bait. Perch and bass are taken by suspending a live prawn over the weed beds under a bubble float; the perch lie in the weeds and grass, looking upwards, and wait for something to swim across their line of vision.

Bemm has long been recognized as the best beach fishing spot in Victoria. Access to the beach is gained around the back of the lake by a gravel road that ends at Pearl Point, a rocky headland with a wide, open beach stretching westward to Cape Conran. On the eastern side of Pearl Point the beach runs right down to Point Hicks, broken by the entrances at Bemm and Tamboon Inlet. The whole area is surrounded by forest and animal life abounds.

Salmon is the main species taken, although at times tailor and mullet can be caught in good numbers and occasionally trevally and flathead appear. Years ago gummy sharks used to be taken from the beach at night, but with the pressure of commercial fishing there are not many now. The best beach fishing can often be had at the mouth of the channel where the river flows into the ocean, but this spot can only be reached by boat.

The best baits off the beach are whitebait on small tarpon 7766 hooks in gangs of three, size 2 or 3 depending on the size of the bait. Pipi seems to be the second choice. The beaches are quite deep with good holes every hundred metres or so. The best time to surf fish is on the rising tide and the most successful rig seems to be the Paternoster rig with two hooks above the sinker. Ball sinkers are preferred as there seems to be no value in using running sinkers for salmon.

Marlo and Cape Conran

The next major estuary west of Bemm River is the Snowy River, with its tributary, the Brodribb River flowing in at the back of the township of Marlo. At the end of the road and about 20 km from the highway, amid lovely coastal views, Marlo has several shops, a pub and camping grounds. This area has access to the ocean and many close reefs which provide excellent fishing. Cape Conran boasts the only launching ramp directly into the ocean on the east coast of Victoria.

The offshore fishing is relatively untapped, although the region is a great fish producer. The 350 km drive from Melbourne is probably the reason why it is not fished more

There was no shortage of variety in this haul from the Bemm River, one of Victoria's best fishing spots, with mullet, luderick, bream and sole amongst the morning's catch.

often. Launching directly into the ocean from Cape Conran, spots such as Beware Reef are only 15 minutes from the ramp. This reef breaks the surface and is an ideal snapper and pike ground. Directly off the Cape and for about 12 km offshore, some of Victoria's best flathead fishing grounds can be found. The area is well provided with pelagic fish in summer when schools of tuna and kingfish come close to shore.

The offshore scene at Marlo is just as good but the open ocean has to be gained by crossing a short, one-wave bar. Usually the waves are not very big at all; boats over 4.3 m can move out comfortably, and there is never any trouble getting back in. The big Marlo Reef is offshore 6.5 km south of the entrance and about 15 minutes out. A depth sounder is necessary. Good snapper and reef fish can be taken here, as well as flathead on the sand areas. For bottom fishing, whitebait on ganged hooks is most effective.

Some of the biggest luderick recorded in Victoria have been taken from the estuary of the Snowy River at Marlo. There are several launching ramps around the estuary, and a well-sited jetty provides good boating facilities as well as making a great fishing platform. At night its lights often allow mullet to be caught in big numbers, and some excellent catches of estuarine perch are taken from under the jetty. The estuary is long and narrow and well protected from strong winds. There are a couple of islands with snags around them that provide shelter for luderick and bream. Close to the entrance salmon often enter the river and can be caught with pilchards on ganged hooks.

If you go far enough upstream into the Brodribb River and then into Cabbage Tree Creek, some excellent bass can be caught amongst the fallen trees. You could spend a month fishing around the rivers and estuary and still not know very much about the area. For anglers who like to get far away from big cities, this area is a delight.

The beach fishing along this section of coastline is almost as good as at Bemm; well-known spots include Point Riccardo and Corringle Beach. The Snowy River flowing into the ocean is a great help to beach anglers, who take good salmon and gummy sharks. Whitebait and pilchards are the best baits, and pipi is suitable for smaller salmon. At Cape Conran itself large schools of garfish often come right in amongst the rocks in autumn and can be caught from the shore on sandworms.

Marlo is one of the best holiday spots along the coast because of its huge variety of fishing, as well as the tourist attractions inland. Although it is only 20 km off the Princes Highway from Orbost, it is often by-passed by holiday-makers who don't realize what a paradise it is for the angler and his family.

Lakes Entrance The Princes Highway runs right down the main street of Lakes Entrance, some 330 km east of Melbourne and about $3\frac{1}{2}$ hours driving time. At the entrance of the Gippsland Lakes, it is a commercial fishing town and tourist resort. All sorts of water sports take place here, fishing being the main one. From Lakes Entrance there is so much water within reach that it is often hard to know where to start.

The once-a-year angler can walk from his motel in the main street, across the highway onto one of the small piers and catch a feed of bream, or can drive up to one of the many rivers and fish for even greater numbers. The best surf beaches in the eastern half of the State start here and they get progressively better towards the New South Wales border. Salmon and tailor can be caught from the shore of Bullock Island just inside the entrance by casting spinners or pilchards and whitebait on ganged hooks into the fast-running tide. These fish are not usually above 1 kg but they provide some great sport in the winter.

Lakes Entrance is the one place in Victoria where there is a luderick fishery with weed under a thin float. Good local weed is hard to get but can be found in some of the drains up the

Lakes Entrance – Westernport Bay

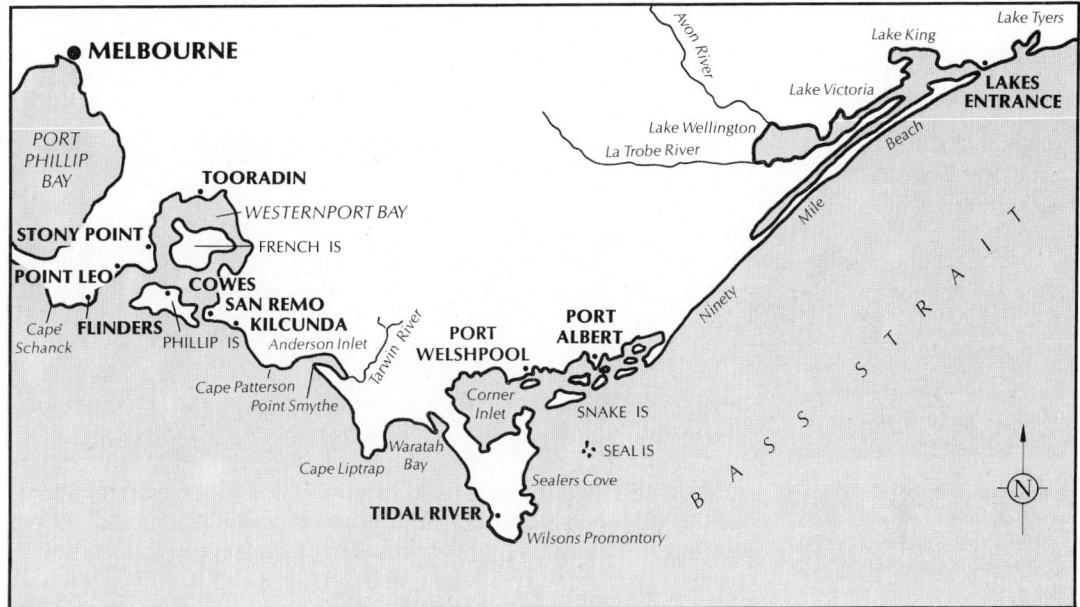

North Arm. This fishing is done from the rocky groynes under Jemmy's Point and at the end of Bullock Island.

The variety of fish is much greater in the Gippsland Lakes, the first place where King George whiting show up in any numbers. They are found near the barrier landing and adjacent islands, and are caught on sandworms. As you move up the lakes past Metung, good catches of bream, flathead, and tailor are taken in Bancroft Bay.

The three big rivers that drain the mountains in central Gippsland—the Tambo, Nicholson and Mitchell—all flow into Jones Bay in Lake King within a few kilometres of each other. Incidentally, this bay is the best producer of sandworms in the area. Worms are pumped commercially and sold locally at many outlets. The Gippsland Lakes are netted by commercial fishermen for bream but no netting is allowed in the rivers. During spring the fish move into the three main rivers in search of water with the right level of salinity in which to spawn and anglers fishing from the river banks take away large hauls.

Further up the lakes at the McLennan Straits near Hollands Landing, some big carp are caught, as they are well established in the upper freshwater section of Lake Wellington. Another species taken around the lakes is garfish. Sandworms are the best bait, and there is a good run of prawns each year not far inside the entrance. Local anglers catch them by the kilo and freeze them for bait for the rest of the year.

The dominant feature of Lakes Entrance is the long, wide bar that has been built up outside the entrance by the vast

V ■ VICTORIA

Looking out through the opening to Lake's Entrance, east of Melbourne, with Jemmy's Point in the foreground. This is a good fishing area for salmon, tailor, bream and luderick.

quantities of water that flow in and out with the tides. Many commercial fishing boats have come to grief, broaching when coming in too slowly, and several lives have been lost. The bar can be very dangerous and the deaths have given it such a bad name that few amateur boat-users attempt the crossing. The small number that do, take good catches on the close reefs to the south called the 'Stockyard' and 'Six Mile' reef. In time, and with care on the bar, a large, offshore amateur fishery may develop.

Port Welshpool A region that is not tourist-orientated but an excellent area for all types of fishing is the Corner Inlet estuary and nearby ocean waters. This very large waterway is strongly tidal and an important nursery for young fish. Port Welshpool township right on the waterfront has a store and a petrol station, but there is not much accommodation in the area. Only 200 km from Melbourne, it is a possible location for a one-day fishing trip, but be prepared for a rather long day. Corner Inlet is a boat fishing spot and although there are a couple of jetties and piers, they only fish at certain times of the year for selected species.

There is so much protected water in this basin with its channels and islands, that you could fish here for years and still have something left to discover. Being right next to Wilsons Promontory adds to its grandeur and scenic splendour. Whiting, snapper, flathead, flounder, garfish, snook and gummy shark are caught in the estuary. The main species on offer is whiting, which are caught along the sides of the channels, while in the deep holes near the wide entrance to the ocean some very large snapper can be taken as well as the occasional gummy shark. But if you are not experienced in this type of fishing it takes a little time to get used to the fast-flowing water.

For whiting, the locals all use yabby, which are plentiful and can be pumped along the banks at low tide. Frozen pilchards and salted whitebait are the most popular baits for the other species. A knowledge of the tides is essential as different fish feed at various stages of the tides. Snapper, for instance, like the rising tide, while whiting prefer the falling tide.

There is no bar as such and access to the ocean is easy. Schools of salmon are sometimes found along the east coast of the Promontory, which protects boats from south and west winds. South-east of the entrance is the Seal Island group, including Cliffy Island where an old lighthouse still stands. On a calm day the islands can be reached in about an hour from the jetty at Welshpool. Around the group school kingfish can be caught in summer, with occasional flathead, snapper and snook thrown in. The flathead beds are around Rabbit Island closer to the Promontory. The best baits out here are pilchards and whitebait fished on ganged hooks.

The only good launching facility is at Port Welshpool, which has an excellent two-car ramp in protected waters. It is important to stick to the channels, which are all well marked with poles and lights or buoys, as it is easy to run aground. Because of its central position, Welshpool gives access to huge amounts of water and nearly all the whiting that appear on the Melbourne market come from this area. Port Welshpool is only 7 km off the South Gippsland Highway with good roads all the way.

Big snook and kingfish can be taken in numbers around the Seal Islands offshore from Welshpool.

Westernport Bay

About 60 km south-east of Melbourne with easy access to most points of the bay, Westernport Bay, unlike Port Phillip Bay, has a wide opening, on each side of Phillip Island. The island protects the bay from the direct ocean swells, but because of the wide openings there is a large tidal rise and fall. In addition, there is not a big freshwater run-off into Westernport as there is into Port Phillip. So although the same fish occur in both bays, the type of fishing is quite different.

Westernport is a series of deep channels and shallow sandbanks, many of the shallow spots being covered by seagrass. For years it was recognized as one of Victoria's top whiting spots, but in the early 1980s the all-over cover of seagrass was reduced by 75 per cent for some unknown reason and this has reduced the whiting catches. The big tidal range makes fishing difficult; the fish tend to feed on one tide or the other, and in some places you cannot fish except at slack water. Large numbers of flathead are not caught in this bay, unlike Port Phillip, because of the cleaning effect of the big tides. Schools of salmon do sometimes come in and great sport can be had from boats, but the main species taken are snapper and whiting. Nearly all the whiting are caught on the falling tide and most near the bottom of the tide. A tide chart is essential for the beginner in this bay.

Good ramps are provided at Stony Point, Hastings, Warneet and Phillip Island. Small boats can be launched at other places, such as Corinalla and Newhaven, if the tide is high. Stony Point and Hastings are the two most-used ramps with the largest populations of big fish nearby. The tide at these places moves about 1 hour *after* Port Phillip heads. Visitors are reminded that all Victorian tide charts are worked out on the tides at Port Phillip heads, and that Victoria has daylight saving in the summer months (you have to add an hour to tide times when it is in operation). Both ramps are right beside the main shipping channel so there are plenty of drop-offs from the banks into the channel. Shipping dominates the bay and you cannot anchor in the channel, but there is plenty of other deep water around. Some whiting about half a kilogram in weight are often described as 'channel' whiting. This has nothing to do with the shipping channel but usually means that they were caught in deep water.

Probably the best place to catch whiting is near the grass beds where the seafloor disappears from visibility. If you can anchor your boat along this line, you are in good whiting country. Whiting come into the bay in September and stay until April, but smaller fish will be found all the year around. The best bait for whiting is freshly shelled mussel, and they are very susceptible to berley containing crushed mussel. There is no season, but there is a minimum size of 27 cm.

Snapper are caught at the top and bottom of the tide and while there are some very large ones, both the run and the fish are usually smaller than in Port Phillip. The tide flow is such

The launching ramp at Stony Point, Westernport Bay, at very low tide. French Island and Tankerton can be seen in the background.

that with any speed in the water and the floating grass snagging the line, the sinker lifts off the bottom and away from the fish. Snapper are always caught in deep water and the holes or trenches fished for snapper often carry big gummy sharks as well. Frozen pilchards are the best bait in these circumstances.

The waterways tend to be narrow because of the large islands in the middle of the bay, and are thus protected from the wind. The seas do not get as rough as in Port Phillip and often it is possible to fish here when Port Phillip is a wipe-out. Other species caught include a few small flathead, snook, salmon and grass whiting. The Danforth anchor carried by most people is almost useless in this bay. There is very little sand and the bottom is mostly mud with weed and grass on which the admiralty anchor holds best.

Port Phillip Bay

Melbourne is at the head of Victoria's biggest estuary, Port Phillip Bay, which is shaped roughly like a huge saucer. The tide difference between the heads and Melbourne is 3 hours because of the narrow entrance. The tidal rise and fall is only about half a metre so there is little current in the northern half of the bay. This bay is the breeding ground for the mighty snapper, which come in spring in their thousands to spawn in the shallows. Other species are very prolific and include large numbers of flathead, garfish and whiting. Each species needs to be fished separately.

Down at the entrance, which is known as the 'heads', Victorians get their first taste of sportfishing with the arrival in summer of big kingfish seeking the schools of garfish. Fish around 15 kg are taken but not in any numbers. Whiting are caught mostly around the western shoreline, while the eastern shoreline is mainly stocked with snapper. Grass beds start near Mount Martha on the eastern side and so the whiting begin to appear in small numbers. Closer to the heads, the numbers of fish increase, and so does the size. When you get down to Sorrento and Portsea you can consistently catch whiting weighing about half a kilogram. On the western side the whiting start right up in the top end of the bay near Altona, and the relatively shallow water along this coast grows good weed and grass and so provides excellent food. These grass beds continue right down to the heads.

Snapper seem to congregate along the eastern shoreline from Mornington right up to Port Melbourne, where the Yarra and Maribyrong Rivers flow into the bay. The fresh water from these rivers provides the right level of salinity for the snapper to spawn along the eastern side. There is quite a long season as they spawn progressively, dribbling out small quantities of eggs at a time over a couple of months. They are caught from September to December and have a late run between February and April.

No sinker is used to catch snapper and the best bait is frozen pilchard. Fast tapered rods such as the 'Barra' variety are the most popular. More fish are caught in the late afternoon than early in the morning, but the middle of the day does not seem to be a good time. There appear to be small snapper all the year round over the inshore reefs from Brighton down to Beaumaris; they are taken mostly just on or after dark on cut pilchards.

Other species that are rather prolific but not much fished are squid and flounder. Victoria has virtually untapped resources of both species. Mussels, and even oysters at one place, are farmed commercially and snapper are taken on long lines for the market place. Fortunately, very little netting is done now as the angling pressure is great.

Melbourne is well off for angling clubs and any newcomer to the State need only contact the Fisheries Department to find the necessary information. Nearly all points of the shoreline in Port Phillip can be reached by road, but the launching facilities are often overcrowded. If you don't own a boat, there are plenty of places around the bay where you can hire one.

Apollo Bay

West of Melbourne, the closest and best fishing area for all types of angling is Apollo Bay, just 2 hours and 174 km from the city. This beautiful fishing village, where the mountains run right down to the ocean, is reached along the Great Ocean Road through Lorne. There is plenty of accommodation, as well as two hotels and a string of shops.

Apollo Bay is known for its beach fishing and offshore fishing. There are a couple of rivers that are rather small but they produce some good bream and estuarine perch in the lower reaches and trout in the mountain sections. The surf beaches provide the best salmon beach fishing in western Victoria. Not only are the fish of a good size but they are taken

Port Phillip Bay

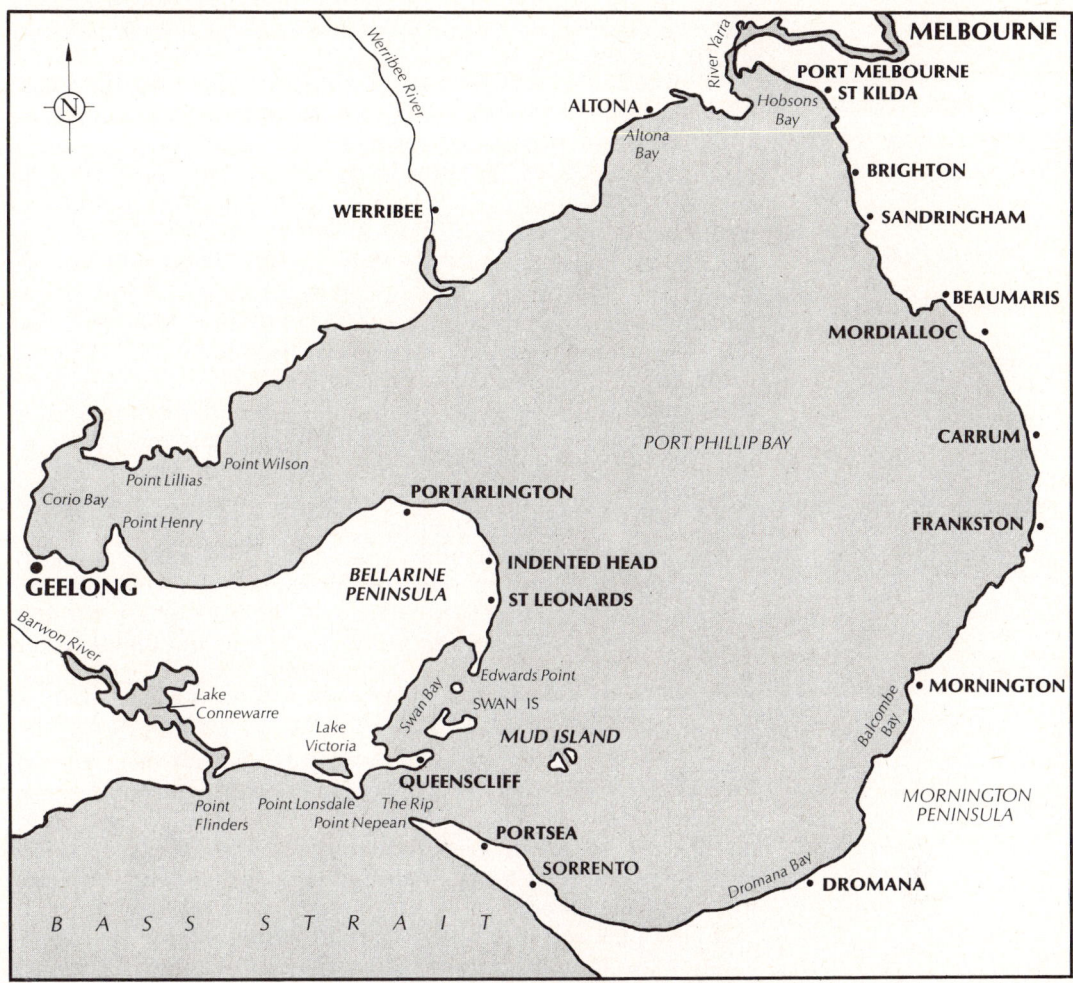

in numbers on the rising tide. They are the only fish available from the beaches apart from occasional trevally. Some very big garfish can be caught from the rocks, using sandfleas and kelp maggots for bait, and a few snapper. Visitors should be warned that rock fishing in Victoria is a very dangerous occupation, best done only when seas are slight with an offshore breeze. While you may hear mention of the occasional sweep being caught in Victoria they are a small fishery and a very specialized one.

Apollo Bay is surrounded by rock and underwater mountains so there are many reefs for bait and fish to feed upon. As there are not many beaches along the western coastline, the bait fish seem to congregate here and other fish follow them. The two big salmon beaches are Wild Dog Creek and Maringo Beach. Both are relatively shallow and have a lot of white water for the bait fish to hide in. Quite often the salmon come right into the beach on the rising tide after dark. Whitebait and pipi are good bait and this is one area of the State where the plastic whitebait seem to work well.

Big schools of salmon come into the corner near the town and feed on the baitfish. You can just drift around and throw lures or frozen pilchards at them. The small snapper flock around the rocky coastline in summer and good bags of more than ten fish from 1 to 2 kg can be taken on an outing. Pike are at the Bay in force as they thrive over inshore reefs and around bomboras. These fish are not to be confused with the snook, which are also present but not in such large numbers. The snook is a long fish that looks similar to a barracouta, whereas the pike is shorter and a little more dumpy.

Other fish include trevally up to 5 kg, which are caught close inshore off the 'Waterfall'. Squid, the occasional flathead and some very large whiting are also taken on quiet days with an offshore breeze when the boats can get in close. Several specimens near 1 kg have been taken and a fish of half a kilogram is considered average.

Apollo Bay can be fished in almost any weather, and fish caught, because of the reefs. Salmon can be taken in good numbers on the rising tide by backing the boat close into the breaking waves and casting a lure back into the white water with a good whippy rod. This produces better results than trolling along behind the breakers, because the lure gets in where the fish are feeding.

A quick way to locate pike is to very slowly troll a bibbed lure such as a Rapala or a Nilsmaster behind the boat close inshore over the reefs. When you catch one, go back and anchor the boat right over the school and then cast to them with the same lure. Both shallow-diving and sinking lures are ideal and the fish do not seem to worry about the colour. You will also pick up snook and salmon while fishing for pike.

Since the launching ramp is in the almost totally enclosed harbour, it is easy to launch in all weathers, and conditions have to be really bad to make it impossible to get out of the boat harbour. The harbour is formed by high granite breakwall that serves as a fishing platform for many anglers who take salmon and trevally. Visitors from Geelong fish this area each weekend, as well as anglers from inland at Colac.

Port Fairy Another town on the Princes Highway, Port Fairy is about 300 km west of Melbourne and is perhaps the best fishing spot in the far west. A town steeped in history—nearly half the houses are classified by the National Trust—it is a typical nineteenth-century fishing village. Built on the Moyne River and being a commercial fishing town, it sports reasonable facilities for anglers, with a good launching ramp into the quiet waters of the river, and two long stone and concrete walls that run out into the protected bay to give easy access in all weathers for all types of boats.

The main catch of the commercial fishing fleet based at Port Fairy is crayfish and shark, but the Moyne River supports a mullet and bream fishery for amateur anglers.

The Moyne is not very long but supports a bream and mullet fishery for the amateur using yabbies pumped from Killarney Beach or worms and shrimps found under the rocks. There is plenty of accommodation of all types, as Port Fairy is a holiday village with long surf beaches and good swimming. The tidal stretch of the river is very short but nearby rivers such as the Fitzroy are larger and support good bream fisheries.

Angling is excellent on the sweeping beach from the mouth of the river right around to Killarney some 10 km away. There is about 2 km of beach on the Warrnambool side of Killarney that is dotted with reefs, and salmon and whiting can be caught from the beach.

The sheltered access to the ocean encourages the use of boats, and a quick trip down to Killarney will put you in sheltered waters where you can fish the sandholes for big whiting. Many small aluminium boats are launched across the beach here and motored out a few hundred metres for whiting fishing. Barracouta, squid and flathead are taken over the mostly sandy bottom out from the Port itself.

About 18 km to the west is Lady Julia Percy Island, a large, flat-topped, volcanic plug sticking up out of the ocean about 5 km offshore. Islands always attract fish and this one is no exception. It is about an hour's run up to the island into the prevailing seas, so it is a downhill run coming home. The water is quite deep around the island except at the northern end where there is a seal colony and parrot fish are found. In summer snapper and warhoo or sea bream are found in good numbers, and pike are always present over the kelp beds beside the island.

Most of the offshore angling is done with the Paternoster rig using two whitebait on ganged hooks. Fish larger than 2 kg are rare, so a whippy rod from the 'Barra' series is as heavy as needed. The Port Fairy side of the island is the lee side and fishing on the Portland side can be dangerous if any sort of a swell is running.

Portland The most westerly town of any size in Victoria, Portland is on the Princes Highway 355 km from Melbourne. It has a large business district and excellent port facilities, but it does lack a river. Estuary fishing is almost non-existent although freshwater is within easy reach at a number of spots. A large aluminium smelter being erected on the foreshores in 1985 is sure to have some effect on the local fishing as there will be some cooling discharge, which usually attracts large numbers of fish to the warmer water.

For anglers, the main activities are shore fishing from piers or rock walls, or offshore fishing from boats. There are some excellent beaches a few kilometres from the town, but access is very restricted being through private property. The area really has not developed from the point of view of recreational angling except in the offshore field. The game fishing clubs have taken a keen interest in the offshore scene because bluefin tuna come in close to the coastline about June each year, well within reach of small boats.

The deep harbour is ideal for the shore-based angler who fishes from the breakwaters and piers. A flush of snapper and sea bream come into the harbour each year and provide great sport. Flathead are also caught in numbers from these walls, as well as occasional trevally. As yet beach fishing is not tapped in the area but the migrating schools of salmon move along this coast on their passage eastwards so the potential is certainly there.

The boat angler has it made for ocean fishing out of Portland. Boat launching is in the inner harbour, which gives direct access to the ocean within a couple of minutes with no bar or big seas to cross. The launching facilities are excellent with wide ramps, and short piers to tie up to when waiting to leave or to retrieve your boat. There is plenty of trailer-parking space and the ramp is right next to the main street. The harbour is on the east side of the headland, sheltered from the prevailing seas of the Southern Ocean.

The catches obtainable offshore from Portland are quite extensive. Salmon, squid, barracouta, flathead, snapper, pike and snook are all present in numbers, with bluefin tuna on

Aireys Inlet – Portland

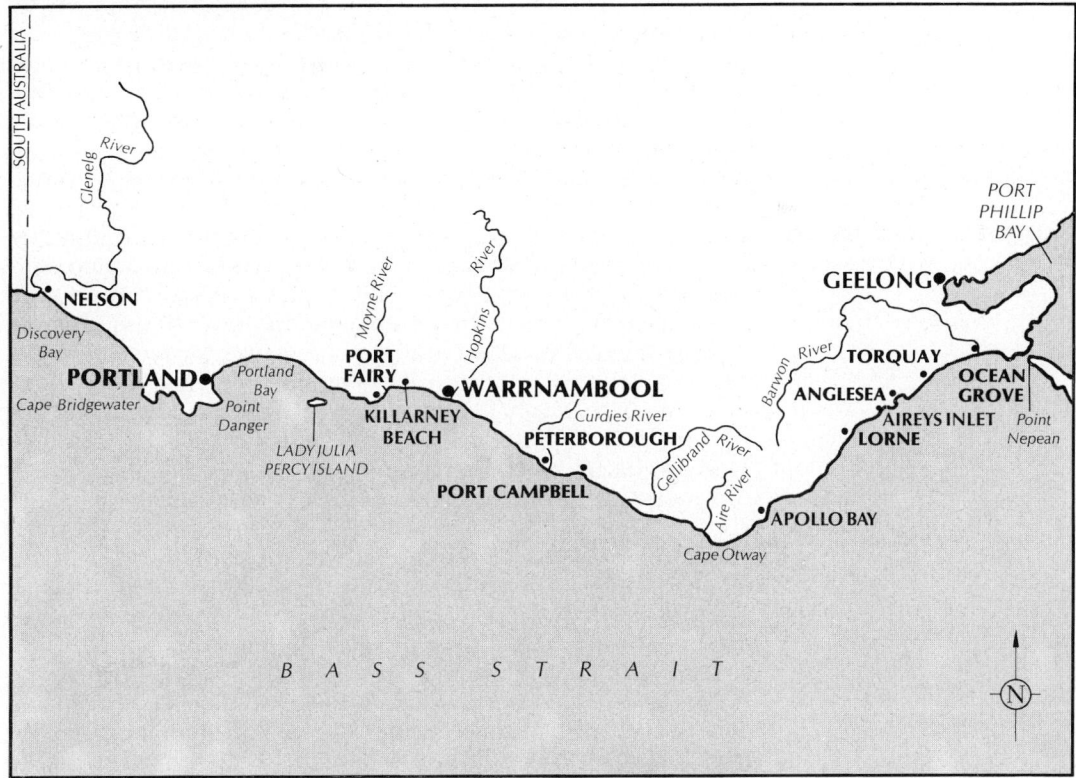

offer for a short period each year. You do not have to go far for this fishing and most of it is in semi-protected waters. Between Port Fairy and Portland are a couple of good bream streams and the Glenelg River, only about 60 km to the west, is a popular water for bream and mulloway.

KEITH FLEMING

Freshwater fishing in Victoria

Freshwater fish, scarce in the sun-parched regions of Australia, flourish in Victoria, where the colder climate and many mountain streams provide the ideal habitat for native and introduced species alike. Of all Australian States, probably only Tasmania can compete with Victoria in the wide variety of freshwater fishing available.

The Victorian Fisheries Department is very progressive and breeds thousands of trout and salmon at the Snobs Creek Hatchery in Central Victoria for release in Victorian streams. Brown and rainbow trout and quinnat salmon have been released in many waters, which now have good stocks of sport and table fish. Over the years survey teams have discovered that quite a number of Victorian rivers are not able to support large populations of fish because of the lack of food, so that both stocking and fishing can be sensibly regulated. In recent years there has been an upsurge of interest in native species. A warm water research station has been built and Murray cod and Macquarie perch have been induced to breed in artificial ponds.

An Inland Angling Licence is required to fish all Victorian fresh waters and anglers should always check closed seasons and bag and size limits, which may vary from time to time.

Tambo River Basin

The Tambo River Basin in north-eastern Victoria is drained by two large rivers, the Tambo and the Nicholson, which discharge separately into Lake King on the east coast. Both flow south from the Great Dividing Range, for most of their length through heavily forested mountain country. Access is difficult but rewarding for fishermen. The estuary regions of both rivers are extensively fished. Brown trout, eels and grayling are the most plentiful species, trout providing most of the catches. The Timbarra River, a tributary of the Tambo, has a big reputation among trout experts and is heavily fished.

Lake King is the most easterly of the Gippsland Lakes, surrounded by farm land to the north, with scrub on the southern side. There are boating facilities for fishermen at Metung and Paynesville and a large number of ocean-going fish with a tolerance to freshwater are available.

The Nicholson River flows through forested country above Deptford, but downstream runs through cleared, open land over gravel and mud bottoms. Access is difficult upstream from Deptford. The Nicholson contains brown trout to 700 g, eels, freshwater catfish and grayling. Below Sarsfield is estuary water, where bream and mullet mix with garfish, European carp and some estuarine perch.

The Tambo River upstream from Ensay carries eels, graying, river blackfish, some brown trout and a few rainbow trout. The headwaters are in private property and permission to fish must be secured from the owners. Downstream from Ensay, the Tambo carries brown trout to 550 g, grayling, eels and crucian carp. The estuary waters below Bruthen carry yellow-eye mullet, estuarine perch, European carp and a few bream and flathead.

La Trobe River Basin

The La Trobe River rises near Warburton, east of Melbourne, and flows east to Lake Wellington, the southernmost of the Gippsland lakes. Eels and river blackfish are common throughout the La Trobe basin, but freshwater crayfish provide the most succulent of the region's catches. Except in the northernmost section, the rivers in this basin flow through open country. Brown trout are plentiful in most waters, but rainbow trout are seldom taken. European carp are well established and abundant in many of the larger, slower waters.

Trout fishing is at its best in early spring and late autumn. The size of the trout is fairly uniform, the big ones coming from the La Trobe River itself. The best fishing for European carp is in the Yallourn Storage Dam and the lower reaches of the La Trobe River.

Above the storage dam, the La Trobe River is a clear, fast-flowing stream with a sand and gravel bottom. The valley has largely been cleared, but there is dense cover on the river bank but here the water is not wadable. Brown trout to 1.3 kg, eels, tench and those delectable crayfish are plentiful. From the Yallourn Power Station wall to Lake Wellington, the La Trobe is subject to flash floods and contains predominantly European carp around 2.7 kg. Eels, English perch to 1 kg, and brown trout to 2.7 kg are taken close to Lake Wellington. The Yallourn Storage Dam is mainly fished from the bank, corn and worms being the best baits for carp that reach as much as 4.5 kg in weight.

Many of the La Trobe's tributaries, including the Moe, Morwell, Tanjil and Tyers Rivers, offer brown trout, blackfish, eels and crayfish.

Mitta Mitta River Basin

Numerous tributaries from the Great Dividing Range run into the Mitta Mitta, which flows north to Lake Hume through extensive areas of mountainous terrain in north-eastern Victoria. Access is limited to four-wheel-drive vehicles or walking, but the fishing makes it worthwhile. Brown trout are abundant, and many are large; rainbow trout are less common and seldom larger than 350 g, the best conditioned fish being caught in autumn.

The Mitta Mitta drainage basin is one of the few regions of Victoria where there are viable populations of Murray cod and Macquarie perch. The best fishing for these native species is from December to April. The best trout rivers are the Cobungra and the Mitta Mitta upstream from the Dart River. Lake Hume provides excellent brown trout and redfin fishing, the brown trout reaching 4.6 kg, the redfin 2.7 kg. Surrounded by cleared land, Hume Lake is a large reservoir, part of which is in New South Wales where a Victorian fishing licence is not valid. The lake is not stocked as fisheries experts believe there is abundant spawning in the inflowing rivers.

Much of the Mitta Mitta River flows through mountainous, forested country over rubble and gravel beds, and upstream of the Gibbo River even four-wheel-drives cannot achieve access. The best part of the river for fishermen is between the town of Mitta Mitta and Lake Hume. Here the river runs over cleared flats, sand, mud and rubble, and redfin average 150 g, and may reach 1.5 kg, and brown trout are common around 400 g. Blackfish to 70 g are caught in a few places and there is a good population of Murray cod up to 19 kg downstream from Eskdale.

V ■ VICTORIA

Dartmouth Dam   In Victoria, mountain storages seem to produce more fish in better condition than the large storages on the open plains. The prime mountain storage is Dartmouth Dam on the Mitta Mitta River. About 400 km from Melbourne, via the Hume Highway to Wodonga then down the Kiewa Highway to shortcut across through the small town of Tangambalanga and then over the 'gap' to rejoin the Omeo Highway near Tallandoon, it is well worth a weekend trip.

When the dam was built (primarily to supply hydro-electricity), the river held an excellent fishery of brown trout and Macquarie perch. Both species have increased naturally over the years, although both brown and rainbow trout have been released by the Fisheries Department. A research station has been established at the dam to study the Macquarie perch, which has been artificially bred, a great breakthrough for a species considered endangered.

The construction township is now developing as a tourist town, fishing being the prime attraction. A modern caravan park with mobile homes as on-site vans has been built, and lodges and houses for up to eight people can be hired by the day. There are also two camping areas, with no facilities and very little flat ground, at Eight Mile Creek and Eustace Creek, but these can only be reached by boat. The large volume of water is between the mountain ranges in very deep gullies and most fishing is done in the dam from boats, but there is plenty of fly fishing water downstream. Boat hire is available and there is an excellent launching ramp.

The main baits are mudeye and worms, but local bait, particularly mudeye, is difficult to obtain. For any serious fishing, anglers are advised to take their own mudeye, scrub worms and flat-tail worms or red wrigglers. The most useful lures are Eildon 99 and Tasmanian Devils, and trolling is most successful with a 'flasher' such as the Ford Fender or Cow Bells in front of the bait or lures.

As closed seasons and bag limits may change from year to year, anglers should check the current rules and regulations. There is a bag limit on all trout of 5 fish per person per day from 1 May until 31 August. This is the breeding season, when the trout move into the shallows of the rivers to spawn and can be caught in large numbers. There is a closed season on Macquarie perch, also during the breeding period, from midnight on Melbourne Cup Day until midnight on the last Friday in January. There is no size limit on trout but the minimum size for Macquarie perch is 25 cm. There are no boating prohibitions.

Trout fishing is largely restricted to bait fishing and trolling or spinning. There is very little fly fishing on the dam, although good trout are still taken on wet flies. The bigger fish, up to 2 kg in weight, are caught in the morning or the evening among the dead trees at the edge of the lake where the water is very deep. The best results are usually had by just tying the

Macquarie perch are an enormous attraction for anglers when they run in large numbers from Lake Dartmouth just before the spawning season in November.

hook on the end of a high quality 4 kg line, hooking the mudeye through, and then dropping it over the side of the boat. Let the line sink slowly until the depth at which the fish are feeding is established. Leave the bail arm of the reel open so that the fish can draw line from the spool without hinderance. Long soft rods like a bream rod can be an advantage for this type of fishing. Quite often perch will also be caught when fishing for trout by this method.

Trolling a flasher with a mudeye, worm or lure some 30 cm behind is done in the open lake but still near the bank. The slower the troll the more fish, so small motors are best. One trick is always to troll into the wind, which slows the boat even further. Smaller fish around 0.5 kg are caught this way.

The best time to fish for Macquarie perch is just before the season closes in early November when the fish move up the rivers and creeks to spawn. It is about 30 km from the dam wall to the flowing water and will take at least an hour in most boats. Quite often a school of fish can be located in the evening, feeding at the base of a tall tree where broken limbs have accumulated. Scrub worms and red worms are the best bait and fish in excess of 1 kg are quite common.

V ■ VICTORIA

Ovens River Basin North of the Divide in eastern Victoria, the rivers of the Ovens basin flow northwards from heavily forested mountain country through extensive river flats to the Murray River. The upper reaches have abundant spawning areas and carry large numbers of rainbow trout. Brown trout are more widely distributed throughout the system and grow to a larger size than rainbows. Small English perch or redfin are common in the lower reaches of rivers and Murray cod appear closer to the Murray River. Small blackfish are common in many rivers of the basin and Macquarie perch are occasionally caught.

The best trout rivers in the region are the King, Buckland and Catherine. The Ovens River itself below the Murray Valley is the best area for redfin.

In the Buckland River at Bright crayfish are abundant and small blackfish and rainbow trout averaging 120 g are found in the headwaters. Fishing is good throughout the year and night fishing with frogs is very popular among the locals. This method is described under Broken River Basin.

The Buffalo River above Lake Buffalo flows through forested country and tobacco fields over gravel and rock beds and offers brown and rainbow trout. There are plenty of redfin to 100 g and occasional Macquarie perch and Murray cod in the larger pools.

Broken River Basin The Broken River drainage basin contains only one major river, the Broken, which rises on the inland slopes of the Great Dividing Range and flows north and west to meet the Goulburn River at Shepparton.

Upstream from Benalla, the Broken River and its tributaries are fast flowing, and provide adequate spawning facilities for trout. But as is fairly common throughout the State, brown trout are more plentiful than rainbow trout and also grow to larger sizes.

Downstream from Benalla, Broken Creek branches off from the river and flows northwards directly to the Murray through extensive river flats with mud and sand bottoms. Trout are rare in this section, but redfin and European carp are being caught there in increasing numbers. Some Murray cod, golden perch and tench occur in the lower reaches, and blackfish, although less plentiful, are widespread.

The best trout water is the Broken River below Lake Nillahcootie and the best redfin waters are Lake Nillahcootie, Lake Mokoan, and Broken Creek between Katamatite and Devenish. Lake Nillahcootie, a State Rivers and Water Supply Commission storage, is surrounded by open farmland. It is mainly very deep but three are a few shallows at the southern end. Camping is prohibited, but there is a boat ramp and toilet facilities. The lake can be fished from the bank, although boat fishing is more productive.

Goulburn River

The most heavily fished and best stocked water in Victoria is the Goulburn River (including the pondage of the Eildon Reservoir), which flows north and west through Seymour and Shepparton on its way to the Murray River. The river has a large number of tributaries, such as the Acheron, Yea and Rubicon Rivers and King Parrot Creek, that are also good fish holding rivers. The Goulburn is used extensively for irrigation. In about April each year, the flow of water to the river is reduced and the fishing goes off until early September when irrigation water is again sent downstream.

Being so close to Melbourne, the Goulburn is heavily fished, but in the late 1970s and early 1980s the Fisheries Departments stocked it with brown trout yearlings of good size. Although larger fish are occasionally taken, most average 250 g in weight and 30 cm in length. There are no bag limits or size limits on the river itself, but there is a bag limit of 5 fish per person per day on the pondage and for 100 m downstream. There are few species other than brown trout in this section of the river.

The pondage, which is filled with water during summer, is not much more than a big gravel pit with its own miniature dam wall below the Eildon Weir. It is here that the brood stock no longer required by the Snobs Creek Hatchery are released each year in late August and early September. Since some of these fish may weigh 4 kg, the pondage becomes a mecca for anglers anxious to land a big trout. The top bait in the pondage is mudeye under a bubble float, but many of the fish are caught on wobblers or on other baits such as scrub worms. Because they are hatchery fish and used to being hand fed, they will take almost anything put in front of them.

There is no camping on the banks of the pondage but the town of Alexandra is nearby. For miles downstream good bitumen roads follow the river on both sides so access is easy.

One interesting method of catching fish in this river is to fish the backwaters at night with frogs. Use an ordinary trout rod, no longer than 2 m, with the last 15 m of line fully greased with line grease, and a small No. 8 or No. 10 hook. Since the fish are small, up to 1 kg at the most, the frogs need be no longer than 4 to 5 cm.

During daylight, walk the river looking for suitable backwaters away from the fast-flowing main stream of the river, but connected to it so that the trout can enter under cover of darkness. Any hole more than about 20 cm deep is suitable and some parts of the main stream can be fished if the water is flowing very slowly. It is important not to shine your torch over the water before fishing the chosen hole.

Quietly approach the hole and stand in the shallows so that the greased line will float on the water and not get tangled in the grass. With the frog hooked very lightly in the mouth, cast across the hole to the water near the other side. If you don't hear a splash you'll know it is either up in a tree or on the far bank. Now comes the difficult part. The rod is held in one hand with the line held between the fingers. With the other hand the line is pulled jerkily through the rod fingers about 15 cm at a time, pausing between pulls, to give the frog the appearance of swimming.

If you have a 'take' you will usually hear it and at this moment it is important to let the line run free so the trout does not feel any resistance. The fish will move off a few metres and stop to swallow the frog. When the initial run stops, start a very slow count to 30, then close the bail arm on the reel and slowly wind up the slack until you are ready to strike. Point the rod at the fish, finish taking up the slack and lift the rod tip smartly. When you land the fish take it well away from the hole before you remove the hook as there may be other fish in the backwater. Work the water over thoroughly before moving to the next hole. This is a very rewarding and exciting method of trout fishing.

Lake Eildon   The closest large body of water to Melbourne is Lake Eildon, some 180 km from the city on the Goulburn River. When full the reservoir covers 13,840 ha with a maximum depth of 79 m and an average depth of 24 m. It is not often at full capacity because the water is used for both hydro-electric power and irrigation. Much of the lake is surrounded by forest, but there is cleared land near the Delatite Arm.

The lake is well stocked with redfin, brown trout and to a lesser degree rainbow trout. Redfin are the main catch during summer and are usually caught from boats. There are still numerous dead trees standing in the water and most fish are caught around them. The best bait for redfin are small yabbies, mudeye, scrub worms and smaller worms. They are often taken on lures, the most famous being the Baltic Bobber, which is lowered down beside a tree trunk and jigged up and down to attract the fish's attention. Redfin are school fish and once they are biting you can catch the whole school. They are very tasty, but because of their tough skin they are skinned instead of scaled. There is no closed season or bag limit on redfin.

Rainbow trout do not match brown trout in weight and are often in poor condition. They are usually found in the deeper parts of the lake and are mostly taken on lures trolled slowly behind paravanes. Keen anglers make a habit of going to the lake at times of very low water in drought years to locate the deep holes and the best dead tree forests where the big rainbows can be caught in the autumn and winter.

Brown trout are the most prolific fish in Lake Eildon and are caught in good numbers during winter and spring. They are generally found in shallow waters, particularly around the mouths of the creeks and rivers that flow into the lake and in areas where dead trees are abundant. In early winter the fish run up into the inflowing waters to spawn and are often taken in good numbers.

Bait anglers have most success using mudeye, and early morning and late afternoon are the best times. Brown trout are also taken on scrub worms and a new artificial bait called 'Catch-it' is proving very successful. Lures can be cast from the shoreline, the best including Tasmanian Devil, the King Cobra and the 14 g Supa Duper in the silver, copper and gold patterns. Celta lures with small blades are also very good in the rivers.

The large township of Alexandra near the weir provides all the necessary services, and house boats can be hired. Most sections of the lake are accessible by road. It is best to take your own bait.

Lake Modewarre

Victoria has many smallish, shallow lakes that are very productive fish breeding grounds. The sun penetrates the shallow water encouraging the growth of weed, which provides an ideal habitat for the tadpoles, mudeye and minnows eaten by the larger fish. The more food, the bigger and faster the trout or salmon will grow.

Only 115 km west of Melbourne, near Winchelsea on the Princes Highway, is Lake Modewarre, a permanent lake about 414 ha in area and 3 to 4 m deep. The aquatic weed in Lake Modewarre is so thick that at times it becomes a pest, growing right up to the surface over large areas and making fishing a little difficult. But such growth is cyclic, and since brown trout of 5 kg are quite common the weed obviously provides plenty of food for the fish. There are some redfin and rainbow trout but brown trout predominate.

The lake is rather exposed to wind, being surrounded by cleared grazing land. It is used for water skiing and a concrete launching ramp is well situated inside an L-shaped man-made lagoon. The best baits are mudeye and live minnow, and because of the weed, lures are not used very often. Live minnows can be obtained from the lake itself, taken in a dip net swept through the weed beds. All the fishing is done under bubble floats with the fishing line greased so that it will float on top of the water. There is some bank angling from the walls of the lagoon, and from the shore at the southern and northern ends. The early morning and late afternoon in winter and spring seem to be the best times to fish this water.

Gellibrand River

One of the most sought-after freshwater native species, and possibly one of the best table fish, are river blackfish *Gadopsis marmoratus*. They do not grow very large, although some as big as 1.3 kg have been recorded from the Gellibrand River in south-western Victoria. This river is the premier blackfish water in the State, but good quality fish can also be found in the Tarwin, Upper Yarra and McKenzie Rivers and Birches Creek. Essentially freshwater fish, blackfish can be caught in the brackish sections of some estuaries.

Blackfish seek out dark places and are always most prolific in tree-lined streams with plenty of snags and usually well away from centres of human population. Although blackfish quickly disappear when snags and logs are removed from a river, they can be encouraged to breed again by placing short lengths of plastic tubing and pipes in the water. They become very active after sundown and angling is most successful from late afternoon until well into the night.

The Gellibrand River rises in the Otway Ranges and flows south to the sea over a distance of 125 km. It is fed by an annual rainfall of 1074 mm, which creates lush growth along the banks, providing an ideal blackfish habitat. The area is not likely to be farmed any more intensively than it is now, so the habitat seems secure. There are a few brown trout in the system, but the Fisheries Department has recognized the importance of this stream as blackfish water and have not stocked it with trout since the 1970s. When there are large numbers of both fish in a water, trout seem to eat more than their fair share of the available food.

All blackfish waters south of the Great Dividing Range are closed from 1 May to midnight on the second Friday in December each year. The Gellibrand River upstream from the Colac-Gellibrand road bridge is totally closed all year round. There is no bag limit but the minimum legal length for blackfish in Victoria is 22 cm.

Blackfish are caught on the usual trout or bream gear. Because they are such light biters, it is important to use very flexible rods and even when fishing in treed areas, a rod of at least 2.4 m is recommended. Experts normally use a 3 kg line, but it may be advisable to use a 4 kg top-quality fine line such as Steelflex. Thin earthworms are the best baits to use on fine No. 6 to No. 8 hooks. Because of the nature of the habitat, nearly all anglers use a quill float and small pieces of splitshot to provide the necessary balance. With this method, the worms can be taken down under overhanging trees right above the snags.

Hopkins River Basin

A large river basin in south-western Victoria with numerous outstanding fishing waters, particularly for brown trout and redfin. The basin is drained by the Hopkins River, which enters the Southern Ocean near Warrnambool. It is tidal for several kilometres upstream from the coast and carries a variety of estuary fish.

The Hopkins River is not worth fishing above Ararat, but between Ararat and Hexham, where it flows over grazing land, it carries abundant redfin, eels and tench, and brown trout up to 3.6 kg. The redfin fishing is particularly good at Willaura. From Hexham to the river mouth, the Hopkins River offers brown trout, blackfish, Australian bass, grayling and redfin.

Restocking is carried out by the Fisheries' Department at many creeks and streams in the region, which usually guarantees reasonable catches for most of the year.

Lakes Alexandra, Beaufort, Bolac, Burrumbeet, Cobrico, Deep and Gillear all carry good numbers of trout and redfin, and some also carry tench. Eels are widespread and are fished commercially in several waters. The best waters for trout are the Merri River, Mount Emu Creek and the best lake for trout is Burrumbeet, which has been regularly stocked with rainbow trout since 1971. Camping facilities are available at this lake and there is a boat launching ramp. The lake has a sand and mud bottom with rocky outcrops along the shore and its main drawback is that the water often becomes discoloured.

Lakes Purrumbete and Bullen Merri

Freshwater salmon have pink flesh that is great eating and they grow to enormous sizes. Quinnat salmon are bred at the Snobs Creek Hatchery and released into the volcanic crater lakes of Purrumbete and Bullen Merri, near Camperdown, about 190 km west of Melbourne. The salmon have made these lakes a very popular fishery, attracting anglers from all over the State. The fish have a life span of about four years and are replaced each year with fresh yearlings. Both lakes are well stocked with food, and the fish grow very fast, reaching 2 kg in only two years. Salmon weighing 6 kg are not uncommon, the State record being 8.4 kg.

The lakes, just off the Princes Highway, also hold some excellent rainbow trout to 5 kg, Bullen Merri growing the heaviest fish, and there is quite a large population of redfin in Lake Purrumbete. Both lakes have an excellent supply of bait and food for the fish, whose eating habits seem to be a little different from those in other localities. All the salmon and the larger trout take whitebait quite readily. Mudeye is the best of the other baits and worms a poor third.

Purrumbete is about 586 ha in area and up to 25 m deep. Most of the salmon seem to feed near the bottom. The usual method is to use a very small running sinker about 1 m above a No. 2 hook on a 4 kg line. The boat is either anchored or allowed to drift if there is very little wind. The rig is lowered to the bottom and then raised about 2 m. A depth sounder is a great asset when fishing these lakes.

Rainbow trout are fished in the more conventional manner, using a bubble float and greased line. There is a new tendency to do away with the float and just lower the mudeye over the side and allow it to sink slowly down until the fish are located. Rainbows are usually found around the edges of the lakes in the vicinity of the drop-off. Both lakes can be fished extensively from the bank, although Bullen Merri is much easier for the bank angler. There is one location on Purrumbete called Hoses Rocks that is reserved for bank angling only.

Each year when the small fish are released, the lakes are

closed to boat fishing for about two months, usually opening on the first Saturday in September. There is a bag limit of five salmon per day but no bag limits on trout. The lakes fish well in summer if it is not too hot.

KEITH FLEMING

MINIMUM LEGAL LENGTHS IN VICTORIA

Bass .... 25 cm	Rock Cod .... 22 cm
Blackfish (except those in streams flowing north from the Great Dividing Range) .. 22 cm	Salmon, Australian (Bay or Salmon Trout) .. 21 cm
	Shark, Gummy .... 45 cm
	Shark, School or Snapper . 40 cm
Bream .... 24 cm	Snapper (Schnapper) .... 27 cm
Eel (except Conger Eels) . 30 cm	Sole .... 20 cm
Estuary perch .... 25 cm	Southern Rock Lobster (Crayfish), saltwater—male ...... 11 cm
Flathead .... 25 cm	
Flounder .... 23 cm	
Garfish (river and sea).... 20 cm	—female .... 10.5 cm
Luderick .... 22 cm	Stranger .... 20 cm
Mullet, flat tail .... 22 cm	Tailor................... 23 cm
Mullet, sea (Poddy) ...... 25 cm	Trout, Brown, Rainbow (in Lakes Hume and Mulwala) .... 25 cm
Mullet, sand............ 22 cm	
Murray Cod (except in Lakes Hume and Mulwala where there is no minimum length) .... 40 cm	
	Trout Cod............. 40 cm
	Whiting, King George, Spotted .... 27 cm
Perch, Macquarie .... 25 cm	

WAHOO

Acanthocybium solandri: Famous game fish of great speed which often broach when trying to free themselves from anglers' hooks. Widely regarded as the finest sport fish of all the mackerel family, they are widely distributed in tropical seas including Lord Howe Island, New Guinea, north-western Australia, Queensland and New South Wales.

Wahoos are not the fastest fish in the sea but are not far from it. They are far in advance of such reputed speedsters as barracuda and Spanish mackerel, and appear more accurately designed for pure speed than dolphin or queenfish. The

Wahoos are known for their speed and fight when first hooked, often ripping the line from the hand of an unwary fisherman.

W ■ WATER beetles

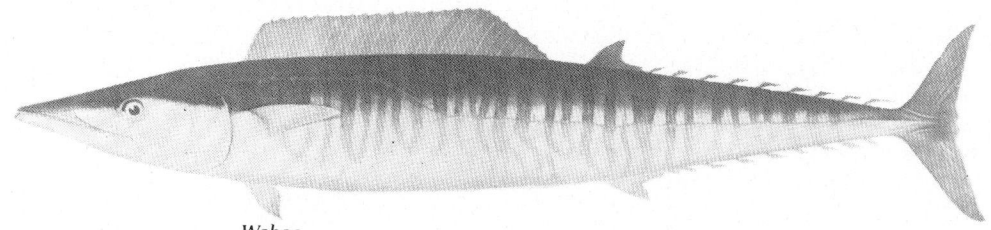

Wahoo

dorsal, tail and all fins would draw praise from any student of hydrodynamics. The underslung lower jaw projects to split the ocean currents easily and the cylindrical body is all muscle.

When hooked, the blistering first run of a wahoo is a true line stripper. However, the body does not resist lateral pressure as well as that of a dolphin or turrum. It is not difficult for a game angler to hold a wahoo within 130 m of a boat on the right tackle. Because of sheer strength and speed they are best fished on light to medium tackle from game boats. Wahoos are elongated, bright navy blue on top, grey to silver on the sides and below, with 20-odd olive or blue cross bars right along the body. The snout is extended. They are highly regarded table fish.

Wahoos are often a nuisance to marlin fishermen, for they are loners which can seize and mutilate a bait in less time than can be believed. Quite often troll baits are pulled in with the tail missing, cut cleanly as if by a knife, without anything having been seen. Apparently wahoo feed by first crippling their food by cutting off the tail and then eating the remainder. Hooks in troll baits aimed at wahoo should be set well back in the bait.

The teeth of the wahoo are one of the sea's wonders. They slash with such speed and power that a bait hardly moves as it is bitten in half. For this reason, anglers treat them with great respect when removing hooks. Troll baits include whole mullet, large garfish and bonito strip on sharp hooks of about 10/0. The fish will take high-speed drones and similar lures, usually weighted for extra trolling depth. In brief, the wahoo is well-named.

Wahoo grow to 1.8 m but are generally caught between 14 and 18 kg. In 1985 the Australian record for the species was 42 kg caught by Tom Scott at Narooma, New South Wales, on a 24 kg line in April 1978. For sport, however, it would be hard to match Tim Simpson's catch of a 35 kg wahoo on only a 6 kg line in Broken Bay in January 1980.

WATER beetles *See Aquatic insects.*

WATER bugs *See Aquatic insects.*

WESTERN Australia

The western half of Australia holds some of the continent's biggest angling challenges. Its remoteness and the sparsity of its population in relation to its great size mean that most of the coastline is seldom fished. To its north lies a coast which only recently has been visited by anglers. The bump of the north Kimberley is still virtually untouched by rod and reel. To its south is a shore rich with ocean fish which already make Western Australians among the keenest boat and shore fishermen in Australia.

The geography of Australia's western coast varies so greatly that it supports several separate populations of fish of distinctive species over the great length of shoreline from the Great Australian Bight in the south to Joseph Bonaparte Gulf near the mouth of the mighty Ord River. The south coast of Western Australia has its massed migrations of pilchard, tommy ruff and Australian salmon or kahawai and its indigenous populations of giant blue groper and 45 kg samson fish.

The west coast has its tailor and Spanish mackerel, whiting and trevally, pink snapper and mulloway. Then round the nose of Western Australia's doggy profile there are sweetlips, bluebone and queenfish. Further north are giant threadfins, great trevallies, cods and gropers; and around the Kimberley, the mystical barramundi.

In Western Australia the name bluebone is rather generally applied to the parrot fish, but is specifically used for the Venus tusk fish or blue-spotted groper *Choerodon venustus*, which

Anglers at Bremer Bay on the south coast of Western Australia using tripods to cast well out from the shore. Tripods are also popular at Trigg, near Perth, and on the south-west coast.

is so well known on the northern New South Wales and Queensland coasts. Queenfish is the local name for the blue morwong *Nemadactylus valenciennesi*, which may be easily recognized by the round patch of bright blue and yellow lines radiating from each eye and running down the snout. It should not be confused with the queenfish *Scomberoides lysan*, a relative of the trevallies, which is found further north.

Western Australian game fishing has come of age, with big marlin and sailfish being caught regularly on regulation tackle. There are some exciting strongholds for marlin and sailfish, for giant narrow banded Spanish mackerel and for wahoo and turrum so big that they break commercial fishermen's best trolling lines.

Freshwater fishing in south-west Western Australian rivers, which has fluctuated since the 1930s is making a comeback from the doldrums of the early 1960s and 1970s. Most suitable streams between Perth and Albany have been regularly stocked with brown and rainbow trout, because this State has no sizeable native freshwater fish except catfish and barramundi. Perch, introduced at the turn of the century, have taken hold in many still rivers and need no stocking. New work being undertaken by the Western Australian Government is helping renew interest in trout. One of the most significant advances is the proof, by one dedicated government scientist, that Western Australian trout do in fact take artificial flies under certain conditions, contrary to earlier belief.

The real surprises in Western Australian freshwater fishing have been in the far north beyond the Great Sandy Desert, where tropical rivers in the rolling Kimberley support barramundi and native perch, oxeye tarpon and big catfish, to mention but a few. The Kimberley is laced with rivers that roar in the wet and retreat into limpid fish-dimpled lagoons in the dry. One single watercourse, the Fitzroy and the Hann rivers, link up to form 650 km of billabong fishing. Accessibility is the main problem of fishing in the north. For every billabong that can be reached by road there are scores that cannot be reached except by four-wheel-drive.

The whole northern Kimberley corner is a fishing enigma. A single four-wheel-drive track leads from the Kimberley beef road to the far northern outpost at Kalumburu Mission, some 300 km. But the gap is steadily being shortened as new beef roads push deeper into the Kimberley each year and new fishing grounds are discovered. Western Australia has been dubbed a State on the move, particularly in its north-west. Many outback fishermen resent this sudden activity. It has already meant the spoiling of good fishing areas by industrial thoughtlessness. It has led to more people and tourists fishing in places northerners once had to themselves. Inevitably, in the end, it will mean fewer fish.

This is one of the sad truths of progress. The only remedy is conservation. Fishermen in Western Australia hope that in remote areas conservation can be applied as a preventative before it has to be used as a cure.

Shore fishing

The long golden beaches of Western Australia make surf fishing a sport for everyone. The long, hot summers encourage thousands of people to the beaches at dawn and dusk, when the best fish are caught. The novice Western Australian angler buying his first fishing rod will invariably learn to use it on beach whiting and tailor in the summer and tommy ruff in the winter. Some anglers on the west coast are perfectly happy to spend their lives catching small tailor, herring and whiting. Others graduate to bigger fish. Shore fishermen in Western Australia today believe that no fish is too big to be landed on a rod and reel from the shore, provided the tackle and the tactics are right.

Western Australia's armies of beach, rock and reef fishermen have chalked up, surprisingly, a more glittering list of State angling records than their boating counterparts, who have the opportunity to get out among the really big ones with heavy handline gear.

On the southern and south-west coast the shore tackle trend is towards longer rods capable of casting farther and reels able to carry big loads of light to medium line so that big fish can be fought with skill and patience instead of with brute force. Most of the record shore captures were made on line with breaking strains between 6.5 and 13 kg. With this long casting, light line trend goes a hook rig now used universally on southern beaches—the flight of hooks; the chain of three or four hooks ganged together, point through eye, to which anglers can bait a whole sardine or pilchard or herring, or a strip of mullet.

Shore fishermen once used the flight of hooks only for catching tailor, to prevent their lines being cut by the tailor's sharp teeth. Today the flight is considered an efficient hook rig for almost any species that will tackle a whole fish or strip bait. Bait is the key to this hooking revolution. The most successful baits on the west coast today are mulies or blue pilchard and whitebait, a species of small white sprat. Both mulies and whitebait are most effectively used on a flight of hooks. The mulie bait on a flight of hooks is deadly for baitcasting with long rods and threadline or sidecast reels. Fish caught by baitcasting include tailor, salmon, mulloway, pike, flathead, trevally, tuna, mackerel and sharks.

Flighted or chain hooks are also used for sinker fishing from the shore for tailor, salmon, mulloway, sharks and other bigger species that occasionally venture within casting distance. Because of the risk of snagging a flight of hooks fished on the bottom, west coast anglers usually attach a cork next to the top hook of the flight to float it a metre or so off the bottom.

W ■ WESTERN Australia

Kalbarri There are fish for every category of angler at Kalbarri, the settlement on the mouth of the Murchison River, 560 km north of Perth. The most capable anglers in Western Australia go there to pit their skill against gamefish from the shore, while holiday fishermen get their quotas of bream and whiting with little effort.

The Murchison River strikes the sea on the northern end of a chain of tall red cliffs. The river mouth is protected on the north by an arm of flat rock known as the Oyster Reef and on the south by a short promontory called Chinaman Rock. Between February and May, fishermen row across the river to fish on Oyster Reef with balloons or bait-casting outfits for narrow-banded Spanish mackerel and tuna.

Some of the biggest tailor on the coast are caught from Oyster and Chinaman. August is usually the month of the 4.5 kg fish, and many up to 6.5 kg are caught there each year. The spring months are best for mulloway, up to 27 kg, which swim in the estuary mouth and off Oyster Reef. About 1 km north of The Oyster—anglers have to walk—is a shelving limestone formation known as Frustration Rock. The name comes from the quantity of rigs snagged and lost there. But the number of big mulloway caught there more than compensate. Sharks, too, are caught at Frustration and occasionally Spanish mackerel are hooked on the bottom at night.

Six kilometres south of the river mouth, the main formation of Red Bluff begins. The flat rock ledges in front of the bluffs

A lone angler fishing for tailor off the rocks at Kalbarri, north of Perth.

drop off into deep water where narrow-banded mackerel come through in runs. Shore fishermen catch many on threadline gear and garfish bait. Snapper and sharks are also caught from the big rocks. On the Bluff Beach, beside the rocks, anglers catch small tailor and big mulloway. In the 6 km stretch between the Red Bluff and the Murchison River mouth are numerous holes and reefs where big tailor hide out. Skindiver Vern Storrey speared an 8.5 kg tailor in this area. In the river mouth small mulloway are caught at night and whiting and bream by day.

Large bream are caught further up the river. They seldom grow to more than 1 kg, possibly because they are so easily caught. These Murchison River bream are a species apart from the brackish water fish of the Swan River and southern estuaries; they do not mind salt water and are quite unsophisticated about baits. Though mullet and bony herring are recognized as the best bream baits here, many fish are caught on red meat, whiting, tailor and other unlikely baits. Small mulloway and javelin fish are occasionally caught up the river on bream lines. Big mulloway, too, are caught up river. The estuarine waters of the Murchison often abound with blue swimmer and pan or mud crabs. They can be caught in drop nets or drawn ashore on baits and scooped.

Other good fishing spots within reasonable driving distance of the Murchison mouth are at Port Gregory, 43 km from Northampton, Sandalwood Bay, Halfway Bay and Lucky Bay. All these spots provide fishing for tailor, mulloway and Spanish mackerel. Big catches of Spanish mackerel, yellowfin and northern bluefin tuna are taken from boats trolling between Lucky Bay and the Murchison River mouth. Drift fishing provides good catches of jewfish, snapper and reef fish.

Cockburn Sound

One of the finest fishing spots in the State, particularly at the height of the north-west 'blow' when the pink salmon are about. Pink snapper, which have a habit of turning up in rough weather and are frequently caught in storms, have a liking for the big grain terminal midway along the Sound. Squid provide plenty of action for dinghy fishermen who drift on the easterly winds off Woodman's Point. Jigs and lures work well, the most popular being a Yo-zuri, which is shaped like a prawn and has an inverted double crown at the base to snare the squid.

Further south at Rockingham, the Garden Island Causeway has become a popular fishing spot. The second opening of the causeway provides anglers with big catches of skipjack or silver trevally. Skipjack bite best in calm conditions on prawns, whitebait or mussels, and are caught from the causeway pylons in the hours just before and just after noon. Herring are plentiful throughout the causeway area, with best results usually coming on the ocean side over weedbanks.

WESTERN Australia

Rottnest Island

One of the most popular fishing playgrounds on the west coast, 19 km by sea from the port of Fremantle. Off its south shore game fishermen catch narrow-banded Spanish mackerel and tuna. The continental shelf off its north shore abounds with jewfish, snapper and other reef fish. Seaward of its West End, about 40 km, game fishermen have a regular marlin fishery with fish attractors in operation, and small-boat and shore fishermen regard it as one of the richest spots for species like tailor, herring, salmon, whiting and trevally.

Rottnest saw the beginning of game fishing in Western Australia and for years anglers had to look no further for all the mackerel and tuna they needed. Parker Point and West End have yielded numerous fish that have been entered for the Australian mackerel record. At one time the all-class Western Australian record for a mackerel caught from a boat was a 32 kg specimen taken off Parker Point.

No deep-sea fish holds more prestige in Western Australia than the Westralian jewfish; and so it enhances the repute of Rottnest that most State record jewies were both hooked there, with many round the 20 kg mark.

Rottnest is also famous as the spawning ground of the west coast tommy ruff or herring. For as long as fishermen can remember, big herring schools that swim around from the Bight each autumn gather at Rottnest at the start of May in

At Parker Point on Rottnest Island there are deep pools ideal for diving or fishing for herring, tailor, whiting, salmon or trevally.

Holiday accommodation at Geordie Bay on Rottnest Island, one of the most popular holiday areas on the Western Australian coast.

such numbers that the sea is often black over large areas. These schools do not bite well until after the spawning and then, bellies empty, they converge ravenously anywhere there is food.

The story of herring biting on bare hooks at Rottnest in May scarcely raises a local eyebrow. Though herring experts on the mainland carefully cultivate their stocks of maggot bait for the herring run, herring at Rottnest bite on red meat, bits of other herring, even on white rag. The old way of catching a lot of herring in a hurry was with a 'Ned Kelly' rod: a long pole with slender tip and a line about 3 m long with a couple of hooks. Fish could be literally ladled out of a school.

August and September are skippy (trevally) months at Rottnest. Fish to 250 g then are tiddlers and anglers look for the schools of 1 to 1.5 kg specimens and fish up to 3 kg are not uncommon. These, incidentally, are not quite the same species of silver trevally which east coast rock fishermen catch. Metropolitan Perth and Fremantle shore fishing clubs spend many weekends in competitive fishing from the rocks and reefs of Rottnest. Their main catches are tailor and trevally.

Jewfish are occasionally caught from the shore where lines can be cast into deep holes. So, too, are big sea kingfish. Mulloway frequent Salmon Bay and anglers can invariably get a catch of tailor up to 1 kg at Natural Jetty.

W ■ WESTERN Australia

Mary Cove on Rottnest Island is an excellent spot for herring, trevally and salmon fishing during winter.

Salmon fishing at Rottnest often becomes hard work at place like Ricey Beach, Radar Reef and Mary Cove when salmon are on the bite. Some fishermen pack up and try another spot because there is a limit to the number they can carry back (there are no cars on the island, only bikes and charabancs when they are available), not to mention the number they can give away. Big schools of salmon take shelter round Rottnest in winter and often stay there until the following summer.

Some of the biggest King George or spotted whiting on the west coast are picked up by fishermen who know the special spots off Rottnest's Parker Point. Though the largest confirmed weight is 1.5 kg they are said to be caught (and quickly eaten) up to and exceeding 2.5 kg.

Outsize cobbler appear at night in weedy Thomson Bay. Pike, too, like the weed beds and fishermen catch them by drifting in boats with unweighted lines baited with whitebait or strips of fish bait. Some splendid cabins for fishermen have been built on Rottnest at Geordie Bay and can be booked through the government tourist offices in each capital city.

Shark Bay The thing southern Western Australian anglers find most exciting about Shark Bay is that its fish and fishing conditions are so different from their own. From the shore you are likely to catch such typically northern fish as long tom and blue bone, barracuda and school mackerel. And yet the southern favourites are there too; the tailor and mulloway, whiting and snapper. Denham, on the Peron Peninsula, is a happy, get-away-from-it-all type of fishing town. The town lives on its

Shark Bay

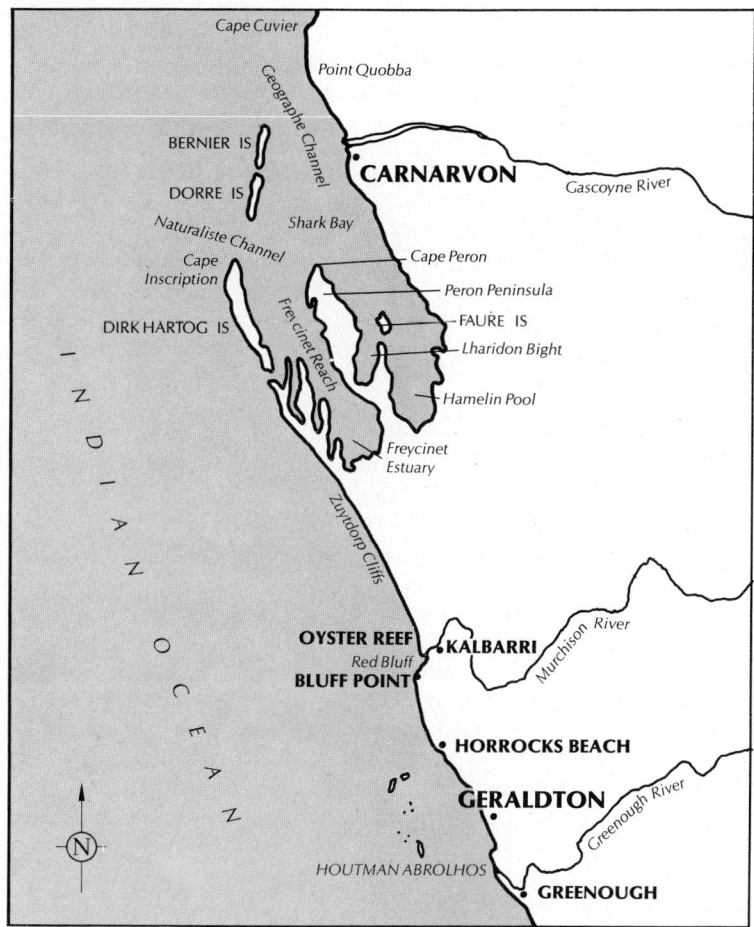

fish—literally. The inhabitants, mostly descendants of Asian pearlers, eat fish, and the town's main industries are mullet, whiting, snapper and fishing tourists.

From the shore in front of the town, whiting, blue bone, flathead and long tom are caught. At the end of the long jetty anglers fish into deep water for mulloway, snapper and big tailor. Eastwards across the peninsula from Denham over 25 km of good road is Monkey Mia where fishermen catch their own bony herring to bait up for big mulloway, snapper, Spanish mackerel, northern trevally and occasional cobia. Sharks and rays are plentiful here, particularly the big shovelnose rays which grow to 90 kg and pull like trains.

Fairly good tracks lead from Denham, 19 km to Eagle Bluff and 37 km to Goulet Bluff for rock fishing for snapper, bream, cod, whiting and tailor. Four-wheel-drive is needed to get to Cape Peron for groper, blue bone, Spanish flag, black snapper, barracuda, northern trevally and Spanish mackerel.

Many anglers take their own boats to Shark Bay to get among the big snapper schools in the deeper offshore channels round Useless Loop and South Passage. Out through South Passage game fishermen may catch Spanish mackerel, sailfish and wahoo. Marlin have been hooked here, too.

Swan River This waterway puts fish on the doorstep of half of Western Australia's anglers. The Swan is more than just a river. It is an estuary which broadens to 3 km in places and meanders through the suburbs for 19 km between Fremantle and the city of Perth. Or rather, the suburbs have grown up around its shores and spread back. In the Swan's estuary there are beaches and rocks, wide flats and sections 18 m deep, channels and spits, jetties and landings. The variety of fish that find sanctuary in the Swan and its estuary, summer and winter, is remarkable.

There are big schools of tailor, wandering groups of old men mulloway, bream, flathead, flounder, whiting, cobbler (catfish), yellowtail and river perch. Small boys catch yellow-eye mullet and trumpeter and when the summer tides turn the estuary as salty as the ocean, anglers even catch tarwhine, trevally, blue mackerel and herring.

The Swan starts to come to life in September as the winter rains ease. Bream fishermen who know the haunts have been catching their feeds all winter, but in September the bream become more interested in bait. A prawn or whitebait on the river bed at Mosman Park and Claremont in September may hook a bream, small mulloway or yellowtail. Cobblers start to run about the same time, but prefer prawn or bloodworm. These species bite until about November, by which time the bream have usually moved past Nedlands and Applecross and are retreating to their summer haunts in the upper reaches of the Swan and Canning rivers.

November sees that start of flounder at Bicton, Blackwall, Mosman Park and Claremont. Small mulloway are running well in these areas too and have reached the Narrows Bridge, a popular mulloway area. Flathead follow in December, spreading across Bicton, Point Walter and Freshwater Bay. By November the boats are out trolling for river tailor at Claremont, Point Walter and as far upstream as Applecross and South Perth. But better tailor trolling follows in the months of January and February, and may stay around until the winter rains start in May. There have been years when the normal whitebait was too small to use for Swan tailor and anglers then took to trolling whole mulies (pilchard), as for ocean fish.

The prawns that have been growing in the Swan all summer begin to swim to sea as adults in March and April. They drift out on the tide through the narrow section of river at Fremantle, usually quite close to the surface. Fishermen anchor in the tide or climb beneath the traffic and railway bridges and

Albany – Perth

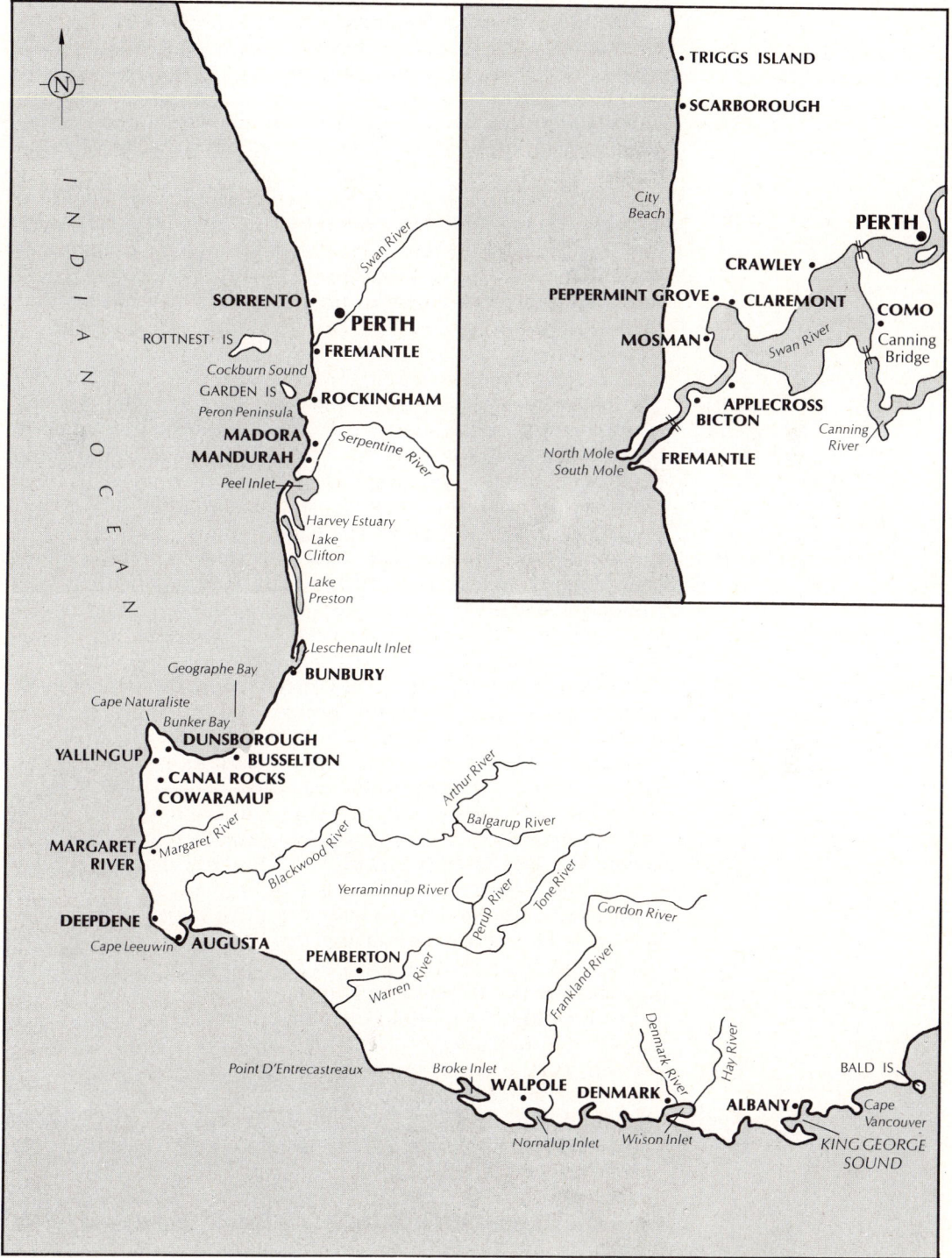

scoop dozens of these big prawns by the light of pressure lamps.

The first winter rains are a sign for the bream to start moving again. They move close to shore, as a rule, feeding ahead of the freshwater around jetties and rocks where fishermen get some of their biggest catches of the year on prawns, mussel, bloodworms, mulletgut and whitebait. Mulloway also move in front of the fresh water and are often caught with the bream.

Swan River bream and those of other southern rivers and estuaries do not go to sea. When the rivers fill with fresh water they take shelter in the deeper sections which remain salt while the fresh flows overhead. The brackish colouring of some big mulloway caught at the end of winter indicates that many mulloway, too, must spend the winter in the river.

Walpole The best shore fishing is at Bellanger Beach, which can be reached on a circuitous road from Walpole or by a shorter boat haul across the estuary. Here fishermen catch salmon, big trevally, mulloway, groper and shark.

Other top spots round Walpole are Mandalay Beach and Point Nuyts for shark, snapper and groper and Rocky Head, at the mouth of the Nornalup Inlet, for sweep, pike, groper, snapper and jewfish. There is excellent black bream fishing up the Frankland and Deep rivers.

Yallingup The angler who goes to Yallingup has such a wide range of fishing spots to choose from that he would need a month to do them all justice. However the fishing on that section of the coast is so good most people do not have to try more than a couple of spots before contacting good fish. Yallingup is on the upturned 'toe' of Western Australia, next door to Cape Naturaliste, which gazes across Geographe Bay at the west coast, disappearing northwards to Busselton, Bunbury, Mandurah and Fremantle.

Recommendation of the Yallingup area needs one qualification. It is much better in the autumn and winter than in spring and summer. From March and April on into winter, the sea around the Cape comes alive, mainly with salmon and herring, but also with tailor, trevally, pike and mulloway. And anglers with heavy gear fish off rocks into deep water for jewfish, snapper, groper, sweep, sharks and sea kingfish.

The salmon run usually hits late in March and big schools pack into resting places at Canal Rocks, Injinup and Cowaramup. At Canal Rocks several hundred anglers may fish side by side from the rocks into a milling mass of salmon packed right to the water's edge. This kind of fishing is frequently wasteful; for some anglers catch many more fish than they can carry home.

Here is a brief guide to surrounding spots:—

Cowaramup
South of Yallingup 25 km. Big bay with rock fishing, surface and sinker, for herring, pike, trevally, salmon, samson fish, groper and sharks. Balloon fishing on offshore wind.

Wyadup
South of Yallingup 12 km. Good roads. Rocky headland; best for surface fishing for herring, pike, trevally, salmon, samson fish. Danger from king waves.

Injinup
Excellent sinker and surface fishing for herring, trevally, salmon, tailor, pike, samson, groper, jewfish, sharks and mulloway.

Canal Rocks
South of Yallingup 8 km. Year-round fishing for trevally, herring, pike, samson fish and sharks. Excellent for winter herring and salmon. Mainly rod fishing, but the use of hand-lines is possible.

Smith's Beach
South of Yallingup 1.5 km. Beach fishing with spoon or star sinker. All year fishing for trevally, tailor, whiting, flathead, herring, flounder, mulloway, sharks. Salmon and herring all winter.

Torpedo Rocks
Surface fishing from southern 'elbow' for herring, tailor, salmon, trevally and sea kingfish. Off deep end for jewfish, groper, sweep, trevally, samson and sharks. Heavy lines required for long haul up rocks. Some danger from king waves.

Yallingup Beach
Reefs for spinning and bait casting. Beach for sinker fishing. Salmon and herring in winter. Trevally, tarwhine, mulloway, tailor, sharks and flathead all year.

Sugarloaf Rock
Twelve kilometres from Dunsborough. Very dangerous when big waves running. Herring, trevally, salmon and samson fish on surface; sweep, jewfish, snapper, sharks and deep-sea species on bottom.

Cape Naturaliste
Rough, sandy 2.5 km track from lighthouse to beach and long walk to fishable rocks or four-wheel-drive. Excellent tailor and salmon fishing, also trevally, herring, samson fish and sharks.

Bunker Bay
Beach and rock fishing off the Docks, Chimneys or Slippery Rocks. Sweep, jewfish, snapper, sharks, pike and deep-sea species as well as other surface fish.

Surf fishing north of Capricorn

Here methods of shore fishing begin to change. Fish are less sophisticated and so is the tackle used. Local anglers have perfected methods of hooking big fish quickly with a minimum of fuss. Because of the profusion of warmer water coral and oysters, simpler rigs are preferred for bottom fishing. Fish come closer to feed along the shoreline on a rising tide and long casts are not necessary. Fine line is often a disadvantage because it allows a fish to take a quick dive around a razor-studded oyster rock and abruptly end the fight. Nothing is more frustrating to the light tackle angler than losing one good fish after another while a northerner next to him calmly pulls up as many as he wants on a heavy handline. Light line fishing can suddenly lose appeal.

Northern anglers prefer handlines with breaking strains between 20 and 60 kg. Thus a fish can be man-handled away from snags and a few scrapes against oysters and coral does little harm. Where there are no snags, in tidal creeks and sandy bays, light line undoubtedly produces more fish. The average north-west handline is equipped with a hook between 4/0 and 10/0, preferably without a sinker. The weight of a fist-size lump of bait is usually sufficient to cast the required distance from shore. If a tide is running, a loose roll of sheet lead on the line is less likely to snag than an angular sinker.

Flights of hooks are not favoured for bottom fishing north of the Tropic of Capricorn. If the hooks do not snag themselves, a fish will. For surface species like longtom, pike, queenfish, mackerel, or threadfin, the flight of hooks with a whole fish or strip fish bait is a deadly rig. But there is always the odd cod, mangrove jack or sweetlips that will flash up and take your flight of hooks around the leg of a tabletop coral.

Reading tides

On the west coast of Australia tides play strange tricks with anglers. At the port of Fremantle, round which is centred the State's heaviest concentration of fishermen, the tide variance is seldom greater than 1.2 m and is so influenced by winds, surf and weather that it is impossible to predict. Anglers on the coast for 480 km on either side of Perth know little about fishing the tide. They fish at other natural fish feeding times; at dawn and at dusk, at the rise of the moon, on the change of wind. A few canny southern anglers are aware that even if there is little water variance, a high tide is still best for mulloway.

When southern anglers go north for the first time they are often lost in a fishing pattern which depends entirely on tide conditions. Broome, at the start of the Kimberley, has a tide variance of between 9 and 12 m. The basic rule of tidal fishing in the north-west is that the fish come in to feed on a rising tide. They are therefore at their biting best on the latter half of a rising tide and once again on change of the high as the ebb begins. This pattern applies to most coastal fishing places.

But in tidal creeks the pattern is just the opposite. You would think that on a high tide fish from the sea would swim up creeks to feed, but it does not happen that way. When the tide rises in a tidal creek it overlaps its banks and spreads out into the mangroves and saltpans for miles around. Mullet and prawns and fodder fish that attract bigger fish into the creeks can hide among the mangroves where predators have little hope of finding them. But when the tide starts to drop all these fish must retreat back into the creeks, eventually to be trapped in the deepest holes left by the ebb tide. This is when the predators are most active.

The best creek fishing is on the latter half of a falling tide and once again at the change, when slack water starts to make. Tides make little difference to bottom fishing from boats in deeper water. Sometimes, however, game fish like mackerel, trevally and queenfish will hide beside reefs to catch small fish swept over on a falling tide. In places where this happens the best time to catch these fish is naturally on a falling tide.

Deep-sea angling

The western coast deep-sea angler is likely to pull aboard anything from a 1.5 kg spotted whiting to a 135 kg spotted cod. In habitat these two fish are 1600 km apart. In habit they are entirely dissimilar. But because both live in the deep water on broken bottom, the tackle used for their capture from deep-sea fishing boats is basically similar.

The Western Australian coastline is so big that the variety of fish changes several times from the South Australian border to the start of the Northern Territory. Yet wherever a boat can find a good offshore patch of bottom fish, a heavy handline with 4.0 to 10.0 hooks and a one pound lead bomb seems to do the trick. Some prefer lighter gear, boat rods and reels, but the common problem of deep-sea fishing seems to be in getting the fish away from the shelter of the bottom before it anchors the tackle there.

Boat fishermen from Esperance to Albany, on the south coast, can expect to catch samson fish, blue groper, jewfish, snapper, sweep, blue morwong or queen snapper and breaksea cod. The state records for blue groper, samson fish and queen snapper all came from boat catches off the south coast. The Western Australian jewfish seems most at home between Cape Leeuwin and the Abrolhos Islands. The above-mentioned queen snapper *Nemadactylus carponemus* is closely related to the eastern jackass fish or New Zealand tarakihi. The breaksea cod *Epinephilides arnatus*, often erroneously called 'black snapper', was originally and is now apparently irremediably known as black-arse snapper on account of the black patch, about the size of a 20 cent piece, neatly centred over its vent.

Sharks are always plentiful in deep-sea fishing areas, but where better scaled fish are plentiful, fishermen use nylon traces which are easily bitten through by a shark. Fishing for

The Westralian jewfish is the most sought-after deep-sea fish along the Western Australian coast, south of Kalbarri.

school sharks is rewarding in the early winter months off the south coast. Anglers in the Fremantle area often use wire traces on their deep-sea handlines so that sharks may be brought aboard. The amateur-caught shark usually ends up in a fish shop and the local saying is that 'sharks pay for boat and petrol'. The most commonly caught around Rottnest are whalers and slim-bodied reef sharks. Small tigers and hammerheads are occasionally boated, but these are not regarded as good eating. Nurse sharks seem to prefer shallower water.

Western Australian small boat fishing

This angling form is finding new horizons on Western Australia's coast. With better seaworthiness, flotation materials, efficient outboards and stringent safety regulations, small boats are venturing 50 km to sea to compete with the launches of deep-sea fishermen. Dinghy fishermen in south-west estuaries and rivers catch black bream, mulloway, trevally and whiting. They troll with moving baits and spinners for tailor, salmon trout, pike and sometimes for salmon.

Though rods and reels have become more popular, most boat fishermen in Western Australia use handlines for whiting, garfish, herring, flathead, mulloway, bream and trevally. Boat rods and centrepin reels are used by dinghy fishermen trolling for small river and coastal tailor. Pike fishermen use lines weighted at intervals with barrel leads so that the bait swims close to the weed banks on which southern pike lie. Preferred baits are whitebait, small whiting, mulies, or strips of whiting, herring or parrot fish. South-west strongholds like Windy Harbour, Hamelin Bay, Cowaramup and Yallingup produce fish up to 3 kg and the occasional 4 to 4.5 kg specimen is brought aboard. Rottnest pike fishermen prefer to drift their boats over the shallow grassweed banks and allow their unweighted whole bait to flick along in the current. Handlines for tailor trolling are usually about 13.5 kg, baited with white-bait on a gang of three No. 2 to 4 limericks or straightened kendall kirby hooks. Halco No. 6 slim chrome plugs are popular, though some prefer imp spoons, Warrnambool spoons and wonder wobblers.

A whole mulie trolled on a set of ganged hooks from a small boat off the metropolitan coast is likely to pick up tailor up to 3 kg or a 4 kg salmon. Big numbers of salmon are caught by small boats trolling Smith jigs when the fish are schooling in March and April.

Dinghy fishermen these days catch almost as many narrow banded Spanish mackerel off the coast as game fishermen in their deep-sea launches. The dinghies can sneak along reef dropaways that could be dangerous for bigger craft. Dinghy mackerel fishermen are a secretive breed. They usually fish one to a boat with a couple of garfish baited lines trolled astern. They know the spots and lumps of the local coast intimately. Sometimes the dinghy man may troll along the coast every morning for a fortnight without a fish. On a good day he might strike three or four 'macks', 4 to 10 kg. When the dinghy fishermen have been striking it rich off the local beaches, the launch men who have not been doing so well in deeper water try to follow their tracks. But somehow the dinghies retain their monopoly on close-to-shore mackerel.

Game fishing off Western Australia

The north-west coast, one of the world's last frontiers of game fishing, is being explored by men who talk in terms of world records and international regulation tackle. Hard-bitten north-west attitudes are changing. The fisherman who uses a rod and line from the back of a boat is no longer suspected of being a wearer of lace underpants.

There are fish on this coast that would amaze Zane Grey, and every year more and more rod and reel men are after them. Today's Australian record chart is liberally sprinkled with fish from this area, whereas ten years ago Western Australian locations seldom were listed. There are places where Spanish mackerel and turrum grow to well over 35 kg, barracudas over 30 kg, queenfish to an amazing 15 kg. No less than eight Australian sailfish records, five Australian turrum records and numerous national tuna records have been set in the region.

At the top of the ladder, of course, is the marlin. Ten years ago marlin were an elusive prize but in the second half of the 1980s blue, black and striped marlin were taken every season off Exmouth, Dampier and the Monte Bello islands, with Julie Cheradi's 1978 catch of a 46.50 kg striped marlin off North West Cape a national record. Further south, marlin are taken regularly on Perth's doorstep off Rottnest Island. There Sir Garrick Agnew's 1983 catch of a 319 kg blue marlin was an Australian record.

For Western Australian game fisherman, the big target is to catch a 1000 lb (453.6 kg) marlin, a prize that would put their area on the map internationally. Several near-misses suggest that such a catch is not far off. When it comes, the sport will owe a lot to Sir Garrick Agnew and Geoff Hammond who first proved the presence of these glamorous fish in Western Australian waters.

Game fishing started in Western Australia in the 1930s, with a local prize offered for the first game fish on regulation gear. A Spanish mackerel caught near Rottnest took the prize and since that day Rottnest Island has been one of the main fishing areas of southern game fishermen. Rottnest is the last southern stronghold of narrow-barred Spanish mackerel. Trolling whole garfish baits, feather jigs and tuna jigs anglers caught mackerel over 30 kg, yellowfin tuna to about the same size, samson fish (in previous times named black tunny), yellowtail kingfish, smaller bluefin tuna and dolphin fish around 5 kg. The 1985 Australian record for narrow-barred Spanish mackerel was a 38.75 kg fish taken off Rottnest by Barry Wrightson in 1978.

Since 1961 when Dr Carl Georgeff started the Nor'West Game Fishing Club on Rosemary Island in the Dampier Archipelago, off Roebourne, this club has challenged Rottnest for headlines. The aim of the club was to catch the marlin or sailfish, billfish which had been sighted but never caught by sportsfishermen. The billfish of Rosemary Island turned out to be sailfish of the Indian Ocean variety, between 20 and 40 kg in weight. They seemed to congregate on a small patch of ocean a couple of kilometres off Rosemary.

When the first sailfish was landed on regulation tackle, there was great jubilation. Soon, as sailfish after sailfish was caught, it became apparent that sailfish were not at all rare in the area, but marlin were. Anglers became bored with catching sailfish, which fought prettily, but without the stamina of more common game fish like mackerel and tuna. To make it worse, once you had killed a sailfish, you could only take its photograph and then throw it away, because unlike marlin, sailfish flesh is not good to eat. They brought in the rule that all sailfish, except obvious records, should be cut off at the hook and set free. The whole exercise became even more pointless—travelling 1600 km from Perth to hook a pretty fish which fought poorly and had to be released.

Japanese longliners were known to be catching big marlin 90 to 140 km further out to sea. Plans to join the longliners were thwarted by the lack of suitable boats. Club members had to be content with sailfish—and an excellent variety of other smaller game fish around the islands. Lighter lines were used to catch sailfish. Finally the sailfish took matters into their own hands and moved headquarters. At one time most Australian sailfish records were held by Rosemary Island captures.

Meanwhile Garrick Agnew was exploring another area off the ocean coast of Dirk Hartog Island at Shark Bay. He found the dark-blue water between South Passage on the south end of the islands and Cape Inscription on the north end contained not only sailfish but the occasional marlin. Agnew worked hard to catch marlin and by 1985 he and his wife Fay both held Australian game fishing records. They have done much to promote game fishing in the west, as Bob and Dolly Dyer did for the east coast. Sailfish are now caught regularly by rod and reel anglers at Steep Point, the most westerly spot in Australia.

The main problem in catching marlin in the Shark Bay area, Agnew found, was that so many other lesser game fish were rearing to bite at his baits. By keeping the baits and lures flapping across the surface Agnew managed to evade most of them, except wahoo. And the wahoo, apparently more plentiful there than anywhere else on the west coast, actually preferred the big flapping baits and lures meant for marlin.

Success at Rosemary Island encouraged anglers to try their skill in new areas. A certain reef near Rosily Island, off Onslow, which houses 45 kg turrum, has been visited by occasional game fishermen. But the dangerous country tests the skill of anglers using anything less than sashcord. The turrum—known locally as black skippy—dwell under a spot where dummy rollers crest and crash. The only way to hook them is for a boat skipper to make a quick pass in the face of a dummy roller. Big fish have been lost on game tackle there because the boatman has had to clear out fast to avoid being swamped. There are other spots round Mauds Landing and Muiron

Islands where 45 kg turrum are hooked occasionally.

Two other spots off the north-west coast which are being talked about by record hunters are the Tryal Rocks, 55 km north-west of the Monte Bello Islands, and Cape Leveque, past Broome, on the seaward tip of King Sound. Both these places are known to produce some of the biggest Spanish mackerel in Australia. Professionals have brought mackerel from the Tryals weighing more than 40 kg dressed, while occasional 55 kg fish have been hooked off Cape Leveque. The Malay crew of a Cape Leveque pearling lugger caught a mackerel which was 2.4 m long and took three men to carry.

Nobody seems to have fished specifically for barracuda, occasionally caught up to 30 kg off Onslow and Roebourne, or queenfish, those quicksilver species with the flat body and nutcracker head. Kilogram-for-kilogram queenfish are better fighters than barracuda or mackerel and more spectacular than the dour trevallies.

Most of the Western Australian smaller game fish have been encountered by southern anglers exploring the coast in search of marlin. These anglers have learnt much from pioneering professionals who have seen billfish and guided the amateurs to these places. In return, the professionals have learnt things from the anglers who are now helping to increase their catches. These days professional fishermen take water temperatures to get their best mackerel catches. Some have also increased their poundage by using whole fresh garfish baits instead of plastic jigs and chrome spoons.

The search for marlin took a dramatic turn in the early months of 1969. After searching the coast from Albany to Port Hedland, suddenly attention was focused on waters close to Perth—the continental shelf due west of Rottnest. It had always been known that marlin swam along the shelf past Rottnest, though anglers doubted they were plentiful enough to fish for consistently. Painstaking probing finally proved the existence of the Rottnest Trench, an underwater canyon about 12 kilometres west of Rottnest. In the past ten years the Trench has produced many marlin between 180 and 22 kg, mainly blues. Perth game fishermen maintain several fish attractor devices over the Trench and in the seasons when marlin are scarce there are always dolphin fish, tuna, mackerel and other smaller game fish as compensation.

The Perth Game Fishing Club had up to seven of these attractor devices (FADS) set up around the Rottnest Trench during the mid-1980s. They did not fulfil hopes and attract big marlin, but stocks of sharks, samson fish and tunas increased. On the opening day of the Perth club's 1985 season, five marlin were hooked, but only one of these came out of the Rottnest Trench area, suggesting either that marlin are aloof to fish attractors or that their appearance runs in cycles.

The Perth club, whose season runs from mid–February for three months, is one of six clubs now affiliated to the Western

Australian Game Fishing Association. The others are King Bay (Dampier), Exmouth, Norwest, Naturaliste, and the club organised within the Fremantle Sailing Club. Of these, Exmouth boasts the most frequent marlin catches, Dampier the most frequent sailfish. Exmouth, of course, owes its prominence in amateur fishing circles to the activities of the professional fisherman, George King, during the 1970s, when he proved beyond doubt there were marlin in the area. King, like most of Western Australia's game fishing addicts is still after that elusive 1000-pounder (imperial weight) which would bring international prestige to his waters.

Crustaceans
Though prawns, crabs and crayfish are hardly considered angling, no summary of Western Australian amateur fishing would be complete without some mention of them.

Thousands of people fill their bags each summer with blue manna crabs—the same blue swimmers found right around the Australian coast. The big southern estuaries, including Perth's home river, the Swan, are gathering points for numbers of these crabs. In recent years Peel Inlet at Mandurah and Leschenault Inlet at Bunbury have produced the richest hauls. The blues and their drabber female counterparts are caught in circular wire frame dropnets, scoopnets and snares. Swan River crabs are for some reason most sought after by seafood gourmets, though in recent years they have been scarce. But in the boom seasons crabs are so plentiful in Leschenault Inlet that professional fishermen cannot set their fishing nets and even line fishermen find they cannot keep bait on the bottom without attracting crabs. Dropnetters and scoopnetters from hundreds of kilometres away throng the estuary every summer weekend, but the crabs remain so plentiful that, according to some, 'they chase you up the beach'.

In the north of the State, mangrove, mud or pan crabs attract most amateur interest. They are dour creatures of up to 2 kg in weight with pincers like small boxing gloves and a love of deep, sloppy mangrove mud. They move into the mangroves on the high tide and dig themselves into deep burrows where they can be caught when the tide recedes. The technique is to hook them out with a long piece of extra stiff wire with a hook on the end. This often involves a prolonged fencing bout with a crab that has no intention of being hooked out. Once caught these big crabs can crush a finger with their powerful claws. Some crabbers paralyze the nipper by spiking the nipper joint with the sharp end of a crab's foot. Northwesterns eat pan crabs, boiled, or grilled on hot coals, native style.

The marron *Cherax tenuimanus* of the south-west inland rivers of Western Australia is one of the largest freshwater crayfish in the world, probably ranking second to the giant freshwater crayfish of Tasmania *Astacopsis gouldi*, which is credited with growing to 40 cm and 6 kg. Some have been caught over 3 kg, though the average size is less than 500 g. Fisheries authorities, realizing the value of the marron as an amateur fishery, have laid down strong laws about sizes and seasons. The marron season opens in January and closes three months later. Set pots, dropnets and scoopnets are allowed.

The old bushman art of snaring marron is slowly being lost. This technique was to stake baits along a river bank and when marron come to feed, to lasso them with a copper wire noose on the end of a long green stick—green because dry wood floats. The noose would be gently slipped over the marron's tail, brought up to the carapace joint, then smartly tugged.

Western Australia's world-famous ocean crayfish, or rock lobsters as the fishing industry prefers to call them, are not very accessible to amateurs. They are taken in numbers by skindivers and amateur boat fishermen are allowed to carry two pots per boat in season.

Prawning in estuaries is a popular pastime on hot summer evenings. Prawn nets stretched between two poles and with a long pocket extending from the middle of the net are dredged along the shallows, a person to either pole.

Probably the least known crustacean of any importance in Western Australia is the cherabin, the northern freshwater shrimp, which grows to about 30 cm in body length and has slender blue nippers almost twice as long as its body. The average cherabin is about 15 cm long. It lives in most northern freshwater rivers and lagoons, can be scooped in some places and responds very well to baited dropnets similar to those used for marron. Cherabin are caught hundreds of kilometres inland in the Kimberley. At the end of the wet season they are most plentiful near dams and natural constrictions, where they congregate while waiting to move upstream.

Anyone using nets for crustaceans, excepting the cherabin, requires an amateur fishing licence, which costs $6 a year. Licence holders must return undersized fish to the water immediately.

Bag limits in Western Australia

No person other than a licensed fisherman may catch, bring on land or into Western Australian waters, any quantity of fish in excess of the following bag limits:

```
* Greenlip Abalone . . . 10 per day      Prawns . . . . . . . . . 9 litres per day
* Brownlip Abalone  . . 10 per day      Rock Lobsters
  Roe's Abalone . . . . . . 20 per day      (all species) . . . . . . . . 8 per day
* Blue Groper . . . . . . . . 1 per day      Trout . . . . . . . . . . . . . 10 per day
* Mud crabs  . . . . . . . . 10 per day    * Salmon, Australian  . 5 per day
  Marron . . . . . . . . . . . 20 per day      Western jewfish . . . . . . 5 per day
```

A total of 10 per day of any combination of the following species: Baldchin groper, Coral Trout, Red Emperor, Snapper, North-West Snapper, Samson Fish and Blue Morwong.

Accumulated bag limits over a number of days spent on board a boat is permitted only for those species—or groups of species—marked with an asterisk. A fisherman who has lived on a boat for three days, for example, may bring ashore three blue groper and a total of 30 snapper and jewfish. Accumulation of bag limits is not permitted on other species. An amateur fishing licence is required for any type of netting of fish, prawns or crabs and for taking rock lobsters by any means. An inland fishing licence, also costing $6, for the taking of marron, barramundi, cherabin, trout, redfin perch and freshwater cobbler, and for the taking of any species of fish from the inland waters of the Kimberley Land Division of the State.

Minimum legal lengths in Western Australia

It is an offence in Western Australia to possess any fish of a size less than the prescribed legal length. It is also an offence to draw a net ashore or into a boat in such a manner that an undersized fish may be killed.

Bream (or Black Bream) . . 25 cm	Nannygai
Bream, Pig-faced	(or King Snapper) . . . . . 23 cm
(or North-West	Pike, Longfin . . . . 33 cm
Snapper) . . . . 28 cm	Red Emperor
Bream, Yellowfin . . . . 25 cm	(or Government Bream) 28 cm
Cobbler . . . . 23 cm	Rock Cod, Red . . . . 25 cm
Flathead, Dusky . . . . 30 cm	Ruff (or Sea Herring) . . . . 18 cm
Flathead, Marbled . . . . 30 cm	Salmon, Australian . . . . . . 30 cm
Flathead, Sand . . . . 30 cm	Samson Fish
Flounder . . . . 23 cm	(or Sea Kingfish) . . . . 60 cm
Garfish . . . . 23 cm	Sergeant Baker . . . . 30 cm
Groper, Baldchin . . . . 40 cm	Snapper (Shark Bay) . . . . 38 cm
Groper, Blue . . . . 40 cm	Snapper, Southern . . . . . . 28 cm
Jewfish, Westralian . . . . . . 50 cm	Snook . . . . 28 cm
Leatherjacket . . . . 25 cm	Sole . . . . 20 cm
Mackerel, Narrow-barred	Sweep . . . . 23 cm
Spanish . . . . 76 cm	Tailor . . . . 25 cm
Mackerel, Broad-barred	Tarwhine
(or grey) Spanish . . . . . . 76 cm	(or Silver Bream) . . . . . . 23 cm
Mackerel, Spotted	Trevally, Silver
Spanish . . . . 50 cm	(or Skipjack) . . . . 20 cm
Mackerel, Wahoo . . . . 76 cm	Trout, Brown . . . . 30 cm
Mackerel, Common . . . . . 15 cm	Trout, Rainbow . . . . 30 cm
Morwong	Whiting, Spotted
(or Queenfish) . . . . 30 cm	(or King George) . . . . 25 cm
Mullet, Sea . . . . 24 cm	Whiting, Western Sand
Mullet, Yellow-eye . . . . . . 23 cm	(or Silver) . . . . 22 cm
Mulloway	Whiting, Transparent
(or River Kingfish) . . . . . 33 cm	(or School) . . . . 22 cm

Garfish are measured from the tip of the upper jaw to the end of the upper half of the tail. Other fish are measured from the point of the snout to the end of the tail.

Legal lengths for crustaceans and molluscs in Western Australia

No licence is required for catching crabs in Western Australia, but an amateur fishing licence is needed for catching any species of lobsters and for the taking of prawns with a net. The official methods for measuring are provided with the licences.

Crabs, Manna	127 mm	Rock Lobster, Western	76 mm
Crabs, Brown Mud	120 mm	Rock Lobster, Southern	98.5 mm
Crabs, Green Mud	150 mm	Roe's Abalone	
Prawns, King	76 mm	(longest diameter)	60 mm
Prawns, School	50 mm	Trochus	65 mm
Marron	76 mm		

It is the fisherman's responsibility to carry accurate measuring gauges when fishing for any of the above.

Freshwater fishing in Western Australia

Between the warm barramundi waters of the north-west and the cold trout and perch streams of the south-west, Western Australia's inland angling is split very definitely in two.

In the hundreds of kilometres of deep, flat-country rivers of the south-west lives a well-stocked, well-fed trout population that is, strange to say, sadly under-fished. The reason seems to be that trout are harder to get at and less popular to eat than Western Australia's more abundant ocean species. Yet east coast trout anglers who know a good trout when they see one travel interstate each season to sample some of this state's unique, big, still-water fish. Browns and rainbows are stocked regularly from Pemberton hatchery. Redfin perch need no stocking and have found the deep pools and dams of slow plains rivers very much to their liking.

Between south and north is a gap of hot, waterless coast where rivers flow spasmodically and inland fish are sparse.

North of the Great Sandy Desert, however, lies the monsoonal Kimberley region with its network of inland rivers, carrying a wide range of native fish, some of them exciting fighters. Unlike the south-west rivers, the waters of the Kimberley are too well supplied with their own inhabitants to require any stocking. Broadly, the north-west Kimberley's inland fish are similar to those of the Northern Territory and north Queensland.

Introduced species dominate in the south-west

When Western Australia was colonized in the last century the only fish of economic significance in its southern rivers was the freshwater eeltail catfish. But settlers from a homeland abounding in inland fish species lost little time in correcting the situation and by the turn of the century were gaily stocking southern rivers with any fish that took their fancy. Murray cod and callop were put in the Helena and Avon Rivers and into the lakes near Albany. Carp, tench, roach and redfin perch were scattered through the south-west. An attempt was made to introduce giant Indian gourami—they grow to 1.2 m—in Mundaring Weir. And, of course, 'salmon trout' or brown trout were stocked in the Canning and other rivers close to Perth. The only ones to thrive were the redfin and the carp. A few brown trout popped up at unusual times, but no serious stocking of trout was attempted in Western Australia until 1930.

Establishing trout in karri country
And then it began by a strange little school experiment in a timber town called Pemberton. The headmaster, Cyril (Sticky) Glew, got his boys interested in hatching trout fry to put in the cold karri country streams around the town. The school experiment turned into a community project in which Pemberton townspeople built holding tanks, traps and the nucleus of a hatchery. Today the State Government runs the Pemberton Trout Hatchery, the heart of freshwater fishing in the south-west.

Trout from Pemberton now stock scores of rivers and streams between Perth and Albany. Most of the early work was done by acclimatization groups of local volunteers who governed trout fishing in their respective areas. But if these societies succeeded in introducing trout in the most enthusiastic way, they failed by not encouraging trout fishing as a popular sport. The concept of the oddball trout connoisseur was cultivated to discourage the mob.

A network of tributaries of the Upper Serpentine River, a mere 48 km from Perth, became the centre of the State's most enthusiastic trout fishermen. But when the Government built the Serpentine Dam in the 1950s and prohibited fishing in what were once choice trout streams, interest in trout fishing fell to rock bottom. In 1965, the State Government dissolved all acclimatization groups and took over the job itself. Two years later it brought in eastern States trout experts to see if they could put some life into the flagging trout fishery. Today things are on the move again. Fisheries research has shown that Western Australia has some of the finest trout fishing in the continent. There are, however, problems to be overcome.

One of the main problems is accessibility. Most of the south-west's best trout waters run through thick State forest. Anglers cannot get to them and when they do, they are so heavily overgrown that casting is almost impossible. Western Australia's trout streams are peculiar in that they do not rise in hills or mountains, but seep out of flat agricultural lands. In other Australian trout streams the best fishing is among the pools and rapids of the headwaters. In Western Australia there are no fishable headwaters; the best trout are in deep pools and under heavy bank scrub. Victoria's trout streams are largely wadable, but Western Australia's are so deep that wading is out of the question.

And so, in the past, accessible streams have been most heavily fished. Canny types did their own exploring and found their own spots and did not like to tell others for fear of the multitude moving in. Eventually these trout streams will all be opened up and then trout fishing must take on new popularity.

Another difficulty encountered by anglers in the south-west trout fishery is the feeding habits of local fish. Western Australian streams have very little insect rise and the trout therefore ignore any flies. They do, however, feed very healthily on a wide diet of marron and jilgies (freshwater crays), shrimps and minnows.

The best Western Australian trout flies
Because of this lack of insect life on south-west streams, fly-fishing in this State became a forgotten art. For years no fishing tackle shop in Perth stocked fly fishing equipment. In recent years, however, it has been proved that western trout bite best on wet flies of the bucktail and matuka varieties, fished to imitate minnows and small jilgies. Other recommended patterns include Mrs Simpson, fuzzy wuzzy, parson's glory and Hamill's killer.

Top Western Australian trout spots
From the early 1980s, Western Australian trout fishermen have been keener to try dry fly fishing, a neglected art in the west. The best dry fly region is the Lefroy Brook at Pemberton, where red tags, greenwell glory and royal coachman work well. Closer to Perth, the most popular trout spots are Logue's Brook Dam, Harvey River, Stirling Dam, Murray River and Collie Gorge. Rainbow trout account for about 75 per cent of all the fish caught in these areas, with the average size around 700 g. The Warren River is the place for big browns, some of which tip the scales at around 4 kg. All of the State's major trout waters are restocked in a continuing conservation programme.

The Blackwood is by far the State's longest trout river, providing about 500 km of angling along its own banks and the banks of its tributaries, the Arthur, Beaufort, Kojonup and Balgarup rivers. Some of Western Australia's best trout fishing is around Pemberton, the home of the western trout. The headwaters of the Warren and the Donnelly rivers put out a network of feeder streams round Pemberton which include such famous names as Treen Brook, Fly Brook, East Brook and Lefroy Brook. Rainbows around 2.5 kg are taken each year in the Donnelly River and in some sections of the Warren anglers may have the curious experience of catching rainbows and redfin perch on alternate casts. Streams closest to Pemberton seem to contain more browns than rainbows.

At Albany a small band of regulars take good catches of rainbows in the upper King and Kalgan rivers. Mostly under 1.5 kg, they make up for their size in numbers and appetite.

The time to fish for Western Australian trout
Though trout fishing is now legal the whole year round there is little point in fishing in winter. The rivers are too fast and full, banks are hard to reach and the fish stay well down. Few start fishing before September, when streams start to slacken pace. Even then the water is often still too dirty for fly or lure and the best bait is fresh live earthworms, rich and odorous, dug from beneath hardened cattle droppings. Vigorous rotating spoons and strong action wobblers produce well early in the season, but as summer approaches and streams clear, less obtrusive lures are preferred.

At the November peak of the trout fishing season, a firm favourite lure is a home-made version of the imp spoon. The gold imp is a top-rate rainbow getter, but in some darker rivers the Great Southern, a longer, more slender spoon, beaten from sheet brass and left to tarnish, seems to attract more fish. Some anglers go so far as to blacken their spoons with paint or boot polish—to give a better imitation of the drab southern freshwater minnow. Flashy, violent-action lures often scare trout in deep, clear rivers.

January and February are the trout fisherman's toughest months. Heat drives the trout to shelter and extreme temperatures kill many fish in shallow streams. Fish hooked are not in prime fighting condition. Fishing picks up again in March and April. The season used to close on 15 April and many a time the season's biggest fish were caught in the last week.

Redfin waters in the south-west
Because it has adopted Western Australian streams with such comfort the English redfin perch is a favourite among southern freshwater fishermen. Restricted by Commonwealth laws from introducing new species of exotic fish into Australian streams, one Perth fishing club diligently stock redfin into the chain of freshwater lakes surrounding Perth.

Redfin are firmly established in many deeper rivers such as the Harvey, Collie, Blackwood, Tone and Warren rivers. They have their good years and their bad. At times the rivers are swarming with juveniles and then in a few years the only fish caught average around 1 kg. The heaviest redfin perch caught in Western Australia weighed 2.5 kg.

Native minnows and pigmy perch are rated top perch baits. Spinners are popular and the most consistent are the rotating spoon types.

Baits for catfish
Wheatbelt creeks and headwater dams are inhabited by freshwater eel-tailed catfish. As far as fishermen can make out, the freshwater eel-tail is the same species as the cobbler that lives in estuaries and along the coast. In freshwater pools its favourite bait is the earthworm and the best time to catch it is after dark. On a good night the farm dam fisherman may catch several dozen cobbler weighing up to 2 kg.

Carp in Western Australia

Years ago, the Western Australian angler admitting to catching a carp would have been laughed at. It was like catching a goldfish from a bowl. The crucian carp or goldfish is abundant in most metropolitan park lakes and drainage streams. Schools of crucian carp swim in the Canning and Helena rivers. Only in recent years have English migrant fishermen made a specialty of carp fishing. In England the giant European carp is keenly hunted by a small but dedicated group of enthusiasts, to whom catching a single 5 kg carp may be the culmination of a year's efforts. There are a few European carp in gravel pits and streams around Perth.

Spangled perch waters

There are several members of the hardy little inland perch family along the Western Australian coast. The one commonly found in the Swan, Canning, Serpentine and Murray rivers is known as the river yellowtail and grows to 700 g, though most would be less than 250 g. They are more a brackish-water fish than a true freshwater fish; however, they are frequently caught in fresh water. They bite hungrily on almost any bait, best on shrimps. A similar freshwater spangled perch, slightly different in species, is caught further north in the upper reaches of the Greenough, Murchison and Gascoyne rivers.

Indigenous species flourish in the north-west

In rivers north of the Great Sandy Desert, the barramundi or palmer perch is king. He has a host of lesser species to pay him court: black grunters, catfish, sleepy cod, longtoms, archer fish, eels, oxeye tarpon and many others. Some are better sporting fish than food fish and vice versa. Most of them are barely known to anglers in Western Australia. Together with sawfish, turtles, freshwater crocodiles and the big freshwater shrimp known as the cherabin, they provide a thriving and balanced inland fishery for the north-west Kimberley.

There are some fish in northern freshwater streams which are really saltwater fish that have been cut off from the tides that brought them, but continue to live well-adjusted lives in the fresh. These include mangrove jacks or red bream, javelin fish and even trevally. Most fish in north-west freshwater streams are lure-takers. Even the forktailed catfish will strike at a slow wobbler, though it responds better to bait. Sleepy cod, black grunters, eels and sawfish are essentially bait-takers.

Kimberley barramundi

Two fish regularly called barramundi cause confusion in some parts of Australia's north. The two are quite dissimilar in appearance. One is the giant perch or palmer perch *Lates calcarifer*, the other the colourful Dawson River salmon or saratoga *Scleropages leichardti*. Other than from reading the arguments that arise in other States, the Western Australian angler has no such problems of identification. Only the giant perch type of barramundi is known to exist in the north-west Kimberley. And it is such an important food fish that nobody gives any other type much thought.

The north-west barramundi may be found in nearly every major river, from the Fitzroy northwards and in many inland lakes and billabongs which only occasionally link with these rivers. The Fitzroy River flows about 550 km through the Kimberley and barramundi are caught right to its source; probably even up into its feeder, the Hann River, which goes 150 km or so further. The most regular freshwater barramundi fishing is in the Fitzroy and Ord rivers, not because these rivers provide the best fishing, but because most of the others around the northern hump of the Kimberley are completely inaccessible.

The best time to catch freshwater river barramundi is in the summer wet, just as the rains begin to stir the rivers into action; and once again as the rivers are settling down after a monsoonal flow. These are times when barramundi are on the move, chasing schools of red-eye mullet, which also travel with the floods. Unfortunately, most southern fishermen stay well away from the Kimberley in the wet. Northerners grow accustomed to catching their best barra hauls when it is raining buckets. Broadly speaking, raining or not, barramundi bite better just after the wet, between March and May. After that, they go quiet until the wet begins again.

Geikie Gorge on the Fitzroy River upstream from Fitzroy Crossing is now a national park. The upper reaches of the river provide freshwater barramundi, black bream, salmon, catfish and ox-eye herring or tarpon.

Anglers continue to catch barras in those 'quiet' months, but a lot more work goes into the catching. Local fishermen who fish during the dry will usually not bother wetting a line unless the temperatures are at least in the thirties. It seems to be a proven theory in the north-west that barras do not bite when it is cold—and anything under 30 degrees C is cold up there.

Just as the mud-eye mullet (shark mullet) is a favourite bait for estuary barramundi, the freshwater red-eye is top bait in freshwater rivers. These are netted or shot. Netting is better because the mullet can then be used alive. A dead mullet may end up down the gullet of a great lump-headed catfish. Other popular baits for freshwater barra are rifle fish, small oxeye herring, hairback (bony) herring, cherabin (large freshwater shrimp) and frogs. All are better if used alive.

Although a skilfully used lure will outfish baits for barramundi during the lean months, local fishermen use lures mainly when the barras are running in the wet. Then these big sporty fish are quite indiscriminate in their choice of food; any interesting object dragged through the water on a line is likely to get a snap. Old-time barramundi fishermen used two brass .303 cartridge cases linked back to back, attaching a hook to one end and a line to the other.

Today there is an excellent range of the type of lures barramundi like best: divers, swaybacks, wobblers, flatfish, flopy, killers—anything with a slow waggling action. Some make their own wooden imitations of these waggling lures with good results. Colours preferred are mixtures of gold with red, brown, green and black. In big rivers and gorges, barramundi are caught by trolling lures and baits behind boats. Big brass spoons are best, trolled slowly, a long way astern.

Sawfish in Western Australia
Though it is hardly classed as a sporting species, the sawfish is a powerful fighter and a freshwater food fish second in importance only to the barramundi within its territory. Its flesh, white and firm, with only the faintest flavour of ray, the family to which it belongs, is preferred by many to the highly rated barra. The sawfish looks like a shovelnose ray with a saw on its snout. The broad flat saw blade is edged on either side with about twenty pointed ivory teeth. The sawfish should not be confused with the saw shark which looks vaguely similar, but is not a known river dweller and can be distinguished by the presence of barbels along its snout.

The murderous-looking saw is designed to attack—not humans, but small fish, on which it feeds. The sawfish is usually much too timid to be accidentally walked on but there are instances of this happening where people have been hacked by the flailing saw.

Sawfish readily take dead fish bait and are often caught by barramundi fishermen after a live bait has died on the hook.

Some say that a wire trace is necessary, but the sawfish's teeth are not sharply edged and a nylon line will not cut against them provided it is gently handled.

Most sawfish caught in freshwater rivers are from 90 to 150 cm long and 5 to 12 kg. Occasionally they are caught to 2.5 m long, but many grow to 6 m and weigh several tonnes when they go to sea in later life.

Black grunter on wallaby liver
Known as the freshwater black bream to most north-westers, this tasty food fish is well established in the Fitzroy and Ord River systems. The black grunter is bronze-black in colour, compressed in shape when young, but becomes very thick shouldered when big. The north-west black bream have been recorded up to 2.5 kg, though a 1 kg specimen is a good one. They bite well on the small sand frogs that live beside most Kimberley rivers and on cherabin bait. Most fishermen, however, use red meat.

In the upper Fitzroy the Kimberley cattlemen swear by salted beef and round the Victoria River, across the Northern Territory border, salted wallaby liver is an oldtimers' favourite. The salt seems to be the clue, because when unsalted baits are fished alongside they never seem to do as well. The bigger specimens put on much of their condition through their omnivorous appetite. Quite often 1 kg fish will be gorged with wild figs, fallen from river-bank trees. They are delicious to eat and cook better skinned.

The Ord River was dammed in 1970–72, forming Lake Argyle which is an increasingly popular fishing spot in northern Western Australia.

Catfish relish grasshoppers

The forktail or salmon catfish is perhaps the commonest large fish of the north-west inland. There are believed to be several species, at least two of them occurring in fresh water. A strong if unspectacular fighter on a light line, the catfish is scorned by most northerners. Its three poison spines are perhaps responsible for much of the prejudice. The flesh tends to be soft if fried like ordinary fish and has a heavy fat content. Cooked on a griddle—with onions or a touch of garlic if you like—it is excellent eating.

Catfish are not fussy feeders. In freshwater they will take most fish or meat baits. Their special favourite, however, is the big khaki grasshopper that in its winged stage becomes the north-west locust. Salted baits are said to be good in fresh water. South of the Kimberley, freshwater catfish are sleek, attractive silver-blue fish. North of the Fitzroy they seem to be a khaki grey. The big Kimberley catfish are often a dull yellow with grotesque black blotches. Bigger specimens are frequently riddled with white flesh worms. The biggest catfish unofficially recorded in Western Australia was 27 kg at Wyndham. This was said to have been the sea-going type of salmon catfish.

The bull-headed river variety is said to exceed 9 kg.

Rifle fish take spoons

This is perhaps the most commonly seen freshwater fish of the Kimberley; mainly because it always swims a whisker away from the surface, where it shoots down its insect prey with unerring jets of water from its mouth. They grow up to about 25 cm and almost 450 g, though most would be less than half this weight. Rifle fish—or archer fish—will readily take a fly or a small spoon, but an effective combination is the very small feathered spoon. They are plucky little fighters and a welcome addition to the pan.

Long-tom in Ord River canals

The freshwater long-tom is related, but of a separate species to the saltwater long-tom. The freshwater variety has the same long, cigar-shaped body, bony head and long alligator jaws. But it is stockier and when first caught has a pinkish tinge with small brown spots, similar to a rainbow trout. The Ord River irrigation project has provided a natural haven for long-tom. Canals that carry water to the cotton fields are patrolled by very large specimens, some 90 cm long and 1 kg or so in weight.

Not many are caught on lines—techniques have yet to be perfected—but when agricultural workers have used weedkiller to clear canals, hundreds of metre-long long-toms have been killed. Freshwater long-tom will slash savagely at live baits, but because of their hard, toothy beaks are more susceptible to small hooks and baits.

A day's spinning in long-tom territory might produce a few score of good bites, perhaps half a dozen leaping, exciting encounters, yet seldom a fish in the bag. Fly fishermen could be luckier, as the long-tom snaps eagerly at any likely object in its path. North-westerners sometimes go 'lashing' long-toms at night with a length of fencing wire and a bright light.

Spearing sleepy cod by torchlight

Also known as rock rod in the Kimberley the sluggish but delicious sleepy cod are common in most of the small feeder streams to the main rivers. A type of giant gudgeon, they look very much like flathead when lying motionless on a creek bed. They respond well to a small bait bounced on a sinker across the bottom. At night they are easily speared by torchlight. They grow to 2 kg and have excellent white, flaky flesh.

Fluttering spoons for ox-eye tarpon

A quick-silver aerial fighter, the ox-eye herring swims right up into the headwaters of northern freshwater rivers. It is found as far south as the River Ashburton and northwards to beyond the Ord. Most ox-eye caught in the Kimberleys are about 30 cm long and weigh less than 450 g. Alive they are excellent barramundi bait. Sometimes schools of bigger fish are found, but 2.5 to 3.5 kg seems to be the limit. At all sizes they are better taken on lures than on baits. Small fluttering spoons like the imp are most successful.

Smaller varieties of the north-west

The commonest and hardiest little freshwater fish of the entire north-west of Western Australia is the orange spotted spangled perch, also known as the poonta and the rock trout. In fact it is a member of the grunter perch family. Any stream or isolated pool be it in desert or mountains, has its poontas. They may be small and bony if the food is scarce or they may grow to 25 cm and be quite meaty. A dry billabong, suddenly filled by rain will soon be alive with poonta. They ravenously attack almost any bait or lure and in hard times have been known to peck at human swimmers.

The mouth almighty is an occasional customer on a lure. A freshwater cardinal fish, related to the southern gobbleguts, the 'mouth' flits around rocks and submerged roots, grows to 15 or 18 cm, is a poor fighter, but not bad to eat.

Small eeltail catfish, much daintier than their forktail cousins, live in the weed of freshwater streams. They are more easily speared at night than caught on a hook.

A small spinner cast into the Ord River diversion dam is likely to be attacked by a shoal of chanda perch. Silver, with black and yellow markings, these flat, oval long-finned fish grow to about 30 cm and when biting can be caught in large numbers. They are good to eat.

PHIL BODEKER AND RAY WILSON

WESTRALIAN jewfish

Glaucosoma hebraicum: A close relative of the eastern epaulette fish or pearl perch, *Glaucosoma scapulare*. Found only off the coast of Western Australia. Grows to 1 m and 27 kg, but 18 kg fish are considered outstanding specimens. Whatever the size, the jewfish is always the top-priced market fish in the West because of its superb edible qualities.

The Westralian jewfish is prevalent on reefs near the coast and is distributed from Cape Naturaliste in the south to Shark Bay in the north. It is mainly caught on handlines in the same fashion as snapper, and is extensively fished for at Rottnest Island, Lucky Bay, Port Gregory, Point Moore and the Albrolhos Islands.

When deep-sea fishermen go out from Busselton, Bunbury, Fremantle and points north, their main quarry is the jewfish. Even one 9 to 13 kg jewie makes up for a day of otherwise poor fishing. Boats frequently come ashore with more jewies than any other fish. The Westralian jewfish is an ungainly grey fish with a dumpy body, big head and enormous jaws. What Whiteley calls a 'shoulder blade bone' grows to a prominent dark round lobe in adult fish. Its colour is silvery or greyish-pearly, with dark longitudinal bands. The dorsal fin increases in height towards the tail, the eyes are pearly. To the deep-sea angler a jewfish coming over the side is a beautiful sight.

Jewfish are caught on the drift with No. 8/0 to 10/0 hooks and big baits of octopus, squid, parrotfish, whiting or other fish. The old saying is: 'If you can't make out what is fiddling with your bait give it more line, because it might be a jewie'. A big jewfish hooked on 35 m of heavy line often feels like the bottom. Half way up the change of pressure stuns it and it comes aboard like a bag of cement. Despite its poor performance on heavy line in deep water, a jewfish hooked from a boat in shallow water gives a good fight. Anglers who have hooked jewfish from the shore are amazed by their fighting ability.

Westralian jewfish

WHITEBAIT

This is considered an epicurean dish in many countries but in Australia few people know much about it. This is because it is scarce and available mainly in tins at a gourmet price. When the tin is opened the contents look like a mess of pickled minnows. These should be drained, rolled in seasoned flour and deep-fried until crisp before eating. The tinned product is rather tasteless when compared with whitebait available from fishmongers overseas.

A London fisherman, Robert Cannon, is credited with first producing and selling whitebait in the year 1780. It was made up of as many as six species of immature fish, taken at the stage where they still were little more than baby minnows. The recipe which he established called for very small herring, smelts, sand-eels, sticklebacks and others, rolled whole in flour and deep-fried until brown and crisp.

The supply was governed by the seasons, for the small fish only were obtainable from February to September, but his business prospered and his descendants carried on after him. It was held in great esteem as a dish in those times and the royal kitchen of King George IV was supplied with it every day during the season for the 10 years of his reign. Ministers of the Crown held an annual Whitebait Dinner and epicures of the Victorian age eulogized it.

Outside England there has been the tendency to nominate one particular species of small fish as 'whitebait'. In America young herrings, sardine, surf-smelt, anchovies and silversides all are marketed under this label. Over there, the Pacific surf-smelt *Allosmerus elongatus* is most prized for making whitebait and in season thousands of people turn out to take them from the surf in small nets.

Whitebait in Australia

There are at least 21 species of whitebait in Australia. It is widely distributed in the south-eastern waters of Australia, where it generally is known as the jollytail or eel-gudgeon. It occurs in its greatest numbers in Tasmania, where it is taken along with two other species of *Galaxias*, but they never have been available in sufficient numbers to excite epicures nor support a whitebait industry. The smelts *Retropinna tasmanica* and a couple of allied species were sought for canning; but of the modest amount of whitebait canned in Tasmania the greater part was made up of the Tasmanian troutlet or Derwent smelt *Lovettia sealii*.

This little fish comes in from the sea at the approximate size of 5 cm to spawn in fresh water, where it deposits its eggs on submerged sticks, piles and weed along the banks of the rivers. They travel in long, narrow shoals and may be taken in long-handled nets from the bank or from boats. They are captured near the river mouths in salt or brackish water while still in roe, for on spawning they lose bulk, darken in colour and deteriorate in appearance. Unfortunately, they never have been so widely distributed as to give any large section of Australian anglers 'whitebait fever' nor to allow the canneries to put this tinned delicacy in every grocer's shop. After an alarming decline in their numbers a total ban on their capture has been introduced by the Tasmanian government to allow stocks to recover.

See Cookery.

WHITING Sillaginidae: Nippy, speedy little fish that spend most of their lives in the channels and shallows of the inlets, along in the surf on the ocean beaches or on the shallower offshore sandflats. Whiting are not big fish—they average about 30 cm and the biggest seldom exceed 45 cm—but they are much sought after by Australian anglers because despite many small bones they are delicious to eat. There are only a few species in Australian waters, all of them exclusive to Australia and unrelated to English whiting. They are quick biters and perhaps the only fish in our waters which the angler is wise to snatch at if he is to hook them.

Whiting have long, soft noses, well rounded mouths with small teeth. They dash at the bait with a rapid threefold nip, nip, nip and are off with some of the bait before the angler can move. They are mostly caught by hooking themselves against the spring of the rod, weight of the sinker or drag on the line. They are fast and guileful and provide excellent sport.

In Victoria in summer months when the trout are not biting, anglers go after whiting on trout tackle. Some veterans prefer a 110 g stiff fly rod with a fixed spool reel and a 2 to 3 kg nylon line, but the majority seem to use the shorter bait-casting rod and a suitable revolving-spool casting reel. A light, stiff spinning rod also makes the basis of an ideal outfit for whiting in the lakes and inlets or when fishing from a boat. The drawback with a long rod is that it cannot be used when fishing with a boatload of companions.

Few whiting anglers agree on the best rigs, but the rigs used certainly depend on the formation of the seabed in the area being fished. Clear nylon which flashes in the sunlight sometimes frightens whiting off a feeding ground and dark green or brown is the best colour in the bays. It is essential that the rig selected should instantly transmit the slightest touch to the rod tip without being blocked by a fixed sinker above the hook. Hook patterns are debatable but for fish with such small, horseshoe-shaped mouths long-shanked hooks are usual.

In the rivers, tidal lakes, estuaries and bays whiting are fished for from beaches, sandspits, jetties and seawalls that give access to sandflats, shallow channels or the edges of deep water. A lot of whiting fishing is done from boats and here the usual procedure is for each angler to drag one line with the drift of the boat and use another to keep a bait moving up and down just above the bottom.

WHITING DRIFTING RIG

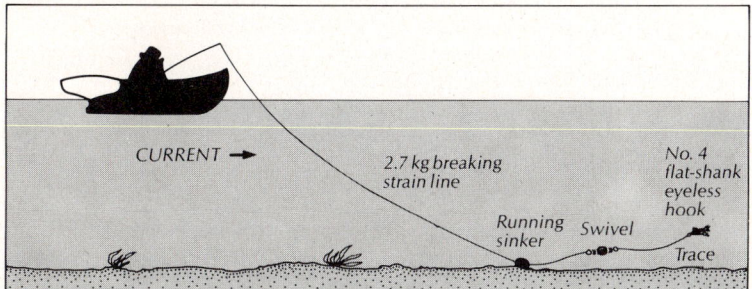

Sometimes a boat may be kellicked on a flat and whiting berleyed around with a mess of chopped-up prawns or smashed pipis. In the estuaries a lot of whiting fishing is done with fine handlines of 1 to 3 kg nylon on cork winders or plastic casting spools. But one of the tubular glass spinning rods and a saltwater resistant threadline reel are most convenient, since this type of tackle is particularly suited to cope with the speedy whiting. They often bite more readily when the bait is being slowly drawn along the bottom.

On the ocean beaches the fish are mostly found in active white water in the more shallow sections of the surf. Here the much heavier type of surf angling tackle is required to cope with the conditions. In the surf, sand whiting often bite better on the ebb than they do on the rise and at times they crowd the potholes and small gutters of the surf at low tide. Owing to the local conditions in South Australia anglers often wade away out into the shallows off the quiet beaches and stand up to their knees to fish for whiting.

Golden-lined whiting

Sillago analis: Often known as 'Tin Can Bay whiting' due to its prevalence in that area. It is the most commonly caught whiting around Fraser Island in the Piabla-Scarness area and Hervey Bay. It is found from Moreton Bay to away up into North Queensland, often in the company of sand whiting.

It closely resembles the sand whiting, but grows to a maximum of only 30 cm. It is easily distinguished from the sand whiting by the absence of the black spot at the base of the pectoral fins and the presence of a bright yellow stripe running along under the lateral line when it is first removed from the water. The overall body colour is more uniformly silver than that of the sand whiting and the anal and ventral fins are bright yellow. It is very good eating, bites well on yabbies and sometimes big catches are made in short times. One hundred at an outing is not unusual.

King George (spotted) whiting

Sillaginodes punctatus: Largest and most notable of the Australian whiting. They are an excellent sporting fish found from the far south coast of New South Wales around Victoria

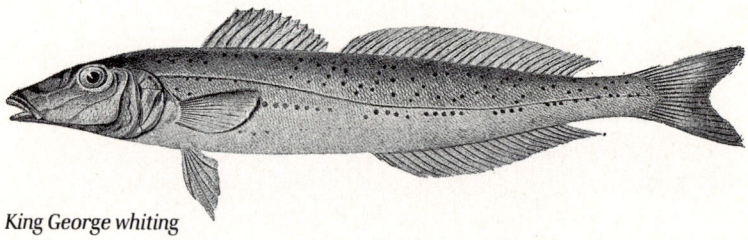

King George whiting

and South Australia and on to southern Western Australia. They are particularly plentiful in South Australia, especially in Spencer Gulf and the Gulf of St Vincent and the waters immediately westward. For a long time it was the most important fish marketed in South Australia and it remains the most sought by anglers.

The King George whiting's upper body is dark brown, almost black sometimes, merging to light brown and reddish-brown on the sides and silver below. The upper part of the body and the sides are well studded with small dark spots. The dorsal fins are decorated with a lot of somewhat larger spots with lighter brown margins. They have been known to grow to 69 cm and 4.8 kg and average, these days, between 700 g and 1 kg. According to South Australian law, in some areas they can only be caught by handlining.

Many Australians regard the King George whiting as the finest eating among Australian fish, partly because the bones are less troublesome than in the smaller fish. Victorians consume big quantities brought from South Australia. In Western Australia the King George whiting is a noted sport-fish, particularly among holidaymakers on the south coast at such places as Oyster Harbour, Irwin Inlet and Wilson Inlet.

King George whiting usually require No. 1 to 4 hooks, depending on the size available. They bite best from November to February and the most successful baits are squid, cockles and pipi. Like all whiting they are selective in their feeding and the range of baits to which they respond is limited. Sand shrimps and pink nippers, taken from the estuary flats with yabby pumps, are soft bait but the whiting relish them. Peeled prawns are used only when the fish are biting well.

Northern whiting *Sillago sihama:* This species is so prevalent in North Australian waters that some almost invariably are taken in the estuaries or along the shallow coastal flats when bait nets or casting nets are used to procure mullet or herring as bait.

It grows to a maximum of 30 cm and is easily distinguishable from the sand whiting through absence of the black mark in front of the pectoral fins. It is of a uniform silvery colour, the first dorsal fin has a black edge along the top of the spine, and there is a somewhat vague silvery-golden stripe running along under the lateral line. The pectoral and caudal

WHITING ■ W

Northern whiting

fins are edged with yellow. It is often erroneously called 'school whiting'.

Sand whiting

Sillago ciliata: The most commonly caught Australian whiting. They can be caught all the year round, but are most plentiful from November to March. They are an eastern Australian species and are found only near the shores of Queensland, New South Wales, Victoria and Tasmania, occurring in greatest numbers in southern Queensland and the New South Wales north coast. When the sand whiting are running they attract remarkable numbers of anglers at Maroochydore, Tweed Heads, Brunswick Heads, Ballina and Iluka-Yamba.

Sand whiting have been known to grow to 50 cm and 1 kg but most of those caught range from 350 to 550 g and a fish of 900 g is rated large. They are olive-green along the back, merging to silver-green, silver and then white below. The lower fins show strong tones of yellow and the dorsal fins are dotted with small dark spots. They live mainly on the sandflats and along the shallow channels in the estuaries, on shallow ocean sandbars and in the surf along the ocean beaches. They often bury themselves.

They spend a lot of time fossicking in the sand for small shellfish and crustaceans, which they break up in the crushers at the back of their palates. They are mainly taken on worms. Probably the best bait for them are the little hard-nipping wriggler worms found under logs and stones along the water's edge in quiet backwaters. Next best are the big

Sand whiting

sand worms taken out of the beaches along the edge of the surf. Blood worms dug from the mudflats in the estuaries are also very good. Squirt worms, ejected out of their tunnels in the estuary sandflats by pressure of an upturned fruit tin, also do well, as do poddy worms dug from under rotting weed on some of the backwater beaches. Earthworms are poor bait for whiting. A lot of fishing is done for sand whiting with cockles and pipis. Pipis are soft but take a lot of sand whiting in the surf. At times a few sand whiting can be caught on off-beat bait such as mullet gut, octopus, garfish or bonito, but this is not customary.

Because it bites so freely and is easily caught, the sand whiting provides more enjoyment in the summer months for once-a-year holiday anglers than any other Australian fish. Inexperienced anglers usually can catch a few. Those who use two or three hooks on their line frequently land fish on each hook. They bite freely by day or night and when they are hungry, at any state of the tide—but generally an early flood tide is best, as this keeps the fish swimming towards the shore in search of food.

To secure most fun, fishing for sand whiting should be done on very light tackle with small hooks, say, sizes No. 3 to 5. A sinker about the size of a small pea is adequate about 60 cm above the hook and the running type are preferred. Only in reasonably strong surf should the breaking strain of the line used—with rod or hand—be increased beyond 3 kg. Sand whiting are seldom caught in water beyond 5.5 m in depth.

School whiting *Sillago bassensis:* Sometimes known as 'Bass Strait whiting' or 'silver whiting'. Prevalent on the south coast of Western Australia and not uncommon in South Australia. Small numbers are taken in prawn trawls off the New South Wales and Queensland coasts. It grows to about 30 cm and the body colours are reddish brown, shading to silver on the belly, with a silvery longitudinal stripe with a narrower brown one above it. Highly edible, it is spattered with blotchy rusty-red to orange-red markings. Mainly taken from deep water and not of much interest to anglers.

School whiting

Other species of little interest to anglers are:—

Yellow-finned whiting

Sillago schomburgkii: A 30 cm grey to sandy-yellow fish from both Western and South Australia and the stout whiting *robusta*, a small creamy-yellow to silvery-white fish with a silver longitudinal stripe and yellow blotches on the cheeks. The last mentioned grows to 27 cm and is mainly taken in prawn trawls on the Queensland coast.

Trumpeter whiting

Sillago maculata: A member of the Australian whiting family which does not rate as highly among anglers as sand whiting, and King George whiting. The trumpeter whiting is a smaller species in which the predominant colour tones are gold and brown, rather than green and silver. It varies from gold to light brown and a series of dark brown blotches is clearly visible on the back and sides. The rear dorsal fin is well marked with a large number of small brown spots. Most of those taken range from 150 to 350 g. Catches of 80 to 100 are common.

The fish does not occur in quantities around Tasmania or South Australia, but is fairly plentiful in the coastal waters of the rest of our States. At times it frequents the estuaries, but its main habitat seems to be in outside waters somewhat deeper than those favoured by the sand whiting.

The trumpeter whiting seems to be more discriminating in choice of haunts. It never seems to penetrate some of our big estuaries and tidal lakes despite the fact that it may be plentiful on the adjacent offshore sandflats. It is invariably found at a longer distance from the shore than sand whiting.

They shoal densely and will bite on almost anything. It is mostly taken by snapper and flathead fishermen drifting outside waters. Doubtless many are missed through the use of unsuitable bait and hooks that are over-large for this species, for this is a fish which demands very light tackle. Commercial fishermen trawl great quantities of them and they are frequently seen in fish shop windows though supplies amount only to about a third of those of sand whiting.

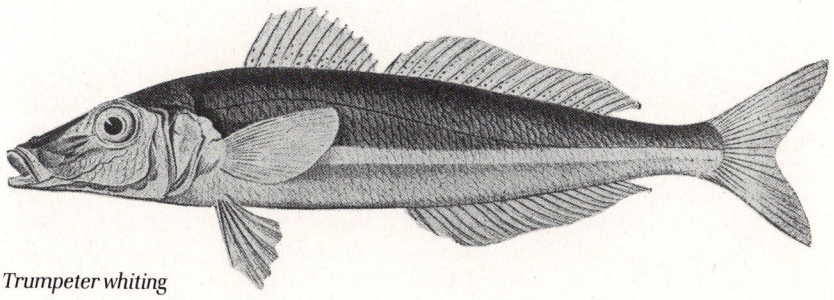

Trumpeter whiting

Wirrah

WIRRAH *Acanthistius serratus:* A tough-skinned inhabitant of rocky foreshores which fights pugnaciously when hooked but has no value whatever as food fish. They are also known as peppermint cod. Wirrah are frequently caught by rock fishermen along the south Queensland coast, right along the New South Wales coast and off Victoria and the south-west of Western Australia. They bite readily on all flesh baits. They are dull green in colour with dozens of black-rimmed bluish spots scattered all over the body, and the dozen or more dorsal spines around 15 rays make them immediately recognizable. They grow to 45 cm and are mostly caught by anglers fishing for drummer and rock blackfish.

WITCHETTY grubs An excellent bait for Murray cod. Throughout the Murray-Darling basin and the western desert country there are numerous varieties of witchetty grub, such as the species gathered at Swan Hill, Victoria, the larvae of the jewel beetle Buprestidae. There are others which are the larvae of various root-feeding and tree-boring insects, such as the ghost moths Hepialdae, goat moths Cassidae and the longicorn beetles Cerambycidea.

The custom of Riverina anglers is to remove the surface soil from under spreading limbs of the gum trees on the river flats to reveal the witchetty holes. These appear to be solely made by the larvae of the jewel beetles. On the lower Lachlan and up the Darling into south-west Queensland the very similar holes under the gums seem to be made mainly by larvae of the cassid moth *Xyleutes amphiplecta*. They have a soft head and are a little more difficult to handle with a wire screw.

The wire corkscrew is the best tool for removing them from their holes. The amount of damage inflicted on them greatly depends on the nature of the tool used. If it is too heavy, most of the witchetties will be injured. Some anglers use a stiff wire shaft with a screw of light springy wire soldered on the end of it. Care should be taken to see that the shaft is co-axial with the screw. Some have wound the screw with a taper so that it tightens on the head of the grub as it is screwed down.

Some anglers claim to have had success in using one of the small alligator clips supplied in some of the women's hair waving outfits. The long thin clip is held open by an improvised trigger which is operated by a thin cord after the clip has been firmly pressed (by a wire handle) onto the grub. There seems to be room for experiment.

Best method of keeping the grubs is to place them in plenty of only slightly moist earth. Some anglers pack them in bran, but this is not as readily available.

See Bait.

WRASSES, parrot fish and rainbow fish

These are grouped in three families in the scientific division Labriformes. There is a huge number of species distributed throughout the oceans of the world and Australia and New Zealand have a very generous share of them. Many of the species prefer warm tropical waters and a great number are specially adapted to living among coral, so the Great Barrier Reef and north Australian waters are particularly well populated with them.

They present a bewildering array of shapes and colours and the latter often are widely variable in the same species, so some may be difficult to identify. The demarcation between families often is not very well marked, so there is a tendency for most to be popularly dubbed 'parrot fish'. One notable characteristic which most have in common is the possession of greenish-blue teeth and/or bones. Most are good eating.

The species are so numerous and their descriptions so involved that herein it only is possible to touch on those most frequently caught by anglers or commonly seen in the fish markets.

Wrasses

These are distinguished from the true parrot-fish through having their peg-like, canine front teeth separate, instead of being fused together. This very numerous family consists of nearly 500 species in more than 60 groups. Australia's Lord Howe Island boasts a large proportion and Queensland alone is well represented in twenty-one of the genera or groups. Some species grow to considerable size and have earned reputations as line breakers. Others are diminutive fish of the coral pools and are prized as aquarium specimens.

Hump-headed or Maori wrasse

Cheilinus undulatus: The largest member of its family in the southern part of the world, commonly growing to 45 kg and more. It is doubtful, but a fish 2.25 m long and weighing 190 kg caught at Hayman Island on the Whitsunday Passage, Queensland, was considered probably to belong to this species. It is variously known in the vernacular as blue-tooth groper, giant wrasse, Maori cod, double-header, double-headed parrot-fish, and so on. The name Maori cod conflicts with that of another species.

W ■ WRASSES, parrot fish and rainbow fish

This Maori wrasse weighed in at 12.7 kg but they commonly grow to 45 kg and have developed a reputation in the north for breaking lines.

Large specimens develop a large fleshy hump at the top of the head, which in due course projects out in front of the eyes and gives rise to the name of 'double-header'. This is a deep-bodied, powerful fish with a particularly long, single dorsal fin and an anal fin of which the rear portions trail back to fill the spaces above and below the peduncle of the decidedly rounded tail fin.

Like many of the wrasses, this is a fish of numerous colour markings, some of which may vary with age. Briefly, it is purple along the top of the head and back, shading to green on the sides and yellowish-green on the belly. The scales on the upper body have at their base a blue-violet bar bordered in orange-yellow. This gives it an overall blue tint. By a fading of the blue and intensification of the yellow the lower body gets its green and yellowish-green tones. Wavy, Maori-like purplish markings on the upper head and snout contrast with similar bright orange lines on the cheeks and gill covers. The front portion of the purplish-grey dorsal fin is thickly spattered with orange-yellow spots, merging to darker orange-yellow or brownish lines on the after portion.

The hump-headed wrasse is a fish of the reefs, particularly the coral reefs, and frequently is taken in fishing for other reef species on the Great Barrier Reef and around North Australia above the Bundaberg-Carnarvon line. Smaller species are outstanding table fare when cooked.

Blue groper

Achoerodus gouldii: Also known as red groper, grey groper and giant pig fish. This species is quite unrelated to the giant groper of the tropics. Its habitat is the more temperate waters and it is found from south Queensland around to South Australia and southern and south-western sections of Western Australia. It is found in its greatest numbers along the ocean rocks and in the kelp beds on the New South Wales coast and from Esperance to Perth in Western Australia. It is not seen around Tasmania or New Zealand.

Like the Maori wrasse, it is a deep-bodied, robust fish with a short, stocky appearance. It has the characteristic thick, heavy lips of the family. There are four large canine-like teeth in the front of the upper and lower jaws which project when the lips are retracted. It has small eyes and a large, powerful tail which assists it to dash to shelter when hooked.

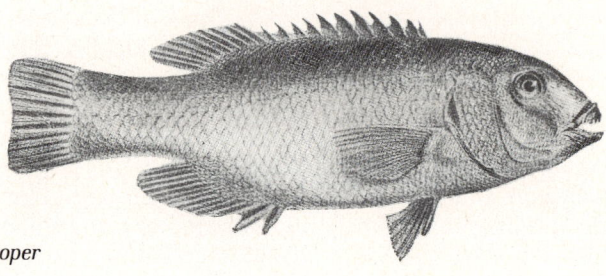

Blue groper

WRASSES, parrot fish and rainbow fish ■ W

W ■ WRASSES, parrot fish and rainbow fish

The red or blue groper are variable in colour according to sex and maturity, whereas the grey groper of Western Australia appear to be mainly female. Young fish are mostly green or olive-grey. The blues grow to the greatest size and Whitley credits one with attaining 1.4 m and 49 kg, though average big specimens range up to 11 kg and particularly large ones are occasionally caught or speared up to 22 kg.

Grant says that recent studies show the form known as *Achoerodus gouldii* is restricted to South Australian and Western Australian waters, and advocates reintroduction of the name *Achoerodus viridis* for the giant pigfish found in Queensland, New South Wales and Victorian waters.

Groper live on crabs, prawns, shellfish, squid, cunje, sea urchins etc. They do not take a flesh bait and mainly are caught on the red crabs *Plagusia carpensis*, which are found under the cunje clumps or in the red moss-weed seen on the rocks at low tide. They are mostly fished for from the rocks with handlines or other heavy gear, for they are powerful fighting fish and make a dash for cover as soon as they are hooked (see *Rock fishing*).

A big groper may take 20 years or more to grow to size. Spearfishing has so depleted them that since early 1969 they have been banned to spearfishermen in New South Wales.

Tusk fish These are a family of colourful wrasses which provide anglers with a lot of sport and some good eating fish. They derive their name from the tusk-like canine teeth in the front of their jaws. They grow a fleshy hump at the top of their heads, similar to that of the adult snapper but with a more rounded profile. Only some are commonly seen by anglers, though the known species include the Venus, blue, black-spot, purple, blue-toothed, orange-dotted, striped, yellow-bellied, bridled, one-spot and harlequin tusk fish.

Venus tusk fish *Choerodon venustus:* Also known as blue-spotted groper, bluebone, blue-parrot, pink-sided tusk fish and roseate tusk fish. It is a tropical species which makes its way down south as far as Port Macquarie on the New South Wales coast and similar latitudes in Western Australia. It is the largest of the group and the species most sought and most often taken by anglers while fishing for snapper or other reef fish.

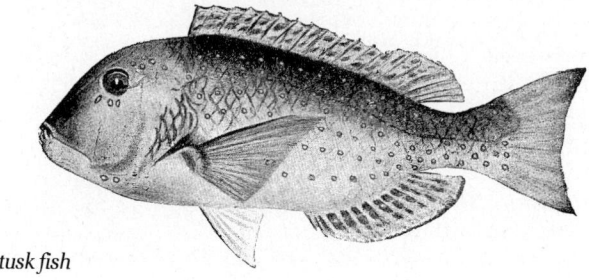

Venus tusk fish

It is extremely variable in colour, the basic tone ranging from green through pale blue to pink and brick-red. The one most permanent colour seems to be the large bright-blue spots well distributed over the head and body. It is credited by Grant with growing to 1.2 m and more than 15 kg, but in anglers' catches good fish range from 1 to 2 kg.

Venus tusk fish take most baits but some anglers regard ghost crabs as being far superior to anything else. It is regarded as very good table fish, the flesh being firm, white, flaky and of very good flavour. But it should be cleaned and iced or cooked soon after capture, for like some other of the wrasses its flesh tends to soften quickly and become mushy.

Black-spot tusk fish

Choerodon shoenleinii: Sometimes called purple groper. It is fairly common in the reef waters of Queensland but is more frequently seen in the north. It takes its name from the large black spot usually present in the base of the fin and on the back at a little behind the middle of the dorsal fin.

This is another colourful species, but again the hues may be very variable. Each scale on the upper body has an upright dark-blue stripe which gives the bright olive-green base a spangled or stippled appearance. The long dorsal fin is bright flame with a blue band running along in its tip and another at its base. Often there is a pale patch on the upper sides, below the middle of the rear soft section of the dorsal. The top lip is orange-yellow and a curved yellow line runs from it to near the bottom edge of the gill cover. There are other yellow marks from the eye down the snout and on the upper part of the gill cover.

The black-spot tusk is credited with growing to 90 cm and 12 kg, but those seen on the party-boats fishing the northern sections of the Great Barrier Reef usually range up to 2 kg. The flesh is white and flaky and it is esteemed as a table fish.

Blue tusk fish

Choerodon albigena: This species is the one most commonly seen in the catches of spearfishermen, particularly in the more northerly waters of the Great Barrier Reef. They have a habit of sheltering under the corals in the pools on the reefs at low tide, where they may be seen lying on their sides to squeeze into limited headroom. It also is frequently taken in the Gulf of Carpentaria, often where there is no sign of coral.

It also is variable, but its general colour is greenish-blue with paler greyish-blue on the cheeks. There are pale blue-green Maori-lines on a dull orange background on the snout, well down from the eyes. The lower lip and beneath the chin are coral pink and there is a blue band running along under the lip and extending back from the corner of the mouth and along the lower edge of the first gill cover. The dorsal fin is heavily marked with blue and orange lines or spots and the anal fin with alternating bands of blue and salmon-pink or yellow.

W ■ WRASSES, parrot fish and rainbow fish

It is credited with growing to 70 cm and 8 kg, but most seen range from 700 g to 2 kg. Its flesh is firm and attractive in appearance, but it is not rated as highly as the previously discussed species. It needs to be cooked or frozen soon after capture, for it deteriorates rapidly. They are very susceptible to trolled baits.

Crimson-banded parrot fish *Pseudolabrus gymnogenis:* A small and very colourful wrasse often taken by fishing from the ocean rocks or from boats over the shallower inshore reefs. It is found in southern Queensland, New South Wales, Western Australia and at Lord Howe Island. It presents a notable case of change of colour pattern with growth. In its younger stages it is brick-red to brown with numerous creamy-white spots. As it grows the spots completely disappear and the pattern changes to brown with bright crimson fins carrying tones of orange and yellow. The most notable feature is a broad, bright-crimson band around the after-body, through the forepart of the soft dorsal fin and the afterpart of the anal fin. It grows only to about 30 cm and is not a very well-flavoured food fish.

Maori fish *Ophthalmolepis cynogramma:* Another small wrasse well known to anglers in our more temperate waters. It is found from the Queensland—New South Wales border around past Victoria, South Australia and Western Australia to about as far north as Geraldton. Sometimes known as banana fish. It has been taken from the rocks, but more often by boatmen and over the shallower reefs.

It takes its name from the Maori-like tattoo markings on its face which, with the gill covers, is olive-green overlaid with numerous pale blue lines, roughly radiating from the red eyes. Its back is red with numerous small pale blue spots. Running along the sides, from the point of the gill cover to the butt of the tail, there is a broad pink band, separated from a lower dusky to black band by a narrower pinkish-white band.

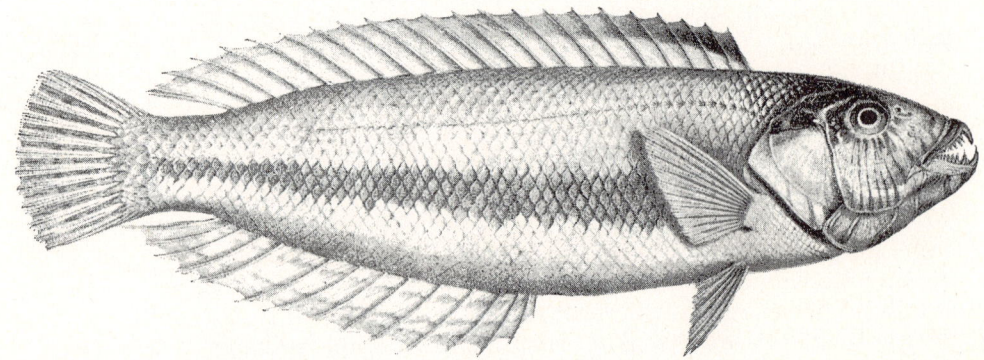

Maori fish

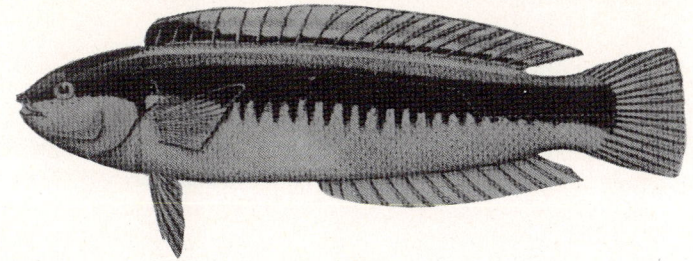

Comb fish

The Maori grows to about 40 cm and although it is small and contains some fine blue bones, it is an excellent food fish.

Comb fish

Coris picta: Often known as banana-fish. Another small wrasse, with the typically long, continuous dorsal fin of the species, well known to rock fishermen and those working the inshore reefs. Its overall colour is cream to banana-yellow. The top of the snout is greyish, giving way to a broad red band which runs back along both sides of the dorsal fin to the butt of the tail. The front end of the dorsal is brown, but this soon recedes and runs as a band in the base of the fin to the rear end. A narrow red band separates this from a broader deep yellow band running along the top.

From the top lip and through the eye, a dark-chocolate band runs back to the front edge of the tail fin. Behind the gill case this band has comb-like teeth extending down from its lower edge and hence the name. The underpart of the body is clear lemon-yellow. This bright little fish is found on the coasts of south Queensland, New South Wales and Lord Howe Island. It is a well flavoured fish, although it is small and carries some fine bones.

Castlenau's wrasse

Dotalabrus aurantiacus: A small, extremely colourful variety with an elongate, moderately compressed body that varies from greyish-black, pale whitish, reddish to yellowish to bright green or orange. The caudal fins are edged in black or violet, the tail and dorsal fins edged in black. Reaches 15 cm. Common in Bass Strait at depths of 45 m. Easily distinguished by the bobbing motion of its head when swimming.

Snakeskin wrasse

Eupetrichthys angustipes: A small but colourful wrasse found in the sandy areas around the edges of reefs in southern Western Australia, South Australia, Tasmania, Victoria and New South Wales. Body white to yellowish, with broad, grey, brown or dark green stripe extending from behind the eye along the upper surface to the caudal fin. The sides carry five blackish bands, paling to brown, pink or purple on the lower half. Head yellowish-brown. Sometimes swims with tail dragging on the bottom. Grows to 12.5 cm.

W ■ WRASSES, parrot fish and rainbow fish

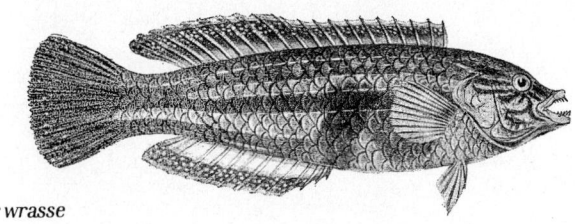

Senator wrasse

Senator wrasse   *Pictilabrus laticlavius:* Also known as the senator fish or the purple-banded wrasse. A reddish-brown fish with a row of dusky spots along the back above the lateral line, often with greyish bars on the body. Fins come in a variety of colours, ranging from brown, green and red to blue. Grows to 30 cm and 620 g. Found throughout southern Australian waters, particularly in Tasmania.

Blue-spotted parrot fish   *Pseudolabrus punctulatus:* Olive green above, pinkish below, spotted with blue eye-like marks. The tail is yellow, the dorsal and anal fins having orange bands. It is fairly common in rock-fishing spots. Found in Victoria, South Australia and Western Australia. Grows to about 40 cm.

Brown-spotted parrot fish   *Pseudolabrus parilus:* The body is greenish, spotted with brown and these spots tend to create irregular bands on the sides. Grows to 30 cm and is a common species in Victoria, South Australia and Western Australia.

Blue-throated parrot fish   *Pseudolabrus tetricus:* The colour of this species varies with growth and some of the young are incorrectly called rosy parrot fish. On adults, two broad bars cross the body. The chin and throat are dark blue. The dorsal, pectoral and ventral fins are bright yellow, the pectoral fin having a noticeable black base. This species grows to a length of 45 cm and is very common in South Australia.

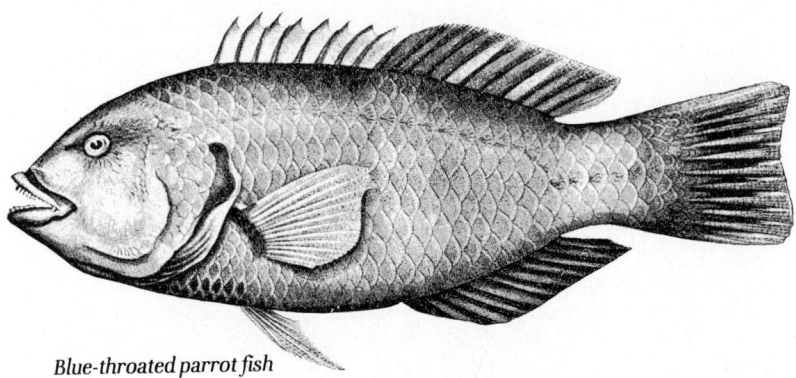

Blue-throated parrot fish

WRASSES, parrot fish and rainbow fish ■ W

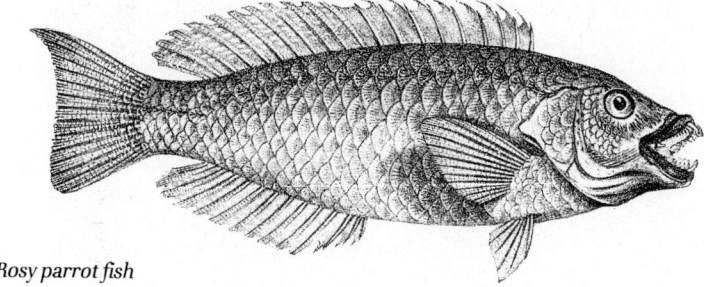

Rosy parrot fish

Rosy parrot fish

Pseudolabrus psittaculus: This species is usually reddish, the centre of each scale having a yellowish spot. It grows to 40 cm and is found in Victoria, New South Wales, Tasmania, South Australia and Western Australia around rocky reefs.

Pigfish

These close relatives of the wrasses are widespread. The banded pigfish *Verreo bellis* is found on the coasts of Queensland, New South Wales, Tasmania and the North Island of New Zealand. It is widely distributed as far as Japan and Hawaii. It is notable for its bright colouring in yellow to orange-red with pink overtones. It is decorated along the back and side with three rows of heavy broken lines which may best be described as bars of uneven length in deep crimson.

Spotted or red pigfish

Is sometimes described as a colour variation of the above species, while some authorities classify it as *Verreo unimaculatus*. It is richer in its brilliant roseate orange-red colouring and has a notable large black spot with a narrow white border at about the centre of the spinous portion of the dorsal fin. It is also unusual in that it has a smattering of pearly-white scales on the upper body, usually in a group towards the rear of the dorsal fin and two or three randomly separated up near its front.

Golden-spot pigfish

A considerably different species is the golden-spot pigfish *Bodianus perditio*, found on the Great Barrier Reef. It is also widely distributed in the North Pacific and Indian Oceans. Its overall colour is bright red, most brilliant at the head and

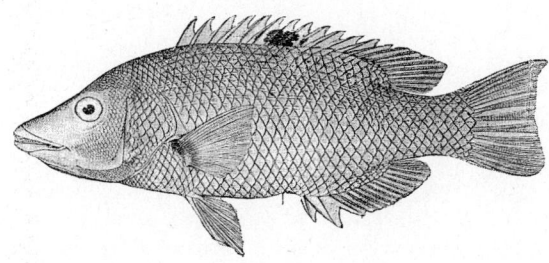

Pigfish

becoming diffused with dusky orange and then violet towards the tail. The head and forepart of the body are speckled with yellow spots. There is a bright yellow patch or heavy bar descending from about the middle of the dorsal fin to about halfway down the side. The spines in the dorsal fin tend to separate out, each with its own attached section of black membrane.

Pig fish grow to 50 cm and more, but are usually seen at 30 to 35 cm. They are very well flavoured but carry too many fine bones for most people's taste.

Rock whiting   *Haletta semifasciata:* Sometimes called grass whiting or stranger. This is another member of the wrasse family which prefers temperate waters. It is found from New South Wales around to Western Australia, though it is taken in greatest quantities in Victoria, South Australia and Tasmania. It is at times taken from the rocks but largest catches are made out over the shallow reefs and particularly where there is a weedy bottom.

This fish has the long, continuous dorsal fin characteristic of the wrasse family and in no way is related to the true whitings, which have two distinctly separate dorsals. It is bright-blue on the back, shading to light greenish-blue below. The body is covered with a network of thin golden lines and there are ten or so somewhat indefinite dark, blotchy vertical bars on the sides. There is a large dark spot a little behind the mid-point in the dorsal fin.

The rock whiting grows to about 40 cm and 800 g and is marketed in Victoria. Nevertheless, it is not by any means as good eating as the more choice members of the wrasse family. The flesh goes soft very quickly and the green bones do not recommend it to the housewife who is used to serving choice species.

Rock whiting

True parrot fish   A parrot is something that anyone immediately visualises and since the demarcation between the two is so small it is no wonder that so many wrasses have come to be called parrot fish. A true parrot fish has the tusk-like front teeth fused together and this gives a beak-like appearance which obviously gave rise to the name. In view of the similarities of the various species otherwise, it is a poor distinction.

Parrot fish have very small mouths and most are coral chewers rather than carnivores. As a result few, if any, are ever taken by anglers on lines. There are many species, some of which grow to more than 60 cm, but they are of little interest to anglers.

Surf parrot fish

Scarus rivulatus: This species is entered here because it is commonly seen by observant anglers and tourists in Great Barrier Reef waters. It may be seen swimming in coral pools on the reefs at low tide, often in schools of two to three dozen. With the rise of the tide they may be observed eagerly trying to get over the lip of the coral barrier to gain entry to pools or a lagoon. To do this they will go over on their sides to swim across the barrier in shallow water. When pursued, one may go over on its side to squeeze under a ledge of coral. Sometimes they may be seen standing on their heads with their tails breaking the surface as they feed.

This is a very pretty fish with numerous markings. The male is pale bright-green on the upper body with the bases of some scales showing through as coral-red. On the undersides the colours shade into dull coral-red and pinkish-red. The face and head are salmon-orange, overlaid with a network of Maori-lines in pale green, particularly around and below the eyes. Other markings are too numerous to detail.

The female is quite different. It is bright greenish-blue, with each scale edged finely with yellow. The face and gill covers are yellow with a series of blue lines radiating from the eye. There is also a blue line along the upper lip and two or three on the chin and throat. The tail fin is yellow, heavily edged and lined with blue. The surf parrot fish is taken by spearing or netting. It grows to 50 cm and 2 kg, but mostly is seen ranging up to 1 kg. The flesh is white, flaky and excellent eating.

Fishing for wrasse

Numbers of wrasse are taken from the rocky and coral coast areas each year, but they are usually caught when the angler is fishing for something else. Only in a few areas are these fish sought as the main quarry and then only because more popular species are not present. At least one of the species found in Australian and New Zealand waters has been dubbed 'the most ferocious of the smaller coastal fish'. This species is so pugnacious it cannot be kept in an aquarium with any other fish, including those of its own species. In fact, nothing is safe from any of the wrasses or parrot fish, not even large crayfish or giant crabs.

The wrasse is an enthusiastic feeder. It finds its food on or among submerged rocks. Tough-shelled molluscs are easily prised off the rocks by the fish's powerful front teeth. It spends part of the time sleeping on the bottom and this has been observed among specimens kept in aquariums.

When the rock fisherman finds a pool that has not been fished before, or has only been lightly fished, he is likely to find that all the parrot fish he hooks will be big ones. However, the average size of the fish caught will gradually become smaller.

Fishing tackle and methods
The tackle used for catching parrot fish differs very little from State to State. A long, fairly heavy Rangoon cane or glass-fibre rod is used, the length being necessary to enable the rock fisherman to keep back from the dangerous edges of rock platforms. Rods measuring from 3 to 5 m are used. Lines need to be strong as parrot fish inhabit rocky pools strewn with sharp coral or rocks and in which there are plenty of snags.

Y

YABBY Freshwater crayfish of the family Parastacidae that provide excellent bait for large numbers of Australian anglers, many of whom unaccountably malign yabbies. They are excellent eating themselves. They inhabit dams, creeks and waterholes and are used to catch cod, yellowbelly, redfin, trout and other inland fish. Yabbies are mostly used as live bait and when the hook is carefully pushed through the tail and about halfway along their bodies, they remain active for long periods. Yabbies are trapped in pots or by a variety of imaginative methods. One of the simplest techniques is to dangle a piece of meat in the water at the end of a piece of string. The yabbies attach themselves to the meat as they attack it and can be brought to the surface and taken in a scoop net. Some anglers build themselves yabby rakes, others take big hauls of them by dragging prawn nets across the bottom of their habitat.

See Bait; Crayfish.

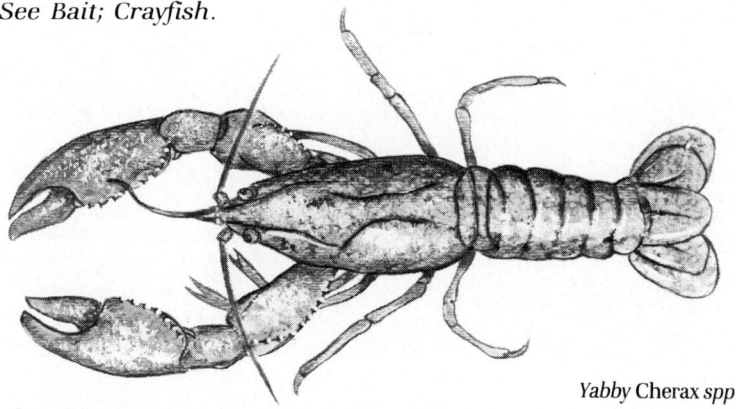

Yabby Cherax *spp.*

YELLOWTAIL kingfish *See Trevallies.*

ACKNOWLEDGEMENTS

The editor and publisher sincerely thank the following for their assistance in compiling the text, illustrations and photographs for this book:

Scientific advisors

Staff at the Australian Museum, particularly Dr John Paxton, Curator of Fishes, for his article on midwater fish and for help with the scientific nomenclature of fish, and Mark McGrouther and Roger Springthorpe for their help with scientific nomenclature; Dr David Pollard, Principal Research Biologist, Fisheries Research Institute, New South Wales Department of Agriculture; Dr Julian Pepperell, Senior Research Biologist, Fisheries Research Institute, for his work on the tagging of fish and on billfish; Dr Bryan Pratt, Assistant Secretary Land Management, Department of Territories, Canberra, for his contributions on fishing in the A.C.T., golden perch and Macquarie perch; Richard Tilzey, former Snowy Mountains biologist, New South Wales Fisheries Department, for his contributions on aquatic insects, freshwater ecology, Lake Eucumbene and stream improvement; Nick V. Ruello, Senior Lecturer, Australian Maritime College, Hobart, for his entry on prawns and shrimps; John Matthews, Fisheries Research Institute, for advice on artificial reefs and fish aggregating devices; Gary Hamer, Fisheries Research Institute, for advice on abalone and scallops; Ted A. Scribner, Water Quality Chemist, Fisheries Research Institute, for his work on water pollution; D. T. Dunstan, Environmental Assessment Officer, Fisheries Research Institute, for advice on habitat pollution; Dr R. D. Sloane and David Scholes of the Tasmanian Inland Fisheries Commission, for the material on freshwater fishing in Tasmania; Dr Ronald V. Southcott, South Australian Museum, for the material on bluebottles; Dr John Glover, Curator of Fishes, South Australian Museum, for a wide variety of advice on fishes and current researches; Peter R. Last, Senior Research Biologist, C.S.I.R.O., Hobart, for advice on Tasmanian species and fishing practices.

Specialist contributors

Dick Lewers, *Sun-Herald* fishing columnist, for his work on rigs, rod building and hairtail; George Brown, editor of *Outdoors & Fishing*, for his contribution on rock fishing; W. R. Heyward for advice on game fishing; the late Athel D'Ombrain for his contribution on photographing the catch; John Turnbull for articles on fly fishing and fishing in the Snowy Mountains.

Contributors

Keith Fleming, Wayne Fulton, Ken Jury, Vic McCristal, Bill Myatt, Ken Roberts, Olaf Ruhen, R. J. Street, Joe Thureau, Lance Wedlick, Ray Wilson.

Illustrations and photographs

The Queensland Government for permission to reproduce the pictures on pages 6, 15, 25, 49, 51, 105, 132, 156–59, 165, 172, 181, 190, 198, 200, 208 (top), 275–76, 299, 307, 321–22, 347, 352, 371, 379, 381, 526, 565, 638, 639, 641, 683, 704, 705, 730, 773–75, 781, 782 (lower), 783 (top), 784 (top), 812, 818, 819 (top), 824, 854, 888, 893 (by the late George Coates and Mr. F. Olsen) from E. M. Grant, *Guide to Fishes*, (Department of Harbours and Marine, Brisbane, 1982); Dr John Glover, Curator of Fishes at the South Australian Museum, for permission to reproduce pictures on pages 18, 44, 62, 99, 107, 134, 203, 204 (top), 205, 210, 279 (lower), 281 (top), 293, 301, 305–06, 375 (top), 485, 561, 778, 902 from T. D. Scott, C. J. M. Glover and R. V. Southcott, *The Marine and Freshwater Fishes of South Australia*, (Government Printer, Adelaide, 1980); Peter R. Last, C.S.I.R.O., Hobart, for permission to reproduce illustrations on pages 73, 81, 103, 167, 192, 202 (top), 280, 292, 301 (top), 491, 670, 751 from P. R. Last, E. O. G. Scott and F. H. Talbot, *Fishes of Tasmania*, (Tasmanian Fisheries Development Authority, Hobart, 1983); Clive Roughley, for permission to reproduce pictures by his father, the late T. C. Roughley, former Superintendent of Fisheries in New South Wales; the Departments of Tourism in A.C.T., New South Wales, South Australia, Tasmania, Victoria and Western Australia for providing photographs of fishing in those States; Bay Picture Library for permission to reproduce the photographs on pages iii, 295, 365, 487, 503, 511, 515, 547; Weldon Transparencies for permission to reproduce the photographs by Gunther Deichmann on pages 3 and 4.

Other photographs are reproduced by permission of the *Canberra Times* (pp. 35, 229, 395), John Fairfax & Sons Ltd (p. 133), West Australian Newspapers Ltd (p. 651), News Ltd (p. 373), government fisheries departments in each State, *Fishing News*, Rapala (p. 608), George Brown, John Carnemolla, Jeff Carter, Don Stephens and Associates (p. 753), R. V. Eussen, Keith Fleming, Mal Florence/Dorado Films, Andrew Jamieson, Stephen Lambert (pp. 359, 361, 883, 885), Dick Lewers, Vic McCristal, Max McIntyre, John Mondora, Owen Stephens Photographers, Bryan Pratt, Steve Starling, John Turnbull, A. H. Weatherley, Ray Wilson Media Services (pp. 855–62).

The practical instructional drawings from the first edition are by Will Mahony. Additional line drawings and maps by Darian Causby and Liz Seymour. Additional drawings of fishes by Sheryll Phelps.

The Division of National Mapping, Canberra, for permission to reproduce the maps between pages 393 and 394.

BIBLIOGRAPHY

Every effort has been made to trace and acknowledge copyright holders of material reproduced in this book and the publishers apologise for any unintended infringement.

Special thanks

This book owes much to the work of the late Wal Hardy, an outstanding fishing writer for more than 30 years; the late John Lake, New South Wales government biologist at Narrandera Research Station and a noted authority on freshwater fishes, who was tireless in his support; David Stead, for his researches into sharks and rays; Gilbert Whitley, for his amazing output of scientific papers on a wide variety of subjects; George Coates, for his outstanding pictorial record of Barrier Reef fishes; Dr Victor Coppleston's studies on sharks and shark attacks; Tom Marshall's work as ichthyologist with the Queensland Department of Harbours and Marine; James Douglas Ogilby's work at the Queensland Museum; A. Dunbavin-Butcher's notable researches on trout and other work as director of the Victorian Fisheries Department; and Trevor D. Scott's cataloguing of marine and freshwater fish in South Australia as Curator of Fishes at the South Australian Museum.

BIBLIOGRAPHY

Sources of reference consulted in the preparation of this book include:

Newspapers and magazines

Advertiser, Adelaide; *Age*, Melbourne; *Australian*, Sydney; *Australian Fisheries Magazine*, Department of Primary Industry; *Bulletin*, Sydney; *Cairns Post*; *Courier-Mail*, Brisbane; *Daily Mirror*, Sydney; *Daily News*, Perth; *Daily Telegraph*, Brisbane; *Daily Telegraph*, Sydney; *Evening News*, Sydney; *Examiner*, Launceston; *Herald*, Melbourne; *Mercury*, Hobart; *Newcastle Herald*; *News*, Adelaide; *Sporting Globe*, Melbourne; *Sun*, Sydney; *Sun News-Pictorial*, Melbourne; *Sunday Mail*, Brisbane; *Sunday Times*, Perth; *West Australian*, Perth.

Periodicals and brochures

Australian Game Fishing Association Record Book; Commonwealth Bureau of Statistics *Reports* on fisheries in Australia; *International Game Fishing Association Year Book*; New South Wales Division of Fisheries' publications including *Gamefish Tagging* (Julian Pepperell), *The Narrandera Story* and *Commercial Fisheries of Australia*; brochures from all States on legal lengths, bag limits and licencing laws for sports fishermen.

Government and official handbooks

Grant, E. M. *Guide to Fishes*, Department of Harbours and Marine, Brisbane, 1982.

Last, P. R., Scott, E. O. G. and Talbot, F. H. *Fishes of Tasmania*, Tasmanian Fisheries Development Authority, Hobart, 1983.

McCulloch, Allan R. *The Fishes of New South Wales*, Royal Zoological Society of New South Wales, Sydney, 1921.

Munro, Ian S. R. "Handbook of Australian Fishes" *Fisheries Newsletter* 1–42, Department of Primary Industry, Canberra, 1960–61.

Scott, T. D., Glover, C. J. M. and Southcott, R. V. *The Marine and Freshwater Fishes of South Australia*, Government Printer, Adelaide, 1980.

Tunbridge, B. R. and Rogan, P. L. *A Guide to the Inland Angling Waters of Victoria*, Fisheries and Wildlife Division, Ministry for Conservation Victoria, Melbourne, 1981.

Waite, Edgar R. *The Fishes of South Australia*, Government Printer, Adelaide, 1923.

General references

Australian Fishes (illustrated by Walter Stackpool), Pollard Publishing, Sydney, 1978.

Bowerman, Martin *Fishing Australia*, Child & Henry, Sydney, 1985.

Carcasson, R. H. *A Field Guide to the Reef Fishes of Tropical Australia*, Collins, Sydney, 1977.

Coppleson, Victor *Killer Sharks*, Angus & Robertson, Sydney, 1962.

Culotta, Nino (John O'Grady) *Gone Fishing*, Ure Smith, Sydney, 1962.

D'Ombrain, Athel *Fish Tales*, Rigby, Adelaide, 1968.

D'Ombrain, Athel *Game Fishing off the Australian Coast*, Angus & Robertson, Sydney, 1957.

Goadby, Peter *Big Fish and Blue Water*, Angus & Robertson, Sydney, 1970.

Gregory's Guides to Fishing, K. G. Murray, Sydney.

Hardy, Wal *The Saltwater Angler*, K. G. Murray, Sydney, 1966.

Hedge, John *A Season on the Monaro*, Abbey, Sydney, 1968.

Hungerford, Rodger *The Junior Angler*, K. G. Murray, Sydney, 1973.

Hungerford, Rodger *The Young Angler*, Angus & Robertson, Sydney, 1981.

Hungerford, Rodger (ed.) *Freshwater Fishing in Australia*, Pollard Publishing, Sydney, 1971.

Hungerford, Rodger (ed.) *The Anglers' Omnibus*, Pollard Publishing, Sydney, 1971.
Lake, John S. *Australian Freshwater Fishes*, Nelson, Melbourne, 1978.
Lewers, Dick *Understanding Fishing Tackle*, A. H. & A. W. Reed, Sydney, 1972.
Marshall, F. D. *Bait for Saltwater Fishing*, Angus & Robertson, Sydney, 1980.
Marshall, F. D. *Let's Go Surf Fishing*, Angus & Robertson, Sydney, 1980.
Marshall, Tom C. *Tropical Fishes of the Great Barrier Reef*, Angus & Robertson, Sydney, 1962.
McCausland, M. E. *Fly Fishing in Australia and New Zealand*, Lothian, Melbourne, 1967.
McCristal, Vic *Freshwater Fighting Fish*, K. G. Murray, Sydney, 1969.
McCristal, Vic *The Family Fisherman*, K. G. Murray, Sydney, 1969.
McDowall, R. M. (ed.) *Freshwater Fishes of South-Eastern Australia*, A. H. & A. W. Reed, Sydney, 1980.
McLane's Standard Fishing Encyclopedia and International Angling Guide, Holt, Rinehart & Winston, New York, 1965.
Parrott, Arthur W. *Sea Anglers' Fishes of Australia*, Hodder & Stoughton, Melbourne, 1959.
Pollard, Jack *The Fisherman Who Laughed*, Hutchinson, Melbourne, 1983.
Pollard, Jack (ed.) *The Scream of the Reel*, Pollard Publishing, Sydney, 1975.
Pratt, Bryan *The Canberra Fisherman*, A.N.U.P., Canberra, 1979.
Ritz, Charles *A Fly Fisher's Life*, Reinhardt, London, 1965.
Roughley, T. C. *Fish and Fisheries of Australia*, Angus & Robertson, Sydney, 1951.
Scholes, David *Fly Fisher in Tasmania*, Jacaranda Press, Brisbane, 1961.
Scholes, David *The Way of An Angler*, Jacaranda Press, Brisbane, 1963.
Stead, David G. *Fishes of Australia*, William Brooks, Sydney, 1906.
Thomson, J. M. *A Field Guide to Common Sea Fishes of Non Tropical Australia*, Collins, Sydney, 1977.
Turnbull, John *A Fly on a Stream*, Angus & Robertson, Sydney, 1968.
Wedlick, Lance *Sixty Ways to Fool a Trout*, Wedneil Publications, Melbourne, 1965.
Wedlick, Lane *Trout on a Fly*, Wedneil Publications, Melbourne, 1968.
Wedlick, Lance *Fishing in Australia*, Angus & Robertson, Sydney, 1962.
Whitley, Gilbert *Freshwater Fishes of Australia*, Jacaranda Press, Brisbane, 1962.
Whitley, Gilbert *Marine Fishes of Australia* 2 vols, Jacaranda Press, Brisbane, 1962.
Whitley, Gilbert *The Sharks of Australia*, Royal Zoological Society of New South Wales, Sydney, 1940.
Williams, W. D. *The Invertebrates of Australian Inland Waters*, Sun Books, Melbourne, 1968.
Zern, Ed (ed.) *Zane Grey's Adventures in Fishing*, Harper, New York, 1952.

INDEX OF SCIENTIFIC NAMES

Acanthistius serratus, 896
Acanthocybium solandri, 853
Acanthopagrus australis, 101, 103
Acanthopagrus berda, 105
Acanthopagrus butcheri, 101, 103
Acanthuridae, 730–1
Acanthurus triostegus, 731
Acanthurus xanthopterus, 730
Achirus pavoninis, 200
Achlyopa nigra, 200
Achoerodus gouldii, 898, 900
Achoerodus viridis, 900
Aetobatis narinari, 557
Agrioposphyraena barracuda, 44, 49
Alabes dorsalis, 188
Albula vulpes, 95
Aldrichetta forsteri, 380, 384
Alectis ciliaris, 782–3
Alima laevis, 524
Allocyttus verruscosus, 177
Alopias caudatus, 662
Alopias superciliosus, 662
Alopiidae, 662
Alpheus spp., 524
Alpheus andouini, 524
Alpheus edwardsi, 524
Alpheus strenuus, 524
Aluteridae, 332–6
Aluterus monoceros, 335
Ambassidae, 131–2
Ambassis castelnaui, 131
Ammotretis lituratus, 204
Ammotretis rostratus, 202
Amniataba percoides, 299
Amusiidae, 642
Anguilla australis, 183
Anguilla bicolor, 183
Anguilla reinhardtii, 183
Anguilliformes, 183–8
Anoplocapros lenticularis, 99
Anthiidae, 306
Antigonia rubicunda, 88
Apasmogaster tasmaniensis, 134
Apogonidae, 280, 378
Aptychotrema rostrata, 562
Arnoglossus bassensis, 203
Arrhamphus sclerolepis, 277
Arripidae, 632–4, 777–8
Arripis esper, 778
Arripis georgianus, 778
Arripis trutta, 632
Asmicridea grisea, 21
Astacopsis gouldi, 166
Asymbolus analis, 668
Atennariidae, 17
Atherinidae, 216–17, 305
Atherinosoma microstoma, 306
Attractoscion aequidens, 770
Atyidae, 525
Atypichthys mado, 732
Atypichthys strigatus, 732
Auxis rochei, 823
Auxis thazard, 822–3

INDEX scientific names

Auxis thynnoides, 823

Barringtonia asiatica, 5
Belonidae, 274, 338–9
Belostomatidae, 23
Berycidae, 399, 684
Bidyanus bidyanus, 298, 670
Bidyanus elliptica, 298, 671
Birgus latro, 160
Blennechis anolius, 82
Blenniidae, 81
Bodianus perditio, 905
Bovichtus variegatus, 771
Brachirus selheimi, 199
Brama brama, 107
Branchiostegus wardi, 776
Bunaka herewerdenii, 300
Buprestidae, 896

Callianassa australiensis, 162, 165, 524
Callorhynchus milii, 188
Cancellus typus, 160
Cantherines trachylepsis, 335
Capropygia unistriata, 99
Carangidae, 171, 779–84
Carangoides emburyi, 816, 824
Carangoides gymnostethoides, 784
Caranx georgianus, 783
Caranx ignobilis, 783
Caranx melampygus, 781
Caranx nobilis, 783
Caranx sexfasciatus, 782, 824
Carassius auratus, 114
Carassius carassius, 113
Carcharhinus brachyurus, 655
Carcharhinus melanopterus, 666
Carcharhinus obscurus, 665
Carcharodon carcharias, 666
Cassidae, 896
Centriscops humerosus, 62
Centroberyx affinis, 399, 684
Centrolophidae, 778
Centropyge bicolor, 17
Cepolidae, 44
Cerambycidea, 896
Ceratias, 18
Ceratiidae, 18
Cetorhinus maximus, 655
Chaetoderma penicilligera, 334
Chaetodontidae, 111
Chaetodontophus duboulayi, 17
Chaetognatha, 26
Chanos chanos, 371
Cheilinus undulatus, 897
Cheilodactylidae, 372
Cheilodactylus fuscus, 565
Cheilodactylus nigripes, 376
Cheilodactylus spectabalis, 375
Chelidonichthys kumu, 300
Cherax spp., 165–6, 908
Cherax tenuimanus, 166, 875
Chironex fleckeri, 85
Chironomidae, 24
Chlorophthalmus nigripinnis, 167
Choerodon albigena, 901

Choerodon shoenleinii, 901
Choerodon venustus, 900
Chrysophrys auratus, 683
Chrysophrys guttulatus, 683
Chrysophrys major, 684
Chrysophrys unicolor, 683
Clinidae, 81
Clinus perspicillatus, 84
Cnidoglanis macrocephalus, 127
Cochleoceps spatula, 134
Coleoptera, 19, 23
Coloburiscoides, 19
Coris picta, 903
Corixidae, 22
Coryphaena hippurus, 175
Crassostrae commercialis, 486
Craterocephalus eyresii, 306
Craterocephalus stercusmuscarum, 306
Creocele cardinalis, 134
Cristiceps australis, 84
Cryptopsaras, 18
Ctenochaetus strigosus, 730
Culicidae, 24
Cybiosarda elegans, 818
Cymbacephalus nematophthalmus, 209, 210
Cynoglossus bilineatus, 200
Cyprinidae, 101
Cyprinus carpio, 113
Cypselurus lineatus, 242
Cypselurus melanocercus, 243
Cyttosoma boops, 177
Cyttus australis, 177

Dactylopagrus macropterus, 376
Dardanus arrosor, 160
Dasyatidae, 558
Dasyatis brevicaudatus, 558
Dasyatis fluviorum, 560
Dasyatis kuhlia, 560
Dasyatis sephen, 554
Dasyatis thetidis, 560
Dasyatis warnak, 560
Derris trifoliolata, 5
Diodon nichthemerus, 518
Diodontidae, 518
Diptera, 19
Donax deltoides, 502
Dotalabrus aurantiacus, 903
Duboisia myoporoides, 5
Dysticidae, 23

Echeneidae, 712
Echeneis, 3, 712
Echeneis naucrates, 712
Echidna nebulosa, 186
Edelia obscura, 496
Eirene menonii, 85
Elagatis bipinnulatus, 624
Eleotridae, 299
Eleutheronema tetradactylum, 773
Emmelichthys nitidus, 43
Engraulis australis, 15
Enoplosus armatus, 485
Ephemeroptera, 18–19
Epigonus lenimen, 280

Eupetrichthys angustipes, 903
Eustacus armatus, 166
Euthynnus alleteratus, 818
Euxiphipops sextriatus, 17
Exocoetidae, 274
Exocoetus volitans, 243

Favonigobius tamarensis, 281
Furgaleus ventralis, 668

Gadidae, 135
Gadopsis marmoratus, 78
Galaxias brevipinnis, 253
Galaxias cleaveri, 253
galaxias johnstoni, 253
Galaxias maculatus, 253
Galaxias truttaceus, 253
Galaxiidae, 253
Galeocerdo cuvieri, 663
Galeorhinus australis, 661
Gambusia affinis, 377
Genypterus blacodes, 135
Genypterus microstomus, 135
Geotria australis, 332
Geotriidae, 332
Gerres argyreus, 670
Gerres ovatus, 670
Gerridae, 22, 670
Girella cyanea, 88
Girella elevata, 80
Girella tricuspidata, 339, 684
Glaucosoma hebraicum, 689, 888
Glaucosoma scapulare, 495
Glossamia aprion aprion, 378
Gnathanodon speciosus, 781
Gobiesocidae, 134, 188
Gobiomoridae, 299
Gobiomorphus coxii, 300
Gonodactylus spp., 524
Gymnosarda unicolor, 818
Gymnothorax, 183
Gymnothorax favagineus, 188
Gymnothorax pictus, 188
Gyrinidae, 23

Haletta semifasciata, 906
Haliotis, 1
Halosaurus pectoralis, 278
Hapalochlaena maculosa, 129, 131
Harpodon translucens, 95
Hemiptera, 18–19, 22
Hemirhamphidae, 274
Hemirhamphus ardelio, 275
Hemirhamphus australis, 276
Hemirhamphus commersoni, 275
Hemirhamphus quoyi, 277
Hemirhamphus regularis ardelio, 276
Hemirhamphus regularis regularis, 276
Hemirhamphus welsbyi, 277
Hephaestus spp., 296
Hepialdae, 896
Heterodontus portusjacksoni, 669
Himantura, 562
Histiopteridae, 88
Holthuisana transversa, 161

INDEX scientific names

Hoplichthyidae, 206
Hydrophilidae, 23
Hyperoglyphe antarctica, 779
Hypnarce subnigra, 558
Hypseleotris galii, 300
Hypseleotris klunzingeri, 300

Ibacus peronii, 165
Ichthyscopus lebeck, 707
Iso rhothophilus, 216, 306
Istiblennius edentulus, 83
Istiophorus albicans, 66
Istiophorus platypterus, 66, 74
Isurus oxyrinchus, 659

Jasus edwardsii, 163
Jasus novaehollandiae, 163
Jasus verreauxi, 164

Katsuwonidae, 822
Katsuwonus pelamis, 817, 821
Kuhlia munda, 493
Kuhlia rupestris, 493
Kuhlia taenuira, 493
Kuhliidae, 496
Kyphosidae, 179
Kyphosus cinerascens, 181
Kyphosus fuscus, 181
Kyphosus gibsoni, 181
Kyphosus sydneyanus, 180
Kyphosus vaigiensis, 181

Labotes surinamensis, 785
Labriformes, 897
Lamna nasus, 660
Lampris guttatus, 485
Lates calcarifer, 51, 640, 882
Latridae, 814
Latridopsis forsteri, 814
Latris lineata, 814
Leionura atun, 44
Leiopotherapon unicolor, 298, 671
Lepidoblennius haplodactylus, 82
Lepidopus caudatus, 251
Leptocephalus wilsoni, 186
Lethrinidae, 189–91
Lethrinus chrysostomus, 190
Lethrinus fletus, 189
Lethrinus nebulosus, 190
Lewinichthys ciconia, 338
Liza diadema, 382
Liza dussumieri, 381
Liza strongylocephalus, 382
Liza vaigiensis, 380
Lophonectes gallus, 203
Lorettia sealii, 889
Lotella callarias, 135
Lutjanidae, 132, 189, 684, 811
Lutjanus argentimaculatus, 351
Lutjanus bohar, 351, 638
Lutjanus sebae, 189, 191

Maccullochella macquariensis, 294, 390, 813
Maccullochella peeli, 389, 813
Macquaria ambigua, 282

Macquaria australasica, 350
Macquaria colonorum, 56, 191
Macquaria novemaculeata, 55–6, 638
Macrobrachium spp., 525
Macrobrachium novaehollandiae, 525
Macrorhamphosidae, 62
Majidae, 160
Makaira inazara, 66
Makaira indica, 66–7
Makaira nigricans, 66, 70
Manta alfredi, 556
Megalops cyprinoides, 307
Melamphaeidae, 167
Melanotaenia fluriatilis, 553
Melanotaenia splendida, 553
Melanotaeniidae, 553
Mendosoma allporti, 814
Mesopristes alligatoris, 299
Metapenaeus bennettae, 519, 522
Metapenaeus dalli, 522
Metapenaeus endeavouri, 521
Metapenaeus macleayi, 519, 521
Meuschenia hippocrepis, 334
Meuschenia trachylepis, 335
Mictyris longicarpus, 158–9
Mobulidae, 556
Mogurnda striata, 300
Mola ramsayi, 714
Molidae, 713
Monacanthidae, 332
Monacanthus chinensis, 333
Monodactylus argenteus, 61
Mordacia mordax, 332
Mordaciidae, 332
Mugil cephalus, 383
Mugil georgii, 381
Mugilidae, 379–87
Muraenesox cinereus, 183, 188
Muraenichthys breviceps, 188
Muraenidae, 186
Mustelus antarcticus, 668
Myliobatidae, 556
Myliobatis australis, 557
Mytilus planulatus, 393
Myxus elongatus, 382
Myxus petardi, 380–1

Nannoperca australis, 496
Narcobatidae, 558
Naucrates ductor, 784
Navodon australis, 335
Navodon ayraud, 336
Nemadactylus douglasii, 374
Nemadactylus macropterus, 375
Nemadactylus valenciennesi, 374
Neoarius australis, 125
Neoceratodus forsteri, 346
Neocyttus rhomboidalis, 177
Neoodax frenatis, 708
Neoodax radiatus, 708
Neopataecus waterhousi, 565
Neoplatycephalus speculator, 210
Neosilurus ater ater, 127
Neosilurus brevidorsalis, 127
Neosilurus hyrtlii, 127

Neosilurus mortoni, 127
Nepidae, 23
Netuma thalassina, 125
Nibea soldado, 387
Nomeidae, 87
Nomeus gronovii, 85
Notesthes robusta, 110
Notographtidae, 175
Notonectidae, 22
Notopogon lilliei, 63
Notorhynchus cepedianus, 661
Nototodarus gouldi, 131

Octopus australis, 129
Octopus pallidus, 129
Ocypode ceratophthalmus, 158
Odacidae, 708
Odonata, 18–21
Odontaspis arenarius, 656
Olisthops cyanomelas, 708
Oncorhynchus tshawytscha, 635
Ophichthidae, 188
Ophiclinidae, 81
Ophiclinops pardalis, 82
Ophiclinops varius, 83
Ophiclinus aethiops, 82
Ophiclinus antarcticus, 82
Ophiclinus gracilis, 82
Ophthalmolepis cynogramma, 902
Opisthognathidae, 673
Orectolobus maculatus, 668
Osbeckia scripta, 333
Ostracioidei, 98
Ostraciontidae, 98
Ostracion tuberculatus, 98
Ostrea angasi, 489
Ostreidae, 486
Otolithes argenteus, 770
Oxymonacanthus longirostris, 333
Oxynotus bruniensis, 175

Pagrus auratus, 683
Paguridae, 159
Palaemonidae, 525
Palinuridae, 162–4
Panulirus cygnus, 162
Panulirus ornatus, 164
Panulirus versicolor, 164
Paragalaxias dissimilis, 253
Paralepididae, 50
Parambassis gulliveri, 131
Parapenaeopsis sculptilis, 522
Parastacidae, 165, 908
Paratrilga papilio, 301
Paratrigla vanessa, 300
Paratya australiensis, 825
Parequula melbournensis, 670
Paristiopterus gallipavo, 89
Paristiopterus labiosus, 88
Pataecidae, 564
Pataecus fronto, 564
Pataecus vincenti, 565
Pecten alba, 642
Pectinidae, 642
Penaeus esculentes, 521

913

INDEX scientific names

Penaeus latisulcatus, 520
Penaeus longistylus, 520
Penaeus merguiensis, 521
Penaeus monodon, 521
Penaeus plebejus, 520
Penicipelta vittiger, 335
Pentaceropsis recurvirostris, 89
Perca fluviatilis, 490
Percichthyidae, 56
Periophthalminae, 378
Peronedys anguillaris, 82
Petraites hepaeolus, 84
Philypnodon grandiceps, 300
Physalia, 84–7
Physiculus bachus, 135, 293
Pictilabrus laticlavius, 904
Planchonia careya, 5
Platacidae, 61
Platax batavianus, 61
Platax pinnatus, 62
Platycephalidae, 206
Platycephalus arenarius, 208
Platycephalus caeruleopunctatus, 210
Platycephalus fuscus, 207
Platycephalus haackei, 210
Platycephalus indicus, 208
Platycephalus laevigatus, 210
Platycephalus longispinis, 209
Platycephalus richardsoni, 209
Plecoptera, 18–20
Plectorhinchidae, 189
Plectorhynchus pictus, 690
Plectropomus leopardus, 811
Plotosidae, 126
Plotosus anguillaris, 126
Poeciliidae, 378
Polydactylus multiradiatus, 774
Polydactylus plebejus, 775
Polydactylus sheridani, 774
Polynemidae, 772
Polyprion americanus, 292
Polyprion moeone, 292
Polyprion oxygeneios, 293
Pomacanthidae, 16
Pomacanthus imperator, 17
Pomacanthus semicirculatus, 17
Pomadasys argyreus, 321
Pomadasys hasta, 321
Pomadasys maculatus, 321
Pomadasys opercularis, 321
Pomatomus saltatrix, 749
Porpita, 84
Portunus pelagicus, 157
Potamonidae, 161
Priacanthidae, 110
Priacanthus macracanthus, 110
priacanthus tayenus, 110
Prionace glauca, 656
Pristidae, 563
Pristiophoridae, 563
Pristiopsis leichhardti, 564
Pristis zijsron, 563
Promicrops lanceolatus, 291
Protonibea diacanthus, 387
Prototroctes maraena, 289

Prototroctidae, 289
Psammoperca waigiensis, 639
Psettodes erumei, 198
Pseudaphritis urvillii, 136
Pseudocarcinus gigas, 160
Pseudohistiophorus angustirostris, 75
Pseudolabrus gymnogenis, 902
Pseudolabrus parilus, 904
Pseudolabrus psittaculus, 905
Pseudolabrus punctulatus, 904
Pseudolabrus tetricus, 904
Pseudomugil signifer, 306
Pseudorhiza haeckeli, 85
Pseudorhombus arsius, 202
Pseudorhombus jenynsii, 204
Pterygotrigla polyommata, 301

Rachycentron canadus, 322
Rajidae, 562
Ranina ranina, 159
Remora remora, 712
Rexea solandri, 44
Rhabdosargus sarba, 106
Rhadinocentrus ornatus, 553
Rhincodon typus, 664
Rhinobatidae, 558, 562
Rhinobatos batillum, 562
Rhombosolea plebeia, 203
Rhombosolea retiaria, 201
Rhombosolea tapirina, 201
Rhynchobatus djiddensis, 562
Rhynchorhamphus georgii, 276
Rhynchostracion nasus, 98
Rouleina eucla, 43

Salmo gairdneri, 800, 802
Salmonidae, 289, 793
Salmo salar, 630, 802
Salmo trutta, 799
Salvelinus fontinalis, 796
Sarda chiliensis australis, 817
Scarus rivulatus, 907
Scatophagus argus, 112
Schindleria praematura, 212
Sciaena antarctica, 387
Sciaenidae, 387, 770
Scleropages leichardti, 51, 640, 882
Scobinichthys granulatus, 335
Scomber australasicus, 349
Scomberesocidae, 274
Scomberoides lysan, 526
Scomberomoridae, 705
Scomberomorus commersoni, 703
Scomberomorus queenslandicus, 705
Scomberomorus semifasciatus, 705
Scombridae, 349, 703, 815, 822
Scorpaenidae, 110, 280
Scorpidae, 731
Scorpis aequipinnis, 731
Scorpis georgianus, 731
Scyllaridae, 164
Scyllarides sculptus, 165
Scylla serrata, 156
Selenotoca multifasciata, 111, 112, 178
  var. aetatevarians, 112

Seriola dumerilii, 6
Seriola hippos, 639
Seriola lalandi, 780
Seriola purpurascens, 6
Seriolella brama, 779
Serranidae, 293
Siganidae, 706
Siganus guttatus, 706
Siganus spinus, 707
Sillaginidae, 890
Sillaginodes punctatus, 891
Sillago analis, 891
Sillago bassensis, 894
Sillago ciliata, 893
Sillago maculata, 895
Sillago robusta, 895
Sillago schomburgkii, 895
Sillago sihama, 892
Siphamia cephalotes, 280
Siphonognathidae, 815
Siphonognathus argyrophanes, 815
Siphonophores, 84
Soleidae, 199
Sparidae, 100–09, 683
Sphyraena jello, 49
Sphyraena novaehollandia, 500
Sphyraena obtusata, 501
Sphyraenidae, 47, 48, 500–02
Sphyrnidae, 657
Stegostoma fasciatum, 669
Stenocaulus kreffti, 339
Stenopus hispidus, 522
Stolephorus carpentariae, 16
Stolephorus devisi, 16
Strophiurichthys robustus, 98
Syngnathidae, 502

Tandanus bostocki, 126
Tandanus rendahli, 127
Tandanus tandanus, 126
Tephrosia purpurea, 5
Tetraodontidae, 777
Tetrapturus spp., 66
Tetrapturus albidus, 66
Tetrapturus angustirostris, 67, 75
Tetrapturus audax, 66, 72
Thalassina squamifera, 165
Thenus orientalis, 165
Thrissa hamiltoni, 16
Thrissa setirostris, 16
Thrissina aestuaria, 16
Thunnidae, 815
Thunnus alalunga, 816
Thunnus albacares, 821
Thunnus maccoyii, 820
Thunnus obesus, 820
Thunnus tonggol, 819
Thyrsoidea macrura, 186
Thysanophrys cironasus, 210
Tinca tinca, 769
Tipulidae, 24
Torpedinidae, 558
Toxotes chatareus, 25
Toxotes jaculator, 26
Trachichthodes gerrardi, 684

Trachinotus anak, 172
Trachinotus bailloni, 172
Trachinotus blochi, 172
Trachinotus russelli, 172
Trachurus declivis, 782
Trachurus novaezelandiae, 782
Triacanthidae, 784
Triacanthus biaculeatus, 784
Triakidae, 668
Trichiuridei, 302
Trichiurus coxii, 302
Trichiurus haemula, 302
Trichiurus savala, 302
Trichoptera, 19, 21–2
Triglidae, 300

Tripterygiidae, 81
Tripterygion spp., 83
Triurus laevis, 714
Trizopagurus strigimanus, 160
Trygonorrhina fasciata, 558
Tylosurus macleayanus, 339
Tylosurus melanotus, 339

Undecimus hendecacanthus, 88
Upeneichthys porosus, 280
Upeneus sulphureus, 279
Upeneus tragula, 279
Uranoscopidae, 707
Urolophus testaceous, 560

Valamugil seheli, 380
Velella, 84
Verreo bellis, 905
Verreo unimaculatus, 905
Vincentiana novaehollandiae, 280

Xiphasia setifer, 83
Xiphias gladius, 66, 76

Yarra singularis, 332

Zeidae, 177
Zenopsis nebulosus, 177
Zeus faber, 177
Zostera, 190, 210, 274–5, 520

INDEX OF COMMON NAMES

abalone, 1–2
albacore, 815–16
   false, 818
amberjack, 6
   yellow banded, 6
anchovy, 14–16
   De Vis', 16
   estuary, 16
   gulf, 16
   Hamilton's, 16
   southern, 15
   whiskered, 16
angelfish, 16–17
   black and gold, 17
   emperor, 17
   scribbled, 17
   six-banded, 17
   zebra, 17
anglerfish, 17–18
   oceanic, 18
   shore, 18
archer fish, 25–6
arrow worms, 26

backswimmers, 22
Balmain bug, 164–5
baitfish, red, 43
baldfish, 43
banana-fish, 903
banana jew, 388
bandfish, 44
barraconda, 44
barracouta, 44–7, 251, 302
   common, 44–5
   king, 44, 46
barracuda, 47–50
   giant, 49
   Jello's, 49
   pick-handle, 49
   striped, 501
barracudina, 50–1
barramundi, 51–5, 640, 856, 877, 882–4
   Dawson, 51

reef, 639
rock, 351
bass, 55–61, 191–2, 282–3
   Australian, 419
   freshwater, 638
   northern hemisphere, 292
   red, 351–2, 504, 505, 638–9
   saltwater, 638–9
   sand, 639
batfish, 61-2
   hump-headed, 61
   long-finned, 62
   silver, 61
beardies, 135
beetles, longicorn, 896
bellowfish, 62–3
   banded, 62
   crested, 63
bidyan, 298, 670
big eye, 110
big eyes, 280
billfish, 65–78, 274
black back, 632
blackfish,
   freshwater, 78
   river, 78–80
   rock, 80–1, 180
black rankin, 135
blenny, 81–4
   Adelaide snake, 82
   black-eyed snake, 82
   dusky snake, 82
   eel, 82
   hairtail, 83
   oyster, 82
   reef, 83
   snake, 82–3
   threefin, 83
   variegated snake, 82–3
blood-worm, 24
bludger, 784
bluebone, 900
bluebottle, 84

bluebottle fish, 87
bluefish, 88
blue-parrot, 900
boarfish, 88–9
   big-spined, 88
   giant, 88–9
   long-snouted, 89
   roseate, 88
   yellow-spotted, 89
bobby, 298
Bombay duck, 95
bonefish, 95–7
bonito, 815, 817–8
   leaping, 818
   New Zealand striped, 817
   oceanic, 821
   Watson's, 818
boxfish, 98–9, 508
   blue-spotted, 98
   robust, 98
   small-nosed, 98
   smooth, 99
   spiny, 99
box-jelly, 85–6
bream, 100–09, 670, 684
   black, 101–3, 298, 339, 351, 670, 866, 877
   bluenose, 101
   bony, 101
   buffalo, 180–1
   Cape Moreton, 101
   Cockney, 101, 688
   coral, 101, 189–90
   creek, 101
   creek red, 351
   dog, 351
   emperor, 101
   freshwater, 101
   freshwater black, 885
   government, 101, 189, 191
   grunter, 101
   hump-headed, 101
   hump-headed ray, 101
   hybrid, 104–5

INDEX common names

Japanese sea, 684
kelp, 101
Murray, 101
pikey, 101, 105
Rays, 101, 107
red, 101, 688
sand, 190
sea, 101, 103, 683
silver, 101, 103
slater, 101
snapper, 101, 189
southern, 101–2
spangled, 101
stinging, 101, 706
surf, 101, 103
thick-lip, 101
yellow-banded butterfly, 101
yellow-lip butterfly, 101
yellowfin, 101, 103–4
bulldogs, 707
bullrout, 110
bullseye, 110
   red, 110
   spotted-finned, 110
bung, 782
butterfish, 111–2
   southern, 112, 178
   spotted, 112
   striped, 112
by-the-wind sailor, 84

caddis fly, 19, 21
callop, 282, 389
cardinal fish, 280, 378
   big-eyed, 280
carp, 113–14, 769, 878–9
   common, 113
   crucian, 113–14, 882
   European, 882
   golden, 113–14
   Prussian, 113
   sea, 373, 565
catfish, 125–9, 856, 864, 882
   blue, 125
   eel-tailed, 126–8, 297
   forktail, 886
   freshwater, 126–9
   freshwater eel-tailed, 881
   marine, 125–6
   salmon, 125
   straight-backed, 127
   striped, 126
cephalopods, 129–31
chanda perch, 131–2
   giant perchlet, 131
   western, 131–2
char, 796
charlia, 526
Chinaman fish, 132, 191, 504
Chinese lantern, 306
chinook, 635
choppers, 750
climbing fish, 378
clingfish, 134, 188
   broad-headed, 134

   cardinal, 134
   Tasmanian, 134
cobbler, 127–8
cobia, 322–3, 780
cockabullies, 81
cocky apple, 5
cod, 135–6
   black rock, 135
   blue, 135
   breaksea, 306
   coral, 135
   estuary rock, 291
   greasy, 291
   humpback, 135
   jumping, 785
   Maori, 897
   Murray, 56, 135, 282, 294, 389–93, 811, 813
   red, 135–6, 293
   scarlet rock, 306
   scorpion, 135
   sleepy, 822, 887
   spotted, 135
   spotted river, 291
   tiger, 306
   white flowered, 135
   wire-netting, 135
coelenterates, 84–5
coffer fish, 98
comb fish, 903
congolli, 136–7
cowanyoung, 782
cowfish, 98, 556
crab, 154–61
   blue manna, 156
   coconut, 160
   freshwater, 161
   frog, 159
   ghost, 158
   giant Tasmanian, 16
   hermit, 159–60
   mangrove, 156–7
   mud, 156–7
   robber, 160
   sand, 157
   soldier, 158
   spanner, 159
   spider, 160
   swift, 158
crane fly, 24
crawfish, 162
crayfish, 162–6, 875–6, 908
   broad-fronted, 165
   freshwater, 162, 165–6, 875–6, 908
   Murray River, 166
   painted, 164
   sea, 162
   southern, 163–5
   western, 162–3
crustaceans, 518, 875–6
crusthead, 167
cucumber fish, 51, 167
cutlass fish, 251, 302
cuttlefish, 129

dab, 203

daddy long legs, 24
darkies, 339
dart, 171–2, 779
   black-spotted, 172
   giant, 526
   snub-nosed, 172
devil fish, 556
dewfish, 126
dially, 750
diamond, 203
diamond fish, 556, 782
dingo fish, 44, 49
dirkfish, 175
doctor fish, 730, 769
dogfish, 175
   prickly, 175
dolphin fish, 175–7
doddy, 131
dory, 177–9
   john, 111, 177–9, 376
   mirror, 177
   ox-eyed, 177
   silver, 177
   spiky, 177
   warty, 177
double-header, 897
dragonet, 771
dragonfly, 19–21
dream fish, 181
drummer, 179–82
   black, 80, 343
   low-finned, 181
   silver, 179–81
   southern, 181
   topsail, 181
dwarf palmer, 639
dynamite plant, 5

eel, 4, 183–8, 297
   clouded reef, 186
   common southern pigmy, 188
   conger, 186
   freshwater, 183–6
   half-banded snake, 188
   long-finned, 183
   long-tailed reef, 186
   marine, 186–8
   moray, 186–8
   painted reef, 188
   pike, 183, 188
   red-banded, 188
   red-banded shore, 188
   reef, 183, 186
   shore, 188
   short-finned, 183–6
   short-headed worm, 188
   snake, 188
   starry reef, 186
   tesselated reef, 188
   worm, 188
eelfish, 126
eel-grass, 274–5, 520
eel-gudgeon, 889
elephant fish, 188
emperor, 189–91, 684

INDEX common names

red, 189, 191
  red-finned, 373
  spangled, 190, 373
  sweetlip, 190
  yellow-tailed, 373
estuarine perch, 191–2
eucalypt, 5

file fish, 332
flagtail, 493
  rock, 493
  silver, 493
flapjack, 164
flasher, 785
flatfish, 198–205
flathead, 206–12
  bar-tailed, 206–7
  black, 210
  deep-sea, 210
  dusky, 206–7
  dwarf, 206
  freshwater, 136
  fringe-eyed, 206, 209
  grassy, 210
  Harris's, 206
  long-headed, 210
  long-spined, 209
  mud, 206–7
  red-spotted, 206, 210
  rock, 209–10
  sand, 206, 208
  spiky, 209
  tiger, 209
flickers, 381
floater, 212
flounder, 198, 201–5
  Bass Strait, 203
  black, 201
  crested, 203
  estuary, 201
  greenback, 201–2
  large-toothed, 202
  long-snouted, 202
  mud, 201
  New Zealand, 198
  river, 201
  sand, 203
  small-toothed, 204
  spotted, 204
  yellowbelly, 201–2
flower of the wave, 216, 306
flying fish, 242–3, 274
  common, 243
  great, 243
forehead fish, 565
frostfish, 251–2

galaxias, 253, 889
  Clarence, 253
  climbing, 253
  mud, 253
  Shannon, 253
garfish, 274–8, 338
  black-barred, 275
  Georgii, 276

long-jawed, 276
river, 275–6
sea, 276
short-nosed, 277
snub-nosed, 277
Welsby's 277
garupa, 293
gastropods, 1
ghost grinner, 95
ghost nipper, 162, 165, 524
giant perchlet, 131
globefish, 518, 777
gnat, 24
goannafish, 278–9
goatfish, 279–80
  mottled, 279
  sunrise, 279, 508
  yellow, 279
gobbleguts, 280
  freshwater, 378
  southern, 280
goblinfish, 280–1
goby, 281
  Tamar, 281
goldfish, 114, 882
goolwa cockle, 502
grasshopper fish, 83
grassy jew, 388
grayling, 289–90
groper, 290–6
  bass, 290, 292
  blue, 290, 898, 900
  blue-spotted, 900
  blue-tooth, 897
  grey, 898, 900
  New Zealand, 293–4
  northern, 291
  purple, 901
  Queensland, 290–2
  red, 898, 900
  southern Australian, 290
grouper, 293
grunter, 296–9, 670
  Barcoo, 296
  bidyan, 298
  black, 882, 885
  black-striped, 299
  bronze, 299
  coal, 297
  leathery, 296
  Norman River, 296
  sooty, 296–8, 670
  spangled, 298
  Welch's, 196
  yellowtail, 296
gruper, 293
gudgeon, 299–300
  checkered, 300
  Cox's, 300
  Daly River, 300
  firetail, 300
  flat-headed, 300
  western carp, 300
guitar fish, 562
gummy, 668

gurnard, 300–1
  butterfly, 300
  flying, 301
  red, 300
  spiny, 301

habuka, 293
haddock, 376
hairtail, 44, 302–5
  Australian, 302
  northern, 302
  spiny, 302
half-beaks, 274
halibut, Queensland, 198–9
happy moments, 706
hapuka, 293
hapuku, 290, 292–3
hardyhead, 305–6
  Lake Eyre, 306
  Mitchellian freshwater, 306
  small-mouthed, 306
harlequin fish, 306
herring, 15, 379, 777–8
  cucumber, 289
  ox-eye, 307
  Perth, 777
  sea, 777
herring cale, 708
hoka, 293

jackass fish, 373, 375–6
Japanese lantern, 306
javelin fish, 321
  blotched, 321
  silver, 321
  small-spotted, 321
  spotted, 321
jellyfish, 85
jewel-eye, 639
jewfish, 126, 387–9
  blotched, 387–8
  silver, 387–8
  spotted, 387–8
  Westralian, 888
jigly, 166
johnny jumper, 378
jollytail, 253, 889
jumping joey, 81–2

kahawai, 276, 632
kamloops, 800
kanae, 383
kangaroo fish, 378
kelp,
  red, 189
kelp bream, 638
kelp fish,
  brown, 189
kelp sea perch, 638
kenaru, 126
kingfish, 779–81
  black, 322–3, 780
  Queensland, 703
  yellowfin, 6
  yellowtail, 6, 780–1

917

INDEX common names

ladyfish, 191
lamprey, 332
  narrow-mouthed, 332
  pouched, 332
  short-headed, 332
  wide-mouthed, 332
landau, 126
langouste, 162
lano, 382
latchet, 301
leadenall, 823
leatherjacket, 332–6
  beaked, 333
  Chinaman, 336
  fan-bellied, 333
  figured, 333
  horseshoe, 334
  prickly, 334
  rough, 335
  silver, 784
  toothbrush, 335
  unicorn, 335
  velvet, 335
  yellow, 336
  yellow-finned, 335
leather johnnies, 332
leatherskin, large-mouthed, 526
lethrinids, 684
ling, 135
  banded, 135
  black, 322
lizard fish, 167
lobby, 162
lobster,
  shovel-nosed, 165
  spiny, 162
long-tom, 27, 338–9
  black-finned, 339
  freshwater, 339, 886–7
  slender, 338
  stout, 339
luderick, 339–46, 684
lungfish, 346–8, 379

mackerel, 349, 703–6, 853
  blotched, 705
  blue, 349, 823
  broad-banded Spanish, 705
  broad-barred Spanish, 705
  common, 349, 823
  doggie, 705
  frigate, 815, 822–3
  horse, 782, 817
  jack, 349, 782
  marine frigate, 823
  narrow-banded Spanish, 703–4
  narrow-barred Spanish, 703
  school, 705
  slimy, 349
  Spanish, 703–6, 816
  spotted, 705
  spotted chubb, 349
mado, 731–2
mahi-mahi, 175
man-eater, 667

mango, 668
mangrove fish, goggle-eyed, 378
mangrove jack, 351–4, 638
maomao, blue, 731
Maori fish, 902–3
marble fish, 136
mariposa, 485
marlin, 65–74, 712
  black, 66–70
  blue, 66, 70–2
  D'Ombrain, 66–7
  Howard, 66
  striped, 66, 72–4
  white, 66
marron, 166, 875–6
mayfly, 19–20
midge, 23–4
midnight fish, 167
milkfish, 371–2
mi mi, 706
minnow, 253
mirror fish, 782–3
moeone, 292
molluscs, 1, 129, 486, 642
moonfish, 485
moora nennigai, 399
Moreton Bay bug, 165
morwong, 190, 372–7
  blue, 373–4
  brown, 189
  brown-banded, 373, 375
  dusky, 373
  grey, 374
  magpie, 373, 376
  red, 565
  red-banded, 373
mosquito, 23–4
mosquito fish, 377–8
mother na di, 399
moths, ghost, 896
  goat, 896
mouth almighty, 378
mudeye, 21
mudskipper, 378–9
mullet, 379–87
  black-spot, 380
  blue-spot, 380
  bully, 383
  diamond-scaled, 380
  fantail, 381
  flat-tail, 381
  freshwater, 380–1
  hardgut, 383
  long-armed, 380–1
  long-finned, 381–2
  mangrove, 383
  New Zealand red, 280
  Ord River, 382
  red, 279
  river, 383
  sand, 382
  sea, 383–4, 508
  silver, 381
  small fantail, 381
  Wide Bay, 382

  yellow-eye, 379–80, 384–7
mulloway, 100, 387–9
mussels, 393

nannygai, 399, 684
narnwai, 181
needle-fish, 338
needle gar, 275
newfish, 632
nicky, 298
niggers, 339
numbfish, 558

octopus, 129, 131
  brown, 129
  blue ringed, 129, 131
  pink, 129
  white, 129
oilfish, 44
old wife, 485
opah, 485–6
opening day fish, 770
oyster, 486–9
  mud, 489
oyster crusher, 669
oyster-eater, 172

paddle-tail, 504
palmer, 51
para, 251
parore, 101, 339
parrot fish, 897–907
  blue-spotted, 904
  blue-throated, 904
  brown spotted, 904
  crimson-banded, 902
  double-headed, 897
  rosy, 905–6
  surf, 907
  true, 906–7
patiki, 203
pennant fish, 782–3
penny fish, 131
perch, 298, 490–6
  black-banded sea, 306
  dusky, 785
  English, 490–3
  estuarine, 56, 191–2
  estuary, 282–3
  giant, 51, 640
  glass-eyed, 639
  golden, 56, 282–9, 811
  jewel, 298
  jungle, 26, 493–5
  Macquarie, 56, 282, 350–1
  mountain, 351, 493
  Murray, 298, 670
  New Zealand black, 101
  Palmer, 882
  pearl, 495–6
  pigmy, 496
  purple sea, 351
  puttynose, 775
  rock, 339
  sand, 639

INDEX common names

silver, 282, 298, 376, 388, 670–3
spangled, 671, 882
squeaker, 376
terapon, 296
Welch's, 296
pigfish, 80, 905–6
  banded, 905
  giant, 898
  golden-spot, 905–6
  red, 905
  spotted, 905
piggy, 190
pike, 500–2
  sea, 44, 49
pilchard, 15
pilot fish, 779, 784
pip, 670
pipefish, 502
piper, 276
pipi, 502–3
pombah, 750
pond-skater, 22
pony fish, 670
porae, 374
porcupine fish, 518
porgies, 683
Portuguese man-o'-war, 84–6
prawn, 518–25
  banana, 521
  bay king, 520
  blue-legged king, 520
  brown, 521
  coral, 522
  eastern king, 520
  endeavour, 521
  greasyback, 522
  greentail, 522
  leader, 521
  red spot king, 520–1
  school, 521
  tiger, 521
  western king, 520
  western school, 522
prawn-killer, 165, 524
prow fish, 564–5
  smooth, 565
  whiskered, 565
puffer fish, 507–8, 777
pu-pi, 67
puttynose, 775

queenfish, 189, 373–4, 526–7, 779

rabbit fish, 706
rainbow fish, 553
  crimson-spotted, 553
  northern, 553
  southern, 553
ranzania, 714
ray, 554–64, 712
  Banks's shovelnose, 562–3
  banjo, 558
  brown fiddler, 558
  bull, 556
  coachwhip, 560

cowtail, 554, 556
devil, 556
eagle, 556–7
electric, 558
fantail, 554
fiddler, 558
leopard, 560
manta, 556
mill, 556
sand, 560
shovelnose, 562
southern, 558
southern shovelnose, 562
thorn-back, 562
whip, 556
whiptail, 560, 562
white-spotted shovelnose, 562
redfin, 490–3
redfish, 399, 684
red indian, 564–5
red throat, 190
remoras, 712
rifle fish, 25–6, 886
roach, 670
rock-lobster, 162–3
roughie, 777
ruff, 777
runner, 779
  rainbow, 624
  sea, 801

saddlefish, 280
sailfish, 66, 74–5
  Atlantic, 66
  Pacific, 66
St Peter's fish, 177, 376–7
salmon,
  Atlantic, 630–2, 811
  Australian, 632–5
  blue, 773
  buck, 632
  Burnett, 774
  Cooktown, 773
  Dawson River, 882
  king, 774
  landlocked, 630
  migratory, 793
  quinnat, 635–8, 793
  sock-eye, 793
salmon trout, 632, 793
saltlicker, 83
sammy dong, 209
samson fish, 639–40, 779
sandy, 136
saratoda, 51
saratoga, 51, 640–2
saratota, 640
sawfish, 563–4, 882, 884–5
  green, 563–4
  Leichhardt's, 564
  narrow-snouted, 563
  Queensland, 564
scabbard fish, 251
scad, 782
scallop, 642

scat, 112
schnapper, 684
sea-pike, short-finned, 500
  striped, 501
sea snake, 183
sea wasp, 85–6
senator fish, 904
sennit, 501
sergeant-fish, 322, 780
Shannon moth, 21
shark, 643–69, 712
  basking, 655
  Beaumaris, 660
  black tip whaler, 666
  black-tipped whaler, 666
  black whaler, 665
  blue, 656
  blue pointer, 659
  blue whaler, 656
  bronze whaler, 655–6
  bullhead, 669
  carpet, 668
  cocktail, 665
  common whaler, 665
  freshwater, 648–9
  ghost, 188
  grey nurse, 656–7
  gummy, 668
  hammerhead, 657–8
  leopard, 669
  mackerel, 660
  mako, 659–60
  porbeagle, 660–1
  Port Jackson, 669
  school, 661
  seven-gilled, 661–2
  snapper, 661
  spinning, 666
  spotted catshark, 668
  Swan River whaler, 665
  sweet william, 668
  thresher, 662
  tiger, 663–4
  whale, 664–5
  whaler, 665–6
  whiskery, 668
  white, 666–7
  white pointer, 666
  wobbegong, 668
  zebra, 669
short bill, 277
shrimp, 518–25
  banded coral, 552
  burrowing, 162, 524
  mantis, 522, 524
sierra, 44
silverbelly, 670
  common, 670
  Darnley Island, 670
  lowfin, 670
  silver, biddy, 670
silvereye, 351
silversides, 305
silver spray, 131
siphon-fish, Wood's, 280

INDEX common names

siphonophores, 84–5
skate, 562
skinny fish, 526
skipjack, 817
skipper, 338, 817
skippy, 817
slimy, 78
slippery, 78
smelt, 15
   Derwent, 889
smiler, 673
snapper, 683–92
   Australian, 101
   black, 684, 690
   golden, 684
   green, 190
   king, 189
   old man, 684
   queens, 373
   red, 351, 399, 684
   reef, 684
   school, 684
   Western Australian black, 684
snoek, 44, 251
snook, 500, 703
snubbie, 277
soapies, 388
soapy, 670
soldier fish, 280
sole, 198–200, 205
   black, 200
   freshwater, 199
   peacock, 200
   tongue, 200
   southern blue-eye, 306
spearfish, 66–7
   Pacific short-billed, 75–6
   short-billed, 67, 75
spinefoot, 706–7
   black, 707
   golden-lined, 706
spinetails, 730
splinter gar, 275
spotted dogfish, 668
spotty, 25
sprat, 15
square, 203
squid, 131
squire, 189
stargazers, 707
steelheads, 800
stingaree, 558, 560
   black, 560
   blue-spotted, 560
   brown, 560
   common, 560
   estuary, 560
   smooth, 558, 560
stonefish, 98
   northern Australian, 281
stonefly, 19–20
stonelifters, 707
stranger, 708, 906
sucker fish, 3, 712

   short, 712
   slender, 712
sunfish, 713–14
   oblong, 714
   ocean, 714
   short, 714
surgeon fish, 730–1
   bristle-toothed, 730
   convict, 731
   ring-tailed, 730
swallowtail, 171
sweep, 731–2
   banded, 731
   sea, 731
sweetlips, 189, 684
   grass, 190
   grey, 190
   netted, 373
   painted, 373, 690
   yellow, 190
swordfish, 65–6
   broadbill, 66, 76–8

tailor, 670, 749–52
takeke, 276
tallegalane, 382
tang, 730
tanguigue, 703
tarakihi, 373, 376–7, 814
tarpon, 307–8
   oxeye, 887
tarwhine, 101, 106
tassel fish, 772
tcheri, 670
tench, 768–70
teraglin, 387, 770–1
   common, 770
   silver, 770–1
thornfish, 771–2
thorntail, 560
threadfin, 772
threadfin salmon, 772–6
   blue, 773–4
   flat, 774
   giant, 773–4
   Sheridan's, 773–4
   striped, 775
three by two, 277
tilefish, 776
tinplate, 203
toadfish, 507–8, 777
toado, 777
   banded, 777
   common, 777
   marbled, 777
   silver, 777
   stars and stripes, 777
   weeping, 777
tommy rough, 777
tommy ruff, 777–8
tope, 661
torpedoes, 558
trevalla, 778–9
   deep-sea, 779
trevally, 779–84, 824

   banded, 781
   black, 706, 779
   diamond, 782–3
   golden, 779, 781
   great, 779, 782, 824
   king, 781
   lowly, 779, 783
   plumed, 782
   rubber-lip, 779
   silver, 783
   skipjack, 783
   snotty, 758
   spotted, 781
   white, 783
   yellow-finned, 779
trigger fish, 332–3
triplespine, 784
tripletail, 785
tripod fish, 784
trout, 793–814, 876–81
   bay, 632
   brook, 793, 796–9, 811
   brown, 21, 793–800, 800–10
   coral, 504, 811–13
   eastern brook, 796
   Kern River, 793, 800
   Loch Leven, 793
   mountain, 253, 493
   Nelson, 800
   rainbow, 793, 800–03, 810
   sand, 136
trout cod, 56, 390, 813–14
troutlet, Tasmanian, 889–90
trumpeter, 814–15
   bastard, 814
   real bastard, 814
   striped, 814
trunk fish, 98
tuatini, 661
tubemouth, 815
tuna, 815–23
   dog-tooth, 818
   little, 818
   mackerel, 818–19
   northern bluefin, 819–20
   Pacific big-eyed, 820
   skipjack, 815, 821
   southern bluefin, 815–16, 820–1
   striped, 815, 817, 821
   yellowfin, 815, 821–2
tunny, 815
tupong, 136
turret fish, 98
turrum, 779, 816, 824
turtle, 712
tusk fish, 290, 900–02
   black-spot, 901, 902
   blue, 901–2
   pink-sided, 900
   roseate, 900
   Venus, 900–01
twisters, 81
tychuree, 381

wahoo, 853–4
warehou, 758, 779
   blue, 758
   silver, 758
   white, 758
water beetle, 23
water-boatmen, 19, 22
water bug, 22–3
   giant, 23
water-scorpion, 23
water-strider, 19, 22
weedfish, 81, 84
   common, 84
   crested, 84
whapuka, 293
whirligig beetle, 23
whitebait, 15, 253, 889–90
white death, 667
white-eye, 351
white fish, 526
whiting, 890–5
   Bass Strait, 894
   bridled rock, 708
   golden-lined, 891
   grass, 906
   King George, 891–2
   long-rayed rock, 708
   northern, 892–3
   rock, 708, 906
   sand, 891, 893–4
   school, 894
   silver, 894
   spotted, 891
   stout, 895
   Tin Can Bay, 891
   trumpeter, 895
   weedy, 708
   yankee, 770
   yellow-finned, 895
Winston Churchills, 707
wire-tooth, 770
wirrah, 896
witchetty grubs, 896–7
wrasse, 290, 897–908
   Castlenau's, 903
   giant, 897
   hump-headed, 897
   Maori, 897–8
   purple-banded, 904
   senator, 904
   snakeskin, 903
wrigglers, 24
wyandotte, English, 296

yabby, 162, 166, 524, 875–6, 908
   black, 166
   white, 166
yellowbelly, 198, 282
yellowtail, 296, 779, 782
yellow-tail, 501